The Pirate Queen

Also by Susan Ronald

The Sancy Blood Diamond
France, The Crossroads of Europe, as Susan Balerdi

The Pirate Queen

QUEEN ELIZABETH I,
HER PIRATE ADVENTURERS,
AND THE DAWN OF EMPIRE

Susan Ronald

HarperCollins*Publishers*

HarperCollins books may be purchased for educational, business, or sales promotional use. For information, please write: Special Markets Department, HarperCollins Publishers, 10 East 53rd Street, New York, NY 10022.

FIRST EDITION

Designed by Leah Carlson-Stanisic

Library of Congress Cataloging-in-Publication Data is available upon request.

ISBN-10: 0-06-082066-7
ISBN: 978-0-06-082066-4

07   08   09   10   /RRD   10   9   8   7   6   5   4   3   2   1

For Doug

There is no jewel, be it of never so rich a price, which I set before this jewel—I mean your loves. For I do more esteem it than any treasure or riches, for that we know how to prize. But love and thanks I count unvaluable [invaluable], and though God hath raised me high, yet this I count the glory of my crown: that I have reigned with your loves. This makes me that I do not so much rejoice that God hath made me to be a queen, as to be a queen over so thankful a people . . . so I trust by the almighty power of God that I shall be His instrument to preserve you from envy, peril, dishonor, shame, tyranny, and oppression, partly by means of your intended helps . . . .

— EXTRACT FROM ELIZABETH I's *Golden Speech* TO PARLIAMENT
NOVEMBER 30, 1601

Contents ❦

Illustrations ❧

The Drake Cup, by kind permission of Plymouth Museums and Art Gallery

The Drake Chair, by permission of the Bodleian Library, University of Oxford, ref. Neg.PR. 1831

Martin Frobisher, by permission of the Bodleian Library, University of Oxford, ref. LP 50

Sir Walter Raleigh, by "H," by permission of the National Portrait Gallery, London

Sir Henry Sidney, by Arnold van Brounckhorst, by permission of the National Portrait Gallery, London

Sir Philip Sidney, by unknown artist, by permission of the National Portrait Gallery, London

Robert Devereux, second Earl of Essex, by unknown artist, by permission of the National Portrait Gallery, London

The Deed of Grant of Virginia to Sir Walter Raleigh, by the kind permission of Plymouth Museums and Art Gallery

View of the Thames, by the Flemish School, by the kind permission of the Museum of London

Troops Arriving in Antwerp, by permission of the British Library

Letter from Elizabeth I to Sir William Cecil in the queen's hand, 1572, by permission of the Bodleian Library, University of Oxford, ref. Ashmole 1729, fol. 13

View of River Thames and the Tower of London, by permission of the British Library

The Armada Tapestry, by the kind permission of Plymouth Museums and Art Gallery

Matthew Baker, shipwright, Designing a Ship, by the kind permission of the Pepsyian Library, University of Cambridge

Baker's design of a ship using a cod to demonstrate the desired shape, by the kind permission of the Pepsyian Library, University of Cambridge

Map of Western Atlantic from Newfoundland to Brazil, by Freducci, by permission of the National Maritime Museum, Greenwich

The Armada Portrait of Queen Elizabeth I, by kind permission of His Grace the Duke of Bedford and the Trustees of the Bedford Estates

Acknowledgments ⚹

To perhaps misquote Sir Isaac Newton, "If I have been able to see as far as I have, it is because I have been able to stand upon the shoulders of giants." Great subjects like Elizabeth Tudor and all her adventurers have survived to be written about from the Elizabethan era to the current day due to the loving attention of so many individuals across the generations—both known and anonymous. They are too numerous to thank individually here, but I would like to thank each and every one of you en masse. I owe you so much above all others for allowing me to glimpse into Elizabeth's world. To the scores of original-manuscript collectors like Sir Thomas Egerton; Sir Thomas Bodley; Robert Cecil, the Marquis of Salisbury, through to Sir Hans Sloane, my thanks for your feverish gathering of letters and papers of national and international importance, and your keeping them safe for later generations. To the Victorian greats like Julian Corbett, Michael Oppenheimer, and all the researchers and painstaking editors of the thousands of letters engrossed into the volumes of the *Calendar of State Papers*, the *Acts of the Privy Council*, the Hakluyt Society, and the Seldon Society for its *Register of the High Court of Admiralty Pleas*, I am truly in your debt. The modern greats like R. B. Wernham, Irene A. Wright, Conyers Read, Professor Kenneth R. Andrews, John Sugden, N. A. M. Rodgers, and David Loades are the true masters of Elizabeth's maritime England, and Geoffrey Parker remains unexcelled in my opinion as the English language's expert on Philip II and the Dutch Revolt. Without the great institutions and their incredibly helpful staffs at the British Library, the National Archives, the Caird Library at the National Maritime Museum, the University of Oxford and the Bodleian Library, the Bank of England, the Folger Shakespeare Library in Washington, D.C., and the most remarkable Archivio de Indias in Seville, this book would simply not have been possible.

I would also like to thank all those who had a hand in making the visual side of the book so very special. To the National Portrait Gallery; the National Maritime Museum Picture Library; the Bodleian Library; the Pepysian Library, Magdalene College,

Cambridge; the British Library; the Walker Gallery and Liverpool Museums; Museum of Plymouth; Museum of London; the Royal College of Arms; the Wallace Collection; and particularly His Grace, the Duke of Bedford, I would like to extend my special thank-you.

My personal thanks to my researcher, Andrew Balerdi, for freeing me up to complete this book by beginning research on the next one for me. To my sons—Matt, Zandy, and Andrew—thanks for putting up with me. To my mother, my heartfelt thanks for your support. To my editor, the extraordinary Hugh Van Dusen at HarperCollins, and the entire HarperCollins team (Marie Estrada, Robert Crawford, and all those behind the scenes), thank you, thank you, thank you. To my agent, Alexander Hoyt: Who would have thought...?

And to my husband, Doug, without whom nothing could ever be possible, this is for you.

Author's Note ✤

For those readers looking for a bodice ripper about Elizabeth's loves, I fear I would disappoint you in *The Pirate Queen*. But if, on the other hand, you always wanted to know *more* about Elizabeth as a person and a monarch, then please read on. Since I was a young child I have been fascinated by Elizabeth Tudor beyond her putative love affairs, and especially how this phenomenal woman had been able to rule with an iron fist in an age of pure male domination. She was the first female ruler of England to rule in her own right. However one speculates about her real reasons, she was determined to remain her own mistress and thereby guarantee England its independence from foreign domination. I especially wanted to know how she was able to achieve this so successfully.

The Pirate Queen, in part, provided me, and hopefully will provide you, with many of the answers. She had the quick intellect of her mother, her father's boldness, and both of their bad tempers. She was hugely vain and courageous; highly educated and gifted; monumentally abused in her youth and shunned by family, church, and society. She at times played her advisors and courtiers consciously off against one another, and more often than not she listened to the sage counsels of William Cecil, Lord Burghley, above all others. Robert Dudley, Earl of Leicester, remained the love of her life, and, as such, it is immaterial if that love was consummated. In the queen's mind, she was a virgin, married to the country, and intent on keeping England independent of foreign princes, come what may. Elizabeth was all these things, and many more.

In her time, the English Renaissance took root and flourished, spawning the great talents of Sidney, Gascoigne, Spenser, Kyd, Marlowe—and killing three of the five in "service of the realm" prematurely. Great poets like Raleigh, the embodiment of courtly love and adventuring, as well as Dyer, a gentleman adventurer, too, help us glimpse behind the curtain of time into Elizabeth's court. Chettle, Nashe, Lodge, and, of course, the remarkable Shakespeare, all found their voice in Elizabeth's England. But why was this so? The reasons are far too varied to do justice to here, other than to say that the writers themselves reflected the times: ordinary people went to the theater to learn about history or England's friends and foes. It was a time of tremendous change, and the queen herself wanted to engage her people (on her side naturally) in the process. That engagement process was a double-edge sword—making and breaking the lives of her most gifted early writers. It also transformed English from a language spoken by very few on the fringes of Europe into the ever-changing, ever-growing world lingua franca that it is today.

In the cauldron brewing between Protestant and Catholic, courtier and adventurer, Spain and the Papacy, Ireland and Scotland, the Dutch and their Spanish overlords, Elizabeth remained constant, imperious, and imperial. She dominated all she surveyed through cunning, wit, loyalty, charm, bad temper, an aura of extreme wealth, and parsimony. It was her parsimony that aggravated her courtiers and councillors to distraction, making her seem weak and indecisive. She was famous for giving her "answer answerless" and wearing her opponents down with her rhetorical arguments. Yet in the end, she became the embodiment of the English psyche and kept the country independent from the Catholic threats posed by Spain and the Papacy. She survived more than twenty assassination attempts, and, with her, England survived, too.

She was above all an incredibly astute businesswoman as head of state. She feared marriage for myriad reasons, and knew instinctively that by naming an heir she would sow the seeds of her own destruction. For forty-four years she successfully evaded this fundamental issue at the heart of her reign. Nonetheless, she was no empire builder. In the simplest terms, if she had been, then she would have wanted a family to keep the Tudor Dynasty alive. But her aversion to empire wouldn't prevent her gentlemen adventurers from embracing the concept.

*

All English foreign interests were, at the outset of Elizabeth's reign, either financial or defensive. Antwerp was the main export and money market since the fall of Calais to the French a year before she came to power. With the growth of Protestantism in the Low Countries, Antwerp's stranglehold on northern trade came under threat, and England needed to look elsewhere for foreign trade, or perish. The mid-1550s saw the first English forays into a faraway commercial entente with Russia through the formation of the

Muscovy Company, in the hope that it would lead to a northerly route to Cathay [China] and direct trade with the Far East. When this failed to materialize, other routes—not already claimed by the Portuguese or Spanish empires—were sought. When both great world empires resisted English "interloping," viewed by the English as attempts at commercial trade, the age of English maritime expansion, or merchant and gentlemen adventuring on a large scale, was born. It is the relationship between Elizabeth and this disparate breed of men and how they worked together for what was believed to be the common "weal"—the enrichment of England and themselves—that is the primary focus of *The Pirate Queen*.

Still, to better understand that focus, it is also vital to understand how weak England was when the twenty-five-year-old Elizabeth became queen. Defense of the realm—and the queen—was the greatest worry on everyone's mind. Throughout her personal writing, the single-minded attention she gives to "security" is quite heartbreaking. And the central theme of security remains the golden thread woven through the intricate fabric of her reign—security for herself before she came to power, supplanted by security for the realm thereafter. In her mind, to create a secure realm, she needed two things: peace and money. When peace was gained at home through deft footwork by the queen and her advisors within the first year of Elizabeth's reign, the disappointed French (under the mother of Mary Queen of Scots), who had tried to invade England, found themselves ousted instead from Scotland. It was through Elizabeth's gentlemen adventurers that the attempt was foiled, and through her merchant adventurers that money was raised to protect the realm and pay for England's soldiers. In those days, plunder was how soldiers and mariners believed they were paid for the risks they took, and it remained common military policy until World War II, to turn a blind eye to the practice.

It was precisely these two groups of adventurers who would eventually deliver the security for the realm that both the queen and the country craved. They would, inadvertently, mind you, transform England into the nascent modern economy and empire that would dominate the world by the end of the eighteenth century. Had Philip II of Spain allowed the English to trade freely in his American dominions and beyond, it is entirely possible that the British Empire would have been quite different.

I have a passion for original sources and, before beginning any research in earnest, go through original manuscripts to get a better feel for the individuals I will be writing about. In Elizabeth's case, I was blessed with a wealth of material. Gentlemen adventurers like Sir Francis Walsingham; Robert Dudley, Earl of Leicester; Sir Walter Raleigh; and Sir Francis Drake provided me with a rich vein to tap into. Merchant adventurers like Sir Thomas Gresham; William Cecil, Lord Burghley; and his second son, Sir Robert Cecil, wrote nearly every day during their tenures in office. Only some of those original manuscripts are detailed in the selected bibliography along with other primary and secondary sources.

Before beginning to read on, there are a number of points that I feel need clarification at the outset. The first relates to dates. In 1582, Pope Gregory XIII introduced the Gregorian calendar that we use today. In October 1582, all Catholic countries moved their dates forward by ten days, which is sometimes termed New Style by authors, with the Julian calendar dates termed Old Style. By 1587, most of Europe used the Gregorian calendar. England, however, refused and did not adopt this calendar until 1751. This meant that when it was March 11 in England, and the first day of spring, the date in France was March 21. In addition, New Year's Day was on March 25 in England. The reasons for England's stubbornness on this matter will become apparent in the course of the book. Since my references are for the most part English, I have converted any New Style dates to Old Style for ease of understanding. Also, I have made New Year's Day January 1, instead of March 25, for the same reason.

Place names were also different from time to time, and after the first usage of those names, I have put the modern equivalent in square brackets [ ]. Thereafter, I use the original name, which has been introduced previously. In quotations, I have also provided modern meanings for obscure words, where I felt the reader would have difficulty, in brackets [ ] next to the offending word. These definitions have, by and large, been provided by the Oxford English

Dictionary entry for that word. Spellings have also been modernized into American English, except where they appear in direct quotations from the period. I have, where appropriate, inserted modern British English spellings in these quotations.

Rates of exchange between currencies are derived from a number of sources ranging from the *Calendar of State Papers*, to merchants' certifications, to the Bank of England. Thanks to the Bank of England I have been able to provide you with a good estimate of what, say, £1,000 in 1599 for example would be worth today. (It's £129,890 by the way.) I must stress, however, that these modern conversion rates are approximate only, and are primarily based on the Retail Price Indices available at the time, again through the Bank of England. Since conversion rates in modern times fluctuate more rapidly than in Elizabeth's era, it's important to remember that a glut or shortage of commodities (gold in particular) in a commercial market would have a greater effect on currencies than, say, what a loaf of bread (a local product) might cost.

When I began writing, the U.S. dollar was struggling to keep below $2 to the pound sterling. By the time I finished the book, the dollar rate had improved to $1.75 to the pound (though still fluctuating). The prognosis from the Bank of England, UBS, CFSB, and Barclays for the coming year is that the dollar-to-sterling exchange rate has been $1.65 to the pound, but the dollar rally would be short lived. To hedge my bets, I've used $1.85 to the pound in my conversions, mainly because I believe that this is the dollar's natural level for the next year. Again, the conversion rates to today's currencies are not exact, and are merely intended to be a representative modern equivalent in dollars and sterling in an effort to aid the reader's understanding.

In an attempt to add clarity for the non-British reader, I have also tried to treat elevations to various aristocratic titles uniformly. Once an individual receives a title, I wrote out his full name, for example, Robert Dudley, Earl of Leicester, and thereafter referred to him as Leicester. This is the way it is normally handled in the United Kingdom. Similarly, since there was a plethora of "Marys" during Elizabeth's reign, I have usually tried to adopt their titles as soon as possible so that they could be more readily differentiated.

There are two terms that are used repeatedly throughout the book: Merchants Adventurers/merchant adventurers. On the former, whenever the words Merchants Adventurers appear, it is intended to signify the Company of Merchants Adventurers or their members. Whenever the term is not capitalized, it means investors or merchants who are traders. Whichever one it is intended to be will be clear in the sentence.

"Pirate" is a word at the heart of the book. The word "privateer" was not coined until the eighteenth century, and I had a terrible objection to using a word that had not as yet been invented, and then to describe someone with that word used for the first time two hundred years into the future. In the 1560s and 1570s, the words "pirate," "corsair," and "rover" are used interchangeably for the queen's illegal traders. An "interloper" was specifically someone who traded illegally in a foreign country either against English interests or foreign ones. (These tended not to be pirates at all.) When a "pirate" raided shipping with the queen's (or another ruler's) approval, they are described as holding "letters of reprisal" or "letters of marque."

As Elizabeth's "pirates" (for that's what many of them were, essentially) evolved into her "adventurers" the word "pirate" is filtered out. An adventurer in Elizabeth's time was anyone who was prepared to take a risk—from the financial entrepreneurs we would recognize today, to an illegal trader ("interloper"), to a merchant trying his luck, or an out-and-out pirate.

Above all, I hope I have lifted the veil on Elizabeth as a leader: her methods of dominating her men; why her famed use of a woman's prerogative to "change her mind" was in most instances a tactical political weapon, astutely wielded to wrong foot the opposition; and why State-sponsored piracy and plunder was the only way England could survive.

Finally, while I have endeavored to be accurate at all times, if there are any errors, I must assure the reader that they are entirely my own.

SUSAN RONALD,
OXFORD, 2006

Introduction ❧

Bilbao, Spain
Six P.M., Wednesday, May 26, 1585

Master Foster gazed upon Bilbao harbor, feasting his eyes on the fine sight of so many Londoners that had heeded the King of Spain's call for help. Philip II had invited English merchants to send cargoes of corn, and assured the Queen's Majesty that her people would have his very own assurance of safe conduct in these troubled times. Payment for the corn would be made by bills of exchange payable to the City of London in Antwerp at fair-market prices. And so, the *Primrose*, a 150-ton Londoner, had been stocked with nearly twenty tons of corn and several ells of broadcloth, and set sail for Bilbao in Biscay.

Master Foster had heard that the country was starving; that the whole of Iberia had had a harsh winter, though the master of the *Primrose* and his men could be no firm judges of that fact for themselves. Bilbao had been bathed in warm sunshine the past two days in port, and the Spaniards they had seen appeared to have been well fed. Indeed, as Foster took in the near idyllic scene with the sun low in the sky, its rays reflecting lazily on the bay, Bilbao seemed a welcoming voice on the wind as she had always been.

It was then that he noted the soft groan of his rigging. A fine southwesterly was stirring. Foster prayed it would still be blowing the following day when they would weigh anchor and head for home. He hunched over the rail of his ship, leaning heavily on his arms, and looked on as a number of sleek Spanish pinnaces darted between his fellow Londoners. It was one of those rare moments of leisure for the captain of an English merchantman. Perhaps that is why he did not spy the pinnace heading for the *Primrose*. When the watch called out the approach of the Spanish vessel, and that there were seven souls aboard, Foster awoke from his reverie and barked his orders to the crew, alerting them that a small party wished to board. What the devil could they want at this time of the evening? the *Primrose*'s cargoes had been unladen. It was most unusual for the Spanish merchants to settle their bills of exchange at this hour of the day. Further, the master of the *Primrose* had already settled the matter of loading the Spanish wines for the return voyage the following day.

It was a wary Foster who greeted the corregidor [magistrate] of Biscay. The hale and hearty fellow presented Foster to the six other men as Biscayan merchants, and claimed that they wished to give him a small token of their esteem. They had brought a hamper full of fresh cherries as a gift—a favorite of the English queen, or so they had understood. Master Foster thanked them and ordered that beef, biscuit, and beer be brought to the impromptu gathering in his cabin. Yet before they sat down to eat, four of the Biscayan merchants made their excuses and announced their intention to return to shore aboard the Spanish pinnace. This lack of common civility made Foster truly smell danger.

He ordered his first mate to accompany the Spaniards back on deck, simultaneously giving him the signal that all was not as it should be. It was a well-rehearsed exercise for English merchantmen in foreign waters, and the first mate knew how to alert the crew in secret to be ready for an assault.

The master of the *Primrose* returned to his unwanted guests, laughing and joking with them in broken Spanish and English, noting all the while through the porthole the pinks and oranges of the setting sun, wondering undoubtedly if it would be his last sunset. After some fifteen minutes, the watch called out again that the pinnace had returned carrying more than twenty men and that a larger vessel with perhaps as many as seventy merchants also followed. Foster silently prayed that God would be English this day.

The master bade the corregidor and his men to return to deck to greet the ships, expecting the worst. They were, after all, only twenty-six men against some ninety or more Spaniards. He could only imagine that these Biscayan merchants meant to board the *Primrose*, capture the crew, and, at best, imprison them all. Many a merchantman had been imprisoned before them, and most had fallen foul of the Inquisition. It was a destiny that he could not wish upon his enemies.

Once above deck, Foster's suspicions were confirmed. Turning to the magistrate and his two friends, he said that he could not allow such a group of men to board his small ship, and the corregidor nodded compliantly. Yet before Foster could give his crew the final signal to repulse an attack, he heard the beat of the battle drum from the Spanish ships below and the unmistakable sound of their swords being unsheathed. The thud of the grappling irons and the roar of the Biscayans wrestling alongside the *Primrose* to board her by force drowned out his orders to his men.

The corregidor and his "merchants" seized Foster with daggers drawn at his throat and cried out above the shouts of the melee, "Yield yourself for you are the king's prisoner!"

Foster narrowed his eyes and bellowed back, "We are betrayed!"

The crew of the *Primrose* had fortunately taken the defensive measures that her master had laid down for circumstances such as these. Within seconds, five calivers were fired through the grates from below decks at the Spaniards scuffling above. There were screams from those Biscayans who had legs blown off, and shouts to abandon their action from others. They could not know that it was the only gunpowder and shot that the *Primrose* had on board. But the few seconds of confusion the blast created was enough to turn the tide. Foster prized himself loose from his captors and gave the order to fight to the death. Many of the Biscayans fled back to the boarding vessels, fearing that they would be blown to smithereens, as several of their number had been seconds before. Others stood their ground. Hand-to-hand battle broke out, and the well-practiced English drill of a skirmish at sea ensued. The English, knowing that if they were forced from the ship, they would die a thousand slow deaths, fought like demons possessed with boar-spears and lances, which whipped through two to three Spaniards at a stroke.[1] Yet, despite the heavy carnage on the Spanish side, the outcome of the battle remained in doubt for a time. The only certainty to Foster and his men was that the deck of the *Primrose* was stained red with the blood of the Spaniards and Englishmen.

Some Spaniards were flung overboard; many of them begged for their lives, since they could not swim. The corregidor once again managed to put a dagger to Foster's throat, demanding that his men cease their fruitless opposition, or Foster would forfeit his own life. The master replied, "Such is the courage of the English nation in defense of their own lives that they would prefer to slay them [the Spanish]."[2] In the heat of the attack, no one had witnessed how Master Foster had freed himself from the corregidor's clutches, and Foster himself never told the tale.

The fighting raged on for another half an hour with many Spanish Biscayans butchered, flung overboard, or drowned before the English could claim victory. Amazingly, only one Englishman, John Tristam, had been killed. Six other members of the crew were injured, but Foster thought they would survive their wounds. He had to presume that his two men, John Burrell and John Broadbank, who had delivered the last of the corn cargo, had been taken into custody ashore. While the master and his crew made ready to set sail, Foster was perplexed why the Biscayan merchants who had escaped in the pinnaces did not bring reinforcements. He could not understand, at the moment of his own victory, why no armed relief for the corregidor had come.

While he decided what should be done with the unfortunates struggling for their lives in the bay, Foster looked out across the harbor for the first time since the assault. All the other Londoners had the King of Spain's flag flying high on their masts. The Spanish treachery was now clear. The English ships had been lured into Spanish harbors for Philip II to confiscate in a master piratical act, and leave England helpless.

As the *Primrose* tacked into the bay, Foster knew that he must reach England in all haste and warn the City of London merchants. He took one last glance down at the Biscayans bobbing upon the water as the *Primrose*'s sails filled with the southwesterly, and spied the corregidor and his "merchants." Foster quickly ordered the crew to fish the Spanish pirates out of the sea.

Once safely away from the Spanish shoreline, Foster demanded that the corregidor and his men be brought to his cabin for questioning. The Spanish officials who had been hale and hearty only two hours earlier now stood trembling and drenched in their bare feet in Foster's quarters. The master ordered the corregidor to answer why he and his men had boarded the *Primrose* and the other

English vessels in harbor—ships that had come in peace at the behest of their king, delivering much needed corn and other sustenance to Spain?

The magistrate replied that it was none of his doing, and that if Master Foster would allow someone to fetch his hose, which were hanging up to dry, the master could see with his very own eyes that he had a commission from the King of Spain himself to seize all ships from "heretic countries."

When the commission was brought back for Foster to read, he scanned the drenched document. While the ink had run somewhat, the words "A great fleet was being prepared. . . . An embargo against foreign shipping is to take place with immediate effect. . . . You must seize all ships in harbor or attempting to come into harbor, and without exception those ships from Holland, Zeeland, Easterland, Germany and England, and any other country not in service of the king, except those ships from France . . . " remained clearly visible. The order had been signed by King Philip II himself in Barcelona a week before.

Foster had the corregidor sent back to the hold with his three "merchants," Francisco de Guevarra, Pedro de Villas Reale, and John de Corale.[3] The crew was ordered to treat their prisoners well, since they may well be worth a ransom. In fact, the corregidor had already offered Foster five hundred crowns to set them free. The master knew they were worth far more than that to the City of London, and that the king's instructions alone would warrant special recognition from the queen herself.

As Foster knew full well, the commission from the King of Spain would be of the greatest interest undoubtedly to the Privy Council. Its discovery might even earn him a place in naval history.

Part One

The Desperate Quest for Security

November 1558–November 1568

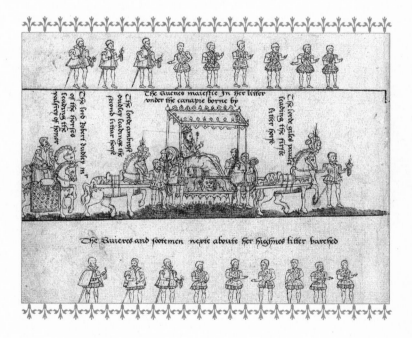

1. The Lord's Doing ✦

November 17, 1558

The dominion of the sea, as it is the ancient and undoubted right of the crown of England, so it is the best security of the land. . . .
The wooden walls [of ships] are the best walls of the kingdom.

—THOMAS COVENTRY, FIRST BARON COVENTRY, 1635

When Elizabeth Tudor inherited the kingdom from her half sister Mary I, in November 1558, England was on the brink of ruin. The feeling of despair among the nobles can only be imagined: not only had the country been torn between the ultra-Protestant reign of Elizabeth's half brother, Edward VI, followed by the fanatically Catholic Mary, but the crown was now proffered to the daughter of the reviled Queen Anne Boleyn. Elizabeth, who had lived her life as an unwelcome reminder of the union of Henry VIII and her mother, would most assuredly have been burned at the stake by Mary without the intervention of the queen's absentee husband, Philip II of Spain. If there was one thing Elizabeth Tudor understood intuitively, it was life on the edge.

Personal security was a luxury of which she must have dreamed as a child and young woman, and barely dared to hope for when her sister was queen. Mary had kept her prisoner, removing the Lady Elizabeth from palace to palace to prevent the next heir to the throne from plotting against her. During Elizabeth's time locked away in the Tower of London, each day could have brought the royal command for her execution, yet each day, the queen hesitated. It was in the Tower that Elizabeth's lifelong devotion to another prisoner, Robert Dudley, blossomed.

Dudley, too, knew life on the edge: his father and grandfather had been executed for high treason, and it looked highly likely that he would follow them to the scaffold for plotting to overthrow Queen Mary. Dudley's loyalty to Elizabeth had been absolute before their imprisonment, often to the detriment of his own security. After their time together in the Tower, Elizabeth could never doubt his loyalty again. It was the only sure thing in her vulnerable life.

When Mary's latest phantom pregnancy in the spring of 1558 did not produce a child, it was obvious to King Philip, the Privy Council, and the court that the swelling in Mary's abdomen was a tumor and not the heir that the king and queen had so desired. With only Mary Stuart, Queen of Scots, remaining as a potential heir apparent, this left Philip in no doubt as to the course of action to be undertaken: Elizabeth must be set free and named as his wife's heir. If Mary Queen of Scots were to take the throne of England, she would have become queen of Scotland, Wales, Ireland, and England. These titles and kingdoms would have been added to her title as Queen of France, since she had lived in the French court since the age of five and had married the Dauphin Francis earlier in the year. Although Catholic, Philip was not prepared to allow the teenagers Mary and Francis to become the powerful pawns to Francis's mother, Catherine de' Medici. At all cost, he must stop the French crown from trying to abscond with Elizabeth's throne.

Besides, Philip could not promote Mary Stuart's claim to the English throne above his own, since he, too, had a direct claim through his mother, Isabelle of Portugal, a descendant of John of Gaunt of Lancaster. No, Elizabeth was a far better alternative as heir presumptive for Philip despite the fact that he had long known that she practiced the Protestant rites in private. This may have been the most important act of religious tolerance and clemency in the history of his long rule.

While Philip was agonizing over his deliberations and eventually paving the road for Elizabeth to take the crown, the English nobility—Protestant and Catholic alike—had already made up their minds. A mood of desperation had crept over the country. As the autumn of 1558 turned chillier in early November, the roads to Hatfield House in Hertfordshire, Elizabeth's childhood home, were gridlocked with those who had served her half sister, as well as others who had been exiled from power. All of them were singular in their purpose: to serve the new queen and better their positions.

For the power brokers like William Cecil, who had served faithfully as secretary of state for Mary and Philip, Elizabeth not only represented the only viable successor, but also a fiercely intelligent one with whom he could do business. Others had different viewpoints. Philip's ambassador, Count Feria, who had also made his way to Hatfield, wrote to the king on November 10 that "she is a very vain and clever woman. She must have been thoroughly schooled in the manner in which her father conducted his affairs and I am very much afraid that she will not be well-disposed in matters of religion. . . . There is not a heretic or traitor in all the kingdom who has not joyfully raised himself from the grave to come to her side. She is determined to be governed by no one."[1]

This was no "news" to Philip. During Elizabeth's imprisonment in the Tower, she had written to Mary that "I so well like this estate [spinsterhood] as I persuade myself there is not any kind of life comparable unto it . . . no though I were offered to the greatest prince of all Europe . . . [I would] rather proceed of a maidenly shamefastness than upon any certain determination."[2] For Elizabeth, who had undergone so many wrongs and near rape at the hands of her uncle, the hapless Thomas Seymour, the future queen had learned all the brutal lessons required of a young, handsome woman that were necessary in the art of sexual politics of the sixteenth century. No man would ever become her master and make her insecure in her position. After all, the Low Countries had eventually become Spanish through the marriage of a female heir. Francis of France was now equally King of Scotland. Moreover, the lessons to be drawn from marriage could never have been very far from her conscious mind with a father like Henry VIII.

While no record remains of her intimate discussions with William Cecil, the Earl of Pembroke, and the Earl of Shrewsbury in the early days of November 1558, these three gentlemen would have "schooled" the future queen in the secrets on the present state of preparedness of England. It was not a pretty picture. To Scotland in the North, the dowager Queen Mary of Guise, who had been ruling Scotland along with the nobles during Queen Mary's minority, had amassed some twenty thousand French troops on the border of England. Since 1557, the nobles had refused to fight under her banner against England, but the war continued nonetheless. From Elizabeth's perspective, bereft of a standing English army and wholly reliant upon her northern, and mostly Catholic nobles' men, the French troops looked more like an invasion force than a defensive one.

In the West, Ireland refused steadfastly to be subdued—either by England or by her own nobility. The country appeared to be in a state of perpetual tribal warfare, and now that Elizabeth wanted England to become a Protestant realm again, she would risk invasion from the West if the fighting in Ireland united her people against a common English Protestant enemy. It did not take her savant mathematician astronomer, John Dee, to tell Elizabeth that trouble could be fomented in Ireland by other Catholic countries like France or Spain through the provision of men or arms.

On the Continent, Philip had dragged Mary's England into his wars with France in the Low Countries. His action against the French not only drained the English coffers of cash, but the country of able men to adequately defend its borders should Mary of England die as expected. In order to fight his war, not only had Philip impoverished his wife's kingdom, but he had also emptied his own treasury, and was effectively bankrupt for the first time in 1557.[3] Philip's rule in the Low Countries had become downright unpopular, not only because the majority of the inhabitants of the seventeen provinces, or states, were Calvinist; but also due to Philip's style of personal rule. Anything that was not Spanish was inferior for Philip, and the people of the Low Countries found their ancient rights eroded under what appeared to be more and more like a foreign occupation.

Yet it was the loss of Calais that represented the greatest threat to Elizabeth's people. Not only was it catastrophic in terms of the national pride, but, more important, Calais was the primary staple town of all English merchant staple exporters, as it was where they had their wool spun. Since broadcloth was England's principal export, made from the wool spun at Calais, trade was at an all-time low. People were starving, imports were scarce, and death rates soared from war, poor hygiene, and famine. And still, Queen

Mary's pyres of Protestant "heretics" burned, their stench wafting throughout the realm.

In fact, the England Elizabeth was about to inherit was downright poor, torn apart by years of religious strife and war. Not only was she a woman in a man's world, but she had been the "bastard" daughter of Henry VIII, whose dynasty held only the most tenuous claim to the throne of England.[4] When or how Elizabeth had decided on her course of action should she become queen is undoubtedly the culmination of many years of statecraft instilled into her by the very life she led, and her progressive tutor, Roger Ascham. It was no accident of fate that on November 17, 1558, Elizabeth Tudor was standing under the great, ancient oak tree at Hatfield House when the royal messengers rode into the park. It is a scene that has been portrayed in most movies and books about Elizabeth, and was the first act of symbolism in her reign. For ancient oaks equated a nation's strength and durability—the ancient Britons worshipped them. The hearts of these oaks became masts for the tall ships that would come to symbolize the greatness of the Empire by the end of her reign. When Elizabeth took the royal ring that had signified Mary's reign and now her death, and slipped it upon her own finger, the new queen kneeled by that gnarled and storm-struck oak and said, "*A domino factum est mirabile in oculis nostris.*"[5]

This is the Lord's doing, and it is marvelous to our eyes.

2. A Realm Exhausted ⚡

Division among ourselves; war with France and Scotland;
The French King bestriding the realm . . . steadfast enmity,
but no steadfast friendship abroad.
CSP—DOMESTIC, ELIZABETH, *vol. 1. no. 66*

Within twenty-four hours of Elizabeth's accession, orders had
gone out to her newly formed Privy Council. On the day of
Queen Mary's death, William Cecil, Elizabeth's principal secretary,
wrote and distributed a memorandum with the form of oath to
be taken by the privy councillors. The following day, Sir Nicholas
Throckmorton wrote to the queen that he had sequestered Cardinal
Pole's house and goods on the queen's instructions.[1] Throckmorton
also confirmed that he had executed Elizabeth's instructions to the
Duke of Norfolk, Elizabeth's uncle Thomas Howard; the Earl of
Bedford, John Russell; and Lord Cobham, William Brooke. All
ships at port would be confined there until a complete audit of
goods, ships, and men could be established.[2] By the time forty-eight
hours had elapsed, Cecil had commissions and instructions for the
"Lords now beyond the sea" and had orders for Thomas Gresham,
the queen's money man and arms dealer in the Low Countries.[3]

Elizabeth's expectations from William Cecil were spelled out
clearly in her first public speech from Hatfield on November 20,
1558:

I give you this charge, that you shall be of my Privy Council and
content yourself to take pains for me and my realm. This judgment I
have of you: that you will not be corrupted with any manner of gift,
and that you will be faithful to the state, and that without respect
of my private will, you will give me that counsel that you think
best, and if you shall know anything necessary to be declared to me
of secrecy, you shall show it to myself only. And assure yourself I

will not fail to keep taciturnity therein, and therefore herewith I charge you.[4]

The following day, Count Feria, Philip's ambassador to England who had married Queen Mary's favorite lady-in-waiting, Jane Dormer, wrote to the king from Hatfield, "our lady the Queen died."[5] Then in his own private code, Feria continued:

I think your Majesty must have a copy of the will … as I have written to your Majesty it is very early yet to talk about marriage … the confusion and ineptitude of these people in all their affairs make it necessary for us to be more circumspect, so as not to miss the opportunities which are presented to us, and particularly in the matter of marriage. For this and other reasons (if there be no objection) it will be well to send me a copy of the [marriage] treaty, which, though it may not be very necessary, will at least serve to post me up as to what would be touched upon, although a new treaty would be different from the last.

The new Queen and her people hold themselves free from your Majesty and will listen to any ambassadors who may come to treat of marriage. Your Majesty understands better than I how important it is that this affair should go through your hands, which as I have said will be difficult except with great negotiation and money. I therefore wish your Majesty to keep in view all the steps to be taken on your behalf, one of them being that the Emperor should not send any ambassador here to treat of this, for it would be inconvenient enough for Ferdinand to marry here even if he took the titbit from your Majesty's hand, but very much worse if it were arranged in any other way. For the present, I know for certain they will not hear the name of the duke of Savoy mentioned as they fear he will want to recover his estates with English forces and will keep them constantly at war. I am very pleased to see that the nobles are all beginning to open their eyes to the fact that it will not do to marry this woman in the country itself.[6]

By the end of November, Elizabeth's Privy Council had been formed save the office of lord keeper, which was eventually taken up by William Cecil's brother-in-law, Sir Nicholas Bacon, in January

1559.[7] A nationwide audit of men and arms was under way for one purpose in mind: to assess how empty the queen's coffers were and how in the devil she could secure her borders.[8]

At the same time, letters were fired off in rapid succession to potential sources of ready cash. On November 27, Cecil wrote on behalf of the Privy Council to London's "lord mayor, Aldermen and Common Council . . . for the sealing of certain bands for the taking up of divers sums of money at Antwerp for the Queen's Majesty by Thomas Gresham, her Highness's Agent there."[9] This was followed up with another letter to the lord mayor, Aldermen, and Common Council to plead for the City of London's merchants in helping to secure funds in Flanders.[10]

No one in England was more acutely aware of the precariousness of her position than Elizabeth herself. For her Catholic population, Mary Queen of Scots held a better claim to the throne as the great-granddaughter of Henry VII through his eldest daughter, Margaret, who was born before Henry VIII. The maternal uncles of Mary Queen of Scots, the powerful French Guise family, ruled Scotland by virtue of the Queen Mother's regency in the name of the French crown, and the common plaint among privy councillors was that Henry II, the French king, was "bestriding the realm, having one foot in Calais and the other in Scotland."[11] This simple fact made the urgency for a religious settlement that could be acceptable to both English Protestants and Catholics essential. Even the Venetian ambassador wrote back to the Doges that the English would be well able "to resist any invasion from abroad, providing there be union within the kingdom."[12]

By autumn 1558 when Elizabeth came to the throne, Philip II and Henry II had begun their peace negotiations. Military operations had ceased, and both realms were determined to make a lasting peace primarily due to their own financial chaos and religious strife in the Spanish-held Low Countries and France. Besides, Philip had wars of religion he was fighting against the Turks in North Africa and the western Mediterranean, and internally, against the Moriscos in Spain. The last thing he could literally afford was to fight a powerful Catholic monarch like the king of France. For Philip, matters of religion always took precedence over temporal matters, and it was essential that Catholic governments unite against the very real expansionist threat of the Turkish Empire and the spread of Calvinism. Elizabeth and Cecil, who both had known Philip well when he had been king consort of England, did not need to listen to the incessant distortions swirling on the winds to know that the greatest danger they faced would be a Catholic League against a Protestant monarchy in England. What they agreed (though few at the time believed that Elizabeth and Cecil could carry out) was to turn Philip's religious zeal into a concern for his empire, by exploiting the opportunities that came their way—or that they could create—with whatever weapons they could conjure for their English arsenal. The potential threat of an invasion from France, or from the French in Scotland, was very real, and the only way Elizabeth saw to forestall this was to pander to Philip's paranoia.

The scene was now set. The negotiators were united at Cateau-Cambrésis to hammer out a lasting peace, and Elizabeth steadfastly held on to the hope of not ceding Calais, ostensibly due to the loss of England's pride and the commercial staple there. Another and more understandable reason was military; with Calais only twenty-six miles across the Narrow Seas, or Straits of Dover, and the French in control of Scotland, Henry and his belligerent dukes represented a potent threat to England's security. The silent reason for her obstinacy—which would later become one of her trademarks—was simply that she was stalling for time to see how best to play upon the mutual jealousies of the Spanish Habsburg and French Valois kings.[13]

She did not have long to wait. It was Henry II who gave her the first breakthrough. Through an Italian merchant of considerable standing and knowledge of England, Guido Cavalcanti, Henry secretly suggested that if Elizabeth would marry someone "of whose friendship France could feel assured," great amity between their realms would ensue.[14] It was understood that the "someone" was Henry's younger son, Henry, Duke of Anjou (later Henry III). Naturally, the queen made Philip II aware of the offer, thereby guaranteeing the King of Spain's protection against the Valois threats, either expressed or implied.

In the meantime, Elizabeth knew that she needed to rally around her people as well as her noble lords to protect her borders. Both groups would understand the force of arms and the potential threat that France represented. It was Cecil's job to ensure that word of the threat was whispered into the right ears at the right time. The queen needed money for soldiers' pay and arms, he explained, and she needed it urgently if the French invasion came. But Elizabeth had just heard that the treasury was virtually empty, thanks in large part to Philip. As king consort to Elizabeth's sister he had made use of England's treasury as if it were his own to fight his Continental wars, and had declared his loans "forfeit" to the merchant bankers in Antwerp only the year before. The use of England's exchequer particularly rankled with the parsimonious Elizabeth since Philip had been expecting two treasure fleets from Tierra Firme, or New Spain, in the Americas, with the first treasure fleet due in March 1558 and the second in May of the same year. This made the loss of Calais in January burn more brightly in her mind: England's exchequer had provided the men, money, and arms for the Spanish war machine in the Low Countries, lost Calais in the process, and had failed to secure any reimbursement from the treasure fleet.[15]

When Elizabeth's new lord treasurer, Sir Walter Mildmay, who took up his post at the end of December 1558, reported that the exchequer was, for all intents and purposes, empty, we can only imagine the queen's despair. The year's consignment of gold and silver from the two treasure fleets had arrived and remained in Spain, and there was no offer to replenish England's depleted coffers.[16] Mildmay's report to the Privy Council showed how deeply the queen's sister had embroiled the country in Philip's wars: in her last year as queen, Mary spent unprecedented sums on her navy alone, amounting to £1,073,844 ($401.3 million or £216.9 million today).[17] Certainly most galling of all for Elizabeth was the fact that she now found herself in a position of relying heavily for the country's security on the very man who bankrupted the realm.

But rely on him she did. She, of course, knew of his intentions. Her court was from its earliest days a beehive of espionage and intrigue, and the queen knew that Philip also feared that the French wanted to make England another province of France as Scotland effectively was. With the Spanish king now firmly on her side, all Elizabeth had to do was wait for an opportunity to press home her advantage. As early as March 1559, Henry II was militating with the pope to declare Elizabeth illegitimate and excommunicate her. On hearing this, the young queen sprang into action, though she hardly needed to prevail upon Philip to impose his will upon the pope to successfully forestall Henry's efforts. Henry retaliated, this time hitting the mark with Elizabeth, by allowing his new seventeen-year-old daughter-in-law, Mary Stuart, Dauphine of France, and his son, Francis, to bear the arms and style of Queen and King of England. While Elizabeth railed against the Stuarts, Guises, and Valoises in a Tudor tirade in England, Philip took more decisive action: he proposed marriage himself to his former sister-in-law. And all this occurred at a dizzying pace, during the peace negotiations at Cateau-Cambrésis in the first quarter of 1559.

Fortunately for Elizabeth, the Count of Feria had the temerity to show his royal instructions to some of the queen's ladies regarding the king's marriage proposal, and Elizabeth knew without doubt from that moment that Philip was a reluctant suitor. Yet she still needed to weigh up the possibility that when she rejected him, Philip, a widower for a second time without an heir to his vast dominions, could well take a Valois bride. This would at a stroke make him England's enemy, and secure a more lasting peace with France. An obvious choice even presented itself: Henry II's daughter, Elisabeth of France.

So, before Mary was cold in her grave, Secretary Cecil and her other councillors were all advising Elizabeth on how she should best play her own marriage card to keep Philip from concluding a Valois pact that would endanger England's very existence. Her first parliament of 1559, on the other hand, was solely urging the queen to marry and have children as was her duty as a woman, thereby putting the Catholic threat of Mary Queen of Scots at one remove from the crown.

Any pretense that Elizabeth had made to marry Philip, or that Secretary Cecil had made on her behalf, was undoubtedly another stalling tactic. The country would not tolerate a return of Philip as their king. The strength of feeling for Elizabeth and against Philip, and even Mary, can best be summed up in a speech believed to have been delivered at York when news of her accession was announced: "Queen Elizabeth, a princess, as you will, of no mingled blood of Spaniard or stranger, but born mere English here among us and therefore most natural unto us."[18] Even setting aside her personal inclinations to remain a "spinster," the last thing England's young and handsome queen needed was a hated husband. What she did need was time, as well as money, and the only way she could prevent Philip from casting around Valois France for a bride was to pretend she was interested herself. The Count of Feria was thus fed a ripe diet of misinformation, and fortunately for the English, swallowed it with gusto.

Philip was, nonetheless, the most powerful monarch in Europe of the day. His father, Charles V, had abdicated as Holy Roman Emperor, splitting his dominions between his brother Ferdinand, who became Holy Roman Emperor in his stead, and Philip, who took direct control of all the lands and provinces outside the borders of the Holy Roman Empire, from the Americas to the Low Countries and much of Italy. Elizabeth had fortunately charmed him during his brief stint at her sister Mary's side; but, more important, had learned a great deal about how he thought, and how best to handle him. She knew better than any other prince alive that Philip was "more Catholic than the Pope"[19] and would not delegate his authority to anyone. She knew that he had his hand in every act, every letter of the Spanish Habsburg Empire; that he gave each order; oversaw all policy; and above all else was paranoid about the jealousy others felt when he wielded his power. Elizabeth and her councillors had been dealing with Philip for five years in England, and had developed a strategy at the outset to help protect her fledgling rule.

Just as Philip's father, Charles V, had been feared and hated, Philip perceived that the world outside Spain, and his Spanish dominions, was to be mistrusted at the very least, and treated as an enemy given the slightest provocation. His weakest—and yet strongest—ally was none other than the pope himself. His dominions surrounded the Papal States, which also depended heavily upon Philip's Habsburg Sicily for its grain. The sack of Rome in 1527 by Charles V was not allowed to become a distant memory, since Philip himself had ruthlessly used force and threatened to starve out Pope Paul IV in 1556–57 to demonstrate his own might. The popes knew to mistrust Philip's temporal power, and much later he wrote to the pope that, "Most of the misfortunes that have befallen my possessions have occurred because I have tried so hard to defend the church and extirpate heresy. But the greater these [misfortunes] have become, the more your Holiness has forgotten them!"[20]

For all these reasons, Philip—and Elizabeth's relationship with him and his Spanish Habsburg Empire—would dominate Elizabethan politics and economic aspirations for her entire forty-four-year reign. Elizabeth's government decisions would be dictated by and large throughout her rule by the ever-pressing considerations of security of the realm (defense), revenue generation, official court favor, and court intrigue.[21] Central to that theme in the early years was trade and plunder, and London was the heartbeat and brain of trade.

The City of London merchants made up about 75 percent of the tax revenues, and paid duties to the queen on goods imported or exported. They comprised different "companies" divided into mercers, staplers, goldsmiths, or merchant adventurers dependent on their specific trade and charter. The West Country ports of Plymouth and Bristol were also active contributors to the treasury, and Southampton with the Isle of Wight had already become an important naval outpost, but even when bundled together, they could not touch the powerhouse that was London.

The members of the twelve great livery companies of London comprised the administrative substructure of the city, and citizenship at London—or the freedom of the City—could only be acquired through membership of one of these companies. Membership, in turn, was gained only through a long period of apprenticeship, even if the new entrants were entitled to join by following the trade of their fathers.[22] This meant that London, unlike Antwerp or other great commercial centers, was run by men who had been engaged in business since they were old enough to work, and virtually always by men who belonged to one of the livery companies. The most powerful of these companies at the time of Elizabeth's accession was the Merchants Adventurers, who derived much of their wealth from the export trade in cloth to Antwerp, and the importation of luxury goods from the East and West Indies.[23] And it was the relationship between the Merchants Adventurers and the crown that would dominate government policy for the next several years.

But trade was only one side of the coin. Treasure, irrespective of its provenance, was the special passport to royal favor, since the queen expected her Merchants Adventurers and other trading corporations and societies to put their ready funds at her disposal for the security of the realm. The same sacrifices were demanded of her gentlemen adventurers at court as well. There was no doubt that Elizabeth's reign was a time when all who wanted power needed to put their money where their ambitions lay, and only then could success be richly rewarded.

And so it was at the beginning of 1559 that the queen found her realm in less than shipshape order. She was literally assailed on all sides and had to unite her country behind her. The first concrete step she took to that end was to set about to create the illusion of power and wealth to dazzle her enemies and give the false impression of a glorious beginning at her coronation in January of that year. It was this illusion that would give the queen her enduring nickname of "Gloriana," and fooled posterity into believing that there had always been some grand mercantile and imperial strategic plan.[24]

But the only "grand plan" that Elizabeth had at that stage was security of the realm. Her vision was clear, and she had the mental acuity and deft touch of a chess grandmaster, always seeing five or six moves ahead of the game, more often than not leading her adversary into the path she wished him, or her, to take. Though she had no money, she had the courage, conviction, advisors, and "stomach of a king" to help her through the task ahead. And at the heart of this illusion in her "grand plan" to save England was the very real world of gentlemen and merchant adventurers, corsairs and pirates. Without them, England could not survive.

3. The Queen, Her Merchants and Gentlemen ⚜

The State may hereafter want such men,
who commonly are the most daring and serviceable
in war of all those kind of people.
—SIR HENRY MAINWARING, ELIZABETHAN PIRATE-TURNED-ADMIRAL

The queen's gentlemen and merchant adventurers—often referred to by England's allies and adversaries alike as her corsairs, rovers, and pirates—were not the stuff of ordinary merchant stock. Indeed, pioneering into new worlds required men who thirsted for knowledge, had tremendous egos, were desperate to make their fortunes, had an acute business sense, and possessed more than a fair portion of intelligence and cunning. Many also claimed a fair degree of patriotism, and all professed undying loyalty to the queen. It was these men who would ultimately save England in ways that no one could begin to imagine in 1559.

Throughout her reign, Elizabeth's court was stuffed to the gunnels with troublesome second sons of gentleman stock, the merchant trades, and the aristocracy. These men had been brought up with "expectations" of wealth, or luxury, but as younger sons they could inherit only the wealth of their wives—should they have the good fortune to marry well—or a portion of their fathers' mercantile enterprises—should their fathers prove generous. If they were unlucky, then they'd have to make their own way in the world, often running foul of strict interpretations of the law and making enemies in their travails and travels. Robert Dudley, John Hawkins, Sir Robert Cecil, Francis Bacon, and Walter Raleigh were some of the most shining examples of Elizabethan younger sons grasping at court power and riches. The jealousy and envy they created was undoubtedly destructive; their contributions to the mainstay of Elizabeth's court, tremendous.

Then there were the great Elizabethan families who dominated the political, economic, and even the intellectual powerhouses of Elizabeth Tudor's England. They were a heady brew of aristocracy, merchant classes, and poorer segments of society. The political and religious changes that were ushered in by Henry VIII's marriage to Anne Boleyn brushed away the cobwebs of the "old" nobility unwilling or unable to follow the king on his new path, and made way for a fresh rising class of merchant aristocrat, such as the Boleyns themselves. Elizabeth's first lord treasurer, the admirably competent and loyal Sir William Paulet, first Marquis of Winchester, was one of Henry's "new men." The queen's administrative and legal tigers, William Cecil and Nicholas Bacon, while both younger than Winchester, were also cut of the same cloth. While the changes toward "meritocracy" began under Henry for loyalty to the king's desires, under Elizabeth, those who demonstrated loyalty to crown and country by wholehearted dedication to work and wisdom would be richly rewarded irrespective of their social pedigree.

And despite much of what has been written, the lines of Elizabethan power were not necessarily drawn with Protestant pitted against Catholic. Where Edward Fiennes de Clinton, Elizabeth's first lord admiral, who later became Earl of Lincoln, was a staunchly Protestant West Countryman, his successor, Lord Charles Howard of Effingham, Earl of Nottingham, was a Catholic. The Earl of Pembroke and the Earl of Arundel, privy councillors under Mary as well as Elizabeth, both professed Catholic leanings. Robert Dudley and Sir Francis Walsingham were staunch Protestants with strong Puritan inclinations. William Cecil, who later became Lord Burghley, was a Protestant; and he, like the queen herself, believed in moderation in religious politics. Only the queen's merchant adventurers and corsairs were virtually all Protestant, and the trades they plied were always tinged with social, religious, or political hidden agendas.

The men who surrounded the court and queen were united not only in their quest for power, knowledge, treasure, adventure, and England's gathering greatness, but they were frequently closely related or in the same golden circle of good friends. Martin

Frobisher, the corsair who would explore the northern latitudes of North America, was jailed for piracy in the first year of Elizabeth's reign.[1] John Dee, Elizabeth's unofficial astrologer and great mathematician, advised Frobisher and most other adventurers on their voyages of discovery. Dee was himself the son of a "mercer" or textile merchant, and his mercantile connections proved invaluable in Dee's rise to political notice. Both Dee and Elizabeth shared the same tutors: Roger Ascham and Sir John Cheke. Ascham, Cheke, and Sir Thomas Smith, another councillor of the queen, were all Cambridge academics and closely associated with the Dutch humanist Desiderius Erasmus, who was credited with bringing the Italian humanist Renaissance to northern Europe. Cheke was a cherished family friend of the East Anglian merchant, Anthony Cooke, whose daughter Anne had married Sir Nicholas Bacon, the queen's lord keeper, while Cooke's eldest daughter, Mildred, had married Sir William Cecil, the queen's principal secretary, a few years earlier. Cooke and Cecil had been affiliated as well to the much-admired humanist clique cultivated by Queen Catherine Parr (Henry VIII's last wife) and the young Prince Edward.[2] Walter Raleigh was the nephew of Elizabeth's beloved governess and lifelong friend, Cat Ashley. His elder half brothers, Humphrey and Adrian Gilbert, the adventurers who promoted the Northwest Passage route to Cathay and settlement of North America, had been introduced at court by Cat Ashley years before Raleigh himself craved the queen's attention. Lady Catherine Knollys, wife of the privy councillor Sir Francis Knollys, was called Elizabeth's cousin but is now thought by some to have been her half sister, born to Henry VIII and Elizabeth's aunt, Mary Boleyn.[3] Catherine Knollys's brother, Henry Carey, Lord Hunsdon, is also believed to be Henry VIII's son by Mary Boleyn, and he, too, would become a stalwart of Elizabethan England and William Shakespeare's patron. By this yardstick of friends and relations, Elizabeth's world was a small one indeed.

But Elizabeth's men were more than close relations and a fractious lot. Her intellectuals brought the Renaissance to England, advancing society and thought beyond what had been believed possible in Henry VIII's time. John Dee traveled extensively throughout Europe, gathering humanist friends abroad, like the phenomenally gifted mapmaker Gerard Mercator. On his return to England, Dee preached to Elizabeth's converted adventurers of great wealth and worlds beyond the horizons that could be theirs for the taking if only they tried.

From a Spanish perspective, Dee's teachings were anathema. The world had been divided between the Portuguese and the Spanish in the previous century, with this division sanctioned by the pope and enshrined in the Treaty of Tordesillas of 1494. Any voyages of discovery were the private reserve of the Iberians, and this precept, coupled with England's economic necessity for survival and security against Spain, provided the catalyst for England's entry into an expansionist world power. In fact, the phrase the "British Empire" wasn't coined in the eighteenth or nineteenth centuries, but by John Dee in his work *The Petty Navy Royal* in 1577.[4] From Spain's and Portugal's perspective, empire was the fundamental principle in the battle to protect Iberian "rights." From an English point of view, any acts of piracy, trade, or war were the basic ingredients needed for survival against the great Catholic powers. And these ingredients would beat at the heart of the clash between Spain, France, and England throughout most of Elizabeth's reign. Yet it would be wrong to think that Elizabeth was ever an imperialist. England's place in history would ultimately be secured by an English Renaissance in thought, science, and the arts by men like Dee, Marlowe, and Shakespeare. Yet her right to rule a Protestant England—and sow the seeds of empire—was secured by her numerous merchant and gentlemen adventurers through trade, plunder, and colonization.

Two other great contributors to expansionist thought and deed were the two Richard Hakluyts. Richard Hakluyt, the elder, and especially the younger Richard Hakluyt, made a lasting record for posterity by writing down the voyages for all the Elizabethan seamen they could find, culminating in the younger Hakluyt's *Principall Navigations*, first published in 1589, and dedicated to Elizabeth's then principal secretary and spymaster, Sir Francis Walsingham.

Among others who helped the revolutionary trains of thought to take hold in England was the queen's keeper of the great seal, Sir Nicholas Bacon, who promoted mass education and funded scholarships for students at Cambridge.[5] Her principal secretary, Sir William Cecil, was the vice chancellor of the University of

Cambridge. Sir Thomas Gresham, Elizabeth's ambassador to the Low Countries, "intelligencer," arms dealer, and London merchant, founded the Royal Exchange in 1572 at his own expense for the promotion of international trade. The Corporation of London and the Mercer's Company, to which he belonged, founded Gresham College for popular education with a strong emphasis on practical subjects connected with commerce.[6]

Some of the most influential merchants belonging to the Mercer's Company or the Staplers (who traded in commodities such as wool rather than finished goods like cloth on the Continent) came from gentry stock like Gresham. Others married into the gentry and acquired their wives' estates and coats of arms. Still others founded noble families by royal favor. Merchants and landed gentlemen who were to shine as Elizabeth's adventurers learned over time to act in concert. Trade and plunder were not obvious commercial or political partners at the outset, but with the political movements of the time, they soon became a united cause. Within ten years of Elizabeth's accession, the blurred distinctions between merchants and gentlemen were the accepted norm. The blurring between their legal trading and illicit plundering activities became a way of life as hostilities with Philip II grew, until, finally, it was virtually impossible to tell trade from plunder or piracy. This naturally created a more fluid society, which while still falling well short of a meritocracy, allowed some cream to rise to the top. And a wealth of hidden talent was not found wanting.

While the hub of the jostling for riches and power took place at court and London, a core of fiercely Protestant southwest gentlemen and merchants had already burst upon the world stage of exploration long before Elizabeth had become queen. John Cabot, an immigrant Italian, had sailed from Bristol in the *Mathew* during the reign of Henry VII.[7] John Cabot's son, Sebastian, who claimed the discovery of Newfoundland for himself, thereby eclipsed his father for posterity. The younger Cabot had masterminded the formation of the first joint stock company for exploration, the Muscovy Company, making its voyages independent of the crown, and provided the money with his small group of peers and high officials for the first Muscovy voyages. William Hawkins of Plymouth, the West Country merchant, had established successful trading with Brazil in the late 1520s, and even brought back an Indian chief aboard ship on his second voyage in 1531 as a sign of the "great favor" that the Indians had shown him. Southampton and Plymouth spawned great adventurers—merchant, gentlemen, and piratical—with such evocative West Country names as Champernowne, Hawkins, Fiennes, Godolphin, Grenville, Gilbert, Killigrew, and Drake.

Yet, the desire for overseas riches that were brought to England by "trade"—whether through legitimate channels or piracy—did not originate with Elizabeth's men. The Tudor courts from Henry VIII's reign simply wallowed in luxury. Luxuries—be they sumptuous clothing, jewels, food, or amusements—were an integral part of Henry's power, and under Elizabeth they became key symbols of her rule. Naturally, her court remained the fashion-setter for the rest of the country, with all the royal status seekers trying to emulate her court in its way of dress, its lavish tastes, and its lust for "the rich trades," or luxury goods, from India and the Orient.

And treasure was the most highly valued prize by the queen herself. It enabled her to pay her bills and spend—carefully—on her aura of wealth, power, and courtly love while, above all else, investing in the security of the realm. Treasure, followed by the rich trades, became the manna of the body politic, attracting royal participation in search of gold.[8] If a lucky adventurer had a cunning plan to find treasure that mitigated risk to the crown, then royal patronage would not be far behind. However, before the queen would commit herself or her ships to dangerous and costly overseas expeditions, she demanded that her men put their own personal fortunes alongside her own at the realm's disposal for most voyages seeking treasure. Even the queen's most cautious ministers of state like Sir William Cecil; Sir Nicholas Bacon; and Sir William Herbert, the Earl of Pembroke, became eager participants in the quest for riches, wagering their own fortunes in the balance. In this way, the precedence was set: anyone wanting royal favor must venture his own wealth for queen and country.

Salaries were notoriously mean, often paid late or not at all, and ministers of state and civil servants alike had to devise ways in which they could serve the realm and earn a good living, while spending their personal fortunes on behalf of the queen. By modern standards, some conflict of interest was expected in their execution of duties, like adding a percentage onto a bid to cover their costs, but loyalty was always demanded. Cecil's and the queen's answer to the conundrum of how to keep these firebrands under control was to promulgate the sale of patents for sweet wines, alum, tin or copper mining, or salt, or even the sale of royal lands. Probably the most lucrative of these patents, or grants, was the ruling in 1560 that Lord Admiral Clinton (and his successors), in adjudicating cases of piracy as well as complaints against holders of legitimate letters of marque, or letters of reprisal, would henceforth be entitled by law to a one-third interest in goods taken from the pirate or legitimate adventurer.[9]

Yet the secret of Elizabeth's success in dealing with this marauding brood of courtiers, merchants, and close relations vying for power, plunder, and riches remained her ability to fuse the colossal and diverging egos of her gentlemen and merchant adventurers while enforcing her personal will for the protection and security of England. Her security and England's undoubtedly took precedence over their greed, their determination to discover "new worlds," faster trade routes to the Indies, or imperialistic visions of settlement. And this "fusion" is a recurrent theme throughout all aspects of her reign. As queen, she masterminded the internal balance of court power, which was mimicked in her international politics by her interminable and often frustrating use of her dog-eared marriage card; the making and breaking of alliances; her prevarication; and her initial tacit, and later overt, acceptance of plunder and piracy as central to state policy.[10]

The queen's crown—her very person—and the essence of her statecraft would depend on the concept of fusion, or compromise. As a Protestant ruler of a mixed Protestant and Catholic country, overpowered by Catholic giants like Spain and France, Elizabeth was all too conscious of the need to appear to be queen of "all the English." The religious settlement culminating in the Act of Supremacy and Uniformity in April 1559, making Elizabeth supreme governor of the Church of England, was neither a Catholic nor Protestant solution. It pleased no one, but offended few. It had been carefully crafted to provide a middle ground to keep the nation at peace. Catholics in her realm were allowed to "opt out" of Anglican Church services for a small recusancy fine to practice their preferred religion without fear of being burned at the stake, so long as they did not engage in treasonous acts against the queen or her government.[11] Even the tightrope walk she endlessly engaged in—that of her feigning interest in marriage to make and break international peace accords—was nothing more than a quest for a balance of power.[12]

Above all other considerations, the golden thread that ran through Elizabeth's domestic and foreign policy was security of the realm. The facts speak for themselves. Her grandfather, Henry VII, had seized power, finally ending generations of royal battles between the Yorks and Lancastrians in their seemingly interminable Wars of the Roses. One of her first memories when she was no more than three would have been her father's reign having been seriously threatened by the popular uprising of the Pilgrimage of Grace. The other enduring fact was the execution of her mother and the invisible scars that had been left on her as a result. When Elizabeth had seen her cousin, Queen Catherine Howard—Henry VIII's fifth wife— dragged through the castle by her hair screaming literally for her very life, it is no wonder that the nine-year-old Elizabeth whispered "I shall never marry" under her breath to Robert Dudley.[13]

These invisible scars continually marred her young and turbulent life until she could become queen. The forced estrangement from her young brother, Edward VI, by Dudley's father, the Earl of Northumberland, began her long years of exile from court and mistrust of privy councillors. Her trauma culminated in the final years of suspicion and imprisonment at the hands of her sister, Mary, as Elizabeth herself best described when writing defiantly with a diamond on a window pane at Woodstock, "Much suspected by me, Nothing proved can be, said Elizabeth the prisoner."[14]

It is little wonder that personal security and security of the realm became her mantras, and that all weapons at her disposal to achieve these goals would be used. Elizabeth's overpowering desire to be personally secure and to ensure the safety of her people and realm was the driving force behind her sanctioning of plunder, promotion of trade, switching allegiances, and eventually giving in to the imperial aims of her intellectuals and adventurers, and creating a nascent British Empire. Piracy and plunder became a vital tool to achieve her goals of security. And yet, for that to become a successful state policy, she would need to successfully "man manage" her merchant adventurers and gentlemen who would make it all possible.

4. The Quest for Cash ❧

*Wherein it may appear that we mean to do to no person
wrong but to provide and foresee how apparent dangers to
our estate may be diverted, and that we might not remain in
this kind of unsurety to have our Calais restored to us . . .*
QUEEN ELIZABETH TO PHILIP II OF SPAIN, SEPTEMBER 30, 1562

By April 1559, the first immediate crises of the queen's reign
had been successfully addressed: the Act of Supremacy and
Uniformity provided a religious solution, and the Treaty of Cateau-
Cambrésis had been agreed. While Elizabeth had ostensibly held
out for the return of Calais, with the treaty providing for the French
to give Calais back to England in eight years' time, or forfeit 500,000
crowns ($186.9 million or £101 million today), there was little doubt
in the queen's or Cecil's minds that Calais was irretrievably lost.[1] Both
the queen and Cecil also understood that the chances of England
ever receiving the forfeit sum entailed in the treaty were slim.

Yet the loss of Calais cut deeper than a loss to Elizabeth's Tudor
pride, as many believe. It had been the home for over a century
to the Staplers, who shipped wool from England to Calais for
spinning and trading on the spun wool. As with all wars, men,
merchandise, money, homes, markets, and confidence were lost
with Calais, too. Furthermore, the security of the realm had
been placed in jeopardy, since without Calais, England no longer
controlled the Straits of Dover, then known as the Narrow Seas,
from both sides of the landmass. This helps to put into perspective,
to some extent, Elizabeth's fixation with regaining Calais, and the
disasters that were to follow as a result of her policy to win her
staple town back.

The treaty of Cateau-Cambrésis merely allowed for the cessation
of hostilities, with a great deal of face saving on both sides. It fell far

short of the ultimate goal of any treaty since it did not eliminate the threat of future wars. The new French king, Francis II, was also by now King of Scotland, and his bride, Mary Queen of Scots, openly defied Elizabeth's personal right to rule by actively claiming the English throne in her own right as a granddaughter of Henry VII.

When Francis's father, Henry II, died from his injuries in a jousting accident in July 1559, things turned from bad to worse for Elizabeth. Even Henry had allowed his son and Mary to sport the insignia of England on their coat of arms, in an overt attempt to goad Elizabeth into premature action against their more powerful kingdom of France. And now that Mary Queen of Scots was also Queen of France, her powerful uncles, the Guises, began actively plotting to put Mary on the throne of England.

At the time, England was by and large rightly regarded as a military and economic backwater by both the French and the Spanish, and there were ample reasons for this perception. What neither crown had yet had the chance to recognize was that Elizabeth Tudor would become the first English monarch adept at playing off one European giant against another in a long game, thereby upsetting the balance of European power and allowing England to step forward onto the world stage. To the north, in France's unofficial vassal realm of Scotland, Elizabeth Tudor warily watched, fearful that it would be only a matter of time before the hostilities between the staunchly Protestant Scottish Lords of the Congregation and the queen dowager, Mary of Guise, would embroil both France and England in their Scottish war. And war was unpredictable and bad for trade.

Any war—aside from the supreme waste of human and economic resources—could not fail to demonstrate, in Elizabeth's eyes, that England was intrinsically weak militarily and economically. The country was simply ill-prepared to face a stronger enemy like France from the Continent, much less a France coupled with Scotland, and potentially Ireland as well. Catholic Ireland had always been viewed as a back door for all Catholic sympathizers, be they French, Spanish, or emissaries from the pope. With a probable war at sea and along the border of Scotland, the thought of having to watch the English flank at Ireland, in addition to the Channel and the North Sea, became a matter for considerable worry. The obvious fact that armies—or for that matter, navies—needed money that the crown did not have seemed to Elizabeth to be an insurmountable problem. Worse still, the young English queen was unproven as a leader. For her councillors, the specter of war was a regrettable diversion so early in the young queen's reign that could well cost the country its freedom.

Yet despite the expensive diversion of war, it was one that they would have to face up to if England were to remain a Protestant nation. To achieve their goals, Elizabeth and her councillors simply had to tackle the economic health of the realm, while simultaneously keeping England out of a conflict that it could ill afford.

The blow inflicted by the French of the loss of the staple at Calais had already impacted England's fledgling modern economy, though the Staplers had removed their business to Antwerp temporarily in the Spanish Low Countries while searching for another city to use as their main staple town. Meanwhile, Scottish and French pirates were marauding the Channel and the Narrow Seas, and the most powerful group of merchants, the Merchants Adventurers, whose international market was located in Antwerp, were deeply concerned that they would be cut off from their Continental source of wealth. They could, by law, only sell their merchandise abroad, and were only licensed to do so at Antwerp. The English queen knew that her merchants were her best chance at securing loans for the crown, and that a war stood to impoverish her best potential source of ready funds.

It was a dilemma she would need to speedily address. But Elizabeth wasn't given to snap decisions. No matter how she tried to evade the issue, at the end of the day, the nation needed to be able to defend itself, and before any loan could be obtained for arms, the queen needed to understand what she could offer up as security and how she could borrow from English or foreign merchants. To do that, Elizabeth needed to know what she owned; what she was owed; what was missing that could be tracked down and restored; and what could be sold for cash or favors. In the first important months of her reign, the Privy Council wrote letters to "the tellers of the exchequer to send hither a perfect book of the names of all such as are behind within the Queen's Majesty's House of the payment of the last Subsidy granted to the late Queen."[2] An inventory was taken of the late Queen Mary's jewels, and note made of those items that were missing or had been sold during her lifetime. A committee of the Privy Council was appointed to examine the grants of crown lands made in the last reign.[3] Under the heading "Debts to the Crown," a letter was sent from the Privy Council "to the lord treasurer to cause speedy certificate to be made to the Queen's Majesty of all manner of debts due in the exchequer to the extent [that] the same being known, [so that] order may be given by such as her Highness hath appointed in Commission to see the same answered with all expedition." In December a letter went out to the Court of Wards [Court of Awards] to a Mr. Damsell requesting him to "certify all manner of debts due in the Court."[4]

No individual, dead or alive, was exempt from the quest for cash. Queen Mary's archbishop, Cardinal Pole, who died the same day as his mistress, was a particular target for Elizabeth's men. Within twelve days of taking power, the Privy Council had issued orders to Sir Nicholas Throckmorton "to suffer certain parcels of the late Cardinal's plate which are thought meet by the officers of the Jewel House for the service of the Queen to be brought hither by some of his own folks to the end that, the same being viewed, he may receive the value thereof or of so much of it as shall be thought meet for her Highness' use, and the rest to be safely returned back again unto him, and that they may be bold in her Majesty's name to assure him."[5]

Then the queen and her ministers instructed the sheriffs to put pressure upon such of the "Collectors of the Subsidy" in each county "as were behindhand in their payments. Letters to the sheriffs of the counties of Buckinghamshire, Yorkshire, Gloucestershire, Nottinghamshire, Oxfordshire, Berkshire, Staffordshire, and Warwickshire and [to] the mayors of the towns of Northampton, Derby, King's Lynn and Southampton, [were expedited] to apprehend the collectors of the fifteenth and [the] tenth [taxes] in the said shires and towns behind of [sic] their collections, and to bind them in good bands in treble the sums to make payment of all that is by them due into the exchequer within fifteen days next after the bands taken, &c., according to the minute in the Council Chest."[6]

Before the end of December, the Privy Council reminded Sir Anthony St. Leger, the Irish treasurer, in the name of the queen—and not for the first time—that the crown must insist on the repayment of the large sums for which he had failed to account during his tenure of office in the treasury in Ireland.[7] Lord Paget received notice that his licence to deal in wine might be reconsidered, and that the Queen reserved the right in the meantime to reasonably demand a share of his profits. Paget was also required to send in an exact statement of the debts due to the late Queen Mary.[8] This was tantamount to an official rebuke, and would have made both St. Leger and Paget unhappy in the extreme. From Berwick in the north to Land's End at the tip of Cornwall, Elizabeth and her privy councillors scoured the country for cash and a true picture of her assets and liabilities. No member of the church or aristocracy, no merchant or yeoman was spared. And most important in this audit of the crown's assets was the queen's navy.

Before March 1559, *The Book of Sea Causes*, the first such register of naval assets and liabilities of its kind, had been compiled by the officers of the queen's navy, giving the names of all the ships, their tonnage, and number of men. It assessed the state of readiness of the queen's navy from the detail of her ships; their state of repair, type and quantity of artillery, the victuals in store, and what would be required at what cost to bring Her Majesty's navy into a fit fighting fleet. The bad-tempered and extremely gifted mariner William Winter, master of the queen's ordnance for the seas and probable main author of *The Book*, also reported on the state of all the ordnance and munitions both aboard ship as well as in the queen's storehouses.[9]

To make matters worse, Scotland's pirates began to make serious inroads into English imports, ravaging the English coastlines from Berwick to Norwich in the East and Carlisle to Liverpool in the West. Even the Spanish king was losing patience with the situation. Elizabeth herself reported to her ambassador in Scotland that the "King of Spain having . . . of late written to us that not only the subjects of the King of Portugal, but also his own of Spain and his Low Countries, are spoiled by pirates, some English, but most Scots, haunting our south and north seas . . . has earnestly renewed the complaint by his ambassador, adding that if the seas were not better preserved under our leagues, he must arm a force himself."[10] Irish pirates also made any passage through Irish waters treacherous, and English smugglers and pirates frequently joined in their escapades.

Then word arrived at court that a significant number of French troops were already garrisoned in Scotland. Invasion from France, where Mary Stuart and her husband, Francis, lived, was feared at any time. Letters poured into the Privy Council begging the queen to fortify the towns of Portsmouth, Southampton, and the towns of the Cinque Ports. The country remained ill prepared for all-out war against France and Scotland, mostly due to lack of funds and trained men to defend the realm. The situation was dire. But not for the first time, nor the last, the dogged English will—whether Catholic or Protestant—to remain independent of a foreign power prevented a civil war, and Englishmen and -women from all walks of life pulled together to defend the country. Scotland's domination by France was a ready example of what could happen in England, and no one wanted a rampaging, invading army to overrun the country and plunder what little they had.

Whether it was luck, or Cecil "making" England's luck on behalf of his queen and country, by April 1559, Scotland's Lords of the Congregation were already engaged in battle against the dowager Queen Mary of Guise's French troops. To the west, Ireland stood steadfastly Catholic and a potential magnet for France, Spain, or even the papacy as a toehold in the British Isles to attack the queen's Protestant England. Elizabeth was undoubtedly wise to see the necessity of preparing England as best she could for war, but without cash, no standing army, a debased coinage that she was in the process of rectifying, and a fleet that was in dire need of urgent repair the prospects of success were bleak.

There is no doubt that the picture was truly grim. Yet despite all the counsel received—both wise and bold—and all the letters issued hastily to better understand the financial state of the realm, it was only the backing of Elizabeth's merchants that gave the queen the breathing room she needed to understand her options and to act upon what she had learned. Sir Thomas Gresham, a member of the Mercers' Company of London and the queen's agent in Antwerp, was the most important of these at the end of 1558 and throughout the early 1560s. Antwerp, which had been on a steady rise in the first half of the sixteenth century, was the hub for all luxury goods for northern Europe. By the spring of 1559, it was easily the northern commercial capital. It was also Gresham's base of operations. Antwerp's other main attraction was that it was the economic powerhouse for Philip II's Spanish Netherlands, and a source of inestimable intelligence on the Habsburg economy and intentions in the New World. And with the loss of Calais, the Staplers had temporarily retreated to Antwerp while seeking new cities to conduct their business for the spinning of their wool into cloth on a more permanent basis.[11]

And so, it was on Thomas Gresham that the queen relied for help. Elizabeth's sister had borrowed £160,000—£100,000 in Antwerp and £60,000 in London—in the final year of her reign ($59.81 million or £32.33 million today).[12] When Elizabeth had come to the throne in November 1558, £69,069 ($25.83 million or £13.96 million today) were still owed to Flanders merchants.[13] Over the next year, Elizabeth would borrow a further £30,000 ($11.14 million or £6.02 million today) from her powerful traders with Antwerp, the Merchants Adventurers, through Gresham's auspices to pay soldiers' wages, buy arms, and refit ships. It was Gresham alone who took charge of the queen's finances with Antwerp, which was still the northern powerhouse of trade and finance. It was also Gresham who advised the queen on how best to consolidate her debt and rebuild confidence in the pound sterling by removing base coins from circulation.

Undoubtedly, not all of what he did was aboveboard. Customs agents were bribed to allow bullion to be exported from the Low Countries, and not all shipments of armaments were openly declared. Gresham rightly feared that, if the Netherlands regent for Philip II, Margaret of Parma, understood that he was arming England for the conflict ahead, a full embargo on exports to England would be put into force. What Gresham also recognized, as a seasoned Channel traveler, was that the queen's navy needed urgent refitting if the country had any hope of staving off the powers of France, Spain, and the papacy. Stealth and rapid deployment of money and materiel were essential.

It was Gresham's echo of other advice already received from Cecil and his fellow privy councillors that helped spring the queen into early action. The first step toward rebuilding her navy was for the princely sum of £14,000 a year ($4.98 million or £2.69 million today) to be advanced half yearly to Sir Benjamin Gonson, treasurer of the

Admiralty, "to be by him defrayed in such sort as shall be prescribed by him the said lord treasurer with the advice of the lord admiral."

The lord treasurer was to

> *cause such of her Majesty's ships as may be made serviceable with caulking and new trimming to be sufficiently renewed and repaired; item to cause such of her Highness's said ships as a must of necessity be made of new to be gone in hand withal and new made with convenient speed; item he to see also her Highness's said ships furnished with sails anchors cables and other tackle and apparel sufficiently; item he to cause a mass of victual to be always in readiness to serve for 1,000 men for a month to be set to the sea upon any sudden; item he to cause the said ships from time to time to be repaired and renewed as occasion shall require; item when the said ships that are to be renewed shall be new made and sufficiently repaired and the whole navy furnished of sails, anchors, cables and other tackle then is the said lord treasurer content to continue this service in form aforesaid for the sum of £10,000 yearly to be advanced as is aforesaid; item the said Benjamin Gonson and Edward Baeshe, surveyor of the victuals of the ships, shall make their several accounts of the defrayment of the said money and of their whole doings herein once in the year at the least and as often besides as shall be thought fit by my lords of the council.[14]*

The Book of Sea Causes detailed the naval preparedness of the realm. Elizabeth's thirty-four ships consisted of eleven great ships (200 tons and upward), ten barks and pinnaces, and one brigantine, which were "meet to be kept," or in satisfactory condition, while the remaining twelve, among which were two galleys, were to be discarded as "of no continuance and not worth repair."[15] Of all the ships surveyed, twenty-four were between 200 and 800 tons, four barks were between 60 and 80 tons, and there were two pinnaces of 40 tons.

But *The Book of Sea Causes* did not stop at its assessment of the Royal Navy. It noted with considerable interest that there were some forty-five "merchant ships which may be put in fashion for war" and another twenty vessels that could serve as victuallers. The commissioners estimated that the enlarged fleet of merchant ships and royal ships could be mobilized within two months, providing there was "ready money for the doing thereof." The recommendation at the end of *The Book* was that "the Queen's Majesty's Navy" (this was the first time the term was employed) should be laid up in the Medway and Gillingham Water below Rochester Bridge in Kent, and that Portsmouth on the south coast should be used as an advanced base of operations in the summer months only.

The Book's main author, William Winter, was a colorful rapscallion who would eventually be knighted for his service to queen and country later in Elizabeth's reign. He had been one of the plotters in the Wyatt's Rebellion against Elizabeth's sister, Queen Mary, the leaders of which had wanted to put the Protestant Elizabeth on the throne. While Winter had been sent to the Tower for his efforts, even Queen Mary of England had to recognize his usefulness at sea when England declared war on Valois France with Spain. She was forced to release him for the good of the realm, and, as expected, Winter proved his mettle. He was undoubtedly the best and most able sea officer of his generation, and would soon prove his worth for Elizabeth, too.

By the time Winter was released into action, Elizabeth had already promoted him from surveyor of the navy to master of naval ordnance. There is every indication that he was most likely the decisive voice in the shaping of the new naval program. During the next few years, he oversaw the building of the 1,200-ton *Triumph* and the 1,000-ton *White Bear*. He also arranged for the 800-ton *Victory* to be purchased from its merchant owners. Yet despite these early advances, the poor state of the royal fleet meant that the total number of great ships in operation by 1565 had fallen to seventeen.[16] Winter found this unacceptable, and was undoubtedly one of the first commanders to believe that England's ships were the best "walls" to protect the realm.

Fortunately, Winter's formidable naval talents extended beyond seamanship and surveying. When war with the Queen of Scots and her French Guise relations to expunge the popular Protestant movement became a certainty, Winter was dispatched by Elizabeth in December 1559, the worst possible time of year to engage in a naval battle in the North Sea. His instructions via the Duke of Norfolk, in charge of the land expedition, were clear: "He [Winter] shall aid the Queen's said friends and annoy their enemies, specially the French, without giving any desperate adventure; and this he must seem to do of his own head as if he had no commission of the Queen or of the Duke of Norfolk. And that the Queen's friends may be the sooner comforted the Duke thinks it not amiss that either the said Winter himself or some of the captains, do forthwith show themselves in the Firth, leaving the rest behind to receive the said five hundred or 600 harquebusiers to follow."[17]

The high winds and swirling icy tides of the North Sea in December did not deter the queen's indomitable sea dog. Not only did he and his fleet of thirty-four ships surprise the French by preventing reinforcements from landing; but the French were driven back all the way to the Spanish Netherlands for shelter. Exhausted and glad to be alive, the French clambered upon the shore, only to be subjected to pillage from pirates of an unknown nationality. Within a few weeks, in January 1560, it was a confident Winter who boldly sailed into the Firth of Forth at Leith, cutting off the French army at Fife. The French troops almost immediately abandoned their weapons, and Winter captured two French galleys as prizes for himself, his men, and the glory of England. When the dispatches reached the queen at court, Elizabeth could hardly believe Winter's phenomenal achievement. An order to attack by land as well was issued, and the courier rode day and night to Berwick to deliver the message. If Winter could do it, then surely the Duke of Norfolk could follow suit and beat the French roundly, she reasoned. Winter's successes had been hailed by the Scottish Lords of the Congregation, and asked only for England's army to help them reclaim their country from Mary Queen of Scots's mother, Mary of Guise.

Meanwhile, in Antwerp, Gresham wrote to Cecil at precisely the same moment that January, declaring, "Here there is very large talk of the Queen's estate, and the weakness of England, which comes in very ill time for the accomplishment of the rest of her affairs."[18] The very real concern for Gresham and his factor, Richard Clough, who were responsible for getting replacement armaments and ammunition to the English fleet and armies, was that credit would not be granted to the queen for a substantial shipment of war materiel worth between £14,000 and £15,000 ($5.38 million and £2.91 million today) and release of Her Majesty's ships from harbor in Antwerp. Yet by the close of business on the very day Gresham wrote his worried letter, the Antwerp authorities and foreign merchant princes agreed to allow the loaded English vessels to depart. Gresham and Clough had already shipped enough copper alone for the queen's ordnance makers to manufacture up to forty cannons.[19]

The success in Gresham's negotiations, as well as the superiority against the French at sea, was due in large part to Winter's ability to keep the French at bay and the Spanish under threat of reprisal if they interfered. By his control of the Narrow Seas, England threatened to cut off communication with Antwerp and French interaction with Scotland. It was the first time in what would become the queen's long reign that her ships would provide her with security from invasion, while ensuring that commerce was allowed to continue, albeit at a greatly reduced level. Gresham, while responsible for procuring the weapons of war, also wanted the peace restored as soon as possible, since for every pirate or adventurer able to capture a valuable prize, there were a thousand Englishmen trying to resume England's main export—the cloth trade to Antwerp.[20]

Once the naval and land battles of the short-lived War of the Insignia against the Guises faded, and the war was declared over (mostly due to the unexpected death of Mary of Guise in June 1560), the French king, Francis II, and his queen, Mary Queen of Scots, were forced to abandon their claims to the English throne— at least on paper in the Treaty of Edinburgh. Yet the English malaise remained great, with councillors and the queen pointing out the repeated failings of Norfolk's armies. There were seemingly endless recriminations as to when, why, and where battles were lost. And the government knew that the country had been extremely lucky to come out of its first test relatively unscathed. The only commander to escape their criticism was William Winter himself. William Cecil, secretary of state, wrapped up government appreciation of Winter when he stated, "but of Mr Winter all men speak so well that I need not mention him."[21]

And it looked as if England's good fortune would hold a little longer. Francis II died unexpectedly in December 1560,[22] and his younger brother became Charles IX under the regency of his omnipotent mother, Catherine de' Medici. Mary Stuart was now a dowager Queen of France, with no power and no presence. While she had never ratified the Treaty of Edinburgh, both France and Spain now wanted peace with England. The near strangulation of trade they had experienced at the hands of Winter and the revitalized English fleet had hardly been expected.

With peace now firmly on the agenda, and the English and French troops out of Scotland, William Winter was once again able to turn his talents to administrative matters. Waste, and more precisely the waste of the queen's exchequer, was a matter dear to Elizabeth's parsimonious heart. Detailed orders regulating the operation of the Navy Board or the "Office of the Admiralty and Marine Affairs" were drawn up based in some part on his advice to tighten up on slack and wasteful accounting, with weekly reporting to the lord admiral or vice admiral instituted. The navy's treasurer had to report monthly as well, giving written accounts quarterly; and the master of naval ordnance was obliged to make a quarterly report from his department. But the real power to spend money on ships, ordnance, and seamen remained in the lord treasurer's hands; and the lord treasurer, the Earl of Winchester, remained at the queen's side in the Privy Council.

The modern naval administration was beginning to take shape. Sir Benjamin Gonson was Winchester's counterpart in the Royal Navy, which disbursed the funds on Gonson's behalf. Gonson, himself a wealthy merchant, had another claim to fame. Within the next few years he would become the father-in-law of the queen's most colorful corsair of the 1560s, John Hawkins.

5. The Merchants Adventurers, Antwerp, and Muscovy ✦

*Our merchants perceived the commodities and wares of
England to be in small request with the countries and
people about us . . . and the price thereof abated . . . and
all foreign merchandises in great account, and their prices
wonderfully raised; certain grave citizens of London . . .
began to think with themselves how this mischief might be
remedied: for seeing that the wealth of the Spaniards and
Portuguese . . . they there upon resolved upon a new and
strange navigation.*

—RICHARD HAKLUYT, *PRINCIPALL NAVIGATIONS*, 1589

Long before and after the wily patriarch of the Hawkins family,
William, had ceded his Spanish trades with Iberia to his two
sons, first Bruges then Antwerp was the center of world trade in the
densely populated north of Europe. Since the last great Dukes of
Burgundy had moved their court to Bruges in the mid-fourteenth
century and aligned themselves to the English crown, the special
relationship between the House of Burgundy and England prevailed
against the common enemy, France. When Marie of Burgundy
married into the Habsburg line around 130 years later, the affinity
between England and Burgundy was automatically transferred to
the House of Habsburg.[1]

The great and powerful London Company of Merchants
Adventurers had profited from the relationship with the House of
Burgundy, then Habsburg, since the late Middle Ages. Its wealth
and power resided not only in maintaining the status quo with
their cloth exports across the Narrow Seas to Antwerp, but also in
keeping ahead of the increasingly cutthroat competition. In the year
before Elizabeth ascended the throne, the foreign merchants of the

north German Hanse towns decided at the Diet of Lübeck to start a commercial war against England, since the Merchants Adventurers were insisting with the crown that Hanse privileges (particularly the waiving of import duties) should be renewed only if the Hanse merchants imported goods solely from their own lands. The value of Hanse imports had already exceeded £200,000 ($73.39 million or £39.67 million today), and so in response, the Hanse merchants gambled that their merchandise from across Europe would mean more to the Elizabethans than the vociferous complaints of her merchant princes.[2]

It was a game played throughout Christendom. The Merchants Adventurers themselves enjoyed special privileges at Antwerp and held similar rights there to the German Hanse merchants based out of the Steelyard in London. So when the English vessels returned to England—importing gems, spices, and other luxuries from the Indies, wines from Italy, or silks—it took little convincing to point out to the queen that it was in her best interests to ensure that they did so on English ships at higher customs duties.[3] But applying diplomatic pressure on the crown wasn't the only way the Merchants Adventurers gained the upper hand against its competition. One of the formidable Hanse towns, Hamburg, had suffered badly from the series of religious edicts made by the pope and Philip of Spain's father, Holy Roman Emperor Charles V, against its predominantly Protestant population. When Elizabeth became queen, her Merchants Adventurers negotiated as trusted Protestant middlemen with the city fathers at Hamburg, and then their queen. The negotiations culminated in the Merchants Adventurers doubling their European market from Antwerp to include henceforth Hamburg. This had the double benefit of also driving a wedge between the northern German cities and contributing largely to breaking up the Hanse trade block.[4]

When Elizabeth ascended the throne, England had been a military and trading backwater compared to Venice, Spain, and especially Portugal. Envy, as well as survival, played an important role in England's premier overseas merchant trading group's quest for alternative markets.[5] The country's Merchants Adventurers had long been the backbone of English export trade, representing

some 90 percent of the cloth exports as well as a strong voice urging
the queen against war and Channel piracy. Both were always bad
for distribution channels and frequently bad for business. The
Merchants Adventurers, like the Hanse merchants, had a great deal
to lose if their overseas markets were difficult to reach, or if they
themselves were embroiled in a war over which they would have
no control. And so, expanding their markets and monopolies made
tremendous sense.

They had their own fleet of ships; their own armaments; their own
treasury; and their own laws, making them a stand alone, powerful
English corporation that could represent an attractive ally to the
inexperienced young queen. They engaged solely in foreign trade,
and were therefore the greatest receivers of foreign exchange, not to
mention foreign intelligence. Strict regulation from "intermeddling"
by interlopers was conferred on them by the crown to protect their
trading outposts.[6] In fact, their royal decree even engaged the Low
Countries in its charter:

> *They have full authority as well from her Majesty as from the
> Princes, States and Rulers of the Low Countries, and beyond the seas,
> without appeal, provocation, or declination, to end and determine
> all civil causes, questions and controversies arising between or
> among the brethren, members and supporters of the said Company,
> or between them and others, either English or Strangers, who either
> may or will prorogate the jurisdiction of the said Company and
> their court, or are subject to the same by privileges and Charters
> thereunto granted.[7]*

Criticism of the court's decision was a punishable offense. Violations
of the ordinary rules of the company were always punishable by
a monetary fine, with repeated violations often culminating in
imprisonment. Any merchant caught "intermeddling" or interloping
on the Merchants Adventurers patch often would be both fined and
imprisoned.[8]

Yet the Merchants Adventurers were still subject to royal decree,
and in order to set sail, export cloth or other commodities, or claim
any monopolies over any territory, they, as all of the crown's subjects,

needed royal assent. And the best way for them to get what they needed to grow their interests was to nurture a symbiotic relationship with the crown. Nothing would have made this more apparent to either party than the brief War of the Insignia, where their cross-Channel business was severely disrupted. Since their freedom to trade was at stake as they were all staunch Protestants, they threw their considerable financial weight behind the queen and facilitated loans through Gresham, the queen's factor in Antwerp, in exchange for royal favor.

The merchants, Gresham, the queen, and the Privy Council all knew the importance of their trade to the realm, and that protecting it was essential to England's balance of payments. If their trade faltered, either in export to the Low Countries or the reexport of English kerseys (a lighter and cheaper cloth sold in southern Europe) over the Alps and back to Italy, Turkey, the Balkans, and Persia, then England's fledgling economy would be ruined.[9] By 1560, the queen had already realized that these powerful London merchants—probably no more than one hundred strong—were her stepping-stones into international finance and world prestige. So she let it be known that if they wanted her royal charter and her protection, there would be a reciprocal price to pay.

For better or worse, they had to agree, and the queen set her man Gresham to work on the plan that would launch England on its own road to empire. His work over the next several years would undoubtedly be fraught with difficulties, but above all else, the queen reminded him that failure was not an acceptable outcome. Gresham wisely counseled the queen that before he could work miracles, and she could strut across the world stage, she and her ministers must undertake a rapid stabilization of the pound sterling.[10] Her father, Henry VIII, had in great part enriched the crown with the Dissolution of the Monasteries, pillaging Church treasures and Church lands for himself and his cronies. Still Henry wanted more, and lowered the gold and silver content of English coins. The king had unwittingly wreaked havoc with the Great Debasement of the English monies, which not only undermined confidence in the pound sterling but also made it virtually impossible in a difficult market—like the one in 1560—to fix a viable exchange rate for sterling against other currencies.

Gresham knew from years of experience that the Antwerp money market was extremely sensitive to change depending on supply and demand, and that it was often so unpredictable that rates could change significantly during the course of two Bourse times. This meant that "easy" money was often followed by a period of a dearth of funds, which would only be made available at astronomical rates of interest.[11] In 1560, both conditions prevailed. Gresham's greatest feats of prestidigitation over the next two years would be to enhance the queen's fiscal management reputation by paying Mary's debts, borrowing fresh funds to cover the Scottish war, assisting with the recoining of English currency, and reestablishing confidence in the pound.

The new shilling (twenty making up one pound sterling) was minted, weighing 96 grains and containing 88 4/5 grains of fine metal. The mint price was fixed at £2.18s.6d. per pound troy of sterling silver. A pound of "angel" gold was coined into £36 by tale, and a pound of crown gold, which was slightly less pure, into £33 by tale. This meant that the rate between silver and gold was slightly more than eleven to one.[12] Elizabeth proclaimed on December 23, 1560, that the deadline to hand in the debased testoons stamped with a greyhound would be extended to April 1, 1561, in order to handle the volume required by the public. Stringent laws were also brought into effect to increase the penalties for "pinching" or "cutting" coins of the realm in order to siphon off silver or gold for personal use. In the event, Elizabeth nearly met her self-imposed deadline, with the old coins ceasing to be legal tender by the end of April. With the recoinage complete within a year of her announcing it, the queen congratulated herself by stating that she had won a victory over "this hideous monster of the base money."

What made this huge undertaking even more sweet was that the government had minted the new coins at a cost of £733,248 ($261.61 million or £141.41 million today), and paid only £683,113 ($250.62 million or £135.47 million today) for the "base monies," giving it a gross profit of £95,000 ($34.85 million or £18.84 million today). After government expenses, a net profit was estimated at £40,000 ($14.67 million or £7.93 million today).[13]

At last, the queen's merchants could put their faith behind the

English pound, assured of a stable standard of weights and measures for the currency. Wild currency exchange rates became a thing of the past, and the English merchants were again in a position to take advantage of the foreign markets. The downside was that while sterling's exchange rates were again stable, the currency had necessarily suffered some devaluation as well. This presented more problems for the smaller merchants, who were also being squeezed by Spanish wool merchants importing merino wool from the high plains of Iberia. The general public was also unhappy, since there was an acute shortage of ready cash at the existing prices. The Elizabethan chronicler, John Stow, wrote that in the fall of 1561, "the citizens of London were plagued with a threefold plague: pestilence, scarcity of money, and dearth of victuals, the misery whereof we hear too long to write."[14]

Still, the competition was bruising. For each English merchant prepared to carry cloth or other English exports like tin to the Continent, there were at least two "strangers," or foreigners, prepared to take his place in any market. London itself, while it had a number of foreign traders, especially from Italy and the German Hanseatic League, never openly welcomed them in the way that Antwerp did. They were mistrusted as "strangers," with the government and competitors alike keeping a close eye on them, making business and living needlessly uncomfortable and at times claustrophobic. In contrast, the openness of Antwerp allowed the city and the whole of the Spanish Netherlands to prosper from its acceptance of foreign traders, and the city burgomasters welcomed "strangers" in its midst in a way that was as yet unheard of in England. In this welcoming attitude, Antwerp was unique, and the city profited from it.[15]

At the beginning of Elizabeth's reign, there were well over 185 Italian firms in Antwerp alone, with more than that number again in German (from both the Hanse cities and Swabia), Spanish, Portuguese, Danish, Swedish, and English trading houses joining the thriving market. The main reason for this extraordinary commercial bustle was that the "Lords of Antwerp," as the English referred to them, were themselves serious players in the luxury trades and excellent businessmen. This contrasted sharply with London, where "citizenship" of London would normally be acquired early in life through an apprenticeship to one of the large medieval City corporations (the Mercers, Merchants Adventurers, Staplers, or others), and even then, the proud possessor would be only one rung above the despised "stranger."[16]

Yet by 1561, Antwerp had passed its heyday. While it still flaunted its ancient privileges handed down from the Burgundy dukes as a free city of the Holy Roman Empire, Philip II had already hatched other ideas.[17] The envisaged changes were spurred on by a number of factors, but the first of these would have been the dishonor of his parlous financial state at the time of becoming King of Spain in 1557. His "bankruptcy" of 1557 had devastated a number of the merchants trading in Antwerp—of all nationalities—and made them wary of taking any further sovereign debt. As if this weren't bad enough, other monarchs, including the Portuguese and French governments, repudiated their financial obligations as well, causing a second wave of bankruptcies among the merchants.[18]

Nothing undermines economies more than a lack of confidence, even war. And Philip of Spain, by his inability to pay the huge war debt inherited from his bellicose father and aggravated in his war against France, promoted the decline of Antwerp unwittingly. He was truly dismayed at the anger of the international merchant community; yet as an absolute monarch, he refused all rebuke. He longed for the warmth and comforts of Spain, and took this opportunity to decide that Seville would become the heart of his world trading operations. He resolved that Spain, which he cherished more than any other of his dominions, would become the center of his personal universe and his political empire. Now that his French war was over, his English wife, Queen Mary, soon to be replaced by Elisabeth of France,[19] Philip needed to get on and build his personal dynasty. Fatefully, the only place to do that, in his mind, was Spain. He left the Low Countries in disarray in July 1559, never to return.

Meanwhile, Elizabeth was ready to turn the economic adversity caused by Philip and his misuse of the Antwerp merchants to her advantage. Her first step was to negotiate through Gresham to buy arms and ammunition for the Scottish war. But more important from Antwerp's viewpoint, Elizabeth sent a clear message through Gresham to reimburse the merchant princes for their loans to her half sister Mary I. At a stroke, Elizabeth of England had set herself above the other monarchs of the time, and especially Philip, by making good her sister's foreign sovereign debt.[20]

Yet despite the queen's ascendancy in Antwerp, England's Merchants Adventurers could not escape unscathed. Philip made his second declaration of "bankruptcy" in 1560, taking down with him some of the top merchant banking families of Europe. Naturally with so many merchants forced to close down operations or tighten their belts as a result of the bankruptcies, there were a number of trades with the English, too, that defaulted. The monumental rise in litigation in Antwerp is a clear indicator of how tricky business dealings had become. English merchants who were not part of the Company of Merchants Adventurers, like the Hawkinses, found that their Spanish and Canaries trades were likewise affected. But most significantly for Elizabeth was if her Merchants Adventurers had dubious royal debtors. In that eventuality, they would be less likely to support her crown with loans in the future unless she could really make it worth their while.

Philip had lost the confidence of his European financiers, relying instead as much as possible in the future on the steady stream of the flota, the Spanish treasure fleet, arriving yearly from New Spain. The Low Countries, and indeed Protestant northern Europe, were proving too great a diversion for him, since the real threat to Spain, or so Philip believed, was the Turkish domination of the Mediterranean, not the heretic English queen. His decision to remove Spanish troops from the defense of the Netherlands against France in the early 1560s was directly linked to his inability to continue to fight European wars on two or more fronts *and* finance them.[21] What Philip had failed to understand was that, at a stroke, he had lost his best chance of taming a young Elizabeth, who, with the Low Countries, would all too soon represent the greatest threat to his empire.

*

While, the Queen of England took the tough decisions to sort out the "base monies," Elizabeth's Merchants Adventurers had seen all too clearly from the Spanish king's actions that Spain was not invincible. Long before the king had made his decision to return to Spain, they had decided to try their hand at plying trade themselves to the Indies, or Cathay, cutting out the middlemen from Iberia, the Arabs, or the Venetians—all of whom had long-established business in the region. But unlike the Spanish and Portuguese, England's Merchants Adventurers would approach the Indies from the Northeast and Russia, or Muscovy, as it was then called.

The idea was the brainchild of the Muscovy Company's first governor, Sebastian Cabot, a Merchant Adventurer himself and self-proclaimed "governor of the mystery and company of the Merchants Adventurers for the Discovery of Regions, Dominions, Islands and Places unknown" as early as 1548, the first year of Edward VI's reign.[22] Cabot, whose father had discovered Newfoundland in an expedition financed by Elizabeth's grandfather in 1497, had been a long-distance sea captain and merchant in his own right since 1508. The company's first voyage to Russia set out in 1553 to tremendous fanfare while the adolescent King Edward VI lay dying at Greenwich.

And it was simply a voyage organized on a scale that had never before been contemplated. The "admiral" or flagship was the *Bona Esperanza* of 120 tons, commanded by Sir Hugh Willoughby and carrying thirty-one men with provisions for eighteen months. His "vice admiral" was the *Edward Bonaventure* of 160 tons, sailing under Richard Chancellor, pilot major of the fleet, with thirty-nine men. The third ship in the tiny flotilla was the *Bona Confidentia* of 90 tons, carrying twenty-five men and the master of the fleet. Each vessel had been "new built," that is, repaired with good planking and timbers with their keels sheathed in lead against sea worm. Each ship had its own pinnace, arms, and victuals. And since this was a trading voyage, there were important merchants, Protestant ministers, and musicians who helped to make up the complement of 116 men in all. There were two hundred subscribers—all the great and the good of the land from peers and privy councillors to wealthy City merchants—whose fully paid-up share capital amounted to the staggering sum of £6,000 ($2.78 million or £1.5 million today). Even the lord high admiral, John Dudley, Duke of Northumberland, and his son-in-law, Henry Sidney, were pivotal investors.[23]

Envy of the luxury trades, so long monopolized by the Spaniards and the Portuguese, was the strongest motive for the enterprise. But it was its component backers—from the common seaman to the lord high admiral and City merchants—that set the blueprint for the future of English maritime expansion. The distinction among England's sea dogs, her merchants, and her rulers would become more and more blurred as the Elizabethan age progressed, with maritime exploits and successes becoming the most certain way of rising quickly in society and in wealth.

Even more extraordinary than the armchair admirals backing the voyage was the privation and degradation that the English would suffer until they could at last call success their own in long-distance voyages. This first voyage of discovery to Russia was, in simple terms, a financial disaster with huge loss of life. The ships were delayed by "fickle winds," and Willoughby, who had been chosen to lead the voyage for his "goodly person" overshot landfall and had to turn south to Arzina on the Lapland coast in September, where they decided to over-winter. He had lost contact with Chancellor in the *Edward* and presumed that Chancellor, the less-experienced man, would not survive. Willoughby's journal abruptly ended with that thought. It was found the following summer by Russian fishermen, who had discovered it among the frozen bodies of seventy men.[24]

Meanwhile, Chancellor had found landfall farther north at Vardo, and, having waited a week (as long as he dared in the enclosing gloom of August near the North Pole), sailed on to the White Sea, where he came ashore near the mouth of the River Dwina. Chancellor and his men made their way overland by sled to Moscow and the Russian czar's "golden" court, presenting King Edward's greetings to Ivan IV, later known as "the Terrible." While the descriptions given of the Russian countryside were of an isolated and desolate icebound wasteland, the court of Ivan IV was much admired by Chancellor and his men:

They go, and being conducted into the Golden Court (for so they call it, although not very fair), they find the Emperor sitting upon a high and stately seat, apparelled with a robe of silver, and with another diadem on his head; our men, being placed over against him, sit down. In the midst of the room stood a mighty

*cupboard upon a square foot, whereupon stood also a round board,
in a manner of a diamond, broad beneath, and towards the top
narrow, and every step rose up more narrow than the other. Upon
this cupboard was placed the Emperor's plate, which was so much
that the very cupboard itself was scant able to sustain the weight of
it. The better part of all the vessels and goblets was made of very
fine gold; and, amongst the rest, there were four pots of very large
bigness, which did adorn the rest of the plate in great measure, for
they were so high, that they thought them at the least five feet long.
Then were also upon this cupboard certain silver casks, not much
differing from the quantity of our firkins wherein was reserved the
Emperor's drink. On each side of the hall stood four tables, each of
them laid and covered with very clean table-cloths . . . [25]*

Ivan, too, was impressed with the English mariners. A general
agreement to commence trading with England was undertaken, and
Ivan wrote back to Edward (who was already long dead), saying:

*In the strength of the twentieth year of our governance, be it
known that at our sea coasts arrived a ship, with one Richard
and his company, and said, that he was desirous to come into our
dominions, and according to his request hath seen our Majesty and
our eyes; and hath declared unto us your Majesty's desire as that
we should grant unto your subjects, to go and come, and in our
dominions, and among our subjects to frequent free marts, with
all sorts of merchandises, and upon the same to have wares for
their return. And they have also delivered us your letters which
declare the same request. And hereupon we have given order,
that wheresoever your faithful servant Hugh Willoughby land or
touch in our dominions, to be well entertained, who as yet is not
arrived as your servant Richard can declare . . . according to your
honourable request and my honourable commandment will not
leave it undone, and are furthermore willing that you send unto us
your ships and vessels, when, and as often as they may have passage,
with good assurance on our part to see them harmless. And if you
send one of your Majesty's council to treat with us, whereby your
country merchants may with all kinds of wares, and where they*

will, make their market in our dominions, they shall have their free
mart with all free liberties through my whole dominions with all
kinds of wares, to come and go at their pleasure, without any let,
damage, or impediment, according to this our letter, our word, and
our seal . . . [26]

Chancellor returned to London in 1554 with the relative good news that the Russians had agreed to trade, and the Muscovy Company was officially incorporated under Queen Mary by royal charter. It was granted the monopoly on trade with Russia and all areas "northwards, northeastwards and northwestwards" which had been unknown to Englishmen prior to 1553.[27] But the hero of the Muscovy Company, Richard Chancellor, drowned two years later in the wreck of the *Edward Bonaventure* after one further voyage to the White Sea. While Chancellor had given his life for dreams of adventure (which he certainly had) and wealth (which he never quite got), the importance of his achievements lay not in the original discoveries made, but rather in the overall drama of his voyages, the royal charter, royal embassies, and its cumulative impact on the English nation. English merchants from the City of London had taken part and witnessed firsthand the impact of long-distance, heavily capitalized trade through a joint stock company involving several strata of society. This made the Muscovy Company the natural patron of geographical science and enterprise well into Elizabeth's reign.

And it was not difficult to find replacements for the Muscovy Company's dead hero. Chancellor's successors were two brothers, Stephen and William Borough, sons of the Devon navigator John Aborough. The Boroughs consolidated Chancellor's northern sea route by turning it into a flourishing commercial highway and increasing important trade in rope, hemp, and Baltic oak to England. By the time the Muscovy Company's Governor Cabot died in 1557, it was believed that the Muscovy trade could travel overland through Russia in a southerly direction to Persia.

Notwithstanding the Borough brothers' achievements by sea, the land route southward through Russia to Persia was trail blazed by a merchant, member of the Mercers' Company, and later royal ambassador of Elizabeth's: Anthony Jenkinson. Jenkinson began his career as an adolescent training in the Levant, and he traveled extensively throughout the Mediterranean, having received a "safe conduct" permitting him to trade freely in Turkish ports from Suleiman the Great in the early days of Mary of England's rule. On his first journey to Russia, he said his trade with the Tartars was "small and beggarly . . . not worth the writing, neither is there any hope of trade in all those parts worth following."[28]

Still, Jenkinson soldiered southward to Bokhara in tremendous danger from the successive marauding caravans who kidnapped him or molested the trading party. When they reached Bokhara some sixteen weeks later, the city was a huge disappointment, with "beggarly and poor" merchants with so few wares to sell that Jenkinson thought that their stocks hadn't been renewed in two, if not three, years. The way to China, he discovered, would take another nine months overland in the most favorable circumstances; but the road was blocked by war, which happened with alarming regularity. Jenkinson continued on to the Caspian region and eventually sold enough goods to make a small profit. But it was his intelligence on the disruption to trade in the region between Russia, Persia, Turkey, and India by war that would prove the commodity of real value to Elizabeth.

In May 1561, Jenkinson was sent out again on his second Muscovy voyage, carrying letters recommending him to Czar Ivan, the Shah of Persia, and other Circassian princes. The purpose of his journey was to establish firm trade with Russia, and to make another trip to the Caspian region to open commercial trade with Persia. On his arrival in Moscow that summer, Jenkinson was shocked that he was denied access to the czar, and refused leave to travel south. After a six-month delay, under effective house arrest, and at a point of giving up all hope of achieving his goal, the former English ambassador "intervened." At last, Jenkinson would be received at the Russian court.[29] But what sort of "intervention" had the English ambassador made?

In the month prior to Jenkinson's departure from England, the Senate of Hamburg wrote to Elizabeth that "certain princes of the Roman Empire" had informed them that "certain large quantities of armour and cannon shipped from their town belong to private persons, and is intended for the use of the Grand Duke of the Russians or Muscovites against the Livonians in contravention to the Imperial decree which forbids any ammunitions of war to be sold for the use of the Muscovites. They therefore beg that she will send them an assurance that these arms are intended for her own service."[30]

This complaint was followed two weeks later by a letter from the Senate of Cologne, that wrote on April 30, "Having heard that a very considerable amount of arms, offensive and defensive, were being shipped by her order (especially of the kind required for men-at-arms, such as hand-guns) they were unwilling to hinder the quiet transportation of the same for her service. It having just now come to their knowledge however that certain English traders convey these arms either into Muscovy direct, or to parts from which they may be carried thither, contrary to the interests of the empire."[31]

Elizabeth naturally denied all knowledge of such goings on and wrote back to the Senate on May 6 that "on her royal word" no arms and munitions *had been* shipped in her name from Hamburg.[32] Eight days later, on May 14, Anthony Jenkinson embarked for Russia. Two weeks after that, on May 31, the Holy Roman Emperor Ferdinand wrote to the Queen of England, telling her that he had heard these "rumors" and that the Muscovites are greatly encouraged in their belligerence against Poland and the Germanic states by the provision of "warlike matters." He has therefore given strict orders that no one shall be allowed to transport arms or victuals into Muscovy, and begged the queen to ensure that none of her subjects would go to the country either.[33]

If Ferdinand had heard rumors that the Queen of England was providing Ivan the Terrible with his dark materiel of war, then most likely Ivan, too, would have expected armaments in the English merchants' wares. There is no precise record of Jenkinson's inventory that survives, but in view of the huge delay in Ivan's receiving him, it seems unlikely that whatever war materiel may (or may not) have been provided at the outset was deemed inadequate by the tempestuous czar. The fact that only upon "the intervention" of the former English ambassador was Jenkinson allowed not only to meet Ivan, but also to become the czar's gem and silk merchant to Persia, indicates that some favors in the form of weaponry were most likely exchanged. Ivan made no secret about his "love" of the English in his struggle against Poland after this, and it is doubtful that this love would have been as steadfast as it became throughout the 1560s in commercial and political terms without an English trade in weaponry.

By June 1562, Jenkinson was finally given a safe conduct from court and allowed once more to journey down the Volga to the Caspian Sea, but aside from a sumptuous welcome and friendly relationship that developed with Abdullah Khan in Shirvan, the trading mission to Persia proved a disaster. He had once again landed himself in a war zone on the turn:

> For the Turk's Ambassador being arrived and the peace concluded, the Turkish merchants there at that time present, declared to the same Ambassador that my coming thither . . . would in great part destroy their trade, and that it should be good for him to persuade the Sophia not to favor me, as his highness meant to observe the league and friendship with the great Turk his master, which request of the Turkish merchants, the same Ambassador earnestly preferred, and being afterwards dismissed with great honor he departed out of the Realm with the Turk's son's head (the rebel Bajazet) as aforesaid, and other presents.[34]

Jenkinson was lucky to escape back to England without being made a "present" himself, and only returned at all through the good auspices of Abdullah Khan, who persuaded the shah that it would bring bad luck to kill a stranger "in that fashion." While Jenkinson made five further voyages to the region, and his voyages were persistently marred by great misfortune, murder, and failure, the overwhelming desire to trade directly with Persia and Cathay would become an English mantra and obsession over the next twenty years. What Jenkinson's adventures highlighted was that England's strengths lie not in overland trade, but in somehow dominating the seas.

Trade had become the promoter of new ideas as well as the generator of economic growth, and helped England to emerge from its mediocrity into the Renaissance. English merchants, mostly Londoners, learned quickly the refined art of the long-distance business gurus, the Italians, combined with the crucial strategy of controlling the Channel and Narrow Seas. Control of the Channel's shipping lanes meant domination—both economic and political—of Spain's trades with the Low Countries, and this in itself became a goal from the beginning of Elizabeth's reign.

By the end of 1560, the English navy was already evolving into an efficient machine. The country's seamen were putting out to sea to "harvest" from England's enemies (and sometimes her friends) while the English Merchants Adventurers often benefited directly from their forays, though often claiming the reverse.

The country's merchant fleet plying the Channel was not only well protected by the queen's ships, as required, but also by a growing breed of fearless and daring seamen out to take prizes from hostile shipping in payment for shepherding the fleet. In the early 1560s many young English adventurers, dreaming most probably of voyages with the Muscovy Company to Cathay rather than mundane Channel crossings, grew up in the hope that some day, they would cross oceans and take "real" prizes. The exploits of English, French Huguenot, or Scottish pirates were whispered on everyone's lips, and the source of persistent complaint to the Queen of England by her neighbors. Their daring raids in smaller, swifter ships were admired and feared by all. In England, these men were the new "Robin Hoods," seeking to redress the previous years of bloody Catholic cruelty under Mary and dreaming of rich prizes to distribute among their friends. Such men hardly saw their own brand of retribution as Protestant corsairs in the same light. One such dreamer in the thick of the trade with the Low Countries and France—a red-haired junior master on a small bark making the run between the Low Countries and Dover—was the then unknown renegade Francis Drake.[35]

Like hundreds, if not thousands, of other young men, Drake's life and career would be made by "harvesting the sea," teetering perilously at times into piracy, while at other times turning his efforts expansively to the legitimate investments of other merchant princes of the day. His career, perhaps more than any other, came to symbolize the synthesis of the English seaman from merchant shipping service to defense of the realm to the type of adventurer who would, in Sir Walter Raleigh's words, "seek new worlds, for gold, for praise, for glory."[36]

Frequently in years to come, it would be difficult to discern the legal endeavors of most of Elizabeth's seamen, statesmen, and gentlemen from out-and-out buccaneering. These men—call them pirates, corsairs, rovers, privateers,[37] mariners, sailors, merchants, adventurers, or gentlemen—would drive the rebirth of an isolated England and transform the island nation into a nascent empire. They would also undermine the fortunes of Catholic Europe, and most notably those of Spain and Portugal.

6. The Politics of Piracy, Trade, and Religion ❧

This is a nation of overwhelming audacity, courageous,
impetuous, unmerciful in war, warm on first acquaintance,
sneering at death, but boastful about it, cunning, and
completely given to dissimulation, whether in word or deed;
above all they possess prudence, along with great
eloquence and hospitality.

—EMANUEL VAN METEREN, ABOUT THE ENGLISH

Before the end of the third year of Elizabeth's reign she had firmly established England as a new force to be reckoned with in the Channel, boosting the country's status and stability, and laying the firm foundations for independence. She had stood up to the troublesome Guise faction in France and Scotland. The whirligig of changing French Valois kings—Henry II, his sons, Francis II, Charles IX— and even their formidable mother, Catherine de' Medici, recognized Elizabeth's achievements and potential danger to France. Philip II admired her and lamented her heresy, and Pope Pius IV wanted her dethroned and even proposed to the Spanish king that he would crown him King of England himself.[1] While the English queen had allied herself with other Protestants in Sweden, Scotland, France, and the Netherlands, she had been careful to maintain a policy of "balance" and "diplomacy" with France, Portugal, the Holy Roman Empire, and Spain. As Philip's ambassador to England so bitterly remarked in April 1562, " . . . now that she has the support of the heretics here and in France, and knows the trouble our affairs are in, in the Netherlands, I am certain that this Queen has thought and studied nothing else since the King sailed for Spain, but how to oust him from the Netherlands, and she believes the best way to effect this is to embroil them over there on religious questions, as I wrote months ago."[2]

Elizabeth did, indeed, keep an intent eye on events in the Low Countries. She knew that England's wealth, security, and ability to borrow and generate foreign exchange depended to a large extent on free trade in the Netherlands. But there were storm clouds on the horizon. Philip's insatiable need for cash to fight his Mediterranean war against the Ottoman Turk had led to the States-General reluctantly agreeing to grant a 3.6 million ducat loan ($326.43 million or £176.45 million today) to their Spanish overlord, but refused to allow disbursements until Spain recalled her crack *tercios* troops home. While Philip may have been apoplectic with rage, he was desperate for the money from the Netherlands to supplement his fortune in gold and silver sent to Seville twice yearly from the Americas. And so he agreed to their terms.[3]

As can be expected from a monarch on whose empire the sun never set, his response to the States-General's economic blackmail was predictably ugly. Philip worked with the pope in secret on a plan to redraw the religious map of the Low Countries, fill the pulpits of the country with his own men of the cloth, and introduce the Inquisition there. Without warning, toward the end of 1561, the pope published the plan, naming the new bishops—all of whom had been personally selected by Philip. Their new primate and cardinal was none other than Philip's trusty minister, Cardinal Antoine Perronet de Granvelle, who later tried to persuade the Netherlander elite that he was one of them. After the first uprisings, he wrote to Philip that "people here universally display discontent with any and all Spaniards in these provinces. It would seem that this derives from the suspicion that one might wish to subject them to Spain and reduce them to the same state as the Italian provinces under the Spanish crown."[4]

Naturally, the situation alarmed the Netherlanders as well as all their trading partners—Protestant and Catholic alike. Unrest in the Low Countries could only spell disaster for the merchant classes. The announcement also created havoc in England, since it was an undisguised fact that two of the most senior Netherlander officials—William of Orange and Count Egmont—knew nothing about the redrawing of the Netherlands map.[5]

To compound the gravity of the situation, English merchants in

Spain had been arrested by Inquisition inspectors under royal edict, and the inquisitors destroyed English "Lutheran books" (the Bible) and merchandise. An English pinnace, the *Fleur de Lys*, had been seized in the Canaries in March 1562, and the inquisitors charged her crew with the dastardly crime of "Lutheranism." Even established English factors were imprisoned under the laws of the Inquisition and charged with heresy.[6] Naturally alarmed, English merchants trading with Spain complained to the queen and the Privy Council, demanding royal intervention and a stop to the seizures. As they were unprotected by a "company," like the Merchants Adventurers, and were without a common organization, English traders in Spain were particularly vulnerable. They had no specific representation with city fathers, or the Spanish court. Not only were they being charged with heresy, but unfair levies were raised against them, and the Spanish courts were patently biased. At the end of the day, the use of English shipping was curtailed for "quarrels of matters of religion without cause."[7]

Still, the English were not the only ones singled out for harsh treatment. When the Netherlanders experienced the same abuse, there was an abrupt souring in relations between England and Spain. This new phase in Anglo-Iberian trade was heralded by unprovoked attacks on Spanish shipping on the high seas in response to the "strange and pitiful" treatment of English merchants in Spain.[8] Trade with "Lutheran" heretics seemed to be no longer respected as a legitimate activity in Spanish waters, so the English had nothing to lose and would no longer act respectably. This naturally provoked outrage from Spain, and the English ambassador met several times with the Duke of Alba to outline what Elizabeth was doing against English piracy in Galicia and Andalusia.

The year when these "provocations" occurred was 1562, and some believed at the time that the escalation of "hostilities" between England and Spain may not have been an accident, irrespective of the King of Spain's troubles in the Low Countries. The Queen of England, some ventured, may have chosen her precise moment to flex her newfound muscles.

Two years earlier, the Ottoman fleet ambushed the Spanish fleet at Djerba off the coast of North Africa, capturing six thousand veteran troops and thirty galleys. Elizabeth chose to believe, rightly, that Philip's withdrawal of the *tercios* from the Low Countries meant that these crack troops were destined for the Mediterranean to replace the captured soldiers, and would be preoccupied in the Mediterranean fighting Islam for some time to come. Her advisors and spies in France had also warned her at the beginning of 1562 that the country was hurtling toward the first of its religious civil wars. The Huguenot commanders, Admiral Gaspard de Coligny and the Prince de Condé were already making overtures to England to help them in their struggle. If she were to take any action against Spain while France was in turmoil, she needn't fear a French reprisal. Trouble in the Low Countries; trouble in France; the confiscation of English merchants, goods, and shipping in Spain; and the restraint of European trade were all important considerations in her decisions. Elizabeth abhorred war. It was a diabolical waste of money and men. If revenge could be had by lightning raids on Spanish shipping, where she could always disown any involvement or tacit approval, then she could keep her dogs of war focused on the enemy at sea, rather than grumbling and troublemaking at home.

There is no doubt that the Queen of England appreciated better than most that Philip's war against the Ottoman Empire had not gone particularly well since Djerba, and in 1562 was at its high tide of danger. Exasperatingly for the King of Spain and the English, Moslem corsairs cruised off the Spanish coast taking any ship they could as their victims—including English vessels at the height of the seizures of English ships by the Spanish themselves! A merchant in Seville reported home, "owing to the Turks and Moors, no ship can come in nor go out."[9] The English ambassador now complained about Spanish and Ottoman depredations, only to be confronted with evidence that English vessels were intruding in Portuguese waters off the Guinea coast of Africa.

Spain and Portugal had long argued against any shipping other than their own being allowed "beyond the line"—that is to say, along the coast of Africa, in the Indies, the Caribbean, the Spanish Main, the Philippines, or Brazil—or for that matter anywhere else where they landed outside of Europe.[10] Now that Portugal had the child king, Sebastian, on its throne, Philip took his duties as the elder statesman protecting their colonies most seriously.[11]

But intrusion by "interlopers" was nothing new to either Spain or Portugal. As early as the 1530s, the Guinea coast had been worried by French and English rovers in search of Ashanti gold and slaves to man the ever-expanding Spanish and Lusitanian empires. The English pirate Thomas Wyndham sailed to the Guinea coast of Africa in 1553—with substantial backing from the City of London— and three ships: the *Primrose*, the *Lion,* and the *Moon.* When their Portuguese pilot fell out with Wyndham, and headed upriver with some gentlemen traders, the crew spat in his face and drew their swords upon his return. The pilot and gentlemen had been blithely trading in human cargo while the crew withered in the "smothering heat with close and cloudy air and storming weather of such putrifying quality that it rotted the coats off their backs."[12] Yellow fever had decimated the crew, and only the *Primrose* returned, with an emaciated crew of a mere forty men. Three-quarters of the men had died, but the ship had over 400 pounds of twenty-two-carat gold in her hold, 36 butts of melegueta peppers, 250 tusks, and the head of one elephant "of huge bigness."[13] Even the queen herself had ventured four royal ships in a failed Guinea voyage in June 1561 as part of a London syndicate.

More worrying to Philip was that he had had reports of English rovers making transatlantic voyages, and demanded that Ambassador Alvarez de Quadra lodge a serious rebuke with the queen. One of the most infamous of these corsairs was a scoundrel called Thomas Stucley, who had been charged with piracy as early as May 1558 for robbing some Spanish ships. Whether Stucley was acquitted due to lack of evidence or the rumor that he was Henry VIII's "base born son" is open to some doubt. Whether Stucley himself started the scurrilous rumor is not beyond the realm of possibility either. Shortly after this incident, Stucley absconded with his own father's property—that is to say, that of Hugh Stucley—and, when those funds ran out, defrauded his four brothers and impoverished his long-suffering wife.

Miraculously, with his past shenanigans, in 1560, Stucley was employed as a tax collector in the county of Berkshire, probably stealing all the money he could get, since a year later he had purchased a captaincy at Berwick. Perhaps more remarkably, Elizabeth more than tolerated the reprobate, and probably attempted to use him as a spy in her "wild" Irish province.

There is no doubt that Stucley was at the heart of a daring plan in 1562 to cross the Atlantic. He had proposed a venture to the Queen of England whereby he, and the French rover Jean Ribault, the Dieppe sailor and "western planter" turned pirate who had previously been in English service, would colonize Florida. Elizabeth was tantalized by the prospect and agreed to supply at least one ship and artillery.[14] All that remained was to recruit the sailors and "planters," or colonists.

There was little that Philip could do, other than protest via his ambassador while he was preoccupied with his war in the Mediterranean and unrest in the Low Countries. Legitimate trade became a precarious way to earn a living in these times, and English piracy flourished with the tacit approval of the state. There was a huge increase in letters of reprisal against injustices perpetrated against English merchants and seamen issued by the Admiralty at the time with the queen's knowledge.

The letter of reprisal was a long-established and useful tool of monarchs throughout Europe. Since medieval times, the letter of reprisal, or *letter de mark*, allowed a merchant, traveler, or ship owner who had been robbed on foreign territory in peacetime by the subjects of a foreign prince to recoup his losses. The letter of reprisal was granted only after the offended party had been unable to obtain justice in the courts of the foreign country, and was, in Elizabethan England, granted by the High Court of the Admiralty in cases of reprisals at sea, and in times of "peace." Peace frequently meant little more than undeclared war, which was for all intents and purposes the situation the English found themselves in now.[15]

The letter of reprisal in the hands of England's merchant navy became a devastatingly blunt instrument. The Channel shipping lanes became positively choked with would-be aggrieved Englishmen boarding, ransacking, maiming, and often destroying any foreign vessel and her crew that they could lay their hands on. It mattered little if the ships were French, Italian, Netherlanders, or indeed Spanish. Since the most numerous—and richest—ships in the Channel were those belonging to Spain and the Netherlands (a neutral), they became the ripest targets for the holders of the letters of reprisal to attack. The English used whatever means they could to obtain their prizes, and we should not doubt their brutality in the exercise of their "duties."[16]

England's seamen were, by and large, a ferocious lot, most of whom had been press-ganged into service. They were rough, undisciplined, and poorly paid. The only thing that sustained many of them and kept them in tow was the promise of prize money or booty—not patriotism or an unswerving loyalty to the authority of the crown, or even their captain—to protect England's shores. Getting wealthy through piracy was their raison d'être, not the icing on the cake. Throughout the 1560s, once pressed into service, these men did not need to be escorted to their ports of embarkation; they went willingly under the command of the recruiting officer and reported for duty wherever they were sent. Their wages were less than fishermen could expect, while the chances of their dying at sea from disease were excellent. Most voyages saw at least half its crew die from disease or starvation. If contact were made with the enemy, then more would die in battle or from infection from their wounds in the weeks that followed. It is little wonder that keeping them in order required excellent leadership skills. As most captains well understood, these men had come for pillage, or, as Drake called it, "some little comfortable dew from heaven."[17] Atrocities carried out by the English were rife. One Spanish crew had even been trussed in their ship's sails and tossed overboard to drown, while their ship—now an English prize—was brought back to an English harbor.[18]

In the words of Captain Luke Ward, a pirate who later became an adventurer of exploration, the English sailor was "great in words and sufficiently crafty, bold as well as hard-working, irascible, inexorable, grasping."[19] The most outstanding of these were the fiercely Protestant West Countrymen like the Hawkinses, the Killigrews, the Champernownes, and the Hawkinses young, and as yet unknown, cousin, Francis Drake, who was trawling the Channel in the early 1560s in a bark that skirted in and out of the waters in the Netherlands, sometimes in legitimate trade, sometimes not. These men represented a new force in English foreign policy, and one that was as unpredictable as it was impossible to resist, or control.

Most significantly, they gave the common folk cause to be proud, and to hope. These "local heroes" were often the difference between survival and starvation. Harvests were frequently poor, and the winter of 1562-63 was bitterly cold. With Elizabethan local government in the hands of this unpaid gentry or nobility, the local heroes' resourcefulness in the quest for prizes often meant employment and food on the table. Men like the elder Sir Walter Raleigh, vice admiral of Devon; and Sir Edward Horsey, captain of the Isle of Wight, were among the more notorious local robber barons who made a fine art of taking prizes and making English markets for their stolen booty. It is little wonder with such sea dogs unleashed in the Channel that the Spaniards and the Netherlanders put their losses at over 2 million ducats ($11.6 billion or £6.27 billion today) by the end of 1563.

In an attempt to cool the rising temperature between Spain and England, Elizabeth had placed herself in the position of honest broker between Spain and the Low Countries, urging Philip to reinstate the "ancient rights"—meaning to stop the Inquisition and allow freedom of religious practice in the Netherlands. She was also heavily involved with the Huguenot cause in France. Naturally, the Spanish king didn't trust her, as she was abrogating "ancient rights" at the same time in Ireland by enforcing English over Celtic law and had instituted recusancy fines against Catholics in England.[20] He resisted all her entreaties to help in his troubled province, and indeed sent Ambassador de Quadra his orders just to drive his own message into Elizabeth's heart. De Quadra inveigled the brutal Ulster Irish malcontent, Shane O'Neill, to come to his embassy in London to hear a Catholic mass. O'Neill, who had come to England to submit to Elizabeth on the understanding that he would be granted rights as the O'Neill chieftain, couldn't resist the temptation. De Quadra wrote to the regent's advisor and Philip's minister, Cardinal de Granvelle, in the Low Countries that, "Shane O'Neill and ten or twelve of his principal followers have received the holy sacrament in my house with the utmost secrecy as he refused to receive the Queen's communion. He has assured me that he is and will be perfectly steadfast on the question of religion. As to the rest, if His Majesty should intend to mend matters here radically as he writes me from Spain, I think this man will be a most important instrument."[21]

Whether O'Neill intended anything other than reserving his political options is open to debate, but certainly de Quadra's actions would have left O'Neill in no doubt whatever that Ireland had a friend in the King of Spain. Equally certain was that any attempt by Spain to stir up trouble in Ireland would have been very dimly viewed by any Tudor monarch, and in particular by the parsimonious queen, who was spending between £20,000 and £26,000 yearly ($8.33 million or £4.5 million today) to "keep the peace" in the rebellious province, in addition to whatever her governors and lord deputy had to shell out of their own pockets.[22]

Fortunately neither de Quadra nor Philip had realized that England was arming itself—just in case—through Gresham's efforts in the Netherlands, Bohemia, Germany, and Hungary through legitimate trade and foreign finance. By April 1562, Gresham had acquired armaments for which he had paid the staggering sum of just under £140,000 ($50.78 million or £27.45 million today). The purchase of weaponry, gunpowder, and other war materiel had become the chief reason for the crown's borrowings at London and Antwerp, and had begun to raise such suspicion in the Low Countries that Gresham had been obliged to bribe customs officers in order to ship the goods out of Antwerp for London.

But things were about to worsen for trade. France erupted into the first in a series of bloody religious civil wars that dogged the Valois dynasty until its end. At the outset the Huguenot factions maintained control broadly of the north and west of the country under the command of Admiral de Coligny as naval commander, and the Prince de Condé leading the land war. When Philip wrote to de Quadra in London in his secret code that the ambassador must advise Elizabeth of his intention to assist the French crown in its time of need, the alarm in the privy chamber was palpable. The argument raged that if Spain were indeed wooing Ireland, and assisting France, then there would be a real risk that England could be surrounded by the Spanish, invaded by her "postern gate," and lose her independence. Spain simply had to be stopped. Yet it was only when Cecil received a communiqué from the English ambassador Throckmorton in France that matters were acted upon. Throckmorton's April 17, 1562, letter stated:

Cecil must work with his friends at home, and especially abroad, so that the King of Spain may have his hand full in case he aid [sic] the Papists in France, for there lies danger. The Queen may make her profit of these troubles as the King of Spain intends to do . . . the Queen must not be idle. I know assuredly that the King of Spain practises to put his foot in Calais. Our friends the Protestants in France must be so handled and dandled that in case the Duke of Guise the Constable, the Marshal St Andre and that sect bring the King of Spain into France, and give them possession of some places and forts, then the Protestants for their defence or for desire of revenge or affliction to the Queen, may be moved to give her possession of Calais, Dieppe, or Newhaven; perhaps all three. This matter must not be moved to any of them or their ministers, for it will fall out more aptly of itself upon their demands of aid and especially when the Prince of Condé and the Protestants perceive the Papists bring strangers into France, and give the King of Spain interest in all things.[23]

By June, Admiral de Coligny and the Prince de Condé had proposed to give the port of Newhaven (Le Havre today) to Elizabeth to help defend France, and the vital shipping artery of the Channel. The Privy Council had had time to examine the repercussions and agree to garrison English troops at Newhaven and Dieppe, with Robert Dudley leading the "hawk" party for immediate support of the Huguenots. The queen and Cecil at last relented, more for tangible security to regain Calais as the longed-after home of the merchant Staplers than out of Protestant sympathy. For the Admiralty, Calais was also strategically important to England, since it was its toehold on the windward side of the Channel. If English shipping could again be harbored there, then the risk of being locked in port was eliminated.

Notwithstanding this, once at Newhaven, the Queen of England categorically refused to allow her soldiers out of the town, since that could be construed as a hostile act against an anointed king. She was keen that her motives should not be misunderstood, so she lost no time in asking her ambassador to Spain, Thomas Challoner, to meet with Philip to set out her concerns, and why she had been obliged to intervene in French affairs. Elizabeth was honing her particular brand of statecraft: wage peace as if it were war. The country could literally ill afford for Philip to turn his heavy guns from his seemingly endless Mediterranean conflicts with the Ottoman Turk onto England.

But before Challoner could arrange the meeting, Elizabeth was struck down with smallpox, and for three weeks lay on what many believed to be her deathbed. She named Robert Dudley as protector of the realm in the event of her death, and the entire country prayed for her survival, remembering with dread the "protectorship" of Dudley's father, Northumberland. The queen knew that Philip's mind had been poisoned by de Quadra, and so one of the first things she did during her recovery was to have a lengthy letter penned to Philip. Her first point made is against the Spanish ambassador:

> We have been in mind now of a long time to impart to you our concept and judgment hereof, wherein we have been occasioned to forbear only by the mutability of the proceedings of our neighbours in France and for that also we have some cause to doubt of the manner of the report of your ambassador, having found him in his negotiations divers times to have more respect towards the weal of others than of us and our country; we have thought not only to give special charge to our ambassador there resident with you to declare plainly and sincerely our disposition and meaning. . . . [24]

Challoner's interview took place at last on November 27, 1562, when the queen was already out of danger. His note of the audience to the Privy Council explained that the queen apologized that she had not written sooner, "not from any want of regard towards [the King of Spain], but because she had imagined that these disturbances in France would long since have ended. As she is compelled to move in the matter, Challoner thought it well to send to His Majesty a paper containing the motives which induced her to act as she has done. These reasons are, the hostility of the house of Guise, their efforts to secure the crown of England for the Queen of Scotland, the assumption of the royal arms of England, the refusal of Queen Mary to ratify the treaty, the Queen's apprehension of a descent on her coasts from the seaports of Normandy, and the retention of Calais."[25]

While the queen had been ill, Dudley had masterminded the deployment of some five thousand men and arms to Newhaven with Privy Council approval under the leadership of his brother, Ambrose, the Earl of Warwick, Robert's elder surviving brother. When the Huguenots lost Rouen in October, they blamed Elizabeth, and her impossible order to remain within the city walls. The garrison had been put in an untenable position—defending an indefensible strategy through an exceptionally harsh winter with semihostile allies in the Huguenots, competent enemies in the French crown, and financial support from the Spanish. Further, with income from the Low Countries more and more precarious, and trade through the Muscovy Company still in its fledgling state, the prospects for peace and economic growth grew dim. It was time for the Queen of England to step up a gear and use the best weapon she had in her arsenal to avoid catastrophe—her adventurers. Some armed with the letter of reprisal, some not.

Elizabeth unleashed Stucley and gave the order for him to raise his army of "planters." She also agreed, at long last, to grant the flamboyant West Countryman, John Hawkins, a passport to go on his first Guinea voyage to sell slaves to the Spanish plantations in the Americas.[26]

7. Raising the Stakes ❧

*Ships from the Indies have arrived . . . very heavily
laden with divers merchandise and with one million and
eight hundred thousand golden ducats, of which about one
hundred eighty thousand belong to the King, and the rest to
private individuals. They brought with them five ships, part
French and part English, captured by them as corsairs;
but the English ambassador declares that his countrymen
were not corsairs, but merchants . . .*

—PAULO TIEPOLO, VENETIAN AMBASSADOR IN SPAIN

With more and more English merchants taken hostage under the draconian legislation of the Inquisition, Elizabeth's resolve to keep her country independent hardened. Every means available to her would be used to that end, and piratical acts and double-dealing by the queen and the Admiralty in the Channel would become some of the sharpest weapons in her arsenal. But there were others, too.

When Elizabeth granted permission to John Hawkins of Plymouth to set sail in October 1562, she was in part responding to the international crisis, and in part to the outcry of her own people for vengeance upon the Inquisition and its perpetrators.[1] In England, popular literature of the day was filled with passionate appeals against the Antichrist, Philip. Pamphleteers depicted the King of Spain as the devil incarnate, while Spanish ballads sung the praises of their king and his undeclared war on the *Luteranos*.[2] In the Inquisition edict published in May 1560, it had been decreed that:

No son or grandson of any person burnt, or reconciled to the Church, can hold office in the King's household, or at the Court.
If he holds a public office in any place he is to lose it.

He cannot be a merchant, apothecary or vendor of spices or drugs.

If any of the aforesaid persons has bought gold or silk, the sale of which had been prohibited them, they are to go to the inquisitors to report themselves within six days; otherwise on the expiration of that term, they will be prosecuted with all rigour, and whoever shall fail to accuse them is to be excommunicated.

No person of this kind can hold office, such as maggiordomo, *accountant, carver, or any other charge in the household of any nobleman.[3]*

With such public declarations of steely will from Spain, and public displays of fabulous Spanish wealth arriving in Seville twice yearly from its American colonies, it is little wonder that English envy and revenge were rapidly becoming the motivations behind the new crusade. Still, it is fair to say that both sides shared the blame of religious intolerance rife in that age, and they reaped the consequences that this would bring. Spain had wealth and an empire to protect. England had its Protestant state to uphold and believed it had every right to trade freely in Spanish territories. These reasons, coupled with religious intolerance, fear of foreigners, envy, greed, and revenge were all behind the escalation of hostilities and the rise of piracy.

Yet within England the reasons for raising the stakes fell broadly into three categories. For the queen and the Privy Council, the reasons were political. For the people, it was a matter of religion and pride. And for most merchants, at the outset, it was commercial. Later on, when piratical acts became a safer bet even for legitimate merchants, their reasons wavered into the political.[4]

But which of these reasons was John Hawkins's motivation as he set sail to Portuguese West Africa on the first of his slaving voyages? The loathsome slave trade had been in existence ever since the conquistadores had decimated the Native American population through forced labor and disease some fifty years earlier. African "imports" were seen as a moral solution, relieving the Native Americans from their work burden, and the "imports" were deemed hardy and good workers for the plantations and the gold or silver mines. A good indication of how the slave business to Spanish America had burgeoned was that, in 1551 alone, no fewer than seventeen thousand licenses were offered for sale.[5] Hawkins, one of the most seasoned English traders in Spain and the Canaries, would have seen the slave trade firstly as an exceptionally good commercial opportunity for any ambitious merchant, and only secondly as a means to curry royal favor.

And what was Elizabeth's motive for raising the stakes? It was obviously economic and political, but was that all? The queen adored symbolic gestures, and sending Hawkins on his first slaving voyage was tantamount to a battle cry that there would be "no peace beyond the lines of amity." The English were simply declaring their right to free trade "beyond the line," meaning in the New World, despite incessant Iberian claims that it was illegal.

Hawkins's backers were enticed into the adventure by the treasurer of the navy, Benjamin Gonson, and the Royal Navy's surveyor and national hero, William Winter. The financial power-houses of the expedition included Londoners like William Garrard, Thomas Lodge, and Lionel Duckett, whose trade had been heavily disrupted by the troubles on the Continent. The undertaking would be purely commercial, thereby allowing the queen to claim loftily in her ambassadorial audiences that it contravened no treaty, and that to the best of her knowledge there was still freedom on the high seas.[6]

Although Hawkins was an excellent navigator, without the benefit of longitude calculations available, accurate maps, and familiarity with the African coast—and later the Caribbean—the voyage could have easily foundered. To ensure success, he needed a competent pilot familiar with the coasts, languages, and people they would encounter. Fortunately, Hawkins's Spanish partner resident in the Canaries, Pedro de Ponte, had provided the wannabe slave trader with this most valuable asset for his long slaving voyage: a Spanish pilot from Cadiz, named Juan Martínez.

Hawkins was intelligent, ambitious, and above all a lateral thinker. The Englishman knew full well that, if he did not plan his voyage diligently, he, like so many others before him, would fail, and possibly die. His greatest strength was that he was a meticulous planner, and he knew that the unhealthy conditions and long voyage would require "buying" the loyalty of his men and commanding them with a steely will. With this uppermost in mind, he willingly offered higher wages to his sailors and the promise of supplementing their pay with pillage and private trade. To further their mutual good health, Hawkins ensured that there would be adequate water, biscuit, beer, salt beef, fresh beef, Newfoundland salt fish, stockfish, herrings, salt, butter, pease,[7] cheese, and live pets that could later serve as food.

And there was cloth—broadcloth stored in packs of ten for trade in cooler climates as well as wool "cotton" and kerseys from the south of England to trade in the tropics. The ship's equipment of buckets, scoops, grinding stones, compasses, ballast, pulleys, ropes, and rat poison was stuffed into the hold prior to setting off.[8] There were carpenters to repair the ships, cooks, a barber-surgeon, and men who could make and repair ropes and sails. The last essentials of the voyage loaded would be the captain's gold and silver plate, then his company of musicians. Once all were aboard, Hawkins was ready to cast off. No one would accuse him of failing in his slaving mission due to a lack of planning.

It was precisely this planning that attracted his investors at home. Gonson, Winter, Duckett, and Lodge paid to equip the 140-ton *Salomon*, the 40-ton *Jonas*, and the 30-ton *Swallow*, with Hawkins as the *Swallow*'s captain. A young, unknown relation of his on board—Francis Drake—sailed with them on this, the first of his long voyages.[9]

While John Hawkins and his crew began their human harvest in the African waters off the coast of Portuguese-"held" Guinea in the winter of 1562–63, they remained blissfully unaware of the changing political climate at home. Communications between the coast of Africa and England were nonexistent. As Hawkins "hunted" slaves—whether stealing them from Portuguese slave traders who had an established business with Spanish America or by "gathering" slaves in the interior aided and abetted by rival tribes[10]—the Flemish regent, Margaret of Parma, and her chief minister, Cardinal de Granvelle, had written to Philip pleading for him to pay attention to the growing unrest in the Low Countries. The English depredations against their shipping in the Channel was a cause of great concern, they noted gloomily. Then there was the not insubstantial matter of the English occupation of Newhaven that worried Margaret, particularly as Philip hadn't responded to any of her letters with his action orders in over four months.[11]

Yet before Philip received the plea, "as if by the hand of God" the English garrison was struck down with a virulent outbreak of plague. The French Huguenots turned against their English allies perhaps for the loss of Rouen to Charles IX, or perhaps because they felt that as Frenchmen, their interests would always remain with other Frenchmen. Whatever the precise reason, Warwick's men, both those in France and those who had already returned to England, were dying the most painful and agonizing deaths while infecting thousands of others.

And all the while, Hawkins plied his loathsome trade for over four months in Africa. Guinea (which meant in Berber "the land of the black men")[12] was a huge expanse of land extending over two thousand miles, from Cape Verde in the north, around Cape Palmas to the south, and bordered by the Niger River Delta and the Bight of Benin in the east. Hawkins's slave "harvest" most likely consisted of a twofold plan of attack. The first, and less successful one, was to hunt down slaves in the interior themselves. It didn't take much reflection for a man of Hawkins's resourcefulness to devise a more fruitful means for this vile trade. It would be far easier to identify other Europeans in the vastness of Guinea and take whatever cargo they had already loaded aboard. After all English ships carried far more artillery and ammunition than their Portuguese or Spanish counterparts, and Englishmen were reputed to be fabulous archers as well. So Hawkins changed tack and set about capturing a number of Portuguese vessels and transferring their slaves and other valuable cargo to his English ships. As Hakluyt wrote, Hawkins "stayed some good time, and got into his possession, partly by the sword and partly by other means, to the number of 300 Negroes at the least, besides other merchandise, which that country yields."[13]

All along the African coast, those merchants who survived the English onslaught naturally wrote furious complaints back to their respective courts about the outrages perpetrated by Hawkins and his men—letters that would take months, if not years, to arrive. Cargoes of ivory, cloves, wax, and nearly four hundred slaves were forcibly obtained, and all merchandise that was deemed unsatisfactory for the Caribbean leg of the journey was returned aboard the smallest ship to England. Among the crew of that ship was a disappointed Drake.[14]

Hawkins, his crew, and his human cargo made the crossing to the Indies in April 1563—the same time that the English occupying force was decimated by plague at Newhaven in France. But the English captain was ignorant of these events, and concerned himself solely with keeping the ship "sweet smelling," his men healthy, and limiting the deaths among his slaves in stinking holds of his ships. But only half the slaves survived the mental anguish and inhumane treatment on their meager diet of beans and water into Caribbean waters. And yet Hawkins had little trouble, at first, in selling the poor wretched souls to the Spaniards to be misused on the Spanish American plantations and in the mines.[15]

Throughout Spanish America the market in slaves at bargain prices was attractive to the Spanish planters. So Hawkins's arrival with his human cargo created a seller's market with brisk trading at Española's ports Puerto de Plata, Monte Christi, and Isabela.[16] Not the first interloper to arrive in the Spanish waters of the Caribbean, Hawkins found a savvy and ready market for his bargain-basement-priced slaves. After all, he had arrived without having been taxed by the Spanish authorities, and his wares represented a significant savings to the colonists. If trading went well there, then Hawkins intended to spread his net wider on future voyages to the Greater Antilles—to Cuba, Jamaica, and Puerto Rico—and beyond to the Spanish Main.[17]

At the region's administrative headquarters, Santo Domingo, rumors and complaints about Hawkins and his methods poured in to the Spanish authorities. It had been claimed that Hawkins had tricked the local governors into trading by a series of plausible lies, coercion, and out-and-out threats. A young and relatively inexperienced officer, Lorenzo Bernáldez, was dispatched to confront Hawkins and halt the Englishman's trading in all Spanish territory—by force, if necessary.

While there had been interlopers for as long as there had been a Spanish empire, it is doubtful that any Spaniard had seen ships bristling with the long and short-range artillery and munitions that Hawkins carried aboard in plain sight. After some bizarre horse-trading, Bernáldez found himself hornswoggled by Hawkins. Violence was avoided when the Spaniard accepted the Englishman's offer of a truce with the receipt of three-quarters of the remaining one hundred forty old or sick slaves, and one of his caravels in exchange for a license to sell the remaining thirty-five slaves and the release of captive Englishmen. An import tax of 7.5 percent was also agreed. The only problem was that Bernáldez hadn't been authorized to grant any license at all.[18]

In spite of all the losses of slaves to death, sickness, and finally ransom, the profits for Hawkins and his backers were phenomenal. His own three ships were so heavily laden with pearls, gold, silver, ginger, hides, sugar, and other trades made with the Spanish colonists in exchange for the unfortunate lives of the West African slaves that he had too much merchandise for the return journey to England. Hawkins, seemingly ever resourceful, chartered two Spanish hulks that were in port and struck a deal for the vessels to take well over fifteen hundred hides and chests of sugar back to Seville. He also gave the captains clear instructions to deliver the goods to the English factor there, Hugh Tipton. While the charter of Spanish ships was depicted as "a bit of luck" by Hawkins, chances are that it had all been prearranged by Pedro de Ponte in the Canaries before Hawkins had left there.[19]

Shipping goods to Spain that the Spaniards classed by virtue of the edict of Inquisition as contraband seems strange, but Hawkins had no choice. The ships (owned by the Seville merchant trading family Martínez) were the only ones available, and Hawkins truly believed that the Spanish authorities would not question the well-established trade of the Martínez family as two of their ships came into port. But Hawkins's luck didn't hold out. A local Basque *licenciado*, Echegoyan, wrote to the Casa de Contractación in Seville about Hawkins's scandalous behavior, finishing with the eye-popping threat, "Tomorrow all this land could become part of England if steps are not taken."[20]

The result was that the Martínez ships and their cargo were impounded, and all Hawkins's men were imprisoned and often tortured under the cruel regime of the Inquisition. Only Thomas Hampton, captain of the first ship to arrive in Seville, managed to escape. The losses—estimated later by Hawkins to be £2,000 ($701,372 or £379,120 today)—were not great when compared with the pearls, other jewels, and luxury goods that had reached England.[21] In fact, though the precise profit was never advertised, shortly after Hawkins arrived back in Plymouth in late summer 1563, he and his backers were already planning their next voyage. William Garrard signed up immediately as a new joint stock backer for the second. He was followed by Sir William Chester, who like Garrard was also a former lord mayor and important merchant in the Canaries. Flattering as their attentions and money were to Hawkins, the big prize came in the form of his powerful new court backers: William Cecil, Lord Admiral Clinton, the Earl of Pembroke, and Robert Dudley.

But they weren't the only ones interested in what John Hawkins had experienced. The queen herself ordered that her quarantine against the plague be broken, and that Hawkins be allowed to join her at Windsor to discuss his journey. It is likely that the queen promised Hawkins the use of the 700-ton *Jesus of Lubeck* for the next Guinea voyage at this time. This was her symbolic gesture that the claim of illegality of English trade "beyond the line" by the Portuguese and Spanish was absurd. The merchant from Plymouth would be able to sail under the queen's colors and reap the benefits that such an honor would entail. But Hawkins was to learn soon that the offer of the *Jesus* was a mixed blessing initially. While the *Jesus* had been deemed as "much worn and of no continuance and not worth repair" in the 1559 *Book of Sea Causes*—it was a public sign of royal approval for both Hawkins and his slaving expeditions.[22]

As if the *Jesus* were not enough, Elizabeth's support for Hawkins was also confirmed by an equally unexpected result of their interview. On September 8, 1563, she wrote to Philip II "in favour of this bearer, John Hawkins . . . our will and pleasure is that your understanding thoroughly the cause, and well-informing yourself of the equity thereof, do take opportunity to communicate the same in our name . . . and to help and assist our said subject in setting forth his said suit."[23]

Hawkins had been tormented by the imprisonment of his men and the merchants who had helped him to so great a success. So, armed in the knowledge that the Queen of England had implored the King of Spain to hear reason and release his crew, Hawkins traveled to Spain. Yet despite his best efforts to have his crew released and to recover his impounded goods, the Spanish would not relent against the *Luteranos*. In fact, Hawkins's own freedom remained in jeopardy so long as he was in Spain. As to his merchandise, he was informed that it had been sold, and the money sequestered under triple lock and key in the king's personal chest.[24]

By English law, Hawkins's attempt to recover the confiscated merchandise in Spain, as well as lodging an official complaint with the High Court of the Admiralty, would most assuredly result in his being granted a letter of reprisal against Spanish and Portuguese shipping to the value of the goods lost. He was now favored by Her Majesty, and knew that he was at last a man of consequence. On the one hand dejected by his failure in Spain, and on the other emboldened by the queen's support and investment, Hawkins returned to England and prepared to embark on his second voyage, secure in the knowledge that in spite of the Spanish seizures, fortune smiled upon him.

Hawkins's interview with the queen would have alerted him in no uncertain terms to the changing tide of English politics, and the favor with which he was viewed as a new protecting force for the realm. Mary, Queen of Scots, the enchanting widow, was seeking a second and powerful husband. She remained poised for action to claim the English throne and seemingly was, at last, in possession of her own country. Elizabeth was determined that Mary should have that husband, but one who would remain loyal to England. And so she ennobled Robert Dudley to the title of Earl of Leicester, granting him vast swathes of land to make him more attractive to the Scottish queen. Only after Hawkins set sail on his second voyage would Mary announce that she would not have the Queen of England's "master of the horse."

Cecil, who had once feared the royal favorite Dudley, particularly when he had been named as "protector" by the queen when she had smallpox, also knew Dudley was dangerous for his intervention in Newhaven. Dudley, too, was a sworn enemy of the Earl of Sussex, Lord Deputy in Ireland, and he backed the charismatic and violent Shane O'Neill, the Ulster Irish chieftain, against Sussex in a bid to extend his influence throughout Ireland. Dudley also looked favorably upon John Hawkins as a merchant engaged in legitimate trade, and a man in whom he could invest for the future.

But what had become of the pirates in the Channel and elsewhere? And what had happened to Stucley and his Huguenot enterprise? While the French pirate Ribault had successfully established the French colony in Florida, perilously close to Philip's empire, Stucley, who had been supplied with one of the queen's ships in his six-vessel force, sailed around the Caribbean with his three hundred men terrorizing merchants and colonists alike.[25] He had been "well furnished with artillery from the queen," according to ambassador de Quadra,[26] so Stucley's exploits rocked the courts of England, France, and Spain, and his piracy on the high seas became the scandal of the day. Stucley had made Elizabeth a fool in her own eyes, something both Catherine de' Medici and Philip II secretly enjoyed, and which the English queen would never forgive.[27] His attacks on Spanish, French, and Portuguese shipping made the English ambassador to Madrid, Chaloner, "hang his head in shame."[28] Elizabeth hesitated a bit, but eventually disowned Stucley and issued a warrant for his arrest. Her hesitation had as much to do with the usefulness of other questionable adventurers' piratical acts, which helped secure England's borders, as it did with a public admission that Stucley had duped her.

But worse was to yet come for England's queen. De Granvelle, with Philip's tacit approval, decided to close Antwerp and all other Low Countries ports to the English, using the excuse of the plague. Stucley was not the only pirate, or adventurer, who was stealing under the legitimate guise of letters of reprisal, and de Granvelle was out to prove the point. As a result, without any other market of equal status, tens of thousands of yards of broadcloth worth over £700,000

($245.48 million or £132.69 million today) lay in the Thames estuary for six months before the lucrative backbone of English trade could be transferred urgently to Emden in Germany.[29]

Just about the only bright spot on the horizon from the English viewpoint was that the universally reviled Spanish ambassador, Alvarez de Quadra, bishop of Aguila, died in poverty in the English countryside, having initially escaped London and the plague. His replacement, Guzmán de Silva, canon of Toledo, was an intellectual, congenial priest with an iron will and understanding of what made the English tick. Philip had, at last, appointed a worthy emissary to oversee events in England. De Silva's insightful and eventful four-year stint in his London embassy would mark an interesting turn of events for both Hawkins and Elizabeth's England.

8. Cunning Deceits ❧

I am a great servant of the majesty of King Philip,
whom I served when he was King of England.
—JOHN HAWKINS TO GOVERNOR BERNÁLDEZ, APRIL 16, 1565

By the time John Hawkins was ready to set sail on his second slaving voyage, the newly appointed Spanish ambassador, Guzmán de Silva, had tapped into the rich vein of his predecessor's spy network in England. Philip himself had directed him to two particularly good sources of information residing in London— Antonio de Guaras and Luis de Paz, to whom the king referred as "persons of entire trust."[1] At first, the picture they had painted of the Hawkins plan was fuzzy, with some of their port spies declaring that the English admiral was making preparations to lead a squadron of pirates into the Channel to capture Spanish and Flemish shipping. But as more reliable intelligence poured in, it became obvious that Hawkins had a grander enterprise in mind. Whenever he sailed, John Hawkins would be flying the queen's royal standard atop his mainmast, confirming his royal commission. Once his destination was rumored to be the West Indies again, Guzmán de Silva penned a hasty warning to Philip that the Spanish Main would again be in grave danger from the great pirate *Aquinas*, as Hawkins was called.

While this may seem an overstatement, even at the time, de Silva was nonetheless outraged that Hawkins would dare a reprise of his first audacious exploit to the West Indies. After advising the king, he lodged an official complaint with the Privy Council and was promptly told that Hawkins was sailing with the queen's commission, and, in what became a familiar refrain, that the high seas were free. De Silva refused to accept their reply as cast in stone, and wrote directly to the queen, asking her to stop Hawkins from sailing, as he was likely to harm the King of Spain's subjects.

This, too, was a familiar tune. Everyone in a position of power in England knew that "harm to Spanish subjects" was a point dear to the ambassador's heart. Since his arrival, he had been successful in pressing for a royal commission to look into piracy in the Channel in a valiant effort to staunch the tide. Failing that, he aimed to get some compensation from the rogues. After several months hammering away on the subject, de Silva seemed to be making progress. On August 7 the Privy Council dashed off several letters on the express desire of the queen and Lord Robert:

> *to Sir William Godolphin, John Arundel, John Killigrew, Sir John Chichester, and William Lower, esquires, that where a ship was spoiled in that parts appertaining to John de Calvette and others, Spaniards, to take order that they may be restored to their goods, or else the offenders to be bound to appear to answer to the laws according to the quality of their faults . . . [and] to make due inquisition of such goods as appertained to John de Calvette and others, which was spoiled upon the seas by John Fleming and Hamond Gifford, requiring them to make restitution of the said goods unto the complaints, or else to take good bands of them . . .*[2]

Satisfied that the queen was acting in good faith, de Silva wrote to Philip that same month that "the proceedings ordered by the queen with the object of redressing the robberies committed on your Majesty's subjects by her pirates, and other injuries inflicted by reason of money owing etc., are still continuing . . . it appears they are doing their best. The fault is not entirely on the part of the judges, although there has been much remissness, but is largely due to false witnesses, of whom there must be a great number in this country, and notwithstanding this, the judges do not consider the evidence strong enough for them to condemn their own countrymen, and are probably not sorry for it."[3]

In the same encrypted letter, de Silva gave Philip a reasonable running account of his discussions with Elizabeth about her pirates: "With regard to the future I have pressed the queen and her council for some measure of security since, if the sea is not free, there will be forever complaints and troubles."[4]

The Spanish ambassador, fully briefed by his king, had used the very excuse with which the queen had defeated—and would defeat—his own argument: freedom of the high seas. Hawkins was, she claimed, not a pirate, but a gentleman and merchant, and one of considerable means. His sole desire was to undertake honest trade; and since one of her leading countrymen, Elizabeth, her merchants, and her gentlemen backed him in his new adventure. The joint stock company formed for this second slaving voyage read like a *Who's Who* of the day, led by the queen herself. As to harming the King of Spain's loyal subjects, what harm could vibrant trade to the West Indies bring? Elizabeth inquired.

What harm indeed. The queen's arguments in favor of her slave trader were at best disingenuous. What attracted her deep interest in the proposition was the real possibility of enriching her treasury by an expanded trade with the Spanish Indies. It is also tempting to imagine that she never considered the true nature that the "harvesting" of his African victims took, despite having warned Hawkins as early as 1563 that "if any African were carried away without his free consent it would be detestable and call down the vengeance of Heaven upon the undertakers."[5] Above all, John Hawkins and his enterprise represented a "get-rich-quick" scheme that appealed to the queen's parsimonious nature, and the business acumen—if not sheer greed—of her merchant and gentlemen adventurers, particularly in light of the debacle at Newhaven and the remorseless rise in the cost of maintaining the peace in English enclaves and plantations in Ireland.

Her Privy Council couldn't see the harm either—it was for the good of the realm. Even Lord Admiral Clinton and Sir William Herbert, now the Earl of Pembroke, were two of Hawkins's prominent gentlemen adventurer investors. The queen's favorite, Robert Dudley—newly elevated as the Earl of Leicester—was not only an investor but also a primary license holder for the export of undyed cloth, which was being loaded onto Hawkins's ships while the queen engaged the Spanish ambassador in the philosophical merits of her case. Even the cautious William Cecil was actively involved in an administrative and supervisory role in the second voyage. And the queen herself, having ventured the *Jesus*, valued at

£4,000 ($1.45 million or £782,800 today) would have been the largest single investor.[6]

Despite Elizabeth's posturing, there was little doubt that the slaving voyage would do someone harm. Hawkins's new fleet of four ships was, of course, headed by the leviathan 700-ton *Jesus of Lubeck*, and in spite of her advanced years, the *Jesus* couldn't fail to impress. With her fabulously ornate poop, four masts of Baltic oak, and formidable forecastle, the *Jesus* was the ultimate symbol of royal favor. While it was known to be in quite poor repair and of questionable seaworthiness since *The Book of Sea Causes* was published on the queen's accession, the *Jesus* still bristled with heavy bronze and iron artillery. As the admiral of the fleet, it had the sort of devastating firepower that befitted a royal Tudor floating fortress. The second ship in the fleet was the 140-ton *Solomon*, now spruced up and ready for action since its first Caribbean voyage under Hawkins's command. The *Solomon*'s companion ships, the 50-ton *Tiger* and new 30-ton pinnace *Swallow*, completed the fleet. All three of the companion ships belonged to Hawkins. All three were heavily armed, carrying as much artillery and shot as they could accommodate readily for their size, while leaving room for the other essentials of the voyage.

What is staggering is that the entire fleet was manned with a mere 170 mariners—far below the norm for the times. Hawkins, ever the meticulous planner, ensured that there would be ample victuals of biscuits and beef, bacon and beer, peas to help keep scurvy at bay, water, and cider. He had also ordered that their holds be filled with enough beans and peas to feed up to four hundred African slaves. There were cots for the Africans to sleep on, and clothing for them to make themselves "respectable" in the slave markets of New Spain. Every contingency had been provided for.

Still, none of the queen's excuses or Hawkins's preparations interested the Spanish ambassador. De Silva was nobody's fool and an exceptionally able diplomat. Since Hawkins was no pirate, then perhaps, de Silva argued, the queen would support an all-out effort to rid the Channel of "this sea of thieves" and make the lanes safe for merchant shipping of all nations.[7] Elizabeth was trapped by her own words this time. On August 4, she was obliged to publish an edict ordering all armed ships to return to port and forbade them to set sail again without a license from the queen herself. Such a license could be granted only on giving an undertaking that they would not harm England's allies, including Spain. All well and good, de Silva reasoned, but without a good show of royal strength in Channel ports, Channel piracy would remain a threat to daily life. The ambassador confirmed the exchange of full and frank views with Elizabeth to his king, closing with the remark, "The queen, so far as her words go, shows great rectitude in matters appertaining to justice."[8] This did not, however, mean that she could succeed in subduing—or indeed wholly wished to subdue—piracy. Maritime theft had become more than a national pastime that neatly exported penniless rogues and thieves away from the towns and cities. When, or rather if, they returned, they were frequently financially better off and posed less of a threat to their fellow countrymen. A successful "adventure" spawned new "adventurers," and so it continued. It was little wonder that Channel piracy had become the national obsession.

Philip, for his part, was greatly preoccupied with these Channel matters—both French and English piracy, as well as what action to take with his own rebellious subjects in the Low Countries. Yet he remained powerless to intervene due to his military commitments against the Turks in the Mediterranean. This is what made de Silva's missive stand out as a shimmering hope on an ever-darkening horizon. The States, as Philip himself referred to the Low Countries, were heading toward open revolt against the king's religious intolerance and decrees. The Dutch nobles like William of Orange and Count Egmont claimed that these decrees served only Spain and infringed on the States' ancient privileges. The regent, Margaret of Parma, had warned the king repeatedly that it would be impossible to rule without the cooperation of the Flemish nobles, and unless something was done to remove the odious influence of Philip's man, Cardinal de Granvelle, the States would erupt in revolt.

There is little doubt that de Granvelle was loathed by everyone in power except the king. Since Antwerp had closed its doors to English merchants on his insistence, the great merchant houses of Antwerp found themselves taken by surprise by the tightening of credit on the Bourse and the "deadness of trade."[9] Payments from the Merchants Adventurers, other English merchants—and even

Elizabeth herself—were suspended at that time, benefiting the English and devastating the Antwerp financiers.[10] What had begun as a punishment for English depredations in the Channel and the English adventure at Newhaven (which was seen as meddling in French affairs), was rapidly becoming a threat to Antwerp's very existence as the main northern hub for the luxury trades.

And worse was still to come. Philip had not had word, as yet, that the trade war with England had escalated. A new "vent" for English cloth had been agreed the previous February at Emden, and when the regent found out and sent word to her brother, she was quick to ban all merchants from the States from trading there on Philip's orders. Yet, from over a thousand miles away in Spain, the king couldn't visualize the hardships at Antwerp, nor could he foresee its waning future. He did, however, take great comfort from Spanish intelligence that the main trading cities of the German Hanse refused to trade with the English at Emden that spring, and would continue to do so until their own ancient trading privileges in England were restored to their pre–1552 favorable status. As their ill luck would have it, the autumn harvest was poor, and the Queen of England decreed, in retaliation, a complete embargo on the shipment of grain from England via any means to the Low Countries.[11]

It was against this backdrop that Hawkins prepared his second voyage. Merchants and the queen who might have otherwise repaid their loans at Antwerp saw a good opportunity to invest in his scheme instead. Others, who had been caught in the wrong end of the financial cycle, having recently repaid their loans in the Low Countries, found themselves unable to sell their goods at the spring or summer markets at Emden, or anywhere else on the Continent. Trapped by the political circumstances, these merchants either went bankrupt or sought new credit and new vents of their own. Whatever their individual situation, Hawkins provided new hope to them all.

By August, de Silva had discovered the truth, and he warned the King of Spain that he had been unable to stop Hawkins sailing. His route had been confirmed by Spanish spies at Plymouth as heading for the Canaries, then on to Guinea and then the West Indies. There was ample time for Philip to intervene with a small squadron, either on the Spanish coast or in the Canaries, which were, after all, Spanish territory. Yet he chose not to do so. For the man who was purported to have the "greatest brain in the world" this was no oversight, but seemingly a cruel calculation.

Philip had not yet become weary of his personal rule—far from it. But he had insisted on ruling his empire from Spain. He saw every missive, every order, every newsletter, and despite his plethora of "councils," the King of Spain handled the details of all correspondence on his own. This meant that instead of direct action, he frequently chose to wield his mighty pen. When the king received word that Hawkins would sail regardless, he speedily wrote to Portugal's boy king, Sebastian, warning him of the voyage to Portuguese-held Guinea. He notified his Council for the Indies in writing—only one of fourteen councils of state in existence at the time—when it met the next morning for its traditional three-hour session. The regent of the Low Countries was informed by letter, as was Cardinal de Granvelle. In fact, it was not uncommon for Philip to dictate and vet more than one hundred letters, licenses, or patents daily in the 1560s, and it was a well-bemoaned fact that no one beside the King of Spain knew for certain what was happening throughout his dominions.[12] Philip often focused down on a single event, and frequently sacrificed the important for the insignificant, as would have certainly been the case concerning Hawkins's fleet.

The Spanish king replied immediately to London to try to stop the voyage at all costs. Philip tempered his request to de Silva, who was, after all, new at his post, by stating that if he couldn't stop Hawkins, the ambassador must at least keep him informed of his efforts at the English court. Interestingly, the intricacies of the financial cycle had dawned on the king. Philip asked de Silva to delve into the queen's finances, and particularly whether she still owed money at Antwerp. On September 4, de Silva penned his reply:

> *I have tried to find out all I could about the finances and the state of the Queen's treasury. She owes to private people in this country lent on her bills 240,000 crowns and in Flanders 200,000 to Belzares and Esquets with whom she ordinarily does business* [a total of $72.41 million or £39.14 million today]. *They tell me that the larger part of this money has been lent to her by the Germans at an interest of 14%, some at 15% and some at 13, according to the value*

of money when the advance was made. The City of London and
certain private merchants guarantee the payment for her.[13]

This was not good news. Philip knew that all the penned protestations
he could devise would never carry sufficient weight to stop Elizabeth
if she had decided on a certain course. Indeed, what was worrying in
the intelligence he was receiving was that Cecil—who had already
declared his dislike for the new school of adventure, which risked
replacing bona fide trade—had some sort of supervisory role in
the Hawkins adventure. It also seemed that Cecil was somehow
involved in another adventure undertaken at the same time to
Guinea—but with a different purpose—by Hawkins's backer and
great London merchant, Sir William Garrard. Robert Dudley, Earl
of Leicester, too, had a foot in each camp. If Philip's spies were right,
there was a considerable shift in the tide of thinking in England, and
Spain would undoubtedly be harmed.[14] Yet still, no direct orders to
physically intervene against the English were given.

Whether it was a cunning deceit to allow the English, through
Hawkins, to steal from the Portuguese in order to provide Spain
with much needed slaves to work plantations and mines in the
New World is a rather tempting thought. It was, nonetheless, in
many ways, Machiavellian. The Spanish king could not be seen
to interfere in Portugal's affairs even though he was second in line
for the Portuguese crown. He may have been an heir to its throne,
but unless or until he was king of that country, all he could do was
covet Portugal's wealth, navy, and territory while professing to be its
closest ally. Through his failure to act and send a squadron to stop
Hawkins, Philip had the perfect platform to use the English outrage
to diplomatic advantage with both Portugal and England.

As for Hawkins personally, he fully expected his competent local
governors in the West Indies to dispatch the troublesome captain
from Plymouth on the spot. In the unlikely event that his governors
failed him, Spain would still benefit from the slave trade; England
would be shamed; Portugal would be thankful for his efforts; and a
Spanish advantage in the Channel and the Low Countries could be
achieved. For Philip, the exploits of a lone sea captain, who had not as
yet achieved any measure of greatness, in Africa and the West Indies,
was only a mild irritant. His main preoccupation remained Channel

piracy and the cessation of trade to the Low Countries. And it was this cessation of trade that would ultimately prove a catastrophe.

Naturally, the Portuguese king felt differently. Portugal had been defending its "colonies" in Africa from French and English interlopers since the 1520s, with the French becoming particularly active over the past ten years, with more than two hundred Portuguese ships seized by French corsairs in that time.[15] These seized ships were stuffed to the gunnels with more than slaves; the Guinea coast of Africa represented wealth in gold and precious stones as well.

To make matters worse, Portugal's hold on the region was tenuous to say the least. The would-be Lusitanian colonizers had already suffered, as well as profited, from African tribal warfare. The ferocious Sumba tribe from central Africa had been displaced westward to the El Mina and Malagueta coasts of Guinea due to drought, leading to the overthrow of smaller peaceful African tribal kingdoms, and the murder and enslavement of these tribes to the Sumba.[16] When Martin Frobisher, who was already well known for his tall tales, was imprisoned in Sao Jorge (El Mina) in 1555–56 for piracy, he claimed that no Portuguese dared to go more than a mile from the forts without first obtaining a "passport" from the local rulers, the Sumba.[17] Still, King Sebastian of Portugal, who loved more than anything else warring against the African infidel—be he black or Muslim—was more concerned for the time being with the English corsairs, and ordered Aires Cardosso to act as ambassador to London to demand satisfaction from the "heretic" English queen. He also alerted his local governors that Hawkins was on his way.

*

And so, amid all this animosity brewing and bubbling over in the courts of Spain and Portugal, on October 18, 1564, in the hope of prosperous winds, John Hawkins gave the order to weigh anchor from Plymouth. Yet before they had cleared port, the strong equinoctial gust lashed the *Jesus* around, and one of the ship's officers was killed by the pulley of a sail in a "sorrowful beginning for them all."[18] But after all his planning, Hawkins couldn't allow the incident to dampen his or his crew's spirits, especially as he knew that there was another small fleet of Londoners also heading for the Guinea coast.

Thirty miles out to sea, the Londoners and Hawkins's fleet met. The *Minion*, the *John the Baptist*, and the *Merlin*—captained by David Cartlet, on behalf of the joint stockholders Sir William Garrard, Benjamin Gonson, Sir William Chester, Thomas Lodge,[19] and the Earl of Leicester—were intent on setting up a base in Guinea and mining for gold under the very noses of the Portuguese. Both admirals agreed that the seven ships should sail on together as a "combined" fleet for greater protection against pirates.

After three days of good progress and fair winds, the wind direction and speed changed. Clouds boiled up and the skies blackened, as a true equinox storm suddenly erupted. Waves battered the ships mercilessly for nearly twelve hours, scattering them. When the skies cleared and the sea swells died down, Hawkins saw that his own ship the *Swallow*, and the entire fleet from London, had been lost from sight.[20] Since no obvious debris from sunken ships could be seen, Hawkins hoped that the ships—and especially the *Swallow*—had simply been separated. It is obvious from Hawkins's distress at the time that he hadn't issued any clear instructions to his company with regard to what they should do in the event of separation, and he blamed himself for this serious omission.

According to the chronicler of the voyage, John Sparke—a merchant and future mayor of Plymouth—there was "no small rejoicing" when they luckily stumbled upon the *Swallow*, becalmed some thirty miles north of Cape Finisterre off the northern coast of Spain. They waited for a wind to carry them around the Iberian peninsula and out into the Atlantic for two days, before turning into shore and sheltering in the Galician port of Ferrol, remembered by the men for its "bleak outlook." There, Hawkins summoned the masters of all his ships and corrected his error. Naturally, there was no semaphore code as yet to ease communication between ships, nor any other sophisticated remote means of warning. Hawkins ordered that the smaller ships would lead the *Jesus*, staying up weather of her. Each ship was ordered to communicate with him twice daily on the *Jesus* without fail. If Hawkins raised his ensign over the poop of the *Jesus*—or lit two lights at night—they were to come in straightaway to "speak with her." Three lights meant that the *Jesus* was casting about, and they were to keep the same distance from the lights. If the bad weather returned, the smaller ships would make a formation tucked in alongside the *Jesus*, or, failing that for whatever reason, alongside the *Solomon*. They were to follow these instructions to the letter until they reached Tenerife. The other ships were also given their own signals: "If any happen to any misfortune, then to show two lights, and shoot off a piece of ordinance. If any lose company, and come in sight again, to make three yaws, and strike the mizzen three times." Finally, Hawkins gave them his benediction order to "serve God daily, love one another, preserve your victuals, beware of fire, and keep good company."[21] It was the same benediction that Elizabeth had given Hawkins on the eve of his sailing.

Hawkins and his mariners had had a narrow escape in the storm. The same cannot be said for the Londoners. Shortly after their arrival in Ferrol, the *Minion* from the Londoners' fleet docked with the dreadful news that the *Merlin* had had an explosion in its powder magazine, burst into flames, and sunk. Only a few mariners had survived in a small boat, and had been towed into port behind the *Minion*. Hawkins quickly added the order to his masters that they would need to put their brigantines astern.[22]

On November 4, the captain mistakenly thought he had reached the Canaries, but he soon realized his error. This was a common enough mistake without the benefit of longitude, even for a reasonably good pilot like Hawkins. Dead reckoning was the only means that Elizabethan sailors had at their disposal to determine longitude, and it would be more than two hundred years before John Harrison discovered an accurate mechanism for its calculation.[23]

Four days later, the fleet arrived at the port of Adeje in Tenerife, finding the *Swallow* awaiting it as Hawkins had previously ordered.[24] After the mishaps in longitude calculation, John Sparke recounted their joy at reaching their first intended port of call with palpable relief. But their happiness soon faded when Hawkins saw that their "welcoming committee" was armed to the teeth and prepared for battle. Hawkins could only assume that they had been taken for corsairs, and called out to the Canarians that they weren't pirates and that he was a good friend of Pedro de Ponte's. Fortunately de Ponte's son, Nicolaso, was one of the armed men, and the confrontation was brought to an end. Hawkins sprang from his landing boat and waded onto the beach to a festive welcome.[25]

After a week of resupplying and making repairs to the fleet—the *Jesus* had sprung its mainmast in the storms and the smaller ships needed minor repairs—Hawkins and his men headed for the Guinea coast. Just north of Cabo Blanco they were spied by several Portuguese fishing boats, which cast about to run ahead of the feared "English pirates." The wind and current were merciless—as it frequently can be near the equatorial coast of Africa—and one of Hawkins's pinnaces capsized. By the time the lookout on the *Jesus* had called out for help, the pinnace was a mile or so back in the admiral's wake, with the English mariners perched unsteadily on its keel. Yet Hawkins kept cool and ordered one of the lifeboats into the sea with two dozen men at oar. Despite the lashing winds and overwhelming currents, the pinnace and her crew were rescued.[26] Hawkins had risked the lives of twenty-four men to save the lives of a handful of others. There is little doubt as to why: he had sailed with few mariners in order to keep his ships "sweet smelling" and avoid pestilence and disease. Each and every soul would be precious in the gathering of his slaves.

While Hawkins was fishing his own men out of the sea, back in England, the queen penned her final reply to the Portuguese ambassador, Aires Cardosso, who had arrived from Lisbon. It mattered not if his arguments had merit, she wrote, the fleet had sailed. Besides, she could see no reason why she should prevent her good subjects from trading in lands subject to the Portuguese, since the two nations had long been allies. Notwithstanding this, she would agree to his demands on the proviso that, "as for sailing into those parts of Africa where the Portuguese king had no more than tacit dominion and where French ships seemed to navigate with impunity, her Majesty finds it not reasonable that she should prohibit her subjects to use their navigation in those parts, otherwise, than the subjects of the French king and other dominions are known yearly to use, offending thereby no dominion, nor country of any Christian prince."[27] Over the ensuing years, this would become Elizabeth's familiar battle cry.

But Hawkins and his men were offending a Christian prince. Having previously been taken for a pirate—and not the honorable merchant he believed himself to be—the queen's adventurer decided to attack a group of Portuguese fishermen and their Moorish protectors in the harbor of Angela de Santa Ana, south of Cabo Blanco. If they were to treat him as a pirate, he would act like one, he reasoned. Armed only with bows and arrows, the fishermen quickly surrendered when Hawkins fired his heavy cannon. In no time at all, the English were free to take all the provisions they wanted before sailing on.[28]

By the end of November, Hawkins had arrived at Cape Verde and had sent his men into the dense jungle in small raiding parties to hunt for slaves. The richest pickings were at the island of Sambula, where the slaves who were captured had been enslaved by another African tribe, the Samboses, nearly three years earlier. Hawkins congratulated himself on a good beginning. So far, the "harvesting" operation had gone well.

On Christmas Day, after prayers, Hawkins bought two caravel loads of slaves from another group of Portuguese traders. When their dealing was over, the Portuguese kindly suggested that the English go farther along the coast to a town called Bymba, where they could easily buy another hundred "fine specimens" as well as Ashanti gold. The English captain thanked them, and sailed on to Bymba expectantly. All seemed peaceful, so Hawkins took around forty men ashore to set his bargain. Suddenly, shots rang out and there were hails of arrows from the jungle. The English took cover, cursing themselves for having fallen so easily into an obvious trap. They escaped back to their boats, dodging poisoned arrows; when Hawkins was aboard, he was surprised to find that he had ten new slaves. Significantly, he also lamented the wounding of nearly thirty of his mariners. Seven others had been killed in the skirmish, including the captain of the *Solomon*. Worse came later in the day, when some sailors were bathing near the ships. They were attacked and mauled by sharks. Another five men were killed, and the one who survived probably wished that he hadn't. All in all, it was a very bad day for the English.[29]

This incident would become infamous years after Hawkins's return, since the Portuguese claimed through official channels that the Englishmen had stolen wax, gold, ivory, and at least sixty slaves from Sierra Leone. Others wanted restitution for their losses when Hawkins and his men had taken their ships and left their sailors on the beaches. One merchant even swore that the English had "confiscated and extorted a ship named the *Cola*, loaded with merchandise to the value of 4,000 ducats [$90,511 or £48,925 today] in the river called Caces."[30] There was certainly some truth in the allegations, but how much was never determined, like so many of the complaints heard by the High Court of the Admiralty.

By the time the English adventurers had left the Guinea coast heading for the West Indies on January 29, 1565, they had four hundred slaves in the hold. Where storms had ravaged the fleet in Europe, they found themselves miserably becalmed mid-Atlantic for a long three weeks, suffocating in the hot, humid, still air, and nearly running out of water. But once the wind filled their sails again, their relief was reasonably short-lived. The fleet had made landfall at La Dominica—called the "Island of Cannibals" by the chronicler Sparke. The English still had three hundred seventy of the four hundred slaves living in the stinking holds of their ships, and "Almighty God" had not allowed his "elect" (meaning the English) to perish so far. But there was such a thing as tempting fate, and with the likelihood of encountering cannibals in their weakened condition, the men filled their water casks and sailed away quickly while the wind was good.

At the next island, Margarita, the inhabitants sold the English beef and mutton, but refused to trade for slaves or other wares. Philip's prohibition to trade had reached the West Indies long before Hawkins. The islanders were relieved when Hawkins's fleet proceeded on its way without coming to grief, but they sent word to the viceroy in Santo Domingo that the Englishmen had arrived among them at last. Before Hawkins reached his next port of call at Santa Fe, word had spread like wildfire ahead of them not to trade with the English. Hawkins, meanwhile, had no qualms about his success. He traded with the Indians for chickens, potatoes, pineapples, and maize cakes in exchange for "beads, pewter whistles, glasses, knives, and other trifles" he carried to bargain with.[31] But he had yet to sell one African.

At this rate, Hawkins would be lucky to break even, much less return to England a rich man. It was time to change tactics. If the low-grade trade continued much longer, the ever-present threat of his men mutinying could become reality, for there was nothing the mariner liked better than plunder. So, on April 3, 1565, when the fleet pulled into harbor at Borburata, and the familiar haggling with local officials began, Hawkins appealed to their better nature. He had been blown off course by contrary winds, he pretended. He sought only legal trade. When he was informed he needed a license, he cajoled the officials that they would surely trade with him while he awaited one from the governor, especially as it might save some of his "lean and sick Negroes." In this way, he'd earn enough to purchase supplies to help the others recover their good health, he reasoned. After three days of bickering, it was agreed to allow the English to sell thirty slaves, but a fair price had not yet been determined. When the governor arrived in town ten days later, Hawkins sensed victory was at hand. He trotted out his well-rehearsed spiel in which he announced he was *el capitán admiral* of Her Majesty, Queen Elizabeth, and that he had been on a mission to Guinea when he was unfortunately driven off course by a devastating contrary wind across the sea. All he wanted to do was sell his slaves so that he—a poor sailor—could pay for supplies and repair his ships before returning home.[32]

Governor Bernáldez (no relation to the officer encountered by Hawkins on his first voyage) wanted to allow Hawkins to trade, but found himself in a serious quandary. The king and the viceroy had ordered that there should be no trading with the *Luteranos*, but his people needed the slaves to keep the plantations running, since the slaves died with alarming regularity. After lengthy discussion with his men and Hawkins, the governor reluctantly agreed to allow the slave trader to proceed with his business after taking several testimonies and on the understanding that he was granting a license only insofar as he had the authority to do so. One of Bernáldez's eyewitnesses swore that he had heard Hawkins threaten to level the entire coast if the governor denied him his trading license. In the event, while the license was issued, the two men couldn't agree on terms, since the governor insisted on the usual royal treasury fee of thirty ducats per slave ($679 or £367 today) and Hawkins refused outright to pay anything. When the license was handed over to the queen's slave trader, he ripped it up, disgusted with the entire proceedings. It was a livid Hawkins who ordered a hundred armed men ashore threatening to destroy the town if Bernáldez wouldn't agree to his terms. Without heavy artillery or guns, the governor had no choice, and he conceded to all Hawkins's demands. Later, John Hawkins would boast that the governor was one of his best customers—so much so that he ran out of ready cash and had to issue a promissory note for six hundred pesos to Hawkins, payable later at Río de la Hacha.

At long last, Hawkins had struck upon a winning formula with the Spanish settlers in Borburata. When officials at his next port of call, Río de la Hacha, had evacuated the town in fear of their lives, Hawkins, after protestations of his innocence and goodwill got him nowhere, fired off his great cannons at the town. When the locals still wouldn't trade, he landed a hundred men armed to the teeth and marched along the beach, threatening in Spanish to burn their homes. Still, the citizens of Río de la Hacha were ostensibly having none of it. Battle drums rolled behind thirty prancing Spanish horsemen carrying the King of Spain's standard. The local inhabitants apparently wanted to join the English in battle. Without hesitation, the admiral gave the signal, and the English ships fired more heavy cannon at the town, taking care not to hit Hawkins and his mariners. Despite all their sound and fury, the Spanish immediately capitulated. The good folk of Río de la Hacha had suddenly become eager customers, purchasing the remaining slaves and anything else the English were selling. The charade was over. Their eagerness to trade even carried over to placing advance orders for Hawkins's next voyage and providing him with a written testimonial of his fair trading practices and friendly conduct. This would later prove the Spaniards' undoing when the matter was investigated by officials back home. They could only conclude that the whole episode was a sham and the town's leaders were severely punished.[33]

A sad, and often lost, part of this story is that the Africans sold as slaves at Río de la Hacha had drawn a particularly harsh lot. They were destined to become pearl divers. And divers had to learn quickly to hold their breath for astounding lengths of time, or die. Even if they succeeded in this feat, the cold waters or the bends often claimed their lives, for they were rumored to dive to depths of twelve fathoms or more. They worked from dawn to dusk with nets strapped to their waists or tied around their necks, breaking the water's surface only to catch their breath and, if they were lucky, eat an odd oyster. Then there were, of course, the sharks. Native American Indians had been banned as divers since the Vera Cruz decree of 1558, when African slaves were ordered in their stead as their official replacements. Their life expectancy was measured in days or months, since they were

> forced to spend their last days in agony, and the nature of the work is such that they perish in any case within a few days, for no man can spend long under water without coming up for air, and the water is so cold that it chills them to the marrow. Most choke on their own blood as the length of time they must stay under water without breathing and the attendant pressure upon their lungs makes them hemorrhage from the mouth; others are carried off by dysentery caused by the extreme cold to which they are subjected.[34]

Their entire human cargo thus disposed of, Hawkins's fleet sailed directly for Curaçao, where they purchased 978 hides valued at 10 reales of silver each ($363 or £196 today). The terms delighted the seller, who had been sure that the English would simply plunder them.[35] After a failed attempt to drop off a Jamaican captive named Llerena, whom Hawkins had freed in Guinea, the fleet stopped briefly for water on the westernmost point of Cuba.

For the next two weeks, Sparke's chronicle becomes remarkably silent, noting only that they reached the French Huguenot enclave at Fort Caroline on the Florida coast safely. Whether this was a scheduled stop or not, Sparke does not venture to say, but it does seem odd that once loaded with riches for his investors and himself, Hawkins and his men would seek out the French, who were notable rovers. It may have been that part of his private discussions with the queen just before leaving home was to better understand the movement of shipping in the area, or that he had decided to scout about for himself. In any event, they were cordially greeted by the Huguenots, and he sold the smallest of his ships to René Laudonnière, the colony's leader in the absence of Jean Ribault, along with shoes for his men, four cannons, and a good supply of powder and shot.

The road home was not arduous, with the fleet stopping off in Newfoundland for fresh water and fish. On September 20, 1565, after eleven months away, Hawkins brought his ships into Padstow harbor in Cornwall. In his note to Elizabeth, he stated that he had "always been a help to all Spaniards and Portuguese that have come in my way without any harm or prejudice by me offered to any of them."[36]

Despite obvious exaggeration on both sides—in terms of actual harm Hawkins had done, his good or bad conduct, and the value of his trades—there is no doubt that John Hawkins had become a national hero. He had also finally attracted the serious attention of King Philip of Spain.

9. The Gloves Are Off ⚜

*We have continued to receive complaints of the Flemish
merchants and mariners of the English robbers, and we
were moved to send many of these letters of complaint to
the Queen of England, both before and after the death
of Bishop Quadra, in the months of August, September,
October, November and December last, begging her to
remedy the evil. . . . Nothing has been done and no answer
given to these letters, and as from day to day the complaints
of people grow, we are now obliged to seek another remedy,
since friendly remonstrance is of no avail.*

—PHILIP II TO AMBASSADOR DE SILVA, FEBRUARY 1565

Despite his protestations of innocence, Ambassador de Silva
had no faith in Hawkins's professed honorable mercantile
intentions. In an encrypted message to Philip, de Silva claimed, "I
do not believe that a ship would be safe, if they were strong enough
to take it."[1] Importantly, de Silva added that he was certain that
Hawkins had been prowling the Indies during his second voyage
for a fortnight to attack the Spanish "plate fleet" known as the flota.

The Spanish ambassador had every right to dread this—as
yet—unfulfilled menace. The English had surpassed the French
as rovers in the Channel, and were aching to burst out of their
financial straitjacket in Europe to trade with Cathay, the Indies,
and the New World. The flota was, indeed, an exceptionally vital
piece of machinery of state, and the threat to it became the Spanish
government's abiding terror throughout the next forty years. Since
the beginning of the century the flota had operated as a government
monopoly, managed by the Casa de Contractacion—or Commercial
House—at Seville. When the fleet sailed up the Guadalquivir River
from the coast, the ships anchored at the Toro del Oro, a magnificent
round stone tower with huge wooden doors two stories high and

360-degree views of the town. There the ships would off-load their treasure chests onto the gently sloping cobbled quay. Ropes were slid through the three-inch-thick solid iron rings studded into the ironmongery of the oak doors, and the treasure was hauled up onto carriages then on about one hundred yards to the Casa de Contractacion.

Two fleets sailed yearly. The flota of New Spain sailed between Mexico and Spain. From 1564, the more important flota of Tierra Firma brought gold and silver from the Potosi mines of Peru via the Pacific (called the Southern Sea at the time) across the Isthmus of Panama to the Atlantic port of Nombre de Díos. Once loaded, the flota of Tierra Firma would head north along the Yucatán Channel then on to Havana. At Havana, always dependent until the last moment on orders received from the king, the flotas could—and frequently did—link up and make their Atlantic crossing together. It would not be an exaggeration to stress that the combined flotas carried the wealth of the Spanish Empire in their holds. Without these treasures, Philip's Spain simply couldn't continue to dominate the world stage, and what made the situation even more tense was the king's utter awareness of this Achilles' heel.[2]

But the English assaults were nothing new for the Spanish. French corsairs had been attacking the treasure trains for decades in the West Indies, and it was only with the appointment of one of Spain's greatest admirals, Pedro de Menéndez de Avilés, that French operations were mostly thwarted. Menéndez had provided three galleons as a permanent escort to the flotas at his own expense, and he was made captain general of the Indian trade in 1561—at his own "request." As a result, hostilities seemed to have settled down at last between the French and Spanish when Hawkins burst upon the scene.

Menéndez's reaction was predictable. He was determined to make both the French and English understand his intentions for the region once and for all. Less than a month after Hawkins and his men had left Fort Caroline in Florida, Menéndez landed soldiers just south of the French colony and massacred nearly all its inhabitants. Jean Ribault had just returned with some raw recruits and supplies, and they, too, were slaughtered. Menéndez, as a lesson to *Luteranos* everywhere, proudly left a plaque under the lifeless bodies of his victims, declaring that the colonists had been hanged as heretics by order of the King of Spain.[3] For Menéndez, there could be no compromise. Any foreign colony would be "most damaging to these kingdoms, because on that coast of Florida, near the Bahama Channel . . . they could establish and fortify themselves so as to be able to maintain galleys and other swift war vessels to capture the flotas and other private ships coming from the Indies. . . . "[4]

Meanwhile, back in Spain, the fact that Hawkins had traded successfully with semiofficial status from the Queen of England had made his intrusion into West Indian waters a very serious matter indeed. Philip's sense of self-preservation, coupled with the unshakable belief that all seagoing *Luteranos*—whether French, Dutch, or English—were hateful scoundrels and pirates, created a sense of imminent danger at the Spanish court that was far greater than the threat the English were capable of delivering.

Yet despite all the attention drawn by the English exploits in the West Indies, it was still the veiled hostilities in the Channel that worried Philip the most. Hawkins was an extension of English Channel piracy in the king's eyes, and all the more dangerous since his return to England when the queen bestowed a knighthood on her new hero. The obvious favor that Elizabeth extended to all her adventurers—and particularly Hawkins—was a clear indication to the Spanish king of the queen's hostile intentions. This, coupled with the unfortunate appointment of Dr. John Man as the English ambassador to Spain in 1566, made discussion of "English affairs" at court a very heated matter.

This was the Spanish viewpoint. For Elizabeth and her privy councillors, the situation was entirely different. England had had its lifeblood of commerce snatched away by Spain, and Emden was proving a very poor replacement for Antwerp. Trade between the Flemish and English was still mutually banned when Hawkins pulled into Padstow harbor in September 1565, and the queen was becoming fretful again for her personal security as well as the security of the realm. Both had been jeopardized by a number of events. Economically, poor trade on the Continent, and the failure of the Muscovy Company (in particular Anthony Jenkinson and others) to prove the stunning successes they had promised long ago, had already led to economic hardship for many. Politically, Elizabeth was weighed down with other grave concerns besides Philip of Spain. The rebellion of Shane O'Neill against colonization in Northern Ireland (Ulster) and the sudden and provocative marriage in the autumn of 1565 of Mary Queen of Scots to the young, handsome, and frequently drunk Lord Henry Darnley had disastrous implications. The Ulster Rebellion proved very costly in human life and hard cash. The Darnley marriage strengthened Mary's claim to the English throne. Mary's actions were also a personal rebuff to the English queen: Elizabeth's choice of husband for the Scottish queen, Leicester, had been spurned as the "keeper of the royal stud." As if this weren't bad enough, Elizabeth's Catholic population reminded her obliquely that failing Mary as queen, Philip II also had a very strong claim in his own right as an heir to the English throne. The only other viable heir, Catherine Grey, was by now locked away in the Tower for marrying without royal consent.

This was the England to which John Hawkins had returned. Security of the realm clung precariously, yet steadfastly, at the top of the Queen of England's agenda, and that security was now seriously compromised by a growing trade war with Spain as well as the constant political machinations of Mary Queen of Scots, who still refused to sign the Treaty of Edinburgh of 1560. Elizabeth's merchant and gentlemen adventurers—whether they were viewed as pirates or not by her friends or foes—represented a private army willing to defend her realm with their wealth and lives, economically, politically, socially, and militarily. And so, she had resolved to nurture them, while appearing to distance herself from their more questionable actions performed in her name.

In most ways, the West Indies was a sideshow. With trade on the Continent in a near shambles, the Holy Grail of riches for Elizabeth's adventurers remained a northeasterly passage to China, or Cathay. No other country had as yet staked a claim to the northeast passage to Cathay, so England was free to maneuver. It was a route that the Portuguese and Spaniards had never frequented. All that remained was to find it. And if the queen's adventurers could find the *northeast* passage—or any other shortcut—to Cathay, the economic wealth of the nation would be preserved.

The Muscovy Company had been founded well over a decade

earlier, and trade with Russia had grown in that time in hemp, cordage, flax, train oil, furs, hides, tallow, and wax. Russian ropes, manufactured by the Muscovy Company's rope makers in Kholmogory and Vologda, supplied most of the crown's naval needs. All these imports were widely used in the burgeoning English merchant navy and were essential in contributing to development of English sea power. The Russians, for their part, were great admirers of English broadcloth, but they were governed by an increasingly unstable Ivan the Terrible. The czar had granted the English privileged trading status, paying no customs duties or tolls, and the English effectively held commercial control over the White Sea for nearly two decades.[5] But for some reason, Ivan had taken a "mislike" of late to Anthony Jenkinson, probably since Jenkinson was trailblazing a path via the Caspian Sea region to Persia, in the hope of opening up a silk trade with the shah.

The czar's "mislike" translated into a high-level personal drama back in England for Sir William Cecil and his protégé, Sir Francis Walsingham. Both were heavy investors in the Russia trade and took an active interest in ensuring that the Muscovy Company prospered. Like many inspired investors since their time, they hadn't viewed Russia as a high-risk investment. Russia was rather an insurance policy for Baltic oak and all the necessities of naval power for the greater good of the English nation. Russia was the first outpost of extra-European trade that had flourished, yet its investors were not reaping real profits.

While Hawkins was establishing his slave trading in the West Indies during his second voyage, Anthony Jenkinson was fighting a rear-guard action with his own Muscovy Company against charges of fraud and misappropriation of funds. To make matters worse for Jenkinson when he had hoped to court royal favor to "scout those seas and to procure to apprehend such pirates as have lately frequented the same," he had angered Elizabeth instead by taking the queen's own ship, the *Aid*, to fulfill this so-called worthwhile task. The hapless adventurer was ordered "in her Highness's name, to repair with the said ship into the river Thames as soon as wind and weather will serve, upon whose arrival Her Majesty will send such smaller vessels thither in his stead as shall be fitter for that service than the *Aid* is."[6]

The *Aid* was, in fact, needed urgently in Ireland, for Sir Henry Sidney, an Elizabethan gentleman adventurer and Ireland's new lord deputy. Sidney had married the Earl of Leicester's sister, Mary, and had been backed by Leicester as a replacement for the Earl of Sussex for the post for some time. Since joining the Privy Council, Leicester had taken a strong, personal interest in Ireland, as he knew that taming the "wild Irish" was the queen's greatest concern for security of the realm and that she remained in constant fear of attack through that "postern gate." Though Sidney had been appointed in the summer, it was October before he was allowed to embark for Dublin to take up his new position as lord deputy.

The intractable problem between England and Ireland had its roots in a papal decree under Henry II, some three hundred years earlier. English plantations that were colonized to replace the power of the church had first begun under Henry VIII when he had dissolved the monasteries. By Elizabeth's reign they had fallen into decay. These plantations were constantly invaded by the Irish clansmen, or septs; and in the North, Shane O'Neill had followed a long-standing Irish tradition and imported Scottish mercenaries, known as "Redshanks," to help him make territorial gains against other Irish septs. To make matters worse, many English colonists, or "planters" as they were called, had gone native, adopting Irish traditions and customs, the most unacceptable of which was "coyne and livery." "Coyne," from the Gaelic *coinmeadh*, meaning the right of the great lord to demand hospitality of whatever nature for his person, had been coupled with the English "livery," by which the lord could demand whatever he needed for his horse. These two demands embodied the worst of both the Irish and English systems and harkened back to the nastiest features of the medieval *droits de seigneur*. It was a uniquely Irish invention, grounded in extortion and intimidation that ran like a sixteenth-century protection racket. The abolition of this pernicious practice became the abiding prime objective of Elizabeth in Ireland.[7] After all, her father, Henry VIII, had made Ireland his own kingdom after his break with Rome, and while the Irish saw matters differently, Elizabeth was determined to colonize the country and tame its wild people. Ireland was in thought and deed the first English colony, and it would become the Queen of England's most spied-on flank—for she feared invasion by this "postern gate" even more than invasion from France, Scotland, or Spain directly.

By the time John Hawkins had returned to England in September 1565, Shane O'Neill's rebellion in the northern part of Ireland was well under way. Sidney's first task would be to find a way to deal with the man diplomatically, if possible, followed very closely by his attempts to settle the long-standing feud between the Earl of Desmond and the Earl of Ormonde. Thomas Ratcliffe, Earl of Sussex, had been lord lieutenant until 1564, when Leicester succeeded through a whispering campaign in having him removed from Ireland. Still, to Leicester's great displeasure, the queen insisted that Sussex remain on the Privy Council. Sidney readily saw that Sussex's policies were by and large just, and with studious topping and tailing, he had these reiterated as his own in his detailed instructions on Tudor Irish policy. The model colony at Laois-Offaly begun several years earlier was to be supported, with "the building of houses and towns and the setting up of husbandry." By settling the northeast coast of the country, it would be the "surest and soonest way" to handle the Scots and "to inhabit between them and the sea whereby . . . all hope of succour may be taken from them." From depriving O'Neill of his fierce Scottish mercenaries, it was only one short step in Sidney's mind to expelling the Scots from Ireland.[8] The disturbing presence of Catholic Scots in Ireland to the queen cannot be overstated. Nothing, except the meddling of the pope or Spain in Irish affairs, drove the message home more clearly to England's queen that she was surrounded by enemies than by the Scots in Ireland.

*

But, momentarily, all these troubles were forgotten. While John Hawkins unveiled the treasure trove to his investors, including the queen, ballads were written and pamphlets distributed recounting his daring adventures. Hawkins had become a national hero. To his investors, he presented a 60 percent profit on their initial stake. Though no precise reckoning of the takings was announced, we can get a fairly accurate picture not only of the profits, but also of the purpose of his voyage by the goods he had sold from the record of the royal treasurer in Borburata:

156 slaves, sold at	*11,055 pesos de oro*
Textiles:	
Paños *(textiles)*	
115 varas *(kerseys)*	
92 varas londras *(London kerseys)*	
10 varas olandas *(Holland linens)*	
90 varas *and 3* ruanes *(Rouen linens)*. . .	*1,473* pesos de oro
Total . . .	*12,528* pesos de oro

Since three *pesos de oro* were equal to one pound sterling at the time, that makes the total value in sterling, £4,176—or $1.51 million or £817,243 today.[9] This receipt shows quite clearly that John Hawkins had only intended for his voyages to open up the slave trade to England. Only 10 percent of the value of the sales were in the traditional export of England, textiles—and even then, most of those came from France and the Low Countries.[10]

It's no wonder that by the time the spoils had been divided, his third voyage was already in the planning. Hawkins should have also not been surprised when Ambassador de Silva took an undue interest in him personally, sidling up to him at court and inviting the new national hero to dinner. De Silva had already warned his king that he believed Hawkins was a danger to Spain, and so during his tête-à-têtes while wine and flattery flowed in equal abundance, the Spanish ambassador tried to "turn" Elizabeth's slave trader and secure Hawkins's allegiance to Spain. There can be little doubt that the mighty mariner sought the advice of William Cecil in the matter, who instructed Hawkins to play along. De Silva's first letter dated October 22, 1565—written in code—recounts their first meeting:

Hawkins, who is the captain, I advised your Majesty had recently arrived from the Indies, conversed with me the day before yesterday at the palace and said that he had been on a long voyage of which he was very tired, and had traded in various parts of the Indies with your Majesty's subjects, but with the permission of the Governors, from whom he brings certificates to show that he has fulfilled the orders given to him by his queen prior to his departure. I said that I should be glad for my own satisfaction and his to see the certificates, and he said he would show them to me. I asked him if it were true that all the Frenchmen who were in Florida had left, and he said they had, and that he had sold them a ship and victuals for their return, as I have already advised. He said the land is not worth much, and that the natives are savage and warlike. . . . I have not thought well to take any steps or make any representations about this voyage until I was well informed of the particulars. I am promised a detailed statement of the voyage—where he went and what he did. . . . The truth will be learnt.[11]

De Silva was determined to stop the English in their tracks and curb their growing passion for roving. Though not as yet as successful, others had already followed Hawkins's lead. In September 1565, Vice Admiral William Winter and his brother, George, had prepared their ship the *Mary Fortune* for a voyage to Guinea, most probably in the hunt for gold rather than slaves. Within the month, the majority of the crew had been killed by the Portuguese, with the remaining few held in captivity in the slave fort at El Mina. Earlier, Thomas Fenner, described as a "pirate gentleman of Sussex" by de Silva, had tried to replicate Hawkins's first voyage, but he, too, alas, failed.[12]

If only, de Silva reasoned, he could get Hawkins to serve his former master, Philip, things might be different. After one of their more amiable dinners, the Spanish ambassador wrote to his king that he may have hit upon a solution:

He [Hawkins] is not satisfied with things here, and I will tell him he is not a fit man for this country, but would be much better off if he went and served your Majesty, where he would find plenty to do as other Englishmen have done; he did not appear disinclined to this. They have again asked him to make another voyage like the last, but he says he will not do so without your Majesty's license. . . . It seems advisable to get this man out of the country, so that he may not teach others, for they have good ships and are greedy folk with more freedom than is good for them.[13]

Hawkins continued to string de Silva along until February 1566, claiming that he would like to serve the King of Spain, when word reached the Spanish ambassador that Hawkins's fleet would be ready to sail as soon as the weather was right. The game of cat and mouse continued between the two men for another six months before de Silva finally confronted the queen. Did she not recall her promises that no Spanish subject should be harmed? Did she not also recall that she had given her word that John Hawkins would not be allowed to return to Spanish ports in the Caribbean? Why were her councillors, her gentlemen, and her merchant adventurers financing yet another slaving voyage? he persevered. The queen couldn't deny any of his arguments. She found herself in the position of ordering Hawkins, George Fenner, John Chichester, and William Coke from sailing to "certain privileged places as is planned." Finally on October 17, the Privy Council wrote to the mayor of Plymouth demanding that they

> *cause a ship that is there prepared to be set to the seas by John Hawkins, which is meant to be sent in voyage to the King of Spain's Indias, to be stayed and not suffered in any wise to go to the seas until the matter be here better considered, charging the owner of the said ship or the setter forth of her, in the Queen's Majesty's name, to repair immediately hither to answer unto that shall be objected against him.*

In early November, Hawkins was ordered to pay a bond of £500 in "sound royal English coinage" and that he must forbear to send any of his ships on a voyage to the West Indies, or lose the bond.[14] In fact, the bond went so far as to specifically prohibit Hawkins from sending "at this time into any place or places of the Indias, which are privileged by the King of Spain to any person, or persons there to traffic, And also if the master and company of the said ship, and the master, and company or any other ship, or ships, to be set further in this voyage by the said John Hawkins do not rob, spoil, or evil handle any of the Queen's majesty's subjects, allies, confederates or friends."[15]

De Silva, scarcely able to conceal his glee, was certain he had won. Yet five days later, on November 9, 1566, four of Hawkins's ships— the *Paul*, the *Solomon*, the *Pascoe*, and the *Swallow*—sailed out of Plymouth harbor under the command of Captain John Lovell. One of Lovell's ordinary seamen aboard the admiral ship, the *Swallow*, was Hawkins's "cousin" Francis Drake.

10. Lovell's Lamentable Voyage ❧

Who seeks by worthy deeds to gain renown for hire,
Whose heart, whose hand, whose purse is pressed to
purchase his desire,
If any such there be, that thirsteth after fame,
Lo! Hear a means to win himself an everlasting name.
—SIR FRANCIS DRAKE, 1583

There can be no doubt that Hawkins never intended to travel on what became known as the Lovell voyage. His plan all along had been to marry Katherine Gonson, the attractive eighteen-year-old daughter of Benjamin Gonson, treasurer of the Navy Board, and move from Plymouth to London. The swashbuckling sea captain now saw himself at the heart of power, and while he cultivated court society, his deputies could continue the slave trade on his behalf.

Not much is known about John Lovell, other than that he was an uncompromising Protestant, and no diplomat. No physical description of Lovell survives, unlike the fiery, bearded, redheaded Hawkins of the 1560s, wearing the finest black velvet, bedecked with a bracelet of diamonds and pearls, jeweled scarf, and three gold rings.

Lovell and his crew had been charged with following the tried and tested method of slave trading pioneered by Hawkins, and there had been every expectation that they would succeed. After all, his fellow commanders, James Raunce in the *Solomon*, James Hampton in the *Paul*, and Robert Bolton in the *Pascoe*, were no novices. But things started badly and got steadily worse. In the Canaries, Lovell flaunted his devout Protestantism and scandalized Hawkins's local partner, de Ponte. He even went so far as to claim to an official in Tenerife that "he had made a vow to God that he would come to these islands, burn the image of Our Lady in Candelaria, and roast a young goat in the coals."[1]

Unlike the pragmatic Hawkins, who often masked his Protestantism to suit the occasion, Lovell obviously felt that his mariners, too, must exercise the "true faith" with the same excess that he did. Our only clear glimpse of Drake on the voyage survives, oddly enough, thanks to Spanish torture. In a confession given by a Welshman, Michael Morgan, after he had been captured and tortured by the Inquisition in Mexico City in 1574, we learn that Drake had converted Morgan to Protestantism on the 1566–67 Lovell voyage. The statement was written down by his inquisitor since Morgan was unable to write:

> He said . . . although at that time he [Morgan] could have found a priest to whom to confess he did not confess but to God in his heart, believing that such a confession was sufficient to be saved, and this he had heard said by Francis Drake, an Englishman and a great Lutheran, who also came on the vessel and who converted him to his belief, alleging the authority of St Paul and saying that those who did not fast should not say evil of those who did, and those who fasted should not speak evil of those who did not, and that in either of those two doctrines, that of Rome and that of England, God would accept the good that they might do; that the true and best doctrine, the one in which man would be saved, was that of England. . . . On the deponent [Morgan] asking the said Drake whether his parents and forefathers would be lost for having kept the doctrines of Rome, he replied 'no,' because the good they had done would be taken into consideration by God, but that the true law and the one whereby they would be saved was that which they now kept in England.[2]

Drake had taught Morgan "the Paternoster and Creed of the Lutheran Law and he had also learned to recite the Psalms from a book."[3] Francis Drake, the eldest son of Edmund Drake, had learned to hate Catholics from his earliest days in Devon, when, according to family legend, the Drakes had been forced to take refuge in Plymouth harbor before fleeing the wrath of the Western Catholic Rebellion against King Edward. The truth of the matter is somewhat different, as we can now see from the entry in the patent rolls of 1548:

December 21, 1548. Whereas Edmund Drake, shearman, and
John Hawking, alias Harte, tailor, late of Tavistock, Devon, are
indicted of having on 25 April, 2 Edward VI [meaning second year
of Edward's reign], at Tavistock, stolen a horse worth £3, of one
John Harte; and whereas William Master, cordyner, and Edmund
Drake, shearman, late of Tavistock, are indicted of having on 16
April 2 Edward VI, at Peter Tavy, Devon, in the king's highway
(via regia) called "Le Crose Lane" assaulted Roger Langisforde
and stolen 21s 7d which he had in his purse.

Pardon to the said Drake, Hawking and Master of all felonies
before 20 Oct. last. By p.s. [privy seal][4]

Still, when Drake gave his family history to the chronicler, William
Camden, it is doubtful that he knew his own father's dark secret. It
would have been easy enough for him to have challenged his father's
story, since the Western Rebellion occurred in the summer of 1549,
not 1548. This doesn't alter the fact that the West Country was a
pretty inhospitable place for those who were staunch supporters of
the "new faith" in the late 1540s. King Edward tried to make the
Protestant toehold in England resemble a much sterner Lutheran
movement. There was no middle ground and no compromise for
Elizabeth's younger brother. So when West Country Catholics had
resisted Edward's new rulings to remove images from all churches
and chapels, withered limbs of one executed Catholic rebel or
another adorned the walls of Tavistock. Body parts of those executed
for disobeying a royal command were frequently exported around
the county to ensure the submission of others. Within the year, the
Cornish peasantry rejected the new Prayer Book—egged on by
the gentry—and all hell broke loose as they marched into Devon,
exercising "the uttermost of their barbarous cruelty." Of course, they
were mercilessly crushed.[5]

It was from their new "home" in the hull of a ship moored or beached
in the River Medway in Kent, the younger Drake brothers were born
and raised until there were twelve surviving sons in all. Edmund
earned his crust of bread by preaching to the sailors of the Royal Navy
at Gillingham. Francis, as the eldest, was expected to find employment
as soon as he was able. Undoubtedly, it was in these mud flats where

the young Francis played, dodging between the king's ships that had been brought in shore for repair. It was in Kent that he absorbed the possibilities of the sea rather than in Devon. It was in Kent that Wyatt's Rebellion to put the Princess Elizabeth on the throne was hatched. It was Kent where the great Londoners passed on their way to the Continent or to Russia or Spain. While Mary's inquisition raged, seizing and burning three hundred innocent mothers, fathers, bakers, butchers, and others of no political significance whatsoever— fifty-four of them were seized and murdered in Kent alone. It is no wonder that Francis Drake hated Philip of Spain, once the king consort of Queen Mary of England.

What is astounding is how his father continued to earn money during the reign of Mary and Philip reading Lutheran prayers to sailors without being counted among those seized for heresy. The family must have lived in constant fear for his life, and their own. What is certain is that Mary's reign would have instilled even greater hatred in Drake for all Catholics. Interestingly, one of the few books Drake carried in his great voyage around the world with him was John Foxe's *Acts and Monuments* from 1563—a history of the Protestant martyrs in the reign of Queen Mary.

While Lovell was sailing on to Guinea, having offended business associates and local officials alike in the Canaries, Elizabeth had other, far more important worries at home. The Queen of Scots had been implicated in the murder of her husband, Lord Darnley, and, it was rumored, had even masterminded the assassination with her lover the Earl of Bothwell. On February 24, 1567, Elizabeth wrote to Mary

> *Madame, My ears have been so deafened and my understanding so grieved and my heart so affrighted to hear the dreadful news of the abominable murder of your mad husband and my killed cousin that I scarcely yet have the wits to write about it. . . . However, I will not at all dissemble what most people are talking about: which is that you will look through your fingers [pretend to ignore] at the revenging of this deed, and that you do not take the measures that touch those who have done as you wished, as if the thing had been entrusted in a way that the murderers felt assurance in doing it.*[6]

There could be little doubt that Mary was plotting again, and that Elizabeth needed to find out what she was up to. Not even de Silva could get the queen's attention in these dark days, so the fate of a small fleet off the coast of Guinea, with no apparent direct investment from the queen herself, would not have hit Elizabeth's radar screen. And so, Lovell sailed on oblivious to the fact that he was of no concern whatsoever to his queen. After two or three months on the Guinea coast "gathering" slaves and merchandise estimated at a value of 30,000 ducats ($10.79 million or £5.83 million) through outright theft, intimidation, or, in a worst case, purchase, Lovell struck out into the Atlantic. Later, the Portuguese would complain that Lovell had attacked the "great ship *Sacharo*, loaded with slaves within sight of the island of Saint James" gravely injuring the captain and slaying many of its crew.[7]

The voyage was not well documented, but it's believed that their first landfall in the West Indies was probably the island of Margarita, off the northern coast of the Spanish Main. Lovell was refused the right to trade, but he was allowed to take on fresh water, wood, and food. At Borburata, on the coast of modern Venezuela, he joined forces with two French pirate fleets that had arrived ahead of him. The more notorious of the pirate captains was Jean Bontemps, with whom Lovell had scraped an acquaintance during his other Hawkins voyages. Bontemps and Lovell sent their agents to Borburata's governor, Pedro Ponce de León, expecting to receive a license to trade as Hawkins had done the previous year. When Ponce de León refused the license, of course under the most strict interdiction from Spain, Lovell sent an armed party ashore. They took two government officials and several other citizens of the town as hostages, and robbed two of the merchants they had kidnapped of the 500 pesos tucked away in their purses.

On reflection, this must have smacked too much of sheer piracy for Lovell, and so the two "robbed" hostages were granted twenty-six slaves in exchange, and everyone was set free. To make everything kosher, the local officials demanded that the merchants—not Lovell or Bontemps—pay a fine to the crown before they would be allowed to take possession of their slaves, thereby settling all tax matters and making everyone happy.[8]

The next we hear of Lovell is on May 18, 1567, when the English fleet—alone—arrived in Río de la Hacha. Again, a representative was sent ashore to ask for a license to trade. The pliable local treasurer, Miguel de Castellanos, who had negotiated the year before with Hawkins, agreed to trade despite Philip's interdiction. But the locals—including de Castellanos's brother Balthasar—refused to trade, since they feared royal retribution from the king. So Lovell simply unloaded around ninety slaves and sailed away in the middle of the night.

When the good citizens of Río de la Hacha had their feet metaphorically put to the fire by the Inquisition a few months later, they changed their tune. One weary inquisitor even commented that he hated to make the colonists testify under oath since they would "only perjure themselves."[9] According to the new story, Bontemps seemed still to be traveling with Lovell, and had arrived first with his fleet. When the colonists had met the French pirate with armed resistance, he had been driven off. When Lovell arrived, claiming he wanted to trade, and was told that it wouldn't be allowed, the Englishman sent a reply threatening to lay waste to the town and kill all the townspeople. The Spaniards claimed that they had defended the town against the interlopers, and had killed or wounded a number of the English. The slaves whom Lovell had off-loaded a few days later were in fact "old and weak and on the point of dying." Being good Christians, they nursed the slaves back to health, so surely, they argued with their inquisitors, they should be rewarded with them as payment for their admirable defense of the town and obeying the king's orders.[10] The investigation concluded that the colonists had probably bought the slaves in one or more midnight trades, but since they all told the same story, there was little the inquisitors could do about it.

Lovell's voyage is chronicled only once more by the good people of Río de la Hacha, when they claim that he had gone on to Española where he "wrought great evil and destruction."[11] If this had been, in fact, true, the voyage would hardly have been largely ignored back home. By the time his fleet pulled into Plymouth harbor in September 1567, Lovell had already been consigned to an anonymous watery history. John Hawkins, on the other hand, had other fish he was frying.

11. The Troublesome Voyage of John Hawkins ✦

An hundred iron pointed darts they fling,
An hundred stones fly whistling by his ears,
An hundred deadly dinted staves they bring,
Yet neither darts, nor stones, nor staves, he fears;
But through the air his plumed crest he rears;
And in derision 'scapes away. . . .
—CHARLES FITZGEFFREY, *Sir Francis Drake*, 1596

While Lovell and his men had been risking life and limb for Hawkins and his investors, the queen had appointed her trailblazing sea captain to the office of clerk of the ships of the Royal Navy, on the condition that his position would be taken up once George Winter retired. Winter understandably clung tightly to his post for another twelve years or so, but the title—and the weight it carried—wielded all the influence Hawkins needed in London's naval society for his next venture.

For this fourth, last, and most impressive slaving voyage, Hawkins's joint stock company investors were even more remarkable than before. The queen; Leicester; the Earl of Pembroke; and Leicester's brother, the Earl of Warwick, were the most prominent from the court itself. But the one astonishing name on the list of investors is that of William Cecil. It seems that even he overcame his habitual "distaste for such ventures" by investing a small sum himself, possibly due to the financial debacle he was facing in his investment in the Muscovy Company.[1] Among the naval backers, the lord admiral, Edward Fiennes de Clinton, invested along with Sir William Winter and William's brother, George. Hawkins's elder brother, William, was a major player, too. The merchants in the syndicate included the usual suspects from the City of London headed by the ubiquitous Sir William Garrard, Sir Lionel Duckett, and Rowland Heyward. In fact, in the confession of one of Hawkins's captured mariners, Thomas Fuller, he claimed that there were thirty merchants in all investing in the voyage, represented by a dozen or so agents aboard the vessels themselves. The most prominent of these seafaring merchants was Anthony Godard from Plymouth, who was fluent in French and Spanish, and of great value to Hawkins aboard his flagship.[2]

While Hawkins was ordering those who had excelled themselves in the Lovell expedition aboard his ships (and there weren't many) for his new adventure, his officers were also busy scouring the port for all the young and fit hopefuls of Plymouth to press-gang into service. Years later, on his return from the West Indies, a young man named William Cornelius, who had been a mariner aboard sardine ships to Flanders until that fateful day in the autumn of 1567, claimed that "one day as he was going along the street unsuspectingly they fell upon him suddenly and hurried him on board as they were short of people owing to the fact that they were going to Guinea which had a reputation of being an unhealthy country where they would die from fever and that they had taken him as many others."[3]

Once again, the queen's own investment in the new adventure was through her ships rather than ready cash. And again, the *Jesus of Lubeck*—newly refitted since her last voyage at Hawkins's own expense—was the fleet's admiral. The queen also ventured the 300-ton *Minion*; and John Hampton, newly returned from the Lovell voyage, became her master, with John Garrett as his mate. The other four ships in the fleet belonged jointly to John Hawkins and his elder brother, William. The aptly named *William and John* was a 150-ton vessel and had the returning Thomas Bolton as her master with the former captain of the *Solomon*, James Raunce, as the ship's mate. The rebuke in this demotion for Raunce was an unspoken warning to all. The 30-ton pinnace *Swallow*, virtually new when she set out on Lovell's voyage, was still in good condition and was also prepared to sail. The last two ships, the 50-ton bark *Judith* and the 32-ton *Angel,* completed the fleet. At the time of sailing, neither the captain of the *Judith* nor that of the *Angel* had been named. Hawkins had at his command some 1,333 tons of shipping positively bristling with firepower in what was, in all but name, a national undertaking.[4]

Aside from the merchants, admiral, his captains, and crew, the fleet also carried an orchestra of sorts: a six-man band with at least two fiddlers, a bass viol player, and organist. Entertainment for the captain and all those who shared his table was essential for the gentlemen adventurers—and as essential as their gold plate to eat off of—especially since they would be gone for a year or more.

And so, within a month of Lovell's return, on October 2, 1567, Hawkins was at sea again. This time, though, it was as a captain of a fleet of state with the flag of St. George hoisted atop his mainmast, the queen's colors alongside the national flag; and the queen's commission in his pocket. But Hawkins hadn't obtained these symbols of national honor lightly. In the queen's presence chamber, he once again faithfully, or perhaps faithlessly, promised Elizabeth that his adventure would not offend England's friends and allies, and that he would not harm any subjects of the King of Spain. The charade was more likely to allow Elizabeth to disavow any knowledge of his actions than be believed by England's savvy queen. Certainly de Silva didn't believe it, and he made Cecil swear "a great oath" that the sea dog Hawkins was not heading back to the West Indies.

Yet despite all Hawkins's preparations and the fair wishes of the great and the good, the voyage was doomed from the outset. Within a few days of putting to sea, the fleet was scattered just north of Cape Finisterre, with only the diminutive *Angel* managing in keeping alongside the *Jesus*. The *Jesus*, despite all the repairs carried out after her last voyage, sprung leaks like a massive colander through her ancient timbers. There was one hole in the ship's stern that was so large it needed to be plugged with chunks of baize. While the ships pitched and rolled, and the *Jesus* listed dangerously in the swelling seas, Hawkins had his mariners man the pumps and prayed they would make it through the night.

By daybreak, all were exhausted and utterly soaked through. They held no hope that they could stay afloat and, for that matter, remain alive. Hawkins gathered his crew together to pray one last time. With clasped hands and bowed heads they begged the Lord to preserve them in their hour of need, and keep the *Jesus*—which was after all named in honor of His own Son—from sinking. Emotions ran high after Hawkins's stirring prayers, and later the crew claimed that there wasn't a dry eye on deck. By midnight of October 10, three days after the storm had started, the winds subsided, and Hawkins knew that the weather was clearing at last. The next morning, with the *Jesus* miraculously still afloat, he led his men in a service of thanksgiving.[5]

Unbeknownst to Hawkins, the tiny *Judith* had sailed on southward in the great storm, and two weeks later Hawkins caught up to her in the roadstead just off Santa Cruz de Tenerife. Still, the *William and John*, the *Swallow*, the *Solomon*, and the *Minion* were missing, feared sunk. To make matters worse, Hawkins had had strained relations with the powers-that-be in Santa Cruz for some time, making it far from the safe haven he needed. When he anchored in the harbor, his great fear was that he was under surveillance, and he couldn't shake the feeling. He was right to be wary. Lovell's shenanigans of the previous year had not been forgotten, and the good people of Santa Cruz feared that they would be attacked by the "thieving English pirates." Nevertheless, it was obvious to the governor that Hawkins's ship had been badly battered in the recent storm, and he was allowed to refit.

Despite being ordered to behave themselves, the confined spaces aboard ship and perhaps their ordeal led two of Hawkins's closest companions, Edward Dudley (captain of the soldiers of the fleet) and George Fitzwilliams, into a violent disagreement. When the men set off to row ashore to fight a duel, Hawkins rushed after them to stop it at once. He wasn't about to allow the Spaniards to have "entertainment" at his men's expense. When Dudley was confronted by his admiral, he struck Hawkins above the eye with his sword in the heat of the moment, and Dudley was clapped in irons on the spot. Striking a senior officer was mutiny even then, and mutiny was punishable by death.

When Dudley heard his death sentence, the hapless captain of the soldiers fell to his knees and begged Hawkins to spare his miserable life. Hawkins told him to say his prayers, and when Dudley babbled to be forgiven yet again, Hawkins helped him to his feet, saying that that would be the end of the matter. The men were relieved, and a thankful Dudley walked away a free, if chastened, man. There would be no rowdiness countenanced on this voyage.[6]

Shortly after this incident, the *Jesus* was finally repaired, and by October 30, Hawkins reached the friendlier southern part of the island where his partner, Pedro de Ponte, greeted him warmly. There he learned that his missing ships—the *Minion*, the *Swallow*, and the *William and John*—were all safe on the island of La Gomera, just fifteen miles west of Tenerife. The *Judith* was dispatched there, and on November 2, the ships were reunited, and their combined companies held a great celebration, firing off their guns and receiving an official welcome from the Spanish governor of the island. Meat, jugs of wine, and fresh oranges were brought on board as a gift from the town of San Sebastian.

Nonetheless, later, the Spanish would complain about "outrages" perpetrated against the Church during Hawkins's sojourn. They may have been right. For whatever reason, this voyage held a strong anti-Catholic bias. There were reports of burning images of the saints, burning the doors to the hermitage at Playa de Santiago, overturning a cross, and shooting at the church and chapel of Santa Cruz. Protestantism had well and truly overshadowed the ethos of the crew. Still, despite their acting like ruffians and pirates, Hawkins and these men thought they were gentlemen and merchant adventurers. They saw themselves as holding a simple, yet burning, piety, often praying three times daily aboard ship. Their adventure was for the good of their realm and queen, in an increasingly hostile world. It never occurred to them that they played a very real role in that increasing hostility.

For that matter, no one had as yet realized that these voyages would change England and, eventually, the world. As they increased over time and in success, their goals would become ever more commercial and, in later years, colonial. They would fundamentally change the very fabric of English society. England's mariners were in a high risk, high reward game. The ships' companies knew that perhaps as many as half of them wouldn't return, but they all calculated that if they did, they would do so as wealthy men. Their adventures would mark the beginning of a new way of expression in the English language, expanding horizons for those more, or perhaps less, fortunate, who stayed at home.

The mariners' diaries are bathed in their workaday chores, the boredom of the Doldrums, the swell of the sea, the stench and the horror of battle, and tales of vast wealth and booty. This was the time when sea shanties were first sung to help pass the long hours at work or while waiting endlessly on a glassy sea for the wind to fill their sails. Their language was rich with the religious fervor of the day and showed their daily hopes and aspirations, their triumphs and their tribulations. And it is their very own words that help us to understand how terrifying, expanding, and exciting the world seemed to them. They themselves were often indentured in some way or another, and suffered greatly just to stay alive. For them slavery was not the heinous crime that we know it to be today, but a means for them to take one step up the social ladder by acquiring the "wealth" that slavery and these "trading" adventures brought.

These were the pioneers who—willingly or not—followed John Hawkins on his fourth slave trading voyage. At Cape Verde, they plundered Portuguese ships for African slaves already "harvested." When this wasn't fruitful enough, he ordered his men to "gather" slaves by direct assaults on their villages. The assaults were a disaster. In one midnight attack, Hawkins and twenty of his men were wounded by poisoned arrows the natives fired at them. Seven or eight of the mariners contracted an illness that may have been lockjaw (tetanus) and died. Considering that they captured only nine slaves, it was a terrible result.

Hawkins and his men couldn't put the Cape Verde Islands behind them quickly enough after this debacle. While they sailed along the Guinea coast, they encountered some French pirates who had taken a Portuguese ship. Hawkins "impounded" the Portuguese *Gratia Dei* (Grace of God) and gave Francis Drake his first command as her captain.

After this, for a while, Hawkins's voyage seemed to be improving. Along the Sierra Leone coast, where numerous rivers flow into the sea, the men set to work in shallow draft, swift ships, and, by the end of November, near Cape Roxo, captured the slaves aboard six Portuguese vessels. But events soon soured again when Drake led an expedition up the Cacheo River, capturing Portuguese ships—which had no slaves. Four Englishmen were killed, and 250 mariners and soldiers were engaged in the fruitless action.

Finally, in January 1568, Hawkins, with the help of the Sapi people, who were the native enemies of the Conga, stormed an indigenous fortified town on the island of Conga off the coast of Sierra Leone. Until that point, the queen's slave trader had "gathered" only 150 slaves despite numerous raids. Through fierce fighting that amazed the English, the town was captured and handed over to the merciless Sapi, and the English "harvested" 250 more slaves. By February, the count had risen to 400, and Hawkins felt he could sail on to the West Indies. He had lost under a dozen men to battle, a few more to disease, and two to drowning when a hippopotamus rammed their ship.[7]

Their Atlantic crossing bode well for the trade ahead, and the English fleet made landfall at Dominica on March 27, where they took on fresh water and wood without incident. At his next port of call, the island of Margarita, the English found the town abandoned and sacked "in a manner all spoiled and burned" with "the walls of a house scrawled in charcoal with the phrase in the French language *Vengeance for La Florida*."[8] What remained of the town's population had escaped into the interior. Hawkins sent a party after them "in peace," and it was soon confirmed that the town had suffered a violent reprisal by the French for the murder of their colonists in Florida three years earlier. Neither Hawkins nor the Spanish had known that the Florida Indians had virtually destroyed the remaining Spanish outposts in Florida by early 1568.[9] Ever the crowd-pleaser, Hawkins vowed to apprehend the French corsairs, after which their Spanish hosts were so grateful that nine days of friendly trading (linen for gold) and feasting followed.

Shortly before Easter, the fleet reached Borburata, only to find that the French had beaten them to it and laid waste to the town. Houses and the church had been destroyed, and most of the inhabitants had fled inland. Soon Hawkins learned that Ponce de Léon and his family had been attacked in Coro, too, the local seat of Spain's government. The Spanish Caribbean had changed for the worse in the two years Hawkins had been absent. But he wouldn't allow French depredations to stop him. As resourceful as ever, Hawkins bribed two men with the reward of an African woman if they could entice the colonists back to town.

Sure enough, the townspeople trickled back in small groups, and a makeshift trading emporium was set up on the beach. Some of the wretched slaves were off-loaded and kept under guard from running away from the Spanish, and probably also from the French.

It did not bode well for a brisk trade, but Hawkins wrote off to governor Ponce de Léon in any event for his license to trade sixty slaves only. Naturally, he hauled out his usual patter that he had blown off course when he wrote that:

> *This voyage on the which I was ordered by the Queen's Majesty of England, my mistress, another way and not to these parts, and the charges being made in England, before I set sail the pretence was forcibly overturned. Therefore I am commanded by the Queen's Majesty my mistress to seek here another traffic with the wares I already had and Negroes which I should procure in Guinea, to lighten the great charges hazarded in the setting out of this navy.*[10]

While he awaited his answer, he ordered his ships to be careened and trimmed. Hawkins even tried to bribe the local bishop to help him get his license by the gift of two Africans and twelve silver spoons. When they were returned at the same time as the negative reply from Governor Ponce de Léon, which said, "before my eyes I saw the governor my predecessor carried away into Spain for giving licence to the country to traffic with you at your last being here, [is] an example for me that I fall not in the like or worse."[11]

The settlers who had been lured back to town to trade now fled again. Hawkins sent a party of sixty men headed by his favorite henchman, Robert Barrett, to bring them back, but Barrett returned only with stolen chickens. The English remained in port, though, hopeful that furtive midnight trades might turn into something more profitable. But when trading didn't pick up enough by the beginning of June 1568 to warrant prolonging their stay, the fleet weighed anchor and headed for Río de la Hacha.

Drake was sent ahead in the *Judith* together with the *Angel* under his command, while Hawkins took on victuals for the fleet at Curaçao. This is the first mention of Drake as captain of an English ship in Hawkins's fleet. But, according to Job Hortop, one of Drake's men:

> *The Spaniards shot three pieces at us from the shore, we requited with two of ours, and shot through the Governor's house: we*

*weighed anchor and anchored again without shot of the town,
where we rode five days in despite of the Spaniards and their
shot. In the mean space there came a carvel of advice from Santo
Domingo, whom with the* Angel *and the* Judith, *we chased and
drove to the shore: we fetched him from thence in spite of 200
Spanish harquebusiers' shot, and anchored again before the town . . .
'till our General's coming, who anchored, landed his men, and
valiantly took the town, with the loss of one man, whose name was
Thomas Surgeon.*[12]

It was only by killing the defenders of Río de la Hacha, burning
half the town, and letting his men loose to plunder that the local
treasurer allowed the English to "trade." The same modus operandi
was used at Santa Marta, the next port west—though at Santa
Marta, the town was taken by "mutual agreement" when a pretense
was instigated to land 150 mariners and "shoot out of the ships half
a score shot over the town for a color [a charade]."[13] Though trade
was brisk, Hawkins still had a number of unsold Africans. And so
he headed to Cartagena.

Where Santa Marta had no hope of resistance, Cartagena was
well fortified and, as a major trading port, well endowed with both
European goods and slaves. There was a heated exchange of views
between Hawkins and Cartagena's governor as well as plenty of
gunfire, but the result remained the same. Cartagena was having
none of the queen's slave trader. The English fleet weighed anchor
on July 24, just before the beginning of the hurricane season. Despite
all their difficulties, the adventure had been a financial success.

They set sail for home and entered the Florida Channel. It
was there that the men claimed they could "smell" the hurricane
coming. Powerless, they watched the clouds darken and swell. As
the winds whipped up to hurricane force, they hoped against hope
that they could outrun the storm. But on August 22, the storm hit
and battered the fleet for several days, threatening to shipwreck
them. As if experiencing déjà vu from the beginning of the voyage,
Hawkins watched the *Jesus* begin to break up. She was "not able to
bear the sea longer, for in her stern on either side of the stern post
her planks did open and shut with every sea [swell], the seas being

without number, and the leaks so big as the thickness of a man's arm, the living fish did swim upon her ballast as in the sea."[14]

This was by far more dangerous than the first storm. Hawkins barked his orders to have the forecastle and the raised poop of the *Jesus* demolished. Anything to make the ship lighter in the turbulent sea. Mariners constantly manned the pumps, while others stuffed anything—and everything—into the gaping holes between her rotted planks to keep the sea at bay. Hawkins thought of giving the "abandon ship" order more than once, but was determined to hold out as long as he possibly could. The disgrace he would face back home for abandoning a royal ship at sea was too much for him to bear. Then, when the hurricane was at its most vicious, he saw that the *William and John* had disappeared, presumed sunk. They tacked round and scoured the coastline for her, and as they did, they also searched for a decent berth for themselves. When the wind died down, their worst fears became reality. Unless the *Jesus* had urgent major repairs, she would not be bringing them back home.

To make things worse, the fleet was running hopelessly short of food and water. They sailed on in light breezes for days on end, lost at sea. None of their pilots had been to these waters, and none knew the geography. It was on September 11 that they realized that they had entered the Gulf of Mexico and were drifting to some reefs off the Yucatán. It was a desperate situation.

Then, as if their prayers had been answered, two Spanish ships were spotted in the distance. Drake was sent in the *Judith* with the *Angel* to overtake them. The faster, sleeker English pinnaces outran the Spaniards with comparative ease, and despite one of the cargo ships escaping Drake's clutches, the other one fortunately was carrying wine and, importantly, a captain who knew the waters well. The Spaniard was questioned and said he was heading for San Juan de Ulúa, the port of Veracruz, the main port in all the Gulf of Mexico. On the one hand, it was lucky that such a major port was within two hundred miles of them; on the other, it was two hundred miles in the wrong direction.

Still Hawkins had no choice, and set sail for San Juan de Ulúa. On their approach, he ordered the flag of St. George to be hauled down three miles from port. The queen's colors on the *Jesus* and the

Minion were so faded and fouled by the weather that they seemed a blank canvas. When the Spaniards realized their mistake in letting the Englishman approach, they immediately banished the tattered English fleet to an island offshore in the harbor. Hawkins tried to be indignant, but as he soon learned, the flota was expected at any moment.

They hadn't long to wait. At first light on September 17, the lookout atop the *Jesus* called down that three sails were nine miles distant. It was the flota's advance guard. By the time the flota was nearing the harbor, its commander, General Francisco de Luxan, could see readily enough that the *Luterano* corsair was blocking the roadstead. What made matters worse was that de Luxan had on board the newly appointed viceroy, Don Martín Enríquez de Almansa. The viceroy ordered that the ships be halted where they were so that the remaining ten ships of the flota could catch up to them while he pondered their predicament. Meanwhile, he arranged for his young son, a gentleman-in-waiting, a horse, and some of his valuables to be taken ashore out of sight of the English rovers.[15]

The situation was potentially explosive and put Hawkins in a "great perplexity of mind." He was powerless to act as he usually did against such a force while his ship slowly sank. And yet his heart must have leapt—along with the hearts of his men—at the thought that the flota carried at least £2 million in riches in gold, silver, and precious gems. Equally well, Hawkins's fleet had its own treasure to protect, and he dared not risk the queen's wrath in such a weighty affair. But there was no time to mull things over. Like his queen, his first thought was of self-defense, and he ordered the Spanish soldiers on the island to sail back into port along with their African slaves. The last thing he wanted was for the "locals" to be at their backs while they faced off the flota. He then ordered the captain of the guard, Anthony Delgadillo, to advise the Spanish fleet of their honorable intentions, and that they simply needed around three weeks time to repair their ships before they could sail home. For once, Hawkins truly *had* been blown off course and was unable to maneuver. Delgadillo was sent like a dove from the ark to deliver the Englishman's ultimatum: let the English fleet stay for repairs, and the flota will be allowed into harbor.

When Enríquez learned from Delgadillo that it was Hawkins who occupied the port, he was incandescent with rage. How dare this rover order *him* around? Hadn't Delgadillo known that Hawkins had "committed serious ravages on these coasts and was . . . little better than a pirate and a corsair on whose word scant reliance could be placed?"[16]

Still, Delgadillo respectfully reminded the viceroy, the English fleet was bristling with heavy guns, demiculverins, and harquebuses, and each ship held the feared English archers in their rigging. There was no doubt that Hawkins had ordered his men to their battle stations. Enríquez agreed that it was an impressive array, and he decided to handle the matter as his king would have done. The flota needed to dock, load, and reach Spain before the weather deteriorated further.

When Delgadillo returned to Hawkins with the viceroy's query as to what he proposed to do to unblock the stalemate, the Englishman was stunned. It was the first he had heard that Philip's representative himself was on board the flota. He quickly clarified his terms:

> *The first was that we might have victuals for our money, and license to sell as much wares as might suffice to furnish our wants.*
>
> *The second, that we might be suffered peaceably to repair our ships.*
>
> *The third, that the island might be in our possession during the time of our abode there.*
>
> *In which island, our General, for the better safety of him and his, had already planted and placed certain ordnance; which were eleven pieces of brass. Therefore he required that the same might so continue; and that no Spaniard should come to land in the said island, having or wearing any kind of weapon about him.*
>
> *The fourth, and last, that for the better and more sure performance and maintenance of peace, and of all the conditions; there might 12 gentlemen of credit be delivered of either part, as hostages.*[17]

Delgadillo carried on the shuttle diplomacy between the viceroy and the Englishman, and when Enríquez learned for certain about the sheer mass of arms the English carried, he knew that he had to agree to the "pirate's terms," despite his fury. After some twenty-four hours of tinkering around the edges of Hawkins's ultimatum, ten hostages were exchanged, a buoy was set afloat to mark the line beyond which neither party should go on pain of death, and the English agreed to pay a fair market rate for any goods or provisions received.

Hawkins played it straight, selecting gentlemen adventurers for the hostage exchange. Christopher Bingham, John Corniel, George Fitzwilliams, Thomas Fowler, William de Orlando, Michael Soul, Richard Temple, and John Varney were chosen for the honor. They were brought out to the Spanish fleet by Delgadillo on Saturday, September 18, at the same time that Enríquez and de Luxan perpetrated their fraud. The Spanish hostages would be random seamen who had been told to draw lots, and then were dressed up "as their betters."

The viceroy, of course, had no intention of allowing a corsair who had ravaged the coasts of New Spain to dictate terms to him. And he certainly would not surrender ten of his gentlemen. But he needed to be in port to do something about the situation. It was only on the following Tuesday that the winds changed and allowed the flota into harbor. An audiencia was held on the Wednesday, and 10,000 *pesos de oro* ($1.19 million or £643,133 today) was handed over to raise an army to fight the *Luteranos*. Spanish horsemen rode up and down the coast, spreading the word to gather all able-bodied Spaniards, African slaves, and Indians to defeat the English upstart. Oblivious to the danger, Hawkins and his men busied themselves with their repairs.

When Hawkins awoke on Thursday, September 23, there was a whiff of treason in the air, as he later wrote, "The treason being at hand, some appearance showed, as shifting of weapons from ship to ship, planting and bending of ordnance from the ships to the island where our men warded [lived], passing to and fro of companies of men more than required for their necessary business, and many other ill-likelihood which caused us to have a vehement suspicion."[18]

Hawkins sent his henchman Barrett to find out what was going on, and went below decks to have breakfast. The Englishman looked out of his cabin window and saw that a Spanish hulk was closing in on the *Minion*, crossing the line of separation marked by the buoy.

He sprang to his feet and saw that the other ships of the fleet were moving as well, and before he could do a thing, warning was given to the flota to attack.

The chaos of a full-scale battle in port ensued. An estimated three hundred Spaniards tried to board the *Jesus*, while others leapt across from the *Jesus* to the *Minion*, and grappled with the English in hand-to-hand combat. An order was given to cut the *Minion*'s head cables so that she could float free from the quayside. The *Minion*'s gunners struck the Spanish vice flagship with her first shot. The next shots ripped through the flagship's broadside, shattering timbers just above the waterline. Seconds later, the ship exploded, taking twenty men with her to the bottom of the harbor. The Spanish vice admiral was in flames. It looked as though God would be Protestant that day.

But it was not to be. Two Spanish ships had grappled aboard the *Jesus* while quite a few of her crew desperately struggled to cut the admiral's cable from the capstan. After nearly an hour, both the *Jesus* and the *Minion* had slipped free of their moorings and turned to fight. Amid the cannon fire, chaos, din, and stench of war, the English inflicted more than sixty direct hits, pummeling the Spanish fleet.

But as reinforcements from the island poured in, the tide of battle turned. The *Angel* was sunk, the *Swallow* and *Grace of God* (the captive Portuguese caravel) were overrun, and the *Jesus* was listing dangerously. Under heavy shore fire, the crew of the *Jesus* transferred as much of its plunder and treasure to the *Minion* as possible. Hawkins hastily ordered in Drake in the *Judith* to take on some of his men, slaves, and other goods. The order was then shouted to abandon ship. The Spanish fire ships were already in the English fleet's midst, separating the *Minion* and the *Judith* from the *Jesus*. Hawkins was the last to climb aboard the *Minion*, only to turn and see the *Jesus* finally sink with much of her treasure still aboard.

To make matters worse, when the fog of battle cleared and the *Minion* had gone beyond the reach of the Spaniards, Hawkins noticed for the first time that the *Judith* had vanished. But that was the least of Hawkins's problems.

England was well on the road to war with Spain.

Part Two

Harvesting the Sea

November 1568–May 1585

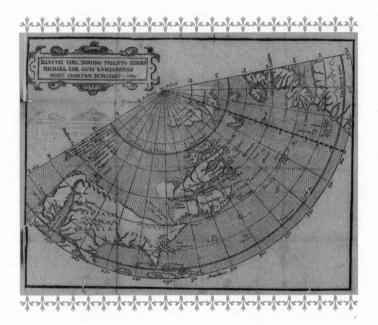

12. The Queen and Alba's Pay Ships ✦

Her Majesty commands all and every, her justices and
officials within her towns, cities, ports, and other places
under her government, to take steps to detain and arrest
with all their goods, chattels, and ships, all subjects born
in the dominions of the King of Spain, in order that they
may be held as security and pledges for the damages and loss
received, without just or apparent cause, by the subjects of
Her Majesty, and for other reasons which may appear. . . .
—ELIZABETH R, ROYAL PROCLAMATION OF JANUARY 1569

Before San Juan de Ulúa, while Hawkins was languishing in the Caribbean waters around Borburata, his world back home had changed dramatically. In May 1568, Mary, Queen of Scots, and her fellow fugitives from Scottish justice stole across the border into England at Solway Firth, fleeing the wrath of their lords of the covenant. With the murder of Shane O'Neill in Ireland a year earlier in June 1567, after nearly two years of a marauding war against the English—and nearly a decade of Shane's deeply humiliating treatment of Elizabeth's government there—the importation of Scottish mercenaries to Ireland had ceased temporarily with Shane's death. In fact, it seemed to many that the Catholic Scottish threat to both England and Ireland—for the time being—was at a standstill.[1] Elizabeth entered her tenth year as England's queen with secure borders at both her "postern" gates, even if the situation with the Low Countries and Spain looked set to explode.

William of Orange and his brother, Louis of Nassau, were both in exile from the States at the head of ineffective mercenary armies, while their maritime supporters—the Sea Beggars—were plundering Spanish shipping at sea. France's Huguenot insurgents held La Rochelle as their base, with the dual result of keeping

Henry III busy in a semiperpetual state of civil war and preventing the French king from becoming interested in foreign affairs. The Huguenots also helped promote English trade inadvertently when, under the pretence of violence against the English wine fleet at Bordeaux, Sir William Winter accompanied the fleet for security—and also ran secret weaponry and victuals ashore to keep supplying France's rebels.[2]

Even Elizabeth's captain of state, William Cecil, saw the benefit of exploiting these improved conditions for England abroad. As long as they lasted, England—and her queen—could breathe easier, and perhaps reflect on the new order, in relative security. While Mary's sudden exile in England was a very tricky matter to handle for myriad reasons, Cecil's calm statecraft in conjunction with Elizabeth's keen desire to see Scotland's rightful monarch restored to the throne saw this as an opportunity to mediate between the Scottish queen and her Protestant lords. So long as Mary—who still had the best claim as heir to the English throne—remained a pawn in Elizabeth's power to play as she willed, the English queen and her councillors held an unexpected trump card against the Catholic League that threatened from Spain and, especially, Rome.

Pope Pius V—as his predecessors Paul IV and Pius IV—had been itching to excommunicate the Queen of England from the fold. To date, it was only Philip's intervention that had stopped the popes from acting in haste. As odd as it may seem, it quite suited Philip in a Machiavellian way to have Mary trussed up in a castle in England. The very last thing that he truly wanted was for her to seize the English throne, which he felt he had almost as good a claim to.[3] Philip knew that there was little doubt that the Scottish queen remained a pawn of her powerful French Guise uncles, and would keep him from recovering his "lost" kingdom, England.

While Elizabeth had become more than a mild irritant, the Spanish king still held out hope that she would marry his cousin, the Austrian Archduke Charles, or another Catholic prince, and at least become subject to her husband's will. That Elizabeth had successfully navigated these waters without finding herself ensnared in a marriage to any prince—Catholic or otherwise—was becoming a serious worry to the Spanish king, and indeed to Elizabeth's parliaments and Privy Council.

Philip's consternation was compounded by the fact that Spanish intelligence had been found woefully lacking. The Spanish ambassador de Silva had claimed that he had the situation under control, that he "understood" Hawkins, and that he had the power to stop the next planned West Indian incursion. De Silva also claimed that he, as spymaster, was "controlling" the renegade Thomas Stucley, who was again throwing his weight around in Ireland by the middle of 1568, unsettling the fragile peace. When the Butlers and the Desmonds renewed their territorial disputes in an open war, Stucley bamboozled de Silva into believing that he could deliver Ireland with just a few thousand men and horse into Spain's eager hands.

All the Spanish ambassador's assertions that he had the situations "under control" couldn't have been further from the truth. So when it was discovered that Hawkins and his fleet had undertaken yet another slaving voyage, Philip glowered with rage at Guzmán de Silva's gullibility and Hawkins's cunning deceits. Something had to be done to improve Spain's intelligence. Since the ambassador had been pleading poverty and wished to return home, the easy solution was at hand. While Hawkins was heading toward the Florida Channel, Philip decided to remove de Silva to a "safer" haven, appointing him ambassador to the signory in Venice.

De Silva's replacement, Guerau de Spes, proved another kettle of fish altogether. Described by his contemporaries as a "fire-eating Catalan soldier," he lacked the finer points of diplomacy so necessary in a good ambassador. Interestingly, Elizabeth's own ambassador to Spain was hardly any better. Dr. John Man had been booted out of Madrid around the same time for calling the pope "a canting little monk" at a dinner party.[4]

But it was the daily bad news from the Channel and the States that continued to preoccupy Philip most. The previous year he had loosed the finest commander of any army in Europe on the Flemings— Don Fernando Álvarez de Toledo, Duke of Alba. Alba had been appointed as general governor of the Low Countries in retaliation to the Flemings' rebellion, called the Iconoclastic Fury. Back in the spring of 1566, the Netherlanders had rioted and destroyed more than four hundred churches and desecrated countless smaller shrines. More than two hundred thousand men had taken up arms against Spain, and when news reached Philip, he shook his head wearily, reportedly saying, "in truth, I cannot understand how such a great evil could have arisen and spread in such a short time."[5] Even when he abolished the Inquisition, the riots continued, and so he rescinded his previous order. Naturally, the Flemings were having none of it.

Alba left Spain in April 1567 and gathered a force of ten thousand crack *tercio* Spanish troops as he marched toward the Low Countries. They crossed the Alps in June and entered Brussels without a fight on August 22, 1567. Today, it is difficult to imagine that this "bloodless" military action was a turning point in northern European history. For the next eighty years, Spain would try to keep trade and communications open to the Spanish Netherlands; whereas the Netherlanders and Spain's enemies would try by any means possible to keep Spain out. The result of the conflict (known as the "Eighty Years' War") would be the United Provinces of the Netherlands and the birth of the Dutch Empire.

In the spring, the Venetian ambassador in Spain wrote to the signory that the Queen of England had written

> to complain of the proclamation published at Antwerp, whereby all English merchants were compelled either to live according to [the] Catholic religion or to abandon commercial pursuits and the country . . . but the King would neither receive the Ambassador nor the letters, and indeed has given the ambassador to understand that if he wishes to remain here, he also must live like a good Christian. . . . I do not know whether his Majesty has lately had any cause for taking this action against the Queen, or whether the result proceeds from his excellent nature . . . the King has told him [the Nuncio] with great distinctness that he may assure the Pope that all the subjects of his Majesty's states must either believe what his Majesty believes, or be utterly destroyed and ruined . . . [6]

By the autumn of 1568, Alba's troops had swollen to over fifty thousand mercenaries. They had been gathered from Italy, Switzerland, Germany, and Spain, and represented a formidable fighting force. It was against these professionals, led by the ruthless Alba, that Elizabeth's merchant and gentlemen adventurers would pitch their lives, fortunes, and wits.[7]

The immediate effect of Alba's arrival was the implementation of the worst excesses of Philip's religious schemes, including a quasi-Inquisition, known by the Spanish as the Council of Troubles. The Flemings called it the "Council of Blood." He pledged to Philip that he would "create a New World" in the troublesome provinces, and there is little doubt that he did, though not in the sense that he had intended.[8] For the Queen of England, and especially Cecil, Alba's arrival shattered the rosier picture from the beginning of the year. A highly disciplined Spanish army was now within a hundred miles of London across a short stretch of the Narrow Seas. De Spes, informed by exiled English Catholics and tutored against the English queen by the Count of Feria, looked increasingly like a fifth column rather than an open avenue for diplomatic discourse. Even William of Orange's resistance was crumbling before Alba's onslaught.

Then, in late November, God became Protestant again. The Channel weather had been appalling, delaying William Winter and the wine fleet at London. On the southern coast, Huguenot rovers had chased four small Spanish ships into port at Falmouth, Plymouth, and Southampton. The customs officers were advised that the ships carried treasure for the Duke of Alba—it was the gold to pay his troops. According to de Spes:

> *Up to the present two cutters and one other vessel have arrived safely in Antwerp, and for the rest of them, Benedict Spinola asked me to intercede. At the same time that I received news of them I requested audience of the Queen, which was granted on the 29th, and the Queen consented to give me a passport for the money to be brought overland, or to lend one of her own ships to convoy the vessels in safety, of which I gave notice to the duke of Alba, from whom I have received no answer. . . . I warned the captains of the vessels not to move, and had letters from the Queen sent to the officials of the ports, ordering them to defend the ships, which was highly necessary as, although in the cases where the ships could get shelter near to the towns, they have done so, the pirates have attacked them, and some of our men have been killed defending their vessels, with a greater loss still on the part of the corsairs. . . . Many people have advised the Queen to seize the money, and the vice admiral has written to this effect from Plymouth. I am in hourly expectation of the Duke's order. . . .*[9]

The Council naturally agreed to the safe conduct overland to Dover, while the queen herself offered a naval squadron to escort the Spanish ships by sea. De Spes dared not decide without Alba, and still awaited word. It is significant that this letter to the king was sent through their usual channels, in Spanish, and certainly not in code. Of course, it was intercepted. Cecil naturally wanted to speak to Benedict Spinola, the great Italian merchant banker residing in London, but he had to tread carefully. Yet little did Cecil know, Spinola had news for Cecil, too.

The merchant had heard through his reliable correspondents in Spain that some great evil had befallen the Hawkins expedition in the West Indies, and that they had all been massacred. Since Spinola had been an investor in the second Hawkins voyage as well as the last one, *and* he was the source of the treasure aboard Alba's pay ships, he had spread the alarm quickly to Sir William Winter, who was guarding Spinola's wine fleet bound for La Rochelle. The last thing Spinola wanted was further losses. When the terrible news reached Winter, he immediately put into Plymouth to protect the treasure ships until some sense could be made of the combined disasters. While he was there, he felt compelled to tell John Hawkins's elder brother, William, the bad news. The date was December 3, the day after the queen had signed the safe conduct for the treasure.

The elder Hawkins lost no time in writing off to Cecil, conveying the dreadful intelligence. He pleaded that Spinola be questioned about the truth of the matter. While de Spes wrangled with the governor of the Isle of Wight (Edward Horsey, a notable rover in his own right) to get the Spanish treasure away from him under the safe conduct dated December 2, Hawkins and Sir Arthur Champernowne, vice admiral of Devon, were battening down the hatches in the West Country. If John Hawkins and his men had been slaughtered, the King of Spain's treasure would make some small recompense under a "letter of patent."

Meanwhile, in London, Spinola and Cecil met at last. Both had reasons for a friendly and frank discussion. The Italian merchant banker told Elizabeth's leading councillor that the treasure had been a loan to the Spanish king, and even told him the terms at 10 percent payable in Antwerp. The queen was consulted forthwith, and it was agreed with Spinola that a loan to the Queen of England was just as advantageous for the Italian, and far less risky, in the circumstances, than a loan to Philip of Spain. Once their transaction was agreed, and sealed, the treasure was brought from its various points on the south coast to the Tower, and locked up securely. When counted, it amounted to a staggering £85,000 ($30.34 million or £16.4 million today).

De Spes was beside himself, sending a panicked missive to Alba on December 21:

> *As Benedict Spinola had put his own money in safety, he has been slack in the dispatch of these other ships, although he was authorised to spend a thousand pounds sterling in the transit. He thought this was inadequate, and sent for authority to spend a larger amount; which authority, he said, he expected hourly, although I believe it has been nothing but a subterfuge. I am now sending to give an account of the matter to the Queen and shall ask for audience in conformity with her reply. . . . It is not for me to advise you but to follow your orders, but I do not like this way of beginning here, and it is my opinion that all English ships and merchandise should be at once seized in the States, and particularly in Antwerp, news of it being also sent swiftly to Spain as there are valuable English ships at Bilbao and Laredo.[10]*

This was followed shortly after by another letter penned by de Spes—also not in code and also panic-stricken—and was received days later at Alba's headquarters:

> *The Queen has taken possession of the boxes of money brought by Lope de la Sierra's ship and 64 boxes from the cutters in Plymouth. She is going to do the same with the other two cutters in Falmouth, notwithstanding her promise and letters, besides the passport she gave. The duke of Alba has ordered all English ships and property to be seized, and informs me thereof in his letter of the 29th ultimo, which was brought by a special courier, who, however, was careless, as with him came four others dispatched by the English. . . . They also tried to raise the mob against foreigners, but the aldermen and constables acted well and took possession of the streets, so that the matter has ended in the seizure of property of Flemish and other*

subjects of your Majesty. All the Spaniards came to my house at night, where most of them still remain. The ports are closed and orders have been issued that no post-horses are to be given to anyone. Cecil was here during the disturbances and returned next day to Hampton Court, where councils are still being held, but nothing yet has been said to me. . . . These heretic knaves of the Council are going headlong to perdition, incited by Cecil, who is indescribably crazy in his zeal for heresy. . . .

The sloops that these pirates have taken are four, with a Spanish ship, all very valuable. They (the English Government) have also seized the property of Portuguese. I send this enclosed in a letter from the French ambassador, with a letter for the Duke and another for Don Francés de Alava. . . . They [the Council] are in consultation every day, and I know not how it will end. . . . [11]

Alba, the great soldier if not the great governor, followed de Spes's ill-conceived advice, though not entirely without reflection. His soldiers hadn't been paid in months, and Alba sensed mutiny in the air. If his men knew why there was further delay, it might stem the tide a while longer. And so, on December 19, 1568—the same day that de Spes officially demanded restitution of the treasure from the queen—Alba ordered all English property in the Low Countries sequestered. This flew in the face of all existing treaties with Spain, where it was clearly stated that no reprisals could be enforced without a distinct refusal or unreasonable delay in returning seized goods. [12]

Elizabeth and Cecil—for once—couldn't have been more delighted. Alba and de Spes had made a serious tactical error that would cost Philip dearly. In retaliation, the queen decreed,

Any merchants born or living under the allegiance of the King of Spain who may be found in towns, ports or other places under suspicion of hiding or disguise, or in any manner of fraud in order to prevent the detention of themselves and their goods, shall be called to account by the officers of justice of such places with the help of all justices of the peace, who shall inquire and examine the said merchants by all legitimate methods and cast them into prison, no matter to what nation they belong, including all those

who may abet or help to hide those who practice such fraud . . .
and especially those who may have concealed such persons or their
property.

　　Her Majesty having also learnt from trustworthy sources that it
was the intention to detain her subjects beyond the sea, under the
pretext that the Queen had detained in one of her ports a certain
ship and three or four small boats in which were certain sums of
money, Her Majesty thinks fit to declare briefly the facts of the
case, by which it will be seen that the detention of her subjects was
unjust and without due cause.[13]

With de Spes now under house arrest, Alba recognized that he would
have to make the first move to defuse the situation. In early January
1569 he sent an emissary, Dr. Christophe d'Assonleville, who was a
member of the Flemish Council of State, to mediate. Elizabeth had
him arrested, too, since he had arrived without proper credentials
from his king.

　　The country was in an uproar against the Spanish knaves. There
was a rising murmur of war or retaliation on everyone's lips in
the streets. The merchants—sickened by the unending stream of
disruptions to trade—longed for new markets, passages to Cathay,
and a world without a dominant Spain.

　　A few days after the public erupted with indignation, on January
20, toward evening, the small weather-beaten 50-ton *Judith* limped
into Plymouth harbor, alone. Francis Drake, overloaded with men
from the *Jesus*, without an ample store of water or victuals, and with
no order given for a rendezvous by Hawkins before he had been
separated by a northerly gale from the *Minion*, had resolved to try to
bring his ship and his men home safely.

13. The Cost of Failure ⚜

If all the miseries and troublesome affairs of this sorrowful voyage should be perfectly and thoroughly written, there should need a painful man with his pen, and as great a time as he had that wrote the lives and deaths of the Martyrs.

—JOHN HAWKINS, COMPARING HIS VOYAGE TO FOXE'S ACCOUNT OF

PROTESTANT MARTYRS UNDER MARY I, MAY 1569

Five days later, the *Minion* careened into harbor at Mounts Bay in Cornwall. John Hawkins and a fraction of the crew had survived the nail-biting Atlantic crossing. Once out of danger from the Spanish fleet, it was a despondent Hawkins who headed for England. With the ship leaking badly and so dangerously overloaded, there was no way any of them could live to tell their tale, he believed, let alone return home. The English admiral had no choice but to take drastic action. More than a hundred men were set ashore in the Gulf of Mexico, never to be seen again. He then tried to head north, but sailed straight into the jaws of a tropical storm in the Bahamas Channel. As he plodded northward, Hawkins watched helplessly as his starving men grew sick and died, one by one. Nearly every rodent, dog, cat, parrot, or monkey aboard ship had long ago been eaten, and while they were still thousands of miles from home, their only sustenance was their leather fittings and abundant salt water.[1] By the time they reached the coast of Galicia in Spain, they were desperate men. Hawkins, dressed in his finest scarlet cloak and doublet, edged with silver and wearing a great gold chain, told the port officials that if they didn't allow him to buy food and wine, he would simply take what they needed without paying. Provisions were, of course, handed over at once, but not without a further cost. The starving mariners were unable to control themselves, and gorged themselves on the fresh food. The result was a spate of further deaths from gluttony. To cover up, Hawkins ordered their emaciated bodies thrown overboard in the dead of night with stones tied to their feet.[2]

When, at long last, they reached port in Mount's Bay in England, word spread like a brushfire that the admiral and some more of his men had returned. In fact, there were only twelve mariners accompanying Hawkins, out of an original complement of four hundred men. William Hawkins, relieved, and fighting fit, quickly wrote off to Cecil demanding the queen issue "letters of reprisal" against the Spanish. Armed with his brother's letter, John Hawkins set off for London. The residue of his entire takings from the West Indies was loaded onto a mere four packhorses for the journey.

But the queen and her councillors refused to be dragged into Hawkins's personal vendetta against Spain. Indeed, though Francis Drake, too, pleaded for "justice," the government was more deeply concerned—and rightly, too—with primary matters of state, which included, among other matters, granting asylum to a huge influx of Protestant refugees from the Netherlands; declaring of a "safe haven" for William of Orange's Sea Beggars at Dover and other southern ports; trying to restore Mary Queen of Scots with some constraints onto Scotland's throne; reconciling the French king to his Huguenot insurgents; negotiating with Alba over the standoff on Spanish and English seizures; fighting the "universal" rebellion in Ireland and the Northern Rising of the Catholic lords Northumberland and Westmoreland in England. Hawkins's timing was, to say the least, poor.

Nonetheless, he persevered. He knew better than anyone else that, with each passing day, the hundreds of Englishmen captured or abandoned in the West Indies were being put to the most brutal torture that the Inquisition had to offer. By March 1569, he and many of the other survivors—save Francis Drake—made their declaration before the High Court of the Admiralty, outlining what had happened.

Drake's reunion with Hawkins had taken place a month earlier, and though no specific record of that encounter survives, it could not have been an easy one. Drake had no formal education, no social standing, no social graces, no previous oceangoing experience as a captain, and no money. But he had proved to both Hawkins and himself that he was one hell of a captain and navigator. Besides, Drake's obvious "excuse" for heading home was a lack of clear orders from Hawkins to rendezvous somewhere. Drake's first duty at that point had been to save as many men and goods as he possibly could. Still, it is intriguing to wonder why Drake never used this argument publicly in his defense. Hawkins, in the end, tempered his criticism of the clearly superior navigator and new captain by reporting only that "the *Judith* . . . forsook us in our great misery."[3]

By the time the High Court of the Admiralty met in March and April, Hawkins had compiled a detailed claim against the Spaniards for the treachery at San Juan de Ulúa, in the hope of negotiating for a letter of reprisal, and for the release of his men from Spanish captivity. His monetary claim was listed as:

1. First, the specified ship, called the *Jesus of Lubeck* With its equipment and accoutrements as sent out from England **£5,000**

2. Item instruments of war, or guns of bronze and iron, which were part of the accoutrements, equipment, and munitions installed in the same ship called the *Jesus* and sent out from England **£2,000**

3. Item gun powder, iron balls, arms and other instruments or guns installed in the same ship and dispatched from England **£2,000**

4. Item two anchors and three anchor lines, called cables, from the equipment of the ship called the *Minion*, which were lost when the said ship escaped from forcible seizure by Spaniards **£200**

5. Item the specified ship called the *Swallow* with its equipment, accoutrements, and munitions sent out from England, and the victuals and seamen's goods carried in it **£850**

6. Item the specified ship called the *Angel*, with its equipment, accoutrements, and munitions sent out from England, as well as the victuals and seamen's goods carried in it **£180**

7. Item the specified ship called the *Grace of God*, with its equipment, apparatus, and munitions, as well as the victuals and seamen's goods placed in it **£400**

8. Item in the specified ship called the *Jesus*, and the three other ships, or some of them, 57 black Ethiopians, commonly called Negroes, of the best sort and stature each of whom is worth gold pesos in the region of the West Indies **£9,120**

9. Item in the said ship called the *Jesus* and the other three ships, or some of them, 30 bales of linen cloth, each worth 3,000 reals **£2,250**

10. Item in the said four ships, or some of them, 1,000 pieces of dyed cloth, each of which is worth 15 shillings sterling **£750**

11. Item in the said four ships, or some of them, 400 pounds of that kind of merchandise commonly called margaritas [trinkets], each pound of which is worth 5 shillings sterling **£100**

12. Item, in the said four ships, or some of them, 300 pounds of pewter, each pound of which is worth 2 shillings sterling **£30**

13. Item, a bale of cambric commonly called taffeta, containing 40 *varas* [ells] **£40**

14. Item four bales of woolen cloth called hampshires and northerns, each of which is worth £8 sterling **£340**

15. Item six bales of cottons **£90**

16. Item a chest containing 30 swords decorated in gold **£120**

17. Item 12 quintals of wax **£120**

18. Item seven tons of manillios, commonly 7 tons of arm and wrist bands [manacles] each of which is worth £50 **£350**

19. Item in the said ship called the *Jesus* a little sack of gold and silver containing 600 pesos of gold and silver **£2,400**

20. Item in the said ship a chest containing various pieces of silver work, commonly called silver plate **£200**

21. Item in the said ship silver called currency **£500**

22. Item in the said four ships, or some of them, twenty jars of Cretan and Spanish wine, commonly 20 butts of malmseys [sweet wines] and secs [dry wines] **£300**

23. Item, in the said four ships or some of them 36 containers of flour, commonly 36 barrels meal, each of which is worth £4 **£144**

24. Item in the said four ships or some of them, other victuals and necessaries to the value of **£150**

25. Item in the said ship called the *Jesus* clothing belonging to the said John Hawkins and other things brought for his personal use **£300**

26. Item in the said ship called the *Jesus* chests and trunks of seamen's belongings **£900**

27. Item in the said ship called the *Jesus* a bale of 20 mantles, commonly called a pack of 20 cloaks, each of which is worth £4, **£80**[4]

The accounting made for a claim of £28,914 ($10.27 million or £5.55 million today). The glaring losses relate to the prime motivation of the voyage, with £9,120 being the loss of the value of 57 "Ethiopians," £320 for their seven tons of manacles, and probably the sterling receipts of £2,400 (600 *pesos de oro*) representing the value of slaves already sold.[5] When the value of the armaments and munitions are added—the very tools required for "harvesting" the Africans—a total of £21,900, or 76 percent, relates directly to so-called losses sustained relating specifically to the slave trade.

Yet this "reckoning" omits the losses of human life. The Africans themselves were doomed either to a curtailed life in misery or an agonizing death from the moment of their capture. Their deaths were never counted. The English sustained losses of 130 dead in the San Juan de Ulúa attack, with a further fifty-two taken prisoner. Hawkins abandoned around 100 more in the Gulf of Mexico, and a further forty-five or so were lost to starvation, disease, or their gluttonous meal on arrival in Galicia.

But still, the High Court of the Admiralty refused to issue a letter of reprisal late in the summer of 1569. According to the French ambassador residing in London at the time, La Mothe Fénélon, "the affairs of the Queen of England are in a condition of peace which appears to be bordering upon war, because the great majority of the English expect to have war. . . . "[6]

The government had bigger fish to fry than the granting of an inflated letter of reprisal to Hawkins. The Northern Rising of two of the country's most prominent Catholic dukes had been quashed—but not without implicating trusted Catholic councillors like the Earl of Pembroke. And to top it all, Spanish forces were gathering a head of steam in the Netherlands. Trade had been suspended between England and Spain, the Netherlands, and Ireland. To make matters worse, Cecil had uncovered a Privy Council–led faction—headed by Leicester—to have Mary Queen of Scots marry the Duke of Norfolk, the queen's cousin.

So when La Mothe Fénélon reported that " . . . money is being raised in every possible way; all the merchandise of Spain is to be sold; new angels are being coined in the Tower in order to pay foreigners, and cash payments to private individuals are being stopped, so that no money is in circulation . . . in truth . . . the queen receives hardly any revenue."[7]

What had started as a promising year had become an *annus horribilis* for the queen. And the only way out, as far as she was concerned, was to wage peace as if it were war.

For that, she needed the services of men like Francis Drake.

14. Undeclared Holy War ✤

I am so keen to achieve the consummation of this enterprise,
I am so attached to it in my heart, and I am so convinced
that God our Saviour must embrace it as His own cause,
that I cannot be dissuaded. Nor can I accept or believe the
contrary.
—PHILIP II TO THE DUKE OF ALBA, SEPTEMBER 14, 1571,
   ON THE INVASION OF ENGLAND

It was obvious to the Privy Council and the queen that Hawkins had not only exaggerated his losses, but also that he had intended to shout his dubious tactics in the West Indies from the rooftops, in an attempt to embarrass the government into action. Hawkins had resolved to make a clear record of the Spanish "treachery," oblivious to the fact that he was hurting his own case for a letter of reprisal. While Hawkins was preparing his "True declaration of the troublesome voyage of M. John Hawkins to the parties of Guinea and the West Indies, in the Years of our Lord 1567 and 1568" in May 1569, Francis Drake had simply vanished. Reprisal was on everyone's lips, and Hawkins's pamphlet outlining in graphic terms the wrongs done to the English was whipping up the general population onto a war footing.

Meanwhile, back in the West Indies, Spain's new viceroy to Mexico, Don Martín Enríquez de Almansa, gave the order to fortify all ports and towns. He sent word to Philip, detailing quite a different picture to the one painted by the aggrieved Hawkins. He, and virtually all of Philip's governors in the West Indies, had become strong proponents for a fleet of galleons to patrol their waters to stop the interlopers before they could come ashore.

Yet while these belated preparations were under way, the Spanish had precious little to fear from the English in 1569. It was the Sea

Beggars and the Huguenots in the Narrow Seas, as well as the Huguenots in the West Indies, who had become active. Instead, England was marshaling its naval resources to protect trade to France (again in a state of civil war) and Germany, bringing troops to and from Ireland, and carrying men and weapons to the north. Still, the rumor machine persisted. "They tell me too," La Mothe Fénélon wrote after citing the movements of the queen's navy, "that Hawkins is pushing forward the armament of seven other good men-of-war, but they want to make me believe that they are for a new voyage he is undertaking to the Indies."[1]

The truth of the matter was that the entire navy—both royal and merchant vessels—was on alert against a potential invasion that had been urged by de Spes, the King of Spain, and lately the pope. In the dark days of the autumn of 1569, Elizabeth knew that the time for prevarication was over. A general muster had been called, and every available man was pressed into service. Ever the wily stateswoman, she also drew upon the services of the fugitive Sea Beggars to help protect England's shores. Their action was particularly appealing to England's parsimonious queen: they defended England, and she bore no expense.

While Hawkins and his personal squadrons were reported in dispatches many times for their activities safeguarding the realm, the only sure sighting we have of Drake in the year was his marriage at St. Budeaux's Church on July 4 to Mary Newman, daughter of seaman Harry Newman, "a great Lutheran who spoke much against the Roman Church and argued for Protestant doctrines" and who had served aboard the *Jesus* in Hawkins's last slaving voyage.[2] Nonetheless, Drake himself claimed to have made a reconnaissance mission back to the West Indies for a future mission with the *Swan*, and he reported that he continued to serve in the queen's navy to his "great advantage."[3] With the Elizabethan penchant for talking in riddles, there may well have been some truth in his boast.

While the queen and her men were protecting the realm from its foes, the Duke of Alba made a pivotal decision. He had no desire to replace Elizabeth with Mary, and he couldn't understand Philip's inclination to replace good military strategy with royal will or religious fervor. Rather than invade England, where Alba ran the double risk of losing his grip in the Netherlands and possibly not succeeding with an invasion force, he resolved to blockade the recalcitrant island nation instead. The wine fleet bound for La Rochelle had been hopelessly delayed at London, and the wool fleet was desperate to sail to Germany. La Mothe Fénélon hit the nail on the head when he claimed that there was a shortage of cash. Without fresh sales of merchandise and healthy international trade, the country's economy would collapse.

So it is entirely likely, that a fabulous navigator and daring captain like Drake would have been among the volunteers in the squadron to protect England's number-one export—wool. It is also likely that Drake, aboard whatever ship he captained, would have been double counted among the forty or so ships roving in the Channel and the Narrow Seas, snapping up the Spanish and Portuguese shipping foolhardy enough to come within his sights.[4]

The ferocious defense of England's shores came as no surprise to Alba, who, alone among Philip's governors and generals, understood and admired the fearlessness of the English. Five months after the Catholic-inspired Northern Rising failed, Pope Pius V at last took measures that had been mooted on the queen's accession—he published the *Regnans in excelsis*, excommunicating England's heretic queen on February 25, 1570. The papal bull radiated from Rome like wildfire and was published throughout Europe. Alba ensured that it was published in the Netherlands in March, especially in the ports for all who dealt with England to see. The main clause that so shocked the queen and her Privy Councillors stated,

> *We declare the said Elizabeth heretic and fautress [patroness] of heretics, and her adherents, to have fallen under sentence of anathema, and to be cut off from the unity of the Body of Christ, and her, Elizabeth, to be deprived of her pretended right to the said realm and of all and every dominion, dignity and privilege; and also the nobles, subjects and peoples of the said realm, and all else who in any manner have made oath to her, to be for ever absolved from such oath, and all duty of liege-fealty and obedience, as by the authority of these presents We absolve them, and deprive the said Elizabeth of her pretended right to the realm and of all else aforesaid,*

and lay upon all and singular nobles, subjects and peoples, and
others aforesaid, our injunction and interdict, that they resume not
to yield obedience to her, or her admonitions, mandates and laws;
otherwise We involve them in the like sentence of anathema.[5]

The effect that the papal bull had on the English—both loyal
Protestants and Catholics—was the decided awareness that the
powers of Rome had declared war on England. For Drake, it
was the declaration of war that he had long awaited. Since Good
Queen Bess had come to the throne, the Spanish and Portuguese
had regarded the English as Lutheran smugglers, interlopers, and
pirates—even if their sole intention had been to engage in legitimate
trade. Elizabeth—now faced with war at home, in the Netherlands,
in France, and in Ireland—had been branded as a common criminal
by the pope, with the hefty price of papal sanction to rebel put on the
queen's head.

It was nothing less than religious imperialism from Pius V. He
hadn't even consulted Philip of Spain, or the man whom he expected
to carry his Catholic arms into war with England, the Duke of Alba.
In fact, by the time the dastardly deed had been pinned to the door
of the Archbishop of Canterbury's residence in London, Lambeth
Palace, that spring, it had become an open invitation for anyone with
a plan to assassinate the English queen.

Certainly, Drake, and in particular. all of his fellow West
Countrymen, were having none of it. The age of hostile commerce
under Hawkins was over. The age of Drake's war had dawned.

15. Drake's War ✦

*As there is a general vengeance which secretly pursues
the doers of wrong and suffers them not to prosper . . . so
is there a particular indignation engraffed [inset] in the
bosom of all that are wronged, which ceases not seeking, by
all means possible, to redress or remedy the wrong received.*
—SIR FRANCIS DRAKE, QUOTED FROM *Sir Francis Drake Revived*

There is an old military adage, "Time spent in reconnaissance
is seldom time wasted." Drake claimed long after the event
that he had spent part of 1570 in the Caribbean on reconnaissance,
and while there is scant surviving evidence to support his claim,
there is no particular reason to disbelieve him. It was a relatively
quiet year in the West Indies, and since the Spanish interchanged
the term *Luterano* freely for either Huguenots or Englishmen, it
is impossible to know for sure whether Drake featured among
the five or so corsair-related incidents on the Spanish Main in that
year. In many ways, the Spaniards were right to mix up the two
peoples. Despite their very different backgrounds, languages, and
countries, English gunners and crossbow archers had long served
aboard Huguenot rovers.[1] What is noteworthy is that until the
arrival of Drake, no Englishman had ever entered the Spanish
colonies of the Main or West Indies intent solely on revenge and
plunder.[2]

But even a reconnaissance mission is not without its rewards.
According to a contemporaneous account entitled *A Summary
Relation of the Harms and Robberies Done by Fr. Drake an Englishman,
with the Assistance and Help of Other Englishmen*:

*In the year 1570, he went to the Indies in a bark of 40 tons, with
whom there went an English merchant of Exeter called Richard*

Dennys and others, and upon the coast of Nombre de Díos they did rob divers barks in the river Chagres that were transporting merchandise of 40,000 ducats [$3.52 million or £1.9 million today] of velvets, and taffetas, beside other merchandise, besides gold and silver in other barks, and with the same came to Plymouth where it was divided amongst his partners.[3]

It is generally assumed that the amount stolen was exaggerated. Yet, this account brings us tantalizingly close to Drake, almost as if we are reading about his daring escapades in a dispassionate newspaper article. Here we see a glimpse of Drake, not as yet in full possession of the cunning that would make him "world famous." Though he was greatly admired by his friends—and even his enemies—he was nonetheless little more than a pirate hell-bent on revenge.

And no man was better suited to the task. Drake had an uncanny genius for sensing his enemy's weakness and, without the need for huge numbers of men and artillery, was able to achieve his nefarious aims. What's more amazing, as with any real genius, he made it all look so easy. San Juan de Ulúa had been etched into his soul and the resultant hatred for Philip, the ignominy of the encounter, and the fire against Catholic injustice in his belly would be stoked by further perceived wrongs until the day he died.

Still, Drake hardly needed excuses or popish threats against England to fulfill his personal quest. The flota had been within his grasp at San Juan de Ulúa, but in following a defensive rather than offensive course—due only in part to circumstances—the English fleet had been well and truly trounced. That flota had belonged to Philip of Spain. Ergo, Philip had humiliated him and his fellow mariners. What's more, Philip had made, in Drake's eyes, a call to arms through the pope against his queen, Elizabeth, by virtue of the excommunication bull. So Drake went to war to protect her, enrich himself, and spread the glory for the realm of England.

While Hawkins, Winter, and Drake's fellow West Countrymen under Devon's Vice Admiral Sir Arthur Champernowne scoured the Narrow Seas in the company of Orange's Sea Beggars, preying on Spanish shipping, Drake headed back to Spanish America. He had seen at firsthand the fabulous wealth there, and his mouth watered at the prospect of Spain's vulnerability. Yet the clear answer to one simple question seemed to elude him. How had the Spanish succeeded in bringing the wealth of its empire back to Seville for over fifty years virtually unscathed?

The reply was obvious. No one had dared to attack the treasure trains or *trajín*. Where San Juan de Ulúa provided a safe haven for the Mexican flota, the treasures of the Spanish Main were brought to Nombre de Díos for transshipment to Seville in a series of complex maneuvers. To reach Nombre de Díos, the gold, silver, pearls, and precious gemstones from Peru, Chile, and Bolivia (all called "Peru" at the time) were first brought to the Pacific by mule train, loaded onto frigates, and shipped northward to Panama City.

From there, another mule train of up to six hundred animals threaded its way through the dense jungle to the isolated settlement of Venta Cruces. In this humid, remote outpost—no more than a wharf and a warehouse rather than a settlement or colony—the bulk of the treasure train was loaded onto shallow draft barks and brought down the Chagres River to Nombre de Díos. The Spanish bullion continued overland from Venta Cruces by mule train to Nombre de Díos. Once there, all the king's riches would be locked up securely in his treasure house, where it awaited the arrival of the flota, which would carry it back to Spain. Without this shipment of gold and silver each and every year, Philip's credibility with his European bankers would evaporate, and so would his funds to keep his empire in a virtual state of perpetual warfare.[4]

Yet, despite its incredible importance, Nombre de Díos was at significant risk of attack. There was no regular garrison stationed there; there were no fortifications to speak of either. It sat a mere twenty-three leagues—around eight miles—across rugged jungle terrain from the Pacific Ocean, and hundreds of miles from anywhere in the Caribbean. It seemed to languish in the stifling equatorial heat, coming to life only when the flota docked. "The treasure house of the world," as Drake called Nombre de Díos in *Sir Francis Drake Revived*, was a ramshackle collection of wooden buildings, a warehouse, a wharf, and the king's treasure house. Its only true defense was its utter isolation.

And so, in late February 1571, Drake had returned. This time, as captain of the tiny forty-ton *Swan*, he anchored off the clear blue coast at Nombre de Díos, timing his arrival to give himself as long as possible for raiding before the hurricane season brewed up again. The information available to Drake prior to these voyages was at best incomplete, and mostly inaccurate. But through studious observation of Panama's coastline and harbors, interrogation of any Spanish prisoners—whom he appeared to have released unharmed—and, most important, the friendship of the *Cimarrones*, or escaped black slaves, Drake garnered an entirely different picture.

The *Cimarrones*, called Cimaroons in sixteenth-century English, were a crucial factor in Drake's ultimate success in the Americas. Only a year earlier, the bishop of Panama had complained that they represented a real threat to Spanish settlements in the area when he wrote to the king that "the human tongue cannot relate the ignominies which both the French and the *cimarrones* [sic] have this year inflicted here on all sorts of persons; and of a thousand Negroes who arrive annually, three hundred or more escape to the wilds."[5] They had the inside knowledge of how the Spanish settlements worked. They knew Spanish habits and ways. They were the ones who confirmed to Drake that the settlements were weakly garrisoned, and frequently fell victim to the depredations of French rovers.

So when Drake's men attacked a vessel from Cartagena traveling to Nombre de Díos in late February at the small port of Pontoons, it is hardly surprising that the Spaniards aboard should have resisted capture. Drake had left the *Swan* safely tucked away in a nearby harbor with "a fine bay . . . safe . . . for all winds,"[6] while he and fifteen or so of his men approached in a pinnace and hailed the Spanish frigate for a "parlay." The English had two small culverins threatening the Spaniards from its bow, and the men were armed to the teeth with swords, crossbows, and harquebuses. According to Spanish accounts, two of the men had their faces powdered with "war paint"—one black, the other red.

The Spaniards never stood a chance. Four were killed, including one African slave, before they cut their own cables and tried to outrun Drake and his men. The frigate inevitably ran aground, and the

Spanish—desperate to escape—waded ashore waist-deep through a mangrove swamp to safety. The frenzied plundering of the first ship was interrupted by the delightfully unexpected capture of a second Spanish frigate. Again its crew fled through the mangrove swamp to shore and watched helplessly. When the Spaniards finally regained the vessel the next day, the English had left a note: " . . . Done by English, who are well disposed if there be no cause to the contrary: if there be cause, we will be devils rather then [sic] men."[7]

While the Spanish were counting their losses, Drake and his men headed up the Chagres River and the fabled route of Spanish gold. Unlike all previous rovers, Drake reached Venta Cruces, and seized 100,000 pesos ($10.55 million or £5.7 million today) worth of clothing and other goods from the wharf as well as three barks. They sank the ships so that the news of their exploits couldn't overtake them. For the next three months, Drake and his men operated between Nombre de Díos and Puerto Bello along the coast, intercepting vessels to and from the mouth of the Chagres, gaining more and more information about the flota each time. In all, around twelve vessels were captured laden with valuables estimated at 150,000 pesos ($17.59 million or £9.51 million today), not including the two prize vessels, slaves, and clothing. These were estimated at another 80,000 pesos ($9.38 million or £5.07 million today).

Drake's next prey was a royal dispatch frigate out of Cartagena, carrying the king's correspondence for the colonies of Panama and Peru. This time, Drake's pinnace was armed with twenty-three men, and the capture took place around May 8, 1571. The ship's owner and another seaman were killed before the prisoners were put ashore on an uninhabited island nearby. Philip's correspondence was tossed irreverently into the sea, and the ship set adrift. When the hapless Spaniards were rescued, tales of "stripping and abusing a friar" identified the new corsair as an unknown *Luterano* pirate from England.

Three expeditions had been sent out to capture the daring Englishman at a cost of 4,000 pesos ($469,110 or £253,573 today) without success. Officials in Panama wrote to Philip on May 25 that this Drake was "so fully in possession of the whole coast of Nombre de Díos, Cartagena, Tolu, Santa Marta and Cabo de la Vela, that traffic dares not sail from Santo Domingo thither, and trade and commerce are diminishing between the windward islands and this Main."[8]

Drake's private war had raked in officially £66,000 ($23.22 million or £12.55 million today) in three months.[9] While the legality of Drake's venture cannot be sustained remotely either morally or in law, it heralded the end of the age of Hawkins's aggressive commercial and illicit trade in the Caribbean. It also meant that Philip II and Sebastian of Portugal would need to redouble their efforts in defending the monopolies they claimed in Africa and the Americas if they were to keep their empires safe from Drake and the new breed of Elizabethan seamen.

16. The Dread of Future Foes ⚘

The doubt[1] of future foes
Exiles my present joy
And wit me warns to shun such snares
As threatens mine annoy.
For falsehood now doth flow
And subjects' faith doth ebb,
Which should not be if reason ruled
Or wisdom weaved the web.

—POEM BY ELIZABETH I, C. 1571[2]

The year 1572 was one of those turning points in history that was comprised not of one momentous event, but of many. The Ridolfi plot to kill Elizabeth and put Mary on England's throne had been uncovered in time, thanks to the astute intelligence work of Sir Francis Walsingham. Implicated in the plot were not only the Duke of Norfolk and his men, but also Mary, Queen of Scots, the Pope, Philip II, Thomas Stucley, and, of course, its author, the Florentine merchant banker Roberto Ridolfi. If Walsingham hadn't communicated the list of all "strangers" arriving from Rome to William Cecil (elevated to the position of lord treasurer and created Lord Burghley in 1571), the machinations of a well-oiled Catholic espionage network could have feasibly succeeded.[3] Elizabeth reacted with notable calm in the middle of the international maelstrom, but still fired off a stinging rebuke to Mary on February 1, 1572, "to consider that it is not the manner to obtain good things with evil speeches," she admonishes her cousin, "nor benefits with injurious challenges, nor to get good to yourself with doing evil to another."[4]

The loss of the Duke of Norfolk, Thomas Howard, as an ally was devastating for Elizabeth in several ways. As her second cousin on the Boleyn side, he was one of her closest surviving family relatives. But more devastating was the fact that since the Northern Catholic

Rising in 1569, Norfolk was the senior noble of the realm. He was also an important Privy Councillor, and a gentleman adventurer whose wealth had been invested in a number of ventures from those of the Muscovy Company to the Hawkins slaving voyages. Yet the most crushing blow to the queen was that only a short time previously, key members of her own Privy Council, led by none other than her favorite, the Earl of Leicester, were behind a marriage negotiation between Norfolk and Mary of Scots. While the earlier negotiation had not, of course, included plans to supplant Elizabeth on the throne, it cast a long shadow of doubt over the motivations of such stalwarts as Leicester, Sir Henry Sidney, and the ever-trusty Earl of Pembroke in these dark days.[5] Pembroke had been implicated previously in the Northern Rising by the Catholic Earls. The possibility that these three most trusted and loyal servants could have been in league to promote the secret marriage plans of the Queen of Scots to Norfolk, which formed the basis for the future Ridolfi plot, was too grotesque for Elizabeth to contemplate. Only when Pembroke protested, "God forbid I should live the hour, now in my old age, to stain my former life with one spot of disloyalty," was the queen's mind put to rest. To prove her confidence in him, Pembroke was put in charge of the queen's personal guard at Windsor.[6]

Norfolk was speedily tried, convicted of treason, and sentenced to death. Meanwhile, his fellow plotters Ridolfi and Stucley had escaped the country. By the time Elizabeth had granted a temporary stay of execution in March 1572, Ridolfi had made good his escape to Rome. Stucley, the queen's former gentleman adventurer in the 1560s, had become one of Philip's heroes in the great battle of Lepanto in October 1571 where the Turkish navy was crushed by the united papal and Spanish forces. Already a resident at the Spanish court, and a great favorite of Jane, Duchess of Feria, former lady-in-waiting to Elizabeth's sister Mary, Stucley remained a wild card in the pack of knaves. Neither the queen nor Lord Burghley knew where he would tip up next, or what forces he would bring to bear on the realm. Stucley's claim on the seneschal [governorship] of Wexford had failed two years earlier, and he was forced to relinquish any claims to plantations in Ireland to his archenemy, Sir Peter Carew. Naturally, this "hand over" didn't pass off smoothly, so Stucley was detained "at Her Majesty's pleasure," imprisoned in

Dublin Castle, until he saw the error of his ways. On the promise of an honorable return to England, Stucley was released, but he fled to Spain instead, much to the embarrassment of Elizabeth's lord deputy, Sir Henry Sidney. Naturally, his escape counted as another black mark on Sidney's record.

And so it came to pass that Stucley, since the time of Ridolfi, had become Philip's "loyal" client. In a joint proposal to the King of Spain and the pope, Stucley had urged, "That there be given him four well equipped ships and a foist and two barks and therewith 3,000 foot and five hundred horse, where he will undertake to raise without for the present any payment on that account; and with that force he will go to Plymouth and burn and take the fleet of Hawkins and thence he will go to Ireland and make himself master of Waterford and Cork."[7]

Though Stucley had personally betrayed Elizabeth, it was the greater Catholic League against her, her troublesome "province" Ireland, and ultimately the defeat of the Turks that truly worried the English queen and Burghley in international politics. These were particularly harsh years for queen and country. Years of upheaval in trade in the Low Countries, the Northern Catholic Rising in England, failed plantations in Ireland coupled with the James Fitzmaurice Fitzgerald and Edmund Butler tribal war there, the loss of "favored nation status" in Ivan the Terrible's Russia for the previous three years, no successful northerly route as yet to Cathay for the growth of the luxury trade to the Orient, Barbary pirates and Spanish wars in the Mediterranean, the papal excommunication and absolution of English subjects from obeying Elizabeth, and the ultimate failure of Hawkins's slaving expeditions all combined to make the early 1570s a time of particular penury and dissatisfaction.

Still, there were, seemingly, some bright rays on the horizon. Peace, though an illusion, had reigned in the more heavily populated, predominantly Protestant south for fifteen years. A compromise had been etched in stone between Protestants and Catholics, and the country was poised to enter a new era of prosperity, if only the rest of the world would let it happen. Some adventurers had dedicated much of their efforts to improving matters at home, despite nursing a penchant for raiding foreign shipping in the Narrow Seas and beyond. Sir Lionel Duckett, master of the Mercers' Company in 1572 and lord mayor of London in that year, was determined to maintain "good order" in the capital by curbing excessive debauchery, drinking, and feasting, despite being labeled a killjoy. He also instituted the system for the issue of writs of habeas corpus to be restricted to cases against those who disturbed the peace. Where Duckett indirectly condoned "lawlessness" at sea through his private investments, he was particularly proud—with good reason—of his efforts at curbing criminality and venal behavior at home.[8]

Sir Thomas Gresham, who would remain the queen's royal factor at Antwerp until May 1573, had found his role increasingly difficult to maintain since the seizure of the Duke of Alba's pay ships. Gresham witnessed the delicate series of negotiations for the return of the money (long ago spent) between the Genoese bankers, the queen and Burghley, and the king's representative, Tomasso Fieschi, but was powerless to contribute positively to talks that were by and large handled at Privy Council level.[9] To complicate matters further, Gresham's great friends were Balthazar and Gaspar Schetz, with whom he often stayed. Life must have been decidedly uncomfortable for the queen's factor since Gaspar was also the King of Spain's royal factor.[10] All of these complications paled into insignificance, though, when, as a result of Philip's naval war against the Turks and his requirement to enhance protection of his colonies, the King of Spain declared bankruptcy in Antwerp yet again in 1572.

And Gresham was unstoppable. He had already turned his attention to a different and positive project. Plans were under way for the pinnacle of his personal achievement. His vision for England's future would become a monument that all merchants and traders could appreciate and enjoy. With Sir Lionel Duckett's able assistance, Gresham began building the physical representation to England's economic future—the Royal Exchange in the City. Modeled on the Antwerp bourse, it was to be Gresham's legacy to the nation, built in large part with his own money.[11]

Yet trade with Antwerp, the greatest pillar of foreign exchange, had long been reduced to a low water mark by international circumstances. Customs and excise duties on imports were at an all time low at the time of building, making the Royal Exchange seem to some like Gresham's great folly. Merchant adventurers had been reduced to becoming "adventurers" harvesting the seas in order to make a living. Naturally, any merchandise brought into port without the proper paperwork—including a "letter of reprisal"—would have been confiscated. And so smuggling became rife everywhere. The result was that most of the crown's receipts now came from the sale of crown lands rather than foreign exchange or excise duty.

Something needed to be done. Sir Thomas Smith, Elizabeth's principal secretary in 1572, had agreed with the Merchants Adventurers stance that, ultimately, only continued trade with the Netherlands could guarantee Anglo-Spanish amity.[12] Perhaps it was for his outspoken, if correct but unpopular, views that Smith was sent to Paris on the embassy with Sir Philip Sidney in 1572 for Henry of Navarre's marriage to the King of France's sister, rather than to the Low Countries to continue the negotiations for the "return" of the money taken from Alba's pay ships in November 1568.

Burghley urged his queen that something had to be done about the international situation if England were to grow and occupy a position of importance in the world. Elizabeth agreed. She knew full well what she would have to do to placate the King of Spain and Alba, and so long as it cost her very little in real financial and face-saving terms, it would seem to show a great willingness on her part to patch things up with the kings of Spain and Portugal. After consultations with Burghley and other Privy Councillors, the queen resolved, firstly, to cease the Guinea and all slave trade;[13] and, secondly, to make a concerted effort to stop Channel piracy. The first of these was handled readily enough through proclamation, though neither Iberian king believed that Elizabeth was sincere. Nor did they believe, rightly, that the Privy Council and the Admiralty could stop privateers from interloping in Spanish and Portuguese colonies.

As to Channel piracy, the ready solution was for the queen to expel Orange's Sea Beggars from their safe haven at Dover. But was this newfound cooperation with Spain all it seemed to be? Or was it, as with so many things with Elizabeth, a masterstroke or "answer answerless" to an intractable problem, another of her gossamer webs that when held up to the lightest of breezes turned round upon itself and became nothing more than broken silken threads?

Captain La Marck, Orange's most robust mariner, had made Dover and the creeks and bays along the south coast his home with his fellow Sea Beggars for several years. English seamen swelled his ranks in the certain expectation that they would share in La Marck's plunder. But La Marck, his men, and even the English who served under or alongside him were expendable in the game of cat and mouse that the Queen of England played with Philip of Spain. They were a cheap and easily disavowed means of making unofficial war. But meanwhile, she persisted—until the spring of 1572—in renewing safe conduct after safe conduct for La Marck and his men. As the Queen of England, it was the only course open to her to show her defiance of Spain. As the patron of these pirates, Elizabeth would never allow their expulsion to mean their extinction.[14]

Alba's view remained skeptical. The Sea Beggars were rebels and pirates, baptized by Elizabeth as Orange's soldiers, but pirates nonetheless.[15] Interestingly, little has been made of the fact that Philip had engaged willingly in the same practice of harboring rebels—but in his case, rebels from English justice. After the collapse of the Northern Rising, the Earl of Westmoreland, Lord Dacre, and others had escaped to the Netherlands and lived comfortably under the protection of the Spanish government *and* on Spanish pensions.[16] These very men would become the backbone for Philip's "Enterprise of England" in 1588. Their activities could not, would not, be tolerated by the queen or her Privy Council without a fight.

And so, in what appeared to the uninitiated to be an act of munificence—the expulsion of Orange's Sea Beggars from England's shores—Elizabeth had, in fact, struck a lethal blow against the King of Spain; she was pulling back the olive branch from his outstretched hand. What followed was vintage Elizabeth.

The expulsion orders handed down from the commissioners of the Cinque Ports on the grounds of "plundering ships belonging to the merchants of the Steelyard and others, and seizing their ships and the goods they had taken or uttered 'to the slander of the realm and impeachment of the haunt and traffic of merchandise'" was only one of the long list of complaints against the Dutch rebels.[17] On March 25, they were ordered to quit Dover and, indeed, England.

When La Marck was still seen hovering off the south coast, Sir John Hawkins was sent with his fleet to ensure La Marck's retreat. A month later, La Marck's fleet landed at the Isle of Wight to sell their captured prizes for victuals. Three days later, they successfully captured one of two deepwater ports in the Netherlands, Brill.

At last, Orange had his toehold on home ground. Brill had been seized by La Marck, but Flushing, the other deepwater port, was beyond his reach. In July 1572, Sir Humphrey Gilbert, Elizabeth's hardened gentleman adventurer fresh from his wars in Ireland, and Gilbert's uncle, the vice admiral of Devon, Sir Arthur Champernowne, led some eleven hundred "pressed" volunteers to capture Flushing and Sluys. Above all, it was Gilbert's duty to ensure that the French would not be able to occupy these ports. There is no doubt that he had the tacit support of the queen and the Privy Council for an undertaking like this: when he failed to take Flushing by November, he returned to England in a feigned "disgrace."[18] Then, in a most transparent effort to prove her good credentials in combating piracy in 1572, Elizabeth refused to grant Sir Richard Grenville a license to voyage into the Pacific since it would "annoy the King of Spain."

Yet even the cunning deceits of the Queen of England were to be outdone in 1572 by another queen—the dowager Queen of France, Catherine de' Medici. In that year Catherine was in the middle of negotiating a marriage between her son, Francis, the Duc d'Alençon, and Elizabeth. She was also responding to the clear and present danger closer to home that the Huguenot leader, Admiral de Coligny, represented. Coligny had, in her eyes and those of the Guises, supplanted Catherine's influence with the weak King Charles, her son. In the summer of 1572, the eyes of the great nations of Europe were on Paris for the wedding of Henry, King of Navarre, to Marguerite de Valois, Catherine's daughter, and sister to King Charles. It was a match that had been championed by Coligny. After years of civil war, Coligny—in an act of conciliation—had become a close advisor of the king, and had been instrumental in the negotiations.

Queen Catherine whispered in her son's ear that as the king of Navarre was a Protestant, she feared the capital could become a killing field if the population were allowed to go about armed. Naturally, Charles concurred, and he issued a royal proclamation forbidding arms and the molestation of any foreigner or Navarre follower. Protestants throughout Europe, and especially in France, took this for a great act of kindness and reconciliation, and they flocked to Paris for the ceremony.

The stark facts were precisely the contrary. The Guises, uncles to Mary, Queen of Scots, along with Queen Catherine, believed that Coligny represented too great an influence on the weak-minded king. Coligny simply had to go. And what better time to assassinate Coligny than when Paris was *en fête* and filled to overflowing with Protestants?

On the morning of Friday, August 22, 1572, after a week of festivities celebrating the elaborate wedding of Henry to Marguerite, Admiral de Coligny wended his way back to his lodgings in the rue de Béthisy. He was returning home from watching the king play Guise at tennis at the Louvre. A would-be assassin fired three shots from a third-floor window as Coligny turned into his street. The first blew off most of Coligny's right-hand index finger. The next lodged in his left arm, and the third missed altogether. The king was notified, and his personal physician was sent to tend to the admiral. Coligny's wounds were not considered grievous, and the Huguenots who had gathered to stand vigil in the street below the admiral's lodgings rejoiced "to see the king so careful as well for the curing of the admiral, as also for searching out of the party that hurt him."[19] Bearing this out, the king and his brothers were so solicitous that they and their mother visited the convalescing admiral.

Yet Henry of Navarre and the Prince de Condé smelled danger in the air. They tried to calm their Huguenot supporters by confirming that Coligny would recover completely. But when the man hired to assassinate the admiral was caught, one Maurevert, it was also discovered that the man who had held the horse for Maurevert's quick getaway was a veteran servant of the Duc de Guise. Maurevert's weapon, a harquebuse, had been "borrowed" from the Duc d'Alençon's armory. And the Duc d'Alençon was the English queen's intended bridegroom.

There was only one option left open to the scheming Valoises and Guises to keep the truth from coming out: exterminate the Huguenots. At four in the morning, the Duc de Guise and his Swiss mercenaries forced their way into the admiral's lodgings. Coligny was already on his knees in prayer. While he knelt, the mercenaries stabbed him repeatedly then tossed his bloodied body out the window. Meanwhile, throughout the capital, Huguenot houses were attacked. Men, women, and children were slaughtered, their bodies thrown into the streets or the River Seine. Huguenots to whom King Charles had granted asylum at the Louvre were murdered, their two hundred or so corpses piled high in the splendid palace courtyard. According to the Spanish ambassador to France, Zuñiga, fanatics had entered the English embassy where Sir Francis Walsingham, Elizabeth's ambassador, resided, and where other English notables like Sir Philip Sidney and Sir Thomas Smith hid along with the ambassador from the mob. Only after the danger had passed had the Duc de Nevers stationed the royal guard outside Ambassador Walsingham's home. In the first blood orgy on St. Bartholomew's Day, conservatively over two thousand Huguenots were slain.

It was the first such massacre of Christian against Christian. Its suddenness, viciousness, and ferocity stunned all who witnessed it and all who heard about it. Elizabeth, after long, hard reflection, wrote to Walsingham in December 1572:

> *We are sorry to hear, first, the great slaughter made in France of noblemen and gentlemen, unconvicted and untried, so suddenly (as it said at his [the king's] commandment), did seem with us so much to touch the honor of our good brother as we could not but with lamentation and with tears of our heart hear it of a prince so well allied to us . . . we do hear it marvelously evil taken and as a thing of a terrible and dangerous example; and are sorry that our good brother was so ready to condescend to any such counsel, whose nature we took to be more humane and noble.*
>
> *But when was added unto it—that women, children, maids, young infants, and sucking babes were at the same time murdered and cast into the river, and that liberty of execution was given to the vilest and basest sort of the popular, without punishment or revenge of such cruelties done afterwards by law upon those cruel*

murderers of such innocents . . . And now since it doth appear by
all doings, both by edicts and otherwise, that the rigor is used only
against them of the religion reformed . . . that his . . . intent doth
tend only to subvert that religion that we do profess and to root
it out of this realm. At least, all the strangers of all nations and
religions so doth interpret it, as may appear by the triumphs and
rejoicing set out as well in the realm of France. . . .[20]

No wonder Elizabeth called off wedding negotiations with Alençon
further along in this same letter. What's more, Elizabeth, from that
moment, questioned who other than Burghley and her merchant
and gentlemen adventurers she could count among her friends and
allies.

A faint smile must have fleeted across her lips when she thought
back to the spring of that year. The most audacious of her adventurers,
Francis Drake, had set sail from Plymouth on Whit Sun Eve, May 24,
1572. He hadn't merely been allowed by the queen and Admiralty to
return to the Spanish Main to ransack the treasure house of the King
of Spain. He was fulfilling her grand plan. Elizabeth of England had
blessed him, and all others like him, in their quests for treasure and
their annoyance of Catholics everywhere who would dare to steal
her crown.

17. Drake at the Treasure House of the World ✦

Some think it true to say he did it in the Devil's name,
And none ever since could do the like again;
But those are all deceived, why should they doubt it,
They know each year there's some that go about it.
—ANONYMOUS, VERSE TO DRAKE C. 1619

It is well nigh impossible for us to imagine how brave, or foolhardy, Drake and his men were—sailing thousands of miles without reliable charts or accurate measurement of longitude into a vast ocean where, on the other side, only hostile forces of the King of Spain awaited them. It is even more impossible to imagine how this voyage eventually led to the hopes of England's becoming a world power.

Nonetheless, as Drake's two small ships left Plymouth Sound that balmy May evening, hope and expectation filled the air. Seventy-three mariners and boys had boarded the 70-ton *Pasco*[1] and the 40-ton *Swan*, each and every one of them a volunteer. Only one sailor was over fifty years of age. The rest were all under thirty. Some, like Drake's younger brother, John, had invested their life savings—in John's case, some £30 ($10,554 or £5,705 today). Aboard the *Pasco*, stored in precut sections, were three pinnaces for shallow, inshore work. Victuals and other provisions for a year were divided between the two ships. "Artificers" (carpenters) with their tools, musicians, and weapons for any eventuality Drake could then imagine were the final necessities added to their complement. Significantly, the *Pasco* had been registered as a Hawkins ship, and word was out that the queen's slave trader had buried the hatchet with Drake and was an investor in the voyage.[2]

According to Drake, they were favored with a "prosperous wind from God" and reached the island of Guadeloupe in twenty-five days, on June 28. On July 12, Drake's ships approached Port Pheasant, the secret cove he had "found" in 1570–71. It was here that Drake had left tools and provisions for his return. Yet as his ship pulled into the cove, a wisp of smoke rose above the treetops near the site of his encampment the year before. Since Drake thought Port Pheasant was uninhabited, he led a small party of heavily armed men ashore at the ready to retake it, only to discover the remains of a smoldering campfire. Nailed to a tree trunk nearby was a lead plaque with its warning etched into it, especially for Drake's eyes:

> *Captain Drake, if you fortune to come to this port, make haste away, for the Spaniards which you had with you here the last year have betrayed this place, and taken away all that you left here. I departed from hence, this present 7 of July, 1572. Your very loving friend John Garret.*[3]

Garret was a fellow West Countryman and ex-slaver like Drake. Obviously, he and doubtless many others had chosen Port Pheasant to emulate Drake's first solo raid. But Drake sloughed off the warning. He ordered his men ashore with the pinnaces and set his carpenters to work on their assembly. His mariners felled trees and erected a huge stockade around their camp for added security—just in case Garret was right.

The following day, three small craft sailed over the horizon. The men were ordered to their battle stations, but they were soon stood down. The admiral, only a bark, had the flag of St. George hoisted on her mainmast, and her captain was none other than James Raunce— the captain of the *William and John*—which had been separated from the Hawkins fleet just before San Juan de Ulúa. Raunce had brought with him two Spanish prizes—one a tiny shallop, the other a caravel called the *Santa Catalina*. He was sailing, he explained to Drake, one of Sir Edward Horsey's barks out of the Isle of Wight in search of treasure. The captured Spanish prize was the *aviso* bound for Nombre de Díos, whose purpose was to bring correspondence and news between the colonies. Raunce lost no time asking Drake if they might not join forces. His old friend was welcomed, Drake said, especially since they had in mind to capture Nombre de Díos and the king's treasure house.[4]

Raunce's captives, some poor slaves who were being freighted across the Spanish Main, happily told Drake and Raunce that they had heard reports that "certain soldiers should come thither shortly, and were daily looked for . . . to defend the town against the Cimaroons."[5] While their intelligence was welcome, their news could not dissuade Drake from his course. He ordered the slaves released, since he wished to "use those Negroes well."[6] Drake had no way of knowing that the slaves' information was false.

By July 28, the three pinnaces—now baptized the *Lion*, *Bear*, and *Minion*—were ready to sail. It was agreed that Raunce would guard their position and keep his bark and the *Santa Catalina*, the *Pasco*, and the *Swan* with him. Drake and his seventy-three men sailed on in the three pinnaces and the shallop toward Nombre de Díos, heavily armed with six shields, six fire pikes (that could double up as torches by night), twelve pikes, twenty-four harquebuses, six spears, sixteen bows with arrows, two drums, and two trumpets. All Drake's men had been briefed. They would sail to Nombre de Díos and attack at dawn.[7]

At the fringes of the bay, Drake and his men lay in wait. They had been drilled and trained for what Drake imagined lay ahead. Nevertheless, they began to fidget and worry about the outcome while they were under strict orders to watch quietly and listen until dawn. Drake was a great observer of nature and men, and he knew that if he waited for daybreak, many of his men would lose their nerve. Fortunately, at some time between two and three in the morning, the clouds cleared, revealing a brilliant full moon. It cast silvery shadows from the masts and rigging onto the deck as if dawn had come early. For Drake it was a clear sign from God. Without hesitation, he gave the order to attack, claiming that dawn was upon them. Once on the move, their mutterings stopped.

As they stole out into the harbor, they saw a wine ship from the Canaries anchored in the bay. Its crew, meanwhile, had already spotted Drake's men skulking in the shadows. Without hesitation, the Spaniards lowered a boat to warn the town, but Drake cut them off and drove them across the bay, where they could do no immediate harm. Drake landed without further skirmishes, and seized the battery of six guns that defended the port. Its sole defender saw Drake approach and ran hell for leather to the town, saving his own life but risking the lives of his fellow Spaniards.

Drake's success would depend solely on the element of surprise, and especially on the Spaniards' belief that they were being attacked by several hundred men rather than several dozen. A few mariners were left in port to guard the pinnaces to secure their retreat, while Drake divided his other men into three groups to storm the town. John Drake and John Oxenham were each given sixteen men to go around the left and right flanks. Drake himself would advance along the main road with the rest. As they marched forward, Nombre de Díos began to stir. The lone sentinel from the battery had raised the alarm. The church bell pealed its anxious cry to the townspeople. Drums beat out an assembly order. Shouts in Spanish called out for every man to defend their town, while the women were begged to hide with their children.

In the midst of all this confusion, Drake advanced steadily, his fire pikes held high, their fierce glow dancing eerily along the walls of the settlement. His drummer and trumpeter heralded his arrival as if he were a caesar, at the head of a huge army. The *alcalde* had already grouped together his nervous militia at the southern corner of the market square when Drake came into view, and ordered his men to fire on the English corsairs. One bullet killed his trumpeter straightaway, the other struck Drake in the leg. All the other shots hit the dust in front of Drake and his men. Then Drake smiled and gave the order for his mariners to attack. The English lunged forward ferociously, waving their pikes, screaming a battle cry, and firing their own shots back at the Spaniards in among a hail of arrows from their crossbows.

Simultaneously, John Drake and John Oxenham arrived in the square with their company of men, brandishing their weapons and firing shot and arrows, too. Terrified, the Spaniards broke ranks and fled, many of them hurling their weapons to the ground behind them.[8] With only one fatality, the English commanded the town. But the Spaniards would soon figure out that they had been duped and would mount a counterattack. As they regrouped in the market square, Drake interrogated some Spanish prisoners, asking for them to lead Drake and his men to the governor's home. If they were intent on trickery, they would not live to tell the tale, he warned. While Drake had come to empty the King of Spain's treasure house, the simple fact of the matter was, he couldn't be exactly sure how best to approach it from shore. The governor would be the most reliable source of that information, Drake had decided. Besides, it may be that the governor himself would be in possession of treasure, too, he reasoned.

Drake would not be disappointed. When the door was pushed open at the governor's house, a candle was lit at the top of the stairs and he saw:

> *a fair jennet [small Spanish horse] ready saddled, either for the Governor himself, or some other of his household to carry it after him. By means of this light, we saw a huge heap of silver in that nether room; being a pile of bars of silver of, as near as we could guess, seventy foot in length, of ten foot in breadth, and twelve foot in height, piled up against the wall. Each bar was between thirty-five and forty pound in weight. At the sight hereof, our captain commanded straightly that none of us should touch a bar of silver, but stand upon our weapons, because the town was full of people, and there was in the King's Treasure House, near the water side, more gold and jewels than all our four pinnaces could carry; which we would presently set some in hand to break open.[9]*

As they were deciding if they should trouble with the silver or head onto the king's treasure house for the gold, an escaped Negro slave, named Diego, rushed forward, begging to be taken on board with Drake and his men. As proof of his good faith the escaped slave claimed that their pinnaces were in danger from the king's soldiers who had been sent to protect the town from the Cimaroons. Drake could ill afford to ignore the warning, and he sent his brother and Oxenham to check. While his cohorts secured the pinnaces, Drake started back into the town toward the king's treasure house, which stood at the westernmost end of the settlement.

Just as they started out, the skies opened in a torrential, tropical, summer thunderstorm, and by the time the main force reached the treasure house, they were soaked through. Worse still, their gunpowder was sodden, and the strings on their crossbows were too wet to use with any degree of accuracy. There was nothing left for them to do but wait. When the rain eased, John Drake, who had rejoined them from securing the pinnaces, was ordered to break down the treasure house door, while Francis and his men held the market square. But as their captain stepped forward, he swooned, and it was then that Drake's men saw for the first time that he had been wounded in the earlier face-off. Blood streaked his footprints in the sand, and the lower part of his leg was stained crimson.

His men gathered around him and decided that they had to get their captain to safety. There would be other opportunities to get treasure, someday. So they bound his leg with one of their scarves and carried him back to the pinnaces, where they made good their escape to the Bastimentos Islands, or Isles of Victuals, about a league west of the town. Still, just so they wouldn't leave empty-handed, they took the Canaries wine ship with them.[10]

Meanwhile, the *alcalde* of Nombre de Díos counted his losses. Thirty-two were dead, according to one eyewitness,[11] though the official complaint to the Queen of England two years later claimed a death toll of eighteen. More worrying to the *alcalde* were his wounded. Had these pirates used poisonous arrows? He needed to know the answer to this, and who these savages were. How else could he make an accurate report to the governor and the king? Since the English had only escaped to a nearby island, the *alcalde* sent a gentleman envoy to Drake to find out the answers to these questions. The English captain proudly told the Spaniard that they had come for the King of Spain's treasure, that they were English and would never use poison arrows, and that his name was Francis Drake. Then, "he advised the governor to hold open his eyes, for before he departed," and Drake nodded at him, "if God lent him life and leave, he meant to reap some of their harvest, which they get out of the earth, and send into Spain to trouble all the earth."[12]

With the "niceties" of the Spaniard's mission completed, Drake ordered that the envoy be "burdened with gifts" as a sign of their personal goodwill.

18. From a Treetop in Darien ⚜

*We came to the height of the desired hill . . . about ten of
the clock; where the chiefest of these Cimaroons took our
Captain by the hand and prayed to him follow him if he
was desirous to see at once the two seas, which he had so
longed for. Here was that goodly and great high tree . . .
and from thence we saw without any difficulty plainly
the Atlantic Ocean, whence now we came, and the South
Atlantic,[1] so much desired . . . .*
—Sir Francis Drake Revived

While Drake was recovering from his wounds during the
course of the next few days, he certainly hatched a plan
for his next raids. During this time, he became friendly with the
former slave, Diego, who had begged to join their company when he
warned them that the pinnaces had been in danger. Drake listened
and learned from Diego. The plan was to involve the Cimaroons in
their attacks, since they knew the jungle and the Spaniards so well.
It took no time at all for Drake to grow to admire Diego greatly. The
English and the Cimaroons had, according to Diego, common cause
in their hatred for the Spanish, and he was sure that these former
slaves turned raiders would prove stalwart allies with important
local knowledge.[2]

By the time they left the Isle of Victuals to rejoin forces with
Captain Raunce, the terrified *alcalde* of Nombre de Díos had
spread the alarm as far as Cartagena, Santa Marta, and Honduras.
Earthworks were thrown up at great speed on the beach, and a new
battery of heavy guns was installed to command the headland. The
alcalde was certain that *El Draco*—the Dragon—or Drake would
return. While Drake and his men had left Nombre de Díos virtually
empty-handed, in Spanish eyes it was an audacious coup. No pirate
had ever come to rob the King of Spain's treasure in its repository.

It struck terror into the hearts of strong men to think that the gold that kept the empire afloat could have so easily been stolen by a mere *Luterano*.[3]

Raunce, on the other hand, was not amused. He decried Drake's antics, fearful that the Caribbean would be crawling with Spanish soldiers in no time at all. When he told Drake that he had had enough, Drake was more than happy to let him go. If Raunce were not made of sterner stuff, he would add nothing to the equation.

Again aware that Raunce's departure might renew grumbling among the ranks, Drake suggested that he and his remaining men should strike while the iron was still hot, and attack the shipping at Cartagena. Though the town itself wasn't particularly well protected, it did have a fortified tower and heavy gun battery in harbor. There would be risks. The crew agreed to give it a whirl, and they set sail. But word had already reached Cartagena that there was an English pirate in the vicinity, and the shipping had moved to the inner harbor. That is, saving one.

This lone ship lay at anchor out of range of the town's great guns— a 240-ton vessel still laden with her cargo of munitions. According to the Spanish complaint two years later, Drake pillaged the prize and burned it.[4] While the attack terrorized the town, it showed Drake that word did indeed travel fast in that part of the world. It also demonstrated that the Spaniards, with all their guns and bluster, remained powerless to stop well-equipped, swift English pinnaces cruising inshore to pillage.

Despite the fact that Drake had sailed with Hawkins, it was rapidly becoming apparent that both he and his men not only valued and liked Diego, treating him as one of their own, but recognized that they were relying heavily upon his local knowledge for the ultimate success of their mission.[5] Diego was his fellow traveler, his friend, who had been sorrowfully mistreated at the hands of the Spanish, and who seemed to sense that Drake was the answer to not only his own, but also the *Cimarrones'* prayers for revenge.

And yet, so far, the voyage had not been a success. Diego was certain that the *Cimarrones* would help Drake. They were, after all, fellow travelers, too. But it was only in his long talks by the campfire with Diego, John Oxenham, and John Drake, that Drake finally thought through a daring scheme where his partnership with the

Cimaroons would benefit them both. Since the Spaniards knew they were there, and were expecting them to raid the towns along the Spanish Main, the English could still have the element of surprise if they attacked the king's treasure *before* it arrived at the treasure house at Nombre de Díos. Drake shared his thoughts with Diego, Oxenham, and his brother, and they all thought it was a brilliant idea.

But they would still need to wait awhile until Spanish vigilance lapsed. And so, Drake dug in for the long haul, allowing the Spaniards to drop their guard over time. With the invaluable assistance of Diego, his men were taught to build shelters and stockades, to make safe havens and depots in which to hide extra provisions along the coast. They would lay low, trim and careen their ships, and gather food and other provisions to place in their storehouses. Meanwhile, John Drake went with Diego to contact the *Cimarrones* in the jungle to ask for their help. It was agreed that they should meet Francis Drake personally, since they had already heard so much about his daring.

On September 14, they met aboard the *Pasco*, and two weeks later, a second group of blacks joined them to seal their bargain "to their great comfort and our content, they rejoicing that they should have some fit opportunity to wreak their wrongs on the Spaniards, we hoping that now our voyage should be bettered."[6]

The *Cimarrones* eagerly told the English that the plan could work by attacking the treasure trains in the middle of the Isthmus of Panama. After all, they had been evading Spanish capture for years in the jungles, and they knew each trail, each tree, and each hazard as their own home. The treasure, they informed the English, always moved after the rainy season, resuming only when the flota was either in port or approaching the port of Nombre de Díos. Drake reckoned that that gave them five months to prepare. He must have also realized at that point that the treasure house at Nombre de Díos had been empty when he first tried to rob it! Drake was always a good judge of men, and he immediately agreed to add the former slaves to his trusted inner circle of "Plymouth lads." They shook hands on a deal and celebrated their partnership aboard the *Pasco*, while they plotted Spain's downfall.

The *Cimarrones* helped Drake and his men to establish a forward base, just to the east of Nombre de Díos, where they built a fort in just over two weeks. Drake, meanwhile, left for Cartagena with two of the pinnaces to try to get more intelligence, victuals, and prizes, leaving his brother John in charge. Throughout October 1572, Francis Drake terrorized the city of Cartagena and nearly blockaded its port. He chased dozens of ships, seized others, taunted his pursuers, and always escaped unharmed. His impudence knew no bounds.

But Drake had had enough fun. They were in dire need of food and had to return to their base with enough to feed their swelling "army." At last, fortune smiled on them when a 90-ton victualing Spaniard came across their path, and Drake found "her laden with victual well powdered and dried, which at that present we received as sent as of God's great mercy."[7]

But their luck didn't hold out. When Drake returned to base, he was told that his brother John had been killed in a skirmish with a Spanish ship. Two months later, his younger brother, Joseph, was the first to die of a mysterious disease that ripped through his crew like no other pestilence they had known before. When the epidemic was over, some 40 percent of the company had perished of yellow fever, and the English had renamed their haven Slaughter Island. While they tried to put their troubles behind them, bury their dead, and keep themselves alive, the *Cimarrone* scouts ran into camp one day to say that the flota had docked at Nombre de Díos.

                    *

Drake, seventeen of his remaining men, and thirty *Cimarrones* headed straightaway toward Panama. The dark and murky jungle floor was lit only by the occasional macaw on the wing or the tropical sun filtering through the canopy of trees. Sounds of their footsteps swishing through the undergrowth became their daily companion, while they kept on the lookout for poisonous snakes, anacondas, and lizards. Their aim was to cut off the *trajín*—or treasure train—near Venta Cruces, where the treasure was divided between the barges and the mule train. But something miraculous happened on their fourth day in the jungle. The leader of the *Cimarrones*, Pedro, pointed to a huge tree and asked Drake to go aloft. The captain and Oxenham exchanged quizzical looks, but he complied. High above the tropical rainforest in the Bay of Darien, in the company of an escaped black slave named Pedro, Drake became the first Englishman to see the massive expanse of the Pacific as he turned his head to the west, and the Caribbean that he knew so well as he wheeled around to the east. Separating the two was a mere twenty leagues of rain forest. We can only imagine Francis Drake's mind clicking into gear, the elation in his heart, and the foundations for his greatest adventure being laid. Later, Drake said that at that moment he "besought almighty God of his goodness to give him life and leave to sail once again in an English ship in that sea."[8]

19. Success at a Cost ✳

*The realm is at the present moment so terrified, and the
spirits of all so disturbed, that we know not in what words
to emphasize to your Majesty the solicitude we make in this
dispatch. . . . These English have so shamelessly opened the
door and a way by which, with impunity, whenever they
desire, they will attack the pack-trains traveling overland
by this highway.*

—MUNICIPAL COUNCIL OF PANAMA TO PHILIP II, FEBRUARY 24, 1573

Drake knew from experience that a surprise assault was critical
to their success. They laid in wait, crouching by the side of
the jungle path for what must have seemed an eternity before the
tinkling of mule bells rang sweetly in their ears. Suddenly, the gallop
of a lone horse coming from the wrong direction warned Drake that
all was not as it should be. Before the rider could be stopped he had
alerted the muleteers to head back, and that the pirate Drake would
pounce on them any moment.[1] The Spanish cleverly separated out
the silver shipment from the more valuable gold—estimated at some
£35,000 ($12.32 million or £6.66 million today)—and sent the mules
carrying the silver on into Drake's arms. Realizing that they had
been discovered, Drake and Pedro decided that it would be too risky
to return to base the same way they had come, and opted instead to
boldly take Venta Cruces. The raiding party marched through the
town, burning and pillaging as they went. Any casualties incurred
were in defense of property, not in brutal murder, according to
reports both Spanish and English. Drake had also ordered his men
that the women must remain "inviolate," and he even entered homes
to reassure the women personally that none of them would be raped.[2]
While there is no excuse for the terror Drake and his raiders inflicted
on their victims, this level of humanity in the sixteenth century—let
alone in the twentieth or twenty-first—is remarkable.

Now that he had made his strike, Drake once again lay low, hoping to trick the Spaniards into believing that he had left the Caribbean with his paltry treasure. While his good "Plymouth lads" grumbled about the heat, humidity, and their ill-luck, the *Cimarrones* tended the sick and injured and made moccasins for the foot-sore rovers. Drake marveled at their strength, their courage, and above all their loyalty. "Yea many times when some of our company fainted with sickness or weariness," Drake wrote later, "two *Cimarrones* would carry him [the sick] with ease between them two miles together, and at other times (when need was) they would show themselves no less valiant than industrious and of good judgement."[3]

After their retreat, there was little else to do than plan their next raid for the spring of 1573, and capture a prize that would hopefully keep them well provided in victuals and water. Then, nearly a month after they had rejoined their ships following the Venta Cruces raids, a large French ship bore down on them just off Cativas Headland near Nombre de Díos. Her captain, who had been looking for Drake for some five weeks, was none other than the Huguenot corsair Guillaume le Testu. Le Testu was no ordinary pirate. He had been the personal protégé of Admiral de Coligny, and was captaining a ship for the merchant adventurer Philippe Strozzi.[4]

Le Testu was well known to Drake. After all, Le Testu had taken part in the French colonial adventure to Brazil, and Drake admired the French challenge in South America to the Spaniards.[5] So when the Frenchman asked for water, and explained some of his men were ill, Drake ordered provisions to be sent aboard; then he asked Le Testu to follow him to one of his storehouses so that they could be fully replenished. When they finally anchored, the Huguenot captain gave Drake a gilt scimitar that had been a gift of his dear, now butchered, leader, Admiral de Coligny. This devastating news, and the carnage that had ensued in France, shocked and angered Drake, making the gift all the more dear.[6]

The two men had already respected each other before they ever met, but once in the same cabin together, that respect grew into mutual admiration. Le Testu showed Drake his invaluable folio atlas of fifty-six maps that he had drawn based on his own experiences, and which had been dedicated to Coligny some years earlier. This treasure of experience would have driven home the fact to Drake of how poor English knowledge of the seas had truly been. Le Testu had been a royal pilot at Le Havre, and had been born and bred with the sea coursing through his soul like Drake. The main difference between the two was that Le Testu had high-level contacts in Coligny and, lately, André Thévet, Catherine de' Medici's chaplain. Drake had to make his own way through hard graft. What is striking from this encounter of great "pirates" is that Le Testu would have not been a corsair or outlaw if he had adhered to the Catholic faith.[7]

Naturally, Drake and Le Testu fell in together, and agreed on how to mount another raid on the *trajín*. Le Testu believed that if they attacked closer to Nombre de Díos, after the gold and silver shipments had been separated at the Chagres River, the soldiers would be more relaxed as their journey was nearing its end. It would be easier to box them in or, preferably, disperse the mule train's defenders more easily, he ventured. Drake agreed.

On March 31, 1573, the combined *Cimarrone*, English, and Huguenot forces stole into the jungle. Cimaroon scouts edged forward in the night, returning to their positions before daybreak. The *trajín* had nearly two hundred mules in all and an escort of around forty-five poorly armed, barefoot soldiers.

The assault was rapid and deadly. The Cimaroons led the charge. Within the first few seconds, a Negro harquebusier fired at Le Testu, wounding him in the stomach, and killing a Cimaroon. The attackers surged forward regardless, shouting fierce battle cries and shooting off their weapons. The Spaniards quickly recognized that if they stayed and defended the *trajín*, it would be a turkey shoot, and they would be the turkeys. While they turned tail and ran, the raiders leapt onto the baggage and prized open the chests. The mules were carrying more than 200,000 *pesos de oro* ($23.24 million or £12.56 million today). What made the prize sweeter was that 18,363 *pesos de oro* ($2.13 million or £1.15 million today) personally belonged to the King of Spain.[8]

The fifteen tons of silver looted was hastily hidden in burrows made by land crabs, or under fallen trees. They had to be quick about it, though, since again, they were only two leagues from Nombre de Díos. Half of the gold was loaded back onto the mules and carried to the mouth of the Francisca River, where their pinnaces were waiting. But Le Testu was mortally wounded, and he knew it. He told Drake to go ahead and leave him, that he would guard the silver until they could return. The last thing Le Testu wanted was for Spanish soldiers to cut off their retreat to the sea, and Drake reluctantly agreed. Two of his men volunteered to keep him company, while the others marched laboriously away.

Two days later, after yet another torrential downpour in the jungle, the raiders arrived at their rendezvous. But instead of their own pinnaces, they found Spanish shallops. Had the pinnaces been captured? How would they escape back to their pirate's haven? the men asked. Had the Spaniards wrecked the *Pasco* and dashed their hopes of returning home? Drake knew from experience that action would keep these worries from overpowering his men. As ever ingenious, he instructed them to make a raft from fallen trees, binding the trunks together and using a slashed biscuit sack for its puny sail. It wasn't pretty, but it just about floated. After the Spaniards rounded the headland, Drake and three men waded out in their ludicrous tree raft, at times sailing waist high in seawater, before they spotted the *Bear* and the *Minion*, nestled in a safe harbor nearby. As Drake boarded the ship, he broke into a sudden smile and brought out a quoit (disc) of gold from his shirt. Their voyage had been made.

After his men had been brought safely on board, the *Cimarrones* came forward with the sad news that captain Le Testu had been killed. Drake said a prayer for the Frenchman's soul and gave the order to weigh anchor. It was unsafe to return for the silver. Their voyage had been made, thanks in large part to the Cimaroons and the Huguenots, with whom he gladly shared their prize. They had been away for more than a year, and more than half of them were dead, including Drake's two brothers.

In an incredibly swift and uneventful crossing of only twenty-three days, Drake and his remaining crew pulled into Plymouth harbor on Sunday, August 9, 1574. All the good men and women of the town were at prayer in St. Andrew's Church, listening to their vicar's sermon, when a murmuring among the parishoners grew into a roar. Drake had returned, they whispered to one another. One by one they left, until finally the entire flock deserted its preacher and raced to the waterfront to welcome home their heroes.

20. Dr. Dee's Nursery and the Northwest Passage ⚜

*I did conjecture the . . . star in Cassiopeia appearing anno
1572 to signify the finding of some great treasure of the
philosopher's stone . . .*
—DR. JOHN DEE, 1582

From the moment Drake returned in August 1574, the floodgates burst open. Adventurers had been champing at the bit for years to explore the western reaches of the globe in search of treasure and a shorter way to the East Indies. Now Drake had returned—not once but twice—with his holds filled with treasure. It mattered little that it was plunder. That he hadn't looked for the fabled Northwest Passage to Cathay meant that there was still vast scope for others to join in the adventures. Soon, it was rumored at court that Drake had seen both great oceans from one vantage point in the high treetop above Darien. Surely, they speculated, this sighting by Drake proved the existence of the passage, and that North America was no more than a trifling obstacle to attain its Holy Grail of Cathay.

They were right certainly about Drake if not the passage. He was interested purely in "singeing the King of Spain's beard" through plunder. He was a man who understood results only. And the result that preoccupied his every waking hour was to execute his private war against Philip of Spain, righting the wrongs perpetrated against all Protestants everywhere. Before Drake had reached his anchorage in Plymouth harbor, the kernel of his most daring exploit had already been hatched.

For the greater West Country public, to say that Drake had become even more famous is absolutely true. But to say that his name was on the lips of very Londoner would still be an exaggeration. This had little to do with Drake's adventure or the boldness of his actions, and everything to do with his timing on returning to England. While he had been plundering the Spanish Main, the Duke of Alba had at last persuaded Philip to come to terms with Elizabeth, and shortly before Drake anchored at Plymouth, the Convention of Bristol of 1574 provided for a settlement over the Spanish pay ships confiscated by the queen in 1568. By mutual agreement neither England nor Spain would harbor aliens who were hostile to the other; and significantly, from the queen's viewpoint, Philip promised to restore the "ancient liberties" previously enjoyed by the Netherlanders. Spain also agreed that the Inquisition would be prevented from harming English sailors on Spanish territory.[1] Nonetheless, since the terms of the Bristol Accord had only been agreed weeks before Drake's return, it is tantalizing to think that the Queen of England could have repaid Philip with her share of the phenomenal booty only recently captured by Drake in the West Indies.

While timing from the queen's perspective may have been a tad bit embarrassing publicly, privately Drake's adventure was the talk of those in the know. He had been singled out by Leicester and Walsingham as an ingenious and handy man to have in a pinch, and Drake was packed off to Ireland to help Walter Devereux, first Earl of Essex, in his Ulster plantation scheme. It was a brilliant coup on their part to distract Drake in the "bog" of Ireland. Leicester knew, probably as one of Drake's backers, that the stout and hardy West Countryman had earned his spurs in the Caribbean. Still, his loyalty to the crown had yet to be proven. When Leicester advised England's most dangerous mariner that the queen had her personal money invested in Essex's Irish venture—£10,000, no less, or some $34.67 million or £18.74 million today—Drake would have readily spotted the opportunity to curry royal favor, and done all he could to ensure Essex's success. Not only would Drake be useful in "the great bog" of Ireland, Leicester reasoned, but also it would keep the dazzlingly bold captain from "annoying the King of Spain" at a time when Elizabeth had become shortsighted again, and was particularly desirous of appeasing the Spanish monarch. But that did not mean that Drake's projects, or indeed others contemplated by a range of adventurers for attacking Spain, had stalled. Though diverted for now, Drake would use his time in Ireland wisely.

And so he planned, and planned. To undertake the greatest voyage of his life, Drake would need powerful and wealthy patrons. John Hawkins and his other West Country backers wouldn't have sufficient resources to back his scheme on their own. Walter Devereux, Earl of Essex, on the other hand, did. Essex was married to the queen's cousin, Lettice Knollys, daughter of the Privy Councillor Sir Francis Knollys, and would recommend Drake to the court if he served the Earl well. Also serving under Essex was Christopher Hatton, a rising star at court. Drake was aiming his sights directly at the queen's personal favorites, and he wanted to prove himself to Leicester, Essex, and Hatton as a capable general at sea.[2]

Ireland had long been the place where an adventurer's fortunes were made, or swallowed up whole, since the time of Henry VII. It was also a vast proving ground for many of the West Countrymen like Drake—most of whom had had some education in Dr. John Dee's nursery for budding adventurers. The most staunchly Protestant West Countrymen like Richard Grenville, Sir Humphrey Gilbert, Walter Raleigh, Sir Peter Carew, and Sir Arthur Champernowne had all served devoted "hard time" in Ireland. The lord deputy of Ireland's son and Renaissance man, Philip Sidney, had engaged in the intellectually stimulating military chatter around the table in Dr. Dee's library at Mortlake near London. And Sir Henry Sidney had come to rely increasingly on Philip's advice during his tenure as Ireland's lord deputy, not only for the geographic and navigational knowledge that Dr. Dee had imparted to England's dogged mariners, but also for his insights into abstract mathematics and science, and how it related to military strategies.[3]

But they were not the only adventurers flocking to Dr. Dee's doors. As early as February 1563, Dee had written to Lord Burghley from an inn in Antwerp aptly named the Golden Angel. Dee had already become a great friend of the Flemish master cartographer Gerard Mercator.[4] Another of his great friends was Abraham Ortelius, a generation younger than Mercator and a brilliant mapmaker in his own right. Dee had known Mercator since his days at Louvain in 1547, when Mercator described him as a "tall, slight youth, looking wise beyond his years, with fair skin, good looks and bright color."[5] Back then, Dee was only nineteen.

By 1563, Dee had come to an "arrangement" with Cecil that in exchange for important information, Cecil and others in positions of power would help him grow his expensive and rare library relating to mathematics, cosmography, astrology, geography, the scientific mysticism of the Cabala, and the writings of the ancients. A voracious reader and devoted correspondent with his Continental friends and luminaries, Dee had already proved to the Privy Council that he could provide them with the crux of a fledgling yet well-oiled espionage network. For Dee, espionage was only one of the end results of the codes and ciphers—a gift from the magical scientific principles of the Cabala—upon which he worked. It was the bigger code, or the unraveling the universe's mysteries for man's understanding, that enthralled him. Espionage was a means to an end, providing him with cash to pursue his travels, to meet more men of thought, to protect the recent Protestant rise, and, above all, to purchase more books.

Dee also accepted government research projects to earn his daily crust. In 1570, Christopher Hatton and Leicester commissioned Dee, through Edward Dyer, to write a "state of the nation" paper. The resulting *Britannicae Republicae Synopsis* is one of the most perceptive and helpful overviews of the realm's political institutions, economy, and defenses.[6] This document clearly identifies the problems besetting Elizabeth's England, from urban degeneration to a declining textile industry, currency debasement to decline in trade, religious strife to unemployment and vagrancy. What is significant, though, is Dee's use of the word "republic." He was emphasizing the ancient need to engage the people in a newfound patriotism, as part of a "common weal" or commonwealth. His philosophy was neoplatonist in approach, and he urged philanthropy from those who could afford it in good works at home in order to promote public prosperity.

But this was not Dee's sole or, indeed, his most important use to the queen. Elizabeth also used Dee's services to interpret signs. He had been hastily summoned to Windsor to explain the sudden appearance of a new star in the constellation Cassiopeia. Surely, it forebode something of great import—either for good or evil, Elizabeth asked. And if there was some means by which evil for the realm could be turned to good, Dee was the only person the queen trusted to tell her how that might best be achieved. Elizabeth had long believed in her own royal "magic," and her highly rated divine royal touch was said to prove her legitimate claim to the throne.

Of course, Dee had already been called to cast her horoscope for the most propitious date for her coronation back in 1559. By this time, Elizabeth had long accepted his advice on the geography, cosmology, or astrology relating to maritime expansion. Dee had read every rare book imaginable on these subjects, and he was increasingly aware of "signs" in the heavens, based on his knowledge of the Hermetic tradition, which blended principles of the ancients with Cabala, early Christianity, and Egyptian philosophical religions. When Dee predicted that the new star was a portent of her rise in the world—in economic, political, and religious terms—the queen was grateful, and pacified.

But Elizabeth was never one to rest on her laurels. She knew that the only way in which Dee's prediction would come true was through shedding her isolationist tendencies, expanding trade, and exploring the new worlds beyond the equinoctial. Burghley was alarmed by the implications of Dee's advice, where the likes of Leicester, Walsingham, Christopher Hatton, and Philip Sidney were entranced.

So when Richard Grenville, the former "sheriff of Cork" in Ireland, had petitioned the queen as well as Lord Admiral Clinton on March 22, 1574, with a proposal to sail to the northwest rather than the northeast to find a passage to Cathay, the paper seemed as if it had surely been written in consultation with Dr. Dee. Grenville's proposed plan, entitled "The Discovery Traffic and Enjoining of Lands South of the Equator Not Already Possessed or Subdued by Any Christian Prince," was at great pains to deny trespass upon any Spanish- or Portuguese-held lands. The expedition's main purpose, Grenville claimed, would be to explore Terra Australis Incognita. At the behest of the lord admiral, who may well have been an investor, the queen granted a letter patent for Grenville to set sail. The 200-ton *Castle of Comfort* was purchased jointly with John Hawkins, and preparations for the voyage began.

Whether Elizabeth heard, or suspected, that Grenville's real objective was to emulate Drake's escapades in the West Indies, is difficult to say. But the new Spanish ambassador, Bernardino de

Mendoza,[7] had certainly had wind of it, and he reminded Elizabeth of how hard they had all worked to bring about this new era of peace. On reflection, the queen, in one of her aggravating "second thoughts," cancelled the letter patent to Grenville and forbade the adventurer from sailing on his first transatlantic voyage. The *Castle of Comfort* was leased out instead to the Prince de Condé for his Huguenot roving, with Grenville and Hawkins receiving a share of any profits.[8] Within the year, Grenville received his knighthood for "services to Ireland," perhaps to assuage his bruised ego.

It would only be in 1579, when John Oxenham was tortured by the Inquisition after his capture in Panama two years earlier, that the true purpose of the Grenville expedition was known. To avoid any further agony, Oxenham avowed that the project was "to come and found a settlement on the River Plate and then pass the Strait [meaning the Magellan Strait] and establish settlements wherever a good country for such could be found."[9] But how would Oxenham have come by that information? Drake is the most likely answer.

The Grenville petition had angered the Muscovy Company, too, which had been granted an exclusive license to explore the Northeast Passage to Cathay. The queen's Letter Patent was an infringement on their rights. And while the lord admiral had supported Grenville, Francis Walsingham, a major shareholder in the Muscovy Company, did not. It wasn't the first time that the company had objected to "interlopers" seeking royal approval. Humphrey Gilbert had run afoul of the Muscovy Company in the 1560s when he had initially mooted a voyage to Cathay via the northwest. He soon realized that he'd have to give up the idea, or undertake his enterprise as a mere servant of the company.

But all this would soon change. A new type of adventurer was appearing on the scene. They were essentially pirates—with little education, and fewer manners still. They were ruthless, hotheaded, and, at heart, fairly unpleasant men. But they often had the backing of the queen's gentlemen adventurers, since they had been rovers for decades. Martin Frobisher was just such a man.

*

Frobisher was a corsair-turned-merchant adventurer who had spent time in jail in England and Guinea for his roving activities. The nephew of Sir John Yorke, one of the Muscovy Company's leading lights and a steward at the Tower of London and the mint, was a pioneer himself in the now defunct Guinea trade. It was Yorke who had arranged for the fourteen-year-old Frobisher to go on Wyndham's ill-fated Guinea voyage. Frobisher was one of the few lucky ones to have survived. A year later, he had returned as part of the Leicester-backed adventure to establish a fort on the Gold Coast. Soon Frobisher fell out with his uncle, but he was clever enough to know that in order to conquer vested interest of any of the "companies," he needed a powerful champion.[10]

Ambrose Dudley, Earl of Warwick and Robert's older brother, was just that man. By the end of 1574, the Muscovy Company was forced to bow to Warwick's pressure with the queen, and stood aside while Frobisher was granted a license, along with the merchant adventurer Michael Lok, to explore the eastern coast of North America for a Northwest Passage to Cathay. Lok, a London member of the Mercers' Company, had previously been agent of the Muscovy Company. When he agreed to provide personal loans of more than £800 cash ($277,382 or £149,936 today) to the expedition, the Letter Patent was granted again.[11] Lok thereby became the major promoter of the voyage. Having traveled widely himself in the services of the company, Lok considered that he was an amateur cosmographer, and he became an avid student at the Dee nursery.

At a meeting in Mortlake with the experienced Muscovy pilot and former Dee pupil Stephen Borough, Lok agreed to a deal with the queen's cosmographer to instruct his partner and fleet captain, Martin Frobisher, in the art of navigation. Dee moved into Muscovy House and began at once to teach Frobisher and his ship's master, Christopher Hall, the navigational experiences of Columbus, and how to keep proper records. He also gave Frobisher, who was after all a novice to transatlantic crossings, a grounding in the importance of frequent depth soundings, how to take and calculate readings for latitude and longitude, how to deal with the natives, and how to ascertain if ores might be valuable. But Frobisher and Hall were, by and large, ignorant, and were unable to understand the importance of the simplest mathematical exercise.

Nonetheless, Dee prevailed as best he could, despite the widely held view that mathematics was "without convenient practise at sea." Where Frobisher found it difficult to see the importance of calculations, the mathematics in Lok's accounts of the Frobisher voyages reveal in wretched detail the huge expectations for success from 1576 to their utter failure to live up to those high hopes in 1579.[12]

While the first voyage was meant to leave England for the east coast of America in 1575, subscribers were like the illusive gold dust they sought on an ill wind, and the expedition had to be delayed. At the end of the day, Lok's and Frobisher's expectations had to be scaled down, and the voyage was limited to two small barks and a pinnace instead of the three larger ships originally contemplated. When Frobisher was looking around later for people to blame, Lok told him that potential investors' reluctance to invest was due to Frobisher's reputation as a pirate. Whatever the truth of the matter, it was Lok's salesmanship that stressed the varied luxury commodities that the road to Cathay might yield, the English woolens the natives might purchase, the precious metals its shores certainly possessed, and the train oil that its oceans held that finally clinched the share purchases. But despite Lok's enthusiasm, the total cash raised was a mere £875 ($303,387 or £163,993 today). Since costs for the expedition had already come to £1,613 19s. 3d. ($561,697 or £303,620 today), Lok had to make good on the rest from his own pocket. Out of the eighteen shareholders, Lord Burghley, Sir Francis Walsingham, Philip Sidney, Thomas Randolph (ambassador to Scotland), and the Earls of Leicester, Warwick, and Sussex were the most prominent, having invested £50 each.

Sir Lionel Duckett was also an active promoter, and it was he who paid for Dee's time and expenses in the technical planning. The Mercator map was provided to Frobisher in place of the Ortelius map that had been favored by Gilbert in the 1560s, but as neither one had any real degree of accuracy, the results could only be based on a fiction. Both maps showed the North American coast at the same latitude as the British Isles, with the legendary Strait of Anian separating Asia and America. During the preparation stage, Lok thought it would be useful for the adventurers to meet with Sir Humphrey Gilbert and arranged the meeting. Naturally, Gilbert expounded on the virtues of the 1564 Ortelius map over the 1569 Mercator map, and the importance of the fabled islands in the North Atlantic called Friesland and Estotiland.[13] It was a case of the blind leading the blind.

Still, at Dee's insistence, the Mercator map prevailed. Dee also ensured that they carry a brass *horologium universale* and an *armilla ptolomei*, among other instruments, to help the mariners get their bearings. Alas, these were better suited to Dee's library than to a transatlantic voyage, particularly in the hands of men like Frobisher and Hall. Dee's influence can also be seen by the library aboard Frobisher's 30-ton bark, *Gabriel*, by the inclusion of André Thevet's *Cosmographie universelle* (in French, of course) and his *New Found World or Antartctike* alongside Pedro de Medina's *Regimiento de Navegación* (in Spanish), Cunningham's *Cosmographical Glasse*, and Robert Recorde's *Castle of Knowledge*. The great navigator, William Borough—who later fell out with Dee publicly—wished Frobisher well by presenting him with an astrolabe, but he still refused to invest in the voyage personally.[14]

Despite all the unpromising financial omens, Frobisher set sail at last from a rainy London in the *Gabriel* with Christopher Hall, and Nicholas Chancellor (son of explorer Richard Chancellor) as his purser on June 7, 1576. There were seventeen men who crewed the ship as well. On the *Michael* (also a 30-ton bark), there was a crew of twelve, and the expedition's unnamed 7-ton pinnace had a crew of three.

The bad omens continued. Before leaving Deptford, the pinnace struck another vessel, losing its bowsprit. The fleet assembled on the Thames in front of Greenwich Palace, and let off its demiculverins in salute to the queen. "Her Majesty," Christopher Hall recorded in the ship's log, "beholding the same, commended it, and bade us farewell, with shaking her hand at us out of the window."[15]

Following Mercator's map, they headed west by north, expecting to land smartly across the Atlantic at the mouth of the Strait of Anian. In the Shetland Isles to the far north of Scotland, the *Michael* began to leak badly, and the ships had to put into shore for repairs. From there Frobisher sent a letter to "the worshipful and our approved good friend, M. Dee," assuring him that "we do remember you, and hold ourselves bound to you as your poor disciples."[16]

Though they had made the crossing in two weeks, of course they couldn't find the strait. In fact, they thought they had landed at the mythical island of Friesland, since Greenland was much farther to the north. (Naturally, it was Greenland.) They had entered the unknown, the far northerly region that Dee called "Thule," being neither land, sea, nor air. As they passed through sheer, spectacular towers of ice, an amazed Frobisher christened them "Dee's Pinnacles" in honor of the teacher he had once shunned.

But nothing had prepared them for the harsh weather, the ice, the thick arctic fogs and snows in mid-summer. By the middle of July, a "great storm" raged, and the pinnace was sunk. The *Michael* stole away from the *Gabriel* and headed straight home for England. The skipper claimed on his return that the *Gabriel* was feared lost in the arctic gales, too. But Frobisher was made of sterner stuff than the *Michael*'s captain. Despite the *Gabriel* capsizing—saved only by Frobisher's "valiant courage" in ordering the mizzen mast to be hacked away while he untangled the rigging and the sails filling with icy water—the ship sailed on. Drenched in freezing saltwater, alone in the desolate heaving sea, Frobisher sailed on for two days more before sighting land.

Where Columbus first sighted sugar sand beaches and swaying palms in his new world, Frobisher spied "a land of ice of marvelous great height." This was "Meta Incognita"—the Limit of the Unknown. To Frobisher, it was Atlantis, the fabled Lost Continent. It was, in fact, the southern tip of Baffin Island. Threading their way through soaring icebergs, frozen seas, and heavy fogs, at around 63 degrees they found an inlet, and sailed into what is known today as Frobisher Bay. For another eight days the *Gabriel* wended its way through the ice blocks unable to see beyond the next bend or the towering ice floes. Finally, Frobisher went ashore, and claimed that,

> there he saw far the two headlands at the furthest end of the straits and no likelihood of any land to the northwards of them and the great open [sea] between them, which . . . they judged to be the West Sea [the Pacific] whereby to pass to Cathay and to the East India.[17]

While this picturesque scene may not have struck a familiar note to Elizabethans, with the benefit of four hundred odd years and twenty-twenty hindsight, Frobisher had intended his claim to rival that of Drake.

But this voyage bore little resemblance to Drake's escapades. They would turn endlessly back on themselves along the Canadian coast of North America with only the mysterious loss of five of his men and one hostile encounter with Inuit kayaks to show for their efforts. Frobisher had also lost two of his boats in the episode (one known to be sunk) and rightly felt that with a story as grand as Drake's—that he had *seen* the passage to Cathay with his own eyes—his investors wouldn't much notice that the only "riches" they were bringing back was the captured Inuit tribesman and a large hunk of black rock given to him by one of the missing mariners, Robert Garrard. At least the unusual rock proved they had hit land.[18]

Frobisher was no Drake, but he knew what he was doing in bringing back the Inuit. The first North American to be paraded ignominiously through London made for great theater with the Elizabethans, who loved their theater. Their "strange man and his boat . . . was such a wonder onto the whole city and to the rest of the realm that heard of it, as seemed never to have happened the like great matter to any man's knowledge."[19] Frobisher was delighted that the Eskimo's Tartar features were suggestive of the Orient, and that Lok and others had made the connection without too much prompting. But it was the mysterious black rock that would eventually cause the greatest stir.

Lok had it assayed by three different experts, each and every one of them declaring that it contained no metal or minerals of note. Finally, in January 1577, the determined Lok took it to an Italian goldsmith in London, who claimed (though how is not clear) that the stone was rich in gold ore. The "secret" of the ore was revealed to Elizabeth by Lok in a letter. When Walsingham replied on the queen's behalf that it seemed odd, since none of the queen's assayers had found any gold, Lok remained adamant that they had discovered gold in the frozen wastelands of Meta Incognita. Even Dee seemed to agree. When no arrangement had been made with the crown for a follow-up expedition, after three more months of negotiations, in March 1577, Frobisher's and Lok's news "bafflingly" leaked out. There was "the hope of more of the same gold ore to be found," they declared, and that this "kindled a greater opinion in the hearts of many to advance the voyage again. Whereupon preparation was made for a new voyage against the year following, and the captain more specially directed by commission for the searching more of this gold ore than for the searching any further of the passage."[20]

Frobisher's fiction—that he had seen the Pacific Ocean from the shores of eastern North America—had brought gold fever to London, and would soon bankrupt his friend and business partner, Michael Lok.

21. Dark Days at Rathlin Island ✦

*Great Framer and Preserver of Things, O God, . . . Free
the country and kingdom most especially from all assault of
war; keep us exempt from the internal and domestic tumults
by which a good part of the Christian world is
now disturbed . . .*

—PRAYER BY ELIZABETH I, C. 1578

While Michael Lok and Martin Frobisher were attempting to entice the great and the good of England to invest in their next Northwest Passage venture, Francis Drake was finishing his harsh service in Ireland under the erratic Walter Devereux, Earl of Essex. Devereux's "plantations" were, like all Tudor projects in Ireland, bogged down in guerrilla warfare. Resistance this time was led primarily by the powerful lord of Tyrone, Turlough O'Neill. But the Scots who had been imported for decades as mercenaries to fight the English were also in revolt. They had decided to stay, and settled in the Glens of Antrim in lands that the O'Neill called their own. Their putative head, Sorley Boy MacDonnell, was the son of the Lord of Islay and Kintyre in Scotland, and had dug in against the English on the jagged L-shaped rock of an island called Rathlin, four miles long by three miles wide. This storm-swept rock in northeastern County Antrim was an oasis for seabirds—razorbills, cormorants, guillemots, puffins, and gulls. The avian population outnumbered the people sheltering there by at least a thousand to one. But its days as a wildlife sanctuary were numbered. In a land that abounds with legend, even a small, craggy outcrop like Rathlin had its moment in ancient lore. It was said that the great Scots king, Robert the Bruce, had centuries earlier taken refuge from the English in the stone castle there. Now, Sorley Boy MacDonnell had followed in the Bruce's footsteps, and he brought his chiefs and their families to Rathlin and to safety.

Strategically, it was a sound move. Rathlin was only thirteen miles from the Scottish coast, and only three from Ireland. The waters surrounding the island had been notorious for centuries for their sudden whirlpools and deadly currents. Rathlin's cliffs remain legendary for attracting shipwrecks over four hundred years on. It is no wonder that when Sorley Boy and his chiefs had retreated to Rathlin with enough food, seed, and animals to last them years, he had every reason to think that he was untouchable. But he hadn't reckoned with Devereux and his new admiral, Francis Drake.[1]

Devereux had made a petition entitled "My Opinion for the Reformation and the Government of Ulster to the Privy Council" in 1574 to provide him with ships for just such an eventuality. Ireland's coast is littered with thousands of safe havens and coves that can be approached only by an invading force by sea. It was Burghley who drafted the Council's reply to Essex in his document "Doubts to Be Resolved by the Earl of Essex," in which the fifteenth item listed queries, "What is to be thought requisite for the having of any shipping upon the sea, besides victuallers, to keep out the Scots, for that no mention is thereof made in the plot [plan]. . . ."[2]

Devereux gave his answer in early 1575, mentioning Drake as the cause for his change of tactic:

> *The shipping was not mentioned in the plot, but yet not unthought of, for I wrote unto my agents to write to my lord admiral [Clinton], that the shipping now here might be converted to buy certain frigates which one Drake brought out of [the] Indies whereof one is in possession of Mr Hawkins [and] one of Sir Arthur Champernowne . . . . They were bought at easy prices. . . . They will brook a sea well and carry 200 soldiers, as I am informed, and yet they draw so little water, as they may pass into every river, island or creek where the Scottish galley may flee, and are of better strength [and] stowage than others, for the galleys are made more slight and thin than the wherries upon the Thames. No shipping therefore [is] so good for this purpose in my opinion as the frigates. . . . Good choice must be made of mariners for these boats, for ordinary sailors love not to pull at an oar.* [3]

Essex's reply lifts the veil of history momentarily. On his return from the West Indies, Drake had evidently sold on his Spanish prizes to Hawkins and Champernowne, who tried immediately to flog them on to Devereux. But ships without a daring captain would only partially fulfill Essex's needs. He had heard of Drake, through the Leicester and Sidney connection, but hadn't the means to attract him into defense of the Irish plantations. After all, Ireland was not Drake's cause célèbre.

Fortunately for Essex, Leicester also took an active interest in Ireland and its affairs. Further ships were bought or leased, and by May 1575, Essex had a squadron with Drake as its admiral. Drake came to Ireland with his own ship, the *Falcon* (probably a frigate), and a pinnace. There were also eighteen mariners, a master, a pilot boatswain, a steward, a carpenter, and a gunner. His thirteen-year-old cousin, also named John Drake, joined the crew as its "boy." Though Drake was the fleet's commander, both he and a Captain James Sydae drew a salary of 42 shillings a month ($690 or £373 today). For the next four months, Drake saw active duty of a kind that was unlike any other he had experienced before. While he commanded the sea operations, he had little to do with land battles, and presumably he didn't like what he saw.

In May 1575, Essex wrote to Burghley, "If the frigates come there shall not be a boat that remain in the Rathlins, or the Glens, or come up that coast."[4] He clearly intended for his fleet to cut off the supplies and communications to Rathlin Island by using Drake. The frigates were ordered to assemble at Carrickfergus, while the Earl mysteriously withdrew toward the Pale around Dublin. Captain John Norris, veteran of the Huguenot civil wars in France, had volunteered with his three hundred foot soldiers and eighty horse to take the island by storm. Where Drake had already become known for his fair treatment of the enemy, and had even gone out of his way to protect the women at Ventas Cruces, Norris had earned a well-deserved reputation as a ruthless soldier who took no prisoners.

But why had Essex withdrawn before Norris had launched his attack? Had his experience of Ireland taught him that the wind had eyes, and that by his sleight of hand, the Scots wouldn't be alerted to the attack? Or was he afraid that whatever brutality Norris would mete out to the Scots might fetch some sturdy rebuke from the queen? Whatever the truth of the matter, Norris ordered Drake to take his army across to Rathlin on July 20.

True to its legend, the winds at Rathlin whipped up and the sea swelled almost immediately, dispersing the fleet. It was two days before they had regrouped and made the three-mile crossing, landing on the eastern side of the island. The troops were disembarked and marched northeasterly toward the castle with such speed that many of MacDonnell's followers had been caught outside. In the inevitable skirmish, one of Norris's men was killed before the Scots reached sanctuary. While Norris and his soldiers pursued them, Drake and his mariners landed two siege guns and brought them within firing distance of the castle. After three days pummeling the castle walls, they finally breached the Scots' defenses. Yet despite this, and an attempted storming of the castle, it took another two days before the Scots asked for a "parlay."

Meanwhile, Drake and his sailors were kept very busy blockading the island from relief vessels or escaping Scots. During the siege of the castle and the next few days, Drake captured and burned eleven Scottish galleys. Any survivors were taken aboard Drake's ships, to be exchanged against English prisoners at a later date. What Drake didn't know was that there would be no exchange.

At the castle, Norris was told by the surrendering Scots that they wanted only to return to Scotland. In the circumstances, their lives, they knew, would depend on Norris's mercy. But they had put their lives into untrustworthy hands. Norris claimed that he would grant clemency to the constable of the castle and his family (who was the son of an Irish chieftain), but that for the Scots, their lives would depend entirely on the "courtesy of the English soldiers," to use the euphemism of the day. What followed was the worst bloodbath in forty years since the Pardon of Maywood in 1535, when English soldiers butchered the garrison at Dengen after its surrender.[5]

Every man, woman, child, and baby on Rathlin Island was slaughtered. More than one hundred horses, three hundred cows, and three thousand sheep were confiscated or killed, and the crops burned, and enough corn to feed two hundred men for a year confiscated. For days the English scoured the island looking in every cave, on every cliff face, in the ditches or undergrowth for any survivors. Several hundred more Scots were brutally slaughtered where they were caught in the days following the surrender.

And yet, when the massacre was reported back to the Privy Council, there was no word of rebuke against Norris or Essex. In fact, the Privy Council congratulated Essex on a successful campaign. Still, it is strange; Elizabeth had expressly warned Essex when he set out for Ireland that he mustn't shed blood unnecessarily. Drake's official reaction is also unrecorded. Where Drake had shown his enemy compassion in the heat of battle, Norris had shown unabated cruelty. It most certainly wasn't the way Drake would have handled things. But the admiral was not without power, as it happened. The events that followed tell their own tale.

When Sir Henry Sidney—a distant relation of Drake through Drake's godfather, the Earl of Bedford—was brought across to Dublin for his renewed tenure as lord deputy, it was Francis Drake who piloted his ship. What words were exchanged between them we can only imagine. Sidney landed on September 7, and the entire English naval squadron in Ireland was disbanded twelve days later. Only Drake remained on the payroll until the end of the month. Essex raged at Sidney's incompetence. After all, Rathlin could be occupied again. In support of Essex, and in a move that was tantamount to mutiny, John Norris complained to the Privy Council that

> *my Lord Deputy that now is presently upon his landing there discharged the frigates which the Scots having intelligence of and of their departure, upon the last voyage that the aforesaid hoy made for the revictualling of the castle, on their return assaulted, took and burnt her. My humble suit to your Honours is not to put this loss upon me . . . for had I not been assured by the Earl of Essex that he understood by certain [of] Her Majesty's letters to himself, her pleasure was the frigates should not have been discharged as long as the place was retained, I would more sufficiently have provided for the safety of the passage.*[6]

Before the end of the year, Sidney ordered the English garrison at Rathlin to be abandoned. The forty soldiers who had remained there had been reduced to eating their own horses for food due to the Scottish reprisals. And without Rathlin, there was no need for a naval squadron. Essex and Drake returned to England, where they both received rewards from the court. By the summer of 1576, Essex had been sent back to Ireland as its earl marshal, but he died within weeks of dysentery, with dreams of yet more bloodshed thankfully unfulfilled.[7]

Drake had shared his own dream from the treetop high above Darien with the earl before his death, as well as his new friend, a gentleman named Thomas Doughty, who had served Essex well as a secretary. Doughty vowed to accompany Drake on his next great voyage, and to help him in any way he possibly could at court.

22. Drake's Perfect Timing ✦

He was sent for unto Her Majesty by Secretary
Walsingham, and she told him that she would gladly be
revenged on the King of Spain for divers injuries and that
Drake was the only man that might do this exploit . . .
—SIR FRANCIS DRAKE, *Sir Francis Drake Revived*

The reappointment of Sir Henry Sidney as lord deputy in Ireland put that troubled province back into a safe pair of hands from the Privy Council's perspective. There was no further need for an Irish navy, and hence no need for Drake to squander his maritime brilliance there.[1]

Where Drake's timing had been decidedly poor on his return from the West Indies, his return from Ireland was blessed in every way. For years, Sir John Hawkins had had an eye on his father-in-law's position as treasurer of the navy, and indeed Benjamin Gonson was grooming him for that post. In February 1577, Hawkins claimed the sums of £100 and £950 from lord treasurer Burghley: the first sum was for clearing "the coast of pirates" and the second, for his provision of ships and losses incurred in Essex's Irish "plantation" scheme. He even listed the £150 costs for recovering his captured mariners from the King of Spain's clutches in sending George Fitzwilliams to meet the king in 1571.[2] In light of what followed, it is fairly clear that Burghley connived with Hawkins in making these demands.

Hawkins's "reasonable suits," so Burghley stated, included information garnered from Gonson's naval accounts as well as discussions with Elizabeth's two master shipwrights, Peter Pett and Matthew Baker. Not satisfied simply to have his losses covered, Hawkins went on to accuse the Winter brothers and the Navy Board of feathering their own nests and avoiding their blindingly obvious inability to deliver a better, sleeker, more efficient navy for less money. The

Winters' annual costs were £6,000 ($2.09 million or £1.13 million today), and Hawkins claimed that a "far better" navy could be maintained for £4,000 yearly. To build seven ships had cost nearly £5,000 in the previous year, and Hawkins predicted that the current year would see a doubling of that sum. His claim, entitled "Abuses in the Admiralty Touching Her Majesty's Navy Exhibited by Mr Hawkins" went on to allege that new ships were being built for £800 too much ($274,658 or £148,464 today) and wood provided for £400 per load too much ($137,329 or £74,232 today). These were serious charges indeed—particularly against a national hero like Sir William Winter—and could not go unaddressed.[3]

The accusation made, Hawkins could only wait out the results of the hornets' nest he had stirred up against the Winter brothers. Though Hawkins had Burghley's trust, the Lord Admiral Clinton, aging, but not without substantial influence, weighed in on the side of William and George Winter. Nonetheless, Hawkins was eventually appointed as the new "treasurer for marine causes," to replace his father-in-law on November 18, 1577. "I shall pluck a thorn out of my foot," an evidently relieved Gonson warned him, "and put it into yours."[4] Hawkins's appointment is a demonstrable change of direction, and an important one in English naval history. Because of, rather than despite, his merchant pirating of the 1560s, a redesign program would be undertaken in his tenure that produced precisely what he had sought: sleeker, swifter, more heavily armed, more efficient ships that would run circles around the Spanish and Portuguese.

Drake's return from Ireland also coincided with the outburst of "gold fever" at court, introduced by Michael Lok and Martin Frobisher. The air was filled with expectation that the gold that had so long filled Philip of Spain's coffers might justly come to England, too, through Frobisher's mining exploits. The only cloud on Drake's horizon was the strong possibility that English merchants—if they knew what he had in mind—could veto his own plans for the future.

Some merchants had already turned to illicit trade and plunder, while others clung precariously to the "old ways" of the merchant companies and government-granted monopolies. But it was the "newer" aggressive English traders who, little by little, had been gnawing away at the fringes of Spain's empire. Yet miraculously, while English depredations against Spanish shipping had been steadily on the rise, so trade with Iberia had risen, too. English trade with the Barbary Coast (largely in the control of the Portuguese or Moors) amounted to some £17,775 ($6.11 million or £3.3 million today) by 1576. England's trade with Portugal in the same year was £8,758 5s. 4d. ($3.01 million or £1.63 million today). While trade had been higher in previous years, there were still some 4,361 English officially resident in Portugal (there were only 7 Portuguese in England in the same period). The treaty of 1572 had also finally come into effect opening trade to the Barbary Coast. All this "progress" led the merchants to hope widely that the English would no longer be viewed as interlopers.[5] It was a slender thread to cling to.

Elizabeth, meanwhile, was never one to pass up a great opportunity to slyly knife Philip in the back. English shipping had once again begun trading in the Mediterranean after the defeat of the Turks at Lepanto, but the war of Cyprus (1570–73) had crippled trade with Venice anew. With Antwerp's trade in chaos since 1569 and the arrival of Alba, the 1570s became a decade of plunder, piracy, and underhanded dealing. A veritable tidal wave of piracy swept the Italian and Iberian peninsulas, with English rovers leading the pack along with the French, Barbary, and Turkish mariners. By the latter part of the decade, the deadly combination of Leicester and Walsingham granted a monopoly to Acerbo Velutelli, a Luccan merchant, to freight imports of currants from the eastern Mediterranean to England aboard English ships. Among the ship owners were Sir John Hawkins, Oliver and Nicholas Stile, Simon Lawrence, and Thomas Cordell.[6]

Still, the most important of the Levant traders would be Sir Edward Osborne. According to Hakluyt,

Sir Edward Osborne and M. Richard Staper seriously considering what benefit might grow to the common wealth by renewing of the foresaid discontinued trade, to the enlarging of Her Majesty's customs [duties], the furthering of navigation, the venting of diverse general commodities of this Realm, and the enriching of the City of London, determined to use some effectual means of re-establishing and augmenting thereof. Wherefore about the year 1575, the foresaid R.W. [Right Worshipful] merchants at their charges and expenses sent John Wight and Joseph Clements by way of Poland to Constantinople, where the said Joseph remained 18 months to procure a safe conduct from the grand signory for Mr William Harborne, then factor for Sir Edward Osborne. . . . The said Mr Harborne the first of July 1578 departed from London by the sea to Hamburg, and thence . . . traveled to Leopolis in Poland . . . he arrived at Constantinople the 28th of October.[7]

Elizabeth was desperate to foster good relations with the Porte (the Sultan's government in Constantinople), as a counterbalance to Spain's open animosity and France's invariable spoiling tactics. Harborne's embassy to Constantinople was not merely a new commercial venture to Spain's old enemy; it was a matter of considerable interest to the state, with state sanction. Walsingham's memorandum to the queen from 1578, entitled "A Consideration of the Trade unto Turkey," sets out how to use this new and important market "to great profit" through direct access to the Levant. He also urged the queen to look at the political advantages to an Anglo-Ottoman entente, thus beginning the long and lucrative chapter in England's history of trade with the Middle East.[8]

It was as if all these excellent signs for his project were conspiring to raise Drake's expectations. But there was more. The single most important development in English thinking of the period, attributable to Dr. John Dee, was about to be published. In August 1576, Dr. Dee wrote his first draft of the incredibly insightful paper "A Petty Navy Royal," which would change English thought on the island nation's relationship to the sea forever. It might have also been aptly entitled "In Defense of the Realm," and it was made available to the public as part of his *General & Rare Memorials Pertaining to the Perfect Art of Navigation*, in 1577.

Dee logically laid out a thirteen-point plan for the development of a standing navy for England's defense. He urged for a navy of seventy-five or more tall ships, well provisioned with supplies to patrol England's coasts, not only to fend off any threat of invasion from her neighbors, but also from Spain and the pope, who had already shown their true colors through the Ridolfi plot and the bull of excommunication. Dee is the first to refer to the "British Empire" and to England's shores as part of a greater Britain. He covers all skills required in such a defensive force from mustering the men to what tasks they would need to be trained to perform ranging from piloting skills in harbor and recognizing landmarks to the greater "art of navigation" and every shade of expertise in between. It is obviously written with an eye to presentation to Elizabeth, since his point 5 lays claim to the intractable problems of vagrancy and crime when he writes, "How many hundreds of lusty and handsome men would be, this way, well occupied, and have needful maintenance, which now are either idle, or want sustenance, or both; in too many places of this renowned Monarchy?"[9]

Not pirate nor prince nor potentate would dare attack a realm so strong, Dee continues, adding that pirates of "good character" would desire to be employed in such an instrument of national pride. Foreign fishermen guilty of invading England's shores for decades could be rebuffed by a standing navy, thereby ensuring enough fish stocks for the common good. But Dee, as an experienced intelligencer, added that humble fishermen may not be fishermen after all:

> *And this sort of people they be, which otherwise by colour [under cover] and pretence of coming about their feat of fishing do subtly and secretly use soundings and searchings of our channels, deeps, shoals, banks, or bars along the sea coasts, and in our haven mouths also, and up in our creeks, sometimes in our bays, and sometimes in our roads, etc.; taking good marks, for avoiding of the dangers, and also trying good landings. And so, making perfect charts of all our coasts round about England and Ireland, are become almost [more] perfect in them, than the most part of our masters, leadsmen or pilots are. To the double danger of mischief in times of war; and also to no little hazard of the State Royal, if maliciously bent, they should purpose to land any puissant army, in time to come.[10]*

Dee concludes his thesis with the correct assertion that "this Petty Navy Royal is thought to be the only Master Key wherewith to open all locks that keep out or hinder this incomparable British Empire from enjoying . . . such a yearly revenue of Treasure . . . with so great ease to . . . yield the like to either king or other potentate . . . "[11]

The timing of Dee's publication was no accident. Frobisher had already left on his second voyage, and adventurers of all sorts were beating a path to his door. Several years earlier, he had presented the queen with his view of the state of the realm that clearly demonstrated that something had to be done to alleviate the perpetual state of near-war abroad so that the people could enjoy their long-earned peace at home. Protestants everywhere—especially in Flanders and the Dutch provinces—were under siege by either the pope, Philip II, or Charles IX of France.

Crucial to this exposé was the simple fact that Elizabeth trusted Dee implicitly. Like Leicester, he was affectionately called her "eyes." While she paid him little by way of money, he was always welcomed at court. His near neighbor, Sir Francis Walsingham, was also a great admirer of his, as was Leicester himself. It would be these three men who would form the core support for Drake and his fellow adventurers, both at court, and in the realm generally. Burghley, on the other hand, had made his views known with regard to partaking in plunder, preferring the integrity of investments through the guise of a joint stock company like the Muscovy Company instead. Though he turned his nose up at booty as a means to become personally wealthy, Burghley welcomed it nonetheless into Elizabeth's purse for the realm.

And now, the final factor came into play to clinch Elizabeth's favor for Drake. Again, Burghley had been urging Elizabeth quite strongly to act at once and marry Francis, the Duke of Alençon. It was the last chance, he thought, for the queen to have a child. There was an edginess at court while power shifted again subtly in favor of Leicester and Walsingham, and away from Burghley. Christopher Hatton had joined ranks with Leicester, and it was their violent opposition to the marriage that won out in the end, temporarily unseating Burghley from pole position.[12]

All this happened just as Drake made his appearance in court. He knew that Grenville had recently presented his own scheme for sailing into the Pacific to Burghley, and he also knew that, although Grenville was regarded as a renegade with little sea experience to cope successfully with the difficult conditions in the Strait of Magellan, he talked a very good game. Drake's old ship's master, John Oxenham, had recently embarked, too, in April on a small voyage of his own— to carry a pinnace across the Isthmus of Panama and raid the Pacific. Oxenham had no means of garnering government support; and if Grenville did, Drake's chances for a major plundering exploit would be at an end.[13]

But the time "wasted" in Ireland had been worthwhile in finding him patronage among the gentlemen adventurers at court as his backers. It had cost him dearly, however, in being the second Englishman ever to reach the Pacific.[14] What Drake had been temporarily unaware of was the delicate change in court power that wafted on the air. When Drake delivered his letter of introduction from Walter Devereux, Earl of Essex, to Sir Francis Walsingham, his timing proved superb.

What followed is shrouded in secrecy, as were all reports that later referred to Drake's voyage of circumnavigation. Walsingham and Leicester were, however, his first and greatest promoters. This "triumvirate" embodied Philip II's most entrenched enemies, and cleverest foes. Drake put up £1,000 ($341,621 or £184,660 today) himself to prove that he believed in his plan. John Hawkins followed with £500 ($170,811 or £92,330 today). William Winter, not to be outdone, contributed £750 ($256,216 or £138,495 today), along with the Lord Admiral Lincoln, Sir Francis Walsingham, the Earl of Leicester, and Christopher Hatton. George Winter, like Hawkins, invested £500. It was now up to Walsingham and Leicester to argue Drake's case before Elizabeth.[15] From the makeup of his investors, it would certainly have been evident to the queen that Drake's voyage had anti-Spanish—and not trading or imperialistic—motivations. In fact, when she met with Drake, she agreed to the captain's terms,

> *that it might please her Majesty to grant . . . her ship the* Swallow *with her tackle, apparel, and only four culverins, with two falcons of brass [that] might be left to the said ship with the ordnance afore named might be valued by indifferent [independent] persons and that sum which the same shall amount unto her Highness to bear*

such portion as she shall like, and for the rest, the same to be born
by the parties that shall be thought . . . Upon good assurances to be
given to the Exchequer . . .

. . . that the Queen's Majesty may be made privy to the truth of
the voyage, and yet the color [cover] to be given out to Alexandria,
which in effect is ready done by a licence procured from the
Turks.[16]

Burghley, though, worried Walsingham and Leicester. If he got
wind of an expedition bent on plunder, he would surely persuade
the notoriously fickle queen against "annoying the King of Spain."
And so, the solution to subvert Burghley was to put about—in a
very convincing manner—that Drake's destination was Alexandria,
since trade to the eastern Mediterranean had been reopened once
more. The queen herself was certainly in the know, for no pen was
ever put to paper to confirm the nature of the highly provocative
escapade other than what she wrote above, and she engaged Drake
in the subterfuge by agreeing to invest on condition that Drake
understood her "special commandment that of all men, my lord
treasurer Burghley should not know about it."[17]

Finally, in July 1577, the queen decided. Drake could go to
"Alexandria." Had John Dee seen into the stars to tell her that the
moment was right? Since Drake's greatest voyage had begun as a
state secret bent on plunder—and ended as a state secret for the
achievements he made—we will never know. Only a remnant of
Drake's instructions and how he readied his fleet survive. The rest is
lost in the fog of history.

What we do know is that on November 15, 1577, his tiny fleet
comprising the 100-ton bark, *Pelican*; the 80-ton *Elizabeth*; the
store ship *Swan;* the puny merchantman, *Marigold*; and the fleet's
scout and messenger ship, *Christopher*, set sail in Plymouth Sound.
Drake and his crew of 164 men were sent almost like "doves from
the ark" to perform miracles. The first miracle was to somehow
beat the King of Spain in his own empire. The second was setting
themselves against the vast and unknown expanses of sea. Despite
being beaten back into harbor virtually straightaway, Drake waited
out the Channel storms, and set sail again on December 13, 1577 on
the historic voyage.

Elizabeth was no fool, and she knew that nothing could be kept a secret for long from Burghley, as he ran his own spy network within court. But she could hope that the dark secret that she, Drake, Leicester, Walsingham, and her main courtiers were going to raid Spanish shipping in the Pacific just might elude him for a time. By then, hopefully, Captain Francis Drake would have returned from the Pacific with his holds filled with gold. England was emerging—whether Elizabeth liked it or not—as the political leader of European Protestants, and a fledgling world power, fighting "old" Catholic Europe with any tools she had at her disposal. And Drake was the sharpest tool in the box.

23. The Northwest and
the Company of Kathai ✦

Ensnared by the enticements of this world or burning with
a desire for riches . . .
—DR. JOHN DEE, C. 1560

D rake's success and his ability to fund his South Seas project was
in small part due to the gold fever that had swept the court and
London after Frobisher's voyage. But who was the "leak" that began
gold fever in the first place? There were many possibilities, with
Michael Lok and Martin Frobisher at the top of the list. Fifty years
after Elizabethan England, the Dutch suffered from Tulipomania,
when a single rare tulip could fetch more than a fine home. While
it's expedient to blame Lok or Frobisher, their investor list for the
second expedition—excluding Elizabeth and Burghley—would
not have been above suspicion as perpetrators of the act. The likes
of the Earls of Leicester, Warwick, and Sussex, any of the West
Countrymen, or Walsingham himself could have been involved to
a greater or lesser extent.

Whatever the truth of the matter, gold fever did hit London and
the court—hard. Anyone who was anyone clamored for shares in
the new joint stock company that Lok was rumored to be setting
up. "Frobisher . . . has given it as his decided opinion," wrote Sir
Philip Sidney to his old friend and courtier Hubert Languet, "that
the island is so productive in metals, as to seem very far to surpass the
country of Peru, at least as it now is. There are also six other islands
near to this, which seem very little inferior."[1]

In response, a grateful Lok launched a new joint stock company
in March 1577, called the Company of Kathai, or Cathay Company,
to manage the discovery and exploitation of gold in North America.

Its chief subscribers were Elizabeth and her court, with a total investment of £5,150 ($1.77 million or £955,737 today). The queen also ventured her 200-ton *Aid*.[2] Unlike the earlier voyage, it was truly a royal expedition with Edward Fenton, the Earl of Warwick's handpicked man, as captain of the *Gabriel*, and Gilbert Yorke, the lord admiral's choice, commanding the *Michael*.[3] Frobisher's lieutenant, George Beste, was Christopher Hatton's representative. The chronicler for the expedition was Dionyse Settle, who was the secretary of George Clifford, the Earl of Cumberland.[4] The admiral, the *Michael*, carried 134 men in total, including 11 gentlemen, 3 "goldfiners" [gold refiners], 20 soldiers, 8 miners, and a number of convicts from the Forest of Dean, brought along as "expendable" colonists for Frobisher to land on the imaginary Friesland. Life in the bleak winter landscape was deemed a reprieve for criminals, and a way for them to redeem themselves back into society. This was the first hint of a policy of "transportation" that would blight the English Empire for forty years of the nineteenth century. Frobisher's instructions regarding these poor souls was to land them on Friesland, and then—if possible—"to speak with them on your return." Fortunately for them, Frobisher off-loaded the convicts at Harwich, claiming that his ship was overloaded.

The orders received in the name of the queen to Frobisher and the other shareholders in the Cathay Company were quite clear:

> *To have regard that there be no spoil of the provisions taken in the ships.*
>
> *To dismiss, before departure or on the way, any that are mutinous.*
>
> *To depart before 12 May and make way north or west to Meta Incognita and the Countess of Warwick's island and sound in the Straight, which we name Frobisher's Strait, having been discovered by yourself two years since. So to order your course that the ships do not lose each other, and if any wilfulness or negligence appear in any person in charge, to punish such offender sharply, to the example of others.*
>
> *On arriving at the Countess of Warwick's island and sound, to harbor your vessels, and repair to the mines and minerals where*

you wrought last year, and set the men to work to gather the ore, seeing they are well placed from danger and malice of the people and any other extremity.

If you find richer mines than those whence you had your last year's lading, you shall remove and work them if convenient.

To search for and consider of an apt place where you may best plant and fortify the 100 men you leave to inhabit there, against the people and all other extremities.

To leave with Capt. Fenton the 100 persons, with orders to keep a journal of proceedings, noting what part of the year is most free from ice, and with him the Gabriel, Michael, *and* Judith *with provisions &c.*

To instruct all the people in any conference with the natives, to behave so as to secure their friendship.

After you have safely harbored your ships, set your miners to work, &c; if time permit, you are to repair with the two barks to the place where you lost your men the first year, to search for mines, and to discover 50 to 100 leagues further westward, as the opening of the strait by water will lead, that you may be certain you are entered the South Sea, called Mer de Sud, *and in your passage to learn all you can; but not to tarry long, that you may be able to return in due time.*

To consider what place is most convenient to fortify for defence of the mines, and possessing of the country, and to bring home perfect notes and maps thereof, to be kept in secret and so delivered to us.

Not to suffer any vessel laden with ore to set sail unto the day fixed in the charter party, except you see good cause, but keep all together till your arrival in the Thames . . .

We chiefly desire to know the temperature of these northwest parts, therefore you shall write an account of how any further discovery of the lands of seas lying within 200 leagues of the place fortified for our people may be achieved . . .

No person is to make an assay of metal or ore in Meta Incog. But those to whom the office is assigned, except yourself, your lieutenant-general, and substitutes; nor is any person to take up or keep for his private use any ore, precious stone &c. found in that

*land but deliver the same to you or your lieutenant, on pain of
forfeiting treble the value out of his wages, and other punishment.*

*To keep a record of all ore and minerals found, as also specimens
thereof in boxes, and the localities of discovery . . . the boxes to be
delivered to the treasurer of the company of Merchant Adventurers
for northwest affairs on your return . . .*

*To bring back 800 tons or more if possible of the said ore, and
return into the Thames . . .*

*You shall have power to punish treason, mutiny, or other disorder
among the persons employed.*[5]

Sailing on May 31, 1577, Frobisher once again reached the southern
tip of the mythical island of Friesland, but was unable to make
landfall due to the weather, rough seas, and ice. He plowed on in the
icy waters to Little Hall's Island and the southern tip of Frobisher
Bay, where some highly unsatisfactory ore samples were taken. The
voyage was beginning to look distinctly unpromising. Since his first
Inuit captive had created such a sensation in London, Frobisher had
in mind to bring others back home; and though it was clearly not
a stated purpose of the journey, it would certainly deflect attention
away from the possibility that they might not find gold. Despite Dr.
Dee's instruction, the statements and audit undertaken after the
voyage show that neither Frobisher nor his gentlemen adventurers
had the remotest inclination or understanding of how good relations
with a native population could have helped make the expedition a
success.

Tentative steps were made to capture some native or other by
what is often called "silent trade" where one group lays down gifts
on the ground and goes away then the other does the same, and so it
continues until they feel confident enough to meet face-to-face. The
English were the first to do this, and the Inuit followed suit. After
several such exchanges, Frobisher and his second in command,
Hall, entered the clearing unarmed. Again the Inuit followed
their example. Presents were exchanged. Then Frobisher, in an
act of unwarranted and cold-blooded treachery, signaled to Hall
to pounce. But the Inuit were too quick and escaped their clutches.
Their kinsmen surged forward from the shadows firing their arrows

and shouting. They chased Frobisher and Hall back to the boats, but in the skirmish, Frobisher justly received the ignominious wound of an arrow in his backside.[6]

His pride had been grievously wounded, and the Inuit were cast as a "base, cruel and man-eating people." When Frobisher was able to fight again, the English mounted a "counterattack" and captured an Inuit male. But Frobisher's blood was up, and nothing short of a proper victory could assuage his ill temper. While ostensibly searching for their five abandoned seamen, they attacked another group of Inuit, brutally slaying several, and capturing a young woman and her baby. The babe had been wounded in the incident, yet there is no record of viewing this as either wrong or of any significance. Still, the three prisoners' behaviors were observed by the expedition's resident artist, probably John White, who would achieve fame later for the Roanoke voyages. White made a series of realistic sketches of the three of them, and they were significant in that they were the first English sketches of native North Americans.

With these three prisoners under his belt, Frobisher had well and truly proved to his fellow adventurers that they had conquered these "crafty villains" in the name of the Queen of England. The mining operation was gaining pace by now, and over 140 tons had been laden onto the *Aid*. They had been away quite long enough, and with winter threatening, Frobisher announced that they had achieved the first two aims of their expedition. What had become of the abandoned English from the earlier voyage, they never asked, and they never learned.[7]

They returned to Countess of Warwick Island, where they finally set up their mining operations after preliminary assays showed that the ore there was "favorable." But they had already squandered four weeks of the arctic summer and, after mining only 140 tons of the black rock, headed smartly home.

As Frobisher expected, the Inuit captives caused a great stir, and at first, the court remained expectant of a windfall. But when the Tower's assayer pronounced that the ore held no gold, Lok had it retested several times until, at last, a Dr. Burchet's opinion had been purchased to state that it was worth at least £40 per ton.[8] Many of the shareholders began to query who Burchet was, and why it had taken so many assays to ascertain the ore's value, so Frobisher and

Lok geared up quickly for a major mining expedition and third voyage. But even before it set sail, the ore's estimated value began to plummet.

Nonetheless, Frobisher and his fleet of fifteen ships sailed on May 31, 1578—exactly one year after the second voyage had set out—from Harwich on what became his last voyage of discovery to the north of America. Sailing northward around the British Isles to the Orkneys, then west past Greenland, the fleet sighted Meta Incognita (the peninsula on Baffin Island) through thick fog. Frobisher and his men were swept into an unknown strait farther to the southwest by the current, prevented from taking any readings whatsoever due to the fog. But, in the confusion, they discovered another "strait" that Frobisher claimed to be the Frobisher Straits of the second voyage. This "Mistaken Straits"—better known today as the Hudson Strait—was undoubtedly Frobisher's greatest discovery. While at first Frobisher pretended that it had been the same strait as he had previously found, Beste wrote in his diary:

> *And truly it was wonderful to hear and see the rushing and noise that the tides do make in this place, with so violent a force that our ships lying a hull were turned sometimes round about even in a moment after the manner of a whirlpool, and the noise of the stream no less to be heard afar off then the waterfall of London Bridge.*[9]

It was July 7, 1578, when the fleet entered the "Mistaken Straits." Three days later, four ships were separated from the advancing fleet in the freezing fog, and decided to turn back. Frobisher and those ships still following him pressed on another estimated sixty leagues between never-ending skyscrapers of ice, whose summits remained perpetually shrouded in the arctic fog. Finally, after nine more days, with no immediate end in sight, he gave the order to return back through the strait, since he "both would and could," Frobisher boasted, "have gone through to the South Sea" if he hadn't had the entire responsibility for the welfare of his fleet and the expedition as a whole to consider.[10]

Frobisher rightly reasoned that it was time to resume the main purpose of the voyage—gold mining. And so they returned to

Friesland (Baffin Island) where the gold mining "colony" was set up by the end of July. Yet it hadn't been smooth sailing through to Baffin. When they were approaching, Baffin was still clogged with ice floes, and after some considerable grinding of wooden hulls against ice, with gentlemen adventurers manning the capstans like common sailors, offering sound advice based on their better education, they finally made landfall. Frobisher trudged across the ice and theatrically raised the flag of St. George, officially claiming the land for England.[11]

But a short while later, the *Dennys*, a 100-ton bark, was struck by an iceberg and sank within sight of the entire, stunned expedition. Fortunately her crew was spared, but the prefabricated "winter" house that had been brought from England partially assembled was lost with the *Dennys*.[12] Instead, stone (partially from ballast) and wooden structures were erected for shelter, and the adventurers settled into their mining operations at long last. What had begun two voyages earlier as the quest for a lucrative trade route to the East Indies and Cathay had clearly become a settlement in its own right searching for gold. By the end of August, over 1,370 tons of ore had been mined and loaded, and they headed for home.

Like Drake on his return from the West Indies, Frobisher had come back to a different England in September than the one he had left in the late spring. Michael Lok had been obliged to submit his accounts for an audit in August, and when the results regarding the value of the ore were other than those desired by Frobisher, he ordered a second official audit to be undertaken. Costs for the three voyages had risen to £20,345 ($6.96 million or £3.76 million today) with two-thirds of that attributed solely to the third voyage and the gold refinery built at Dartford. This was equivalent to one tenth of the national budget. Yet the investors had stumped up only £17,630 6s. 8d. ($6.03 million or £3.26 million today). The list of unpaid subscriptions read like a *Who's Who* of Elizabethan England: Lord Burghley; Lord Admiral Clinton; the Earl of Sussex; the Earl of Warwick; Henry Carey, Lord Hunsdon; Sir Francis Knollys; the Earl of Pembroke; Philip Sidney; Edward Dyer; Anthony Jenkinson; Dr. John Dee; and Thomas Randolph, to name just a few.

It wasn't until January 1579 that the wages for the mariners and others involved in the voyage were settled, leaving an outstanding deficit of £3,658 14s. 3d.—that is, until the refined gold could be sold. Frobisher distanced himself from Lok, rounding on him that he was a fraud, a knave, and a bankrupt. "I daily instructed him," Lok ventured in his defense, "making my house his home, my purse his purse at his need, and my credit his credit to my power, when he was utterly destitute both of money, credit and friends."[13]

Even more damning was Lok's description of his business partner after the initial ore discovery, while gold fever still swept the court: "Frobisher grew into such a monstrous mind that a whole kingdom could not contain it but already, by discovery of a new world, he was become another Columbus."[14] Though Lok was putting up a spirited defense, the debts kept piling in, with claims from the ship owners mounting. When William Boroughs demanded £200 for his ship loaned to the Company of Kathai for the last voyage, and Lok was unable to pay, he was left no alternative but to declare bankruptcy. This had the effect of throwing the Company of Kathai into receivership—pending the sale of the ore—not to mention Lok's spending a spell in the dreaded Fleet Prison as an undischarged bankrupt.

The only problem in selling the ore was that from the haul of well over a thousand tons of black, gleaming rock from North America, the total amount of gold that was extracted remains imbedded today in the sealing wax appended to the report that it was completely worthless. The entire gold extraction could be placed upon the head of a pin.

24. In the Shadow of Magellan ⚓

*And now, my masters, let us consider what we have
done. We have now set together by the ears three mighty
princes, as first Her Majesty [then] the Kings of Spain and
Portugal, and if this voyage should not have good success,
we should not only be a scorning or a reproachful scoffing
spoke unto our enemies, but also a great blot to our whole
country forever . . .*

—FRANCIS DRAKE, PORT ST. JULIAN, AUGUST 1578

Frobisher was preparing for his third voyage when Drake sailed
November 15, 1577. Within days the queen's favorite, Christopher
Hatton, had been knighted for his services to the queen. Aside from
his known courtly duties as the head of her guard, Hatton had also
contributed the *Pelican* and the *Marigold* to Drake's journey. The
Christopher was named after him.

As far as hugely historic voyages go, Drake had made a rather
inauspicious beginning. In the days between his initial and final
sailing from Plymouth, Drake accused James Sydae, who had served
with him and Thomas Doughty in Ireland, of provisioning the ships
poorly for the months at sea that lay ahead. This was a famous trick
of many ships' masters, when they underspent on their budget for
victuals, substituting poorer quality foodstuffs or providing less, and
pocketing the surplus. Doughty muttered his unhappiness to the crew
that Drake had dismissed an "essential member" of their company,
and that their hotheaded captain might even dismiss him, Doughty,
who had been instrumental in ensuring that the voyage happened
in the first place. When Doughty found he had a ready audience,
he even claimed that Drake had been ordered to consult him at all
times by their investors, and that he shared Drake's authority. None
of Drake's men told him while they were still on English soil what

Doughty had been getting up to. If they had, matters may have turned out differently.

They were past the entry to the Mediterranean before the mariners learned that Alexandria was not their intended destination. Naturally there was grumbling, like, "Mr. Drake had hired them for Alexandria," one mariner complained, "and if he had known that *this* had been Alexandria, he would have been hanged in England rather than have come on this voyage."[1] But still, Drake recorded no incident in his own narrative up to this point, despite the fact that he must have been on his guard for malcontents among his men.

As they steered past the Cape Verde Islands, Drake held up the old English tradition of plundering the coast. A pinnace was sent in hot pursuit after a ship off Santiago and captured her. The *Santa Maria*, as she was then called, was filled with fresh victuals, fresh fruit, other everyday necessities, an astrolabe, and the most valuable commodity yet—a Portuguese pilot named Nuño da Silva, who was the proud owner of several nautical charts of the coasts and ocean between Europe and South America. Nuño da Silva, Drake resolved, would pilot their way to South America.

Drake rechristened the prize ship the *Mary*, after his wife, and appointed his good friend Doughty as her skipper. Soon after Doughty came aboard, there was an argument with some of the men, and two contradictory stories of that dispute survive. The first supporting Doughty's actions has it that Drake's brother, Thomas, was found rifling through the Portuguese booty, and Doughty threatened to report it to the commander. When Drake was told, he flew into a rage against Doughty, accusing him of undermining his authority. The second version, from the ship's preacher, Francis Fletcher, puts an entirely different slant on the matter. Though Fletcher could be considered a "hostile witness" for Drake, he claimed that it was Doughty who was stealing some of the prize goods. Drake looked into it—since fisticuffs about booty often ended in injury or death among sailors, and always ended in discord. He found that Doughty had indeed some Portuguese gloves, a ring, and some Portuguese coins upon his person. Doughty explained this away, claiming that it was the Portuguese prisoners who had given these tokens to him for preferential treatment aboard ship. Drake considered this to be a plausible explanation, but he thought it wiser to remove Doughty from the crew, who might readily slit his throat in his sleep. And so, Drake made Doughty captain of the *Pelican*—the admiral ship.

Only Drake knew the probable length of their voyage, and the ability of any commander to keep the peace among rough men at sea was always a risky business. No one knew better than Drake how much his sailors looked for "some little comfortable dew from heaven," and how his mariners "rejoiced in things stark naughty, bragging in sundry piracies."[2] Transferring Doughty seemed the most sensible and amicable course, but Drake hadn't bargained on Doughty's colossal ego.

Doughty had been well educated, had powerful connections at court, and was an insufferable snob—all things that Drake was not. It rankled with him that Drake, and men like Hawkins and Winter, used their sea captaincies as a means of stepping up the social ladder. Little else can explain his path to self-destruction, even his later assertion that he was secretly in the pay of Lord Burghley. He couldn't fathom Drake's strict discipline with his lawless mariners, nor why he, Doughty, had to abide by the same rules and play second fiddle to an uneducated sailor like Drake. But even Drake's prisoners saw the point, and they remarked on the special relationships he had with his men. In a statement to Don Martín Enríquez from Drake's former prisoner Francisco de Zátate, "He treats them [his men] with affection, and they treat him with respect."[3]

With Doughty aboard the *Pelican* and Drake now captaining the *Mary*, Thomas Doughty's ego inflated beyond his ability to use any tact in his accusations against Drake. John Doughty, Thomas's younger brother, boasted that both he and his brother could summon up the powers of witchcraft, and bring "the Devil to bear down upon the ship's company" as a bear or a lion, if they so desired. The superstitious seamen were evidently in fear of their lives and dared not, at first, to tell their captain. But matters came to a head when Thomas Doughty sent a mysteriously threatening missive to Drake that he would shortly "have more need of me than I shall have of the voyage."[4]

Drake finally snapped. He sent his trumpeter John Brewer, Hatton's faithful servant, to fetch Doughty back to the *Mary*.[5] When Brewer delivered the general's message, Doughty started a scuffle and refused. Brewer returned, eventually, without the reprobate in tow, so Drake beat the *Mary* round to join the *Pelican*, calling Doughty aboard. While Doughty climbed the ladder, Drake exclaimed "Stay there, Thomas Doughty! For I must send you to another place."[6] The oarsmen were commanded to remove Doughty to the fly boat, the *Swan*, and he was compelled to go. Doughty complained bitterly to the *Swan*'s captain, John Chester, that he was being treated as a prisoner, but Chester—like Drake—made no reply.

With Doughty under wraps, the fleet slowly headed across the vast Atlantic on its southwesterly route. They would spend sixty days and nights without the sight or smell of land until on April 5, 1578, they breathed in the familiar "very sweet smell" at 31°30' south. At last, they had reached the coast of Brazil. They sailed straight past the well-trodden trading posts surrounding the River Plate, while Drake concentrated on the main task at hand—consulting Nuño's charts and comparing them to the coastline. Only one European ship had ever passed through the Strait of Magellan before— fifty-eight years earlier—and Magellan, its captain, was killed before the circumnavigation voyage had been completed. Whether or not Drake had seriously intended to go around the world at this stage has been a subject of hot debate, but what was in no doubt was that he was planning to bring his personal war against Philip of Spain to the Pacific. Understanding Nuño's charts, how the currents worked, the reversal of the magnetic pole in the Southern Hemisphere were all critical not only to Drake keeping himself and his crew alive, but also to eventual success.

As the Southern Hemisphere's autumn gripped the tiny flotilla in its clutches, the seas swelled, and the likelihood of finding fresh supplies dwindled. The fleet was scattered, but Drake had appointed a rendezvous with Nuño's help. When Drake's ships reassembled at Bahia Nodales (Argentina) at 47°57' he learned that Doughty was still making mischief. One of Drake's men, John Saracold, bluntly remarked to the commander in front of Doughty that there "were traitors aboard" and that Drake would do well to deal with them as Magellan had done, as an example to the others. Doughty cried out that Drake had no authority to hang him, or even put him on trial. But since Doughty had made it clear to the gentlemen adventurers aboard the *Swan* that mucking in alongside rough sailors was beneath them, he left Drake with little choice as to the outcome. Mutiny was only a short step away.

Drake gave the order to break up the *Swan* to consolidate the fleet, ordering the Doughty brothers aboard the *Christopher*. When they refused to go, Drake cut their dramatics short by telling his men to hoist them aboard with the ship's tackle. It was obvious to Drake that the men were beginning to take sides, and unless Doughty changed his ways immediately, his disobedience could no longer go unpunished. With the seas continually swelling the farther south they sailed, Drake realized that he would need to scuttle the *Christopher* as well, or else they would lose the weather, wasting time waiting to reassemble the fleet. He boarded the *Elizabeth* and warned his men that "a very bad couple of men" would be sent to them, "the which he did not know how to carry along with him . . . Thomas Doughty is a conjuror, a seditious fellow . . . and his brother . . . a witch, a poisoner and such a one as the world can judge of. I cannot tell from whence he came, but from the Devil I think."[7] Then he reminded his men that they were on a quest for treasure beyond their wildest dreams. He could only hope they would remain focused on the last part of his message.

Not far north of the Strait of Magellan stood a ghostlike relic of doom and foreboding—the fifty-eight-year-old wooden scaffold erected by Ferdinand Magellan when he hanged one of his men for mutiny. Whether or not the eerie sight of Magellan's gallows stirred Drake into action as they finally entered the harbor of Port St. Julian was never recorded, but the fact remains that at Port St. Julian, Thomas Doughty would be put on trial at last. But first Drake needed to secure their anchorage, for shortly after they arrived, a fatal skirmish with the local Indians saw two of Drake's men killed. To avoid further attacks by the hostile natives, the Englishmen were ordered to pitch their tents on a rocky island in the harbor. And still, in the midst of grave danger, Doughty continually criticized their commander. The following day, they were all summoned before Drake. He was mightily fed up. Thomas Doughty would be tried for mutiny and witchcraft.

Doughty, a clever, trained lawyer, claimed that Drake had no jurisdiction to put him on trial and that he would answer only to the "Queen's court" in England. He was, strictly speaking, right. Unless

Drake could produce a written commission signed by the queen herself, he had no authority to act *in loco reginae*. But how could Drake produce such a document when Elizabeth had sworn him to secrecy, even from Burghley? He, like so many "spies" and agents provocateurs before and after him, had no papers for the express reason that the queen could disown their actions if they were captured. All Drake carried with him was his written instructions, unendorsed by queen or council. Doughty must have known this, and his claim that Drake did not have a royal commission almost had the proceedings go his way.

Drake blustered that Doughty had poisoned the Earl of Essex, that he was poisoning his men against him, too. Doughty, instead of staying on strong ground, allowed himself to get diverted into a shouting match with Drake, claiming that he was in the pay of Lord Burghley, who had knowledge of the voyage from none other than Doughty himself. "Lo, my masters," Drake declared, "what this fellow hath done! God will have his treacheries all known for Her Majesty gave me special commandment that of all men my lord treasurer should not know it, but to see his own mouth hath betrayed him!"[8]

Now it was made generally known to the sailors that Burghley disapproved of plundering and would have stopped their voyage from setting sail if he had known their true purpose. Drake produced some papers for his men, presumably his written instructions. They were, after all, now sworn in properly as jurors of the kangaroo court. Eventually, Drake prevailed, and they supported him in his assertion that he had the queen's blessing. Witnesses for and against Doughty were heard. Then, Drake set out the alternatives to the jurors once all the evidence had been heard for and against Doughty:

> *And now my masters, consider what a great voyage we are like to make, the like was never made out of England, for by the same the worst in this fleet shall become a gentleman, and if this voyage go not forward, which I cannot see how possible it should if this man live, what a reproach it will be, not only unto our country but especially unto us, the very simplest here may consider of. Therefore, my masters, they that think this man worthy to die, let them with me hold up their hands.*[9]

The choices were stark. If they returned home to have Doughty tried, they would incur the wrath of the queen, who Drake maintained to his men, had ventured a thousand crowns. And that was before their other powerful backers like Hatton, Walsingham, and Leicester sank their teeth into them. To send Doughty back home with a ship, and in the company of some men (for Doughty was no sailor), would weaken the expedition too much and put their own lives at risk. To leave Doughty at Port St. Julian would guarantee him a slow and lingering death at the hands of hostile natives. The men voted unanimously to execute Doughty.

In the end, Doughty met his maker with great courage befitting an Elizabethan gentleman. He chose to die by the axe, and made his will. He shared the sacrament with Drake, and then they had a last dinner together. At the end, they had a few moments together, but their conversation was never recorded. He begged all the men to forgive him, and Drake promised that there would be no further reprisals—specifically against Doughty's younger brother, John. Doughty's head was severed in one blow then held aloft by Drake as the head of a mutineer.

Drake reminded his men of the huge task ahead of them. There would be no arbitrary class distinctions between them any longer. Each life would depend in future upon the goodwill of the others. Old wounds from the Doughty business could not be allowed to fester, and they must all work together for queen and country. If they failed to sail on, "what triumph it would be to Spain and Portugal, and again the like would never be attempted." Having said his piece, Drake begged the men to take a vote on whether or not they wanted to continue. He had been relying on promise of Spanish treasure and plunder, of riches beyond their wildest imaginings, not upon any twentieth century notion of patriotism. They agreed to follow their commander to the ends of the world.

And so, on August 17, 1578, nearly two months to the day after they reached Port St. Julian, that desolate site of two executions for mutiny, Drake and his men burned the *Mary* to reduce the squadron to just the *Pelican*, the *Elizabeth*, and the *Marigold*, and sailed into the unknown.

25. Into the Jaws of Death 彡

But escaping from these straits and miseries, as it were
through the needle's eye . . . we could now no longer
forbear, but must needs find some place of refuge . . . thus
worn out by so many and so long intolerable toils; the
like whereof, it is supposed, no traveler hath felt, neither
hath there ever been such a tempest, so violent and of such
continuance since Noah's flood. . . .

—SIR FRANCIS DRAKE, OCTOBER 1579

Three days later, the ships were confronted with the Cape of Virgins some four leagues off, rising sharply as sheer, gray peaks in the distance. These were the sentinels that guarded the entry to the Strait of Magellan "full of black stars against which the sea beating, showed as it were, the spoutings of whales."[1] It was a terrifying and solemn moment, and breathtakingly momentous for Drake and his men. The seas swelled and rocked them off their feet, as if in warning that they should not dare to enter the forbidden territory. The moment of awe had to pass if they were to become masters of their destiny, Drake's instinct told him, so he ordered the fleet to strike their topsails in homage to their Sovereign Lady, Queen Elizabeth. Then in remembrance of Christopher Hatton, the *Pelican* was rechristened The *Golden Hind*.[2] With Doughty's demise still fresh in his mind, it was a necessary demonstration of respect for his patron.

The ceremonies had the desired effect of whipping up the men's lust for plunder and glory. But until they were favored with a good wind from the northeast, entering the straits would be impossible. And so they waited in the shadows of the Cape of Virgins beating back and forth against the current. And then they waited more. Finally, two long days later, the ships entered the yawning mouth of the Strait of Magellan, which must have seemed biblical to the preaching side of Drake, reminding him of Jonah and the "great fish." No one aboard any of the ships—including their Portuguese pilot, Nuño da Silva—had ever passed through the forbidding straits before. No one even knew that it was a three-hundred-mile-long twisting waterway. All charts were hopelessly inaccurate. All they knew is that it was riddled with false trails and turns and had claimed the lives of hundreds of sailors before them. They also knew—falsely, as it turns out—that the Strait of Magellan was the channel between the tip of South America and "Terra Australis." They could only pray that the winds would remain at their backs, and the currents run steadily from east to west by northwest.

Drake ordered that they keep to midchannel to avoid any unknown shoals, which at first was relatively easy, for "the ebbings and flowings [there] being as orderly as on other coasts."[3] The shores to either side were flat and low at this point, but the general knew better than to breathe any sighs of relief. On August 24, St. Bartholomew's Day, they "fell with three islands bearing triangle-wise one from another; one of them was very fair and large and of fruitful soil, upon which, being next unto us and the weather very calm, our general with his gentlemen and certain of his mariners, then landed, taking possession thereof in Her Majesty's name, and to her use, and called the same Elizabeth Island."[4] They christened the other two islands St. George, after England's flag, and St. Bartholomew, to mark the day. Since the weather was so good, Drake gave the order to reprovision and scavenge for food and wood. The discovery of a human skeleton on St. George's drove home to them again the dangerous nature of their expedition.

Their main source of fresh food was penguins, described as having a "body less than a goose and bigger than a mallard." An estimated three thousand inhabited the islands before the arrival of the Englishmen, when several hundred were bludgeoned and stored aboard ship. After reprovisioning, Drake ordered them to sail on while the weather and wind remained with them. "From these islands to the entrance into the South Sea," Drake later remarked, "the fret is very crooked, having many turnings, and so it were shuttings up, as if there were no passage at all, by means whereof we were often troubled with contrary winds, so that some of our ships recovering a cape of land, entering another reach, the rest were forced to alter their course and come to anchor where they might."[5]

As they progressed, the land to both sides soared again to dizzying heights, like gray basalt columns of glass covered in snow. Drake remarked that to the northerly side of the straits lay the continent of America, and to the south and east "nothing but islands, among which lie innumerable frets or passages into the South Seas."[6] Until now, the current had by and large been with them, but when the winds varied, the sea was whipped up into eddies and whirlpools and it became impossible for Drake to sound for depth or too dangerous or deep to anchor. When they found anchorage, the rock face was so jagged that it frayed the hemp cables. The landscape was foreign and difficult to describe. Drake later called it a land of "congealed cloud" and "frozen meteors."

Then, about 150 miles into the channel, as they wended their way to the northwest, through the myriad islands scattered in the straits, the wind swung around to a strong gusting westerly. It funneled between the mountains, howling a gale and churning up the sea. For the next 150 miles, they battled the weather emerging, in only fourteen days, on September 6, 1578, into the South Seas. It had taken Magellan thirty-seven.[7]

But Drake had no time to rest on his laurels. His instructions ordered him to head along the Chilean coast to Peru. Consulting the charts again, they turned northwesterly, but after two or more days of good progress, all they could see from every horizon was the stunning blue sea. The charts, he reasoned, had to be wrong. And so, with heavy hearts, they luffed around and headed back to where they had been disgorged into the Pacific. The Chilean coast had to lie to the north, not to the northwest. This, too, was a significant geographical discovery, though not the purpose of the voyage.

Terrible weeks ensued. Instead of finding the Chilean coast where they expected to, they mistakenly reentered the Strait of Magellan. Screaming winds and torrential rain remorselessly pummeled the ships, threatening hourly to crash them upon the rocks. When it wasn't raining, it was so foggy they could barely see the bow of the ship, much less between ships, and all they could hear was the eerie roar of the waves echoing as they broke on the rocks. At times they beat southwesterly toward the open sea between South America and

Antarctica; at other times they simply clawed their way along the northern shore of the straits. Finally, at some time toward the end of September, the *Marigold* was lost with all twenty-nine hands on board. Drake pretended for a time that they had merely lost sight of her, but he couldn't deny the "fearful cries" they had all heard the night she vanished.

They were most likely within reach of Cape Horn when Captain Winter, aboard the *Elizabeth*, had had enough and turned his ship back to England. He later claimed that he had no choice in the "fog and outrageous winter" if he were to avoid shipwreck. The fact remains that Winter and his men reentered the Magellan Strait, found shelter for a few weeks to recover from their ordeal, then knowingly, willingly sailed for England. Winter disclaimed authorship of the idea, but his men insisted that the decision had been his and his alone.[8] When the *Elizabeth* anchored in Ilfracombe, Devon, in June 1579, it was the first news that Plymouth and the court had had of Drake and his successful passage into the South Seas. The important question that Winter was unable to answer though was if Drake had survived the storms that had made them turn back.

Of course, Drake had survived. He had also made his second great geographic discovery. The Strait of Magellan was not the tip of South America. And he was the first European commander to sail around the southernmost tip of South America from the Atlantic into the Pacific.[9] But Drake was not an explorer. His mission was to plunder the western coast of Spanish America, and to bring the treasure back to England.

26. The Famous Voyage ✣

You will say that this man who steals by day and prays by night in public is a devil. . . . I would not wish to take anything except what belongs to King Philip and Don Martín Enríquez. . . . I am not going to stop until I collect two millions which my cousin, John Hawkins, lost at San Juan d'Ulúa.

—FRANCIS DRAKE, NOVEMBER 1578

While Drake was turning north toward the Chilean coast into the vast unknown, Elizabeth was facing a greater enemy at home. Men like Drake were rare, and while most of her courtiers and other adventurers rallied round to the greater threat imposed by an ever-stronger Spain, few had the daring and bravado to get under Philip's skin in the way *El Draco* did. And none other than Drake understood the element of surprise. The queen had come to the realization that her adventurers were her only defensive and offensive weapons of any importance, and there were precious few of them. England's merchant navy was small, with fewer than twenty ships above 200 tons. "Officially" between 1578 and 1581, they would snaffle no more than ten Spanish ships in the entire world. And Drake alone took at least twelve of them.[1]

Europe teetered once again on the brink. In the Low Countries, Alexander Farnese, the Duke of Parma and Philip's nephew, had been appointed to execute the King of Spain's will with intolerable brutality and cruelty against the Dutch. While the Spanish Fury raged in the Low Countries, Henry of Guise, uncle to Mary, Queen of Scots, had become Philip's puppet and had the ear of the French king. As if the neutralization of France wasn't bad enough, Walsingham's and Burghley's spies reported that something was afoot in Munster again, this time backed by the pope. And while King Sebastian of Portugal had been killed along with the ubiquitous Thomas

Stucley in the Battle of the Three Kings at Alcazar in Morocco, his uncle Henry d'Evora, the sickly, elderly cardinal and head of the Inquisition in Portugal, was crowned Portugal's new king. Worse still, Philip of Spain, according to Henry, had the next best claim to the Portuguese throne on his death. If Spain united with Portugal, all hope of checking Philip's pernicious anti-Protestant influence against Elizabeth would be lost forever.[2]

This was the queen's view of the tempests brewing in Europe. Of the Pacific and Drake, she could only wonder how they were faring, if she thought of them at all. Still God hadn't abandoned them, in Drake's words. After fifty days of a raging storm that had cost him his tiny fleet, the commander headed toward the rendezvous at 30° south and anchored twelve fathoms off the island of Mocha. But Drake had misjudged the animosity of the natives against the Spanish. As they rowed ashore, they were met with a shower of darts and arrows whistling directly at them, forcing them to retreat, while the natives splashed through the waves in pursuit. Drake was struck twice in the head, with one arrow narrowly missing his right eye. Their barber-surgeon was dead. Two of his best masters had been captured and butchered by the time Drake reached the *Hind*. They had been mistaken for Spaniards, clearly, and it was a salutary lesson to Drake for the future.[3] They were left with little choice but to weigh anchor, and abandon all further hope of meeting up with the *Elizabeth*.

Four days later, on November 30, they came across an Indian in a canoe and cajoled him into becoming their pilot along the coast of Chile in exchange for trinkets. He led them to Valparaiso, where the *Captain of Moriall*, admiral of the fleet of the Solomon Islands, was moored in harbor. They certainly saw the windswept, barnacled ship pulling alongside, for they drummed her in as a sign of welcome. Despite the fact that they didn't recognize the ship or her colors, it didn't matter—there were no strangers in the South Seas—also affectionately called the Spanish Lake. It was only when the *Captain of Moriall* was boarded that the truth finally became apparent.

The Spanish were herded into the hold, barring one who jumped overboard and swam toward shore to raise the alarm. He needn't have bothered. Drake loaded two boats with his men armed to the teeth and captured the town without a shot being fired. All the inhabitants had abandoned it, fearing for their lives. In their first encounter against Spain's "forces," the English had been triumphant. As their reward, they ransacked the port of Valparaiso in an orgy of looting.

They had resolved to take along the Spanish ship's pilot, naturally hoping that he would be useful in sailing farther north. The *Captain of Moriall* had also been laden with alcohol and "a certain quantity of fine gold of Baldinia, and a great cross of gold beset with emeralds," the memoirs of the voyage tells us, and "we spent some time in refreshing ourselves, and easing [plundering] this ship of so heavy a burden on the 8th day of the same month [December] having in the meantime sufficiently stored ourselves with necessaries, as wine, bread, bacon, etc., for a long season."[4]

Drake and his men loaded four chests containing an estimated 25,000 *pesos de oro* worth of gold ($3.46 million or £1.87 million today), as well as some fine Spanish wine.[5] The port's warehouses and homes provided them with food, and its church with some silver. As they said their good-byes to Valparaiso, it was undoubtedly a grateful crew who bathed themselves in the glory of their first real prize in over a year at sea. All of Drake's promises could be believed, and the hardships they had endured were worth it. They were already wealthy men.[6]

But Drake knew that this was only the beginning, providing he could stay ahead of the news announcing his arrival in the South Seas. If word reached Lima before he did, then Spanish shipping would scatter at sea, and an offensive would be mounted against their lone ship. Still, the immediate problem he had to cope with was to see to the repairs the *Golden Hind* so desperately needed, mounting the full complement of her heavy guns, and building the pinnace they had brought along for their plundering and inshore work.

Drake still hoped against hope that he might find the *Elizabeth* and perhaps even the *Marigold*, and he decided to start work on the *Hind* near the appointed rendezvous at 30° south. On December 19, 1578, a party of Spanish horse and foot attacked a dozen of his men who were working onshore collecting fresh water. One Englishman was killed before the rovers were rescued by boats launched hastily

from the *Hind*. The dead man, Richard Minivy, had his heart carved
out and was beheaded in full view of the general and crew. The
rewards of their labors might be high, but so were the risks.

They moved on to Salada Bay, near Coquimbo, where they
completed their preparations to raid the treasure fleet from Peru,
which had been Drake's long-held dream since Darien. A pinnace
large enough to take forty men and a culverin in its bow was built,
while essential repairs for leaks and the full complement of the *Hind*'s
heavy guns were mounted. As they headed north toward Lima, two
more barks were taken with forty odd bars of silver "the bigness
and fashion of a brick bat" and each weighing twenty pounds,
not to mention the thirteen bars of silver from a Spaniard asleep
on the beach valued at 4,000 ducats ($338,217 or £182,820 today).
Fortunately for the Spaniard, he was a sound sleeper, though poorer
when he awoke.[7]

At Arica, on February 9, 1579, the English corsairs fell upon
another bark in the middle of loading thirty-seven bars of silver
and a chest of silver coin that they simply had to help themselves to,
followed shortly after by another bark laden with fresh linen and
wine. It was too tempting a prize for men who had been at sea for
fifteen months to ignore.[8] Still, it was a rather disappointing haul,
since Arica was the port for the legendary Potosi mines.

But worse was yet to come. After Arica, they headed to the
small port of Chule, where they took on a little water. They soon
learned that the news of their piracy had traveled fast—two hours
before they had anchored, a bullion vessel had left fully loaded.
The locals jeered at them from the quayside, hurling verbal abuse
and laughing at them for being so slow. The element of surprise
had been squandered on meager prizes, while overland messengers
carried the word that *El Draco*—Drake, the dragon—had found his
way into the South Seas. The time for pinpricks to Spain's empire
was at an end.

Drake set the prize ships adrift and released all his prisoners, save
two Spanish pilots who set their course for Callao, the port for Lima.
More prizes were taken en route, more with a view to intelligence
than capturing gold, and at last Drake was rewarded for his diligence.
There was a silver vessel bound for Panama at Callao and another

ship, *Nuestra Señora de la Concepcíon*—irreverently rebranded the *Cacafuego* or "Shitfire"[9] by her crew—that had just left Callao for Panama. The Spanish captain thought that the *Cacafuego* was richly laden with silver, and had overheard that she would be stopping at several ports to take on consignments of flour.

The problem for Drake was both ships had silver and not gold, making his choice of which one to go for more difficult. Callao was nearest, so he plumbed for the port, reasoning that the overland couriers hadn't reached there yet. Quite late in the night of February 15, 1579, Drake snuck into the harbor of Callao between the island of San Lorenzo and the mainland. The port was full of sail, and all seemed quiet. He ordered his pinnace to steal between the ships at anchor and have his men see if they were laden with treasure, and he was disappointed to learn that all of the ships had not as yet taken their cargoes on board. Rather than attack the customs house carrying an estimated 200,000 pesos in silver and risk word leaking out to Lima quickly, he gave the order to cut the cables of all the ships and hack down the main masts of the two largest vessels in harbor, escaping only with some silk and a chest containing some Spanish *reals*.[10] They would instead, he resolved, give chase to the *Cacafuego*.

But while they were amassing their plunder, another ship sailed innocently into harbor. The *San Cristobal* had arrived from Panama with her merchandise for Peru. The customs officials boarding the *San Cristobal* first noticed the activity aboard the *Hind*, and rowed across, hailing to her to identify herself. A Spanish voice replied from the *Hind* that she was Miguel Angel's ship from Chile (the one that had made a narrow escape in Arica). As the customs officer hauled himself aboard, he stared directly into the mouth of an English brass culverin. He immediately realized his mistake, fell back into his boat, and rowed as fast as he could to save his life. The crew of the *San Cristobal* saw—and, importantly, heard—what had happened, but before they could do anything, Drake's pinnace had captured her. Her crew either swam to safety, or escaped in lowered boats, allowing Drake's rovers to invade and take control.

The *Hind*'s sails filled and she tacked about. While the militia was being raised in the town, witnesses could see the *San Cristobal* in the distance being plundered by the pirates. But before they could attack, Drake and his pirates had sailed after the *Cacafuego*. All along the coast northward, they had news of their prey. From their next prize they learned that she was three days ahead of them. When they raided the port at Paita, the *Cacafuego*'s lead had been cut to two days. Their next two vessels attacked brought the rovers gold, silver, food, and new ships' tackle that its owner later valued at 24,000 *pesos de oro* ($3.31 million or £1.79 million today).[11]

A golden reward was offered to the first mariner to spot the *Cacafuego* on the horizon. On March 1st at around three in the afternoon, young John Drake, aloft in the crow's nest, claimed the gold chain, spying their prey around four leagues to the south. Naturally, the *Cacafuego* had no knowledge whatsoever of the danger she was in. In order not to scare her into flight, it would be impossible to strike the sails, so Drake ordered pots to be filled with water, tied to ropes, then thrown astern. This would put a great drag on the *Hind* and lull the *Cacafuego* into believing that the *Hind* was just a small merchantman on the same heading, and moving at a normal speed for a Spanish ship.

The Spanish ship's owner and captain, San Juan de Anton, spied the *Hind* and thought at first she might be from Chile. According to Drake's plan, they gained slowly on the *Cacafuego* without her taking fright. By nine in the evening, when the *Hind* was virtually alongside, her captain rang a salute, but there was no answer from the strange vessel. Anton came over to the side to investigate. But by then it was too late.

The English were already grappling alongside from the pinnace. Drake's drum and trumpet sounded the attack from the opposite side. After this, Drake's narrative reports that:

> *what seemed to be about sixty harquebuses were shot, followed by many arrows, which struck the side of the ship, and chainballs shot from a heavy piece of ordnance carried away the mizzen [mast] and sent it into the sea with its sail and lateen yard. After this the English shot another great gun, shouting again, "Strike sail!" and simultaneously a pinnace laid aboard to port and about forty archers climbed up the channels of the shrouds and entered [the]*

ship while, at the opposite side, the English ship laid aboard. It was
thus that they forced San Juan's ship to surrender . . . they seized
him and carried him to the English ship where he saw the corsair
Francis Drake, who was removing his helmet and coat of mail.
Drake embraced [him] saying "Have patience, for such is the usage
of war," and immediately ordered him to be locked up in the cabin
in the poop.[12]

And what a prize she was! Much needed fresh fruits, conserves, sugars, meal, and other victuals were pounced upon by Drake's ravenous men. The general himself, with his masters, went immediately below to see the reason for the *Cacafuego*'s slow sailing. There was "a certain quantity of jewels and precious stones, 13 chests of *reals* of plate, 80 pounds weight in gold, 26 tons of uncoined silver, two very fair gilt silver drinking bowls, and the like trifles, valued in all at about 360,000 pesos."[13] This represents $49.62 million or £26.82 million today. An estimated half of the prize had belonged to Philip of Spain. It took them six days to secure the booty aboard the *Hind*, before leaving San Juan de Anton and his crew behind to beat a path to Panama to sound the alarm.

Drake knew that he hadn't fooled any of the Spaniards into believing that he would be stupid enough to return along the South American coast through the straits to home, but he tried to dissemble with them anyway. What the Spaniards hadn't realized was that Drake had promised the queen, Hatton, Leicester, and Walsingham that he would search for the western entry to the fabled Strait of Anian, mark the entry to the Northwest Passage, and, if possible, head back to England that way. But Drake knew better than anyone that if he hugged the coast, it would mean suicide. So his first move was to strike out to sea again, heading in a northwesterly direction "by guess and by God." But by the time they had reached somewhere around modern Vancouver they had been so engulfed in icy fogs and fierce northwesterlies that the *Hind*, squatting badly on the seas with her spectacular treasure, began leaking. They had been at sea again for fifty days, and food and fresh water were once more running low. There was no alternative but to turn back. Finally, they reached a haven somewhere between 38° and 48° north.[14]

The *Hind* was finally hauled ashore for careening and trimming around June 5, 1579. The natives, immediately friendly toward the Englishmen, were obviously intrigued by their vessel, clothing, trinkets, and skin color. Evidently, it was their first encounter with Europeans. On June 29, 1579, the tribal chief came down the mountain, followed by hundreds of men and women all dancing and singing in celebration, and bearing gifts for the English. The chief bade them all to be silent while he made a speech, which, of course, Drake and his men were unable to understand, but they surmised that "it was their intent, the king himself, with all the singing a song, set a crown upon his [Drake's] head, enriched his neck with all their chains, and offering unto him many other things, honoured him by the name *Hyóh* . . . because they were not only visited of the gods (for so they still judged us to be), but the great and chief God was now become their God, their king and patron. . . . "[15]

Drake, duly crowned God, was now expected to speak. And so, he raised his newly hewn scepter and proclaimed this land New Albion, on behalf of Her Most Excellent Sovereign Majesty. After that, they begged their new God, Drake, to heal their sick or infirm with his "royal touch." All the English could do was to apply the same balms they ministered to themselves, and from that day until their last ashore, in what many assume to be modern day Drake's Bay, their devoted "subjects" rarely left them.

Before leaving the coast, Drake says that a "plate of brass" was struck and "fast nailed to a great and firm post whereon is engraven her Grace's name, and the day and year of our arrival there, and of the free giving up of the province and kingdom, both by the king and people, into Her Majesty's hands."[16]

On July 23, 1579, Drake struck out into the vastness of the Pacific Ocean, singularly ill prepared for the voyage ahead in the *Golden Hind*, which was after all a tiny ship measuring no more than a hundred feet in length and twenty in the beam, and heavily laden with fabulous treasure. While their number had dwindled to about sixty-five, the bare minimum Drake believed necessary to attempt a voyage around the world, he was certain it was the only course left to steer. His men had become well disciplined under his strict command, and they wanted only to get home safely to enjoy their new wealth. But Drake was no fool, and he realized that the length of time they might spend out of sight of land could lead to anything. The charts and sailing directions he had purloined showed him that the distance was greater than any shown on any map that had been made available to him previously. He therefore provisioned the ship for a longer voyage to stave off any privation or talk of mutiny, and kept his discovery to himself. Drake was thus able to avoid the problems that beset Magellan.

For sixty-eight days they sailed west, out of sight of land or man. Fortunately the winds and seas were favorable. Yet all they could hear was the swishing of the bow as it plowed through the ocean, the creaking of the *Hind*'s rigging and timbers, and the steady whir of the wind in its sails. The English made landfall in Micronesia, somewhere in the Carolinian archipelago on September 30, 1579. Naturally, they were glad to see land again, and apparently relieved at the "friendly" reception that awaited them. Hordes of natives in their dugout canoes paddled out to greet them, chattering and smiling, then clambering aboard the *Hind*. But all was not as it seemed. Soon they began arguing among themselves, taking the Englishmen's possessions when they refused to trade with them. Drake fired a warning shot, but that only scattered them temporarily. Though he was saddened and ashamed by it, he was compelled to fire directly at an approaching canoe, and blew it and its occupants to smithereens. Meanwhile, the order had been given to tack about, and the *Hind* and her men sailed away from the isle that Drake had already named the "Island of Thieves."[17] It was the ancestors of these same natives who had killed Magellan.

They next touched briefly at Mindanao in the Philippines, and sailed on to the legendary Spice Islands of the Moluccas. We can hardly imagine the tremendous sense of accomplishment Drake felt as he reached the Far Eastern frontier of the Spanish and Portuguese empires, for in that single moment, he had fulfilled the dreams of all explorers and navigators since Columbus more than eighty years earlier.

All his Spanish maps were now utterly useless. This was Portuguese territory, and Spain had relinquished her claim to the precious Spice Islands fifty years earlier. It also meant that Drake should change his tactics, especially if he wanted to create a toehold for his queen in the East. Fortunately for Drake, the bulk of the rich trade in cloves was in the hands of the Sultan of Ternate when he arrived. And the sultan had not been enamored with the Portuguese. Drake was assured of a warm welcome by the sultan's emissary.

The sultan was true to his word. The English were met with tremendous pomp and ceremony, with the *Hind* being towed into the best anchorage by the sultan's galley. The sultan himself, Babu, accompanied by three galleys rowed by eighty oarsmen each and soldiers lining the decks armed to the eyeballs, boarded the *Hind* to extend his personal welcome to Drake and his men. Babu, statuesque and imperious, bedecked in cloth of gold and red leather shoes with jewels strewn about his person, greeted the sea weary, stocky redheaded West Country Englishman as an equal. Drake ordered some of their treasure on deck so that he could show Babu that they truly were in possession of a fortune. The formalities at an end, Drake followed Babu to his fortress, where an agreement was hammered out for England to expel Portugal from the area if Babu would concede his trade in cloves to the Queen of England. In exchange, Drake gave his word that within two years "he would decorate that sea with ships for whatever purpose might be necessary . . . and gave [Babu] a gold ring set with a precious stone, a coat of mail, and a very fine helmet."[18]

Drake, of course, had no power to commit the queen to such an undertaking and the complications in international diplomacy it could unleash, but it did "buy" him six tons of top quality cloves that were laden into the *Hind*. Still, Drake certainly didn't trust Babu's effusion, nor did Babu completely trust Drake.[19] Three days later, with even more treasure—this time spices—in its hold, the *Hind* set out into the Indian Ocean. Somewhere off the northeastern coast of the Celebes, they found an uninhabited island with abundant wood and water, and all the victuals they could want. There Drake left three Negroes, including a woman named Maria, who had been brought from South America and had conceived a child aboard ship. By the narratives, and contrary to Drake's many detractors' theories, it seems that they wanted to establish a colony there, since it was "rich in all the necessities of life." Drake's faithful friend, Diego, of course, remained at his master's side.

As they sailed around into the Celebes Sea, the warm green waters hid the last great danger that Drake would have to face—a long, steep, coral reef only seven feet below the surface. The winds were driving them southward rather than west, and soon they found themselves lost in a maze of shallows and islands along the fingerlike east coast of the Celebes. Without any charts, maps, or personal knowledge, they had to navigate their way through—constantly beating back and forth—with "extraordinary care and circumspection."[20] Then, on January 9, 1580, at nine P.M., the unmistakable and spectacular grinding of the ship's wooden hull against the reef rocked the *Hind*. She had run aground and was listing perilously on the rocks.[21] In that single moment, all could have been lost, and no one was more acutely aware of that fact than the commander. Drake and his men began bailing the water out of the hold to inspect the damage. Somehow, most of the timbers were still intact and able to be repaired, if only they could work the ship loose from the reef. Drake took soundings, and only a single length away from the ship, the sea was so deep that he could find no sea floor. There was, however, no safe ground for the men to stand upon to haul the *Hind* off, and the nearest land, by their reckoning, was almost twenty miles away. Their pinnace could take only a third of their crew.

In the morning, Drake took his soundings again with no better results. Then he prayed, and his recalcitrant preacher Fletcher gave them the sacrament. The only alternative left to them, Drake said, was to lighten the *Hind*'s load. Three tons of cloves, victuals, ammunition, and two pieces of artillery were eventually tossed overboard, yet still the ship held fast. Then, as if by divine will, in the late afternoon the wind changed, and the *Hind* slid like an ungainly whale into deep water.[22]

Understandably, the next leg of the *Hind*'s voyage is not easily decipherable since the geography was completely unknown to Drake. Nonetheless, the *Hind* found itself at sea again, and was able to refit and recover from their ordeal at an island, avoiding the Malacca Strait, somewhere south of Java. Drake, despite the Portuguese presence in the region, was the first European to navigate successfully Java's southern coast, proving it was an island, separate from Terra Australis.

From the tip of Java, Drake and his men sailed out into the Indian Ocean on March 26, 1580, reaching the Cape of Good Hope in June. By the time they made landfall along the western coast of Africa at Sierra Leone, their water supplies were dangerously low, with only a half a pint to share between three men. Amazingly this 9,700-mile stretch of the voyage—from the tip of Java to Sierra Leone—is barely documented, though it must feature among Drake's greatest achievements, for even in the eighteenth century, it was "a thing hardly to be credited, and which was never performed by any mariner before his time or since."[23] His navigation of these waters in the tiny *Hind* without a safe base or any reliable map is tantamount to being launched to the moon out of a cannon, orbiting without instruments or ground control, then returning safely home.

Sierra Leone was no less spectacular a place to them than New Albion. The Englishmen were delighted and overawed at the sight of their first elephant, and the fabled "oyster tree" (the mangrove) of travelers' tales. More important, fresh water abounded, as did lemons and other fruits. Though it would be nearly two hundred years more before citrus fruits would be credited with staving off the deadly swelling, extreme muscular distension, and weakness of scurvy, Drake intuitively knew that it was keeping him and his men healthy. There were no recorded deaths from scurvy on his voyage.

From Sierra Leone, the Cape Verde Islands were only a stone's throw away comparatively speaking. As they headed on the final leg of their journey, Drake could but wonder if Elizabeth still was queen, or if Philip of Spain had at last succeeded in planting Mary Queen of Scots upon the English throne. Had the queen married? he wondered. Was the country at peace or at war? After all they had been through, he worried at last about what kind of reception they might receive at home.

On September 26, 1580, some local fishermen in the Channel spied a small, weather worn, heavily lying ship making her approach past them into Plymouth Sound. A stocky man with curly red hair hailed them and asked, "Is Elizabeth still queen?" Later they recalled that they thought it was a very odd question for an Englishman flying the flag of St. George to ask. One of them piped up proudly though in reply, "Aye, and in fine health, too!" Little did they know that they had been the welcoming party for one of the world's greatest adventures ever recorded.[24]

27. The World Is Not Enough ❧

When Captain Winter had returned in June 1579 with the *Elizabeth*, there was more than a fluttering of butterflies' wings at court and in the City of London. The country, then Europe, was thrown into utter disbelief. Bernardino de Mendoza, the Spanish ambassador to England, had been caught completely unaware. "The adventurers who provided money and ships for the voyage," he blustered in a report to Philip, "are beside themselves for joy, and I am told that there are some councillors amongst them. The people here are talking of nothing else but going out to plunder in a similar way."[1] Only Burghley remained calm. What else could he do? The expedition had left without his express knowledge of its final destination, and whatever his relationship with Doughty had been, that was at an end as well.

Three weeks before Drake returned, news reached the City from Seville merchants trading with London in the new Spanish Company that Drake had captured several prizes and taken 600,000 ducats ($50.47 million or £27.28 million today). The investors in the voyage—including Elizabeth—waited expectantly, hoping for an enormous windfall. The Portuguese ambassador had already petitioned the queen for restitution to Nuño da Silva for his losses, and in June 1580 the lord admiral, an investor in the expedition, too, ordered that goods "piratically taken on the seas by Francis Drake and his accomplices to be restored to the Portuguese."[2] But the only person guilty of the crimes and capable of any restoration at that point was Captain Winter, who had returned to England, abandoning his commander.

But Philip II knew more than he was letting on to others. In August 1579, the letters began arriving, and they did not stop for over a year. The South Seas colonies had been ravaged by "the boldness of this low man." The "Spanish Lake" that cosseted Philip's western empire, he knew, had become a vast Pacific Ocean where any corsair could become "lost" from reprisals. Still, putting things into perspective, Drake's thefts, though huge, were insignificant in the greater scheme of things. What mattered was that the navigational feat was colossal, and would not fail to inspire others. All Philip could do was to wait and see the extent of the damage before acting. In the meantime, he felt justified in the shift in his grand strategy by creating a Catholic League against England's heretic queen.

Drake, too, waited. Plymouth had had an outbreak of the plague, and he was deeply unsure how matters would stand with the queen. All he could hope was that the vastness of the treasure would please her. He remained ignorant of any changes in the political, social, or economic landscape that might affect his reception, and until John Brewer, Sir Christopher Hatton's trumpeter who had accompanied them on the voyage, returned, there would be no certainty. Drake's wife, Mary, and the mayor of Plymouth, John Blitheman, rowed out to the *Hind*, but whether they had a grasp of international affairs, or the queen's present frame of mind, is doubtful. And so Drake wrote to Leicester, Hatton, Walsingham, and the other backers to tell them he had safely returned with riches.

When Elizabeth learned that her pirate had returned with fabulous treasure, a quorum of privy councillors was immediately convened, but only the lord admiral was among the five members present who openly supported Drake. Burghley and Sussex concluded that Drake's booty should be registered at the Tower of London in preparation for its return. When the restitution order was put before Leicester, Walsingham, and Hatton, they refused to sign it. Why should they lose a fortune to please Philip of Spain? And so, while the gentlemen argued, Elizabeth quietly sent word to Drake that he needn't fear. She was summoning him to court and asked him to kindly bring her some samples from his great adventure.

Drake sprang into action, loading several packhorses with some gold and silver, and all of the precious jewels. When he arrived at court at Richmond, he was admitted immediately to the queen's privy chamber, where they remained quite alone for six hours. What was said between them was never recorded in full, but certainly the queen told Drake about the dreadful turn of events in Europe, while he pledged to do as she wished to help.

In 1579, the queen most likely explained, Philip had backed the papal expedition to Munster to foment an Irish uprising against England. An English expedition to Munster was under way, but the outcome remained uncertain. Charles IX of France had died, and his brother Henry was now King Henry III. The French king was under the influence of Henry of Guise who was both the uncle of Mary, Queen of Scots, and the puppet of Philip of Spain. Worse still, in January 1580, King Henry of Portugal had died, and Philip was claiming his right as heir to the Portuguese crown. The Portuguese wanted the natural nephew of King Henry, Dom Antonio de Crato, as their king, but Philip had successfully invaded Portugal both by land and by sea in the summer, and had declared himself king in Antonio's place. The Spanish and Portuguese empires were now one, and Philip was king of the largest empire that the world had ever known. In a sound bite that Drake could readily comprehend, Philip now had twelve oceangoing galleons from the Portuguese Royal Navy, doubling the size of his Indian guard and ocean fleet. The total combined shipping that he now held exceeded 250,000 tons—over six times that of England—and his great admiral, the Marquis of Santa Cruz, had branded Elizabeth "the pirate queen."[3]

In these circumstances, Drake's adventurous tales and evident vast plunder would have been like "heaven's dew" to the beleaguered queen. The Elizabeth Islands in the Strait of Magellan, New Albion in the South Seas, and a trade agreement with the Spice Islands would have made her recognize that there was no going back, no handing over, and certainly no abandoning her renegade captain. No matter what, Drake would not suffer, for he had served her loyally and extremely well.

While Drake left for home with orders to register the treasure aboard the *Hind* with Edmund Tremayne, clerk to the Privy Council and a former Member of Parliament for Plymouth, the court was electric with anticipation around him. Mendoza was outraged that the queen had received the pirate. Would the queen send him to the Tower? Or would she reward him? Rumors of the spectacular hoard grew, and soon all London knew about the great adventure.

Back in Plymouth, Drake did as his queen had requested. He took £10,000 ($3.42 million or £1.82 million today) for himself and £14,000 ($4.72 million or £2.55 million today) for his men, though it is entirely likely that he took more. Then Tremayne and his assistant began the arduous task of counting the treasure for registration and eventual transportation by land to the Tower. Tremayne's orders in the queen's hand, "To assist Francis Drake in sending up certain bullion brought into the realm by him, but to leave so much of it in Drake's hands as shall amount to the sum of £10,000, the leaving of which sum in his hands is to be kept most secret to himself alone" were carried out with part of the treasure remaining in custody in Plymouth, and the vast majority shipped overland to the Tower.[4]

In London, Elizabeth categorically refused to grant the Spanish ambassador an audience, writing instead to the outraged Mendoza that she had made a personal investigation of Drake's voyage and had determined that no harm had been done to the King of Spain. While the victims of Drake's depredations had begun submitting the dossiers relating to their losses, the alleged amounts pillaged skyrocketed. Many Spanish merchants had tried to avoid duties by shipping unregistered cargoes and blaming Drake for fictitiously high losses. English merchants in the new Spanish Company pressed the queen for restitution, fearing reprisals against their own businesses. Burghley complained bitterly to the queen that Drake had committed several acts of war. Elizabeth replied that so had Philip and Pope Gregory XIII in invading Ireland. The massacre of the papal troops at Smerwick had shown that Philip was garnering support against her, and she would not placate him by returning the treasure.

But why? Elizabeth was never so steadfast toward anyone except Leicester before this. The answer is simple really. After years of near-war with Spain, of balancing Spain's power against that of France, of weighing the possibilities of one marital match against another to protect England, of protecting England's borders from Scotland and Ireland while helping to support the Netherlanders in their bid to return to their ancient rights, the queen's coffers were emptying too rapidly for the continued security of the realm. Wars were "easily begun, but not so soon ended," to use one of her favorite expressions, and yet for the millions that the queen had poured into securing the realm, it was all she could do to tread water and not drown. And now Drake—coupled with Antonio de Crato, who had brought her the fabulous Portuguese crown jewels to help pay for an English expedition to reclaim his country—offered the parsimonious queen a real opportunity to stop handling by half measures the most dangerous situation she faced. Spain needed to be checked, and by restoring Drake's plunder, she would only succeed in limiting her possibilities to maneuver.[5]

And, to add to the mystery, there were literally tons of swag that had not been registered either at Plymouth or at the Tower of London. Tremayne's official report of what had been sent to the Tower from Plymouth's Saltash Castle shows "forty-six parcels of treasure average over two hundred-weight each," or almost five tons. This was, of course, after Drake had siphoned off the £24,000 for himself and his men. Another account in Burghley's State Papers states that there were ten tons of silver bullion delivered.[6] What of the twenty-six tons of uncoined silver alone that Drake himself claimed to have taken?

Then there were the Royal Warrants for coins refined. In this manner, Sir Christopher Hatton received £2,300; Sir Francis Walsingham, £4,000; and the Earl of Leicester, £4,000 in newly minted coins. A further £29,635 was refined into "clean ingots" in their names.[7] The truth of the matter is that the backers were happy to admit to a windfall profit of 4,700 percent on their investment, but, officially, millions went unaccounted for.

Unofficially, it has been estimated that the queen's share exceeded a full year's expenditure for the entire realm. This is backed up by the fact that she gave over £100,000 to Francis, now Duke of Anjou, and again a suitor for Elizabeth's hand, to help the Dutch in their struggle against Spain shortly after Drake's return. By early 1581, Leicester had accompanied Anjou to the Low Countries with hundreds of courtiers as a sign of the queen's goodwill, and also negotiated with Francisco Rodriguez (a former victim of Hawkins's thefts) for the pawning of some of the finest of the Portuguese crown's diamonds.[8] Without Drake, Elizabeth simply would have been unable to support the Dutch or defend the realm in full measure as she would do over the coming years. Harvesting the sea was beginning to have its distinct attractions.

Still, the Queen of England could never admit in official circles that this was the case. She dissembled with Philip as she had done with Mendoza, feigning disbelief at his "*Memoria de los Cossarios Ingleses que han hecho robas en las Indias*" ("Memorandum concerning the robberies of the English Corsairs in the Indies").[9] Her "engagement" to Anjou neutralized any French action against her, and effectively made Anjou her puppet in the Low Countries. Her sweet talking Antonio de Crato was to keep possible invasion of Portugal open as an option in the event of a full-fledged war with Spain. And the agreement hammered out by William Harborne in Turkey ushered in a new era of legitimate trade with Sultan Murad III and the beginning of the Levant Company through its special Charter of Privileges.

Coded messages to her enemies were the golden thread stringing all her disparate foreign policies together. While the queen's enemies and her more conservative advisors like Burghley may have been dismayed at her behavior, she had read the mood of the nation perfectly: the country was puffing out its chest with pride at Drake's exploits. England would no longer kowtow to Spain's demands that she ignore the sea.

And so, on April 1, 1581, the queen decided to give her enemies the key to her cipher. The *Golden Hind* had made the voyage from Plymouth to Deptford to show her to the queen, as requested. Naturally, much of London rushed to the quayside to glimpse a view of the ship that had given them hope for the future. The throng was huge, with a hundred or so well wishers collapsing the plank across which the queen had walked to climb aboard the *Hind* moments earlier. They scrabbled in the mudflats below, uninjured, and entertaining other onlookers with their antics in trying to escape. The queen was entertaining, too, losing one of her garters, which was fetched back to her by Monsieur de Marchaumont, the French ambassador. It was purple and gold, and Elizabeth raised her skirts, placing it upon her leg in front of the crowd, promising, like the coquette she was, that she would send it on to the ambassador as a keepsake when she had finished with it. After the royal banquet on deck, Drake was made to stoop before her. She mused aloud to the assembled audience if she should strike off his head with her gilded sword she held aloft. Naturally, there were defiant howls of "NO!" The queen smiled, lowering her eyes and nodding to her people, then passed the golden sword to de Marchaumont and asked him to kindly perform the ceremony of knighthood. The queen now had France, and Sir Francis Drake to protect her realm and harvest the seas.

As if to prove her right, Drake ordered a present of 1,200 crowns to be divided among the queen's officers aboard the *Golden Hind*, and presented a large silver tray with a diamond frog to Elizabeth herself, to symbolize their understanding with France.[10]

28. Elizabeth Strikes Back in the Levant ✦

One must be a fox in order to recognize traps, and a lion to frighten off wolves.
—NICCOLÒ MACHIAVELLI, *The Prince*, 1531[1]

Until the early 1580s, foreign policy was underpinned by the three-legged stool of trade, plunder, and, in the case of Ireland, settlement. This period experienced a metaphorical tug-of-war between bona fide merchants seeking fresh outlets for legitimate trade, Elizabethan corsairs looking to get rich, and the new imperialists like Walter Raleigh, who had a vision to make colonization enrobe and dominate trade and plunder. Elizabeth, despite what her detractors may say, was not an imperialist. But like Drake with Doughty, she, too, had had enough poking and prodding by the pope and the King of Spain. Her difficulty remained in controlling the various factions at home to the benefit of England abroad.

Elizabeth's deeply Protestant—even puritanical—party, led by Leicester and Walsingham, wanted her to protect the Dutch, at almost any cost. By agreeing to finance the Duke of Anjou's elected rule in the Low Countries, her commitment was clear, and her risks were small.[2] Trade had been so erratic in the previous decade that the Low Countries had ceased to be the powerhouse it had been twenty years before, and had become instead a symbol of Spain's might or religious freedom or persecution, depending on the point of view. But the queen was adamant, the Netherlands was not a colony or province of England, nor would it ever become one. To go down that weary road would mean all out war with Spain. Indeed, William of Orange paid dearly for welcoming Anjou as their leader in 1582 by an assassination attempt on his life funded by Philip of Spain. What did interest Elizabeth were the opportunities to renew trade in places that had been a blank canvas until recent years, like the Levant. Walsingham, too, saw the merit of trade and recommended that

> *the first thing that is to be done to withstand their fines [customs duties] is to make choice of some apt man to be sent with her Majesty's letters unto the Turk to procure an ample safe conduct, who is always to remain there at the charge of the merchants, as agent to impeach the indirect practises of the said Ambassadors, whose repair thither is to be handled with great secrecy, and his voyage to be performed rather by land than by sea.*[3]

William Harborne was just the man whom the leaders of the Levant Company, Osborne and Staper, identified for the job. He could promise precisely what the Turks wanted, and what the pope had forbidden as an export from Christendom—munitions. By allying herself with the Ottoman Empire, Philip's main enemy, and contravening an edict from the pope, Elizabeth knew she could not only reap the rewards of the Levant trade but also annoy her two main enemies while adopting her favorite stance: feigning innocence. In May 1580, Harborne succeeded in procuring a complex charter of privileges from Sultan Murad III, which took the form of a unilateral treaty. It offered fabulous trading privileges merely for the friendship of the English queen. The reason for his munificence was, of course, a complete work of fiction. But it wasn't all smooth sailing.

In April 1581, shortly after Drake had been knighted, an English ship called *Bark Roe* had been blissfully unaware of the importance of the new entente with the sultan and, after spending some time with Harborne at Chios, seized and plundered two merchantmen belonging to Greek subjects of Murad III. Harborne was arrested and locked up for piracy, and all English privileges were summarily withdrawn. Two months later, the queen was obliged to humbly apologize, and she offered to send a permanent ambassador to Constantinople to avoid such terrible misunderstandings of their amity.[4]

Harborne was released and, after a brief sojourn in England, returned as the queen's ambassador from 1583 to 1588. In that time, he set up a network of consulates in Egypt, Syria, Algeria, Tunisia, Lebanon, and Libya. One of the Levant Company's most forward thinking traders, John Newbery, set up trading posts stretching from Aleppo in Syria to India. English traders plied the Mediterranean freely bringing back Turkish carpets, Persian silk, sweet oils and wines, currants, and other delicacies from the Levant. They also traded in pepper, and other rare spices like cloves, nutmeg, ginger, and cinnamon, cutting out the middlemen between the Levant and England. England had more choice at cheaper prices in its luxury markets. The Levant Company at last fulfilled the trading aspirations that so many other trading companies, including the Muscovy Company, had simply failed to do. Undoubtedly Newbery, more than any other merchant so far, understood how the system in the Middle East worked. His journal took account of commodity prices, customs duties, cultural differences, transport costs, local caravan trading routes and much more.[5] And the more he succeeded, the angrier Philip II became. But the king was not the only one.

The temptation to link the Middle East to the East was huge, particularly since Newbery had been so successful in setting up his trading posts as far as India. In Newbery's 1583 voyage to the East, he not only carried the queen's letters of introduction to Akbar the Great and "the king of China," but sailing with him in the *Tiger* were the merchants Ralph Fitch (who would later become famous for his involvement in the East India Company), Ralph Allen, John Eldred, William Shales, and William Skinner, along with a jeweler, William Leeds, and a painter named James Story. The queen herself had "lent" 10,000 pounds in weight in silver to Osborne, Staper, and their partners for the journey—silver certainly looted from Spain's empire by Drake. While all the merchants except Fitch and Newbery were to be left at Baghdad and Basra to set up their trading posts, Newbery, Fitch, the jeweler, and the painter went on to India. But why?

India was, until the mid-eighteenth century, the only place where diamonds of any quality could be found. It was also where rubies, emeralds, and pearls abounded along with gold. John Dee had been consulted by Newbery before leaving London, and it was evident that the intention of their reconnaissance into India was to acquire "great quantities of diamonds, pearls and rubies, etc. to which end they brought with them a great sum of money and gold, and that very secretly."[6]

In August, within ten days of setting up their trading post in Hormuz, Newbery and Fitch were arrested and shipped to prison in Goa. According to Newbery, "there were two causes which moved the captain of Hormuz to imprison us and afterwards to send us hither. The first was because Michael Stropene had accused us of many matters, which were most false. And the second was for that Mr Drake at his being at Moluccas, caused two pieces of his ordinance to be shot at a galleon of the king of Portugal. . . . "[7]

While it was all well and good for the Portuguese—who had been governing Hormuz and Goa for nearly eighty years—to allege offense at Drake's actions, Newbery was probably aware of the queen's fascination with Dom Antonio de Crato (and even more aware of her fixation on acquiring his crown jewels), and her surreptitious support for him. Undeterred, he disavowed any dealings with either Drake or Antonio de Crato, and he blamed his imprisonment on the Venetian Stropene, who, Newbery claimed, "did presently invent all the subtle means they could to hinder them [the English]: and to that end they went unto the Captain of Hormuz . . . telling him that there were certain English men come into Hormuz, that were sent only to spy the country; and said further, that they were heretics."[8] What hadn't occurred to either Newbery or Fitch was that the middlemen whom they were cutting out of the Levant trade with England were the Venetians.

Fortunately for the hapless English merchants, two Jesuit priests and a Dutch trader intervened on their behalf, and they were released after three desperate weeks in the Goan prison. The lesson was salutary but unfortunately wasn't automatically transferable between adventurers. Like children, Elizabeth's adventurers rarely learned from the mistakes of their brothers. It would be at least another fifty years before English traders realized that if they didn't know the local system and understand the politics, legal trade would be virtually impossible.

29. Katherine Champernowne's Sons Take Up the American Dream 🪶

Brother, I have sent you a token from Her Majesty, an anchor guided by a Lady as you see, and farther Her Highness willed me to send you word that she wished as great good hap and safety to your ship as if herself were there in person. . . .

—WALTER RALEIGH TO SIR HUMPHREY GILBERT, MARCH 18, 1582

Closer to home, the gentlemen adventurers fared better, at least in terms of the political upheavals of Elizabeth's reign. Humphrey Gilbert had been a soldier of fortune since 1562, first at Newhaven in France, then, from 1566 in Ireland, involving himself in myriad plantation schemes. Between his stint at Newhaven and his time in Ireland, he had proposed to the queen that he set out and search for the Northwest Passage.

But Ireland was where he would make his name. His uncle, Sir Arthur Champernowne, embroiled him further in that unfortunate country with his personal vision for Irish "plantings" in Ulster and Munster between 1566 and 1572. Gilbert even became involved with Sir Thomas Smith, Elizabeth's secretary of state, in his privately financed plantation schemes in Ulster from 1571 to 1575, and led English "volunteers" as their hardened military commander in the Low Countries in 1572. Knighted for services to the crown in Ireland in 1570, Sir Humphrey Gilbert was of that breed of highly volatile younger sons of gentle birth in Elizabethan England who saw gold in colonization, rather than in piracy.[1]

The queen, for her part, needed Gilbert and men like him to extend her authority in Ireland. Allowing her gentlemen to pillage and spoil the land of its rich natural timber resources and prolific fishing grounds was the only pay she could afford to give. Still Gilbert, much like his much younger half brother, Walter Raleigh, seemed expert at snatching defeat from the jaws of victory. The eldest Gilbert was Sir John, followed by Sir Humphrey, then Adrian. Walter Raleigh and his elder brother Carew were their half brothers by their mother's marriage to Walter Raleigh senior. Never before had five sons from one gentlewoman dominated foreign expansion. But such was the lot for Katherine Champernowne's sons. They had each been introduced in their turn at court by their aunt, Cat Ashley, Elizabeth's faithful governess. For each, their early days held tremendous promise, but they were ultimately destroyed by their own arrogance, poor judgment of their courtly rivals, scant knowledge of the lands they wanted to explore, and, in Walter's case, an inability to assess the situation dispassionately and roll with the tides of change.

Gilbert's early successes as a brutal military captain in Ireland fed his vision of transplanting Englishmen to foreign shores. Unlike Drake, Gilbert delighted in inflicting massive casualties in as vile a manner as possible. Deliberately killing as many women and children along with their men, his particular specialty was to lay waste to the land, cut off his victims' heads, and use them as markers forming a gruesome path to his tent. He brought "great terror to the people when they saw the heads of their dead fathers, mothers, sisters, brothers, children, kinsfolk and friends lie on the ground before their faces." Gilbert himself boasted to Sir Henry Sidney that "after my first summoning of any castle or fort, if they would not presently yield it, I would not afterwards take it of their gift [accept their surrender], but won it perforce, how many lives soever it cost, putting man, woman and child of them to the sword."[2]

For some reason, Humphrey Gilbert thought that his fearsome conduct in Ireland qualified him to go in search of the Northwest Passage, as if this perilous sea voyage of discovery was a natural extension to his previous credentials. When the Muscovy Company refused to allow Gilbert to "interlope," he continued to build on his knowledge base for North America, reading everything he could find on the subject and consulting with the Hakluyts and Dee. By concentrating his energies on the colonization of America, he believed that he would be in the forefront of what would become, at some point, a necessity to England's survival. On the plus side of his highly volatile character, Gilbert's enthusiasm for North American colonies was infectious and spread to young Walter (sixteen years his junior). It would be their spectacular failures that would pave the way for the seventeenth-century successes.[3]

With the assistance of both the Richard Hakluyts and John Dee, a huge body of correspondence and firsthand accounts of life in the Americas was building up, and Humphrey Gilbert had access to most of it. He conjectured that the failure of the Company of Kathai, and Drake's secret departure on his voyage of circumnavigation, meant the time was right to press the queen for a royal patent for Norumbega—that swathe of North America between the Hudson River and Cape Breton in Newfoundland.

Since Gilbert was so well connected, and had Leicester's support to search for the Northwest Passage and settle America, Elizabeth granted a royal patent on June 11, 1578, "to discover and inhabit some strange place not actually possessed of any Christian prince or people."[4] It is tantalizing to hope that the queen did not want such a violent adventurer to wreak havoc on any people, but this was hardly her worry. Her limitation on the patent to a term of six years in which to settle Englishmen in these lands in order to retain the title from the crown was, however, a stroke of genius. Elizabeth could appear to comply with his scheme, while not venturing a penny herself, and if the venture came to nothing, then she would have lost nothing.

While Gilbert's own substantial family of brothers and uncles involved their fortunes in the undertaking, Gilbert himself understood the benefit of royal patronage, and tried to enthuse others at court, including Elizabeth, with the prospect of discovering gold. But he found that Lok and Frobisher had tied up the wafer-thin royal investment market with their final voyage, and his pleas fell on deaf ears. Only young Henry Knollys, son of Sir Francis Knollys, treasurer of the queen's household and cousin to the queen, became a major participant. While Sir Humphrey was gathering together his fleet for the Norumbega expedition, he talked of rescuing Oxenham from Panama; capturing all the shipping of France, Spain, and Portugal; fishing at the Newfoundland fisheries; and eventually seizing the whole of the West Indies for England. He wrote off memorandum after memorandum trying to enlist the same level of support Drake had done so successfully, but to no avail.

While the word "madness" springs to mind for this as well as other Gilbert projects, in his defense, these rantings fit more into the realm of trying to make dreams come true. Most of the queen's western adventurers were facing the complete unknown, with Spanish America their sole compass for "how things worked." And if Spain could fashion an empire from nothing and become wealthier than any other European nation could imagine, then so could England . . . if only the queen would back *their* voyages of exploration to North America.

But before the expedition sailed from Plymouth, Gilbert and Henry Knollys fell out, and Knollys set off with three of the ten ships in the expedition to capture "rich prizes" through opportunistic piracy. Gilbert, meanwhile, with his brothers and half brothers set off in the seven remaining ships for North America. Before they were past Ireland, the fleet was dispersed by heavy squalls and storms. Gilbert alone made landfall there. That was the closest he would get to America.

His half brothers, Carew and Walter Raleigh, however, each in command of his own ship, fared only slightly better. Walter's navigator was the exiled Portuguese pilot, Simon Fernandez, who would play an important role in Raleigh's own dreams of settlement. After the storms, Fernandez argued that it would be best to head south instead of north by northwest to the Canaries, taking the more familiar route favored by Hawkins and Drake.[5] They made it as far as the Cape Verde Islands, where they had a "confrontation" with some Spanish and Portuguese ships and escaped back home, with the *Falcon*, a leased ship from John Hawkins, now badly in need of repairs. Understandably, any plunder taken in the fracas was shared out with the ship owner.

In one sense, their timing was fortunate. The court and Privy Council had no time to immediately address issues of gentlemen adventurers engaging in piracy. The proposed French marriage with Alençon was "on again" in 1580–81, consuming all of the court's energies, and forcing all of the queen's gentlemen to take sides. Burghley, a proponent of the match, was in disfavor, and Walsingham with Leicester, on the rise. Whose patronage a gentleman followed would determine which side of the argument he would be on. Walter Raleigh was the exception. Originally under the patronage of the vituperative Earl of Oxford, Raleigh "jumped ship" and made his search for a new patron. He wrote to the Earl of Leicester, declaring that "I will be found as ready and dare do as much in your service as any man you may command."[6] Of course, Raleigh hadn't recognized that Leicester's heir, Sir Philip Sidney, was being groomed as the earl's younger replacement for the queen's affections, and if for any reason Sidney failed, Leicester's stepson, Robert, Earl of Essex, would most assuredly do well. Despite Raleigh's brief encounter with the sea, remembered by many as a dubious chapter in his young career, by 1581, he had already shown great promise as a soldier in Munster. And Leicester wanted to keep him there, out of court, and out of harm's way.

In the meantime, the tenacious Spanish ambassador, Bernardino de Mendoza, was unrelenting in trying to get recompense for the piracy in which Knollys, and later Raleigh, had been engaged during the failed first Gilbert voyage. But the queen was not minded to hear the pleadings of Philip's servant in England until such time as he came forward with a reasonable explanation or apology for the king's financing the papal mercenary troops in Ireland. He had invaded her sovereign soil and committed a clear act of war, she argued. Mendoza's position had been so severely compromised that no one dared to speak to him. When he walked along the street, children hooted and stoned him. In his audience with the queen in October 1581 at Richmond, he lashed out at Elizabeth that whatever she might think of Spain, she had brought these tribulations upon herself; that she was extending herself far too much to the Portuguese pretender, Dom Antonio de Crato; and that if she didn't change tack, "cannons would bring her to reason."[7]

Elizabeth was livid. She told Mendoza that he need "not think to threaten or frighten her, for if he did, she would put him in a place where he could not say a word." He was within an ace of being expelled, and he knew it. He had gone too far, and he tried to appease the English queen with flattery, telling her that she was "a lady so beautiful that even lions would crouch before her."[8] Elizabeth answered that she would ignore the Spanish ambassador's pleas for restitution from her gentlemen adventurers, including Drake, until the King of Spain could answer for his invasion of Ireland.[9]

Yet despite the heated exchange, when Gilbert requested another passport to go to his "lands" in America, the queen forbade him to sail, claiming that he was "noted of not good hap by sea" as his recent voyage clearly showed. Disgruntled, Humphrey Gilbert sold part of his "concession" of lands north of the fiftieth parallel in Norumbega to Dr. John Dee.[10] After all, he had "by his former preparation [been] enfeebled of ability and credit to perform his designments . . . whereby his estate was impaired." He had been left no alternative but to dispose of "certain assignments out of his commission to sundry persons of mean ability desiring the privilege of his grant, to plant and fortify in the North parts of America about the river of Canada."[11]

Gilbert assigned rights to a Southampton merchant, Edward Cotton, to exploit whaling in the Gulf of St. Lawrence; but his venture soon ended in failure, too. Then in 1581, Gilbert took advantage of a change in the political atmosphere with the first Throckmorton assassination attempt on Elizabeth's life and subsequent clamping down on Catholics and recusancy fines. He agreed on a deal to grant rights of settlement to some 8.5 million acres to Catholics led by Sir George Peckham and Sir Thomas Gerrard to offset some of his losses.[12]

When the Spanish ambassador got wind of the Catholic "transportation" scheme, which would effectively export all opposition to Protestant policies in England, he set in motion a campaign to discredit both Gilbert and the Peckham/Gerrard undertaking. It would be disastrous for Spain's designs on England if Gilbert and his Catholic subtenants overcame the odds stacked against them.[13] Gilbert predictably ignored the Spanish threat and formed his own Southampton-based company called "The Merchant Adventurers with Sir Humphrey Gilbert," which would be imbued with the exclusive rights of trade with Gilbert's North American colony. The new company included all of Katherine Champernowne's five sons, thirty-nine Southampton merchants, and, notably, Francis Walsingham, who ventured £50.[14]

Prior to this, in preparation for Gilbert's own second expedition, Simon Fernandez was sent to the New England coast in an 8-ton frigate, the *Squirrel*, on a reconnaissance mission. On his return, Hakluyt, Gilbert, Dee, and Peckham all met at Dee's Mortlake home to discuss Fernandez's findings. But myths, not hard facts about terrain, the native Americans, and threats to settlement generally abounded. In their desperation, an Englishman named David Ingram, who had been put ashore in the Gulf of Mexico by John Hawkins back in 1568, was also interrogated by Gilbert and his partners. Ingram had miraculously walked across North America to Newfoundland, where he was eventually picked up and returned to England. Still Ingram's tale was so fabulous to the adventurers that they were unable to decipher his facts from fantasy.[15]

Predictably, money began to dwindle, as always in these costly expeditions, and many of Peckham's backers pulled out when it became apparent that the queen would still demand the vast recusancy fines from her Catholic subjects even if they emigrated to America. Still, the lack of enthusiasm for the project can be largely attributable to Francis Throckmorton, who had initially been arrested in 1581 for plotting against the queen. In early 1583, he was unexpectedly taken into custody again.[16] Walsingham, who may have invested in the Catholic venture to North America to get to know his "enemies" better, had had Throckmorton seized as one of "the chief agents of the Queen of Scots," and who was also in the pay of the King of Spain. Seditious pamphlets published abroad were found in his possession, and he was put under excruciating torture for six months before he finally confessed all.

Meanwhile, Mendoza had been expelled to Paris in 1582, after the first Throckmorton affair, and had instigated this second and far more dangerous plot in 1583.[17] The assassination plots translated into draconian measures by the crown, and a waning willingness on the part of Catholics to poke their heads above the metaphorical parapet of English politics for any risky venture.

Finally, and mysteriously, Walsingham's stepson, Christopher Carleill, seemed to redeem the situation somewhat for Gilbert. He had interested the city of Bristol in Gilbert's plans, and in the spring of 1583, the Bristol merchants agreed to give 1,000 marks ($153,550 or £83,000 today) and a bark to be captained by Carleill.

Even better news was yet to come. Walter Raleigh had somehow stepped forward from the mass of young men itching to grab the queen's attention at court. He not only grabbed her attention, but he retained it. Since Gilbert was the "new favorite's" brother, the voyage now seemed to have a royal seal of approval.

After all the delays, a small fleet of five vessels set sail at last. On this second voyage, Gilbert commanded the admiral ship, the *Delight* (120 tons), that was part-owned by William Winter and his brother John. Other ships in the fleet were the *Golden Hind* (40 tons), owned and captained by Edward Hayes; Raleigh's *Bark Ralegh* (200 tons); the *Swallow* (40 tons), belonging to a Scottish merchant; and the *Squirrel*. The voyage of 1583 was taken for one reason only: to retain Gilbert's six-year patent and thus prevent its expiry. But this voyage, too, to recoin Elizabeth's own words, was of "little hap." Within two days, the *Bark Ralegh* had returned to Plymouth, presumably due to disease. The *Swallow* split off from the rest of the fleet during their seven-week voyage to Newfoundland, in search of plunder. Yet somehow the fleet regrouped in St. John's harbor, where, despite the presence of thirty-six other ships with Spanish, Portuguese, and French flags hoisted proudly aloft their mainmasts, Gilbert claimed the land for the queen with great ceremony.

Yet, in their two weeks at St. John's prospecting for gold, disease spread like a brushfire among the men. So many had died and others were too ill to work that Gilbert was reluctantly compelled to order the *Swallow* to return to England with the sick and dying. The few who weren't sick refused to carry on, and Gilbert knew he was beaten. He claimed that the following spring he would send out two new fleets, one for the north of America, and the other for the south, and that "Her Majesty will be so gracious, to lend me 10,000 pounds."[18]

Then in a storm near Cape Breton Island, the *Delight* was shipwrecked. Eighty of her crew were killed, and, of the twenty survivors, only a handful ever saw England again. Gilbert was aboard the *Squirrel*, and on Monday, September 9, "the frigate [the *Squirrel*] being ahead of us . . . suddenly her lights were out, whereof as it were in a moment, we lost sight, and withal our watch cried, the General was cast away, which was too true."[19]

The first patent granted for North America had ended in fiasco. Humphrey Gilbert and his youngest brother, Walter Raleigh, had thought of their colonization schemes as a good means to injure Spain and enrich themselves and England. Carleill, and probably Peckham, until the issue of recusancy fines loomed large again, viewed it as an economically sound colonial enterprise. None gave any thought to the indigenous population of America. And Elizabeth herself thought of it as a sideshow to the pressing requirements for containing Spain, and getting more gold quickly.

Still, Walter Raleigh would persuade his queen that America would be worth another try.

30. The Defeats of 1582–84 ❧

Tell me what has become of Drake and what you
hear of arming of ships. . . . It is most important
that I should know all this.

—PHILIP II TO BERNARDINO DE MENDOZA

Drake had made good use of his time since he returned from his around-the-world voyage. He had become mayor of Plymouth in 1581 and began a major infrastructure project to bring a fresh water supply to the town. The queen and Leicester had ensured that he received just reward and standing for his phenomenal accomplishment that had to remain a state secret, due to its very nature. A proposal was put forward by Leicester that Drake should head a company as its life governor to search for new territories, and to spearhead a fruitful trading relationship with the Moluccas. Most important for Sir Francis, he would never again sail as a rover. From 1580 onward, he would always have the queen's commission.

Drake was the most famous, most feared mariner in the world. Everyone everywhere wanted to know him. And as the most accomplished seaman of his day he was nicknamed "The Fortunate" by popular acclaim. Even royalty sought Drake out, and Antonio de Crato, the dethroned king of Portugal, was no exception. Where Drake had been dubbed "The Fortunate," Antonio was called "The Determined." It was Antonio's determination, his theft of the Portuguese crown jewels, and his ability to embroil men and women of greatness in his affairs that prevents him from being a mere footnote in history.

Antonio, hearing of Drake's successes, and counting on the long-standing friendship of Portugal and England, entrusted much of the Portuguese crown jewels in pawn to Elizabeth to try to win back his kingdom through the back door of the Azores. He should have known better than to believe that Elizabeth would involve herself in certain war with Spain. After all, she had by and large ignored his earlier plea for help when Spain overran the Portuguese mainland in 1580.[1]

But Drake was of another mind altogether. He carried grudges for his lifetime. Philip had invaded sovereign English territory in 1580 through the papal troops who ended up massacred on the southwest coast of Ireland at Smerwick. Any action he might take with or on behalf of Antonio would be justifiable retaliation for that act of war by Spain. Antonio's plan was to have a combined English and French fleet sailing under Antonio's flag to Terceira in the Azores, with Drake as his general. The plan was discussed at the highest levels of government with Leicester, Walsingham, Hawkins, Winter, and with the ailing Lord Admiral Clinton. Frobisher and Edward Fenton were named by the politicians as possible vice admirals for Drake. The financial deal was that the English would receive 75 percent of the Spanish prizes, and keep any Portuguese ships that refused allegiance to Antonio de Crato.[2] Naturally privileged trading status would also be on offer to England if they succeeded.

Still, to put out to sea without the queen's commission, the Privy Council would need to agree to these terms. Elizabeth and Burghley quickly vetoed Antonio's demand that the fleet would also need to intervene on mainland Portugal in the event that "the Kingdom of Portugal needs succouring." From that moment on, the proposed voyage was doomed. Munster was still in rebellion, and Elizabeth rightly feared that Philip might send more troops to her rebellious province Ireland in retaliation for any overt support for Antonio's cause. The fact that she had already financed Anjou's rule in the Low Countries conveniently escaped her view. A Portuguese invasion was too risky a business for her. Voyages of exploration, while treacherous for their mariners, could always be disowned. And nothing could prevent her from obfuscating about her involvement in the future as she had done so adeptly in the past.

Yet Drake believed that part of the plan might still be worth resurrecting. If the English fleet accompanied Antonio back to the Azores, and waited there to intercept the Spanish flota on its return, there would be no need to attack the West Indies later. Leicester and Walsingham agreed that money, or, more precisely, the lack of it, was the King of Spain's weak point. Any attack on his treasure trains would wound Philip more deeply than any other exploit they could undertake. His incessant wars, the costs of subduing the rebellious Dutch, the annexation of Portugal, had meant that his solvency relied increasingly on every single treasure ship making a safe return to the Casa in Seville.

The plan made sense, but all they could hope for from a watchful queen who had just been told that there was yet another plot against her life (the second Throckmorton plot) was an "indirect" participation. Even then Elizabeth made England's involvement reliant on the joining in, too. If Catherine de' Medici, who had also been a claimant to the Portuguese throne, would not agree, then neither would the Queen of England. Drake, Hawkins, and Leicester were called to meet with Burghley, where the lord treasurer laid down clearly the queen's objections. The mission, in its present form, would need to be scuttled. Unbeknownst to them at the time, Philip had written to Mendoza only a week earlier that any voyage sailing from England undertaken on behalf of Antonio would be considered an act of war.

Yet Drake, ever the man of action, appealed to Leicester for another mission—a braver and more dangerous one, but one that would bring them all great wealth. Drake had pushed the door ajar to the East in his dealings with Babu, and now proposed a trading mission to the East Indies. Leicester, Walsingham, Hatton, Christopher Carleill, and Lord Admiral Lincoln agreed to the idea along with the Muscovy Company and adventurers like Frobisher. Drake himself invested £666 13s. 4d. ($211,805 or £114,489 today). As the voyage's inspiration and advisor, not to mention the only man who had actually sailed those seas, Drake was instrumental in the nitty-gritty of navigation, mapping out the best watering holes, planning how to victual the ship (including the provision of fresh fruit) and determining how to keep the ships "sweet smelling" to preserve health on board. More than a dozen of his own men agreed to join the expedition. Even Drake's young cousin, John, would sail in the 40-ton *Bark Francis* belonging to Sir Francis.

While the planning was meticulous by the standards of the day, the ultimate choice of captain was a disaster. Martin Frobisher, somehow relatively unscathed from the Northwest Passage debacle, was mooted as the expedition's general. But Drake, at least, had the foresight to veto his selection on the grounds that he was too cantankerous a man to command a voyage that required both naval cunning and diplomatic prowess. Instead, Edward Fenton proposed himself as a replacement for Frobisher. Frobisher was more senior, but Drake's earlier point having been taken meant that Fenton eventually had himself accepted by the gentlemen adventurers. Fenton's vice admiral was the seasoned veteran Captain Luke Ward. The fact that Drake had been outvoted in the Council on these choices mattered little at the end of the day. He remained confident that he could inspire and educate the commanders adequately for the task that lay ahead, especially since many of his own highly skilled men were also participating.

When Drake blew in to Plymouth to give his final encouragement to the fleet, he saw immediately that the ships were light on tackle, and he ordered more to be delivered straightaway to the admiral with his compliments, along with some wine. Drake had been promoted to a position of standing and power, but there were—at least on this voyage—no more "Drakes" to replace his ingenuity, bravado, and flair in mastering the sea.

Fenton, who had proved himself a soldier of fortune only on land, was quite simply not up to the task. Virtually all others taking part in the expedition were better sailors and knew the sea better than he. His motivation for putting himself forward as commander of the fleet was to "get rich quick" and to advance to the place that Drake already occupied. The result was disastrous. In the vast expanse of the Atlantic Ocean, Fenton became alienated from his men and reality. As the Atlantic winds became unfavorable for sailing around the Cape of Good Hope, as originally planned, his professional mariners demanded that Fenton toss away his instructions and make for the Strait of Magellan to plunder Peru as Sir Francis had done. Powerless to resist, Fenton complied but not without ample bluster. Only some of Fenton's fleet reached the Brazilian coast, where they made a frenzied attack on three Spanish ships, sinking one. Trade was refused to them by everyone they encountered, and they were forced to return home to England none the richer, and none the wiser. Fenton, by now leading an uncontrolled crew, demanded that they take the island of St. Helena, where he would be crowned "king," and from which they would plunder all ships passing to and from the Cape of Good Hope. The loneliness of command and the sea coupled with the demands of the voyage had made him lose the touchstones that grounded all men to their daily life ashore. Doubtless, Fenton had experienced some sort of mental breakdown.

By the time the fleet returned to England in June 1583—thirteen months after sailing—Fenton had lost most of his men and ships. He discovered that his vice admiral, Luke Ward, had reached England before him and had reported to the backers, and therefore the better part of the Privy Council, about Fenton's wanting to become "King of St. Helena." When his crazed attack against William Hawkins became common currency, Fenton was dealt with judiciously and told to retire to obscurity or face the consequences. Sadly, Sir Francis's young cousin, John Drake, had been captured near the River Plate, where the *Bark Francis* was shipwrecked and never returned to England.[3]

This was the nadir of the English maritime expansion. To make matters worse, Sir John Hawkins and Sir William Winter were at each other's throats, each claiming that the other was lining his pockets and that other naval officials were misappropriating funds. When Hawkins complained to Burghley that "the officers have taken courage and hardness to oppose themselves against me . . . divers [sic] matters have been omitted, delayed and hindered by many subtle practises," the queen ordered Burghley to set up a commission to investigate. The five commissioners were Lord Howard of Effingham (a Catholic and lord chamberlain at the time), the Earl of Lincoln (lord admiral), Sir Walter Mildmay, Sir Francis Walsingham, and, of course Burghley himself.[4] Four members of the Navy Board were to assist them in their deliberations: William Winter, surveyor of the ships; John Hawkins, treasurer; William Borough, clerk of ships; and William Holstocke, comptroller of ships. The master shipwrights, Peter Pett and Matthew Baker, were also called upon to assist the commissioners in their inquiries.

Elizabeth knew that each and every one of these men was vital to the navy, and that no fault must be discovered against any of them. Burghley had been ordered to investigate thoroughly, resolve their differences, and make certain that they knew that she wanted this to be the end of the matter. But the facts spoke for themselves. Hawkins was right. The ships were being repaired with inferior products at inflated prices. Unseasoned oak was used for planking causing excessive leaking and time in dry dock. All the ships had at last been put in good order since 1578, but at a price. All ships built at Woolwich, Chatham, or Portsmouth seemed to be clear of the inflated charges against the ships built at Deptford. This laid the blame squarely on Matthew Baker, though the inspectors were most careful to omit his name from any documentation. Pett signed the report signifying his agreement to its findings, whereas Baker did not. Nor did Winter or the other Navy Board members.[5] As if to rub salt in their fresh wounds, Hawkins went on to offer the Privy Council a shipbuilding program that would not only be systematic, but would also include all ordinary and extraordinary repairs at an annualized savings of £3,200 ($956,968 or £517,280 today) to the crown. The proposal would eventually be accepted by mid-1585, when war with Spain had become inevitable.

In the interim, Philip's naval forces had gone from strength to strength. His brilliant admiral, the Marquis of Santa Cruz, annihilated any Portuguese resistance in the Azores, crushing forces loyal to Antonio in July 1582.[6] At the same time, Alba's troops in Portugal solidified Philip's stranglehold on his new dominion. In the Low Countries, the Duke of Parma's vicious campaign against the Dutch insurgents went on unabated, despite Elizabeth's support for Anjou's puppet government. In 1583, Parma retook Nieupoort and Dunkirk on the North Sea, establishing his Spanish naval squadron there as a bridgehead to an invasion of England. Still, these were not deepwater ports, and only ships of up to 200 tons could dock from Spain there.

Inevitably, Anjou had been routed from the Netherlands, and died a month later on May 31, 1584. Two months after that, William of Orange was assassinated in his own home. And Philip's flotas continued to pour gold, silver, and precious gems into his coffers unabated, while Elizabeth sold her crown lands, took part in risky maritime adventures, and prayed for deliverance. She must have feared on more than one occasion that God had become Catholic again. Pope Gregory XIII had already reinforced the point with the adoption of the Gregorian calendar in October 1582. Naturally, the queen refused to adopt it (despite its being more accurate) from an institution that called her "the patroness of heretics and pirates." From 1582 until 1751, England would lag ten days behind the Catholic empires.

There was only one option left in 1584 to the queen and England. The country must recover from its nadir, and it would have to call upon the resources and tenacity of her adventurers.

31. Water! ⚜

Whosoever commands the sea commands the trade;
whosoever commands the trade of the world commands the
riches of the world, and consequently the world itself.
— SIR WALTER RALEIGH

Clearly something needed to be done to reverse the tide. The old tried-and-true methods of daring plunder didn't seem to work any longer. Unless Elizabeth gave up all hope of peace, and surrendered to the horror of war with Spain, she could see no clear way through the impasse. Spain or the papacy would continue to fund assassination plots until one day, Lord forbid, they would succeed. Over £3.3 million ($1.11 billion or £600 million today) had been shipped from the Americas to Philip's coffers in the ten years between 1570 and 1580. That figure, unbeknown to Elizabeth, would rise nearly sixfold to £18.7 million ($5.42 billion or £2.93 billion today) by 1590.[1]

While the King of Spain's financial affairs were a closely guarded state secret, the obvious benefit he enjoyed from his American colonies was difficult to disguise. Now that he had successfully overrun Portugal and subsumed its navy into his own, it seemed to most minds of every persuasion that the King of Spain was unstoppable. That is to most minds except the great commanders of the past like Drake, Hawkins, and Winter. Sharing their point of view was the new adventurer of the future, Walter Raleigh. The queen's great political mainstays Leicester, Walsingham, and Burghley were also unwilling to look at the situation through defeatist eyes. Even Burghley had overcome his aversion to plunder, since to date it had been the only effective weapon against Spain. If England were to remain Protestant, ruled by their Virgin Queen, then it required the queen to be realistic and see that war was already inevitable.

Though she never openly admitted that they were right, Elizabeth would agree by the autumn of 1584 to give financial and military assistance to the Dutch rebels. The top priority was to try to save Antwerp from extermination at the hands of Parma. And with Parma now in charge of two Low Countries' ports, capable of making rendezvous with a larger invasion force from Spain, Walsingham's spy network clicked into high gear.

It is no wonder that with war looming heavily upon the horizon Elizabeth, now aged fifty-one, would find such pleasure in the sweet and lilting banter of the charismatic Walter Raleigh. His strong sense of power, his almost Machiavellian energy in his quest of fortune, mesmerized the aging queen. While Elizabeth had sent him packing to Ireland in 1582, on his return a year later with hard proof of his "better experience in martial affairs" for his role in the massacre at Smerwick, the dashing, handsome, and well-spoken Raleigh radiated that confidence and courtly eloquence that the queen so admired.[2] Within the year, she had given him the first of his nicknames, "Water," and pretended to die of thirst every time he left her sight. Soon her "Pug" Walter would follow—her lap dog—giving her courtly love and the intellectual stimulation she so craved.

After the nicknames came the showering of wealth. Elizabeth gave her new favorite Scotney (Bletching Court) at Lydd in Kent and Newlands Farm in Romney Marsh, Hampshire, recently received from All Souls College Oxford.[3] The medieval pile Durham House, in London, followed; and though it was in dire need of remedial work, Raleigh's position with its commanding view over the Thames could not leave anyone wondering about his commanding position in the queen's affections. To help with his upkeep, and his necessarily ruinous court expenses, Elizabeth granted him by royal patent, a license for the farm of wine. This provided him with a basic income of somewhere between £700 and £800 annually (approximately $222,000 or £120,000 today). In the spring of 1584, he was also granted a number of profitable licenses from the queen for the export of broadcloth without any of the standard statutory restrictions, making him a perceived enemy of the Merchants Adventurers, the Levant Company, the Spanish Company, and the Muscovy Company combined. Extensive plantations in Ireland would come later, as would the estates belonging to the Babington Plotters. He had become the Member for Parliament for Devonshire, vociferously defending royal prerogatives. Indubitably, the impoverished youngest son of Katherine Champernowne had finally arrived. But it still wasn't enough for the ambitious West Countryman.

Elizabeth was clearly entranced by him. Leicester, Walsingham, Burghley, and all her merchants and other adventurers were incensed by his colossal ego and the sway he held over the queen. No other favorite, aside from Leicester himself in the 1560s, had been shown such preferential treatment. Leicester's own chosen successor to the queen's heart through poetry and courtly deeds, Sir Philip Sidney, had been more or less spurned, though Elizabeth had made him Master of the Ordnance of the Tower in recompense. And so, Leicester resolved, probably with the connivance of both Walsingham and Burghley for a time, to supplant the upstart Raleigh in the queen's affections with his own stepson Robert, Earl of Essex. But timing, as Leicester knew, was everything, and for now, he would allow Raleigh his moment of glory.[4]

Raleigh was nothing if not monumentally ambitious. Like his friend, John Dee, he saw colonization and a British Empire spanning all the world's seas and continents as the queen's, and by extension, his rightful place in the world. His half brothers Adrian and Sir John Gilbert were eager to retain Sir Humphrey's grant of lands in the north of the North American continent, while the lands sold to Peckham and Gerrard were adjoining these to the south in modern New England. That only left Raleigh the "Mediterranean" coast north of Florida, which was far more to his personal liking in any event. This preference wasn't only driven by the hazards of the voyage and climate. Raleigh, like Dee before him, believed that gold only "grew" in warmer climates.

On March 25, 1584, Raleigh's application to take over some of his dead half brother's patent was granted by the queen. He "owned" exclusive rights to control the settlement and access to land in North America within six hundred miles to the north and south of any plantation he could establish and maintain within the next six years.[5]

Raleigh wouldn't make the same mistake that his half-brother had made, and prepared two barks to sail from the West Country on a reconnaissance voyage to the east coast of North America the moment the patent was granted. His servants, Philip Amadas and Arthur Barlow, captained the two ships, with Simon Fernandez as their pilot.[6] Raleigh edited Barlow's narrative with an exceedingly heavy hand prior to its publication, yet the excitement Barlow felt on first sight of America remains breathtaking today:

> We viewed the land about us, being, whereas we first landed, very sandy and low towards the water's side, but so full of grapes as the very beating and surge of the sea overflowed them of which we found such plenty, as well there as in all places else, both on the sand and on the green soil on the hills, as in the plains, as well on every little shrub, as also climbing towards the tops of high cedars, that I think in all the world the like abundance is not to be found.
>
> We passed from the sea side towards the tops of those hills next adjoining, being but of mean height, and from thence we beheld the sea on both sides. Under the bank or hill whereon we stood, we beheld the valleys replenished with goodly cedar trees, and having discharged our harquebus-shot, such a flock of cranes (the most part white) arose under us, with such a cry redoubled by many echoes, as if an army of men had shouted all together.[7]

Three days after making landfall at Hatteras on the Carolina Outer Banks, their first contact with Native Americans was made by three men rowing a canoe. They communicated through the use of sign language, with one of the Native Americans receiving presents of food, drink, a hat, and a shirt. He returned a short while later with a boatload of fish for the Englishmen. Soon, brisk bartering took place. The English exchanged their pots, pans, tools, and weaponry for skins, furs, and pearls. Fresh meat, vegetables, and fruit were brought as gifts. Some of the food in the cornucopia of delights, like potatoes, had never been tasted before. It was on a clear summer's day that Barlow remarked their "maize" that was "very white, fair and well tasted."[8]

Their friendship thusly sealed, the Englishmen were shown the way to Roanoke, an island lying between the reef and the shore near the mouth of the Albemarle Sound. There, the tribal village of "nine houses, built of cedar, and fortified round about with sharp trees, to keep out their enemies, and the entrance into it made like a turnpike very artificially" greeted them. Their hosts were "kind and loving people," the likes of which "there can not be found in the world."[9]

Barlow omitted all reference to their other encounter—that time with hostile natives, where some of the English were certainly killed and possibly eaten. Instead, he depicted the natives as "very handsome and goodly people, and in their behaviour as mannerly and civil as any of Europe . . . void of all guile, and treason, and such as lived after the manner of the golden age."[10]

The ships returned to England in September, with two Native Americans named Manteo and Wanchese from Roanoke in tow along with their Indian wares. Raleigh was presumably informed of the full details of the expedition by Barlow, Amadas, and Fernandez—from the tricky crossing in the Florida Channel to the difficult navigation around the Outer Banks. But Raleigh was the most expert Elizabethan salesman to date, and knew that all of the negative and more truthful remarks would need to be crossed out of any account of the voyage outside of their inner circle if he were to succeed in funding and forming a colony. Perhaps by the time his settlers had been recruited he actually believed that "Virginia" was indeed the land of milk and honey, but, more likely, he had his eyes firmly focused on the need to get official and royal backing for the voyage that lay ahead.

Raleigh doctored the Barlow narrative, redesigning it to attract the greatest support possible among the people who would ultimately be his settlers, but also in large measure to assure royal backing. With his poetic ability and rosy picture of a promised land, he by and large achieved his wishes. Where five years earlier the court had been gripped with gold fever, it now saw the merit—despite its general and strong dislike for the swaggering Raleigh—of his Western Plantation scheme.

The queen was truly excited about the new possibilities Raleigh's scheme offered after an era of prolonged ignominious failures. When his bill was passed by the House of Commons to confirm his title to the appropriately named "Wyngandacoia" (the Native American expression for "you wear good clothes"), Elizabeth knighted Raleigh in January 1585, authorizing the change of name for his lands to the also appropriate moniker, "Virginia."[11]

There was nothing more to lose. Any vestige of the old amity between Spain and England was in tatters, and for the queen, attacking Spain "beyond the equinoctial," where she stood a good chance of enriching herself without risking outright war, somehow held out a perverse hope for the future. It also had the merit of being consistent with her foreign policy since the 1560s.

For Raleigh, it meant that he could better anything Drake had achieved so far.

32. Roanoke ❧

No, no, my Pug, though Fortune were not blind,
Assure thyself she could not rule my mind.
Fortune, I know, sometimes doth conquer kings,
And rules and reigns on earth and earthly things,
But never think Fortune can bear the sway,
If virtue watch, and will her not obey.[1]

—ELIZABETH I TO WALTER RALEIGH, C. 1587

Raleigh had manipulated the Elizabethan propaganda machine into working overtime. At his behest and specific commission, Hakluyt published his *Discourse of Western Planting* in 1584 in support of Raleigh's Virginia project for the queen's and Walsingham's eyes only. His conclusion that "a brief collection of certain reasons to induce her Majesty and the State to take in hand the western voyage and the planting there" was clearly aimed at garnering crown support for the Raleigh scheme.[2] Hakluyt, as a practicing clergyman, doubtless wanted to save souls that had no hope of salvation through Christianity (the beginning of the misplaced British colonial philosophy of "White Man's Burden"). Yet Hakluyt's not-so-hidden message urged the queen to merge entrepreneurial activity with state sponsorship, harnessing her adventurers' apparent boundless energy for the good of the realm.

What both Raleigh and Hakluyt failed to notice was that Europe was again in crisis, and where the crisis following the St. Bartholomew's massacre in 1572 ended in peace, the crisis of 1585 would most assuredly end in war.[3] Elizabeth had to amass her ever-dwindling resources to address the Spanish threat closer to home. Naturally, Raleigh had her emotional support, and she gave him authority to impound shipping, supplies, and men in Devon, Cornwall, and in the Bristol Channel, but he would need to make his own way in financing and provisioning his expedition.[4] Still, fortune smiled on the sweet-talking Raleigh, and his subscribers were drawn from the likes of Sir Francis Walsingham; the new lord admiral following Clinton's death, Lord Charles Howard; Thomas Cavendish; and Sir Richard Grenville. His second expedition to Virginia would be the best-equipped voyage to North America so far.

In the end, the queen ventured her 160-ton ship the *Tiger* and ordered Sir Philip Sidney to release £400 ($119,510 or £64,600 today) worth of gunpowder from the Tower's stores. Four other ships with two pinnaces for inshore work under Grenville's command carried six hundred men in all. The seasoned Irish commander Ralph Lane was granted leave from Ireland to lead the soldiers who would form the mainstay of the Virginia settlement. Raleigh, of course, would be their armchair admiral, for the queen simply disallowed any talk of her favorite accompanying his men on their dangerous mission. Raleigh knew he was more than fortunate to have this level of support, given his jealous enemies at court. With the threat that loomed in the Low Countries (despite his political arguments in Hakluyt's treatise that he could inflict a major blow against Spain with his colony), Raleigh was lucky to attract any finance at all.[5]

He threw himself into the enterprise both financially and intellectually. His London home, Durham House, was turned into an alternative center of naval excellence to Dee's Mortlake home, and Raleigh was rumored to have also put over £3,000 ($919,450 or £497,000 today) of his personal fortune toward the venture. But even this staggering sum meant little to the vastly wealthy Raleigh. The queen had been remarkably generous to her new favorite, and his income from various appointments far exceeded his lavish spending. Described as "very sumptuous in his apparel . . . he is served at his table [with] silver with his own [coat of] arms on the same. He has attending on him at least 30 men whose liveries are chargeable [paid for by Raleigh], of which half be gentlemen, very brave fellows, [with] divers having chains of gold."[6]

From his vantage point high atop his turreted study overlooking the Thames, Raleigh and his disciples plotted the voyage and eventual settlement of Virginia. They pored over the existing sea charts, discussed the navigational aspects, and gleaned new ideas on how effectively to begin a nascent civilization. Anyone who Raleigh thought might be able to contribute to the body of knowledge to make the colony a success was called upon, irrespective of race or religion. Dutch émigrés were welcome, as were Jews and Catholics. In a largesse that was uncharacteristic of the age, Raleigh stressed that what mattered was their intellect and facts or skills at their disposal, not their beliefs. Foremost among Raleigh's "savant disciples" was Thomas Hariot—a "white wizard" or conjurer expert in mathematics and algebra. Unlike Dee, Hariot didn't dabble in the occult, but like Dee, he saw the world as a complex mathematical equation that held the secrets of God's great design.[7]

Whether Raleigh subscribed to Dee's emphasis on mathematics, or felt that he had "reinvented the wheel" with Hariot's system, matters little. Hariot, with the benefit of Raleigh's munificent salary, threw himself into his work with vigor. He was responsible for teaching the mariners the art of navigation while Raleigh read anything he could relating to the Spanish conquest of America. Fortune smiled on him once again, since in the previous year *The Spanish Colonie* had been translated into English and published. It detailed the killing machinery of the conquistadors.

But for Raleigh, his first hurdle would be against time: the longer he waited to sail, the greater the risk would be of the queen changing her mind in light of the deteriorating political scene in Europe. The ships were well victualed (not only with meats and fish that could be stored for longer periods, but also with livestock), and ample supplies of ciders, beers, wines, and aqua vitae bought and loaded for the colonists' unquenchable thirsts. Seeds for planting were stowed away carefully in the holds, and Raleigh and his captains prayed that the victuals would last until the first crops came in.

But Raleigh was naïve if he thought his adventure had escaped the ever-watchful King of Spain. Mendoza—even from his enforced exile in Paris—had managed to slip a spy in among the dockworkers, and he sent a factual and copious report to Philip relating the number of ships, victuals, guns mounted on deck, and mariners.

Again, Fortune played her part: Mendoza had wildly overestimated the number of ships and underestimated the number of men. This misinformation led the King of Spain to the slightly false conclusion that the primary purpose of the expedition was plunder.

And so, on April 9, 1585, Raleigh's squadron sailed at daybreak of a fine spring morning. Ten days out to sea, the sky to the west darkened, and the sun was reduced to a thin sliver. The superstitious mariners hadn't seen an eclipse before, and muttered that it was an omen of evil. Luckily, Hariot had accompanied the voyage, and he explained that it wasn't an evil omen, but a near total eclipse of the sun, a natural and recurring phenomenon. Across the Atlantic in Virginia, though, the Native Americans at Roanoke saw a total eclipse, and definitely viewed it as the foreshadowing of a great disaster.

Then a storm blew up near the Canaries and the *Tiger*'s pinnace sank. Grenville tried to keep his squadron together, but in vain. Unlike Hawkins's ill-fated voyage, Sir Richard had appointed a rendezvous at Puerto Rico for his dispersed ships, and spent no time looking for them. The crossing to the warm, welcoming waters of the Caribbean took only twenty-one days. But their victuals had become infected with weevils in the tropical heat, and the humidity encased most of the food in a thick, stinking, furry mold. They had failed to take on fresh fruits or food that had kept Drake's men healthy on much longer voyages, and by the time they reached the rendezvous harbor at Guayanilla Bay in Puerto Rico, they had to go ashore—into hostile Spanish territory—to find food and clean water, or perish. The experienced soldier and future governor of the first Virginia colony, Ralph Lane, ordered a vast battlement to be built to protect the men, while they waited for the other ships to arrive. By the time the *Elizabeth* appeared over the horizon several days later, they were predictably fending off an attack of Spanish horsemen.

When the Spanish governor saw the second ship, he asked for a "parlay" which, thanks to Grenville's arrogance, turned into a dangerous standoff. Despite this, the Spaniards promised to return with food, but when they failed to appear at the appointed time, Grenville ordered the men to cast off and sail. He smelled a trap, and he was right. All they could do to relieve themselves from starvation and dehydration was to sink into piracy, and so they fell upon the first two prize ships they could master to relieve their plight. Nonetheless, other problems beset them. Lane's and Grenville's command structure was badly frayed, with Lane complaining of Grenville's "intolerable pride and insatiable ambition." Thomas Cavendish, captain of the *Elizabeth*, and Captain Clarke of the *Roebuck* agreed.[8] But things would deteriorate even further.

Toward the end of June, the fleet made landfall at the Carolina Outer Banks. When the *Tiger* tried to navigate her way through into the inner channel, she ran aground and was damaged. Much of the stores for the colony were destroyed by the seawater gushing through her torn planks. The ship's master, Simon Fernandez, should have known better, since he was the expert navigator who knew those waters. What neither Grenville nor Lane had come to realize as yet was that Roanoke simply did not afford a safe anchorage for ships the size of the *Tiger*.[9]

Repairs to the damaged queen's ship began, while the rest of the squadron pressed on with their settlement plan. By the end of July, the four ships and pinnace anchored at Port Ferdinando on Hatarask Island, opposite Roanoke. The two Native Americans whom Barlow had brought back to London, Manteo and Wanchese, returned with the second expedition acting as their interpreters. After the statutory exchange of gifts and other trading formalities were finished, the English were granted the right to build a fort and cottages at the northern tip of the island. Lane ordered that one hundred men make their settlement there while he and the others explored up-country for food and fresh water sources before winter closed in.

Sir Richard Grenville, to the palpable relief of the colonists, departed back to England in late August with a letter from Lane to Richard Hakluyt that belied any notion of hardship or friction:

If Virginia had but horses and [their] kind in some reasonable proportion, I dare assure myself being inhabited with English, no realm in Christendom were comparable to it. For this already we find, that what commodities soever Spain, France, Italy, or the

*East parts do yield unto us in wines of all sorts, in oils, in flax,
in resins, pitch, frankincense, currants, sugars and such like, these
parts do about with it growth of them all, but being Savages that
possess the land, they know no use of the same. And sundry other
rich commodities, that no parts of the world, be they West or East
Indies, have, here we find great abundance of.*[10]

Raleigh couldn't have written a better piece of propaganda himself.

⁕c Part Three ɔ⁕

The Spanish War

*And if you suppose that princes' causes be veiled covertly
that no intelligence may bewray [reveal] them, deceive
not yourself: we old foxes can find shifts [cracks] to save
ourselves by others' malice, and come by knowledge of
greatest secret, specially if it touch our freehold.*

—ELIZABETH I, JULY 1585

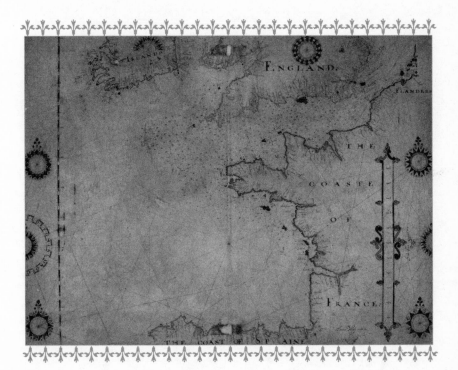

33. The Queen Lets Loose Her Dragon ✴

With this corsair at sea in such strength, we cannot protect any island or coast, nor predict where he may attack, so it is not clear what we can do to stop him.

— BERNARDINO DE ESCALANTE FROM SANTO DOMINGO TO PHILIP II

Since the autumn of 1583, Philip had been plotting and planning the "Enterprise of England" that had been urged for so long by his admiral, the Marquis of Santa Cruz, and other mariners. But it was only in the spring of 1585 that most of the pieces on the chessboard had been moved into place. Parma's merciless war of attrition against the Dutch rebels was entering its endgame. Antwerp would buckle. The powerful Guise faction in France was in the King of Spain's pay, and had mounted another failed attempt on Elizabeth's life in 1583, increasing the pressure on the heretic queen by stoking the fires of Catholic discontent at home with her harsh retaliatory measures. The year 1584 progressed Santa Cruz's scheme through the assassination of William of Orange, along with the rout and death of Anjou. Still, Philip was nervous. There had been little, if any, news of Drake. What was he up to? What was the she-devil Elizabeth planning? Since the expulsion of Mendoza in 1582, he had to admit that the quality of his intelligence had suffered dramatically.

Mountains of official papers littered his desk, among them Santa Cruz's plan for the Armada. Though well advanced in age, nothing happened anywhere in Spain's empire without Philip reviewing it on his gigantic desk. Into the small hours of the morning, the King of Spain pored over his papers, looking for alternative strategic plans. As he rustled through them with his arthritic hands, he hoped fruitlessly to discover a panacea for the Queen of England's dragon, Drake, hidden somewhere in their texts. All he needed to do was to give the order. And yet he waited. Santa Cruz must be ready. Or was he? How could he allow Santa Cruz to sail from Lisbon with the Armada without backup from Parma in Holland? Surely it would be useful to make a two-pronged attack to include the Duke of Parma? But Parma was slow in subduing the Dutch, and Antwerp had not as yet fallen. What would the Queen of England do about her Dutch Protestant brethren? Philip worried these issues whether strolling in his gardenia fragranced gardens at the Escorial, or by candlelight among his masses of dispatches. Still, a clear and divine reply would not answer his myriad questions.

· But he needn't have worried long. Word soon reached Philip that Elizabeth had suspended trade with the Spanish Netherlands. It was a small sign, but a sign nonetheless of her intentions. It is easy to imagine the wily king smiling to himself at her poor timing. A plea for help had gone out to provide food for his people who had had yet another year of failed harvests followed by a harsh winter. The French, English, and many countries that had Baltic ports had responded generously with grain shipments. But with the number of English ships in Spanish-held harbors, Philip could take much of Elizabeth's merchant shipping, and weaken any response she might make to him back home. Philip believed the time was ripe to flex his muscles, and he gave the order to seize all foreign shipping.

But he hadn't reckoned on the escape of the *Primrose* in May, or her master's seizure of two of his henchmen in Galicia. They were, of course, interrogated by Walsingham's finest men and sang like canaries. Not only did they sing, but they also held a copy of the king's orders. When these were shown to Elizabeth, endorsed personally by the King of Spain, her rage must have been felt throughout the court. She had dithered about war since, in Machiavelli's words, "it was a gamble," but she could no longer shy away from its inevitability.

The Privy Council discussed little else over the coming weeks, and when the Dutch envoys appeared at court begging for the queen and her men to send relief hurriedly to Antwerp, she agreed. She also invited Philip's "thorn," Dom Antonio, to return to England in June. Drake had suggested—not for the first time—that they take the battle to Spain and invade first, and the thought no doubt titillated the queen and many of her adventurers.[1] But her courtiers knew that

Drake's entreaties wouldn't be heard. The Queen of England almost never acted rashly or decisively, and yet, at least this time, she had acted. While she negotiated suitable terms to support the Dutch, she unleashed Drake along the Galician coast to try to recover as many Englishmen and ships as he possibly could. Her royal commission was signed on July 1, 1585, granting him and any merchants who had experienced losses in the latest treachery the "right of reprisal." It was a royal warrant to plunder—not only along the northern coast of Spain—but anywhere, anytime, and against anyone on Spanish territory.

Meanwhile, Philip had perhaps realized his error in acting so hastily. By August, the Treaty of Nonsuch was signed for the English to relieve the beleaguered Dutch, but by then it was too late for Antwerp. Parma had razed the once great city to the ground in what became known quickly as the Spanish Fury. Virtually every nobleman in the realm put together their own forces under the queen's banner in the month that followed, and over three hundred noble gentlemen adventurers led thousands of their troops into the Low Countries and war by the end of the year.

Drake, for his part, had devised a calculated, ambitious plan that— if successful—could rip apart the Spanish Empire. He planned to attack the Galician coast of Spain, then head into the West Indies, and capture Santo Domingo, Cartagena, Nombre de Díos, Río de la Hacha, and Santa Marta before heading north to Raleigh's new colony of Virginia to ensure that the "western planters" wanted for nothing. Not only would he bring well over twenty-three hundred men with him, but he also planned to free around five thousand Cimaroons from their Spanish overlords to fight alongside his own men.[2]

Drake's first task was to raise money for the joint stock company that would fund his exploit, and ensure that the stockholders would understand that the mission had more than the purpose of plunder at its heart. The queen needed money to finance the Netherlands war, and Drake had undertaken to provide it with his adventure. In doing so, he would also deprive Philip of his American treasure. Leicester thought it was a splendid plan, and he told Burghley "that is the string that toucheth him [Philip] indeed, for whiles his riches of the Indies continue, he thinketh he will be able with them to weary out all other princes. And I know by good means that he more feareth this action of Sir Francis than he ever did anything that hath been attempted against him."[3]

Drake's fleet would be the largest England had ever sent to foreign waters. Its ships were evidently on a fully sanctioned royal mission, comprising:

Ship	Captain	Owner
The *Elizabeth Bonaventure*	Sir Francis Drake	Elizabeth I
The *Aid*	Edward Winter	Elizabeth I
The *Talbot Bark*	*	Earl of Shrewsbury
The *Galleon Leicester*	Francis Knollys	Robert, Earl of Leicester
The *Sea Dragon*	*	Sir William Winter
The *White Lion*	James Erisey	Lord Admiral Howard
The *Bark Bond*	Robert Crosse	William and John Hawkins
The *Hope*	William Hawkins	William and John Hawkins
The *Bark Hawkins*	William Hawkins, younger	William and John Hawkins
The *Galliot Duck*	Richard Hawkins	Richard Hawkins
The *Bark Bonner*	George Fortescue	Richard Hawkins
The *Thomas Drake*	Thomas Moone	Francis Drake
The *Francis*	*	Francis Drake
The *Elizabeth Drake*	John Varney	Francis Drake
The *Tiger*	Christopher Carleill	City of London
The *Primrose*	Martin Frobisher	City of London

Elizabeth I in *The Pelican Portrait*, thought to be painted by Nicholas Hilliard, c. 1578. The pelican is a symbol of purity, but given the year of painting, it could also have been a symbolic and secret tribute to Sir Francis Drake, who was circumnavigating the globe aboard the *Pelican*, later renamed the *Golden Hind*.

Robert Dudley, Earl of Leicester, painted roughly the same time as Elizabeth's *Pelican Portrait* opposite.

King Philip II of Spain, who had a sneaking admiration for Elizabeth, despite being her nemesis for over forty years.

Lord Admiral Charles Howard followed in the Howard family tradition when he became lord admiral. A Catholic, and a close cousin of the queen, he remained her devoted servant during her lifetime.

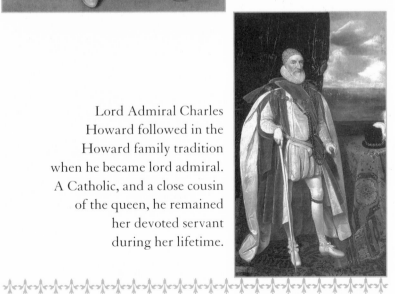

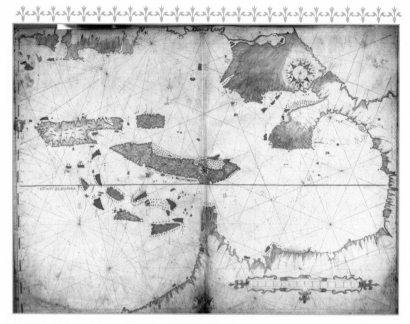

Map of the Gulf of Mexico and the Caribbean by Jacques Dousaigo that was available to Philip's Spanish navigators, and stolen by Elizabethan adventurers.

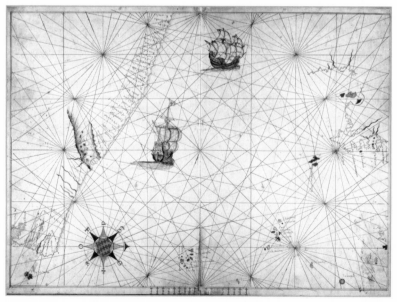

An Elizabethan chart of the Virginia Coast.

Sir William Cecil, Lord Burghley, the queen's lord chancellor and longest-serving minister, famously riding his donkey.

Sir Francis Walsingham, Elizabeth's loyal spymaster.

Sir John Hawkins, Elizabeth's slave trader and later treasurer of the navy. Hawkins had a vision of making England a world power by elbowing his way into the Spanish American Empire through trade.

Sir Francis Drake was Elizabeth's most gifted and audacious mariner. While his ship was the second to circumnavigate the globe, it is unlikely that this had been his original intent. The lure of American gold and rich prizes from Spanish vessels were most likely his target, but to bring these home safely, his only hope of eluding Spanish capture was to strike out across the Pacific. Fortunately for Drake and his men, he also captured valuable Spanish charts and a Portuguese pilot who knew the Pacific.

The priceless jeweled Drake Cup (right) that was given to Drake by Elizabeth with her gratitude for his achievements at the time he was knighted aboard the *Golden Hind* (formerly called the *Pelican*).

The Drake Chair (pictured at University of Oxford's Divinity School) is one of three known chairs that remain in existence today. After Drake was knighted aboard ship, the *Hind* remained in London for several years, until she had begun to rot. Eventually, she was broken up for scrap, and the only known remnants of the ship are these three chairs.

Martin Frobisher, like Drake, was essentially a pirate, though he lacked Drake's navigational and strategic abilities. Frobisher's Northwest Passage venture ended in failure, with his business partner and many gentlemen adventurers financially ruined.

While Sir Walter Raleigh was highly favored by the queen, and granted his half brother's lands in North America—over a million acres of "Northern" and "Southern" Virginia—he failed to make a viable settlement work in Virginia and dreamed of the gold of "El Dorado." On Elizabeth's death, he was implicated in a plot to put Arabella Stuart on the throne instead of James Stuart and, after many years in the Tower and a doomed expedition to "El Dorado," was executed for treason.

Sir Henry Sidney, lord deputy of Ireland and close confidante of Sir William Cecil, Lord Burghley. He married Robert Dudley's sister, Mary.

Sir Philip Sidney, courtier and poet. Sidney was the most influential and gifted poet of his day and was Robert Dudley's heir until his violent death in the Netherlands in 1586.

Robert Devereux was Robert Dudley's stepson. After his time in Holland, and throughout his campaigns in Ireland, he grew a beard and apparently cared far less about his personal appearance. He was willed Philip Sidney's "two best swords" and was a patron of the arts and a friend of Shakespeare. Devereux, despite being one of the queen's favorites, masterminded an ill-fated rebellion in London and was beheaded as a traitor.

The Deed of Grant for Virginia to Sir Walter Raleigh from Elizabeth. Note that the official Privy Seal is still attached.

This is how the Thames looked at Greenwich from Elizabeth's reign through to the 1630s.

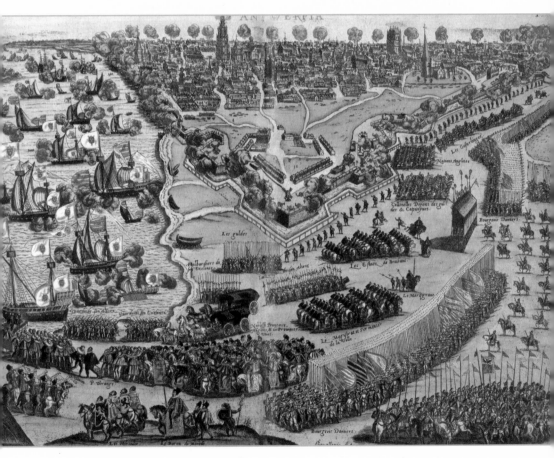

An artist's impression of troops arriving for the Siege of Antwerp. The city fell and was razed to the ground in what became known as "the Spanish Fury."

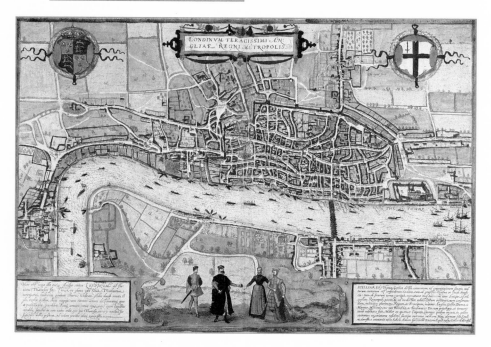

A letter written in Elizabeth's own hand around two A.M. to Sir William Cecil, demanding a stay of execution for her cousin, Thomas Howard, who had been found guilty of treason and of plotting to marry Mary Queen of Scots, against Elizabeth's will. The letter has little of Elizabeth's exceptionally fluid penmanship, and her agitated state of mind is reflected in her handwriting.

A map of London and the Thames to the Tower of London showing the detail of the river and streets.

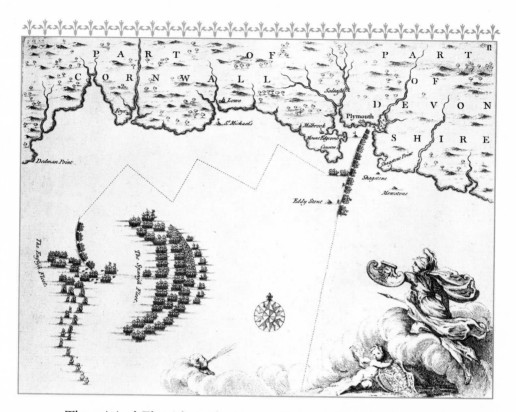

The original Flemish-made Armada Tapestry hung in the Houses of Parliament at Westminster but was destroyed by fire in the nineteenth century. This is a copy made to commemorate the single most important battle in British history, and is historically accurate.

Matthew Baker, one of Elizabeth's most trusted shipwrights, is designing a ship.

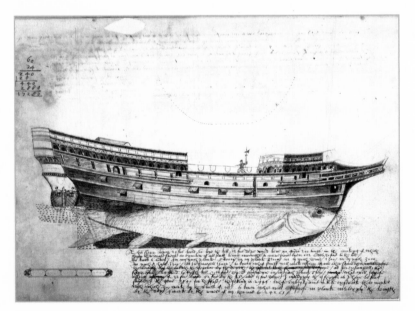

The cod in the belly of the ship depicts the ideal design for one of Baker's ships.

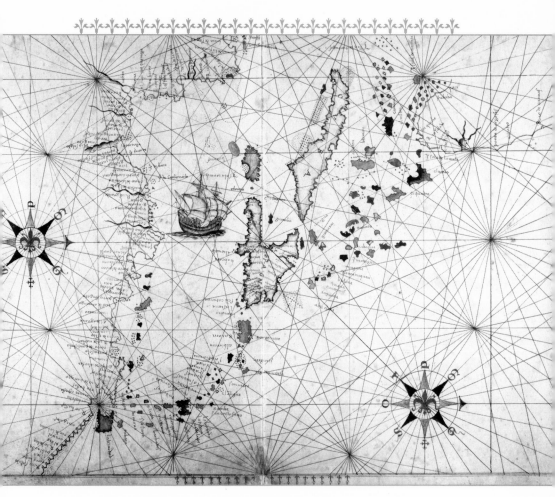

A contemporary chart of the North Atlantic, Newfoundland to
Brazil, by Angelo de Conte Freducci. It shows the challenges that
navigators faced in sailing on the eastern seaboards of North and
South America.

The Armada Portrait of Queen Elizabeth I is the most iconic image of England's naval strength from her reign. Her hand is placed on the globe, she is wearing the de' Medici pearls that had been given as a wedding present to Mary Queen of Scots by Catherine de' Medici, and her English navy, flying the flag of St. George, has just defeated the Spanish Armada. There are three "Armada Portraits," but it is believed that the one in the Duke of Bedford's collection is the first to have been painted by the artist.

In all, some twenty-five ships and eight pinnaces made up the fleet. Sir Francis's lieutenant general, Sir Christopher Carleill (Walsingham's stepson), was a professional soldier and had fought valiantly in Ireland. While the military contingent aboard was unseasoned, Drake was glad to leave their training in Carleill's capable hands. Though Frobisher had had more "experience" at sea, and remained as cantankerous as ever, he bowed graciously to Carleill's superior position, unlike Leicester's upstart brother-in-law Knollys. Drake had no time for prima donnas aboard ship, and demanded that his gentlemen make themselves useful in the same everyday chores as his lowest mariners.

On September 14, 1585, the same day that Drake managed to rid himself of Sidney and his entourage, he hastily set sail, though the ships hadn't been fully victualed, and one of his captains had to be hustled aboard to avoid missing the sailing. Drake knew his queen well enough to know that Sidney might have blighted the entire mission, and that Elizabeth, in a fit of pique, might recall the fleet at any moment. This, of course, was an unacceptable risk for Sir Francis, but they still needed the food they had been compelled to leave behind. As he sailed away, Drake also knew in his heart that it would be unsafe to finish his victualing at any English port.

Incredibly, Drake's phenomenal good luck held, and within the week he came upon a Biscayan ship laden with fish. Three vessels from the English fleet pursued her and, with their weatherly design, had no trouble in snaring her. It was Carleill who won the game, and he snatched the prize for the fleet. Once brought aboard there was

* There was some last minute confusion regarding these captains with the unscheduled, and unwanted, arrival of Sir Philip Sidney, Sir Fulke Greville, and their entourages—including Dom Antonio. Sidney insisted that Greville be made captain of the *Hope*. Sidney was trying to escape to America, angered by Elizabeth's failure to agree to acknowledge him as governor for Flushing. He and Fulke Greville tried to sail with Drake, but were outwitted by the admiral, and ordered to return to London. The *Tiger* should not be confused with the queen's ship *Tiger*, which had just returned home from Virginia under Greville.[4]

now enough food for the fleet to run to Spain and take shelter at the mouth of the Vigo River and replenish their stocks with clean water.

Once safely ensconced at anchor, Sir Francis sent word to the local governor at Bayona asking if Spain was at war with England, and why the King of Spain had impounded the English merchant fleet. Don Pedro Bermudez, Bayona's hapless governor, could not have mistaken the intent of the Englishmen, and was undoubtedly overawed. He took a thousand Spanish horse with him to personally confront *El Draco*. Meeting face-to-face midriver in a tiny rowboat, Bermudez told Drake that they were not at war with each other; that Philip had recently released the impounded vessels; and that if Drake left Bayona and Vigo alone, he would give them all the water and food they needed. And so it was agreed.

By mid-October, the English left Spain, having had an unusually friendly and hospitable exchange with the Spanish. Meanwhile, Philip fulminated at the Escorial. But things could have been much worse for the King of Spain. Drake had narrowly missed capturing the *flota* as it returned from the West Indies. It had passed within twelve hours of Drake while the fleet was sailing off the Portuguese coast, just out of sight over the line of the horizon.[5]

After plundering the Cape Verde Islands, most likely in retaliation for an old complaint by William Hawkins as well as resupplying the fleet, the English headed west across the Atlantic, only to be stricken with a virulent disease (possibly typhus) on their voyage. Somewhere between two and three hundred men died within days, and hundreds of others were left weak and debilitated. When landfall was made at St. Kitts (then uninhabited), the mariners who could went ashore so that the sick could recover, and the fetid ships be cleaned and fumigated. Where Drake had so successfully kept his men healthy in his voyage of circumnavigation by keeping the numbers down, on a military adventure like this, it simply was not possible. After a few weeks ashore recovering, the fleet plowed through the green-fringed Caribbean waters to Santo Domingo, the oldest city in the New World.[6]

Its elegant whitewashed buildings spoke of its ancient pride, though a closer glimpse revealed that it was merely faded glory. Santo Domingo was no longer on the bullion route, and, while rich in sugar and cattle, it had by and large become an administrative center for the Audiencia, or high court of the region.

While closing in on the town, Drake and his men took three frigates also heading for its port. Drake's luck was almost uncanny, since one of these carried the letters from King Philip warning the Audiencia that *El Draco* was heading in their direction to destroy them. Naturally, the town was metaphorically caught sleeping, despite a lone fisherman describing an impressive fleet in the waters off the island. The English attacked on New Year's Eve. Santo Domingo was theirs on New Year's Day 1586, but not before a cannonball crashed through the side of the *Elizabeth Bonaventure*, and another fell on deck and rolled between Drake's legs while he paced back and forth with Carleill and Frobisher.[7]

The English overran the once great city, plundering and pillaging at will. Still, Drake's estimates of vast mountains of plunder and gold were hopelessly optimistic: all the fleet had to show for their capture was sixteen thousand hides, victuals, wine, vinegar, and oil. The cash they found was so insignificant that it was not even specified. Their only alternative was to "ransom" the city itself.

Twelve days later, the high sheriff met Drake to negotiate their release. Drake asked for a million ducats (the amount at which he had originally valued the plunder). The *alcalde* muttered that such a sum was impossible, that there wasn't that much money in the whole of his jurisdiction. So Drake told him that they would be compelled to burn the town down, building by building, until his demands were met. At this point, the king's factor, García Fernández de Torrequemada, took over the negotiations while Santo Domingo burned. In the end, Drake was forced to compromise on the not so paltry figure of 25,000 ducats, raising their total takings to £11,275 ($3.27 million or £1.77 million today). Nonetheless, the figure was still disappointing to Sir Francis and his men.

Afterward, Fernández de Torrequemada wrote to Philip, "Drake is a man of medium stature, blond, rather heavy than slender, merry, careful. He commands and governs imperiously. He is feared and obeyed by his men. He punishes resolutely. Sharp, restless, well-spoken, inclined to liberality and to ambition, vainglorious, boastful, not very cruel."[8] Considering that Drake had ordered the destruction of over a third of Santo Domingo—from the lowliest houses to its churches, monastery, and castle—this was high praise indeed. While Torrequemada watched the English fleet weigh anchor leaving behind the smoldering ruin of the New World's oldest settlement, he couldn't help but wonder aloud that "this thing must have had Divine sanction as punishment for the people's sins."[9]

While the fall of Santo Domingo sent an aftershock through the Caribbean and beyond, Grenville was counting his cash back in London. After he had sailed from Roanoke on August 25, 1585, he had had the good fortune to fall in behind the flota and give chase. Of the thirty-three ships that had left Havana in July, only the 300-ton unarmed *Santa Maria* straggled behind the rest, squatting heavily on the rolling sea cradling treasure in her hold. The English pirate adventurers had long ago uncovered the unmistakable and ungainly gait of a ship laden with treasure, and gave chase. When the *Tiger* overcame her, the *Santa Maria* had no alternative but to surrender to the faster, sleeker vessel bristling with firepower, flying the flag of St. George, and the queen's colors.

Once aboard his Spanish prize, Grenville could hardly believe his good luck. He held up the passengers at gunpoint and ordered them to pass across their valuables. The ship's manifest confirmed that a rich cargo of gold, silver, and pearls, calf hides, sugar, ginger, and cochineal was stowed aboard. In all, it was valued at 120,000 ducats—roughly £30,000, or $8.70 million or £4.7 million today. Grenville ordered the treasure to be removed to the *Tiger*, while he captained the prize back to Plymouth. Not only was the ship worth a great deal more, but there was also the good possibility of ransoming his hostages. The first voyage to colonize North America had been made, not by a "western planting" but by plunder. Grenville knew, as did any good sea captain in Elizabeth's reign, that his duty was not only to accompany the colonists to safety on foreign shores, but also to ensure the financial aspects— profit to the joint stockholders—remained uppermost in their minds. And plunder was the surest way of making exploration pay quickly. On their return to Plymouth on October 18, 1585—one month after Drake's fleet had sailed—Elizabeth was said to have been so delighted with the quality of the pearls that she kept a whole cabinet filled with them for her own use.[10]

In the closing months of 1585, while Sir Richard Grenville basked in the glory of his haul in the comfort of an excited London, Ralph Lane and his 107 settlers were toiling to try to make their colony work. Lane, an exceptionally strict disciplinarian who had recommended keelhauling as punishment on the outbound voyage, was not above meting out the harshest sentences imaginable on land to keep his "riff raff" in check.[11] There were carpenters, metallurgists like the German Jewish expert Joachim Ganz, former soldiers from Ireland, "drones and grumblers" masquerading as gentlemen, and a few who knew how to till the soil, though they weren't specialist gardeners or farmers. Lane wrote that most "had little or no care for any other thing but to pamper their bellies," then adding, "Because there were not to be found any English cities, nor such fair houses, nor at their own wish any of their old accustomed dainty food, nor any soft beds of down or feathers, the country was to them miserable."

Of his second in command, Philip Amadas, Lane extolled rare praise when he said "he was the gentleman that never spared labour or peril either by land or water, fair weather or foul, to perform any service committed unto him." Thomas Hariot had accompanied Lane as the chief mathematician, but his observations pale into insignificance (as do Lane's) when compared to the amazing body of drawings provided to posterity by the expedition's accredited artist, John White. White had already made his name in England for his stunning portraits of the Inuit tribesmen on Baffin Island during Frobisher's 1577 voyage, and his drawings in Virginia remain our most poignant reminders today of that ill-fated colony.[12]

The critical task ahead, aside from staying alive, was to find a better natural harbor than the one Roanoke afforded. Their "scouts" Manteo and Wanchese suggested exploring to the north, where they believed the ideal harbor existed. Lane and a small party of settlers discovered Chesapeake Bay and spent part of their first American winter inland there, making friends with the Chesapeake tribe. Lane reported that "a good harbor being found to the northward . . . you shall clear yourself from all those dangers and broad shallow sounds . . . and gain within four days travel into the heart of the Main

200 miles at the least . . . the territory and soil of the Chesepians was for pleasantness of seat, for temperature of climate, of fertility of soil and for the commodity of the sea . . . not to be excelled by any other whatsoever."[13]

In the spring, Lane took another expedition to the west, exploring the Albemarle Sound. From there, they headed north again, this time up the Chowan River, where they met the Chowan "king," who showed them samples of his "wassador"—a metal deemed by Lane to be copper, or perhaps a different quality of gold. The Chowan chief also told Lane that there were pearls to be had in plentiful supply at the Chesapeake Bay. Lane did not question the Native American "king" and informed his settlers that their firm intention should be to remove themselves to the better harbor at Chesapeake, as soon as relief finally arrived from England. "The discovery of a good mine," Lane remarked, "by the goodness of God, or a passage to the South Sea, or some way to it, and nothing else can bring this country in request to be inhabited by our nation."[14] But he could do nothing until his English support arrived. On more than one occasion, Lane must have asked himself, where in the blazes was their relief from England?

That was the spring of 1586, when Drake's name rang throughout Spanish America and Catholic Europe like a death knell. In England, the Low Countries, and other Protestant nation-states, it brought cascades of joy. Rumors, most based on the incredible truth, abounded with Drake said to have liberated twelve thousand slaves on Hispaniola. Some said he had been defeated at Havana, others that he had taken the flagship of the Peruvian flota and 300,000 ducats booty. But these rumors were at variance with the truth.

The Spanish colonies in the New World were thrown into terror, confusion, and disarray by the news of Drake's fleet and the ransoming of Santo Domingo. While the cash prize for the city was miniscule to Spaniard and Englishman alike, the catastrophic blow to Spain's prestige was irrecoverable. Though ill-prepared to mount a defense against the faster, more weatherly, more heavily armed, and more brazen English fleet, they had little choice. Either defend Spanish America, or lose it entirely. Their greatest dilemma was, however, to answer the burning question: Where would Drake strike next?

During the night of February 9–10, Sir Francis landed Carleill with around a thousand men near the fort of La Caleta, where Cartagena's battery guns were located. Carleill's men had to pick their way through the darkness, carefully avoiding the poisoned stakes driven into the path by the Indians. The Caleta's defenses were not strong, but they could inflict serious damage on the English fleet if Carleill were unable to overcome them. Unlike sleepy Santo Domingo, Cartagena—as all of Spain's important cities and towns in the New World now—was on high alert. While Carleill and his men advanced, the three hundred Spanish soldiers and two hundred Indians tried to ambush the advancing English but, when they failed, scurried for cover. Around an hour before dawn, Carleill and his men had snaked their way within reach of the Caleta. The attack order was given, and as the English sprang forth from the brush on the far side of the fort from the harbor, the Spaniards opened fire roaring, "Come on, heretic dogs!" Galleys in the port fired high, but as Carleill was out of range, their shot was useless. Also on the far side of the fort, the wall had been ravaged by poor maintenance and time, and all the English had to do was to kick in the flimsy thirty-foot-wide wine-butt barricade that had been erected in haste to keep them out. After the briefest pike battle, most of the Spaniards fled to the town, hotly pursued by the English.[15] In the meantime, two galleys ran aground as they attempted to escape, and the order was given by their admiral to destroy them at once so Drake could not benefit from the disaster. But Drake was never one to come up empty-handed. He had already seized the *Santa Clara* and the *Napolitana*, as well as the few remaining vessels in harbor.[16] And so, a day later, Sir Francis Drake was master of Cartagena.

Drake turned his attention to the business of administering his prize while also trying to stave off the unwelcome reappearance of the "fever" in his fleet. Fresh wells were dug for clean water; "Frenchmen, Turks and Negroes"—to a man Spanish prisoners— were released and ordered by Drake to be treated with the greatest civility. The Turks were so thankful that more than one hundred of them begged to accompany Drake's fleet back to England. Sir Francis, of course, complied.

The business of ransom was undertaken with decorum on both sides. Sir Francis demanded 5,000 ducats ransom for Alonso Bravo to cover the preservation of his home and neighborhood ($362,138 or £195,750 today). When he heard that Bravo's wife was terminally ill, Drake agreed that the Spaniard could return home to keep her company for as long as necessary and until the agreed ransom was paid. When his wife, Elvira, died, Drake and his men attended her funeral, and provided the pomp and ceremony at which the English so excel, with their muffled drums, flags drawn up high, and a proper military volley shot off as befitted a brave soldier's wife. As he had demanded a further 3,000 ducats for the priory where Elvira was buried, in an incongruous act of generosity, Sir Francis reduced the demand to a nominal 600 ducats, and a promise to Bravo that no one would disturb Elvira's final resting place.

As negotiations progressed for the release of Cartagena, Drake's initial demand for 400,000 ducats ($28.97 million or £15.66 million today) was whittled down. After 248 homes were destroyed by arson, a ransom of 107,000 ducats was finally secured in early March 1586. This brought the total yield for Cartagena to 113,000 gold ducats ($32.75 million or £17.7 million today), including the ransom paid by Bravo, the priory, and another small estate. But this small gain was offset by great personal loss. Half of the men who had survived the voyage of circumnavigation with him had lost their lives at Cartagena. Men like Thomas Moone and John Varney who had been with him from the beginning, had fallen. A hundred more men had died of the "fever," including George Fortescue. Only seven hundred men remained fit for service—an attrition of sixteen hundred men from the original complement. Even Drake had to admit it was a grossly inadequate force to attack Havana. Notwithstanding this change in plan, there was no time to linger. Drake knew he was late in supporting Raleigh's colony, and since the pickings were hopelessly poorer in the West Indies than anticipated, he did not want to fail in that important task as well.

At Cuba, they dug wells for fresh water, with Sir Francis mucking in with his sailors "up to his armpits" carrying the barrels of clean water aboard ship. Once replenished, the fleet sailed along the east coast of Florida to St. Augustine, Spain's oldest city in Florida. Sir Francis called a "war council," and Carleill and Frobisher agreed that the Spanish watchtower there posed a severe threat to Raleigh's settlement. The next day, after a few bullets were fired (that hit nothing) Sir Francis and his men took the town. To their delight, the governor had deserted so quickly that he fled without the £2,000 worth of money brought to the fort for safekeeping ($579,420 or £313,200 today). By May 29, two days after their siege, the town and fort were utterly destroyed.

Though Lane had no idea where Drake was—or even if it was Drake who had been still designated to come—and Drake was uncertain where to find Roanoke since Grenville hadn't returned before Drake had left (thanks to the Philip Sidney incident), Sir Francis supposed that the colony lay at about 36° north. Amazingly he found Roanoke on June 9, and immediately saw that it didn't offer any safe anchorage within the Outer Banks. Drake and a party of his men rowed ashore, to Lane's immense relief. Relations between the Native Americans and the inept, unskilled settlers had deteriorated dramatically over the issue of the Englishmen badgering the natives for both food and water. Grenville had failed to return with fresh provisions at Easter, and now the natives were literally starving them out. Sir Francis offered that all of the settlers were welcome to return to England with the fleet, but Lane demurred. He wanted to stay. So Drake offered him the *Francis* and some small boats and food for four months and a hundred men to navigate the ships. Lane agreed to the second proposal and preparations began at once. But a huge June thunderstorm bubbled up and raged on for three solid days, driving the *Francis*, the *Sea Dragon*, the *White Lion*, and the *Talbot* out to sea.

Now, all Sir Francis could offer Lane was the *Bark Bonner* and whatever food he could spare. But Lane realized that the *Bark Bonner* could never bring them all to safety. It was as if the heavens were sending Lane a message, and he announced after consultation with his colonists that he had changed his mind and wanted to return home. The colonists stampeded to get aboard the ships that had rowed into the shallows to rescue them, upsetting maps, books, and detailed accounts of their story. The three colonists who had gone up-country in search of food and an alternate settlement site were abandoned, never to be seen again. Finally, on June 18, 1586, Sir Francis Drake had embarked the Roanoke settlers and sailed for England. Five weeks later, on July 27, they anchored safely at Portsmouth.[19]

Two weeks after that, Sir Richard Grenville returned to Roanoke, finding it abandoned. He searched the country surrounding the settlement and explored the coastline in the vain hope of finding the men he had come to relieve. He was "desolate yet unwilling to lose possession of the country," and so he landed fifteen men on the "Isle of Roanoke," plentifully provisioned for two years, and sailed away. Grenville, of course, left them to certain death.

34. The Camel's Back

Considering that the English have done so much damage in
so short a time to the merchant men trading in these waters,
it is likely that they will do the same to the India fleets;
accordingly it would be as well to give orders that at least
two more ships besides the Captain and the Admiral should
be armed in each fleet . . . all these preparations are directed
solely against the English fleet. . . .

—MARQUIS OF SANTA CRUZ TO PHILIP II

In January 1585, the pope published another bull against Elizabeth, giving Philip of Spain 1.8 million crowns annually ($1.15 billion or £623 million today) over a five-year period to eradicate the "heretical state" of England. Effectively, the pope agreed to forfeit papal concessions to the crown of Spain. Proceeds would be collected in special chests at the mint in Madrid for the king's use to rid himself of the demon Elizabeth. He raised an additional 900,000 crowns for his enterprise.[1]

Philip had tired by the end of 1585 with English meddling in the Low Countries. Had he not had William of Orange assassinated to bring the Netherlands back under control? And what for? So that Robert Dudley, Earl of Leicester, should become its effective king! Little did Philip know that Dudley's rise to a quasi-kingship offered by the Dutch had stirred almost as much consternation at Elizabeth's court as it had at Philip's. The queen was so angry that she wrote a personal letter to Leicester and had it brought to him by Sir Thomas Heneage in the Low Countries. She intuitively knew that Leicester's actions drove England ever closer to the final confrontation. Her stinging words to Leicester (though not the finest she had written) were these:

We hold our honour greatly touched by the said acceptation of that government, and least as we may not with our honour endure, or that it carries a manifest appearance of repugnancy to our protestation set out in print, by the which we declare that our only intent in sending him over to those parts was to direct and govern the English troops that we had granted to the States for their aid and to assist them with his advice and counsel for the better ordering both of their civil and martial courses, as is contained in the late contract passed between us and their commissioners that were here, so as the world may justly thereby conceive . . . [that] a minister [of] ours sent thither to execute and hold such a course of government as was contained in the said contract—should without our assent be pressed to assent to accept of more large and absolute authority over the said countries than was accorded by virtue of the said contract, especially seeing that we ourself, being oftentimes pressed by their commissioners to accept of the absolute government, did always refuse the same. . . .[2]

Despite the rebuke, Leicester, never a great commander in the field, didn't stand a chance against the superior Spanish troops honed into a crack fighting force by Parma. At the end of 1586, Leicester, and what was left of his army, had been brought back to England, defeated. Sir Philip Sidney, along with thousands of others, had been killed in a fruitless, chaotic attempt to free the Dutch from the yoke of the Spanish.

Then, in February 1587 at the Earl of Shrewsbury's home, Fotheringhay Castle, the final act in the twenty-year drama between the two British queens was played out. Despite having been thrust into the rarified atmosphere of the French and Scottish courts her entire life, Mary had allowed her heart to rule her head. Now she would lose even that. Her execution for her role in the Babington plot would serve as a symbol for all Catholics that "stubborn disobedience . . . Incitement to insurrection . . . against the life and person of her Sacred Majesty" would end in a guilty verdict for high treason and death. When Mary's auburn wig and head were held aloft for the executioner to utter the customary words for traitors, "Long live the queen," in Elizabeth's name, all-out war was inevitable.

Or perhaps not. Elizabeth always made a good show of saying
what she didn't mean, and meaning what she didn't say. She lashed
out at her Councillors, singling out Walsingham, for tricking her
into signing Mary's death warrant. Her former agent in the Low
Countries, William Davison, now one of her secretaries, was judged
to be the most culpable and was thrown unceremoniously into the
Tower through its notorious Traitor's Gate. Yet, for Davison, the
Traitor's Gate swung both ways, and he was later released upon a
bond of £10,000. For now Elizabeth had written the script, and for
the time being, Davison would need to be sacrificed for the good of
the realm. Elizabeth, meanwhile, put on the best performance of her
life to avoid any backlash from Scotland. She wailed for a solid three
weeks, then wrote a heartfelt letter of apology and explanation to
the King of Scotland, James, blaming her secretary and begging the
King's personal forgiveness. James was no fool and felt he was a step
closer to becoming Elizabeth's heir. If the queen asked forgiveness
he would comply. With the throne of England dangled in front of
his nose, how could he refuse?[3]

When the dramatic news reached the King of Spain on March
23, Philip recognized that he, too, could dither no longer. Aside
from Mary's Calvinist son, James VI of Scotland, he believed (as
did Mendoza, by his genealogical chart showing Philip directly
descended from Edward III) that he had the best claim to England's
throne, and would need to seize it for Catholicism.[4]

Orders were sent out to Don Alvaro de Bazán, the Marquis of
Santa Cruz, to prepare the fleet for the "Enterprise of England"
he had so long wanted to undertake. Santa Cruz's estimate was for
150 great ships, which included all Spain's galleons and most of her
merchantmen. Over forty *urcas*—round tublike freighters used for
provisions—would also be required. Some 320 dispatch boats and
cruisers would also be needed, bringing the total estimate to 510 sail,
along with 30,000 mariners and 64,000 soldiers. The naval ordnance
alone would cost around 3.8 million ducats ($4.20 billion or £2.27
billion today). Such a force was as far beyond Philip's reach as it
would have been beyond Elizabeth's. And so, the king came up with
an alternative plan for Santa Cruz to meet up with Parma's troops
in the Low Countries and for them to invade England together. It
was a perfect solution for the armchair strategist: marry his premier

naval commander with the ruthless and skilled Parma.[5] But as preparations progressed through the spring of 1587, costs soared, making Philip feel literally ill. Spending rose to 10,000,500 *reals* per day for his officers' commissions alone ($1.06 billion or £570,322 million). Yet Santa Cruz required another 3 million *reals* in gold urgently.[6]

Almost as bad as the financial strain that the Enterprise was putting on Spain's coffers were the blithe remarks from his officers that an invasion of England would be a dawdle. *Disparo!* (Nonsense!) Philip scrawled on these papers before he would toss them aside, or into the fire. After all, *he* had been King of England, and he knew something of English stubbornness and character. The uncertainty of the outcome of the Enterprise weighed heavily on his conscience. But as Mendoza wrote to Philip and later shared his thoughts with the Pope, "since God in His wisdom has ordained otherwise [than for Mary to rule England], He will raise up other instruments for the triumph of His cause. . . . So it would seem to be God's obvious design to bestow upon your majesty the crowns of these two kingdoms."[7]

Yet Philip's "Enterprise of England" was the worst-kept secret in Europe, and Elizabeth, too, was left no alternative but to try to cut it off at the knees. She would unleash Drake again, and pray.

35. Cadiz ✦

I've Singed the beard of the King of Spain.
— SIR FRANCIS DRAKE

Philip II had been in his sickbed crippled by gout and self-doubt for the past six months. Though ill, he knew decisive action had to be taken that spring to hold out any palpable hope to be rid of his great demons—Elizabeth and Drake—once and for all. More recently, Raleigh and his Virginia colony troubled his aching mind. The man Davis had already made two voyages in search of the Northwest Passage, and would soon undertake a third! And now he had been advised that a certain Thomas Cavendish had sailed for Peru in his ship the *Desire*.[1] Desire . . . it was a word that haunted him. He now desired peace. Even Aranjuez, his oasis of calm, could not provide him with the balm to soothe his troubled thoughts. The undeclared war against "that Englishwoman" continued to escalate despite his best efforts. Still, he often wondered how things had degenerated to such an impasse. How had he gone from brother to would-be suitor to her persecutor in twenty-eight years? But when the nostalgia cleared, Philip remembered that Elizabeth often claimed no knowledge of her adventurers' undertakings, while simultaneously counting her third of the cash they plundered.

The king was, as ever, well informed. Since 1585, her firsthand knowledge of the two hundred vessels sailing each year carrying out her business of piracy and plunder had made her, at the very least, an accessory. The rules of these naval engagements had been well defined by the English Admiralty: the queen received a one-third share of the registered plunder, the investors a third, and the crew a third. The Admiralty would get a 10 percent slice off the top, after customs officials (who also paid out to the queen and her councillors) were paid on the ships' arrivals into harbor.[2]

What good were all the riches of the world, Philip asked his councillors, if none of his Indiamen reached Spanish or Portuguese ports? He knew full well that not one treasure ship had docked in Spain the previous year, and prayed that the Queen of England's intelligencers had not been informed. Her sailors would be the ruin of him. Yet Elizabeth had been her own worst enemy, and left him with no alternative once she had eliminated the Queen of Scots.

And so, it had been with some reluctance that Philip gave the order to his great admiral, Santa Cruz, to press ahead with a Spanish Armada to invade England to claim the throne for Spanish interests. It was a matter of self-defense, a matter of national pride. It was also an economic necessity.

While Philip II shambled through the perfumed gardens in the afternoons of April 1587, he mused repeatedly, "Clearly God must be allowing her waywardness on account of her sins and unfaithfulness, so that she will be lost." As ever, the Spanish monarch sought the financial—as well as spiritual—support from Pope Sixtus V for his enterprise against England. However, this time, the pope's offer of a million ducats was conditional on the successful invasion of England, ordering that "your Majesty would not maintain the throne for yourself." When the pope—through his own spy network— learned about Philip's plan to keep England as part of his enlarged empire, Sixtus fulminated against the king with threats of divine vengeance unless he "repented of his great sin, and obeyed the Vicar of Christ."[3]

Meanwhile, Elizabeth, of course, knew everything. Drake begged to be allowed to sail and attack Philip on his home territory. Walsingham and Leicester agreed. A plan was hatched to use Antonio, the dethroned Portuguese king, as their decoy, and Walsingham spread as much disinformation as he could to keep the object of Drake's mission an utter secret.[4] For the job ahead, Drake was given six of the queen's ships: her four best galleons—the *Elizabeth Bonaventure*, the *Golden Lion*, the *Dreadnought*, and the *Rainbow*—and two of her swiftest pinnaces. Elizabeth personally authorized Drake to "obtain as many ships as would join him from the London merchants," and the lord admiral offered his own galleon and pinnace. Drake invested four of his own ships in the venture.[5] By March 27, 1587, Drake had obtained a total of forty-two vessels for his secret mission.

To help keep Philip's spies off the scent, Drake stayed behind in London for twenty-four hours for an unrecorded meeting with his great friend, Sir Francis Walsingham, before joining the Londoners at Dover and boarding the *Elizabeth Bonaventure* with his wife, Lady Elizabeth.[6] Walsingham then leaked the latest disinformation to Philip's newest spy—the English ambassador in Paris—Sir Edward Stafford. As an excellent spymaster, Walsingham knew that Stafford had accepted 8,000 crowns from Philip only weeks earlier, and he chose specifically to leave the traitor in place so that he could better serve the English crown by his treachery. Stafford did not disappoint him.[7]

Mendoza was told immediately, and he penned an urgent advice to Philip that "the Queen of England's secretary writes to the new confidant [Stafford] telling him to be careful what reports he sends from here . . . the Queen had not decided anything about sending out the fleet, as the intelligence sent by her ambassador here had cooled her."[8]

Ten days later "true advices from England" were received by Mendoza that proclaimed:

> On the 27th March proclamation was made in London ordering the instant embarkation of the crews and troops of the 10 ships with Francis Drake. Of these 10 ships, four belonged to the Queen, their burden being respectively 400, 300 and 120 tons; very well armed with bronze guns. The others are merchantmen, the largest 200 tons, but most of them 120 to 150 tons, with iron pieces. The queen's flagship took out 200 men . . . Drake went on board near Dover, and sailed with the ships to Plymouth, where the fleet was to rendezvous. Off the Isle of Wight he was joined by 12 merchant ships which had been sent by the Queen, and they all proceeded together to Plymouth. They take victuals for over four months . . . Drake took orders for the ships which might be in the Western ports, or at sea with letters of marque [letters of reprisal], to accompany him . . . so that altogether they hoped to enter Spanish waters with 60 sail and about 3,000 men, besides those who might be in the

ships bearing the letters of marque . . . they are going to prevent the junction of his Majesty's fleet in Spain, destroying a portion of it, as it will have to be fitted out in various ports. Others say the design is to intercept the Indian flotillas, and this seems the most probable.[9]

But it was too late. *El Draco* had set sail two weeks before with his fleet to "singe the beard of the King of Spain." It was an exercise that Drake embraced with relish, as he did every opportunity for retribution in his personal war. As had become her custom, Elizabeth set about to publicly disassociate herself from Drake's secret mission, despite the fact that she had just sent him out with sealed orders "to impeach the purpose of the Spanish fleet and stop their meeting at Lisbon, distressing their ships within their havens, and returning to England with the plunder."[10]

By now Drake knew that the queen's decisions could be transitory, and for this reason he fled London with the Portuguese pretender, literally riding on his coattails, begging to come along. But Drake knew that it was no time to get diverted by Antonio's wild assertions that all of Portugal would rise up behind him. Sir Francis and his combined fleet set sail on April 12, 1587, from Plymouth, leaving the Portuguese pretender to kick his heels in the West Country of England.

It did not take Drake's naval genius to know that the rumors of Philip's Armada were true, and that the time for diplomacy had passed. As prime defender of the Catholic faith, Philip had had his hand forced with the swing of the Queen of Scots' executioner's blade, and everyone—including his vacillating queen—knew that England was already at war. Elizabeth's counter-orders, written in her own hand, to "forbear to enter forcibly into any of the said king's ports or havens, or to offer violence to any of his towns or shipping within harboring, or to do any act of hostility upon the land. And yet, notwithstanding this direction, her pleasure is that both you and such of her subjects as serve there under you should do your best endeavour (avoiding as much as may lie in you the effusion of Christian blood) to get into your possession such shipping of the said king or his subjects as you shall find at sea" were rushed out to the admiral on one of her finest remaining pinnaces.[11]

It was vintage Elizabeth. And it encapsulated her desire to have her cake and eat it, to wage peace as if it were war, and to try to lull her enemies into believing that she would not knowingly take up arms against them. Yet, the amended order was sent out a full nine days after Drake had sailed. Her intended subterfuge now complete, all Elizabeth—and the country—could do was wait and pray. Walsingham tried to throw oil on troubled waters by claiming that Drake was heading for the West Indies to "harry" the West Indies fleet of Spain. The queen herself enhanced the misinformation when she dismissed these rumors as fantasy, confirming to the Venetian ambassador that Drake had not "left London for Plymouth to gather a powerful fleet with a view to meeting and fighting the Peruvian flotilla, but had sailed instead for Constantinople."[12]

While Philip tried to enjoy his fragrant garden, Elizabeth, in her turn, rambled through her chilly palace at Whitehall, more ill-tempered than usual. Only her daily horseback riding and hunting brought her some relief from the tension. Perhaps she had acted rashly? Had she played her cards well? Would Drake let her down? She was both empowered and powerless. Elizabeth was now fifty-four. All she had worked for her entire life was in play. Worst of all, she hated being backed into a corner almost as much as she loathed war.

Drake, in the meantime, was making good progress. Aside from a storm off Finisterre, where at least one ship was lost, the voyage had gone swiftly and smoothly, and Drake had arrived off the coast of Cadiz within eighteen days without alerting the Spaniards. The bulk of the flotilla still lagged badly behind the *Elizabeth Bonaventure* due to the Finisterre storm when Drake called in his seasoned second in command, William Burroughs, to his cabin for a council of war. Cadiz lay just over the horizon ahead, Drake pointed, and the flotilla at the horizon behind them. Burroughs waited before replying. Unbeknown to Drake he had become his lieutenant general at Burghley's specific request. Drake explained that the time to attack was now. Burroughs was of the opinion that their number was dangerously low, and it was best to wait for the fleet to catch up to them before attacking the Spanish port. First thing in the morning would be better. Drake railed at him that it was tactically wrong to lose the crucial element of surprise, and categorically overruled Burroughs. The order for attack was given at four P.M. on the afternoon of April 29.

At precisely that moment, Philip was shambling through his sweet-scented gardens at Aranjuez, ignoring the urgent dispatch from Mendoza in Paris. It warned the king that Drake "was to try to prevent the junction of your Majesty's fleet, which had to be equipped in various ports, and if they succeed in breaking up a portion of it, then to proceed on the Indian route and encounter the flotillas. To this end they had let out a few words to Drake about Cadiz being a good port to burn the shipping in, if a good fleet were taken thither."[13] Even if Philip had read the urgent message, he would have been unable to stop Elizabeth's admiral.

As the favorable winds blew Drake's fleet within view of Cadiz harbor, its inhabitants were enjoying some street players performing a comedy in the large central town square. A tumbler measured his muscles against the comedians', to the general amusement of the crowd, while the surrounding shops burst to breaking point with customers who had had too much to drink. Someone pointed to the approaching ships. It must be the valiant fleet of Juan Martínez de Recalde and his Biscayans, another replied. Only when the ships were counted did the people of Cadiz begin to think that it could be their enemies, the *Luteranos*, perhaps even *El Draco*.

Despite the relaxed atmosphere, the harbor was not unguarded. Six galleys of the Spanish fleet had docked from Gibraltar a few days earlier, and had spread themselves across the upper bay, in the shadow of the old castle. Their commander, Don Pedro de Acuña, drew these ships across the entrance to the bay, oars glinting in the late afternoon sunlight, in preparation for the attack. Another ship broke ranks and, with its harquebusiers and pikemen at their battle stations in the forecastle, prepared to stop the hostile fleet. Drake's long-distance guns struck them midships in response. The English banners were broken out, and Drake's trumpets and drum hailed their presence from the quarterdeck of the *Elizabeth Bonaventure*.

The townspeople watched in utter disbelief. Whispers of *El Draco* became shrieks of "Drake, the Dragon!" in no time. Orders were shouted for the women, children, and the aged to take refuge in the castle. Pandemonium broke out as the people of Cadiz fled for their lives. Fearful of the terrified "mob" running toward him, the captain of the guard in the castle shut his gates to the panicked crowd. Twenty-five women and children were trampled to death before he came to his senses and let them in.

Meanwhile, the men of the town formed themselves into companies to defend the port in the event of Drake landing, but without adequate harbor defenses they couldn't have held out much hope of winning. Murmurs between the frightened men claimed that the formidable galleys of the Spanish empire were superior to Drake's sailing ships. But the Spanish galleons were huge hulks, with forecastles overflowing with soldiers and short-range cannon, unable to maneuver swiftly in rolling seas or close combat. What they had not appreciated was that any of Drake's seven heaviest sailing ships could heave more firepower at them in a single broadside than all of the Spanish galleons put together—and that they could heave it much more accurately and a great deal further. Even if their number had been greater, the Spaniards could never have beaten the more technically advanced, more heavily armed English vessels. Hawkins's redesign of the English fleet would stand up admirably to the battlefield conditions.

The Spanish galleys limped into anchor between the old fort of Cadiz and St. Mary's Port, some four miles to the northeast of Cadiz harbor. There the waters were shallow, and the defenders regrouped and mounted skirmishes against the plundering English throughout the night. The Spanish shore guns pounded the harbor waters, with not an Englishman nor English ship injured. Excuses for this appalling lack of force were later said to be due to the fact that Spanish gunpowder was expensive and unreliable, and the men firing the weapons were inexperienced.

Even in these threatening circumstances, and against direct orders from the queen, Drake did not seek to destroy the remaining merchant vessels in harbor. Instead, he huddled the ships together and had most of the sixty vessels boarded to take their cargo as plunder. Evidently, it was hard to break old habits. Some of these cargo ships were destined to join the Armada at Lisbon, including five *urcas* fully laden with wine and biscuit, and a number of Dutch hulks. The Dutch vessels had been confiscated by the Spanish and pressed into Philip's service for his great invasion force. There were also ships waiting to join the fleet sailing for the Americas. Instead, Drake ordered his men to remove the Xerez wine (sherry) from the ships as well as all the other provisions they could load.

Throughout the night the Spanish took aim at Drake's fleet, but cornered only Burroughs's ship, the *Golden Lion*, when a cannon ball hit her hull. Drake sent the *Rainbow* with six merchantmen and his own pinnace to protect her and bring her to safety, cursing Burroughs for his "treachery." By morning, the wind had died away, leaving Drake and his men pathetically becalmed and in real danger. At midday, the Duke of Medina Sidonia and his men arrived to rescue Cadiz. For twelve hours he tried with fire ships to pierce Drake's defenses, but to no avail. Then the wind picked up again shortly after midnight, and Drake's fleet sailed from the harbor with the Spanish in pursuit. Drake turned and lay anchor, and again, despite heavy fire from the Spaniards, the *Elizabeth Bonaventure* remained unscathed. At dawn, prisoners were exchanged, Medina Sidonia gave the English admiral a present of wine and sweetmeats, and Drake sailed off in the direction of Cape St. Vincent and the Azores.[14]

An estimate prepared by the Duke of Medina Sidonia, for Philip's eyes only, listed twenty-four vessels lost, valued at 172,000 ducats, including their cargoes ($11.90 million or £6.43 million today). "The loss," Philip said, "was not very great, but the daring of the attempt was very great indeed." Drake believed that he had sunk thirty-seven ships. But even this estimate doesn't tell the full story.[15]

Sir Francis's solemn vow to Elizabeth was to defeat the Spanish fleet and to reward the private investors and crew through plunder. Until this point, neither had really been achieved. Although the Spanish estimated some twenty-four ships destroyed—including an impressive fighting galleon belonging to the Armada commander, the Marquis of Santa Cruz—some sixty ships remained seaworthy at Cadiz. Considering that the English looted, burned, and sank the ships at will, it remains a mystery why Drake didn't destroy the entire fleet. If only he had scuttled them . . .

So why did Drake flagrantly disregard his commitment to Elizabeth? Surely Drake had learned in Cadiz that the *urcas* and the other merchant ships were there to join the rest of the Armada in Lisbon before sailing to England. Why did he not destroy these ships, too? Like so many skirmishes clouded by the fog of war, the answers remain unclear. Most likely, it was because Drake had a sniff of greater glory to come. He had learned from his prisoners that Juan Martínez de Recalde, Spain's most able naval officer after the great Santa Cruz himself, was somewhere off Cape St. Vincent with a squadron half the size of Drake's. And so, after ten days in an orgy of plunder in and around Cadiz, Drake's fleet sailed west toward Recalde and glory. It was a unique opportunity for Sir Francis to face off the legendary Recalde with the odds stacked in his favor and perhaps seize the flota he was rumored to be accompanying. Yet even if the flota hadn't sailed under Recalde, if he could neutralize the talented Spaniard, Drake must have thought that the threat imposed by Spain later would be greatly reduced.

Since Cape St. Vincent was not on the strategic map for the naval campaign agreed with Elizabeth, Burroughs objected strongly to Drake's disobeying the queen's orders. Drake countered accusing Burroughs of mutiny and treason, and ordering him put under arrest on the *Golden Lion*. But in an exceptional turn of events, Burroughs's men mutinied against Drake, and released their captain, who hightailed it back to London in the queen's ship. While sailing southward to Cape St. Vincent, Drake had him tried in abstentia for desertion and treason, sentencing him to death. But by the time Drake would catch up with Burroughs again in London, Burghley had ensured that his man was well beyond Drake's wrath.

At Cape St. Vincent, the English fleet destroyed fishing boats and coasters bringing barrel staves for the Armada's water barrels. From a twenty-first century vantage point, this may seem petty; yet it was the most successful portion of the Spanish raid in strategic terms. Without the staves to hold the water barrels together, it was impossible to store water and food for any long voyage. Through this single act of piracy, Drake had ensured that the Armada would be doomed to yet another lengthy delay, and escaped Elizabeth's promised retribution.

Yet where was Recalde? While waiting for his answer, Drake wrote to Walsingham: "I assure your honour the like preparation [at Cadiz] was never heard of nor known as the King of Spain hath and daily maketh to invade England. . . . I dare not almost write of the great forces we hear the King of Spain hath. Prepare in England strongly and most by sea!"[16]

Drake's tendency to lawlessness had always been overlooked because of his sheer brilliance as a commander. Cadiz was the first time the English lower, sleeker ships had been used against the Spanish vessels in "skirmish" tactics. It was also the first time that smaller ships had outgunned the towering Spanish galleons. But even Drake knew that unless he could bring back chests of swag, he would *be* history, rather than finding his place in it.

As luck would have it, by the time Drake sailed from Cadiz, Recalde had already anchored in Lisbon harbor. Drake pursued him, sailing north along the Portuguese coast, and landed unopposed at Lagos. Columns of Spanish horsemen shadowed the English invaders and opened fire, and the English made a dash to the rather unimpressive Sagres Castle and captured it. Drake probably never realized that it was the castle of Prince Henry the Navigator, the first royal ever to promote maritime exploration. Nonetheless, he wrote in his ship's log that day, "continuing to the end, yields the true glory."

Then, as ever, his luck changed. On June 1, the whole fleet weighed anchor, and ships carrying Drake's dispatches and diseased or disabled turned northward, while the fleet sailed south for the Azores. Drake had had news that the king's own carrack, the lumbering *San Felipe*, was homeward-bound from Goa with its annual cargo of spices, jewels, and other oriental goods that were fruits of Portugal's eastern empire.

By now Philip II was apoplectic with rage at Drake's ignominious escapades along the Portuguese coast and Cadiz. He already feared that *El Draco* had heard of the approaching *San Felipe* from caravels in the Guinea trade before the bad news had reached him. After all, the *San Felipe* was the vessel worth 3 million *reals* that Philip needed badly to fit out the Armada in its final stages. Most of all he needed her treasure.

On June 18, at São Miguel in the Azores, the *Elizabeth Bonaventure* "engaged" Philip's carrack and easily seized her. The *San Felipe*'s guns were so jammed with precious cargo that she was unable to use them against the English marauders. The carrack was stuffed with pepper, cinnamon, cloves, calicoes, silks, ivories, gold, silver, and caskets of jewels. The total value was £114,000 ($32.01 million or £17.3 million today) and three times the value of all the ships' cargoes he had sunk, seized, or burned in Cadiz Bay. Considering that the queen's ship, the *Elizabeth Bonaventure*, could be provisioned for £175 monthly, and that £40,000 put an entire army in the field, this was a colossal booty—even for Drake.

Its capture also meant that Sir Francis needed to set sail immediately for England to save his prize, forfeiting all the unfinished goals set by his queen back home. The loss of the *San Felipe* would aggravate Philip's precarious financial position and lead him to make ever more desperate deals with his enemies and allies alike in order to launch his Armada. While Drake, as admiral, had not destroyed the Armada fleet, he had so confused and disrupted Spanish and Portuguese shipping that he had bought Elizabeth's England another year to prepare for the enterprise. In Drake's own words, "there must be a beginning of any good matter."[17]

36. The Plundering of the Spanish Armada ⚜

*If the late Queen would have believed her men of war
as she did her scribes, we had in her time beaten that
great empire in pieces and made their kings kings of
figs and oranges as in old times.*

—SIR WALTER RALEIGH

The country was in an uproar when Drake returned with the
treasure from King Philip's carrack. Not only was Drake's name
on everyone's lips, in every pamphlet, and blessed in every church in
an exultation of joy, but he had provided a boost of confidence to the
court and the people. The queen was delighted with her portion of
the takings, but again threw the court into dismay against her when
she steadfastly refused to prepare for the inevitable war. Drake
cajoled and begged Elizabeth, having written to Walsingham while
still in pursuit of Recalde and the flota: "I dare not almost write unto
your Honour of the great forces we hear that the King of Spain hath
out. . . . Prepare in England strongly, and most by sea. Stop him now,
and stop him ever."[1]

From that moment until the time he was finally let loose, Drake
sang the same song, over and over. He longed to capture the fleet, in
port, at Lisbon while it was still assembling its victuals and forces.
"The advantage of time and place," Drake wrote to the queen on
April 13, 1588, "in all martial actions is half the victory."[2] He had
certainly convinced Lord Admiral Howard that his tactics were
right, but the queen remained unmoved. England possessed the
most sophisticated mobilization system of the age, and could muster
and load men and supplies aboard ship in weeks, as opposed to the
Spanish method that seemed to take years. Though she didn't want
to let on to Drake, his latest escapade had done more damage than
the taking of the *San Felipe* and the destruction and plundering of

ships and critical supplies. Philip had been obliged to suspend the silver fleets for 1588 and, in addition to his astronomical papal loans, borrow money from the merchant banking houses of Fugger and Spinola.[3] The blow to Spanish pride had been colossal.

Yet the queen knew that her own system, while finely tuned, was also fragile. Unlike Philip, her borrowing capability was restricted to small sums and for short periods of time. Parliament had voted an increase in her expenditure to £72,000 a year at the beginning of 1588, and, thanks to her parsimonious nature, she still had a further £154,000 in her reserves ($41.94 million or £22.67 million today). Considering that the first year of Dutch financial assistance had cost her £160,000, and that the navy's best estimate for a partial naval mobilization would cost £15,000 a month, Elizabeth simply couldn't afford the luxury of granting Drake his "advantage of time and place" until—possibly—the very last second.[4] Her parsimony has been blamed for much of what went wrong in the preparations for the Spanish Armada battle, but even with all the money in the world, it would have been unwise to prepare and man the fleet. It was virtually impossible to keep ships manned for combat at sea for any length of time without sickness—scurvy or dysentery—ravaging the crews. The lack of funds, in this case, saved English lives.

In addition to her financial woes, the queen also had to assuage any number of bruised egos in the formation of her fighting force. Her dear "Water" had been begging to send relief to his second group of colonists newly installed in Virginia, but she dared not allow any of her expert captains to sail with men and provisions for such a task. England needed all its resources to hand. Raleigh also could not understand why his West Country cousin had been selected as the lieutenant general of the fleet when *he* was the queen's obvious favorite! Frobisher, too, cut up rough when she had selected Drake as Howard's second in command, but he was swiftly reminded of his numerous failures at sea and Drake's phenomenal successes to keep him in check. William Burroughs, too, had been offended by Drake's appointment, especially as his "case" had not as yet been settled by the High Court of the Admiralty. Henry Knollys had taken a dislike to the upstart Drake after their run-in during the 1585 West Indies voyage, and he let his feelings be known as well. The only naval man not to make his ego felt was Drake himself, who never made any reference to the Lord High Admiral Howard's having no sea battle experience whatsoever.[5]

Philip, too, had a number of worries beyond the obvious financial double whammy of no fleets arriving with treasure, combined with past depredations coupled with the threat of future ones. Then, of course, Santa Cruz had done the unthinkable. He died. It was with an extremely heavy heart that Philip named the soldier and "hero" of Cadiz, Medina Sidonia, as Santa Cruz's replacement. Medina Sidonia was the next most high-ranking peer of the realm, and, as such, his appointment was "God's obvious design." Philip may have been obliged to make him admiral of the fleet, but he was not obliged to trust him. Medina Sidonia made his lack of confidence in the undertaking clear to his king, and all Philip could urge was, "sail . . . sail." Parma, too, had lost any enthusiasm for Philip's hybrid scheme devised to save money, since it would most likely lose lives. Like Elizabeth, the King of Spain had no conception of how wars were actually fought at sea, and the difficulty that his generals would have in meeting up with the English baying at their heels. No practical suggestions were forthcoming either as to how Parma's forces could board from their two hundred or so skiffs onto the Spanish galleons without being attacked by the Dutch, who still controlled the deepwater ports. Above all, Spanish mutinies could be brought on by lack of prompt pay. This would mean that the Armada would need to travel with treasure for her mariners, and keep them loyal.[6]

Philip also had to play a treacherous double game—persuading Protestant nations of the north of Europe (and thereby ones which could inconveniently intervene in his battle plan) that his invasion of England was strictly political, while reassuring the Catholic countries that his motivations were purely religious. Such conceits could be kept "secret" for only a short period. Time was, as a result, his enemy as well.[7]

And so, through a series of half-measures, concessions on the part of the monarchs and their nobility, and the disparate voices of their adventurers, Elizabeth and Philip prepared to have their fleets meet in what would become the first modern naval battle in history. Pitted against the imperious, high-castled Spanish galleons were Hawkins's smaller, sleeker, more heavily armed warships and pinnaces. Yet the notorious English weather conspired against each of them, preventing Medina Sidonia from reaching England until the end of July and keeping Drake and Howard from sailing out beyond France to attack Lisbon. It would become an engagement simplistically remembered by history as won by "a great wind." It was, in fact, no such thing.

The formation of England's fleet was divided into seven types: the queen's ships; merchant ships serving "westward under Sir F. Drake"; those "set forth and paid for by the City of London"; merchant ships and barks in the queen's pay; coasters under the lord admiral paid for by the queen; coasters under Lord Henry Seymour; and volunteers that joined the fleet after the attack by the Armada.[8] In all, some 182 ships and 15 victualing ships. Six ships only were 300 tons or more—the *Galleon Leicester*, the *Edward Bonaventure*, the *Merchant Royal*, the *Roebuck*, the *Hercules,* and the *Sampson*. Another twenty were between 200 and 300 tons, and proven fighters, like John Watts's *Margaret and John*, a merchant ship from the City of London. Also on England's side was a superior naval efficiency in victualing and in repairs, with the long established royal dockyards at Deptford, Woolwich, and Chatham.[9]

Spain, amazingly, had no royal dockyards, which made their preparations ponderous and extremely inefficient. Through attrition, by the time the Spaniards reached the Channel, their fleet had already lost over twenty ships. While the 127 vessels sailing toward England were slightly fewer than the total English contingent, they were dramatically impressive in their tightly knit crescent formation, and vastly outweighed the English ships. Twenty were warships, or armed merchantmen of considerable stature and force. Four of these were galleasses (mixed oared and sail vessels that had helped Philip to win at Lepanto over sixteen years earlier). All the rest were transports, the tubby *urcas* for victuals or small craft for communications and distribution. In the spring storms that drove them back to Corunna in May, they had lost four other galleys.

When Medina Sidonia finally sailed again from Corunna on July 12, 1588, with his remaining 131 vessels manned with 7,000 mariners and 17,000 soldiers, he had a fraction of the 510 ships and 35,000 men demanded by Santa Cruz. Philip's plan was to have Medina

Sidonia "join hands" with Parma from Dunkirk and Nieuwport, and invade England. Parma's assault force was around seventeen thousand men, whom he would somehow embark on the fly boats and skiffs to join Medina Sidonia.[10] If for any reason the "joining hands" did not succeed, the Spanish fleet was to take the Isle of Wight, secure it, and communicate with Parma from there for an alternative plan.[11]

Elizabeth has frequently been criticized by many strategists and historians for her intrusive, and at times contradictory, orders to her fleet. In part, this is because Drake finally persuaded her (with the active connivance of Howard) that it was foolhardy to divide the English ships, with Howard guarding the Narrow Seas, and Drake the entry to the Channel at Plymouth, called the Western Approaches. Yet after the order had been given in the spring to attempt to catch Philip sleeping in Lisbon, the queen's "interference" was minimal, particularly in comparison with the King of Spain, who had an alternative plan for nearly any contingency. If there was one thing the Queen of England did at this point, it was to trust her commanders once they had put out to sea. Burghley, now quite old and gnarled with gout and arthritis, wrote gloomily at the time, "a man would wish, if peace cannot be had, that the enemy would no longer delay, but prove (as I trust) his evil fortune."[12] The wait was getting to everyone.

But Burghley was always a pessimist. Sir William Winter wrote, "Our ships doth show themselves like gallants here. . . . I assure you, it would do a man's heart good to behold them." Lord Admiral Howard, too, remained confident, boasting, "I have been aboard of every ship that goeth out with me and in every place where any may creep, and I thank God that they be in the estate they be in, and there is never a one of them that knows what a leak means. . . . "[13]

The entire country prepared for war in its own way. Across the south coast, bonfires were erected on all the high peaks leading from Land's End to London and manned around the clock. At the first sight of the Spaniards, the order to light the first beacon would be given from a salvo let off at Plymouth, and it would take under fifteen minutes for the torchlight warnings to carry the news to court. It was a tried and tested method used since ancient times, and it would be used again and again until the advent of telecommunications.[14]

Then, suddenly, on the morning of July 19, 1588, a seaman named Captain Thomas Fleming was cruising with his ship, the *Golden Hind,* off the coast at the Lizard when he spied a massive line of ships in the distance off the Isles of Scilly with their sails struck, as if in wait for more ships. It must have been an incredibly impressive sight. Despite a royal warrant for his detention as a pirate, Fleming headed into port to warn the fleet at Plymouth.

Legend has it that Drake was playing a game of bowls on Plymouth Hoe when Fleming broke the news, and that he allegedly said that there was more than enough time to finish the game and beat the Spaniards. There is no evidence from any English source at the time or later that anything of the sort happened. After fifteen months of waiting to engage the enemy, it is highly unlikely that Drake, in particular, did anything other than scramble his men to their ships and their battle stations, while ordering the beacons to be lit to carry word to London. While, strictly speaking, Fleming should have been clapped in irons, since a warrant had been issued for his arrest for piracy, it is more likely that he had, in fact, been engaged by Howard and Drake to act as their scout. [15]

The Armada made for a formidable sight. The Spanish ships ranged two miles in breadth, and with their huge fore and after castles towered over the English. In the six battles that followed, the history of naval combat evolved into the modern era. Gone forever were the days of oarpowered ships over sail. Grappling and boarding, too, was replaced by superior firepower and long-range weaponry. The death knell was also tolled for the English crossbow archers as the country's most lethal fighting force aboard ship. [16]

Yet despite superior maneuverability and firepower, the English made little, if any headway, on the first day of battle (July 20). The next day, though, the English got lucky. One of the Spanish warships, the *Nuestra Señora del Rosario*, was lost. The *Rosario*, a colossal 1,150 ton *nao*, a multipurpose ship armed for war with fifty-two guns and a crew of over four hundred men, lost its bowsprit, foreyard, halyards, and forecourse after a series of collisions in the fleet due to their tight formation. Her commander, Don Pedro de Valdes, fired off his guns to let Medina Sidonia know his plight, but all efforts to save her failed. Valdes watched helplessly as the Armada slowly pulled away to the east, leaving him to his destiny. This was a huge blow to the Spaniards, since she was one of the largest ships in the Armada, and carried a third of the treasure taken along to pay the mariners and soldiers.[17]

While the English had seen that the *Rosario* had been left behind, at their council of war that night, Howard gave the order to keep their formation and follow the main body of the Spanish fleet. It was Drake's turn to lead the watch that night, and so his poop lantern was lit at his stern for the other ships to follow. Nonetheless, Watts's Londoner, the *Margaret and John*, broke formation and ranged alongside the *Rosario*. His arrows and muskets at close range met with the ferocious reply of several Spanish guns, and the *Margaret and John*'s captain replied with a broadside. They were so close that they could hear the Spaniards whispering after the crash of the cannonball into the *Rosario*'s hull. Though disabled, she was still over four times the English ship's size, and the men voted to return to the English fleet.[18]

Meanwhile, Howard blithely followed the lantern, unaware that all was not as it should be. The lookout had lost sight of Drake's lantern, and instead of advising the admiral, who had gone below, he waited and strained his eyes into the dark distance before he saw the lantern again, but this time much farther forward than expected. Fogs suddenly bubbled up all the time in the Channel, and so the watch thought nothing more of the episode until morning. Drake, meanwhile, had sailed away. His own watch aboard his ship, the *Revenge*, had reported that there were three or four ships sailing abreast of them. Could it be the Spaniards working to windward in the dark? Drake ordered his lantern extinguished to surprise the ships that dogged him, and to avoid taking the whole of the fleet on a wild-goose chase, and lose the Armada.

His prey turned out to be German freighters, and Drake claimed to be rejoining the fleet when he spied the *Rosario* and pulled up alongside her. He summoned her captain to surrender, and when the Spaniard asked for terms, Drake replied that he had no time to parlay, but that they had the word of Sir Francis Drake that they wouldn't be harmed. Twenty years later, when Drake's heirs were arguing over his estate, testimony from his sailors that night reported:

The said Sir Francis entertained the said Don Pedro in his cabin, and there, in the hearing of the deponent, the said Sir Francis did will his own interpreter to ask the said Don Pedro in the Spanish tongue whether he would yield unto him or no and further to tell him if he would not yield he would set him aboard again. Whereupon the said Don Pedro paused a little while with himself, and afterwards yielded unto the said Sir Francis Drake and remained with him as a prisoner.[19]

The Spaniards were transferred to the *Revenge* and her sister ship, the *Roebuck*, while the *Rosario*'s treasure was lowered into the *Revenge*, where Drake could keep his eye on it. It is believed that the haul amounted to some 55,000 ducats ($3.74 million or £2.02 million today) as well as jewels, silver plate, and fine apparel, though no one knew for sure how much was truly there. When the treasure passed into the lord admiral's hands, only half that sum was counted. When Frobisher later learned of the incident, he was incandescent with rage. Frobisher's rescue by Drake near the Isle of Wight was a even more bitter pill to swallow.

But on that day, Drake hadn't returned as yet by dawn, and it was only when Howard came above decks that he quickly saw that he hadn't been following Drake's poop lantern after all, but the one of the Spanish Armada instead! The English account of how he extricated himself and what, if anything, he said to Drake when he rejoined him is ambiguous. All we know for sure is that Drake did rejoin, Howard did take possession of the treasure, and that Drake was again on several occasions entrusted to act as lead ship with his poop lantern alight to guide the fleet.

That same day, Howard himself peeled off from the fleet and picked up the *San Salvador*, which was sinking after an explosion in her gunpowder stores ripped through the ship. She should have been scuttled, but Howard ordered instead that Captain Fleming (the pirate who gave the first alert) should bring her into harbor at Weymouth, Dorset.[20]

After the first two battles, the Spaniards were already very low on powder and shot. The gunpowder magazine's explosion aboard the *San Salvador* spelled further disaster. Frobisher in the largest English ship, the *Triumph*, was nearly cornered at the Isle of Wight, but rescued at the end of the day by Drake's sharp maneuvering. By the time the Armada had reached the Calais Roads, it was seriously depleted of food and water as well. The English had learned from their battles to stay just out of gun range while the Spaniards tried to sink them. English rates of fire were only one or one and a half rounds per gun per hour, where the Spanish managed only one to one and a half rounds per day. With its superior firepower, the English ships slowly made inroads into the invincible Armada. But it was Philip's strict order to Medina Sidonia not to make any independent landing without Parma that committed the Spanish Armada to failure—not the English fleet.

Parma had too few armed vessels to protect his army sailing out of harbor to meet the Armada, and he knew he and his soldiers would be sitting ducks for the Dutch, who had now joined the English side. On the Sunday night, the English loosed eight fire ships into the tightly packed Armada and watched the Spaniards grapple themselves free while they stood out to sea. Despite incredible Spanish courage, the elements were against them. A great storm brewed up, allowing the English to herd them toward the Zealand Banks—shallows that could shipwreck the entire fleet.

Then as Tuesday dawned, the wind changed direction to southward, allowing the entrapped Armada to escape to the north. No one believed that it would be the end of the action. In fact, Howard wrote to Walsingham, "Their force is wonderful great and strong, yet we pluck their feathers by little and little. I pray to God that the forces on the land be strong enough to answer so puissant a force."[21]

But it was the end. The Spanish Armada sailed around to the north of the British Isles, and west again around Ireland, with several of their galleons shipwrecked there. At least one-third of the men were dead, and half of those who returned were sick or dying. Only Recalde landed safely in Ireland with a small squadron, and got away to tell the gruesome tale of the Armada's destruction on Ireland's western coast. But even the great Recalde fell victim to sickness on his return to Spain, dying within weeks, it was claimed, of a broken heart. Spain fell into deep mourning, for the loss of the Armada was a national catastrophe. The loss of her men was irreplaceable. The loss of the treasure and the ships was barely considered in the public psyche. Where Spain mourned, England rejoiced. Even at the time, there were many who claimed that the defeat of the Armada was the moment when Spanish maritime expansion ceased, and the English were on the rise.

For the Queen of England, it was a vindication by God of all she represented. In the ten days that the Spanish Armada threatened England, God had smiled down on His Protestant queen.

37. America Again . . . and Again? ✺

As Salomon said, "Riches are a stronghold, in the
imagination of the rich man." But this is excellently
expressed that it is in imagination, and not always in fact.
—SIR FRANCIS BACON, *Essays*, NO. 34 "OF RICHES"

Raleigh's role in the Armada campaign was largely supportive, even selling the *Ark Ralegh* to the queen to use as the renamed *Ark Royal* for Admiral Howard. After it was all over, he somehow was charged with selling the captured Armada wines as agent to his half brother, Sir John Gilbert. While it must have been a highly profitable transaction for both men, Raleigh's real interest was with the casks. "I must also pray you to set aside twenty-five tons of the iron hooped cask for me," he asked Sir John, "priced in such reasonable sort as you may, for I shall have great use of them. And if my Lord of Cumberland or any other make means to have them, you may answer that they are priced and sold, or that Her Majesty has given them to me. . . . "[1]

Cumberland and any other adventurer would have probably figured that Raleigh needed so many casks for his wine trade. This was not the case remotely. Raleigh earnestly put about the fact that having been prevented from reprovisioning his colonists (who had sailed to Virginia in April 1587), due to the Armada threat, he was absolutely determined to ensure their safety—and his grant of twelve hundred miles of North America—by supporting them with fresh supplies in 1588–1589.

Virginia was, after all, his best opportunity to find his own gold supply. And so, while Frobisher and the other disgruntled commanders from the Armada fleet argued with the Admiralty over the prizes and ransoms to be obtained for ships and men, Raleigh rose above the petty squabbling and stepped up his efforts for Virginia.

Raleigh had set up an innovative scheme to attract settlers in the third Virginia colony by offering them five hundred acres of land to farm on the strength of their signing up for the adventure. If they invested funds, then they would get more again. His Virginia company, unusually, was organized as one enjoying the right of self-government under their own officials, with representatives in England to ensure the chain of supply until they could provide for themselves in America.[2] Raleigh's chosen governor and his twelve assistants were granted their charter on January 7, 1587, as "Governor and Assistants of the City of Raleigh in Virginia." The charter did not delegate powers to the colonists, but merely made them paid servants of Raleigh and any other adventurers or promoters residing in England. After all, Raleigh's planters were markedly "middle class." Their only claim to any aristocracy, whatsoever, was the false coat of arms that Raleigh had bribed the chief officer of arms, William Dethick, to bestow upon White and each of his twelve assistants.[3]

What Raleigh didn't know, of course, was that all was not well. Only he would continue to employ Simon Fernandez, nicknamed "the swine" by other adventurers. Fernandez's interest was plunder, and, as a former pirate, the temptation to revert to his old trade was far too great. Raleigh's simple instructions to collect plants and water in the West Indies, then to purchase livestock for the colony, resulted in Fernandez going after Spanish prizes and ignoring the 110 men and women in his charge. If their captain acted like this in the West Indies, then how would Fernandez carry out his further orders to pick up the fifteen-man contingent left by Grenville at Roanoke in 1586, then drop the settlers off at the more fertile landing and good harbor of Chesapeake? Evidently this wasn't a question that had occurred to Raleigh's appointed governor, John White. White was undoubtedly a splendid artist but, as it turned out, a truly dreadful leader of men. Instead of asking himself some basic questions, White harangued and shamed Fernandez until they finally sailed north to Virginia.[4]

By the time they reached Roanoke, Fernandez was spoiling for a fight. While White equipped a pinnace with forty of his best men to go search for the fifteen men Grenville had left behind, Fernandez hailed them from the *Lion*, shouting orders that he prepared to abandon them. All the colonists were hastily ordered ashore. Only White and two or three others were allowed to return to the *Lion* to make the necessary arrangements to offload provisions.[5] Amazingly, White, though angry, was not unhappy. He knew Roanoke very well and, with anglicized Manteo as Raleigh's personal representative at his side, most likely felt that they could not come to any harm. After some haggling, White finally agreed with Fernandez that the *Lion* should return shortly to take aboard the men left by Grenville, and that, in the interim, Fernandez would ensure that the fly boat carrying the rest of the "planters" would be able to disembark in safety.

Thus at the end of July the planters were reunited in Lane's abandoned fort, having found no trace of Grenville's men. When Manteo, recently converted to Christianity and dubbed Lord of Roanoke and Dasemunkepeuc, returned with the news from his own people at Croatoan that Grenville's men had been driven off Roanoke by the hostile mainland tribes, razing the earthworks and fort in the process, White did nothing. A short while later, one of White's assistants was ambushed while fishing for crabs. And still White did nothing.[6]

Trusting that all would somehow be all right, White tried to make amends for the wrongs that Lane had committed, and to correct the label the previous planters had acquired of "stealers of corn." When White failed to get the mainland chiefs and elders to come to some sort of accommodation with his settlers, the planters mistakenly ambushed the friendly Croatoans in their village, killing one native.[7] Relations between the Native Americans and planters were still strained when, on August 18, Virginia Dare, a healthy baby girl, became the first child born to Europeans in North America. She was also White's first grandchild.

Meanwhile, Fernandez had returned and remained within sight of the colonists two miles from shore, waiting. Fernandez's hovering offshore frankly unnerved the colonists. His sinister actions, combined with the repeated native attacks, made them doubt their ability to withstand the winter and the wisdom of planting any fields at Roanoke to harvest in the spring. Chesapeake had become a perceived haven in this hostile land in the colonists' eyes, and White's resistance to any move there utterly undermined his authority. After a number of discussions, White was at last compelled to go by his assistants, and, on August 25, was given a certificate asserting that he had been selected to "the present and speedy supply of certain our known and apparent lacks and needs most requisite and necessary for the good planting of us, or any other in this land of Virginia."[8]

And so Raleigh's governor left eighty-four men, seventeen women, and eleven children with Manteo and his assistant, Towaye. White understood that they intended to move fifty miles or so farther up into the mainland, where the land was fertile and the risk of hostile natives was lower. To this day, we are unsure if it was to the mouth of the Chesapeake or the Albemarle Sound. What we do know is that a pinnace and some boats were left behind with them. On August 27, White was allowed to board the fly boat, leaving behind his daughter, Elenora; her husband, Ananias Dare; and baby, Virginia, with the rest of the planters entrusted to his care. Before they had sailed over the horizon, a disastrous accident at the capstan injured most of the crew. Many died, and others became ill with fever and the bloody flux, reducing their number so dramatically that they couldn't sail beyond Smerwick in southwest Ireland, where Raleigh had first made his name. White alone continued to London, arriving only in early November, three weeks after the *Lion* had returned from its fruitless privateering voyage.[9] Even White could not help noticing that the country was on a war footing, and that the queen wouldn't allow any ships to sail that might weaken the defense of the realm.

For Raleigh it was a double disaster. He could not possibly lose face and do nothing. To do nothing would be to abandon his fellow "adventurers" who had invested their money alongside him. Yet all he could muster on behalf of White and the planters was for two pinnaces to sail—the 30-ton *Brave* and 24-ton *Roe*—from Grenville's home port of Bideford. But the Atlantic was teaming with pirates, adventurers, and Spaniards all aching for a brawl, and the *Roe*'s captain decided to break off and join in. Alone now, the *Brave* was attacked by a Huguenot ship out of La Rochelle, and by the end of May 1588, White was back in Bideford. Raleigh tried time and time again to get Grenville to sea on his behalf to provide support for the fledgling colony, but he was overruled by the Privy Council. It was this harsh and necessary decision in the face of the real threat to England that sealed the colonists' fates.[10]

Richard Hakluyt, in the meantime, had published his *Principall Navigations* at the beginning of 1590, stinging Walter Raleigh with his bitter preface that "the plantations were founded at the charges of Sir Walter Raleigh, whose entrance upon those new inhabitations had been happy, if it had been as seriously followed, as it was cheerfully undertaken."[11] The threat of the Armada had passed, yet throughout 1589, Raleigh, who himself had men-of-war in the Atlantic, made no effort to rescue his planters. His attention, like thousands of other adventurers, had been grabbed by the real chance for riches beyond even his greedy dreams, and the destruction of Spain's empire. The casks that he had written to his half brother Sir John about would serve just as well aboard his men-of-war. The planters would simply have to wait.

38. The Last Gasp of the Early Roaring '90s ⨳

Tis England's honor that you have in hand,
Then think thereof, if you do love our land.
The gain is yours, if millions home you bring,
Then courage take, to gain so sweet a thing.
The time calls on, which causes me to end,
Wherefore to God, I do you all commend . . .
That Philip's Regions may not be more stored,
With Pearl, Jewels and the purest Gold.

—HENRY ROBERTS, ADVENTURER POET, *The Trumpet of Fame*

The only ones who could afford to continue the war against Spain were Elizabeth's adventurers. Where they dreamed of riches and empire, Elizabeth longed to consolidate her England, and stop her ruinous expenditure in Ireland. Little did she realize then that the 1590s would see her spend £2 million ($480.63 million or £259.8 million today) in the defense of her postern gate. She had built her image of Gloriana on the peace and security of the realm, and continually hoped for the day when the myth would become a reality. It was precisely these desires that the adventurers pandered to throughout the 1590s. Under the guise of a new nationalism they would enrich themselves, leading the queen to believe that only by destroying Spain's wealth could England ever find peace. But the queen was no fool. The death of her beloved "Robin," Earl of Leicester, a month after the Armada was defeated in 1588 had left her personally rudderless. The advice of the equally aging Walsingham and Burghley may have seemed faint as the younger generation energetically pressed itself forward first at court, then in the Privy Council. Certainly, years of loyal service had worn them out. So when the queen's spymaster, Sir Francis Walsingham, died in

April 1590, Elizabeth simply relied more heavily on Lord Burghley, and his chosen successor and second son, Robert Cecil. Only the two Cecils had the overview in the same way the queen had, and only *they* now shared her most intimate strategies. Cecil's "hold" over the old queen became the source of tremendous friction between him and Robert, Earl of Essex, and Cecil's appointment would prove to be one of the more controversial appointments Elizabeth would make.

But Robert Cecil did not necessarily mean "bad news" for the queen's adventurers. When Sir John Hawkins came to the Council with his brilliant plan for a Silver Blockade of Spain, Cecil not only listened to him, Cecil believed he was right. The Hawkins plan was simple and cheap. Six major galleons would need to be maintained between Spain and the Azores, and kept at sea for four months. At the end of that time, they would be replaced with another fleet of the same strength. England had proved that it could keep ships at sea—so long as they were not heavily manned—in reasonable condition and "healthy and sweet-smelling" for that period. Young Cecil was still an unknown quantity beyond the dizzying heights of the queen's personal company, despite his rapidly growing power. Perhaps it was for that reason that Hawkins had made no statement about commercial gain possible in his scheme. Whatever his reasons, the plan was, alas, never fully enacted. More is the pity, since it made complete sense. The best way to level the playing field would be for Philip to have access to the same amounts of gold—or preferably less—than Elizabeth. Only her adventurers could achieve that task, and both the queen and Cecil knew it.

There is also the possibility that the plan was put on hold with the first failure ever of Sir Francis Drake as commander of his own fleet. In 1589, Drake undertook to land Dom Antonio in Portugal to reestablish him on the throne, investing £1,000 himself in the adventure ($268,250 or £145,000 today) and "setting himself forth with twenty men and muskets."[1] The soldiers were led by the brutal veteran of the Irish and Dutch campaigns, Sir John "Black Jack" Norris, and the exuberant rising star Robert, Earl of Essex. Drake should have known better than to be associated with either, but he had had little choice. He also should have known better than to believe that the Portuguese would rise up spontaneously for Dom Antonio after living peacefully under Philip's rule for nine years. Notwithstanding all this, the 1589 voyage was doomed to failure for the same reason that most adventuring voyages in the 1590s failed: Elizabeth had sent adventurers to do the job of a professional, government-controlled Royal Navy, blurring her "war aims." Granted, the queen did not have the money to develop a true Royal Navy, and so private adventurers who invested in ships and manpower for the queen (with their own commercial plans for plundering) ruined Drake's chances along with Antonio's overinflated view of his people's love for him.[2] For Drake, the result was an apparent fall from favor.

Drake would spend the better part of the next six years in what many called his "disgrace." But the term is inaccurate. A disgraced general is not constantly called upon by his political superiors for his advice and handling of matters ashore as Drake had been. By November 1590, the Privy Council commissioned Sir Francis as a justice of the Admiralty to help resolve regular episodes involving the plundering of neutral ships by English adventurers, and making an inventory of their proceeds. Since the bulk of adventurers or pirates were West Countrymen, and the lord admiral received a portion of all registered prizes, this was a position of extreme importance. Drake was also responsible for the safe stowage of the loot until the case could be heard in the High Court of the Admiralty. The job of recovering, securing, and handling the accounting for questionable cargoes and examination of these "foul outrages" became the mainstay of his work until 1596.[3]

And while Drake built up his fortunes ashore, Philip rebuilt his navy. English spies reported the king's naval strength from Spain in 1591:

> *At Ferroll: thirty-two sail, ready, small and great.*
> *At Santander: Eight new galleons, the least eight hundred tons. Four already launched, four to be launched within a month.*
> *At Bilbao: ten ships pressed for the king.*
> *At the River of Portugal [Lisbon]: Nine new galleons and ships. Four about one thousand tons, the rest from eight hundred to seven hundred tons each. Eight already launched, the other to be launched in a month.*

At Passages: Fifteen great ships of which thirteen were in the
Armada of three hundred to five hundred tons.
In all about seventy-five to rendezvous at Ferrol.[4]

Raleigh, meanwhile, was back at his plantations in Ireland, making mansions for himself at Youghal and Lismore. Among his frequent houseguests were the out-of-royal-favor poet and neighbor Edmund Spenser, and Raleigh's cousin Sir George Carew, who was also Ireland's master of the ordnance. Unlike the queen, Raleigh saw adventuring only in terms of empire. And while in Ireland, he had taken to building his own personal empire, thanks in no small part to the queen's extreme generosity of 42,000 acres of prime farmland at a rent of £233 6s. 3d. ($62,583 or £33,829 today) annually after the first three rent-free years.[5]

At Youghal he introduced novelty crops as early as 1595, planting potatoes and tomatoes—from the New World—around the same time. While it had been Drake who brought the first tobacco back to England from the West Indies (and Ralph Lane, an officer of Drake's at the time, who would teach Raleigh how to smoke), it would be Raleigh who would popularize the habit of social smoking while drinking mugs of ale. An invitation to smoke and drink ale with Raleigh was the most welcomed of private male gatherings in the 1590s.[6]

Even so, while his smoking parties took place primarily at his London home, Durham House, Ireland remained the main source of his revenue. He had grand plans to import New World foods on a large scale and to commercialize the planting of tobacco. Still, as with so many things in Raleigh's life, plans were all they would remain.

Elizabeth had also allowed Raleigh to muster an extra company of cavalry to help protect his intended "planters" there. But as in England, he quickly gained the reputation for being full of himself, falling out with Ireland's lord deputy, Sir William Fitzwilliam, through an unnecessary lawsuit against Lady Stanley, wife of Sir William Stanley the traitor, but nonetheless a vastly popular figure in Catholic Ireland. Raleigh continued to alienate those around him who viewed him as a "pushing and selfish adventurer."[7] In a typical fit of pique, Raleigh complained in a veiled threat to George Carew that, "if in Ireland they think I am not worth respecting, they shall much deceive themselves."[8] And while Raleigh played in Ireland, his ships still sailed under the command of his masters, enriching their owner.

It was said at the time by the queen's intelligencers that "traitors murderers, thieves, cozeners, cony catchers, shifting mates, runners away with other men's wives, some having two or three wives, persons divorced living loosely, bankrupts, carnal gospellers, Papists, Puritans, and Brownists," all flocked in droves from England to Munster. In the hundred years between 1580 and 1680, over a hundred thousand English—though not all reprobates by a long shot—emigrated to Ireland. It naturally attracted those who had nothing to lose and pure adventurers. All of them were looking to pluck a prime piece of land from the Irish for themselves in the same way that frontiersmen of America did.[9]

At sea, the English adventurers were led by the queen's "rogue" George Clifford, third Earl of Cumberland, off the Azores in 1591, in what became known as the Islands Voyage. Cumberland and his squadron cruised that summer in the Azores aboard the queen's *Victory*, plundering dozens of ships and netting tens of thousands of ducats (official reports varying wildly). Still, their aim wasn't a blockade as Hawkins had suggested. It was a plunder mission. Had they adopted the Hawkins plan, they could have probably captured the passing Portuguese carracks laden with gold and precious gems, as well as several West Indiamen. Nonetheless, Cumberland was happy with his takings, and remained at sea through September when the queen sent out Frobisher with a small squadron to reconnoiter Seville and Lisbon. Frobisher took four prize ships, much to his own delight, but the bulk of the flota had arrived in port safely.

Yet, as expected, this did nothing to deter Philip in his determination to rebuild his fleet to use against England again. To make matters worse, a more concerted effort to blockade Spain had failed in 1590, with the East Indiamen this time eluding twelve of the queen's ships under the joint command of Frobisher and

Hawkins. Reprisal ships still abounded, with John Watts's ships in the West Indies making a killing in understated loot to avoid taxation.

Gold and silver was flowing into the queen's and Admiralty's coffers, but still, Philip's rebuilding program remained on track. By the spring of 1592, Lord Admiral Howard finally managed to launch a squadron back to sea to meet up with other adventurers, including Cumberland. While details of their mission have not been preserved, it seems that suffered too from the double-headed coin of plunder to pay for the voyage while ensuring state security. Elizabeth certainly knew Philip well enough by now to be acutely aware that he would not take the defeat of the "Invincible" Armada lying down. What she didn't know is that Don Alonso de Bazán's fleet had been relaunched in the hope of catching John Watts's fleet as it returned from its plunder operation in the West Indies.

The King of Spain had ordered that all Spanish ships remain in the West Indies until further notice, but, unknown to Philip, many had already stolen homeward and lay at anchor near Terceira in the Azores and cursed the English corsairs repeatedly for their misfortunes. Frobisher, Hawkins, and his son Richard were all under sail in different squadrons, all trying to encircle the Iberian coast like a school of sharks. And Philip was unable to send gold or reinforcements to Parma in the Netherlands. At last the English blockade seemed to be working.[10]

Still, Elizabeth wasn't convinced. Reluctantly, she sent Lord Admiral Howard with Sir Richard Grenville as his lieutenant to Spanish waters. The Earl of Cumberland planned to join them to lead the "jackal" squadron that roved tightly against the Iberian coast. They were lucky in taking a Lubecker off the Finisterre coast with £10,000 worth of masts and timber ($2.41 million or £1.3 million today) destined to provision Philip's new fleet.[11] Their prisoners told them that the Indian fleet they were looking to plunder had arrived some weeks earlier at the Azores, and were out of their reach by now.

Howard wasn't having any of that! The Lubecker was sent back to England while he headed the ships belonging to the queen and Raleigh to the Azores. Back home, the queen had received alarming reports of the Spanish king's new naval strength, and the possibility of a new Armada. Raleigh was ordered to hasten down to Plymouth to organize a fleet, while Cumberland sailed quickly out to rendezvous with Howard.

When Cumberland met up with some of his cruising ships along the Spanish coast, his worst fears were confirmed. The Marquis of Santa Cruz's brother, Don Alonso de Bazán, had sailed to accompany the Indian fleet to safety from the Azores. Howard was in mortal danger. But with the luck of "the gifted amateur" that England spawned throughout its rise to empire, Howard remained blissfully unaware of the danger, claiming that he was "almost famished for want of prey, or rather like a bear robbed of her whelps."[12] Fortunately, a squadron of sixteen ships (including the *Bark Raleigh*) had met up with the lord admiral before he could come to harm. Don Alonso, however, was closing in with his fifty sail—thirty of which were great ships and galleons. Nonetheless, the English fleet was caught by surprise reprovisioning with water at Flores.

Orders were shouted to "heave ho!" by the English, but the Spaniards blocked the roadstead as their sails began to fill with wind. Still, Howard's luck held, and despite most ships slipping their cables, they sailed away. That is, all except Sir Richard Grenville aboard the *Revenge* who resolved to stay and engage the enemy. It was an act of sheer madness. The *Revenge*, the queen's pride and joy as her prototype for a sleeker, more yar vessel, was lost after twelve long hours of battle, and Grenville with many of his men were needlessly killed. All others were spared.

The loss of the *Revenge* was a harsh blow for the queen—until now (or *ever*, for that matter)—it was the only royal ship to be lost in the Spanish War.[13] "Sir Richard utterly refused to turn from the enemy," Walter Raleigh wrote in a scathing verbal attack against Grenville, "alleging that he would rather chose [sic] to die, then to dishonor himself, his country, and Her Majesty's ship, persuading his company that he would pass through the two squadrons [of Spaniards] in despite of them: and enforce those of Seville to give him way."[14] But Raleigh had other motives for being so angry at the needless loss of life and property aboard the *Revenge*. Grenville was dead, and so were Raleigh's dreams of sending him to Virginia to rescue his colonists.

Raleigh knew that he had to concentrate on either his quest for gold or his colony in Virginia, and so he agreed to terms with the London merchants Thomas Smythe and William Sanderson to send nineteen new colonists to Roanoke. In exchange for their investment of money, shipping, victuals, and so on, Raleigh relinquished some of his rights of trade. It seemed an ideal solution to the Elizabethan entrepreneur. When John Watts, the London merchant and greatest owner and promoter of adventuring ships, was involved by Sanderson, it looked as though White's "lost colonists" would at last be rescued. But this was a false hope, since in the end the three ships were not allowed to sail, as the Privy Council expected yet another Armada.[15] Undaunted, Raleigh used his famous charm with Elizabeth, and succeeded in obtaining a license for another private ship, the *Hopewell*, to sail with John White aboard, together with some more "western planters" and provisions.

When they anchored at last off Hatarask on August 15, 1590, they found the Roanoke fort three days later, deserted. Carved into one of the trees marking out the former fort was the word CROATOAN and another tree had "CRO" etched into its trunk. This was the agreed signal between the planters and White for his return. If the word of their destination also had a Maltese cross beneath, then that would mean that they had decamped under duress. White was overjoyed at finding "a certain token of their safe being at Croatoan, which is the place where Manteo was born, and the Savages of the land our friends."[16]

The captain of the *Hopewell* began his run south to Croatoan but was taken by surprise in what must have been the beginning of a hurricane. They were unable to recover their water casks, and lost two anchors trying to clear the Outer Banks. With only a single cable and anchor, few victuals, and no pinnace in vastly deteriorating weather, the captain decided, with White's consent, to head for the West Indies and outrun the storm. A few days later, after a further pounding, the *Hopewell* was forced to turn east toward the Azores and home. It proved to be the last real attempt to rescue the colonists at Roanoke.

By the time Howard and Cumberland were planning their mission against Spain, Raleigh had engrossed himself in his new role as the leader of Elizabeth's adventurers, organizing Atlantic plunder on a gigantic scale. Yet he never gave up hope of finding treasure in the New World, and had long dreamed of "El Dorado," the mythical golden kingdom whispered in Indian folklore. In Hakluyt's *Discourse of Western Planting*, he describes a tract of twenty-one hundred miles that "is neither Spaniard, nor Portuguese, nor any Christian man, but only the Caribs, Indians and savages. In which places is great plenty of gold, pearl and precious stones."[17] For years he had been querying explorers returning from South America about El Dorado, and particularly French corsairs who had traveled up the Amazon. He was so hungry for real knowledge about El Dorado that Raleigh exchanged with these men the intelligence they craved about Raleigh's own difficulties in establishing colonies in Virginia for facts about Patagonia and the Spanish Main.[18]

But Raleigh's inquisitiveness and hopes to launch an all-out investigation of the region were interrupted with the sudden discovery by Elizabeth that he had secretly married her lady-in-waiting, Bess Throckmorton. Their son, Wat, was living proof of their relationship, yet Raleigh lied and bluffed about his involvement with the queen's lady. When Raleigh was finally compelled to confess, Elizabeth thundered at him in rage and unceremoniously packed him off to the Tower to cool his silken heels for a while. The queen had to approve all court marriages by law, and Raleigh should have known better. After all, he followed Leicester's own public debacle in secretly marrying Lettice Knollys, Walter Devereux's widow, by a number of years, as well as Robert Devereux's (second Earl of Essex) own crime two years earlier.

Elizabeth's efforts in the early 1590s were also absorbed by Philip's change of tactic. Henry of Navarre had inherited the French throne, and as the Protestant king of predominantly Catholic France, this made his efforts in the Spanish Netherlands even more futile. That is, until the Spanish took Calais. Now Henry, financed as well by Elizabeth, was fighting a rear-guard action, trying to keep the Spanish from fanning out from the Pas de Calais and beyond. For her part, Elizabeth did what she could by sending Essex and his volunteers to relieve Rouen at the French king's side, but her frayed purse strings were near breaking point. It is intriguing to speculate if her lack of capital might have been the main reason why she had allowed the adventurers out to sea in the vast numbers that she did at the time. A percentage of their takings—even after pilferage by the crews and hangers-on at port—was better than absolutely nothing. She had become bitter that things had come to such an impasse, for if there was one thing above all else that Elizabeth loathed, it was being backed into a corner.[19]

It seems odd that Drake was the only great adventurer who was not at sea, and may well have held a warmer place in her heart as a result. He, at least, was making an attempt to capture the ill-gotten gains of her pirates and adventurers. Even more interesting is that Elizabeth used his wondrous reputation to full advantage, often claiming within earshot of the Venetian ambassador that Drake was due to sail with fifty ships. Here we can still see the young queen teasing and taunting her enemies, and telling lies as if they were truths.[20]

No longer fettered by Elizabeth as her indispensable favorite, Raleigh along with Cumberland came up with a scheme to capture the Isthmus of Panama in reprisal for the loss of the *Revenge*. The plan appealed to the queen's devious side, and it was a way for Raleigh to show his allegiance. Without too much cajoling Elizabeth ventured two ships and £3,000 in cash ($720,890 or £389,670 today). Raleigh contributed the *Roebuck* and money he said was his own, but many think it had really been borrowed from his friends. In the event, they never made it past the Azores. There Captain Crosse (who was a Drake veteran mariner) in one of Cumberland's ships took the Portuguese carrack *Madre de Díos* after a hard fight. It was the largest ship afloat at the time, with seven decks and a cargo in gold, spices, and precious gemstones worth a staggering £150,000 ($36.08 million or £19.5 million today).[21] At least that was the official figure.

But by the time the treasure was brought back to England, much had been pilfered along the way. Stories of disorderliness among the English sailors filled the official and popular press. Drake himself heard how the swarm of English pirates (for he could describe them as nothing else) ran wild with excitement, rummaging through the passengers' cabins, breaking open chests with their weapons, and running off with much of what belonged by law to the adventurers' ship owners and the Admiralty. He spent much of his time taking depositions of how Cumberland's mariners were literally at one another's throats, staving off sailors from the other adventuring ships and keeping them from partaking in their ecstatic orgy of booty.

Still, that wasn't the end of the affair. London jewelers clamored aboard diligences and rushed to Plymouth where the sailors disembarked. Every cutpurse and thief gathered around the pier in the hope of something to steal while the treasure was unloaded. "We cannot look upon anything here," the harassed receiver of customs, Thomas Middleton, opined, "except we should keep a guard to drive away the disordered pilfering bystanders that attend but a time to carry away somewhat when any chest is opened." It took Drake and several other commissioners several weeks to gain control of the situation—restoring order, taking witness statements, examining mariners, taking inventory, and finally, thankfully, sending £141,000 worth of the cargo to London.[22] Drake had yet again more than proved his weight in gold.

The taking of the *Madre de Dios* had a devastating effect on Philip's reputation. The gossipy Venetian ambassador in Spain wrote in cipher to the doges that "the King must be relieved from the weight of so many debts . . . he has debts of about thirteen millions [ducats] in gold . . . in the air as they say." And it was true that "the West India fleet has never at any time of its history been so harried by the English and exposed to such danger of capture as at this present moment."[23]

But in truth, enough gold and silver made its way to Philip's coffers, and his rebuilding program continued unabated. There would be another Armada.

❧✦ Part Four ✦❧

Dawn of Empire

*I myself will venture my royal blood; I myself will be
your general, judge, and rewarder of your virtue in the
field. I know that already for your forwardness you have
deserved rewards and crowns, and I assure you in the
word of a prince you shall not fail of them. . . .*

—ELIZABETH I, ARMADA SPEECH AT TILBURY, AUGUST 9, 1588

39. The Alchemy That Turned Plunder into Trade ✦

Ambition is like choler, which is an humour that maketh men active, earnest, full of alacrity, and stirring if not stopped . . . . So ambitious men, if they find the way open for their rising, and still get forward, they are rather busy than dangerous . . .

—SIR FRANCIS BACON, *Essays, Of Ambition*

By the mid-1590s, Spain's naval rebirth was not only rumored, but also evident from the turning tide of her adventurers at sea. While Philip's health continued to deteriorate, his anger against England remained hearty. Drake had been a landlubber for six years, and he longed to feel the boards beneath his feet, the stiff sea breezes in his face, and the thrill of the attack again. The ghost of Thomas Doughty had finally been laid to rest, though his younger brother, John, still rotted in prison for his attempt on Drake's life.[1] Now in his mid-fifties, with the help of his cousin, Sir John Hawkins (in his sixties himself), the two veteran sea dogs persuaded the queen to allow them a nostalgic revival of their "troublesome" 1568 adventure, but this time the purpose was to capture Panama. If Hawkins's blockade couldn't stop the silver shipments, surely their landing at Panama would. The queen allowed them to go, wanting to believe in them more than *truly* believing. Perhaps this was why she wanted them to adopt the tactics that had been so successful in their youths—the surprise smash-and-grab raids that had so inspired her younger, ambitious adventurers. And so, after much preparation, they set sail with the old queen's blessing.

The result was catastrophic. When the two former pirates heard that a great silver carrack had been crippled in Puerto Rico, they naturally attacked. It had been over ten years since Drake had last seen the West Indies, and in that time, Spain's fortifications against the return of *El Draco* proved more than effective. Hawkins was killed by a direct hit in November 1595. Two months later, in January 1596, Drake had his stool shot out from under him while eating dinner. But his luck would not hold this time. Within weeks, he was dead of the bloody flux, probably brought on by an infection of his wounds.[2] Starved of the threat of *El Draco*—whether real or imagined—all looked lost to the despondent queen.

But just as this devastating news reached court, worse was yet to come. Henry IV of France had decided that "Paris was worth a mass" and converted to Catholicism, ending decades of civil war. The effect on Elizabeth was profound since Henry had been her hope for a Protestant, and thereby benign, France. In reply to this, she urgently sent Gilbert Talbot, seventh Earl of Shrewsbury, to obtain Henry's oath to observe the conditions of their league against Spain and to invest him in the Order of the Garter. "And by this means you will shade if not cover my error," she wrote to Henry, "if such I may call it, who was the first to present to you my faith, assuring you that if all pacts were as inviolate as this one will be on my side, everyone would be astonished to see such constant friendship in this century."[3] Her words still ring true today. Catholic France and Catholic Spain would assuredly form a league against England, the queen feared. Time was of the essence if Philip, France, the pope, and any other takers of her crown were to be stopped.

Elizabeth knew that her only alternative was to continue to prosecute her war against Spain, and so she agreed to send out an expedition from Plymouth bound for the Spanish coast and bent on capturing and destroying as many ships as it could at Cadiz, then Lisbon.[4] Leading the voyage was the lord admiral himself with the queen's charismatic favorite, the handsome, hotheaded Robert, Earl of Essex. Raleigh, freshly returned from his Guiana voyage (which had not been successful in finding the mythical El Dorado, nor had it been of any real significance as a voyage of discovery), had been asked to join the fleet as its rear admiral. Funding for the expedition came directly from the queen, with Howard and Essex as her joint shareholders. A stunning fleet of around 150 sail with 18 of the queen's ships among them, along with 18 Dutchmen and 12 outsized Londoners all bristling with the latest firepower. A landing force of ten thousand soldiers of England's "choisest men" was mustered and taken aboard. They would be led by Essex, Vere, Blount, Gerrard, and Cumberland.[5]

As with Drake nine years earlier, Cadiz was miraculously caught sleeping. Two of the king's galleons were destroyed and two others captured. When the town surrendered to the swashbuckling Essex for an agreed ransom of 125,000 ducats ($7.59 million or £4.1 million today) the best terms they could get from the English was to allow all but the top 150 citizens of the town leave, along with all the women, before the sack began. In addition, the Spaniards had to leave all their worldly possessions behind.[6] As soon as the women left town the queen's soldiers sacked it, in an ecstatic, raging free-for-all lasting two weeks. So far as they were concerned, their voyage was made.

Incredibly, while the sack of the town was taking place, the lord high admiral and his men did not have their eyes on the richly laden India fleet in port. To prevent them from stealing it and using the proceeds against Spain, Don Luis Alfonso Flores, the admiral of the flota, ordered the ships to be destroyed. The estimated value of the ships' cargoes alone amounted to around 4 million ducats ($240.32 million or £129.9 million today) according to Medina Sidonia, but the Spanish merchants would later claim 12 million ducats in losses.[7] As to personal effects of the townspeople and churches, no accurate estimate of either the value, or the inventory of what was taken or destroyed, survives. Loot was, after all, how all nations paid their soldiers for the risks they took.

What had originally been intended as an act of war with strict instructions by the queen was again sidetracked by private interest and plunder. The lord admiral had persuaded the queen that a mission entirely funded by her as a royal expeditionary force, and not as a joint stock company, would stop the increasing lawlessness of her mariners and achieve her war aims. Indeed, his instructions ordered, "by burning of ships of war in his [the King of Spain's] havens before they should come forth to the seas, and therewith also destroying his magazines of victuals and his munitions for the arming of his navy, to provide that neither the rebels in Ireland should be aided and strengthened, nor yet the king be able, of long time, to have any great navy in readiness to offend us."[8]

Still, it was Essex's shining hour—a brilliant, magnificent knight at the head of an army defeating the queen's greatest foe. He was like a fire-breathing dragon in the face of the enemy, demanding the council of war to hold on to the port of Cadiz to stop trade from the Mediterranean and both the East and West Indies, "whereby we shall cut his [Philip's] sinews and make war upon him with his own money."[9] More is the pity that he was overruled by "wiser" heads since by occupying the port—even for a short period of time—all shipments by sea could have been halted, turning the thorn in Philip's side into a massive bellyache. This was Essex's first and best moment as a soldier. Even his great rivalry with the disgraced Walter Raleigh (who famously cried *Entramos!* while attacking the town) showed Essex to be an inspirational leader of men at Cadiz, while Raleigh was shown to be a great talker at them.

Yet this "great" victory did not achieve Elizabeth's aims. The Indies fleet was in harbor—some forty to fifty vessels fully laden and ripe for the plucking—but while the soldiers ravaged Cadiz, the Spanish captains were given all the time they needed to destroy the fleet themselves to prevent an English capture. To compound their error, no attempt was made to take Lisbon or any other Iberian port, and no thought was given to try to intercept the incoming treasure fleet. Essentially, the "famous victory" pointed up in red-letter terms that soldiers were not mariners, and that Lord Admiral Howard was no sailor. To make matters worse, their booty was embezzled by underlings at the cost of the adventure's promoters. The queen, naturally, was left distinctly unamused, despite the fleet's returning to England with two new Spanish warships, some 1,200 Spanish pieces of ordnance and £12,838 in gold, plate, sugar, hides, silks, and jewels ($3.09 million or £1.67 million today).[10]

She was all the more angry since her spies reported that the next Armada was now ready to sail from Lisbon. But no one seemed to know for certain if the plan was to reach England, or to land a force to fight and meddle in the continuing troubles in Ireland. Half of her advisors felt that Philip could not let the defeat of the "Invincible" lie, especially as it was compounded by the ignominy of Cadiz for a second time. Other voices were certain that the King of Spain meant to attack her at her rebellious postern gate. Then, mercifully, word came through that the fleet had sailed from Lisbon, but had been shipwrecked by Atlantic storms off Finisterre that October. Again, the weather seemed to conspire in England's favor, at least for a little while.

Essex, never one to miss a fresh rush of blood to the head, felt invincible himself after Cadiz. In a quickly cobbled together action, he embarked his forces to meet the remnants of the failed second armada—the "Invisible"—scattered along the coast at Ferrol and Corunna. But Essex was essentially a soldier and not a sailor—a common error in thinking among Elizabethan fighters—and he had paid little attention to the time of year for launching such an ill-conceived attack. Naturally, the weather had turned again, and Essex's army was driven back to Plymouth by the autumn equinoctial storms, his ships battered and troops dreadfully seasick.

The year 1596 was another watershed in the prosecution of the war against Spain: there was Essex's role as national hero, taking over Drake's position, the end of France's wars of religion by the conversion to Catholicism by Henry IV, and Philip's second failed Armada attempt. Nonetheless, it was apparent that England could not deliver a knockout blow to Spain unless it had a base in the heart of the enemy's territory. And England's last chance of doing this ended when Essex was overruled by his own council of war at Cadiz.

Yet in many ways, it was probably the right decision to abandon Cadiz. The unruliness of the soldiers and seamen fighting seemingly endless years of war had produced an expectation of mountains of plunder as their just payment for serving their country. This expectation in turn had created an underclass of English seaman who, when viewed through the eyes of their superior officers, did not make a pretty picture in the light of day. "They rejoiced in things stark naughty, bragging in his [sic] sundry piracies." The only thing that kept their officers safe from attack was a strict disciplinarian regime. Whipping at the capstan, keelhauling, or hanging were always options. Drake hanged a man for sodomy, and Cumberland a member of his crew for rape. Crews of less well-regimented vessels were not above murdering their own masters for victuals or casting their captains adrift to die in despair—as happened later to the explorer Henry Hudson.[11]

From the sailors' standpoint, however, they deserved better. "What is a piece of beef of half a pound among four men to dinner," one seaman asked, "or half a dry stockfish for four days in the week, and nothing else to help withal: yea, we have help—a little beverage more than pump water. We were pressed by Her Majesty's press to have her allowance [take her pay], and not to be thus dealt withal—you make no men of us, but beasts."[12] Still, the better ships allowed the men to swim and play music to help wile away the lonely hours in healthy undertakings rather than drinking and gambling. Music became part of the daily routine to help the men perform their chores, and their sea shanties had begun to be sung ashore in taverns.

What emerged as the Royal Navy then was a group of men who were not born to the gentleman class, serving alongside gentlemen and noblemen of the realm. For those lucky enough to survive, and wanting to better themselves socially and financially, the navy was their respectable "leg up" into the higher echelons of society. For those who thought only of plunder and swag—irrespective of their social standing—their place was frequently found lashed at the mizzen mast or clapped in irons before being killed or escaping into out-and-out piracy. Above all, there was evidently truth on both sides of the argument.

The harsh reality was that there were no more Drakes after 1596. Instead, private interests investing in joint stock companies continued to dominate not only Elizabethan foreign trade but also Elizabethan adventuring. Though still alive, the ailing William Cecil, Lord Burghley, had by now ceded most of his duties to his intelligent younger son, Robert. Unlike his father, the ambitious Robert Cecil was a strong proponent of adventuring; and he, like the queen, was as guilty as the seagoing adventurers in hoping that treasure would come his way. As a younger son, Cecil, like all adventurers, was looking to build up his personal fortune, and he succeeded admirably.[13] Elizabeth was trying to keep the country afloat, praying (as it turns out in vain) to avoid the further sale of crown lands. Both Elizabeth and Cecil invested heavily in the Earl of Cumberland's adventures of 1589 and 1593, but it was their support of the lord admiral and the Admiralty that brought them their most lucrative source of income.[14]

The Admiralty, under Charles Howard, had turned plunder into quite a business. Not only did it receive 10 percent on all registered prizes—and it is estimated that only 10 percent of prizes were registered—but the High Court of the Admiralty sold reprisal letters to adventurers, took bonds from them, sold plundered goods in order to make "cash restitutions," and levied and collected customs. Its officers, from the admiral to its high court judge, Sir Julius Caesar, to the individuals in charge of every department or activity, were all involved in adventuring. In this way, the queen's navy had become a navy of private interests that encouraged Elizabeth to invest in plundering expeditions whenever her navy was not engaged in defense of the realm.[15] And whenever a matter of particular interest to "Mr. Secretary Cecil" came before the High Court of the Admiralty, Lord Howard was quick to dash a note off to Sir Julius Caesar reminding him of Cecil's personal interest. It was an exceedingly well-oiled machine, with Sir Julius Caesar taking a "twentieth" of the lord admiral's "tenth." [16] Still, these men who made the Admiralty work should not be judged too harshly. By the standards of the time, they worked efficiently and honestly, taking what was expected by way of recompense since salaries were often not paid at all, or paid late. When compared to Spain's naval administration, England's Admiralty was a paragon of virtue.

In truth, by the late 1590s, it had become so difficult to discern the machinations of the Admiralty that it was left to Cecil to oversee its activities on behalf of the Privy Council. The "pirates" were dealt with harshly by the High Court of the Admiralty, and usually forced to give restitution for a portion of what had been stolen. In 1600 alone, there were eighty-nine cases of men arrested as pirates. It mattered little if they were the lowly Captain Diggory Piper (of the famed galliard) or a peer of the realm. Only Sir George Carey, governor of the Isle of Wight, and heir to Lord Hunsdon and future patron of William Shakespeare, seemed to escape unscathed. But then again, he was the lord admiral's brother-in-law. What mattered were the circumstances of the seizure, and whether the so-called "pirates" could bribe their way out of trouble.[17]

Sir Julius Caesar, too, had a position of unprecedented power. It was he who sat at the High Court of the Admiralty and issued the letters of reprisal, often accepting fiction as fact. It was said that Drake's adventures had "inflamed the whole country with a desire to adventure unto the seas, in the hope of the like good success," and it was Caesar's duty to ensure that they could. Reprisal ships usually accompanied "royal" missions, though others chose to sail independently if the queen's expeditions seemed too tame for their needs. The 1590s were therefore the decade where John Hagthorpe's statement that there were "never less than two hundred sail of voluntaries and others on Spanish Coasts" has generally been accepted. Even if it were an exaggeration, there were probably never any less than a hundred English ships of reprisal sailing on the seas at any one time in the whole decade. And most of these ships went "unregistered" for a fee, thanks to Sir Julius and the Admiralty officers. Others were logged in at low values for their cargoes.[18]

Taking the Admiralty, merchants, and the adventurers as "the queen's adventurers," it is easy to see why the queen's share of the purse in pure percentage terms continued to dwindle. But it wasn't the unfair distribution of the spoils that strained the economy. It was Ireland, as well as the war with Spain, that was ruining her. Each year, more and more crown lands needed to be sold to keep "Battleship England" afloat, and the old queen was reduced to finding as many creative ways as possible, assisted by her "elf" (also called her "pygmy") Cecil, to plug the leaks. Raleigh, somewhat unkindly but nonetheless truthfully, accused the queen of not recognizing the power of her "private navy."

Still, even the outspoken Raleigh hadn't recognized that the real power had almost imperceptibly shifted from the gentlemen adventurers back into the hands of the queen's merchant adventurers. These men, like John Watts of London and alderman Paul Bayning with his *Golden Phoenix*, worked at times for the queen, and at other times, strictly for their own commercial interests. Any joint stock companies that they engaged in had clear objectives, and these were cast in stone. Heavily armed for defensive and offensive action, the

Londoners in particular who specialized in building and owning ships that could double up for "warfare" were awesome weapons. There was no longer any room on their ships for the amateur adventurer, or the queen's objectives when they were engaged in trade. These were businessmen in the modern sense. Friends were friends, but business was business.

There were still smaller vessels hankering for plunder, too. These were usually owner captains, much as young Drake had been aboard his bark plying the Channel ports. Often they grouped together, sharing expenses and creating small squadrons, especially when they ventured farther afield like the West Indies. Those who had done well sometimes lent money to the great adventures of Drake, Raleigh, Essex, and Cumberland, but, by and large, they knew their place among the second rung of merchant adventurers, combining trade and plunder when they could.

And yet the "trade" of plunder consumed many more fortunes and lives than it made. "The numbers of sailors and seamen," Admiral Monson complained, "are increased treble by it [plunder] to what they are in the navigations of peaceable voyages."[19] True pirates became the more respectable "adventurers" thanks in no small part to the lining of Sir Julius Caesar's pockets. Often a peaceful voyage would deteriorate into an exercise in piracy as a result. Naturally, this made foreigners reluctant to trade with the English, never quite knowing their real intentions. And, in turn, it created a trade depression that compounded the intractable problem of unemployment and poverty to a level unknown since the Wars of the Roses a century earlier. The 1590s became known as a decade of high inflation, failed harvests, renewed bouts of plague in London in particular, and the decade where the aging queen (now in her sixties) seemed to be losing her tight grip on her divergent factions at court. It is no wonder that the reputation Englishmen gained abroad was as a rambunctious lot of pirates.

But Elizabeth hadn't by any stretch of the imagination "lost the plot." She, and of course Robert Cecil, encouraged pamphleteers singing the praises of her seafaring men. Adventuring writers like Henry Roberts became more popular than Shakespeare. Nationalism and patriotism were attributed to the acts of daring-do by the queen's adventurers, and the average Englishman swelled with pride that their tiny country had seen off the greatest empire in the world—not once or twice, but three times, with the third armada attempt meeting the same fate as the second.

Spain's economy had suffered, too. Not so much from the direct plundering of ships but more from the secondary and tertiary effects of the English (and by now to a lesser extent the French) and Dutch depredations. Ships lost added enormously to the cost of maintaining the flow of treasure. Increased fortifications in the West Indies and elsewhere consumed real time, money, and men. Lives of Spain's finest soldiers and mariners were lost, with their number severely depleted after the failed "Invincible" campaign of 1588. Scurvy (the plague of the sea), ships sunk at sea, poor wages, and poorer campaigns of attack meant that Spain's men were dying in droves. Its population began to slump. Defense of the Atlantic had to be added to the price tag of trying to reconquer the Netherlands in its unrelenting rebellion. Famine and plague at home also took their toll, in part caused by private fortunes being wasted on protection of their West Indian plantations and mines. Others began to feel that the Atlantic trade was too risky and sought other ways of making a living.

And still, England's merchants continued their onslaught. Talented captains like James Lancaster successfully raided Pernambuco in 1595, with Watts, Bayning, and other former merchants of England's Spanish Company joining forces with him. The arms trade to Morocco flourished, as did the sale of metals for weaponry to the Ottoman sultans. Robert Cecil was a particularly active backer of Mediterranean plunder, and he became involved with Thomas Cordell's and William Garraway's plundering operations there, while also investing with the lord admiral's own reprisal fleet.

The outports of England suffered if, like Bristol, they didn't possess ship owners who had built vessels for the purposes of war, trade, and plunder. The ports of Plymouth, Weymouth, and Southampton fared better than most with their merchant and gentlemen adventurers, who frequently put their ships to sea under the queen's banner either on the Continent or in Ireland. Yet while the great merchants and the adventurers were not inflicting the long-hoped-for "knockout blow," they were amassing gigantic personal fortunes. Watts, Bayning, Thomas Smythe, and Thomas Middleton all cast around for how best to turn those gigantic fortunes into monumental ones. To do that, they had to ensure a steady flow of merchandise of extreme worth and high quality, and a buoyant home market to sell it in. That would mean fishing in new grounds. These men had refined the skill of trade and plunder to a new art form and could engage in either or both at will. And so, without a strictly fixed idea as to which of their activities would prevail, they turned their eyes from the Atlantic eastward.

The East Indies had always been their Holy Grail, after all.

40. Essex, Ireland, and Tragedy ❧

Eyes of youth have sharp sights, but commonly not so
deep as those of older age. . . . I see as in a crystal the right
figure of my folly . . . foreseen haps breeds no wonder;
no more doth your short-returned post before his time.
—ELIZABETH I TO ROBERT DEVEREUX, JULY 1597

R obert Devereux, Earl of Essex, like so many adventurers and
courtiers of the younger Elizabethan generations, began his
military career in the Low Countries at Leicester's side. It was there
that he inherited two of Sir Philip Sidney's "best swords" and made
his most steadfast friends in combat. With Sidney's death, Essex
became the queen's favorite on his return home in 1587, and took
Sidney's place as well as darling of the court's literati. The other
"pretender" to both those titles, Walter Raleigh, would remain
his bitter enemy for the duration of their lives. When Raleigh had
himself painted with pearls under a crescent moon, Essex replied
with Hilliard's *Young Man among Roses*. Poetry, too, became a
weapon of choice, as did—nearly—swords. With the loss of his own
heir, Sir Philip Sidney, in the Low Countries, Leicester himself had
encouraged their rivalry from the outset, seeing his stepson Essex
as his natural successor for the queen's heart over the upstart West
Countryman Raleigh.[1]

And Leicester's wishes, during his lifetime, were never ignored.
Essex's rise was meteoric. Within the year, he was a knight of the
Garter, had been given the attainted Sir Francis Englefield's lands,
and the smashing London pad York House (which he'd rename Essex
House). The young Earl's servants boasted that even into the small
hours of the morning "my lord is at cards or one game or another
with her [the queen], that he comes not to his own lodging until
the birds sing in the morning."[2] When Leicester died unexpectedly

on September 4, 1588, Essex took over his offices as lord steward and master of the horse. Elizabeth, deeply bereaved without her Leicester, saw him again daily in his stepson, Essex, and soon would not be parted from the young man. Though undoubtedly charismatic and brilliant, he had become the young Robert Dudley in Elizabeth's eyes, lavishing gifts and appointments on him as she had done for Dudley in their youth. Even Leicester's farm on sweet wines became Essex's, and remained his until October 1600.

Yet, despite all the promise and all the love and gifts Elizabeth showered upon him, Essex's worst enemy remained himself. His arrogance was colossal. He would do as he wished, and he would bring the "old" queen to heel. Possessing the pride of a man whose nature refused to be ruled would prove his epitaph.

Well aware of the queen's disfavor for "secret" marriages among her men and women at court, Essex nonetheless contracted to marry Philip Sidney's widow, Frances Walsingham Sidney, sometime in 1590. While Elizabeth's attachment to Essex meant that her fury soon subsided, his constant string of women—from her maid of honor Elizabeth Southwell to the Countess of Derby—stretched the queen's patience more than once to breaking point. The queen frowned upon overt infidelity as it reflected poorly on her court. But the queen's feelings mattered little at the end of the day to Essex. While his wife had given him an heir, she lacked the money that the queen's most ostentatious courtier craved and demanded. And with Sir Francis Walsingham now dead, there was nothing to keep him in check. Essex found himself boasting "overly grandly" how he would handle matters, while plotting to make daring adventures in the hope of plunder and the position he believed he deserved.[3]

But Essex was a transparent boy compared to Robert Cecil, and he could never plumb the depths of Cecil's Machiavellian thoughts and deeds. Essex's own impatience and desperate wishes always seemed to interfere. So when he shined like a brilliant gemstone at Cadiz, and still did not get his way, he suffered a deep depression for the first part of 1587. The only thing that pulled him out of it was Elizabeth's approval for him to take part in the Silver Blockade scheme devised by Hawkins. Instead of cruising off the Spanish coast, Essex and his men sailed for the Azores in the hope of catching the flota, despite his criticism that this kind of expedition was "idle wanderings upon the sea" only a year before.[4] Disgrace followed, when, on his return home, he discovered that the Spaniards had nearly succeeded in launching their fleet in an assault on Falmouth in Cornwall. And despite these setbacks, it never once dawned on Essex that he was a soldier of fortune and adventurer, not a naval commander.

Essex was sworn in as a privy councillor before the end of 1593, an honor that eluded Raleigh altogether. He threw himself into his work on the council in the vain hope that he could take over Burghley's role as the queen's chief advisor, since it was rumored that "their chief hour glass [Burghley] has little sand left in it."[5] As if to prove his unswerving loyalty, Essex wrongly accused, and had convicted, the queen's physician, Roderigo Lopez, of plotting to assassinate the queen in 1594. Still, whenever the queen ridiculed him (as she derided all her councillors) for his flights of fancy or other pretensions, he would shut himself away in his rooms for days on end, like a spoiled child, until she made a gesture to show her favor. He lived in the mistaken hope that, on Burghley's death, Elizabeth would choose his counsel over that of Robert Cecil.

By 1598, Essex had become known as a "man of great designs." Elizabeth had become weary of his constant haranguing and demands for more gifts, more favors, more power. To boot, Essex had made powerful enemies—Burghley, Cecil, Nottingham, Cobham, and Raleigh—all of whom had been strengthened by their own successes. As if that were not enough to count against him, he insisted on trying to make peace between his mother and Elizabeth, whose "mislike" for her cousin Lettice (who had secretly married Leicester) had not lessened since Leicester's death. Again and again, he taunted the queen, famously turning his back on her in her presence chamber, dumbfounding all onlookers. The incident in which he drew his sword on the queen had been smoothed over, but it was not entirely forgiven or forgotten.

He angered Elizabeth, yet moments later could make her laugh. No other subject had treated her in this way, but an explanation for the queen's remarkable patience was that she saw in him the rambunctious Robert Dudley instead of the prideful Essex, and felt somehow that she couldn't live without him at her side. When Essex became highly critical of all previous campaigns in Ireland—

including his dead father's—his bluff was eventually called, and despite the queen's hesitation at putting such a man at the head of her army there, she at last relented. The Privy Council agreed that he should prosecute the war against the rebellious Hugh O'Neill, Earl of Tyrone, and bring the Irish troubles to an end. His instructions clearly stated that he should head for Ulster after landing at Dublin, and defeat Tyrone.

Crushing Tyrone would be Essex's greatest challenge. Ireland had been in "revolt" in one form or another for most of Elizabeth's long reign, with Tyrone's own uncle, Shane O'Neill, being massacred at the hands of the English. The Earl of Ormond had been the queen's staunchest ally though, for a long while, he was wrongly viewed as treacherous to England by the machinations of the Earl of Desmond, and the misinformation that Hugh O'Neill himself had sown among English nobles. Sir Henry Sidney claimed that he had "bred" the young O'Neill (at the time the third Baron of Dungannon) "from a little boy, then very poor of goods, and full feebly friended" between 1556 and 1559. In 1567, Sir Henry brought the young Dungannon to court along with other sons from other Irish noble houses to fully educate them in the English ways. He had gone from having no chance of inheriting the title of the "O'Neill" as the third defenseless son of the man deprived of his inheritance by Shane O'Neill, to the all-powerful Earl of Tyrone, who used his knowledge of England and its customs against itself to his own ends.[6]

The situation in Ireland was desperate. When the English hadn't been trying to dominate the Irish chieftains, the chieftains themselves warred endlessly with one another. Cattle raids, scorched-earth policies, rape, murder, and tribal allegiances dominated the country. The only constant was the Catholic religion, which after Henry VIII's break with Rome meant that Catholic interests viewed it as a launch pad into England. The more Protestant England fought to retain its "Irish plantations" (confiscated, of course, from dissident Irish chieftains) and its Irish sovereignty, the more the Irish revolted.[7]

When Tyrone returned to Ulster in 1585, it was with the single purpose to make himself master of his own lands yet again, then to free Ireland from England's yoke. He was a consummate general and, unusually for the times, had oodles of patience. For the next ten years; he honed his Ulster guerrilla raids into a well-run rebellion, until at last in 1595 open warfare was declared. These tactics had been the undoing of Sir John "Black Jack" Norris, returned from the Low Countries and Cadiz to give the Irish yet another drubbing. The current lord deputy, Sir William Russell, too, had been confounded by Tyrone. When Russell was replaced by Lord Burgh in 1597, Elizabeth hoped that at last she had found the military and administrative combination to bring Ireland to heel. Within eight months, both Norris and Burgh were dead.

Nothing and no one seemed capable of stopping Tyrone. He leveled one English plantation after another, and the queen feared that even the Pale surrounding Dublin might be in jeopardy. Other parts of the country were beginning to adopt Tyrone's tactics, and no matter what forces or commanders the queen threw at them, the Irish were victorious. Tyrone's famous victory against Sir Henry Bagenal at Yellow Ford gave heart to all Ireland, and created a number of other uprisings around the Pale in Leinster and in Munster in the Southwest. Walter Raleigh's own vast forty-two-thousand-acre plantation was washed away in a sea of blood. As if this wasn't bad enough, what Elizabeth truly feared with considerable dread was that Tyrone was expecting assistance at any moment from Spain or the pope, not only to take her troubled province from her realm, but also to invade England itself.[8]

It was into this tricky situation that the new lord lieutenant, the hotheaded Essex, arrived in April 1599. Instead of following the queen's directions to head at once for Ulster, Essex attacked Munster, in the Southwest, claiming that he needed to make the South safe first against possible Spanish support. With each passing week, the queen wrote more and more vitriolic letters to her new lord lieutenant. Ireland was bankrupting her. Why wasn't he meeting Tyrone's forces in Ulster? Finally, she snapped, and on July 19, 1599, wrote to Essex:

We have perceived by your letters to our Council brought by Henry Carey, that you are arrived at Dublin after your journey into Munster, where though it seemeth by the words of your letter that you had spent divers days in taking an account of all that have passed since you left that place, yet have you in this dispatch given us small light either when or in what order you intend particularly to proceed to the northern action. Wherein if you compare the time that is run on and the excessive charges that is spent with the effects of anything wrought by this voyage (howsoever we may remain satisfied with your own particular cares and travails of body and mind), yet you must needs think that we that have the eyes of foreign princes upon our actions and have the hearts of people to comfort and cherish—who groan under the burden of continual levies and impositions which are occasioned by these late actions—can little please ourself hitherto with anything that hath been effected.[9]

Against the queen's specific command, instead of engaging Tyrone's troops in the North, he proceeded to make peace with Tyrone, who had after all been Essex's good friend at court. The English had been decimated by disease and fruitless war in Munster thanks to Essex. When the two old friends met, talking midstream so that they wouldn't be overheard, their horses belly-deep in the fast-flowing current, the history of Ireland would be changed forever. At the end of their half-hour talk, Essex came away feeling that he had made an honorable peace. He believed that his Irish friend had agreed to lay down his arms. Tyrone, meanwhile, reported back to Spain that he had nearly persuaded Essex to turn against Elizabeth![10] It is one of the more mysterious chapters in the history of the two countries since what happened next doesn't clearly follow, and proved a tragedy to both sides.

Elizabeth's letters continued to arrive—each one angrier than the last. No longer trusting his written word to calm her, Essex was certain that his detractors—of which there were many—were poisoning the queen against him. Only a personal appearance at court could make her see that he had, in fact, acted for the good of her realm. And so, again, the prideful Essex ignored royal commandment, left his post as lord lieutenant without leave, and hastened to Nonsuch, where on September 24, he barged in on the old queen, who was not fully dressed. To say that his demeanor startled her is more than an English understatement. Elizabeth felt distinctly threatened by her soldier, still muddy from his travels and carrying his sword in his hand. She famously sweet-talked him, asking him to give her leave to dress before they spoke in earnest. She begged him to go wash the dirt from his travels from him, and rejoin her later in the day. By afternoon, her sails had filled with a good head of wind again, and she blasted him as only Queen Elizabeth could do, in front of the entire Council. It would be the last time that they would ever see each other.

Essex was confined to his chambers before being sent to Essex House under house arrest. He was in a state of near mental and physical collapse. Treason charges were drawn up against him, and perhaps for the first time, he realized that his short life could end in total failure, though by now his paranoia was near complete. He was, however, in one way fortunate: his breakdown did spare him a judgment by the Star Chamber at the end of November 1602 since it was believed Essex would die of his malady. If, after all, he would die, then why make a martyr of him, the Star Chamber argued.

And yet, Essex did recover, though he never fully in strength or sound reasoning again. Though disgraced, a number of young and disaffected noblemen flocked to his side, like the heartthrob Henry Wriothesley, third Earl of Southampton; while others, Sir Francis Bacon being the most notable, deserted and betrayed him. Eventually, Elizabeth settled on the best solution: allow Essex his freedom, but continue to bar him from court. His political career was at an end, but she would not otherwise harm him.[11]

*

Had she left matters like that, then things might have turned out differently. In the end, though, the queen's pride and parsimony got the better of her. When Essex's sweet wines farm came up for renewal in October 1600, she refused to renew it. From her vantage point, it was an extremely valuable royal gift, and one that had continually shown exceptional royal favor since it was first bestowed in the 1560s onto Robert Dudley. How could she allow a man who had failed to tame Tyrone or even fight him to retain this treasure?

Essex's reaction was predictably harebrained. He wrote to James VI of Scotland pleading for help. James, the only child of Mary, Queen of Scots, had been Elizabeth's putative heir since the time of

Mary's execution—so long as no one pushed the English queen into making it official. Naturally, the queen's "intelligencers" knew all. Essex had naturally been put under constant surveillance. Finally, in February 1601, Essex and his followers had hatched a scheme to take over control of court and oust Essex's enemies by denouncing them to the queen. But their plans were preempted by a summons to appear before the queen on Saturday, February 7. On the one hand, they panicked, resolving to throw themselves on the mercy of the City. On the other, they sought refuge in a final act of defiance, and paid Shakespeare and his players to put on a specially commissioned performance of *Richard II* at the Globe Theater, instead of responding to the summons.

The following morning, Essex led around three hundred men, all wearing their swords and doublets but no armor, on a march into the City. Some of the men carried firearms. Notable among them were the Earls of Southampton, Rutland, Bedford, Sandys, Cromwell, and Monteagle, as well as Sir Christopher Blount. When Essex's march came to the house of the sheriff of London, Sir Thomas Smythe, they soon realized the folly of their action. Smythe and the lord mayor had ordered the City gates shut, and Essex's support evaporated. By nine P.M., Essex had surrendered, spending the night as a prisoner at Lambeth Palace (the archbishop of Canterbury's London home) before being transported to the Tower through Traitor's Gate.

Ten days later, Essex and Southampton were tried for treason. Southampton's sentence was commuted to imprisonment, but Essex was to die on the scaffold, thanks in no small part to the testimony of his former intimate friend, Sir Francis Bacon.[12] It could be claimed that Essex, more than any other adventurer, lost everything in Ireland. He certainly lost his father to the interminable Irish wars, and may have lost his sanity in the guerrilla warfare so expertly practiced by the Irish rebels. Still, at the end of the day, Robert Devereux, Earl of Essex, had ideas beyond his station in life. He was no Leicester. He was no Francis Drake. He was no Burghley, nor even a Robert Cecil. But if wishing made it so, he had all their cunning and fortunes rolled into one, and the ability to make himself the queen's master where all the others had failed.

❧

And what of Tyrone and Ireland? Tyrone's insistence that Ireland could only free itself completely from England's rule with the help of the Spanish proved a tremendous weakness in his otherwise fine strategy. The notorious contrary winds between Spain and England in the Bay of Biscay shipwrecked Philip's last two armadas. When the third armada landed at Kinsale with four thousand men, under the leadership of Don Juan de Aguilla, instead of on Ulster's shores, Irish hopes for a Gaelic Ireland were dashed. In a country full of myth and legend, they claim that early modern Irish had thirty-two words that meant fool, idiot, moron, or imbecile. That is until Tyrone began his insults against Aguilla: "that misbegotten son of a tree stump . . . that baboon's droppings . . . that, that *Spaniard!*"[13]

It must be said that Essex's desertion was another blessing for England and curse of Ireland at the end of the day. For Essex was replaced by the unbelievably tenacious Charles Blount, Lord Mountjoy, who proved to be the right man—at last—for the job of taming the "wild" Irish. Through Mountjoy's phenomenal energy and generalship (not unlike Wellington's two centuries later), Tyrone's plans were anticipated, and he was stopped at every turn. Raleigh's cousin, Sir George Carew (also Essex's mortal enemy), was put in charge of settling Munster, which he did with diplomacy and tact more than by force of arms. New forts at Derry near Lough Foyle provided a base camp near Tyrone's own lands, from which Sir Henry Docwra could tackle the disaffected O'Neills, Maguires, and O'Donnells for the English as Carew had done in Munster, and Mountjoy had done in Connaught.

Tyrone's epithets aside, when the Spaniards finally landed their four thousand crack infantrymen at Kinsale in September 1601, it was too late. Naturally, with Tyrone's strength in the North, there was no chance of victory. The Munster Irish and Tyrone's supporters were already depleted by Mountjoy's tactics, and the combined Irish and Spanish forces faced a complete rout. De Aguilla made an honorable surrender in January 1602, while O'Neill fled to Spain. Tyrone was eventually captured in March 1603, and with him died the expectation of Irish independence for nearly a century and a half.[14]

Though there are many who would disagree, England's conquest of Ireland wasn't entirely bad for the country. It extinguished tribal warfare on the island, making blood feuds, murder, and cattle raiding illegal. In conquest came the birth of the Irish nation, rising like the phoenix from its ashes. Pride in being Irish, as opposed to an O'Neill or O'Toole, with the accompanying patriotism against the archenemy England, swelled in its people as a whole, and was allowed to take hold and flourish.

41. Raleigh, Virginia, and Empire ❧

A maze wherein affection finds no end
A ranging cloud that runs before the wind
A substance like the shadow of the sun
A goal of grief for which the wisest run.
—SIR WALTER RALEIGH, "Farewell False Love," 1588

Raleigh's income had been severely curtailed as a result of the Munster uprising in the wake of Tyrone's guerrilla exploits. He had acquired the largest seignory in the country through the English conquest of the Irish chieftains, and had spent a great deal of time in 1589 renovating his mansion and plantation near Youghall. To his friends, he claimed he was retreating "from Court . . . to take order for my prize."[1] The vast forests there provided much of the wooden staves for barrels, which was one of his main trading businesses, selling to the Admiralty and other shipowners. When his estate fell victim to the same scorched earth policy as others had done in the rebellion, the pinch he felt was most certainly real. After Tyrone's supporters had laid waste to his lands, he was lucky to sell them to Sir Richard Boyle, secretary for Munster, for £1,500 ($360,750 or £195,000 today).

Other than Essex, Walter Raleigh was only other courtier vying for the perfect vision of courtly love at the sunset of Elizabeth's reign. Essex had been born into the new nobility, and was the handsome portrait of the highly educated, suave, hot-tempered, quick-tempered, and arrogant nobleman until his premature death on the scaffold. Raleigh, too, had bagfuls of arrogance and charm, was quick to anger and slow to forgive. He had been educated at Oxford, but he came down to London without obtaining a degree. Yet Raleigh, despite his pretensions, was only a West Countryman of gentle birth, and he spoke his whole life with a thick West Country accent. And accents in England, until recently, determined one's place in society.

Both were adventurers in the true sense of the word—Raleigh earned a fortune several times over from his escapades, while Essex lost his principal capital. Aside from these main points of their lives, Raleigh and Essex would share the reason for their deaths, too: treason.

But that is for the future.

Elizabeth could not live without either of them. Some believed that when Essex was executed, much of the life, vigor, and good humor went out of her. She sank into what can only be described as a deep depression, where even her "Water" could not quench her thirst and bring her back to life. While Raleigh continued to live high on the hog, his expenses far exceeded his income. After Essex's execution, when the queen didn't give Raleigh any new and beneficial grants to relieve his often-bemoaned penury, it was clear that Raleigh would not profit from Essex's demise.[2] The thought of tightening his belt and living within his means was not an option that Raleigh could stomach. And so he fell back again on his adventuring with renewed passion.

He had planned a campaign with Cumberland and Frobisher to capture the West Indies flota in 1592. Yet, shortly before setting sail with the impressive fleet, Elizabeth recalled him to London. Raleigh ignored the order and accompanied his ships until he could give his orders to his new commander Sir John Burgh, at sea. Frobisher was to keep guard on the Spanish coast, while the rest of the adventuring fleet were led by Cumberland to the Azores. There, Cumberland encountered two Portuguese East Indies carracks, the *Santa Cruz* and the *Madre de Díos*. The *Santa Cruz* was burned after her richly laden cargo was taken, while the *Madre de Díos* was sailed back to England.[3]

This "campaign" became known as the Islands Voyage to the Azores. Under normal circumstances, Raleigh stood every chance of making good his losses in Ireland and Virginia, and by normal calculations should have cleared around £80,000 for his troubles ($19.24 million or £10.4 million today). Instead, this would be the queen's ransom. To his abiding anger, it was not meant to be. After

the shares of the spoils were divided, Raleigh complained bitterly to
Lord Burghley that

> *the City of London is to have £6,000 profit by Her Majesty's order.*
> *Then they are to have Her Majesty's allowance of £2,000 upon all*
> *and £4,000 profit as well out of our principal. By that means we*
> *are to lose £4,000 of money disbursed. . . . The Earl of Cumberland*
> *is allowed £36,000 and his account came but to £19,000, so he has*
> *£ 17,000 profit, who adventured for himself, and we that served the*
> *Queen and assisted her service [fitting out her ships] have not our*
> *own again. Besides I gave my ship's sails and cables to furnish the*
> *carrack and bring her home or else she [would] have perished. . . .*
> *I was the cause that all this came to the Queen and that the King*
> *of Spain spent £300,000 [in] the last year. And I lost in the last*
> *year in the voyage of my Lord Thomas Howard, £1,600, besides*
> *the interest of £11,000 which I have paid ever since this voyage*
> *began.*[4]

All of the figures, and certainly reference to his being solely responsible
for the expenditure of the King of Spain, are incorrect. Raleigh's
summary of woe is right, however, when he states that he earned
very little from England's largest adventuring haul. The reason for
this was simple: in between the time when Raleigh had initially
intended to sail on the voyage and the date of the final accounting in
January 1593, Raleigh had been committed to the Tower for lying to
the queen about his secret marriage to Bess Throckmorton and the
birth of his son Wat.

Still, it is difficult to feel sorry for the man. He was immensely
talented, a great strategist, a gifted poet and historian, and he had
other varied sources of income. He was an Admiralty officer, and
earned a great deal from his declared—as well as undeclared—
dealings in this professional capacity. He advised other, more sea
loving, admirals and captains about where to go in search of plunder,
and duly received his fair portion for his trouble. While vice admiral
for both Devon and Cornwall since 1585, his undeclared earnings
would have been huge.

Then there was the not insubstantial matter of the Virginia grant.

Some adventurers had pointed out to the Privy Council that Raleigh's patent of 1584 had expired since no colony had been successfully established within six years. Raleigh argued, with the support of Richard Hakluyt, that they were wrong. There was no evidence that his colony at Roanoke had perished, only that they had moved to Croatoan. Indeed, two children—Virginia Dare and a boy to the Harvies—had been born in Virginia.[5] So long as he could argue that point successfully (which he did), then the twelve hundred miles of prime North American coastline belonged exclusively to him. Still, the fact remained that there were no documented voyages to Virginia in the decade between 1591 and 1602, and certainly Raleigh appeared to have abandoned Virginia in favor of adventure and the quest for gold.

Indeed, Raleigh spent the 1590s busily looking for the fabled El Dorado. Virginia, according to his surveyors and experts, held no gold. And if England were to become the great empire to supplant Spain, Raleigh argued, it was gold that the country needed. It would also be the only salvation for Raleigh's dwindling resources. In order to exploit any gold deposits or mines that he may be fortunate enough to find during his voyages of exploration in the 1590s, Raleigh needed to promote the concept of colonies and empire strongly. Without the manpower to take charge of these new lands, there would be no means of extracting, protecting, or shipping the gold back to England.

Yet, as hard as he tried, after his 1595 voyage to Trinidad and the Orinoco, where no concrete sign of El Dorado had been discerned, it remained impossible for Raleigh to attract finance to his proposed adventures. Other adventurers like Sir Robert Dudley, the "base-born" son of Leicester and Lady Douglas Sheffield, searched as well, but they did not join in Raleigh's expedition. Even Raleigh's *Discoverie of the Large Rich, and Beautiful Empire of Guiana*, published in 1596, failed to renew the gold fever at court that had prevailed at the time of Frobisher's attempts at finding the Northwest Passage.[6] When this was followed a year later with his *Of the Voyage for Guiana*, outlining his proposed methods for settlement, and the attributes of converting the "heathens" to Christianity, few realized what an insightful work it was. Even Hakluyt's preaching in intellectual circles and at court produced no result for him. It was a pity, but the country wasn't ready for an all out push into the great unknown while Ireland remained in revolt, and Spain continually—or so it seemed—sent out repeated armadas through the 1590s. *Of the Voyage for Guiana* set out clearly—and for the first time—the foundations necessary for the development of a tropical colony, arguing at length about how to use the local population to advantage, while importing English settlers to bring in the rule of English law and mastermind the export of goods and supplies back to England.[7]

Despite Cecil's agreement to send out two ships to Guiana to look for El Dorado, the level of interest in the region in the late 1590s was exceedingly limited. In addition to the Irish and Spanish problems (Spain had taken Calais and threatened Rouen), France had a Catholic king again with the conversion of Henry IV. The queen could die at any time, and the succession was not assured. The tropical jungles of the Orinoco or the Amazon were too far away and too dangerous for anyone to venture their money in when matters in Europe remained so unsettled.

Then a new adventure happened to refresh Raleigh's interests in Virginia, though he had no part in the expedition. In 1597, a separatist Puritan sect, mistakenly called Brownists by the Privy Council, asked for a license to emigrate to the St. Lawrence region of North America. The queen agreed, providing that they never returned to England while still practicing their faith. She deeply mistrusted Puritans, as did Cecil. But Raleigh would have preferred they attempt to settle in Virginia, and cleverly wrote to Cecil "not to meddle with the state of Ireland (where Cecil had substantial holdings) nor that of Guiana. There is under our noses the great and ample country of Virginia."[8]

The letter continued, urging Cecil to advise the queen that if they proceeded to make a colony in Virginia, "if upon a good and godly peace obtained, it shall please the Almighty to stir up her majesty's heart to continue with her favourable countenance . . . with transporting of one or two thousand of her people . . . she shall by God's assistance, in short space, work many great and unlooked-for effects, increase her dominions, enrich her coffers, and reduce many pagans to the father of Christ."[9]

But the "Brownists" sailed under the auspices of two London

merchants, Alexander van Harwick and Charles Leigh, for the island of Ramea on the St. Lawrence River. The *Hopewell* and *Chancewell* set out in April 1597 but, on their arrival, were confronted by hostile Breton and Basque fishermen who had already laid claim to the territory. In the end, Leigh, who led the expedition in the *Hopewell*, had to return to England with his pioneers still aboard due to French and Spanish resistance to the formation of an English colony at the site of their fisheries.[10]

Finally, in 1602, Raleigh sent two ships and a pinnace under Captain Samuel Mace to renew trade with North America. Mace was under strict orders that if the "lost colonists" had survived, then he must bring some of them back to England. They would be his best instruments for selling his ideas of empire at home after all. But while Mace worked up the coast of North America to Cape Fear, there was no serious effort to find the "lost colonists" of 1587. Instead, Mace loaded sassafras wood and china root (sarsaparilla). While sarsaparilla had no medicinal value despite reports to the contrary, sassafras fetched 3s. to 20s. for a pound weight in London (between $7 and $240 or £20 to £130 today) and was the new "miracle" cure for "the French pox" or syphilis.[11]

At the same time, Bartholomew Gosnold, Bartholomew Gilbert, and John Brereton sailed a small expedition to the New England coast in the hope of establishing a trading settlement there. As frequently happened in these early voyages, though, food was in short supply, planters were poorly advised, and, as a result, serious arguments threatening survival broke out. In the end, within three months, on June 18, 1602, they had all sailed again for England, anchoring at Weymouth three weeks later.

Significantly, Raleigh was there to meet them that July 1602—hopping mad. It seems that the first he had heard of their voyage had been after they left. Since he held the exclusive rights to settle and trade in that part of North America—or so he believed—he was not prepared to abide their interloping. Still, it wasn't his plantation rights that truly concerned him: if Bartholomew Gilbert and his partners sold their sassafras on the open market, it would become flooded, wiping out the considerable profit that Raleigh himself had intended to claim from his own earlier shipment. The hapless merchant agreed that this would not be any good for either of them, and so Raleigh sent him to Cecil in London with a letter warning, "I have a patent that all ships and goods are confiscate that shall trade there without my leave. . . . Gilbert went without my leave, and therefore *all* is confiscate . . . [yet Gilbert] shall have his part again."[12]

Raleigh was acting with pure economics at the heart of his argument. He merely wanted to control market flow and ensure that there would not be a glut. There were obviously no hard feelings since the group later dedicated their *Brief and True Relation of the Discovery of the North Part of Virginia*, published shortly after, to Raleigh.

Economics even ruled Raleigh's head in the quest for the "lost colonists," too. His interest in their survival was twofold: to protect his exclusive patent and to tempt others to follow in their footsteps. Yet, Raleigh would not be remembered for his callousness toward his "western planters." He would be credited with far greater things: the "introduction" of tobacco and potatoes to England (both false); the embodiment of chivalry and courtly love; and the founding of Virginia.

It was an appropriate way for the queen's favorite adventurer to be remembered. Still, it would have been more appropriate perhaps if he had been more widely seen for what he had really been: a promoter of empire and a poet. Interestingly, nearly the last surviving letter of Elizabeth's reign is from Raleigh: it was the first piece of direct spin doctoring to attract planters to the American colonies in the early days of the seventeenth century.

42. The East and the East India Company ❧

I cannot tell you where you should look for me because I
live at the devotion of the winds and seas.

—SIR JAMES LANCASTER TO THE GOVERNORS OF

THE EAST INDIA COMPANY, 1603

When Thomas Cavendish sailed up the Channel in the autumn of 1588—his mariners sporting silken doublets and his topsails trimmed with gold—a new era in maritime adventuring was ushered in, though no one knew it at the time. Cavendish, the second Englishman to circumnavigate the globe had also returned home with treasure, some £100,000, in fact ($2.41 billion or £1.3 billion today).

No sooner did he step ashore than Cavendish wrote to his old friend, the lord chamberlain, Lord Hunsdon, "I sailed along the islands of the Moluccas where our countrymen may have trade as freely as the Portuguese if they themselves will."[1] Not only had he reiterated Drake's message of eight years before, but he also proved that the size of ship or fleet no longer mattered. Nor, indeed, did the pope's division of the world between Spain and Portugal of a hundred years earlier.

Yet what did matter was the machinery of state that had been put in place for the queen's adventurers to serve the crown. Elizabeth held the ultimate sanction to allow her mariners to sail. As a result, England's merchants had been taking a backseat to the queen and her gentlemen adventurers for the past eighteen years while affairs of state intermingled with their trading aims.

In those heady days after the defeat of the "Invincible," a huge shift in overseas trade would take place, much to the queen's satisfaction. The better-maintained fleets belonging to the merchants doubled up as men-of-war to serve the queen. When security of the realm allowed for them to be employed by their owners in the single objective of trade, they were phenomenally successful in most adventurers that they undertook. In turn, their vast wealth garnered from those years of freebooting and trade created their moment to reemerge as the premier economic force of the country. Whenever their trading ships anchored at faraway ports in the aftermath of July 1588, sultans and potentates were uniformly impressed to meet the men who had put Philip of Spain in his rightful place.

By the late 1590s, Londoners realized that there was no longer any need to rely solely on mariners of varying skills and honesty, or on seas that could dash their fortunes without warning. Cavendish's second voyage in 1591, Richard Hawkins's in 1594, followed by Dudley's, Chidley's, and Wood's had all ended in disaster. No, the merchants agreed. Their thrust would be different. Their undertaking would resemble the colony "forts" of Portuguese India. The foreign rulers now wanted to trade with them, in part as protection against Spain, in part, to make more money. The London merchants envisaged huge emporia—cities and towns— from which they could turn their fortunes into a power that the world had not as yet seen. The time had come to seize the Holy Grail: trade with the East Indies.

Sir James Lancaster, a former merchant and English factor who had lived in Lisbon until the union of Portuguese and Spanish crowns in 1580, made a reconnaissance mission lasting from 1591 to 1594 to the East in the *Edward Bonaventure*—the same Levant Company ship he had captained during the armada campaign. He was shadowed by the Dutch fleet reconnoitering the same waters to develop the Netherlands' spice trade; and where their voyage was a phenomenal success, Lancaster's was a financial disaster. Yet despite this dismal beginning, it was by watching and drooling over the Dutch successes that the London merchants thought that they must seize their chance at once or their last opportunity to enter the spice race would be squandered. They were determined not to lose out again—this time to the Dutch, who England had saved from Spain.[2]

The rivalry between Dutch and English merchants came to a head when the Dutch petitioned Elizabeth in July 1599 to purchase a number of English ships for their Eastern colonization purposes.

The Londoners protested angrily. It was a matter of national interest to hold on to its own spice trade, they argued. Then, on September 22, 1599, 101 London merchants signed a petition promising a total of £30,133 6s. 8d. ($7.23 million or £3.91 million today) "to venture in the pretended voyage to the East Indies,"[3] and set it before the queen for her consideration. Within weeks, the demand came back from court that their venturing must be suspended at once—and that the company should not be formed under any circumstances.

It seemed that Robert Cecil had finally penetrated the queen's deep mistrust of the Spaniard, and had begun peace talks. From Elizabeth's and Cecil's viewpoint, the formation of a company to plunder the rich East Indies could only bring bad news to those negotiations. Philip II had died the year before, as had Lord Burghley, but it was feared that Philip's son and heir, Philip III, harbored a venomous loathing for the English, too. After de Aguilla's failed invasion of Ireland, naturally, these talks failed.

In the meantime, the London merchants argued their case compellingly, producing vast lists and maps of cities and towns occupied by the Portuguese, and even greater lists and maps of places where "no Christian prince" had a fort or trade. Still, they didn't fool the old queen. She knew full well that the Portuguese were far more than "merchants" in the East—the *Estado da India* controlled huge trading forts in Mozambique, Hormuz, Goa, and Malacca, and had fended off Arab and Venetian traders there for nearly a century.[4]

Nonetheless, the merchants were right to stress the vast gaps in Portugal's dominance between Indonesia and China. Where the Portuguese were strongest was, of course, from the western coast of India, encompassing Ceylon (Sri Lanka) to the Persian Gulf. But the Dutch, too, had consulted their maps and drawn the same conclusions. They knew that the eastern Portuguese trading empire was vulnerable. Their voyages to Bantam and Java were so successful that several new Dutch companies were formed to exploit the spice trade. There was widespread agreement among the queen's merchants: if the English Levant Company merchants could not make the queen budge from her position, then England's access to spices and the other rich trades was in jeopardy.

Elizabeth was tempted, but it was only when the talks with Spain were truly at an irrevocable impasse that she consented to allow their plan to go ahead. It was an ever-familiar pattern of "stop start" that dogged Elizabeth's reign, at times caused by her natural caution for security of the realm, while at other times caused by lack of funds.[5] Still, the Londoners remained tenacious. By New Year's Day 1600, the 101 names had grown to 218 merchants, incorporating as the "Company of London Merchants trading to the East Indies." One of the leading merchants, Alderman Paul Bayning, headed the committee, and his close colleague, Thomas Smythe, became the new company's governor. The only "titled" member they had was George Clifford, third Earl of Cumberland.

While most gentlemen adventurers had not as yet realized that their day had passed and that the future would need to be won by hard work and cunning rather than plunder, Cumberland and the London merchants were well aware of the changes in the world. Protestantism had spread; Spain had lost its terrier Philip II; and the Dutch with their States General had set themselves up as an alternative government to Spain's, and they had taken control of their destiny. It was right that trade should change as a result, and the Londoners would remain single-minded in their eastern undertakings, agreeing universally not to muddle affairs of state with their trading objectives. Or so they thought.

The company charter of 1600 allowed the company a monopoly to the countries beyond the Cape of Good Hope and Strait of Magellan for a period of fifteen years, subject to the usual exclusion of places possessed by any Christian prince. Exceptionally, they were also allowed to export silver to a value of up to £30,000 annually ($7.22 million or £3.9 million today) to facilitate their trading activities. This was an incredible concession for a crown that scrimped to find cash at the best of times. The £30,000 represented an astounding sixth of the queen's annual purse for the realm. Conversely, it demonstrated clearly to all participants in the new company that it had Elizabeth's seal of approval.

But the Londoners would not allow the queen's "seal" to keep them from running their company as they saw fit. They categorically refused one of Essex's soldiers, Sir Edward Michelbourne, to command the first venture, opting instead to continue backing James Lancaster as their commander. There remained a mistrust of gentleman adventurers' ability to distinguish trade from plunder, whereas they knew that Lancaster would obey his orders and maintain trade as his primary concern.

Lancaster's flagship, the 600-ton *Red Dragon*, had been recently purchased from the Earl of Cumberland (formerly called the *Malice Scourge*) at the inflated price of £3,700 ($889,092 or £480,590 today). The 240-ton *Susan*, which had belonged to Paul Bayning; the 260-ton *Ascension*, built for William Garraway (Cecil's partner); the 300-ton *Hector*, and the 120-ton *Gift* comprised the rest of the fleet.[6] The *Red Dragon* would set the standard for all subsequent English East Indiamen—a real man-of-war bristling with firepower (thirty-eight guns in all), large yet sleek, weatherly, and, importantly, graced with a large cargo hold. She was as much a warship as a trader.

Each ship also had its merchants aboard. John Middleton, John Havard, and William Brund were the main factors aboard the *Hector*, *Susan*, and *Ascension*, respectively. Lancaster had a crew of two hundred, but the entire fleet had around five hundred men for 1,520 tons of shipping. Importantly, Lancaster's chief pilot, the veteran of three arctic voyages, John Davis, had been to the East Indies before—sailing with the Dutch commander Cornelius Houtman van Hoorn, after whom Cape Horn is named.

A prerequisite of the voyage by Lancaster was that the ships be provisioned with enough lemon juice until they made landfall at the Cape in South Africa. He demanded that three spoonfuls of lemon juice be doled out to the men of all ranks daily to avoid the "plague of the sea"—scurvy. By the time they reached the Cape six months later, all men had remained "in rude health."[7]

The *Red Dragon* and her squadron were off the coast of Madagascar on Christmas Day 1601, only anchoring off Achin (Sumatra) the following June. Here was the major source of pepper, and a people hostile to Portugal. But pepper wasn't the spice they sought: nutmeg and cloves fetched the highest prices in London, and that was what they intended to bring home. So they pressed on to Bantam, where they were allowed to trade freely, and left several of their factors there, thereby founding the first English "factory" in the East.[8] But this did not bring the members of the company their Holy Grail, at least not yet.

After a fifteen-month outward bound journey, several months in the Far East, and a seven-month return stretch, Lancaster only reached England in September 1603, with his cargo that consisted, despite all his efforts, primarily of pepper.

The England he returned to was not the same place he had left, as Drake had found before in his time.

Plague ravaged the realm, and the queen was dead.

※

Many had believed that it was Essex's tragic end that brought on the queen's depression in 1602. But was Essex's life worth more than that of Burghley, Walsingham, Hatton, Drake, Winter, Hawkins, Hunsdon, Knollys, or her most beloved Leicester? There were perhaps no more Drakes, but Drake, like so many Elizabethans, would be an anachronism in the seventeenth century. There was no more Philip II either. Protestantism had taken root and flourished at last, and Elizabeth knew that she had been instrumental in ensuring that its new shoots hadn't withered.

In the third week of March 1603, the queen became progressively more reflective, standing for long hours simply staring out the window. She had been at her privy chamber window embrasure for two solid days, refusing food, running her index finger along her sore gums, staring. The sixty-nine-year-old Elizabeth, queen for over forty-four years, by the grace of God, turned, so it's believed, to listen to the entreaties of her advisors to lie down and rest. Worn out from the burdens of office, illness, and age, and especially the loss of all those she had loved and who had died before her, the old queen made to turn and collapsed.

In the gray hours of Thursday, March 24, 1603, Tudor England expired with Elizabeth. On her deathbed, too weak to talk, she communicated with her privy councillors by signs. They read out the names of her possible successors, and when the King of Scots's name was uttered, she slowly brought her hand to the crown of her head and nodded. James VI of Scotland, son of Mary Queen of Scots, would become James I of England. Having at last made her choice of successor official, Elizabeth Tudor allowed herself to slip away quietly.[9]

Given her symptoms, medical historians suggest that she died of septicemia caused by extensive tooth and gum decay, perhaps brought on by her great penchant for candied cherries, lovingly brought back from warmer seas by her adventurers to please their pirate queen.

Epilogue ❧

*France and England cannot be debarred from meddling
with the aforesaid trade and navigation: their power is
great, their seamen many, their seas large, their merchants
with their captains and soldiers over greedy of money and
booty and their subjects and servants never trusting. . . .*
—PHILIP II'S INSTRUCTIONS TO HIS SON, PHILIP III, IN 1596,
BEFORE SLIPPING INTO A COMA AND DYING

Though forbidding any formal naming of her successor, or even any discussion of the matter, from the moment Elizabeth wrote to James VI of Scotland after the execution of his mother in 1587, King James had always been treated as her heir. It wasn't a perfect or tidy solution, but for Elizabeth it was the only one. She had been right to believe that in choosing an heir, the seeds of destruction would be sown. Where Tudor statecraft had raised England from little more than a tribal community in her grandfather's time, Elizabeth's talent, perseverance, and skill had honed England into the beginnings of the nation state we recognize today. Though not officially united for another hundred years, the United Kingdom of Great Britain and Northern Ireland found its roots in her time. Much of our treasured English language and literature flourished—despite or perhaps because of censorship—in Elizabeth's England. In James Stuart, an intelligent but untrustworthy pair of hands, Elizabeth had inadvertently sown the seeds of the English Civil War and a century of upheaval.

Robert Cecil went on to become the great Jacobean statesman, elevated in James's reign to the title of Marquis of Salisbury. Sir Francis Bacon's betrayal of his good friend Essex was soon forgotten. By 1621 he had risen to become Lord Verulam Viscount St. Albans. King James treasured him, giving him a knighthood in 1603, then ultimately promoting his rise to Privy Councillor, lord keeper and, finally, lord chancellor in 1618. Bacon was, of course, also the accomplished Jacobean writer and philosopher. Both the Cecils and Bacons, along with many other great Elizabethan aristocratic families like the Stanleys, Herberts, and Sidneys, remain influential in Britain today.

Elizabeth died knowing that the Earl of Tyrone, who had cost her so dearly in lives of her adventurers and hard cash, had been captured, though fortunately she did not live to see his fate. King James I ultimately pardoned and restored him to power in 1607, but Tyrone fled to Rome, where he lived out his life peacefully until its end in 1616.

Walter Raleigh, though, did not fare as well. No sooner had James reached London than he was advised by none other than Robert Cecil that Raleigh was championing a scheme to put James's cousin Arabella Stuart on the throne of England. Raleigh once again found himself incarcerated in the Tower and was found guilty of high treason. Though initially slated for execution, at the pleading of James's wife, Anne of Denmark, and eldest son, Prince Henry, Raleigh's sentence was commuted. It was in these dreary days that Raleigh wrote his *History of the World* and some of his best poetry, including "The Lie." Desperate to restore his fortune and favor at court, Raleigh was given one last chance by the king to find El Dorado. The voyage naturally failed, with Raleigh also losing his eldest son Wat in the escapade. The sixty-three-year-old adventurer returned to England a broken man, and readied himself for the scaffold that awaited him, famously pronouncing as the axe touched his neck, "Tis a sharp remedy, but a sure one for all ills."

James naturally had revoked any claim that Raleigh had to the "country of Virginia." In 1607 the colony of Jamestown was founded. In 1609 the Virginia Company was granted its new charter by the king, with funding by many of the London merchants and their heirs who had also been involved in the East India Company. Its governor, John Rolfe—the husband of the Native American princess Pocahontas— began the exploitation of tobacco for sale back in London in 1612. But the Virginia Company's government was too rigid, and despite a revamping of its operations in 1616, company control of the enlarged Virginia colony was never adequate to ensure its survival. Though Raleigh lived long enough to hear of its expansion before his death, he never saw Virginia again. Also, the Virginia Company was never profitable like the East India Company, thus dooming it to failure. After an attack by the natives in 1622 that wiped out Jamestown, the Virginia Company was dissolved in favor of a royal government.

A few years earlier, the self-imposed exiles, the Brownists of Elizabethan England, had returned from Leiden in the Netherlands after a lifetime abroad. Better known today as the Pilgrim Fathers, these Puritan Separatists chartered the 180-ton merchant ship *Mayflower* used in the wine trade from a London adventurer, settling in December 1620 in Massachusetts Bay. While only thirty-seven of the colonists were "Leiden Separatists," there were an additional sixty-five passengers plus crew who hopefully had the varied skills required for success in northern Virginia . The closely knit religious community founded on the Puritan work ethic prospered where nearly all other religiously motivated attempts at colonization had failed.

The Catholic "transportation policy" originally envisaged for northern Virginia (Norumbega) headed farther south, where the "great city" of Baltimore was founded as a Catholic enclave promoting Catholic ideals under Lord Baltimore in Charles I's reign. The state of Maryland was named after Charles I's queen, Henrietta Maria, the youngest child of Henry IV of France and a staunch Catholic.

As for the plea for Catholic toleration in England, the aversion to having Catholics in power never faded. The Gunpowder Plot to kill the king and all of Parliament failed in November 1605, and ruined any potential for religious toleration or the restoration of Catholicism to the crown. By the end of the seventeenth century, it became "illegal" for the reigning monarch to be Catholic after James II's enforced abdication. England preferred to import other Stuart cousins—William III and Mary II—from the Netherlands as their new monarchs over James II, their rightful Catholic king.

And the East India Company? After a very shaky start in violent competition with the VOC, or the Dutch East India Company, the Honourable Company, as it was frequently called, more than fulfilled the Londoners' most fanciful dreams. It was the Netherlands' time first for its Golden Age and empire built on the fortunes of the VOC, and throughout the first half of the seventeenth century the

Honourable Company had only a few hard-fought successes. Yet through their tenacity, as much as their cunning and wit, the East India Company ruled over what later became the English colonies or spheres of influence from India through to China, and its efforts, trials, and tribulations evolved into the British Empire spanning two-fifths of the world's landmass. Had Britain not made the mistakes it did in its "western plantings"—the United States—its empire would have been substantially larger.

What had begun as a means of survival in what some today might call state-sponsored terrorism, England's "wooden walls" were, in fact, the only means left open to the country to stay independent and financially solvent. Had Philip II allowed trade with his colonies, perhaps things would have been different. Perhaps not. In any event, it didn't happen. What did occur, though, was a series of events over decades that made Elizabeth and her adventurers fundamental to the formation of the British Empire.

Appendix I ✴

Doctor John Dee.
The Petty Navy Royal.

(extract from *General & Rare Memorials*, published in August 1577)

Whom also I have heard often and most heartily wish, that all manner of persons passing or frequenting our seas appropriate, and many ways next environing England, Ireland, and Scotland, might be in convenient and honourable sort, at all times, at the commandment and order, by beck or check, of a Petty Naval Royal of three-score tall ships or more, but in no case fewer; and they to be very well appointed, thoroughly manned, and sufficiently victualled.

The public commodities whereof ensuing are, or would be so great and many, as the whole commons, and all the subjects of this noble Kingdom would for ever bless the day and hour wherein such good and politic order was, in so good time and opportunity, taken and established: and esteem them not only most worthy and royal Councillors, but also heroical Magistrates, who have had so fatherly care for the commonalty; and most wisely procured so general British security,

1. That, henceforth, neither France, Denmark, Scotland, Spain, nor any other country can have such liberty for invasion, or their mutual conspiracies or aids, anyway transporting, to annoy the blessed state of our tranquillity; is either they have in times past had, or else may have whensoever they will forget or contemn the observing of their sworn or pretended amity.

2. Besides that, I report me to all English merchants, said he, *of how great value to them, and consequently to the public weal of this Kingdom, such a security were? (a) Whereby, both outward and homeward, continually their merchantlike ships, many or few, great or small, may in our seas and somewhat further, pass quietly unpilled, unspoiled, and untaken by pirates or others in time of peace. (b) What abundance of money now lost by assurance [marine insurance] given or taken, would by this means also, be greatly out of danger?*

3. And thirdly, (a) how many men, before time of urgent need, would thus be made very skilful in all the foresaid seas and sea coasts; in their channels knowing, in soundings all over, in good marks taking for avoiding dangers, in good harbors trying out, in good landings essaying, in the order of ebbs and floods observing, and all other points advisedly learning, which to the perfect Art of Navigation are very necessary: whereby they may be the better able to be divided and distributed in a greater Navy, with charge of Mastership or Pilotage, in time of great need. (b) They of this Navy should oftentimes espy or meet the privy sounders and searchers of our channels, flats, banks, pits &c.; and so very diligently deciphering our sea coasts, yea, in the river of Thames also; otherwhile up to the station of the Grand Navy Royal. (c) And likewise, very often meet with the abominable thieves that steal our corn and victuals from sundry our coasts, to the great hindrance of the public plenty of England. And these thieves are both subjects and foreigners; and very often and to to [far to] evidently seen, and generally murmured at, but as yet not redressed; for all the good and wise order by the most honourable Senate of the Privy Council taken therein.

4. Fourthly, how many thousands of soldiers of all degrees, and apt ages of men, would be, by this means, not only hardened well to brook all rage and disturbance of sea, and endure healthfully all hardness of lodging and diet there; but also would be well practised and easily trained up to great perfection of understanding all manner of fight and service at sea? So that, in time of great need, that expert and hardy crew of some thousands of sea soldiers [Marines] would be to this realm a treasure incomparable. And who knoweth, not, what danger it is, in time of great need, either to use all fresh water soldiers; or to be a fortnight in providing a little company of omni-gatharums, *taken up on the sudden to serve at sea? For our ordinary Land Musters are generally intended, or now may be spared to be employed otherwise, if need be.*

5. *How many hundreds of lusty and handsome men would be, this way, well occupied, and have needful maintenance, which now are either idle, or want sustenance, or both; in too many places of this renowned Monarchy?*

6. *Moreover, what a comfort and safeguard will it, or may it be to the whole Realm, to have the great advantage of so many warlike ships, so well manned and appointed for all assays, at all hours, ready to affront straightway, set on and overthrow, any sudden or privy foreign treachery by sea, directly or indirectly, attempted against this Empire, in any coast or part thereof. For sudden foreign attempts (that is to say, unknown or unheard of to us, before their readiness) cannot be done with great power. For great navies most commonly are espied or heard somewhat of, and that very certainly while they are in preparing; though in the meanwhile, politically, in divers places, they distribute their ships and their preparations appertaining.*

7. *And by reason of the foresaid Petty Navy Royal, it shall at all times, not only lie in our hands greatly to displease and pinch the petty foreign offender at sea; but also, if just occasion be given, on land to do very valiant service and that speedily: as well against any of the foresaid foreign possible offenders, as also against such of Ireland or England, who shall or will traitorously, rebelliously, or seditiously assemble in troops or bands within the territories of Ireland or England; while greater armies, on our behalf, shall be in preparing against them, if further need be. For skilful sea soldiers are also on land far more trainable to all martial exploits executing; and therein to be more quick-eyed and nimble at hand strokes or scaling; better to endure all hardness of lodging or diet; and less to fear all danger near or far: that the land soldier can be brought to the perfection of a sea soldier.*

8. *By this Navy also, all pirates—our own countrymen, and they be no small number—would be called, or constrained to come home. And then (upon good assurance taken of the reformable and men of choice, for their good abearing from henceforth) all such to be*

*bestowed here and there in the foresaid Navy. For good account is
to be made of their bodies, already hardened to the seas; and chiefly
of their courage and skill for good service to be done at the sea.*

9. *Ninthly, Princes and potentates, our foreign friends or privy
foes, the one for love and the other for fear, would not suffer any
merchant or others, subjects of the Queen's Majesty, either to have
speedy wrong in their Courts; or by unreasonable delays or trifling
shifts to be made weary and unable to follow their rights. And
notwithstanding such our friends or privy foes, their subjects would
be glad most reverently to become suitors and petitioners to the
royal State of this Kingdom for just redress, if, any kind of way, they
could truly prove themselves by any subject of this realm injured;
and they would never be so stout, rude and dishonourably injurious
to the Crown and Dignity of this most sacred Monarchy as, in such
cases, to be their own judges, or to use against this Kingdom and the
royal chief Council thereof, such abominable terms of dishonour as
our to to great lenity and their to to barbarous impudency might in a
manner induce them to do. And all this would come to pass through
the Royalty and Sovereignty of the seas adjacent or environing this
Monarchy of England, Ireland, and (by right) Scotland and the
Orkneys also, very princely, prudently, and valiantly recovered
(that is to say, by the Petty Navy Royal); duly and justly limited;
discreetly possessed; and triumphantly enjoyed.*

10. *Should not Foreign Fishermen (overboldly now, and to to
injuriously abusing such fishings about England, Wales and Ireland)
by the presence, oversight power and industry of this Petty Navy
Royal be made content; and judge themselves well apaid to enjoy,
by our leave, some great portion of revenue to enrich themselves
and their countries by, with fishing within the seas appertaining to
our ancient bounds and limits? Where now, to our great shame and
reproach, some of them do come in a manner home to our doors;
and among them all, deprive us yearly of many hundred thousand
pounds, which by our fishermen using the said fishings as chief,
we might enjoy; and at length, by little and little, bring them (if
he would deal so rigorously with them) to have as little portion of
our peculiar commodity (to our Islandish Monarchy, by GOD and
Nature assigned) as now they force our fishermen to be contented*

with: and yearly notwithstanding, do at their fishing openly and ragingly use such words of reproach to our Prince and realm, as no true subject's heart can quietly digest. And besides that, offer such shameful wrongs to the good laboursome people of this land, as is not by any reason to be borne withal, or endured any longer: destroying their nets; cutting their cables to the loss of their anchors, yea, and often-times of barks, men and all.

And this sort of people they be, which otherwhile by colour and pretence of coming about their feat of fishing, do subtly and secretly use soundings and searchings of our channels, deeps, shoals, banks, or bars along the sea coasts, and in our haven mouths also, and up in our creeks, sometimes in our bays, and sometimes in our roads; &c.; taking good marks, for avoiding of the dangers, and also trying good landings. And so, making perfect charts of all our coasts round about England and Ireland, are become almost perfecter in them, than the most part of our Masters, Leadsmen, or Pilots are. To the double danger of mischief in times of war; and also to no little hazard of the State Royal, if, maliciously bent, they should purpose to land any puissant army, in time to come.

And as concerning those fishings of England, Wales and Ireland, of their places, yearly seasons, the many hundreds of foreign fisherboats yearly resorting, the divers sorts of fish there taken, with appurtenances: I know right well that long ago all such matter concerning these fishings was declared unto some of the higher powers of this Kingdom, and made manifest by R[obert]. H[itchcock]. another honest gentleman of the Middle Temple, who very discreetly and faithfully hath dealt therein; and still travaileth, and by divers other ways also, to further the weal public of England so much as in him lieth.

But note, I pray you, this point very advisedly. That as by this Plat [tract] *of our said fishing commodities, many a hundred thousand pounds of yearly revenue might grow to the Crown of England more than now doth, and much more the commons of this Monarchy also; besides the inestimable benefit of plentiful victualling and relieving of both England and Ireland; the increasing of many thousands of expert, hard, and hardy mariners; the abating of the sea forces of our foreign neighbours and unconstant friends; and contrariwise; the increasing of our own power and force at sea; so it is most evident and certain that* principium *in this case is,* Plus quam dimidium totius, *as I have heard it verified proverbially in many other affairs.*

Wherefore, the very entrance and beginning towards our Sea Right recovering, and the foresaid commodities enjoying at length; yea, and the only *means of our continuance therewith, can be no other; but by the dreadful presence and power, with discreet oversight and due order, of the said Petty Navy Royal; being— wholly sometimes, sometimes a part thereof—at all the chief places of our fishings; as if they were Public Officers, Commissioners, and Justiciers, by the supreme authority royal of our most renowned Queen Elizabeth, rightfully and prudently thereto assigned.*

So that this Petty Navy Royal is thought to be the only Master Key wherewith to open all locks that keep out or hinder this comparable British Empire from enjoying by many reasons, such a yearly Revenue of Treasure, both to the Supreme Head and the subjects thereof—as no plat of ground of sea in the whole world else, being of no greater quantity—can with more right, greater honour, with so great ease and so little charges, so near at hand, in so short time, and in so little danger, any kind of way, yield the like to either King or other potentate and absolute Governor thereof whosoever. Besides, the Peaceable Enjoyment to enjoy all the same, for ever; year, yearly and yearly, by our wisdom and valiantness duly used, all manner of our commodities to arise greater and greater; as well in wealth and strength as of foreign love and fear, where it is most requisite to be: and also of Triumphant Fame the whole world over, undoubtedly.

Also this Petty Navy Royal will be the perfect means of very many other and exceeding great commodities redounding to this Monarchy; which our fishermen and their fisher-boats only, can never be able to compass or bring to pass: and those being such as are more necessary to be cared for presently [instantly] than wealth.

Therefore, the premise well weighed, above and before all other, this Plat [plan] of a Petty Navy Royal will, by GOD's grace, be found the plain and perfect A.B.C., most necessary for the commons and every subject in his calling to be carefully and diligently musing upon, or exercising himself therein; till, shortly, they may be able in effect to read before their eyes, the most joyful and pleasant British histories by that Alphabet only deciphered, and so brought to their understanding and knowledge that ever to this or any kingdom in the whole world else, was known or perceived.

11. Furthermore, how acceptable a thing may this be to the Ragusyes [Argosies], *Hulks, Caravels, and other foreign rich laden ships, passing within or by any of the sea limits of Her Majesty's royalty; even there to be now in most security where only, heretofore, they have been in most jeopardy: as well by the ravin of the pirate, as the rage of the sea distressing them, for lack of succour, or good and ready pilotage! What great friendship in [sic the] heart of foreign Prince and subject! And what liberal presents and foreign contributions in hand will duly follow thereof, who cannot imagine?*

12. Moreover, such a Petty Navy Royal, said he, *would be in such stead, as though (a) one [fleet] were appointed to consider and listen to the doings of Ireland; and (b) another to have as good an eye, and ready hand for Scottish dealings; (c) another to intercept or understand all privy conspiracies, by sea to be communicated; and privy aids of men, munition or money be sea to be transported; to the endamaging of this kingdom, any way intended (d) another against all sudden foreign attempts: (e) another to oversee the foreign fishermen: (f) another against all pirates haunting our seas: and therewith as well to waft and guard our own merchant fleets as they shall pass and repass between this realm, and wheresoever else they may best be planted for their ordinary marts' keeping; if England may not best serve that turn. And also to defend, help, and direct many of our foreign friends, who must needs pass by or frequent any of those seas, whose principal royalty, undoubtedly, is to the Imperial Crown of these British Islands appropriate.*

One such Navy, said he, *by royal direction, excellently well manned, and to all purposes aptly and plentifully furnished and appointed;* and now, in time of our peace and quiet everywhere, yet beforehand set forth to the foresaid seas *with their charges and commissions (most secretly to be kept from all foes and foreigners) would stand this common wealth in as great stead as four times so many ships would or could do; if, upon the sudden and all at once, we should be forced to deal for removing the foresaid sundry*

principal matters of annoyance: we being then utterly unready
thereto, and the enemy's attempt requiring speedy, and admitting
of no successive, defeating.

13. To conclude herein. This Petty Navy Royal undoubtedly will
stand the realm in better stead than the enjoying of four such forts
or towns as Calais and Boulogne only could do. For this will be
as great strength, and to as good purpose in any coast of England,
Ireland, or Scotland, between us and the foreign foe, as ever Calais
was for that only one place that it is situated in; and will help to
enjoy the Royalty and Sovereignty of the Narrow Seas throughout,
and of other our seas also, more serviceable than Calais or Boulogne
ever did or could do: if all the provisos hereto appertaining be duly
observed. Forasmuch as we intend now peace only preserving,
and no invasion of France or any enemy on that main inhabiting;
toward whom by Calais or Boulogne we need to let in our land
forces &c. Much I know may be here said, Pro et Contra, *in this*
case: but GOD hath suffered such matters to fall so out; and all to us
for the best, if it be so, thankfully construed and duly considered.

For when all foreign Princes, our neighbours, doubtful friends,
or undutiful people, subjects or vassals to our Sovereign, perceive
such a Petty Navy Royal hovering purposely here and there, ever
ready and able to overthrow any of their malicious and subtle secret
attempts intended against the weal public of this noble Kingdom in
any part or coast thereof: then every one of them will or may think
that, of purpose, that Navy was made out only to prevent them, and
none other; and for their destruction being bewrayed [betrayed]
as they would deem. So that not one such foreign enemy would
adventure, first, to break out into any notable disorder against us;
nor homish subject or wavering vassal, for like respects, durst, the,
privily muster to rebellion, or make harmful rodes [inroads] *or*
dangerous riots in any English or Irish Marches.

But such matter as this, I judge you have, or might have heard
of, ere now, by worshipful Master DYER; and that abundantly:
seeing Synopsis Reipublicae Britanicae, *was, at his request, six*
years past [i.e., in 1570] *contrived; as by the methodical author*
thereof, I understand. Whose policy for the partings, meetings,
followings, circuits &c., of the ships (to the foresaid Petty Navy

Royal belonging) with the alterations both of times, places, and numbers &c., is very strange to hear.

So that, in total sum of all the foresaid considerations united in one, it seemeth to be almost a mathematical demonstration, next under the merciful and mighty protection of GOD, for a feasible policy to bring and preserve this victorious British Monarchy in a marvellous security. Whereupon, the revenue of the Crown of England and Wealth public will wonderfully increase and flourish; and then, thereupon, sea forces anew to be increased proportionally, &c. And so the Fame, Renown, Estimation, and Love or Fear of this British Microcosmus, *all the whole and great World over, will be speedily be spread, and surely be settled, &c.*

It is most earnestly and carefully to be considered that our herring fishings, against [over] Yarmouth chiefly, have not (so notably, to our great injury and loss and been traded, but from Thirty-six years ago hitherward.) [This fixes the commencement of the Dutch herring fishery on the English coasts about 1540.] *In which time, as they have in wealth, and numbers of boats and men, by little and little increased, and are now become very rich, strong, proud, and violent; so, in the race [course] of the selfsame time running, the coasts of Norfolk and Suffolk next to those fishing-places adjacent, are decayed in their navy to the number of 140 sail, and they [of] from threescore to a hundred tons and upwards [each]; besides Crayers and others. Whereupon, besides many other damages thereby sustained publicly, these coasts are not able to trade to Iceland, as in times past they have done; to no little loss yearly to the wealth public of this kingdom.*

But the Herring Busses hither yearly restoring out of the Low Countries, under King PHILIP his dominion, are above five hundred.

Besides 100 or such a thing, of Frenchmen.

The North Seas fishing, within the English limits, are yearly possessed of 300 or 400 sail of Flemings [Dutch]; so accounted.

The Western fishings of Hake and Pilchards are yearly possessed by a great navy of Frenchmen; who yearly do great injuries to our poor countrymen, Her Majesty's faithful subjects.

Strangers also enjoy at their pleasure the Herring fishing of Allonby, Workington, and Whitehaven on the coast of Lancashire.

And in Wales, about Dyfi [the Dyfed] and Aberystwyth, the plentiful Herring fishing is enjoyed by 300 Sail of strangers.

But in Ireland, Baltimore [near Cape Clear] is possessed yearly, from July to Michaelmas most commonly, with 300 Sail of Spaniards, entering there into the fishing at a Strait [passage] not so broad as half the breadth of the Thames against [over] Whitehall. Where, our late good King EDWARD VI's most honourable Privy Council was of the mind once to have planted a strong bulwark [fort]; for other weighty reasons, as well as His Majesty to be Sovereign Lord of the fishing of Millwin and Cod there.

Black Rock [co. Cork?] is yearly fished by 300 or sometimes 400 sail of Spaniards and Frenchmen.

But to reckon all, I should be too tedious to you; and make my heart ache for sorrow, &c.

Yet surely I think it necessary to leave to our posterity some remembrance of the places where our rich fishings else are, about Ireland. As at Kinsale, Cork, Carlingford, Saltesses, Dungarven, Youghal, Waterford, La Foy, The Band, Calibeg [Killibegs] &c. And all chiefly enjoyed, as securely and freely from us by strangers, as if they were within their own Kings' peculiar sea limits: nay rather as if those coasts, seas, and bays &c., were of their private and several purchases. To our unspeakable loss, discredit, and discomfort; and to no small further danger in these perilous times, of most subtle treacheries and fickle fidelity.

Dictum, Sapienti sat esto.

Appendix II ⚜

Since much of the book is spent in discussion of the flota and the treasure it carried, I thought the reader would be interested to see what a typical (though not large) flota from New Spain brought back to Seville, according to the Venetian Ambassador. This is what arrived at the *casa* in the same year as Drake's plundering of the *San Felipe*.

Report of all that the *Flotilla of New Spain* brings with it, August 1587

For the King

Eight thousand bars of silver.
Twelve cases of gold.
Three hundred thousand reals.
Twenty cases of pearls.
One case of emeralds.

For Private Individuals

Five millions of fused silver.
One thousand five hundred marks* of pearls.
A great case of emeralds.

From San Domingo

Thirty-five thousand pieces of stamped leather.
Two hundred cases of sugar.
Twenty-two thousand quintals of ginger.
Four thousand quintals of guaiacum (lignum vitae).
Fifty quintals of sarsaparilla.

Forty-eight quintals of cassia.
Sixty-four cases of linen.

From New Spain

One million nine hundred thousand pesos of silver for the King.
Two millions for private merchants.
One thousand one hundred marks* of gold.
Five thousand six hundred cases of cochineal.
Sixty-four thousand pieces of stamped leather.
Twenty-five thousand pounds of indigo.

The value of the above, sixteen millions [ducats] in gold.

($4.42 billion or £2.39 billion today)

---

*1 mark = 8 ounces

Endnotes ✄

Abbreviations:

AI	Archivio de Indias, Seville, Spain
APC	*Acts of the Privy Council*
BL	British Library
CPR	*Calendar of Patent Rolls*
CSP	*Calendar of State Papers*
DNB	*Dictionary of National Biography*
FSL	Folger Shakespeare Library, Washington, D.C.
HMC	Historic Manuscripts Commission
KL	Kervyn Lettenhove, *Les Relations des Pays Bas et L'Angleterre*
NA	National Archive
OED	*Oxford English Dictionary*
SP	State Papers

Introduction

1. Richard Hakluyt, *Tudor Venturers* (London, 1970), p. 201
2. Ibid., p. 200.
3. SP 94/2 fol. 78, 100.

Chapter 1. *The Lord's Doing*

1. *CSP—Spain*, vol. 1, p. 334.
2. Simon, Schama, *A History of Britain* (London, 2000), p. 285
3. G. Parker, *The Grand Strategy of Philip II*, (New Haven, 2000), p. 2; also see, J. Denucé, *Lettres Marchandes d'Anvers*, (Brussels, 1961), Chapter 9, pp. 164–168
4. Owen Tudor, grandfather of Henry VII, was the second husband of Queen Katherine, the widow of Henry V and mother of Henry VI, the last Lancastrian king in the Wars of the Roses. Victorian historians claimed that there was never any proof of their marriage, but this

has since been refuted. See S. B. Chrimes, *Henry VII* (New Haven, 1999).

5. Simon Schama, *A History of Britain*, p. 285.

Chapter 2. *A Realm Exhausted*

1. Throckmorton was soon to be appointed as the queen's ambassador to France. This particular news would have given Elizabeth great pleasure, since it was Cardinal Pole who had been her nemesis throughout Mary's reign, and it was he who had carried out an Anglicized version of the Spanish Inquisition in the previous five years.

2. *CSP—Domestic*, vol. 1, p. 115, nos. 2, 4.

3. Ibid., no. 5.

4. National Archives, SP Domestic, Elizabeth 12/1/7.

5. *CSP—Spain*, vol. 1, p. 1.

6. Ibid.

7. The office of lord keeper (of the privy seal) was one of extreme trust. The lord keeper kept the queen's seals required to engross an act into law and made the signatory personally responsible for the contents of any document under seal. Nicholas Bacon is most noted as a solid stalwart of early Elizabethan rule, as he set about modernizing the legal system to make it more just and was a firm believer in universal education (for men).

8. *CSP—Domestic*, vols 2, 3, pp. 120–129

9. *APC*, p. 9, no. 38.

10. Ibid.

11. National Archives, SP Domestic., Elizabeth I/77.

12. R. B. Wernham, *Before the Armada* (London, 1966), p. 240; also see *CSP—Venice*, vol. 6, 1049.

13. R. B. Wernham, *Before the Armada*, p. 245

14. Ibid.

15. AI, Indice General de los Papeles del Consejos de Indias, p. 128.

16. *CSP—Foreign*, vol. 1, p. xvi.

17. *CSP—Domestic*, p. 118.

18. *CSP—Foreign*, vol. 1, p. ix.

19. A repeated complaint of all popes between 1558 and Philip's death in 1596. It is found time and time again in the *CSP—Rome*, *CSP— Spain*, G. Parker's *The Grand Strategy of Philip II* (New Haven, 2000), and many other sources.

20. G. Parker, *The Grand Strategy of Philip II*, p. 7.

21. Ibid., p. 14.

22. G. D. Ramsay, *The City of London* (Manchester, 1964), p. 34.

23. I refer to them by their correct name and not Merchant Adventurers as is commonly the case today, in order to avoid any confusion with "merchant adventurers" (a generic term) and the Merchants Adventurers, the specific corporation.

24. Kenneth R. Andrews, *Trade, Plunder & Settlement*, p. 16.

Chapter 3. *The Queen, Her Merchants and Gentlemen*

1. DNB Biographical sketch on Martin Frobisher

2. R. Tittler, *Nicholas Bacon: The Making of a Tudor Statesman* (London, 1966), pp. 48-50.

3. See bibliographical sketches in the DNB for further details.

4. Benjamin Woolley's recent biography of Dr. John Dee, *The Queen's Conjurer* (New York, 2001) makes for riveting reading.

5. Robert Tittler's *Nicholas Bacon* is the best biography of this exceptionally egalitarian man dedicated to the law and justice.

6. Kenneth Andrews, *Trade, Plunder & Settlement* (Cambridge, 1999), p. 32.

7. John Cabot's voyage of discovery in 1497 had been funded by Elizabeth's grandfather, Henry VII, who had refused money to Columbus for his "West Indies" expedition only five years earlier in 1492.

8. Kenneth Andrews, *Trade, Plunder & Settlement*, p. 14.

9. Lord Admiral Clinton and later Lord Admiral Howard became accomplices before and after the fact in many instances of piracy by virtue of this ruling. They took a keen interest in who would be issued with letters of reprisal, or "letters of marque," making the bearer a bona fide mariner seeking reprisal granted from a head of state at the beginning of Elizabeth's reign. Yet as the years rolled on, virtually anyone requesting a letter of reprisal was granted one. They became direct beneficiaries of the pirates' prosperity. Please note that the term "privateer" did not exist in Elizabethan times, and was used only from the eighteenth century onward.

10. Ibid.

11. Again, this is an area that has been explored very well by Susan Brigen in *New Worlds, Lost Worlds* (New York, 2001). The recusancy fines were tolerated by Catholics, but increased significantly after 1570 when the pope sent out a communiqué that all Catholics were exempt from any loyalty to the "heretic queen."

12. This is the topic of many books on Elizabeth, and I could never do the subject justice here. It was an important tactic in her international politics that she would use as long as she decently could (until the early

1580s), but not something she probably seriously entertained in light of her childhood traumas, desire to rule in her own right, and deep devotion to Robert Dudley. Despite all the protestations of "courtly love" and a long list of admirers and scandalous behavior, Elizabeth only ever loved Robert Dudley, and never seriously entertained any marriage—except perhaps in old age—to the Duke of Alençon. With Robert Dudley disgraced by the inconvenient and suspicious "accidental" death of his wife, Amy Robsart, any chance Elizabeth could have had in marrying him had ended. In fictional works there are hints that William Cecil could have been behind a plot to murder Amy and thereby ruin Robert's chances with the queen. The theory is historically possible, perhaps even probable, but there is no proof.

13. Derek Wilson, *Sweet Robin* (London, 1981), pp. 81–87.

14. John Foxe, *Foxe's Book of Martyrs* (London, 1888), 1714; also Raphael Holinshed, *Chronicles of England, Scotland, and Ireland* (London, 1808), vol. 3, p. 1158; and *Elizabeth I Collected Works*, L. S. Marcus, J. Mueller, and M.B. Rose (eds.), p. 48.

Chapter 4. *The Quest for Cash*

1. *APC*, 1558–1559, p. 1. Note that the documents are silent on whether these are Continental crowns or English crowns. One Continental crown was equal to 4 English crowns, and there were 5 shillings to a crown, or 4 crowns to a pound. I have taken the crowns as being Continental crowns since it was a payment due from France, or 2 million English crowns.

2. *APC*, p. 38, January 5, 1559.

3. Ibid., p. 28.

4. Ibid.

5. Ibid., p. 11, no. 15.

6. Ibid.

7. Ibid., pp. 14–15.

8. Ibid., pp. 22, 25, viii, ix.

9. *CSP—Domestic* 1559, p. 126, nos. 44 and 45. The use of the word "cause" in this instance means a fact or condition of matters or consideration moving a person to action [OED].

10. *CSP—Scotland*, p. 546, no. 1008.

11. Staplers were those who had the wool woven or spun into cloth or another finished product. A staple was the market town for its sale.

12. *CSP—Spain*, vol. 1, p. ix.

13. Raymond de Roover, *Gresham on Foreign Exchange* (Cambridge USA, 1949), p. 26.

14. M. Oppenheim, *A History of the Administration of the Royal Navy, 1509–1660* (London, 1896), p. 112.

15. N. A. M. Rodger, *Safeguard of the Sea* (London, 2004), p. 229.

16. Ibid.

17. *CSP—Foreign*, 1559–1565, p. 313, no. 623.

18. Ibid., pp. 308–310.

19. Ibid.

20. N. A. M. Rodger, *Safeguard of the Sea,* p. 196.

21. Ibid., p. 230.

22. When the Bishop of Ross, Confessor of Mary Queen of Scots, was interrogated after the Babington Plot was uncovered, he claimed that Mary had poisoned her husband, Francis.

Chapter 5. *The Merchants Adventurers, Antwerp, and Muscovy*

1. Margaret of York, sister of Edward IV, was the third wife of Marie's father, Duke Charles of Burgundy. While the marriage was childless, it was also a further bond.

2. W. E. Lingelbach, *The Merchant Adventurers of England: Their Laws and Ordinances with Other Documents* (New York, 1971), p. xxix.

3. Kenneth Andrews, *Trade, Plunder & Settlement* (Cambridge, 1999), p. 6.

4. W. E. Lingelbach, *The Merchant Adventurers of England*, p.xxix.

5. Kenneth Andrews, *Trade, Plunder & Settlement*, p. 63.

6. W. E. Lingelbach, *The Merchant Adventurers of England*, pp. xvi, 6.

7. Wheeler, *Treatise of Commerce* (London, 1601), p. 25.

8. W. E. Lingelbach, *The Merchant Adventurers of England*, p. 6.

9. G. D. Ramsay, *The City of London* (Manchester, 1964), pp. 6-7.

10. Raymond de Roover, *An Elizabethan Manuscript: Text of Gresham on The Understanding of Foreign Exchange* (London, 1949), p. 22.

11. Ibid., pp. 8-9. See also Chaloner to Cecil, August 31, 1559 and KL, II, 8–9.

12. Ibid., p. 68.

13. Ibid., p. 69. See also Albert Feavearyear, *The Pound Sterling* (Oxford, 1963), p. 79.

14. Ibid.

15. The key to Antwerp's commercial success was the atmosphere of tolerance that had been guaranteed as an ancient right. Europe's oppressed peoples, like the Jews, flocked there and rebuilt their fortunes.

16. Kenneth Andrews, *Trade, Plunder & Settlement*, p. 68. Also see William Cunningham, *Growth of English Industry and Commerce*, vol. 2 (Cambridge, UK, 1882), p. 136, n. 2.

17. Baron Kervyn Lettenhove has calendared the State Papers of the Low-Countries in *Les Relations des Pays Bas et l'Angleterre*, which shows in fine detail the erosion of these privileges of tolerance.

18. J. Denucé, *Les Lettres des Marchands d'Anvers* (Brussels, 1961), pp. 267–268

19. Philip II's "proposal" to Elizabeth shortly after her accession was at best halfhearted. The defender of the Catholic faith, and according to Gregory XIII, "more Catholic than the pope," could barely bring himself to issue the offer of marriage to the heretic Queen Elizabeth.

20. At the time of Mary's death, her debt was £65,069; this was much more than existed in England's exchequer. This equates approximately to £10.09 million or $18.66 million today.

21. Philip also rightly believed that by marrying Elisabeth of France that the French threat against the Spanish Netherlands had naturally receded.

22. W. E. Lingelbach, *The Merchant Adventurers of England*, p. xviii.

23. Richard Hakluyt, *Principall Navigations*, vol. 2, pp. 212–214; Kenneth Andrews, *Trade, Plunder & Settlement*, p. 64.

24. Kenneth Andrews, *Trade, Plunder & Settlement*, p. 65.

25. Ibid., p. 68.

26. Richard Hakluyt, *Discoveries of Muscovy,* London (1589 edition), pp. 26–32.

27. Ibid.

28. Kenneth Andrews, *Trade, Plunder & Settlement*, pp. 19-20.

29. Ibid., pp. 68, 81.

30. *CSP—Foreign*, p. 59, no 112, April 14, 1561.

31. Ibid., p. 90, no 156, April 30, 1561.

32. Ibid., p.102, no 184, May 6, 1561.

33. Ibid., pp. 126–127, no. 217

34. Richard Hakluyt, *Principall Navigations*, vol. 3., p. 38.

35. Julian A. Corbett, *Drake and the Tudor Navy* (London, 1988), pp. 71-72

36. Raleigh quoted from A. G. Lee, *The Son of Leicester: The Story of Sir Robert Dudley*, (London, 1964), p. 61.

37. The term "privateer" was not invented until the eighteenth century. Despite the trend since the nineteenth century to use it to describe Elizabethan seamen, I try to avoid it for a more accurate historical depiction.

Chapter 6. The Politics of Piracy, Trade, and Religion

1. G. Parker, *The Grand Strategy of Philip II* (New Haven, 2000), p. 150.

2. *CSP—Spain*, vol. 1, 1558–1567, p. 234, no. 158. Bishop Quadra to Cardinal de Granvelle, London, April 2, 1562.

3. G. Parker, *The Grand Strategy of Philip II*, p. 118

4. Ibid., p. 117. See also Groen van Prinsterer, *Archives*, 1st series, I, 152, Granvelle to Philip II, March 10, 1563.

5. G. Parker, *The Grand Strategy of Philip II*, pp. 120–123.

6. Ibid.

7. G. D. Ramsay, *The City of London* (Manchester, 1964), p. 137.

8. Ibid.

9. Ibid. c.f. SP 70/39/200. Tipton to Chaloner, July 4, 1562.

10. The "lines of amity" meant European waters. While the pope had divided the world between Portugal and Spain in the previous century, successive Tudor monarchs had never bought into the idea that all other nations, and especially England, should not be allowed to trade in Portuguese and Spanish waters.

11. This becomes more comprehensible when we consider that Philip II had the best claim to the Portuguese throne should Sebastian die childless. Also see, G. Parker, *The Grand Strategy of Philip II,* p. 123.

12. Nick Hazlewood, *The Queen's Slave Trader* (New York, 2005), p. 53

13. Ibid.

14. *CSP—Foreign*, 1562, no. 18.

15. N. A. M. Rodger, *Safeguard of the Sea* (London, 2004), pp. 199-200.

16. Ibid., p. 195.

17. N. Hazlewood, *The Queen's Slave Trader* (New York, 2005), p. 199.

18. N. A. M. Rodger, *Safeguard of the Sea,* p. 198.

19. Ibid.

20. R. B.Wernham, *Before the Armada* (London, 1966), p. 279.

21. *CSP—Spain*, vol. 1, p. 322 (de Quadra to Philip)

22. G. D. Ramsay, *The City of London,* p. 116.

23. *CSP—Spain*, vol. 1, p. 239, no. 31.

24. National Archives, SP Foreign, Elizabeth, 70/41/503, fols. 239r-241r. Written in Cecil's secretary's hand, though definitely Elizabeth's words. Postscript written by Cecil.

25. *CSP—Spain*, vol. 1, 1558–1567, p. 234, no. 158.

26. Ibid.

Chapter 7. *Raising the Stakes*

1. N. Hazlewood, *The Queen's Slave Trader*, p. 54.

2. J.A., Corbett, *Drake and the Tudor Navy* (Aldershot, England, 1988 Centenary imprint), p. 71.

3. *CSP—Venice*, vol. 2, pp. 207–208.

4. J.A. Corbett, *Drake and the Tudor Navy*, p. 75

5. Ibid., p. 79.

6. N. A. M. Rodger, *Safeguard of the Sea* (London, 2004), p. 322.

7. "Pease" were dried lentils made into porridge. The nursery rhyme, "Pease porridge hot, pease porridge cold, pease porridge in the pot, nine days old," may well have had its origins among the sea shanties that were sung at this time.

8. N. A. M. Rodger, *Safeguard of the Sea*, p. 198.

9. Ibid., p. 199.

10. Nick Hazlewood, *The Queen's Slave Trader* (New York, 2005), p. 54.

11. G. Parker, *The Grand Strategy of Philip II* (New Haven, 2000), pp. 117–119.

12. Nick Hazlewood, *The Queen's Slave Trader*, p. 53.

13. Richard Hakluyt, *Principall Navigations* (London, 1598), p. 522. Also see H. Kelsey, *Sir John Hawkins* (New Haven, 2003), p. 12.

14. Ibid.

15. Slave trading, begun and heavily taxed by the Spanish and the Portuguese, was considered not only a legitimate but also humane activity to replace the Native American populations decimated by war, famine, and disease. For a brilliant account of the reasons for conquest of southern America by the Spanish, read Jared Diamond's Pulitzer Prize-winning book, *Guns, Germs and Steel* (New York, 1997).

16. Kenneth Andrews, *Trade, Plunder & Settlement* (Cambridge, 1999), p. 117.

17. Nick Hazlewood, *The Queen's Slave Trader*, p. 57.

18. Ibid.

19. H. Kelsey, *Sir John Hawkins*, p. 15. See also N. Hazelwood, *The Queen's Slave Trader*, pp. 50–51. Agreed taxes in Corbett, *Drake and the Tudor Navy*, p. 88.

20. *CSP—Foreign*, no 1136, pp. 497–498.

21. H. Kelsey, *Sir John Hawkins*, p. 17.

22. William Monson, *Sir William Monson's Tracts* (London, 1625), vol. 2, pp. 247–248.

23. Kenneth Andrews, *Trade, Plunder & Settlement*, pp. 107–108. See also *CSP—Foreign*, 1562, no. 18.

24. H. Kelsey, *Sir John Hawkins*, p. 16.

25. *DNB* (biography on Stucley).

26. *CSP—Spain*, vol. 1, p. 322 (de Quadra to Philip).

27. *CSP—Spain*, vol. 3, p. 349.

28. *CSP—Foreign*, 1564–1565, p. 272.

29. G. D. Ramsay, *The City of London*, chapter 8 relating to Emden.

Chapter 8. *Cunning Deceits*

1. *CSP—Spain*, vol. 1, p. 352.

2. *APC*, p. 146.

3. Ibid., pp. 373–374.

4. Nick Hazlewood, *The Queen's Slave Trader* (New York, 2005), p. 91.

5. Julian A. Corbett, *Drake and the Tudor Navy* (Aldershot, England, 1988 Centenary imprint), p. 84.

6. *CSP—Spain,* vol. 1, pp. 373–374.

7. Ibid.

8. G. D. Ramsay, *The City of London* (Manchester, 1964), p. 238.

9. See Ibid., chapter 8, pp. 251–283.

10. *APC*, pp. 154–156. There were eight securities that were "canceled" by the queen, some of which were on behalf of the City of London. At the time of cancellation, the queen owed well in excess of 800,000 Fl, or £200,000 ($6.87 billion or £4.04 billion today) or a year's entire exchequer receipts.

11. *APC*, pp. 157–158.

12. G. Parker, *The Grand Strategy of Philip II* (New Haven, 2000), p. 28. This grew to over 2,000 by the 1590s.

13. *CSP—Spain*, vol.1, pp. 383–384. The sums owed by the queen far exceeded what de Silva had gleaned, but the rates of interest did not exceed 10 percent.

14. J.S. Corbett, *Drake and the Tudor Navy*, pp. 84–85. See also N. Hazlewood, *The Queen's Slave Trader*, pp. 94–95.

15. John W. Blake, *West Africa, Quest for God and Gold—1454–1578* (London, 1977), p. 107.

16. Ibid., p. 138.

17. BL, Lansdowne MS 171, ff. 148–9.

18. Nick Hazlewood, *The Queen's Slave Trader*, p. 95 as quoted from Richard Hakluyt's *Principall Navigations* (London, 1598).

19. Lodge had been caught at the wrong end of the financial cycle in Antwerp, and had been propped up by the queen herself to join in on this expedition in the hope of avoiding bankruptcy.

20. Nick Hazlewood, *The Queen's Slave Trader,* p. 97.

21. H. Kelsey, *Sir John Hawkins* (New Haven, 2003), p. 20.

22. Ibid. The brigantines, small light craft, usually carried explosives and other highly flammable and unstable stores at sea, and were used for close onshore work in unfamiliar harbors since they had a very shallow draft.

23. See Dava Sobel's fabulous book *Longitude* (London, 1998). On page 14, she explains for the uninitiated "dead reckoning" better than anyone else when she writes, "The captain would throw a log overboard and observe how quickly the ship receded from this guidepost. He noted the crude speedometer reading in his ship's logbook, along with the direction of travel, which he took from the stars or a compass, and the length of time on a particular course, counted with a sandglass or a pocket watch. Factoring in the effects of ocean currents, fickle winds, and errors in judgment, he then determined his longitude. He routinely missed the mark."

24. H. Kelsey, *Sir John Hawkins*, p. 20.

25. Ibid., p. 21.

26. In Richard Hakluyt's *Principall Navigations*, see John Sparke, "Voyage Made by the Worshipful J. Hawkins," p. 523.

27. H. Kelsey, *Sir John Hawkins*, p. 22.

28. H. Kelsey, *Sir John Hawkins*, p. 23.

29. Ibid.

30. *CSP—Foreign*, pp. 15–20.

31. Ibid., p. 24. See also National Archives, MS SP 70/99, fols. 4–5v.

32. In Richard Hakluyt's *Principall Navigations*, see John Sparke, "Voyage Made by the Worshipful J. Hawkins," p. 523.

33. H. Kelsey, *Sir John Hawkins*, p. 26. See also letter from Hawkins to Alonso Bernáldez dated April 16, 1565, AGI Justicia 93, fol. 88v.

34. Ibid. See also John Sparke, "Voyage Made by the Worshipful J. Hawkins," in Richard Hakluyt's *Principall Navigations*.

35. Ibid., p. 28. See also N. Hazlewood, *The Queen's Slave Trader*, pp. 122–130 for a detailed account.

36. Nick Hazlewood, *The Queen's Slave Trader*, p. 127–128.

Chapter 9. *The Gloves Are Off*

1. J. S. Corbett, *Drake and the Tudor Navy* (Aldershot, England, 1988 Centenary imprint), p. 89.

2. Ibid., p. 90.

3. Nick Hazlewood, *The Queen's Slave Trader* (New York, 2005), p. 139.

4. Kenneth Andrews, *The Spanish Caribbean* (London, 1978), p. 91.

5. Kenneth Andrews, *Trade, Plunder & Settlement* (Cambridge, 1999), p. 76.

6. *APC*, October 11, 1565, p. 267.

7. C. Brady, *The Chief Governors of Ireland* (Dublin, 2004), pp. 6–7.

8. Ibid., p. 118. See also Henry Sidney's *Articles*, May 20, 1565, SP 63/13/46.

9. Kenneth Andrews, *The Spanish Caribbean*, p. 109.

10. James Williamson's *Sir John Hawkins* (Oxford, 1927) believes that the goal was for a less reprehensible trade in textiles. Many experts believe that Professor Williamson's slant on matters could be colored by the fact that he is a descendant of Hawkins's.

11. *CSP—Spain*, vol. 1, p. 494.

12. Nick Hazlewood, *The Queen's Slave Trader,* p. 145.

13. Ibid., p. 148.

14. Ibid., pp. 152–153.

15. H. Kelsey, *Sir John Hawkins* (New Haven, 2003), p. 39. See also, SP 12/40/99, f.211.

Chapter 10. *Lovell's Lamentable Voyage*

1. H. Kelsey, *Sir John Hawkins* (New Haven, 2003), p. 41.

2. John Sugden, *Sir Francis Drake* (London, 1996), p. 19. See also, Conway Papers Manuscript, "Confession of Michael Morgan, January 1574." Add MS 7235.

3. Ibid., p. 20.

4. *CPR*, Edward, Second Year of his Reign, No. 893. Dated Westminster. 18 Dec 1548.

5. H. Kelsey, *Sir John Hawkins,* p. 43.

6. L. S. Marcus, *Elizabeth I Collected Works*, *c.f.* SP Scotland, Elizabeth 52/13/17, f. 30r (copy of the French original).

7. H. Kelsey, *Sir John Hawkins*, p. 44.

8. Ibid.

9. Ibid., p. 45. See also N. Hazlewood, *The Queen's Slave Trader* (New York, 2005), pp. 157–158.

10. Ibid., p. 46.

11. Ibid.

Chapter 11. *The Troublesome Voyage of John Hawkins*

1. John Sugden, *Sir Francis Drake* (London, 1996), p. 23.

2. In the testimonies of the captured sailors given before the Inquisition, Godard frequently appears as "Antonio Tejida," since he was a dealer in woollen cloth, or *tejido*. Most of the Englishmen who were captured, or of whom the prisoners spoke, had their names corrupted through Spanish transcription. Aside from the obvious Juan Aquinas—John

Hawkins—there were names like Juan Brun (easily identifiable as John Brown) and the more esoteric Enrique Quince (Henry Quin) and Jorge Fizullens (George Fitzallen).

3. Nick Hazlewood, *The Queen's Slave Trader* (New York, 2005), p. 181.

4. Kenneth Andrews, *The Spanish Caribbean* (London, 1978), pp. 122–123.

5. There are so many great accounts of this incident. See N. Hazlewood's *The Queen's Slave Trader*, p. 185, for the most detailed account. Also see H. Kelsey's *Sir John Hawkins* (New Haven, 2003), p. 57 and J. Sugden's, *Sir Francis Drake*, p. 24. It is also recounted in Richard Hakluyt's *Principall Navigations* (London, 1598).

6. In N. Hazlewood's *The Queen's Slave Trader*, pp. 188–189. In J. Sugden's *Sir Francis Drake*, pp. 24–25.

7. John Sugden, *Sir Francis Drake*, pp. 26–27.

8. N. Hazlewood, *The Queen's Slave Trader*, p. 214

9. Kenneth Andrews, *The Spanish Caribbean*, p. 101. Although Hawkins and the Spanish didn't know about the Spanish being massacred in Florida, the French under Dominique de Gourgues certainly did. De Gourgues left the message behind at St Johns, "je ne fais ceci comme aux Espagnols, ni comme aux Marranos, mais comme aux traitres, voleurs et meurtriers." (I am not doing this either to Spaniards or Marranos, but to traitors, thieves and murderers.)

10. Nick Hazlewood, *The Queen's Slave Trader*, pp. 215–216.

11. Ibid., p. 217.

12. Richard Hakluyt, *Principall Navigations*, vol. 9, p. 449. See also Kenneth Andrews, *The Spanish Caribbean*, p. 124.

13. BL, Cotton MSS, Otho E. VIII, f. 36. Otho E VIII is the most fabulous source of West Indian exploits of the 1560s.

14. Nick Hazlewood, *The Queen's Slave Trader*, pp. 233–239.

15. Ibid.

16. Ibid., p. 240. See also Kenneth Andrews, *The Spanish Caribbean*, pp. 125–126.

17. Ibid., p. 241. See also, Julian Corbett, *Successors of Drake* (London, 1900), pp. 56-133.

18. Ibid., p. 246. See also Kenneth Andrews, *Elizabethan Privateering* (Cambridge, UK, 1964), pp. 32–34.

Chapter 12. *The Queen and Alba's Pay Ships*

1. Shane O'Neill had been importing Scots mercenaries known as "red-shanks" to populate the northeast coast of Ulster and fight alongside him. So long as Mary remained on Scotland's throne, this represented a double danger to England's borders.

2. Julian A. Corbett, *Drake and the Tudor Navy* (Aldershot, England, 1988 Centenary imprint), p. 121.

3. Philip II did, in fact, have a very legitimate claim to the English throne. His next ambassador, Bernardino de Mendoza, penned a rather over-zealous defense of Philip's claim as a direct descendant from John of Gaunt, which did nothing to endear either of them to Elizabeth or her Councillors.

4. G. Parker, *The Grand Strategy of Philip II* (New Haven, 2000), pp. 120–122.

5. *CSP—Spain*, vol. 2, p. 29.

6. *CSP—Venice*, vol. 3, p. 423, dated May 7, 1568.

7. R. B. Wernham, *Before the Armada*, pp. 290–292.

8. G. Parker, *The Grand Strategy of Philip II*, p. 123. (Alba to Philip II, January 6, 1568).

9. *CSP—Spain*, vol. 2, p. 83.

10. Ibid., p. 90.

11. Ibid., p. 95.

12. Julian A. Corbett, *Drake and the Tudor Navy*, p. 124.

13. *CSP—Spain*, vol. 2, p. 99–100.

Chapter 13. *The Cost of Failure*

1. AGI Patronato 265, Ramo, 13, fol. 25v. Testimony of Juan de la Torre, February 28, 1569.

2. J. Hawkins, *Troublesome Voyadge,* fol. B. vii.

3. J. Hampden (ed.), *Francis Drake Privateer*, (London, 1972), p. 45. Hawkins's reasons for tempering his criticism by not mentioning Drake by name are many. It is tempting to hope that one of them was that for Drake's silence about Hawkins's lack of clear course of action to follow in the event of attack, the young Drake again found favor with his more "experienced" cousin. This early stain on Drake's record, however, stuck, and was trotted out many years later by both Martin Frobisher and William Borough as an alleged "proof" of cowardice. Drake's subsequent record speaks volumes for itself.

4. SP 12/53, f. iv-7. See also printed version in E. Arber's *An English Garner*, (London, 1903), pp. 104–126.

5. Hawkins, naturally, exaggerated his losses in several ways. The most glaring and provable of which is the fact that the *peso de oro* was exchanged at 3 to the pound sterling, not 25p to the pound, as he accounts here.

6. *CSP—Foreign*, vol. 5, p. 436.

7. Ibid., pp. 437–438.

Chapter 14. *Undeclared Holy War*

1. J. Corbett, *Drake and the Tudor Navy* (Aldershot, England, 1988 Centenary reprint), vol. 1, p. 148.
2. J. Hampden (ed.), *Sir Francis Drake Privateer*, (London, 1972), p. 46.
3. J. Corbett, *Drake and the Tudor Navy*, vol. 1, p. 126.
4. Ibid., pp. 126–127.
5. *CSP—Rome*, vol. 1, p. 328.

Chapter 15. *Drake's War*

1. J. Corbett, *Drake and the Tudor Navy* (Aldershot, England, 1988 Centenary reprint), vol. 1, p. 146.
2. John Sugden, *Sir Francis Drake* (London, 1996), p. 45.
3. MS Ashmole 830, unnumbered folio. See also Irene A. Wright's *Documents Concerning English Voyages to the Spanish Main 1569–1580* (London, 1973) vol. 1, docs. 5-13. In Kelsey's biographical sketch in the *DNB*, he claims that this voyage was funded by William Winter and his brother, George. Sugden believes it was Hawkins. In light of this original manuscript, coupled with Irene Wright's meticulous translations in *Documents*, and Drake's mini-celebrity status in Plymouth at the time, there is little reason to disbelieve that Richard Dennys and other Devon merchants backed this relatively inexpensive voyage. Taken into consideration with Drake's dubious reputation on his return in 1569, it makes sense.
4. John Sugden, *Sir Francis Drake*, pp. 45–46.
5. J. Hampden (ed.), *Sir Francis Drake Privateer*, (London, 1972), pp. 46–47.
6. John Sugden, *Sir Francis Drake*, (London, 1996), p. 48.
7. Ibid., p. 50.
8. Ibid., p. 51. See also Irene A. Wright, *Documents Concerning English Voyages*, vol. 1, docs. 31–35.
9. It is safer to take this estimate rather than the sum of the other estimates provided earlier in the chapter by Drake, and also the estimate of £100,000 provided in the *DNB*. The lord admiral, Customs & Excise, and Drake's crew and partners received their shares based on the £66,000.

Chapter 16. *The Dread of Future Foes*

1. "Doubt" in this instance, per the *OED*, means "dread."
2. FSL, MS V.b. 317, fol. 20 vol. 1. It is assumed that this poem was written on the discovery of the Ridolfi plot, the betrayal by the queen's cousin, the Duke of Norfolk, and Mary's involvement from her castle prison.

3. *CSP—Rome*, pp. 337, 379.

4. BL, MS Cotton Caligula, C. III, fol. 145r.

5. A. Stewart, *Philip Sidney*, (London, 2004), p. 200.

6. *DNB*, William Herbert, Earl of Pembroke biography. He had been an investor in Hugh Willoughby's northeast passage adventure in the 1550s, the Hawkins voyages, and was a principal shareholder in the mines royal and mineral and battery companies. Note that later, Sir Henry Sidney's daughter, Mary, would become the second wife of the Earl's son and heir.

7. *CSP—Rome*, p. 374.

8. *DNB*, Sir Lionel Duckett.

9. Raymond de Roover, *Gresham on Foreign Exchange*, (Cambridge, USA, 1999), p. 27.

10. Ibid.

11. Ibid. See pages 22–25 for an explanation of the Gresham accounts. His accounts hadn't been audited for the eleven years prior to his retirement as the queen's factor, and were estimated to be £10,000 ($3.4 million or £2 million today) understated. In order to get around the potential problem of reimbursement—since the money had already been earmarked for the Royal Exchange—Gresham cleverly approached the queen through Leicester during her Kenilworth visit in the summer of 1573, where the queen magnanimously (and uncharacteristically) wrote off the amount.

12. R. B. Wernham, *The Making of Elizabethan Foreign Policy* (Berkeley, 1980), p. 33.

13. England voluntarily abandoned all Guinea trade and slave trade from 1572 until it was resumed in 1650.

14. A. F. Pollard, *History of England 1547–1603*, pp. 305, 331–332.

15. C. W. Previté-Orton (ed.), *The English Historical Review*, vol. XLVI, 1931, "Queen Elizabeth, The Sea Beggars, and the Capture of Brill, 1572," p. 38.

16. Ibid.

17. Ibid., p. 39.

18. *DNB*, sketch biography of Sir Humphrey Gilbert.

19. A. Stewart, *Sir Philip Sidney* (London, 2004), p. 84.

20. BL, MS Additional 30156, fol. 437r-440r.

Chapter 17. *Drake at the Treasure House of the World*

1. The *Pasco* is sometimes referred to as the *Pascha*.

2. Whether his investment took the form of giving the *Pasco* to Drake, or in the fitting out costs, is unclear.

3. J. Hampden (ed.), *Sir Francis Drake Revived* (London, 1954), p. 55.

4. Ibid., p. 57. Also see J. Sugden, *Sir Francis Drake* (London, 1996), p. 55.

5. John Sugden, *Sir Francis Drake*, p. 55.

6. Ibid., pp. 55–56. Drake always treated his hostages and prisoners as well as possible, but there is no doubt that he felt truly badly for the lives that the Negro slaves were made to endure, as evidenced by his subsequent behavior.

7. Ibid.

8. J. Hampden (ed.), *Sir Francis Drake Revived*, pp. 60–61. Drake's wound was most likely a flesh wound, but he did lose a large amount of blood.

9. Ibid., p. 64.

10. Ibid.

11. John Sugden, *Sir Francis Drake*, p. 58. The testimony of the eyewitness García de Paz is generally now thought to have been exaggerated.

12. Ibid., p. 65.

Chapter 18. *From a Treetop in Darien*

1. The Pacific Ocean was interchangeably called the South Atlantic, West Sea, the Southern Sea, the South Sea, or even the Spanish Lake, but never, as yet, the Pacific.

2. J. Hampden, (ed.), *Sir Francis Drake Revived* (London, 1954), p. 64. Diego is mentioned more in J. Hamden's *Sir Francis Drake Revived* than anyone else, save the captain himself and his brother, John.

3. John Sugden, *Sir Francis Drake* (London, 1996), p. 59.

4. Ibid., p. 62, quoted from J. Hampden's *Sir Francis Drake Revived.*

5. Ibid., p. 64, quoted from J. Hampden's *Sir Francis Drake Revived.*

6. J. Hampden (ed.), *Sir Francis Drake Revived*, p. 85. The momentous date was February 11, 1573. While the Spaniards and some Portuguese had long known the significance of the Isthmus of Panama, this "open secret" hadn't been seen by any other European before this date.

7. Ibid.

8. Ibid.

Chapter 19. *Success at a Cost*

1. John Sugden, *Sir Francis Drake* (London, 1996), p. 68. The rider had seen one of Oxenham's men, a fellow named Robert Pike, stand up in the undergrowth. Pike had allegedly drunk too much neat aqua vitae the night before.

2. J. Hampden (ed.), *Sir Francis Drake Revived* (London, 1954), p. 91.

3. Ibid., p. 92.

4. J. Corbett, *Drake and the Tudor Navy* (Aldershot, England, 1988 Centenary reprint), p. 184. Also see J. Sugden, *Sir Francis Drake*, p. 71. Strozzi was more than a "mercenary soldier" as depicted in these texts. The family had been merchant princes for at least a hundred years, and the Strozzi were bankers to Henry III, who succeeded Charles IX as King of France. See S. Ronald, *The Sancy Blood Diamond* (New York, 2004), pp. 48, 62, 87, 88, 92, 93.

5. Kenneth Andrews, *Trade, Plunder & Settlement* (Cambridge, 1999), p. 131.

6. John Sugden, *Sir Francis Drake*, p. 72.

7. Ibid.

8. Ibid., p. 73.

Chapter 20. *Dr. Dee's Nursery and the Northwest Passage*

1. John Sugden, *Sir Francis Drake* (London, 1996), p. 79.

2. Sir Francis Knollys held a position of great trust with Elizabeth. Married to her beloved cousin, Catherine, he had been chosen to guard Mary, Queen of Scots, when she fled to England in 1568. His daughter, Lettice, married Robert Dudley, Earl of Leicester, shortly after Walter Devereux's death. It was an open secret that Lettice, reputed to be the greatest beauty at court, and Leicester were lovers while Essex was bogged down in Ireland.

3. B. Woolley, *The Queen's Conjurer* (New York, 2001), pp. 97–123. The entire chapter relates to Dee's position within the adventurer community and how important his influence was.

4. The Mercator Principle is still used by NASA today.

5. N. Crane, *Mercator* (London, 2003), p. 164. Cf. R. Deacon, *John Dee Scientist, Geographer, Astrologer and Secret Agent to Elizabeth I* (London, 1968). Nicholas Crane's *Mercator* is a marvelously good read, even for those bored by geography.

6. BL, MS Cotton Charter XIII, art. 39.

7. Ambassador de Spes had been recalled hastily in January 1570 since he had failed miserably as an "ambassador" in England. Whether this was to protect him from his reported involvement in the Ridolfi plot or not is open to interpretation.

8. *DNB*, biography on Richard Grenville. Interestingly, Grenville's father was the master aboard the *Mary Rose*, which sank in July 1545 as she was launched in the Solent, and had been built as Henry VIII's greatest battleship.

9. Kenneth Andrews, *Trade, Plunder & Settlement* (Cambridge, 1999), p. 140.

10. Ibid., p. 168. Walsingham had most likely been an investor since 1562, when he married Anne Carleill, daughter of Sir George Barnes, who was one of the founding counselors in 1555, the year the Muscovy Company was founded. Anne's first husband, Alexander Carleill, held stock in the company in his own name prior to his death, and these shares, along with any that Sir George Barnes would leave to her, would have been controlled by Walsingham.

11. DNB, biography of Michael Lok.

12. R. Collinson, Stefansson and McCaskill, *The Three Voyages of Martin Frobisher* (London, 1938), vol. 2, pp. 215–223, Cf. State Papers E/351. Also see B. Woolley, *The Queen's Conjurer*, pp. 102–103.

13. Kenneth Andrews, *Trade, Plunder & Settlement,* pp. 169–170.

14. Ibid., p. 171.

15. B. Woolley, *The Queen's Conjurer*, Cf. E. G. Taylor's *Tudor Geography*, (London, 1930), p. 97.

16. Ibid., p. 105. Cf. *Tudor Geography* (London, 1930), document ix, pp. 262–263.

17. Kenneth Andrews, *Trade, Plunder & Settlement*, p. 172. Cf. R. Collinson (ed.), *Three Voyages of Frobisher*, p. 83.

18. The passage does exist, but is iced over most of the time. In 1845, the best-equipped expedition to date set out, and all its mariners died in the attempt. It was successfully navigated only between June 13, 1903, and August 26, 1905, by Norwegian explorer Roald Amundsen, in a small fishing boat, *The Jonah*, along with a crew of seven men.

19. Ibid., p. 173. Cf. R. Collinson (ed.), *Three Voyages of Frobisher* (London, 1867), p. 87.

20. Richard Hakluyt, *Principall Navigations* (London, 1598), vol. 7, p. 283.

Chapter 21. *Dark Days at Rathlin Island*

1. C., Brady, *The Chief Governors of Ireland* (Dublin, 2004), pp. 259–260.

2. BL MS Additional 48015, f. 319–320.

3. Ibid., f. 329.

4. NA SP63/51, f. 19, 20.

5. John Sugden, *Sir Francis Drake* (London, 1996), p. 85.

6. NA SP 63/54, f. 126.

7. When Essex died so rapidly and so violently on his return to Ireland, many whispered that Leicester had somehow perpetrated the heinous crime—just as he was alleged to have killed his first wife, Amy Robsart. Nothing was ever proven, and history has not given Essex's death any nefarious postmortem.

Chapter 22. *Drake's Perfect Timing*

1. Elizabeth had been deeply wounded by Leicester's affair with Lettice Devereux, née Knollys, and had most likely heard the rumors spread at court by Mendoza, the Spanish ambassador, and others, that Lettice had had two illegitimate children by Leicester during Devereux's first term in Ireland. I haven't been able to find that Devereux himself had made any such discovery. It is, however, significant that after the two failed French matches (with Henry III of France and his younger brother Francis), which Leicester opposed, the queen should be extremely jealous of his attentions wandering elsewhere. Lettice Devereux, Countess of Essex, and Robert Dudley, Earl of Leicester, were married in 1580, and she gave birth to Leicester's first legitimate male heir in April 1581.

2. H. Kelsey, *Sir John Hawkins* (New Haven, 2003), pp. 150–152. Interestingly, the episode with Fitzwilliams shows how Hawkins misled the very man who had been sent to do his bidding with Philip II, giving us great insight into how loyalties in Elizabethan England were subject to the prevailing wind.

3. BL MS Lansdowne 113, no. 14, f. 45–47. The manuscript is undated, but describes repairs made in 1577.

4. H. Kelsey, *Sir John Hawkins*, p. 153.

5. V. M. Shillington and A. B. W. Chapman, *Commercial Relations of Portugal* (London, 1907), pp. 140–144.

6. Kenneth Andrews, *Trade, Plunder & Settlement*, pp. 88–89.

7. Richard Hakluyt, *Principall Navigations* (London, 1598), vol. 5, pp. 168–169.

8. Kenneth Andrews, *Trade, Plunder & Settlement*, p. 90.

9. John Dee, *A Petty Navy Royal* (printed version from E. Arber's *An English Garner* [London, 1903]), p. 47.

10. Ibid., p. 49.

11. Ibid.

12. Derek Wilson, *Sweet Robin* (London, 1981), p. 224.

13. John Sugden, *Sir Francis Drake*, pp. 93–94.

14. Magellan's master gunner was English, and John Oxenham would have preceded him.

15. Derek Wilson, *Sweet Robin*, p. 94.

16. John Sugden, *Sir Francis Drake*, pp. 95-96.

17. Francis Drake, *Sir Francis Drake Revived* (London, 1954), pp. 112–113.

Chapter 23. *The Northwest and the Company of Kathai*

1. S. A. Pears (ed.), *Correspondence of Sir Philip Sidney* (London, 1845), p. 144.

2. Kenneth Andrews, *Trade, Plunder & Settlement* (Cambridge, 1999), pp. 174–175.

3. It is probably significant that the names of the ships were the *Michael* and *Gabriel*, both of whom were, of course, archangels. By this time, Dr. Dee's occult experiments had already progressed, and both names would become increasingly important to his work in the ensuing decades.

4. George Clifford, third Earl of Cumberland, was affectionately referred to by Elizabeth as her "rogue."

5. *CSP—Domestic*, 1547–1580, pp. 536–538, no. 81, undated but presumed to be March or April 1577.

6. Kenneth Andrews, *Trade, Plunder & Settlement* (Cambridge, 1999), p. 175.

7. As part of local folklore, the Inuit verbally passed down from generation to generation that the Englishmen built themselves a kayak, and rowed away.

8. Dr. Burchet is a figure of some mystery. His name is spelled in very different ways—even for Elizabethans—and some believe that he may not have even existed.

9. Richard Hakluyt, *Principall Navigations* (London, 1598), vol. 7, 284–286. Also see E164/35.

10. Ibid., vol. 7, p. 334.

11. Ibid., vol. 7, p. 336. Frobisher had been accused at the time of never reaching the coast of North America. The remnants of the Frobisher expeditions were found in the 1861–2 expedition of American explorer Charles Francis Hall, though the artifacts Hall found have since vanished. Hall also documented an Inuit legend handed down from generation to generation that the five lost Englishmen built themselves a boat, and sailed away. See Kenneth Andrews, *Trade, Plunder & Settlement*, p. 177, note 26.

12. G. Beste, *A True Discourse of the Late Voyages of Martin Frobisher . . .* (London, 1578), p. 236.

13. *CSP—Colonial*, p. xii.

14. Ibid., p. 58, no. 142.

Chapter 24. *In the Shadow of Magellan*

1. Samuel Taylor Coleridge, *More Light on Drake* (London, 1907), p. 150, report of Robert Winter, June 2, 1579.

2. N. A. M. Rodger, *Safeguard of the Sea* (London, 2004), p. 322.

3. J. Calvar Gross, *La Batalla del Mar Oceáno* (Madrid, 1988), I, p. 155.

4. John Sugden, *Sir Francis Drake* (London, 1996), p 104. C.f. W.S.W Vaux, *The World Encompassed by Sir Francis Drake* (London, 1854), p. 173.

5. Trumpeters had special functions aboard ships. All ships that Drake was on had a drum, fife, and at least one trumpeter. The trumpeter "should have a silver trumpet, and himself and his noise to have banners of silk of the admiral's colours. His place is to keep the poop, to attend to the general's going ashore and coming aboard, and all other strangers or boats, and to sound as an entertainment to them, as also when they hail a ship, or when they charge, board or enter her . . . " Cf. William Mason, *Sir William Monson's Tracts,* vol.4, p. 57.

6. John Sugden, *Sir Francis Drake*, p. 104.

7. Ibid., Cf. W. S. W. Vaux, *The World Encompassed by Sir Francis Drake* (London, 1854), p. 199.

8. Ibid., p. 110.

9. Ibid., pp. 113–114.

Chapter 25. *Into the Jaws of Death*

1. Francis Drake's account in *The World Encompassed* (London, 1628), p. 150.

2. Ibid. The hind was in the family crest of the Hatton family. There is an interesting aside I would like to make here. The beautiful portrait of Elizabeth known as *The Pelican Portrait* was painted c. 1576. It is possible, according to the Liverpool Museum of Art, that this was painted the following year. If this is, in fact, the case, then I would argue that the queen—the greatest lover of symbolism of her age—had this portrait painted as a symbol of purity, while she had sent Drake forth in the *Pelican* to plunder the King of Spain.

3. Ibid., p. 152.

4. Ibid.

5. Ibid.

6. Ibid.

7. John Sugden, *Sir Francis Drake* (London, 1996). It was the fastest time through the straits that century. Loyasa took four months, Thomas Cavendish forty-nine days, and Richard Hawkins forty-six days.

8. Ibid., pp. 116–117.

9. It was William Cornelius Shouten Van Hoorn who would name Cape Horn in 1616.

Chapter 26. *The Famous Voyage*

1. J. Calvar Gross, *La Batalla del Mar Oceáno* (Madrid, 1988), vol. 1, pp. 319–320. During this same period, on his voyage of circumnavigation alone, Drake took a minimum of eleven ships by the time he plundered the *Cacafuego*. It is difficult to estimate the exact number, since in the harbor of Callao there were between nine and thirty ships, depending on which account you read. For the purposes of simplicity, I am counting *all* the ships in Callao harbor and Paita harbor as one ship in each of those ports. This, of course, means that the original State Paper source from Spain clearly underestimates Drake's depredations and any possible undocumented English piracies in the Channel.

2. S. Ronald, *The Sancy Blood Diamond* (New York, 2004), pp.76–79.

3. John Sugden, *Sir Francis Drake* (London, 1996), p. 120.

4. F. Drake, *The World Encompassed*, p. 164.

5. According to Sugden, the exchange rate between the GBP and the *peso de oro* was 8 shillings 3 pence (prior to decimalization). This rounds off to .4075 pence today. Since rates of exchange vacillated then, as now, the rate of exchange between foreign currency and sterling had changed too.

6. F. Drake, *The World Encompassed* (London, 1996), pp. 165-166.

7. Ibid., p. 167.

8. Drake refers to the vessel as the *Cacafuego* in his narrative, and so I call it that, too, in mine to obviate confusion. Apparently after she was taken, one of the Spaniards renamed her the *Cacaplata*—or the "shits plate," meaning gold.

9. John Sugden, *Sir Francis Drake*, p. 125.

10. Ibid.

11. For the last of these prizes, Drake agreed with the Spanish owner that he would only take the cargo since the ship was all he had.

12. F. Drake, *The World Encompassed*, additional notes, p. 213.

13. Ibid., p. 170. While this formed the vast majority of the booty, it wasn't all.

14. The huge debate over whether this was San Francisco or not is not discussed here. The controversy rages on, and there are many scholars who are better placed than I to pronounce on this point. What I would say is that this mooring was most likely within the boundaries of what is today the continental United States.

15. W.S.W. Vaux (ed.), *The World Encompassed*, p. 237.

16. F. Drake, *The World Encompassed*, p. 184.

17. John Sugden, *Sir Francis Drake*, pp. 136–138.

18. Ibid., p. 140. Cf. Henry Wagner, *Sir Francis Drake's Voyage Around the World* (Mansfield Center, CT, 2005), p. 180.

19. According to Spanish sources like Antonio de Herrera's *Historia General de Mundo* (Madrid, 1606), Babu had plotted to kill Drake since he had traded without his permission.

20. Ibid., p. 141.

21. Zelia Nuttall (ed.), *New Light on Drake* (London,1914), pp. 383–384.

22. Julian Corbett and Henry Wagner both feel that the incident probably took place near Tomori Bay or Vesuvius Reef nearby.

23. Zelia Nuttall (ed.), *New Light on Drake*, p. 142.

24. Ibid., p.143. Cf. W. Anderson, *The Whole of Captain Cook's Voyages* (London, 1784).

Chapter 27. *The World Is Not Enough*

1. *CSP—Spain*, vol. 2, pp. 694–695.

2. Zelia Nuttall (ed.), *New Light on Drake*, pp. 385–386. Of all those who claimed money back from Drake, Nuño da Silva alone met with Drake privately, and dropped any claims he had against the commander following on that meeting. Drake clearly gave credit where it was due, and he treated his former captive with generosity.

3. J. Calvar Gross, *La Batalla del Mar Oceáno* (Madrid, 1988), vol. 1, no. 395.

4. *CSP—Domestic*, the queen to Tremayne, October 25, 1580, no. 30.

5. S. Ronald, *The Sancy Blood Diamond* (New York, 2004), pp. 74–81, for a brief financial history of the takeover of Portugal by Spain and Elizabeth's reaction.

6. J. S. Corbett, *Drake and the Tudor Navy* (Aldershot, England, 1988 Centenary reprint), pp. 408–409.

7. Ibid.

8. S. Ronald, *The Sancy Blood Diamond*, pp. 82–105. Also see J. S. Corbett, *Drake and the Tudor Navy,* p. 332. After completing the book, I found specific references in the de Lisle papers regarding Leicester's mission while accompanying Anjou to the Low Countries.

9. J. S. Corbett, *Drake and the Tudor Navy,* p. 402.

10. The knighthood of Sir Francis Drake is recounted in all his biographies, and in film. My favorite "rendition" is J. Corbett's in *Drake and the Tudor Navy*, pp. 315–318, followed by J. Sugden's *Sir Francis Drake*, pp. 150–151. It's vintage Elizabeth.

Chapter 28. *Elizabeth Strikes Back in the Levant*

1. *The Prince* was, of course, in Elizabeth's personal library. It is also the only book besides the Bible I know of that has never been out of popular print since it was first published 500 years ago. Dedicated to

the Magnificent Lorenzo de' Medici, it was published posthumously. Machiavelli, who had no formal education as a child due to the family's extreme poverty, died in 1527.

2. Francis, Duke of Anjou, had been the Duke of Alençon until his brother, King Charles IX, died. On Henry of Anjou's accession to the French throne as Henry III, Francis dropped the title of Alençon and became Francis, Duke of Anjou.

3. Kenneth Andrews, *Trade, Plunder & Settlement* (Cambridge, 1999), p. 90. Cf. Walsingham's memo headed "A Consideration of the Trade into Turkey."

4. Ibid., pp. 91–92.

5. S.A. Skilliter *Harborne* (London, 1977), pp. 159–200. Also see Richard Hakluyt's *Principall Navigations* (London, 1598), vol. 5, pp. 189–191, and *CSP—Foreign*, p. 781.

6. Kenneth Andrews, *Trade, Plunder & Settlement,* p. 94.

7. Richard Hakluyt, *Principall Navigations*, vol. 5, p. 459.

8. Ibid., vol. 5, p. 507.

Chapter 29. *Katherine Champernowne's Sons Take Up the American Dream*

1. D. B. Quinn, *Ralegh and the British Empire* (London, 1973), pp. 36–37.

2. Kenneth Andrews, *Trade, Plunder & Settlement* (Cambridge, 1999), pp. 184–185. Cf. Thomas Churchyard, *Churchyard's Choice* (London, 1587), p. 128, and Richard Chope, *A New Light on Grenville* (London, 1918), p. 214.

3. D. B. Quinn, *Ralegh and the British Empire*, p. 38.

4. Ibid.

5. Kenneth Andrews, *Trade, Plunder & Settlement*, p. 187.

6. D. B. Quinn, *Ralegh and the British Empire*, p. 39.

7. BL, Harl. 6993, f.5. Letter from Walter Raleigh to the Earl of Leicester from Lismore, August 26, 1581.

8. *CSP—Spain*, vol. 3, pp. xxxiii, 186.

9. Ibid.

10. Ibid., pp. xxxiv, 193.

11. Kenneth Andrews, *Trade, Plunder & Settlement*, p. 190.

12. Ibid., Cf. D.B. Quinn, *Sir Humphrey Gilbert* (Liverpool, 1983), pp. 49–53.

13. D. B. Quinn, *England and the Discovery of America* (London, 1974), pp. 364-397.

14. Ibid.

15. Ibid.

16. Ibid., p. 217.

17. A. Beer, *Bess: The Life of Lady Ralegh* (London, 2003), pp. 45–47. This plot did indeed involve Mary Queen of Scots, and was a vicious attempt on Elizabeth's life. Burghley and Walsingham put in place a set of draconian laws that were intended to safeguard the queen, but only punished her Catholic subjects. Though the Babington Plot, for which Mary lost her life, was barely anything more than entrapment, she certainly had acted to kill the Queen of England in the Throckmorton Plot. Francis Throckmorton's cousin, Elizabeth Throckmorton, would later become Walter Raleigh's wife.

18. Richard Hakluyt, *Principall Navigations* (London, 1598), vol. 8, pp. 34–77.

19. Ibid., p. 77.

Chapter 30. *The Defeats of 1582–84*

1. S. Ronald, *The Sancy Blood Diamond* (New York, 2004), pp. 87–88.

2. John Sugden, *Sir Francis Drake* (London, 1996), p. 165, also pp. 166–168.

3. John Drake was captured and brought to Lima where he was "interrogated" and tortured by the Inquisition. Seven years later, it is presumed that he was made to walk in the *auto-da-fé* at Lima, repenting his Lutheranism, since another eighty-eight-year-old John Drake was made to walk another *auto-da-fé* at Cartagena in December 1650.

4. H. Kelsey, *Sir John Hawkins* (New Haven, 2003), p. 166.

5. Ibid., p. 168.

6. N. A. M. Rodger, *Safeguard of the Sea* (London, 2004), p. 246.

Chapter 31. *Water!*

1. N. A. M. Rodger, *Safeguard of the Sea* (London, 2004), p. 248.

2. A. Latham and J. Youings (eds.), *The Letters of Sir Walter Ralegh* (London, 2001), p. 13.

3. D. B. Quinn, *Ralegh and the British Empire* (London, 1973), p. 17.

4. D. Wilson, *Sweet Robin (London, 1981),* pp. 272–273.

5. D. B. Quinn, *Ralegh and the British Empire*, p. 52.

6. Ibid., p. 53.

7. Ibid.

8. Ibid., p. 54.

9. Ibid.

10. Richard Hakluyt (ed.), *Virginia Voyages*, pp. 8–12.

11. D. B. Quinn, *Ralegh and the British Empire*, p. 61.

Chapter 32. *Roanoke*

1. This is a portion of a poem reply to Raleigh's poem from BL, MS Add. 63742, f. 116r, oddly included in a vellum-bound tome described as *Letters from Henry, fourth Earl of Derby*. Pug was another of Elizabeth's nicknames for Raleigh.

2. E. G. R. Taylor, *Writings of the Hakluyts* (London, 1935), p. 326. Also see Charles Deane (ed.), *Discourse on Western Planting* (London, 1877).

3. R. B. Wernham, *The Making of Elizabethan Foreign Policy* (Berkeley, 1980), p. 55.

4. Kenneth Andrews, *Trade, Plunder & Settlement* (Cambridge, 1999), p. 205.

5. D. B. Quinn, *Ralegh and the British Empire* (London, 1973), p. 59.

6. G. Milton, *Big Chief Elizabeth* (London, 2000), pp. 46–47.

7. Dee was the first to systematically use the mathematical signs of equals, plus, minus, divide, and multiply, and he wrote a treatise on using these universally in the 1560s.

8. Ibid., p. 103.

9. Kenneth Andrews, *Trade, Plunder & Settlement*, p. 205.

10. Richard Hakluyt, *Virginia Voyages* (London, 1888), pp. 22–23.

Chapter 33. *The Queen Lets Loose Her Dragon*

1. G. Parker, *The Grand Strategy of Philip II* (New Haven, 2000), p. 175.

2. D. Loades, *The Tudor Navy* (Aldershot, England, 1992), p. 234.

3. John Sugden, *Sir Francis Drake*, p. 178. Cf. *CSP—Foreign*, pp. 330–332.

4. Ibid., pp. 178–181.

5. Ibid., p. 182.

6. Ibid., p. 186.

7. Ibid., p. 187.

8. Ibid., p. 189. Cf. *García Fernández de Torrequemada's Letter to the Spanish Crown 4th February 1587*, Irene A. Wright, ed. (London, 1951), pp. 200–205.

9. Ibid., p. 190. Cf. *Rodrigo Fernández de Ribera to the Crown*, in Wright, *Further Voyages to Spanish America* (London, 1951), pp. 178–180.

10. D. B. Quinn, *Ralegh and the British Empire* (London, 1973), p. 68.

11. See G. Milton's *Big Chief Elizabeth* (London, 2000), for a description of the character and recruitment criteria for the first colonists, pp. 83–92.

12. D. B. Quinn, *Ralegh and the British Empire*, pp. 70–71. The White drawings are at the British Library and can be seen in the two-volume set, *The American Drawings of John White*.

13. Richard Hakluyt, *The Virginia Voyages*, pp. 33-34.

14. Kenneth Andrews, *Trade, Plunder & Settlement*, p. 208, Cf. Richard Hakluyt, *Principall Navigation* (London, 1598), vol. 8, p. 331.

15. John Sugden, *Sir Francis Drake* (London, 1996), p. 194. There were two examples of great courage by the Spaniards: Captain Alonso Bravo, a captain of the infantry, was taken prisoner only after six wounds had been inflicted; and the Spanish standard bearer stood his ground until Carleill himself had to kill him.

16. Ibid., p. 196.

17. Ibid.

18. Ibid., p. 198.

19. Richard Hakluyt, *The Virginia Voyages*, pp. 42–45.

Chapter 34. *The Camel's Back*

1. S. Ronald, *The Sancy Blood Diamond* (New York, 2004), p. 95.

2. L. Marcus, J. Mueller, and M. B. Rose, *Elizabeth I: Collected Works* (Chicago, 2000), pp. 268–272.

3. G. Mattingly, *The Defeat of the Spanish Armada* (London, 1959), pp. 17–28 carries the full account.

4. S. Ronald, *The Sancy Blood Diamond*, pp. 100–101.

5. G. Mattingly, *The Defeat of the Spanish Armada*, pp. 72–74. This book is the most compelling one written about the Armada in my opinion, putting it beautifully into historical context and making the characters of Philip and Elizabeth blaze with life. Though first published in 1959, it is still in print.

6. Ibid., p. 78.

7. *CSP—Spain*, vol. 4, p. 61.

Chapter 35. *Cadiz*

1. The *CSP—Spain* and *Venice* carry numerous references to Philip's torment about Drake, Elizabeth, Raleigh, Leicester, and the newer generation of seaman "explorer" like Raleigh and Cavendish. For a good overview of Cavendish's accomplishments and voyage, see Derek Wilson's *The Circumnavigators* (London, 1989).

2. R. W. Kenny, *Elizabeth's Admiral* (Baltimore, 1970), pp. 38–42.

3. *CSP—Spain*, vol. 4, pp. xix-xx.

4. John Sugden, *Sir Francis Drake* (London, 1996), pp. 204–205.

5. SP 12/193, F. 26-28, 42.

6. Drake's first wife, Mary, had died several years earlier. His second wife was Lady Elizabeth Sydenham, whose father was a wealthy Somerset merchant.

7. *CSP—Spain*, vol.4, p. 62, no. 62. In Stafford's defense, he had been complaining of penury for quite some time, begging the queen to give him a financial reward commensurate with his position. Elizabeth naturally demurred.

8. Ibid.

9. Ibid., p. 65, no. 65, and p. 69, no. 67.

10. BL, MS Cotton Otho E, VIII, 192–195.

11. BL, MS Cotton Vespasian, CVIII, f. 207.

12. *CSP—Venice*, vol. 8, p. 254–258.

13. *CSP—Spain*, vol. 3, p. 368.

14. G. Mattingly, *The Defeat of the Spanish Armada* (London, 1959), pp. 91–106.

15. Ibid.

16. Ibid.

17. Ibid.

Chapter 36. *The Plundering of the Spanish Armada*

1. J. S. Corbett, *The Spanish War*, p. 109. Cf. *A Letter from Sir Francis Drake to Sir Francis Walsingham*, April 27, 1587.

2. J. K. Laughton (ed.), *State Papers Relating to the Defeat of the Spanish Armada* (London, 1898), vol. 1, p. 148.

3. N. A. M. Rodger, *Safeguard of the Sea* (London, 2004), p. 260. Also see J. Corbett, *The Spanish War*, p. 280.

4. R. Wernham, *Before the Armada* (London, 1966), pp. 377–378. Cf. SP12/143, f. 20.

5. N. A. M. Rodger, *Safeguard of the Sea*, pp. 260–261. Also see G. Mattingly, *The Defeat of the Spanish Armada* (London, 1959), pp. 107–109; J. S. Corbett, *The Spanish War*, pp. 277–280; W. T. MacCaffrey, *The Shaping of the Elizabethan Regime* (Princeton, 1908), p. 299; R. B. Wernham, *The Making of Elizabethan Foreign Policy* (Berkeley, 1980), p. 59; and Dietz, *The Exchequer under Elizabeth* (New Haven, 2000), pp. 100–103.

6. G. Parker, *The Grand Strategy of Philip II* (New Haven, 2000), pp. 182–84. Also see N. A. M. Rodger, *Safeguard of the Sea* (London, 2004) pp. 258–259.

7. N. A. M. Rodger, *Safeguard of the Sea*, p. 259.

8. J. K. Laughton (ed.), *State Papers Relating to the Defeat of the Spanish Armada*, vol. 2, pp. 324–331.

9. N. A. M., Rodger, *Safeguard of the Sea*, p. 263–264.

10. Kenneth Andrews, *Trade, Plunder & Settlement* (Cambridge, 1999), p. 233.

11. F. Duro, *Armada Invencible* (Madrid, 1884), vol. 2, pp. 5–10.

12. N. A. M. Rodger, *Safeguard of the Sea*, p. 264.

13. J. K. Laughton (ed.), *State Papers Relating to the Defeat of the Spanish Armada*, vol. 1, pp. 79–81.

14. Bonfires play an important part in British military and social history. There is a great book about them called *Bonfires to Beacons* by Nick Kumons (London, 1990).

15. See J. Sugden, *Sir Francis Drake* (London, 1996), pp. 234–235, for details.

16. Ibid., pp. 238–239. Also see Kenneth Andrews, *Trade, Plunder & Settlement*, pp. 232–233.

17. J. Sugden, *Sir Francis Drake*, pp. 241-246. Also see N. A. M. Rodger, *Safeguard of the Sea*, pp. 265–266.

18. J. Sugden, *Sir Francis Drake*, p. 246.

19. Ibid., pp. 243–244. The National Archives has the depositions ref. E 133/47. The lawsuit related to the Drakes of Esher being dissatisfied with their share of the family spoils and their lawsuit against Drake's heir, Thomas Drake.

20. G. Mattingly, *The Defeat of the Spanish Armada*, p. 288.

21. N. A. M. Rodger, *Safeguard of the Sea*, p. 270. Cf. G. Mattingly, *The Defeat of the Spanish Armada*, vol. 1, p. 341.

Chapter 37. *America Again . . . and Again?*

1. A. Latham and J. Youings (eds.), *The Letters of Sir Walter Ralegh* (London, 2001), pp. 45–46, dated September 13, 1588, from court. My Lord Cumberland to whom he refers is George, third Earl of Cumberland.

2. D. B. Quinn, *Ralegh and the British Empire* (London, 1973), p. 89.

3. G. Milton, *Big Chief Elizabeth* (London, 2000), p. 203.

4. For a splendid profile of White and his colonists, read G. Milton's *Big Chief Elizabeth*.

5. D. B. Quinn, *Ralegh and the British Empire*, p. 92.

6. Kenneth Andrews, *Trade, Plunder & Settlement* (Cambridge, 1999), pp. 216–217.

7. D. B. Quinn, *Ralegh and the British Empire*, p. 93.

8. Ibid., p. 94.

9. Kenneth, Andrews, *Trade, Plunder & Settlement*, p. 217.

10. Ibid., p. 218.

11. Richard Hakluyt, *Principall Navigations* (London, 1598), p. 4.

Chapter 38. *The Last Gasp of the Early Roaring '90s*

1. Kenneth Andrews, *Elizabethan Privateering* (Cambridge, 1964), p. 206.

2. Ibid., pp. 236–239. For the best account of the 1589 voyage, see J. Sugden, *Sir Francis Drake* (London, 1996), chapter XX, pp. 263–284.

3. John Sugden, *Sir Francis Drake* (London, 1996), pp. 300–301.

4. J. S. Corbett, *Drake and the Tudor Navy* (Aldershot, England, 1988 Centenary reprint), vol. 2, p. 340. Cf. SP Spain, xxix, no. 2.

5. D. B. Quinn, *Ralegh and the British Empire* (London, 1973), pp. 109–114.

6. D. Akenson, *An Irish History of Civilization* (London, 2005), vol. 1, pp. 160–162.

7. J. S. Corbett, *Successors of Drake* (London, 1900), p. 27.

8. D. B. Quinn, *Ralegh and the British Empire,* pp. 114–115.

9. D. Akenson, *An Irish History of Civilization*, vol. 1, p. 160.

10. J. S. Corbett, *Drake and the Tudor Navy*, pp. 350–351.

11. Ibid., p. 357.

12. Ibid.

13. Kenneth Andrews, *Trade, Plunder & Settlement*, p. 242.

14. Ibid., p. 240.

15. Ibid., p. 219.

16. Ibid.

17. D. B. Quinn, *Ralegh and the British Empire*, p. 126.

18. Ibid.

19. Ibid., p. 131.

20. *CSP—Venice*, vol. 9, no. 121, pp. 53–54.

21. J. S. Corbett, *Drake and the Tudor Navy* (Aldershot, England, 1988 Centenary reprint), vol.2, pp. 366–369.

22. J. Sugden, *Sir Francis Drake*, pp. 302–303.

23. *CSP—Venice*, vol. 9, no. 153, pp. 67–68.

Chapter 39. *The Alchemy That Turned Plunder into Trade*

1. Corbett goes into some significant detail on how poor John Doughty,

on his return from the voyage of circumnavigation, first tried to have Drake brought to trial for the murder of his brother, and, when that failed, he attempted to kill him. He was thrown into jail unceremoniously—without trial—and the last we see of him is a letter to the Earl of Leicester, Robert Dudley, begging for his release. He undoubtedly died a dreadful and agonizing death in the most undemocratic way repugnant to all great democracies.

2. Kenneth Andrews, *Trade, Plunder & Settlement* (Cambridge, 1999), p. 241.

3. BL, MS Additonal 24023, f.1 [in French in Elizabeth's hand] with the date provided by MS Additional 48212, f.13 as September 13, 1596.

4. Kenneth Andrews, *Trade, Plunder & Settlement*, p. 241.

5. J. S. Corbett, *Successors of Drake* (London, 1900), pp. 89–90.

6. Ibid., pp. 100–101.

7. Ibid., pp. 102–103.

8. N. A. M. Rodger, *Safeguard of the Sea* (London, 2004), p. 284.

9. Ibid., p. 285.

10. Ibid.

11. Kenneth Andrews, *The Elizabethan Seaman* (London, 1982), p. 322.

12. M. Oppenheim, *A History of the Administration of the Royal Navy* (London, 1896), p. 384.

13. By 1596, Elizabeth had entrusted much of her government's workings to Robert Cecil, her hunchbacked "Elf." Cecil, like many Elizabethan children, had a spinal deformity: as a result of the constant taunting he endured while growing up, he was more Machiavellian than any other of the queen's Privy Councillors. See his entry in the *DNB*.

14. By the end of Elizabeth's reign, Cecil's farm of "silks" netted him £7,000 annually—$1.77 million or £909,200 today. His "takings" through his adventures with Charles Howard amounted to significantly more.

15. R. W. Kenny, *Elizabeth's Admiral* (Baltimore, 1970), pp. 37–40.

16. Ibid. Also see Hatfield MSS 4:358, 375.

17. N. A. M. Rodger, *Safeguard of the Sea*, pp. 343–344. Also see Kenneth Andrews, *Trade, Plunder & Settlement*, p. 245, and K. R. Kenny, *Elizabeth's Admiral*, pp. 67–87.

18. Kenneth Andrews, *Elizabethan Privateering* (Cambridge, 1964), pp. 32–34.

19. William Monson, *Sir William Monson's Tracts* (London, 1625), vol. 4, p. 21.

Chapter 40. *Essex, Ireland, and Tragedy*

1. *DNB*, Robert Devereux biography, p. 4.

2. FSL, L.a.39.

3. For details, see *DNB* biography.

4. BL, MS Additional 74287, f.13v.

5. Salisbury MSS, 4, 116.

6. *DNB*, Hugh O'Neill biography, p. 1.

7. G. R. Elton, *England Under the Tudors* (London, 1993), pp. 379–385.

8. Ibid., pp. 386–387.

9. FSL, MS V.b.214, f.229v–230v.

10. *CSP—Spain* vol.4, p. 685.

11. *DNB*, biography, p. 18. One of Essex's many rows with the queen was over the appointment of Bacon as attorney-general. The queen steadfastly refused.

12. D. Akenson, *An Irish History of Civilization* (London, 2005), vol. 1, pp. 165–166.

13. G. R. Elton, *England Under the Tudors*, pp. 388–389.

Chapter 41. *Raleigh, Virginia, and Empire*

1. A. Latham and J. Youings (eds.), *The Letters of Sir Walter Ralegh* (London, 2001), pp. 50–51, no. 33.

2. Elizabeth's final illness was more complex than that, and was as much due to old age and depression at the loss of so many of her contemporaries, poor understanding of medical matters, and the feeling that she had served her time on earth.

3. D. B. Quinn, *Ralegh and the British Empire* (London, 1973), pp. 134–135.

4. A. Latham and J. Youings (eds.), *The Letters of Sir Walter Ralegh* p. 87, no. 56.

5. D.B. Quinn and A.M. Quinn, *The First Colonists* (Raleigh, NC, 1982), p. 108.

6. D. B. Quinn, *Ralegh and the British Empire*, p. 149.

7. Ibid., p. 151.

8. Ibid., p. 158.

9. Ibid.

10. Ibid., p. 157.

11. *HMC Salisbury* (London, 1888), vol. 9, p. 311. Also see A. Latham and J. Youings, *The Letters of Sir Walter Raleigh*, pp. 240–241, letter no. 161.

12. Ibid.

Chapter 42. *The East and East India Company*

1. G. Milton, *Nathaniel's Nutmeg* (New York, 1999), p. 41.

2. This is a distinctly English perspective, I'm sure, though not without foundation.

3. Kenneth Andrews, *Trade, Plunder & Settlement* (Cambridge, 1999), p. 256.

4. J. Keay, *The Honourable Company* (London, 1993), pp. 10–13.

5. There were other reasons as well for Elizabeth to hesitate as she did: it was a favorite game to wrong-foot her courtiers, at times pandering to one faction or another, as well as a way of keeping her enemies (foreign ambassadors and unseen traitors in her midst) guessing as to her true purpose. Sometimes she would change her mind simply for the fun of it. But when it came to matters of national or international importance, she invariably hesitated for one of the two reasons I give.

6. Kenneth Andrews, *Trade, Plunder & Settlement*, pp. 258–259.

7. Ibid., p. 263.

8. J. Keay, *The Honourable Company*, pp. 14–15.

9. S. Ronald, *The Sancy Blood Diamond* (New York, 2004), p. 137.

Glossary ⚜

Sources for this glossary were provided primarily by the *Oxford English Dictionary*, Kenneth R. Andrews's *The Spanish Caribbean*, N. A. M. Rodgers's *The Safeguard of the Sea*, and David Loades's *The Tudor Navy*. My sincerest thanks to them all.

abeam, (adj.) at right angles to the ship's center line.

admiral, 1. the officer commanding a squadron of ships; 2. the Lord (High) Admiral, an officer of the crown in charge of Admiralty and naval affairs; 3. a flagship in a fleet (16th and 17th centuries).

adviso, announcement.

afore, same as fore.

aft, abaft, towards the stern or rear of a ship.

aftercastle, the tower or fighting platform built at the stern of a ship from the 13th century.

agreeing, (as in climate), becoming acclimatized.

alcaide, Spanish governor.

aloft, 1. relating to the masts and rigging upwards, or 2. on deck.

amidship(s), relating to the middle or centerline of a ship.

anatomy, a skeleton or mummy.

ancient, 1. an ensign or standard; 2. an ensign or standard-bearer.

annoy, injure.

appointed, equipped or armed.

armada, any fleet of warships, or if large enough, a single warship. Used in this book solely for Spanish warships.

arquebuse (also harquebuse), a portable fire-arm with a box-like fire lock of variable size, but usually a large, cumbersome kind of musket.

artificial, skillful, workmanlike.

ashore, towards or on the shore.

assay, assault. (Term "at all assays," meaning "in any attack," or "any danger.")

astern, behind the ship, in the direction from which she is moving.

astrolabe, a navigational instrument used for measuring the altitude of heavenly bodies and thereby the ship's latitude.

asiento, a Spanish commercial contract or licence.

audiencia, the high court of a region within Spain's jurisdiction.

back, 1. to trim sails so that they catch the wind from ahead; 2. (of the wind) to change in a counter-clockwise direction.

ballast, stones, gravel, or other weight stowed low in a ship to improve her stability.

banquet, dessert; sweetmeats and wine.

bar, a shoal across the mouth of a tidal estuary.

Barbary, from the northwest coast of Africa (as in barbary pirate, or barbary trade).

barbican, a man-made structure defending the gate of a castle.

barge, an oared sailing vessel used for war and trade (14th–16th centuries).

bark, any seagoing sailing ship of moderate size (16th century).

barrel, 1. a cask of specified capacity, usually between 30–34 gallons; 2. the muzzle of a gun.

base, a very small cannon, probably firing a six-ounce shot.

basilisk, a type of long heavy gun, usually breech-loading (15th–16th century).

battery, 1. the broadside guns mounted on one deck or the side of the ship; 2. a group of guns mounted ashore to fire on ships.

beach, to run a ship aground or ashore.

beam, 1. the width of the ship; 2. the direction at right angles to the center line of the ship; 3. a timber running from side to side of the ship to support the deck.

bear, 1. to enter names in the ships book as part of the ship's company; 2. to lie or point in a certain direction; 3.—**away,** to bear up or turn downwind; 4.—**room,** to bear up (16th–17th century); 5.—**up,** to turn downwind.

beat, (of a ship), to work windward by several tacks (turnings).

behoveful, advantageous.

bill, halberd (see *halberd*).

block, a pulley.

boatswain, 1. a ship's officer responsible for sails, rigging, and ground tackle; 2. boatswain's mate, the petty officer assisting the boatswain.

bolt, a short arrow fired from a crossbow.

bonaventure mizzen, see mizzen.

boom, 1. a light running spar, especially one at the foot of a sail; 2. a floating barrier protecting a harbor.

bow, verb, 1. to bend; 2. to cant a broadside gun as far forward as possible (16th century).

bowline, a line or tackle led forward from the leach of a square sail to haul the weather leach taut when beating to windward.

bow-shoot, bow-shot, a distance of about 240 yards.

bowspirit, a spar projecting over the bows, spreading various riggings and one or more sails.

brave, beautiful, fine, decorated.

Brazil, a wood used for dyeing cloth. (Brazil was named after its wood.)

breach, the breaking of the sea on the shore.

breech, the inner or rear end of a gun.

breeching, a rope attaching the breech of the gun to the ship's side to restrain the recoil or movement of the gun.

brigantine, a small vessel equipped for sailing or rowing, swifter and more easily maneuverable than large ships, frequently used for piracy, espionage, or reconnoitering.

brow, a portable bridge for crossing from dockside to the ship or from ship to ship

brownbill, a burnished axe.

brustling, crackling, rustling, roaring.

buff, buffalo.

buskin, a boot reaching to the calf or the knee.

by and by, at once.

cable, 1. a thick long rope, particularly the anchor cable; 2. a measure of distance originally 120, then later 100 fathoms or one-tenth of a nautical mile.

cabrito, goat (Spanish).

cacique, an Indian chieftain.

caliver, a long, light musket.

cannon, the English cannon was probably a 7-inch gun firing a 40 pound round of shot. The Spanish cannon was larger, firing a 50 pound round of shot.

cant, to turn or change the heading or direction of the ship.

capitana, Spanish flagship.

caravel, a small, light, fast lateen-rigged ship, originally a Portuguese type.

carvel, adj. Of the "skeleton-first" method of shipbuilding in which a frame of timbers is clad with planking laid edge to edge.

cargason, cargo, bill of lading.

carrack, a large "round ship" used as a merchant ship, (merchantman) with a high superstructure fore and aft (15th–16th century) particularly to transport cargo from the East Indies.

castle, 1. a structure erected forward (forecastle) or aft (aftercastle).

caulk, to make seams watertight on a ship.

cause, causeway or raised roadway across water.

chamlet or camlet, presumed to be a type or mohair or camel hair cloth mixed with wool, silk, or cotton (*A Handbook of English Costume in the Sixteenth Century*).

chamber, a detachable breech containing the explosive charge of a gun (15th–16th century); 2. the inner end of the bore of a muzzle-loading gun which is bored to a smaller diameter than the rest to accept a reduced charge.

chargeable, responsible, expensive, or troublesome.

charged, high or having tall castles fore and aft.

chase, the bow of a ship.

chirurgeon, surgeon.

Cimarróne, Cimarroon, a runaway slave.

Cipango, Japan.

clift, split wood.

clinker (clench), a system of shipbuilding where the hull is made of overlapping strakes of planking built up from the keel with light frames inserted later for stiffening.

close-hauled, steering as close to the wind as possible.

cock-boat, a small boat or dinghy.

cod, pod

cog, a type of merchant ship with a flat bottom and high freeboard rigged with a single mast and sail.

commodious, convenient, advantageous or profitable.

composition, agreement, treaty, compromise.

conceits, ideas or fancies.

contagious, foul.

contractátion house, a commercial exchange center.

cooper, 1. a skilled repairer of casks; 2. a rating employed to assist the purser to dispense beer and other liquids.

cordovan skin, fine leather from Cordova, Spain, or in the style of Cordova.

corinths, currants.

corregidor, a magistrate or sheriff.

coxswain, a petty officer in charge of a boat's crew.

crossbar, cross-shot, cannon shot in the form of a bar or a cross.

cross-staff, an instrument for observing the altitude of the sun or star in order to fix latitude. John Dee made vast improvements to the cross-staff.

cruet, a small vessel holding wine or water for the celebration of the Eucharist.

crumbs, to gather up or pick up strength.

culverin, the longest range gun in use in the 16th century. A long, muzzle-loading smooth bore gun, usually firing a round of shot of about 17 pounds in weight. The demi-culverin shot was about half that weight at 9 pounds.

cunning, skillful or clever.

customer, a customs house officer.

cut out, to take as a prize a ship from its fleet.

daw, to revive, bring back to consciousness.

dead reckoning, the captain would throw a log overboard and observe how quickly the ship receded from this guidepost. Noting the speed reading in his ship's logbook, along with the direction of travel, which he took from the stars or a compass, and the length of time on a particular course, he then determined his longitude. He routinely missed the mark.

defend, to forbid.

deliver, quick to, active, or nimble.

demurrage, a payment made by a shipper to the ship owner in compensation for unreasonably detaining the ship on her voyage.

detract, to withdraw from.

dight, dressed, dressed up, or decorated.

disbock, to flow out of or into.

draft, chart.

drake, a short gun of the culverin type.

drumbler, a small fast vessel used as a transport or a fighting ship.

ducat, a Spanish coin worth about 5 shillings and 10 pence in Elizabethan times.

Easterland, the territory of the Hanse merchants on the Baltic.

elchie, ambassador.

ell, 45 inches, the standard width of cloth.

equinoctial, of the equator.

factor, an agent for a merchant or monarch in a foreign country.

factory, trading station for the factor.

falchion, a broad curved sword (as used by the Turks and Barbary pirates).

falconet, a gun about 6½ feet long firing a 1½ pound shot.

fat, cask.

fencible, easy to defend.

figu, plantain banana.

fine, end.

firkin, a small cask containing between eight to nine gallons.

fish, to mend a mast or spar by binding it to a splint.

flead, fleane, flayed, or skinned.

flux, dysentery.

fly-boat, fast sailing vessel usually traveling between ships in a squadron with provisions and messages.

foist, a small light galley with 18-20 oars aside and two masts.

foot, foot soldiers, infantry.

freeboard, the minimum height of the ship's side above the waterline.

frumenty or furmenty, a dish of wheat boiled in milk and seasoned to taste.

furicane, hurricane.

furniture, equipment.

gable, cable.

galleass, a large long sailing vessel with a flush deck, auxiliary oars, and broadside guns.

galleon, a sailing warship of fine lines, with high upperworks aft and a galley bow with heavy battery of chasers (16th century).

galley, 1. a type of warship propelled by oars; 2. the kitchen aboard ship.

galliard, a kissing dance.

galliot, a small galley.

gallizabra, a type of Spanish sailing warship that was small, fast and equipped with oars.

general, 1. commander of any expedition, either maritime or military; 2. a flagship.

glass, gloss.

goose-wing, "one of the clews or lower corners of a ship's mainsail or foresail when the middle part is furled or tied up to the yard" (*SOED*).

grave, v. to clean a ship's bottom by burning off the accretions and paying it over with tar while aground on a beach or placed in a dock (*SOED*).

groat, an English four penny piece.

grommet, an Elizabethan apprentice seaman.

guards, stripes (blue and green).

Guinea, Coast of, the west coast of Africa from Sierra Leone to Benin where the Portuguese had initially set up slaving forts.

gunwale, a heavy timber forming the top of the ship's side.

halberd, a kind of spear approximately six feet long with a head that could be used either for cutting or thrusting.

handy, easily maneuverable.

hardly, with difficulty.

harquebus, see arquebus.

harping iron, harpoon.

hawser, a large rope or tackle.

hold, fort.

horse, cavalry.

hound, projection at the mast-head.

hoy, a flat bottomed sailing vessel.

ingenio, sugar mill.

intend to, to attend to.

jealousy, suspicion, mistrust.

jennet, a small Spanish horse.

jut, a push or knock.

kemb, comb.

kern, v. to make into grains, to granulate.

kintal, see *quintal*.

larboard, now known as the port side.

large (of the wind), on the quarter.

lateen, 1. a fore-and-aft rig where triangular sails are bent to yards which are set so that the foot is made fast on deck and the middle hoisted to the masthead; 2. a triangular sail rigged ship.

latitude, a position lying on a line around the earth parallel to the equator.

league, approximately three miles.

leese, lose.

letters patent, a document under the Great Seal of England appointing the person(s) to act on behalf of the Crown.

lewd, unprincipled, vulgar, evil, foolish.

ligier, resident ambassador or commercial representative.

list, strip, edging.

longitude, a position lying on a line around the earth from pole to pole.

lowbell, a small bell used in fowling.

luff, to bring the ship closer to the wind.

maguey, American aloe.

main, mainland.

main to, v., to lower sails.

mammee, a large tropical tree bearing huge yellow fruit when ripe.

mankind, male stags.

mark, thirteen shillings and eight pence in Elizabethan money.

mart, market.

master, 1. the commanding officer of a merchant ship; 2. an officer responsible for the navigation and pilotage of a warship.

match, a slow burning fuse for firing guns.

mean, moderate or medium.

mess, a group of seamen.

millio, millet.

mizzen, 1. the foremost mast of a ship; 2. bonaventure—, the fourth and aftermost mast of a great ship of the 16th century.

morse, walrus.

musket, a breech-loading gun in a swivel mounting (16th century).

occupy, 1. to follow one's occupation; 2. to have sexual intercourse.

open, in view of.

overseen, mistaken.

painful, diligent.

pantofles, overshoes like slippers.

part, partisan.

partisan, a kind of spear approximately nine feet long with a broad blade.

patache, "a small boat used for communications between the vessels of a fleet" (*SOED*).

peason, peas.

peso, a piece of eight, worth about four shillings and three pence in Elizabethan money.

pilled, pillaged.

pilot, navigator.

pine, pineapple.

pinnace, a small ship or boat, usually with oars as well as sails and fairly fast. It is able to navigate in the shallows.

pintado, a cloth painted or printed in colors.

pipe, (of wine or water for example), a very large cask, about half a ton.

plant, v., to colonize.

plantano, plantain.

policy, crafty device, strategem, trick.

politically, craftily, falsely.

pompion, pumpkin.

posy, a short inscription or motto.

purchase, capture, plunder, or prize.

purveyance, the sovereign's right to obtain supplies for the royal household at a fixed price.

quintal, a one hundred pound weight.

race-built ship, a ship built low in the water designed for speed.

real of plate, a Spanish coin, worth about six and a half pennies of Elizabethan money.

receipt, capacity.

reckoning, 1. a calculation of a ship's position; 2. dead-, an estimation of the ship's position without the benefit of observations, by calculating course, speed, and drift from a known point of departure.

regiment, rule or government.

road, anchorage or port.

roan cloth, a kind of linen made at Rouen.

rowbarge, a small oared warship (16th century).

royal of plate, see real of plate above.

rude, untutored, barbarous.

rummage, v., to stow cargo or clean a ship thoroughly.

St. Laurence, island of, believed to be Madagascar.

seron, "a bale or package of exotic products (such as almonds cocoa) made up from an animal's hide" (*SOED*).

shallop, a small, sleek cruising warship in the 16th century.

shift, v. to change clothes.

sith, sithens, since.

sleeveless, useless.

sodden, boiled.

sort (of files), a number of different kinds.

span, approximately nine inches.

spend, v., to lose (as a mast, etc).

spoiled, despoiled, pillaged.

states, men of importance.

stead, help.

stirk, a young bullock or heifer.

stock, the crossbar of an anchor.

stone bow, a kind of crossbow or catapult for shooting stones (*SOED*).

success, fortune, either good or bad.

suckets, fruits preserved in syrup or candied.

sumach, a preparation used in tanning or dyeing leather.

swimmer (of a fish), a dorsal fin.

tabard, a surcoat bearing the arms of the wearer or his lord.

tables, pictures, flat surfaces.

tack, 1. to shift tack or go about, to turn into the wind and so onto the opposite tack; 2. to beat to windward by successive tacks.

tally, an accounting device, usually a notched stick or note recording a sum of money owed.

target, shield.

tierce, one third.

towardly, promising.

trade, trail, footprints, tread.

trajín, the portage of Spanish treasure across the isthmus of Panama to Nombre de Díos, a trap for catching wild animals, a decoy, a snare.

troterro, a messenger.

tuberones, sharks.

turkey, turquoise.

turnout, to launch a ship.

twelve tide, the twelve days of Christmas.

unstocked (of an anchor), without a crossbar.

utter, 1. outer; 2. to offer for sale, to sell.

utterance, sale.

vail, v. to go down stream with the tide.

victual, v., to provide good and drink for a ship or the navy; n. good and drink.

waft, v. 1. to beckon; 2. to wave something as a signal; 3. to protect a convoy of merchant ships (16th century).

want, mole.

warp, 1. to tow a ship with boats; 2. to move a ship by hauling on warps to make fast to shore.

watchet, light or sky blue.

weatherly, (of a ship) tending to drift little to leeward when close-hauled.

wood, mad.

worm, snake, serpent, dragon.

zabra, a small vessel used off the coasts of Spain and Portugal (*SOED*).

Zeilan, (Ceylon) Sri Lanka.

Zocotoro, Socotra.

Select Bibliographical Essay and Suggested Reading ⅍

Abbreviations:

BL   British Library

DNB   *Dictionary of National Biography*

MS   Manuscript

Manuscripts

The handwritten and printed manuscripts of the British Library, the Guildhall Library, The Caird Library at the National Maritime Museum, and the National Archives in London, as well as those at the Archivio de Indias in Seville, Spain, and Folger Shakespeare Library in Washington, D.C., have formed the crux of my original research.

From the British Library, the most useful manuscripts were Titus B XIII and MS 48015 relating to Ireland. Harleian MSS 168, 398, 598, 1546, 1877 and 6990; Lansdowne MSS 14, 16, 26, 113 [Burghley papers] and 43 [regarding Spain]; Additional MS 33,271; 11405; 33592, 36316; 36317; Egerton 2541; Sloane MSS 1786, 2292, 3289; Titus F I and Titus 107/46; Caligula C, II relating to English affairs were essential reading. Cotton Ortho VIII; Stowe 303; and Tiberius D VIII relating to the adventurers and the Turkey/Levant Company were indispensable; Cotton Galba B, XI; Cotton Galba D; Additional MSS 12497; 12503; 12504; 28,702 and 28,357 regarding relations with Spain were particularly useful. Stowe 159 relating to Portugal made fascinating reading, too.

From the National Archives, I relied heavily on the State Papers pertaining to Spain, Ireland, and the Low Countries, with the most helpful documents being SP 43 [English adventurers against Spain]; SP 12/78, 12/3, 12/7, 12/12 [Elizabeth's reign]; SP46/16, SP46/17, SP46/27, SP 941 [relating to Spain]; SP 94 [Walsingham's spies]; SP 84/4, 5, 6, 7, 8, 9, 10 [the Dutch Revolts]; and SP 99 [proclamations to pirates].

From the Archivio de Indias I found the testimonies contained in the manuscripts *Justicia* 908, Indiferente General 742, 1866 and the Casa de Contratacion 5109, 5110 illuminating.

At the Folger Shakespeare Library the most helpful original manuscripts were MS V.a. 197, L.d. 66; L.d. 406; L.d. 403; L.d. 483; L.b. 516; V.b. 142 [Ireland], x.d. 200 [victualing] and L.d. 612. The printed manuscript DA. 35089, representing a collection of state papers for the Tudor children's reigns, edited by Samuel Haynes (London, 1740), was also useful.

From the Caird Library at the National Maritime Museum, Samuel Purchas's *Purchas His Pilgrims,* vols. 1–2 (Glasgow, 1905), Sebastian Cabot's *Memoirs* and Philip Barbour (ed.), *The Complete Works of Captain John Smith,* vol. 1 (Chapel Hill, 1986), were my primary sources.

General

I have also relied on the *Calendar of State Papers—Spain*, vols. 1–4, Martin A. S. Hume (ed.); *Rome*, vols. 1–2, J. M. Rigg (ed.) (1926); *Venice*, vols. 7–9, R. Brown and H. Brown (eds.) (London, 1890-1894); *Foreign*, Joseph Stevenson (ed.) (London, 1865-1870) and *Foreign*, Allan James Crosby (ed.) (London, 1871–1895). R. B. Wernham was the editor for the years 1596 until the end of Elizabeth's reign. *The Calendar of State Papers—Scotland*, vols. 1–2, Joseph Bain (ed.) (Edinburgh, 1898); *Ireland*, 8 vols., H. C. Hamilton (ed.) (London, 1877) and E. G. Atkinson (ed.) (London, 1885–1903); *Colonial*, vol. 1; and *Domestic*, vols. 1–3, Mary Anne Everett Green (ed.) (London, 1867–1870). These State Papers, as well as the *Acts of the Privy Council*, J. R. Dasent (ed.) (London, 1886–1900), all were exceptionally valuable in increasing my understanding of the fears and diplomacy of the time, as well as in discerning Elizabeth's true motivations—but frequently, when read in juxtaposition with one another (for example, by cross-referencing the same incident in three or more of the calendars, a different image would emerge than from reading a certain ambassador's report to his king). All proved fascinating reading, particularly in relation to the growing concerns about English piracy, and putting these into context with the piratical acts of other nations.

The works of Richard Hakluyt, and in particular his *Principall Navigations* (London, 1598) in 26 volumes, gave clarity to the main voyages during Elizabeth's long reign.

I found the works of Kenneth R. Andrews—*Trade, Plunder & Settlement: Maritime Enterprise and the Genesis of the British Empire 1480–1630* (Cambridge, 1999), *The Spanish Caribbean* (London, 1978), *Elizabethan Privateering: English Privateering During the Spanish War 1585–1603* (Cambridge, 1964), *The Elizabethan Seaman* (Mariner's Mirror, 69, London, 1982), and *Ships, Money & Politics* (Cambridge, 1991)— illuminating, fun, and essential reading. N. A. M. Rodger's *The Safeguard of the Sea* (London, 2004) was both invaluable and reliable, and could hardly be considered a secondary source. Michael Oppenheim's *A History of the Administration of the Royal Navy and Merchant Shipping in Relation to the Navy* (London, 1896); the six-volume *Sir William Monson's*

Tracts by Sir William Monson (London, 1625); Richard Hakluyt's *Fighting Merchantman* (1927 printed edition) and his *Elizabethan Adventurers upon the Spanish Main* (1912 printed edition) were equally core sources. Without the fabulous groundbreaking (though now in parts somewhat out of date) work of Julian S. Corbett in his *Drake and the Tudor Navy* (Aldershot, England, 1988 Centenary reprint of vols. 1–2 of 1888) and his *Successors of Drake* (London, 1900), I would have undoubtedly had to dig much harder.

For general accounts and understanding how commerce worked, H. S. Cobb (ed.), *Corporation of London Records Office—The Overseas Trade of London: Exchequer Customs Accounts* (London, 1990); R. R. Sharpe (ed.), *Calendar of Letter Books Preserved Among the Archives of the City of London*, 11 vols. (London, 1899–1912); *Calendar of MSS Marquis of Salisbury*, 18 vols. (London, 1883); C. M. Clode (ed.), *Memoirs of the Merchant Taylors' Company* (London, 1875); *Accounts for the Merchant Taylors' Company* (London, 1875); Victor van Klarwill (ed.), *The Fugger News-letters: Second Series* (London, 1926); Henry Machlyn's *The Diary of Henry Machlyn, Citizen and Merchant Taylor of London* (J. G. Nichols, ed.) (London, 1848); John Wheeler's *A Treatise on Commerce* (London, 1601); William of Orange's *A Discourse Consisting of Motives for the Enlargement and Freedom of Trade* (London, 1645), and Dudley Digges (ed.), *The Compleat Ambassador* (London, 1655) proved invaluable.

For Spanish sources, I widely consulted Irene A. Wright's translations of original Spanish papers in *Documents Concerning English Voyages to the Spanish Main 1569–1580*, vol. 1 (London, 1932); J. Calvar Gross (ed.), *La Batalia del Mar Océano: Génesis de la Empressa de Inglaterra de 1588*, vol. 1 (Madrid, 1988); and Geoffrey Parker's *The Grand Strategy of Philip II* (New Haven, 2000), as well as *The Dutch Revolt* (London, 2002). I also referred to the *Archivio de Indias* in Seville, the *Legajos* from the *Casa de Contratacion* 5109, 5110; *Justicia* 908; the *Indiferente General* 742, 1866; Panama 44, 45; and Santo Domingo 15, 51, 73, 81, 129, 184, and 186. In addition, I found Andrew Wheatcroft's *The Hapsburgs* (London, 2004) fascinating reading.

Specific to the Low Countries, the works of Baron Kervyn de Lettenhove *Les Relations des Pays Bas et l'Angleterre*, vols. 1–4 of 11 volumes (Brussels, 1882) is equivalent to the Calendar of State Papers relating to English affairs for the period. John Stow's *Survey of London* (London, 1598) is a fabulous research tool. The French ambassador's letters expertly edited by A. Teulet, *Correspondance diplomatique de la Mothe Fénélon*, 7 vols. (Paris, 1838–1840), gives a different viewpoint that is illusive in English documents. Also, the *Correspondence du Cardinal de Granvelle 1565–1586*, 12 vols., E. Poullet and C. Piot (eds.) (Brussels, 1877-96) gave great insight.

Conyers Read's *Mr Secretary Cecil and Queen Elizabeth* (New York,

1955), *Mr Secretary Walsingham and the Policy of Queen Elizabeth*, vols. 1–3 (Oxford, 1925), *The Seizure of Alva's Payships* in the Mariner's Mirror (London, no. 21), *Lord Burghley and Elizabeth* (Oxford, 1925), and his *Walsingham and Burghley in Queen Elizabeth's Privy Council* in the English Historical Review (London, no. xxvii, January 1913) are essential reading. Susan Brigden's *New Worlds, Lost Worlds: The Rule of the Tudors 1485-1603* (London, 2001) provided a great overview of the period and helped to put me into the mind-set of the "ruling" Elizabethan classes (merchant and gentlemen adventurers or courtiers). John Guy's *Tudor England* (Oxford, 1990) remains essential Tudor reading. J. E. Neale's *Elizabeth I* (London, 2005 reprint) gives a highly readable overview of the queen and her dilemma regarding security, marriage, and Mary, Queen of Scots. Raphael Holinshed's *Chronicles of England, Scotland, Ireland* (London, 1577), though widely seen as historically inaccurate today, provides again a good understanding of the Elizabethan mind-set.

Finally, the two great national resources, *The Dictionary of National Biography* (Oxford, 2003) and the *Oxford English Dictionary* (Oxford, 1998–2003) were widely consulted online. I cross-referenced virtually every person I wrote about in the *DNB*, and checked my sixteenth century meanings in the *OED*, both of which I subscribe to online.

Introduction

I consulted original papers from the High Court of the Admiralty, H.C.A. 24, Letters of Marque, Bonds, etc., 3, 1585, as well as State Papers, SP 46/179/32-31; SP 46/180/59A; SP 46/179/36-38; SP 94/2/78, 100. J. H. Parry's *The Discovery of the Sea* (London, 1974) was most helpful in better understanding technical aspects of seamanship. Both Garett Mattingly's *Defeat of the Spanish Armada* (London, 1959) and Felipe Fernàndez-Armesto's *The Spanish Armada* (London, 2003) also provided source material. I also used the Folio Society's edition of Richard Hakluyt's *Tudor Venturers* (London, 1970).

Chapter 1. *The Lord's Doing*

Martin A. S. Hume (ed.), vol. 1 of the *Calendar of State Papers Relating to English Affairs with Spain* (London, 1892); Richard Starkey's *Elizabeth* (London, 2000); Simon Schama's *History of Britain* (London, 2000); and Geoffrey Parker's *The Grand Strategy of Philip II* (London, 1998) were the main sources for this introductory chapter. J. Denucé's original *Lettres Marchandes d'Anvers* (Brussels, 1961) was particularly helpful in my understanding of the concerns of everyday merchants in Antwerp at the time.

Chapter 2. A Realm Exhausted

Aside from the general sources mentioned above, and in particular all of the *Calendar of State Papers*, for the relevant years, and *Acts of the Privy Council*, R. B. Wernham's *Before the Armada* (1966) and *The Making of Elizabethan Foreign Policy 1558–1603* (1980) were particularly insightful; as was G. D. Ramsay's *The City of London in International Politics at the Accession of Elizabeth Tudor* (Manchester, 1964) and W. E. Lingelbach's *The Merchants Adventurers: Their Laws and Ordinances with Other Documents* (New York, 1971 edition).

Chapter 3. The Queen, Her Merchants and Gentlemen

Again, aside from the specific and general sources above as well as the relevant *Calendars* and *Acts of the Privy Council*, Benjamin Woolley's *The Queen's Conjurer* (New York, 2001), Richard Deacon's *John Dee: Scientist, Geographer, Astrologer and Secret Agent to Elizabeth I* (London, 1968), and Dee's own *Diaries* and *The Perfecte Arte of Navigation* (London, 1577) provided the basis of the information on Dee in this chapter and others. Regarding Thomas Gresham, I referred to J. W. Burgon's two- volume *The Life and Times of Sir Thomas Gresham* (London, 1839) and Raymond de Roover's *Gresham on Foreign Exchange* (Cambridge, USA, 1949), as well as Ann Saunders's (ed.) *The Royal Exchange London* (London, 1997). The best books on Sir Nicholas Bacon and his family are *The Golden Lads* by Daphne du Maurier (London, 1977), *The Winding Stair* (London, 1976) also by du Maurier, and especially Robert Titler's *Nicholas Bacon: The Making of a Tudor Statesman* (Athens, OH, 1976). J. A. Williamson's *The Cabot Voyages & Bristol Discovery Under Henry VIII* (London, 1962) helped, too, to put the pre-Elizabethan voyages of "discovery" into context. Derek Wilson's highly readable *Sweet Robin* (London, 1981) gives great insight into Robert Dudley's relationship with Elizabeth and the greater world.

Chapter 4. The Quest for Cash

On the value of English money at the time, and the effects of the debasement under Henry VIII, I consulted the definitive work by J. D. Gould, *The Great Debasement* (Oxford, 1970). In addition to naval texts mentioned above, Michael Oppenheim's *A History of the Administration of the Royal Navy, 1509–1660* sheds interesting light on the problems facing the country, though I relied more heavily upon N. A. M. Rodger's *Safeguard of the Sea* for the contents of this chapter, as well as appropriately dated *Calendars*, *APC*, letters from de Granvelle and Mothe Fénélon, and books on Gresham and Burghley.

Chapter 5. The Merchants Adventurers, Antwerp, and Muscovy
T. S. Willan's *Studies in English Foreign Trade* (London, 1959), and S. L. Thrupp's *The Merchant Class of Medieval London* (Chicago, 1948) supplemented W. E. Lingelbach's *The Merchant Adventurers of England* (New York, 1971), W. T. MacCaffrey's *The Shaping of the Elizabethan Regime 1558–72* (Princeton, 1968), and A. B. Beaven's two-volume book *The Aldermen of the City of London* (London, 1908–13). G. D. Ramsay's *City of London* and Kenneth Andrew's *Trade, Plunder & Settlement* were also consulted.

Chapter 6. The Politics of Piracy, Trade, and Religion
Geoffrey Parker's books on the interdiction of trade with England (*Grand Strategy of Philip II,* most especially) and the *Lettres* of Cardinal de Granvelle give the crux of the Spanish perspective here. I consulted, too, Julian Corbett's (ed.) *Naval Records Society Archives*, vols. I-XIII (London, 1898). F. C. Danvers's *The Portuguese in India* (London, 1894) and H. Stevens and G. Birdwood's (eds.) *The Dawn of Trade to the East Indies, 1599–1603* (London, 1886) provided background to the Portuguese position. J. W. Elliot's *The Old World and the New, 1492–1650* (Cambridge, 1972) was perceptive. Nick Hazlewood's *The Queen's Slave Trader* (New York, 2005) and Harry Kelsey's *Sir John Hawkins* (New Haven, 2003) are essential reading for anyone wanting to study John Hawkins.

Chapter 7. Raising the Stakes
All books previously used relating to the economy and naval matters, John Hawkins, the appropriately dated *Calendars* and *APC* were also used in this chapter. Also, I consulted G. D. Ramsay's *City of London*.

Chapter 8. Cunning Deceits
In this chapter, I used the aforementioned *Calendars* books relating to economics and politics, Elizabeth's and Philip II's strategies, John Hawkins, and Hakluyt's *Principall Navigations*. Additionally, I also consulted Dava Sobel's marvelous *Longitude* (London, 1998); vol. 8 of J. A. Froude's *History of England* (London, 1872); John Blake's *West Africa, Quest for God and Gold, 1454–1578* (London, 1977); and, of course, Julian Corbett's *Drake and the Tudor Navy* (Aldershot, England, 1988).

Chapter 9. The Gloves Are Off
Again, I used the appropriate *Calendars* and *APC* in this chapter. I also consulted C. Brady's *The Chief Governors of Ireland* (Dublin, 2004) and

his edition of *A Viceroy's Vindication* (Cork, 2002). Julian Corbett, Nick Hazlewood, and Harry Kelsey provided the detail on the Hawkins voyages.

Chapter 10. *Lovell's Lamentable Voyage*

Harry Kelsey's and Nick Hazlewood's Hawkins biographies formed the basis of this chapter, along with John Sugden's amazing biography *Sir Francis Drake* (London, 1996). I also consulted the original manuscripts listed above, regarding privateering.

Chapter 11. *The Troublesome Voyage of John Hawkins*

Original testimonies from the Inquisition contained in the Spanish-affairs manuscripts highlighted above, as well as Ortho E VIII formed the basis of this chapter. Richard Hakluyt's *Principall Navigations* was a core source. Kenneth Andrews's *The Spanish Caribbean*, N. Hazlewood's *The Queen's Slave Trader*, H. Kelsey's *Sir John Hawkins*, and J. Sugden's *Sir Francis Drake* were also used.

Chapter 12. *The Queen and Alba's Pay Ships*

I consulted the *Calendar of State Papers—Spain*, as well as Richard Hakluyt's *The Tudor Venturers* and J. Calvar Gross's (ed.) *La Batalla del Mar Océano* (Madrid, 1988), vols 1–3. Conyers Read's *Seizure of Alba's Payships* (Mariner's Mirror, London, no. 21, pp. 450–452) provides a succinct interpretation of the events. Charles Wilson's *Queen Elizabeth and the Revolt of the Netherlands* (London, 1970) was very useful, as was Geoffrey Parker's *The Grand Strategy of Philip II* (London, 1998). Julian Corbett's above referenced works were also used.

Chapter 13. *The Cost of Failure*

I consulted Spanish manuscripts, in particular AGI Patronato 265, containing eyewitness accounts and statements. I relied on John Hawkins's own *Troublesome Voyadge* (London, 1571), which recounts events of the 1568 voyage, as well as *Francis Drake Privateer*, John Hampden (ed.) (London, 1972), which incorporates Drake's own testimony from *Sir Francis Drake Revived*. In addition, I consulted English *Calendars* for the appropriate dates and E. Arber's (ed.) *An English Garner*, 10 vols. (London, 1903) was particularly useful.

Chapter 14. *Undeclared Holy War*

I referred to the same sources I used for Chapter 13, with the addition of J. S. Corbett's *Drake and the Tudor Navy* and the *Calendar* for Rome.

Chapter 15. *Drake's War*
MS Ashmole 830 from the Bodleian Library, John Sugden's *Sir Francis Drake*, Irene A. Wright's superb translation of *Documents Concerning English Voyages to the Spanish Main 1569–1580*, vol. 1 (London, 1973), and John Hampden's (ed.) *Francis Drake Privateer* were the main sources I consulted for this chapter. I also used *Calendars* and the other general histories outlined in the beginning of the bibliography.

Chapter 16. *The Dread of Future Foes*
In addition to consulting the *Calendars* for Rome and Spain, the English manuscripts I consulted included MS Cotton Caligula, C. III and MS Additional 30156. I checked the *DNB* for the biographies of those who appear in the chapter, and used Alan Stewart's highly readable *Philip Sidney, A Double Life* (London, 2004). On the queen and the Sea Beggars, I relied upon *The English Historical Review*, vol. XLVI 1931, "Queen Elizabeth, The Sea Beggars, and the Capture of Brill, 1572," in addition to Ellis's *Original Letters Illustrative of English History* (London, 1824). Raymond de Roover's *Gresham on Foreign Exchange* was also useful.

Chapter 17. *Drake at the Treasure House of the World,* and
Chapter 18. *From a Treetop in Darien*
All of the Drake biographies, and especially his own version of events, I relied upon heavily when working on this chapter. Additionally, Harry Kelsey's *Sir Francis Drake: The Queen's Pirate* (New York, 1998) was also useful.

Chapter 19. *Success at a Cost*
I relied on all the Drake biographies again here, as well as Julian Corbett's *Drake and the Tudor Navy*, and my book, *The Sancy Blood Diamond* (New York, 2004), specifically relating to previous research regarding Drake, Queen Elizabeth, and Dom Antonio of Portugal. Kenneth R. Andrew's *Trade, Plunder & Settlement* proved invaluable.

Chapter 20. *Dr. Dee's Nursery and the Northwest Passage*
Few of us today appreciate just how pivotal Dr. John Dee was to the exploration process. This becomes quite apparent in this chapter through his own writings in his *Private Diaries* (London, 1842 reprint) and *The British Monarchy or General & Rare Memoria* (London 1577), in which his treatise on the *Petty Navy Royal* first appears. Benjamin Woolley's *The Queen's Conjurer* and Nicholas Crane's exceptional *Mercator* (London, 2003) are gripping and wonderful reads, and I used them both in this chapter. I referred to George Beste's *A True*

Discourse of the Late Voyages of Martin Frobisher . . . (London, 1578), as well as Hakluyt's *Principall Navigations* and the Exchequer E351 State Papers.

Chapter 21. Dark Days at Rathlin Island

The Drake biographies (particularly Sugden), Sir Henry Sidney's *A Viceroy's Vindication*, C. Brady (ed.), and C. Brady's *The Chief Governors of Ireland* were my prime sources here. MS Additional 48015 and SP 63/51 and 63/54 (Ireland) were also useful. *The Correspondence of Sir Philip Sidney and Hubert Languet*, S. A. Pears (ed.) (London, 1845) was also illuminating.

Chapter 22. Drake's Perfect Timing

Drake's own account in *Sir Francis Drake Revived* forms the primary source for this chapter. Derek Wilson's *Sweet Robin*, about Robert Dudley, Earl of Leicester; Harry Kelsey's *Sir John Hawkins*; John Sugden's *Sir Francis Drake,* and Kenneth R. Andrews's *Trade, Plunder & Settlement* were used to corroborate some of Drake's assertions. Also BL MS Lansdowne 113, and John Dee's *A Petty Navy Royal* were integral parts of my research. I also referred to Thomas Greepe's account *The True and Perfect News of the Worthy and Valiant Exploits Performed and Done by That Valiant Knight, Sir Francis Drake* (London, 1587).

Chapter 23. The Northwest and the Company of Kathai

George Best's original *A True Discourse of the Late Voyages of Martin Frobisher . . .* was my primary source for this chapter. The appropriately dated *Calendar of State Papers—Domestic* and *Colonial* were also useful. I relied upon Richard Hakluyt's *Principall Navigations* and Andrews's *Trade, Plunder & Settlement*, too.

Chapter 24. In the Shadow of Magellan

The chapter in Samuel Taylor Coleridge's *More Light on Drake* (London, 1907), which in turn was based on Robert Winter's June 1579 report, was one source here. However, John Sugden's *Sir Francis Drake*, *Monson's Tracts,* J. Calvar Gross's *La Batalla del Mar Oceáno*, and N. A. M. Rodger's *Safeguard of the Sea* were my primary sources. Some of these sources relied heavily, in turn, on W. S. W. Vaux, *The World Encompassed* (London, 1628).

Chapter 25. Into the Jaws of Death

I consulted all of the Drake biographies here in order to determine a consensus of the actual events.

Chapter 26. The Famous Voyage

La Batalla del Mar Océano, which is a Spanish Calendar of State Papers, provides illuminating reading, and it was fascinating to see what the Spanish were or were not able to glean about Drake's circumnavigation. In today's age we often lose sight of truly historic events accomplished by the grit and determination of one man, and Drake's circumnavigation—though still appreciated by mariners everywhere—seems somehow not to be earth-shattering in the twenty-first century. I consulted all books relating to the period here, in particular the Drake biographies, Drake's own account in *The World Encompassed*, and de Herrera's *Historia General de Mundo* (Madrid, 1606). For reasons that were apparent in the book, this had to remain a secret.

Chapter 27. The World Is Not Enough

I referred to the *Calendar* of Spanish and Domestic State Papers—*Spain* and *Domestic* for the relevant years, but Julian Corbett's insight from *Drake and the Tudor Navy*, as well as the Drake biographies, made up the core of my research for this chapter. The *La Batalla del Mar Océano* also provided further insight.

Chapter 28. Elizabeth Strikes Back in the Levant

I say in this chapter that Elizabeth (as other monarchs in her time and after) held a copy of Niccolò Machiavelli's *The Prince* and his *Discourses* in her library. These would have both been essential reading for any ruler, and remained in print as Penguin Classics to this day. Hakluyt's *Principall Navigations*, S. A. Skilliter's *Harborne* (London, 1977), and Kenneth Andrews's *Trade, Plunder & Settlement* provided the core of my research for this chapter, double-checked against their own sources and the State Papers highlighted above.

Chapter 29. Katherine Champernowne's Sons Take Up the American Dream

When it comes to the early colonization of America, David B. Quinn is the acknowledged expert. His books—*England and the Discovery of America, 1481–1620* (London, 1974), *European Approaches to North America, 1450–1640* (Aldershot, 1998), *Some Spanish Reactions to Elizabethan Colonial Enterprise* (London, 1976), *The First Colonists* (London, 1978), *Ralegh and the British Empire* (London, 1973)—were extremely useful to this and subsequent chapters, with his *Ralegh and the British Empire* being the most widely quoted. Anna Beer's highly readable *Bess: The Life of Lady Ralegh* (London, 2003) gives an unusual insight into Raleigh, and especially his long-suffering wife. Of course the requisite Calendars and manuscripts also formed part of my research. In addition, I consulted D. B. Chidsey's *Sir Humphrey Gilbert, Elizabeth's Racketeer* (New York, 1932), Benjamin Dutton's *Navigation and Nautical Astronomy* (Annapolis, 1951), Richard Hakluyt's *Divers Voyages Touching on the Discovery of America* (London, 1598), A. L. Rowland's *Studies in English Commerce and Exploration* (London, 1924), and J. E. D. Williams's *From Sails to Satellites, the Origin and Development of Navigational Science* (Oxford, 1992).

Chapter 30. The Defeats of 1582–84

I had previously written about the Dutch Revolt as part of *The Sancy Blood Diamond*, and so much of my background research was based on those sources. In addition, the John Sugden biography *Sir Francis Drake* and Harry Kelsey's *Sir John Hawkins* proved useful too. Spanish State Papers in *Justicia* 908 were also part of my core research.

Chapter 31. Water!

All D. B. Quinn's works formed my primary research for this chapter, as well as the collection of *The Letters of Sir Walter Ralegh*, Agnes Latham and Joyce Youings (eds.) (London, 2001). Richard Hakluyt's *Virginia Voyages* (London, 1973) and Derek Wilson's *Sweet Robin* (London, 1981) were also useful.

Chapter 32. Roanoke

E. G. R. Taylor's *Writings of the Hakluyts*, 2 vols. (London, 1935); Charles Deane's (ed.) *Discourse on Western Planting* (London, 1877); R. B. Wernham's *The Making of Elizabethan Foreign Policy* (Berkeley, 1980); Kenneth Andrews's *Trade, Plunder & Settlement*; D. B. Quinn's *Ralegh and the British Empire*; Richard Hakluyt's *Virginia Voyages*; and Giles Milton's highly informative and readable *Big Chief Elizabeth* (London, 2000) were all source material for this chapter.

Chapter 33. The Queen Lets Loose Her Dragon

I referred to the same sources I used in chapter 32, with the addition of David Loade's *The Tudor Navy* (Aldershot, 1992), which is a long overdue update of Julian Corbett's great work *Drake and the Tudor Navy*. I also widely consulted Geoffrey Parker's *The Grand Strategy of Philip II*, John Sugden's *Sir Francis Drake*, and the *Calendar of State Papers*.

Chapter 34. The Camel's Back

My *Sancy Blood Diamond* and its sources, as well as Garrett Mattingly's timeless *The Defeat of the Spanish Armada* (London, 1959) were my primary sources for this chapter.

Chapter 35. Cadiz

There were so many different accounts of the Cadiz expedition that I felt it wisest to revert to original sources here, then double-check against trustworthy secondary sources. I consulted the relevant *Calendars of State Papers—Spain* and *Venice*, as well as SP 12/193; BL MS Cotton Otho E VIII; BL MS Cotton Vespasian, CVIII; and the books mentioned throughout chapter 35.

Chapter 36. The Plundering of the Spanish Armada

I reviewed Julian Corbett's *The Spanish War* for this chapter and subsequent chapters. J. K. Laughton (ed.), *State Papers Relating to the Defeat of the Spanish Armada*, vol. 1 (London, 1898) carries a huge number of original letters and orders. N. A. M. Rodger's *Safeguard of the Sea*, Kenneth Andrews's *Trade, Plunder & Settlement,* R. Wernham's *The World Before Armada*, and of course Garrett Mattingly's *The Defeat of the Spanish Armada* were also primary research sources. R. W. Kenny's biography *Elizabeth's Admiral*, about Lord Admiral Charles Howard (Baltimore, 1970), also provided great background material, and is highly readable.

Chapter 37. America Again . . . and Again?

Raleigh's *The Letters of Sir Walter Ralegh*, Agnes Latham and Joyce Youings (eds.); D. B. Quinn's *Ralegh and the British Empire*; Kenneth Andrews's *Trade, Plunder & Settlement*; Richard Hakluyt's *Principall Navigations*; T. S. Willan's *Studies in Foreign Trade* (London, 1959); A. L. Rowse's *Sir Richard Grenville of the* Revenge (London, 1937) and *The Elizabethans and America* (London, 1959); and Giles Milton's *Big Chief Elizabeth* were my main sources used in this chapter.

Chapter 38. The Last Gasp of the Early Roaring '90s

All the books I used in chapters 36 and 37 I used in this chapter, too. Additionally, I consulted Julian Corbett's *Successors of Drake* and his edition of *Papers Relating to the Spanish War*. The *Calendar of State Papers—Venice* was particularly useful, providing an "unbiased" view of the rampant English adventuring. D. Akenson's Talmudic *An Irish History of Civilization*, vol. 1 (London, 2005) provides a fascinating insight into the English in Ireland, incorporating a tremendously innovative, highly entertaining style.

Chapter 39. The Alchemy That Turned Plunder into Trade

All books used in the previous four chapters were again primary sources for this chapter. Additionally, Kenneth Andrews's *The Elizabethan*

Seaman; Michael Oppenheim's *A History of the Administration of the Royal Navy*; the *DNB* entry on Robert Cecil; Lord Burghley's *Advice to a Son*, Louis Wright (ed.) (New York, 1961); J. W. Shirley's *The Scientific Experiments of Sir Walter Ralegh: The Wizard Earl and the Three Magi in the Tower, 1603–1617* (London, 1949); A. Tenenti's *Naufrages, Corsaires et Assurances Maritimes à Venise, 1592–1609* (Paris, 1959); and V. M. Shillington's and A. B. W. Chapman's *The Commercial Relations of England and Portugal* (New York, 1970) proved extremely useful. R.W. Kenny's *Elizabeth's Admiral*, Kenneth Andrews' *Elizabethan Privateering and Trade, Plunder & Settlement*, and N. A. M. Rodger's *Safeguard of the Sea* were also widely used and often quoted.

Chapter 40. Essex, Ireland, and Tragedy

The *DNB* entries for Robert Devereux, 2nd Earl of Essex, and Hugh O'Neill were useful, though it was D. Akenson's *An Irish History of Civilization* that I found the most refreshing. Original manuscripts from the Folger Shakespeare Library (especially FSL, MS V.b.214) and the British Library's MS Additional 74287 were also useful. The relevant *Calendars of State Papers—Ireland*, *Spain*, and *Domestic* papers were also source material. Finally, G. R. Elton's *England Under the Tudors* (London, 1993) provided me with an overview.

Chapter 41. Raleigh, Virginia, and Empire

Again here, D. B. Quinn's books proved invaluable, particularly *Ralegh and the British Empire*. *The Letters of Sir Walter Ralegh*, by Agnes Latham and Joyce Youings (eds.) were incredibly helpful, too.

Chapter 42. The East and the East India Company

John Keay's *The Honourable Company* (London, 1993) was a prime source for this chapter, as well as James Lancaster's *Voyages to Brazil and the East Indies, 1591–1603*, W. Foster (ed.) (London, 1943); E. M. Jacobs, *In Pursuit of Pepper and Tea* (London, 1996); *Calendar of State Papers— Colonial* (vol. 1); W. Foster's *England's Quest of Eastern Trade* (London, 1933); *East India Company: The Dawn of British Trade to the East Indies . . . 1599-1603*, Steven and Birdwood (eds.); and K. N. Chaudhuri's essential tome, *The English East India Company 1600-1640* (London, 1945).

Index

LECTURES ON
THE RELIGION OF THE SEMITES

THE LIBRARY
OF
BIBLICAL STUDIES

Edited by

Harry M. Orlinsky

LECTURES ON
THE RELIGION OF
THE SEMITES

THE FUNDAMENTAL INSTITUTIONS

BY THE LATE

WILLIAM ROBERTSON SMITH, M.A, LL.D.

SIR THOMAS ADAMS'S PROFESSOR OF ARABIC IN THE UNIVERSITY OF CAMBRIDGE

THIRD EDITION

WITH AN INTRODUCTION AND ADDITIONAL NOTES

BY

STANLEY A. COOK, Litt.D.

FELLOW OF GONVILLE AND CAIUS COLLEGE, CAMBRIDGE
UNIVERSITY LECTURER IN HEBREW AND ARAMAIC

PROLEGOMENON BY

JAMES MUILENBERG

KTAV PUBLISHING HOUSE, Inc.
1969

FIRST PUBLISHED 1927

Library of Congress Catalog Card Number: 69-11428
Manufactured in the United States of America

CONTENTS

CONTENTS

CONTENTS

NOTES TO THE THIRD EDITION

PROLEGOMENON

The second half of the nineteenth century was a period of widespread intellectual and cultural ferment. It found expression not only in the fields of philosophy and the natural sciences, but also in the social and historical disciplines and in the study of religion in its diverse phenomenological and confessional manifestations. The thinking of the time was not infrequently dominated by the philosophy of Hegel (1770-1831), particularly by his delineation of the structures and patterns of history; by the positivism of August Comte (1798-1857), and by the evolutionary theories of Charles Darwin (1809-1882) and Herbert Spencer (1820-1903). It was during this period that cultural anthropology achieved the status of a major academic discipline, thanks to the labors, above all, of Edward B. Tylor, whose two volumes on *Primitive Culture* (1871) marked an epoch in the history of the study of primitive folkways and religion. Not unrelated to Tylor's work were the sociological and ethnological researches of Sir James Frazer (1854-1941), whose monumental work on *The Golden Bough* extended the study of primitive religion to the whole of antiquity, of the French School, whose most eminent representatives were Émile Durkheim (1858-1917) and Lévy-Bruhl (1857-1939), and, not least of all, Max Weber (1864-1920) in Germany. The comparative methodology reflected

1

in all these works had been anticipated to a degree by the
monograph of John Spencer, Master of Corpus Christi College in Cambridge, on *De legibus Hebraeorum ritualibus
et earum rationibus* (1695) and Johann Gottfried von
Herder's *Vom Geist der Ebräischen Poesie* (1782-83), but
received fresh impetus in the investigations of Adolf Bas-
tian (1826-1905), who has sometimes been called the
founder of social anthropology, and of Albert Eichhorn
(1856-1926), whose influence was later reflected in the
writings of Hermann Gunkel, Hugo Gressmann, and others.
The comparative study of religion came to a head in the
two volumes of Wolf Wilhelm Baudissin (1847-1926), *Studien zur semitischen Religionsgeschichte* (1876-78).

Of particular importance for our present purpose was
the rise and development of historical criticism of the Old
Testament, most notably in the work of Julius Wellhausen
(1844-1918) whose great book *Prolegomena zur Geschichte Israels* (1878; English translation, *Prolegomena to the
History of Israel* 1885) has remained a classic to this day,[1]
and of the brilliant Dutch scholar, Abraham Kuenen
(1828-91).[2] Wellhausen had his predecessors in Karl H.
Graf (1815-69) and Eduard Reuss (1804-09) and others,
but his influence has always been primary. His work represented a radical departure from the traditional view of
the composition of the biblical materials and consequently
resulted in a radically different construction of the origin
and history of Israel's religion. He was ably supported by
many of his contemporaries—in Germany by such eminent
scholars as Bernhard Duhm, Bernhard Stade, Karl Budde,
Alfred Bertholet, and Karl Steuernagel; in England, by S.
R. Driver, John Skinner, T. K. Cheyne, G. Buchanan Gray,
A. B. Davidson, George Adam Smith, C. F. Burney, and
not least of all by W. Robertson Smith, who wrote the pref-

[1] Hans-Joachim Kraus, *Geschichte der historisch-kritischen Erforshung
des Alten Testaments von der Reformation bis zur Gegenwart*, Neukir-
chen, 1956, pp. 222-49.

[2] Simon J. De Vries, *Bible and Theology in the Netherlands*, Wagen-
ingen, 1968.

ace to the English edition of the *Prolegomena* (1885).
During the period from 1835 to 1885 the records of the
major peoples of the ancient Near East, notably those from
Egypt and Mesopotamia, were recovered and subjected to
intensive scrutiny. Adolf Erman composed his *Neuägyp-
tische Grammatik* in 1880, and Sir Flinders Petrie laid the
foundations for excavating technique on the basis of his
excavations at Naucratis (1884-85). A long succession of
scholars contributed to the field of cuneiform studies,
among them Friedrich Delitzsch, Heinrich Zimmern, and
Paul Haupt.[3]

It is within this cultural context that we are to understand and assess the academic career and scientific contributions of one of the most gifted, versatile, and creative
scholars of the period—William Robertson Smith. The
learning of the age exerted a cumulative effect upon his
fertile and many-faceted mind. Heir to the achievements
of his predecessors and early contemporaries, he was destined, in turn, to influence the course of biblical and Semitic studies in the generations succeeding his own. He could
count among his friends some of the foremost scholars of
his age, most notably Julius Wellhausen, Sir James Frazer,
and A. B. Davidson. But there were forces of another kind
that were to exert a fateful, even tragic influence upon
Robertson Smith—the theological situation in Scotland
during his lifetime.[4] The Church of Scotland was torn by
internal dissensions, and in 1843 the Free Church, the dis-
senting party, came into existence by ascribing to the Act
of Separation. Among the 396 ministers who broke with the
Church was William Pirie Smith, the father of William
Robertson, who had been for some time headmaster of a
prominent school in Aberdeen, but now accepted a call
from the two small parishes of Keig and Tough in Aber-

[3] W. F. Albright, *History, Archaeology, and Christian Humanism*, New
York, 1964, pp. 106-07, 130 ff.

[4] John Sutherland Black and George Chrystal, *The Life of William
Robertson Smith*, London, 1912; James B. Pritchard, "W. Robertson
Smith, Heretic," *Crozer Quarterly*, (1947), pp. 146-160.

deenshire. On November 8, 1846 William Robertson Smith was born. He was a frail child, but precocious. He did not attend school, but received instruction from his father until the time that he was to leave home for the university. It is reported of him that he mastered the Hebrew alphabet and was able to read the Hebrew words before the age of six.[5] His father was a rigid disciplinarian and taught the boy Latin and Greek, mathematics, and "rational conversation." At the unprecedented age of fifteen years (1861), he entered the University of Aberdeen, having won the Bursary Competition with a stipend of thirty pounds. In 1865 he was awarded the degree of Master of Arts and the Town Council Medal. In 1866 he entered New College, Edinburgh, where he studied under A. B. Davidson, Professor of Hebrew and Old Testament exegesis, who had published his great commentary on the Book of Job in 1862. He took young Robertson Smith under his wing and made a profound impression upon him, as he was to do in later years upon George Adam Smith and John Skinner. At the end of his first year at New College (1867) Robertson Smith went to Germany to study under Kamphausen, Köhler, and Lange at the University of Bonn. During this period he was deeply interested in physics.

His first teaching experience came in 1868-69 when he served as assistant to P. G. Tait, Professor of Physics at the University of Edinburgh. He wrote a number of articles on physics, but also on philosophy, theology, and biblical studies.[6] In the spring of 1869 he returned to Germany, this time to Göttingen, where he responded to the stimulating

---

[5] Black and Chrystal, pp. 11-12.

[6] Note *inter alia* his letters on "Newton and Hegel" in the *Edinburgh Courant*, December 29, 1869; January 18 and 21, 1870; his paper "On the Flow of Electricity in Conducting Surfaces," in *Proceedings of R.S.E.*, vol. II, 1870; "The Question of Prophecy in the Critical Schools of the Continent," *British Quarterly Review*, April, 1870. His lectures on the Nazirites, Habakkuk, and on the prophets were given in the same year.

influence of Albrecht Ritschl[7] but also pursued his interests in physics and mathematics. The year following his return to Scotland marked a turning point in his career. Professor Sachs, the occupant of the chair of Hebrew at the Free Church College at Aberdeen, died, and A. B. Davidson persuaded him to apply for the position and pressed his candidature. On May 25, 1870 he was elected to the chair of Oriental Languages and Old Testament exegesis. In the summer of 1872 he returned to Germany at the University of Göttingen where he studied Arabic poetry under the aegis of Paul de Lagarde. Here he was exposed again to higher criticism, as he had been before at Bonn and Edinburgh, and acquired many friends among his German colleagues.[8]

After teaching at Aberdeen for some six years (1870-76) the question of his orthodoxy was raised in the Free Church. He had contributed several articles to the ninth edition of the *Encyclopaedia Britannica,* among them one on "Bible," which scandalized the orthodox leaders of the church.[9] He was accused of heresy, and he asked for a formal trial when the General Assembly of the Church gave an adverse report on him. While the indictment was dropped at the time, he was harassed by charges of heresy for years, until in 1881 he was formally removed from his chair.[10] Shortly thereafter he became editor-in-chief of the

[7] Black and Crystal, *op. cit.,* p. 111: "His [Ritschl's] lectures were indeed the most important experience of the summer, and the beginning of a friendship to which they led is a landmark in the history of Smith's theological views even more important than the first impressions of the German school which he had received at Bonn in 1867."

[8] Black and Chrystal, pp. 146-153. Heinrich Ewald had already retired and was succeeded by de Lagarde. Robertson Smith visited other university centers such as Halle, Leipzig, and Dresden.

[9] For the numerous contributions to the ninth edition of the *Encyclopaedia Britannica,* during the years 1875-1888, see Black and Chrystal, *op. cit.,* pp. 620-24. The article on "Bible" was written in 1875.

[10] For a detailed report of the heresy trials, see Black and Chrystal, Chapters VI-X. See also J. B. Pritchard, *op. cit.,* pp. 150-58.

Encyclopaedia Britannica. He served in this capacity until
the completion of the work in 1888.

While Robertson Smith had defended himself eloquently
and courageously, and at times caustically, throughout the
long years of the heresy trials, the experience exacted great
physical and mental strain and no little inward grief from
a man of frail constitution and sensitive temper. But he
was sustained and buoyed up by the support he received
not only from the greatest scholars of his day, from men
like Wellhausen and Kuenen and others of similar stature,
but also from many of his own countrymen with whom he
always felt himself on terms of interior rapport and, what
is more, by many of the best minds of the Church.[11] Mass
meetings were held in his support, and he was invited to
give a series of popular lectures at Edinburgh and Glasgow. These were attended by large and enthusiastic audiences and were published under the title *The Old Testament in the Jewish Church* (first edition, 1881; second
edition, 1892). A second series followed in the next winter, this time on the prophets of Israel, and again with the
same enthusiastic response. The lectures were published
under the title *The Prophets of Israel and Their Place in
History to the Close of the Eighth Century* B. C. (first edition, 1882; second edition, 1885).[12] When President Eliot
of Harvard University learned of the verdict against Robertson Smith, he inquired through Lord Bryce whether he
would accept appointment to his institution.[13]

We have referred to Robertson Smith's studies in Arabic
under Lagarde at Göttingen (1872). Three years later he
himself offered a course in the subject to a small class of

---

[11] Black and Chrystal, 404 ff.

[12] Smith's work was a great classic for his time and belongs in the great
succession of those who have contributed most fruitfully to our under-
standing of the prophets: in Scotland scholars like A. B. Davidson,
George Adam Smith, John Skinner, and Adam Welch; in Germany,
Bernhard Duhm, *Theologie der Propheten* (1875) and his successors: C.
H. Cornill, Gustav Hölscher, Hermann Gunkel, and others.

[13] Black and Chrystal, pp. 340 ff., 406; J. B. Pritchard, pp. 155 f.

advanced students. But he was determined to gain a thorough mastery of the language. In the winter of 1878-79, during a lull in the heresy trial, he spent an enforced leave from his teaching by going to Cairo. Here he made rapid progress, and had time to visit some of the famous archaeological ruins in the neighborhood of the city. He also spent some time in visiting Palestine where he made friends among the people. The following year he returned to Egypt, and traveled extensively throughout the Middle East, spending some two months at Jeddah and visiting Palestine, Syria, Tunis, and southern Spain. He acquired an intimate knowledge of the literature of the Near East, but more especially a first-hand acquaintance with the manners and customs and daily life of the people. This experience was to stand him in good stead for his future work, both for his knowledge of the language and for his anthropological studies.

Throughout these years Robertson Smith continued to cultivate his intimate friendship with John Ferguson M'Lennan (1827-1881), who had contributed an article on "Law" to the eighth edition of the *Encyclopaedia Britannica* and had composed a monograph on *Inquiry into the Origin of Capture in Marriage Ceremonies,* better known as *Primitive Marriage* (1865) and *Studies in Ancient History* (1867). He had also contributed an essay on "The Worship of Plants and Animals" to *The Fortnightly Review* (1866) in which he supported the thesis that from earliest times and among widely separated races, animals were worshipped by tribes who were named after them and which were believed to belong to the same stock or breed as themselves.[14] M'Lennan's studies exerted a strong influence upon him. He had written a long letter to M'Lennan on totem warfare in Coptos and Tentyra, and on sorcery in the Old Testament.[15] But his first important contribution to

[14] Black and Chrystal, p. 369.
[15] *Ibid.,* pp. 143-45.

this field was his article on "Animal Worship and Animal Tribes among the Arabs and in the Old Testament," which was published in *Journal of Philology,* No. 17, June, 1880. Robertson Smith's interests had become increasingly directed to the comparative study of primitive customs and their meaning, which were to find expression first of all in his article on "Sacrifice" in the *Encyclopaedia Britannica,* but then later in the two major classical works on *Kinship and Marriage in Early Arabia* (1885) and *The Religion of the Semites* (first edition, 1889; second edition, 1894).

In view of his expulsion from his academic chair at Aberdeen and of his mastery of Arabic during the years of the long drawn out trials, it was Robertson Smith's good fortune to receive an appointment in 1883 as Lord Summoner's Professor of Arabic at the University of Cambridge. In 1885 he was elected to a professorial fellowship at Christ's College, and in 1886 he became university librarian. In 1889 he was appointed to the chair of Professor of Arabic. In 1888-91 he delivered the Burnett lectures on *The Religion of the Semites* at Aberdeen. His health was very precarious at the time. His last years were full of suffering, yet to the end he continued his labors and was particularly active in laying the groundwork for the *Encyclopaedia Biblica,* which he had hoped to edit. This was unfortunately denied him, but when the work appeared under the aegis of John Sutherland Black, his intimate friend and biographer, and T. K. Cheyne, it was appropriately dedicated to him. He died at Cambridge at the age of forty-eight on March 31, 1894 and was buried at his birthplace at Keig.

William Robertson Smith lived on in the life of his pupils, among whom he could count such eminent scholars as A. A. Bevan, F. C. Burkitt, R. H. Kennett, Norman McLean, and S. A. Cook. Without question he was one of the foremost scholars of his generation. He vindicated the right of free and untrammeled critical historical inquiry of the Old Testament scriptures. He was a man of great originality with an almost encyclopaedic range of knowledge and astonishing brilliance. The General Assembly of the Church, which had pronounced him a heretic during his lifetime, adopted a formal resolution at his death:[16]

> His brilliant career as a student, distinguished alike in classics, in science, and in philosophy, and the rapid steps by which he advanced to a foremost place among the Biblical scholars of Europe, are still fresh in the memory of the Church and of the community. His intellectual energy and industry, his quick apprehension, his singular command of his varied knowledge, along with a rare power of clear and felicitous expression, combined to rank him among the most remarkable men of his time.

His numerous contributions to the ninth edition of the *Encyclopaedia Britannica* reveal not only the range of his intelligence, but also his precision and competence along a wider frontier. His study of the prophets continued for many years to be a classic. But surely not least of his achievements was his research into what we may appropriately style cultural anthropology, to which he made a singularly illuminating contribution, above all in his Burnett lectures on *The Religion of the Semites*. Its limitations have often been pointed out by later scholars, but he would have been among the first to recognize the defects in his work. In the context of his own time, he loomed large as a commanding figure. Moreover, it is not impossible that in certain respects his work may serve as a corrective to some of the excesses of our time.

In April, 1887 the Burnett Trustees of the University of Aberdeen issued an invitation to Robertson Smith to deliver three courses of lectures on "the primitive religions of the Semitic peoples, viewed in relation to other ancient religions, and to the spiritual religion of the Old Testament

---

[16] Black and Chrystal, p. 560.

and Christianity." The subject was congenial to him because it provided him the opportunity to bring together in
orderly and coherent fashion the results of many years of
study and research and, more particularly, to bring his anthropological studies to bear upon the literature and religion of the Old Testament. Indeed, all of his previous
investigations seemed somehow to converge upon this
momentous task. Without any understanding of the development and growth of the Old Testament records and a
proper recognition of their temporal sequence such an undertaking would have been impossible. More than any other
scholar of his time he had made the achievements of the
Wellhausen school familiar in Great Britain, most notably
by his appreciative preface to the *Prolegomena to the History of Israel*,[17] and by his early work on *The Old Testament in the Jewish Church*. In the former work Wellhausen
had studied the religious institutions of Israel in a thorough
and penetrating manner from the data provided only by
the Old Testament; Robertson Smith was to center his interest upon Israel's institutions also, but in the context of
Semitic religion in general. In another way his work bore
affinities with Wellhausen's. In the third volume of his
Skizzen und Vorarbeiten, on *Reste arabischen Heidentumes*
(1887), Wellhausen had made a detailed study of the
religious conceptions of the Arabs, gathering together for
the first time all the remains of primitive beliefs in the surviving Arabic literature. Robertson Smith was similarly
interested in primitive Arabian religion and worship,
though his stress was quite different from Wellhausen's. For
him "religion was a part of the organized social life into
which a man was born and to which he conformed through
life in the same unconscious way in which men fall into

[17] Cf. pp. ix-x: "The reader will find that every part of the *Prolegomena*
is instinct with historical interest, and contributes something to a vivid
realization of what Old Israel really was, and why it has so great a
part in the history of spiritual faith . . . Here the reader will learn how
close are the bonds that connect the critical study of the Old Testament
with the deepest and unchanging problems of living faith."

any habitual practice of the society in which they live."[18] Wellhausen laid greater emphasis upon the individual and upon spontaneity.

Robertson Smith's previous work on "Animal Worship and Animal Tribes among the Arabs and in the Old Testament" (see above), his important study on *Kinship and Marriage in Early Arabia* (1885), and his article on "Sacrifice" in the *Encyclopaedia Britannica* equipped him to an exceptional degree for his fresh undertaking. He was indebted to others besides Wellhausen. He paid tribute to John Spencer's work, to which we have already made reference, and especially to his contemporary, M'Lennan, whose monograph on marriage had stimulated his own work on *Kinship and Marriage in Early Arabia*. He was indebted also to E. B. Tylor, the social anthropologist, whose interests coincided much with his own, and, above all others in this area, to Sir James Frazer, who was quick to recognize his own indebtedness to Robertson Smith. He had profited from Lagarde in his Arabic studies. His travels in the Near East had given him such a mastery of spoken Arabic that he could speak it fluently, and, what is more, an unusually intimate contact with the life of the people. All of these influences played a role in the preparation for the *Lectures on the Religion of the Semites*. But there was another force which made itself felt in the lectures, *viz.*, Robertson Smith's personality. He was open and receptive to all that he saw about him in his journeys in Arabia. He came to know the common people intimately. He not only mastered their language, but was also a keen observer of their customs, practices, and religious rites. One of the most impressive features of his work is the extraordinary detail of his discussion, teeming, as it does, with innumerable concrete first-hand observations. This is quite consistent with the burden of his thought: "it is of the first importance to realize clearly from the outset that ritual and practical

[18] *Lectures on the Religion of the Semites: the Fundamental Institutions.* Third edition, 1927, p. 21.

usage were, strictly speaking, the sum-total of ancient religions" (p. 20). While Robertson Smith from his earliest years had a keen interest in theology,[19] it is as an anthropologist and a student of comparative religion that he speaks. It is probable that his third series of lectures were devoted to theological concerns, but the first two series have quite another character. He was the first to apply the anthropological approach to the study of the Old Testament, and it was his design to view the Old Testament in the context of the ancient Semitic religion that he believed to lie behind it and to accompany its early stages.

Robertson Smith sets out at once to delineate the purpose and design of his lectures. He is not concerned to give an account of the religions that have a Semitic origin, but rather of "Semitic religion as a whole in its common features and general type" (p. 1). He seeks to gain an insight into that sphere of Semitic culture which will cast maximum light upon the religion of ancient Israel. Originally the Semites represented a clearly defined linguistic and ethnic unity, a cultural homogeneity, and a geographical region determined by the limits of the Arabian Peninsula, which Smith assumed to be the original home of all the Semitic peoples. The origins of the religions of these peoples he finds in the Arabs. It is among them that we encounter the most primitive forms of religion; in their records we see a reflection of nomadic mentality and the unchanging character of nomadic life. So he availed himself of the pre-Islamic literary records and the references to Semitic life and practice in the classical literature. The criticism that has been most frequently launched against *The Religion of the Semites,* present already in the first reviews of his work, is its neglect of the Babylonian and Assyrian sources. It is probable that he anticipated the objection, but he avers that the latter represent a relatively late stage of cultural and religious development. They reflect an established monarchical form of govern-

[19] James D. Smart, *The Interpretation of Scripture,* Philadelphia, 1961, pp. 39, 242.

ment, an organized pantheon, and an elaborate mythology. Mythology takes the place of dogma and belief. It was not an essential part of ancient religion and had no binding force upon the worshippers. It was only later that it acquired great importance. The ancient religions of the Babylonians and Assyrians presuppose a long period of social and religious growth. The Arabian sources, on the contrary, while admittedly late, preserve the primitive culture emanating from a much earlier age. We must not confuse *ancient* and *primitive*. Moreover, the Babylonians and Assyrians were not pure Semites; there was a strong infusion of early, non-Semitic culture in their veins, and their literature reflects cultural borrowing. In the light of our contemporary knowledge of the ancient Near Eastern peoples, much of this will sound precarious and alien, but it must be remembered that Near Eastern scholarship in the nineteenth century was poles removed from what it is today. Nevertheless, even in the time of Robertson Smith, voices were raised in protest against this neglect of the cuneiform monuments from Babylonia and Assyria. Be that as it may, the criticism does not invalidate all that Robertson Smith has to say; on the contrary, his work is a monument of scholarship, a great work for its own day and not without importance for our own. It is a vast storehouse of phenomenology of Arabian folkways and religion, and much of it is relevant to many Old Testament contexts, though, perhaps not to the degree assumed in a previous generation.

For a proper understanding of *The Religion of the Semites,* it is essential that we not only recognize its purpose or intention, but also that we take note of its methodology. The writer employs a vast canvas upon which to sketch or portray what he considers to be the primitive religion of the Semites, and he draws his materials from a vast variety of sources, both within the Semitic quadrilateral and outside it. He is at pains to stress again and again the unity which persists beyond all the diversities of the practices and rituals of the Semitic tribes. Like his contemporary, Tylor, he writes as an anthropologist and, like him and like Renan, Baudissin, Wellhausen, Sayce, M. J. Lagrange, and others before and after him, he is intent upon comparing the cultural and social phenomena that are common to all the Semitic tribes and even to the communities lying outside the orbit of the Arabian Peninsula. But more than that, after all has been said, it is a more specific and basic comparison that comes within his range of vision: the relation of primitive Semitic religion with the religion of the ancient Hebrews. The significance of Robertson Smith in the history of scholarship is that he belongs at one and the same time to the students of anthropology, to the pioneers of comparative religion, and to the company of those Old Testament scholars who, like B. Duhm, B. Stade, Karl Budde, and others, were among the first to compose a history of Israel's faith on the basis of historico-critical presuppositions.

We may press our inquiry into the methodology of the book more concretely and succinctly, especially since it emerges as the major topic of the opening lecture. When we undertake to gain a synoptic view of the entire work with its spacious panorama, is it possible to subsume the long and detailed discussion under a single rubric? The author is very clear and emphatic in his reply to our query. As we have had occasion to observe before, it is not with mythology that we are here first of all concerned, for, as the writer contends, mythology represents a developed stage in the history of religion. Nor is it with beliefs or doctrines that we have in the first instance to do, for they, too, are derivative. Primitive religion is not a system of beliefs with practical applications; rather it is a body of traditional practices which were the common possession of early society. What is essential in primitive religion is the proper observance of rites and customs, of rituals and cultic activities, obedience to which is regarded as piety and is believed to secure the favor of the gods. Rules of conduct antecede

general principles formulated in words. "Religious institutions are older than religious theories" (p. 20). In the popular religions of antiquity, all religious relationships are in-
extricably bound to fixed institutions, such as cult, sacrifice, and precedent. In a word, the methodology of the book
is to sketch the life history of early religious institutions,
to engage in an inquiry into "the religious institutions
which governed the lives of men of Semitic race" (p. 22).

It may be observed that this stress on institutions is not
remote from our contemporary study of the Old Testament,
as is illustrated, on the one hand, by such works as those of
Johannes Pedersen[20] and Roland de Vaux, O.P.,[21] and, on
the other, by the many studies of the religion and theology
of ancient Israel.

The fundamental principle and basic presupposition of
Semitic religion is the solidarity of the community. It is
not the family but the clan or tribe which is the elemental
social unit. The primary religious fact is the relationship
of the god and his worshippers. Together they form an
organic society, a single community of kinship. It is blood
relationship that determines the bond, not only between
members of the clan, but also between the members of the
clan and its god. Every clan has its own god, who is understood as its progenitor. The only bond which has binding
force, which unites men into a single social and cohesive
whole, is the community of blood. The ancient conception
of kinship is participation in one blood, which flows
through the veins of parent and child and through every
member of the clan or tribe. The relationship is therefore
viewed as physical, and this holds too for the relationship
between men and gods.

The god, as we have said, is the progenitor of the tribe
who lives on friendly and human terms with his descendants.
He is their protector against a common enemy and the
participant in all their fortunes. As their ancestor, he is con-

[20] *Israel: Its Life and Culture* I-II, Copenhagen, 1926; III-IV, 1940.
[21] *Ancient Israel: its Life and Institutions,* Translated by John McHugh,
New York, 1961.

cerned for their welfare and survival. According to the social organization of the particular clan, he is originally viewed as mother under the primitive matriarchate, later as father, as is illustrated in the *'ab* preformatives of proper names, such as Abiel, "el is my father," or Abibaal, "Baal is my father." The relationship of the father to his descendants is moral as well as physical, and it is here that we may discern the origin of ethics. It is not fear that motivates the minds of the worshippers of the clan, but rather reverence and loyalty. Robertson Smith, therefore, rejects the ancient dictum of Statius, *primus in orbe deos fecit timor,* commonly supported by the anthropologists of his day. In the religion of the Hebrews and in Christianity, the divine fatherhood is quite central, but it is completely dissociated from a physical relationship (cf. Hos. 11:1; Deut. 32:6). "Man was created in the image of God, but he was not begotten; God sonship is not a thing of nature, but a thing of grace" (p. 41). With the breaking of the old tribal system among the northern Semites, the idea of the divine descent was necessarily altered. The bonds which united them were not political, and the god was now no longer father but king. Yet the father-son kinship survived among the more eminent and influential families, who traced their origin to a common ancestor. But as king, he was addressed as lord, and his worshippers were his servants. Here too, we find the proper names illuminating: 'Abd-Eshmun, "servant of Eshmun," 'Abd Baal, 'Abd Osir, etc. This usage survives in not a few Old Testament contexts. Yahweh's worshippers are his servants, and Israel is his servant too. The idea is not so much one of authority or of slavery, but of allegiance and loyalty.

It is not surprising that in his discussion of Semitic religion Robertson Smith should give priority to the conception of *holiness.* More than any other term, holiness expresses the nature of what is uniquely divine. It is a *sui generis* word and manifests itself wherever and whenever men sense themselves to be in the presence of divinity. It

is at once the most important and most comprehensive
conception for the sacred. The writer is acutely aware of
the difficulties of definition, especially in relation to the
primitive materials that are at his disposal. He has little
to say of the sense of the numinous, so much stressed by
Rudolf Otto in his study on *The Idea of the Holy,* although
he does speak repeatedly of the sense of awe, reverence,
and dread of the worshippers. He takes as his starting
point the connection of the gods with certain places or areas.
In ancient religion, gods, like men, have a physical environment in and through which they act and manifest
themselves. The god has a natural life and a natural habitation which must not be violated or infringed upon. Originally holiness is entirely without ethical significance; it
has nothing to do with morality or purity of life. The activity and dominion of the gods are conceived as being
bound by certain physical limits; they have their abodes in
certain "holy places" or sanctuaries. Holy persons, things,
and times presuppose the existence of sacred areas where
men minister or celebrate. The basic conception underlying the conception of holiness is restriction or prohibition.
A holy place is one which is prohibited to common use.
The contrast between what is *common* and what is *holy* is
present in all primitive religion. The Hebrew root *ḥerem*
is an expression of this prohibition; it is that which is reserved or devoted to the god. The same idea is found in the
root חמי, which denotes a sacred enclosure protected from
encroachment (p. 150). Sanctuaries come into existence
and altars are erected where the divinity makes himself
known, as in the numerous theophanies preserved in the
Old Testament, especially in the patriarchal traditions. The
system of restrictions and the rules of holiness are expressed
by the Polynesian word *tabu.* To this subject Robertson
Smith devotes an extended discussion (pp. 153 ff., and the
two "additional notes" on "holiness, uncleanness and taboo"
and "taboos on the intercourse of the sexes," pp. 446-56).
In his discussion of various holy areas or regions the writer

has been strongly influenced by the animistic theories of
E. B. Tylor. All nature is alive and animated, but there
are certain spots which are the favorite haunts of animate
life, to which reverence was attached. The fifth chapter is
devoted to a discussion of holy waters (pp. 165-184),
sacred trees (pp. 185-197), sacred caves and pits, (pp.
197-200), and sacred stones or altars (pp. 200-212).
Altars, shrines, or sanctuaries were subsequently often
erected at or near these sites, and the persons associated
with them become holy."

In the context of his discussion of the primitive religion
of the clans, Robertson Smith enters into a long discussion
of baalism and the land of the Baal. The worship of the Baal
is the religion of the Semitic culture lands; it has as its
presuppositions the pursuit of agriculture and private
property. The title *baal* = "possessor" already points to
changed economic and legal relationships. Agriculture
which is carried on by individuals leads to private possession. The baal is the possessor of a particular district;
every district has its baal. So we hear of Melcarth, the Baal
of Tyre, of Astarte, the Baalath of Byblus, of the Baal of
Lebanon, of Mount Hermon, of Mount Peor; etc. The baals
are associated with the soil that requires no irrigation; they
are its fertilizers, the owners of its produce, and are entitled
to its natural gifts. According to the author, baal worship
was never known to the pastoral bedouins except in so far
as they came under the influence of the inhabitants of the
agricultural oases, who had borrowed from neighboring
culture lands. Through his character as lord of the ground
the baal is spatially bound. Yahweh in the Old Testament
is the baal of the land of Palestine, and the title was employed in the proper names, such as those of Saul's son
Ishbaal and his grandson Meribaal. Hosea thinks of Yahweh as Israel's Baal, the giver of grain, wine, and oil
(Hosea 2). He becomes the creator and embodiment not
only of all plant life, but of all fertility, both animal and
human. The author refers to the influence which the con-

ception of the baals as the productive and reproductive powers exercised in the development of a highly sensuous mythology, where the gods are divided into sexes and the Baal is conceived as the male principle of reproduction, but he does not elaborate since it falls outside the scope of his immediate interest and concern.

The solidarity of the clan or tribe in the kinship of its members and the holiness of certain restricted places or areas form the prolegomena to the major theme of *The Religion of the Semites,* viz., the ritual of sacrifice among the early Semites and the Hebrews. To this subject more than half of the book is devoted. Sacrifice is the oldest and most essential of all primitive religious rites and is antecedent to every other form of religion. All religion is the activity of the community and finds its most concrete embodiment and expression in sacrifice. It is our best key to an understanding of the interior character of the primitive nomadic religion.

The primary significance of sacrifice is that it is a communal meal in which the god and his worshippers participate. Together they eat the flesh and drink of the blood of the sacred animal. In their eating and drinking they are bound in a mystic communion. The form that the sacrifice takes then is that of a sacramental meal of the tribe. Its purpose is to renew and celebrate the "natural" community of blood within the tribe and its father god. The sacrificial offering is the totem animal of the tribe, which may be slaughtered only on the occasion of the sacramental meal.[22] In Semitic antiquity there is no sharp distinction between the nature of gods, of men, and of beasts. "The kinship between gods and their worshippers, on the one hand, and

---

[22] The stress on totemism and of its importance in the origins of early Semitic religion and in its survivals in the Old Testament pervades a large part of the book, including its appendices. Perhaps no single feature has received greater discussion, both favorable, especially from the anthrolopogists, and unfavorable. For an extended comment, see the *Introduction* to the third edition by Stanley A. Cook.

kinship between the gods and certain kinds of animals, on the other, are deep-seated principles of Semitic religion" (p. 289). In the sacramental meal the god and his worshippers are *commensals,* and every aspect of their mutual relationship is included in what this involves. They who eat and drink together are united for all social relationships. Hospitality is one of the basic institutions of the primitive nomadic Semite. Covenants are sealed by partaking of the same food, the deity probably to be understood as the third party.

Closely related to the view of sacrifice as a ritual of communion between the god and his worshippers is the conception of atonement. From very early times the two were intimately connected. Atonement is the act of communion which is meant or designed to wipe out all previous estrangement. In it the community is restored to its former relationship of harmony and peace with the deity. To the author communion and atonement are the two basic realities of early Semitic religion. The ceremonies attendant upon the celebration of the sacrifice are intended "to establish a life-bond between the worshipper and his god, but are dissociated with the death of the victim and from every idea of penal satisfaction" (p. 336). In the sin-offerings which date from the time of national distress of the seventh century B. C. the victim is slain "before Yahweh," and only the priests may eat of its flesh. On this circumstance, the author comments (p. 350):

> I am not aware that anything quite parallel to the ordinary Hebrew sin-offering occurs among the other Semites; and indeed no other Semitic religion appears to have developed to the same extent the doctrine of the consuming holiness of God, and the consequent need for priestly intervention between the laity and the most holy things.

The historical movement of Israel's religion is intimately associated with the development of piacular or expiatory offerings, a subject to which the author devotes an extended discussion with the intention of discerning their origin and religious significance. He regards these as going back to a very early period, but as attaining great significance in the period of national decline and stress of the seventh century B. C. During this period the old sense of friendly rapport with the deity gave way to a feeling of malaise and a need to conciliate the favor of Yahweh, who had hidden his face from the house of Israel. The ancient piaculum to our author was not a means of gaining forgiveness for sins; rather it was founded on a myth expressed in the ritual. Thus, among the Cathaginians and the Arabs of Dumaetha the sacrifice was often a human victim. The piaculum, in short, was a communion of blood, that is, of life, between man and his god, and is derived from the old conception of kinship and of nature between the deity and his worshippers.

To evaluate or assess the importance of the contribution of Robertson Smith to our understanding of ancient Semitic religion, it is essential that we distinguish between its significance in the context of his own time and its relevance in the context of contemporary Semitic and biblical scholarship. The publication of the *Lectures* received a mixed response. To those who could not accept its historical-critical presuppositions concerning the composition of the Old Testament, especially of the Pentateuch, the work carried little or no weight and was, indeed, roundly condemned. The reaction of many of the leading Churchmen was much the same and resulted in years of heresy trials. Yet everywhere, in conservative as well as radical quarters, it was recognized that it was indeed a *magnum opus*, an achievement of great learning and monumental range. The evolutionary presuppositions which underlay the exposition were, of course, rejected by not a few. On the other hand, the book was enthusiastically received by others throughout Britain and in Germany. It was translated into German, and edited by Professor R. Stübe, who placed it in the

very first rank of religious scientific presentations and considered it epoch-making in the history of the study of Semitic religion. Karl Budde wrote a long critical review in the
Theologische Literaturzeitung (1890, No. 22, pp. 528-44).
In general the most enthusiastic reviews came from anthropologists like Sir James Frazer, E. B. Tylor, F. B. Jevons,
and others. Smith's work has left its impression upon all
subsequent literature, even when the name of the original
author had ceased to be mentioned. He was one of the
founders, if not preeminently *the* founder of the modern
study of Semitic and other religions, according to one of
his most distinguished reviewers. Similar encomia were
composed by many others in literary and scientific journals.

The third edition of the *Lectures* was published in 1927
and edited by Stanley A. Cook. Professor Cook provides
an appreciative, illuminating, and perceptive introduction
in which he undertakes to assess and interpret the importance and value of the work in the context of the scholarship of his time. He devotes a substantial section to a
criticism of the totemic theory, but his sympathies with
that view are stronger than that of any scholar today. More
important are the detailed and exhaustive notes of more
than two hundred finely printed pages appended at the
end of the book. Whatever judgments one may register concerning the judgments that are there expressed, they offer
us an encyclopaedic body of anthropological data, cultural
phenomenology, and primitive religon to which it would be
difficult to find a parallel.

It is not quite so easy to assess the significance of *The
Religion of the Semites* for contemporary scholarship. The
whole direction of our approach to the Semitic world has
altered radically. For it is not to the desert of Arabia that
we now look, but rather to the great Semitic and non-
Semitic cultures of the ancient Near East. We have already
called attention to the major defect of Robertson Smith's
work, viz., its total neglect of these cultures. There are

not a few who take quite a different view of the value and relevance of the Arab tribes and their religion and folkways for an understanding of the religion of Ancient Israel. Exception has often been taken, too, to the evolutionary doctrine which doubtless influences the exposition of the development of Semitic religion. It has been averred that there is an implicit positivism in the interpretation of the sources, both written and unwritten, from the desert clans. It is certain that Robertson Smith was deeply influenced by the animistic theories of E. B. Tylor; there is no scholar today who would attempt to write the early history of Israel's religion from this point of view, though it must be added that Robertson Smith had his successors as, for example, in the work on *Hebrew Religion* (1930) by W. O. E. Oesterley and T. H. Robinson. Similarly, the view that Israel's religion, like that of the Arab clansmen, was in its origin *totemic* is rejected by all scholars today. Yet, despite all these caveats *The Religion of the Semites* is not only a monument in the history of Semitic studies, but also a vast storehouse of anthropological data of great interest, an extraordinary gathering together of cultural and religious phenomena, a work of colossal learning from a mind that was fertile, perceptive, creative, and open. The emphasis upon the importance of institutions in the study of religions would receive widespread acceptance today. It is a salutary, even necessary approach to an understanding of religion. Finally, we have often been too exclusive in our stress upon the great Near Eastern cultures in their relation to the Old Testament records. We may be confident that powerful nomadic influences continued to exert themselves upon Israel's religion throughout its history.

We initiated our discussion with a general account of the intellectual and cultural environment of the second half of the nineteenth century, the period of Robertson Smith's scholarly activity and the background against which he pursued his researches into Semitic and biblical religion.

It is our intention now to discern, as best we can, some of
the major trends since his day in the area of his greatest
interest and concern. First of all we may mention a substantial number of works devoted to nomadism and "the
nomadic ideal."[23] Chief among these are A. Musil's, *The
Manners and Customs of the Rwala Bedouins* (1928),
M. von Oppenheim's, *Die Beduinen* (1939–1952; three
volumes thus far), and J. R. Kupper's *Les nomades en
Mésopotamie au temps des rois de Mari* (1957).[24] Related
to these works are the studies on tribal organization by A.
Causse, *Du groupe ethnique à la communauté religieuse*
(1937) and S. Nyström, *Beduinentum und Jahwismus*
(1946). We have remarked repeatedly that the most serious
defect of Robertson Smith's *magnum opus* was its neglect of
the inscriptional materials from the peoples of the ancient
Near East. Although archaeology was still a budding
science in his day, the Egyptian hieroglyphic and Mesopotamian cuneiform had been deciphered and numerous inscriptions translated. It is not surprising, therefore, that
practically all subsequent research has to one degree or
another taken account of the revelations from the mounds
and of the literary remains or archives of the Near Eastern
peoples. For example, Rudolf Kittel in his monumental
work, *Geschichte des Volkes Israel* (I. seventh edition,
1932; II. 1925; III. Second edition, 1927-29), utilized the
ancient records in his discussion of the institutions of Israel
as did many others, among whom were I. Benzinger,
Hebräische Archäologie (1894; third edition, 1927);
later A. G. Barrois,, *Manuel d'Archéologie Biblique* (vol. I,
1939; vol. II, 1953), and most recently, R. de Vaux in
his excellent work on *Les Institutions de l'Ancien Testament* (vol. I, 1958; vol. II, 1960.) Translated by John

---

[23] Karl Budde, "Das nomadische Ideal im Alten Testament," *Preussische
Jahrbücher,* v. 85, 1896, pp. 57-79; A. Causse, *Les "pauvres" d'Israël,*
1922, Chap. V; J. W. Flight, "The Nomadic Idea and Ideal in the
Old Testament," *JBL,* XLII (1923), pp. 158-226.
[24] For detailed bibliography, see R. de Vaux, *Ancient Israel: Its Life and
Institutions,* 1961, pp. 519-20.

McHugh under the title *Ancient Israel: Its Life and Institutions,* 1961) and in his important article on "Les Patriarches hébreux et les découvertes modernes" *RB,* LVI (1949), 5-36; preceded by LIII (1946), 321-48; LV (1948), 321-47).[25] W. F. Albright from the beginning of his career to the present has taken account of the ancient Near Eastern records; for the period under our inspection, and see now his *Yahweh and the Gods of Canaan* (1968).[26] The life and culture of Israel are discussed by A. Bertholet, *Kulturgeschichte Israels* (1919; English translation, by A. K. Dallas, *A History of Hebrew Civilization* 1926), with more than occasional references to the great cultures of the Near East. A work which addresses itself to the same subject, but more expansive in its range and more perceptive in its grasp of Semitic and biblical mentality, is Johannes Pedersen's *Israel: Its Life and Culture* (Vol. I, 1926; Vol. II, 1940), which is replete with anthropological data. Like Robertson Smith, Pedersen makes use of the nomadic materials and understands Israel's cultural history largely in their setting. The clan or tribal organization of Israel has been carefully studied by Causse, Nyström, and de Vaux in the works already mentioned, and by Ed. Meyer (and B. Luther) in *Die Israeliten und ihre Nachbarstämme* (1906) and by Martin Noth's influential work on *Das System der Zwölf Stämme Israels* (1930).

The ancient Semitic sanctuaries and the rites associated with them have been subjected to scrutiny in several substantial works by Robertson Smith's contemporaries, such as W. W. von Baudissin, *Studien zur semitischen Religionsgeschichte* (vol. II, 1878), Friedrich Baethgen, *Beiträge zur semitischen Religionsgeschichte* (1888), and M. J.

[25] For the best compilation of texts from the ancient Near East, including *inter alia* the laws, myths, rituals, incantations, hymns, and prayers, see James B. Pritchard, *Ancient Near Eastern Texts Relating to the Old Testament,* Princeton, 1950.

[26] Note also his three earlier works: *From the Stone Age to Christianity: Monotheism and the Historical Process,* Baltimore, 1940; *Archaeology and the Religion of Israel,* Baltimore, 1942; *History, Archaeology, and Christian Humanism,* New York, 1964.

Lagrange, *Études sur les Religions sémitiques* (1903; second edition, 1905), and a smaller work by T. Canaan, *Mohammedan Saints and Sanctuaries in Palestine* (1927). Among the most recent studies of the sanctuary is the series of essays on "The Significance of the Temple in the Ancient Near East" in *The Biblical Archaeologist Reader* (vol. I, edited by D. N. Freedman and G. Ernest Wright, Anchor Books, 1961, pp. 145-200): Part I, "The Egyptian Temple," by Harold H. Nelson; Part II, The Mesopotamian Temple," by A. Leo Oppenheim; Part III, "The Temple in Palestine-Syria," by G. Ernest Wright; Part IV, "Temple Synagogue, and Church," by Floyd V. Filson. Note also the essay which follows by Frank M. Cross, Jr. on "The Priestly Tabernacle." The rites of sacrifice among the Assyrians and Babylonians have been treated *inter alios* by E. Dhorme, "Le sacrifice accadien à propos d'un ouvrage récent" in *Revue de l'histoire des Religions,* CVII, no. 2-3, 1933 pp. 107-25 and in his "Les religions de Babylonie et d'Assyrie," in *Mana: Introduction à l'Histoire des Religions,* (1945, pp. 220-233). Sacrificial rituals among the Arabs were described by J. Wellhausen in his *Reste arabischen Heidentumes* (1887; second edition, 1897), and later by J. Henninger, "Das Opfer in den altsüdarabischen Hochkulturen" in *Anthropos,* XXXVII-XL, 1942-45, pp. 779-810 and "Le sacrifice chez les Arabes" in *Ethnos* (Stockholm), XIII (1948), pp. 1-16. Henninger also has treated the Nilus evidence in "Ist der sogenannte Nilus-Bericht eine brauchbare religionsgeschichtliche Quelle?" in *Anthropos,* I, 1955, pp. 81-148. Canaanite sacrifice has also received much attention. Among the contributions to this important area of Semitic and biblical study are the works of Theodor Gaster, "The Service of the Sanctuary: a Study in Hebrew Survivals," in *Mélanges Syriens offerts à R. Dussaud,* II, 1939, pp. 577-82; R. Dussaud, *Les origines cananéennes du sacrifice israélite*[2] (1941) and *Les découvertes de Ras Shamra (Ugarit) et l'Ancien Testament* (1937; 2nd ed. 1941) John Gray, *The*

Legacy of Canaan (Supplements to *VT,* V, 1957); and R. de Vaux, *Studies in Old Testament Sacrifice,* Cardiff, 1964.

What directions our future study of the Old Testament and the literatures of the other peoples of the ancient Near East will take is not easy to say. It is probable, however, that we shall continue to find numerous affinities between the culture of Israel and that of her Semitic and non-Semitic neighbors. The materials from Ugarit and Mari and the other mounds will continue to reveal disclosures of different kinds which bear either directly or indirectly upon the Old Testament, whether one thinks of the linguistic and philological data, or of the literary styles and genres, or of the social practices and institutions, or of the historical information provided by references and records, or of religious phenomenology. We shall probably come to see ever more clearly that much of the Old Testament goes back to a very early period, that its literary expression has many parallels to that of other peoples, that its social institutions are related to those of her neighbors, and that its religion was much less "primitive" than has sometimes been supposed. Our knowledge of the history of the transmission of the Old Testament text will continue to produce fruitful results in the light of the records from Qumran. Finally, the sociology of religion will come to assume an ampler place in our future study and will serve as a corrective to some of the views now widely held in this field of inquiry. The influences from the Arabian desert and from the great empires and peoples will be more properly assessed, and a better understanding of the uniqueness of Israel in the ancient world will be achieved.

James Muilenburg
Seminary Professor
San Francisco Theological
Seminary and Graduate
Theological Union

May 1969

PREFACE TO THE THIRD EDITION

*THE continuous demand for the " Religion of the Semites"
induced the publishers, when the necessity for another reprint
drew near, to consider the possibility of a new edition. Many
years have passed since the second edition, revised by Robertson
Smith himself—the last of his labours—was seen through the
press by his friend and subsequent biographer, the late Dr. John
Sutherland Black (1894). But for nearly three decades continental scholars have had, in Stübe's German translation, what
is in several respects virtually a new edition ; and for this and
other reasons a mere reprint seemed undesirable. Needless to
say, a work that in its day was regarded as epoch-making for
the powerful stimulus it gave to the study of Semitic religion,
and indeed of religion in general, could be revised only by its
author. It touched upon so many delicate and controversial
subjects, and the treatment was so incisive and characteristic,
that what Robertson Smith thought and wrote must remain
unchanged. Accordingly, apart from the correction of a few
trifling misprints, the text has been left unaltered. In the foot-
notes references to various classical works (by Frazer, Wellhausen, and others) have been tacitly brought up to date, and a
few new references added, with sundry other minor changes that
could be made on the plates.*

*Besides this, the present edition contains a number of new
notes to which the attention of readers is drawn by asterisks
in the margin of the text. For these and for the Introduction I*

*am wholly responsible. Naturally, the notes could have been
enlarged and multiplied. What has been done was suggested
(1) by Robertson Smith's MS. notes in his copies of the first
edition both of this work and of Wellhausen's great " Reste
Arabischen Heidentums," now in the library of Christ's College,
Cambridge* [1] *; (2) by the additions in the German translation* [2] *;
(3) by the work of Baudissin, Frazer, Lagrange, and others
since 1894 ; and (4) by what I conceive to be the trend of
Robertson Smith's work.*

*Criticism, since his day, has forced an entire reconsideration
of his arguments and theories, and many of the topics with
which he deals now appear in another light. This fact has
shaped the Introduction and the Notes. Robertson Smith has
often been regarded as the founder of the modern Comparative
Study of Religion—he was, I venture to think, the founder of
what I would call the Science and Theory of Religion. He
opened up in a new way questions of religion and magic ; of
ritual, theology, and myth ; of personality, human and divine ;
of sin and atonement ; of sacramentalism, immanence, and
transcendence ; and even of production and property. Whereas
theologians naturally discuss such subjects as these within the
limits of Christian theology, Robertson Smith went farther
afield, to the most essential ideas, and those not of Christianity
alone. Western thought is throughout indebted to Christianity
and to Greek and Roman civilization ; Robertson Smith went
down deeper, to the more primitive modes of thought of mankind.
His temperament and his profound personal faith, coupled
with marvellous erudition, gave him an insight into the funda-*

---

[1] A certain amount of Robertson Smith's unpublished material was
utilized in the *Encyclopædia Biblica.*

[2] R. Stübe, *Die Religion der Semiten*, with preface by E. Kautzsch ;
Freiburg i. B. 1899.   This edition, with thirteen illustrations, modifies
the " lecture " form and expands numerous references and citations ; it
has various additions and a few omissions. A Comparative Table of
Pagination will be found at the end of this volume (p. 693).

mental theories of Religion which, it seems safe to affirm, has never been surpassed.

It would be difficult, if not impossible, to find elsewhere so stimulating an approach to the serious study of Religion ; and if enthusiastic disciples have sometimes gone too far and wandered from the track he blazed, there is no doubt that his critics have not always understood either the man himself, or the problems of Religion as they presented themselves to him. It must, indeed, be frankly admitted that some of his arguments now appear too difficult, and are sometimes unnecessary for his position as a whole ; but no less frankly may the belief be expressed that his position is far more significant than has often been thought, and that he has much to offer those who at the present day are interested in religious problems. It is with such convictions as these that the Introduction and Notes have been prepared.

In this task I have to express grateful thanks to many for advice and help, including Prof. A. A. Bevan (especially for the notes signed with his initials), Sir James Frazer (for the references on p. xli n.), Dr. Alan Gardner and Prof. Eric Peet (on some Egyptological points), Prof. Halliday (on some points of Greek religion), Mr. W. T. Vesey (for the information on p. 519 n. 1), Dr. A. S. Tritton, and Dr. and Mrs. Seligman. My indebtedness to the works of Stübe (viz. the German translation), Baudissin, Durkheim, Lagrange, G. F. Moore, Westermarck, and very many others, will be evident in the course of the notes.

The reproduction, after all these years, of a photograph of Robertson Smith will, it is hoped, gratify those to whom he is still more than a name.[1] To me he and his work have been an unfailing inspiration since 1894–5, when I dimly began to feel that the " Religion of the Semites " revealed a new world

---

[1] The original hangs in the Combination Room of Christ's College.

*to be explored.   Years of exploration have only convinced me
that the study of Religion along the lines he laid down is destined
in the future to inaugurate a new era in the history of religious
thought ; and if in this tribute to his memory an enthusiastic
disciple has strayed from the path, the fault is not the master's.*

STANLEY A. COOK.

CAMBRIDGE, *August* 1927.

PREFACE TO THE FIRST EDITION

In April 1887 I was invited by the trustees of the Burnett Fund to deliver three courses of lectures at Aberdeen, in the three years from October 1888 to October 1891, on "The primitive religions of the Semitic peoples, viewed in relation to other ancient religions, and to the spiritual religion of the Old Testament and of Christianity." I gladly accepted this invitation; for the subject proposed had interested me for many years, and it seemed to me possible to treat it in a way that would not be uninteresting to the members of my old University, in whose hall the Burnett Lectures are delivered, and to the wider public to whom the gates of Marischal College are opened on the occasion.

In years gone by, when I was called upon to defend before the courts of my Church the rights of historical research, as applied to the Old Testament, I had reason to acknowledge with gratitude the fairness and independence of judgment which my fellow - townsmen of Aberdeen brought to the discussion of questions which in most countries are held to be reserved for the learned, and to be merely disturbing to the piety of the ordinary layman; and I was glad to have the opportunity of commending to the notice of a public so impartial and so intelligent the study of a branch of comparative religion which, as I venture to think, is indispensable to the future progress of Biblical research.

In Scotland, at least, no words need be wasted to prove that a right understanding of the religion of the Old Testament is the only way to a right understanding of the Christian faith; but it is not so fully recognised, except in the circle of professed scholars, that the doctrines and ordinances of the Old Testament cannot be thoroughly comprehended until they are put into comparison with the religions of the nations akin to the Israelites. The value of comparative studies for the study of the religion of the Bible was brought out very clearly, two hundred years ago, by one of the greatest of English theologians, Dr. John Spencer, Master of Corpus Christi College in Cambridge, whose Latin work on the ritual laws of the Hebrews may justly be said to have laid the foundations of the science of Comparative Religion, and in its special subject, in spite of certain defects that could hardly have been avoided at the time when it was composed, still remains by far the most important book on the religious antiquities of the Hebrews. But Spencer was so much before his time that his work was not followed up; it is often ignored by professed students of the Old Testament, and has hardly exercised any influence on the current ideas which are the common property of educated men interested in the Bible.

In modern times Comparative Religion has become in some degree a popular subject, and in our own country has been treated from various points of view by men of eminence who have the ear of the public; but nothing considerable has been done since Spencer's time, either in England or on the Continent, whether in learned or in popular form, towards a systematic comparison of the religion of the Hebrews, as a whole, with the beliefs and ritual practices of the other Semitic peoples. In matters of detail valuable work has been done; but this work has been too special, and for the most part too technical, to help the circle to whom the Burnett Lectures are addressed , which I take to be a circle of cultivated and thinking men and women who have no special acquaintance with Semitic lore, but are interested in everything that throws light on their own religion, and are prepared to follow a sustained or even a severe argument, if the speaker on his part will remember that historical research can always be made intelligible to thinking people, when it is set forth with orderly method and in plain language.

There is a particular reason why some attempt in this direction should be made now. The first conditions of an effective comparison of Hebrew religion, as a whole, with the religion of the other Semites, were lacking so long as the historical order of the Old Testament documents, and especially of the documents of which the Pentateuch is made up, was unascertained or wrongly apprehended; but, thanks to the labours of a series of scholars (of whom it is sufficient to name Kuenen and Wellhausen, as the men whose acumen and research have carried this inquiry to a point where nothing of vital importance for the historical study of the Old Testament religion still remains uncertain), the growth of the Old Testament religion can now be followed from stage to stage, in a way that is hardly possible with any other religion of antiquity. And so it is now not only possible, but most necessary for further progress, to make a fair comparison between Hebrew religion in its various stages and the religions of the races with which the Hebrews were cognate by natural descent, and with which also they were historically in constant touch.

The plan which I have framed for my guidance in carrying out the desires of the Burnett trustees is explained in the first lecture. I begin with the institutions

of religion, and in the present series I discuss those
institutions which may be called fundamental, particularly
that of sacrifice, to which fully one half of the volume
is devoted.   It will readily be understood that, in the
course of the argument, I have found it convenient to
take up a good many things that are not fundamental, at
the place where they could most naturally be explained;
and, on the other hand, I daresay that students of the
subject may sometimes be disposed to regard as fundamental certain matters which I have been compelled to
defer.   But on the whole I trust that the present volume
will be found to justify its title, and to contain a fairly
adequate analysis of the first principles of Semitic worship.
It would indeed have been in some respects more satisfactory to myself to defer the publication of the first
series of lectures till I could complete the whole subject
of institutions, derivative as well as primary.   But it
seemed due to the hearers who may desire to attend the
second series of lectures, to let them have before them in
print the arguments and conclusions from which that
series must start; and also, in a matter of this sort, when
one has put forth a considerable number of new ideas, the
value of which must be tested by criticism, one is anxious
to have the judgment of scholars on the first part of one's
work before going on to further developments.

I may explain that the lectures, as now printed, are
considerably expanded from the form in which they were
delivered; and that only nine lectures of the eleven were
read in Aberdeen, the last two having been added to
complete the discussion of sacrificial ritual.

In dealing with the multiplicity of scattered evidences
on which the argument rests, I have derived great assistance from the researches of a number of scholars, to whom
acknowledgment is made in the proper places.   For Arabia

I have been able to refer throughout to my friend
Wellhausen's excellent volume, *Reste arabischen Heiden-
thumes* (Berl. 1887), in which the extant material for this
branch of Semitic heathenism is fully brought together,
and criticised with the author's well-known acumen. For
the other parts of Semitic heathenism there is no standard
exposition of a systematic kind that can be referred to
in the same way.   In this country Movers's book on
Phœnician religion is often regarded as a standard
authority for the heathenism of the Northern Semites;
but, with all its learning, it is a very unsafe guide, and
does not supersede even so old a book as Selden, *De diis
Syris.*

In analysing the origin of ritual institutions, I have
often had occasion to consult analogies in the usages of
early peoples beyond the Semitic field.   In this part of
the work I have had invaluable assistance from my friend,
Mr. J. G. Frazer, who has given me free access to his
unpublished collections on the superstitions and religious
observances of primitive nations in all parts of the globe.
I have sometimes referred to him by name, in the course
of the book, but these references convey but an imperfect
idea of my obligations to his learning and intimate
familiarity with primitive habits of thought.   In this
connection I would also desire to make special acknowledgment of the value, to students of Semitic ritual and
usage, of the comparative studies of Dr. Wilken of Leyden;
which I mention in this place, because Dutch work is too
apt to be overlooked in England.

In transcribing Oriental words, I have distinguished the
emphatic consonants, so far as seemed necessary to preclude
ambiguities, by the usual device of putting dots under the
English letters that come nearest to them in sound.   But
instead of *k* (ק) I write *c*, following a precedent set by

b

eminent French Orientalists.   In Eastern words both *c* and
g are always to be pronounced hard.   But where there is
a conventional English form for a word I retain it; thus
I write " Caaba," not " Ka'ba ; " " Caliph," not " Khalīfa " ;
" Jehovah," not " Yahveh " or " Iahwé."[1] As regards the
references in the notes, it may be useful to mention that
CIS. means the Paris *Corpus Inscriptionem Semiticarum*,
and *ZDMG.* the *Zeitschrift* of the German Oriental Society ;
that when Wellhausen is cited, without reference to the
title of a book, his work on Arabian Heathenism is meant ;
and that *Kinship* means my book on *Kinship and Marriage
in Early Arabia* (Cambridge, University Press, 1885).[2]

Finally, I have to express my thanks to my friend, Mr.
J. S. Black, who has kindly read the whole book in proof
and made many valuable suggestions.

W. ROBERTSON SMITH.

CHRIST'S COLLEGE, CAMBRIDGE,
1st *October* 1889.

---

[1] [In the new notes *k* has commonly been employed in the place of *c*,
and other spellings—*e.g.* Yahweh—adopted in conformity with modern
usage.]

[2] [See now the List of Abbreviations, etc., on pp. xxi *sqq.*]

NOTE TO THE SECOND EDITION

THE failure of Professor Smith's health from 1890 onwards made it impossible for him to prepare for publication the Second and Third Series of Burnett Lectures, delivered in March 1890 and December 1891 ; but the subject never ceased to interest him, and the comparatively manageable task of embodying in a new edition of the First Series the results of further reading and reflection, as well as of criticisms from other workers in the same field, was one of his latest occupations. On March 17th, only a fortnight before his lamented death, he handed over to my care the annotated print, and also the manuscript volume of new materials, with the remark that, apart from some adjustments in detail, which he hoped he might yet find strength to make as the work passed through the press, he believed the revision was practically complete. In making the adjustments referred to, it has been my endeavour to carry out with absolute fidelity the author's wishes so far as I knew or could divine them ; and in the majority of instances the task has not been difficult. My best thanks are due to Mr. J. G. Frazer, and also to Professor Bevan (both of Cambridge), for much valuable help in correcting the proofs.

J. S. B.

EDINBURGH, *3rd October* 1894.

xix

LIST OF ABBREVIATIONS AND BIBLIOGRAPHY

This list is confined to an explanation of abbreviations and of works often cited in abbreviated form. Unless otherwise specified, English and French books are printed in London and Paris respectively.

A. A. B. : A. A. Bevan.
Abelson, J. : *The Immanence of God in Rabbinical Literature.* 1912.
Agh. : *Kitāb al-Aghānī.* Bulac, 1285.
AR. : *Archiv für Religionswissenschaft.*

B. : Banū (sons) (p. 127, n. 1, etc.).
B. B : Bar Bahlūl.
B. B. : Bābā Bathrā (p. 102, n. 2).
Bancroft, H. H. : *The Native Races of the Pacific States of North America.* 1875–6.
Barton, G. A. : *Sketch of Semitic Origins, Social and Religious.* New York, 1902.
Baudissin : *Adonis und Esmun; Eine Untersuchung zur Geschichte des Glaubens an Auferstehungsgötter und an Heilgötter.* Leipzig, 1911.
Studien zur semitischen Religionsgeschichte. Leipzig, 1876.
" Der gerechte Gott in altsemit. Relig.," in *Festgabe* to A. von Harnack, 1 *sqq.* Tübingen, 1921.
Black, J. S., and G. W. Chrystal : *The Life of W. Robertson Smith and Lectures and Essays.* 1912.
Bousset-Gressmann : *Die Religion des Judentums im Spät-hellenistischen Zeitalter,* by W. Bousset. 3rd ed by Hugo Gressman. Tübingen, 1926.
Breasted, James Henry : *Ancient Records of Egypt: Historical Documents.* 5 vols. Chicago, 1906.
Development of Religion and Thought in Ancient Egypt. 1912.
Büchler, Adolph : *Types of Jewish-Palestinian Piety from 70 B.C.E. to 70 C.E. The Ancient Pious Men.* 1922.

CAH. : *The Cambridge Ancient History.* Cambridge, i. 1923.
Canaan, T. : Articles in the *Journal of the Palestine Oriental Society,* on Palestinian religion, custom, and folklore.

Cesnola, Palma di : *Antiquities of Cyprus.* 1873.
Chwolson, D. : *Die Ssabier und der Ssabismus.* 2 vols. St. Petersburg, 1856.
CIGr. : *Corpus Inscriptionum Græcarum.* Berlin, 1828.
CIL. : *C. Inscr. Latinarum.* Berlin, 1863.
CIS. : *C. Inscr. Semiticarum.* Paris, 1885. (Where the volume is not indicated, the reference is to Vol. I. Phœnician Inscriptions.)
Clermont-Ganneau : *Recueil d'Archéologie Orientale.* 8 vols. 1888–1907.
Cook, Arthur Bernard (Queens' College, Cambridge) : *Zeus: A Study in Ancient Religion.* i. 1914 ; ii. 1 and 2, 1925. Cambridge.
Cook, Stanley Arthur (Gonville and Caius College, Cambridge) : *The Laws of Moses and the Code of Hammurabi.* 1903.
The Study of Religions. 1914.
Cooke, George Albert (Regius Professor of Hebrew, Christchurch, Oxford) : *A Text-Book of North-Semitic Inscriptions.* Oxford, 1903. (The references, when not to the number of the inscription, are to the page.)
Cornford, F. M. : *From Religion to Philosophy: A Study in the Origins of Western Speculation.* 1912.
CR. : *Comptes Rendus.*
Crawley, A. E : *The Mystic Rose: A Study of Primitive Marriage* (1902). (2nd ed. revised and enlarged by T. Besterman, has since appeared. 2 vols. 1927.)
The Tree of Life. 1905.
The Idea of the Soul. 1909.
Curtiss, S. I. : *Primitive Semitic Religion To-day.* 1902.
Cumont, F. : *The Oriental Religions in Roman Paganism.* Chicago, 1911.
Études Syriennes. 1917.

Dhorme, P. : *La Religion Assyro-Baby-lonienne.* 1910.

Döller, J. : *Die Reinheits- und Speise-gestze des Alten Testaments.* Münster i. W., 1917.

Doughty, C. M. : *Travels in Arabia Deserta.* 2 vols. Cambridge, 1888.

Driver, G. R. : " The Modern Study of the Hebrew Language," in *People and the Book.* See Peake.
' The Psalms in the Light of Babylonian Research," in *The Psalmists.* See Simpson.

Driver, S. R. : Commentary on *Deuteronomy.* 1895.

Durkheim, E. : *The Elementary Forms of the Religious Life.* 1919. (Transl. of *Les Formes Élémentaires de la Vie Religieuse: le Système Totémique en Australie.* 1912.)

Dussaud, René : *Les Origines Cananéennes du Sacrifice Israélite.* 1921.

EBi. : *Encyclopædia Biblica.* 4 vols. 1899–1903.

Eitrem, S : *Opferritus und Voropfer der Griechen und Römer.* Christiania, 1915.

Ency. Brit. : *Encyclopædia Britannica,* 11th ed., 1910–11. (To the 9th ed. W. R. S. made valuable contributions, and of the last part of it he was the editor, 1875–89.)

ERE. : *Encyclopædia of Religion and Ethics.* 12 vols. 1908–21. Index. 1926.

Euting, J. : *Nabatäische Inschriften aus Arabien.* Berlin, 1885.
Sinäitische Inschriften. Berlin, 1891.

Farnell, L. R. : *The Cults of the Greek States.* 5 vols. Oxford, 1896.
Greece and Babylon : A Comparative Sketch of Mesopotamian, Anatolian, and Hellenic Religions. Edinburgh, 1911.
The Evolution of Religion. 1905.

FHG. : *Fragmenta Hist. Graec.* ed. Müller.

Fihrist : Ed. Flugel and Rödiger and P. Müller. Leipzig, 1871–2.

FOT. : See Frazer.

Fränkel, S. : *Die aramäischen Fremd-wörter im arabischen.* Leiden, 1886.

Frazer, Sir James George : *The Golden Bough : A Study in Magic and Religion.* 3rd ed. 1911–20.
GB. i. *The Magic Art and the Evolution of Kings,* vol. i.
ii. *The Magic Art and the Evolution of Kings,* vol. ii.
iii. *Taboo and the Perils of the Soul.*
iv. *The Dying God.*
v. *Adonis, Attis, Osiris,* vol. i.

Frazer, Sir James George :
GB. vi. *Adonis, Attis, Osiris,* vol. ii.
vii. *Spirits of the Corn and of the Wild,* vol. i.
viii. *Spirits of the Corn and of the Wild,* vol. ii.
ix. *The Scapegoat.*
x. *Balder the Beautiful,* vol. i.
xi. *Balder the Beautiful,* vol. ii.
xii. *Bibliography and General Index.* (Abridged edition in one vol. 1925.)
Tot. Ex. : *Totemism and Exogamy : A Treatise on Certain Early Forms of Superstition and Society.* 4 vols. 1910.
FOT. : *Folklore in the Old Testament.* 3 vols. 1918.
Pausanias's Description of Greece : Translation and Commentary. 6 vols. 1898.
Belief in Immortality and the Worship of the Dead, i.–. 1913–.
Psyche's Task. 2nd ed. 1913.
The Worship of Nature, vol. i. 1926.

Garstang, J. : *The Syrian Goddess, a translation of Lucian's " De Dea Syria,"* with a Life of Lucian, by H. A. Strong. 1913.

Gaudefroy-Demombynes : *Pèlerinage à la Mekke.* 1923.

GB : See Frazer, *Golden Bough.*

Gennep, Arnold Van : *Les Rites de Passage.* 1909.
L'État actuel du Problème Totémique. 1920.

Gl(ossary) Belādhorī (p. 99 n.).

Goldziher, I. : *Muhammedanische Studien,* i. 1889 ; ii. 1890. Halle a. S.
Abhandlungen zur arabischen Philologie, i. Leiden, 1896.

Gray, G. B. : Commentary on *Numbers.* Edinburgh, 1903.
Sacrifice in the Old Testament : Its Theory and Practice. (Posthumous.) Oxford, 1925.

Gressmann, Hugo : *Mose und seine Zeit. Ein Kommentar zu den Mose-sagen.* Göttingen, 1913.
Altorientalische Texte zum Alten Testament. 2nd ed. Leipzig, 1926. (Egyptian texts by H. Ranke, Bab.-Ass. by E. Ebeling, Old South Arabian by Rhodokanakis.)
" Die Paradiessage " in *Festgabe* to A. von Harnack, 24 *sqq.* Tübingen, 1921.

Guarmani, Carlo : *Il Neged Settentrionale* (p. 99 n.). Jerusalem, 1866.

Halliday, W. R. : *Greek Divination : A Study of its Methods and Principles.* 1913.

Harnack : *Festgabe.* Tübingen, 1921.

Harrison, Miss Jane : *Themis: A Study of the Social Origins of Greek Religion.* Cambridge, 1912.

Hartland, E. S. : *Primitive Paternity: The Myth of Supernatural Birth in Relation to the History of the Family.* 2 vols. 1909.
Ritual and Belief: Studies in the History of Religion. 1914.
Primitive Law. 1924.

Hartmann, M. : *Der islamische Orient,* ii. Leipzig, 1909.

Head, B. W. : *Historia Numorum.* Oxford, 1887.

Hehn, J. : *Die biblische und die babylonische Gottesidee.* Leipzig, 1913.

Hermann : *Gottesdienstliche Altertümer.*

Hobhouse, L. T., G. C. Wheeler, and M. Ginsberg : *The Material Culture and Social Institutions of the Simpler Peoples.* 1915.
Morals in Evolution : A Study in Comparative Ethics. 1915.

Hoffman, J. G. E. : *Auszüge aus syrischen Akten persischer Märtyrer.* Leipzig, 1880.
Julianos der Abtrünnige. Leiden, 1881.
Über einige phœn. inschr. Göttingen, 1890.

Hommel, Fritz : *Ethnologie und Geographie des Alten Orients.* Munich, 1926.

Hubert and Mauss : *Mélanges d'Histoire des Religions* (1909). [A translation by A. J. Nelson, *The Open Court,* xl. (1926), 33 *sqq.* 93 *sqq.* 169 *sqq.*]

Ibn Doreid : *Kitābu 'l-ishtiḳaḳ,* ed. Wüstenfeld. 1854.

Isaac : Isaac of Antioch, ed. Bickell, 1873–6 ; and Bedjan, 1903.

Jacob, G. : *Altarabische Parallelen zum Alten Testament.* Berlin, 1897.
Altarabisches Beduinenleben. 2nd ed. Berlin, 1897.

Jahnow, Hedwig : *Das hebräische Leichenlied im Rahmen der Völkerdichtung.* Giessen, 1923.

JAOS. : *Journal of the American Oriental Society.*

JAs. : *Journal Asiatique.*

Jastrow, M. : *Die Religion Babyloniens und Assyriens.* 2 vols. Giessen, 1905–12.
Rel. Bel.: Aspects of Religious Belief and Practice in Bab. and Ass. New York, 1911.

Jaussen, Antonin : *Coutumes des Arabes au pays de Moab.* 1908.

JBL. : *Journal of Biblical Literature.*

JEA. : *Journal of Egyptian Archæology.*

Jeremias, Alfred : *Handbuch der altorientalischen Geisteskultur.* Leipzig, 1913.
The Old Testament in the Light of the Ancient East. 1911.

Jevons, F. B. : *Introduction to the History of Religion.* 7th ed. 1896.
Introduction to the Study of Comparative Religion. New York, 1908.
The Idea of God in Early Religions. Cambridge, 1910.
Comparative Religion. Cambridge, 1913.

Joannes Lydus : See Lydus.

Johns, C. H. W. : *Babylonian and Assyrian Laws, Contracts and Letters.* Edinburgh, 1904.

JPOS. : *Journal of the Palestine Oriental Society.*

JQR. : *Jewish Quarterly Review.*

JRAI. : *Journal of the Royal Anthropological Institute.*

JRAS. : *Journal of the Royal Asiatic Society.*

JSOR. : *Journal of the Society of Oriental Research.*

JTS. : *Journal of Theological Studies.*

KAT. : *Die Keilinschriften und das Alte Testament.* 3rd ed. by H. Zimmern and H. Winckler. Berlin, 1903.

King, Irving : *The Development of Religion : A Study in Anthropology and Social Psychology.* New York, 1910.

King, L. W. : *History of Sumer and Akkad.* 1910.
History of Babylon. 1915.

Kinship : See Smith, W. R.

Knudtzon, J. A. : *Die El-Amarna-Tafeln mit Einleitung und Erläuterungen.* With notes, etc., by O. Weber and E. Ebeling. 2 vols. Leipzig, 1915.

Kreglinger, R. : *Études sur l'Origine et le Développement de la Vie Religieuse,* i. Brussels, 1919.

Kremer, A. von : *Studien zur vergleichenden Kulturgeschichte. Sitzungs-berichte.* Vol. cxx. Vienna, 1890.

Kuenen, A. : *Gesammelte Abhandlungen zur biblischen Wissenschaft aus dem Holländischen übersezt,* by K. Budde. Freiburg i. B., 1894.

Lagrange, P. Marie-Joseph : *Études sur les Religions Sémitiques.* 2nd ed. Paris, 1905.

Landberg, C. Graf von : *Arabica,* iv. v. Leiden, 1897–8.
Études sur les dialectes de l'Arabe méridionale. i, ii, 1–3. Leiden, 1901–13.

Lectures and Essays : See Smith, W. R.

Lidzbarski, M. : *Handbuch der nord-semitischen Epigraphik nebst aus-gewählten Inschriften. Text und Tafeln.* Weimar, 1898.
Ephemeris für semitische Epigraphik, i. (1900–2) ; Giessen, 1902. ii. (1903–7) ; 1908. iii. (1909–15) ; 1915.
Lisān al-'Arab : Cairo, 1308.
Loisy, A. : *Essai Historique sur le Sacrifice.* 1920.
Lydus, Joannes (*c.* 490–570 A.D.) : On the editions by Wachsmuth, Leipzig, 1897 ; Wuensch, *ibid.* 1898, etc.; see Stübe's note, p. 337, n. 764.

Macculloch, J. A. : *Comparative Theology.* 1902.
McLennan, J. F. : *Primitive Marriage.* Edinburgh, 1865 ; reprinted in *Studies in Ancient History.* 2nd ed. 1886.
Studies in Ancient History : Second Series, Comprising an Inquiry into the Origin of Exogamy. 1896.
Mader, E. : *Die Menschenopfer der alten Hebräer und der benachbarten Völker.* Freiburg i. B., 1909.
Malinowski, B. : " Magic, Science and Religion," in *Science, Religion and Reality,* ed. Joseph Needham (1925), pp. 20–84.
Myth in Primitive Psychology. 1926.
Articles in *Psyche.*
Marett, R. R. : *Anthropology and the Classics.* Oxford, 1908.
The Threshold of Religion. 2nd ed. London, 1914.
Psychology and Folklore. 1920.
Marti-Festschrift : Ed. Budde. Giessen, 1925.
Meek, C. K. : *The Northern Tribes of Nigeria.* 2 vols. 1925.
Meyer, Ed., and B. Luther : *Die Israeliten und ihre Nachbarstämme.* Halle a. S. 1906.
Meyer, Eduard : *Geschichte des Altertums.* 3rd ed.
i. 1. *Einleitung. Elemente der Anthropologie.*
i. 2. *Die ältesten geschichtlichen Völker und Kulturen bis zum sechzehnten Jahrhundert.* Stuttgart and Berlin, 1907, 1913. (References are made to the sections.)
MGWJ. : *Monatsschrift für Gesch. u. Wiss. d. Judentums.*
Moore, G. F. : Articles in *Encyclopædia Biblica* on Asherah, High Place, Idolatry and Primitive Religion, Molech, Nature-Worship, Queen of Heaven, etc., and especially Sacrifice.
History of Religions, i. 1914 ; ii. 920.

Mordtmann, J. H., and D. H. Müller : *Sabäische Denkmäler.* Vienna, 1882.
Morgenländische Forschungen : Festschrift für Fleischer. Leipzig, 1875.
Morgenstern, J. : " The Doctrine of Sin in the Babylonian Religion," *MVAG.,* 1905, iii. (to which reference is always made, except on pp. 558, 577).
Muh. i. Med. : See Wellhausen.
MVAG. : *Mitteilungen der vorderasiatischen Gesellschaft.*

Needham : See Malinowski.
Nielsen, D. : *Der dreieinige Gott in religionshistorischer Beleuchtung.* Copenhagen, 1922. (The references are, unless stated, to this volume.)
Handbuch der Altarabischen Altertumskunde (with Hommel and Rhodokanakis), i. Copenhagen, 1927.
Nilsson, N. M. P. : *A History of Greek Religion.* Transl. by F. J. Fielden, with a preface by Sir J. G. Frazer. Oxford, 1925.
Nilus : See Migne, *P.Gr.* lxxix. Citations in Zapletal, p. 99 *sq.,* Lagrange, 258.
Nöldeke-Festschrift : Ed. Bezold. Giessen, 1906.

Oesterley, W. O. E. : *Immortality and the Unseen World : A Study in Old Testament Religion.* 1921.
OLZ. : *Orientalistische Literaturzeitung.*
OTJC. : See Smith, W. R.

Peake, A. S. : *The People and the Book.* (Essays on the O.T. by various scholars.) Oxford, 1925.
PEF. : *Palestine Exploration Fund.*
PEF. Qy. St. : *Palestine Exploration Fund Quarterly Statements.*
PGr. : *Patrologia Græca* (Migne).
Pietschmann, R. : *Geschichte der Phönizier.* Berlin, 1889.
Pilter, W. T. : Index of the South Arabian Proper-names in *CIS.* iv. fasc. 1–5. *Proc. of the Soc. of Biblical Archæology,* xxxix. 99–112, 115–132.
Potter, M. A. : *Sohrab and Rustem.* 1902.
PRE. : *Real-Encyklopädie für Protestantische Theologie und Kirche.*
Prophets : See Smith, W. R.
PSBA. : *Proceedings of the Society of Biblical Archæology.*
PW. : Pauly-Wissowa, *Real-Encyclopädie der classischen Altertumswissenschaft.*

Rasmussen : *Additamenta ad hist. Arabum ante islamismum.* Copenhagen, 1921.

Reinach, Salomon : *Cultes, Mythes et Religions.* 4 vols. 1905–12.

REJ. : *Revue des Études Juives.*

Revue Biblique.

Revue de l'Historie des Religions.

Ridgeway, Sir William : *Essays and Studies Presented to,* ed. E. C. Quiggin. Cambridge, 1913.

Robinson, E. : *Biblical Researches in Palestine, Mt. Sinai, and Arabia.* 3 vols. 1841; 2nd ed. 1846.

Robinson, H. Wheeler : " Hebrew Psychology " in *People and the Book,* ed. Peake (*q.v.*).

Sachau-Festschrift : Ed. by G. Weil. Berlin, 1915.

SB. : *Sitzungs-berichte.*

Seligman, C. G. : " Some Aspects of the Hamitic Problem in the Anglo-Egyptian Sudan," *Journal of the Royal Anthropological Institute,* xliii. (1913), 593–705.

Seligman, Mrs. Brenda Z. : " Studies in Semitic Kinship," *Bulletin of the School of Oriental Studies, London Institution,* iii. 1924–5.

Seligman, C. G. and B. Z. : " The Kabābīsh. A Sudan and Arab Tribe," *Harvard African Studies,* ii. 105–186. Cambridge, U.S.A., 1918.

Simpson, D. C. : *The Psalmists.* (Essays by various scholars.) Oxford, 1926.

Skizzen iv. : See Wellhausen.

Smith, W. Robertson : " Animal Worship and Animal Tribes among the Arabs and the Old Testament," *Journal of Philology,* ix. (1880) ; reprinted in *Lectures and Essays* (below).

  Kinship : Kinship and Marriage in Early Arabia. 2nd ed. 1894.

  OTJC. : The Old Testament in the Jewish Church. 2nd ed. 1892.

  Prophets : The Prophets of Israel. 2nd ed. 1902.

  Lectures and Essays : Ed. J. S. Black and G. W. Chrystal. 1912.

Spencer, Sir Baldwin, and F. J. Gillen : *The Native Tribes of Central Australia.* 1899.

  The Northern Tribes of Central Australia. 1904.

Spencer, John : *De Legibus Hebraeorum Ritualibus et earum Rationibus.* 1st ed. Cambridge. 1685.

Sprenger : *Das Leben und die Lehre des Mohammads.* 2nd ed. 3 vols. Berlin, 1861–5 and 1869.

Stübe, R. : *Die Religion der Semiten* (German translation of *Religion of the Semites*), with 13 illustrations, and a preface by Professor E. Kautzsch. Freiburg i. B., 1899.

Stade's *Zeitschrift* : See *ZATW.*

Thompson, R. Campbell : *Semitic Magic : Its Origins and Development.* 1908.

  The Devils and Evil Spirits of Babylonia. 2 vols. 1903–4.

Thomson, Joseph : *Through Masai-Land.* 1885.

Tot. Ex. : See Frazer.

Toy, C. H. : *Introduction to the History of Religions.* U.S.A , 1913.

Tylor, Sir Edward B. : *Primitive Culture.* 4th ed. 1903.

Van Gennep : See Gennep.

Vincent, H. : *Canaan d'après l'Exploration Récente.* 1907.

Vogüé, Vicomte de : *Syrie Centrale : Inscriptions Semitiques.* 1868–77.

Waddington, W. H. (and le Bas.) : *Voyage archéologique.* (The proper names in the Greek and Latin inscriptions are indexed by Chabot in the *Revue Archéologique,* 1896.)

Webster, Hutton : *Primitive Secret Societies : A Study in Early Politics and Religion.* New York. 1908.

Wellhausen, J. : *Reste Arabischen Heidentums.* 1st ed. Berlin, 1887 (=*Skizzen und Vorarbeiten,* iii.) ; 2nd ed. Berlin, 1897, to which all references are made, unless otherwise specified.

  Muh. i. Med. : Muhammed in Medina. Berlin, 1882.

  Skizzen iv. : (1) *Medina vor dem Islam ;* (2) *Muhammads Gemeindeordnung von Medina,* etc. Berlin, 1889.

  Ein Gemeinwesen ohne Obrigkeit. Göttingen, 1900.

Wellhausen-Festschift : Ed. Marti. Giessen, 1914.

Westermarck, Edward A. : *The Origin and Development of the Moral Ideas.* 2 vols. 1906.

  Ritual and Belief in Morocco. 2 vols. 1926. (Invaluable.)

  The History of Human Marriage. 3 vols. 1921.

  A Short History of Marriage. 1926.

  Festskrift tillegnad Westermarck. Helsingfors, 1912.

Wheeler, G. C. W. C. : *The Tribe and Intertribal Relations in Australia.* 1910.

Wrede, A. v. : *Reise in Hadhramaut*, ed. Maltzan. Brunswick, 1870.

Wright, William : *Notulæ Syricæ*. Cambridge, 1887.

Apocryphal Acts of the Apostles. 1871.

W. R. S. : See Smith, W. R.

WZKM. : *Wiener Zeitschrift für die Kunde des Morgenlandes.*

Yakūt : *Geog. Wörterbuch*, ed. Wüstenfeld.

ZA. : *Zeitschrift für Assyriologie.*

Zapletal, Vinc., O. P. : *Der Totemismus und die Religion Israels.* Freiburg i. S. 1901.

ZATW. : *Zeitschrift für die alttestamentliche Wissenschaft.*

ZDMG. : *Z. der deutschen Morgenländischen Gesellschaft.*

ZDPV. : *Z. des deutschen Palästina-Vereins.*

ZNTW. : *Z. für d. neutestamentliche Wissenschaft.*

INTRODUCTION

THIS book grew out of a small monograph on " Animal Worship and Animal Tribes among the Arabs and in the Old Testament," published in 1880.[1] It was followed by lectures on *Kinship and Marriage in Early Arabia* (1885), and by an article on " Sacrifice " in the Ninth Edition of the *Encyclopædia Britannica* (1886), wherein Robertson Smith began to develop those views which were to make the book a landmark.[2] *The Religion of the Semites* had an immediate effect upon the critical study of religion ; and, exercising powerful influence upon a host of scholars—one may mention Sir James Frazer and Principal F. B. Jevons, Salomon Reinach in France, and the German scholar Stade—left its impression upon all subsequent literature, even where the name of the original author ceased to be mentioned. If Dr. John Spencer, once Master of Corpus Christi College, " may justly be said to have laid the foundations of the science of Comparative Religion " (p. xiv above), Robertson Smith, by reason of his comprehensive and stimulating treatment, came to be regarded in many quarters as one of the founders,

---

[1] Reprinted in *Lectures and Essays*, edited by J. S. Black and G. W. Chrystal, 1912.

[2] It is interesting to recall that already in *The Old Testament in the Jewish Church* (First Ed. 1881), his doctrine of sacrifice was recognized by one of his opponents as involving " a new theory of the essential character of the Old Testament religion," one which " cut away the basis on which the whole doctrine of salvation rests " (see *Life of W. R. Smith*, by Black & Chrystal, 1912, p. 417 *sq.*). Strangely enough, this was not pursued in the controversy which was then raging about his writings.

if not pre-eminently as *the* founder, of the modern study of Semitic and other religions.[1]

The volume, the first of a series, is admittedly incomplete. Originally three courses of lectures were planned, to culminate in an inquiry into the part played by Semitic religion in the general progress of humanity. The second series was delivered, from notes, in March 1890 ; and in three lectures covered Feasts, Priests, Prophecy, and Divination.[2] Publication was proposed, but failing health forbade all hopes. Of the third series (three lectures given in December 1891), apart from fragmentary notes and meagre press reports, little survived, but enough to emphasize the profound spiritual difference which he had always maintained between the Old Testament and other literature.[3] We know that in 1893 he was anxious to finish the second and third series of lectures, and " complete his argument," but this was not granted him. He lived to finish the preparation of the second edition of this volume, and perhaps the very considerable difference between the two editions and the more decisive exposition of his main principles which he was able to furnish may reconcile us to the loss of what one of the most powerful of intellects would have given had he been spared to round off his argument as he desired.

As it is, *The Religion of the Semites* is, as the biographers acknowledge—one of them a friend of many years' standing —a fragment. " The arrangement is not so methodical as could be wished, the canvas is overcrowded, and there are repetitions and digressions." The book contains, as its author says, " a considerable number of new ideas," and the biographers remark rightly : " He expected much help—

---

[1] Spencer's interpretation of the " Red Heifer " in *De Legibus Hebraeorum Ritualibus et earum Rationibus* (1685), marks an epoch. See H. P. Smith, *Essays in Biblical Interpretation* (Boston, U.S.A., 1921), pp. 106 *sqq.*

[2] See the Synopsis, *Life*, pp. 525 *sqq.*

[3] See *Life*, pp. 535 *sqq.*

perhaps more than he ultimately received—from his critics."
Looking back, we are bound to admit that he laid down
principles, some of which have hardly received the attention
they deserve ; he opened out a new field of research, or
rather, he opened it out in a new manner ; and his life-work,
taken as a whole, has a significance which perhaps may be
more readily understood now than when he wrote as a pioneer.[1]
While, on the one hand, attention has commonly been directed
to particular and more sensational theories—notably to
sacramental communion as the fundamental idea in ancient
sacrifice and its totemic origin ; on the other, the problems
with which he was occupied are now studied in the light of
a far greater wealth of material than was accessible in his
day. The whole subject has become more intricate, and the
differences among experts, as concerns attitude, treatment,
and conclusions, more confusing. The mass of data which
he collected has been increased, and occasionally modified
or corrected ; his most conspicuous theories have been
closely criticized, but—one may venture to assert—they have
not been replaced by better ones. It is true that it would
now be agreed that the course of religious development did
not run so simply as he thought ; but all theories of the
evolution of culture are under consideration. Again, the
problems of totemism no longer stand where they did when
J. F. M'Lennan revealed to him the value of anthropological
research ; but totemism is immensely more complex than it
once seemed. Robertson Smith's central theory of sacrifice
as primarily a communion is sometimes felt to be exaggerated ; but subsequent study on this subject has only shown
that we are still far from an adequate treatment of the
network of questions with which sacrifice is intertwined.

Robertson Smith's temperament, religion, and standpoint

---

[1] The present writer may refer in this connexion to his notice in the
Hibbert Journal, xi. (1912) pp. 211 *sqq.*

are so characteristic of him as man and scholar that it is not easy, particularly for those who would not share his religious convictions, to understand either his attitude or the nature of his achievement. In the critical or scientific study of religions it is obvious that unprejudiced inquiry inevitably affects the growth of a man's religious or philosophical outlook; also, that a man's religious or philosophical convictions inevitably influence his attitude to and treatment of his data. This invariable interaction of personal conviction and the data of religion—which so often become data only as the result of a *bona fide* though subjective interpretation of the material—will, it may perhaps be found, explain Robertson Smith's most characteristic and most permanent work. Our most pressing task, then, is to understand him; and the aim of this Introduction is, in the first instance, to indicate what seems to be the genetic connexion between his life-work as a whole and his theories of religion.

In Robertson Smith there was a man of really astonishing erudition and acute speculative ability. Brilliant in conversation and dexterous in argument, his letters reveal that to the very end he was a man of the deepest religious feelings. Moreover, he was, at least as a young man, profoundly interested in theology. In *The Old Testament in the Jewish Church* (1881) he did more than any one else to interpret to English-speaking readers the new stage in Old Testament criticism, the importance of which for the study of Semitic religion he has described in his Preface (p. xv). In his highly technical studies, first on Semitic sociology, later on Semitic religion and religious institutions, he might seem to have outgrown the theologian and the biblical critic. Yet he attracted attention as much by his uncompromising treatment of the *minutiæ* of Israelite and Oriental life, seriously offending those who would sever the Bible from the world which gave birth to it and in which it grew up, as by his insistence to the last upon the real difference between Biblical Religion and all else.

He was born in November 1846, and, when barely turned twenty-two, in a paper on "Christianity and the Supernatural" he comes before us as a keen reformer : "It is the business of Christianity to conquer the whole universe to itself and not least the universe of thought."[1] He desires a new Reformation, for, as he found occasion to complain, in many respects "the first promise of the Reformation was not fulfilled in the sequel" (p. 401). The Reformers gradually departed from their own principles and began to explain and justify themselves to themselves. But they had had a new way of looking at the Bible—in contrast to the unhistorical intellectualism of their opponents ; and he upholds the "historical treatment" of Scripture, asserting that "just as it requires a historic sense to understand profane history, it requires a spiritual sense to understand sacred history." So he would restore the Reformation principles of Biblical criticism, and readers of *The Old Testament in the Jewish Church* will remember how, especially in his opening chapter, he is at pains to combine the principles of a thorough-going criticism with the principles which permeated Western Europe at the Reformation.

Throughout he takes his stand upon the Bible. The Bible is not a Book of Infallible Truth, nor is it mainly a Divine Body of Doctrine, or a supernatural communication of Doctrines. It has the Holy Spirit behind it ; it is the historic manifestation of God in Christ, and speaks from the heart and to the heart : this is a cardinal point in the genuine Reformation which Protestant theology has almost forgotten (p. 406). The Bible when diligently studied is "the true manual of a Catholic religious life." He looked for a new Catholicity, and

[1] *Lectures*, p. 135, dated January 1869. The quotations that follow are, of course, of different dates.

by this he did not mean " toleration and compromise " (p. 332) —that would have been unlike the man he ever was ! Current theology dissatisfied him. As early as 1869 he was asserting that it was necessary " frankly to recognize the need of progress in our theological conceptions," for to cling to an unchangeable dogma is to cease to cling to the Christ of the Gospels who transcends the theology of every age (pp. 151, 162).

Current theology, he complained, had not rightly defined its relation to Scripture and its relation to human thought ; and, in a striking, though little known, essay on " The Place of Theology in the Work and Growth of the Church " (1875), he laments the lack of advance in the Church and the inability of theology to speak " any decisive and convincing word in the questions of the day." As he says in one of his trenchant remarks, " a Church which ceases to theologize ceases in the same moment to grow." He demands a " vigorous theology " : " a religion without theology means, for the most part, a religion without God." Theology is a safeguard against the mysticism which regards with complacency a degree of ignorance in the laity which is inconsistent with truly moral growth. Loose unshaped knowledge is a hindrance, and side by side with Christian experience there must go " an exercise of real hard thought before our knowledge takes scientific shape and is really worthy to be called theology " (p. 160). Accordingly, a theology of permanent value is not to be shaped with reference to the present attitude of unbelief, the cause of which he finds in the "actual imperfection of the existent state of the Church " (p. 314, dated 1875).

He maintained that the relation between practical religion and theology requires serious consideration. Christian knowledge should be in direct contact with faith and practice ; and if inarticulate, it is " deep inarticulate knowledge elaborated in practice." The true function of theology is to make explicit and elaborate truths which " in the shape of practical tact and insight lie at the root of untheological wisdom " (pp. 321 *sqq.*). "The theology of a living Church," he had said earlier, "does not start from the mere outward form and vehicle of Christianity "; there can be no true theology where there is no true Christian life (pp. 152, 155 ; cf. 133). It is religious experience which makes us believe in the authority of Scripture and not the reverse. So writes the young theologian, insisting upon the difference between the practical religious life, on the one side, and on the other, the theology which once alive has become defective and moribund.

As we read his early addresses it is very difficult not to perceive that the way is being paved for his subsequent recognition of the superior significance, for the study of the world's religions, of the unspoken ideas embodied in traditional ritual (cf. below, pp. 25 foot, 26 top). Hence, just as theology is of varying value according to its relation to the circumstances of the age, so myth in turn is commonly of secondary importance.[1] The theology of a living Church, he had asserted (in 1869), comes when the Church is conscious that she holds the true substance of Christianity (*Lectures*, p. 155) ; and we shall miss the point of Robertson Smith's later researches if we ignore the fact that the man who hoped for a new Catholicity was, consciously or unconsciously, looking for the factors which are creative in religious development, and that in years to come he was to turn from the contrast between a living Christian faith and an imperfect theology to the contrast between the practical, working religion of primitive peoples and the secondary myths.

[1] We must recognize that sweeping condemnation of all myth is not intended, and that some myths may be of immediate value (see below, p. 501).

c

Theology, he declares, is needed in order to make Christianity a social thing; it implies a knowledge which can be put into words and imparted to a man who has not shared the experience of him who imparts it. It is a *social* bond; for a Christian society is not the sum of its individuals but an organic unity, and the fellowship or the corporate spirit which makes such a unity is a moral, not a physical fact. No outward sign but an invisible bond unites the Church invisible, the mystic body of Christ; and we cannot tell what partakers of the sacraments are true members of Christ.[1] Repeatedly he returns to the *personal* intercourse between God and man; and he quotes with approval Luther's saying that Faith unites the soul to Christ as a bride to her bridegroom (pp. 115, 225 *sq.*). This conviction of a close personal relationship is central in his early essays on Christian religion and theology, and it becomes of cardinal importance in *The Religion of the Semites*. It is, therefore, of the highest interest to perceive how the theologian was reaching out towards his pregnant generalization of the significance of the social unit—of the group and group-religion—which subsequent writers have developed further along different lines.

Hebrew Prophecy interested him from the first, and his great book on the *Prophets of Israel* (first ed. 1882; second ed. 1902) is still a great classic. True prophecy, he laid down, rests upon the conviction of a personal and living power, the utterance of a new life, which sprang from the infinite source of all life (*Lectures*, pp. 189, 365). In what he has to say of the prophets, of Christ, and of the Reformers, and in his own religious idealism—throughout there peers the germ of his fine theory that the consciousness of communion is the most vital phenomenon in all religion. Not that all

---

[1] Pp. 325 *sqq.*, cf. 275, 319. There is no grace *ex opere operato* (p. 223, cf. p. 152).

else is unessential, but that it vitalizes religion, and without
it the progressive development of religion would be inexplicable. It is in this sense that the idea of communion is
original or primary, and much confusion has been caused
because this has not been fully realized.

Religion has its ebb and flow, and different stages have
their distinctive criteria. The Reformation was marked by
the new growth of the religious spirit, a new self-consciousness
separates the Reformers from their fore-goers ; a new stage
was reached, and it was of supreme importance for the
dynamics of religion. From time to time there comes the
stage when a distinction can be drawn between the sign and
the signified, between the word and its real meaning, between
the outward letter and the experiences demanding expression.
" With the Reformation begins a great awakening into new
self-conscious personal life " (p. 225). So it came to pass
that while acknowledging himself a son of the Reformation,
he was profoundly dissatisfied with the conditions in which
he found himself, and gradually passed from his arresting
treatment of current religion and theology to the inquiry
into the systematic treatment of Semitic religion. The task
of restating religious truths gave way to the distinctly
specialised study of ancient religion, and almost at the close
of his life we find this surely noteworthy admission, " I
begin to think I never can have been a theologian " (*Life*,
p. 535).

But throughout he placed the Bible by itself, and insisted that Christianity must be supernatural. Yet as early
as 1869 he was saying that the significance of the supernatural falls away when man's redemption ceases to be
imperfect (p. 119). More precisely, this means that the
fellowship of God and Man, with its implication of divine
" immanence," is accompanied with the consciousness of
the gulf between the human and the divine. Prophets

were filled with the conviction of a " personal " communion
with God ; they were inspired by something distinct from
themselves and not by " the immanent spirit of the universe
working in their own hearts " (p. 365). Their supreme
consciousness of the nearness and immediacy of the Divine
was of " a transcendent," not an " immanent " power, and
it is essential to remember that wholly characteristic of
Robertson Smith's position is his denial of Semitic monotheism and his recognition that " immanence " no less than
" transcendence " distinguishes Semitic religion generally.
The significance of this has hardly been sufficiently realized,
and demands a few words.

In a very notable essay on " Prophecy and Personality "
January 1868) the young scholar pointed out how the
prophet's personality builds up the vision which he sees
(p. 98). The *subjective* side is vital—we have only to compare the " varieties of religious experience " and observe
the difference in content and value due to the difference in
training and temperament of each prophet, seer, or mystic.
But, as he himself says a little later, " a consciousness
originally subjective in character, is not . . . purely subjective in origin." There is no " dictation from on high of
truths about God and man " ; and he is as anxious to avoid
false ideas of inspiration and revelation as to escape " the
no less dangerous extreme of mysticism giving an unbounded
play to an unrestrained subjectivity " (p. 157 *sq.*). In a
remarkable essay on the " Poetry of the Old Testament,"
written in 1877, he takes a wider view of religion. Com-
menting upon the absence of calm, disciplined, and intellectual effort among primitive peoples, he lays stress upon
the intensely practical nature of their religion. " All
thought stands in immediate contact with living impressions
and feelings, and so, if incapable of rising to the abstract,
is prevented from sinking to the unreal," Religious truths

centre in human life and human interests. There was no "dreamy unpractical sentimentalism," and he has the profound observation that it is the preponderance of the emotional rather than of the rational part of a man's nature that makes a strong personality able to conquer all difficulties, whereas intellectual acuteness is often associated with a restlessness of purpose that can attain nothing great (p. 443). It is a remark which one is tempted to take as an unconscious self-revelation.

Now to the Semites and other primitive peoples the Universe is "a complex of living powers" with which man enters into a fellowship; he is awed by their might, or he boastfully bends them to his service. All nature is "instinct with life which vibrates responsive to each change in his personal feelings and spiritual relations" (p. 421 *sq.*). Everywhere man sees in nature life bearing directly upon him. All life has a meaning for man, the fascination for the Semitic mind of the idea of practical lordship over powers mightier than himself "finds a loftier and truer, but not less characteristic, expression in the Old Testament." His ethical monotheism alone saved the Israelite. In vivid sentences Robertson Smith paints "the nature-worship of the heathen Semites," the "religion of passionate emotion," the worship "of those inner powers, awful because unseen, of which outer things are only the symbol," the "sombre horror" and "wildest sensuality." "The very tone of mind which makes Semitic heathenism the most hideous of false worships, enabled the Hebrew nation to grasp with unparalleled tenacity and force the spiritual idea of Jehovah." These are weighty words, and they must be before us when some writers with the best intentions draw idyllic pictures of religion prior to the prophets, and unwittingly make of these majestic figures an unintelligible phenomenon in the history of religion, unintentionally accusing them of grossest exaggeration.

" To the Hebrew, force is life and life is personality "
(*ib.*) ; and we come to perceive that what we call " religion "
is, as it were, woven upon a texture of beliefs and customs
which cannot be called by that name, and that a social-
religious system is the safeguard against the dangerous
kinship of Magic with Religion. The lofty spiritual heights
of the Israelite prophets are a reaction against the crudest
physical and material depths ; and in the darkness, cruelty
and coarsest orgies of the Semite—ever prone to extremes—it
was left for the few to enunciate truths of spiritual intimacy
with the Divine and of man's place in the Universe. One
has only to read the pages on Hebrew poetry and on the
Semite's sense of personal fellowship with the life of all that
surrounds him—animate and inanimate—to realize how
natural was the transition from the theologian writing in
1877 on the " Poetry of the Old Testament," to the anthropologist who, in July 1880, had begun to view the Old Testament and the Semites in the light of M'Lennan's researches
on totemism.

The merit of M'Lennan's totem-hypothesis lies, according
to Robertson Smith, in the fact that " it does justice to the
intimate relation between religion and the fundamental
structure of society which is so characteristic of the ancient
world." [1] It threw new light upon the history of religion
as a social system ; and it is not surprising, when we consider his readiness to recognize both the lighter and darker
sides of primitive religion, that his own theory of totem-
sacrament seemed to him to provide the key to the development of religion from its lowest to its highest forms. The
theory was justly called by Reinach " one of the most
brilliant discoveries of modern science " ; [2] and in spite of

---

[1] *Kinship and Marriage*, p. 258 *sq.*

[2] S. Reinach, *Cultes, Mythes et Religions*, iv. 23 (cited in *Life*, p. 567).
Reinach's well-known *mot* concerning Robertson Smith—" *genuit Frazerum* "

the extent to which totemism has been abused, this rudimentary type of cult still provides one of the most intricate problems of the modern study of religion.[1] The reasons for this can be briefly summarized. (1) There are the extremely difficult technical problems of distinguishing between the varieties of totemism and totemic, totemistic and theriomorphic beliefs and practices. (2) Animal deities and animal imagery prevail even among advanced peoples. (3) There is a persistence or recrudescence of the animal features (whether totemic or not) by the side of and in spite of distinctly high forms of cult. (4) Besides the obvious and essential points of contrast between totemic (and all related) features and anthropomorphic religion, there are no less essential points of contact and a genetic connexion can apparently be traced between them. At all events, no theory of the phenomena of religion can be entertained which does not do adequate justice to these beliefs and practices which seem to be so remote from our way of thinking. For (5) totemism involves a way of thinking which it is difficult or impossible for us to grasp ; and in the attempt to understand the true relation between it and higher modes of thought we immensely enlarge our knowledge of mental processes and the lines along which they have developed.

To put the fundamental problem otherwise, we have to determine (1) whether the most rudimentary types of religion were (a) anthropomorphic or (b) theriomorphic, and specifically totemic ; (2) whether the latter type (b) can reasonably be derived from the former (a); and (3) into what did the latter develop, if at all. If theriomorphism is, as at times it seems to be, a refuge from an inadequate or impoverished anthropomorphism, was it—was totemism—normal before

—can be supplemented by the remarks of his biographers in the *Life*, p. 494 *sq.*, and by Sir James Frazer's own Preface to *The Golden Bough*.

[1] See especially A. van Gennep, *L'État actuel du Problème Totémique* (1920). For a recent definition of totemism, see below, p. 535 n. 1.

there was anthropomorphic religion ? Such questions cannot be ignored by those who are interested in the line of development which religion has taken hitherto.

Sir James Frazer, who dedicated *The Golden Bough* to his friend Robertson Smith, "in gratitude and admiration," refers in the Preface of the Second Edition (1900) to the famous discoveries made in Central Australia by Sir Baldwin Spencer and Mr F. J. Gillen which revolutionized ideas of totemism, and indeed of rudimentary religion in general. He points out that while these have proved that there were indeed—as Robertson Smith had surmised—clans who killed and solemnly ate their totem animal, this fact did not make the rite either a universal one or the origin of animal sacrifice in general. More than that, the totem was not a god, but on a more equal relationship ; and the rites were not "religious" but "magical." Hence, if Robertson Smith's insight was thus triumphantly justified in some essential particulars, it now appeared that totemism was not the sort of cult that he had supposed. Naturally no one would wish to minimize the importance of Sir James Frazer's candid admissions in *The Golden Bough* and elsewhere, but several points have certainly to be taken into consideration. Jevons, Marett, and Durkheim, all most highly equipped and competent observers, and writing from rather different standpoints, do not agree that Robertson Smith is refuted by the character of the Australian evidence. And Malinowski, in the course of a valuable study of primitive religion, while speaking of Central Australian totemism as "a system of *magical* co-operation," emphasizes its survival value, and observes that "totemism appears . . . as a blessing bestowed by *religion* on primitive man's efforts in dealing with his useful surroundings." [1] Obviously

[1] In *Science, Religion and Reality* (ed. J. Needham, 1925), p. 46. The italics are ours.

our conceptions of " religion " and " magic " are at stake.

Further, the totem is not, after all, precisely the equal of man, and in totemism we find ruder forms of what is familiar in anthropomorphic religion : imitation of and identification with the sacred being, appeal to it, and value attached to its name. Nay, more, with his usual courtesy and invariable loyalty to facts, Sir James Frazer has drawn the attention of the present writer to certain cases where the totem is actually the object of a cult.[1] The importance of the new evidence is undeniable, and it brings to the front two urgent questions. The first is, is it desirable to have only the two pigeon-holes—*either* Religion *or* Magic— wherein to distribute the relevant data ? Do we not also need the description Magico-Religious ? The second concerns degrees of Religion and the varying quality of Deity. Even in anthropomorphic religion gods often stand in a very close relationship to their worshippers, and, as frequently in personal religion and mysticism, the attitude of dependence upon the god is by no means the only one. Again, there are both near and remote gods ; and they vary in status, even as at the present day saints or Eastern *welis* are not " gods " from the point of view of the orthodox and national religion, though they are apt to be very adequate deities from that of the inhabitant of the locality wherein they are commanding figures.

Further, as a general rule, religion is much more " practical " than is recognized by writers who have adversely criticized Robertson Smith's leading positions ; and the

---

[1] In a letter of April 27, 1925, Sir James Frazer states that the cases which he had lately noticed of worship or sacrifices regularly offered to totems are (1) in the Bombay Presidency, R. E. Enthoven, *Folklore of Bombay* (Oxford, 1924), pp. 19, 209–211 ; (2) in the Ivory Coast, L. Tauxier, *Nègres Gouro et Gagou* (Paris, 1924), pp. 145, 160, 183, 205, 223, 256, 257 ; and (3) in the Solomon Islands, C. E. Fox, *The Threshold of the Pacific* (London, 1924), pp. 10 *sq.*, 72, 73, 74, 75, 275.

extent to which directness, intimacy, and a confidence verging on compulsion colour much that is remote from "magic," and can only be regarded as "religion," is as significant as it is surprising. Long ago an acute critic remarked that Robertson Smith's idea of a primitive communion " seemed too theologically abstract to be at the basis of savage rites of sacrifice." [1] But, as has been seen, Smith had already insisted upon the practical nature of primitive, and especially of Semitic religion.[2] The longing for Atonement and the rites which brought together gods and worshippers were ultimately for the "material" as for the "spiritual" well-being of men. This is both Biblical and primitive religion, and students, compelled to formulate the difference between Religion and Magic, and between degrees of Deity, may yet find themselves compelled to consider what shall be the criterion of "spiritual" religion (see pp. 676 *sqq.*).

If the objection just referred to appears to rest on the frequent confusion of the perception of metaphysical or theological facts with the capacity for metaphysical or theological reasoning—on which, see p. 655 and n.2—a more forcible criticism is that which objects, and not unjustly, that Robertson Smith carried simplification too far and formulated too simple a theory of the history of religion.[3]

In his theory of the totem-sacrament, while freely recognizing the prominence of the gift-idea in all religion, he gave the priority to the communion idea. The most recent study of the subject emphasizes the strength and persistence of the gift idea, but clearly recognizes that it does not explain all the data.[4] The eminent Dominican, Father Lagrange,

[1] Jos. Jacobs, *Studies in Biblical Archæology* (1894), p. 33 *sq.*

[2] Cf. *Lectures*, p. 443 (above, p. xxxvi *sq.*), and *Old Testament in the Jewish Church*, p. 441 (cited below, p. 671).

[3] See *Life*, p. 517 *sq.*

[4] G. Buchanan Gray, *Sacrifice in the Old Testament* (Oxford, 1925), p. 352, etc. This posthumous volume covers a very wide field ; and it is much to be deplored that so splendid a scholar, who made so many

author of a work which in many respects is scarcely less indispensable than *The Relgiion of the Semites,* makes many valuable criticisms ; but he agrees that communion is a constitutive element in sacrifice, and that the *do ut des* element does not explain the *horror sacer.*[1] Rather is it that the author, like all pioneers, is deemed to have exaggerated the prevalence and significance of the communion idea. So, Hubert and Mauss in their important monograph on sacrifice, while agreeing with Robertson Smith's general treatment of taboos and the ideas of holy and unclean, decisively reject his genealogical explanation of the history of sacrifices.[2] And Durkheim, too, who perhaps more than any other writer has most powerfully supplemented his treatment of religion as a social institution, points out that ideas of gift, renunciation, and expiation are very early.[3]

Earnest heed must be paid to these criticisms ; yet, when all has been said, is it not true that every profound religious act is, in a sense, an act of communion ? So, as G. F. Moore has pointed out, the sacrificial feast at the sanctuary must have strengthened the bond of religion by the sense of God's presence and friendliness.[4] Malinowski speaks of the gifts of food to the gods as " communion in beneficent abundance."[5] To be sure, a more careful study might lead us to attempt to draw the lines between friendliness, fellowship, communion,

permanent contributions to Biblical Studies, was not spared to give unity and completeness to this admirable collection of lectures.

[1] *Études des Religions Sémitiques,* p. 267. The value of this work will be evident from the many references to it in the new notes to this edition. Its attitude can be gauged from the statement in the Preface that *The Religion of the Semites* " est constamment dominé par une idée fausse, l'importance exagérée du totémisme dans l'histoire de la religion."

[2] *Mélanges d'Hist. des Religions,* Preface, p. iv.

[3] *The Elementary Forms of the Religious Life : a Study in Religious Sociology* (London, 1915), pp. 343, 406.

[4] *Ency. Biblica,* art. "Sacrifice" (§ 42 end); still the completest synopsis of the subject from the Biblical point of view.

[5] *Op. cit.,* p. 43.

and identity.[1] In this way it might be possible to discuss
" the degree of at-one-ment present in the various Sacrifices,"
how far, for example, " any sense of Divine indwelling " was
conveyed by the Jewish Peace Offering.[2] Buchanan Gray
himself, in the volume already referred to, is at pains to
discuss the different nuances of the sacrificial ceremonies.
Undoubtedly much could be done along such lines. One
could compare and contrast the relative psychological effect
of sacred stones (and other inanimate objects), sacred
animals (varying in utility or in character), and sacred men
(ancestors, saints, divine rulers, etc.). One could consider
the sort of ideas which would naturally be symbolized, suggested, or carried by each of these. One could discuss the
possible place of each in the social group. In this way much
light could be thrown upon the self-evident effects—social,
moral, intellectual—which different sorts of sacred persons,
things, or rites could have upon a religion and its vicissitudes.
But there would remain ultimate problems which, even if
they are not handled, cannot be dismissed.

The difficulty of interpreting rites is notorious ; they may
not retain their apparently obvious meaning, and may
perhaps have acquired a new one. The most solemn of rites
may have only a transitory value for the worshipper, and the
most simple of commemorative occasions may be charged
with the profoundest meaning. Further, the study of the
history of religion reveals the essential fact that at certain
periods religion has lost that reality which had once made
it a force in the life of a people ; or a line is drawn between
the existing religion and new spiritual tendencies, and the
standard of real and true religion is set so high that it cannot

---

[1] See the criticisms of M. H. Pinard de la Boullaye, S.J., in his elaborate
work, *Étude Comparée des Religions : Essai Critique* (Paris, 1922 and 1925),
ii. 58.

[2] S. C. Gayford, *Sacrifice and Priesthood* (London, 1914), pp.
33, 39.

be ignored in an estimate of religion in general.   The inquiry into the vicissitudes of religious beliefs and practices is that into men's convictions concerning what to them were supreme realities, and it cannot be indifferent to the great periods which force the question whether and in what way the ultimate realities of the Universe are themselves involved in those convictions which are explicit or implicit in religion.

The student who has grasped the spirit of the Bible knows that in the last analysis no human being or human institution can determine the real value of convictions of the relations between man and God.   Robertson Smith wrote in 1871 that men cannot judge who are true members of Christ (above, p. xxxiv).   There are Biblical passages which imply that the Deity may be in fellowship with men who do not recognize Him, and that He does not necessarily operate in accordance with the ways in which He has been apprehended.   Such are among the data of religion, and no impartial student can refuse to find a place for them in the final synthesis.   It is this transcendence of the ultimate realities, and the knowledge that convictions and theories are approximations, and that the progress of thought enables us to test these approximations, which combine to make the newer study of the world's religions a landmark in the history of religion.

Views are extensively held to the effect that Magic is absolutely prior to Religion, that Fear is primary, and that Sacrifice served originally to propitiate gods and avert their anger—and so forth.   One's own personal religion may make it impossible to accept such views ; one's experience may convince one that familiarity certainly breeds indifference, and that it is natural to seek to placate the anger only of one who is *known*.   But, quite apart from one's personal religion, it is puzzling to see how ideas could ever arise in the first instance of a supersensuous being with particular attributes ; and the views in question labour under the double disadvan-

tage of surreptitiously introducing all the question-begging
elements and of doing scanty justice to their rivals. On the
other hand, on the assumption of the relative priority of
Religion certain tendencies are seen to be normal and inevitable. On the assumption of certain conceptions of the
Ultimate Realities the variation and vicissitudes of ideas of
gods and men can be more or less intelligibly traced, and the
interrelation between the religious (magical, etc.) and the
non-religious spheres can be fruitfully studied. When what is
called " religion," in its divers forms, makes its appearance in
an individual's life and thought it becomes so fused with the
" non-religious," that the really vital problem for modern
research is not the Conflict of Science and Religion, so called,
but the varying relations between the " religious " and
" non-religious " phases of life and their mutual interaction.
Thus there quickly arises the need for a more theoretical
treatment of religion which is able to do justice to those
views, on the one side or the other, which are pronounced
improbable or impossible ; and of this theoretical treatment
Robertson Smith, because of his line of approach, may be
claimed as the founder.

It is of the utmost importance that we should distinguish
between actual historical origins and whatever inaugurates
new lines of development. Robertson Smith is concerned
with creative ideas, with those that recur and govern the
evolution of faith and worship. It is an inquiry, as he
himself admits, of real interest to the " philosophical student "
(p. 15). And when he argues that the communion of the
group with their god stands at the head of all developments
it is easy to see how extraordinarily impressive the theory
is from the theistic standpoint, but how delicate, directly we
perceive that of the great variety of experiences which can be
classed as "numinous," only some are of definite "religious"
significance, and these, after what has been said, differ in

quality and value.[1] Now Robertson Smith is not merely concerned with creative ideas and creative experiences—the factors that make for new developments in religion—he takes a very definite Christian standpoint, and the question is really a very important one, whether this has prejudiced or facilitated his researches.

His peculiar interest in the Reformation and Protestantism, his desire for some new formulation of theology, and his pioneering work in the criticism of the Old Testament, in particular the function of the prophets, and finally his invariable distinction between " natural " and " supernatural " religion have recognizably influenced the lines he has taken. Accordingly, the ebb and flow of beliefs and the vicissitudes of cults are not so significant for him as that progressive development which would undoubtedly strike him as he looked back upon the " heathenism " of the Semites and the more rudimentary cults of primitive peoples, and looked forward to a further development in religion. The problems as they presented themselves to him were necessarily other than those that confront scholars whose main work has lain in other fields, or whose deepest sympathies are perchance differently directed. The training which might have encouraged the most hesitating and mediating of inquiries made him at all events the most uncompromising of investigators ; and if *The Religion of the Semites* marks an epoch, it was because it came from the hands of a man who combined with unequalled knowledge a sympathetic insight into the most advanced and the most rudimentary religions in a way which has not been equalled by his successors, and whose genius saw new prospects opening out in the world of thought. With him : *la théorie c'est l'homme.*

[1] According to Hubert and Mauss the sacrifice establishes a communication between the sacred sphere and the profane (cf. Toy's summary, *Introduction to the History of Religion*, § 1049). This is much more generalized than Robertson Smith's theory of the communion of worshippers

That Robertson Smith's arguments were influenced by current evolutionary ideas was inevitable, and one can but say that the study of beliefs and customs as such can only be pursued along evolutionary lines, and that those writers who object to one theory of development usually prove to be cherishing another of their own. In point of fact, we pass from the "comparative" treatment of the data of religion to the best method of presenting them, and enter upon the most difficult part of the subject. In the first place, then, it may be observed that the main argument of *The Religion of the Semites* does not require us to believe that the communion idea is some absolutely prior abstraction. His recognition of aberration, degradation, etc. (pp. 354, 394), indicates that by the "origin" of sacrifice is not meant that which characterized the earliest prehistoric religion alone. It is rather that this idea, although it operated from the very first, lies at the back of the new and significant stages in the development of sacrificial ritual. On the same analogy, it can be seen that similar tendencies explain initiation, in one place into a tribal group, in another into important secret societies, and in a third into small guilds or unions (cf. p. 607 *sq.*). Further, revolutionary aims and methods, very similar in several respects, will differ everywhere according to current conditions. And even as regards the "animal" features in totemism, there are significant analogies not only in "totemistic" rites (those that are not strictly "totemic"), but also in those that can only be called "theriomorphic" (cf. p. 538 *sq.*). Thus, there are similar recurrent elements which take different forms peculiar to each age, land, and community, and a Science of Religion must do justice alike to the essential resemblances and the equally essential differences.

with their *god* ; but less so than the more recent conception of experiences of the "numinous," see p. 554.

In the present state of knowledge, ambiguity and vagueness are here unavoidable. None the less we can understand Robertson Smith's meaning when he speaks of " the more ancient idea of a living communion " and its " element of permanent truth " (p. 396). He has in mind the recurrence of the idea at different stages ; and its " truth " is proved by the fact that it is constantly reappearing, though reshaped, and evidently answers to some vital need. Again, when both ordinary and extraordinary sacrifices go back to the same principle (p. 312), we may use symbols and say that the x which is found in l reappears in m and n. But, we ask, do n and m go back to l, or to the common factor x ? Analysis takes us back to what Buchanan Gray suggestively calls the " actual creative idea." [1] But instead of inaugural or creative ideas—or experiences—we can go back to an initiator or originator, to an *arkhē*.[2] Or else we arrive at the embodiment of an idea, or some system or some stage which, by reason of its evident primary position, is commonly regarded as the true " origin." Thus it is easy to see how confusion can arise when the attempt is made to account for recurring tendencies or to trace back things to their " beginnings."

Indeed, when sacrificial rites—or aught else for that matter—are traced back to a single ancestor, it is easier to criticize the fallaciousness of this simple procedure than to find a better one that is not too intricate.[3] We cannot intelligently conceive any absolute beginning : our most ancient data are relatively recent, considering the antiquity of man ; the most primitive communities have a history behind them ; and repeatedly it can be seen that ancient evidence is not necessarily prior—sociologically speaking—

---

[1] Gray, *Sacrifice*, p. 359 n.

[2] See especially J. L. Myres, *The Political Ideas of the Greeks* (1927), Index, *s.v.*

[3] Cf. p. 499. Instead of seeking a single ancestor, the attempt is often made to find a single ancestral home, cf. p. 497.

d

to that which is later.   As a general rule one must be guided
by a knowledge of actual known processes in the vicissitudes
of religious and other thought, and by "methodological
necessity"—the most effective treatment of the data.   Many
cases will be found in these pages where we gradually pass
from mere "comparison" to "methodology," and problems
arise which are much too technical for discussion here.
Some of them may be mentioned as illustrations.

The theory of the absolute priority of mother-right—
of which there are several varieties—was adopted by Robertson Smith, and after being under a cloud, has again become
respectable.   We must recognize that certain conditions
would give mother-right prominence at certain periods and—
what is no less interesting—they can also make the theory
itself more attractive !   Thus the Arabian evidence belongs
on the whole to a transitional period, after the decline of
the great cultures to which the South Arabian inscriptions
testify ;   and while it is arguable that in prehistoric times
mother-right would completely overshadow father-right, it
is a little difficult to see why it should be given absolute
priority.[1]   Next, if we consider the theory of a primitive
promiscuity—now fallen into the background—it can be
argued that promiscuity is likely to lead to the inauguration
of some social *régime*, even as rampant lawlessness will force
the effort to institute order.   Promiscuity and lawlessness
can hardly be regarded as a stage of evolution "prior" to
the "introduction" of social order and justice, but rather
as a step leading thereto, and doubtless often following upon

---

[1] It may be noticed that the question of the relative priority of gods as
"brothers" or as "fathers" (pp. 510, 512) is complicated by such an
observation as Oswald Spengler's on the Russian tendency away from the
Father-God to a fraternal relationship ; see *Decline of the West*, i. 201 n. 2
("Christ, even, is conceived as a Brother"). The tendencies which affect
conceptions of (*a*) supreme gods, and (*b*) those near at hand and more
closely associated with men, cannot be treated as stages in any single
development.

the collapse of some earlier system. In other words, we can only deal effectively with systems, and although the social group is made up of individuals, the group rather than the *socius* is the more effective unit.

Individual religion and individual property are secondary (p. 247 *sq.*), though it is obvious that to men of personality all the great changes are due. Among rudimentary peoples both personal religion and personal property can be traced, but the cases are often irrelevant, just in the same way as the social equality which we discern among primitive peoples disappears on closer inspection, but the inequalities are negligible for the particular purpose of our initial inquiry. Again, in tracing back the development of life and thought, we go from our modern highly differentiated and specialized conditions to conditions so extremely simple as to appear absolutely undifferentiated. But the most homogeneous clan-units and the simplest elements which we reach prove to be integral parts of some larger system or organism. It is perfectly true that development is *towards* specialization and complexity ; but the facts that can be adduced in support of this must be balanced with the facts that point back to societies or systems possessing a differentiation and specialization peculiar to themselves.[1] It would be safer to say that the process of development or evolution is from one *system* to another.

Some important developments may preferably be regarded as alternations, or as extreme forms of transition which are otherwise so normal as not to attract attention. Such, for example, is the change from happy (or confident) to gloomy (and pessimistic) types of religion. Some writers find evidence enough to prove that primitive man must

---

[1] For example, the dichotomies good and bad, the sacred and profane, and the supernatural and natural are clearly recognized, but the contents are differently arranged.

have lived in a state of fear, oppressed by unknown terrors ; whereas Robertson Smith is more concerned with the creative moments, the confidence and assurance which make for progressive development (see p. 519 *sq.*). Again, while it is indubitably suggestive to conceive of an absolute development from the " childhood " of humanity to its adolescence or maturity (p. 257), there is an increase or growth of consciousness which is of immense importance for the history of separate peoples or of individuals, and this in turn differs qualitively from many less epoch-making changes. The transition from the " natural " to the " conscious " state will mark eras ; but it is precisely the new awakening, awareness, and rebirth which cause discontinuity and shatter facile theories of a continuous development.[1]

The " childish unconsciousness " of inexorable laws (p. 257) is, unfortunately, by no means confined to primitive peoples, but it is only another example of a perfectly intelligible statement which is extremely helpful, though its limitations are evident. It is legitimate to speak of the " triumph of the gods over the demons " (p. 122), or to say that gods " become " demons, or that Baal was " changed " from a god of rain to one of springs, or even that totems " become " gods. The words express intelligibly enough certain vicissitudes in ideas concerning gods or supernatural beings ; but it is necessary to observe that this simple terminology is really hindering more fruitful ways of handling the events in the world of thought, and that the alternative to this " mythology " would take us away from Comparative Religion to a department of Mental Science.[2]

---

[1] This is not to say that the " evolutionary " *façon de penser* is wrong, but that it stands in need of a more careful application.

[2] Instinctively, and surely with some justification, we said at the beginning of this Introduction that *The Religion of the Semites* " grew out " of certain preliminary work; but the process, it will now be seen, is much more complex and difficult to describe. On the other hand, the more

Next we observe that Robertson Smith's main theories have far-reaching implications which have yet to be worked out. His theory of the communion of gods and men leads back to the "naturally holy," to an inherent sanctity which is more primary than any process of sanctification. The unity of gods and men is primary, the unity is always being broken, and the compact or covenant is secondary. The unity is potential, and the rite which actualizes it really cements it afresh. The facts of aberration and deterioration, and the consciousness of a higher ideal from which one has lapsed, have gone to create the conception of a "Fall" as some original event in human history, as distinct from the many occasions when one is painfully conscious of one's lapses and of the terrible difference between the ordinary self and the harmony which, in theistic experience, is the fellowship of God and Man. Another similar translation of psychological experience into an historical event is the "Primitive Revelation." Without the consciousness of the Holy or Sacred there could be neither religion of social importance nor any great steps in the development of religion ; but inasmuch as every experience of a Sacred Power will be determined by contemporary conditions of knowledge, mode of life, and so forth, the farther back we travel in human history, the more difficult is it to imagine the content of prehistoric religion. And though, from the solely intellectual point of view, "God" is also a methodological necessity and prior to all things, the meaning it had for the most primitive social-religious cult can be set down only in the most abstract terms.

We may agree with Robertson Smith that the terrestrial Baal is older than the cosmic, for ideas of the remote are

tangible and intelligible cases of development, such as the genesis of Robertson Smith's volume, may perhaps enable one to apprehend and illustrate those which are more complicated (cf. p. 499, near foot), and to discover that a similar sort of process rules throughout.

based upon a knowledge of the near. An experience of a transcendent power will bring about the development of the positive knowledge of the day ; but such an experience will, in the first instance, be limited by ordinary experience. Ideas concerning the gods are influenced by men who themselves have been influenced by transcendent experiences ; men have learnt that they must imitate the gods, but they have also had to learn what it was they had to imitate. A curious complexity manifests itself as we follow the mutual interaction of the religious and the non-religious spheres of life and thought; but the facts of social development and the facts of religious experience, when taken together, point to a development from the totem-stage upwards by the side of a gradually deepening theism under the influence of outstanding men and their more " ethical " ideas and " anthropomorphic " type of religion (see p. 670). In a word, the data of " theistic " development do not by any means exclude Robertson Smith's theory which takes back sacrifice to the " theriomorphic " totem-stage.

His theory of the unity of group and its god has another very important issue. This group-unit has its ordinary, secular or " profane " interests, and it can therefore be said that the social system includes within itself both the " sacred " (*e.g.* the gods, sacred ceremonies, etc.) and the " secular." The social group is a practical working system, a " natural " one, and the god and other supernatural beings form a " natural " part of it. Indeed, so much so is this the case that there is a tendency for men to take their gods for granted and the result is detrimental to the religious and social development of the group. The occasions when the group and gods come together, and usually for the practical purposes of life, are specifically " sacred," and—psychologically —they are essentially different from the " secular," even as the " sacred " and " secular " states of the individual are

two essentially different phases in one and the same individual. Hence the gods are a "natural" part of the social
unit. But they are also "supernatural"; and at a higher
stage of development it becomes more clear that the god
is a natural part of the natural environment, and therefore
"immanent." At the same time, he is felt to be on another
and higher plane of existence, and the gulf between him
and man makes him "transcendent." To the genuine
theist God is a Transcendent Being, but He is also a
natural part of the Universe (i.e. of the *ultimate* whole
of which man knows only a part). Hence there are two
senses of the "natural"—(a) that which is opposed to the
supernatural, and (b) that which includes this dichotomy;
and already in the primitive religions of the practical group-
unit of gods and men there are implicit those paradoxical
facts of personal experience which are fundamental for
theology.

Analysis takes us back to personal experiences of a
religious or spiritual order; but no less to impersonal processes which are self-vindicating, a power or a mechanism
which men use or misuse, and agencies such that the failure
to do right or the deed that is positively wrong has inevitable
consequences. Again, we are led back to single origins;
whence it comes to pass that religion is very often supposed
to be derived from a single factor. But one also gets back
to complementary ideas: Transcendence and Immanence,
Rights and Duties; they are dynamic, and upon them our
conception of the typical working social-religious unit can
be constructed.[1] The familiar processes of scission, isolation,
and disintegration, which we so readily trace in history,
point back to a system; and a working social system can
be regarded as a system of interrelated sentiments, ideas,
and aims. With all this, however, it does not follow that

[1] See *Encyc. of Religion and Ethics*, art. "Religion," §§ 29, 31 (1).

the ideal system which we logically construct existed ; but the system so constructed forms an ideal type whereby to evaluate social religious facts.[1]

Now in the course of differentiation of society and thought, new structures—whether sects or theories—are frequently built upon the narrowest bases, and at this point the question arises whether Robertson Smith has not been guilty of a gross methodological error in the use he has made of Nilus's Saracens. The student who is already acquainted with *The Religion of the Semites* will be aware of the prominence which is given to them and their bloody rite. Since Smith's day a little quiet fun has sometimes been poked at his Saracens, and we have to meet a typical criticism expressed in Lagrange's words that the rite is admittedly barbaric, but " *c'est trop isolé* pour qu'on tire de ce seul cas toute la théorie du sacrifice " (*Études*, p. 258). In reply to this, we are entitled at the outset to ask whether it is sound method to start from the normal rites, or at least those which correspond to ordinary instincts (*ib.* p. 259 n.). Are we to cry, " Mais cette sauvagerie n'a rien de religieux " ? Are we to take our stand upon some definition : " When I mention religion, I mean . . ." ? On the contrary, no science or philosophy of religion can start from any division into what is and what is not religious, even as science cannot at the outset rule out mongrels or weeds.

Further, although human sacrifice has been common enough, Robertson Smith treats it as exceptional (p. 394) ; whereas old Nilus, however isolated, gives us " a very typical embodiment of the main ideas that underlie Semitic sacrifices " (p. 345). And this is entirely justified if we analyse

---

[1] Inevitably one passes from " comparative " religion to the more theoretical treatment of the data ; and the history of comparison in the world of organic life will warn us to avoid such an error as the single abstract generalized type conceived by Geoffroy Saint-Hilaire (E. W. Hobson, *The Domain of Natural Science,* p. 385 *sq.*).

the rite and observe the parallels which can be found for every element. A more careful reading of *The Religion of the Semites* should have shown opponents that the communion-theory is not based upon and does not start from Nilus—as we have seen, it has a much profounder inception. The unprejudiced reader will discover for himself that it is part of a network of ideas which are common to mankind, even as every religion can be viewed as a particular structure of the numerous beliefs and practices which make up the world of religion. It must, of course, be granted that Robertson Smith has given every prominence to Nilus, but the value of his work does not rest upon Nilus, and he and his Saracens are no longer so vital. His evidence is still extremely important, but we do not need it as a clue.[1] We are assured that " even in its details it probably comes nearer " the primitive form of Semitic sacrifice (see p. 345) : that is to say, Robertson Smith, so far from starting from it, considers that he has found in it the most rudimentary embodiment of the main sacrificial ideas which he has discovered elsewhere.

Late and isolated Nilus may be, but an advanced stage of culture never excludes gross barbaric ide   or rites, either outside or—at certain periods at least—within ; nor does it exclude the emergence of " primitive " types of thought, however we may choose to evaluate them.[2] Hence while, on the one hand, the evidence of Nilus is an isolated example of a combination of tpyical ideas, human sacrifice, on the other hand, affords numerous examples of ideas which, for

[1] How a clue may come to be of secondary value is well seen in the literary criticism of the Pentateuch and the book of Joshua, where the difference in the Divine Names led to very important discoveries, which are of permanent value, whereas this particular criterion was soon found to be of relatively secondary importance.

[2] That is to say, the " primitive " is barbaric or it is spiritual, and it is a false conception of evolution which tends to regard it as necessarily the former.

reasons given, are not representative of the main development of religion. And here we have to remember the essential difference between Robertson Smith and some of his critics : human sacrifice, licentious cults, and so forth abound, and—like what Renan said of the Arabic Lexicon—the student of comparative religion can pick and choose the evidence for the theory he prefers ; but from first to last Smith is concerned with the factors that make for the progressive development of religion, and he is distinguishing between a systematic arrangement of the mere *data* of religion and the crucial facts of the *history* of religion.[1]

Exceptional and isolated are also the peculiar ceremonies of the totem clans in Central Australia, which partly confirm Robertson Smith, while putting his problems in a new light (above, p. xl). They afford most rudimentary examples of the pregnant ideas that mark the higher religions—as Durkheim in particular has shown—and there is no necessity to suppose that they correspond to, or even in their details approximate primitive prehistoric cults. It seems impossible to conceive more primitive *systems* ; and the totem cults bring to a head the problems of primitive religion in a way that is far more important for the Science of Religion than— and this must be admitted—for the ordinary theologian. The evidence is so remarkable as to demand some explanation. For, as " Mana " accounts for the unusual or abnormal (cf. p. 553), or as Religion is supposed, on one view, to fill the " gaps " in knowledge, so we are compelled to find a way of co-ordinating the more extraordinary phenomena of re-

---

[1] After all, Nilus is not quite isolated. Van Gennep (*Totémisme*, pp. 249 *sqq.*) cites from E. Doutté, *Les 'Aïssâoua à Tlemcen* (1900), who claims to have found a modern parallel. The evidence is certainly striking, and Van Gennep is hardly convincing when he disputes its value because of the interval of space and time which severs it from Nilus, and because the rite can be explained on the principles that actuate the brotherhood who practise it.

ligion and the more ordinary. The fact that various unusual, superstitious, or even abnormal beliefs seem to satisfy tribes is as important as the fact that the animal or plant species is, for very rudimentary peoples, a sufficient embodiment of profound ideas. Indeed, totemism enlarges the range of facts upon which we base our inductions, it widens our conception of the development of human personality ; and it enables us to consider, on the one side, the place of rude stone cults in the development of religion, and, on the other, the relations between theriomorphic and anthropomorphic supernatural beings who stand in a personal relationship to men. Robertson Smith took totemism more seriously than most other workers in the field, and, to judge from the influence this volume has had upon the study of religions, most would agree that his insight more than justified itself.

There are phenomena in the history of religion that are of pre-eminent value to others than theologians. They raise questions which do not occur to the students of current theology and philosophy, but upon the answer to them the future development of theology and philosophy seems to rest. It commonly happens that as new religions arise they ignore— perhaps inevitably, perhaps rightly—beliefs and practices which had been of no little value and efficacy, and had been efficacious and " true " for normal men. But in religious as in other thought men will strike off on a new line, and only in course of time is it found necessary to come to terms with that which had been ignored, if not condemned. So, as regards the lengthy history of religion, when one has attentively read the work of Sir James Frazer on the sacred man and the slain god, or of MM. Hubert and Mauss on the function of sacrifice, or of M. Émile Durkheim on the significance of social religious systems for the vicissitudes of mental development, it is impossible to resist the conviction that, not only the great religions of history other than the " highest," but even the very rudimentary religions, with their naïve experiences of the Universe, have something of permanent value to contribute to modern knowledge and western types of experience and thought (see pp. 683 *sqq.*).

Robertson Smith's insistence upon the social-religious unit, upon the working *systems* as distinct from less organized peoples—Pygmies and others, even with their " Supreme Gods "—is entirely characteristic of the man who in his early years demanded a *systematized* theology. He fully realized the necessity for organizing knowledge—as befitted an Editor of the *Encyclopædia Britannica* !—but he did not live to attempt the task of undertaking a fresh systematization of the results which he had reached. Such a task awaits the future. Questions arise concerning the relation between communion, fellowship, and the like (p. xliii *sq.* above), between totemic, totemistic, and theriomorphic cults, between gods (of varying degree of divinity), heroes, and saints, between friendly and unfriendly supernatural beings, between " religious," " magical," and " magico-religious " beliefs and practices. This is no exaggerated statement of the task that already confronts the student of the religions ; and as he proceeds to systematize his definitions he will discover that the Science of Religion is reaching out towards, we will not say a " Theology," but, an interpretation of the data of religion far more " Catholic " than even Robertson Smith himself divined. Nor is this all. Repeatedly the interpretation of the evidence can only be " mystical," in the sense that a sympathetic understanding of religious and mystical types of experience alone enables one man to interpret and another to test the interpretation. This will be one of the difficulties—perhaps one of the embarrassments —of the future, for there is much that is ambiguous in religion, that *seems* " religious," or is only subjectively so ;

and on this account less question-begging terms should perhaps be employed.[1]

Our Theology and Philosophy, if not specifically Christian, is Western, whereas Robertson Smith combined the keenest Christian sympathies with a profound knowledge of Semitic, or rather Oriental, modes of thought—and the consequences were far-reaching. Prediction is idle work, but whereas the rise of Christianity led to the theology and philosophy which characterize western thought, the tendency of the study of the world's religions is to lay new foundations upon which the thinkers and systematizers of the future will build. One need not commit oneself to the " phenomenology of religion," or any other specific school or tendency of to-day, but the deeper inquiry into the way in which we ourselves have come to think as we do and to hold the beliefs that we do, and of the relation between different types of thinking, is opening out new lines of research, and fashioning new and powerful tools for the future. More fundamental than any given religious or scientific inquiry is the inquiry into the processes of differentiation, development, and systematization of ideas, and at the present day the precise relationship between Religion and Science is of less *primary* importance than the critical study of the interrelation between religious and non-religious experience and expression.

The Religion of the Semites, when we consider the author and his work, is a veritable symptom. Some there are who do not find it difficult to foreshadow the " Decline of the West ": the point has been reached where all that is creative has exhausted itself, serious thought has found itself in a

---

[1] Thus, M. Pinard de la Boullaye (ii. p. 11 *sq.* ; see p. xliv n., above) suggests the terms *hierography* (the history of religion), *hierology* (comparative religion and scientific generalization of the data), and *hierosophy* (metaphysical speculation) ; cf. also Count Goblet d'Alviella (*Oxford Congress of Religions*, 1908, ii. p. 365), who proposes *hierography* (analysis and description) and *hierology* (synthesis).

cul-de-sac, and the confidence which beheld a world picture, a scheme of history culminating in one's own personal or national standpoint, has given place to the chill yet not unjust realization that a more objective survey of man, his history and his religion, must base its theology and philosophy upon a far wider synthesis. But Robertson Smith is concerned with the physiology rather than the morphology of cultures ; and, instinctively a prophet, he is dynamic, feeling out towards the future, to a Reformation, a Rebirth or a Renaissance. The past shows us dying and dead cultures, but also new developments and progress ; and those who realize that vast movements in history lie behind the Bible will agree that, although there can be no assurance that any particular line of development *must* be continued, there is no justification for the conviction that there can *not* be a further development embodying the best of all that has gone before and creating a new continuity with the past. And it may be claimed that when Robertson Smith, the theologian and the anthropologist, went down to primitive and ancient religion, he took up the past and carried it forward, indicating the lines upon which further progress might most fruitfully be made.

A vast amount has been written upon Semitic and other religions, but the independence of his position is still astonishing. Much of the literature does not touch the central problems of religion. Much is out of sympathy with the mystical or transcendental element in religion, which it is crass obscurantism to reject and intellectual suicide to accept uncritically. Again, much ignores the religions at either end of the scale. Not as slavish copyists of what Robertson Smith wrote, but as sympathetic and critical students of the greatest of all subjects, can one find in his life and work a new source of inspiration. And since a man is more than his theories, and this man's standpoint so eminently character-

istic, no more interesting subject for the study of personal
evolution can well be found when we consider his life, his
work, and his influence—for evolution in human personality
and that in the world which the scientist has constructed
cannot, on philosophical grounds, be ultimately separated.[1]

As explained in the Preface, Robertson Smith has been
left to speak for himself, and for the new notes, which are
printed apart by themselves, the present writer is entirely
responsible. These notes give bibliographical information,
and contain additional illustrative matter, especially from
modern Palestine and the ancient surrounding civilizations.
No attempt is made to refer to all available sources, the aim
being merely to emphasize afresh the fact that Palestine and
the Semites cannot be treated in isolation, and that the
religion—or, as some would prefer to say, the religions—of
the Semites must be viewed in the light of our knowledge of
religion in general. Accordingly, attention is drawn to the
close interrelation between the lower and the higher religions,
between various types of religious and related experiences,
and between the religious and non-religious spheres of life
and thought. Some notice is taken of criticisms of Robertson Smith's theories, and fuller evidence has been given for
the different sorts of beliefs and practices expressing contact,
fellowship, communion, or at-one-ment with the supernatural
or divine. The " practical " and often quasi-" magical "
element in religion has been illustrated, in view of its importance for the development of ideas concerning man's place
in and control over Nature, and for the relationship between
the " physical " and " spiritual " phases in the history of

[1] The reference is to the Right Hon. J. C. Smuts on the importance of
" personology," see *Holism and Evolution* (1926), pp. 284 *sqq.* The present
writer may perhaps be permitted to refer to his *Study of Religions* (1914),
pp. 64 *sqq.*, 338 *sq.*, and his review of the *Life of Robertson Smith* in the
Hibbert Journal, xi. p. 214.

religion. The significance of group-units and systems has been developed, for the problem is not to explain the variation of belief and practice—this must be taken as given—but to co-ordinate the systematizing and regulating tendencies throughout the Cosmos. Further, as will have been seen in this Introduction, the immense importance of specifically "religious" data for studies which, in a sense, are "non-religious" can no longer be ignored, and the problem of "evolution" in the world of thought has become of the first importance for the presentation of the data of religion.

Owing partly to lack of space, archæological material has rarely been introduced ; the writer hopes to utilize it in his Schweich Lectures on *The Religion of Palestine in the Light of Archæology.* Moreover, since the Second Edition of *The Religion of the Semites* omits on p. 414 a very striking paragraph which appeared in the First Edition, p. 393, on the death of the God-man and the "germ" of John xvii. 19,[1] it seemed undesirable to develop the bearing of comparative religion upon the interpretation of Christianity. But although Robertson Smith evidently preferred to omit the paragraph, his volume not merely opens out a treatment of religion more systematic than others which might be named, it also inaugurates a theoretical study of all religions, from the varieties of Christian belief and practice to the humblest cults of totemic and other rude communities, and it is, perhaps, no exaggeration to see in his work the foundation of the Science and Theory of Religion.

STANLEY A. COOK.

CAMBRIDGE, *August* 1927.

---

[1] On this omission, see also Sir James Frazer, in his essay on Robertson Smith, reprinted in *The Gorgon's Head and other Literary Pieces* (1927), pp. 278–290.

LECTURE I

THE subject before us is the religion of the Semitic peoples,
that is, of the group of kindred nations, including the Arabs,
the Hebrews and Phœnicians, the Aramæans, the Babylonians and Assyrians, which in ancient times occupied the
great Arabian Peninsula, with the more fertile lands of ★
Syria Mesopotamia and Irac, from the Mediterranean
coast to the base of the mountains of Iran and Armenia.
Among these peoples three of the great faiths of the
world had their origin, so that the Semites must always
have a peculiar interest for the student of the history of
religion.   Our subject, however, is not the history of the
several religions that have a Semitic origin, but Semitic
religion as a whole in its common features and general
type.   Judaism, Christianity and Islam are *positive* religions,
that is, they did not grow up like the systems of ancient
heathenism, under the action of unconscious forces operating silently from age to age, but trace their origin to the
teaching of great religious innovators, who spoke as the
organs of a divine revelation, and deliberately departed
from the traditions of the past.   Behind these positive
religions lies the old unconscious religious tradition, the

I

body of religious usage and belief which cannot be traced
to the influence of individual minds, and was not propagated
on individual authority, but formed part of that inheritance
from the past into which successive generations of the
Semitic race grew up as it were instinctively, taking it as
a matter of course that they should believe and act as their
fathers had done before them.   The positive Semitic
religions had to establish themselves on ground already
occupied by these older beliefs and usages; they had to
displace what they could not assimilate, and whether they
rejected or absorbed the elements of the older religion,
they had at every point to reckon with them and take up
a definite attitude towards them.   No positive religion that
has moved men has been able to start with a *tabula rasa*,
and express itself as if religion were beginning for the first
time; in form, if not in substance, the new system must
be in contact all along the line with the older ideas and
practices which it finds in possession.   A new scheme of
faith can find a hearing only by appealing to religious
instincts and susceptibilities that already exist in its
audience, and it cannot reach these without taking account
of the traditional forms in which all religious feeling is
embodied, and without speaking a language which men
accustomed to these old forms can understand.   Thus to
comprehend a system of positive religion thoroughly, to
understand it in its historical origin and form as well as
in its abstract principles, we must know the traditional
religion that preceded it.   It is from this point of view
that I invite you to take an interest in the ancient religion
of the Semitic peoples; the matter is not one of mere
antiquarian curiosity, but has a direct and important bearing on the great problem of the origins of the spiritual
religion of the Bible.   Let me illustrate this by an example.
You know how large a part of the teaching of the New

Testament and of all Christian theology turns on the ideas of sacrifice and priesthood.   In what they have to say on these heads the New Testament writers presuppose, as the basis of their argument, the notion of sacrifice and priesthood current among the Jews and embodied in the ordinances of the Temple.   But, again, the ritual of the Temple was not in its origin an entirely novel thing; the precepts of the Pentateuch did not create a priesthood and a sacrificial service on an altogether independent basis, but only reshaped and remodelled, in accordance with a more spiritual doctrine, institutions of an older type, which in many particulars were common to the Hebrews with their heathen neighbours.   Every one who reads the Old Testament with attention is struck with the fact that the origin and *rationale* of sacrifice are nowhere fully explained; that sacrifice is an essential part of religion is taken for granted, as something which is not a doctrine peculiar to Israel but is universally admitted and acted on without as well as within the limits of the chosen people.   Thus, when we wish thoroughly to study the New Testament doctrine of sacrifice, we are carried back step by step till we reach a point where we have to ask what sacrifice meant, not to the old Hebrews alone, but to the whole circle of nations of which they formed a part.   By considerations of this sort we are led to the conclusion that no one of the religions of Semitic origin which still exercise so great an influence on the lives of men can be completely understood without enquiry into the older traditional religion of the Semitic race.

You observe that in this argument I take it for granted that, when we go back to the most ancient religious conceptions and usages of the Hebrews, we shall find them to be the common property of a group of kindred peoples, and not the exclusive possession of the

tribes of Israel. The proof that this is so will appear
more clearly in the sequel; but, indeed, the thing will
hardly be denied by any one who has read the Bible with
care. In the history of old Israel before the captivity,
nothing comes out more clearly than that the mass of the
people found the greatest difficulty in keeping their
national religion distinct from that of the surrounding
nations. Those who had no grasp of spiritual principles,
and knew the religion of Jehovah only as an affair of
inherited usage, were not conscious of any great difference
between themselves and their heathen neighbours, and fell
into Canaanite and other foreign practices with the greatest
facility. The significance of this fact is manifest if we
consider how deeply the most untutored religious sensi-
bilities are shocked by any kind of innovation. ·Nothing
appeals so strongly as religion to the conservative instincts;
and conservatism is the habitual attitude of Orientals
The whole history of Israel is unintelligible if we suppose
that the heathenism against which the prophets contended
was a thing altogether alien to the religious traditions of
the Hebrews. In principle there was all the difference in
the world between the faith of Isaiah and that of an
idolater. But the difference in principle, which seems so
clear to us, was not clear to the average Judæan, and the
reason of this was that it was obscured by the great
similarity in many important points of religious tradition
and ritual practice. The conservatism which refuses to
look at principles, and has an eye only for tradition and
usage, was against the prophets, and had no sympathy with
their efforts to draw a sharp line between the religion of
Jehovah and that of the foreign gods. This is a proof
that what I may call the natural basis of Israel's
worship was very closely akin to that of the neighbouring
cults.

The conclusion on this point which is suggested by the
facts of Old Testament history, may be accepted the more
readily because it is confirmed by presumptive arguments
of another kind. Traditional religion is handed down from
father to child, and therefore is in great measure an affair
of race. Nations sprung from a common stock will have
a common inheritance of traditional belief and usage in
things sacred as well as profane, and thus the evidence
that the Hebrews and their neighbours had a large common
stock of religious tradition falls in with the evidence
which we have from other sources, that in point of race
the people of Israel were nearly akin to the heathen
nations of Syria and Arabia. The populations of this
whole region constitute a well-marked ethnic unity, a fact
which is usually expressed by giving to them the common
name of Semites. The choice of this term was originally
suggested by the tenth chapter of Genesis, in which most
of the nations of the group with which we are concerned
are represented as descended from Shem the son of Noah.
But though modern historians and ethnographers have
borrowed a name from the book of Genesis, it must be
understood that they do not define the Semitic group as
coextensive with the list of nations that are there reckoned
to the children of Shem. Most recent interpreters are
disposed to regard the classification of the families of
mankind given in Genesis x. as founded on principles
geographical or political rather than ethnographical; the
Phœnicians and other Canaanites, for example, are made
to be children of Ham and near cousins of the Egyptians.
This arrangement corresponds to historical facts, for, at a
period anterior to the Hebrew conquest, Canaan was for
centuries an Egyptian dependency, and Phœnician religion
and civilisation are permeated by Egyptian influence.
But ethnographically the Canaanites were akin to the

Arabs and Syrians, and they spoke a language which is hardly different from Hebrew. On the other hand, Elam and Lud, that is Susiana and Lydia, are called children of Shem, though there is no reason to think that in either country the mass of the population belonged to the same stock as the Syrians and Arabs. Accordingly it must be remembered that when modern scholars use the term Semitic, they do not speak as interpreters of Scripture, but include all peoples whose distinctive ethnical characters assign them to the same group with the Hebrews, Syrians and Arabs.

The scientific definition of an ethnographical group depends on a variety of considerations; for direct historical evidence of an unimpeachable kind as to the original seats and kindred of ancient peoples is not generally to be had. The defects of historical tradition must therefore be supplied by observation, partly of inherited physical characteristics, and partly of mental characteristics, habits and attainments such as are usually transmitted from parent to child. Among the indirect criteria of kinship between nations, the most obvious, and the one which has hitherto been most carefully studied, is the criterion of language; for it is observed that the languages of mankind form a series of natural groups, and that within each group it is possible to arrange the several languages which it contains in what may be called a genealogical order, according to degrees of kinship. Now it may not always be true that people of the same or kindred speech are as closely related by actual descent as they seem to be from the language they speak; a Gaelic tribe, for example, may forget their ancient speech, and learn to speak a Teutonic dialect, without ceasing to be true Gaels by blood. But, in general, large groups of men do not readily change their language, but go on from generation to generation speaking the ancestral dialect, with such gradual modification as the lapse of time brings about. As a rule, therefore, the classification of mankind by language, at least when applied to large masses, will approach pretty closely to a natural classification ; and in a large proportion of cases the language of a mixed race will prove on examination to be that of the stock whose blood is predominant. Where this is not the case, where a minority has imposed its speech on a majority, we may safely conclude that it has done so in virtue of a natural pre-eminence, a power of shaping lower races in its own mould, which is not confined to the sphere of language, but extends to all parts of life. Where we find unity of language, we can at least say with certainty that we are dealing with a group of men who are subject to common influences of the most subtle and far-reaching kind ; and where unity of speech has prevailed for many generations, we may be sure that the continued action of these influences has produced great uniformity of physical and mental type. When we come to deal with groups which have long had separate histories, and whose languages are therefore not identical but only cognate, the case is not so strong ; but, on the whole, it remains true that the stock which is strong enough, whether by numbers or by genius, to impress its language on a nation, must also exercise a predominant influence on the national type in other respects ; and to this extent the classification of races by language must be called natural and not artificial. Especially is this true for ancient times, when the absence of literature, and particularly of religious books, made it much more difficult than it has been in recent ages for a new language to establish itself in a race to which it was originally foreign. All Egypt now speaks Arabic—a Semitic tongue—and yet the population is very far from having assimilated itself to the Arabic type. But this could not have happened without the Coran and the religion of the Coran.

The Semitic nations are classed together on the ground of similarity of language; but we have every reason to recognise their linguistic kinship as only one manifestation of a very marked general unity of type. The unity is not perfect; it would not, for example, be safe to make generalisations about the Semitic character from the Arabian nomads, and to apply them to the ancient Babylonians. And for this there are probably two reasons. On the one hand, the Semite of the Arabian desert and the Semite of the Babylonian alluvium lived under altogether different physical and moral conditions; the difference of environment is as complete as possible. And, on the other hand, it is pretty certain that the Arabs of the desert have been from time immemorial a race practically unmixed, while the Babylonians, and other members of the same family settled on the fringes of the Semitic land, were in all probability largely mingled with the blood of other races, and underwent a corresponding modification of type.

But when every allowance is made for demonstrable or possible variations of type within the Semitic field, it still remains true that the Semites form a singularly well marked and relatively speaking a very homogeneous group. So far as language goes the evidence to this effect is particularly strong. The Semitic tongues are so much alike that their affinity is recognised even by the untrained observer; and modern science has little difficulty in tracing them back to a single primitive speech, and determining in a general way what the features of that speech were. On the other hand, the differences between these languages and those spoken by other adjacent races are so fundamental and so wide, that little or nothing can be affirmed with certainty as to the relation of the Semitic tongues to other linguistic stocks.   Their nearest kinship seems to be with the languages of North Africa, but even here the common features are balanced by profound differences. The evidence of language therefore tends to show that the period during which the original and common Semitic speech existed apart, and developed its peculiar characters at a distance from languages of other stocks, must have been very long in comparison with the subsequent period during which the separate branches of the Semitic stock, such as Hebrew Aramaic and Arabic, were isolated from one another and developed into separate dialects.   Or, to draw the historical inference from this, it would appear that before the Hebrews, the Aramæans, and the Arabs spread themselves over widely distant seats, and began their course of separate national development, there must have been long ages in which the ancestors of all these nations lived together and spoke with one tongue.   And as this was in the infancy of mankind, the period of human history in which individuality went for nothing, and all common influences had a force which we moderns can with difficulty conceive, the various swarms which ultimately hived off from the common stock and formed the Semitic nations known to history, must have carried with them a strongly marked race character, and many common possessions of custom and idea, besides their common language.

And further, let us observe that the dispersion of the Semitic nations was never carried so far as the dispersion of the Aryans.   If we leave out of account settlements made over the seas,—the South Arabian colonies in East Africa, and the Phœnician colonies on the coasts and isles of the Mediterranean,—we find that the region of Semitic occupation is continuous and compact.   Its great immovable centre is the vast Arabian peninsula, a region naturally isolated, and in virtue of its physical characters almost exempt from immigration or change of inhabitants. From this central stronghold, which the predominant opinion of modern scholars designates as the probable starting-point of the whole Semitic dispersion, the region of Semitic speech spreads out round the margin of the Syrian desert till it strikes against great natural boundaries, the Mediterranean, Mount Taurus, and the mountains of Armenia and Iran. From the earliest dawn of history all that lies within these limits was fully occupied by Semitic tribes speaking Semitic dialects, and the compactness of this settlement must necessarily have tended to maintain uniformity of type. The several Semitic nations, when they were not in direct contact with one another, were divided not by alien populations, but only by the natural barriers of mountain and desert. These natural barriers, indeed, were numerous, and served to break up the race into a number of small tribes or nations; but, like the mountains of Greece, they were not so formidable as to prevent the separate states from maintaining a great deal of intercourse, which, whether peaceful or warlike, tended to perpetuate the original community of type. Nor was the operation of these causes disturbed in ancient times by any great foreign immigration. The early Egyptian invasions of Syria were not followed by colonisation; and while the so-called Hittite monuments, which have given rise to so much speculation, may afford evidence that a non-Semitic people from Asia Minor at one time pushed its way into Northern Syria, it is pretty clear that the Hittites of the Bible, *i.e.* the non-Aramaic communities of Cœle-Syria, were a branch of the Canaanite stock, though they may for a time have been dominated by a non-Semitic aristocracy. At one time it was not uncommon to represent the Philistines as a non-Semitic people, but it is now generally recognised that the arguments for this view are inadequate, and that, though they came into Palestine from across the sea, from Caphtor, *i.e.* probably from Crete, they were either mainly of Semitic blood, or at least were already thoroughly Semitised at the time of their immigration, alike in speech and in religion.

Coming down to later times, we find that the Assyrian Babylonian and Persian conquests made no considerable change in the general type of the population of the Semitic lands. National and tribal landmarks were removed, and there were considerable shiftings of population within the Semitic area, but no great incursion of new populations of alien stock. In the Greek and Roman periods, on the contrary, a large foreign element was introduced into the towns of Syria; but as the immigration was practically confined to the cities, hardly touching the rural districts, its effects in modifying racial type were, it would seem, of a very transitory character. For in Eastern cities the death-rate habitually exceeds the birth-rate, and the urban population is maintained only by constant recruital from the country, so that it is the blood of the peasantry which ultimately determines the type of the population. Thus it is to be explained that, after the Arab conquest of Syria, the Greek element in the population rapidly disappeared. Indeed, one of the most palpable proofs that the populations of all the old Semitic lands possessed a remarkable homogeneity of character, is the fact that in them, and in them alone, the Arabs and Arab influence took permanent root. The Moslem conquests extended far beyond these limits; but, except in the old Semitic countries, Islam speedily took new shapes, and the Arab dominations soon gave way before the reaction of the mass of its foreign subjects.

Thus the whole course of history, from the earliest date to which authentic knowledge extends down to the time of

the decay of the Caliphate, records no great permanent
disturbance of population to affect the constancy of the
Semitic type within its original seats, apart from the
temporary Hellenisation of the great cities already spoken
of.   Such disturbances as did take place consisted partly
of mere local displacements among the settled Semites,
partly, and in a much greater degree, of the arrival and
establishment in the cultivated lands of successive hordes
of Semitic nomads from the Arabian wilderness, which on
their settlement found themselves surrounded by populations so nearly of their own type that the complete
fusion of the old and new inhabitants was effected without
difficulty, and without modification of the general character
of the race.   If at any point in its settlements, except
along the frontiers, the Semitic blood was largely modified
by foreign admixture, this must have taken place in
prehistoric times, or by fusion with other races which
may have occupied the country before the arrival of the
Semites.   How far anything of this sort actually happened
can only be matter of conjecture, for the special hypotheses
which have sometimes been put forth—as, for example, that
there was a considerable strain of pre-Semitic blood in the
Phœnicians and Canaanites—rest on presumptions of no
conclusive sort.   What is certain is that the Semitic
settlements in Asia were practically complete at the first
dawn of history, and that the Semitic blood was constantly
reinforced, from very early times, by fresh immigrations
from the desert.   There is hardly another part of the
world where we have such good historical reasons for
presuming that linguistic affinity will prove a safe indication of affinity in race, and in general physical and mental
type.   And this presumption is not belied by the results
of nearer enquiry.   Those who have busied themselves
with the history and literature of the Semitic peoples, bear

uniform testimony to the close family likeness that runs through them all.

It is only natural that this homogeneity of type appears to be modified on the frontiers of the Semitic field. To the West, if we leave the transmarine colonies out of view, natural conditions drew a sharp line of local demarcation between the Semites and their alien neighbours. The Red Sea and the desert north of it formed a geographical barrier, which was often crossed by the expansive force of the Semitic race, but which appears to have effectually checked the advance into Asia of African populations. But on the East, the fertile basin of the Euphrates and Tigris seems in ancient as in modern times to have been a meeting-place of races. The preponderating opinion of Assyriologists is to the effect that the civilisation of Assyria and Babylonia was not purely Semitic, and that the ancient population of these parts contained a large pre-Semitic element, whose influence is especially to be recognised in religion and in the sacred literature of the cuneiform records.

If this be so, it is plain that the cuneiform material must be used with caution in our enquiry into the type of traditional religion characteristic of the ancient Semites. That Babylonia is the best starting-point for a comparative study of the sacred beliefs and practices of the Semitic peoples, is an idea which has lately had some vogue, and which at first sight appears plausible on account of the great antiquity of the monumental evidence. But, in matters of this sort, ancient and primitive are not synonymous terms; and we must not look for the most primitive form of Semitic faith in a region where society was not primitive. In Babylonia, it would seem, society and religion alike were based on a fusion of two races, and so were not primitive but complex. Moreover, the official system of Babylonian and Assyrian religion, as it is known

to us from priestly texts and public inscriptions, bears clear
marks of being something more than a popular traditional
faith; it has been artificially moulded by priestcraft and
statecraft in much the same way as the official religion of
Egypt; that is to say, it is in great measure an artificial
combination, for imperial purposes, of elements drawn from
a number of local worships. In all probability the actual
religion of the masses was always much simpler than the
official system; and in later times it would seem that, both
in religion and in race, Assyria was little different from the
adjacent Aramæan countries. These remarks are not meant
to throw doubt on the great importance of cuneiform studies
for the history of Semitic religion; the monumental data
are valuable for comparison with what we know of the
faith and worship of other Semitic peoples, and peculiarly
valuable because, in religion as in other matters, the
civilisation of the Euphrates-Tigris valley exercised a great
historical influence on a large part of the Semitic field.
But the right point of departure for a general study of
Semitic religion must be sought in regions where, though
our knowledge begins at a later date, it refers to a simpler
state of society, and where accordingly the religious
phenomena revealed to us are of an origin less doubtful and
a character less complicated. In many respects the religion
of heathen Arabia, though we have little information concerning it that is not of post-Christian date, displays an
extremely primitive type, corresponding to the primitive
and unchanging character of nomadic life. With what
may be gathered from this source we must compare, above
all, the invaluable notices, preserved in the Old Testament,
of the religion of the small Palestinian states before their
conquest by the great empires of the East. For this
period, apart from the Assyrian monuments and a few
precious fragments of other evidence from inscriptions, we

have no contemporary documents outside the Bible.   At a
later date the evidence from monuments is multiplied, and
Greek literature begins to give important aid; but by
this time also we have reached the period of religious
syncretism—the period, that is, when different faiths and
worships began to react on one another, and produce
new and complex forms of religion.   Here, therefore, we
have to use the same precautions that are called for in
dealing with the older syncretistic religion of Babylonia
and Assyria; it is only by careful sifting and comparison
that we can separate between ancient use and modern
innovation, between the old religious inheritance of the
Semites and things that came in from without.

Let it be understood from the outset that we have
not the materials for anything like a complete comparative history of Semitic religions, and that nothing of
the sort will be attempted in these Lectures.   But a careful
study and comparison of the various sources is sufficient
to furnish a tolerably accurate view of a series of general
features, which recur with striking uniformity in all parts
of the Semitic field, and govern the evolution of faith and
worship down to a late date.   These widespread and
permanent features form the real interest of Semitic
religion to the philosophical student; it was in them,
and not in the things that vary from place to place and
from time to time, that the strength of Semitic religion
lay, and it is to them therefore that we must look for help
in the most important practical application of our studies,
for light on the great question of the relation of the
positive Semitic religions to the earlier faith of the race.

Before entering upon the particulars of our enquiry, I
must still detain you with a few words about the method
and order of investigation that seem to be prescribed by
the nature of the subject.   To get a true and well-defined

picture of the type of Semitic religion, we must not only study the parts separately, but must have clear views of the place and proportion of each part in its relation to the whole. And here we shall go very far wrong if we take it for granted that what is the most important and prominent side of religion to us was equally important in the ancient society with which we are to deal. In connection with every religion, whether ancient or modern, we find on the one hand certain beliefs, and on the other certain institutions ritual practices and rules of conduct. Our modern habit is to look at religion from the side of belief rather than of practice ; for, down to comparatively recent times, almost the only forms of religion seriously studied in Europe have been those of the various Christian Churches, and all parts of Christendom are agreed that ritual is important only in connection with its inter-pretation. Thus the study of religion has meant mainly the study of Christian beliefs, and instruction in religion has habitually begun with the creed, religious duties being presented to the learner as flowing from the dogmatic truths he is taught to accept. All this seems to us so much a matter of course that, when we approach some strange or antique religion, we naturally assume that here also our first business is to search for a creed, and find in it the key to ritual and practice. But the antique religions had for the most part no creed ; they consisted entirely of institutions and practices. No doubt men will not habitually follow certain practices without attaching a meaning to them ; but as a rule we find that while the practice was rigorously fixed, the meaning attached to it was extremely vague, and the same rite was explained by different people in different ways, without any question of orthodoxy or heterodoxy arising in conse-quence. In ancient Greece, for example, certain things

were done at a temple, and people were agreed that it
would be impious not to do them.　But if you had asked
why they were done, you would probably have had several
mutually contradictory explanations from different persons,
and no one would have thought it a matter of the least
religious importance which of these you chose to adopt.
Indeed, the explanations offered would not have been of
a kind to stir any strong feeling ; for in most cases they
would have been merely different stories as to the circumstances under which the rite first came to be established,
by the command or by the direct example of the god.
The rite, in short, was connected not with a dogma but
with a myth.

　　In all the antique religions, mythology takes the place
of dogma ; that is, the sacred lore of priests and people,　★
so far as it does not consist of mere rules for the performance of religious acts, assumes the form of stories about
the gods ; and these stories afford the only explanation
that is offered of the precepts of religion and the prescribed rules of ritual.　But, strictly speaking, this
mythology was no essential part of ancient religion, for
it had no sacred sanction and no binding force on the
worshippers.　The myths connected with individual sanctuaries and ceremonies were merely part of the apparatus
of the worship ; they served to excite the fancy and
sustain the interest of the worshipper ; but he was often
offered a choice of several accounts of the same thing,
and, provided that he fulfilled the ritual with accuracy,
no one cared what he believed about its origin.　Belief
in a certain series of myths was neither obligatory as a
part of true religion, nor was it supposed that, by believing,
a man acquired religious merit and conciliated the favour
of the gods.　What was obligatory or meritorious was the
exact performance of certain sacred acts prescribed by

2

religious tradition.　This being so, it follows that mythology ought not to take the prominent place that is too often assigned to it in the scientific study of ancient faiths.　So far as myths consist of explanations of ritual, their value is altogether secondary, and it may be affirmed with confidence that in almost every case the myth was derived from the ritual, and not the ritual from the myth; for the ritual was fixed and the myth was variable, the ritual was obligatory and faith in the myth was at the discretion of the worshipper.　Now by far the largest part of the myths of antique religions are connected with the ritual of particular shrines, or with the religious observances of particular tribes and districts.　In all such cases it is probable, in most cases it is certain, that the myth is merely the explanation of a religious usage; and ordinarily it is such an explanation as could not have arisen till the original sense of the usage had more or less fallen into oblivion. As a rule the myth is no explanation of the origin of the ritual to any one who does not believe it to be a narrative of real occurrences, and the boldest mythologist will not believe that.　But if it be not true, the myth itself requires to be explained, and every principle of philosophy and common sense demands that the explanation be sought, not in arbitrary allegorical theories, but in the actual facts of ritual or religious custom to which the myth attaches. The conclusion is, that in the study of ancient religions we must begin, not with myth, but with ritual and traditional usage.

Nor can it be fairly set against this conclusion, that there are certain myths which are not mere explanations of traditional practices, but exhibit the beginnings of larger religious speculation, or of an attempt to systematise and reduce to order the motley variety of local worships and beliefs.　For in this case the secondary character of the

myths is still more clearly marked. They are either products of early philosophy, reflecting on the nature of the
universe; or they are political in scope, being designed to
supply a thread of union between the various worships of
groups, originally distinct, which have been united into
one social or political organism; or, finally, they are due
to the free play of epic imagination. But philosophy
politics and poetry are something more, or something less,
than religion pure and simple.

There can be no doubt that, in the later stages of
ancient religions, mythology acquired an increased importance. In the struggle of heathenism with scepticism on
the one hand and Christianity on the other, the supporters
of the old traditional religion were driven to search for
ideas of a modern cast, which they could represent as the
true inner meaning of the traditional rites. To this end
they laid hold of the old myths, and applied to them an
allegorical system of interpretation. Myth interpreted by
the aid of allegory became the favourite means of infusing
a new significance into ancient forms. But the theories
thus developed are the falsest of false guides as to the
original meaning of the old religions.

On the other hand, the ancient myths taken in their
natural sense, without allegorical gloss, are plainly of great
importance as testimonies to the views of the nature of the
gods that were prevalent when they were formed. For
though the mythical details had no dogmatic value and no
binding authority over faith, it is to be supposed that
nothing was put into a myth which people at that time
were not prepared to believe without offence. But so far
as the way of thinking expressed in the myth was not
already expressed in the ritual itself, it had no properly
religious sanction; the myth apart from the ritual affords
only a doubtful and slippery kind of evidence. Before we

can handle myths with any confidence, we must have some definite hold of the ideas expressed in the ritual tradition, which embodied the only fixed and statutory elements of the religion.

All this, I hope, will become clearer to us as we proceed with our enquiry, and learn by practical example the use to be made of the different lines of evidence open to us. But it is of the first importance to realise clearly from the outset that ritual and practical usage were, strictly speaking, the sum-total of ancient religions. Religion in primitive times was not a system of belief with practical applications; it was a body of fixed traditional practices, to which every member of society conformed as a matter of course. Men would not be men if they agreed to do certain things without having a reason for their action; but in ancient religion the reason was not first formulated as a doctrine and then expressed in practice, but conversely, practice preceded doctrinal theory. Men form general rules of conduct before they begin to express general principles in words; political institutions are older than political theories, and in like manner religious institutions are older than religious theories. This analogy is not arbitrarily chosen, for in fact the parallelism in ancient society between religious and political institutions is complete. In each sphere great importance was attached to form and precedent, but the explanation why the precedent was followed consisted merely of a legend as to its first establishment. That the precedent, once established, was authoritative did not appear to require any proof. The rules of society were based on precedent, and the continued existence of the society was sufficient reason why a precedent once set should continue to be followed.

Strictly speaking, indeed, I understate the case when

I say that the oldest religious and political institutions present a close analogy. It would be more correct to say that they were parts of one whole of social custom. Religion was a part of the organised social life into which a man was born, and to which he conformed through life in the same unconscious way in which men fall into any habitual practice of the society in which they live. Men took the gods and their worship for granted, just as they took the other usages of the state for granted, and if they reasoned or speculated about them, they did so on the presupposition that the traditional usages were fixed things, behind which their reasonings must not go, and which no reasoning could be allowed to overturn. To us moderns religion is above all a matter of individual conviction and reasoned belief, but to the ancients it was a part of the citizen's public life, reduced to fixed forms, which he was not bound to understand and was not at liberty to criticise or to neglect. Religious nonconformity was an offence against the state; for if sacred tradition was tampered with the bases of society were undermined, and the favour of the gods was forfeited. But so long as the prescribed forms were duly observed, a man was recognised as truly pious, and no one asked how his religion was rooted in his heart or affected his reason. Like political duty, of which indeed it was a part, religion was entirely comprehended in the observance of certain fixed rules of outward conduct.

The conclusion from all this as to the method of our investigation is obvious. When we study the political structure of an early society, we do not begin by asking what is recorded of the first legislators, or what theory men advanced as to the reason of their institutions; we try to understand what the institutions were, and how they shaped men's lives. In like manner, in the study of Semitic eligion, we must not begin by asking what was

told about the gods, but what the working religious
institutions were, and how they shaped the lives of the
worshippers.   Our enquiry, therefore, will be directed to
the religious institutions which governed the lives of men
of Semitic race.

In following out this plan, however, we shall do well
not to throw ourselves at once upon the multitudinous
details of rite and ceremony, but to devote our attention
to certain broad features of the sacred institutions which
are sufficiently well marked to be realised at once.   If we
were called upon to examine the political institutions of
antiquity, we should find it convenient to carry with us
some general notion of the several types of government
under which the multifarious institutions of ancient states
arrange themselves.   And in like manner it will be useful
for us, when we examine the religious institutions of the
Semites, to have first some general knowledge of the types
of divine governance, the various ruling conceptions of the
relations of the gods to man, which underlie the rites and
ordinances of religion in different places and at different
times.   Such knowledge we can obtain in a provisional
form, before entering on a mass of ritual details, mainly by
considering the titles of honour by which men addressed
their gods, and the language in which they expressed their
dependence on them.   From these we can see at once, in a
broad, general way, what place the gods held in the social
system of antiquity, and under what general categories
their relations to their worshippers fell.   The broad
results thus reached must then be developed, and at the
same time controlled and rendered more precise, by an
examination in detail of the working institutions of
religion.

The question of the metaphysical nature of the gods, as
distinct from their social office and function, must be left

in the background till this whole investigation is completed.   It is vain to ask what the gods are in themselves
till we have studied them in what I may call their public
life, that is, in the stated intercourse between them and
their worshippers which was kept up by means of the
prescribed forms of cultus.   From the antique point of
view, indeed, the question what the gods are in themselves
is not a religious but a speculative one ; what is requisite
to religion is a practical acquaintance with the rules on
which the deity acts and on which he expects his
worshippers to frame their conduct—what in 2 Kings
xvii. 26 is called the " manner " or rather the " customary
law " (*mishpāṭ*) of the god of the land.   This is true
even of the religion of Israel.   When the prophets
speak of the knowledge of God, they always mean a
practical knowledge of the laws and principles of His
government in Israel,[1] and a summary expression for
religion as a whole is " the knowledge and fear of
Jehovah," [2] *i.e.* the knowledge of what Jehovah prescribes,
combined with a reverent obedience.   An extreme scepticism towards all religious speculation is recommended in
the Book of Ecclesiastes as the proper attitude of piety, for
no amount of discussion can carry a man beyond the plain
rule to " fear God and keep His commandments." [3]   This
counsel the author puts into the mouth of Solomon, and so
represents it, not unjustly, as summing up the old view of
religion, which in more modern days had unfortunately
begun to be undermined.

The propriety of keeping back all metaphysical questions
as to the nature of the gods till we have studied the
practices of religion in detail, becomes very apparent if we
consider for a moment what befel the later philosophers
and theosophists of heathenism in their attempts to con-

---

[1] See especially Hosea, chap. iv.   [2] Isa. xi. 2.   [3] Eccles. xii. 13.

struct a theory of the traditional religion. None of these thinkers succeeded in giving an account of the nature of the gods from which all the received practices of worship could be rationally deduced, and those who had any pretensions to orthodoxy had recourse to violent allegorical interpretations in order to bring the established ritual into accordance with their theories.[1] The reason for this is obvious. The traditional usages of religion had grown up gradually in the course of many centuries, and reflected habits of thought characteristic of very diverse stages of man's intellectual and moral development. No one conception of the nature of the gods could possibly afford the clue to all parts of that motley complex of rites and ceremonies which the later paganism had received by inheritance, from a series of ancestors in every state of culture from pure savagery upwards. The record of the religious thought of mankind, as it is embodied in religious institutions, resembles the geological record of the history of the earth's crust; the new and the old are preserved side by side, or rather layer upon layer. The classification of ritual formations in their proper sequence is the first step towards their explanation, and that explanation itself must take the form, not of a speculative theory, but of a rational life-history.

I have already explained that, in attempting such a life-history of religious institutions, we must begin by forming some preliminary ideas of the practical relation in which the gods of antiquity stood to their worshippers. I have now to add, that we shall also find it necessary to have before us from the outset some elementary notions of the relations which early races of mankind conceived to subsist between gods and men on the one hand, and the material universe on the other. All acts of ancient

---

[1] See, for example, Plutarch's *Greek* and *Roman Questions.*

worship have a material embodiment, the form of which
is determined by the consideration that gods and men
alike stand in certain fixed relations to particular parts
or aspects of physical nature.   Certain places, certain
things, even certain animal kinds are conceived as holy, *i.e.*
as standing in a near relation to the gods, and claiming
special reverence from men, and this conception plays
a very large part in the development of religious institutions.   Here again we have a problem that cannot be
solved by *à priori* methods ; it is only as we move onward
from step to step in the analysis of the details of ritual
observance that we can hope to gain full insight into the
relations of the gods to physical nature.   But there are
certain broad features in the ancient conception of the
universe, and of the relations of its parts to one another,
which can be grasped at once, upon a merely preliminary
survey, and we shall find it profitable to give attention to
these at an early stage of our discussion.

I propose, therefore, to devote my second lecture to
the nature of the antique religious community and the
relations of the gods to their worshippers.   After this we
will proceed to consider the relations of the gods to physical
nature, not in a complete or exhaustive way, but in a
manner entirely preliminary and provisional, and only so
far as is necessary to enable us to understand the material
basis of ancient ritual.   After these preliminary enquiries
have furnished us with certain necessary points of view, we
shall be in a position to take up the institutions of worship
in an orderly manner, and make an attempt to work out
their life - history.   We shall find that the history of
religious institutions is the history of ancient religion
itself, as a practical force in the development of the human
race, and that the articulate efforts of the antique intellect
to comprehend the meaning of religion, the nature of the

gods, and the principles on which they deal with men, take their point of departure from the unspoken ideas embodied in the traditional forms of ritual praxis. Whether the conscious efforts of ancient religious thinkers took the shape of mythological invention or of speculative construction, the raw material of thought upon which they operated was derived from the common traditional stock of religious conceptions that was handed on from generation to generation, not in express words, but in the form of religious custom.

In accordance with the rules of the Burnett Trust, three courses of lectures, to be delivered in successive winters, are allowed me for the development of this great subject. When the work was first entrusted to me, I formed the plan of dividing my task into three distinct parts. In the first course of lectures I hoped to cover the whole field of practical religious institutions. In the second I proposed to myself to discuss the nature and origin of the gods of Semitic heathenism, their relations to one another, the myths that surround them, and the whole subject of religious belief, so far as it is not directly involved in the observances of daily religious life. The third winter would thus have been left free for an examination of the part which Semitic religion has played in universal history, and its influence on the general progress of humanity, whether in virtue of the early contact of Semitic faiths with other systems of antique religion, or— what is more important—in virtue of the influence, both positive and negative, that the common type of Semitic religion has exercised on the formulas and structure of the great monotheistic faiths that have gone forth from the Semitic lands. But the first division of the subject has grown under my hands, and I find that it will not be possible in a single winter to cover the whole field of religious institutions in a way at all adequate to the fundamental importance of this part of the enquiry.

It will therefore be necessary to allow the first branch of the subject to run over into the second course, for which I reserve, among other matters of interest, the whole history of religious feasts and also that of the Semitic priesthoods. I hope, however, to give the present course a certain completeness in itself by carrying the investigation to the end of the great subject of sacrifice. The origin and meaning of sacrifice constitute the central problem of ancient religion, and when this problem has been disposed of we may naturally feel that we have reached a point of rest at which both speaker and hearers will be glad to make a pause.

THE NATURE OF THE RELIGIOUS COMMUNITY, AND THE RELATION OF THE GODS TO THEIR WORSHIPPERS

WE have seen that ancient faiths must be looked on as matters of institution rather than of dogma or formulated belief, and that the system of an antique religion was part of the social order under which its adherents lived; so that the word " system " must here be taken in a practical sense, as when we speak of a political system, and not in the sense of an organised body of ideas or theological opinions. Broadly speaking, religion was made up of a series of acts and observances, the correct performance of which was necessary or desirable to secure the favour of the gods or to avert their anger; and in these observances every member of society had a share, marked out for him either in virtue of his being born within a certain family and community, or in virtue of the station, within the family and community, that he had come to hold in the course of his life. A man did not choose his religion or frame it for himself; it came to him as part of the general scheme of social obligations and ordinances laid upon him, as a matter of course, by his position in the family and in the nation. Individual men were more or less religious, as men now are more or less patriotic; that is, they discharged their religious duties with a greater or less degree of zeal according to their character and temperament; but there was no such thing as an absolutely irreligious man. A certain amount of religion was required of everybody; for the due performance of religious acts was a social obligation in which every one had his appointed share.   Of intolerance in the modern sense of the word ancient society knew nothing; it never persecuted a man into particular beliefs for the good of his own soul.   Religion did not exist for the saving of souls but for the preservation and welfare of society, and in all that was necessary to this end every man had to take his part, or break with the domestic and political community to which he belonged.

Perhaps the simplest way of putting the state of the case is this.   Every human being, without choice on his own part, but simply in virtue of his birth and upbringing, becomes a member of what we call a *natural* society.   He belongs, that is, to a certain family and a certain nation, and this membership lays upon him definite obligations and duties which he is called upon to fulfil as a matter of course, and on pain of social penalties and disabilities, while at the same time it confers upon him certain social rights and advantages.   In this respect the ancient and modern worlds are alike; but there is this important difference, that the tribal or national societies of the ancient world were not strictly natural in the modern sense of the word, for the gods had their part and place in them equally with men.   The circle into which a man was born was not simply a group of kinsfolk and fellow-citizens, but embraced also certain divine beings, the gods of the family and of the state, which to the ancient mind were as much a part of the particular community with which they stood connected as the human members of the social circle.   The relation between the gods of antiquity and their worshippers was expressed in the language of human relationship, and this language was not taken in a figurative sense but with strict literality.   If a god was spoken of as father and his wor-

shippers as his offspring, the meaning was that the worshippers were literally of his stock, that he and they made up
one natural family with reciprocal family duties to one
another.   Or, again, if the god was addressed as king, and
the worshippers called themselves his servants, they meant
that the supreme guidance of the state was actually in his
hands, and accordingly the organisation of the state included provision for consulting his will and obtaining his
direction in all weighty matters, and also provision for
approaching him as king with due homage and tribute.

Thus a man was born into a fixed relation to certain
gods as surely as he was born into relation to his fellow-
men ; and his religion, that is, the part of conduct which
was determined by his relation to the gods, was simply
one side of the general scheme of conduct prescribed for
him by his position as a member of society.   There was no
separation between the spheres of religion and of ordinary
life.   Every social act had a reference to the gods as well
as to men, for the social body was not made up of men
only, but of gods and men.

This account of the position of religion in the social
system holds good, I believe, for all parts and races of the
ancient world in the earlier stages of their history.   The
causes of so remarkable a uniformity lie hidden in the mists
of prehistoric time, but must plainly have been of a general
kind, operating on all parts of mankind without distinction
of race and local environment; for in every region of the
world, as soon as we find a nation or tribe emerging from
prehistoric darkness into the light of authentic history, we
find also that its religion conforms to the general type
which has just been indicated.   As time rolls on and
society advances, modifications take place.   In religion as
in other matters the transition from the antique to the
modern type of life is not sudden and unprepared, but is

gradually led up to by a continuous disintegration of the old structure of society, accompanied by the growth of new ideas and institutions. In Greece, for example, the intimate connection of religion with the organisation of the family and the state was modified and made less exclusive, at a relatively early date, by the Pan-Hellenic conceptions which find their theological expressions in Homer. If the Homeric poems were the Bible of the Greeks, as has so often been said, the true meaning of this phrase is that in these poems utterance was given to ideas about the gods which broke through the limitations of local and tribal worship, and held forth to all Greeks a certain common stock of religious ideas and motives, not hampered by the exclusiveness which in the earlier stages of society allows of no fellowship in religion that is not also a fellowship in the interests of a single kin or a single political group. In Italy there never was anything corresponding to the Pan-Hellenic ideas that operated in Greece, and accordingly the strict union of religion and the state, the solidarity of gods and men as parts of a single society with common interests and common aims, was characteristically exhibited in the institutions of Rome down to quite a late date. But in Greece as well as in Rome the ordinary traditional work-a-day religion of the masses never greatly departed from the primitive type. The final disintegration of antique religion in the countries of Græco-Italian civilisation was the work first of the philosophers and then of Christianity. But Christianity itself, in Southern Europe, has not altogether obliterated the original features of the paganism which it displaced. The Spanish peasants who insult the Madonna of the neighbouring village, and come to blows over the merits of rival local saints, still do homage to the same antique conception of religion which in Egypt animated the feuds of Ombos and Tentyra, and made hatred for each ✦

other's gods the formula that summed up all the local jealousies of the two towns.

The principle that the fundamental conception of ancient religion is the solidarity of the gods and their worshippers as part of one organic society, carries with it important consequences, which I propose to examine in some detail, with special reference to the group of religions that forms the proper subject of these lectures. But though my facts and illustrations will be drawn from the Semitic sphere, a great part of what I shall have to say in the present lecture might be applied, with very trifling modifications, to the early religion of any other part of mankind. The differences between Semitic and Aryan religion, for example, are not so primitive or fundamental as is often imagined. Not only in matters of worship, but in social organisation generally—and we have seen that ancient religion is but a part of the general social order which embraces gods and men alike—the two races, Aryans and Semites, began on lines which are so much alike as to be almost indistinguishable, and the divergence between their paths, which becomes more and more apparent in the course of ages, was not altogether an affair of race and innate tendency, but depended in a great measure on the operation of special local and historical causes.

In both races the first steps of social and religious development took place in small communities, which at the dawn of history had a political system based on the principle of kinship, and were mainly held together by the tie of blood, the only social bond which then had absolute and undisputed strength, being enforced by the law of blood revenge. As a rule, however, men of several clans lived side by side, forming communities which did not possess the absolute homogeneity of blood brotherhood, and yet were united by common interests and the habit of friendly association. The origin of such associations, which are found all over the world at a very early stage of society, need not occupy us now. It is enough to note the fact that they existed, and were not maintained by the feeling of kindred, but by habit and community of interests. These local communities of men of different clans, who lived together on a footing of amity, and had often to unite in common action, especially in war, but also in affairs of polity and justice, were the origin of the antique state. There is probably no case in ancient history where a state was simply the development of a single homogeneous clan or gens, although the several clans which united to form a state often came in course of time to suppose themselves to be only branches of one great ancestral brotherhood, and were thus knit together in a closer unity of sentiment and action. But in the beginning, the union of several clans for common political action was not sustained either by an effective sentiment of kinship (the law of blood revenge uniting only members of the same clan) or by any close political organisation, but was produced by the pressure of practical necessity, and always tended towards dissolution when this practical pressure was withdrawn. The only organisation for common action was that the leading men of the clans consulted together in time of need, and their influence led the masses with them. Out of these conferences arose the senates of elders found in the ancient states of Semitic and Aryan antiquity alike. The kingship, again, as we find it in most antique states, appears to have ordinarily arisen in the way which is so well illustrated by the history of Israel. In time of war an individual leader is indispensable ; in a time of prolonged danger the temporary authority of an approved captain easily passes into the lifelong leadership at home as well as in the field, which

3

was exercised by such a judge as Gideon; and at length the advantages of having a permanent head, both as a leader of the army and as a restraint on the perennial feuds and jealousies of clans that constantly threaten the solidity of the state, are recognised in the institution of the kingship, which again tends to become hereditary, as in the case of the house of David, simply because the king's house naturally becomes greater and richer than other houses, and so better able to sustain the burden of power.

Up to this point the progress of society was much alike in the East and in the West, and the progress of religion, as we shall see in the sequel, followed that of society in general. But while in Greece and Rome the early period of the kings lies in the far background of tradition, and only forms the starting-point of the long development with which the historian of these countries is mainly occupied, the independent evolution of Semitic society was arrested at an early stage. In the case of the nomadic Arabs, shut up in their wildernesses of rock and sand, Nature herself barred the way of progress. The life of the desert does not furnish the material conditions for permanent advance beyond the tribal system, and we find that the religious development of the Arabs was proportionally retarded, so that at the advent of Islam the ancient heathenism, like the ancient tribal structure of society, had become effete without having ever ceased to be barbarous.

The northern Semites, on the other hand, whose progress up to the eighth century before Christ certainly did not lag behind that of the Greeks, were deprived of political independence, and so cut short in their natural development, by the advance from the Tigris to the Mediterranean of the great Assyrian monarchs, who, drawing from the rich and broad alluvium of the Two Rivers resources which none of their neighbours could rival, went on from conquest to conquest till all the small states of Syria and Palestine had gone down before them. The Assyrians were conquerors of the most brutal and destructive kind, and wherever they came the whole structure of ancient society was dissolved. From this time onwards the difference between the Syrian or Palestinian and the Greek was not one of race alone; it was the difference between a free citizen and a slave of an Oriental despotism. Religion as well as civil society was profoundly affected by the catastrophe of the old free communities of the northern Semitic lands; the society of one and the same religion was no longer identical with the state, and the old solidarity of civil and religious life continued to exist only in a modified form. It is not therefore surprising that from the eighth century onwards the history of Semitic religion runs a very different course from that which we observe on the other side of the Mediterranean.

The ancient Semitic communities were small, and were separated from each other by incessant feuds. Hence, on the principle of solidarity between gods and their worshippers, the particularism characteristic of political society could not but reappear in the sphere of religion. In the same measure as the god of a clan or town had indisputable claim to the reverence and service of the community to which he belonged, he was necessarily an enemy to their enemies and a stranger to those to whom they were strangers. Of this there are sufficient evidences in the way in which the Old Testament speaks about the relation of the nations to their gods. When David in the bitterness of his heart complains of those who " have driven him out from connection with the heritage of Jehovah," he represents them as saying to

him, "Go, serve other gods."[1] In driving him to seek
refuge in another land and another nationality, they
compel him to change his religion, for a man's religion
is part of his political connection. "Thy sister," says
Naomi to Ruth, "is gone back unto her people and unto
her gods"; and Ruth replies, "Thy people shall be my
people, and thy God my God":[2] the change of nationality
involves a change of cult. Jeremiah, in the full consciousness of the falsehood of all religions except that of Israel,
remarks that no nation changes its gods although they be
no gods:[3] a nation's worship remains as constant as its
political identity. The Book of Deuteronomy, speaking in
like manner from the standpoint of monotheism, reconciles
the sovereignty of Jehovah with the actual facts of
heathenism, by saying that He has "allotted" the various
objects of false worship "unto all nations under the whole
heaven."[4] The "allotment" of false gods among the
nations, as property is allotted, expresses with precision
the idea that each god had his own determinate circle of
worshippers, to whom he stood in a peculiar and exclusive
relation.

The exclusiveness of which I have just spoken naturally
finds its most pronounced expression in the share taken
by the gods in the feuds and wars of their worshippers.
The enemies of the god and the enemies of his people are
identical; even in the Old Testament "the enemies of
Jehovah" are originally nothing else than the enemies
of Israel.[5] In battle each god fights for his own people,
and to his aid success is ascribed; Chemosh gives victory
to Moab, and Asshur to Assyria;[6] and often the divine

---

[1] 1 Sam. xxvi. 19.　　　　　[2] Ruth i. 14 *sqq.*

[3] Jer. ii. 11.　　　　　[4] Deut. iv. 19.

[5] 1 Sam. xxx. 26, "the spoil of the enemies of Jehovah"; Judg. v. 31.

[6] See the inscription of King Mesha on the so-called Moabite Stone, and
the Assyrian inscriptions, *passim.*

image or symbol accompanies the host to battle. When
the ark was brought into the camp of Israel, the Philistines
said, " Gods are come into the camp; who can deliver us
from the hand of these mighty gods?"[1]   They judged from
their own practice, for when David defeated them at Baal-
perazim, part of the booty consisted in their idols which
had been carried into the field.[2]   When the Carthaginians,
in their treaty with Philip of Macedon,[3] speak of " the gods
that take part in the campaign," they doubtless refer to
the inmates of the sacred tent which was pitched in time ★
of war beside the tent of the general, and before which
prisoners were sacrificed after a victory.[4]   Similarly an
Arabic poet says, " Yaghūth went forth with us against
Morād ";[5] that is, the image of the god Yaghūth was
carried into the fray.   You observe how literal and
realistic was the conception of the part taken by the
deity in the wars of his worshippers.

When the gods of the several Semitic communities
took part in this way in the ancestral feuds of their
worshippers, it was impossible for an individual to change
his religion without changing his nationality, and a whole
community could hardly change its religion at all without
being absorbed into another stock or nation.   Religious
like political ties were transmitted from father to son;
for a man could not choose a new god at will; the gods of
his fathers were the only deities on whom he could count
as friendly and ready to accept his homage, unless he
forswore his own kindred and was received into a new

[1] 1 Sam. iv. 7 *sqq*.   [2] 2 Sam. v. 21.
[3] Polybius, vii. 9.   [4] Diodorus, xx. 65.
[5] Yācūt, iv. 1023.   A survival of the same idea is seen in the portable
tabernacle of the Carmathians (Ibn al-Jauzī, *ap.* De Goeje, *Carmathes* [1886],
pp. 180 220 *sq*.) from which victory was believed to descend.   De Goeje
compares the portable sanctuary of Mokhtār (Ṭabari, ii. 702 *sqq*.) and the
'*otfa* still used by Bedouin tribes (Burckhardt, *Bed. and Wah.* i. 145 ; Lady
Anne Blunt, *Bedouin Tribes*, ii. 146 ; Doughty, i. 61, ii. 304).

circle of civil as well as religious life.   In the old times
hardly any but outlaws changed their religion ; ceremonies
of initiation, by which a man was received into a new
religious circle, became important, as we shall see by and
by, only after the breaking up of the old political life of
the small Semitic commonwealths.

On the other hand, all social fusion between two
communities tended to bring about a religious fusion also.
This might take place in two ways.   Sometimes two gods
were themselves fused into one, as when the mass of the
Israelites in their local worship of Jehovah identified Him
with the Baalim of the Canaanite high places, and carried
over into His worship the ritual of the Canaanite shrines,
not deeming that in so doing they were less truly Jehovah-
worshippers than before.   This process was greatly facilitated by the extreme similarity in the attributes ascribed
to different local or tribal gods, and the frequent identity
of the divine titles.[1]   One Baal hardly differed from another,
except in being connected with a different kindred or a
different place, and when the kindreds were fused by
intermarriage, or lived together in one village on a footing
of social amity, there was nothing to keep their gods
permanently distinct.   In other cases, where the several
deities brought together by the union of their worshippers
into one state were too distinct to lose their individuality,
they continued to be worshipped side by side as allied

[1] It will appear in the sequel that the worship of the greater Semitic
deities was closely associated with the reverence which all primitive pastoral
tribes pay to their flocks and herds.   To a tribe whose herds consisted of
kine and oxen, the cow and the ox were sacred beings, which in the oldest
times were never killed or eaten except sacrificially.   The tribal deities
themselves were conceived as closely akin to the sacred species of domestic
animals, and their images were often made in the likeness of steers or heifers
in cow-keeping tribes, or of rams and ewes in shepherd tribes.   It is easy to
see how this facilitated the fusion of tribal worships, and how deities
originally distinct might come to be identified on account of the similarity
of their images and of the sacrifices offered to them.   See p. 297 *sqq*.

divine powers, and it is to this kind of process that we must apparently ascribe the development of a Semitic pantheon or polytheistic system. A pantheon, or organised commonwealth of gods, such as we find in the state religion of Egypt or in the Homeric poems, is not the primitive type of heathenism, and little trace of such a thing appears in the oldest documents of the religion of the smaller Semitic communities. The old Semites believed in the existence of many gods, for they accepted as real the gods of their enemies as well as their own, but they did not worship the strange gods from whom they had no favour to expect, and on whom their gifts and offerings would have been thrown away. When every small community was on terms of frequent hostility with all its neighbours, the formation of a polytheistic system was impossible. Each group had its own god, or perhaps a god and a goddess, to whom the other gods bore no relation whatever. It was only as the small groups coalesced into larger unities, that a society and kinship of many gods began to be formed, on the model of the alliance or fusion of their respective worshippers; and indeed the chief part in the development of a systematic hierarchy or commonwealth of Semitic deities is due to the Babylonians and Assyrians, among whom the labours of statesmen to build up a consolidated empire out of a multitude of local communities, originally independent, were seconded by the efforts of the priests to give a corresponding unity of scheme to the multiplicity of local worships.[1]

Thus far we have looked only at the general fact, that in a Semitic community men and their gods formed a social and political as well as a religious whole. But to

---

[1] In the eighth century B.C. some of the Western Semitic states had a considerable pantheon, as appears most clearly from the notices of the "gods of Ya'di" on the inscriptions found (in 1890) at Zenjirli in North-West Syria, at the foot of Mount Amanus. See Cooke, Nos. 61–63.

make our conceptions more concrete we must consider what place in this whole was occupied by the divine element of the social partnership. And here we find that the two leading conceptions of the relation of the god to his people are those of fatherhood and of kingship. We have learned to look on Semitic society as built up on two bases—on kinship, which is the foundation of the system of clans or gentes, and on the union of kins, living intermingled or side by side, and bound together by common interests, which is the foundation of the state. We now see that the clan and the state are both represented in religion : as father the god belongs to the family or clan, as king he belongs to the state ; and in each sphere of the social order he holds the position of highest dignity. Both these conceptions deserve to be looked at and illustrated in some detail.

The relation of a father to his children has a moral as well as a physical aspect, and each of these must be taken into account in considering what the fatherhood of the tribal deity meant in ancient religion. In the physical aspect the father is the being to whom the child owes his life, and through whom he traces kinship with the other members of his family or clan. The antique conception of kinship is participation in one blood, which passes from parent to child and circulates in the veins of every member of the family. The unity of the family or clan is viewed as a physical unity, for the blood is the life,—an idea familiar to us from the Old Testament,[1]—and it is the same

---

[1] Gen. ix. 4 ; Deut. xii. 23. Among the Arabs also *nafs* is used of the life-blood. When a man dies a natural death his life departs through the nostrils (*māta ḥatfa anfihi*), but when he is slain in battle "his life flows on the spear point" (Ḥamāsa, p. 52). Similarly *lā nafsa lahu sāïlatun* means *lā dama lahu yajrī* (*Miṣbāḥ, s.v.*). To the use of *nafs* in the sense of blood, the Arabian philologists refer such expressions as *nifās*, childbirth ; *nafsā*, puerpera. The use of *nafisat* or *nufisat* in the sense of *ḥādat* (Bokhārī, i. 72, l. 10) appears to justify their explanation.

blood and therefore the same life that is shared by every descendant of the common ancestor. The idea that the race has a life of its own, of which individual lives are only parts, is expressed even more clearly by picturing the race as a tree, of which the ancestor is the root or stem and the descendants the branches. This figure is used by all the Semites, and is very common both in the Old Testament and in the Arabian poets.

The moral aspect of fatherhood, again, lies in the social relations and obligations which flow from the physical relationship—in the sanctity of the tie of blood which binds together the whole family, and in the particular modification of this tie in the case of parent and child, the parent protecting and nourishing the child, while the child owes obedience and service to his parent.

In Christianity, and already in the spiritual religion of the Hebrews, the idea of divine fatherhood is entirely dissociated from the physical basis of natural fatherhood. Man was created in the image of God, but he was not begotten ; God-sonship is not a thing of nature but a thing of grace. In the Old Testament, Israel is Jehovah's son, and Jehovah is his father who created him ;[1] but this creation is not a physical act, it refers to the series of gracious deeds by which Israel was shaped into a nation. And so, though it may be said of the Israelites as a whole, " Ye are the children of Jehovah your God,"[2] this sonship is national, not personal, and the individual Israelite has not the right to call himself Jehovah's son.

But in heathen religions the fatherhood of the gods is physical fatherhood. Among the Greeks, for example, the idea that the gods fashioned men out of clay, as potters fashion images, is relatively modern. The older conception is that the races of men have gods for their ancestors, or

---

[1] Hos. xi. 1 ; Deut. xxxii. 6.   [2] Deut. xiv. 1.

are the children of the earth, the common mother of gods
and men, so that men are really of the stock or kin of the
gods.[1] That the same conception was familiar to the older
Semites appears from the Bible. Jeremiah describes
idolaters as saying to a stock, Thou art my father; and to a
stone, Thou hast brought me forth.[2] In the ancient poem,
Num. xxi. 29, the Moabites are called the sons and
daughters of Chemosh, and at a much more recent date the
prophet Malachi calls a heathen woman "the daughter of
a strange god."[3] These phrases are doubtless accommoda-
tions to the language which the heathen neighbours of
Israel used about themselves; they belong to an age when
society in Syria and Palestine was still mainly organised
on the tribal system, so that each clan, or even each complex
of clans forming a small independent people, traced back its
origin to a great first father; and they indicate that, just
as in Greece, this father or $ἀρχηγέτης$ of the race was
commonly identified with the god of the race. With this
it accords that in the judgment of most modern enquirers
several names of deities appear in the old genealogies of
nations in the Book of Genesis. Edom, for example, the
progenitor of the Edomites, was identified by the Hebrews
with Esau the brother of Jacob, but to the heathen he was
a god, as appears from the theophorous proper name
Obededom, "worshipper of Edom."[4] The remains of such

---

[1] See details and references in Preller-Robert, *Griechische Mythol.* (1887)
i. 78 *sqq.*

[2] Jer. ii. 27. [3] Mal. ii. 11.

[4] Bäthgen, *Beiträge zur Semitischen Religionsg.* p. 10, objects that not
all names compounded with עבד are theophorous. And it is true that on
the Nabatæan inscriptions we find names of this form in which the second
element is the name of a king; but this is in a state of society where the
king was revered as at least quasi-divine, and where the apotheosis of dead
kings was not unknown. Cf. Wellh. p. 2 *sq.*; Euting, *Nabat. Inschr.* p.
32 *sq.*; and especially Clermont-Ganneau, *Rec. d'Archéol. Or.* i. 39 *sqq.* It
must, however, be admitted that in questions of the history of religion,
arguments derived from names are apt to be somewhat inconclusive; it is

mythology are naturally few in records which have come to us through the monotheistic Hebrews. On the other hand, the extant fragments of Phœnician and Babylonian cosmogonies date from a time when tribal religion and the connection of individual gods with particular kindreds was forgotten or had fallen into the background. But in a generalised form the notion that men are the offspring of the gods still held its ground. In the Phœnician cosmogony of Philo Byblius it does so in a confused shape, due to the author's euhemerism, that is, to his theory that deities are nothing more than deified men who had been great bene-factors to their species. But euhemerism itself can arise, as an explanation of popular religion, only where the old gods are regarded as akin to men, and where, therefore, the deification of human benefactors does not involve any such patent absurdity as on our way of thinking. Again, in the Chaldæan legend preserved by Berosus,[1] the belief that men are of the blood of the gods is expressed in a form too crude not to be very ancient; for animals as well as men are said to have been formed out of clay mingled with the blood of a decapitated deity. Here we have a blood-kinship

---

possible, though surely very improbable, that the national name אדום (always written *plene*) means "men," Arabic *anām*, and is different from the god-name אדם ; see Nöldeke in *ZDMG*. xlii. 470.

As examples of god-names in the genealogies of Genesis, I have elsewhere adduced Uz (Gen. xxii. 21, xxxvi. 28; LXX, Ωζ, Ωξ, Ωs : and in Job i. 1, Αὐσιτις='Aud (*Kin.* 59–61) and Yeush (Gen. xxxvi. 14)=Yaghûth. The second of these identifications is accepted by Nöldeke, but rejected by Lagarde, *Mitth.* ii. 77, *Bildung der Nomina*, p. 124. The other has been criticised by Nöldeke, *ZDMG*. xl. 184, but his remarks do not seem to me to be conclusive. That the Arabian god is a mere personification of Time is a hard saying, and the view that 'auḍo or 'auḍa in the line of al-A'shā is derived from the name of the god, which Nöldeke finds to be "doch etwas bizarr," has at least the authority of Ibn al-Kalbī as cited by Jauharī, and more clearly in the *Lisān*. A god קינן bearing the same name as the ante-diluvian Cainan (Gen. v. 9) appears in Himyaritic inscriptions : *ZDMG*. xxxi. 86 ; *CIS*. iv. p. 20.

[1] Müller, *Fr. Hist. Gr.* ii. 497 *sq.*

of gods men and beasts, a belief which has points of contact with the lowest forms of savage religion.

It is obvious that the idea of a physical affinity between the gods and men in general is more modern than that of affinity between particular gods and their worshippers; and the survival of the idea in a generalised form, after men's religion had ceased to be strictly dependent on tribal connection, is in itself a proof that belief in their descent from the blood of the gods was not confined to this or that clan, but was a widespread feature in the old tribal religions of the Semites, too deeply interwoven with the whole system of faith and practice to be altogether thrown aside when the community of the same worship ceased to be purely one of kinship.

That this was really the case will be seen more clearly when we come to speak of the common features of Semitic ritual, and especially of the ritual use of blood, which is the primitive symbol of kinship. Meantime let us observe that there is yet another form in which the idea of divine descent survived the breaking up of the tribal system among the northern Semites. When this took place, the worshippers of one god, being now men of different kindreds, united by political bonds instead of bonds of blood, could not be all thought of as children of the god. He was no longer their father but their king. But as the deities of a mixed community were in their origin the old deities of the more influential families, the members of these families might still trace their origin to the family god, and find in this pedigree matter of aristocratic pride. Thus royal and noble houses among the Greeks long continued to trace their stem back to a divine forefather, and the same thing appears among the Semites. We are told by Virgil and Silius Italicus,[1] that the royal house of Tyre

---

[1] *Æn.* i. 729 ; *Punica*, i. 87.

and the noblest families of Carthage claimed descent from
the Tyrian Baal; among the Aramæan sovereigns of
Damascus, mentioned in the Bible, we find more than one
Ben-hadad, "son of the god Hadad," and at Zenjirli the
king Bar-RKB seems from his name to claim descent from
the god RKB-EL.[1] Among the later Aramæans names
like Barlāhā, "son of God," Barbaʿshmīn, "son of the Lord
of Heaven," Barate, "son of Ate," are not uncommon. At
Palmyra we have Barnebo, "son of Nebo," Barshamsh,
"son of the Sun-god"; and in Ezra ii. the eponym of a
family of temple slaves is Barkos, "son of the god Caus."
Whether any definite idea was attached to such names in
later times is doubtful; perhaps their diffusion was due to
the constant tendency of the masses to copy aristocratic
names, which is as prevalent in the East as among
ourselves.[2]

[1] For the god-sonship of Assyrian monarchs, see Tiele, *Babylonisch-Assyr.
Gesch.* p. 492.

[2] Among the Hebrews and Phœnicians personal names of this type do
not appear; we have, however, the woman's name בתבעל, "daughter of
Baal," *CIS.* pt. i. Nos. 469, 727, etc. On the other hand, the worshipper is
called brother (that is, kinsman) or sister of the god in such names as
the Phœnician חתלת, חתמלקרת, חתמלכת, חתמלכת; חרם, חתמלך, חמלכת, חמלך,
חתנת, "sister of Tanith," and the Hebrew אחיה, חיאל. A singular and
puzzling class of theophorous names are those which have the form of an
Arabic *konya*; as Abibaal, "father of Baal." It has been common to evade
the difficulty by rendering "my father is Baal"; but this view breaks down
before such a woman's name as אמאשמן (*CIS.* No. 881), "mother of the
god Eshmun." See Nöldeke in *ZDMG.* xlii. (1888) p. 480, who seems disposed to believe that "father" has here some metaphorical sense, comparing
Gen. xlv. 8. For my own part I hazard the conjecture that the *konya* was
in practice used as equivalent to the patronymic; the custom of calling the
eldest son after the grandfather was so widespread that M, son of N, was
pretty sure to be known also as M, father of N, and the latter, as the more
polite form of address, might very well come to supersede the patronymic
altogether. I think there are some traces of this in Arabic; the poet ʿAmr b.
Kolthum addresses the king ʿAmr b. Hind as Abu Hind (Moall. 1. 23). In
Hebrew the prefixes אבי, אחי, חמו are used in forming names of women as
well as men, and so in Phœnician Abibaal may be a woman's name (*CIS.*
No. 378), as אבעלי, אבמלך are in Ḥimyaritic (*CIS.* pt. iv. Nos. 6, 85);
but for this linguistic peculiarity Nöldeke has adduced satisfactory analogies.

The belief that all the members of a clan are sons and
daughters of its god, might naturally be expected to survive
longest in Arabia, where the tribe was never lost in the
state, and kinship continued down to the time of Mohammed
to be the one sacred bond of social unity.   In point of
fact many Arabian tribes bear the names of gods, or of
celestial bodies worshipped as gods, and their members are
styled " sons of Hobal," " sons of the Full Moon," and the
like.[1]   There is no adequate reason for refusing to explain
these names, or at least the older ones among them, on
the analogy of the similar clan-names found among the
northern Semites; for Arabian ritual, as well as that of
Palestine and Syria, involves in its origin a belief in the
kinship of the god and his worshippers.   In the later ages
of Arabian heathenism, however, of which alone we have
any full accounts, religion had come to be very much dissociated from tribal feeling, mainly, it would seem, in
consequence of the extensive migrations which took place
in the first centuries of our era, and carried tribes far away
from the fixed sanctuaries of the gods of their fathers.[2]
Men forgot their old worship, and as the names of gods
were also used as individual proper names, the divine
ancestor, even before Islam, had generally sunk to the rank
of a mere man.   But though the later Arabs worshipped
gods that were not the gods of their fathers, and tribes of
alien blood were often found gathered together on festival

---

[1] See *Kinship*, p. 241 *sqq.*, and Wellhausen, *Heidenthum*, p. 7 *sqq.*, who
explains all such names as due to omission of the prefix *'Abd* or the like.
In some cases this probably is so, but it must not be assumed that because
the same tribe is called (for example) 'Auf or 'Abd 'Auf indifferently, Banu
'Auf is a contraction of Banu 'Abd 'Auf.   It is quite logical that the sons
of 'Auf form the collective body of his worshippers; cf. Mal. iii. 17 ; and
for the collective use of *'abd* cf. *Ḥamāsa*, p. 312, first verse.   Personal names
indicating god-sonship are lacking in Arabia ; see on supposed Sabæan
examples, D. H. Müller, *ZDMG.* xxxvii. 12 *sq.*, 15.

[2] See Wellhausen, *ut supra*, p. 215 *sq.*, and compare 1 Sam. xxvi. 19.

occasions at the great pilgrim shrines, there are many evidences that all Arabic deities were originally the gods of particular kins, and that the bond of religion was originally coextensive with the bond of blood.

A main proof of this lies in the fact that the duties of blood were the only duties of absolute and indefeasible sanctity. The Arab warrior in the ages immediately preceding Islam was very deficient in religion in the ordinary sense of the word ; he was little occupied with the things of the gods and negligent in matters of ritual worship. But he had a truly religious reverence for his clan, and a kinsman's blood was to him a thing holy and inviolable. This apparent paradox becomes at once intelligible when we view it in the light of the antique conception, that the god and his worshippers make up a society in which the same character of sanctity is impressed on the relations of the worshippers to one another as on their relations to their god. The original religious society was the kindred group, and all the duties of kinship were part of religion. And so even when the clan-god had fallen into the background and was little remembered, the type of a clan-religion was still maintained in the enduring sanctity of the kindred bond.[1]

Again, the primitive connection of religion with kindred is attested by the existence of priesthoods confined to men of one clan or family, which in many cases was of a

---

[1] When the oracle at Tabāla forbade the poet Imraulcais to make war on the slayers of his father, he broke the lot and dashed the pieces in the face of the god, exclaiming with a gross and insulting expletive, "If it had been thy father that was killed, thou wouldst not have refused me vengeance." The respect for the sanctity of blood overrides respect for a god who, by taking no interest in the poet's blood-feud, has shown that he has no feeling of kindred for the murdered man and his son. Imraulcais's act does not show that he was impious, but only that kinship was the principle of his religion. That with such principles he consulted the oracle of a strange god at all, is perhaps to be explained by the fact that his army was a miscellaneous band of hirelings and broken men of various tribes.

different blood from the class of the worshippers.   Cases
of this sort are common, not only among the Arabs,[1] but
among the other Semites also, and generally throughout
the ancient world.   In such cases the priestly clan may
often represent the original kindred group which was once
in exclusive possession of the *sacra* of the god, and continued to administer them after worshippers from without
were admitted to the religion.

And further, it will appear when we come to the
subject of sacrifice, that when tribes of different blood
worshipped at the same sanctuary and adored the same
god, they yet held themselves apart from one another and
did not engage in any common act that united them in
religious fellowship.   The circle of worship was still the
kin, though the deity worshipped was not of the kin, and
the only way in which two kindreds could form a religious
fusion was by a covenant ceremony, in which it was
symbolically set forth that they were no longer twain, but
of one blood.   It is clear, therefore, that among the Arabs
the circle of religious solidarity was originally the group
of kinsmen, and it needs no proof that, this being so, the
god himself must have been conceived as united to his
worshippers by the bond of blood, as their great kinsman,
or more specifically as their great ancestor.

It is often said that the original Semitic conception
of the godhead was abstract and transcendental; that
while Aryan religion with its poetic mythology drew
the gods down into the sphere of nature and of human
life, Semitic religion always showed an opposite tendency,
that it sought to remove the gods as far as possible from
man, and even contained within itself from the first the
seeds of an abstract deism.   According to this view, the
anthropomorphisms of Semitic religion, that is, all expres-

---

[1] Wellhausen, p. 130 *sq.*

sions which in their literal sense imply that the gods have
a physical nature cognate to that of man, are explained
away as mere allegory, and it is urged, in proof of the
fundamental distinction between the Aryan and Semitic
conceptions of the divine nature, that myths like those of
the Aryans, in which gods act like men, mingle with men
and in fact live a common life with mankind, have little
or no place in Semitic religion. But all this is mere
unfounded assumption. It is true that the remains of
ancient Semitic mythology are not very numerous ; but
mythology cannot be preserved without literature, and an
early literature of Semitic heathenism does not exist.
The one exception is the cuneiform literature of Babylonia,
and in it we find fragments of a copious mythology. It is
true, also, that there is not much mythology in the poetry
of heathen Arabia ; but Arabian poetry has little to do
with religion at all : it dates from the extreme decadence
of the old heathenism, and is preserved to us only in the
collections formed by Mohammedan scholars, who were
careful to avoid or obliterate as far as possible the traces
of their fathers' idolatry. That the Semites never had a
mythological epic poetry comparable to that of the Greeks
is admitted ; but the character of the Semitic genius, which
is deficient in plastic power and in the faculty of sustained
and orderly effort, is enough to account for the fact. We
cannot draw inferences for religion from the absence of
an elaborate mythology ; the question is whether there are
not traces, in however crude a form, of the mythological
point of view. And this question must be answered in
the affirmative. I must not turn aside now to speak at
large of Semitic myths, but it is to the point to observe
that there do exist remains of myths, and not only of
myths but of sacred usages, involving a conception of the
divine beings and their relation with man which entirely

4

justifies us in taking the kinship of men with gods in its literal and physical sense, exactly as in Greece. In Greece the loves of the gods with the daughters of men were referred to remote antiquity, but in Babylon the god Bel was still, in the time of Herodotus, provided with a human wife, who spent the night in his temple and with whom he was believed to share his couch.[1] In one of the few fragments of old mythology which have been transplanted unaltered into the Hebrew Scriptures, we read of the sons of gods who took wives of the daughters of men, and became the fathers of the renowned heroes of ancient days. Such a hero is the Gilgamesh of Babylonian myth, to whom the great goddess Ishtar did not disdain to offer her hand. Arabian tradition presents similar legends. The clan of ʿAmr b. Yarbūʿ was descended from a siʿlāt, or she-demon, who became the wife of their human father, but suddenly disappeared from him on seeing a flash of lightning.[2] In this connection the distinction between gods and demi-gods is immaterial; the demi-gods are of divine kind, though they have not attained to the full position of deities with a recognised circle of worshippers.[3]

There is then a great variety of evidence to show that the type of religion which is founded on kinship, and in which the deity and his worshippers make up a society united by the bond of blood, was widely prevalent, and

[1] Herod. i. 181 *sq.* This is not more realistic than the custom of providing the Hercules (Baal) of Sanbulos with a horse, on which he rode out to hunt by night (Tac. *Ann.* xii. 13 ; cf. *Gaz. Archéol.* 1879, p. 178 *sqq.*).

[2] Ibn Doreid, *Kitāb al-ishticāc*, p. 139. It is implied that the demoniac wife was of lightning kind. Elsewhere also the *siʿlāt* seems to be a fiery scorching being. In Ibn Hishām, p. 27, l. 14, the Abyssinian hosts resemble *Saʿālī* because they ravage the country with fire, and the green trees are scorched up before them. See also Rasmussen, *Addit.* p. 71, l. 19 of the Ar. text.

[3] Modern legends of marriage or courtship between men and jinn, Doughty, ii. 191 *sq.* ; *ZDPV.* x. 84. Whether such marriages are lawful is solemnly discussed by Mohammedan jurists.

that at an early date, among all the Semitic peoples. But
the force of the evidence goes further, and leaves no
reasonable doubt that among the Semites this was the
original type of religion, out of which all other types
grew. That it was so is particularly clear as regards
Arabia, where we have found the conception of the circle
of worship and the circle of kindred as identical to be
so deeply rooted that it dominated the practical side of
religion, even after men worshipped deities that were not
kindred gods. But among the other branches of the
Semites also, the connection between religion and kinship
is often manifested in forms that cannot be explained
except by reference to a primitive stage of society, in
which the circle of blood relations was also the circle
of all religious and social unity. Nations, as distinguished from mere clans, are not constructed on the
principle of kinship, and yet the Semitic nations
habitually feigned themselves to be of one kin, and
their national religions are deeply imbued, both in
legend and in ritual, with the idea that the god and
his worshippers are of one stock. This, I apprehend,
is good evidence that the fundamental lines of all
Semitic religion were laid down, long before the beginnings of authentic history, in that earliest stage of
society when kinship was the only recognised type of
permanent friendly relation between man and man, and
therefore the only type on which it was possible to
frame the conception of a permanent friendly relation
between a group of men and a supernatural being.
That all human societies have been developed from
this stage is now generally recognised; and the evidence
shows that amongst the Semites the historical forms of
religion can be traced back to such a stage.

Recent researches into the history of the family render

it in the highest degree improbable that the physical
kinship between the god and his worshippers, of which
traces are found all over the Semitic area, was originally
conceived as fatherhood. It was the mother's, not the
father's, blood which formed the original bond of kinship
among the Semites as among other early peoples, and in
this stage of society, if the tribal deity was thought of
as the parent of the stock, a goddess, not a god, would
necessarily have been the object of worship. In point
of fact, goddesses play a great part in Semitic religion,
and that not merely in the subordinate *rôle* of wives of
the gods; it is also noticeable that in various parts of
the Semitic field we find deities originally female changing
their sex and becoming gods, as if with the change in the
rule of human kinship.[1] So long as kinship was traced
through the mother alone, a male deity of common stock
with his worshippers could only be their cousin, or, in the
language of that stage of society, their brother. This in
fact is the relationship between gods and men asserted by
Pindar, when he ascribes to both alike a common mother
Earth, and among the Semites a trace of the same point
of view may be seen in the class of proper names which
designate their bearers as "brother" or "sister" of a deity.[2]
If this be so, we must distinguish the religious significance
belonging to the wider and older conception of kinship
between the deity and the race that worshipped him, from
the special and more advanced ideas, conformed to a higher
stage of social development, that were added when the
kindred god came to be revered as a father.

Some of the most notable and constant features of
all ancient heathenism, and indeed of all nature-religions,

[1] See *Kinship*, p. 298 *sqq.*, note E. I hope to return to this subject on
a future opportunity.
[2] See above, p. 45, note 2.

from the totemism of savages upward, find their sufficient
explanation in the physical kinship that unites the human
and superhuman members of the same religious and social
community, without reference to the special doctrine of
divine fatherhood. From this point of view the natural
solidarity of the god and his worshippers, which has been
already enlarged upon as characteristic of antique religion,
at once becomes intelligible; the indissoluble bond that
unites men to their god is the same bond of blood-fellowship which in early society is the one binding link
between man and man, and the one sacred principle of
moral obligation. And thus we see that even in its
rudest forms religion was a moral force; the powers
that man reveres were on the side of social order and
tribal law; and the fear of the gods was a motive to
enforce the laws of society, which were also the laws of
morality.

But though the earliest nature-religion was fully
identified with the earliest morality, it was not fitted
to raise morality towards higher ideals; and instead of
leading the way in social and ethical progress, it was often
content to follow or even to lag behind. Religious feeling
is naturally conservative, for it is bound up with old
custom and usage; and the gods, who are approached
only in traditional ritual, and invoked as giving sanction
to long-established principles of conduct, seem always to
be on the side of those who are averse to change. Among
the Semites, as among other races, religion often came to
work against a higher morality, not because it was in
its essence a power for evil, but because it clung to the
obsolete ethical standard of a bygone stage of society.
To our better judgment, for example, one of the most
offensive features in tribal religion is its particularism;
a man is held answerable to his god for wrong done to

a member of his own kindred or political community, but
he may deceive, rob, or kill an alien without offence to
religion ; the deity cares only for his own kinsfolk.   This
is a very narrow morality, and we are tempted to call it
sheer immorality.   But such a judgment would be altogether false from an historical point of view.   The larger
morality which embraces all mankind has its basis in
habits of loyalty, love, and self-sacrifice, which were
originally formed and grew strong in the narrower circle
of the family or the clan ; and the part which the religion
of kinship played in the development and maintenance
of these habits, is one of the greatest services it has
done to human progress.   This service it was able to
render because the gods were themselves members of
the kin, and the man who was untrue to kindred duty
had to reckon with them as with his human clansmen.

An eloquent French writer has recently quoted with
approval, and applied to the beginnings of Semitic religion,
★ the words of Statius, *Primus in orbe deos fecit timor,*[1]
" Man fancied himself surrounded by enemies whom he
sought to appease."   But however true it is that savage
man feels himself to be environed by innumerable dangers
which he does not understand, and so personifies as invisible
or mysterious enemies of more than human power, it is not
true that the attempt to appease these powers is the foundation of religion.   From the earliest times, religion, as distinct
from magic or sorcery, addresses itself to kindred and
friendly beings, who may indeed be angry with their people
for a time, but are always placable except to the enemies
of their worshippers or to renegade members of the community.   It is not with a vague fear of unknown powers,
but with a loving reverence for known gods who are knit
to their worshippers by strong bonds of kinship, that

[1] Renan, *Hist. d'Israel,* i. 29.

religion in the only true sense of the word begins.
Religion in this sense is not the child of terror; and
the difference between it and the savage's dread of unseen foes is as absolute and fundamental in the earliest
as in the latest stages of development.   It is only in
times of social dissolution, as in the last age of the
small Semitic states, when men and their gods were
alike powerless before the advance of the Assyrians, that
magical superstitions based on mere terror, or rites
designed to conciliate alien gods, invade the sphere of
tribal or national religion.   In better times the religion
of the tribe or state has nothing in common with the
private and foreign superstitions or magical rites that
savage terror may dictate to the individual.   Religion
is not an arbitrary relation of the individual man to a
supernatural power, it is a relation of all the members
of a community to a power that has the good of the
community at heart, and protects its law and moral
order.   This distinction seems to have escaped some
modern theorists, but it was plain enough to the common
sense of antiquity, in which private and magical superstitions were habitually regarded as offences against morals
and the state.   It is not only in Israel that we find the
suppression of magical rites to be one of the first cares of
the founder of the kingdom, or see the introduction of
foreign worships treated as a heinous crime.   In both
respects the law of Israel is the law of every well-ordered
ancient community.

In the historical stage of Semitic religion the kinship
of the deity with his or her people is specified as fatherhood or motherhood, the former conception predominating,
in accordance with the later rule that assigned the son to
his father's stock.   Under the law of male kinship woman
takes a subordinate place; the father is the natural head

of the family, and superior to the mother, and accordingly
the chief place in religion usually belongs, not to a mother-
goddess, but to a father-god.   At the same time the conception of the goddess-mother was not unknown, and seems
to be attached to cults which go back to the ages of
polyandry and female kinship.   The Babylonian Ishtar in
her oldest form is such a mother-goddess, unmarried, or
rather choosing her temporary partners at will, the queen
head and firstborn of all gods.[1]   She is the mother of the
gods and also the mother of men, who, in the Chaldæan
flood-legends, mourns over the death of her offspring.
In like manner the Carthaginians worshipped a "great
mother," who seems to be identical with Tanith-Artemis,
the "heavenly virgin," [2] and the Arabian Lāt was
★ worshipped by the Nabatæans as mother of the gods, and
must be identified with the virgin-mother, whose worship
at Petra is described by Epiphanius.[3]

[1] Tiele, *Babylonisch-Assyrische Gesch.* p. 528.

[2] אם רבת, *CIS.* Nos. 195, 380; cf. No. 177.   The identification of
Tanith with Artemis appears from No. 116, where עבדתנת =ʼΑρτεμίδωρος, and
is confirmed by the prominence of the *virgo cœlestis* or *numen virginale* in
the later cults of Punic Africa.   The identification of the mother of the gods
with the heavenly virgin, *i.e.* the unmarried goddess, is confirmed if not
absolutely demanded by Aug. *Civ. Dei,* ii. 4.   At Carthage she seems also
to be identical with Dido, of whom as a goddess more in another connection.
See Hoffmann, *Ueb. einige Phœn. Inschrr.* p. 32 *sq.*   The foul type of worship
corresponding to the conception of the goddess as polyandrous prevailed at
Sicca Veneria, and Augustin speaks with indignation of the incredible
obscenity of the songs that accompanied the worship of the Carthaginian
mother-goddess ; but perhaps this is not wholly to be set down as of Punic
origin, for the general laxity on the point of female chastity in which such a
type of worship originates has always been characteristic of North Africa (see
Tissot, *La Prov. d'Afrique,* i. 477).

[3] De Vogüé, *Syr. Centr.* Inscr. Nab. No. 8 ; Epiph., *Panarium* 51 (ii. 483,
Dind.), see *Kinship,* p. 298 *sq.*   I am not able to follow the argument by
which Wellh.[1], pp. 40, 46, seeks to invalidate the evidence as to the worship
of a mother-goddess by the Nabatæans. He supposes that the Χααβου, which
Epiphanius represents as the virgin-mother of Dusares, is really nothing
more than the cippus, or betyl, out of which the god was supposed to have
been born, *i.e.* the image of the god himself, not a distinct deity.   But from
the time of Herodotus downwards, al-Lāt was worshipped in these regions

Originally, since men are of one stock with their gods, the mother of the gods must also have been, like Ishtar, the mother of men ; but except in Babylonia and Assyria, where the kings at least continued to speak of themselves as the progeny of Ishtar, it is not clear that this idea was present to the Semitic worshipper when he addressed his goddess as the great mother.   But if we may judge from analogy, and even from such modern analogies as are supplied by the cult of the Virgin Mary, we can hardly doubt that the use of a name appropriated to the tenderest and truest of human relationships was associated in acts of worship with feelings of peculiar warmth and trustful devotion.   " Can a woman forget her sucking child, that she should not have compassion on the son of her womb ? Yea, they may forget, yet will I not forget thee." [1] That such thoughts were not wholly foreign to Semitic heathenism appears, to give a single instance, from the

side by side with a god, and the evidence of De Vogüé's inscription and that of Epiphanius agree in making Lāt the mother and the god her son.   Epiphanius implies that the virgin-mother was worshipped also at Elusa ; and here Jerome, in his life of S. Hilarion, knows a temple of a goddess whom he calls Venus, and who was worshipped "ob Luciferum," on account of her connection with the morning star.   Wellhausen takes this to mean that the goddess of Elusa was identified with the morning star; but that is impossible, for, in his comm. on Amos v., Jerome plainly indicates that the morning star was worshipped as a god, not as a goddess. This is the old Semitic conception ; see Isa. xiv. 12, "Lucifer, son of the Dawn " ; and in the Arabian poets, also, the planet Venus is masculine, as Wellhausen himself observes.   I see no reason to believe that the Arabs of Nilus worshipped the morning star as a goddess ; nor perhaps does the worship of this planet as a goddess (Al-'Ozzā) appear anywhere in Arabia, except among the Eastern tribes who came under the influence of the Assyrian Ishtar-worship, as it survived among the Aramæans.   This point was not clear to me when I wrote my *Kinship*, and want of attention to it has brought some confusion into the argument.   That the goddess of Elusa was Al-'Ozzā, as Wellh., p. 48, supposes, is thus very doubtful. Whether, as Tuch thought, her local name was Khalasa is also doubtful, but we must not reject the identification of Elusa with the place still called Khalasa ; see Palmer, *Desert of the Exodus*, p. 423, compared with p. 550 *sqq.*

[1] Isa. xlix. 15.

language in which Assurbanipal appeals to Ishtar in his time of need, and in the oracle she sends to comfort him.[1]

But in this, as in all its aspects, heathenism shows its fundamental weakness, in its inability to separate the ethical motives of religion from their source in a merely naturalistic conception of the godhead and its relation to man. Divine motherhood, like the kinship of men and gods in general, was to the heathen Semites a physical fact, and the development of the corresponding cults and myths laid more stress on the physical than on the ethical side of maternity, and gave a prominence to sexual ideas which was never edifying, and often repulsive. Especially was this the case when the change in the law of kinship deprived the mother of her old pre-eminence in the family, and transferred to the father the greater part of her authority and dignity. This change, as we know, went hand in hand with the abolition of the old polyandry; and as women lost the right to choose their own partners at will, the wife became subject to her husband's lordship, and her freedom of action was restrained by his jealousy, at the same time that her children became, for all purposes of inheritance and all duties of blood, members of his and not of her kin. So far as religion kept pace with the new laws of social morality due to this development, the independent divine mother necessarily became the subordinate partner of a male deity; and so the old polyandrous Ishtar reappears in Canaan and elsewhere as Astarte, the wife of the supreme Baal. Or if the supremacy of the goddess was too well established to be thus undermined, she might change her sex, as in Southern Arabia, where Ishtar is transformed into the masculine

---

[1] George Smith, *Assurbanipal*, p. 117 *sqq.; Records of the Past*, ix. 51 *sqq.*

'Athtar. But not seldom religious tradition refused to move forward with the progress of society; the goddess retained her old character as a mother who was not a wife bound to fidelity to her husband, and at her sanctuary she protected, under the name of religion, the sexual licence of savage society, or even demanded of the daughters of her worshippers a shameful sacrifice of their chastity, before they were permitted to bind themselves for the rest of their lives to that conjugal fidelity which their goddess despised.

The emotional side of Semitic heathenism was always very much connected with the worship of female deities, partly through the associations of maternity, which appealed to the purest and tenderest feelings, and partly through other associations connected with woman, which too often appealed to the sensuality so strongly developed in the Semitic race. The feelings called forth when the deity was conceived as a father were on the whole of an austerer kind, for the distinctive note of fatherhood, as distinguished from kinship in general, lay mainly in the parental authority, in the father's claim to be honoured and served by his son. The honour which the fifth commandment requires children to pay to their fathers is named in Mal. i. 6 along with that which a servant owes to his master, and the same prophet (iii. 17) speaks of the considerate regard which a father shows for " the son that serveth him." To this day the grown-up son in Arabia serves his father in much the same offices as the domestic slave, and approaches him with much the same degree of reverence and even of constraint. It is only with his little children that the father is effusively affectionate and on quite easy terms. On the other hand, the father's authority had not a despotic character. He had no such power of life and death over his sons as

Roman law recognised,[1] and indeed, after they passed
beyond childhood, had no means of enforcing his authority
if they refused to respect it. Paradoxical as this may
seem, it is quite in harmony with the general spirit of
Semitic institutions that authority should exist and be
generally acknowledged without having any force behind
it except the pressure of public opinion. The authority
of an Arab sheikh is in the same position; and when an
Arab judge pronounces sentence on a culprit, it is at the
option of the latter whether he will pay the fine, which is
the invariable form of penalty, or continue in feud with
his accuser.

★ Thus, while the conception of the tribal god as father
introduces into religion the idea of divine authority, of
reverence and service due from the worshipper to the
deity, it does not carry with it any idea of the strict and
rigid enforcement of divine commands by supernatural
sanctions. The respect paid by the Semite to his father
is but the respect which he pays to kindred, focussed
upon a single representative person, and the father's
authority is only a special manifestation of the authority
of the kin, which can go no further than the whole kin is
prepared to back it. Thus, in the sphere of religion, the
god, as father, stands by the majority of the tribe in
enforcing tribal law against refractory members: outlawry,
which is the only punishment ordinarily applicable to
a clansman, carries with it excommunication from religious
communion, and the man who defies tribal law has to fear

---

[1] See Deut. xxi. 18, where the word "chastened" should rather be
"admonished." The powerlessness of Jacob to restrain his grown-up sons is
not related as a proof that he was weak, but shows that a father had no means
of enforcing his authority. The law of Deuteronomy can hardly have been
carried into practice. In Prov. xxx. 17 disobedience to parents is cited as
a thing which brings a man to a bad end, not as a thing punished by law.
That an Arab father could do no more than argue with his son, and bring
tribal opinion to bear on him, appears from *Agh.* xix 102 *sq.*

the god as well as his fellow-men. But in all minor
matters, where outlawry is out of the question, the long-
suffering tolerance which tribesmen in early society
habitually extend to the offences of their fellow-tribesmen
is ascribed also to the god; he does not willingly break
with any of his worshippers, and accordingly a bold and
wilful man does not hesitate to take considerable liberties
with the paternal deity. As regards his worshippers at
large, it appears scarcely conceivable, from the point of
view of tribal religion, that the god can be so much
displeased with anything they do that his anger can go
beyond a temporary estrangement, which is readily
terminated by their repentance, or even by a mere change
of humour on the part of the god, when his permanent
affection for his own gets the better of his momentary
displeasure, as it is pretty sure to do if he sees them to
be in straits, *e.g.* to be hard pressed by their and his
enemies. On the whole, men live on very easy terms
with their tribal god, and his paternal authority is neither
strict nor exacting.

This is a very characteristic feature of heathen religion,
and one which does not disappear when the god of the
community comes to be thought of as king rather than as
father. The inscription of King Mesha, for example, tells
us that Chemosh was angry with his people, and suffered
Israel to oppress Moab; and then again that Chemosh
fought for Moab, and delivered it from the foe. There is
no explanation offered of the god's change of mind; it
appears to be simply taken for granted that he was tired
of seeing his people put to the worse. In like manner
the mass of the Hebrews before the exile received with
blank incredulity the prophetic teaching, that Jehovah was
ready to enforce His law of righteousness even by the
destruction of the sinful commonwealth of Israel. To the

prophets Jehovah's long-suffering meant the patience with which He offers repeated calls to repentance, and defers punishment while there is hope of amendment; but to the heathen, and to the heathenly-minded in Israel, the long-suffering of the goos meant a disposition to overlook the offences of their worshippers.

To reconcile the forgiving goodness of God with His absolute justice, is one of the highest problems of spiritual religion, which in Christianity is solved by the doctrine of the atonement. It is important to realise that in heathenism this problem never arose in the form in which the New Testament deals with it, not because the gods of the heathen were not conceived as good and gracious, but because they were not absolutely just. This lack of strict justice, however, is not to be taken as meaning that the gods were in their nature unjust, when measured by the existing standards of social righteousness; as a rule they were conceived as sympathising with right conduct, but not as rigidly enforcing it in every case. To us, who are accustomed to take an abstract view of the divine attributes, this is difficult to conceive, but it seemed perfectly natural when the divine sovereignty was conceived as a kingship precisely similar to human kingship.

In its beginnings, human kingship was as little absolute as the authority of the fathers and elders of the clan, for it was not supported by an executive organisation sufficient to carry out the king's sentence of justice or constrain obedience to his decrees. The authority of the prince was moral rather than physical; his business was to guide rather than to dictate the conduct of his free subjects, to declare what was just rather than to enforce it.[1]

---

[1] In Aramaic the root MLK (from which the common Semitic word for "king" is derived) means "to advise"; and in Arabic the word *Amîr*, "commander," "prince," also means "adviser"; 'Orwa b. al-Ward, i. 16, and *schol.*

Thus the limitations of royal power went on quite an opposite principle from that which underlies a modern limited monarchy. With us the king or his government is armed with the fullest authority to enforce law and justice, and the limitations of his power lie in the independence of the legislature and the judicial courts. The old Semitic king, on the contrary, was supreme judge, and his decrees were laws, but neither his sentences nor his decrees could take effect unless they were supported by forces over which he had very imperfect control. He simply threw his weight into the scale, a weight which was partly due to the moral effect of his sentence, and partly to the material resources which he commanded, not so much *quâ* king as in the character of a great noble and the head of a powerful circle of kinsfolk and clients. An energetic sovereign, who had gained wealth and prestige by successful wars, or inherited the resources accumulated by a line of kingly ancestors, might wield almost despotic power, and in a stable dynasty the tendency was towards the gradual establishment of absolute monarchy, especially if the royal house was able to maintain a standing army devoted to its interests. But a pure despotism of the modern Eastern type probably had not been reached by any of the small kingdoms that were crushed by the Assyrian empire, and certainly the ideas which underlay the conception of divine sovereignty date from an age when the human kingship was still in a rudimentary state, when its executive strength was very limited, and the sovereign was in no way held responsible for the constant maintenance of law and order in all parts of his realm. In most matters of internal order he was not expected to interfere unless directly appealed to by one or other party in a dispute, and even then it was not certain that the party in whose favour he decided would not be left to make good his rights with the aid of his own family connections. So loose a system of administration did not offer a pattern on which to frame the conception of a constant unremitting divine providence, overlooking no injustice and suffering no right to be crushed; the national god might be good and just, but was not continually active or omnipresent in his activity. But we are not to suppose that this remissness was felt to be a defect in the divine character. The Semitic nature is impatient of control, and has no desire to be strictly governed either by human or by divine authority. A god who could be reached when he was wanted, but usually left men pretty much to themselves, was far more acceptable than one whose ever watchful eye can neither be avoided nor deceived. What the Semitic communities asked, and believed themselves to receive, from their god as king lay mainly in three things: help against their enemies, counsel by oracles or soothsayers in matters of national difficulty, and a sentence of justice when a case was too hard for human decision. The valour, the wisdom, and the justice of the nation looked to him as their head, and were strengthened by his support in time of need. For the rest it was not expected that he should always be busy righting human affairs. In ordinary matters it was men's business to help themselves and their own kinsfolk, though the sense that the god was always near, and could be called upon at need, was a moral force continually working in some degree for the maintenance of social righteousness and order. The strength of this moral force was indeed very uncertain, for it was always possible for the evil-doer to flatter himself that his offence would be overlooked; but even so uncertain an influence of religion over conduct was of no little use in the slow and difficult process of the consolidation of an orderly society out of barbarism.

As a social and political force, in the earlier stages of
Semitic society, antique religion cannot be said to have
failed in its mission ; but it was too closely modelled on
the traditional organisation of the family and the nation
to retain a healthful vitality when the social system was
violently shattered.   Among the northern Semites the
age of Assyrian conquest proved as critical for religious
as for civil history, for from that time forward the old
religion was quite out of touch with the actualities of
social life, and became almost wholly mischievous.   But
apart from the Assyrian catastrophe, there are good reasons
to think that in the eighth century B.C. the national
religion of the northern Semites had already passed its
prime, and was sinking into decadence.   The moral springs
of conduct which it touched were mainly connected with
the first needs of a rude society, with the community's
instinct of self-preservation.   The enthusiasm of religion
was seen only in times of peril, when the nation, under
its divine head, was struggling for national existence.   In
times of peace and prosperity, religion had little force to
raise man above sensuality and kindle him to right and
noble deeds.   Except when the nation was in danger, it
called for no self-denial, and rather encouraged an easy
sluggish indulgence in the good things that were enjoyed
under the protection of the national god.   The evils that
slowly sap society, the vices that at first sight seem too
private to be matters of national concern, the disorders
that accompany the increase and unequal distribution of
wealth, the relaxation of moral fibre produced by luxury
and sensuality, were things that religion hardly touched
at all, and that the easy, indulgent god could hardly be
thought to take note of.   The God who could deal with
such evils was the God of the prophets, no mere Oriental
king raised to a throne in heaven, but the just and jealous

5

God, whose eyes are in every place, beholding the evil and
the good, who is of purer eyes than to behold evil, and
cannot look upon iniquity.[1]

In what precedes I have thought it convenient to
assume for the moment, without breaking the argument
by pausing to offer proof, that among the Semitic peoples
which got beyond the mere tribal stage and developed a
tolerably organised state, the supreme deity was habitually
thought of as king. The definitive proof that this was
really so must be sought in the details of religious practice,
to which we shall come by and by, and in which we shall
find indicated a most realistic conception of the divine
kingship. Meantime some proofs of a different character
may be briefly indicated. In the Old Testament the kingship of Jehovah is often set forth as the glory of Israel, but
never in such terms as to suggest that the idea of divine
kingship was peculiar to the Hebrews. On the contrary,
other nations are " the kingdoms of the false gods." [2] In
two exceptional cases a pious judge or a prophet appears
to express the opinion that Jehovah's sovereignty is inconsistent with human kingship,[3] such as existed in the
surrounding nations ; but this difficulty was never felt by
the mass of the Israelites, nor even by the prophets in the
regal period, and it was certainly not felt by Israel's
neighbours. If a son could be crowned in the lifetime of
his father, as was done in the case of Solomon, or could act
for his father as Jotham acted for Uzziah,[4] there was no
difficulty in looking on the human king as the viceroy of
the divine sovereign, who, as we have seen, was often
believed to be the father of the royal race, and so to lend
a certain sanctity to the dynasty. Accordingly we find
that the Tyrian Baal bears the title of Melcarth, " king of

---

[1] Prov. xv. 3 ; Hab. i. 13.   [2] Isa. x. 10.
[3] Judg. viii. 23 ; 1 Sam. xii. 12.   [4] 1 Kings i. 32 *sqq.*; 2 Kings xv. 5.

the city," or more fully, " our lord Melcarth, the Baal of
Tyre," [1] and this sovereignty was acknowledged by the
Carthaginian colonists when they paid tithes at his temple
in the mother city ; for in the East tithes are the king's
due.[2] Similarly the supreme god of the Ammonites was
Milkom or Malkam, which is only a variation of Melek,
" king." The familiar Moloch or Molech is the same thing
in a distorted pronunciation, due to the scruples of the
later Jews, who furnished the consonants of the word
MLK with the vowels of *bosheth,* " shameful thing," whenever it was to be understood as the title of a false god.
In Babylonia and Assyria the application of royal titles to
deities is too common to call for special exemplification.
Again, we have Malakhbel, " King Bel," as the great god
of the Aramæans of Palmyra ; but in this and other
examples of later date it is perhaps open to suppose
that the kingship of the supreme deity means his sovereignty over other gods rather than over his worshippers.
On the other hand, a large mass of evidence can be
drawn from proper names of religious significance, in
which the god of the worshipper is designated as king.
Such names were as common among the Phœnicians and
Assyrians as they were among the Israelites,[3] and are

---

[1] *CIS.* No. 122.

[2] Diod. xx. 14 ; and for the payment of tithes to the king, 1 Sam. viii.
15, 17 ; Aristotle, *Œcon.* ii. p. 1352 *b* of the Berlin ed., cf. p. 1345 *b.*

[3] אהלמלך, *CIS.* No. 50, cf. אהלבעל, No. 54 ; יחומלך, King of Byblus,
No. 1, cf. יחובעל, No. 69 ; מלכיתן, Nos. 10, 16, etc., cf. בעליתן, No. 78 ; רשפיתן,
No. 44 ; עבדמלך, No. 46, cf. עבדאסר, עבדאשמן, עבראשמן, etc. ; עזמלך, Nos. 189, 219,
386, cf. עזבעל, on a coin of Byblus, Head, p. 668. The title of מלכת,
" queen," for Astarte is seen probably in חמלכת, חתמלכת (*supra,* p. 45,
note 2), and more certainly in מתמלכת, "handmaid of the queen," cf.
מתעשתרת, No. 83, and in נעמלכת, " favour of the queen," No. 41. For
Assyrian names of similar type see Schrader in *ZDMG.* xxvi. 140 *sqq.,*
where also an Edomite king's name on a cylinder of Sennacherib is read
Malik-ramu, " the (divine) king, is exalted."   ★

found even among the Arabs of the Syrian and Egyptian frontier.[1]

Where the god is conceived as a king, he will naturally be addressed as lord, and his worshippers will be spoken of as his subjects, and so we find as divine titles Adōn, "lord" (whence Adonis = the god Tammuz), and Rabbath, "lady" (as a title of Tanith), among the Phœnicians, with corresponding phrases among other nations,[2] while in all parts of the Semitic field the worshipper calls himself the servant or slave ('abd, 'ebed) of his god, just as a subject does in addressing his king. The designation "servant" is much affected by worshippers, and forms the basis of a large number of theophorous proper names—'Abd-Eshmun "servant of Eshmun," 'Abd-Baal, 'Abd-Osir, etc. At first sight this designation seems to point to a more rigid conception of divine kingship than I have presented, for it is only under a strict despotism that the subject is the slave of the monarch ; nay, it has been taken as a fundamental distinction between Semitic religion and that of the Greeks, that in the one case the relation of man to his god is servile, while in the other it is not so. But this conclusion rests on the neglect of a nicety of language, a refinement of Semitic politeness. When a man addresses any superior he calls him "my lord," and speaks of himself and others as "thy servants,"[3] and this form of politeness is

---

[1] *E.g.* Κοσμαλαχος, Ἐλμαλαχος, "Cos, El is king," *Rev. Arch.* 1870, pp. 115, 117 ; Schrader (see *KAT.* p. 473) reads Kausmalak as the name of an Edomite king on an inscription of Tiglathpileser. For the god Caus, or Cos, see Wellhausen, *Heidenthum,* p. 67 ; cf. *ZDMG.* 1887, p. 714.

[2] *E.g.* Nabatæan *Rab*, "Lord," in the proper name רבאל (Euting, 21. 3, 21. 14 ; Waddington, 2152, 2189, 2298), and at Gaza the god Marna, that is, "our Lord," both on coins (Head, p. 680), and in M. Diaconus, *Vita Porphyrii,* § 19 ; also at Kerak, Wadd. 2412 g.

[3] This holds good for Hebrew and Aramaic ; also for Phœnician (Schröder, *Phön. Spr.* p. 18, n. 5) ; and even in Arabia an old poet says : "I am the slave of my guest as long as he is with me, but save in this there is no trace of the slave in my nature" (*Ḥamāsa,* p. 727).

naturally *de rigueur* in presence of the king ; but where the king is not addressed, his " servants " mean his courtiers that are in personal attendance on him, or such of his subjects as are actually engaged in his service, for example, his soldiers. In the Old Testament this usage is constant, and the king's servants are often distinguished from the people at large. And so the servants of Jehovah are sometimes the prophets, who hold a special commission from Him ; at other times, as often in the Psalms, His worshipping people assembled at the temple ; and at other times, as in Deutero-Isaiah, His true servants as distinguished from the natural Israel, who are His subjects only in name. In short, both in the political and in the religious sphere, the designation *'abd, 'ebed,* " servant," is strictly correlated with the verb *'abad,* " to do service, homage, or religious worship," a word which, as we have already seen, is sufficiently elastic to cover the service which a son does for his father, as well as that which a master requires from his slave.[1] Thus, when a man is named the servant of a god, the implication appears to be, not merely that he belongs to the community of which the god is king, but that he is specially devoted to his service and worship. Like other theophorous names, compounds with *'abd* seem to have been originally most common in royal and priestly families, whose members naturally claimed a special interest in religion and a constant nearness to the god ; and in later times, when a man's particular worship was not rigidly defined by his national connection, they served to specify the cult to which he was particularly attached, or the patron to whom his parents dedicated him. That the use of such names was not connected with the

---

[1] *Supra,* p. 60. Primarily עבד is " to work," and in Aramaic " to make, to do." Ancient worship is viewed as work or service, because it consists in material operations (sacrifice). The same connection of ideas appears in the root פלח and in the Greek ῥέζειν θεῷ.

idea of slavery to a divine despot is pretty clear from their
frequency among the Arabs, who had very loose ideas of
all authority, whether human or divine.   Among the
Arabs, indeed, as among the old Hebrews, the relation of
the subject to his divine chief is often expressed by names
of another class.   Of King Saul's sons two were named
Ishbaal and Meribaal, both meaning "man of Baal," *i.e.* of
Jehovah, who in these early days was called Baal without
offence ; among the Arabs of the Syrian frontier we have
Amriel, "man of El," Amrishams, "man of the Sun-god,"
and others like them ;[1] and in Arabia proper Imraulcais,
"the man of Cais," Shai' al-Lāt, "follower, comrade of
Lāt," Anas al-Lāt, all expressive of the relation of the free
warrior to his chief.

That the Arabs, like their northern congeners, thought
of deity as lordship or chieftainship is proved not only by
such proper names, and by the titles *rab, rabbi*, " lord,"
" lady," given to their gods and goddesses, but especially
by the history of the foundation of Islam.   In his quality
of prophet, Mohammed became a judge, lawgiver, and
captain, not of his own initiative, but because the Arabs of
different clans were willing to refer to a divine authority
questions of right and precedence in which they would not
yield to one another.[2]   They brought their difficulties to
the prophet as the Israelites did to Moses, and his decisions
became the law of Islam, as those of Moses were the
foundation of the Hebrew Torah.   But up to the time of
the prophet the practical development of the idea of divine
kingship among the nomadic Arabs was very elementary
and inadequate, as was to be expected in a society which
had never taken kindly to the institution of human king-

[1] Nöldeke, *Sitzungsb. Berl. Ak.* 1880, p. 768 ; Wellhausen, *Heidenthum,*
p. 5.

[2] For the god as giver of decisions, compare the name *farrāḍ*, borne by an
idol of the Sa'd al-'ashira (Ibn Sa'd, ed. Wellh. No. 124 *b*).

ship.　In the prosperous days of Arabian commerce, when
the precious wares of the far East reached the Mediterranean chiefly by caravan from Southern Arabia, there were
settled kingdoms in several parts of the peninsula.　But
after the sea-route to India was opened, these kingdoms
were broken up and almost the whole country fell back
into anarchy.　The nomads proper often felt the want
of a controlling authority that would put an end to the
incessant tribal and clan feuds, but their pride and impatience of control never permitted them to be long faithful
to the authority of a stranger ; while, on the other hand,
the exaggerated feeling for kindred made it quite certain
that a chief chosen at home would not deal with an even
hand between his own kinsman and a person of different
blood.　Thus, after the fall of the Yemenite and Nabatæan
kingdoms, which drew their strength from commerce, there
was no permanently successful attempt to consolidate a
body of several tribes into a homogeneous state, except
under Roman or Persian suzerainty.　The decay of the
power of religion in the peninsula in the last days of
Arab heathenism presents a natural parallel to this condition of political disintegration.　The wild tribesmen had
lost the feeling of kinship with their tribal gods, and had
not learned to yield steady submission and obedience to
any power dissociated from kinship.　Their religion sat
as loose on them as their allegiance to this or that human
king whom for a season they might find it convenient to
obey, and they were as ready to renounce their deities in a
moment of petulance and disgust as to transfer their service
from one petty sovereign to another.[1]

[1] Religion had more strength in towns like Mecca and Ṭâif, where there
was a sanctuary, and the deity lived in the midst of his people, and was
honoured by stated and frequent acts of worship.　So under Islam, the
Bedouins have never taken kindly to the laws of the Coran, and live in
entire neglect of the most simple ordinances of religion, while the townsmen

Up to this point we have considered the conception, or rather the institution, of divine sovereignty as based on the fundamental type of Semitic kingship, when the nation was still made up of free tribesmen, retaining their tribal organisation and possessing the sense of personal dignity and independence engendered by the tribal system, where all clansmen are brothers, and where each man feels that his brethren need him and that he can count on the help of his brethren. There is no principle so levelling as the law of blood-revenge, which is the basis of the tribal system, for here the law is man for man, whether in defence or in offence, without respect of persons. In such a society the king is a guiding and moderating force rather than an imperial power; he is the leader under whom men of several tribes unite for common action, and the arbiter in cases of difficulty or of irreconcilable dispute between two kindreds, when neither will humble itself before the other. The kingship, and therefore the godhead, is not a principle of absolute order and justice, but it is a principle of higher order and more impartial justice than can be realised where there is no other law than the obligation of blood. As the king waxes stronger, and is better able to enforce his will by active interference in his subjects' quarrels, the standard of right is gradually raised above the consideration which disputant has the strongest kin to back him, for it is the glory of the sovereign to vindicate the cause of the weak, if only because by so doing he shows himself to be stronger than the strong. And as the god, though not conceived as omnipotent, is at least conceived as much stronger than man, he becomes in a special measure the champion of right against might, the protector

are in their way very devout. Much of this religion is hypocrisy; but so it was, to judge by the accounts of the conversion of the Thacif at Täif, even in the time of Mohammed. Religion was a matter of custom, of keeping up appearances.

of the poor, the widow and the fatherless, of the man who has no helper on earth.

Now it is matter of constant observation in early history that the primitive equality of the tribal system tends in progress of time to transform itself into an aristocracy of the more powerful kins, or of the more powerful families within one kin. That is, the smaller and weaker kins are content to place themselves in a position of dependence on their more powerful neighbours in order to secure their protection; or even within one and the same kin men distinguish between their nearer and more distant cousins, and, as wealth begins to be unequally distributed, the great man's distant and poor relation has to be content with a distant and supercilious patronage, and sinks into a position of inferiority. The kingship is the one social force that works against this tendency, for it is the king's interest to maintain a balance of power, and prevent the excessive aggrandisement of noble families that might compete with his own authority. Thus even for selfish reasons the sovereign is more and more brought into the position of the champion of the weak against the strong, of the masses against the aristocracy. Generally speaking, the struggle between king and nobles to which these conditions give rise ended differently in the East and in the West. In Greece and Rome the kingship fell before the aristocracy; in Asia the kingship held its own, till in the larger states it developed into despotism, or in the smaller ones it was crushed by a foreign despotism. This diversity of political fortune is reflected in the diversity of religious development. For as the national god did not at first supersede tribal and family deities any more than the king superseded tribal and family institutions, the tendency of the West, where the kingship succumbed, was towards a divine aristocracy of many gods, only modified by a weak

reminiscence of the old kingship in the not very effective
sovereignty of Zeus, while in the East the national god
tended to acquire a really monarchic sway. What is
often described as the natural tendency of Semitic religion
★ towards ethical monotheism, is in the main nothing more
than a consequence of the alliance of religion with
monarchy. For however corrupt the actual kingships of
the East became, the ideal of the kingship as a source of
even-handed justice throughout the whole nation, without
respect of persons, was higher than the ideal of aristocracy,
in which each noble is expected to favour his own family
even at the expense of the state or of justice ; and it is on
the ideal, rather than on the actual, that religious conceptions are based, if not in ordinary minds, at least in the
minds of more thoughtful and pious men. At the same
time the idea of absolute and ever-watchful divine justice,
as we find it in the prophets, is no more natural to the
East than to the West, for even the ideal Semitic king is,
as we have seen, a very imperfect earthly providence, and
moreover he has a different standard of right for his own
people and for strangers. The prophetic idea that Jehovah
will vindicate the right even in the destruction of His own
people of Israel, involves an ethical standard as foreign to
Semitic as to Aryan tradition. Thus, as regards their
ethical tendency, the difference between Eastern and Western
religion is one of degree rather than of principle ; all that
we can say is that the East was better prepared to receive
the idea of a god of absolute righteousness, because its
political institutions and history, and, not least, the enormous gulf between the ideal and the reality of human
sovereignty, directed men's minds to appreciate the need of
righteousness more strongly, and accustomed them to look
to a power of monarchic character as its necessary source.
A similar judgment must be passed on the supposed mono-

theistic tendency of the Semitic as opposed to the Hellenic
or Aryan system of religion.   Neither system, in its natural
development, can fairly be said to have come near to
monotheism ; the difference touched only the equality or
subordination of divine powers.   But while in Greece the
idea of the unity of God was a philosophical speculation,
without any definite point of attachment to actual religion,
the monotheism of the Hebrew prophets kept touch with
the ideas and institutions of the Semitic race by conceiving
the one true God as the king of absolute justice, the
national God of Israel, who at the same time was, or
rather was destined to become, the God of all the earth,
not merely because His power was world-wide, but because
as the perfect ruler He could not fail to draw all nations
to do Him homage (Isa. ii. 2 *sqq.*).

When I speak of the way in which the prophets conceived of Jehovah's sovereignty, as destined to extend itself
beyond Israel and over all the earth, I touch on a feature
common to all Semitic religions, which must be explained
and defined before we can properly understand wherein
the prophets transcended the common sphere of Semitic
thought, and which indeed is necessary to complete our
view of the ultimate development of the Semitic religions
as tribal and national institutions.

From a very early date the Semitic communities embraced, in addition to the free tribesmen of pure blood
(Heb. *ezrāḥ*, Arab. *ṣarīḥ*) with their families and slaves, a
class of men who were personally free but had no political
rights, viz. the protected strangers (Heb. *gērīm*, sing. *gēr* ;
Arab. *jīrān*, sing. *jār*), of whom mention is so often made
both in the Old Testament and in early Arabic literature.
The *gēr* was a man of another tribe or district, who, coming
to sojourn in a place where he was not strengthened by
the presence of his own kin, put himself under the pro-

tection of a clan or of a powerful chief. From the earliest
times of Semitic life the lawlessness of the desert, in which
every stranger is an enemy, has been tempered by the
principle that the guest is inviolable. A man is safe in
the midst of enemies as soon as he enters a tent or even
touches the tent rope.[1] To harm a guest, or to refuse him
hospitality, is an offence against honour, which covers the
perpetrator with indelible shame. The bond of hospitality
among the Arabs is temporary ; the guest is entertained
for a night or at most for three days,[2] and the protection
which the host owes to him expires after three days
more.[3] But more permanent protection is seldom refused
to a stranger who asks for it,[4] and when granted by any
tribesman it binds the whole tribe. The obligation thus
constituted is one of honour, and not enforced by any
human sanction except public opinion, for if the stranger
is wronged he has no kinsmen to fight for him. And for
this very reason it is a sacred obligation, which among the
old Arabs was often confirmed by oath at a sanctuary, and
could not be renounced except by a formal act at the same
holy place,[5] so that the god himself became the protector
of the stranger's cause. The protected stranger did not
necessarily give up his old worship any more than he gave
up his old kindred, and in the earliest times it is not to be
supposed that he was admitted to full communion in the
religion of his protectors, for religion went with political
rights. But it was natural that he should acknowledge in
some degree the god of the land in which he lived, and
indeed, since the stated exercises of religion were confined

---

[1] See further, *Kinship*, pp. 48–52.

[2] This is the space prescribed by the traditions of the prophet, Ḥarīrī (De
Sacy's 2nd ed. p. 177 ; cf. Sharīshī, i. 242). A viaticum sufficient for a
day's journey should be added ; all beyond this is not duty but alms.

[3] Burckhardt, *Bedouins and Wahábys*, i. 336.

[4] Burckhardt, *op. cit.* i. 174.

[5] Ibn Hishām, p. 243 *sqq.; Kinship*, p. 51.

to certain fixed sanctuaries, the man who was far from his
old home was also far from his own god, and sooner or
later could hardly fail to become a dependent adherent of
the cult of his patrons, though not with rights equal to
theirs.   Sometimes, indeed, the god was the direct patron
of the *gēr*, a thing easily understood when we consider
that a common motive for seeking foreign protection was
the fear of the avenger of blood, and that there was a
right of asylum at sanctuaries.   From a Phœnician inscription found near Larnaca, which gives the monthly accounts
of a temple, we learn that the *gērīm* formed a distinct
class in the *personnel* of the sanctuary, and received certain
allowances,[1] just as we know from Ezek. xliv. that much
of the service of the first temple was done by uncircumcised foreigners.   This notion of the temple-client, the man
who lives in the precincts of the sanctuary under the
special protection of the god, is used in a figurative sense
in Ps. xv., " Who shall sojourn (*yāgūr, i.e.* live as a *gēr*)
in Thy tabernacle ? " and similarly the Arabs give the
title of *jār allāh* to one who resides in Mecca beside the
Caaba.

   The importance of this occasional reception of strangers
was not great so long as the old national divisions remained
untouched, and the proportion of foreigners in any community was small.   But the case became very different
when the boundaries of nations were changed by the
migration of tribes, or by the wholesale deportations that
were part of the policy of the Assyrians towards conquered
countries where their arms had met with strenuous resistance.   In such circumstances it was natural for the new-
comers to seek admission to the sanctuaries of the " god of
the land," [2] which they were able to do by presenting
themselves as his clients.   In such a case the clients of

---

[1] *CIS.* No. 86.   [2] 2 Kings xvii. 26.

the god were not necessarily in a position of political
dependence on his old worshippers, and the religious sense
of the term *gēr* became detached from the idea of social
inferiority. But the relation of the new worshippers to
the god was no longer the same as on the old purely
national system. It was more dependent and less permanent; it was constituted, not by nature and inherited
privilege, but by submission on the worshipper's side and
free bounty on the side of the god; and in every way it
tended to make the relation between man and god more
distant, to make men fear the god more and throw more
servility into their homage, while at the same time the
higher feelings of devotion were quickened by the thought
that the protection and favour of the god was a thing of
free grace and not of national right. How important this
change was may be judged from the Old Testament, where
the idea that the Israelites are Jehovah's clients, sojourning
in a land where they have no rights of their own, but are
absolutely dependent on His bounty, is one of the most
characteristic notes of the new and more timid type of
piety that distinguishes post-exilic Judaism from the
religion of Old Israel.[1] In the old national religions a
man felt sure of his standing with the national god, unless
he forfeited it by a distinct breach of social law; but the
client is accepted, so to speak, on his good behaviour, an
idea which precisely accords with the anxious legality of
Judaism after the captivity.

In Judaism the spirit of legality was allied with genuine
moral earnestness, as we see in the noble description of the
character that befits Jehovah's *gēr* drawn in Ps. xv.; but
among the heathen Semites we find the same spirit of
legalism, the same timid uncertainty as to a man's standing

[1] Lev. xxv. 23; Ps. xxxix. 12 [Heb. 13]; Ps. cxix. 19; 1 Chron.
xxix. 15.

with the god whose protection he seeks, while the conception of what is pleasing to the deity has not attained
the same ethical elevation. The extent to which, in the
disintegration of the old nationalities of the East and
the constant movements of population due to political
disturbance, men's religion detached itself from their local
and national connections, is seen by the prevalence of names
in which a man is designated the client of the god.   In
Phœnician inscriptions we find a whole series of men's
names compounded with *Gēr*,—Germelkarth, Gerastart, and
so forth,—and the same type recurs among the Arabs of
Syria in the name Gairelos or Gerelos, " client of El." [1]   In ★
Arabia proper, where the relation of protector and protected
had a great development, and whole clans were wont to
attach themselves as dependants to a more powerful tribe,
the conception of god and worshipper as patron and client
appears to have been specially predominant, not merely
because dependent clans took up the religion of the patrons
with whom they took refuge, but because of the frequent
shiftings of the tribes.   Wellhausen has noted that the
hereditary priesthoods of Arabian sanctuaries were often in
the hands of families that did not belong to the tribe of
the worshippers, but apparently were descended from older
inhabitants ; [2] and in such cases the modern worshippers
were really only clients of a foreign god.   So, in fact, at
the great Sabæan pilgrimage shrine of Riyām, the god
Ta'lab is adored as " patron," and his worshippers are called
his clients. [3]   To the same conception may be assigned the
proper name Salm, " submission," shortened from such
theophorous forms as the Palmyrene Salm al-Lāt, " sub-

[1] See Nöldeke, *Sitzungsb. Berl. Ak.* 1880, p. 765.

[2] Wellhausen, *Heidenthum*, p. 131 ; cf. p. 215.

[3] Mordtmann u. Müller, *Sab. Denkm.* p. 22, No. 5, l. 2 *sq.* (שימהמו), l.
8 *sq.* (אדמהו) *etc.*   Cf. No. 13, l. 12, אדמה, the clients of the goddess
Shams.

mission to Lat," [1] and corresponding to the religious use
of the verb *istalama*, " he made his peace," to designate the
ceremony of kissing, stroking, or embracing the sacred
stone at the Caaba; [2] and perhaps also the numerous
names compounded with *taim*, which, if we may judge
by the profane use of the word *motayyam*, applied to a
deeply attached lover, seems to have some such sense as
" devotee." [3]   But above all, the prevalence of religion
based on clientship and voluntary homage is seen in the
growth of the practice of pilgrimage to distant shrines,
which is so prominent a feature in later Semitic heathenism.
Almost all Arabia met at Mecca, and the shrine at Hierapolis drew visitors from the whole Semitic world.   These
pilgrims were the guests of the god, and were received
as such by the inhabitants of the holy places.   They
approached the god as strangers, not with the old joyous
confidence of national worship, but with atoning ceremonies
and rites of self-mortification, and their acts of worship
were carefully prescribed for them by qualified instructors,[4]
the prototypes of the modern Meccan *Motawwif*.   The

---

[1] De Vogüé, No. 54.

[2] Ibn Doraid, *Kit. al-ishticāc*, p. 22.   The same idea of a religion accepted
by voluntary submission is expressed in the name *Islām*.   We shall see later
that much the same idea underlies the designation of the Christian religion
as a "mystery."

[3] *Taim* is generally taken to be a mere synonym of *'Abd*; but in Arabic
the word is quite obsolete, except as an element in old theophorous names,
and the other forms derived from the root give no clear insight into its
original sense.   In the dialect of the Sinaitic inscriptions, where proper
names like Taimallāhī, Taimdhūsharā are common, *taim* seems to occur as
a common noun in Euting, *Sinaitische Inschriften*, No. 431, where the editor
renders תימה by "sein Knecht."   But the Arabic uses of the root seem to
point to a somewhat more special sense, perhaps "captive," which might
be figuratively applied to a devotee, or, when the name compounded with
taim is a clan-name, as is the usual Arabian case, to a subject tribe that
had adopted the worship of their conquerors.   On the other hand, *tīma*
is a sheep not sent forth to pasture, but kept at the homestead to be milked,
and on this analogy *taim* may mean *domestic*.

[4] Lucian, *De Dea Syria*, lvi.

progress of heathenism towards universalism, as it is displayed in these usages, seemed only to widen the gulf
between the deity and man, to destroy the naïve trustful-
ness of the old religion without substituting a better way
for man to be at one with his god, to weaken the moral ideas
of nationality without bringing in a higher morality of universal obligation, to transform the divine kingship into a
mere court pageant of priestly ceremonies without permanent influence on the order of society and daily life.   The
Hebrew ideal of a divine kingship that must one day draw
all men to do it homage offered better things than these,
not in virtue of any feature that it possessed in common with
the Semitic religions as a whole, but solely through the
unique conception of Jehovah as a God whose love for His
people was conditioned by a law of absolute righteousness.
In other nations individual thinkers rose to lofty conceptions of a supreme deity, but in Israel, and in Israel
alone, these conceptions were incorporated in the accepted
worship of the national god.   And so of all the gods of
the nations Jehovah alone was fitted to become the God of
the whole earth.

At the end of these remarks on the relations of the
gods to their worshippers, it may not be amiss to advert to
an objection to the whole course of our investigation that
will possibly occur to some readers.   Most enquirers into
Semitic religion have made it their first business to discuss
the nature of the gods, and with this view have sought to
determine a particular class of natural phenomena or moral
actions over which each deity presides.   Persons trained in
this school may remark on reading the foregoing pages that
they are not a whit the better for knowing that the gods

6

were conceived as parents kings or patrons, since these relationships do not help us to understand what the gods could do for their worshippers. The ancients prayed to their gods for rain and fruitful seasons, for children, for health and long life, for the multiplication of their flocks and herds, and for many other things that no child asked from his father, no subject from his king. Hence it may be argued that fathership and kingship in religion are mere forms of words; the essence of the thing is to know why the gods were deemed able to do for their worshippers things that kings and fathers cannot do. So far as this objection is a general challenge to the method of the present volume, I must leave the sequel to answer it; but the point that the gods did for their worshippers things that human fathers kings and patrons were not expected to do, demands and may receive some elucidation at the present point. And first I will remark that the help of the gods was sought in all matters, without distinction, that were objects of desire and could not certainly be attained by the worshipper's unaided efforts. Further, it appears that help in all these matters was sought by the worshipper from whatever god he had a right to appeal to. If a Semitic worshipper was sick he called upon his national or tribal god, and the same god was addressed if he desired rain or victory over enemies. The power of a god was not conceived as unlimited, but it was very great, and applied to all sorts of things that men could desire. So far as primitive Semitic heathenism is concerned, it is quite a mistake to suppose that a god to whom men prayed for rain was necessarily a god of clouds, while another deity was the god of flocks, and the proper recipient of prayers for increase in the sheepfold. The gods had their physical limitations, as we shall see in the next lecture, but not in the sense that each deity presided over

a distinct department of nature; that is a conception much
too abstract for the primitive mind, and proper to an
advanced stage of polytheism which most of the Semitic
nations never fully reached. In early heathenism the
really vital question is not what a god has power to do,
but whether I can get him to do it for me, and this
depends on the relation in which he stands to me. If I
have a god who is my king, I ask him for things that I do
not ask from a human chief, simply because he is able to do
them, and as his subject I have a claim to his help in all
matters where my welfare belongs to the welfare of the
state over which he presides. And in fact it is by no
means true that in asking the god for rain the Semites went
quite beyond what could be asked of a human king; for,
strange as it may seem to us, almost all primitive peoples
believe that rain-making is an art to which men can
attain, and some of them expect their kings to exercise
it.[1] To peoples in this stage of development a rainmaker
is not a cosmical power, but merely a person, human or
divine, possessed of a certain art or charm. To say that
a god who can make rain is necessarily an elemental power
associated with the clouds and the sky, is as absurd as to
say that Hera was the goddess of Love when she borrowed
the girdle of Aphrodite. This is a very obvious remark,
but it knocks on the head a great deal that has been
written about Semitic religion.

---

[1] Frazer, *The Golden Bough*, i. 247 *sqq.*, 342 *sqq.*, 396, 416, gives sufficient
proofs of this. See below, p. 231.

LECTURE III

In the last lecture I endeavoured to sketch in broad outline the general features of the religious institutions of the
Semites in so far as they rest on the idea that gods and
men, or rather the god and his own proper worshippers,
make up a single community, and that the place of the
god in the community is interpreted on the analogy of
human relationships. We are now to follow out this
point of view through the details of sacred rite and
observance, and to consider how the various acts and
offices of religion stand related to the place assigned to the
deity in the community of his worshippers. But as soon
as we begin to enter on these details, we find it necessary
to take account of a new series of relations connecting man
on the one hand, and his god on the other, with physical
nature and material objects. All acts of ancient worship
have a material embodiment, which is not left to the choice
of the worshipper but is limited by fixed rules. They must
be performed at certain places and at certain times, with
the aid of certain material appliances and according to
certain mechanical forms. These rules import that the
intercourse between the deity and his worshippers is
subject to physical conditions of a definite kind, and this

again implies that the relations between gods and men are not independent of the material environment. The relations of a man to his fellow-men are limited by physical conditions, because man, on the side of his bodily organism, is himself a part of the material universe; and when we find that the relations of a man to his god are limited in the same way, we are led to conclude that the gods too are in some sense conceived to be a part of the natural universe, and that this is the reason why men can hold converse with them only by the aid of certain material things. It is true that in some of the higher forms of antique religion the material restrictions imposed on the legitimate intercourse between gods and men were conceived to be not natural but positive, that is they were not held to be dependent on the nature of the gods, but were looked upon as arbitrary rules laid down by the free will of the deity. But in the ordinary forms of heathenism it appears quite plainly that the gods themselves are not exempt from the general limitations of physical existence; indeed, we have already seen that where the relation of the deity to his worshippers is conceived as a relation of kinship, the kinship is taken to have a physical as well as a moral sense, so that the worshipped and the worshippers are parts not only of one social community but of one physical unity of life.

It is important that we should realise to ourselves with some definiteness the primitive view of the universe in which this conception arose, and in which it has its natural place. It dates from a time when men had not learned to draw sharp distinctions between the nature of one thing and another. Savages, we know, are not only incapable of separating in thought between phenomenal and noumenal existence, but habitually ignore the distinctions, which to us seem obvious, between organic and inorganic nature, or within the former region between animals and plants. Arguing altogether by analogy, and concluding from the known to the unknown with the freedom of men who do not know the difference between the imagination and the reason, they ascribe to all material objects a life analogous to that which their own self-consciousness reveals to them. They see that men are liker to one another than beasts are to men, that men are liker to beasts than they are to plants, and to plants than they are to stones; but all things appear to them to live, and the more incomprehensible any form of life seems to them the more wonderful and worthy of reverence do they take it to be. Now this attitude of savage man to the natural things by which he is surrounded is the very attitude attested to us for ancient times by some of the most salient features of antique religion. Among races which have attained to a certain degree of culture, the predominant conception of the gods is anthropomorphic; that is, they are supposed on the whole to resemble men and act like men, and the artistic imagination, whether in poetry or in sculpture and painting, draws them after the similitude of man. But at the same time the list of deities includes a variety of natural objects of all kinds, the sun moon and stars, the heavens and the earth, animals and trees, or even sacred stones. And all these gods, without distinction of their several natures, are conceived as entering into the same kind of relation to man, are approached in ritual of the same type, and excite the same kind of hopes and fears in the breasts of their worshippers. It is of course easy to say that the gods were not identified with these natural objects, that they were only supposed to inhabit them; but for our present purpose this distinction is not valid. A certain crude distinction between soul and body, combined with the idea that the soul may act where the body is not, is suggested to the most savage races by familiar psychical phenomena, particularly by those of dreams; and the unbounded use of analogy characteristic of pre-scientific thought extends this conception to all parts of nature which becomes to the savage mind full of spiritual forces, mcre or less detached in their movements and action from the material objects to which they are supposed properly to belong. But the detachment of the invisible life from its visible embodiment is never complete. A man after all is not a ghost or phantom, a life or soul without a body, but a body with its life, and in like manner the unseen life that inhabits the plant, tree, or sacred stone makes the sacred object itself be conceived as a living being. And in ritual the sacred object was spoken of and treated as the god himself; it was not merely his symbol but his embodiment, the permanent centre of his activity in the same sense in which the human body is the permanent centre of man's activity. In short, the whole conception belongs in its origin to a stage of thought in which there was no more difficulty in ascribing living powers and personality to a stone, tree, or animal, than to a being of human or superhuman build.

The same lack of any sharp distinction between the nature of different kinds of visible beings appears in the oldest myths, in which all kinds of objects, animate and inanimate, organic and inorganic, appear as cognate with one another, with men, and with the gods. The kinship between gods and men which we have already discussed is only one part of a larger kinship which embraces the lower creation. In the Babylonian legend beasts as well as man are formed of earth mingled with the life-blood of a god; in Greece the stories of the descent of men from gods stand side by side with ancient legends of men sprung from trees or rocks, or of races whose mother was a tree

and their father a god.[1]   Similar myths, connecting both
men and gods with animals plants and rocks, are found all
over the world, and were not lacking among the Semites.
To this day the legend of the country explains the name
of the Beni Sokhr tribe by making them the offspring of
the sandstone rocks about Madāin Ṣāliḥ.[2]   To the same
stage of thought belong the stories of transformations of
men into animals, which are not infrequent in Arabian
legend.   Mohammed would not eat lizards because he
fancied them to be the offspring of a metamorphosed
clan of Israelites.[3]   Macrīzī relates of the Ṣeiʿar in
Ḥaḍramaut that in time of drought part of the tribe
change themselves into ravening were-wolves.   They have
a magical means of assuming and again casting off the
wolf shape.[4]   Other Hadramites changed themselves into
vultures or kites.[5]   In the Sinai Peninsula the hyrax and
the panther are believed to have been originally men.[6]
Among the northern Semites transformation myths are
not uncommon, though they have generally been preserved
to us only in Greek forms.   The pregnant mother of
Adonis was changed into a myrrh tree, and in the tenth
month the tree burst open and the infant god came forth.[7]
The metamorphosis of Derceto into a fish was related both
at Ascalon and at Bambyce, and so forth.   In the same
spirit is conceived the Assyrian myth which includes
the lion, the eagle, and the war-horse among the lovers of

[1] *Odyssey*, xviii. 163 ; Preller-Robert, i. 79 *sq*.

[2] Doughty, *Travels in Arabia*, i. 17 ; see Ibn Doraid, p. 329, l. 20.
Conversely, many stones and rocks in Arabia were believed to be transformed
men, but especially women.   Dozy, *Israeliten te Mekka*, p. 201, gives
examples.   See also Yācūt, i. 123.

[3] Damīrī, ii. 87 ; cf. Doughty, i. 326.   A similar *ḥadīth* about the
mouse, Damīrī, ii. 218.

[4] *De valle Hadhramaut* (Bonn 1866), p. 19 *sq*.

[5] *Ibid*. p. 20.   See also Ibn Mojāwir in Sprenger, *Post-routen*, p. 142.

[6] See *Kinship*, p. 238 *sq*., where I give other evidences on the point.

[7] Apollodorus, iii. 14. 3 ; Servius on *Æn* v. 72.

Ishtar, while in the region of plastic art the absence of any sharp line of distinction between gods and men on the one hand and the lower creation on the other is displayed in the predilection for fantastic monsters, half human half bestial, which began with the oldest Chaldæan engraved cylinders, gave Phœnicia its cherubim griffins and sphinxes,[1] and continued to characterise the sacred art of the Babylonians down to the time of Berosus.[2]   Of course most of these things can be explained away as allegories, and are so explained to this day by persons who shut their eyes to the obvious difference between primitive thought, which treats all nature as a kindred unity because it has not yet differentiated things into their kinds, and modern monistic philosophy, in which the universe of things, after having been realised in its multiplicity of kinds, is again brought into unity by a metaphysical synthesis.   But by what process of allegory can we explain away the belief in werewolves?   When the same person is believed to be now a man and now a wolf, the difference which we recognise between a man and a wild beast is certainly not yet perceived.   And such a belief as this cannot be a mere isolated extravagance of the fancy; it points to a view of nature as a whole which is, in fact, the ordinary view of savages in all parts of the world, and everywhere produces just such a confusion between the several orders of natural and supernatural beings as we find to have existed among the early Semites.

The influence of these ideas on early systems of religion may be considered under two aspects: (1) On the one hand, the range of the supernatural is so wide that no

[1] See Menant, *Glyptique Orientale*, vol. i.

[2] Berosus (*Fr. Hist. Gr.* ii. 497) refers to the images at the temple of Bel which preserved the forms of the strange monsters that lived in the time of chaos.   But the peculiar prevalence of such figures on the oldest gems shows that the chaos in question is only the chaotic imagination of early man.

antique religion attempts to deal with all its manifestations. The simplest proof of this is that magic and
sorcery, though they lay outside of religion and were
forbidden arts in all the civilised states of antiquity, were
yet never regarded as mere imposture. It was not denied
that there were supernatural agencies at work in the world
of which the public religion took no account. Religion
dealt only with the gods, *i.e.* with a definite circle of great
supernatural powers whose relations to man were established on a regular friendly basis and maintained by stated
rites and fixed institutions. Beyond the circle of gods
there lay a vast and undetermined mass of minor supernatural agencies, some of which were half-incorporated in
religion under the name of demi-gods, while others were
altogether ignored except in private popular superstition,
or by those who professed the art of constraining demoniac
powers to do them service and obey their commands.
(2) On the other hand, the gods proper were not sharply
marked off, *as regards their nature,* from the lower orders of
demoniac beings, or even from such physical objects as
were believed to possess demoniac attributes. Their
distinctive mark lay in their relations with man, or, more
exactly, with a definite circle of men, their habitual worshippers. As these relations were known and stable, they
gave rise to an orderly and fixed series of religious institutions. But the forms of religious service were not determined merely by the fact that the god was considered in
one case as the father, in another as the king, in yet
another as the patron of his worshippers. In determining
how the god was to be approached, and how his help could
be most fully realised, it was necessary to take account of
the fact that he was not an omnipotent and omnipresent
being standing wholly outside of nature, but was himself
linked to the physical world by a series of affinities con-

necting him not merely with man but with beasts trees and inanimate things. In antique religion gods as well as men have a physical environment, on and through which they act, and by which their activity is conditioned.

The influence of this idea on ancient religion is very far-reaching and often difficult to analyse. But there is one aspect of it that is both easily grasped and of fundamental importance; I mean the connection of particular gods with particular places. The most general term to express the relation of natural things to the gods which our language affords is the word " holy "; thus when we speak of holy places, holy things, holy persons, holy times, we imply that the places things persons and times stand in some special relation to the godhead or to its manifestation. But the word " holy " has had a long and complicated history, and has various shades of meaning according to the connection in which it is used. It is not possible, by mere analysis of the modern use of the word, to arrive at a single definite conception of the meaning of holiness; nor is it possible to fix on any one of the modern aspects of the conception, and say that it represents the fundamental idea from which all other modifications of the idea can be deduced. The primitive conception of holiness, to which the modern variations of the idea must be traced back, belonged to a habit of thought with which we have lost touch, and we cannot hope to understand it by the aid of logical discussion, but only by studying it on its own ground as it is exhibited in the actual working of early religion. It would be idle, therefore, at this stage to attempt any general definition, or to seek for a comprehensive formula covering all the relations of the gods to natural things. The problem must be attacked in detail and for many reasons the most suitable point of attack will be found in the connection that ancient religion conceived to exist between particular deities and particular "holy" places. This topic is of fundamental importance, because all complete acts of ancient worship were necessarily performed at a holy place, and thus the local connections of the gods are involved, explicitly or implicitly, in every function of religion.

The local relations of the gods may be considered under two heads. In the first place the activity power and dominion of the gods were conceived as bounded by certain local limits, and in the second place they were conceived as having their residences and homes at certain fixed sanctuaries. These two conceptions are not of course independent, for generally speaking the region of divine authority and influence surrounds the sanctuary which is the god's principal seat; but for convenience of exposition we shall look first at the god's *land* and then at his *sanctuary* or dwelling-place.

Broadly speaking, the land of a god corresponds with the land of his worshippers; Canaan is Jehovah's land as Israel is Jehovah's people.[1] In like manner the land of Assyria (Asshur) has its name from the god Asshur,[2] and in general the deities of the heathen are called indifferently the gods of the nations and the gods of the lands.[3] Our natural impulse is to connect these expressions with the divine kingship, which in modern states of feudal origin is a sovereignty over land as well as men. But the older Semitic kingdoms were not feudal, and before the captivity we shall hardly find an example of a Semitic sovereign being called king of a land.[4] In fact the relations of

---

[1] Hos. ix. 3 ; cf. Reland, *Palæstina*, vol. i. p. 16 *sqq.*

[2] Schrader, *KAT.* 3rd ed. p. 351 ; cf. Micah v. 6 (Heb. 5), where the "land of Asshur" stands in parallelism with "land of Nimrod." Nimrod is a god, see his article in *Enc. Brit.*, 9th ed., and Wellhausen, *Hexateuch* (2nd ed. 1889), p. 308 *sqq.*

[3] 2 Kings xviii. 33 *sqq.*

[4] The Hebrews say "king of Asshur" (Assyria), Edom, Aram (Syria), etc.,

a god to his land were not merely political, or dependent on his relation to the inhabitants. The Aramæans and Babylonians whom the king of Assyria planted in northern Israel brought their own gods with them, but when they were attacked by lions they felt that they must call in the aid of "the god of the land," who, we must infer, had in his own region power over beasts as well as men.[1] Similarly the Aramæans of Damascus, after their defeat in the hill-country of Samaria, argue that the gods of Israel are gods of the hills and will have no power in the plains; the power of the gods has physical and local limitations. So too the conception that a god cannot be worshipped outside of his own land, which we find applied even to the worship of Jehovah,[2] does not simply mean that there can be no worship of a god where he has no sanctuary, but that the land of a strange god is not a fit place to erect a sanctuary. In the language of the Old Testament foreign countries are unclean,[3] so that Naaman, when he desires to worship the God of Israel at Damascus, has to beg for two mules' burden of the soil of Canaan, to make a sort of enclave of Jehovah's land in his Aramæan dwelling-place.

In Semitic religion the relation of the gods to particular places which are special seats of their power is usually expressed by the title Baal (pl. *Baalim*, fem. *Baalath*).

---

but these are names of nations, the countries being properly the "land of Asshur," etc. The local designation of a king is taken from his capital, or royal seat. Thus the king of Israel is king of Samaria (1 Kings xxi. 1), Sihon, king of the Amorites, is king of Heshbon (Deut. iii. 6). Hiram, whom the Bible calls king of Tyre, appears on the oldest of Phœnician ★ inscriptions (*CIS*. No. 5) as king of the Sidonians, *i.e.* the Phœnicians (cf. 1 Kings xvi. 31), Nebuchadrezzar is king of Babylon, and so forth. The only exception to this rule in old Hebrew is, I think, Og, king of Bashan (Deut. i. 4 ; 1 Kings iv. 19), who is a mythical figure, presumably an old god of the region.

[1] 2 Kings xvii. 24 *sqq.* [2] 1 Sam. xxvi. 19 ; Hos. ix. 4.
[3] Amos vii. 17 ; Josh. xxii. 19.

★ As applied to men *baal* means the master of a house, the owner of a field cattle or the like; or in the plural the *baalim* of a city are its freeholders and full citizens.[1] In a secondary sense, in which alone the word is ordinarily used in Arabic, *baal* means husband; but it is not used of the relation of a master to his slave, or of a superior to his inferior, and it is incorrect to regard it, when employed as a divine title, as a mere synonym of the titles implying lordship over men which came before us in the last lecture. When a god is simply called "the Baal," the meaning is not "the lord of the worshipper" but the possessor of some place or district, and each of the multitude of local Baalim is distinguished by adding the name of his own place.[2] Melcarth is the Baal of Tyre, Astarte the Baalath of Byblus;[3] there was a Baal of Lebanon,[4] of Mount Hermon,[5] of Mount Peor, and so forth. In Southern Arabia Baal constantly occurs in similar local connections, *e.g.* Dhū Samāwī is the Baal of the district Bācir, ʿAthtar the Baal of Gumdān, and the sun-goddess the Baalath of several places or regions.[6]

[1] So often in the Old Testament, and also in Phœnician. *Baalath* is used of a female citizen (*CIS.* No. 120).

[2] Cf. Stade in *ZATW.* 1886, p. 303.

[3] *CIS.* Nos. 1, 122.   [4] *CIS.* No. 5.

[5] See Judg. iii. 3, where this mountain is called the mountain of the Baal of Hermon. Hermon properly means a sacred place. In the Old Testament place-names like Baal-peor, Baal-meon are shortened from Beth Baal Peor, "house or sanctuary of the Baal of Mount Peor," etc.

[6] Hence we read in the Himyaritic inscriptions of sun-goddesses in the plural (*e.g.* אשמסהמו, *CIS.* pt. iv. No. 46), as in Canaan we have a plurality of local Baalim. Special forms of Baal occur which are defined not by the name of a place or region but in some other way, *e.g.* by the name of a sacred object, as Baal-tamar, "lord of the palm-tree," preserved to us only in the name of a town, Judg. xx. 33. So too Baal-hammān, on the Carthaginian Tanith inscriptions, may be primarily "lord of the sun-pillar"; yet compare אל חמן, "the divinity of (the place) Hammōn" (*CIS.* No. 8, and the inscr. of Maʿsūb); see G. Hoffmann in the *Abhandlungen* of the Göttingen Academy, vol. xxxvi. (4 May 1889). Baal-zebub, the god of Ekron, is "owner of flies," rather than Βάαλ Μυῖα, the fly-god. In one or two cases the title of Baal

As the heathen gods are never conceived as ubiquitous
and can act only where they or their ministers are present,
the sphere of their permanent authority and influence is
naturally regarded as their residence. It will be observed
that the local titles which I have cited are generally derived
either from towns where the god had a temple, or (as the
Semites say) a house, or else from mountains, which are
constantly conceived as the dwelling-places of deities. The
notion of personal property in land is a thing that grows
up gradually in human society, and is first applied to a
man's homestead. Pasture land is common property,[1] but
a man acquires rights in the soil by building a house, or by
"quickening" a waste place, i.e. bringing it under cultiva-

seems to be prefixed to the name of a god; thus we have Baal-zephon as a
place-name on the frontiers of Egypt, and also a god צפן (*CIS.* Nos. 108,
265). Similarly the second element in Baal-gad, a town at the foot of
Mount Hermon, is the name of an ancient Semitic god. The grammatical
explanation of these forms is not clear to me. Another peculiar form is
Baal-berith at Shechem, which in ordinary Hebrew simply means "possessor
of covenant," i.e. "covenant ally," but may here signify the Baal who
presides over covenants, or rather over the special covenant by which the
neighbouring Israelites were bound to the Canaanite inhabitants of the city.
Peculiar also is the more modern Baal-marcod, κοίρανος κωμῶν (near Bairūt),
known from inscriptions (Wadd. Nos. 1855, 1856; Ganneau, *Rec. d'Arch. Or.*
i. 95, 103). The Semitic form is supposed to be בעל מרקד, "lord of
dancing," i.e. he to whom dancing is due as an act of homage; cf. for the
construction, Prov. iii. 27. In later times Baal or Bel became a proper
name, especially in connection with the cult of the Babylonian Bel, and
entered into compounds of a new kind like the Aglibol and Malakhbel of
Palmyra. Baal Shamaim, "the lord of heaven," belongs to the class of
titles taken from the region of nature in which the god dwells or has sway.
בעל מרפא (*CIS.* No. 41) and בעלת החדרת (*ibid.* No. 177) are of doubtful
interpretation. In the Panamu inscription of Zenjirli, l. 22, בעל בית can
hardly mean "patron of the royal family," as Sachau takes it, but rather
designates RKB-El as the local Baal of the sanctuary, or perhaps of the
royal city. On the whole there is nothing in these peculiar forms to shake
the general conclusion that Baal is primarily the title of a god as inhabitant
or owner of a place.

[1] Common, that is, to a tribe, for the tribes are very jealous of encroachments on their pastures. But, as we have here to do with the personal
rights of the Baal within his own community, the question of intertribal
rights does not come in.

tion. Originally, that is, private rights over land are a mere consequence of rights over what is produced by private labour upon the land.[1] The ideas of building and cultivation are closely connected—the Arabic 'amara, like the German bauen, covers both—and the word for house or homestead is extended to include the dependent fields or territory. Thus in Syriac "the house of Antioch" is the territory dependent on the town, and in the Old Testament the land of Canaan is called not only Jehovah's land but his house.[2] If the relation of the Baal to his district is to be judged on these analogies, the land is his, first because he inhabits it, and then because he "quickens" it, and makes it productive.

That this is the true account of the relations of the name Baal appears from what Hosea tells us of the religious conceptions of his idolatrous contemporaries, whose nominal Jehovah worship was merged in the numerous local cults of the Canaanite Baalim. To the Baalim they ascribed all the natural gifts of the land, the corn the wine and the oil, the wool and the flax, the vines and fig-trees,[3] and we shall see by and by that the whole ritual of feasts and sacrifices was imbued with this conception. We can, however, go a step further, and trace the idea to an earlier form, by the aid of a fragment of old heathen phraseology which has survived in the language of Jewish and Arabian agriculture. In the system of Mohammedan taxation land irrigated by the water-wheel or other laborious methods pays five per cent. of its produce in the name of charity-tax, whereas land

---

[1] The law of Islam is that land which has never been cultivated or occupied by houses becomes private property by being "quickened" (bil-ihyā). See Nawawī, Minhāj, ed. Van den Berg, ii. 171. This is in accordance with pre-Islamic custom. Cf. Wellhausen, Heidenthum, p. 108.

[2] Hos. viii. 1, ix. 15, compared with ix. 3.

[3] Hos. ii. 8 sqq.

that does not require laborious irrigation pays a full tithe. The latter, according to Arabian jurists, is of various kinds, which are designated by special names; but all these are summed up in the general expression "what the sky waters and what the Ba'l waters." Similarly the Mishna and Talmud draw a distinction between land artificially irrigated and land naturally moist, calling the latter the "house of Baal" or "field of the house of Baal." It must be remembered that in the East the success of agriculture depends more on the supply of water than on anything else, and the "quickening of dead ground" (*ihyā al-mawāt*), which, as we have seen, creates ownership, has reference mainly to irrigation.[1] Accordingly what the husbandman irrigates is his own property, but what is naturally watered he regards as irrigated by a god and as the field or property of this god, who is thus looked upon as the Baal or owner of the spot.

It has generally been assumed that Baal's land, in the sense in which it is opposed to irrigated fields, means land watered by the rains of heaven, "the waters of the sky" as the Arabs call them, and from this again it has been inferred that the Baal who gives his name to land naturally moist and fertile is the god of the sky (*Baal-shamaim*), who plays so great a part in later Semitic religion, and is identified by Philo Byblius with the sun. But, strictly regarded, this view, which is natural in our climate and with our meteorological notions, appears to be inconsistent with the conditions of vegetable growth in most parts of the Semitic lands, where the rainfall is precarious or confined to certain seasons. so that the face of the earth is bare and lifeless for the greater part of the year except where it is kept fresh by irrigation or by the natural

[1] See, for example, Abū Yūsuf Ya'cūb, *Kitāb al-Kharāj*, Cairo, A.H. 1302, p. 37.

7

percolation of underground water. To us, of course, it is plain that all fertility is ultimately due to the rains which feed the springs and watery bottoms, as well as the broad corn-fields; but this is a knowledge beyond the science of the oldest Semites;[1] while on the other hand the distinction between favoured spots that are always green and fruitful and the less favoured fields that are useless during the rainless season, is alike obvious and essential to the most primitive systems of husbandry.

In Arabia the rainfall is all-important for pasture,[2] but except in the far south, which comes within the skirts of the monsoon region, it is too irregular to form a basis for agriculture. An occasional crop of gourds or melons may be raised in certain places after copious showers; and on low-lying plains, where the rain sinks into a heavy soil and cannot flow away, the palm-tree will sometimes live and produce a dry tough fruit of little value.[3] But on the whole the contrast between land naturally productive and land artificially fertilised, as it presents itself to the Arabian husbandman, has no direct connection with rainfall, but depends on the depth of the ground-water. Where the roots of the date-palm can reach the subterranean flow, or where a fountain sends forth a stream whose branches fertilise an oasis without the toil of the

---

[1] Cf. the remarks of Dillmann in his comm. on Gen. i. 6–8.

[2] Ibn Sa'd, No. 80. Here Wellhausen introduces a reference to agriculture, but in rendering *janābunā*, "our palm gardens," he departs from the traditional interpretation. (See Lane.)

[3] Such palms and the land they grow on are called *'idhy*, pl. *a'dhā* ; the dates are *saḥḥ* or *casb*; see Al-Azhari's luminous account of the different kinds of date-palms in the *Lisān*, s.v. *ba'l*. In the traditions that require a whole tithe to be paid on crops watered by rain the *'idhy* seems to be mainly contemplated ; for in Ibn Sa'd, No. 68, the prophet exacts no tithe on such precarious crops as cucumbers raised on ground watered by rain. I rode in 1880 through a desolate plain of heavy soil some miles to the S.-E. of Mecca, and was told that after good rain the waste would be covered with patches of melons and the like. (See *Lectures and Essays*, p. 508 *sqq.*)

water-wheel, the ground is naturally fertile, and such land
is "watered by the Ba'l." The best Arabian authorities
say expressly that ba'l palm-trees are such as drink by
their roots, without artificial irrigation and without rain,
"from the water which God has created beneath the
earth," [1] and in an exact specification of what is liable
to the full tithe the *ba'l* and the sky are mentioned
together, not used interchangeably.[2]

[1] Al-Aṣma'ī and Al-Azharī in the *Lisān*, s.v. *ba'l*. This article and the
materials collected in the Glossary to De Goeje's *Belādhorī* give almost all
the evidence. I may add a ref. to Ibn Sa'd, No. 119, compared with No.
73, and Macrīzī *Khiṭaṭ*, ii. 129, and in the next note I will cite some of the
leading traditions, which are very inaccurately given by Sprenger in *ZDMG.*
xviii.

[2] The fullest expressions are, Bokhārī, ii. 122 (Būlāc vocalised ed.),
"what is watered by the sky and the fountains or is *'atharī*"; *Mowaṭṭa*
(Tunis ed.), p. 94, "what is watered by the sky and the fountains and the
ba'l"; *ibid.* p. 95, "what is watered by the sky and the fountains or is *ba'l.*"
Shorter phrases are, *Belādh.* p. 70, "what is watered by the *ba'l* and what is
watered by the sky," with such variants as "the surface flow [*ghail, saih*] ★
and the sky" (*ib.* p. 71), "the fountains and the sky" (B. Hishām, 956),
"the rivers and the clouds" (Moslim, ed. of A.H. 1290, i. 268). These
variations are intelligible if we bear in mind the aspect of the cultivated
patches in such a valley as the Baṭn Marr. The valley is a great watercourse, but for the most part the water flows underground, breaking out in
powerful springs where there is a sharp fall in the ground, and sometimes
flowing for a few hundred yards in a visible stream, which is soon led off in
many branches through the palms and tiny corn-fields and presently disappears again under the sand and stones. Where the hard bottom is level
and near the surface, the palms can drink from their roots where there is no
visible stream ; but where the bottom lies deep (as in the neighbourhood of
Ṭāif) cultivation is possible only by the use of the water-wheel, and then the
tithe is reduced to 5 per cent. Where irrigation can be effected by gravita-
tion through a pipe or channel, without pumping, the land is still regarded
as naturally fertile and pays full tithe ; see *Gl. Bel.* and Ibn Sa'd, No. 119.
According to one interpretation, the obscure word *'atharī*, which I have not
met with in any tradition except that cited above, means land watered by
an artificial channel (*'āthūr*). This may be a mere guess, for the oldest and
best Arabian scholars seem to have had no clear understanding of the word ;
but at least it is preferable to the view which identifies *'atharī* and *'idhy*.
For a comparison of the traditions given above indicates that *'atharī* is
either a synonym for *ba'l* or some species thereof ; moreover, the oasis in
W. Sirhān which Guarmani (p. 209) calls Etera, and Lady Anne Blunt
(*Nejd*, i. 89 *sqq.*) writes Itheri, can hardly be anything else than *'Atharī* in a
modern pronunciation. (Huber writes it with initial *alif*, but his ortho-

The Arabian evidence therefore leads us to associate the life-giving operation of the Baʿl or Baal, not with the rains of heaven, but with springs, streams and underground flow. On the other hand it is clear (*e.g.* from Hosea) that among the agricultural peoples of Canaan the Baalim were looked upon as the authors of all fertility, including the corn crops, which are wholly dependent on rain in most parts of Palestine. And it is here that we find the sky-Baal (*Baal-shamaim*) with such local forms as Marna "the lord of rains" at Gaza.[1] Thus the question arises whether the original Semitic conception of the sphere of the Baal's activity has been modified in Arabia to suit its special climate, or whether, on the other hand, the notion of the Baal as lord of rain is of later growth.

It would be easier to answer this question if we knew with certainty whether the use of Baal (Baʿl) as a divine title is indigenous to Arabia or borrowed from the agricultural Semites beyond the peninsula. On the former alternative, which is accepted by some of the first scholars of our day, such as Wellhausen and Nöldeke, Baal-worship must be held to be older than the Semitic dispersion, and

graphy, as the editors warn us, is not greatly to be trusted.) ʿAtharī, for which some good authorities give also ʿaththarī (see *Lisān*), seems to mean "belonging to Athtar," the S. Arabian god, who corresponds in name, but not in sex, to the Babylonian Ishtar, the Phœnician Astarte, and the Aramaic ʿAttar or Athar. Athtar is one of the S. Arabian gods who preside ★ over irrigation (*CIS.* pt. 4 ; cf. *ZDMG.* xxxvii. 371) ; cf. also the place ʿAththar, described as a jungly haunt of lions (*Bānat Soʿād*, 46).

The crops dependent on rain are so unimportant in most parts of Arabia that some of the prophet's decrees pass them by altogether, and simply say that the *saih* pays full tithe (Ibn Saʿd, No. 68). Thus it is easy to understand how, in less precise speech, the term *baʿl* is applied *à potiori* to all crops not artificially irrigated ; and so, when the empire of Islam was extended to lands of more copious rain, confusion arose and the true meaning of *baʿl* was obscured. The corn crops of Palestine, which strictly speaking are *aʿdhā* (Abulf. ed. Reinaud, p. 227), and those near Alexandria, which are sown on the retiring of the Nile, are alike said by Mocaddasī to be "on the *baʿl*"; but this is not in accordance with the old classical usage.

[1] Procopius of Gaza, iii. 19, in Galland, vol. ix. — "dominus imbrium."

to belong to an age when all the Semites were still
nomadic. And in that case it can hardly be doubted
that the Arabs, as the nearest representatives of ancient
Semitic life, held most closely to the original conception
of the Baal. Personally I think it most probable that
Baal as a divine title entered Arabia with the date-palm,
whose culture is certainly not indigenous to the peninsula.
There is direct proof from inscriptions of the worship of
" the Baal " among the Nabatæans of the Sinaitic desert
to the north, and among the Sabæans and Himyarites
in the south of the peninsula; but for central Arabia
Baal-worship is only an inference from certain points
of language, of which the most important is the phrase
we have been considering.[1] Thus, to say the least, it is
possible that Baal - worship was never known to the
pastoral Bedouins except in so far as they came under
the influence of the denizens of the agricultural oases,
who had borrowed their art from Syria or Irac, and,
according to all analogy, could not have failed to borrow
at the same time so much of the foreign religion as was
deemed necessary to secure the success of their husbandry.
But even on this hypothesis I conceive it to be in the
highest degree improbable that Baal on entering Arabia
was changed from a god of rain to a god of springs and
watery bottoms. We have here to do mainly with the
culture of the date-palm, and I find no evidence that this
tree was largely grown on land watered by rain alone in
any part of the Semitic area. And even in Palestine,
which is the typical case of a Semitic country dependent
on rain, there is so vast a difference between the pro-
ductiveness of lands that are watered by rain alone and
those which enjoy natural or artificial irrigation, that we
can hardly conceive the idea of natural fertility, expressed

[1] See Nöldeke in *ZDMG.* xl. 174 ; and Wellhausen[1], p. 170.

by the term Baal's land, to have been originally connected
with the former.   For my own part I have no doubt that
Semitic agriculture began, as it has always most flourished,
in places naturally watered by springs and streams, and
that the language of agricultural religion was fixed by the
conditions prevailing in such places.[1]

I see an important confirmation of this view in the
local character of the Baalim, which has always been a
hopeless puzzle to those who begin with the conception
of the Baal as a sky god, but is at once intelligible if
the seats of the gods were originally sought in spots of
natural fertility, by springs and river-banks, in the groves
and tangled thickets and green tree-shaded glades of
mountain hollows and deep watercourses.   All the Semites,
as we shall presently see, attached a certain sanctity to
such places quite apart from agriculture; and as agriculture
must have begun in naturally productive spots, it is
inevitable to infer that agricultural religion took its
starting-point from the sanctity already attaching to
waters groves and meadows.[2]   The difficulty which we

[1] A good conception of the material conditions of Palestinian agriculture
may be got from an article by Anderlind in *ZDPV.* ix. (1886).   The following illustration from *Belādhorî*, p. 151, may be helpful.   The district of
Bāho (Baibalissus) was dependent on rain alone, and paid the usual tithes.
The inhabitants proposed to Maslama that he should make them an irrigation
canal from the Euphrates, and offered to pay him one-third of their crops in
addition to the tithe.

[2] In this argument I have not ventured to lay any weight on the Mishnic
use of the term, "Baal's field."   In Palestine, many centuries before the
Mishna was composed, the Baalim were certainly regarded as fertilising the
corn crops, and must therefore have been viewed as givers of rain ; thus it is
only natural that Baal's land, as opposed to land artificially irrigated, should
include corn-lands wholly dependent on rain, as it plainly does in *B. B.* iii. 1.
On the other hand, there are clear indications that even in Palestine the word
was sometimes used in a sense corresponding to the Arabic usage ; in other
words, that crops which cannot be raised in Palestine except in spots
naturally moist or artificially watered are divided into בעל and שׁקי.   This
distinction, for example, is applied to such vegetables as onions and cabbages
(*Terūm.* x. 11 ; *Shebî.* ii. 9), and in *Suc.* iii. 3 we read of a water-willow
(*populus Euphratica*) grown on the *ba'l.*   Moreover, in *Shebî.* ii. 9 there is a

feel in accepting this view arises mainly from the totally
different climate in which we live.   When a man has
journeyed in the Arabian wilderness, traversing day after
day stony plateaus, black volcanic fields, or arid sands
walled in by hot mountains of bare rock and relieved by
no other vegetation than a few grey and thorny acacias or
scanty tufts of parched herbage, till suddenly, at a turn of
the road, he emerges on a Wady where the ground-water
rises to the surface, and passes as if by magic into a new
world, where the ground is carpeted with verdure, and a
grove of stately palm-trees spreads forth its canopy of shade
against the hot and angry heaven, he does not find it
difficult to realise that to early man such a spot was
verily a garden and habitation of the gods.   In Syria the
contrasts are less glaring than in the desert; but only in
the spring time, and in many parts of the country not even
then, is the general fertility such that a fountain or a
marshy bottom with its greensward and thicket of natural
wood can fail strongly to impress the imagination.   Nor
are the religious associations of such a scene felt only by
heathen barbarians.   " The trees of the Lord drink their
fill, the cedars of Lebanon which He hath planted : Where
the birds make their nests; as for the stork, the fir-trees
are her house " (Ps. civ. 16).   This might pass for the
description of the natural sanctuary of the Baal of
Lebanon, but who does not feel its solemn grandeur ?
Or who will condemn the touch of primitive naturalism

clear statement that vegetables grown on the *ba'l* were irrigated, so that the
contrast with שַׁקְי can only be maintained by supposing that the latter term,
as is the case in Arabia, is restricted to laborious irrigation (*e.g.* by water
drawn from a cistern), and that vegetable gardens lying beneath a spring on
the hillside, such as still common in Palestine, were reckoned to the *ba'l*.
The only vegetables that were and are commonly grown in Palestine on the
open field before the summer sun has dried up the ground are those of the
gourd and cucumber kind ; see *Shebi.* ii. 1 ; Klein in *ZDPV.* iv. 82, and
cf. Isa. i. 8.

that colours the comparison in the first Psalm : " He shall
be like a tree planted by watercourses, that bringeth forth
his fruit in his season ; his leaf also shall not wither, and
whatsoever he doeth shall prosper " (Ps. i. 3) ?

When the conception of Baal's land is thus narrowed to
its oldest form, and limited to certain favoured spots that
seem to be planted and watered by the hand of the gods,[1]
we are on the point of passing from the idea of the land of
the god to that of his homestead and sanctuary. But
before we take this step it will be convenient for us to
glance rapidly at the way in which the primitive idea was
widened and extended. Ultimately, as we see from Hosea,
all agricultural produce was regarded as the gift of the
Baalim, and all the worshippers who frequented a particular sanctuary brought a tribute of first-fruits to the
local god, whether their crops grew on land naturally moist
and fertile, or on land laboriously irrigated, or on fields
watered by the rain of heaven. The god therefore had
acquired certain proprietary rights, or at least certain
rights of suzerainty, over the whole district inhabited by his
worshippers, far beyond the limits of the original Baal's land.

The first step in this process is easily understood from
the fundamental principles of Semitic land-law. Property
in water is older and more important than property in
land. In nomadic Arabia there is no property, strictly so
called, in desert pastures, but certain families or tribes
hold the watering-places without which the right of pasture
is useless. Or, again, if a man digs a well he has a preferential right to water his camels at it before other camels
are admitted ; and he has an absolute right to prevent
others from using the water for agricultural purposes
unless they buy it from him. This is Moslem law ; but

[1] To the same circle of ideas belongs the conception of the Garden of
Eden, planted by God, and watered not by rain but by rivers.

it is broadly in accordance with old Arabian custom, and
indeed with general Semitic custom, as appears from many
passages of the Old Testament.[1] On these principles it
is clear that even in the nomadic stage of society the god
of the waters may be held to exercise certain vague rights
over the adjoining pasture lands, the use of which depends
on access to the watering-places. And with the introduction of agriculture these rights become definite. All
irrigated lands are dependent on him for the water that
makes them fertile, and pay him first-fruits or tithes in
acknowledgment of his bounty. So far all is clear, and
in many parts of the Semitic area—notably in the alluvium
of the Euphrates and Tigris, the granary of the ancient
East—agriculture is so completely dependent on irrigation
that no more than this is needed to bring all habitable
land within the domain of the gods who send forth from
the storehouse of subterranean waters, fountains and
rivers to quicken the dead soil, and so are the authors of
all growth and fertility. But in Palestine the corn crops,
which form a chief source of agricultural wealth, are
mainly grown without irrigation on land watered by rain
alone. Yet in Hosea's time the first-fruits of corn were
offered at the shrines of the Baalim, who had therefore
become, in Canaan, the givers of rain as well as the lords
of terrestrial waters. The explanation of this fact must
be sought in the uncontrolled use of analogy characteristic
of early thought. The idea that the Baalim were the
authors of all fertility can only have taken shape among
communities whose agriculture was essentially dependent
on irrigation. But a little consideration will convince

[1] Gen. xxi. 25 sqq., xxvi. 17 sqq. ; Judg. i. 15 ; joint ownership in a well,
Gen. xxix. 8 ; Ex. ii. 16. Traces of a water law stricter than that of Islam
appear in Deut. ii. 6, 28 ; but the Arabian law, that the wayfarer and his
beasts were allowed to drink freely, but not to anticipate the owners of
the water, must always have been the general rule. (Cf. *Lectures*, p. 520.)

us that even in Palestine the earliest agriculture was necessarily of this type. Cultivation begins in the most fertile spots, which in that climate means the spots watered by streams and fountains. In such places agricultural villages must have existed, each with its worship of the local Baal, while the broad plains of Sharon or Esdraelon were still abandoned to wandering herdsmen. As husbandry spread from these centres and gradually covered the whole land, the worship of the Baalim spread with it; the gods of the springs extended their domain over the lands watered by the sky, and gradually added to their old attributes the new character of "lords of rain." The physical notions of the early Semites lent themselves readily enough to this development. Men saw with their own eyes that clouds rise from the sea (1 Kings xviii. 44) or from " the ends of the earth," *i.e.* the distant horizon (Jer. x. 13 ; Ps. cxxxv. 7), and so they had no reason to doubt that the rain came from the same storehouse as the fountains and streams of the Baalim.[1] In the oldest poetry of the Hebrews, when Jehovah rides over His land in the thunderstorm, His starting-point is not heaven but Mount Sinai; a natural conception, for in mountainous regions storms gather round the highest summits. And on this analogy we may infer that when the rainclouds lay heavy on the upland glens and wooded crown of Lebanon, where the great Baalim of Phœnicia had their most famous seats at the sources of sacred

---

[1] I cannot follow Dillmann in regarding the cosmology of Gen. i., with its twofold storehouse of water above and beneath the firmament, as more primitive than the simpler conception of rising clouds (נְשִׂאִים). The cosmology of Gen. i. is confined to post-exilic writings (for 2 Kings vii. 2, 19 is not to the point), and involves a certain amount of abstract thought ; while the other view merely represents things as they appear to the eye. It is quite a mistake to find a doctrine of evaporation in passages like Jer. x. 13 ; the epithet *nesi'im* refers to the visible movements of the clouds ; cf. such Arabic epithets as *ḥabī,* "a cloud crouching on the horizon."

streams, their worshippers would see a visible proof that
the gods of the fountains and rivers were also the givers
of rain.   In the latest stage of Phœnician religion, when
all deities were habitually thought of as heavenly or astral
beings, the holiest sanctuaries were still those of the primitive fountains and river gods, and both ritual and legend
continued to bear witness to the original character of these
deities.   Many examples of this will come before us in
due course ; for the present, it may suffice to cite the case
of Aphaca, where the Urania or heaven goddess was worshipped by casting gifts into the sacred pool, and where it
was fabled that once a year the goddess descended into the
waters in the shape of a falling star.[1]   ★

Finally the life-giving power of the god was not limited
to vegetative nature, but to him also was ascribed the
increase of animal life, the multiplication of flocks and
herds, and, not least, of the human inhabitants of the
land.   For the increase of animate nature is obviously
conditioned, in the last resort, by the fertility of the soil,
and primitive races, which have not learned to differentiate
the various kinds of life with precision, think of animate
as well as vegetable life as rooted in the earth and sprung
from it.   The earth is the great mother of all things in
most mythological philosophies, and the comparison of the
life of mankind, or of a stock of men, with the life of a
tree, which is so common in Semitic as in other primitive
poetry, is not in its origin a mere figure.   Thus where
the growth of vegetation is ascribed to a particular divine
power, the same power receives the thanks and homage of
his worshippers for the increase of cattle and of men.
Firstlings as well as first-fruits were offered at the shrines

[1] Sozomen, ii. 5 ; cf. the fallen star which Astarte is said to have
consecrated at the holy isle of Tyre (Philo Byblius in *Fr. Hist. Gr.* iii.
569).

of the Baalim,[1] and one of the commonest classes of personal names given by parents to their sons or daughters
designates the child as the gift of the god.[2]

In this rapid sketch of the development of the idea of
the local Baalim I have left many things to be confirmed
or filled out in detail by subsequent reference to the
particulars of their ritual, and I abstain altogether from
entering at this stage into the influence which the conception of the Baalim as productive and reproductive
powers exercised on the development of a highly sensual
mythology, especially when the gods were divided into
sexes, and the Baal was conceived as the male principle
of reproduction, the husband of the land which he
★ fertilised,[3] for this belongs rather to the discussion of the
nature of the gods.

---

[1] We shall see as we proceed that the sacrifice of firstlings is older than
agricultural religion, and was not originally a tribute like the first-fruits.
But in religions of the Baal type firstlings and first-fruits were brought
under the same general conception.

[2] To this class belong primarily the numerous Hebrew and Phœnician
names compounded with forms of the root נתן or יתן, "to give" (Heb.
Jonathan, Phœn. Baaliathon; Heb. Mattaniah, Phœn. Mutumbal [masc.
and fem.], etc.; Nabatæan, Cosnathan [Euting, No. 12]); and Arabic names
formed by adding the god's name to Wahb, Zaid (perhaps also Aus), "gift
of." Cognate to these are the names in which the birth of a son is recognised as a proof of the divine favour (Heb. Hananiah, Johanan; Phœn.
Hannibal, No'ammilkat [CIS. No. 41], etc.; Edomite, Baal-Hanan [Gen.
xxxvi. 38]; Ar. Ναμηλη [Wadd. 2143], "favour of El," Auf-el, "[good]
augury from El," Ουαδδηλος [Wadd. 2372], "love of El"), or which express
the idea that he has helped the parents or heard their prayers (Heb. Azariah,
Shemaiah; Phœn. Asdrubal, Eshmunazar, etc.); cf. Gen. xxix. xxx.,
1 Sam. i. Finally there is a long series of names such as Yehavbaal
(CIS. No. 69), Kemoshyehī (De Vogüé, Mélanges, p. 89), "Baal, Chemosh
gives life." The great variety of gods referred to in Phœnician names of
these forms shows that the gift of children was ascribed to all Baalim, each
in his own sphere; cf. Hosea, chap. i.

[3] This conception appears in Hosea and underlies the figure in Isa. lxii. 4,
where married land (be'ūlāh) is contrasted with wilderness; Wellhausen,
Heidenthum[1], p. 170. It is a conception which might arise naturally
enough from the ideas above developed, but was no doubt favoured by the
use of baal to mean "husband." How baal comes to mean husband is not

You will observe also that the sequence of ideas which I have proposed is applicable in its entirety only to agricultural populations, such as those of Canaan, Syria, and Irac on the one hand and of Yemen on the other. It is in these parts of the Semitic field that the conception of the local gods as Baalim is predominant, though traces of Ba'l as a divine title are found in Central Arabia in various forms.[1]

In the central parts of Arabia agriculture was confined to oases, and the vocabulary connected with it is mainly borrowed from the northern Semites.[2]   Many centuries before the date of the oldest Arabic literature, when the desert was the great highway of Eastern commerce, colonies of the settled Semites, Yemenites, and Aramæans occupied the oases and watering-places in the desert that were suitable for commercial stations, and to these immigrants must be ascribed the introduction of agriculture and even of the date-palm itself. The most developed cults of Arabia belong not to the pure nomads, but to these agricultural and trading settlements, which the Bedouins visited only as pilgrims, not to pay stated homage to the lord of the land from which they drew their life, but in fulfilment of vows. As most of our knowledge about Arabian cults refers to pilgrimages and the visits of the Bedouins, the impression is produced that all offerings were vows, and that fixed tribute of the fruits of the earth, such as was paid in the settled lands

perfectly clear ; the name is certainly associated with monandry and the appropriation of the wife to her husband, but it does not imply a servile relation, for the slave-girl does not call her master ba'l. Probably the key is to be found in the notion that the wife is her husband's tillage (Coran ii. 233), in which case private rights over land were older than exclusive marital rights.

[1] For the evidence see Nöldeke in *ZDMG.* vol. xl. (1886) p. **174**; and Wellhausen, *Heidenthum*[1], p. **170** ; [2] p. 146.

[2] Fränkel, *Aram. Fremdww.* p. 125.

to local Baalim, was unknown ; but this impression is not accurate. From the Coran (vi. 137) and other sources we have sufficient evidence that the settled Arabs paid to the god a regular tribute from their fields, apparently by marking off as his a certain portion of the irrigated and cultivated ground.[1]   Thus as regards the settled Arabs the parallelism with the other Semites is complete, and the only question is whether cults of the Baal type and the name of Baal itself were not borrowed, along with agriculture, from the northern Semitic peoples.

This question I am disposed to answer in the affirmative ; for I find nothing in the Arabic use of the word *ba'l* and its derivatives which is inconsistent with the view that they had their origin in the cultivated oases, and much that strongly favours such a view. The phrase " land which the Baal waters " has no sense till it is opposed to " land which the hand of man waters," and irrigation is certainly not older than agriculture. It is questionable whether the idea of the godhead as the permanent or immanent source of life and fertility—a very different

[1] All the evidence on this point has been confused by an early misunderstanding of the passage in the Coran : "They set apart for Allāh a portion of the tilth or the cattle he has created, and say, This is Allāh's—as they fancy—and this belongs to our partners (idols) ; but what is assigned to idols does not reach Allāh, and what is assigned to Allāh really goes to the idols." It is plain that the heathen said indifferently " this belongs to Allāh," meaning the local god (cf. Wellh. *Heid.* p. 217 *sq.*), or this belongs to such and such a deity (naming him), and Mohammed argues, exactly as Hosea does in speaking of the homage paid by his contemporaries to local Baalim, whom they identified with Jehovah, that whether they say " Allah " or " Hobal," the real object of their homage is a false god. But the traditional interpretation of the text is that one part was set aside for the supreme Allah and another for the idols, and this distortion has coloured all accounts of what the Arabs actually did, for of course historical tradition must be corrected by the Coran. Allowance being made for this error, which made the second half of the verse say that Allah was habitually cheated out of his share in favour of the idols, the notices in Ibn Hishām, p. 53, Sprenger, *Leb. Moh.* iii. 358, Pocock, *Specimen,* p. 112, may be accepted as based upon fact. In Pocock's citation from the *Nazm al-dorr* it appears that irrigated land is referred to.

thing from the belief that the god is the ancestor of his
worshippers—had any place in the old tribal religion of
the nomadic Arabs.   To the nomad, who does not practise
irrigation, the source of life and fertility is the rain that
quickens the desert pastures, and there is no evidence that
rain was ascribed to tribal deities.   The Arabs regard rain
as depending on the constellations, *i.e.* on the seasons,
which affect all tribes alike within a wide range; and so
when the showers of heaven are ascribed to a god, that
god is Allah, the supreme and non-tribal deity.[1]   It is to
be noted also that among the Arabs the theophorous
proper names that express religious ideas most akin to
those of the settled Semites are derived from deities
whose worship was widespread and not confined to the
nomads.   Further it will appear in a later lecture that
the fundamental type of Arabian sacrifice does not take
the form of a tribute to the god, but is simply an act of
communion with him.   The gift of firstlings, indeed, which
has so prominent a place in Canaanite religion, is not
unknown in Arabia.   But this aspect of sacrifice has very
little prominence; we find no approach to the payment
of stated tribute to the gods, and the festal sacrifices at
fixed seasons, which are characteristic of religions that
regard the gods as the source of the annual renovation
of fertility in nature, seem to have been confined to the
great sanctuaries at which the nomads appeared only as
pilgrims before a foreign god.[2]   In these pilgrimages the
nomadic Arabs might learn the name of Baal, but they

---

[1] Wellhausen, *Heid.* p. 210; cf. Ibn Sa'd, No. 80; *Diw. Hodh.* cxiii. 18.
Note also that rain is not one of the boons prayed for at 'Arafa (Agh. iii. 4 ;
cf. xix. 132. 6), though charms to produce rain were used (Wellh. p. 167).
These evidences do not prove that the gods were never appealed to as rain-
makers, but they render it very improbable that they were habitually
thought of as such.

[2] Cf. Wellhausen, *Heid.*[1] p. 116; [2] p. 121 *sq.*

could not assimilate the conception of the god as a land-owner and apply it to their own tribal deities, for the simple reason that in the desert private property in land was unknown and the right of water and of pasturage was common to every member of the tribe.[1] But in estimating the influence on Arabian religion of agriculture and the ideas connected with settled life, we must remember how completely, in the centuries before Mohammed, the gods of the *madar* ("glebe," *i.e.* villagers and townsfolk) had superseded the gods of the *wabar* ("hair," *i.e.* dwellers in haircloth tents). Much the most important part of the religious practices of the nomads consisted in pilgrim-ages to the great shrines of the town Arabs, and even the minor sanctuaries, which were frequented only by particular tribes, seem to have been often fixed at spots where there was some commencement of settled life. Where the god had a house or temple we recognise the work of men who were no longer pure nomads, but had begun to form fixed homes ; and indeed modern observation shows that, when an Arab tribe begins to settle down, it acquires the elements of husbandry before it gives up its tents and learns to erect immovable houses. Again there were sanctuaries without temples, but even at these the god had his treasure in a cave, and a priest who took care of his possessions, and there is no reason to think that the priest was an isolated hermit. The presumption is that

---

[1] We shall see in the next lecture that the institution of the *ḥimā* or sacred pasture-land is not based on the idea of property but on a principle of taboo. A main argument for the antiquity of Baal religion in Arabia is drawn from the denominative verb *ba'ila = aliha*, which means "to be in a state of helpless panic and perplexity," literally "to be Baal-struck." But such results are more naturally to be ascribed to the influence of an alien god than of a tribal divinity, and the word may well be supposed to have primarily expressed the confusion and mazed perplexity of the nomad when he finds himself at some great feast at a pilgrim shrine, amidst the strange habits and worship of a settled population ; cf. Æthiopic *ba'āl*, feast."

almost every holy place at the time of Mohammed was a little centre of settled agricultural life, and so also a centre of ideas foreign to the purely nomadic worshippers that frequented it.[1]

The final result of this long discussion is that the conception of the local god as Baal or lord of the land, the source of its fertility and the giver of all the good things of life enjoyed by its inhabitants, is intimately bound up with the growth of agricultural society, and involves a series of ideas unknown to the primitive life of the savage huntsman or the pure pastoral nomad. But we have also seen that the original idea of Baal's land was limited to certain favoured spots that seem to be planted and watered by the hand of the god, and to form, as it were, his homestead. Thus in its beginnings the idea of the land of the god appears to be only a development, in accordance with the type of agricultural life, of the more primitive idea that the god has a special home or haunt on earth. Agricultural habits teach men to look on this home as a garden of God, cultivated and fertilised by the hand of deity, but it was not agriculture that created the conception that certain places were the special haunts of

---

[1] In Arabia one section of a tribe is often nomadic while another is agricultural, but in spite of their kinship the two sections feel themselves very far apart in life and ways of thought, and a nomad girl often refuses to stay with a village husband. In this connection the traditions of the foreign origin of the cult at Mecca deserve more attention than is generally paid to them, though not in the line of Dozy's speculations. To the tribes of the desert the religion of the towns was foreign in spirit and contrasted in many ways with their old nomadic habits ; moreover, as we have seen, it was probably coloured from the first by Syrian and Nabatæan influences. Yet it exercised a great attraction, mainly by appealing to the sensual part of the Bedouin's nature ; the feasts were connected with the markets, and at them there was much jollity and good cheer. They began to be looked on as making up the sum of religion, and the cult of the gods came to be almost entirely dissociated from daily life, and from the customs associated with the sanctity of kinship, which at one time made up the chief part of nomad religion. Cf. Wellh., *Heid.* p. 215 *sq.*

8

superhuman powers. That the gods are not ubiquitous
but subject to limitations of time and space, and that they
can act only where they or their messengers are present,
is the universal idea of antiquity and needs no explanation.
In no region of thought do men begin with transcendental
ideas and conceive of existences raised above space and
time.   Thus whatever the nature of the gods, they were
doubtless conceived from the first as having their proper
homes or haunts, which they went forth from and returned
to, and where they were to be found by the worshippers
with whom they had fixed relations.   We are not entitled
to say à priori that this home would necessarily be a spot
on the surface of the earth, for, just as there are fowls of
the heaven and fish of the sea as well as beasts of the
field, there might be, and in fact were, celestial gods and
gods of the waters under the earth as well as gods
terrestrial.   In later times celestial gods predominate, as
we see from the prevalence of sacrifice by fire, in which
the homage of the worshipper is directed upwards in the
pillar of savoury smoke that rises from the altar towards
the seat of the godhead in the sky.   But all sacrifices are
not made by fire.   The Greeks, especially in older times,
buried the sacrifices devoted to gods of the underworld,
and threw into the water gifts destined for the gods of
seas and rivers.   Both these forms of fireless ritual are
found also among the Semites; and indeed among the
Arabs sacrifices by fire were almost unknown, and the gift
of the worshipper was conveyed to the deity simply by
being laid on sacred ground, hung on a sacred tree, or, in
the case of liquid offerings and sacrificial blood, poured over
a sacred stone.   In such cases we have the idea of locality
connected with the godhead in the simplest form.   There
is a fixed place on the earth's surface, marked by a
sacred tree or a sacred stone, where the god is wont to

be found, and offerings deposited there have reached their address.

In later times the home or sanctuary of a god was a temple, or, as the Semites call it, a "house" or "palace." But as a rule the sanctuary is older than the house, and the god did not take up his residence in a place because a house had been provided for him, but, on the contrary, when men had learned to build houses for themselves, they also set up a house for their god in the place which was already known as his home. Of course, as population increased and temples were multiplied, means were found to evade this rule, and new sanctuaries were constituted in the places most convenient for the worshippers; but even in such cases forms were observed which implied that a temple could not fitly be erected except in a place affected by the deity, and the greatest and holiest sanctuaries were those which, according to undisputed tradition, he had been known to frequent from time immemorial.

That the gods haunted certain spots, which in consequence of this were holy places and fit places of worship, was to the ancients not a theory but a matter of fact, handed down by tradition from one generation to another, and accepted with unquestioning faith. Accordingly we find that new sanctuaries can be formed and new altars or temples erected, only where the godhead has given unmistakable evidence of his presence. All that is necessary to constitute a Semitic sanctuary is a precedent; it is assumed that where the god has once manifested himself and shown favour to his worshippers he will do so again, and when the precedent has been strengthened by frequent repetition the holiness of the place is fully established. Thus in the earlier parts of the Old Testament a theophany is always taken to be a good reason for sacrificing on the spot. The deity has manifested himself either visibly or

by some mighty deed, and therefore an act of worship
cannot be out of place. Saul builds an altar on the site
of his victory over the Philistines,[1] the patriarchs found
sanctuaries on the spot where the deity has appeared
to them,[2] Gideon and Manoah present an offering where
they have received a divine message.[3] Even in the Hebrew
religion God is not equally near at all places and all times,
and when a man is brought face to face with Him he
seizes the opportunity for an act of ritual homage. But
the ordinary practices of religion are not dependent on
extraordinary manifestations of the divine presence ; they
proceed on the assumption that there are fixed places
where the deity has appeared in the past and may be
expected to appear again. When Jacob has his dream of
a divine apparition at Bethel, he concludes not merely that
Jehovah is present there at the moment, but that the
place is " the house of God, the gate of heaven." And
accordingly Bethel continued to be regarded as a sanctuary
of the first class down to the captivity. In like manner
all the places where the patriarchs were recorded to have
worshipped or where God appeared to them, figure as
traditional holy places in the later history, and at least
one of them, that of Mamre, was a notable sanctuary
down to Christian times. We are entitled to use these
facts as illustrative of Semitic religion in general, and not
of the distinctive features of the spiritual religion of the
Old Testament ; for the worship of Bethel, Shechem, Beersheba, and the other patriarchal holy places, was mingled
with Canaanite elements and is regarded as idolatrous by
the prophets ; and the later ritual at Mamre, which was
put down by the Christian emperors, was purely heathenish.

[1] 1 Sam. xiv. 35.
[2] Gen. xii. 7, xxii. 14, xxviii. 18 *sqq.* ; cf. Ex. xvii. 15.
[3] Judg. vi. 20, xiii. 19.
[4] The evidence is collected by Reland, *Palæstina*, p. 711 *sqq.*

This law of precedent as forming a safe rule for ritual institutions is common to the Old Testament religion and to the surrounding heathenism; the difference lies in the interpretation put on it. And even in this respect all parts of the Old Testament are not on the same level By a prophet like Isaiah the residence of Jehovah in Zion is almost wholly dematerialised. Isaiah has not risen to the full height of the New Testament conception that God, who is spirit and is to be worshipped spiritually, makes no distinction of spot with regard to His worship, and is equally near to receive men's prayers in every place; but he falls short of this view, not out of regard for ritual tradition, but because, conceiving Jehovah as the king of Israel, the supreme director of its national polity, he necessarily conceives His kingly activity as going forth from the capital of the nation. The ordinary conception of the Old Testament, in the historical books and in the Law, is not so subtle as this. Jehovah is not tied to one place more than another, but He is not to be found except in the places where " He has set a memorial of His name," and in these He " comes to His worshippers and blesses them " (Ex. xx. 24). Even this view rises above the current ideas of the older Hebrews in so far as it represents the establishment of fixed sanctuaries as an accommodation to the necessities of man. It is obvious that in the history of Jacob's vision the idea is not that Jehovah came to Jacob, but that Jacob was unconsciously guided to the place where there already was a ladder set between earth and heaven, and where, therefore, the godhead was peculiarly accessible. Precisely similar to this is the old Hebrew conception of Sinai or Horeb, " the Mount of God." It is clear that in Ex. iii. the ground about the burning bush does not become holy because God has appeared to Moses. On the contrary, the theophany takes place there because

it is holy ground, Jehovah's habitual dwelling-place.   In Ex.
xix. 4, when Jehovah at Sinai says that He has brought
the Israelites unto Himself, the meaning is that He has
brought them to the Mount of God ; and long after the
establishment of the Hebrews in Canaan, poets and prophets describe Jehovah, when He comes to help His people,
as marching from Sinai in thundercloud and storm.[1]

This point of view, which in the Old Testament appears
only as an occasional survival of primitive thought, corresponds to the ordinary ideas of Semitic heathenism.   The
local relations of the gods are natural relations ; men
worship at a particular spot because it is the natural home
or haunt of the god.   Holy places in this sense are older
than temples, and even older than the beginnings of settled
life.   The nomad shepherd or the savage hunter has no
fixed home, and cannot think of his god as having one, but
he has a district or beat to which his wanderings are
usually confined, and within it again he has his favourite
lairs or camping-places.   And on this analogy he can
imagine for himself tracts of sacred ground habitually
frequented by the gods, and special points within these
tracts which the deity particularly affects.   By and by,
under the influence of agriculture and settled life, the
sacred tract becomes the estate of the god, and the special
sacred points within it become his temples ; but originally
the former is only a mountain or glade in the unenclosed
wilderness, and the latter are merely spots in the desert
defined by some natural landmark, a cave, a rock, a fountain
or a tree.

We have seen that, when a sanctuary was once constituted, the mere force of tradition and precedent, the

[1] Deut. xxxiii. 2 ; Judg. v. 4 *sqq.* ; Hab. iii. 3.   That the sanctity of Sinai
is derived from the law-giving there is not the primitive idea.   This appears
most clearly from the critical analysis of the Pentateuch, but is sufficiently
evident from the facts cited above.

continuous custom of worshipping at it, were sufficient
to maintain its character.   At the more developed
sanctuaries the temple, the image of the god, the whole
apparatus of ritual, the miraculous legends recounted by
the priests, and the marvels that were actually displayed
before the eyes of the worshippers, were to an uncritical
age sufficient confirmation of the belief that the place
was indeed a house of God.   But in the most primitive
sanctuaries there were no such artificial aids to faith, and
it is not so easy to realise the process by which the
traditional belief that a spot in the wilderness was the
sacred ground of a particular deity became firmly established.   Ultimately, as we have seen, the proof that the
deity frequents a particular place lies in the fact that he
manifests himself there, and the proof is cumulative in
proportion to the frequency of the manifestations.   The
difficulty about this line of proof is not that which
naturally suggests itself to our minds.   We find it hard
to think of a visible manifestation of the godhead as an
actual occurrence, but all primitive peoples believe in
frequent theophanies, or at least in frequent occasions of
personal contact between men and superhuman powers.
When all nature is mysterious and full of unknown
activities, any natural object or occurrence which appeals
strongly to the imagination, or excites sentiments of awe
and reverence, is readily taken for a manifestation of
divine or demoniac life.   But a supernatural being as such
is not a god, he becomes a god only when he enters into
stated relations with man, or rather with a community of
men.   In the belief of the heathen Arabs, for example,
nature is full of living beings of superhuman kind, the
Jinn or demons.[1]   These *jinn* are not pure spirits but ⋆

---

[1] For details as to the *jinn* in ancient times, see Wellhausen, *Heidenthum*,
p. 148 *sqq.* The later form of the belief in such beings, much modified by

corporeal beings, more like beasts than men, for they are ordinarily represented as hairy, or have some other animal shape, as that of an ostrich or a snake. Their bodies are not phantasms, for if a *jinnī* is killed a solid carcase remains ; but they have certain mysterious powers of appearing and disappearing, or even of changing their aspect and temporarily assuming human form, and when they are offended they can avenge themselves in a supernatural way, *e.g.* by sending disease or madness. Like the wild beasts, they have, for the most part, no friendly or stated relations with men, but are outside the pale of man's society, and frequent savage and deserted places far from the wonted tread of men.[1] It appears from several poetical passages of the Old Testament that the northern Semites believed in demons of a precisely similar kind, hairy beings (*sĕʿīrīm*), nocturnal monsters (*lilīth*), which haunted waste and desolate places, in fellowship with jackals and ostriches and other animals that shun the abodes of man.[2]

In Islam the gods of heathenism are degraded into *jinn*, just as the gods of north Semitic heathenism are called *sĕʿīrīm* [3] in Lev. xvii. 7, or as the gods of Greece and Rome became devils to the early Christians. In all these cases the adherents of a higher faith were not prepared to deny that the heathen gods really existed, and

Islam, is illustrated by Lane in Note 21 of the Introduction to his version of the *Arabian Nights*. In the old translation of the *Arabian Nights* they are called Genii. See also Van Vloten in *Vienna Or. Jour.* 1893, p. 169 *sqq.*, from Al-Jāḥiẓ.

[1] Certain kinds of them, however, frequent trees and even human habitations, and these were identified with the serpents which appear and disappear so mysteriously about walls and the roots of trees. See Nöldeke, *Ztschr. f. Völkerpsych.* 1860, p. 412 *sqq.* ; Wellh. *ut sup.* p. 152 *sq.* For the snake as the form of the *jinn* of trees, see Rasmussen, *Addit.* p. 71, compared with Jauharī and the *Lisān, s. rad.* ﺟﻦ .

[2] Isa. xiii. 21, xxxiv. 14 ; cf. Luke xi. 24.

[3] " Hairy demons," E.V. " devils," but in Isa. xiii. 21 " satyrs."

did the things recorded of them ; the difference between
gods and demons lies not in their nature and power—
for the heathen themselves did not rate the power of
their gods at omnipotence—but in their relations to man.
The *jinn* would make very passable gods, for the cruder
forms of heathenism, if they only had a circle of human
dependants and worshippers ; and conversely a god who
loses his worshippers falls back into the ranks of the
demons, as a being of vague and indeterminate powers
who, having no fixed personal relations to men, is on
the whole to be regarded as an enemy. The demons,
like the gods, have their particular haunts which are
regarded as awful and dangerous places. But the haunt
of the *jinn* differs from a sanctuary as the *jinn* themselves
differ from gods. The one is feared and avoided, the
other is approached, not indeed without awe, but yet with
hopeful confidence; for though there is no essential physical
distinction between demons and gods, there is the fundamental moral difference that the *jinn* are strangers and
so, by the law of the desert, enemies, while the god, to
the worshippers who frequent his sanctuary, is a known
and friendly power. In fact the earth may be said to be
parcelled out between demons and wild beasts on the one
hand, and gods and men on the other.[1] To the former
belong the untrodden wilderness with all its unknown
perils, the wastes and jungles that lie outside the familiar
tracks and pasture grounds of the tribe, and which only
the boldest men venture upon without terror ; to the
latter belong the regions that man knows and habitually
frequents, and within which he has established relations,
not only with his human neighbours, but with the super-

---

[1] The close association between demons and wild beasts is well brought ★
out in a scholion to Ibn Hishām (ii. 9, l. 20, 23), where wild beasts and
serpents swarm round a ruin, and every one who seeks to carry anything
away from it is stricken by the *jinn*.

natural beings that have their haunts side by side with
him. And as man gradually encroaches on the wilderness
and drives back the wild beasts before him, so the gods in
like manner drive out the demons, and spots that were
once feared, as the habitation of mysterious and presumably malignant powers, lose their terrors and either
become common ground or are transformed into the seats
of friendly deities. From this point of view the recognition of certain spots as haunts of the gods is the religious
expression of the gradual subjugation of nature by man.
In conquering the earth for himself primitive man has
to contend not only with material difficulties but with
superstitious terror of the unknown, paralysing his energies
and forbidding him freely to put forth his strength to
subdue nature to his use. Where the unknown demons
reign he is afraid to set his foot and make the good things
of nature his own. But where the god has his haunt he
is on friendly soil, and has a protector near at hand; the
mysterious powers of nature are his allies instead of his
enemies, " he is in league with the stones of the field, and
the wild beasts of the field are at peace with him." [1]

The triumph of the gods over the demons, like the
triumph of man over wild beasts, must have been effected
very gradually, and may be regarded as finally sealed and
secured only in the agricultural stage, when the god of the
community became also the supreme lord of the land and
the author of all the good things therein. When this
stage was reached the demons—or supernatural beings
that have no stated relations to their human neighbours—
were either driven out into waste and untrodden places,
or were reduced to insignificance as merely subordinate

[1] Job v. 23. The allusion to the wild beasts is characteristic; cf. Hos.
ii. 20 (18); 2 Kings xvii. 26. An Arabian parallel in Ibn Sa'd, No. 145
with Wellhausen's note, *Skizzen*, iv. 194.

beings of which private superstition might take account
but with which public religion had nothing to do.
Within the region frequented by a community of men
the god of the community was supreme ; every phenomenon that seemed supernatural was ordinarily referred to
his initiative and regarded as a token of his personal
presence, or of the presence of his messengers and agents ;
and in consequence every place that had special supernatural associations was regarded, not as a haunt of
unknown demons, but as a holy place of the known god.
This is the point of view which prevailed among the
ancient Hebrews, and undoubtedly prevailed also among
their Canaanite neighbours.   Up to a certain point the
process involved in all this is not difficult to follow.   That
the powers that haunt a district in which men live and
prosper must be friendly powers is an obvious conclusion.
But it is not so easy to see how the vague idea of supernatural but friendly neighbours passes into the precise
conception of a definite local god, or how the local power
comes to be confidently identified with the tribal god of
the community.   The tribal god, as we have seen, has very
definite and permanent relations to his worshippers, of a
kind quite different from the local relations which we
have just been speaking of; he is not merely their
friendly neighbour, but (at least in most cases) their
kinsman and the parent of their race.   How does it come
about that the parent of a race of men is identified with
the superhuman being that haunts a certain spot, and
manifests himself there by visible apparitions, or other
evidence of his presence satisfactory to the untutored
mind ?   The importance of such an identification is
enormous, for it makes a durable alliance between man
and certain parts of nature which are not subject to his
will and control, and so permanently raises his position in

the scale of the universe, setting him free, within a certain range, from the crushing sense of constant insecurity and vague dread of the unknown powers that close him in on every side. So great a step in the emancipation of man from bondage to his natural surroundings cannot have been easily made, and is not to be explained by any slight à priori method. The problem is not one to be solved off-hand, but to be carefully kept in mind as we continue our studies.

There is one thing, however, which it may be well to note at once. We have seen that through the local god, who on the one hand has fixed relations to a race of men, and on the other hand has fixed relations to a definite sphere of nature, the worshipper is brought into stated and permanent alliance with certain parts of his material environment which are not subject to his will and control. But within somewhat narrow limits exactly the same thing is effected, in the very earliest stage of savage society, and in a way that does not involve any belief in an individual stock-god, through the institution of totemism. In the totem stage of society each kinship or stock of savages believes itself to be physically akin to some natural kind of animate or inanimate things, most generally to some kind of animal. Every animal of this kind is looked upon as a brother, is treated with the same respect as a human clansman, and is believed to aid his human relations by a variety of friendly services.[1] The importance of such a permanent alliance, based on the indissoluble bond of kinship, with a whole group of natural beings lying outside the sphere of humanity, is not to be measured by our knowledge of what animals can and cannot do. For

[1] See J. G. Frazer, *Totemism* (Edinburgh : A. & C. Black, 1887), p. 20 *sqq.*, reprinted in his monumental work *Totemism and Exogamy* (London, 1910), i. 1–87, with numerous additions, iv. 173–266.

as their nature is imperfectly known, savage imagination clothes them with all sort of marvellous attributes; it is seen that their powers differ from those of man, and it is supposed that they can do many things that are beyond his scope.   In fact they are invested with gifts such as we should call supernatural, and of the very same kind which heathenism ascribes to the gods—for example with the power of giving omens and oracles, of healing diseases and the like.

The origin of totemism is as much a problem as the origin of local gods.   But it is highly improbable that the two problems are independent; for in both cases the thing to be explained is the emancipation of a society of men from the dread of certain natural agencies, by the establishment of the conception of a physical alliance and affinity between the two parts.   It is a strong thing to suppose that a conception so remarkable as this, which is found all over the world, and which among savage races is invariably put in the totem form, had an altogether distinct and independent origin among those races which we know only in a state of society higher than savagery. *The belief in local nature-gods that are also clan-gods may not be directly evolved out of an earlier totemism, but there can be no reasonable doubt that it is evolved out of ideas or usages which also find their expression in totemism, and therefore must go back to the most primitive stage of savage society.* It is important to bear this in mind, if only that we may be constantly warned against explaining primitive religious institutions by conceptions that belong to a relatively advanced stage of human thought.   But the comparison of totemism can do more than this negative service to our enquiry, for it calls our attention to certain habits of very early thought which throw light on several points in the conception of local sanctuaries.

In the system of totemism men have relations not with individual powers of nature, *i.e.* with gods, but with certain classes of natural agents. The idea is that nature, like mankind, is divided into groups or societies of things, analogous to the groups or kindreds of human society. As life analogous to human life is imagined to permeate all parts of the universe, the application of this idea may readily be extended to inanimate as well as to animate things. But the statistics of totemism show that the natural kinds with which the savage mind was most occupied were the various species of animals. It is with them especially that he has permanent relations of kinship or hostility, and round them are gathered in a peculiar degree his superstitious hopes and fears and observances. Keeping these facts before us, let us look back for a moment at the Arabian *jinn*. One difference between gods and *jinn* we have already noted; the gods have worshippers, and the *jinn* have not. But there is another difference that now forces itself on our attention; the gods have individuality, and the *jinn* have not. In the *Arabian Nights* we find *jinn* with individual names and distinctive personalities, but in the old legends the individual *jinnī* who may happen to appear to a man has no more a distinct personality than a beast.[1] He is only one of a group of beings which to man are indistinguishable from

---

[1] This may be illustrated by reference to a point of grammar which is of some interest and is not made clear in the ordinary books. The Arab says "the *ghūl* appeared," not "a *ghūl* appeared," just as David says "the lion came and the bear" (1 Sam. xvii. 34; Amos iii. 12, v. 19). The definite article is used because in such cases definition cannot be carried beyond the indication of the species. The individuals are numerically different, but qualitatively indistinguishable. This use of the article is sharply to be distinguished from such a case as האיש in 1 Sam. ix. 9, where the article is generic, and a general practice of men is spoken of; and also from cases like הפליט (Gen. xiv. 13), גאל הדם, האיב, etc., where the noun is really a verbal adjective implying an action, and the person is defined by the action ascribed to him.

one another, and which are regarded as making up a nation or clan of superhuman beings,[1] inhabiting a particular locality, and united together by bonds of kinship and by the practice of the blood-feud, so that the whole clan acts together in defending its haunts from intrusion or in avenging on men any injury done to one of its members.[2] This conception of the communities of the *jinn* is precisely identical with the savage conception of the animal creation. Each kind of animal is regarded as an organised kindred, held together by ties of blood and the practice of blood revenge, and so presenting a united front when it is assailed by men in the person of any of its members. Alike in the Arabian superstitions about the *jinn* and in savage superstitions about animals it is this solidarity between all the members of one species, rather than the strength of the individual *jinnī* or animal, that makes it an object of superstitious terror.

These points of similarity between the families of the *jinn* in Arabia and the families of animals among savages are sufficiently striking, but they do not nearly exhaust the case. We have already seen that the *jinn* usually appear to men in animal form, though they can also take the shape of men. This last feature, however, cannot be regarded as constituting a fundamental distinction between

---

[1] A curious local story about two clans of *jinn*, the B. Mālik and the B. Shaiṣabān may be read in Yācūt, iii. 476 *sqq.* It is a genuine Bedouin tale, but like most later stories of the kind is not strictly mythical, but a free invention on the lines of current superstition. The oldest case of a clan of the *jinn* which is defined by a patronymic and not merely by a local name is perhaps that of the B. Ocaish, Nābigha, xxix. 10 ; cf. Ibn Hish. p. 282. But Tha'lab makes the B. Ocaish a human race, and the words of Nābigha are quite consistent with this view. Jinn with personal names appear in several traditions of the prophet, but only, so far as I can see, in such as are manifestly " weak," *i.e.* spurious.

[2] For the blood-feud of the *jinn* the classical example is that in Azracī, p. 261 (see below). But see also Damīrī, *s.v. arcam* (vol. i. p. 23), where we learn that the slayer of a serpent-demon was likely to die or go mad, and this was held to be the revenge of the kin of the slain. Cf. Wellh. 149.

them and ordinary animals in the mind of the Arabs, who believed that there were whole tribes of men who had the power of assuming animal form.   On the whole it appears that the supernatural powers of the *jinn* do not differ from those which savages, in the totem stage, ascribe to wild beasts.   They appear and disappear mysteriously, and are connected with supernatural voices and warnings, with unexplained sickness or death, just as totem animals are ; they occasionally enter into friendly relations or even into marriages with men, but animals do the same in the legends of savages ; finally, a madman is possessed by the *jinn* (*majnūn*), but there are a hundred examples of the soul of a beast being held to pass into a man.[1]   The accounts of the *jinn* which we possess have come to us from an age when the Arabs were no longer pure savages, and had ceased to ascribe demoniac attributes to most animals ; and our narrators, when they repeat tales about animals endowed with speech or supernatural gifts, assume as a matter of course that they are not ordinary animals but a special class of beings.   But the stories themselves are just such as savages tell about real animals ; the blood-feud between the Banu Sahm and the *jinn* of Dhū Ṭawā is simply a war between men and all creeping things, which, as in the Old Testament, have a common name [2] and are regarded as a single species or kindred ; and the " wild beast of the wild beasts of the *jinn*," which Taabbaṭa Sharran slew in a night encounter and carried home under his arm, was as concrete an animal as one can well imagine.[3]   The proper form of the *jinn* seems to be

---

[1] The widespread belief in this form of possession ought to be cited by commentators on Dan. iv. 16.

[2] *Ḥanash* = Heb. שׂרץ, רמשׂ.   For the story see Azracī, p. 261 *sqq.*; Wellh. p. 154.

[3] *Agh.* xviii. 210 *sqq.*   Taabbaṭa Sharran is an historical person, and the incident also is probably a fact.   From the verses in which he describes his

always that of some kind of lower animal, or a monstrous composition of animal forms, as appears even in later times in the description of the four hundred and twenty species that were marshalled before Solomon.[1]   But the tendency to give human shape to creatures that can reason and speak is irresistible as soon as men pass beyond pure savagery, and just as animal gods pass over into anthropomorphic gods, figured as riding on animals or otherwise associated with them, the *jinn* begin to be conceived as manlike in form, and the supernatural animals of the original conception appear as the beasts on which they ride.[2]   Ultimately the only animals directly and constantly identified with the *jinn* were snakes and other noxious creeping things.   The authority of certain utterances of the prophet had a share in this limitation, but it is

foe it would seem that the supposed *ghūl* was one of the feline carnivora.   In Damīrī, ii. 212, last line, a *ghūl* appears in the form of a thieving cat.

[1] Cazwīnī, i. 372 *sq.*   Even when they appear in the guise of men they have some animal attribute, *e.g.* a dog's hairy paw in place of a hand, Damīrī, ii. 213, l. 22.

[2] The stories in which the apparition takes this shape are obviously late. When a demon appears riding on a wolf or an ostrich to give his opinion on the merits of the Arabian poets (*Agh.* viii. 78, ix. 163, cited by Wellh. p. 152), we have to do with literary fiction rather than genuine belief; and similarly the story of a *ghūl* who rides on an ostrich in Cazwīnī, i. 373 *sq.*, is only an edifying Moslem tale.   These stories stand in marked contrast with the genuine old story in Maidānī, i. 181, where the demon actually is an ostrich.   The transition to the anthropomorphic view is seen in the story of Taabbaṭa Sharran, where the monster *ghūl* is called one of the wild beasts of the *jinn*, as if he were only their animal emissary.   The riding beasts of the *jinn* are of many species; they include the jackal, the gazelle, the porcupine, and it is mentioned as an exceptional thing that the hare is not one of them (*Ṣiḥāḥ, s.v.*; Rasmussen, *Addit.* p. 71, l. 14), for which reason amulets are made from parts of its body (cf. *ZDMG.* xxxix. 329).   Prof. De Goeje supplies me with an interesting quotation from Zamakhsharī, *Fāic*, i. 71: "Ignorant people think that wild beasts are the cattle of the *jinn*, and that a man who meets a wild beast is affected by them with mental disorder." The paralysing effect of terror is assigned to supernatural agency.   Cf. Arist. *Mir. Ausc.* 145: "In Arabia there is said to be a kind of hyæna, which when it sees a beast first (*i.e.* before being seen, **Plato**, *Rep.* i. p. 336 D; Theocr. xiv. 22; Virgil, *Ecl.* 9. 54) or treads on a man's shadow, renders it or him incapable of voice and movement."

9

natural enough that these creatures, of which men everywhere have a peculiar horror and which continue to haunt
and molest men's habitations after wild beasts have been
driven out into the desert, should be the last to be stripped
of their supernatural character.[1]

It appears then that even in modern accounts *jinn*
and various kinds of animals are closely associated, while
in the older legends they are practically identified, and
also that nothing is told of the *jinn* which savages do not
tell of animals. Under these circumstances it requires a
very exaggerated scepticism to doubt that the *jinn*, with all
their mysterious powers, are mainly nothing else than more
or less modernised representatives of animal kinds, clothed
with the supernatural attributes inseparable from the
savage conception of animate nature. A species of *jinn*
allied by kinship with a tribe of men would be indistinguishable from a totem kind, and instead of calling the
jinn gods without worshippers, we may, with greater precision, speak of them as potential totems without human
kinsfolk. This view of the nature of the *jinn* helps us to
understand the principle on which particular spots were
viewed as their haunts. In the vast solitudes of the
Arabian desert every strange sound is readily taken to be
the murmuring of the *jinn*, and every strange sight to be
a demoniac apparition. But when certain spots were fixed
on as being pre-eminently haunted places, we must necessarily suppose that the sights and sounds that were deemed
supernatural really were more frequent there than elsewhere. Mere fancy might keep the supernatural reputation
of a place alive, but in its origin even the uncontrolled

[1] The snake is an object of superstition in all countries. For superstitions
connected with "creeping things" in general among the northern Semites,
see Ezek. viii. 10. An oath by all the creeping things (*ḥanash*) between the
two Ḥarras appears in Ibn Hish. 10, l. 14, Tab. i. 911. 20, in a spurious
imitation of the style of the heathen soothsayers.

imagination of the savage must have some point of contact with reality. Now the nocturnal sights and sounds that affray the wayfarer in haunted regions, and the stories of huntsmen who go up into a mountain of evil name and are carried off by the *ghūl*, point distinctly to haunted spots being the places where evil beasts walk by night. Moreover, while the *jinn* frequent waste and desert places in general, their special haunts are just those where wild beasts gather most thickly—not the arid and lifeless desert, but the mountain glades and passes, the neighbourhood of trees and groves, especially the dense untrodden thickets that occupy moist places in the bottoms of the valleys.[1]

These, it is true, are the places where the spontaneous life of nature is most actively exhibited in all its phases, and where therefore it may seem self-evident that man will be most apt to recognise the presence of divine or at least of superhuman powers. But so general an explanation as this is no explanation at all. Primitive religion was not a philosophical pantheism, and the primitive deities were not vague expressions for the principle of life in nature. What we have to explain is that the places where the life of nature is most intense—or rather some of these places— appeared to the primitive Semite to be the habitations, not

---

[1] All this, and especially the association of the *jinn* with natural thickets, is well brought out by Wellhausen, *Heid.*[1], p. 136 ; [2] p.150 *sqq.* ; though he offers no explanation of the reason why " the direct impression of divine life present in nature " is associated with so bizarre a conception. In Southern Arabia natural jungles are still avoided as the haunts of wild beasts ; no Arab, according to Wrede, willingly spends a night in the Wady Ma'īsha, because its jungles are the haunts of many species of dangerous carnivora (Wrede's *Reise in Hadhramaut*, ed. Maltzan, p. 131). The lions of Al-Sharā and of the jungles of the Jordan valley (Zech. xi. 3) may be compared, and it is to be remembered that in savage life, when man's struggle with wild beasts is one of life and death, the awe associated with such places is magnified tenfold. Even in the old Mohammedan literature no sharp line is drawn between danger from wild beasts and danger from *jinn* ; see the scholion cited *supra*, p. 121, note.

of abstract divine powers, but of very concrete and tangible beings, with the singular attributes which we have found the *jinn* to possess, and that this belief did not rest on mere general impressions, but was supported by reference to actual demoniac apparitions. The usual vague talk about an instinctive sense of the presence of the deity in the manifestations of natural life does not carry us a whit nearer the comprehension of these beliefs, but it is helpful to note that spots of natural fertility, untouched by man's hand and seldom trodden by his foot, are the favoured haunts of wild beasts, that all savages clothe wild beasts and other animals with the very same supernatural qualities which the Arabs ascribe to the *jinn*, and that the Arabs speak of Baccār as a place famous for its demons in exactly the same matter-of-fact way in which they speak of Al-Sharā and its famous lions.

While the most marked attributes of the *jinn* are plainly derived from animals, it is to be remembered that the savage imagination, which ascribes supernatural powers to all parts of animate nature, extends the sphere of animate life in a very liberal fashion. Totems are not seldom taken from trees, which appear to do everything for their adherents that a totem animal could do. And indeed that trees are animate, and have perceptions, passions and a reasonable soul, was argued even by the early Greek philosophers on such evidence as their movements in the wind and the elasticity of their branches.[1] Thus while the supernatural associations of groves and thickets may appear to be sufficiently explained by the fact that these are the favourite lairs of wild beasts, it appears probable that the association of certain kinds of *jinn* with trees must in many cases be regarded as primary, the trees themselves being conceived as animated demoniac beings.

[1] Aristotle, *De plantis*, i. p. 815 ; Plutarch, *Plac. Philos.* v. 26.

In Ḥaḍramaut it is still dangerous to touch the sensitive Mimosa, because the spirit that resides in the plant will avenge the injury.[1]   The same idea appears in the story of Ḥarb b. Omayya and Mirdās b. Abī 'Amir, historical persons who lived a generation before Mohammed.   When these two men set fire to an untrodden and tangled thicket, with the design to bring it under cultivation, the demons of the place flew away with doleful cries in the shape of white serpents, and the intruders died soon afterwards.   The *jinn* it was believed slew them " because they had set fire to their dwelling-place." [2]   Here the spirits of the trees take serpent form when they leave their natural seats, and similarly in Moslem superstition the *jinn* of the *'oshr* and the *ḥamāṭa* are serpents which frequent trees of these species.   But primarily supernatural life and power reside in the trees themselves, which are conceived as animate and even as rational.   Moslim b. 'Ocba heard in a dream the voice of the *gharcad* tree designing him to the command of the army of Yazīd against Medina.[3]   Or again the value of the gum of the acacia (*samora*) as an amulet is connected wth the idea that it is a clot of menstruous blood (*ḥaiḍ*), *i.e.* that the tree is a woman.[4] And similarly the old Hebrew fables of trees that speak and act like human beings [5] have their original source in the savage personification of vegetable species.

---

[1] Wrede's *Reise*, ed. Maltzan, p. 131.

[2] *Agh.* vi. 92, xx. 135 *sq.*   [3] *Agh.* i. 14 ; Wellh. 205.

[4] Rasmussen, *Add.* p. 71; Zamakhsharī, *Asās, s.v.* حيض.   New-born children's heads were rubbed with the gum to keep away the *jinn*, just as they used to be daubed with the blood of the sacrifice called '*acīca* (see my *Kinship*, p. 179 *sq.*).   The blood of menstruation has supernatural qualities among all races, and the value of the hare's foot as an amulet was connected with the belief that this animal menstruates (Rasm. *ut sup.*). The same thing was affirmed of the hyæna, which has many magical qualities and peculiar affinities to man (*Kinship*, p. 231 *sq.*).

[5] Judg. ix. 8 *sqq.* ; 2 Kings xiv. 9.

In brief it is not unjust to say that, wherever the spontaneous life of nature was manifested in an emphatic way, the ancient Semite saw something supernatural. But this is only half the truth; the other half is that the supernatural was conceived in genuinely savage fashion, and identified with the quasi-human life ascribed to the various species of animals or plants or even of inorganic things.

For indeed certain phenomena of inorganic nature directly suggest to the primitive mind the idea of living force, and the presence of a living agent. Thus, to take a trivial example, the mediæval Arabs associate a definite class of demons with sand-whirlwinds and apply the name *zawābiʿ* indifferently to these phenomena and to the *jinn* that accompany or cause them.[1] More important is the widespread belief that the stars move because they are alive, which underlies the planet and constellation worship of the Semites as of other ancient nations. Volcanic phenomena, in like manner, are taken for manifestations of supernatural life, as we see in the Greek myths of Typhoeus and in the Moslem legend of the crater of Barahūt in Ḥadramaut, whose rumblings are held to be the groans of lost souls;[2] probably also in the legend of the "fire of Yemen" in the valley of Ḍarawān which in heathen times is said to have served as an ordeal, devouring the guilty and sparing the innocent;[3] and again,

---

[1] See the lexx. and also Jāḥiẓ as cited by Vloten, *Vien. Or. J.* vii. 180. In several Arabian legends the eccentric movements of dust-whirlwinds are taken to be the visible signs of a battle between two clans of Jinn (Ibn Hish. ii. 42, Yācūt, iii. 478; cf. Ibn Hish. 131 *sq.*). Cf. Goldz. *Abh.* i. 205, ii. cviii.

[2] See Yācūt, i. 598; De Goeje, *Ḥadramaut,* p. 20 (Rev. Col. Intern. 1886). Does this belief rest on an early myth connected with the name of Ḥadramaut itself ? See Olshausen in *Rhein. Mus.* Ser. 3, vol. viii. p. 332 ; *Sitzungsb. d. Berliner Ak.* 1879, p. 751 *sqq.*

[3] Ibn Hishām, p. 17, with the scholia ; Bekri, p. 621 ; Yācūt, iii. 470. Yācūt describes the valley as accursed ; no plant grew there, no man could traverse it, and no bird fly across it.

mephitic vapours rising from fissures in the earth are taken to be potent spiritual influences.[1]   But remote phenomena like the movements of the stars, and exceptional phenomena like volcanoes, influence the savage imagination less than mundane and everyday things, which are not less mysterious to him and touch his common life more closely. It seems to be a mistake to suppose that distant and exceptional things are those from which primitive man forms his general views of the supernatural; on the contrary he interprets the remote by the near, and thinks of heavenly bodies, for example, as men or animals, like the animate denizens of earth.[2]   Of all inanimate things that which has the best marked supernatural associations among the Semites is flowing (or, as the Hebrews say, " living ") water. In one of the oldest fragments of Hebrew poetry [3] the fountain is addressed as a living being; and sacred wells are among the oldest and most ineradicable objects of reverence among all the Semites, and are credited with oracular powers and a sort of volition by which they receive or reject offerings.   Of course these superstitions often take the form of a belief that the sacred spring is the dwelling-place of beings which from time to time emerge from it in human or animal form, but the fundamental

---

[1] It may be conjectured that the indignation of the *jinn* at the violation of their haunts, as it appears in the story of Harb and Mirdās, would not have been so firmly believed in but for the fact that places such as the *jinn* were thought to frequent are also the haunts of ague, which is particularly active when land is cultivated for the first time.   According to a Mohammedan tradition, the Prophet assigned the uplands (*jals*) to the believing jinn, and the deep lowlands (*ghaur*) to the unbelieving.   The latter are in Arabia the homes of fever and plague (Damīrī, i. 231).

[2] See Lang, *Myth, Ritual and Religion*, chap. v.   Among the Semites the worship of sun, moon and stars does not appear to have had any great vogue in the earliest times.   Among the Hebrews there is little trace of it before Assyrian influence became potent, and in Arabia it is by no means so prominent as is sometimes supposed ; cf. Wellhausen, p. 209 *sqq.*

[3] Num. xxi. 17, 18 : " Spring up, O well ! sing ye to it ! "   See p. 183, n. 2.

idea is that the water itself is the living organism of a demoniac life, not a mere dead organ.[1]

If now we turn from the haunts of the demons to sanctuaries proper, the seats of known and friendly powers with whom men maintain stated relations, we find that in their physical character the homes of the gods are precisely similar to those of the *jinn*—mountains and thickets, fertile spots beside a spring or stream, or sometimes points defined by the presence of a single notable tree. As man encroaches on the wilderness, and brings these spots within the range of his daily life and walk, they lose their terror but not their supernatural associations, and the friendly deity takes the place of the dreaded demons. The conclusion to be drawn from this is obvious. The physical characters that were held to mark out a holy place are not to be explained by conjectures based on the more developed type of heathenism, but must be regarded as taken over from the primitive beliefs of savage man. The nature of the god did not determine the place of his sanctuary, but conversely the features of the sanctuary had an important share in determining the development of ideas as to the functions of the god. How this was possible we have seen in the conception of the local Baalim. The spontaneous luxuriance of marshy lands already possessed supernatural associations when there was no thought of bringing it under the service of man by cultivation, and when the rich valley bottoms were avoided with superstitious terror as the haunts of formidable natural enemies. How this terror was first broken through, and the transformation of certain groups of hostile demons into friendly and kindred powers was first effected, we cannot tell; we can only say

[1] For the details as to sacred waters among the Semites, see below in Lect. V.

that the same transformation is already effected, by means
of totemism, in the most primitive societies of savages, and
that there is no record of a stage in human society in
which each community of men did not claim kindred
and alliance with some group or species of the living
powers of nature. But if we take this decisive step for
granted, the subsequent development of the relation of the
gods to the land follows by a kind of moral necessity,
and the transformation of the vague friendly powers that
haunt the seats of spontaneous natural life into the
beneficent agricultural Baalim, the lords of the land
and its waters, the givers of life and fertility to all
that dwell on it, goes naturally hand in hand with the
development of agriculture and the laws of agricultural
society.

I have tried to put this argument in such a way as
may not commit us prematurely to the hypothesis that the
friendly powers of the Semites were originally totems, *i.e.*
that the relations of certain kindred communities of men
with certain groups of natural powers were established
before these natural powers had ceased to be directly
identified with species of plants and animals. But if my
analysis of the nature of the *jinn* is correct, the conclusion
that the Semites did pass through the totem stage can be
avoided only by supposing them to be an exception to the
universal rule, that even the most primitive savages have
not only enemies but permanent allies (which at so early a
stage in society necessarily means kinsfolk) among the
non-human or superhuman animate kinds by which the
universe is peopled. And this supposition is so extrava-
gant that no one is likely to adopt it. On the other hand,
it may be argued with more plausibility that totemism, if
it ever did exist, disappeared when the Semites emerged
from savagery, and that the religion of the race, in its

higher stages, may have rested on altogether independent
bases.   Whether this hypothesis is or is not admissible
must be determined by an actual examination of the
higher heathenism.   If its rites usages and beliefs really
are independent of savage ideas, and of the purely savage
conception of nature of which totemism is only one aspect,
the hypothesis is legitimate ; but it is not legitimate if the
higher heathenism itself is permeated in all its parts by
savage ideas, and if its ritual and institutions are throughout in the closest contact with savage ritual and institutions of totem type.   That the latter is the true state of
the case will I believe become overwhelmingly clear as we
proceed with our survey of the phenomena of Semitic
religion ; and a very substantial step towards the proof that
it is so has already been taken, when we have found that
the sanctuaries of the Semitic world are identical in physical
character with the haunts of the *jinn*, so that as regards
their local associations the gods must be viewed as simply
replacing the plant and animal demons.[1]   If this is so we
can hardly avoid the conclusion that some of the Semitic
gods are of totem origin, and we may expect to find the
most distinct traces of this origin at the oldest sanctuaries.
*But we are not to suppose that every local deity will have
totem associations, for new gods as well as new sanctuaries
might doubtless spring up at a later stage of human
progress than that of which totemism is characteristic.*
Even holy places that had an old connection with the
demons may, in many instances, have come to be looked
upon as the abode of friendly powers and fit seats of
worship, after the demons had ceased to be directly
identified with species of plants and animals, and had

---

[1] The complete development of this argument as it bears on the nature of
the gods must be reserved for a later course of lectures ; but a provisional
discussion of some points on which a difficulty may arise will be found
below : see *Additional Note* A, *Gods, Demons, and Plants or Animals.*

acquired quasi-human forms like the nymph and satyrs of the Greeks. *It is one thing to say that the phenomena of Semitic religion carry us back to totemism, and another thing to say that they are all to be explained from totemism.*

LECTURE IV

I HAVE spoken hitherto of the physical characters of the sanctuary, as the haunt of divine beings that prove, in the last resort, to be themselves parts of the mundane universe, and so have natural connections with sacred localities; let us now proceed to look at the places of the gods in another aspect, to wit in their relation to men, and the conduct which men are called upon to observe at and towards them. The fundamental principle by which this is regulated is that the sanctuary is holy, and must not be treated as a common place. The distinction between what is *holy* and what is *common* is one of the most important things in ancient religion, but also one which it is very difficult to grasp precisely, because its interpretation varied from age to age with the general progress of religious thought. To us holiness is an ethical idea. God, the perfect being, is the type of holiness; men are holy in proportion as their lives and character are godlike; places and things can be called holy only by a figure, on account of their associations with spiritual things. This conception of holiness goes back to the Hebrew prophets, especially to Isaiah; but it is not the ordinary conception of antique religion, nor does it correspond to the original sense of the Semitic words that we translate by " holy." While it is not easy to fix the exact idea of holiness in ancient Semitic religion, it is quite certain that it has nothing to do with morality and purity of life. Holy persons were such, not in virtue of their character but in virtue of their race, function, or mere material consecration; and at the Canaanite shrines the name of "holy" (masc. *cĕdeshīm*, fem. *cĕdeshōth*) was specially appropriated to a class of degraded wretches, devoted to the most shameful practices of a corrupt religion, whose life, apart from its connection with the sanctuary, would have been disgraceful even from the standpoint of heathenism. But holiness in antique religion is not mainly an attribute of persons. The gods are holy,[1] and their ministers of whatever kind or grade are holy also, but holy seasons holy places and holy things, that is, seasons places and things that stand in a special relation to the godhead and are withdrawn by divine sanction from some or all ordinary uses, are equally to be considered in determining what holiness means. Indeed the holiness of the gods is an expression to which it is hardly possible to attach a definite sense apart from the holiness of their physical surroundings; it shows itself in the sanctity attached to the persons places things and times through which the gods and men come in contact with one another. The holiness of the sanctuary, which is the matter immediately before us, seems also to be on the whole the particular form of sanctity which lends itself most readily to independent investigation. Holy persons things and times, as they are conceived in antiquity, all presuppose the existence of holy places at which the persons minister, the things are preserved, and the times are celebrated. Nay the holiness of the god-head itself is manifest to men, not equally at all places, but specially at those places where the gods are immediately present and from which their activity proceeds. In fact

---

[1] The Phœnicians speak of the "holy gods" (האלנם הקדשם, *CIS.* No. 3, l. 9, 22), as the Hebrews predicate holiness of Jehovah.

the idea of holiness comes into prominence wherever the gods come into touch with men; it is not so much a thing that characterises the gods and divine things in themselves, as the most general notion that governs their relations with humanity; and, as these relations are concentrated at particular points of the earth's surface, it is at these points that we must expect to find the clearest indications of what holiness means.

At first sight the holiness of the sanctuary may seem to be only the expression of the idea that the sanctuary belongs to the god, that the temple and its precincts are his homestead and domain, reserved for his use and that of his ministers, as a man's house and estate are reserved for himself and his household. In Arabia, for example, where there were great tracts of sacred land, it was forbidden to cut fodder, fell trees, or hunt game;[1] all the

[1] Wellh., *Heidenthum*, p. 106, and refs. there given to the ordinances laid down by Mohammed for the *Ḥaram* of Mecca and the *Ḥimā* of Wajj at Ṭāif. In both cases the ordinance was a confirmation of old usage, and similar rules were laid down by Mohammed for his new *Ḥaram* at Medina (Belādhorī, p. 7 *sq.*). At Mecca the law against killing or chasing animals did not apply to certain noxious creatures. The usually received tradition (Bokhārī, ii. 195, of the Būlāc vocalised ed.) names the raven and the kite, the rat, the scorpion and the "biting dog," which is taken to cover the lion, panther, and wolf, and other carnivora that attack man (Mowaṭṭa, ii. 198). The serpent also was killed without scruple at Minā, which is within the Ḥaram (Bokh. ii. 196, l. 1 *sqq.*). That the protection of the god is not extended to manslaying animals and to the birds of prey that molest the sacred doves is intelligible. The permission to kill vermin is to be compared with the story of the war between the Jinn and the B. Sahm (*supra*, p. 128). From the law against cutting plants the *idhkhir* (*Andropogon schœnanthus*, or lemon-grass) was excepted by Mohammed with some hesitation, on the demand of Al-Abbās, who pointed out that it was the custom to allow it to be cut for certain purposes. Here unfortunately our texts are obscure and vary greatly, but the variations all depend on the reading of two words of which one is either "smiths" or "graves" and the other "purification" or "roofs" of houses. In the Arabic the variations turn on small graphical points often left out by scribes. I take it that originally the two uses were either both practical, "for the smiths and the (thatching of) house-roofs," or both ceremonial, "for entombment and the purification of houses." As the lemon-grass was valued in antiquity for its perfume, and the fragrant *ḥarmal* was also

natural products of the holy soil were exempt from human appropriation.   But it would be rash to conclude that what cannot be the private property of men is therefore the private property of the gods, reserved for the exclusive use of them or their ministers.   The positive exercise of legal rights of property on the part of the gods is only possible where they have human representatives to act for them, and no doubt in later times the priests at the greater Semitic sanctuaries did treat the holy reservations as their own domain.   But in early times there was no privileged class of sacred persons to assert on their own behalf the doctrine of divine proprietorship, and in these times accordingly the prohibition of private encroachment was consistent with the existence of public or communal rights in holy places and things.   In nomadic Arabia sanctuaries are older than any doctrine of property that could possibly be applied to a tract like the *ḥaram* at Mecca or the *ḥimā* of Ṭāif.   To constitute private property, according to the ancient doctrine still preserved in Moslem law, a man must build on the soil or cultivate it; there is no property in natural pastures.   Every tribe indeed has its own range of plains and valleys, and its own watering-places, by which it habitually encamps at certain seasons and from which it repels aliens by the strong hand.   But this does not constitute property, for the boundaries of the tribal land are merely maintained by force against enemies, and not only every tribesman but every covenanted ally has equal and unrestricted right to pitch his tent and drive his cattle where he will.   This is still the rule among nomadic tribes, but where there are

used in old Arabia to lay the dead in, and is still used to fumigate houses, the second reading is the better.   The lemon-grass might be cut for purposes of a religious or quasi-religious character.   Mohammed probably hesitated because these uses were connected with heathen superstition.   Cf. *Muh. in Medina*, p. 338.

fixed villages the inhabitants claim an exclusive right to a certain circuit of pasture round the township. Claims of this description are older than Islam, and are guaranteed by Mohammed in several of his treaties with new converts, in varying terms, which evidently follow the variations of customary law in different parts of the peninsula. In such cases we may legitimately speak of *communal* property in pasture-lands, but *private* property in such has never been known to Arabian law.[1]

From this statement it is obvious that the Arabs might indeed conceive the temple to be the personal property of the god, but could not bring the rules affecting sacred pastures under the same category. On the analogies that have just come before us we can readily understand that the haunts of unfriendly demons would be shunned for fear of their enmity, but the friendly god could have no exclusive right to hold waste lands against his worshippers. At Mecca the Coraish built houses or dug wells and enjoyed the full right of property in the work of their hands, and the open Ḥaram was free to every man's cattle like an ordinary tribal or communal pasture-ground. These rules are so obviously in accordance with the whole spirit of ancient Arabian institutions that they can hardly have been peculiar to Mecca. About other sacred tracts, which lost their religious prerogative through the spread of Islam, our information is too scanty to permit a positive statement, yet it seems probable that at most sanctuaries embracing a stretch of pasture-ground, the right of grazing was free to the community of the god, but not to outsiders. It appears to me that this formula covers all the known facts if we make a reasonable allowance for local variations

[1] See Ibn Sa'd, Nos. 21, 23, 121, with Wellhausen's refs. to Doughty, ii. 245, and especially Ibn Hishām, p. 955. In two cases the reserved pasture is called a *ḥimā*, and this is the term still used. Cf. on the law of pasture, Abū Yūsuf, *Kit. al-Kharāj* (Būlāc, A.H. 1302), p. 58 *sq.* See Wellh. 108, n. 3.

in the definition of outsiders. Where the sacred tract was attached to the sanctuary of a town, it might be an open question whether the privileged religious community was limited to the townsmen or included a wider circle of the surrounding Bedouins who were accustomed to pay occasional homage at the shrine. On the other hand, a sanctuary that lay between the waters of several tribes and was equally visited by all would afford a common pasture-ground where enemies could meet and feed their flocks in security under the peace of the god. And finally, there seem to have been some Arabian sanctuaries that were neither attached to a town nor intertribal, but practically were in the hands of a single family of hereditary priests. At such sanctuaries all worshippers were in some sense outsiders, and the priests might claim the *ḥimā* as a *quasi*-private domain for themselves and the god. All these cases seem to find more or less clear exemplification in the fragmentary details that have come down to us. At the *ḥimā* of Wajj, attached to the sanctuary of al-Lāt at Ṭāif, the rules are practically identical with those at Mecca ; and when we observe that Mohammed confirmed these rules, in the interest of the inhabitants,[1] at the same time that he destroyed al-Lāt and did away with the ancient sanctity of the spot, it is natural to infer that in other cases also the *ḥimā* which he allowed to subsist as a communal pasture-ground round a village or town was originally a sacred tract, protected from encroachment by the fear of the god rather than by any civil authority. It is indeed plain that with such a property-law as has been described, and in the absence of any intertribal authority, religion was the only power, other than the high

[1] According to Bekrī, p. 838, the treaty of Mohammed with the Thacīf, or people of Ṭāif, contained the clause *wathacīfun aḥaccu 'n-nāsi biwajjin,* so ★ that the confirmation of the old taboos was clearly meant to benefit them. And so it did ; for to cut down the wood is the quickest way to ruin a pasture-ground for camels. See the interesting remarks of Floyer in *Journ. R. A. Soc.*

hand, that could afford any security to a communal pasture, and we are not without evidence as to how this security was effected. The privileges of the Ḥaram at Mecca and Medina are still placed under a religious sanction; on those who violated the latter Mohammed invoked the irrevocable curse of God and the angels and all men.[1] The restrictions on the use of other *ḥimās* have under Islam only a civil sanction, but the punishments appointed by Mohammed for those who violate them are manifestly based on old religious customs exactly parallel to the *taboos* prevalent among savage nations whose notions of property are still imperfectly developed. If a wood-cutter intruded on the *ḥimā* of Wajj or Nacī‘, he forfeited his hatchet and his clothes; if a man unlawfully grazed his cattle on the *ḥimā* of Jorash, the cattle were forfeit.[2] To us these seem to be arbitrary penalties, attached by the will of the lawgiver to a breach of civil law; but to the Arabs, just emerged from heathenism, this was not so. We shall presently see that the ancient Semites, like other early races, deemed holiness to be propagated by physical contagion, so that common things brought into the sanctuary became holy and could not be safely withdrawn again to common use. Thus the forfeiture of clothes in Islamic law is only a continuation of the old rule, attested for the sanctuary of Mecca, that common raiment worn in the sacred place had to be cast off and left behind;[3] while the forfeiture of cattle at Jorash follows the rule recorded for the sanctuary of Al-Jalsad, that cattle straying from outside into the *ḥimā* become sacred and cannot be reclaimed. By students of primitive society these rules will at once be recognised as belonging to the sphere of *taboo* and not of

---

[1] Belādhorī, p. 8.

[2] Ibn Hishām, p. 918 ; Belādhorī, p. 9 ; Ibn Hishām, p. 955.

[3] For the details on this point see below, *Additional Note* B.

property-law; those who are not familiar with the subject will find it further elucidated at the end of this volume in *Additional Note* B.

Hitherto we have been speaking of a type of sanctuary older than the institution of property in land. But even where the doctrine of property is fully developed, holy places and holy things, except where they have been appropriated to the use of kings and priests, fall under the head of public rather than of private estate. According to ancient conceptions, the interests of the god and his community are too closely identified to admit of a sharp distinction between sacred purposes and public purposes, and as a rule nothing is claimed for the god in which his worshippers have not a right to share. Even the holy dues presented at the sanctuary are not reserved for the private use of the deity, but are used to furnish forth sacrificial feasts in which all who are present partake. So too the sanctuaries of ancient cities served the purpose of public parks and public halls, and the treasures of the gods, accumulated within them, were a kind of state treasure, preserved by religious sanctions against peculation and individual encroachment, but available for public objects in time of need. The Canaanites of Shechem took money from their temple to provide means for Abimelech's enterprise, when they resolved to make him their king; and the sacred treasure of Jerusalem, originally derived from the fruits of David's campaigns, was used by his successors as a reserve fund available in great emergencies. On the whole, then, it is evident that the difference between holy things and common things does not originally turn on ownership, as if common things belonged to men and holy things to the gods. Indeed there are many holy things which are also private property, images, for example, and the other appurtenances of domestic sanctuaries.

Thus far it would appear that the rights of the gods in holy places and things fall short of ownership, because they do not exclude a right of user or even of property by man in the same things. But in other directions the prerogatives of the gods, in respect of that which is holy, go beyond what is involved in ownership. The approach to ancient sanctuaries was surrounded by restrictions which cannot be regarded as designed to protect the property of the gods, but rather fall under the notion that they will not tolerate the vicinity of certain persons (*e.g.* such as are physically unclean) and certain actions (*e.g.* the shedding of blood). Nay, in many cases the assertion of a man's undoubted rights as against a fugitive at the sanctuary is regarded as an encroachment on its holiness; justice cannot strike the criminal, and a master cannot recover his runaway slave, who has found asylum on holy soil. In the Old Testament the legal right of asylum is limited to the case of involuntary homicide;[1] but the wording of the law shows that this was a narrowing of ancient custom, and many heathen sanctuaries of the Phœnicians and Syrians retained even in Roman times what seems to have ★ been an unlimited right of asylum.[2] At certain Arabian

---

[1] Ex. xxi. 13, 14. Here the right of asylum belongs to all altars, but it was afterwards limited, on the abolition of the local altars, to certain old sanctuaries—the cities of refuge (Deut. xix.).

[2] This follows especially from the account in Tacitus, *Ann.* iii. 60 *sqq.*, of the inquiry made by Tiberius into abuses of the right of asylum. Among the holy places to which the right was confirmed after due investigation were Paphos and Amathus, both of them Phœnician sanctuaries. The asylum at the temple of Melcarth at Tyre is mentioned by Diodorus, xvii. 41. 8. There was also a right of asylum at Daphne near Antioch (Strabo, xvi. 2. 6; 2 Macc. iv. 33), and many Phœnician and Syrian towns are designated as asylums on their coins; see Head, *Hist. Num.*, Index iv., under ΑΣΥΛΟΣ and ΙΕΡΑΣ ΑΣΥΛΟΥ. The Heracleum at the fishcuring station near the Canobic mouth of the Nile (Herod. ii. 113) may also be cited, for its name and place leave little doubt that it was a Phœnician temple. Here the fugitive slave was dedicated by being tattooed with sacred marks—a Semitic custom; cf. Lucian, *Dea Syria*, lix., and *Aghāni,*

sanctuaries the god gave shelter to all fugitives without distinction, and even stray or stolen cattle that reached the holy ground could not be reclaimed by their owners.[1] What was done with these animals is not stated; possibly they enjoyed the same liberty as the consecrated camels which the Arabs, for various reasons, were accustomed to release from service and suffer to roam at large. These camels seem to be sometimes spoken of as the property of the deity,[2] but they were not used for his service. Their consecration was simply a limitation of man's right to use them.[3]

We have here another indication that the relations of holiness to the institution of property are mainly negative. Holy places and things are not so much reserved for the use of the god as surrounded by a network of restrictions and disabilities which forbid them to be used by men except in particular ways, and in certain cases forbid them to be used at all. As a rule the restrictions are such as to prevent the appropriation of holy things by men, and

vii. 110, l. 26, where an Arab patron stamps his clients with his camel mark. I owe the last reference to Prof. de Goeje.

[1] Yācūt, *s.v. Jalsad* and *Fals*; Wellhausen, pp. 52–54.

[2] See the verse from Ibn Hishām, p. 58, explained by Wellh. p. 107. The grounds on which Wellhausen concludes that these consecrated camels formed a sacred herd grazing on the holy pasture of the god are not quite satisfactory. The story in Mofaḍḍal, *Amthāl*, p. 19, shows that sometimes at least they remained with their old herd; and this agrees best with the statement of the Arabian philologists.

[3] *E.g.* their milk might be drunk only by guests (Ibn Hishām, p. 58). Similarly, consecration sometimes meant no more than that men might eat the flesh but not women, or that only particular persons might eat of it (Sura, vi. 139 *sq.*). Above all, the consecrated camel might not be ridden, whence the name *ḥāmī*. It is recorded on the authority of Laith (*Lisān*, xix. 341) that in certain cases the back of the camel was so injured that it could not be ridden; but this certainly was not the universal rule, for in an emergency a man mounts a sacred camel to pursue robbers (Mofaḍḍal, *Amthāl*. p. 19; Freytag, *Ar. Provv.* i. 352). The *immissio hirudinum in tergum* (Rasmussen, *Add.* p. 70) is only a corruption of what Laith tells. In Rasmussen's text read اغلتی for اعلتی, and سناسن for سنا من, in accordance with the *Lisān*, xix. 341, l. 20 *sq.* (see We. 114 n. 1).

sometimes they cancel existing rights of property. But they do so only by limiting the right of user, and in the case of objects like idols, which no one would propose to use except for sacred purposes, a thing may be holy and still be private property. From this point of view it would appear that common things are such as men have licence to use freely at their own good pleasure without fear of supernatural penalties, while holy things may be used only in prescribed ways and under definite restrictions, on pain of the anger of the gods. That holiness is essentially a restriction on the licence of man in the free use of natural things, seems to be confirmed by the Semitic roots used to express the idea. No stress can be laid on the root קדש, which is that commonly used by the northern Semites, for of this the original meaning is very uncertain, though there is some probability that it implies "separation" or "withdrawal." But the root חרם, which is mainly employed in Arabic but runs through the whole Semitic field, undoubtedly conveys the notion of prohibition, so that a sacred thing is one which, whether absolutely or in certain relations, is prohibited to human use.[1] The same idea of prohibition or interdiction associated with that of protection from encroachment is found in the root חמי, from which is derived the word *ḥimā,* denoting a sacred enclosure or *temenos.*[2]

We have already found reason to think that in Arabia

---

[1] In Hebrew this root is mainly applied to such consecration as implies absolute separation from human use and association, *i.e.* the total destruction of an accursed thing, or in more modern times excommunication. Somewhat similar is the sense of *ḥarām* in the Arabic form of oath "*ana ḥarāmum in . . .,*" *Agh.* xix. 27. 18.

[2] Hence perhaps the name of Hamath on the Orontes; Lagarde, *Bildung der Nomina,* p. 156. The primary sense of the root, as Nöldeke has remarked, is "to watch over," whence in Palestinian Aramaic it comes to be the usual word for "to see," while in Hebrew again the word חומה, "a wall," is derived from it.

the holiness· of places is older than the institution of
property in land, and the view of holiness that has just
been set forth enables us to understand why it should be
so. We have found that from the earliest times of savagery
certain spots were dreaded and shunned as the haunts of
supernatural beings. These, however, are not holy places
any more than an enemy's ground is holy; they are not
hedged round by definite restrictions, but altogether avoided
as full of indefinite dangers. But when men establish
relations with the powers that haunt a spot, it is at once
necessary that there should be rules of conduct towards
them and their surroundings. These rules moreover have
two aspects. On the one hand, the god and his worshippers
form a single community—primarily, let us suppose, a
community of kinship—and so all the social laws that
regulate men's conduct towards a clansman are applicable
to their relations to the god. But, on the other hand, the
god has natural relations to certain physical things, and
these must be respected also; he has himself a natural life
and natural habits in which he must not be molested.
Moreover the mysterious superhuman powers of the god—
the powers which we call supernatural—are manifested,
according to primitive ideas, in and through his physical
life, so that every place and thing which has natural
associations with the god is regarded, if I may borrow a
metaphor from electricity, as charged with divine energy
and ready at any moment to discharge itself to the destruction of the man who presumes to approach it unduly.
Hence in all their dealings with natural things men must
be on their guard to respect the divine prerogative, and
this they are able to do by knowing and observing the
rules of holiness, which prescribe definite restrictions and
limitations in their dealings with the god and all natural
things that in any way pertain to the god. Thus we see

that holiness is not necessarily limited to things that are the property of the deity to the exclusion of men ; it applies equally to things in which both gods and men have an interest, and in the latter case the rules of holiness are directed to regulate man's use of the holy thing in such a way that the godhead may not be offended or wronged.

Rules of holiness in the sense just explained, *i.e.* a system of restrictions on man's arbitrary use of natural things, enforced by the dread of supernatural penalties,[1] are found among all primitive peoples.   It is convenient to have a distinct name for this primitive institution, to mark it off from the later developments of the idea of holiness in advanced religions, and for this purpose the Polynesian term *taboo* has been selected.[2]   The field covered by taboos among savage and half-savage races is very wide, for there is no part of life in which the savage does not feel himself to be surrounded by mysterious agencies and recognise the need of walking warily.   Moreover all taboos do not belong to religion proper, that is, they are not always rules of conduct for the regulation of man's contact with deities that, when taken in the right way, may be counted on as friendly, but rather appear in many cases to be precautions against the approach of malignant enemies—against contact with evil spirits and the like.   Thus alongside of taboos that exactly correspond to rules of holiness, protecting the inviolability of idols and sanctuaries, priests and chiefs, and generally of all persons and things pertaining to the gods and their worship, we find another kind of taboo which in

[1] Sometimes by civil penalties also.   For in virtue of its solidarity the whole community is compromised by the impiety of any one of its members, and is concerned to purge away the offence.

[2] A good account of taboo, with references to the best sources of informa-
tion on the subject, is given by Mr. J. G. Frazer in the 9th ed. of the *Encycl. Britan.* vol. xxiii. p. 15 *sqq.*

the Semitic field has its parallel in rules of uncleanness. Women after child-birth, men who have touched a dead body and so forth, are temporarily taboo and separated from human society, just as the same persons are unclean in Semitic religion. In these cases the person under taboo is not regarded as holy, for he is separated from approach to the sanctuary as well as from contact with men; but his act or condition is somehow associated with supernatural dangers, arising, according to the common savage explanation, from the presence of formidable spirits which are shunned like an infectious disease. In most savage societies no sharp line seems to be drawn between the two kinds of taboo just indicated, and even in more advanced nations the notions of holiness and uncleanness often touch. Among the Syrians, for example, swine's flesh was taboo, but it was an open question whether this was because the animal was holy or because it was unclean.[1] But though not precise, the distinction between what is holy and what is unclean is real; in rules of holiness the motive is respect for the gods, in rules of uncleanness it is primarily fear of an unknown or hostile power, though ultimately, as we see in the Levitical legislation, the law of clean and unclean may be brought within the sphere of divine ordinances, on the view that uncleanness is hateful to God and must be avoided by all that have to do with Him.

The fact that all the Semites have rules of uncleanness as well as rules of holiness, that the boundary between the two is often vague, and that the former as well as the latter present the most startling agreement in point of detail with savage *taboos*,[2] leaves no reasonable doubt as to the origin and ultimate relations of the idea of holiness.

[1] Lucian, *Dea Syr.* liv.; cf. Antiphanes, *ap.* Athen. iii. p. 95 [Meineke, *Fr. Com. Gr.* iii. 68].
[2] See *Additional Note* B, *Holiness, Uncleanness, and Taboo.*

On the other hand, the fact that the Semites—or at least the northern Semites—distinguish between the holy and the unclean, marks a real advance above savagery. All taboos are inspired by awe of the supernatural, but there is a great moral difference between precautions against the invasion of mysterious hostile powers and precautions founded on respect for the prerogative of a friendly god. The former belong to magical superstition—the barrenest of all aberrations of the savage imagination—which, being founded only on fear, acts merely as a bar to progress and an impediment to the free use of nature by human energy and industry. But the restrictions on individual licence which are due to respect for a known and friendly power allied to man, however trivial and absurd they may appear to us in their details, contain within them germinant principles of social progress and moral order. To know that one has the mysterious powers of nature on one's side so long as one acts in conformity with certain rules, gives a man strength and courage to pursue the task of the subjugation of nature to his service. To restrain one's individual licence, not out of slavish fear, but from respect for a higher and beneficent power, is a moral discipline of which the value does not altogether depend on the reasonableness of the sacred restrictions; an English schoolboy is subject to many unreasonable taboos, which are not without value in the formation of character. But finally, and above all, the very association of the idea of holiness with a beneficent deity, whose own interests are bound up with the interests of the community, makes it inevitable that the laws of social and moral order, as well as mere external precepts of physical observance, shall be placed under the sanction of the god of the community. Breaches of social order are recognised as offences against the holiness of the deity, and the development of law and morals is made

possible, at a stage when human sanctions are still wanting,
or too imperfectly administered to have much power, by
the belief that the restrictions on human licence which
are necessary to social well-being are conditions imposed
by the god for the maintenance of a good understanding
between himself and his worshippers.

As every sanctuary was protected by rigid taboos it
was important that its site and limits should be clearly
marked.   From the account already given of the origin of
holy places, it follows that in very many cases the natural
features of the spot were sufficient to distinguish it.   A
fountain with its margin of rich vegetation, a covert of
jungle haunted by lions, a shaggy glade on the mountain-
side, a solitary eminence rising from the desert, where
toppling blocks of weather-beaten granite concealed the
dens of the hyæna and the bear, needed only the support
of tradition to bear witness for themselves to their own
sanctity.   In such cases it was natural to draw the border
of the holy ground somewhat widely, and to allow an
ample verge on all sides of the sacred centre.   In Arabia,
as we have seen, the _ḥimā_ sometimes enclosed a great tract
of pasture land roughly marked off by pillars or cairns,
and the _ḥaram_ or sacred territory of Mecca extends for
some hours' journey on almost every side of the city.
The whole mountain of Horeb was sacred ground, and so
probably was Mount Hermon, for its name means "holy,"
and the summit and slopes still bear the ruins of many
temples.[1]   In like manner Renan concludes from the
multitude of sacred remains along the course of the
Adonis, in the Lebanon, that the whole valley was a
kind of sacred territory of the god from whom the river
had its name.[2]   In a cultivated and thickly-peopled land

---

[1] For the sanctity of Hermon see further Reland, _Palæstina_, p. 323.   ★
[2] Renan, _Mission de Phénicie_ (1864), p. 295.

it was difficult to maintain a rigid rule of sanctity over a wide area, and strict taboos were necessarily limited to the temples and their immediate enclosures, while in a looser sense the whole city or land of the god's worshippers was held to be the god's land and to participate in his holiness. Yet some remains of the old sanctity of whole regions survived even in Syria to a late date. Iamblichus, in the last days of heathenism, still speaks of Mount Carmel as " sacred above all mountains and forbidden of access to the vulgar," and here Vespasian worshipped at the solitary altar, embowered in inviolable thickets, to which ancient tradition forbade the adjuncts of temple and image.[1]

The taboos or restrictions applicable within the wide limits of these greater sacred tracts have already been touched upon. The most universal of them was that men were not allowed to interfere with the natural life of the spot. No blood might be shed and no tree cut down; an obvious rule whether these living things are regarded as the protected associates of the god, or—which perhaps was the earlier conception—as participating in the divine life. In some cases all access to the Arabian ḥimā was forbidden, as at the sacred tract marked off round the grave of Ibn Ṭofail.[2] For with the Arabs grave and sanctuary were

[1] Iamblichus, *Vit. Pyth.* iii. (15); Tacitus, *Hist.* ii. 78. From 1 Kings xviii. it would be clear, apart from the classical testimonies, that Carmel was a sacred mountain of the Phœnicians. It had also an altar of Jehovah, and this made it the fit place for the contest between Jehovah-worship and Baal-worship. Carmel is still clothed with thickets as it was in Old Testament times (Amos i. 2 ; Mic. vii. 14 ; Cant. vii. 5) ; and Amos ix. 3, Mic. vii. 14, where its woods appear as a place of refuge, do not receive their full force till we combine them with Iamblichus's notice that the mountain was an ἄβατον, where the flocks, driven up into the forest in autumn to feed on the leaves (as is still done, Thomson, *Land and Book* [1860], pp. 204 *sq.*, 485), were inviolable, and where the fugitive found a sure asylum. The sanctity of Carmel is even now not extinct, and the scene at the Festival of Elijah, described by Seetzen, ii. 96 *sq.*, is exactly like an old Canaanite feast.

[2] *Agh.* xv. 139 ; Wellh. p. 184. This is not the place to go into the

kindred ideas, and famous chiefs and heroes were honoured ★
by the consecration of their resting-place. But an absolute
exclusion of human visitors, while not unintelligible at a
tomb, could hardly be maintained at a sanctuary which
contained a place of worship, and we have seen that some
himās were open pastures, while the *haram* at Mecca even
contained a large permanent population.[1] The tendency
was evidently to a gradual relaxation of burdensome restrictions, not necessarily because religious reverence declined,
but from an increasing confidence that the god was his
servants' well-wisher and did not press his prerogative
unduly. Yet the "jealousy" of the deity—an idea
familiar to us from the Old Testament—was never lost
sight of in Semitic worship. In the higher forms of
religion this quality, which nearly corresponds to self-
respect and the sense of personal dignity in a man, readily
lent itself to an ethical interpretation, so that the jealousy
of the deity was mainly conceived to be indignation against
wrong-doing, as an offence against the honour of the
divine sovereign;[2] but in savage times the personal

general question of the worship of ancestors. See Wellhausen, *ut supra*;
Goldziher, *Culte des Ancêtres chez les Arabes* (Paris, 1885), and *Muh. Studien*,
p. 229 *sqq.*; and some remarks, perhaps too sceptical, in my *Kinship*,
p. 20, n. 2.

[1] Yācūt, iii. 790 (We. p. 105 *sq.*, cf. p. 43), says that marks, called "scare-
crows" (*akhyila*), were set up to show that a place was a *himā*, and must not
be approached. But to "approach" a forbidden thing (*cariba*) is the
general word for violating a taboo, so the expression ought not perhaps to
be pressed too closely. The Greek ἄβατον is also used simply in the sense of
inviolable (along with ἄσυλον). It is notable, however, that in the same
passage Yācūt tells us that two of the marks that defined the *himā* of Faid
were called "the twin sacrificial stones" (*ghariyān*). He did not know the
ritual meaning of *ghariy*, and may therefore include them among the
akhyila by mere inadvertence. But if the place of sacrifice really stood on the
border of the sacred ground, the inevitable inference is that the worshippers
were not allowed to enter the enclosure. This would be parallel to the
sacrifice in Ex. xxiv. 4, where the altar is built outside the limits of
Sinai, and the people are not allowed to approach the mountain.

[2] This, it will be remembered, is the idea on which Anselm's theory of the
atonement is based.

diginity of the god, like that of a great chief, asserts itself mainly in punctilious insistence on a complicated etiquette that surrounds his place and person. Naturally the strictness of the etiquette admits of gradations. When the god and his worshippers live side by side, as in the case of Mecca, or still more in cases where the idea of holiness has been extended to cover the whole land of a particular religion, the general laws of sacred observance, applicable in all parts of the holy land, are modified by practical considerations. Strict taboos are limited to the sanctuary (in the narrower sense) or to special seasons and occasions, such as religious festivals or the time of war; in ordinary life necessary actions that constitute a breach of ceremonial holiness merely involve temporary uncleanness and some ceremonial act of purification, or else are condoned altogether provided they are done in a particular way. Thus in Canaan, where the whole land was holy, the hunter was allowed to kill game if he returned the life to the god by pouring it on the ground; or again the intercourse of the sexes, which was strictly forbidden at temples and to warriors on an expedition, entailed in ordinary life only a temporary impurity, purged by ablution or fumigation.[1] But in all this care was taken not to presume on the prerogative of the gods, or trench without permission on the sanctity of their domain; and in particular, fresh encroachments on untouched parts of nature—the breaking up of waste lands, the foundation of new cities, or even the annual cutting down of corn or gathering in of the vintage—were not undertaken without special precautions to propitiate the divine powers. It was felt that such encroachments were not without grave danger, and it was often thought necessary to accompany them with expiatory

[1] See *Additional Note* C, *Taboos on the Intercourse of the Sexes.*

ceremonies of the most solemn kind.[1] Within the god's
holy land all parts of life are regulated with constant
regard to his sanctity, and so among the settled Semites,
who live on Baal's ground, religion entered far more
deeply into common life than was the case among the Arabs,
where only special tracts were consecrated land and the wide
desert was as yet unclaimed either by gods or by men.

Some of the restrictions enforced at ancient sanctuaries
have already been touched upon ; but it will repay us to
look at them again more closely under the new light which
falls upon the subject as soon as we recognise that all
such restrictions are ultimately of the nature of taboos.
The simplest and most universal of these taboos is that
which protects the trees of the *temenos* or *ḥimā*, and all
the natural life of the spot.   In the more advanced forms
of Semitic religion the natural wood of the sanctuary is
sometimes represented as planted by the god,[2] which would

---

[1] The details, so far as they are concerned with the yearly recurring ritual
of harvest and vintage, belong to the subject of Agricultural Feasts, and
must be reserved for a future course of lectures.   The danger connected with
the breaking up of waste lands is illustrated for Arabia by the story of
Ḥarb and Mirdās (*supra*, p. 133).   Here the danger still comes from the
jinn of the place, but even where the whole land already belongs to a
friendly deity, precautions are necessary when man lays his hand for the
first time on any of the good things of nature.   Thus the Hebrews ate the
fruit of new trees only in the fifth year ; in the fourth year the fruit was
consecrated to Jehovah, but the produce of the first three years was "uncircumcised," *i.e.* taboo, and might not be eaten at all (Lev. xix. 23 *sqq.*).   A
similar idea underlies the Syrian traditions of human sacrifice at the foundation of cities (Malalas, Bonn ed. pp. 37, 200, 203), which are not the less
instructive that they are not historically true.   In Arabia the local *jinn* or
earth-demons (*ahl al-arḍ*) are still propitiated by sprinkling the blood
of a sacrifice when new land is broken up, a new house built, or a new well
opened (Doughty, i. 136, ii. 100, 198).   Kremer, *Studien*, p. 48, cites a
passage from Abū ʿObaida, *ap.* Damīrī, i. 241, which shows that such
sacrifices to the *jinn* follow an ancient custom, forbidden by the prophet.

[2] The cypresses at Daphne were planted by Heracles (Malalas, p. 204) ;
cf. Ps. civ. 16.

of course give him a right of property in it. But for the most part the phenomena of tree and grove worship, of which we shall learn more in Lect. V., point to a more ancient conception, in which the vegetation of the sanctuary is conceived as actually instinct with a particle of divine life. Equally widespread, and to all appearance equally primitive, is the rule exempting the birds, deer and other game of the sanctuary from molestation.[1] These wild creatures must have been regarded as the guests or clients rather than the property of the god, for Semitic law recognises no property in *feræ naturæ.* But in the oldest law the client is only an artificial kinsman, whose rights are constituted by a ceremony importing that he and his patron are henceforth of one blood ; and thus it is probable that, in the beginning, the beasts and birds of the sanctuary, as well as its vegetation, were conceived as holy because they partook of the pervasive divine life. We may conceive the oldest sanctuaries as charged in all their parts and pertinents with a certain supernatural energy. This is the usual savage idea about things that are *taboo,* and even in the higher religions the process of subsuming all taboos under the conception of the holiness of the personal god is always slow and often imperfectly carried out. In particular there is one main element in the doctrine of *taboo,* perfectly irrational from the standpoint of any religion that has clear views as to the

---

[1] The cases of Mecca and Wajj have already been cited ; for the former compare the verses in Ibn Hishām, p. 74, ll. 10, 11. Birds found sanctuary at the temple of Jerusalem (Ps. lxxxiv. 3). At Curium in Cyprus, where religion is full of Semitic elements, dogs did not venture to follow game into the sacred grove, but stood outside barking (Aelian, *N. A.* xi. 7), and the same belief prevailed in the Middle Ages with regard to the mosque and tomb of Ṣiddīcā (Al-Shajara) in the mountains E. of Sidon (Mocaddasī, p. 188). In the sacred island of Icarus in the Persian Gulf the wild goats and gazelles might be taken for sacrifice only (Arrian, vii. 20) ; or, according to Aelian (*N. A.* xi. 9), the huntsman had to ask permission of the goddess ; otherwise the hunt proved vain and a penalty was incurred.

personality of the gods, which was never eliminated from the Semitic conception of holiness, and figures even in the ritual parts of the Old Testament. Holiness, like taboo, is conceived as infectious, propagating itself by physical con-tact. To avoid complicating the present argument by a multitude of details, I reserve the full illustration of this matter for a note,[1] and confine myself to the observation that even in Hebrew ritual common things brought into contact with things very sacred are themselves "sanctified," so that they can be no longer used for common purposes. In some cases it is provided that this inconvenient sanctity may be washed out and purged away by a ceremonial process; in others the consecration is indelible, and the thing has to be destroyed. In the Old Testament these are mere fragmentary survivals of old rules of sanctity; and the details are to some extent peculiar. The idea that things which fall under a taboo, and so are withdrawn from common use, must be destroyed, is far more prominent among the Hebrews than among other Semites; but the general principle applies to all Semitic religions, and at once explains most of the special taboos applicable to sanctuaries, e.g. the right of asylum, the forfeiture of camels that stray on holy ground, and the Meccan rule that strangers who worship at the Caaba in their common dress must leave it behind them at the door of the sanctuary. All such rules are governed by the principle that common things brought into contact with the holy place become holy and inviolable, like the original pertinents of the sanctuary. Naturally this principle admits of many varieties in detail. Holiness acquired by contact is not so indelible as inborn sanctity. In many rituals it can be removed from clothes by washing them, and from the person of a worshipper by ablution. As a rule the con-

[1] See *Additional Note* B, *Holiness, Uncleanness, and Taboo.*

II

secration of persons by holy things is only temporary; thus
the Syrian who touched a dove, the holiest of birds, was
taboo for a single day, and at most ancient asylums the
fugitive was no longer inviolable when he left the sacred
precincts (Num. xxxv. 26 *sq.*).

The ultimate sanction of these rules lay in the intrinsic
power of holy things to vindicate themselves against encroachment; or according to the higher heathenism in the
jealousy of the personal god, who resents all undue violation
of his environment.   But when the rules were once established, they tended to maintain themselves without the
constant intervention of supernatural sanctions by the
action of ordinary social forces.   A bold man might
venture to violate a taboo and take his risk of supernatural danger; but if his comrades were not equally bold
they would immediately shun him lest the danger should
spread to them.[1]   On this principle most ancient societies
attached the penalty of outlawry or death to impious
offences, such as the violation of holy things, without
waiting for the god to vindicate his own cause.[2]   The
argument of Joash, "If he be a god, let him plead for
himself, because one hath cast down his altar," does not
commend itself to a firm faith.   The deity is not put to
such a proof till his power begins to be doubted.[3]   The

---

[1] Cf. the case of Achan, Josh. vi. 18, vii. 1, 11 *sq.*, where Achan's breach
of a taboo involves the whole host.

[2] Cf. Lev. xx. 4, 5; if the people of the land do not slay the impious
person, Jehovah will destroy him and all his clan.   In the Pentateuch it is
sometimes difficult to decide whether the penalty invoked on impious
offences is civil or supernatural, *e.g.* Lev. xvii. 4, xix. 8.

[3] Judg. vi. 31. An Arabian parallel in Ibn Hishām, p. 303 *sq.*—
'Amr's domestic idol has been repeatedly defiled by unknown Moslems.
At length the owner girds the god with a sword, and bids him defend himself if he is good for anything.   Of course conversion follows.   Similarly in
Yācūt, iii. 912 *sq.*, a daring man reclaims a stolen camel from the sanctuary
of Al-Fals. A bystander exclaims, "Wait and see what will happen to him
this very day!"; when several days pass and nothing happens, he renounces

principle that it is not safe to wait till the god vindicates his own holiness, has enormous historical importance as one of the chief bases of early criminal law.   In the oldest type of society impious acts or breaches of taboo were the only offences treated as crimes; *e.g.* there is no such crime as theft, but a man can save his property from invasion by placing it under a taboo, when it becomes an act of impiety to touch it.[1]   Among the Hebrews such taboos are created by means of a curse (Judg. xvii. 2), and by the same means a king can give validity to the most unreasonable decrees (1 Sam. xiv. 24 *sqq.*).   But unreasonable taboos, as we see in the case of Saul and Jonathan, are sure to be evaded in the long run because public opinion goes against them, whereas taboos that make for the general good and check wrong-doing are supported and enforced by the community, and ultimately pass into laws with a civil sanction.   But no ancient society deemed its good order to be sufficiently secured by civil sanctions alone; there was always a last recourse to the curse, the ordeal, the oath of probation at the sanctuary—all of them means to stamp an offender with the guilt of impiety and

---

idols and becomes a Christian. I suspect that in Judg. vi. the original text expressed a similar belief that the god's vengeance must fall on the very day of the offence. The clause אשר יריב לו יומת עד הבקר gives a very unsuitable sense. But the true Septuagint text (which in this book is better represented by A than by B) indicates a reading בו for כי. Accepting this and reading ימות (which in the old orthography is not distinguished for יומת) we get good sense: "The man who strives with the Baal dies before (the next) morning." The common belief was that supernatural judgments came swiftly on the offence, or not at all. That Jehovah does not overlook sin because He is long-suffering and gives time for repentance (Ex. xxxiv. 6, 7), is one of the distinctive points of O. T. doctrine which the prophets had special difficulty in impressing on their hearers.

[1] I believe that in early society (and not merely in the very earliest) we may safely affirm that every offence to which death or outlawry is attached was primarily viewed as a breach of holiness; *e.g.* murder within the kin, and incest, are breaches of the holiness of tribal blood, which would be ★ supernaturally avenged if men overlooked them.

bring him under the direct judgment of the supernatural powers.

Very noteworthy, in this connection, is the representation in Deut. xxvii., Josh. viii. 30 *sqq.*, according to which the Israelites, on their first entry into Canaan, placed a number of the chief heads of public morality under the protection of a solemn taboo by a great act of public cursing. I use the word taboo deliberately as implying a more mechanical sequence of sin and punishment than we associate with the idea of divine judgment ; ⋆ see the description of the operation of the curse in Zech. v. 1–4.[1]

[1] Among the Arabs the operation of a curse is purely mechanical ; if a man falls on his face it may pass over him ; see Wellhausen[1], p. 126. For the oath of purgation among the Arabs, see *Kinship*, p. 64 and note ; among the Hebrews, Deut. xxi. 7 and Num. v. 11 *sq.*, where the connection with very primitive ideas of taboo is unmistakable (cf. p. 180, *infra*). A late Syriac survival of the use of a curse to protect (or perhaps to create) an exclusive right of property (as in Judg. xvii. 2) is found in Jacob of Edessa, *Qu.* 47, "concerning a priest who writes a curse and hangs it on a tree that no man may eat of the fruit." Various examples of the operation of a curse to vindicate rights of property, etc., in the lawless society of Arabia before Islam are collected in *Div. Hodh.* No. 245, in the form of anecdotes of the Times of Ignorance related to the Caliph ' Omar I. Omar observes that God granted temporal judgments, in answer to prayer, when there was no knowledge of a future state ; but in Islam divine retribution is reserved for the day of judgment.

LECTURE V

SANCTUARIES, NATURAL AND ARTIFICIAL. HOLY WATERS, TREES, CAVES, AND STONES

WE have seen that holiness admits of degrees, and that within a sacred land or tract it is natural to mark off an inner circle of intenser holiness, where all ritual restrictions are stringently enforced, and where man feels himself to be nearer to his god than on other parts even of holy ground. Such a spot of intenser holiness becomes the sanctuary or place of sacrifice, where the worshipper approaches the god with prayers and gifts, and seeks guidance for life from the divine oracle. As holy tracts in general are the regions haunted by divine powers, so the site of the sanctuary *par excellence*, or place of worship, is a spot where the god is constantly present in some visible embodiment, or which has received a special consecration by some extraordinary manifestation of deity. For the more developed forms of cultus a mere vague *himā* does not suffice; men require a special point at which they may come together and do sacrifice with the assurance that the god is present at the act. In Arabia, indeed, it seems to be not incredible that certain sacrifices were simply laid on sacred ground to be devoured by wild beasts. But even in Arabia the *himā* usually, probably always, contained a fixed point where the blood of the offering was directly presented to the deity by being applied to sacred stones, or where a sacred tree was hung with gifts. In

the ordinary forms of heathenism, at any rate, it was
essential that the worshipper should bring his offering
into the actual presence of the god, or into contact with
the symbol of that presence.[1]

The symbol or permanent visible object, at and through
which the worshipper came into direct contact with the
god, was not lacking in any Semitic place of worship, but
had not always the same form, and was sometimes a
natural object, sometimes an artificial erection. The usual
natural symbols are a fountain or a tree, while the
ordinary artificial symbol is a pillar or pile of stones;
but very often all three are found together, and this was
the rule in the more developed sanctuaries, particular
sacred observances being connected with each.

The choice of the natural symbols, the fountain and
the tree, is no doubt due in part to the fact that the
favourite haunts of animate life, to which a superstitious
reverence was attached, are mainly found beside wood and
running water. But besides this we have found evidence
of the direct ascription to trees and living waters of a life
analogous to man's, but mysterious and therefore awful.[2]
To us this may seem to be quite another point of view;
in the one case the fountain or the tree merely marks
the spot which the deity frequents, in the other it is
the visible embodiment of the divine presence. But
the primitive imagination has no difficulty in combining
different ideas about the same holy place or thing. The
gods are not tied to one form of embodiment or manifestation; for, as has already been observed,[3] some sort
of distinction between life and the material embodiment

---

[1] This rule is observed even when the god is a heavenly body. The
sacrifices of the Saracens to the morning star, described by Nilus, were celebrated when that star rose, and could not be made after it was lost to sight
on the rising of the sun (*Nili op. quædam* [Paris, 1639], pp. 28, 117).

[2] *Supra*, p. 135 *sqq.*   [3] *Supra*, pp. 86, 87.

of life is suggested to the rudest peoples by phenomena
like those of dreams.   Even men, it is supposed, can
change their embodiment, and assume for a time the
shape of wolves or birds ;[1] and of course the gods with
their superior powers have a still greater range, and the
same deity may quite well manifest himself in the life
of a tree or a spring, and yet emerge from time to time
in human or animal form.   All manifestations of life at
or about a holy place readily assume a divine character
and form a religious unity, contributing as they do to
create and nourish the same religious emotion ; and in all
of them the godhead is felt to be present in the same
direct way.   The permanent manifestations of his presence,
however, the sacred fountain and the sacred tree, are likely
to hold the first place in acts of worship, simply because
they are permanent and so attach to themselves a fixed
sacred tradition.   These considerations apply equally to
the sanctuaries of nomadic and of settled peoples, but among
the latter the religious importance of water and wood
could not fail to be greatly reinforced by the growth of
the ideas of Baal-worship, in which the deity as the giver
of life is specially connected with quickening waters and
vegetative growth.   ★

    With this it agrees that sacred wells, in connection
with sanctuaries, are found in all parts of the Semitic area,
but are less prominent among the nomadic Arabs than
among the agricultural peoples of Syria and Palestine.
There is mention of fountains or streams at a good many
Arabian sanctuaries, but little direct evidence that these
waters were holy, or played any definite part in the ritual.
The clearest case is that of Mecca, where the holiness of
the well Zamzam is certainly pre-Islamic.   It would even
seem that in old time gifts were cast into it, as they were

---

[1] *Supra*, pp. 87, 88.

cast into the sacred wells of the northern Semites.[1] Some
kind of ritual holiness seems also to have attached to the
pool beneath a waterfall at the Dausite sanctuary of
Dusares.[2] Again, as healing springs and sacred springs
are everywhere identified, it is noteworthy that the south
Arabs regard medicinal waters as inhabited by *jinn*, usually
of serpent form,[3] and that the water of the sanctuary at
the Palmetum was thought to be health-giving, and was
carried home by pilgrims[4] as Zamzam water now is. In
like manner the custom of pilgrims carrying away water
from the well of ʿOrwa[5] is probably a relic of ancient
sanctity. Further, on the borders of the Arabian field, we
have the sacred fountain of Ephca at Palmyra, with which
a legend of a demon in serpent form is still connected.
This is a sulphurous spring, which had a guardian

[1] So Wellhausen, p. 103, concludes with probability from the story that
when the well was rediscovered and cleaned out by the grandfather of
Mohammed, two golden gazelles and a number of swords were found in it.
Everything told of the prophet's ancestors must be received with caution,
but this does not look like invention. The two golden gazelles are parallel
to the golden camels of Sabæan and Nabatæan inscriptions (*ZDMG*. xxxviii.
143 *sq.*).

[2] Ibn Hishām, p. 253 ; Wellhausen, p. 48 *sq.* A woman who adopts
Islam breaks with the heathen god by " purifying herself " in this pool. This
implies that her act was a breach of the ritual of the spot ; presumably a
woman who required purification (viz. from her courses) was not admitted to
the sacred water ; cf. Yācūt, i. 657, l. 2 *sqq.*; iv. 651, l. 4 *sqq.*; Ibn Hishām,
p. 15 ult. In Ṭabarī, i. 271 *sq.*, we read that the water of Beersheba shrank
when a woman in her courses drew from it. Cf. also Bērūnī, *Chron.* p. 246,
l. 8 *sqq.* Under ordinary circumstances to bathe in the sacred spring would
be an act of homage to the heathen god : so at least it was in Syria.

[3] Mordtmann in *ZDMG*. xxxviii. 587, cites a modern instance from
Maltzan, *Reise in Südarabien*, p. 304, and others from Hamdānī's *Iklīl*, *ap.*
Müller, *Burgen*, i. 34. Maltzan's spring, the hot well of Msaʿide, has every
feature of an ancient sanctuary except that the serpent-god, who is invoked
as Msaʿud, and sends hot or cold water at the prayer of the worshipper, has
been degraded to the rank of a demon. There is an annual pilgrimage to
the spot in the month Rajab, the ancient sacred month of Arabia, which
is accompanied by festivities and lasts for several days.

[4] Agatharchides, *ap.* Diod. Sic. iii. 43.

[5] Yācūt, i. 434; Cazwīnī, i. 200.

appointed by the god Yarhibol, and on an inscription ★
is called the " blessed fountain." [1]   Again, in the desert
beyond Bostra, we find the Stygian waters, where a great
cleft received a lofty cataract.   The waters had the power
to swallow up or cast forth the gifts flung into them, as a
sign that the god was or was not propitious, and the oath
by the spot and its stream was the most horrible known
to the inhabitants of the region.[2]   The last two cases
belong to a region in which religion was not purely
Arabian in character, but the Stygian waters recall the
waterfall in the Dausite sanctuary of Dusares, and
Ptolemy twice mentions a Stygian fountain in Arabia
proper.

Among the northern Semites, the agricultural Canaanites and Syrians, sacred waters hold a much more prominent
place.   Where all ground watered by fountains and streams,
without the aid of man's hand, was regarded as the Baal's
land, a certain sanctity could hardly fail to be ascribed to
every source of living water ; and where the divine
activity was looked upon as mainly displaying itself in
the quickening of the soil, the waters which gave fertility
to the land, and so life to its inhabitants, would appear
to be the direct embodiment of divine energies.   Accordingly we find that Hannibal, in his covenant with Philip
of Macedon, when he swears before all the deities of
Carthage and of Hellas, includes among the divine powers
to which his oath appeals " the sun the moon and the
earth, rivers, meadows (?) and waters." [3]   Thus when we ★
find that temples were so often erected near springs and

---

[1] Wadd., No. 2571 *c*; De Vog., No. 95.   For the modern serpent myth
see Mordtmann, *ut supra* ; Blunt, *Pilgr. to Nejd*, ii. 67.

[2] Damascius, *Vita Isidori*, § 199.

[3] Polybius, vii. 9.   The word "meadows" is uncertain, resting on a
conjecture of Casaubon: λειμώνων for δαιμόνων.   Reiske conjectured λιμνῶν.
In Palestine to this day all springs are viewed as the seats of spirits, and the

rivers, we must consider not only that such a position was convenient, inasmuch as pure water was indispensable for ablutions and other ritual purposes, but that the presence of living water in itself gave consecration to the place.[1] The fountain or stream was not a mere adjunct to the temple, but was itself one of the principal *sacra* of the spot, to which special legends and a special ritual were often attached, and to which the temple in many instances owed its celebrity and even its name. This is particularly the case with perennial streams and their sources, which in a country like Palestine, where rain is confined to the winter months, are not very numerous, and form striking features in the topography of the region. From Hannibal's oath we may conclude that among the Phœnicians and Carthaginians all such waters were held to be divine, and what we know in detail of the waters of the Phœnician coast goes far to confirm the conclusion.[2] Of the eminent sanctity of certain rivers, such as the Belus and the Adonis, we have direct evidence, and the grove and pool of Aphaca at the source of the latter stream was the most famous of all Phœnician holy places.[3] These rivers are named from gods, and so also, on the same coast, are the Asclepius, near Sidon, the Ares (perhaps identical with the Lycus), and presumably the Kishon.[4] The river of Tripolis, which descends from the famous cedars, is still called the Cadīsha

---

peasant women, whether Moslem or Christian, ask their permission before drawing water (*ZDPV.* x. 180); cf. Num. xxi. 17.

[1] For the choice of a place beside a pool as the site of a chapel, see Waddington, No 2015, εὐσεβίης τόπος οὗτος ὃν ἔκτισεν ἐγγύθι λίμνης.

[2] The authorities for the details, so far as they are not cited below, will be found in Baudissin, *Studien*, ii. 161.

[3] Euseb., *Vit. Const.* iii. 55; Sozomen, ii. 5.

[4] River of קיש, Ar. Cais. Prof. De Goeje, referring to Hamdānī, p. 3
★ l. 9, and perhaps p. 221, L 14, suggests to me by letter that Cais is a title "dominus."

or holy stream, and the grove at its source is sacred to Christians and Moslems alike.[1]

In Hellenic and Roman times the source of the Jordan at Paneas with its grotto was sacred to Pan, and in ancient days the great Israelite sanctuary of Dan occupied the same site, or that of the twin source at Tell al-Cādi. It is evident that Naaman's indignation when he was told to bathe in the Jordan, and his confidence that the rivers of Damascus were better than all the waters of Israel, sprang from the idea that the Jordan was the sacred healing stream of the Hebrews, as Abana and Pharpar were the sacred rivers of the Syrians, and in this he probably did no injustice to the belief of the mass of the Israelites. The sanctity of the Barada, the chief river of Damascus, was concentrated at its nominal source, the fountain of El-Fiji, that is, $\pi\eta\gamma\alpha\acute{\iota}$. The river - gods Chrysorrhoa and Pegai often appear on Damascene coins, and evidently had a great part in the religion of the city. That the thermal waters of Gadara were originally sacred may be inferred from the peculiar ceremonies that were still observed by the patients in the time of Antoninus Martyr (*De locis Sanctis*, vii.). The baths were used by night; there were lights and incense, and the patient saw visions during the pernoctation. To this day a patient at the natural bath of Tiberias must not offend the spirits by pronouncing the name of God (*ZDPV.* x. 179).

The river of Cœle-Syria, the Orontes, was carved out, according to local tradition, by a great dragon, which disappeared in the earth at its source.[2] The connection

---

[1] Robinson, iii. 590. On Carthaginian soil, it is not impossible that the Bagradas or Majerda, Macaros or Macros in MSS. of Polybius, bears the name of the Tyrian Baal-Melcarth.

[2] Strabo, xvi. 2. 7. Other sacred traditions about the Orontes are given by Malalas, p. 38, from Pausanias of Damascus.

of *jinn* in the form of dragons or serpents with sacred or healing springs has already come before us in Arabian superstition, and the lake of Cadas near Emesa, which is regarded as the source of the river (Yācūt, iii. 588), bears a name which implies its ancient sanctity. Among Syrian waters those of the Euphrates played an important part in the ritual of Hierapolis, and from them the great goddess was thought to have been born; while the source of its chief Mesopotamian tributary, the Aborrhas or Chaboras, was reverenced as the place where Hera (Atargatis) bathed after her marriage with Zeus (Bel). It gave out a sweet odour, and was full of tame, that is sacred, fishes.[1]

The sacredness of living waters was by no means confined to such great streams and sources as have just been spoken of. But in cultivated districts fountains could not ordinarily be reserved for purposes exclusively sacred. Each town or village had as a rule its own well, and its own high place or little temple, but in Canaan the well was not generally within the precincts of the high place. Towns were built on rising ground, and the well lay outside the gate, usually below the town, while the high place stood on the higher ground overlooking the human habitations.[2] Thus any idea of sanctity that might be connected with the fountain was dissociated from the temple ritual, and would necessarily become vague and attenuated.[3] Sacred springs in the full sense of the word

---

[1] Ælian, *Nat. Ann.* xii. 30; Pliny, *H. N.* xxxi. 37, xxxii. 16.

[2] Gen. xxiv. 11 ; 1 Sam. ix. 11 ; 2 Sam. ii. 13, xxiii. 16 ; 2 Kings ii. 21 ; 1 Kings xxi. 13, 19, compared with chap. xxii. 38.

[3] There are, however, indications that in some cases the original sanctuary was at a well beneath the town. In 1 Kings i. 9, 38, the fountains of En-rogel, where Adonijah held his sacrificial feast, and of Gihon, where Solomon was crowned, are plainly the original sanctuaries of Jerusalem. The former was by the "serpent's stone," and may perhaps be identified with the "dragon well" of Neh. ii. 13. Here again, as in Arabia and at the Orontes, the dragon or serpent has a sacred significance.

are generally found, not at the ordinary local sanctuaries, but at remote pilgrimage shrines like Aphaca, Beersheba, Mamre, or within the enclosure of great and spacious temples like that at Ascalon, where the pool of Atargatis was shown and her sacred fishes were fed. Sometimes, as at Daphne near Antioch, the water and its surrounding groves formed a sort of public park near a city, where religion and pleasure were combined in the characteristic Syriac fashion.[1]

The myths attached to holy sources and streams, and put forth to worshippers as accounting for their sanctity, were of various types; but the practical beliefs and ritual usages connected with sacred waters were much the same everywhere. The one general principle which runs through all the varieties of the legends, and which also lies at the basis of the ritual, is that the sacred waters are instinct with divine life and energy. The legends explain this in diverse ways, and bring the divine quality of the waters into connection with various deities or supernatural powers, but they all agree in this, that their main object is to show how the fountain or stream comes to be impregnated, so to speak, with the vital energy of the deity to which it is sacred.

Among the ancients blood is generally conceived as the principle or vehicle of life, and so the account often given of sacred waters is that the blood of the deity flows in them. Thus as Milton writes—

> Smooth Adonis from his native rock
> Ran purple to the sea, supposed with blood
> Of Thammuz yearly wounded.[2]

---

[1] A similar example, Wadd., No. 2370. A sacred fountain of Eshmun "in the mountain" seems to appear in *CIS.* No. 3, l. 17 ; cf. G. Hoffmann, *Ueber einige Phœn. Inschrr.* p. 52 *sq.* See also Baudissin, *Ad.* p. 244 *sq.*

[2] *Paradise Lost*, i. 450, following Lucian, *Dea Syria*, viii.

The ruddy colour which the swollen river derived from
the soil at a certain season [1] was ascribed to the blood of
the god who received his death-wound in Lebanon at that
time of the year, and lay buried beside the sacred source.[2]
Similarily a tawny fountain near Joppa was thought to
derive its colour from the blood of the sea-monster slain
by Perseus,[3] and Philo Byblius says that the fountains and
rivers sacred to the heaven-god (Baalshamaim) were those
which received his blood when he was mutilated by his
son.[4]　In another class of legends, specially connected
with the worship of Atargatis, the divine life of the waters
resides in the sacred fish that inhabit them.　Atargatis
and her son, according to a legend common to Hierapolis
and Ascalon, plunged into the waters—in the first case
the Euphrates, in the second the sacred pool at the temple
near the town—and were changed into fishes.[5]　This is
only another form of the idea expressed in the first class
of legend, where a god dies, that is ceases to exist in
human form, but his life passes into the waters where he
is buried; and this again is merely a theory to bring the
divine water or the divine fish into harmony with anthro-

[1] The reddening of the Adonis was observed by Maundrell on March $\frac{1}{4}\frac{7}{4}$,
169$\frac{4}{5}$, and by Renan early in February.　Cf. Frazer, *GB.* v. 225.

[2] Melito in Cureton, *Spic. Syr.* p. 25, l. 7.　That the grave of Adonis
was also shown at the mouth of the river has been inferred from *Dea Syr.*
vi. vii.　The river Belus also had its Memnonion or Adonis tomb (Josephus,
B. J. ii. 10. 2.)　In modern Syria cisterns are always found beside the
graves of saints, and are believed to be inhabited by a sort of fairy.　A
pining child is thought to be a fairy changeling, and must be lowered into
the cistern.　The fairy will then take it back, and the true child is drawn
up in its room.　This is in the region of Sidon (*ZDPV.* vol. vii. p. 84 ; cf.
ib. p. 106).

[3] Pausanias, iv. 35. 9.

[4] Euseb. *Præp. Ev.* i. 10. 22 (*Fr. Hist. Gr.* iii. 568).　The fountain of
the Chabōras, where Hera μετὰ τοὺς γάμους . . ἀπελούσατο, belongs to the
same class.

[5] Hyginus, *Astr.* ii. 30 ; **Manilius,** iv. 580 *sqq.*; Xanthus in Athenæus,
viii. 37.　I have discussed these legends at length in the *English Hist.
Review,* April 1887, to which the reader is referred for details.

pomorphic ideas.[1] The same thing was sometimes effected in another way by saying that the anthropomorphic deity was born from the water, as Aphrodite sprang from the sea-foam, or as Atargatis, in another form of the Euphrates legend, given by the scholiast on Germanicus's Aratus, was born of an egg which the sacred fishes found in the Euphrates and pushed ashore. Here, we see, it was left to the choice of the worshippers whether they would think of the deity as arising from or disappearing in the water, and in the ritual of the Syrian goddess at Hierapolis both ideas were combined at the solemn feasts, when her image was carried down to the river and back again to the temple. Where the legend is so elastic we can hardly doubt that the sacred waters and sacred fish were worshipped for their own sake before the anthropomorphic goddess came into the religion, and in fact the sacred fish at the source of the Chaboras are connected with an altogether different myth. Fish were *taboo*, and sacred fish were found in rivers or in pools at sanctuaries, all over Syria.[2] This superstition has proved one of the

---

[1] The idea that the godhead consecrates waters by descending into them appears at Aphaca in a peculiar form associated with the astral character which, at least in later times, was ascribed to the goddess Astarte. It was believed that the goddess on a certain day of the year descended into the river in the form of a fiery star from the top of Lebanon. So Sozomen, *H. E.* ii. 4, 5. Zosimus, i. 58, says only that fireballs appeared at the temple and the places about it, on the occasion of solemn feasts, and does not connect the apparition with the sacred waters. There is nothing improbable in the frequent occurrence of striking electrical phenomena in a mountain sanctuary. We shall presently find fiery apparitions connected also with sacred trees (*infra*, p. 193). "Thunders, lightnings and light flashing in the heavens," appear as objects of veneration among the Syrians (Jacob of Edessa, *Qu.* 43) ; cf. also the fiery globe of the Heliopolitan Lion-god, whose fall from heaven is described by Damascius, *Vit. Is.* § 203, and what Pausanias of Damascus relates of the fireball that checked the flood of the Orontes (Malalas, p. 38).

[2] Xenophon, *Anab.* i. 4. 9, who found such fish in the Chalus near Aleppo, expressly says that they were regarded as gods. Lucian, *Dea Syr.* xlv., relates that at the lake of Atargatis at Hierapolis the sacred fish

most durable parts of ancient heathenism ; sacred fish are
still kept in pools at the mosques of Tripolis and Edessa.
At the latter place it is believed that death or other
★ evil consequences would befall the man who dared to eat
them.[1]

The living power that inhabits sacred waters and gives
them their miraculous or healing quality is very often held
to be a serpent, as in the Arabian and Hebrew cases which
have been already cited,[2] or a huge dragon or water monster,
such as that which in the Antiochene legend hollowed out
the winding bed of the Orontes and disappeared beneath
its source.[3]   In such cases the serpents are of course
supernatural serpents or *jinn*, and the dragon of Orontes
was identified in the Greek period with Typhon, the enemy
of the gods.[4]   But the demon may also have other forms ;
thus at Rāmallāh in Palestine there are two springs, of
which one is inhabited by a camel, the other by a bride ;
while the spring at ʿArtās is guarded by a white and a
black ram.[5]

In all their various forms the point of the legends is
that the sacred source is either inhabited by a demoniac
being or imbued with demoniac life.   The same notion
appears with great distinctness in the ritual of sacred

wore gold ornaments, as did also the eels at the sanctuary of the war-god
Zeus, amidst the sacred plane-trees (Herod. v. 119) at Labraunda in Caria
(Pliny, *H. N.* xxxii. 16, 17 ; Ælian, *N. A.* xii. 30).   Caria was thoroughly
permeated by Phœnician influence.

[1] Sachau, *Reise*, p. 197.   [2] *Supra*, p. 168 *sqq.*

[3] The Leviathan (תַּנִּין) of Scripture, like the Arabian *tinnīn*, is probably
a personification of the waterspout (Masʿūdī, i. 263, 266 ; Ps. cxlviii. 7).
Thus we see how readily the Eastern imagination clothes aquatic phenomena with an animal form.

[4] Hence perhaps the modern name of the river Nahr al-ʿÂṣī, "the rebel's
stream" ; the explanation in Yācūt, iii. 588, does not commend itself.   The
burial of the Typhonic dragon at the source of the Orontes may be compared
with the Moslem legend of the well at Babylon, where the rebel angels
Hārūt and Mārūt were entombed (Cazwīnī, i. 197).

[5] *ZDPV.* x. 180 ; *PEF. Qu. St.* 1893, p. 204.

waters. Though such waters are often associated with temples, altars, and the usual apparatus of a cultus addressed to heavenly deities, the service paid to the holy well retained a form which implies that the divine power addressed was in the water. We have seen that at Mecca, and at the Stygian waters in the Syrian desert, gifts were cast into the holy source. But even at Aphaca, where, in the times to which our accounts refer, the goddess of the spot was held to be the Urania or celestial Astarte, the pilgrims cast into the pool jewels of gold and silver, webs of linen and byssus and other precious stuffs, and the obvious contradiction between the celestial character of the goddess and the earthward destination of the gifts was explained by the fiction that at the season of the feast she descended into the pool in the form of a fiery star. Similarly, at the annual fair and feast of the Terebinth, or tree and well of Abraham at Mamre, the heathen visitors, who reverenced the spot as a haunt of " angels," [1] not only offered sacrifices beside the tree, but illuminated the well with lamps, and cast into it libations of wine, cakes, coins, myrrh, and incense.[2] On the other hand, at the sacred waters of Karwa and Sāwid in S. Arabia, described by Hamdānī in the *Iklīl* (Müller, *Burgen*, p. 69), offerings of bread, fruit or other food were deposited beside the fountain. In the former case they were believed to be eaten by the serpent denizen of the water, in the latter they were consumed by beasts and birds. At Gaza bread is still thrown into the sea by way of offering.[3]

---

[1] *I.e.* demons. Sozomen says "angels," and not "devils," because the sanctity of the place was acknowledged by Christians also.

[2] Sozomen, *H. E.* ii. 4.—As all "living waters" seem to have had a certain sanctity in N. Semitic religion, the custom of throwing the Ἀδώνιδος κῆποι into springs (Zenobius, *Cent.* i. 49) may probably belong to this chapter.

[3] *PEF. Qu. St.* 1893, p. 216.

In ancient religion offerings are the proper vehicle of prayer and supplication, and the worshipper when he presents his gift looks for a visible indication whether his prayer is accepted.[1] At Aphaca and at the Stygian fountain the accepted gift sank into the depths, the unacceptable offering was cast forth by the eddies. It was taken as an omen of the impending fall of Palmyra that the gifts sent from that city at an annual festival were cast up again in the following year.[2] In this example we see that the holy well, by declaring the favourable or unfavourable disposition of the divine power, becomes a place of oracle and divination. In Greece, also, holy wells are connected with oracles, but mainly in the form of a belief that the water gives prophetic inspiration to those who drink of it. At the Semitic oracle of Aphaca the method is more primitive, for the answer is given directly by the water itself, but its range is limited to what can be inferred from the acceptance or rejection of the worshipper and his petition.

The oracle of Daphne near Antioch, which was obtained by dipping a laurel leaf into the water, was presumably of the same class, for we cannot take seriously the statement that the response appeared written on the leaf.[3] The choice of the laurel leaf as the offering cast into the water must be due to Greek influence, but Daphne was a sanctuary of Heracles, i.e. of the Semitic Baal, before the temple of Apollo was built.[4]

----

[1] Cf. Gen. iv. 4, 5.

[2] Zosimus, i. 58. At Aphaca, as at the Stygian fountain, the waters fall down a cataract into a deep gorge.

[3] Sozomen, v. 19. 11. Cf. the ordeal by casting a tablet into the water at Palici in Sicily. The tablet sank if what was written on it was false (*Mir. Ausc.* § 57).

[4] Malalas, p. 204. A variant of this form of oracle occurs at Myra in Lycia, where the omen is from the sacred fish accepting or rejecting the food offered to them (Pliny, *H. N.* xxxii. 17 ; Ælian, *N. A.* viii. 5 ; Athenæus,

An oracle that speaks by receiving or rejecting the worshipper and his homage may very readily pass into an ordeal, where the person who is accused of a crime, or is suspected of having perjured himself in a suit, is presented at the sanctuary, to be accepted or rejected by the deity, in accordance with the principle that no impious person can come before God with impunity.[1] A rude form of this ordeal seems to survive even in modern times in the widespread form of trial of witches by water. In Ḥaḍramaut, according to Macrīzī,[2] when a man was injured by enchantment, he brought all the witches suspect to the sea or to a deep pool, tied stones to their backs and threw them into the water. She who did not sink was the guilty person, the meaning evidently being that the sacred element rejects the criminal.[3] That an impure person dare not approach sacred waters is a general principle—whether the impurity is moral or physical is not a distinction made by ancient religion. Thus in Arabia we have found that a woman in her uncleanness was afraid, for her children's sake, to bathe in the water of Dusares; and to this day among the Yezīdīs no one may enter the valley of Sheik Adi, with its sacred fountain, unless he has first purified his body and clothes.[4] The sacred oil-spring of the Carthaginian sanctuary, described in the book of *Wonderful Stories* that passes under the name of Aristotle,[5] would not flow except for persons ceremonially pure. An ordeal at a sacred spring based on

---

viii. 8, p. 333). How far Lycian worship was influenced by the Semites is not clear.

[1] Cf. Job xiii. 16 ; Isa. xxxiii. 14.

[2] *De Valle Ḥadhramaut*, p. 26 *sq.*

[3] The story about Mojammi' and Al-Ahwaṣ (*Agh.* iv. 48), cited by Wellhausen, *Heid.* p. 160, refers to this kind of ordeal, not to a form of magic. A very curious story of the water test for witches in India is told by Ibn Batuta, iv. 37.

[4] Layard, *Nineveh*, i. 280.   [5] *Mir. Ausc.* § 113.

this principle might be worked in several ways,[1] but the
usual Semitic method seems to have been by drinking the
water. Evidently, if it is dangerous for the impious person
★ to come into contact with the holy element, the danger
must be intensified if he ventures to take it into his system,
and it was believed that in such a case the draught produced disease and death. At the Asbamæan lake and
springs near Tyana the water was sweet and kindly to
those that swore truly, but the perjured man was at once
smitten in his eyes, feet and hands, seized with dropsy and
wasting.[2] In like manner he who swore falsely by the
Stygian waters in the Syrian desert died of dropsy within
a year. In the latter case it would seem that the oath
by the waters sufficed; but primarily, as we see in the
other case, the essential thing is the draught of water at
the holy place, the oath simply taking the place of the
petition which ordinarily accompanies a ritual act. Among
the Hebrews this ordeal by drinking holy water is preserved
even in the pentateuchal legislation in the case of a woman
suspected of infidelity to her husband.[3] Here also the
belief was that the holy water, which was mingled with
the dust of the sanctuary, and administered with an oath,
produced dropsy and wasting; and the antiquity of the

---

[1] See, for example, the Sicilian oracle of the Palic lake, where the oath of
the accused was written on a tablet and cast into the water to sink or swim
(*Mir. Ausc.* § 57).

[2] *Mir. Ausc.* § 152; Philostr., *Vit. Apollonii*, i. 6. That the sanctuary
was Semitic I infer from its name; see below, p. 182.

[3] Num. v. 11 *sqq.* In *Agh.* i. 156, l. 3 *sqq.*, a suspected wife swears
seventy oaths at the Caaba, to which she is conducted with circumstances
of ignominy—seated on a camel between two sacks of dung. This was
under Islam, but is evidently an old custom. In heathen Arabia the decision
in such a case was sometimes referred to a diviner, as we see from the story
of Hind bint 'Otba ('*Icd*, iii. 273; *Agh.* viii. 50). An ordeal for virgins
accused of unchastity existed at the Stygian water near Ephesus. The
accused swore that she was innocent; her oath was written and tied round
her neck. She then entered the shallow pool, and if she was guilty the
water rose till it covered the writing (Achilles Tatius, viii. 12).

ceremony is evident not only from its whole character, but because the expression " holy water " (ver. 17) is unique in the language of Hebrew ritual, and must be taken as an isolated survival of an obsolete expression. Unique though the expression be, it is not difficult to assign its original meaning; the analogies already before us indicate that we must think of water from a holy spring, and this conclusion is certainly correct. Wellhausen has shown that the oldest Hebrew tradition refers the origin of the Torah to the divine sentences taught by Moses at the sanctuary of Kadesh or Meribah,[1] beside the holy fountain which in Gen. xiv. 7 is also called " the fountain of judgment." The principle underlying the administration of justice at the sanctuary is that cases too hard for man are referred to the decision of God. Among the Hebrews in Canaan this was ordinarily done by an appeal to the sacred lot, but the survival of even one case of ordeal by holy water leaves no doubt as to the sense of the " fountain of judgment " (En-Mishpaṭ) or " waters of controversy " (Meribah).

With this evidence before us as to the early importance of holy waters among the Hebrews, we cannot but attach significance to the fact that the two chief places of pilgrimage of the northern Israelites in the time of Amos were Dan and Beersheba.[2] We have already seen that there was a sacred fountain at Dan, and the sanctuary of Beersheba properly consisted of the " Seven Wells," which gave the place its name. It is notable that among the Semites a special sanctity was attached to groups of seven wells.[3] In the canons of Jacob of Edessa (Qu. 43) we read of nominally Christian Syrians who bewail their diseases to

---

[1] *Prolegomena*, viii. 3 (Eng. trans. p. 343).
[2] Amos viii. 14 ; cf. 1 Kings xii. 30.
[3] See Nöldeke in *Litt. Centralblatt*, 22 Mar. 1879, p. 363.

the stars, or turn for help to a solitary tree or a fountain
or *seven springs* or water of the sea, etc.   Among the
Mandæans, also, we read of mysteries performed at seven
wells, and among the Arabs a place called "the seven
wells" is mentioned by Strabo, xvi. 4. 24.[1]   The name of
the Asbamæan waters seems also to mean "seven waters"
(Syr. *shab'ā mayā*); the spot is a lake where a number of
sources bubble up above the surface of the water.   Seven
is a sacred number among the Semites, particularly affected
in matters of ritual, and the Hebrew verb "to swear"
means literally "to come under the influence of seven
things."   Thus seven ewe lambs figure in the oath between
Abraham and Abimelech at Beersheba, and in the Arabian
oath of covenant described by Herodotus (iii. 8), seven
stones are smeared with blood.   The oath of purgation at
seven wells would therefore have peculiar force.[2]

It is the part of a divine power to grant to his
worshippers not only oracles and judgment, but help in
trouble and blessing in daily life.   The kind of blessing
which it is most obvious to expect from a sacred spring is
the quickening and fertilisation of the soil and all that
depends on it.   That fruitful seasons were the chief object
of petition at the sacred springs requires no special proof,
for this object holds the first place in all the great religious
occasions of the settled Semites, and everywhere we find
that the festal cycle is regulated by the seasons of the

---

[1] Cf. also the seven marvellous wells at Tiberias (Cazwīnī, i. 193), and
the Thorayyā or "Pleiad waters" at Darīya (Yācūt, i. 924, iii. 588 ; Bekrī,
214, 627) ; also the modern Syrian custom of making a sick child that is
thought to be bewitched drink from seven wells or cisterns (*ZDPV.*
vii. 106).

[2] In Amos viii. 14 there is mention of an oath by the way (ritual ?) of
Beersheba.   The pilgrims at Mamre would not drink of the water of the
well.   Sozomen supposes that the gifts cast in made it undrinkable ; but
at an Oriental market, where every bargain is accompanied by false oaths
and protestations, the precaution is rather to be explained by fear of the
divine ordeal.

agricultural year.[1]　Beyond doubt the first and best gift
of the sacred spring to the worshipper was its own life-
giving water, and the first object of the religion addressed
to it was to encourage its benignant flow.[2]　But the life-
giving power of the holy stream was by no means confined
to the quickening of vegetation.　Sacred waters are also
healing waters, as we have already seen in various examples,
particularly in that of the Syrians, who sought to them for
help in disease.　I may here add one instance which, though
it lies a little outside of the proper Semitic region, is connected with a holy river of the Syrians.　In the Middle
Ages it was still believed that he who bathed in the spring-
time in the source of the Euphrates would be free from
sickness for the whole year.[3]　This healing power was not
confined to the water itself, but extended to the vegetation
that surrounded it.　By the sacred river Belus grew the
colocasium plants by which Heracles was healed after his
conflict with the Hydra, and the roots continued to be used
as a cure for bad sores.[4]　At Paneas an herb that healed
all diseases grew at the base of a statue which was
supposed to represent Christ, evidently a relic of the old
heathenism of the place.[5]　Thus when Ezekiel describes

[1] A myth of the connection of sacred waters with the origin of agriculture
seems to survive in modernised form in the mediæval legend of 'Ain al-
bacar, "the oxen's well," at Acre.　It was visited by Christian, Jewish and
Moslem pilgrims, because the oxen with which Adam ploughed issued from
it (Cazwīnī, Yācūt).　There was a *mashhed*, or sacred tomb, beside it,
perhaps the modern representative of the ancient Memnonium.

[2] In Num. xxi. 17 we find a song addressed to the well exhorting it to ★
rise, which in its origin is hardly a mere poetic figure.　We may compare
what Cazwīnī, i. 189, records of the well of Ilābistān.　When the water
failed, a feast was held at the source, with music and dancing, to induce
it to flow again.　See also the modern Palestinian usage cited above, p.
169, n. 3.

[3] Cazwīnī, i. 194.　I may also cite the numerous fables of amulets, to be
found in the Tigris and other rivers, which protected their wearers against
wild beasts, demons and other dangers (*Mir. Ausc.* § 159 *sq.*).

[4] Claudius Iolaus, *ap.* Steph. Byz. *s.v.* Ἄκη.

[5] Theophanes, quoted by Reland, *Antiq. Hebr.* ii. 922.

the sacred waters that issue from the New Jerusalem as giving life wherever they come, and the leaves of the trees on their banks as supplying medicine, his imagery is in full touch with common Semitic ideas (Ezek. xlvii. 9, 12).

The healing power of sacred water is closely connected with its purifying and consecrating power, for the primary conception of uncleanness is that of a dangerous infection. Washings and purifications play a great part in Semitic ritual, and were performed with living water, which was as such sacred in some degree. Whether specially sacred springs were used for purification, and if so under what restrictions I cannot make out; in most cases, I apprehend, they were deemed too holy to be approached by a person technically impure. It appears, however, from Ephræm Syrus that the practice of bathing in fountains was one of the heathen customs to which the Syrians of his time were much addicted, and he seems to regard this as a sort of heathen consecration.[1] Unfortunately the rhetoric of the Syrian fathers seldom condescends to precise details on such matters.

From this account of the ritual of sacred wells it will, I think, be clear that the usages and ceremonies are all intelligible on general principles, without reference to particular legends or the worship of the particular deities associated with special waters. The fountain is treated as a living thing, those properties of its waters which we call natural are regarded as manifestations of a divine life, and the source itself is honoured as a divine being, I had almost said a divine animal. When religion takes a form decidedly anthropomorphic or astral, myths are devised to reconcile the new point of view with the old usage, but the substance of the ritual remains unchanged.

[1] *Opp.* iii. 670 *sq.*; *H. et S.*, ed. Lamy, ii. 395, 411.

Let us now pass on from the worship of sacred waters to the cults connected with sacred trees.[1]

That the conception of trees as demoniac beings was ★ familiar to the Semites has been already shown by many examples,[2] and there is also abundant evidence that in all parts of the Semitic area trees were adored as divine.

Tree worship pure and simple, where the tree is in all respects treated as a god, is attested for Arabia (but not on the best authority) in the case of the sacred date-palm at Nejrān.[3] It was adored at an annual feast, when it was all hung with fine clothes and women's ornaments. A similar tree, to which the people of Mecca resorted annually, and hung upon it weapons, garments, ostrich eggs and other gifts, is spoken of in the traditions of the prophet under the vague name of a *dhāt anwāt*, or "tree to hang things on." It seems to be identical with the sacred acacia at Nakhla in which the goddess Al-ʿOzzā was believed to reside.[4] The tree at Ḥodaibiya, mentioned in Sura xlviii. 18, was frequented by pilgrims who thought to derive a blessing from it, till it was cut down by the Caliph ʿOmar lest it should be worshipped like Al-Lāt and Al-ʿOzzā.[5] By the modern Arabs sacred trees are called *manāhil*, places where angels or *jinn* descend and are heard dancing and singing. It is deadly danger to pluck

---

[1] On sacred trees among the Semites, see Baudissin, *Studien*, ii. 184 *sqq.*; for Arabia, Wellhausen, *Heid.* p. 104. Compare Bötticher, *Baumcultus der Hellenen* (Berl. 1856), and Mannhardt, *Wald- und Feld-Culte* (Berl. 1875, 77).

[2] *Supra*, p. 133.

[3] Tabarī, i. 922 (Nöldeke's trans. p. 181); Ibn Hish. 22. The authority is Wahb b. Monabbih, who, I fear, was little better than a plausible liar.

[4] Wellhausen, pp. 36 *sq.*, 38 *sq.*

[5] Yāḳūt, iii. 261. At Ḥodaibiya there was also a well whose waters were miraculously increased by the prophet (Ibn Hish. 742 ; *Moh. in Med.* 247). I suspect that the sanctity of tree and well are older than Mohammed, for the place is reckoned to the Ḥaram but juts out beyond the line of its border (Yāḳūt, ii. 222).

so much as a bough from such a tree ; they are honoured
with sacrifices, and parts of the flesh are hung on them,
as well as shreds of calico, beads, etc.   The sick man who
sleeps under them receives counsel in a dream for the
restoration of his health.[1]

Among the heathen Syrians tree worship must have
had a large place, for this is one of the superstitions which
Christianity itself was powerless to eradicate.   We have
already met with nominal Christians of Syria who in their
sicknesses turned for help to a solitary tree, while zealous
Christians were at pains to hew down the " trees of the
demons." [2]   As regards the Phœnicians and Canaanites we
have the testimony of Philo Byblius that the plants of
the earth were in ancient times esteemed as gods and
honoured with libations and sacrifices, because from them
the successive generations of men drew the support of their
life.   To this day the traveller in Palestine frequently
meets with holy trees hung like an Arabian *dhāt anwāṭ*
with rags as tokens of homage.

What place the cult of trees held in the more
developed forms of Semitic religion it is not easy to
determine.   In later times the groves at the greater
sanctuaries do not seem to have been direct objects of
worship, though they shared in the inviolability that
belonged to all the surroundings of the deity, and were
sometimes—like the ancient cypresses of Heracles at
Daphne—believed to have been planted by the god
himself.[3]   It was not at the great sanctuaries of cities
but in the open field, where the rural population had
continued from age to age to practise primitive rites
without modification, that the worship of " solitary

[1] Doughty, *Arabia Deserta*, i. 448 *sqq.*

[2] See the citations in Kayser, *Jacob v. Edessa*, p. 141.

[3] Similarly the tamarisk at Beersheba was believed to have been planted
by Abraham (Gen. xxi. 33).

trees " survived the fall of the great gods of Semitic heathenism.[1]

There is no reason to think that any of the greater Semitic cults was developed out of tree worship. In all of them the main place is given to altar service, and we shall see by and by that the beginnings of this form of worship, so far as they can be traced back to a time when the gods were not yet anthropomorphic, point to the cult of animals rather than of trees. That trees are habitually found at sanctuaries is by no means inconsistent with this view, for where the tree is merely conceived as planted by the god or as marking his favourite haunt, it receives no direct homage.

When, however, we find that no Canaanite high place was complete without its sacred tree standing beside the altar, and when we take along with this the undoubted fact that the direct cult of trees was familiar to all the Semites, it is hardly possible to avoid the conclusion that some elements of tree worship entered into the ritual even of such deities as in their origin were not tree-gods. The local sanctuaries of the Hebrews, which the prophets regard as purely heathenish, and which certainly were modelled in all points on Canaanite usage, were altar-sanctuaries. But the altars were habitually set up " under green trees," and, what is more, the altar was incomplete unless an *ashera* stood beside it. The meaning of this word, which the Authorised Version wrongly renders " grove," has given rise to a good deal of controversy. What kind of object the *ashera* was appears from Deut. xvi. 21 : " Thou shalt not plant an *ashera* of any kind of

---

[1] The solitary tree may in certain cases be the last relic of a ruined heathen sanctuary. What Mocaddasi relates about the place called Al-Shajara ("the Tree "; *supra*, p. 160) points to something of this kind ; for here there was an annual feast or fair. At the Terebinth of Mamre in like manner an altar at least can hardly have been lacking in heathen times.

wood (or, an *ashera*, any kind of tree) beside the altar of
Jehovah"; it must therefore have been either a living
tree or a tree-like post, and in all probability either form
was originally admissible. The oldest altars, as we gather
from the accounts of patriarchal sanctuaries, stood under
actual trees; but this rule could not always be followed,
and in the period of the kings it would seem that the
place of the living tree was taken by a dead post or pole,
planted in the ground like an English Maypole.[1] The
ashera undoubtedly was an object of worship; for the
prophets put it on the same line with other sacred
symbols, images cippi and Baal-pillars (Isa. xvii. 8; Micah
v. 12 *sqq.*), and the Phœnician inscription of Maṣ'ūb
speaks of "the Astarte in the Ashera of the divinity of
Hammon." The *ashera* therefore is a sacred symbol, the
seat of the deity, and perhaps the name itself, as G.
Hoffmann has suggested, means nothing more than the
"mark" of the divine presence. But the opinion that
★ there was a Canaanite goddess called Ashera, and that
the trees or poles of the same name were her particular
symbols, is not tenable; every altar had its *ashera*, even
such altars as in the popular, pre-prophetic forms of
Hebrew religion were dedicated to Jehovah.[2] This is

---

[1] It is a thing made by man's hands; Isa. xvii. 8, cf. 1 Kings xvi. 33,
etc. In 2 Kings xxi. 7 (cf. xxiii. 6) we read of the Ashera-image. Similarly
in 1 Kings xv. 13 there is mention of a "grisly object" which Queen Maacah
made for an Ashera. These expressions may imply that the sacred pole
was sometimes carved into a kind of image. That the sacred tree should
degenerate first into a mere Maypole, and then into a rude wooden idol, is
in accordance with analogies found elsewhere, *e.g.* in Greece; but it seems
quite as likely that the *ashera* is described as a kind of idol simply because
it was used in idolatrous cultus. An Assyrian monument from Khorsābād,
figured by Botta and Layard, and reproduced in Rawlinson, *Monarchies*,
ii. 37, and Stade, *Gesch. Isr.* i. 461, shows an ornamental pole planted beside a
portable altar. Priests stand before it engaged in an act of worship, and touch
the pole with their hands, or perhaps anoint it with some liquid substance.

[2] The prohibition in Deut. xvi. 21 is good evidence of the previous
practice of the thing prohibited. See also 2 Kings xiii. 6.

not consistent with the idea that the sacred pole was the
symbol of a distinct divinity; it seems rather to show
that in early times tree worship had such a vogue in
Canaan that the sacred tree, or the pole its surrogate,
had come to be viewed as a general symbol of deity which
might fittingly stand beside the altar of any god.[1]

[1] If a god and a goddess were worshipped together at the same sanctuary,
as was the case, for example, at Aphaca and Hierapolis, and if the two sacred
symbols at the sanctuary were a pole and a pillar of stone, it might naturally
enough come about that the pole was identified with the goddess and the
pillar with the god. The worship of Tammuz or Adonis was known at
Jerusalem in the time of Ezekiel (viii. 14), and with Adonis the goddess
Astarte must also have been worshipped, probably as the "queen of heaven"
(Jer. vii., xliv.; cf. on this worship Kuenen in the *Verslagen*, etc., of the
Royal Acad. of Amsterdam, 1888). It is not therefore surprising that in
one or two late passages, written at a time when all the worship of the high
places was regarded as entirely foreign to the religion of Jehovah, the
Asherim seem to be regarded as the female partners of the Baalim ; *i.e.*
that the *ashera* is taken as a symbol of Astarte (Judg. iii. 7). The prophets
of the *ashera* in 1 Kings xviii. 19, who appear along with the prophets of
the Tyrian Baal as ministers of the foreign religion introduced by Jezebel,
must have been prophets of Astarte. They form part of the Tyrian queen's
court, and eat of her table, so that they have nothing to do with Hebrew
religion. And conversely the old Hebrew sacred poles can have had nothing
to do with the Tyrian goddess, for Jehu left the *ashera* at Samaria standing
when he abolished all trace of Tyrian worship (2 Kings xiii. 6). There is
no evidence of the worship of a divine pair among the older Hebrews ; in
the time of Solomon Astarte worship was a foreign religion (1 Kings xi. 5),
and it is plain from Jer. ii. 27 that in ordinary Hebrew idolatry the tree
or stock was the symbol not of a goddess but of a god. Even among the
Phœnicians the association of sacred trees with goddesses rather than with
gods is not so clear as is often supposed. From all this it follows that the
"prophets of the Ashera" in 1 Kings, *l.c.*, are very misty personages, and
that the mention of them implies a confusion between Astarte and the
Ashera, which no Israelite in Elijah's time, or indeed so long as the
northern kingdom stood, could have fallen into. In fact they do not
reappear either in ver. 22 or in ver. 40, and the mention of them seems to be
due to a late interpolation (Wellh., *Hexateuch*, 2nd ed. (1889), p. 281).
　The evidence offered by Assyriologists that Ashrat = Ashera was a
goddess (see Schrader in *Zeitschr. f. Assyriologie*, iii. 363 *sq.*) cannot overrule the plain sense of the Hebrew texts. Whether it suffices to show that
in some places the general symbol of deity had become a special goddess is a
question on which I do not offer an opinion ; but see G. Hoffmann, *Ueber
einige Phœn. Inschrr.* (1889), p. 26 *sqq.*, whose whole remarks are noteworthy. In *Cit.* 51 (*ZDMG.* xxxv. 424) the goddess seems to be called the

The general adoption of tree symbols at Canaanite sanctuaries must be connected with the fact that all Canaanite Baalim, whatever their original character, were associated with naturally fertile spots (Baal's land), and were worshipped as the givers of vegetable increase. We have seen already in the case of sacred streams how the life-blood of the god was conceived as diffused through the sacred waters, which thus became themselves impregnated with divine life and energy. And it was an easy extension of this idea to suppose that the tree which overshadowed the sacred fountain, and drew perennial strength and freshness from the moisture at its roots, was itself instinct with a particle of divine life. With the ancients the conception of life, whether divine or human, was not so much individualised as it is with us; thus, for example, all the members of one kin were conceived as having a common life embodied in the common blood which flowed through their veins. Similarly one and the same divine life might be shared by a number of objects, if all of them were nourished from a common vital source, and the elasticity of this conception made it very easy to bring natural holy things of different kinds into the cult of one and the same god. Elements of water tree and animal worship could all be combined in the ritual of a single anthropomorphic deity, by the simple supposition that the life of the god flowed in the sacred waters and fed the sacred tree.

As regards the connection of holy waters and holy trees, it must be remembered that in most Semitic lands self-sown wood can flourish only where there is underground water, and where therefore springs or wells exist beside the trees. Hence the idea that the same life is

mother of the sacred pole (אם האשרה), but the editors of the *CIS* (No. 13) read האזרת. See Cooke, No. 14.

manifested in the water and in the surrounding vegetation could hardly fail to suggest itself, and, broadly speaking, the holiness of fountains and that of trees, at least among the northern Semites, appear to be parts of the same religious conception, for it is only in exceptional cases that the one is found apart from the other.[1]

Where a tree was worshipped as the symbol of an anthropomorphic god we sometimes find a transformation legend directly connecting the life of the god with the vegetative life of the tree. This kind of myth, in which a god is transformed into a tree or a tree springs from the blood of a god, plays a large part in the sacred lore of Phrygia, where tree worship had peculiar prominence, and is also common in Greece. The Semitic examples are not numerous, and are neither so early nor so well attested as to inspire confidence that they are genuine old legends independent of Greek influence.[2] The most important of them is the myth told at Byblus in the time of Plutarch, of the sacred *erica* which was worshipped in the temple ★ of Isis, and was said to have grown round the dead body of Osiris. At Byblus, Isis and Osiris are really Astarte and Adonis, so this may possibly be an original Semitic legend of a holy tree growing from the grave of a god.[3]

[1] An interesting example of the combination may here be added to those cited above. The Syriac text of Epiphanius, *De pond. et mens.* § 62 (Lagarde, *V. T. Fragm.* p. 65 ; *Symmicta,* ii. 203), tells us that Atad of Gen. l. 11 was identified with the spring and thorn-bush of Beth-haglā near Jericho, and the explanation offered of the name Beth-haglā seems to be based on a local tradition of a ritual procession round the sacred objects. See also the *Onomastica, s.v.* Area Atath. In Greece also it is an exception to find a sacred tree without its fountain ; Bötticher, p. 47.

[2] Cf. Baudissin, *op. cit.* p. 214.

[3] Plut. *Is. et Os.* §§ 15, 16. One or two features in the story are noteworthy. The sacred erica was a mere dead stump, for it was cut down by Isis and presented to the Byblians wrapped in a linen cloth and anointed with myrrh like a corpse. It therefore represented the dead god. But as a mere stump it also resembles the Hebrew *ashera*. Can it be that the rite of draping and anointing a sacred stump supplies the answer to the unsolved

I apprehend, however, that the physical link between trees and anthropomorphic gods was generally sought in the sacred water from which the trees drew their life. This is probable from the use of the term *ba'l* to denote trees that need neither rain nor irrigation, and indeed from the whole circle of ideas connected with Baal's land. A tree belonged to a particular deity, not because it was of a particular species, but simply because it was the natural wood of the place where the god was worshipped and sent forth his quickening streams to fertilise the earth. The sacred trees of the Semites include every prominent species of natural wood—the pines and cedars of Lebanon, the evergreen oaks of the Palestinian hills, the tamarisks of the Syrian jungles, the acacias of the Arabian wadies, and so forth.[1] So far as these natural woods are concerned, the attempts that have been made to connect individual species of trees with the worship of a single deity break down altogether; it cannot, for example, be said that the cypress belongs to Astarte more than to Melcarth, who planted the cypress trees at Daphne.

Cultivated trees, on the other hand, such as the palm, the olive and the vine, might *à priori* be expected, among the Semites as among the Greeks, to be connected with the special worship of the deity of the spot from which their culture was diffused; for religion and agricultural

---

question of the nature of the ritual practices connected with the Ashera? Some sort of drapery for the *ashera* is spoken of in 2 Kings xxiii. 7, and the Assyrian representation cited on p. 188, note 1, perhaps represents the anointing of the sacred pole.

[1] In modern Palestine the carob tree is peculiarly demoniac, the reddish hue of the wood suggesting blood (*ZDPV.* x. 181). According to *PEF. Qu. St.* 1893, p. 203 *sq.*, fig, carob and sycamore trees are haunted by devils, and it is dangerous to sleep under them, whereas the lotus tree (*sidr*) and the tamarisk appear to be inhabited by a *wely* (saint). But a tree of any species may be sacred if it grows at a Macâm or sacred spot.

arts spread together and the one carried the other with it Yet even of this there is little evidence; the palm was a familiar symbol of Astarte, but we also find a "Baal of the palm-tree" (Baal-tamar) in a place-name in Judg. xx. 33. The only clear Semitic case of the association of a particular deity with a fruit tree is, I believe, that of the Nabatæan Dusares, who was the god of the vine. But the vine came to the Nabatæans only in the period of Hellenic culture,[1] and Dusares as the wine-god seems simply to have borrowed the traits of Dionysus.

At Aphaca at the annual feast the goddess appeared in the form of a fiery meteor, which descended from the mountain-top and plunged into the water, while according to another account fire played about the temple, presumably, since an electrical phenomenon must have lain at the foundation of this belief, in the tree-tops of the sacred grove.[2] Similarly it was believed that fire played about the branches of the sacred olive tree between the Ambrosian ★ rocks at Tyre, without scorching its leaves.[3] In like manner Jehovah appeared to Moses in the bush in flames of fire, so that the bush seemed to burn yet not to be consumed. The same phenomenon, according to Africanus [4] and Eustathius,[5] was seen at the terebinth of Mamre; the whole tree seemed to be aflame, but when the fire sank again remained unharmed. As lights were set by the well under the tree, and the festival was a nocturnal one, this was probably nothing more than an optical delusion exaggerated by the superstitious imagination, a mere artificial contrivance to keep up an ancient belief which must once have had wide currency in connection with

[1] Diodorus, xix. 94. 3.   [2] *Supra*, p. 175, note 1.

[3] Achilles Tatius, ii. 14 ; Nonnus, xl. 474 ; cf. the representation on a coin of Gordian III. figured in Pietschmann, *Phœnizier*, p. 295.

[4] Georg. Syncellus, Bonn ed. p. 202.

[5] Cited by Reland, p. 712.

13

sacred trees, and is remarkable because it shows how a tree might become holy apart from all relation to agriculture and fertility. Jehovah, "who dwells in the bush" (Deut. xxxiii. 16), in the arid desert of Sinai, was the God of the Hebrews while they were still nomads ignorant of agriculture; and indeed the original seat of a conception like the burning bush, which must have its physical basis in electrical phenomena, must probably be sought in the clear dry air of the desert or of lofty mountains. The apparition of Jehovah in the burning bush belongs to the same circle of ideas as His apparition in the thunders and lightnings of Sinai.

When the divine manifestation takes such a form as the flames in the bush, the connection between the god and the material symbol is evidently much looser than in the Baal type of religion, where the divine life is immanent in the life of the tree; and the transition is comparatively easy from the conception of Deut. xxxiii. 16, where Jehovah inhabits (not visits) the bush, as elsewhere He is said to inhabit the temple, to the view prevalent in most parts of the Old Testament, that the tree or the pillar at a sanctuary is merely a memorial of the divine name, the mark of a place where He has been found in the past and may be found again. The separation between Jehovah and physical nature, which is so sharply drawn by the prophets and constitutes one of the chief points of distinction between their faith and that of the masses, whose Jehovah worship had all the characters of Baal worship, may be justly considered as a development of the older type of Hebrew religion. It has sometimes been ★ supposed that the conception of a God immanent in nature is Aryan, and that of a transcendental God Semitic; but the former view is quite as characteristic of the Baal worship of the agricultural Semites as of the early faiths

of the agricultural Aryans. It is true that the higher
developments of Semitic religion took a different line, but
they did not grow out of Baal worship.

As regards the special forms of cultus addressed to
sacred trees, I can add nothing certain to the very scanty
indications that have already come before us. Prayers
were addressed to them, particularly for help in sickness,
but doubtless also for fertile seasons and the like, and they
were hung with votive gifts, especially garments and
ornaments, perhaps also anointed with unguents as if
they had been real persons. More could be said about
the use of branches, leaves or other parts of sacred trees
in lustrations, as medicine, and for other ritual purposes.
But these things do not directly concern us at present;
they are simply to be noted as supplying additional
evidence, if such be necessary, that a sacred energy, that
is, a divine life, resided even in the parts of holy trees.

The only other aspect of the subject which seems to
call for notice at the present stage is the connection of
sacred trees with oracles and divination. Oracles and
omens from trees and at tree sanctuaries are of the commonest among all races,[1] and are derived in very various
ways, either from observation of phenomena connected
with the trees themselves, and interpreted as manifestations of divine life, or from ordinary processes of
divination performed in the presence of the sacred object.
Sometimes the tree is believed to speak with an articulate
voice, as the *gharcad* did in a dream to Moslim;[2] but
except in a dream it is obvious that the voice of the
tree can only be some rustling sound, as of wind in the
branches, like that which was given to David as a token

---

[1] Cf. Bötticher, *op. cit.* chap. xi.

[2] *Supra*, p. 133. The same belief in trees from which a spirit speaks
oracles occurs in a modern legend given by Doughty, *Ar. Des.* ii. 209.

of the right moment to attack the Philistines,[1] and requires
a soothsayer to interpret it. The famous holy tree near
Shechem, called the tree of soothsayers in Judg. ix. 37,[2]
and the "tree of the revealer" in Gen. xii. 6, must have
been the seat of a Canaanite tree oracle.[3] We have no
hint as to the nature of the physical indications that
guided the soothsayers, nor have I found any other case
of a Semitic tree oracle where the mode of procedure is
described. But the belief in trees as places of divine
revelation must have been widespread in Canaan. The
prophetess Deborah gave her responses under a palm near
Bethel, which according to sacred tradition marked the
grave of the nurse of Rebekah.[4] That the artificial sacred
tree or *ashera* was used in divination would follow from
1 Kings xviii. 19, were it not that there are good grounds
for holding that in this passage the prophets of the
ashera are simply the prophets of the Tyrian Astarte.
But in Hos. iv. 12 the "stock" of which the prophet's
contemporaries sought counsel can hardly be anything else
than the *ashera*.[5] Soothsayers who draw their inspiration

[1] 2 Sam. v. 24.

[2] A.V. "plain of Meonenim."

[3] It was perhaps only one tree of a sacred grove, for Deut. xi. 30 speaks
of the "trees of the revealer" in the plural. Sam. and LXX read "oak."

[4] Gen. xxxv. 8. There indeed the tree is called an *allōn*, a word
generally rendered oak. But *allōn*, like *ēlāh* and *ēlōn*, seems to be a name
applicable to any sacred tree, perhaps to any great tree. Stade, *Gesch. Is.*
i. 455, would even connect these words with *ēl*, god, and the Phœnician
alonīm.

[5] As the next clause says, "and their rod declareth to them," it is
commonly supposed that rhabdomancy is alluded to, *i.e.* the use of divining
rods. And no doubt the divining rod, in which a spirit of life is supposed
to reside, so that it moves and gives indications apart from the will of the
man who holds it, is a superstition cognate to the belief in sacred trees ; but
when "their rod" occurs in parallelism with "their stock" or tree, it lies
nearer to cite Philo Byblius, *ap.* Eus. *Pr. Ev.* i. 10. 11, who speaks of
rods and pillars consecrated by the Phœnicians and worshipped by annual
feasts. On this view the rod is only a smaller *ashera*. Drusius therefore
seems to hit the mark in comparing Festus's note on *delubrum*, where the

from plants are found in Semitic legend even in the Middle Ages.[1]

To the two great natural marks of a place of worship, the fountain and the tree, ought perhaps to be added grottoes and caves of the earth. At the present day almost every sacred site in Palestine has its grotto, and that this is no new thing is plain from the numerous symbols of Astarte worship found on the walls of caves in Phœnicia. There can be little doubt that the oldest Phœnician temples were natural or artificial grottoes, and that the sacred as well as the profane monuments of Phœnicia, with their marked preference for monolithic forms, point to the rock-hewn cavern as the original type that dominated the architecture of the region.[2] But if this be so, the use of grottoes as temples in later times does not prove that caverns as such had any primitive religious significance. Religious practice is always conservative, and rock-hewn temples would naturally be used after men had ceased to live like troglodytes in caves and holes of the earth. Moreover, ancient temples are in most instances not so much houses where the gods live, as storehouses for the vessels and treasures of the sanctuary. The altar, the sacred tree, and the other divine symbols to which acts of worship are addressed, stand outside in front of the temple, and the whole service is carried on in the open air. Now all over the Semitic world caves and pits are the primitive storehouses, and we know that in Arabia

---

Romans are said to have worshipped pilled rods as gods. See more on rod worship in Bötticher, *op. cit.* xvi. 5. Was the omen derived from the rod flourishing or withering? We have such an omen in Aaron's rod (Num. xvii.); and Adonis rods, set as slips to grow or wither, seem to be referred to in Isa. xvii. 10 *sqq.*, a passage which would certainly gain force if the withering of the slips was an ill omen. Divination from the flourishing and withering of sacred trees is very common in antiquity (Bötticher, ★ ɔhap. xi.).

[1] Chwolsohn, *Ssabier*, ii. 914.   [2] Renan, *Phénicie*, p. 822 *sq.*

a pit called the *ghabghab*, in which the sacred treasure was stored, was a usual adjunct to sanctuaries.[1] But there are weighty reasons for doubting whether this is the whole explanation of cave sacrifices. In other parts of the world, *e.g.* in Greece, there are many examples of caves associated with the worship of chthonic deities, and also with the oracles of gods like Apollo who are not usually regarded as chthonic or subterranean; and the acts performed in these caves imply that they were regarded as the peculiar seats of divine energy. The common opinion seems to be that Semitic gods were never chthonic, in the sense that their seats and the source of their influence were sought

★ underground. But we know that all branches of the Semites believed in chthonic demons, the Hebrew *ōb*, the Syrian *zakkūrē*, the Arabian *ahl al-arḍ* or "earth-folk,"[2] with whom wizards hold fellowship. Again, the ordinary usages of Semitic religion have many points of contact with the chthonic rites of the Greeks. The Arabian *ghabghab* is not a mere treasury, for the victim is said to be brought to it, and the sacrificial blood flows into the pit.[3] Similarly the annual human sacrifice at Dumætha (Duma) was buried under the altar-idol.[4] As regards the northern Semites the chthonic associations of the Baalim as gods of the subterranean waters are unquestionable, particularly at sanctuaries like Aphaca, where the tomb of the Baal was shown beside his sacred stream;[5] for a buried god is a god that dwells underground. The whole N. Semitic area was dotted over with sacred tombs, Memnonia, Semiramis

[1] Wellhausen, p. 103.

★ [2] For the *ōb* see especially Isa. xxix. 4; for the *zakkūrē*, *Julianos*, ed. Hoffmann, p. 247, and *ZDMG.* xxviii. 666. For the *ahl al-arḍ* the oldest passage I know is Ibn Hishām, p. 258, l. 19, where these demons appear in connection with witchcraft, exactly like the *ōb* and the *zakkūrē*.

[3] Yācūt, iii. 772 *sq.*; Ibn Hishām, p. 55, l. 18; cf. Wellhausen, *ut supra*

[4] Porphyry, *De Abst.* ii. 56.

[5] *Supra,* p. 174, note.

mounds and the like, and at every such spot a god or
demigod had his subterranean abode.[1]   No part of old
Semitic belief was more deeply graven on the popular
imagination than this, which still holds its ground among
the peasantry, in spite of Christianity and Islam, with the
merely nominal modification that the ancient god has been
transformed into a wonder-working *sheikh* or *wely*.   In
view of these facts it can hardly be doubted that remarkable caves or passages, leading into the bowels of the earth,
were as likely to be clothed with supernatural associations
among the Semites as among the Greeks.   And there is at
least one great Semitic temple whose legends distinctly
indicate that the original sanctuary was a chasm in the
ground.   According to Lucian, this chasm swallowed up
the waters of the Flood (Deucalion's flood, as the Hellenised ★
form of the legend has it), and the temple with its altars
and special ritual of pouring water into the gulf was
erected in commemoration of this deliverance.[2]   According
to the Christian Melito, the chasm, or " well," as he calls it,
was haunted by a demon and the water-pouring was
designed to prevent him from coming up to injure men.[3]
Here the primitive sanctity of the chasm is the one fixed
point amidst the variations and distortions of later
legend ; and on this analogy I am disposed to conjecture
that in other cases also a cavern or cleft in the earth may
have been chosen as a primæval sanctuary because it marked
the spot where a chthonic god went up and down between
the outer world and his subterranean home, and where he

---

[1] That the Semiramis mounds were really tomb-sanctuaries appears from
the testimony of Ctesias cited by Syncellus, i. 119 (Bonn), and John of
Antioch (*Fr. Hist. Gr.* iv. 589), compared with Langlois, *Chron. de Michel
le Grand* (Venice, 1868), p. 40.   See also my article on "Ctesias and the
Semiramis legend " in *Eng. Hist. Rev.* April 1887, pp. 303 *sqq.*

[2] *De Dea Syria*, § 13, cf. § 48.

[3] Melito, *Spic. Syr.* p. 25.

could be best approached with prayers and offerings. What seems particularly to strengthen this conjecture is that the adytum, or dark inner chamber, found in many temples both among the Semites and in Greece, was almost certainly in its origin a cave ; indeed in Greece it was often wholly or partially subterranean and is called μέγαρον—a word which in this application can hardly be true Greek, and mean " hall," but is rather to be identified with the Semitic מערה, " a cave." The adytum is not a constant feature in Greek temples, and the name ★ μέγαρον seems to indicate that it was borrowed from the Semites.[1] Where it does exist it is a place of oracle, as the Holy of Holies was at Jerusalem, and therefore cannot be looked upon in any other light than as the part of the sanctuary where the god is most immediately present.

From this obscure topic we pass at once into clearer light when we turn to consider the ordinary artificial ★ mark of a Semitic sanctuary, viz. the sacrificial pillar, cairn or rude altar. The sacred fountain and the sacred tree are common symbols at sanctuaries, but they are not invariably found, and in most cases they have but a secondary relation to the ordinary ritual. In the more advanced type of sanctuary the real meeting-place between man and his god is the altar. The altar in its developed form is a raised structure upon which sacrifices are presented to the god. Most commonly the sacrifices are fire-offerings, and the altar is the place where they are burned ; but in another type of ritual, of which the Roman *lectisternium* and the Hebrew oblation of shewbread are familiar examples, the altar is simply a table on which a meal is spread before the deity. Whether fire is used or not is a

---

[1] The possibility of this can hardly be disputed when we think of the temple of Apollo at Delos, where the holy cave is the original sanctuary. For this was a place of worship which the Greeks took over from the Phœnicians.

detail in the mode of presentation and does not affect the essence of the sacrificial act. In either case the offering consists of food, " the bread of God " as it is called in the Hebrew ritual,[1] and there is no real difference between a table and altar. Indeed the Hebrew altar of burnt-offering is called the table of the Lord, while conversely the table of shewbread is called an altar.[2]

The table is not a very primitive article of furniture,[3] and this circumstance alone is enough to lead us to suspect that the altar was not originally a raised platform on which a sacrificial meal could be set forth. In Arabia, where sacrifice by fire is almost unknown, we find no proper altar, but in its place a rude pillar or heap of stones, beside which the victim is slain, the blood being poured out over the stone or at its base.[4] This ritual of the blood is the essence of the offering; no part of the flesh falls as a rule to the god, but the whole is distributed among the men who assist at the sacrifice. The sacred stones, which are already mentioned by Herodotus, are called *ansāb* (sing. *noṣb*), *i.e.* stones set up, pillars. We also find the name *gharīy*, " blood-bedaubed," with reference to the ritual just described. The meaning of this ritual will occupy us later; meantime the thing to be noted is that the altar is only a modification of the *noṣb*, and that the rude Arabian usage is the primitive type out of which all the elaborate altar ceremonies of the more cultivated Semites grew. Whatever else was done in connection with a sacrifice, the primitive rite of sprinkling

---

[1] Lev. xxi. 8, 17, etc.; cf. Lev. iii. 11.

[2] Mal. i. 7, 12 ; Ezek. xli. 22 ; cf. Wellhausen, *Prolegomena* (Eng.), p. 71. The same word (עָרַךְ) is used of setting a table and disposing the pieces of the sacrifice on the fire-altar.

[3] The old Arabian *sofra* is merely a skin spread on the ground, not a raised table. Cf. *E. Bi.* col. 2991.

[4] Wellhausen, *Heid.* pp. 43, 101, 116 ; cf. *Kinship*, p. 258.

or dashing the blood against the altar, or allowing it to flow down on the ground at its base, was hardly ever omitted;[1] and this practice was not peculiar to the Semites, but was equally the rule with the Greeks and Romans, and indeed with the ancient nations generally.

As regards fire sacrifices, we shall find reason to doubt whether the hearth on which the sacred flesh was consumed was originally identical with the sacred stone or cairn over which the sacrificial blood was allowed to flow. It seems probable, for reasons that cannot be stated at this point, that the more modern form of altar, which could be used both for the ritual of the blood and as a sacred hearth, was reached by combining two operations which originally took place apart. But in any case it is certain that the original altar among the northern Semites, as well as among the Arabs, was a great stone or cairn at which the blood of the victim was shed. At Jacob's covenant with Laban no other altar appears than the cairn of stones beside which the parties to the compact ate together; in the ancient law of Ex. xx. 24, 25, it is prescribed that the altar must be of earth or of unhewn stone; and that a single stone sufficed appears from 1 Sam. xiv. 32 *sqq.*, where the first altar built by Saul is simply the great stone which he caused to be rolled unto him after the battle of Michmash, that the people might slay their booty of sheep and cattle at it, and not eat the flesh with the blood. The simple shedding of the blood by

---

[1] There were indeed altars at which no animal sacrifices were presented. Such are, among the Hebrews, the altar of incense and the table of shewbread, and among the Phœnicians the altar at Paphos (Tac., *Hist.* ii. 3); perhaps also the "altar of the pious" at Delos (Porph., *De Abst.* ii. 28) was of Phœnician origin. In later times certain exceptional sacrifices were burned alive or slain without effusion of blood, but this does not touch the general principle.

the stone or altar consecrated the slaughter and made it a legitimate sacrifice. Here, therefore, there is no difference between the Hebrew altar and the Arabian *noṣb* or *ghariy*.

Monolithic pillars or cairns of stone are frequently mentioned in the more ancient parts of the Old Testament as standing at sanctuaries,[1] generally in connection with a sacred legend about the occasion on which they were set up by some famous patriarch or hero. In the biblical story they usually appear as mere memorial structures without any definite ritual significance; but the penta-teuchal law looks on the use of sacred pillars (*maṣṣēbōth*) as idolatrous.[2] This is the best evidence that such pillars had an important place among the appurtenances of Canaanite temples, and as Hosea (iii. 4) speaks of the *maṣṣēba* as an indispensable feature in the sanctuaries of northern Israel in his time, we may be sure that by the mass of the Hebrews the pillars of Shechem, Bethel, Gilgal and other shrines were looked upon not as mere memorials of historical events, but as necessary parts of the ritual apparatus of a place of worship. That the special ritual acts connected with the Canaanite *maṣṣēba* were essentially the same as in the case of the Arabian *noṣb* may be gathered from Philo Byblius, who, in his pseudo-historical manner, speaks of a certain Usous who consecrated two pillars to fire and wind, and paid worship to them, pouring out libations to them of the blood of beasts taken in hunting.[3] From these evidences, and especially from the fact that libations of the same kind

---

[1] At Shechem, Josh. xxiv. 26 ; Bethel, Gen. xxviii. 18 *sqq.*; Gilgal, [Ramoth-gilead), Gen. xxxi. 45 *sqq.*; Gilgal, Josh. iv. 5 ; Mizpah, 1 Sam. vii. 12 ; Gibeon, 2 Sam. xx. 8 ; En-rogel, 1 Kings i. 9.

[2] Ex. xxxiv. 13 ; Deut. xii. 3 ; cf. Mic. v. 13 (12). For pillars A.V. generally gives, incorrectly, 'images."

[3] Euseb. *Præp. Ev.* i. 10. 10. Libations of blood are mentioned as a heathenish rite in Ps. xvi. 4.

are applied to both, it seems clear that the altar is a
differentiated form of the primitive rude stone pillar, the
noṣb or *maṣṣēba*.[1]　But the sacred stone is more than an altar,
for in Hebrew and Canaanite sanctuaries the altar, in its
developed form as a table or hearth, does not supersede
the pillar; the two are found side by side at the same
sanctuary, the altar as a piece of sacrificial apparatus, and
the pillar as a visible symbol or embodiment of the presence
of the deity, which in process of time comes to be fashioned
and carved in various ways, till ultimately it becomes a
statue or anthropomorphic idol of stone, just as the sacred
tree or post was ultimately developed into an image of
wood.[2]

It has been disputed whether the sacred stone at
Semitic sanctuaries was from the first an object of
worship, a sort of rude idol in which the divinity was
somehow supposed to be present.　It is urged that in
the narratives of Genesis the *maṣṣēba* is a mere mark
without intrinsic religious significance.　But the original
significance of the patriarchal symbols cannot be concluded
from the sense put on them by writers who lived many
centuries after those ancient sanctuaries were first founded;
and at the time when the oldest of the pentateuchal
narratives were written, the Canaanites and the great
mass of the Hebrews certainly treated the *maṣṣēba* as a
sort of idol or embodiment of the divine presence.　Moreover Jacob's pillar is more than a mere landmark, for it
is anointed, just as idols were in antiquity, and the
pillar itself, not the spot on which it stood, is called

---

[1] *Noṣb* and *maṣṣēba* are derived from the same root (NṢB, "set up").
Another name for the pillar or cairn is נְצִיב, which occurs in place-names,
both in Canaan and among the Aramæans (Nisibis, "the pillars").

[2] From this point of view the prohibition of a graven image (פֶסֶל) in the
second commandment stands on one line with the prohibition of an altar of
hewn stone (Ex. xx. 25).

"the house of God,"[1] as if the deity were conceived actually to dwell in the stone, or manifest himself therein to his worshippers. And this is the conception which appears to have been associated with sacred stones everywhere. When the Arab daubed blood on the *noṣb* his object was to bring the offering into direct contact with the deity, and in like manner the practice of stroking the sacred stone with the hand is identical with the practice of touching or stroking the garments or beard of a man ★ in acts of supplication before him.[2] Here, therefore, the sacred stone is altar and idol in one; and so Porphyry (*De Abst.* ii. 56) in his account of the worship of Duma in Arabia expressly speaks of "the altar which they use as an idol."[3] The same conception must have prevailed among the Canaanites before altar and pillar were differentiated from one another, otherwise the pillar would have been simply changed into the more convenient form of an altar, and there could have been no reason for retaining both. So far as the evidence from tradition and ritual goes, we can only think of the sacred stone as consecrated by the actual presence of the godhead, so that whatever touched it was brought into immediate contact with the deity. How such a conception first obtained currency is a matter for which no direct evidence is available, and which if settled at all can be settled only by inference and conjecture. At the present stage of our inquiry it is not possible to touch on this subject except in a provisional

---

[1] Gen. xxviii. 22.

[2] Wellhausen, p. 109; *ibid.* p. 56. Conversely a holy person conveys a blessing by the touch of his hand (Ibn Sa'd, Nos. 90, 130), or even by touching something which others touch after him (Ibn Hishām, 338. 15).

[3] So in the well-known line of Al-A'shā the god to whom the sacred stone belongs is himself said to be *manṣūb*, " set up " (Ibn Hish. 256, 8; *Morg. Forsch.* p. 258). The Arabian gods are expressly called " gods of stone " in a verse cited by Ibn Sa'd, No. 118.

way. But some things may be said which will at least
tend to make the problem more definite.

Let us note then that there are two distinct points to
be considered—(1) how men came to look on an artificial
structure as the symbol or abode of the god, (2) why the
particular artificial structure is a stone or a cairn of stones.

(1.) In tree worship and in the worship of fountains
adoration is paid to a thing which man did not make,
which has an independent life, and properties such as to
the savage imagination may well appear to be divine.
On the same analogy one can understand how natural
rocks and boulders, suited by their size and aspect to affect
the savage imagination, have acquired in various parts of
the world the reputation of being animated objects with
power to help and hurt man, and so have come to receive
religious worship. But the worship of artificial pillars
and cairns of stones, chosen at random and set up by man's
hand, is a very different thing from this. Of course not
the rudest savage believes that in setting up a sacred stone
he is making a new god; what he does believe is that the
god comes into the stone, dwells in it or animates it, so
★ that for practical purposes the stone is thenceforth an
embodiment of the god, and may be spoken of and dealt
with as if it were the god himself. But there is an
enormous difference between worshipping the god in his
natural embodiment, such as a tree or some notable rock,
and persuading him to come and take for his embodiment
a structure set up for him by the worshipper. From the
metaphysical point of view, which we are always tempted
to apply to ancient religion, the worship of stocks and
stones prepared by man's hand seems to be a much cruder
thing than the worship of natural life as displayed in a
fountain or a secular tree; but practically the idea that
the godhead consents to be present in a structure set for

him by his worshippers implies a degree of intimacy and permanency in the relations between man and the being he adores which marks an advance on the worship of natural objects.   It is true that the rule of Semitic worship is that the artificial symbol can only be set up in a place already consecrated by tokens of the divine presence; but the sacred stone is not merely a token that the place is frequented by a god, it is also a permanent pledge that in this place he consents to enter into stated relations with men and accept their service.

(2.) That deities like those of ancient heathenism, which were not supposed to be omnipresent, and which were commonly thought of as having some sort of corporeal nature, could enter into a stone for the convenience of their worshippers, seems to us a fundamental difficulty, but was hardly a difficulty that would be felt by primitive man, who has most elastic conceptions of what is possible. When we speak of an idol we generally think of an image presenting a likeness of the god, because our knowledge of heathenism is mainly drawn from races which had made some advance in the plastic arts, and used idols shaped in such a way as to suggest the appearance and attributes which legend ascribed to each particular deity.   But there is no reason in the nature of things why the physical embodiment which the deity assumes for the convenience of his worshipper should be a copy of his proper form, and in the earliest times to which the worship of sacred stones goes back there was evidently no attempt to make the idol a simulacrum.   A cairn or rude stone pillar is not a portrait of anything, and I take it that we shall go on altogether false lines if we try to explain its selection as a divine symbol by any consideration of what it looks like. Even when the arts had made considerable progress the Semites felt no need to fashion their sacred symbols into

likenesses of the gods.   Melcarth was worshipped at Tyre
in the form of two pillars,[1] and at the great temple of
Paphos, down to Roman times, the idol was not an
anthropomorphic image of Astarte, but a conical stone.[2]
These antique forms were not retained from want of
plastic skill, or because there were not well-known types
on which images of the various gods could be and often
were constructed ; for we see from the second commandment that likenesses of things celestial terrestrial and
aquatic were objects of worship in Canaan from a very
early date.   It was simply not thought necessary that the
symbol in which the divinity was present should be like
the god.

Phœnician votive cippi were often adorned with rude
figures of men, animals and the like, as may be seen in the
series of such monuments dedicated to Tanith and Baal
Hammān which are depicted in the *Corpus Inscr. Sem.*
These figures, which are often little better than hierogly-
phics, served, like the accompanying inscriptions, to indicate
the meaning of the cippus and the deity to which it was
devoted.   An image in like manner declares its own
meaning better than a mere pillar, but the chief idol of a
great sanctuary did not require to be explained in this
way ; its position showed what it was without either figure
or inscription.   It is probable that among the Phœnicians
and Hebrews, as among the Arabs at the time of Mohammed,
portrait images, such as are spoken of in the second com-

[1] Herod. ii. 44.   Twin pillars stood also before the temples of Paphos
and Hierapolis, and Solomon set up two brazen pillars before his temple at
Jerusalem (1 Kings vii. 15, 21).   As he named them "The stablisher" and
"In him is strength," they were doubtless symbols of Jehovah.
[2] Tac., *Hist.* ii. 2.   Other examples are the cone of Elagabalus at Emesa
(Herodian, v. 3. 5) and that of Zeus Casius.   More in Zoega, *De obeliscis*,
p. 203.   The cone at Emesa was believed to have fallen from heaven,
like the idol of Artemis at Ephesus and other ancient and very sacred
idols.

mandment, were mainly small gods for private use.[1]   For public sanctuaries the second pillar or *ashera* sufficed.

The worship of sacred stones is often spoken of as if it belonged to a distinctly lower type of religion than the worship of images.   It is called fetichism—a merely popular term, which conveys no precise idea, but is vaguely supposed to mean something very savage and contemptible. And no doubt the worship of unshapen blocks is from the artistic point of view a very poor thing, but from a purely religious point of view its inferiority to image worship is not so evident.   The host in the mass is artistically as much inferior to the Venus of Milo as a Semitic *masṣēba* was, but no one will say that mediæval Christianity is a lower form of religion than Aphrodite worship.   What seems to be implied when sacred stones are spoken of as fetiches is that they date from a time when stones were regarded as the natural embodiment and proper form of the gods, not merely as the embodiment which they took up in order to receive the homage of their worshippers. Such a view, I venture to think, is entirely without foundation.   Sacred stones are found in all parts of the world and in the worship of gods of the most various kinds, so that their use must rest on some cause which was operative in all primitive religions.   But that all or most ancient gods were originally gods of stones, inhabiting natural rocks or boulders, and that artificial cairns or pillars are imitations of these natural objects, is against evidence and quite incredible.   Among the Semites the sacred pillar is universal, but the instances of the worship of rocks and stones *in situ* are neither numerous

---

[1] Of the common use of such gods every museum supplies evidence, in the shape of portable idols and amulets with pictured carving. Compare 2 Macc. xii. 40, where we read that many of the army of Judas Maccabæus— Jews fighting against heathenism—wore under their shirts ἱερώματα τῶν ἀπὸ Ἰαμνίας εἰδώλων.

14

nor prominent, and the idea of founding a theory of the
origin of sacred stones in general upon them could hardly
occur to any one, except on the perfectly gratuitous
supposition that the idol or symbol must necessarily be
like the god.[1]

The notion that the sacred stone is a simulacrum of
the god seems also to be excluded by the observation that
several pillars may stand together as representatives of a
single deity. Here, indeed, the evidence must be sifted
with some care, for a god and a goddess were often
worshipped together, and then each would have a pillar.[2]
But this kind of explanation does not cover all the cases.
In the Arabian rite described in Herod. iii. 8, two deities
are invoked, but seven sacred stones are anointed with

---

[1] The stone of al-Lāt at Ṭāïf, in which the goddess was supposed to dwell,
is identified by local tradition with a mass which seems to be a natural block
in situ, though not one of unusual size or form. See my *Kinship*, p. 299,
and Doughty, ii. 515. At 'Okāz the sacred circle was performed round
rocks (*ṣokhūr*, Yācūt, iii. 705), presumably the remarkable group which I
★ described in 1880 in a letter to the *Scotsman* newspaper. "In the S.E.
corner of the small plain, which is barely two miles across, rises a hill of
loose granite blocks, crowned by an enormous pillar standing quite erect and
flanked by lower masses. I do not think that this pillar can be less than
50 or 60 feet in height, and its extraordinary aspect, standing between two
lesser guards on either side, is the first thing that strikes the eye on nearing
the plain." The rock of Dusares, referred to by Steph. Byz., is perhaps the
cliff with a waterfall which has been already mentioned (*supra*, p. 168), and
so may be compared with the rock at Kadesh from which the fountain
gushed. The sanctity of rocks from which water flows, or of rocks that
form a sacred grotto, plainly cannot be used to explain the origin of sacred
cairns and pillars which have neither water nor cavern.

That the phrase "Rock of Israel," applied to Jehovah, has anything to
do with stone worship may legitimately be doubted. The use of baetylia,
or small portable stones to which magical life was ascribed, hardly belongs
to the present argument. The idol Abnîl at Nisibis is simply "the cippus
of El" (Assem. i. 27).

[2] Cf. *Kinship*, pp. 60 n., 299 *sqq.* Whether the two gharī at Ḥira and
Faid (Wellh. p. 43) belong to a pair of gods, or are a double image of one
deity, like the twin pillars of Heracles-Melcarth at Tyre, cannot be decided.
Wellhausen inclines to the latter view, citing *Ḥamāsa*, 190. 15. But in
Arabic idiom the two 'Ozzās may mean al-'Ozzā and her companion
goddess al-Lāt. Mr. C. Lyall suggests the reading *gharīyaini.*

blood, and a plurality of sacred stones round which the worshippers circled in a single act of worship are frequently spoken of in Arabian poetry.[1] Similarly in Canaan the place-name Anathoth means images of 'Anath in the plural; and at Gilgal there were twelve sacred pillars according to the number of the twelve tribes,[2] as at Sinai twelve pillars were erected at the covenant sacrifice.[3] Twin pillars of Melcarth have already been noticed at Tyre, and are familiar to us as the " pillars of Hercules " in connection with the Straits of Gibraltar.

Another view taken of sacred pillars and cippi is that they are images, not of the deity, but of bodily organs taken as emblems of particular powers or attributes of deity, especially of life-giving and reproductive power. I will say something of this theory in a note; but as an explanation of the origin of sacred stones it has not even a show of plausibility. Men did not begin by worshipping emblems of divine powers, they brought their homage and offerings to the god himself. If the god was already conceived as present in the stone, it was a natural exercise of the artistic faculty to put something on the stone to indicate the fact; and this something, if the god was anthropomorphically conceived, might either be a human figure, or merely an indication of important parts of the human figure. At Tabāla in Arabia, for

---

[1] Wellh., *Heid.* p. 102. The poets often seem to identify the god with one of the stones, as al-'Ozzā was identified with one of the three trees at Nakhla. The *anṣāb* stand beside the god (*Tāj*, iii. 560, l. 1) or round him, which probably means that the idol proper stood in the midst. In the verse of al-Farazdac, *Agh.* xix. 3, l. 30, to which Wellhausen calls attention, the Oxford MS. of the Nacāiḍ and that of the late Spitta-Bey read, '*alā ḥini lā tuḥyā 'l-banātu wa-idh humū 'ukūfun 'alā 'l-anṣābi ḥawla 'l-mudawwari*, and the ★ scholia explain *al-mudawwar* as *ṣanam yadūrūna ḥawlahu*. It is impossible to believe that this distinction between one stone and the rest is primitive.

[2] Josh. iv. 20. These stones are probably identical with the stone-idols (A.V. " quarries ") of Judg. iii. 19, 26.

[3] Ex. xxiv. 4.

instance, a sort of crown was sculptured on the stone of al-Lāt to mark her head. In like manner other parts of the body may be rudely designated, particularly such as distinguish sex. But that the sacred cippus, as such, is not a sexual emblem, is plain from the fact that exactly the same kind of pillar or cone is used to represent gods and goddesses indifferently.[1]

On a review of all these theories it seems most probable that the choice of a pillar or cairn as the primitive idol was not dictated by any other consideration than convenience for ritual purposes. The stone or stone-heap was a convenient mark of the proper place of sacrifice, and at the same time, if the deity consented to be present at it, provided the means for carrying out the ritual of the sacrificial blood. Further than this it does not seem possible to go, till we know why it was thought so essential to bring the blood into immediate contact with the god adored. This question belongs to the subject of sacrifice, which I propose to commence in the next lecture.[2]

---

[1] See *Additional Note* D, *Phallic Symbols*.

[2] One or two isolated statements about sacred stones, not sufficiently important or well attested to be mentioned in the text, may deserve citation in a note. Pliny, *H. N.* xxxvii. 161, speaks of an ordeal at the temple of Melcarth at Tyre by sitting on a stone seat, *ex qua pii facile surgebant.*— Yācūt, iii. 760, has a very curious account of a stone like a landmark near Aleppo. When it was thrown down the women of the adjoining villages were seized by a shameful frenzy, which ceased when it was set up again. Yācūt had this by very formal written attestation from persons he names ; but failed to obtain confirmation of the story on making personal inquiry at Aleppo.

LECTURE VI

WE have seen in the course of the last lecture that the practices of ancient religion required a fixed meeting-place between the worshippers and their god. The choice of such a place is determined in the first instance by the consideration that certain spots are the natural haunts of a deity, and therefore holy ground. But for most rituals it is not sufficient that the worshipper should present his service on holy ground: it is necessary that he should come into contact with the god himself, and this he believes himself to do when he directs his homage to a natural object, like a tree or a sacred fountain, which is believed to be the actual seat of the god and embodiment of a divine life, or when he draws near to an artificial mark of the immediate presence of the deity. In the oldest forms of Semitic religion this mark is a sacred stone, which is at once idol and altar; in later times the idol and the altar stand side by side, and the original functions of the sacred stone are divided between them; the idol represents the presence of the god, and the altar serves to receive the gifts of the worshipper. Both are necessary to constitute a complete sanctuary, because a complete act of worship implies not merely that the worshipper comes into the presence of his god with gestures of homage and words of prayer, but also that he lays before the deity some material oblation. In antiquity an act of

worship was a formal operation in which certain prescribed
rites and ceremonies must be duly observed.   And among
these the oblation at the altar had so central a place that
among the Greeks and Romans the words ἱερουργία and
sacrificium, which in their primary application denote
any action within the sphere of things sacred to the gods,
and so cover the whole field of ritual, were habitually used,
like our English word sacrifice, of those oblations at the
altar round which all other parts of ritual turned.   In
English idiom there is a further tendency to narrow the
word sacrifice to such oblations as involve the slaughter
of a victim.   In the Authorised Version of the Bible
★ " sacrifice and offering " is the usual translation of the
Hebrew *zébah uminha*, that is, " bloody and bloodless
oblations."   For the purposes of the present discussion,
however, it seems best to include both kinds of oblation
under the term " sacrifice "; for a comprehensive term is
necessary, and the word " offering," which naturally suggests itself as an alternative, is somewhat too wide, as it
may properly include not only sacrifices but votive offerings,
of treasure images and the like, which form a distinct
class from offerings at the altar.

   Why sacrifice is the typical form of all complete acts
of worship in the antique religions, and what the sacrificial
act means, is an involved and difficult problem.   The
problem does not belong to any one religion, for sacrifice
is equally important among all early peoples in all parts
of the world where religious ritual has reached any considerable development.   Here, therefore, we have to deal
with an institution that must have been shaped by the
action of general causes, operating very widely and under
conditions that were common in primitive times to all
races of mankind.   To construct a theory of sacrifice
exclusively on the Semitic evidence would be unscientific

and misleading, but for the present purpose it is right to put the facts attested for the Semitic peoples in the foreground, and to call in the sacrifices of other nations to confirm or modify the conclusions to which we are led. For some of the main aspects of the subject the Semitic evidence is very full and clear, for others it is fragmentary and unintelligible without help from what is known about other rituals.

Unfortunately the only system of Semitic sacrifice of which we possess a full account is that of the second temple at Jerusalem ;[1] and though the ritual of Jerusalem as described in the Book of Leviticus is undoubtedly based on very ancient tradition, going back to a time when there was no substantial difference, in point of form, between Hebrew sacrifices and those of the surrounding nations, the system as we have it dates from a time when sacrifice was no longer the sum and substance of worship. In the long years of Babylonian exile the Israelites who remained true to the faith of Jehovah had learned to draw nigh to their God without the aid of sacrifice and offering, and, when they returned to Canaan, they did not return to the old

---

[1] The detailed ritual laws of the Pentateuch belong to the post-exilic document commonly called the Priestly Code, which was adopted as the law of Israel's religion at Ezra's reformation (444 B.C.). To the Priestly Code belong the Book of Leviticus, together with the cognate parts of the adjacent Books, Ex. xxv.–xxxi., xxxv.–xl., and Num. i.–x., xv.–xix., xxv.–xxxvi. (with some inconsiderable exceptions). With the Code is associated an account of the sacred history from Adam to Joshua, and some ritual matter is found in the historical sections of the work, especially in Ex. xii., where the law of the Passover is mainly priestly, and represents post-exilic usage. The law of Deuteronomy (seventh cent. B.C.) and the older codes of Ex. xx.–xxiii., xxxiv., have little to say about the rules of ritual, which in old times were matters of priestly tradition and not incorporated in a law-book. A just view of the sequence and dates of the several parts of the Pentateuch is essential to the historical study of Hebrew religion. Readers to whom this subject is new may refer to Wellhausen's *Prolegomena* (Eng. trans., Edin. 1883), to the article "Pentateuch," *Encycl. Brit.*, 9th ★ ed., to my *Old Test. in the Jewish Church* (2nd ed. 1892), or to Professor Driver's *Introduction*.

type of religion.   They built an altar, indeed, and restored
its ritual on the lines of old tradition, so far as these could
be reconciled with the teaching of the prophets and the
Deuteronomic law—especially with the principle that there
was but one sanctuary at which sacrifice could be accept-
ably offered.   But this principle itself was entirely
destructive of the old importance of sacrifice, as the stated
means of converse between God and man.   In the old
time every town had its altar, and a visit to the local
sanctuary was the easy and obvious way of consecrating
every important act of life.   No such interweaving of
sacrificial service with everyday religion was possible
under the new law, nor was anything of the kind attempted.   The worship of the second temple was an
antiquarian resuscitation of forms which had lost their
intimate connection with the national life, and therefore
had lost the greater part of their original significance.
The Book of Leviticus, with all its fulness of ritual detail,
does not furnish any clear idea of the place which each
kind of altar service held in the old religion, when all
worship took the form of sacrifice.   And in some particulars there is reason to believe that the desire to avoid
all heathenism, the necessity for giving expression to new
religious ideas, and the growing tendency to keep the
people as far as possible from the altar and make sacrifice
the business of a priestly caste, had introduced into the
ritual features unknown to more ancient practice.

The three main types of sacrifice recognised by the
Levitical law are the whole burnt-offering (*'ōla*), the
sacrifice followed by a meal of which the flesh of the victim
formed the staple (*shélem, zébah*), and the sin-offering
(*hattāth*), with an obscure variety of the last named called
asham (A.V. " trespass-offering "). Of these *'ōla* and *zébah*
are frequently mentioned in the older literature, and they

are often spoken of together, as if all animal sacrifices
fell under one or the other head.　The use of sacrifice as
an atonement for sin is also recognised in the old literature,
especially in the case of the burnt-offering, but there is
little or no trace of a special kind of offering appropriated
for this purpose before the time of Ezekiel.[1]　The formal
distinctions with regard to Hebrew sacrifices that can be
clearly made out from the pre-exilic literature are—

(1) The distinction between animal and vegetable
oblations, *zébaḥ* and *minḥa*).

(2) The distinction between offerings that were consumed
by fire and such as were merely set forth on the sacred
table (the shewbread).

(3) The distinction between sacrifices in which the
consecrated gift is wholly made over to the god, to be
consumed on the altar or otherwise disposed of in his
service, and those at which the god and his worshippers
partake together in the consecrated thing.　To the latter
class belong the *zebahīm*, or ordinary animal sacrifices, in
which a victim is slain, its blood poured out at the altar,
and the fat of the intestines with certain other pieces
burned, while the greater part of the flesh is left to the
offerer to form the material of a sacrificial banquet.

These three distinctions, which are undoubtedly ancient,
and applicable to the sacrifices of other Semitic nations,
suggest three heads under which a preliminary survey of
the subject may be conveniently arranged.　But not till
we reach the third head shall we find ourselves brought
face to face with the deeper aspects of the problem of the
origin and significance of sacrificial worship.

[1] See Wellhausen, *Prolegomena*, chap. ii.　The Hebrew designations of
the species of sacrifices are to be compared with those on the Carthaginian
tables of fees paid to priests for the various kinds of offerings, *CIS*. Nos.
165, 164 *sqq.*, but the information given in these is so fragmentary that it is
difficult to make much of it.　See below, p. 237 n.

1. *The material of sacrifice.* The division of sacrifices
into animal and vegetable offerings involves the principle
that sacrifices—as distinct from votive offerings of garments,
weapons, treasure and the like—are drawn from edible
substances, and indeed from such substances as form the
ordinary staple of human food. The last statement is
strictly true of the Levitical ritual; but, so far as the
flesh of animals is concerned, it was subject, even in the
later heathen rituals, to certain rare but important exceptions, unclean or sacred animals, whose flesh was ordinarily
forbidden to men, being offered and eaten sacramentally on
very solemn occasions. We shall see by and by that in
the earliest times these extraordinary sacrifices had a very
great importance in ritual, and that on them depends the
theory of the oldest sacrificial meals; but, as regards later
times, the Hebrew sacrifices are sufficiently typical of the
ordinary usage of the Semites generally. The four-footed
animals from which the Levitical law allows victims to be
selected are the ox the sheep and the goat, that is, the
" clean " domestic quadrupeds which men were allowed to
eat. The same quadrupeds are named upon the Carthaginian inscriptions that give the tariff of sacrificial fees to
be paid at the temple,[1] and in Lucian's account of the
Syrian ritual at Hierapolis.[2] The Israelites neither ate nor
sacrificed camels, but among the Arabs the camel was
★ common food and a common offering. The swine, on the
other hand, which was commonly sacrificed and eaten in
Greece, was forbidden food to all the Semites,[3] and occurs
as a sacrifice only in certain exceptional rites of the kind
already alluded to. Deer, gazelles and other kinds of
game were eaten by the Hebrews, but not sacrificed, and
from Deut. xii. 16 we may conclude that this was an

---

[1] *CIS.* Nos. 165, 167.   [2] *Dea Syria,* liv.
[3] Lucian, *ut sup.* (Syrians); Sozomen, vi. 38 (all Saracens).

ancient rule. Among the Arabs, in like manner, a gazelle was regarded as an imperfect oblation, a shabby substitute for a sheep.[1] As regards birds, the Levitical law admits pigeons and turtle-doves, but only as holocausts and in certain purificatory ceremonies.[2] Birds seem also to be mentioned in the Carthaginian sacrificial lists; what is said of them is very obscure, but it would appear that they might be used either for ordinary sacrifices (*shelem kalîl*) or for special purposes piacular and oracular. That the quail was sacrificed to the Tyrian Baal appears from Athenæus, ix. 47, p. 392*d*. See p. 469.

Fish were eaten by the Israelites, but not sacrificed ; among their heathen neighbours, on the contrary, fish—or certain kinds of fish—were forbidden food, and were sacrificed only in exceptional cases.[3]

Among the Hebrew offerings from the vegetable kingdom, meal wine and oil take the chief place,[4] and these were also the chief vegetable constituents of man's daily food.[5]

---

[1] Wellh. p. 115; Hārith, *Mo'all.* 69 ; especially *Lisān*, vi. 211. The reason of this rule, and certain exceptions, will appear in the sequel.

[2] Lev. i. 14, xii. 6, 8, xiv. 22, xv. 14, 29 ; Num. vi. 10. Two birds, of which one is slain and its blood used for lustration, appear also in the ritual for cleansing a leper, or a house that has been affected with leprosy (Lev. xiv. 4 *sq.*, 49 *sq.*). Further, the turtle-dove and nestling (pigeon) appear in an ancient covenant ceremony (Gen. xv. 9 *sqq.*). The fact that the dove was not used by the Hebrews for any ordinary sacrifice, involving a sacrificial meal, can hardly be, in its origin, independent of the sacrosanct character ascribed to this bird in the religion of the heathen Semites. The Syrians would not eat doves, and their very touch made a man unclean for a day (*Dea Syria*, liv.). In Palestine also the dove was sacred with the Phœnicians and Philistines, and on this superstition is based the common Jewish accusation against the Samaritans, that they were worshippers of the dove (see for all this Bochart, *Hierozoicon*, II. i. 1). Nay, sacred doves that may not be harmed are found even at Mecca. In legal times the dove was of course a "clean" bird to the Hebrews, but it is somewhat remarkable that we never read of it in the Old Testament as an article of diet—not even in 1 Kings v. 2 *sqq.* (A.V. iv. 22 *sqq.*)—though it is now one of the commonest table-birds all over the East.

[3] See below, p. 292 *sq.*   [4] Cf. Mic. vi. 7 with Lev. ii. 1 *sqq.*

[5] Ps. civ. 14 *sq.*

In the lands of the olive, oil takes the place that butter and other animal fats hold among northern nations, and accordingly among the Hebrews, and seemingly also among the Phœnicians,[1] it was customary to mingle oil with the cereal oblation before it was placed upon the altar, in conformity with the usage at ordinary meals. In like manner no cereal offering was complete without salt,[2] which, for physiological reasons, is a necessary of life to all who use a cereal diet, though among nations that live exclusively on flesh and milk it is not indispensable and is often dispensed with. Wine, which as Jotham's parable has it, " cheereth gods and men," [3] was added to whole burnt-offerings and to the oblation of victims of whose flesh the worshippers partook.[4] The sacrificial use of wine, without which no feast was complete, seems to have ★ been well-nigh universal wherever the grape was known,[5] and even penetrated to Arabia, where wine was a scarce and costly luxury imported from abroad. Milk, on the other hand, though one of the commonest articles of food among the Israelites, has no place in Hebrew sacrifice, but libations of milk were offered by the Arabs, and also at Carthage.[6] Their absence among the Hebrews may perhaps be explained by the rule of Ex. xxiii. 18, Lev. ii. 11, which excludes all ferments from presentation at the altar; for in hot climates milk ferments rapidly and is generally eaten sour.[7] The same principle covers the

[1] In *CIS.* No. 165, l. 14, the בלל is to be interpreted by the aid of Lev. vii. 10, and understood of bread or meal moistened with oil.

[2] Lev. ii. 13.   [3] Judg. ix. 13.   [4] Num. xv. 5.

[5] For some exceptions see Aesch., *Eum.* 107 ; Soph., *Oed. Col.* 100, with Schol. ; Paus. ii. 11. 4 ; v. 15. 10 (Greek libations to the Eumenides and to the Nymphs) ; and Athen. xv. 48 (libations to the sun at Emesa).

[6] Wellh. p. 114 *sq.* ; *CIS.* No. 165, l. 14 ; No. 167, l. 10.

[7] The rule against offering fermented things on the altar was not observed in northern Israel in all forms of sacrifice (Amos iv. 5), and traces of greater freedom in this respect appear also in Lev. vii. 13, xxiii. 17. It seems strange that wine should be admitted in sacrifice and leaven excluded, for

prohibition of "honey,"[1] which term, like the modern ★ Arabic *dibs*, appears to include fruit juice inspissated by boiling—a very important article of food in modern and presumably in ancient Palestine.   Fruit in its natural state, however, was offered at Carthage,[2] and was probably admitted by the Hebrews in ancient times.[3]   Among the

leaven is a product of vinous fermentation, and leavened bread equally with wine is to the nomad a foreign luxury (*al-khamr wal-khamir, Agh.* xix. 25), so that both alike must have been wanting in the oldest type of Hebrew sacrifices.   Thus the continued prohibition of leaven in sacrifice, after wine was admitted, can hardly be regarded as a mere piece of religious conservatism, but must have some further significance.   It is possible that in its oldest form the legal prohibition of leaven applied only to the Passover, to which Ex. xxiii. 18, xxxiv. 25, specially refer.   In this connection the prohibition of leaven is closely associated with the rule that the fat and flesh must not remain over till the morning.   For we shall find by and by that a similar rule applied to certain Saracen sacrifices nearly akin to the Passover, which were even eaten raw, and had to be entirely consumed before the sun rose.   In this case the idea was that the efficacy of the sacrifice lay in the living flesh and blood of the victim.   Everything of the nature of putrefaction was therefore to be avoided, and the connection between leaven and putrefaction is obvious.

The only positive law against the sacrificial use of milk is that in Ex. xxiii. 19, xxxiv. 26: "Thou shalt not seethe a kid in its mother's milk." ★ Mother's milk is simply goat's milk, which was that generally used (Prov. xxvii. 27), and flesh seethed in milk is still a common Arabian dish ; sour milk is specified as the kind employed in *PEF. Qu. St.* 1888, p. 188. The context of the passages in Exodus shows that some ancient form of sacrifice is referred to ; cf. Judg. vi. 19, where we have a holocaust of sodden flesh.   A sacrificial gift sodden in sour milk would evidently be of the nature of fermented food ; but I do not feel sure that this goes to the root of the matter.   Many primitive peoples regard milk as a kind of equivalent for blood, and thus to eat a kid seethed in its mother's milk might be taken as equivalent to eating "with the blood," and be forbidden to the Hebrews along with the bloody sacraments of the heathen, of which more hereafter.

[1] Lev. ii. 11.   [2] *CIS.* No. 166.

[3] The term *hillulim*, applied in Lev. **xix.** 24 to the consecrated fruit ★ borne by a new tree in its fourth year, is applied in Judg. ix. 27 to the Canaanite vintage feast at the sanctuary.   The Carthaginian fruit-offering consisted of a branch bearing fruit, like the "ethrog" of the modern Jewish feast of Tabernacles.   The use of "goodly fruits" at this festival is ordained in Lev. xxiii. 40, but their destination is not specified.   In Carthage, though the inscription that speaks of the rite is fragmentary, it seems to be clear that the fruit was offered at the altar, for incense is mentioned with it ; and this, no doubt, is the original sense of the Hebrew rite also.

Hebrews vegetable or cereal oblations were sometimes presented by themselves, especially in the form of first-fruits, but the commonest use of them was as an accompaniment to an animal sacrifice. When the Hebrew ate flesh, he ate bread with it and drank wine, and when he offered flesh on the table of his God, it was natural that he should add to it the same concomitants which were necessary to make up a comfortable and generous meal.

Of these various oblations animal sacrifices are by far the most important in all the Semitic countries. They are in fact the typical sacrifice, so that among the Phœnicians the word *zébaḥ*, which properly means a slaughtered victim, is applied even to offerings of bread and oil.[1] That cereal offerings have but a secondary place in ritual is not unintelligible in connection with the history of the Semitic race. For all the Semites were originally nomadic, and the ritual of the nomad Arabs and the settled Canaanites has so many points in common that there can be no question that the main lines of sacrificial worship were fixed before any part of the Semitic stock had learned agriculture and adopted cereal food as its ordinary diet. It must be observed, however, that animal food—or at least the flesh of domestic animals, which are the only class of victims admitted among the Semites as ordinary and regular sacrifices— was not a common article of diet even among the nomad Arabs. The everyday food of the nomad consisted of milk, of game, when he could get it, and to a limited extent of dates and meal—the latter for the most part being attainable only by purchase or robbery. Flesh

Cf. the raisin-cakes (A.V. "flagons of wine"), Hos. iii. 1, which from the context appear to be connected with the worship of the Baalim.

[1] *CIS.* No. 165, l. 12 ; 167, l. 9. In the context צד can hardly mean game, but must be taken, as in Josh. ix. 11 *sqq.*, of cereal food, the ordinary "provision" of agricultural peoples,

of domestic animals was eaten only as a luxury or in
times of famine.[1] If therefore the sole principle that
governed the choice of the material of sacrifices had been
that they must consist of human food, milk and not flesh
would have had the leading place in nomad ritual, whereas
its real place is exceedingly subordinate.   To remove this
difficulty it may be urged that, as sacrifice is food offered
to the gods, it ought naturally to be of the best and most
luxurious kind that can be attained; but on this principle
it is not easy to see why game should be excluded, for a
gazelle is not worse food than an old camel.[2]   The true
solution of the matter lies in another direction.   Among
the Hebrews no sacrificial meal was provided for the
worshippers unless a victim was sacrificed; if the oblation
was purely cereal it was wholly consumed either on the
altar or by the priests, in the holy place, *i.e.* by the
representatives of the deity.[3]   In like manner the only
Arabian meal-offering about which we have particulars,
that of the god Ocaisir,[4] was laid before the idol in
handfuls.   The poor, however, were allowed to partake
of it, being viewed no doubt as the guests of the deity.

---

[1] See the old narratives, *passim*, and compare Doughty, i. 325 *sq.*   The
statement of Fränkel, *Fremdwörter*, p. 31, that the Arabs lived mainly on
flesh, overlooks the importance of milk as an article of diet among all the
pastoral tribes, and must also be taken with the qualification that the flesh used
as ordinary food was that of wild beasts taken in hunting.   On this point
the evidence is clear; Pliny, *H. N.* vi. 161, "nomadas lacte et ferina carne
uesci"; Agatharchides, *ap.* Diod. Sic. iii. 44. 2; Ammianus, xiv. 4, 6,
"uictus uniuersis caro ferina est lactisque abundans copia qua sustentantur";
Nilus, p. 27.   By these express statements we must interpret the vaguer
utterances of Diodorus (xix. 94. 9) and Agatharchides (*ap.* Diod. iii. 43. 5)
about the ancient diet of the Nabatæans: the "nourishment supplied by
their herds" was mainly milk.   Certain Arab tribes, like the modern Sleyb,
had no herds and lived wholly by hunting, and these perhaps are referred
to in what Agatharchides says of the Banizomenes, and in the Syriac life
of Simeon Stylites (Assemani, *Mart.* ii. 345), where, at any rate, *besrā
d'ḥaiwāthā* means game.

[2] Cf. Gen. xxvii. 7.   [3] Lev. ii. 3, v. 11, vi. 16 (E.V. 22).

[4] Yācūt, *s.v.* ; Wellh. p. 62 *sqq.*

The cereal offering therefore has strictly the character of
a tribute paid by the worshipper to his god, as indeed is
expressed by the name *minḥa*, whereas when an animal
is sacrificed, the sacrificer and the deity feast together, part
of the victim going to each. The predominance assigned in
ancient ritual to animal sacrifice corresponds to the predominance of the type of sacrifice which is not a mere payment
of tribute but an act of social fellowship between the
deity and his worshippers. Why this social meal always
includes the flesh of a victim will be considered in a subsequent lecture.

All sacrifices laid upon the altar were taken by the
ancients as being literally the food of the gods. The
Homeric deities "feast on hecatombs,"[1] nay, particular
Greek gods have special epithets designating them as the
goat-eater, the ram-eater, the bull-eater, even "the cannibal,"
with allusion to human sacrifices.[2] Among the Hebrews
the conception that Jehovah eats the flesh of bulls and
drinks the blood of goats, against which the author of
Ps. l. protests so strongly, was never eliminated from
the ancient technical language of the priestly ritual, in
which the sacrifices are called לחם אלהים, "the food of the
deity." In its origin this phrase must belong to the same
circle of ideas as Jotham's "wine which cheereth gods and
men." But in the higher forms of heathenism the crass
materialism of this conception was modified, in the case of
fire-offerings, by the doctrine that man's food must be
etherealised or sublimated into fragrant smoke before the
gods partake of it. This observation brings us to the
second of the points which we have noted in connection
with Hebrew sacrifice, viz. the distinction between sacrifices
that are merely set forth on the sacred table before the
deity, and such as are consumed by fire upon the altar.

---

[1] *Iliad*, ix. 531.   [2] αἰγοφάγος, κριοφάγος, ταυροφάγος, Διόνυσος ὠμηστής.

2. The table of shewbread has its closest parallel in the *lectisternia* of ancient heathenism, when a table laden with meats was spread beside the idol. Such tables were set in the great temple of Bel at Babylon,[1] and, if any weight is to be given to the apocryphal story of Bel and the Dragon in the Greek Book of Daniel, it was popularly believed that the god actually consumed the meal provided for him,[2] a superstition that might easily hold its ground by priestly connivance where the table was spread inside a temple. A more primitive form of the same kind of offering appears in Arabia, where the meal-offering to Ocaisir is cast by handfuls at the foot of the idol mingled with the hair of the worshipper,[3] and milk is poured over the sacred stones. A narrative of somewhat apocryphal colour, given without reference to his authority by Sprenger,[4] has it that in the worship of 'Amm-anas in Southern Arabia, whole hecatombs were slaughtered and left to be devoured by wild beasts. Apart from the exaggeration, there may be something in this; for the idea that sacred animals are the guests or clients of the god is not alien to Arabian thought,[5] and to feed them is an act of religion

---

[1] Herod. i. 181, 183 ; Diod. Sic. ii. 9. 7.

[2] The story, so far as it has a basis in actual superstition, is probably drawn from Egyptian beliefs ; but in such matters Egypt and Babylon were much alike ; Herod. i. 182.

[3] The same thing probably applies to other Arabian meal-offerings, *e.g.* the wheat and barley offered to Al-Kholaṣa (Azrācī, p. 78). As the dove was the sacred bird at Mecca, the epithet *Moṭ'im al-ṭair*, "he who feeds the ★ birds," applied to the idol that stood upon Marwa (*ibid.*), seems to point to similar meal-offerings rather than to animal victims left lying before the god. The "idol" made of *hais*, *i.e.* a mass of dates kneaded up with butter and sour milk, which the B. Ḥanīfa ate up in time of famine (see the *Lexx. s.v.* تباعة ; Ibn Coteiba, ed. Wüst. p. 299 ; Bīrūnī, *Chron.* p. 210), probably belonged to the widespread class of cereal offerings, shaped as rude idols and eaten sacramentally (Liebrecht, *Zur Volkskunde*, p. 436 ; *ZDMG.* xxx. 539).

[4] *Leb. Moh.* iii. 457.

[5] See above, p. 142 *sqq.*, and the god-name Mot'im al-ṭair in the last

in many heathen systems, especially where, as in Egypt,[1]
★ the gods themselves are totem-deities, *i.e.* personifications
or individual representations of the sacred character and
attributes which, in the purely totem stage of religion,
were ascribed without distinction to all animals of the
holy kind. Thus at Cynopolis in Egypt, where dogs were
honoured and fed with sacred food, the local deity was the
divine dog Anubis, and similarly in Greece, at the sanctuary
of the Wolf Apollo (Apollo Lycius) of Sicyon, an old tradition preserved—though in a distorted form—the memory of
a time when flesh used to be set forth for the wolves.[2] It
is by no means impossible that something of the same sort
took place at certain Arabian shrines, for we have already
learned how closely the gods were related to the *jinn* and
the *jinn* to wild animals, and the list of Arabian deities
includes a Lion-god (Yaghūth) and a Vulture-god (Nasr),[3]
to whose worship rites like those described by Sprenger
would be altogether appropriate.

But while it cannot be thought impossible that sacrificial victims were presented on holy ground and left to be
devoured by wild beasts as the guests or congeners of the
gods, I confess that there seems to me to be no sufficient
evidence that such a practice had any considerable place
in Arabian ritual. The leading idea in the animal sacrifices
of the Semites, as we shall see by and by, was not that of
a gift made over to the god, but of an act of communion,

note but one; also Hamdānī's account of the offerings at Sāwid, *supra*,
p. 177.

[1] Strabo, xvii. 1. 39 *sq.* (p. 812).

[2] Pausanias, ii. 9. 7. The later rationalism which changed the Wolf-god
into a Wolf-slayer gave the story a corresponding twist by relating that the
flesh was poisoned, under the god's directions, with the leaves of a tree whose
trunk was preserved in the temple, like the sacred erica at Byblus.

[3] See *Kinship*, pp. 223, 242 ; Nöldeke, *ZDMG.* 1886, p. 186. See also,
★ for the Himyarite Vulture-god, *ZDMG.* xxix. 600, and compare the eagle
standard of Morra, Nābigha, iv. 7, Ahlw. = xxi. 7, Der.

in which the god and his worshippers unite by partaking together of the flesh and blood of a sacred victim. It is true that in the case of certain very solemn sacrifices, especially of *piacula*, to which class the sacrifices cited by Sprenger appear to belong, the victim sometimes came to be regarded as so sacred that the worshippers did not venture to eat of it at all, but that the flesh was burned or buried or otherwise disposed of in a way that secured it from profanation; and among the Arabs, who did not use burning except in the case of human sacrifices, we can quite well understand that one way of disposing of holy flesh might be to leave it to be eaten by the sacred animals of the god. Or again, when a sacrifice is expressly offered as a ransom, as in the case of the hundred camels with which 'Abd-al-Moṭṭalib redeemed his vow to sacrifice his son, it is intelligible that the offerer reserves no part of the flesh, but leaves it to anyone who chooses to help himself; or even (according to another reading) leaves it free to man and beast.[1] On the whole, however, all the well-authenticated accounts of Arabian sacrifice seem to indicate that the original principle, that the worshippers must actually eat of the sacred flesh, was very rigorously held to.[2] Wellhausen indeed is disposed to think that the practice of slaughtering animals and leaving them beside the altar to be devoured by wild beasts was not confined to certain exceptional cults, but prevailed generally in the case of the *'atāïr* (sing. *'atīra*) or annual sacrifices presented by the Arabs in the month Rajab, which originally corresponded to the Hebrew Passover-month (Abib, Nisan).[3]

---

[1] Ibn Hish. p. 100, l. 7; Ṭabarī, i. 1078, l. 4.   (Wellh. 116.)

[2] The evidence of Nilus is very important in this connection; for the interval between his time and that of the oldest native traditions is scarcely sufficient to allow for the development of an extensive system of sacrifice without a sacrificial meal; *infra*, p. 338.

[3] Cf. Wellh.[1] p. 94 *sq.*, [2] 98 *sq.* To complete the parallelism of the Passover

" It is remarkable," says Wellhausen, " how often we hear of the 'atāïr lying round the altar-idol, and sometimes in poetical comparisons the slain are said to be left lying on the battlefield like 'atāïr." [1] But on the Arabian method of sacrifice the carcases of the victims naturally lie on the ground, beside the sacred stone, till the blood, which is the god's portion, has drained into the *ghabghab*, or pit, at its foot, and till all the other ritual prescriptions have been fulfilled. Thus at a great feast when many victims were offered together, the scene would resemble a battlefield ; indeed, it is impossible to imagine a more disgusting scene of carnage than is still presented every year at Minā on the great day of sacrifice, when the ground is literally covered with innumerable carcases. It is not therefore necessary to suppose that the 'atāïr at Rajab were left to the hyæna and the vulture ; and, as the name *atīra* seems to be also used in a more general sense of any victim whose blood is applied to the sacred stones at the sanctuary, it is hardly to be thought that there was anything very exceptional in the form of the Rajab ceremony.

In the higher forms of Semitic heathenism offerings of the shewbread type are not very conspicuous ; in truth the idea that the gods actually consume the solid food deposited

with the Rajab offerings, Wellhausen desiderates evidence connecting the 'atāïr of Rajab with the sacrifice of firstlings. The traditionists, *e.g.* Bokhārī, vi. 207 (at the close of the *Kit. al-'acīca*), distinguish between firstlings (*fara'*) and 'atīra, but the line of distinction is not sharp. The lexicons apply the name *fara'*, not only to firstlings sacrificed while their flesh was still like glue (*Lisān*, x. 120), but also to the sacrifice of one beast ★ in a hundred, which is what the scholiast on Ḥarith's *Moall.* 69 understands by the 'atīra. Conversely the *Lisān*, vi. 210, defines the 'atīra as a firstling (*awwal mā yuntaj*) which was sacrificed to the gods. If we could accept this statement without reserve, in the general confusion of the later Arabs on the subject, it would supply what Wellhausen desiderates.

[1] Wellh.[1] p. 115, cf. [2] 121 ; cf. the verses cited *ibid.* pp. 18, 61 ; and, for the poetical comparisons, Ibn Hishām, 534. 4 ; Alcama, vi. 3, Soc.

at their shrines is too crude to subsist without modification beyond the savage state of society; the ritual may
survive, but the sacrificial gifts, which the god is evidently
unable to dispose of himself, will come to be the perquisite
of the priests, as in the case of the shewbread, or of the
poor, as in the meal sacrifice to Ocaisir. In such cases
the actual eating is done by the guests of the deity, but
the god himself may still be supposed to partake of food
in a subtle and supersensuous way. It is interesting to
note the gradations of ritual that correspond to this modification of the original idea.

In the more primitive forms of Semitic religion the
difficulty of conceiving that the gods actually partake of
food is partly got over by a predominant use of liquid
oblations; for fluid substances, which sink in and disappear,
are more easily believed to be consumed by the deity than
obstinate masses of solid matter.

The libation, which holds quite a secondary place in the
more advanced Semitic rituals, and is generally a mere
accessory to a fire offering, has great prominence among the
Arabs, to whom sacrifices by fire were practically unknown
except, as we shall see by and by, in the case of human
sacrifice. Its typical form is the libation of blood, the
subtle vehicle of the life of the sacrifice; but milk, which
was used in ritual both by the Arabs and by the Phœnicians, is also no doubt a very ancient Semitic libation. In
ordinary Arabian sacrifices the blood which was poured
over the sacred stone was all that fell to the god's part, the
whole flesh being consumed by the worshippers and their
guests; and the early prevalence of this kind of oblation
appears from the fact that the word נסך, "to pour," which
in Hebrew means to pour out a drink-offering, is in Arabic
the general term for an act of worship.

In the North Semitic ritual the most notable feature in

the libation, which ordinarily consisted of wine, is that it was not consumed by fire, even when it went with a fire-offering.   The Greeks and Romans poured the sacrificial wine over the flesh, but the Hebrews treated it like the blood, pouring it out at the base of the altar.[1]   In Ecclesiasticus the wine so treated is even called " the blood of the grape," [2] from which one is tempted to conclude that here also blood is the typical form of libation, and that wine is a surrogate for it, as fruit-juice seems to have been in certain Arabian rites.[3]   It is true that the blood of the sacrifice is not called a libation in Hebrew ritual, and in Ps. xvi. 4 " drink-offerings of blood " are spoken of as something heathenish.   But this proves that such libations were known ; and that the Hebrew altar ritual of the blood is essentially a drink-offering appears from Ps. l. 13, where Jehovah asks, " Will I eat the flesh of bulls or drink the blood of goats ? " and also from 2 Sam. xxiii. 17, where David pours out as a drink-offering the water from the well of Bethlehem, refusing to drink " the blood of the men that fetched it in jeopardy of their lives." Putting all this together, and noting also that libations were retained as a chief part of ritual in the domestic heathenism of the Hebrew women in the time of Jeremiah,[4] and that private service is often more conservative than

---

[1] Ecclus. l. 15 ; Jos. *Antt.* iii. 9. 4.   Num. xv. 7 is sometimes cited as proving that in older times the wine was poured over the sacrificial flesh, but see against this interpretation Num. xxviii. 7.

[2] The term αἷμα βοτρύων occurs in the Tyrian legend of the invention of wine, Ach. Tatius, ii. 2, and may possibly be the translation of an old Phœnician phrase.

[3] *Kinship*, p. 59 n. ; Wellh. p. 125.

[4] Jer. xix. 13, xxxii. 29, xliv. 17, 18.   With this worship on the house-tops, cf. what Strabo, xvi. 4. 26, tells of the daily offerings of libations and incense presented to the sun by the Nabatæans at an altar erected on the house-tops.   The sacrificial act must be done in the presence of the deity (cf. Nilus, pp. 30, 117), and if the sun or the queen of heaven is worshipped, a place open to the sky must be chosen.   See Wellh. 41.

public worship, we are led to conclude (1) that the
libation of blood is a common Semitic practice, older than
fire-sacrifices, and (2) that the libation of wine is in some
sense an imitation of, and a surrogate for, the primitive
blood-offering.

Whether libations of water can properly be reckoned
among the drink-offerings of the Semites is very doubtful.
David's libation is plainly exceptional, and in the Levitical
ritual offerings of water have no place.　In the actual
practice of later Judaism, however, water drawn from the
fountain of Siloam, and carried into the Temple amidst the
blare of trumpets, was solemnly poured out upon the altar
on seven days of the Feast of Tabernacles.[1]　According
to the Rabbins, the object of this ceremony was to secure
fertilising rains in the following year.　The explanation
is doubtless correct, for it is a common belief all over the
world that pouring out water is a potent rain - charm.[2] ★
This being so, we can well understand that the rite derives
no countenance from the law ; in truth it does not belong
to the sphere of religion at all, but falls under the category of sympathetic magic in which natural phenomena
are thought to be produced by imitating them on a small
scale.　In some forms of this charm thunder is imitated
as well as rain ;[3] and perhaps the trumpet-blowing at the
Temple is to be explained in this way.

The closest parallel to the water-pouring of the Feast

---

[1] See *Succa*, iv. 9 ; Lightfoot on John vii. 37 ; Reland, *Ant. Heb.* p.
448 *sq.*, with the refs. there given. The water was poured into a special
channel in the altar.

[2] Numerous examples are given by Frazer, *Golden Bough*, i. 248 *sqq.*,
to which I may add the annual " water-pouring " at Ispahan (Bīrūnī,
Chron. p. 228 *sqq.* ; Cazwīnī, i. 84).

[3] Frazer, i. 303 : a very curious Arabian rain-charm, where cattle (or
perhaps antelopes) are driven into the mountains with firebrands attached
to their tails, seems to be an imitation of lightning. See Wellhausen,
p. 167 ; *Lisān*, v. 140 ; Rāghib, i. 94.

of Tabernacles is found in the rite of Hierapolis, described
by Lucian.[1] Twice a year a great concourse of worshippers
assembled at the Temple bearing water from " the sea "
(*i.e.* the Euphrates [2]), which was poured out in the Temple
and flowed away into a cleft which, according to tradition,
absorbed the waters of Deucalion's flood, and so gave occasion to the erection of a sanctuary, with commemorative
services on the spot.[3]

★ In Hebrew ritual oil is not a libation, but when used
in sacrifice serves to moisten and enrich a cereal offering.
The ancient custom of pouring oil on sacred stones [4] was
presumably maintained at Bethel according to the precedent
set by Jacob; and even in the fourth Christian century the
Bordeaux pilgrim speaks of the " lapis pertusus " at Jerusalem " ad quem ueniunt Iudæi singulis annis et ungunt
eum "; but, as oil by itself was not an article of food, the
natural analogy to this act of ritual is to be sought in the
application of unguents to the hair and skin. The use of
unguents was a luxury proper to feasts and gala days, when
men wore their best clothes and made merry; and from
Ps. xlv. 8 (E.V. 7) compared with Isa. lxi. 3, we may con-

---

[1] *Dea Syria*, § 13, cf. § 48. The same rite is alluded to by Melito in
Cureton, *Spic. Syr.* p. 25.

[2] To the dwellers in Mesopotamia the Euphrates was "the sea"; Philo-
stratus, *Vita Apollonii*, i. 20.

[3] The ritual of pouring water into the cleft has its parallel in the modern
practice at the fountain of water before the gates of Tyre, when in September
the water becomes red and troubled, and the natives gather for a great feast
and restore its limpidity by pouring a pitcher of sea-water into the source
(Volney, *État pol. de la Syrie*, chap. viii.; Mariti, ii. 269). Here the
ceremony takes place at the end of the dry season when the water is low,
and may therefore be compared with the legend that Mohammed made
the empty well of Ḥodaibiya to overflow by causing it to be stirred with
one of his arrows after a pitcher of water had been poured into it (*Moh.
in Med.* p. 247). As a rule the pouring out of water in early superstition
is, as we have already seen, a rain-charm, and possibly the rite of Hierapolis
was really designed to procure rain, but only in due measure.

[4] Gen. xxviii. 18, xxxv. 14.

clude that the anointing of kings at their coronation is part
of the ceremony of investing them in the festal dress and
ornaments appropriate to their dignity on that joyous day
(cf. Cant. iii. 11). To anoint the head of a guest was a
hospitable act and a sign of honour; it was the completion
of the toilet appropriate to a feast. Thus the sacred stone
or rude idol described by Pausanias (x. 24. 6) had oil poured
on it daily, and was crowned with wool at every feast.
We have seen that the Semites on festal occasions dressed
up their sacred poles, and they did the same with their
idols.[1] With all this the ritual of anointing goes quite
naturally; thus at Medīna in the last days of heathenism
we find a man washing his domestic idol, which had been
defiled by Moslems, and then anointing it.[2] But apart
from this, the very act of applying ointment to the sacred
symbol had a religious significance. The Hebrew word
meaning to anoint (*mashah*) means properly to wipe or
stroke with the hand, which was used to spread the unguent
over the skin. Thus the anointing of the sacred symbol
is associated with the simpler form of homage common in
Arabia, in which the hand was passed over the idol
(*tamassoh*). In the oath described by Ibn Hishām, p. 85,
the parties dip their hands in unguent and then wipe them
on the Caaba. The ultimate source of the use of unguents
in religion will be discussed by and by in connection with
animal sacrifice.

The sacrificial use of blood, as we shall see hereafter,
is connected with a series of very important ritual ideas,
turning on the conception that the blood is a special seat of
the life. But primarily, when the blood is offered at the
altar, it is conceived to be drunk by the deity. Apart from
Ps. l. 13 the direct evidence for this is somewhat scanty,
so far as the Semites are concerned; the authority usually

---

[1] Ezek. xvi. 18.　　　　[2] Ibn Hishām, p. 303.

appealed to is Maimonides, who states that the Ṣabians looked on blood as the nourishment of the gods. So late a witness would have little value if he stood alone, but the expression in the Psalm cannot be mere rhetoric, and the same belief appears among early nations in all parts of the globe.[1] Nor does this oblation form an exception to the rule that the offerings of the gods consist of human food, for many savages drink fresh blood by way of nourishment, and esteem it a special delicacy.[2]

Among the Arabs, down to the age of Mohammed, blood drawn from the veins of a living camel was eaten—in a kind of blood pudding—in seasons of hunger, and perhaps also at other times.[3] We shall find, however, as we proceed, that sacrificial blood, which contained the life, gradually came to be considered as something too sacred to be eaten, and that in most sacrifices it was entirely made over to the god at the altar. As all slaughter of domestic animals for food was originally sacrificial among the Arabs as well as among the Hebrews, this carried with it the disuse of blood as an article of ordinary food; and

---

[1] See Tylor, *Primitive Culture*[4], ii. 381 *sq.* The story told by Yācūt, ii. 882, of the demon at the temple of Riām to whom bowls of sacrificial blood were presented, of which he partook, seems to have a Jewish origin. According to one version this demon had the form of a black dog (cf. Ibn Hish. p. 18, l. 3).

[2] See, for America, Bancroft, *Native Races,* i. 55, 492, ii. 344. In Africa fresh blood is held as a dainty by all the negroes of the White Nile (Marno, *Reise*, p. 79); it is largely drunk by Masai warriors (Thomson, p. 430); and also by the Gallas, as various travellers attest. Among the Hottentots the pure blood of beasts is forbidden to women but not to men; Kolben, *State of the Cape*, i. 205, cf. 203. In the last case we see that the blood is sacred food. For blood-drinking among the Tartars, see Yule's *Marco Polo*, i. 254, and the editor's note. Where mineral salt is not used for food, the drinking of blood supplies, as Thomson remarks, an important constituent to the system.

[3] Maidānī, ii. 119; *Ḥamāsa*, p. 645, last verse. From *Agh.* xvi. 107. 20, one is led to doubt whether the practice was confined to seasons of famine, or whether this kind of food was used more regularly, as was done, on the other side of the Red Sea, by the Troglodytes (Agatharchides in *Fr. Geog. Gr.* i. 153). See further the *Lexx. s.vv. faṣada, ʿilḥiz, bajja, musawwad.*

even when slaughter ceased to involve a formal sacrifice, it was still thought necessary to slay the victim in the name of a god and pour the blood on the ground.[1] Among the Hebrews this practice soon gave rise to an absolute prohibition of blood-eating; among the Arabs the rule was made absolute only by Mohammed's legislation.[2]

The idea that the gods partake only of the liquid parts of the sacrifice appears, as has been already said, to indicate a modification of the most crassly materialistic conception of the divine nature. The direction which this modification took may, I think, be judged of by comparing the sacrifices of the gods with the oblations offered to the dead. In the famous νέκυια of the *Odyssey*[3] the ghosts drink greedily of the sacrificial blood, and libations of gore form a special feature in Greek offerings to heroes. Among the Arabs, too, the dead are thirsty rather than hungry; water and wine are poured upon their graves.[4] Thirst is a subtler appetite than hunger, and therefore more appropriate to the disembodied shades, just as it is from thirst rather than from hunger that the Hebrews and many other nations borrow metaphors for spiritual longings and intellectual desires. Thus the idea that the gods drink, but do not eat, seems to mark the feeling that they must be thought of as having a less solid material nature than men.

---

[1] Wellh.[1] 113 *sq.*, [2] 117. In an Arab encampment slaves sleep beside " the blood and the dung " (*Agh.* viii. 74. 29) ; cf. 1 Sam. ii. 8.

[2] Whether the blood of game was prohibited to the Hebrews before the law of Lev. xvii. 13 is not quite clear ; Deut. xii. 16 is ambiguous. In Islām as in Judaism the prohibition of blood-eating and the rule that carrion must not be eaten go together (Lev. xvii. 15; Ibn Hish. p. 206, l. 7).

[3] Bk. xi. ; cf. Pindar, *Ol.* i. 90, where the word αἱμακουρίαι is explained by Hesychius as τὰ ἐναγίσματα τῶν κατοιχομένων ; Pausan. v. 13, § 2 ; Plut., *Aristides*, 21.

[4] Wellhausen, p. 182.

A farther step in the same direction is associated with
the introduction of fire sacrifices ; for, though there are
valid reasons for thinking that the practice of burning
the flesh or fat of victims originated in a different line
of thought (as we shall by and by see), the fire ritual
readily lent itself to the idea that the burnt flesh is simply
a food-offering etherealised into fragrant smoke, and that
the gods regale themselves on the odour instead of the
substance of the sacrifice.   Here again the analogy of gifts
to the dead helps us to comprehend the point of view ;
among the Greeks of the seventh century B.C. it was, as
we learn from the story of Periander and Melissa, a new
idea that the dead could make no use of the gifts buried
with them, unless they were etherealised by fire.[1]   A
similar notion seems to have attached itself to the custom
of sacrifice by fire, combined probably at an early date
with the idea that the gods, as ethereal beings, lived in the
upper air, towards which the sacrificial smoke ascended in
savoury clouds.   Thus the prevalence among the settled
Semites of fire sacrifices, which were interpreted as offerings of fragrant smoke, marks the firm establishment of a
conception of the divine nature which, though not purely
spiritual, is at least stripped of the crassest aspects of
materialism.

3. The distinction between sacrifices which are wholly
made over to the god and sacrifices of which the god and
the worshipper partake together requires careful handling.
In the later form of Hebrew ritual laid down in the
Levitical law, the distinction is clearly marked.   To the
former class belong all cereal oblations (Heb. *minḥa* ; A.V.
" offering " or " meat-offering "), which so far as they are not
burned on the altar are assigned to the priests, and among

---

[1] Herodotus, v. 92 ; cf. Joannes Lydus, *Mens.* iii. 27, where the object of
burning the dead is said to be to etherealise the body along with the soul.

animal sacrifices the sin-offering and the burnt-offering or
holocaust.   Most sin-offerings were not holocausts, but the
part of the flesh that was not burned fell to the priests.
To the latter class, again, belong the *zebahīm* or *shelamīm*
(sing. *zébah, shélem,* Amos v. 22), that is, all the ordinary
festal sacrifices, vows and freewill offerings, of which the
share of the deity was the blood and the fat of the
intestines, the rest of the carcase (subject to the payment
of certain dues to the officiating priest) being left to the
worshipper to form a social feast.[1]   In judging of the
original scope and meaning of these two classes of sacrifice,
it will be convenient, in the first instance, to confine our
attention to the simplest and most common forms of
offering.   In the last days of the kingdom of Judah, and
still more after the Exile, piacular sacrifices and holocausts
acquired a prominence which they did not possess in
ancient times.   The old history knows nothing of the
Levitical sin-offering; the atoning function of sacrifice is
not confined to a particular class of oblation, but belongs to

[1] In the English Bible *zebahīm* is rendered "sacrifices," and *shelamīm*
"peace-offerings." The latter rendering is not plausible, and the term
shelamīm can hardly be separated from the verb *shillem,* to pay or discharge,
e.g. a vow. *Zébah* is the more general word, including (like the Arabic
dhibh) all animals slain for food, agreeably with the fact that in old times all
slaughter was sacrificial. In later times, when slaughter and sacrifice were
no longer identical, *zébah* was not precise enough to be used as a technical
term of ritual, and so the term *shelamīm* came to be more largely used than
in the earlier literature.

On the sacrificial lists of the Carthaginians the terms corresponding to
עלה and זבח seem to be כלל and צועת. The former is the old Hebrew כליל
(Deut. xxxiii. 10 ; 1 Sam. vii. 9), the latter is etymologically quite obscure.
In the Carthaginian burnt - sacrifice a certain weight of the flesh was
apparently not consumed on the altar, but given to the priests (*CIS.* 165),
as in the case of the Hebrew sin-offering, which was probably a modification
of the holocaust. The שלם כלל, which appears along with כלל and צועת
in *CIS.* 165 (but not in *CIS.* 167), is hardly a third co-ordinate species of
sacrifice. The editors of the *Corpus* regard it as a variety of the holocaust
(*hol. eucharisticum*), which is not easily reconciled with their own restitution
of l. 11 or with the Hebrew sense of שלם. Perhaps it is an ordinary sacrifice
accompanying a holocaust.

all sacrifices.[1]   The holocaust, again, although ancient, is
not in ancient times a common form of sacrifice, and unless
on very exceptional occasions occurs only in great public
feasts and in association with *zebaḥīm*.   The distressful
times that preceded the end of Hebrew independence drove
men to seek exceptional religious means to conciliate the
favour of a deity who seemed to have turned his back on
his people.   Piacular rites and costly holocausts became,
therefore, more usual, and after the abolition of the local
high places this new importance was still further accentuated by contrast with the decline of the more common
forms of sacrifice.   When each local community had its
own high place, it was the rule that every animal slain for
food should be presented at the altar, and every meal at
which flesh was served had the character of a sacrificial
feast.[2]   As men ordinarily lived on bread fruit and milk,
and ate flesh only on feast days and holidays, this rule was
easily observed as long as the local sanctuaries stood.
But when there was no altar left except at Jerusalem, the
identity of slaughter and sacrifice could no longer be maintained, and accordingly the law of Deuteronomy allows
men to slay and eat domestic animals everywhere, provided
only that the blood—the ancient share of the god—is
poured out upon the ground.[3]   When this new rule came
into force men ceased to feel that the eating of flesh was
essentially a sacred act, and though strictly religious meals
were still maintained at Jerusalem on the great feast days,
the sacrificial meal necessarily lost much of its old signifi-

---

[1] To *zébaḥ* and *minḥa*, 1 Sam. iii. 14, xxvi. 19, and still more to the
holocaust, Mic. vi. 6, 7.

[2] Hos. ix. 4.

[3] Deut. xii. 15, 16 ; cf. Lev. xvii. 10 *sq.*   The fat of the intestines was
also from ancient times reserved for the deity (1 Sam. ii. 16), and therefore
it also was forbidden food (Lev. iii. 17).   The prohibition did not extend to
the fat distributed through other parts of the body.

cance, and the holocaust seemed to have a more purely
sacred character than the *zébaḥ*, in which men ate and
drank just as they might do at home.

But in ancient times the preponderance was all the
other way, and the *zébaḥ* was not only much more frequent
than the holocaust, but much more intimately bound up
with the prevailing religious ideas and feelings of the
Hebrews. On this point the evidence of the older literature is decisive; *zébaḥ* and *minḥa*, sacrifices slain to provide
a religious feast, and vegetable oblations presented at the
altar, make up the sum of the ordinary religious practices
of the older Hebrews, and we must try to understand these
ordinary rites before we attack the harder problem of
exceptional forms of sacrifice.

Now, if we put aside the *piacula* and whole burnt-
offerings, it appears that, according to the Levitical ritual,
the distinction between oblations in which the worshipper
shared, and oblations which were wholly given over to the
deity to be consumed on the altar or by the priests, corresponds to the distinction between animal and vegetable
offerings. The animal victim was presented at the altar
and devoted by the imposition of hands, but the greater
part of the flesh was returned to the worshipper, to be
eaten by him under special rules. It could be eaten only
by persons ceremonially clean, *i.e.* fit to approach the
deity; and if the food was not consumed on the same day,
or in certain cases within two days, the remainder had to
be burned.[1] The plain meaning of these rules is that the
flesh is not common but holy,[2] and that the act of eating
it is a part of the service, which is to be completed before
men break up from the sanctuary.[3] The *zébaḥ*, therefore, is

[1] Lev. vii. 15 *sqq.*, xix. 6, xxii. 30.

[2] Hag. ii. 12; cf. Jer. xi. 15, LXX.

[3] The old sacrificial feasts occupy but a single day (1 Sam. ix.), or at most
two days (1 Sam. xx. 27).

not a mere attenuated offering, in which man grudges to give up the whole victim to his God. On the contrary, the central significance of the rite lies in the act of communion between God and man, when the worshipper is admitted to eat of the same holy flesh of which a part is laid upon the altar as "the food of the deity." But with the *minḥa* nothing of this kind occurs; the whole consecrated offering is retained by the deity, and the worshipper's part in the service is completed as soon as he has made over his gift. In short, while the *zébaḥ* turns on an act of communion between the deity and his worshippers, the *minḥa* (as its name denotes) is simply a tribute.

I will not undertake to say that the distinction so clearly laid down in the Levitical law was observed before the Exile in all cases of cereal sacrifices. Probably it was not, for in most ancient religions we find that cereal offerings come to be accepted in certain cases as substitutes for animal sacrifices, and that in this way the difference between the two kinds of offering gradually gets to be obliterated.[1] But in such matters great weight is to be attached to priestly tradition, such as underlies the Levitical ritual. The priests were not likely to invent a distinction of the kind which has been described, and in point of fact there is good evidence that they did not invent it. For there is no doubt that in ancient times the ordinary source of the *minḥa* was the offering of first-fruits—this is, of a small but choice portion of the annual produce of the ground, which in fact is the only cereal oblation prescribed in the oldest laws.[2] So far as can be seen, the first-fruits were always a tribute wholly made

---

[1] So at Rome models in wax or dough often took the place of animals. The same thing took place at Athens: Hesychius, *s.vv.* βοῦς and ἴβδομος βοῦς; cf. Thucyd. i. 126 and *schol.* At Carthage we have found the name *zébaḥ* applied to vegetable offerings (p. 222 **n.**).

[2] Ex. xxii. 29, xxiii. 19, xxxiv. 26.

over to the deity at the sanctuary. They were brought by
the peasant in a basket and deposited at the altar,[1] and so
far as they were not actually burned on the altar, they
were assigned to the priests [2]—not to the ministrant as a
reward for his service, but to the priests as a body, as the
household of the sanctuary.[3]

Among the Hebrews, as among many other agricultural
peoples, the offering of first-fruits was connected with the
idea that it is not lawful or safe to eat of the new fruit
until the god has received his due.[4] The offering makes
the whole crop lawful food, but it does not make it holy
food; nothing is consecrated except the small portion
offered at the altar, and of the remaining store clean
persons and unclean eat alike throughout the year. This,
therefore, is quite a different thing from the consecration
of animal sacrifices, for in the latter case the whole flesh
is holy, and only those who are clean can eat of it.[5]

In old Israel all slaughter was sacrifice,[6] and a man
could never eat beef or mutton except as a religious act,
but cereal food had no such sacred associations; as soon
as God had received His due of first-fruits, the whole
domestic store was common. The difference between
cereal and animal food was therefore deeply marked, and
though bread was of course brought to the sanctuary to be

[1] Deut. xxvi. 1 *sqq.*

[2] Lev. xxiii. 17 ; Deut. xviii. 4. For the purpose of this argument it is
not necessary to advert to the distinction recognised by post-Biblical
tradition between *rēshīth* and *bikkūrīm,* on which see Wellh., *Prolegomena,*
3rd ed., p. 161 *sq.* (Eng. trans., p. 157 *sq.*).

[3] This follows from 2 Kings xxiii. 9. The tribute was sometimes paid
to a man of God (2 Kings iv. 42), which is another way of making it over
to the deity. In the Levitical law also the *minḥa* belongs to the priests
as a whole (Lev. vii. 10). This is an important point. What the ministrant receives as a fee comes from the worshipper, what the priests as a
whole receive is given them by the deity.

[4] Lev. xxiii. 14 ; cf. Pliny, *H. N.* xviii. 8.

[5] Hos. ix. 4 refers only to animal food.

[6] The same thing is true of Old Arabia ; Wellh. p. 117.

16

eaten with the *zebaḥīm*, it had not and could not have the
same religious meaning as the holy flesh.   It appears from
Amos iv. 4 that it was the custom in northern Israel to
lay a portion of the worshipper's provision of ordinary
leavened bread on the altar with the sacrificial flesh, and
this custom was natural enough : for why should not the
deity's share of the sacrificial meal have the same cereal
accompaniments as man's share ?   But there is no indication that this oblation consecrated the part of the bread
retained by the worshipper and made it holy bread.   The
only holy bread of which we read is such as belonged to
the priests, not to the offerer.[1]   In Lev. vii. 14, Num. vi.
15, the cake of common bread is given to the priest
instead of being laid on the altar, but it is carefully
distinguished from the *minḥa*.   In old times the priests
had no altar dues of this kind.   They had only the first-
fruits and a claim to a piece of the sacrificial flesh,[2] from
which it may be presumed that the custom of offering
bread with the *zébaḥ* was not primitive.   Indeed Amos
seems to mention it with some surprise as a thing not
familiar to Judæan practice.   At all events no sacrificial
meal could consist of bread alone.   All through the old
history it is taken for granted that a religious feast
necessarily implies a victim slain.[3]

---

[1] 1 Sam. xxi. 4.   [2] Deut. xviii. 3, 4 ; 1 Sam. ii. 13 *sqq.*

[3] What has been said above of the contrast between cereal sacrificial gifts
and the sacrificial feast seems to me to hold good also for Greece and Rome,
with some modification in the case of domestic meals, which among the
Semites had no religious character, but at Rome were consecrated by a
portion being offered to the household gods. This, however, has nothing to do
with public religion, in which the law holds good that there is no sacred feast
without a victim, and that consecrated *aparchœ* are wholly given over to
the sanctuary.   The same thing holds good for many other peoples, and
seems, so far as my reading goes, to be the general rule.   But there are
exceptions.   My friend Mr. J. G. Frazer, to whose wide reading I never
appeal without profit, refers me to Wilken's *Alfoeren van het eiland Beroe*,
p. 26, where a true sacrificial feast is made of the first-fruits of rice.   This

The distinction which we are thus led to draw between the cereal oblation, in which the dominant idea is that of a tribute paid to the god, and animal sacrifices, which are essentially acts of communion between the god and his worshippers, deserves to be followed out in more detail. But this task must be reserved for another lecture.

is called "eating the soul of the rice," so that the rice is viewed as a living creature. In such a case it is not unreasonable to say that the rice may be regarded as really an animate victim. Agricultural religions seem often to have borrowed ideas from the older cults of pastoral times.

LECTURE VII

FIRST-FRUITS, TITHES, AND SACRIFICIAL MEALS

IT became apparent to us towards the close of the last lecture that the Levitical distinction between *minḥa* and *zébaḥ*, or cereal oblation and animal sacrifice, rests upon an ancient principle; that the idea of communion with the deity in a sacrificial meal of holy food was primarily confined to the *zébaḥ* or animal victim, and that the proper significance of the cereal offering is that of a tribute paid by the worshipper from the produce of the soil. Now we have already seen that the conception of the national deity as the Baal, or lord of the land, was developed in connection with the growth of agriculture and agricultural law. Spots of natural fertility were the Baal's land, because they were productive without the labour of man's hands, which, according to Eastern ideas, is the only basis of private property in the soil; and land which required irrigation was also liable to the payment of a sacred tribute, because it was fertilised by streams which belonged to the god or even were conceived as instinct with divine energy. This whole circle of ideas belongs to a condition of society in which agriculture and the laws that regulate it have made considerable progress, and is foreign to the sphere of thought in which the purely nomadic Semites moved. That the *minḥa* is not so ancient a form of sacrifice as the *zébaḥ* will not be doubted, fo nomadic life is older than agriculture. But if the foregoin argument

is correct, we can say more than this; we can affirm that
the idea of the sacrificial meal as an act of communion is
older than sacrifice in the sense of tribute, and that the
latter notion grew up with the development of agricultural
life and the conception of the deity as Baal of the land.
Among the nomadic Arabs the idea of sacrificial tribute
has little or no place; all sacrifices are free-will offerings,
and except in some rare forms of piacular oblation—
particularly human sacrifice—and perhaps in some very
simple offerings such as the libation of milk, the object
of the sacrifice is to provide the material for an act of
sacrificial communion with the god.[1]

In most ancient nations the idea of sacrificial tribute is
most clearly marked in the institution of the sacred tithe,
which was paid to the gods from the produce of the soil,
and sometimes also from other sources of revenue.[2]   In
antiquity tithe and tribute are practically identical, nor is
the name of tithe strictly limited to tributes of one-tenth,
the term being used to cover any impost paid in kind
upon a fixed scale.   Such taxes play a great part in the
revenues of Eastern sovereigns, and have done so from a
very early date.   The Babylonian kings drew a tithe from
imports,[3] and the tithe of the fruits of the soil had the
first place among the revenues of the Persian satraps.[4]
The Hebrew kings in like manner took tithes of their
subjects, and the tribute in kind which Solomon drew
from the provinces for the support of his household may

[1] Some points connected with this statement which invite attention, but
cannot be fully discussed at the present stage of the argument, will be
considered in *Additional Note* E, *Sacred Tribute in Arabia.*
[2] See the instances collected by Spencer, Lib. iii. cap. 10, § 1 ; Hermann,
Gottesdienstliche Alterth. d. Griechen, 2nd ed., § 20, note 4 ; Wyttenbach in ✱
the index to his edition of Plutarch's *Moralia, s.v.* ʻΗραχλῆς.
[3] Aristotle, *Œcon.* p. 1352*b* of the Berlin edition.   A tithe on imports
is found also at Mecca (Azracī, p. 107 ; Ibn Hish. p. 72).
[4] Aristotle, *Œcon.* p. 1345*b*.

be regarded as an impost of this sort.[1] Thus the institution
of a sacred tithe corresponds to the conception of the
national god as a king, and so at Tyre tithes were paid to
Melcarth, "the king of the city." The Carthaginians, as
Diodorus [2] tells us, sent the tithe of produce to Tyre
annually from the time of the foundation of their city.
This is the earliest example of a Semitic sacred tithe of
which we have any exact account, and it is to be noted
that it is as much a political as a religious tribute; for the
temple of Melcarth was the state treasury of Tyre, and it
is impossible to draw a distinction between the sacred
tithe paid by the Carthaginians and the political tribute
paid by other colonies, such as Utica.[3]

The oldest Hebrew laws require the payment of first-
fruits, but know nothing of a tithe due at the sanctuary.
And indeed the Hebrew sanctuaries in old time had not
such a splendid establishment as called for the imposition
of sacred tributes on a large scale. When Solomon erected
his temple, in emulation of Hiram's great buildings at
Tyre, a more lavish ritual expenditure became necessary;
but, as the temple at Jerusalem was attached to the palace,
this was part of the household expenditure of the sovereign,
and doubtless was met out of the imposts *in natura* levied
for the maintenance of the court.[4] In other words, the
maintenance of the royal sanctuary was a charge on the
king's tithes; and so we find that a tenth directly paid
to the sanctuary forms no part of the temple revenues

---

[1] 1 Sam. viii. 15, 17 ; 1 Kings iv. 7 *sqq.* The "king's mowings" (Amos
vii. 1) belong to the same class of imposts, being a tribute in kind levied
on the spring herbage to feed the horses of the king (cf. 1 Kings xviii. 5).
Similarly the Romans in Syria levied a tax on pasture-land in the month
Nisan for the food of their horses : see Bruns and Sachau, *Syrisch-Röm.
Rechtsbuch*, Text L, § 121 ; and Wright, *Notulæ Syriacæ* (1887), p. 6.

[2] Lib. xx. cap. 14.

[3] Jos., *Antt.* viii. 5. 3, as read by Niese after Gutschmid.

[4] Cf. 2 Kings xvi. 15 ; Ezek. xlv. 9 *sqq.*

referred to in 2 Kings xii. 4. In northern Israel the royal sanctuaries, of which Bethel was the chief,[1] were originally maintained, in the same way, by the king himself; but as Bethel was not the ordinary seat of the court, so that the usual stated sacrifices there could not be combined with the maintenance of the king's table, some special provision must have been made for them. As the new and elaborate type of sanctuary was due to Phœnician influence, it was Phœnicia, where the religious tithe was an ancient institution, which would naturally suggest the source from which a more splendid worship should be defrayed; the service of the god of the land ought to be a burden on the land. And the general analogy of fiscal arrangements in the East makes it probable that this would be done by assigning to the sanctuary the taxes in kind levied on the surrounding district;[2] it is therefore noteworthy that the only pre-Deuteronomic references to a tithe paid at the sanctuary refer to the "royal chapel" of Bethel.[3]

The tithes paid to ancient sanctuaries were spent in various ways, and were by no means, what the Hebrew tithes ultimately became under the hierocracy, a revenue appropriated to the maintenance of the priests; thus in South Arabia we find tithes devoted to the erection of sacred monuments.[4] One of the chief objects, however, for which they were expended was the maintenance of feasts and sacrifices of a public character, at which the worshippers were entertained free of charge.[5] This element

---

[1] Amos vii. 13.

[2] Cf. the grant of the village of Bætocæce for the maintenance of the sanctuary of the place, Waddington, No. 2720a.

[3] Gen. xxviii. 22 ; Amos iv. 4.

[4] Mordtm. und Müller, *Sab. Denkm.* No. 11 (*CIS.* iv. 19, 1. 7).

[5] Xen., *Anab.* v. 3. 9 ; Waddington, *ut supra.* Similarly the tithes of incense paid to the priests at Sabota in South Arabia were spent on the feast which the god spread for his guests for a certain number of days (Pliny,

cannot have been lacking at the royal sanctuaries of the Hebrews, for a splendid hospitality to all and sundry who assembled at the great religious feasts was recognised as the duty of the king even in the time of David.[1] And so we find that Amos enumerates the tithe at Bethel as one of the chief elements that contributed to the jovial luxurious worship maintained at that holy place.

If this account of the matter is correct, the tithes collected at Bethel were strictly of the nature of a tribute gathered from certain lands, and payment of them was doubtless enforced by royal authority. They were not used by each man to make a private religious feast for himself and his family, but were devoted to the maintenance of the public or royal sacrifices. This, it ought to be said, is not the view commonly taken by modern critics. The old festivities at Hebrew sanctuaries before the regal period were maintained, not out of any public revenue, but by each man bringing up to the sanctuary his own victim and all else that was necessary to make up a hearty feast, with the sacrificial flesh as its *pièce de resistance*.[2] It is generally assumed that this description was still applicable to the feasts at Bethel in Amos's time, and that the tithes were the provision that each farmer brought with him to feast his domestic circle and friends. At first sight this view looks plausible enough, especially when we find that the Book of Deuteronomy, written a century after Amos prophesied, actually prescribes that the annual tithes should be used by each householder to furnish forth a family feast before Jehovah. But it is not safe to argue back from the reforming ordinances of Deuteronomy to the practices of the northern sanctuaries, without checking the

H. N. xii. 63). M. R. Duval (*Rev. d'Assyriologie*, etc., 1888, p. 1 *sq.*)
★ argues that at Taimā, in N. Arabia, there was a tithe on palm trees from which grants were made to the priest. But this is very doubtful.
[1] 2 Sam. vi. 19.   [2] 1 Sam. i. 21, 24, x. 3.

inference at every point. The connection between tithe
and tribute is too close and too ancient to allow us to
admit without hesitation that the Deuteronomic annual
tithe, which retains nothing of the character of a tribute,
is the primitive type of the institution. And this difficulty
is not diminished when we observe that the Book of
Deuteronomy recognises also another tithe, payable once
in three years, which really is of the nature of a sacred
tribute, although it is devoted not to the altar but to
charity. It is arbitrary to say that the first tithe of
Deuteronomy corresponds to ancient usage, and that the
second is an innovation of the author ; indeed, some indications of the Book of Deuteronomy itself point all the
other way. In Deut. xxvi. 12, the third year, in which
the charity tithe is to be paid, is called *par excellence*
" the year of tithing," and in the following verse the
charity tithe is reckoned in the list of " holy things,"
while the annual tithe, to be spent on family festivities
at the sanctuary, is not so reckoned. In the face of these
difficulties it is not safe to assume that either of the
Deuteronomic tithes exactly corresponds to old usage. *
And if we look at Amos's account of the worship at
Bethel as a whole, a feature which cannot fail to strike us
is that the luxurious feasts beside the altars which he
describes are entirely different in kind from the old rustic
festivities at Shiloh described in 1 Samuel. They are not
simple agricultural merry-makings of a popular character,
but mainly feasts of the rich, enjoying themselves at the
expense of the poor. The keynote struck in chap. ii. 7, 8,
where the sanctuary itself is designated as the seat of
oppression and extortion, is re-echoed all through the book ;
Amos's charge against the nobles is not merely that they
are professedly religious and yet oppressors, but that their
luxurious religion is founded on oppression, on the gains of

corruption at the sacred tribunal and other forms of extortion.   This is not the association in which we can look
for the idyllic simplicity of the Deuteronomic family feast
of tithes.   But it is the very association in which one
expects to find the tithe as I have supposed it to be; the
revenues of the state religion, originally designed to maintain a public hospitality at the altar, and enable rich and
poor alike to rejoice before their God, were monopolised by
a privileged class.

   This being understood, the innovations in the law of
tithes proposed in the Book of Deuteronomy become
sufficiently intelligible.   In the kingdom of Judah there
was no royal sanctuary except that at Jerusalem, the
maintenance of which was part of the king's household
charges, and it is hardly probable that any part of the
royal tithes was assigned to the maintenance of the local
sanctuaries.   But as early as the time of Samuel we find
religious feasts of clans or of towns, which are not a mere
agglomeration of private sacrifices, and so must have been
defrayed out of communal funds; from this germ, as
religion became more luxurious, a fixed impost on land
for the maintenance of the public services, such as was
collected among the Phœnicians, would naturally grow.
Such an impost would be in the hands, not of the priests,
but of the heads of clans and communes, *i.e.* of the rich,
and would necessarily be liable to the same abuses as
prevailed in the northern kingdom.   The remedy which
Deuteronomy proposes for these abuses is to leave each
farmer to spend his own tithes as he pleases at the central
sanctuary.   But this provision, if it had stood alone, would
have amounted to the total abolition of a communal fund,
which, however much abused in practice, was theoretically
designed for the maintenance of a public table, where
every one had a right to claim a portion, and which was

doubtless of some service to the landless proletariate, however hardly its collection might press on the poorer farmer.[1] This difficulty was met by the triennial tithe devoted to charity, to the landless poor and to the landless Levite. Strictly speaking, this triennial due was the only real tithe left—the only impost for a religious purpose which a man was actually bound to pay away—and to it the whole subsequent history of Hebrew tithes attaches itself. The other tithe, which was not a due but of a mere voluntary character, disappears altogether in the Levitical legislation.

If this account of the Hebrew tithe is correct, that institution is of relatively modern origin—as indeed is indicated by the silence of the most ancient laws—and throws very little light on the original principles of Semitic sacrifice. The principle that the god of the land claims a tribute on the increase of the soil was originally expressed in the offering of first-fruits, at a time when sanctuaries and their service were too simple to need any elaborate provision for their support. The tithe originated when worship became more complex and ritual more splendid, so that a fixed tribute was necessary for its maintenance. The tribute took the shape of an impost on the produce of land, partly because this was an ordinary source of revenue for all public purposes, partly because such an impost could be justified from the religious point of view, as agreeing in principle with the oblation of first-fruits, and constituting a tribute to the god from the agricultural blessings he bestowed. But here the similarity between tithes and first-fruits ends. The first-fruits constituted a private sacrifice of the worshipper, who brought

---

[1] The same principle was acknowledged in Greece, ἀπὸ τῶν ἱερῶν γὰρ οἱ πτωχοὶ ζῶσιν (*Schol.* on Aristoph. *Plutus*, 596, in Hermann *op. cit.* § 15, note 16). So too in the Arabian meal-offering to Ocaisir (*supra*, p. 223).

them himself to the altar and was answerable for the payment only to God and his own conscience. The tithe, on
the contrary, was a public burden enforced by the community for the maintenance of public religion. In principle
there was no reason why it should not be employed for any
purpose, connected with the public exercises of religion,
for which money or money's worth was required ; the way
in which it should be spent depended not on the individual
tithe-payer but on the sovereign or the commune. In
later times, after the exile, it was entirely appropriated to
the support of the clergy. But in old Israel it seems to
have been mainly, if not exclusively, used to furnish forth
public feasts at the sanctuary. In this respect it entirely
differed from the first-fruits, which might be, and generally
were, offered at a public festival, but did not supply any
part of the material of the feast. The sacred feast, at
which men and their god ate together, was originally quite
unconnected with the cereal oblations paid in tribute to
the deity, and its staple was the *zébaḥ*—the sacrificial
victim. We shall see by and by that in its origin the
zébaḥ was not the private offering of an individual householder but the sacrifice of a clan, and so the sacrificial
meal had pre-eminently the character of a public feast.
Now when public feasts are organised on a considerable
scale, and furnished not merely with store of sacrificial
flesh, but—as was the wont in Israel under the kings—
with all manner of luxurious accessories, they come to be
costly affairs, which can only be defrayed out of public
moneys. The Israel of the time of the kings was not a
simple society of peasants, all living in the same way, who
could simply club together to maintain a rustic feast by
what each man brought to the sanctuary from his own
farm. Splendid festivals like those of Bethel were evidently not furnished in this way, but were mainly banquets

of the upper classes in which the poor had a very subordinate share.   The source of these festivals was the tithe,
but it was not the poor tithe-payer who figured as host at
the banquet.   The organisation of the feast was in the
hands of the ruling classes, who received the tithes and
spent them on the service in a way that gave the lion's
share of the good things to themselves ; though no doubt,
as in other ancient countries, the principle of a public feast
was not wholly ignored, and every one present had something to eat and drink, so that the whole populace was kept
in good humour.[1]   Of course it is not to be supposed that
the whole service was of this public character.   Private
persons still brought up their own vows and free-will
offerings, and arranged their own family parties.   But
these, I conceive, were quite independent of the tithes,
which were a public tax devoted to what was regarded
as the public part of religion.   On the whole, therefore, the
tithe system has nothing to do with primitive Hebrew
religion ; the only point about it which casts a light backwards on the earlier stages of worship is that it could
hardly have sprung up except in connection with the idea
that the maintenance of sacrifice was a public duty, and
that the sacrificial feast had essentially a public character.
This point, however, is of the highest importance, and must
be kept clearly before us as we proceed.

Long before any public revenue was set apart for the
maintenance of sacrificial ritual, the ordinary type of
Hebrew worship was essentially social, for in antiquity all
religion was the affair of the community rather than of the

---

[1] The only way of escape from this conclusion is to suppose that the rich
nobles paid out of their own pockets for the more expensive parts of the
public sacrifices ; and no one who knows the East and reads the Book of
Amos will believe that.   Nathan's parable about the poor man's one lamb,
which his rich neighbour took to make a feast (necessarily at that date
sacrificial), is an apposite illustration,

individual. A sacrifice was a public ceremony of a township or of a clan,[1] and private householders were accustomed
to reserve their offerings for the annual feasts, satisfying
their religious feelings in the interval by vows to be discharged when the festal season came round.[2] Then the
crowds streamed into the sanctuary from all sides, dressed
in their gayest attire,[3] marching joyfully to the sound of
music,[4] and bearing with them not only the victims
appointed for sacrifice, but store of bread and wine to set
forth the feast.[5] The law of the feast was open-handed
hospitality; no sacrifice was complete without guests, and
portions were freely distributed to rich and poor within
the circle of a man's acquaintance.[6] Universal hilarity
prevailed, men ate drank and were merry together, rejoicing before their God.

The picture which I have drawn of the dominant
type of Hebrew worship contains nothing peculiar to the
religion of Jehovah. It is clear from the Old Testament
that the ritual observances at a Hebrew and at a Canaanite
sanctuary were so similar that to the mass of the people
Jehovah worship and Baal worship were not separated by
any well-marked line, and that in both cases the prevailing

---

[1] 1 Sam. ix. 12, xx. 6. In the latter passage "family" means "clan,"
not "domestic circle." See below, p. 276, note.

[2] 1 Sam. i. 3, 21.   [3] Hos. ii. 15 (E. V. 13).

[4] Isa. xxx. 29.   [5] 1 Sam. x. 3.

[6] 1 Sam. ix. 13; 2 Sam. vi. 19, xv. 11; Neh. viii. 10. The guests of
the sacrifice supply a figure to the prophets (Ezek. xxxix. 17 *sqq.*; Zeph.
i. 7). Nabal's refusal to allow David to share in his sheep-shearing feast
was not only churlish but a breach of religious custom; from Amos iv. 5 it
would appear that with a free-will offering there was a free invitation to all
to come and partake. For the Arabian usuage in like cases, see Wellhausen,
p. 117 *sq.* A banqueting hall for the communal sacrifice is mentioned as
early as 1 Sam. ix. 22, and the name given to it (*lishka*) seems to be identical
with the Greek λέσχη, from which it may be gathered that the Phœnicians
had similar halls from an early date; cf. Judg. ix. 27, xvi. 23 *sqq.* For
the communal feasts of the Syrians in later times, see Posidon. Apam *ap.*
Athen. xii. 527 (*Fr. Hist. Gr.* iii. 258).

tone and temper of the worshippers were determined by
the festive character of the service. Nor is the prevalence of the sacrificial feast, as the established type of
ordinary religion, confined to the Semitic peoples; the
same kind of worship ruled in ancient Greece and Italy,
and seems to be the universal type of the local cults of
the small agricultural communities out of which all the
nations of ancient civilisation grew. Everywhere we find
that a sacrifice ordinarily involves a feast, and that a feast
cannot be provided without a sacrifice. For a feast is not
complete without flesh, and in early times the rule that
all slaughter is sacrifice was not confined to the Semites.[1]
The identity of religious occasions and festal seasons may
indeed be taken as the determining characteristic of the
type of ancient religion generally; when men meet their
god they feast and are glad together, and whenever they
feast and are glad they desire that the god should be of
the party. This view is proper to religions in which the
habitual temper of the worshippers is one of joyous confidence in their god, untroubled by any habitual sense of
human guilt, and resting on the firm conviction that they
and the deity they adore are good friends, who understand
each other perfectly and are united by bonds not easily
broken. The basis of this confidence lies of course in the
view that the gods are part and parcel of the same natural
community with their worshippers. The divine father or
king claims the same kind of respect and service as a
human father or king, and practical religion is simply a
branch of social duty, an understood part of the conduct

---

[1] It is Indian (Manu, v. 31 *sqq.*) and Persian (Sprenger, *Eranische
Alterth.* iii. 578 ; cf. Herod. i. 132 ; Strabo, xv. 3. 13, p. 732). Among
the Romans and the older Greeks there was something sacrificial about every
feast, or even about every social meal ; in the latter case the Romans paid
tribute to the household gods. On the identity of feast and sacrifice in
Greece, see Athenæus, v. 19 ; Buchholz, *Hom. Realien*, II. ii. 202, 213 *sqq.*

of daily life, governed by fixed rules to which every one
has been trained from his infancy.   No man who is a good
citizen, living up to the ordinary standard of civil morality
in his dealings with his neighbours, and accurately following
the ritual tradition in his worship of the gods, is oppressed
with the fear that the deity may set a higher standard
of conduct and find him wanting.   Civil and religious
morality have one and the same measure, and the conduct
which suffices to secure the esteem of men suffices also to
make a man perfectly easy as to his standing with the
gods.   It must be remembered that all antique morality
is an affair of social custom and customary law, and that
in the more primitive forms of ancient life the force of
custom is so strong that there is hardly any middle course
between living well up to the standard of social duty
which it prescribes, and falling altogether outside the
pale of the civil and religious community.   A man who
deliberately sets himself against the rules of the society
in which he lives must expect to be outlawed ; but minor
offences are readily condoned as mere mistakes, which may
expose the offender to a fine but do not permanently lower
his social status or his self-respect.   So too a man may
offend his god, and be called upon to make reparation to
him.   But in such a case he knows, or can learn from a
competent priestly authority, exactly what he ought to do
to set matters right, and then everything goes on as before.
In a religion of this kind there is no room for an abiding
sense of sin and unworthiness, or for acts of worship that
express the struggle after an unattained righteousness, the
longing for uncertain forgiveness.   It is only when the old
religions begin to break down that these feelings come in.
The older national and tribal religions work with the
smoothness of a machine.   Men are satisfied with their
gods, and they feel that the gods are satisfied with them.

Or if at any time famine, pestilence or disaster in war appears to shew that the gods are angry, this casts no doubt on the adequacy of the religious system as such, but is merely held to prove that a grave fault has been committed by some one for whom the community is responsible, and that they are bound to put it right by an appropriate reparation. That they can put it right, and stand as well with the god as they ever did, is not doubted; and when rain falls, or the pestilence is checked, or the defeat is retrieved, they at once recover their old easy confidence, and go on eating and drinking and rejoicing before their god with the assurance that he and they are on the best of jovial good terms.

The kind of religion which finds its proper æsthetic expression in the merry sacrificial feast implies a habit of mind, a way of taking the world as well as a way of regarding the gods, which we have some difficulty in realising. Human life is never perfectly happy and satisfactory, yet ancient religion assumes that through the help of the gods it is so happy and satisfactory that ordinary acts of worship are all brightness and hilarity, expressing no other idea than that the worshippers are well content with themselves and with their divine sovereign. This implies a measure of *insouciance*, a power of casting off the past and living in the impression of the moment, which belongs to the childhood of humanity, and can exist only along with a childish unconsciousness of the inexorable laws that connect the present and the future with the past. Accordingly the more developed nations of antiquity, in proportion as they emerged from national childhood, began to find the old religious forms inadequate, and either became less concerned to associate all their happiness with the worship of the gods, and, in a word, less religious, or else were unable to think of the divine

17

powers as habitually well pleased and favourable, and so
were driven to look on the anger of the gods as much
more frequent and permanent than their fathers had
supposed, and to give to atoning rites a stated and
important place in ritual, which went far to change the
whole attitude characteristic of early worship, and substitute for the old joyous confidence a painful and
scrupulous anxiety in all approach to the gods. Among
the Semites the Arabs furnish an example of the general
decay of religion, while the nations of Palestine in the
seventh century B.C. afford an excellent illustration of
★ the development of a gloomier type of worship under the
pressure of accumulated political disasters. On the whole,
however, what strikes the modern thinker as surprising is
not that the old joyous type of worship ultimately broke
down, but that it lasted so long as it did, or even that it
ever attained a paramount place among nations so advanced
as the Greeks and the Syrians. This is a matter which
well deserves attentive consideration.

First of all, then, it is to be observed that the frame
of mind in which men are well pleased with themselves,
with their gods, and with the world, could not have
dominated antique religion as it did, unless religion had
been essentially the affair of the community rather than
of individuals. It was not the business of the gods of
heathenism to watch, by a series of special providences,
over the welfare of every individual. It is true that
individuals laid their private affairs before the gods, and
asked with prayers and vows for strictly personal blessings.
But they did this just as they might crave a personal
boon from a king, or as a son craves a boon from a father,
without expecting to get all that was asked. What the
gods might do in this way was done as a matter of
personal favour, and was no part of their proper function

as heads of the community. The benefits which were
expected from the gods were of a public character, affecting the whole community, especially fruitful seasons,
increase of flocks and herds, and success in war. So long
as the community flourished the fact that an individual
was miserable reflected no discredit on divine providence,
but was rather taken to prove that the sufferer was an
evil-doer, justly hateful to the gods. Such a man was out
of place among the happy and prosperous crowd that
assembled on feast days before the altar; even in Israel,
Hannah, with her sad face and silent petition, was a strange
figure at the sanctuary of Shiloh, and the unhappy leper,
in his lifelong affliction, was shut out from the exercises
of religion as well as from the privileges of social life.
So too the mourner was unclean, and his food was not
brought into the house of God; the very occasions of life
in which spiritual things are nearest to the Christian, and
the comfort of religion is most fervently sought, were in
the ancient world the times when a man was forbidden
to approach the seat of God's presence. To us, whose
habit it is to look at religion in its influence on the life
and happiness of individuals, this seems a cruel law; nay,
our sense of justice is offended by a system in which
misfortunes set up a barrier between a man and his God.
But whether in civil or in profane matters, the habit of
the old world was to think much of the community and
little of the individual life, and no one felt this to be
unjust even though it bore hardly on himself. The god
was the god of the nation or of the tribe, and he knew
and cared for the individual only as a member of the
community. Why, then, should private misfortune be
allowed to mar by its ill-omened presence the public
gladness of the sanctuary?

Accordingly the air of habitual satisfaction with themselves, their gods and the world, which characterises the worship of ancient communities, must be explained without reference to the vicissitudes of individual life. And so far as the thing requires any other explanation than the general *insouciance* and absorption in the feelings of the moment characteristic of the childhood of society, I apprehend that the key to the joyful character of the antique religions known to us lies in the fact that they took their shape in communities that were progressive and on the whole prosperous. If we realise to ourselves the conditions of early society, whether in Europe or in Asia, at the first daybreak of history, we cannot fail to see that a tribe or nation that could not hold its own and make headway must soon have been crushed out of existence in the incessant feuds it had to wage with all its neighbours. The communities of ancient civilisation were formed by the survival of the fittest, and they had all the self-confidence and elasticity that are engendered by success in the struggle for life. These characters, therefore, are reflected in the religious system that grew up with the growth of the state, and the type of worship that corresponded to them was not felt to be inadequate till the political system was undermined from within or shattered by blows from without.

These considerations sufficiently account for the development of the habitually joyous temper of ancient sacrificial worship. But it is also to be observed that when the type was once formed it would not at once disappear, even when a change in social conditions made it no longer an adequate expression of the habitual tone of national life. The most important functions of ancient worship were reserved for public occasions, when the whole community was stirred by a common emotion, and among agricultural nations the stated occasions of

sacrifice were the natural seasons of festivity, at harvest
and vintage.   At such times every one was ready to cast
off his cares and rejoice before his god, and so the
coincidence of religious and agricultural gladness helped
to keep the old form of worship alive, long after it had
ceased to be in full harmony with men's permanent view
of the world.   Moreover it must be remembered that the
spirit of boisterous mirth which characterised the oldest
religious festivals was nourished by the act of worship
itself.   The sacrificial feast was not only an expression of
gladness but a means of driving away care, for it was set
forth with every circumstance of gaiety, with garlands,
perfumes and music, as well as with store of meat and
wine.   The sensuous Oriental nature responds to such
physical stimulus with a readiness foreign to our more
sluggish temperament; to the Arab it is an excitement
and a delight of the highest order merely to have flesh to
eat.[1]   From the earliest times, therefore, the religious
gladness of the Semites tended to assume an orgiastic
character and become a sort of intoxication of the senses,
in which anxiety and sorrow were drowned for the moment.
This is apparent in the old Canaanite festivals, such as the
vintage feast at Shechem described in Judg. ix. 27, and not
less in the service of the Hebrew high places, as it is characterised by the prophets.   Even at Jerusalem the worship
must have been boisterous indeed, when Lam. ii. 7 compares
the shouts of the storming party of the Chaldæans in the
courts of the temple with the noise of a solemn feast.
Among the Nabatæans and elsewhere the orgiastic character of the worship often led in later times to the
identification of Semitic gods, especially of Dusares, with

---

[1] A current Arabic saying, which I have somewhere seen ascribed to
Ta'abbaṭa Sharran, reckons the eating of flesh as one of the three great
delights of life.   In Maidānī, ii. 22, flesh and wine are classed together as
seductive luxuries.

the Greek Dionysus. It is plain that a religion of this
sort would not necessarily cease to be powerful when it
ceased to express a habitually joyous view of the world
and the divine governance; in evil times, when men's
thoughts were habitually sombre, they betook themselves
to the physical excitement of religion, as men now take
refuge in wine. That this is not a fancy picture is clear
from Isaiah's description of the conduct of his contemporaries during the approach of the Assyrians to Jerusalem,[1]
when the multiplied sacrifices that were offered to avert
the disaster degenerated into a drunken carnival—"Let
us eat and drink, for to-morrow we die." And so in
general when an act of Semitic worship began with
sorrow and lamentation—as in the mourning for Adonis,
or in the great atoning ceremonies which became common
in later times—a swift revulsion of feeling followed, and
the gloomy part of the service was presently succeeded by
a burst of hilarious revelry, which, in later times at least,
was not a purely spontaneous expression of the conviction
that man is reconciled with the powers that govern his life
and rule the universe, but in great measure a mere orgiastic
excitement. The nerves were strung to the utmost tension
in the sombre part of the ceremony, and the natural reaction
was fed by the physical stimulus of the revelry that followed.

This, however, is not a picture of what Semitic religion
was from the first, and in its ordinary exercises, but of the
shape it tended to assume in extraordinary times of national
calamity, and still more under the habitual pressure of
grinding despotism, when the general tone of social life
was no longer bright and hopeful, but stood in painful
contrast to the joyous temper proper to the traditional
forms of worship. Ancient heathenism was not made for
such times, but for seasons of national prosperity, when its

---

[1] Isa. xxii. 12, 13, compared with i. 11 *sqq.*

joyous rites were the appropriate expression for the happy
fellowship that united the god and his worshippers to
the satisfaction of both parties. Then the enthusiasm of
the worshipping throng was genuine. Men came to the
sanctuary to give free vent to habitual feelings of thankful
confidence in their god, and warmed themselves into excitement in a perfectly natural way by feasting together, as
people still do when they rejoice together.

In acts of worship we expect to find the religious ideal
expressed in its purest form, and we cannot easily think
well of a type of religion whose ritual culminates in a
jovial feast. It seems that such a faith sought nothing
higher than a condition of physical *bien être*, and in one
sense this judgment is just. The good things desired of
the gods were the blessings of earthly life, not spiritual
but carnal things. But Semitic heathenism was redeemed
from mere materialism by the fact that religion was not
the affair of the individual but of the community. The ★
ideal was earthly, but it was not selfish. In rejoicing
before his god a man rejoiced with and for the welfare
of his kindred, his neighbours and his country, and, in
renewing by a solemn act of worship the bond that united
him to his god, he also renewed the bonds of family social
and national obligation. We have seen that the compact
between the god and the community of his worshippers
was not held to pledge the deity to make the private cares
of each member of the community his own. The gods had
their favourites no doubt, for whom they were prepared to
do many things that they were not bound to do; but no
man could approach his god in a purely personal matter
with that spirit of absolute confidence which I have
described as characteristic of antique religions; it was the
community, and not the individual, that was sure of the
permanent and unfailing help of its deity. It was a

national not a personal providence that was taught by ancient religion. So much was this the case that in purely personal concerns the ancients were very apt to turn, not to the recognised religion of the family or of the state, but to magical superstitions. The gods watched over a man's civic life, they gave him his share in public benefits, the annual largess of the harvest and the vintage, national peace or victory over enemies, and so forth, but they were not sure helpers in every private need, and above all they would not help him in matters that were against the interests of the community as a whole. There was therefore a whole region of possible needs and desires for which religion could and would do nothing; and if supernatural help was sought in such things it had to be sought through magical ceremonies, designed to purchase or constrain the favour of demoniac powers with which the public religion had nothing to do. Not only did these magical superstitions lie outside religion, but in all well-ordered states they were regarded as illicit. A man had no right to enter into private relations with supernatural powers that might help him at the expense of the community to which he belonged. In his relations to the unseen he was bound always to think and act with and for the community, and not for himself alone.

With this it accords that every complete act of worship —for a mere vow was not a complete act till it was fulfilled by presenting a sacrifice—had a public or quasi-public character. Most sacrifices were offered on fixed occasions, at the great communal or national feasts, but even a private offering was not complete without guests, and the surplus of sacrificial flesh was not sold but distributed with an open hand.[1] Thus every act of

[1] See above, p. 254. In Greece, in later times, sacrificial flesh was exposed for sale (1 Cor. x. 25).

worship expressed the idea that man does not live for himself only but for his fellows, and that this partnership of social interests is the sphere over which the gods preside and on which they bestow their assured blessing.

The ethical significance which thus appertains to the sacrificial meal, viewed as a social act, received particular emphasis from certain ancient customs and ideas connected with eating and drinking. According to antique ideas, those who eat and drink together are by this very act tied to one another by a bond of friendship and mutual obligation. Hence when we find that in ancient religions all the ordinary functions of worship are summed up in the sacrificial meal, and that the ordinary intercourse between gods and men has no other form, we are to remember that the act of eating and drinking together is the solemn and stated expression of the fact that all who share the meal are brethren, and that the duties of friendship and brotherhood are implicitly acknowledged in their common act. By admitting man to his table the god admits him to his friendship; but this favour is extended to no man in his mere private capacity; he is received as one of a community, to eat and drink along with his fellows, and in the same measure as the act of worship cements the bond between him and his god, it cements also the bond between him and his brethren in the common faith.

We have now reached a point in our discussion at which it is possible to form some general estimate of the ethical value of the type of religion which has been described. The power of religion over life is twofold, lying partly in its association with particular precepts of conduct, to which it supplies a supernatural sanction, but mainly in its influence on the general tone and temper

of men's minds, which it elevates to higher courage and
purpose, and raises above a brutal servitude to the
physical wants of the moment, by teaching men that their
lives and happiness are not the mere sport of the blind
forces of nature, but are watched over and cared for by
a higher power.   As a spring of action this influence is
more potent than the fear of supernatural sanctions, for
it is stimulative, while the other is only regulative.   But
to produce a moral effect on life the two must go together;
a man's actions must be not only supported by the feeling
that the divine help is with him, but regulated by the
conviction that that help will not accompany him except
on the right path.   In ancient religion, as it appears
among the Semites, the confident assurance of divine help
belongs, not to each man in his private concerns, but to
the community in its public functions and public aims; and
it is this assurance that is expressed in public acts of
worship, where all the members of the community meet
together to eat and drink at the table of their god, and
so renew the sense that he and they are altogether at one.
Now, if we look at the whole community of worshippers
as absolutely one, personify them and think of them as a
single individual, it is plain that the effect of this type
of religion must be regarded as merely stimulative and
not regulative.   When the community is at one with
itself and at one with its god, it may, for anything that
religion has to say, do exactly what it pleases towards
all who are outside it.   Its friends are the god's friends,
its enemies the god's enemies; it takes its god with it in
whatever it chooses to do.   As the ancient communities
of religion are tribes or nations, this is as much as to say
that, properly speaking, ancient religion has no influence
on intertribal or international morality—in such matters
the god simply goes with his own nation or his own tribe.

So long as we consider the tribe or nation of common religion as a single subject, the influence of religion is limited to an increase of the national self-confidence—a quality very useful in the continual struggle for life that was waged between ancient communities, but which beyond this has no moral value

But the case is very different when we look at the religious community as made up of a multitude of individuals, each of whom has private as well as public purposes and desires. In this aspect it is the regulative influence of ancient religion that is predominant, for the good things which religion holds forth are promised to the individual only in so far as he lives in and for the community. The conception of man's chief good set forth in the social act of sacrificial worship is the happiness of the individual in the happiness of the community, and thus the whole force of ancient religion is directed, so far as the individual is concerned, to maintain the civil virtues of loyalty and devotion to a man's fellows at a pitch of confident enthusiasm, to teach him to set his highest good in the prosperity of the society of which he is a member, not doubting that in so doing he has the divine power on his side and has given his life to a cause that cannot fail. This devotion to the common weal was, as every one knows, the mainspring of ancient morality and the source of all the heroic virtues of which ancient history presents so many illustrious examples. In ancient society, therefore, the religious ideal expressed in the act of social worship and the ethical ideal which governed the conduct of daily life were wholly at one, and all morality—as morality was then understood—was consecrated and enforced by religious motives and sanctions.

These observations are fully applicable only to the typical form of ancient religion, when it was still strictly

tribal or national.   When nationality and religion began
to fall apart, certain worships assumed a character more
or less cosmopolitan.   Even in heathenism, therefore, in
its more advanced forms, the gods, or at least certain gods,
are in some measure the guardians of universal morality,
and not merely of communal loyalty.   But what was thus
gained in comprehensiveness was lost in intensity and
strength of religious feeling, and the advance towards
ethical universalism, which was made with feeble and
uncertain steps, was never sufficient to make up for the
decline of the old heroic virtues that were fostered by the
narrower type of national faith.

LECTURE VIII

THE ORIGINAL SIGNIFICANCE OF ANIMAL SACRIFICE

ENOUGH has been said as to the significance of the sacrificial feast as we find it among ancient nations no longer barbarous. But to understand the matter fully we must trace it back to its origin in a state of society much more primitive than that of the agricultural Semites or Greeks.

The sacrificial meal was an appropriate expression of the antique ideal of religious life, not merely because it was a social act and an act in which the god and his worshippers were conceived as partaking together, but because, as has already been said, the very act of eating and drinking with a man was a symbol and a confirmation of fellowship and mutual social obligations. The one thing directly expressed in the sacrificial meal is that the god and his worshippers are *commensals*, but every other point in their mutual relations is included in what this involves. Those who sit at meat together are united for all social effects; those who do not eat together are aliens to one another, without fellowship in religion and without reciprocal social duties. The extent to which this view prevailed among the ancient Semites, and still prevails among the Arabs, may be brought out most clearly by reference to the law of hospitality. Among the Arabs every stranger whom one meets in the desert is a natural enemy, and has no protection against violence except his own strong hand or the fear

that his tribe will avenge him if his blood be spilt.[1] But
if I have eaten the smallest morsel of food with a man,
I have nothing further to fear from him; "there is salt
★ between us," and he is bound not only to do me no harm,
but to help and defend me as if I were his brother.[2] So
far was this principle carried by the old Arabs, that Zaid
al-Khail, a famous warrior in the days of Mohammed,
refused to slay a vagabond who carried off his camels,
because the thief had surreptitiously drunk from his
father's milk bowl before committing the theft.[3] It does
not indeed follow as a matter of course that because I have
eaten once with a man I am permanently his friend, for
the bond of union is conceived in a very realistic way, and
strictly speaking lasts no longer than the food may be
supposed to remain in my system.[4] But the temporary
bond is confirmed by repetition,[5] and readily passes into a
permanent tie confirmed by an oath. "There was a sworn
alliance between the Lihyān and the Moṣṭalic, they were

[1] This is the meaning of Gen. iv. 14 *sq.* Cain is "driven out from the
face of the cultivated land" into the desert, where his only protection is
the law of blood revenge.

[2] The *milḥa*, or bond of salt, is not dependent on the actual use of mineral
salt with the food by which the bond is constituted. Milk, for example,
will serve the purpose. Cf. Burckhardt, *Bedouins and Wahabys*, i. 329, and
Kāmil, p. 284, especially the verse of Abu 'l-Ṭamaḥān there cited, where salt
is interpreted to mean "milk."

[3] *Agh.* xvi. 51 ; cf. *Kinship*, p. 176 *sq.*

[4] Burton, *Pilgrimage*, iii. 84 (1st ed.), says that some tribes "require to
renew the bond every twenty-four hours," as otherwise, to use their own
phrase, "the salt is not in their stomachs" (almost the same phrase is used
in the verse of Abu 'l-Ṭamaḥān referred to above). But usually the protection extended to a guest lasts three days and a third after his departure
(Burckhardt, *op. cit.* i. 136) ; or, according to Doughty, i. 228, two nights
and the day between. A curious example of the degree to which these
notions might be pushed is given in the *Amthāl* of Mofaḍḍal al-Ḍabbī,
Const. A. H. 1300, p. 46, where a man claims and obtains the help of Al-
Ḥārith in recovering his stolen camels, because the water that was still in
their stomachs when they were taken from him had been drawn with the
help of a rope borrowed from Al-Ḥārith's herdsmen.

[5] "O enemy of God, wilt thou slay this Jew ? Much of the fat on thy
paunch is of his substance" (Ibn Hishām, p. 553 *sq.*).

wont to eat and drink together." [1]　This phrase of an Arab
narrator supplies exactly what is wanted to define the
significance of the sacrificial meal.　The god and his
worshippers are wont to eat and drink together, and by
this token their fellowship is declared and sealed.

The ethical significance of the common meal can be
most adequately illustrated from Arabian usage, but it was
not confined to the Arabs.　The Old Testament records
many cases where a covenant was sealed by the parties
eating and drinking together.　In most of these indeed the
meal is sacrificial, so that it is not at once clear that two
men are bound to each other merely by partaking of the
same dish, unless the deity is taken in as a third party to
the covenant.　The value of the Arabian evidence is that
it supplies proof that the bond of food is valid of itself,
that religion may be called in to confirm and strengthen it,
but that the essence of the thing lies in the physical act of
eating together.　That this was also the case among the
Hebrews and Canaanites may be safely concluded from
analogy, and appears to receive direct confirmation from
Josh. ix. 14, where the Israelites enter into alliance with
the Gibeonites by taking of their victuals, without consulting Jehovah.　A formal league confirmed by an oath
follows, but by accepting the proffered food the Israelites
are already committed to the alliance.

But we have not yet got to the root of the matter.
What is the ultimate nature of the fellowship which is
constituted or declared when men eat and drink together ?
In our complicated society fellowship has many types and
many degrees ; men may be united by bonds of duty and
honour for certain purposes, and stand quite apart in all

---

[1] *Diw. Hodh.* No. 87 (Kosegarten's ed. p. 170).　In Sukkari's account of
the battle of Coshāwa (William Wright, *Nacā'iḍ*, p. 20) a captive refuses
to eat the food of his captor who has slain his son, and thus apparently
keeps his right of blood revenge alive.

other things. Even in ancient times—for example, in the
Old Testament—we find the sacrament of a common meal
introduced to seal engagements of various kinds. But in
every case the engagement is absolute and inviolable; it
constitutes what in the language of ethics is called a duty
of perfect obligation. Now in the most primitive society
there is only one kind of fellowship which is absolute and
inviolable. To the primitive man all other men fall under
two classes, those to whom his life is sacred and those to
whom it is not sacred. The former are his fellows; the
latter are strangers and potential foemen, with whom it is
absurd to think of forming any inviolable tie unless they
are first brought into the circle within which each man's
life is sacred to all his comrades.

But that circle again corresponds to the circle of
kinship, for the practical test of kinship is that the
whole kin is answerable for the life of each of its
members. By the rules of early society, if I slay my
kinsman, whether voluntarily or involuntarily, the act
is murder, and is punished by expulsion from the kin;[1]
if my kinsman is slain by an outsider I and every other
member of my kin are bound to avenge his death by
killing the manslayer or some member of his kin. It
is obvious that under such a system there can be no
inviolable fellowship except between men of the same
blood. For the duty of blood revenge is paramount, and
every other obligation is dissolved as soon as it comes into
conflict with the claims of blood. I cannot bind myself
absolutely to a man, even for a temporary purpose, unless
during the time of our engagement he is put into a
kinsman's place. And this is as much as to say that a

---

[1] Even in Homeric society no bloodwit can be accepted for slaughter
within the kin; a point which is commonly overlooked, *e.g.* by Buchholz,
Hom. Real. II. i. 76.

stranger cannot become bound to me, unless at the same time he becomes bound to all my kinsmen in exactly the same way.   Such is, in fact, the law of the desert; when any member of a clan receives an outsider through the bond of salt, the whole clan is bound by his act, and must, while the engagement lasts, receive the stranger as one of themselves.[1]

The idea that kinship is not purely an affair of birth, but may be acquired, has quite fallen out of our circle of ideas; but so, for that matter, has the primitive conception of kindred itself.   To us kinship has no absolute value, but is measured by degrees, and means much or little, or nothing at all, according to its degree and other circumstances.   In ancient times, on the contrary, the fundamental obligations of kinship had nothing to do with degrees of relationship, but rested with absolute and identical force on every member of the clan.   To know that a man's life was sacred to me, and that every blood-feud that touched him involved me also, it was not necessary for me to count cousinship with him by reckoning up to our common ancestor; it was enough that we belonged to the same clan and bore the same clan-name. What was my clan was determined by customary law, which was not the same in all stages of society; in the earliest Semitic communities a man was of his mother's clan, in later times he belonged to the clan of his father. But the essential idea of kinship was independent of the particular form of the law.   A kin was a group of persons whose lives were so bound up together, in what must be called a physical unity, that they could be treated as parts

---

[1] This of course is to be understood only of the fundamental rights and duties which turn on the sanctity of kindred blood.   The secondary privileges of kinship, in matters of inheritance and the like, lie outside of the present argument, and with regard to them the covenanted ally had not the full rights of a kinsman (*Kinship*, p. 55 *sq.*).

18

of one common life. The members of one kindred looked
on themselves as one living whole, a single animated mass
of blood, flesh and bones, of which no member could be
touched without all the members suffering. This point
of view is expressed in the Semitic tongues in many
familiar forms of speech. In a case of homicide Arabian
tribesmen do not say, "The blood of M. or N. has been
spilt," naming the man; they say, "Our blood has been
spilt." In Hebrew the phrase by which one claims
kinship is "I am your bone and your flesh."[1] Both in
Hebrew and in Arabic "flesh" is synonymous with "clan"
or kindred group.[2] To us all this seems mere metaphor,
from which no practical consequences can follow. But
in early thought there is no sharp line between the metaphorical and the literal, between the way of expressing a
thing and the way of conceiving it; phrases and symbols
are treated as realities. Now, if kinship means participation in a common mass of flesh blood and bones, it is
natural that it should be regarded as dependent, not
merely on the fact that a man was born of his mother's
body, and so was from his birth a part of her flesh, but
also on the not less significant fact that he was nourished
by her milk. And so we find that among the Arabs there
is a tie of milk, as well as of blood, which unites the
★ foster-child to his foster-mother and her kin. Again,
after the child is weaned, his flesh and blood continue to
be nourished and renewed by the food which he shares
with his commensals, so that commensality can be thought
of (1) as confirming or even (2) as constituting kinship in
a very real sense.[3]

Judg. ix. 2; 2 Sam. **v. 1.** Conversely in acknowledging kinship the
★ phrase is "Thou art my bone and my flesh" (Gen. xxix. 14; 2 Sam. xix. 12);
cf. Gen. xxxvii. 27, "our brother and our flesh."

[2] Lev. xxv. 49; *Kinship*, p. 175.

[3] Cf. *Kinship*, p. 176 *sq.*

As regards their bearing on the doctrine of sacrifice
it will conduce to clearness if we keep these two points
distinct. Primarily the circle of common religion and of
common social duties was identical with that of natural
kinship,[1] and the god himself was conceived as a being of
the same stock with his worshippers. It was natural,
therefore, that the kinsmen and their kindred god should
seal and strengthen their fellowship by meeting together
from time to time to nourish their common life by a
common meal, to which those outside the kin were not
admitted. A good example of this kind of clan sacrifice,
in which a whole kinship periodically joins, is afforded by
the Roman *sacra gentilicia*. As in primitive society no
man can belong to more than one kindred, so among the
Romans no one could share in the *sacra* of two gentes—
to do so was to confound the ritual and contaminate the
purity of the gens. The *sacra* consisted in common anniversary sacrifices, in which the clansmen honoured the
gods of the clan and after them the " demons " of their
ancestors, so that the whole kin living and dead were
brought together in the service.[2] That the earliest sacrificial feasts among the Semites were of the nature of *sacra
gentilicia* is matter of inference rather than of direct
evidence, but is not on that account less certain. For
that the Semites form no exception to the general rule
that the circle of religion and of kinship were originally
identical, has been shown in Lecture II. The only thing,
therefore, for which additional proof is needed is that the
sacrificial ritual of the Semites already existed in this
primitive form of society. That this was so is morally
certain on general grounds ; for an institution like the

[1] *Supra*, p. 50.
[2] For proofs and further details see the evidence collected by Marquardt,
Röm. Staatsverwaltung, 2nd ed., iii. 130 *sq.*

sacrificial meal, which occurs with the same general
features all over the world, and is found among the most
primitive peoples, must, in the nature of things, date
from the earliest stage of social organisation. And the
general argument is confirmed by the fact that after several
clans had begun to frequent the same sanctuary and
worship the same god, the worshippers still grouped themselves for sacrificial purposes on the principle of kinship.
In the days of Saul and David all the tribes of Israel
had long been united in the worship of Jehovah, yet the
clans still maintained their annual gentile sacrifice, at
which every member of the group was bound to be
present.[1] But evidence more decisive comes to us from
Arabia, where, as we have seen, men would not eat
together at all unless they were united by kinship or by
a covenant that had the same effect as natural kinship.
Under such a rule the sacrificial feast must have been
confined to kinsmen, and the clan was the largest circle
that could unite in a sacrificial act. And so, though the
great sanctuaries of heathen Arabia were frequented at
the pilgrimage feasts by men of different tribes, who met
peaceably for a season under the protection of the truce
of God, we find that their participation in the worship of
the same holy place did not bind alien clans together in
any religious unity; they worshipped side by side, but
not together. It is only under Islam that the pilgrimage

---

[1] 1 Sam. xx. 6, 29. The word *mishpaḥa*, which the English Bible here
and elsewhere renders "family," denotes not a household but a clan. In
verse 29 the true reading is indicated by the Septuagint, and has been restored by Wellhausen (הֵא צִוּוּ לִי אֶחָי). It was not David's brother, but
his brethren, that is his clansmen, that enjoined his presence. The annual
festivity, the duty of all clansmen to attend, the expectation that this
sacred duty would be accepted as a valid excuse for absence from court
even at the king's new-moon sacrifice, are so many points of correspondence
with the Roman gentile worship; cf. Gellius, xvi. 4. 3, and the other passages
cited by Marquardt, *Röm. Staatsverwaltung*, 2nd ed., iii. 132, note 4.

becomes a bond of religious fellowship, whereas in the times of heathenism it was the correct usage that the different tribes, before they broke up from the feast, should engage in a rivalry of self-exaltation and mutual abuse, which sent them home with all their old jealousies freshly inflamed.[1]

That the sacrificial meal was originally a feast of kinsmen, is apt to suggest to modern minds the idea that its primitive type is to be sought in the household circle, and that public sacrifices, in which the whole clan united, are merely an extension of such an act of domestic worship as in ancient Rome accompanied every family meal. The Roman family never rose from supper till a portion of food had been laid on the burning hearth as an offering to the Lares, and the current opinion, which regards the gens as nothing more than an enlarged household, naturally looks on the gentile sacrifice as an enlargement of this domestic rite. But the notion that the clan is only a larger household is not consistent with the results of modern research. Kinship is an older thing than family life, and in the most primitive societies known to us the family or household group was not a subdivision of the clan, but contained members of more than one kindred. As a rule the savage

[1] See Goldziher, *Muh. Stud.* i. 56. The prayer and exhortation of the leader of the procession of tribes from 'Arafa (*Agh.* iii. 4 ; Wellh.[1] p. 191) seems to me to be meant for his own tribe alone. The prayer for " peace among our women, a continuous range of pasture occupied by our herdsmen, wealth placed in the hands of our most generous men," asks only blessings for the tribe, and indeed occurs elsewhere as a form of blessing addressed to a tribe (*Agh.* xix. 132. 6). And the admonition to observe treaties, honour clients, and be hospitable to guests, contains nothing that was not a point of tribal morality. The *ijāza*, or right to give the signal for dissolving the worshipping assembly, belonged to a particular tribe ; it was the right to start first. The man who gave the sign to this tribe closed the service for them by a prayer and admonition. This is all that I can gather from the passage, and it does not prove that the tribes had any other religious communion than was involved in their being in one place at one time.

man may not marry a clanswoman, and the children are of the mother's kin, and therefore have no communion of blood religion with their father. In such a society there is hardly any family life, and there can be no sacred household meal. Before the family meal can acquire the religious significance that it possessed in Rome, one of two things must take place : either the primitive association of religion with kinship must be dissolved, or means must have been found to make the whole household of one blood, as was done in Rome by the rule that the wife upon her marriage was adopted into her husband's gens.[1] The rudest nations have religious rules about food, based on the principle of kinship, viz. that a man may not eat the totem animal of his clan ; and they generally have some rites of the nature of the sacrificial feast of kinsmen ; but it is not the custom of savages to take their ordinary daily food in a social way, in regular domestic meals. Their habit is to eat irregularly and apart, and this habit is strengthened by the religious rules, which often forbid to one member of a household the food which is permitted to another.

We have no direct evidence as to the rules and habits of the Semites in the state of primitive savagery, though there is ample proof of an indirect kind that they originally reckoned kinship through the mother, and that men often, if not always, took their wives from strange kins. It is to be presumed that at this stage of society the Semite did not eat with his wife and children, and it is certain that if he did so the meal could not have had a religious character, as an acknowledgment and seal of kinship and adherence

---

[1] In Greece, according to the testimony of Theophrastus, *ap.* Porph., *De Abst.* ii. 20 (Bernays, p. 68), it was customary to pay to the gods an *aparche* of every meal. The term ἀπάρχεσθαι seems to place this offering under the head of gifts rather than of sacrificial communion, and the gods to whom the offering was made were not, as at Rome, family gods.

to a kindred god. But in fact the family meal never became a fixed institution among the Semites generally. In Egypt, down to the present day, many persons hardly ever eat with their wives and children,[1] and, among the Arabs, boys who are not of full age do not presume to eat in the presence of their parents, but take their meals separately or with the women of the house.[2] No doubt the seclusion of women has retarded the development of family life in Mohammedan countries; but for most purposes this seclusion has never taken much hold on the desert, and yet in northern Arabia no woman will eat ★ before men.[3] I apprehend that these customs were originally formed at a time when a man and his wife and family were not usually of one kin, and when only kinsmen would eat together.[4] But be this as it may, the fact remains that in Arabia the daily family meal has never been an established institution with such a religious significance as attaches to the Roman supper.[5]

The sacrificial feast, therefore, cannot be traced back to the domestic meal, but must be considered as having been

[1] Lane, *Mod. Egyptians*, 5th ed., i. 179 ; cf. *Arabian Nights*, chap. ii. note 17.

[2] Burckhardt, *Bed. and Wah.* i. 355 ; Doughty, ii. 142.

[3] Burckhardt, *op. cit.* i. 349. Conversely Ibn Mojāwir, *ap.* Sprenger, *Postrouten*, p. 151, tells of southern Arabs who would rather die than accept food at the hand of a woman.

[4] In Arabia, even in historical times, the wife was not adopted into her husband's kin. The children in historical times were generally reckoned to the father's stock ; but there is much reason to think that this new rule of kinship, when it first came in, did not mean that the infant was born into his father's clan, but that he was adopted into it by a formal act, which did not always take place in infancy. We find that young children follow their mother (*Kinship*, p. 137 *sq.*), and that the law of blood revenge did not prevent fathers from killing their young daughters (*ibid.* p. 153 *sq.*). Of this more hereafter.

[5] The naming of God, by which every meal is consecrated according to Mohammed's precept, seems in ancient times to have been practised only when a victim was slaughtered ; cf. Wellh. p. 117. Here the *tahlil* corresponds to the blessing of the sacrifice, 1 Sam. ix. 13.

from the first a public feast of clansmen. That this is true not only for Arabia but for the Semites as a whole might be inferred on general grounds, inasmuch as all Semitic worship manifestly springs from a common origin, and the inference is confirmed by the observation that even among the agricultural Semites there is no trace of a sacrificial character being attached to ordinary household meals. The domestic hearth among the Semites was not an altar as it was at Rome.[1]

Almost all varieties of human food were offered to the gods, and any kind of food suffices, according to the laws of Arabian hospitality, to establish that bond between two men which in the last resort rests on the principle that only kinsmen eat together. It may seem, therefore, that in the abstract any sort of meal publicly partaken of by a company of kinsmen may constitute a sacrificial feast. The distinction between the feast and an ordinary meal lies, it may seem, not in the material or the copiousness of the repast, but in its public character. When men eat alone they do not invite the god to share their food, but when the clan eats together as a kindred unity the kindred god must also be of the party.

Practically, however, there is no sacrificial feast according to Semitic usage except where a victim is slaughtered. The rule of the Levitical law, that a cereal oblation, when offered alone, belongs wholly to the god and gives no occasion for a feast of the worshippers, agrees with the older history, in which we never find a sacrificial meal of which flesh does not form part. Among the Arabs the usage is the same; a religious banquet implies a victim. It appears, therefore, to look at the matter from its merely human side, that the slaughter of a victim must have been

---

[1] The passover became a sort of household sacrifice after the exile, but was not so originally. See Wellhausen, *Prolegomena*, chap. iii.

in early times the only thing that brought the clan together for a stated meal. Conversely, every slaughter was a clan sacrifice, that is, a domestic animal was not slain except to procure the material for a public meal of kinsmen. This last proposition seems startling, but it is confirmed by the direct evidence of Nilus as to the habits of the Arabs of the Sinaitic desert towards the close of the fourth Christian century. The ordinary sustenance of these Saracens was derived from pillage or from hunting, to which, no doubt, must be added, as a main element, the milk of their herds. When these supplies failed they fell back on the flesh of their camels, one of which was slain for each clan (συγγένεια) or for each group which habitually pitched their tents together (συσκηνία)—which according to known Arab usage would always be a fraction of a clan—and the flesh was hastily devoured by the kinsmen in dog-like fashion, half raw and merely softened over the fire.[1]

To grasp the force of this evidence we must remember that, beyond question, there was at this time among the Saracens private property in camels, and that therefore, so far as the law of property went, there could be no reason why a man should not kill a beast for the use of his own family. And though a whole camel might be too much for a single household to eat fresh, the Arabs knew and practised the art of preserving flesh by cutting it into strips and drying them in the sun. Under these circumstances private slaughter could not have failed to be customary, unless it was absolutely forbidden by tribal usage. In short, it appears that while milk, game, the fruits of pillage were private food which might be eaten in any way, the

---

[1] *Nili opera quædam nondum edita* (Paris, 1639), p. 27.—The συγγένεια answers to the Arabic *baṭn*, the συσκηνία to the Arabic *ḥayy*, in the sense of encampment. See *Kinship*, p. 41 *sq.*

camel was not allowed to be killed and eaten except in a public rite, at which all the kinsmen assisted.

This evidence is all the more remarkable because, among the Saracens of whom Nilus speaks, the slaughter of a camel in times of hunger does not seem to have been considered as a sacrifice to the gods. For a couple of pages later he speaks expressly of the sacrifices which these Arabs offered to the morning star, the sole deity that they acknowledged. These could be performed only when the star was visible, and the whole victim—flesh, skin and bones—had to be devoured before the sun rose upon it, and the day-star disappeared. As this form of sacrifice was necessarily confined to seasons when the planet Venus was a morning star, while the necessity for slaughtering a camel as food might arise at any season, it is to be inferred that in the latter case the victim was not recognised as having a sacrificial character. The Saracens, in fact, had outlived the stage in which no necessity can justify slaughter that is not sacrificial. The principle that the god claims his share in every slaughter has its origin in the religion of kinship, and dates from a time when the tribal god was himself a member of the tribal stock, so that his participation in the sacrificial feast was only one aspect of the rule that no kinsman must be excluded from a share in the victim. But the Saracens of Nilus, like the Arabs generally in the last ages of heathenism, had ceased to do sacrifice to the tribal or clan gods with whose worship the feast of kinsmen was originally connected. The planet Venus, or Lucifer, was not a tribal deity, but, as we know from a variety of sources, was worshipped by all the northern Arabs, to whatever kin they belonged. It is not therefore surprising that in case of necessity we should meet with a slaughter in which the non-tribal deity had no part; but it is noteworthy that, after the victim had lost its sacrificial character, it was still deemed necessary that the slaughter should be the affair of the whole kindred. That this was so, while among the Hebrews, on the other hand, the rule that all legitimate slaughter is sacrifice survived long after householders were permitted to make private sacrifices on their own account, is characteristic of the peculiar development of Arabia, where, as Wellhausen has justly remarked, religious feeling was quite put in the shade by the feeling for the sanctity of kindred blood. Elsewhere among the Semites we see the old religion surviving the tribal system on which it was based, and accommodating itself to the new forms of national life; but in Arabia the rules and customs of the kin retained the sanctity which they originally derived from their connection with the religion of the kin, long after the kindred god had been forgotten or had sunk into quite a subordinate place. I take it, however, that the eating of camels' flesh continued to be regarded by the Arabs as in some sense a religious act, even when it was no longer associated with a formal act of sacrifice; for abstinence from the flesh of camels and wild asses was prescribed by Simeon Stylites to his Saracen converts,[1] and traces of an idolatrous significance in feasts of camels' flesh appear in Mohammedan tradition.[2]

The persistence among the Arabs of the scruple against private slaughter for a man's own personal use may, I think, be traced in a modified form in other parts of Arabia and long after the time of Nilus. Even in modern times,

---

[1] Theodoret, ed. Nösselt, iii. 1274 *sq.*

[2] Wellh. p. 117; *Kinship*, p. 60. These traces are the more worthy of notice because we also find indications that, down to the time of the prophet, or even later, the idea prevailed that camels, or at all events certain breeds of camels, were of demoniac origin; see Cazwīnī, ii. 42, and other authorities cited by Vloten in the *Vienna Oriental Journal*, vii. 239.

when a sheep or camel is slain in honour of a guest, the
good old custom is that the host keeps open house for his
neighbours, or at least distributes portions of the flesh as
far as it will go.   To do otherwise is still deemed churlish,
though not illegal, and the old Arabic literature leaves the
impression that in ancient times this feeling was still
stronger than it is now, and that the whole encampment
was considered when a beast was slain for food.[1]   But be
this as it may, it is highly significant to find that, even in
one branch of the Arabian race, the doctrine that hunger
itself does not justify slaughter, except as the act of the
clan, was so deeply rooted as to survive the doctrine that
all slaughter is sacrifice.   This fact is sufficient to remove
the last doubt as to the proposition that all sacrifice was
originally clan sacrifice, and at the same time it puts the
slaughter of a victim in a new light, by classing it among
the acts which, in primitive society, are illegal to an
individual, and can only be justified when the whole clan
shares the responsibility of the deed.   So far as I know,
there is only one class of actions recognised by early nations
to which this description applies, viz. actions which involve
an invasion of the sanctity of the tribal blood.   In fact, a
life which no single tribesman is allowed to invade, and
which can be sacrificed only by the consent and common
action of the kin, stands on the same footing with the life
of the fellow-tribesman.   Neither may be taken away by
private violence, but only by the consent of the kindred

---

[1] Compare especially the story of Māwīya's courtship (*Agh.* xvi. 103 *sq.*;
Caussin de Perceval, ii. 613).   The beggar's claim to a share in the feast is
doubtless ultimately based on religious and tribal usage rather than on
personal generosity.   Cf. Deut. xxvi. 13.   Similarly among the Zulus,
"when a man kills a cow—which, however, is seldom and reluctantly done,
unless it happens to be stolen property—the whole population of the hamlet
assemble to eat it without invitation ; and people living at a distance of ten
miles will also come to partake of the feast" (Shaw, *Memorials of South
Africa*, p. 59).

and the kindred god. And the parallelism between the two cases is curiously marked in detail by what I may call a similarity between the ritual of sacrifice and of the execution of a tribesman. In both cases it is required that, as far as possible, every member of the kindred should be not only a consenting party but a partaker in the act, so that whatever responsibility it involves may be equally distributed over the whole clan. This is the meaning of the ancient Hebrew form of execution, where the culprit is stoned by the whole congregation.

The idea that the life of a brute animal may be protected by the same kind of religious scruple as the life of a fellow-man is one which we have a difficulty in grasping, or which at any rate we are apt to regard as more proper to a late and sentimental age than to the rude life of primitive times. But this difficulty mainly comes from our taking up a false point of view. Early man had certainly no conception of the sacredness of animal life as such, but neither had he any conception of the sacredness of human life as such. The life of his clansman was sacred to him, not because he was a man, but because he was a kinsman; and, in like manner, the life of an animal of his totem kind is sacred to the savage, not because it is animate, but because he and it are sprung from the same stock and are cousins to one another.

It is clear that the scruple of Nilus's Saracens about killing the camel was of this restricted kind; for they had no objection to kill and eat game. But the camel they would not kill except under the same circumstances as make it lawful for many savages to kill their totem, *i.e.* under the pressure of hunger or in connection with exceptional religious rites.[1] The parallelism between the Arabian custom and totemism is therefore complete except

[1] Frazer, *Totemism and Exogamy*, iv. pp. 19 *sq.*, 45.

in one point. There is no direct evidence that the scruple
against the private slaughter of a camel had its origin in
feelings of kinship. But, as we have seen, there is this
indirect evidence, that the consent and participation of
the clan, which was required to make the slaughter of a
camel legitimate, is the very thing that is needed to make
the death of a kinsman legitimate. And direct evidence
we cannot expect to find, for it is most improbable that
the Arabs of Nilus's time retained any clear ideas about
the original significance of rules inherited by tradition
from a more primitive state of society.

The presumption thus created that the regard paid by
the Saracens for the life of the camel sprang from the
same principle of kinship between men and certain kinds
of animals which is the prime factor in totemism, would
not be worth much if it rested only on an isolated statement about a particular branch of the Arab race. But it
is to be observed that the same kind of restriction on the
private slaughter of animals must have existed in ancient
times among all the Semites. We have found reason to
believe that among the early Semites generally no slaughter
was legitimate except for sacrifice, and we have also found
reason, apart from Nilus's evidence, for believing that all
Semitic sacrifice was originally the act of the community.
If these two propositions are true, it follows that all the
Semites at one time protected the lives of animals proper
for sacrifice, and forbade them to be slain except by the
act of the clan, that is, except under such circumstances
as would justify or excuse the death of a kinsman. Now,
if it thus appears that the scruple against private slaughter
of an animal proper for sacrifice was no mere individual
peculiarity of Nilus's Saracens, but must at an early period
have extended to all the Semites, it is obvious that the
conjecture which connects the scruple with a feeling of

kinship between the worshippers and the victim gains
greatly in plausibility.   For the origin of the scruple
must now be sought in some widespread and very primitive habit of thought, and it is therefore apposite to point
out that among primitive peoples there are no binding
precepts of conduct except those that rest on the principle
of kinship.[1]   This is the general rule which is found in
operation wherever we have an opportunity of observing
rude societies, and that it prevailed among the early
Semites is not to be doubted.   Indeed among the Arabs
the rule held good without substantial modification down
to the time of Mohammed.   No life and no obligation
was sacred unless it was brought within the charmed
circle of the kindred blood.

   Thus the *prima facie* presumption, that the scruple in
question had to do with the notion that certain animals
were akin to men, becomes very strong indeed, and can
hardly be set aside unless those who reject it are prepared
to show that the idea of kinship between men and beasts,
as it is found in most primitive nations, was altogether
foreign to Semitic thought, or at least had no substantial
place in the ancient religious ideas of that race.   But I
do not propose to throw the burden of proof on the
antagonist.

   I have already had occasion in another connection to
shew by a variety of evidences that the earliest Semites,
like primitive men of other races, drew no sharp line of
distinction between the nature of gods, of men, and of
beasts, and had no difficulty in admitting a real kinship
between (*a*) gods and men, (*b*) gods and sacred animals,
(*c*) families of men and families of beasts.[2]   As regards

---

[1] In religions based on kinship, where the god and his worshippers are
of one stock, precepts of sanctity are, of course, covered by the principle of
kinship.

[2] *Supra*, pp. 41 *sqq.* 85 *sqq.*

the third of these points, the direct evidence is fragmentary and sporadic ; it is sufficient to prove that the idea of
kinship between races of men and races of beasts was not
foreign to the Semites, but it is not sufficient to prove
that such a belief was widely prevalent, or to justify us
in taking it as one of the fundamental principles on which
Semitic ritual was founded.   But it must be remembered
that the three points are so connected that if any two of
them are established, the third necessarily follows.   Now,
as regards (a), it is not disputed that the kinship of gods
with their worshippers is a fundamental doctrine of Semitic
religion ; it appears so widely and in so many forms and
applications, that we cannot look upon it otherwise than
as one of the first and most universal principles of ancient
faith.   Again, as regards (b), a belief in sacred animals,
which are treated with the reverence due to divine beings,
is an essential element in the most widespread and
important Semitic cults.   All the great deities of the
northern Semites had their sacred animals, and were
themselves worshipped in animal form, or in association
with animal symbols, down to a late date ; and that this
association implied a veritable unity of kind between
animals and gods is placed beyond doubt, on the one hand,
by the fact that the sacred animals, *e.g.* the doves and
fish of Atargatis, were reverenced with divine honours ;
and, on the other hand, by theogonic myths, such as that
which makes the dove-goddess be born from an egg, and
transformation myths, such as that of Bambyce, where
it was believed that the fish-goddess and her son had
actually been transformed into fish.[1]

---

[1] Examples of the evidence on this head have been given above ; a fuller
account of it will fall to be given in a future course of lectures.   Meantime
the reader may refer to *Kinship*, chap. vii.   I may here, however, add a
general argument which seems to deserve attention.   We have seen (*supra*,
p. 142 *sqq.*) that holiness is not based on the idea of property.   Holy

Now if kinship between the gods and their worshippers, on the one hand, and kinship between the gods and certain kinds of animals, on the other, are deep-seated principles of Semitic religion, manifesting themselves in all parts of the sacred institutions of the race, we must necessarily conclude that kinship between families of men and animal kinds was an idea equally deep-seated, and we shall expect to find that sacred animals, wherever they occur, will be treated with the regard which men pay to their kinsfolk.

Indeed in a religion based on kinship, where the god and his worshippers are of one stock, the principle of sanctity and that of kinship are identical. The sanctity of a kinsman's life and the sanctity of the godhead are not two things, but one; for ultimately the only thing that is sacred is the common tribal life, or the common blood which is identified with the life. Whatever being partakes in this life is holy, and its holiness may be described indifferently, as participation in the divine life and nature, or as participation in the kindred blood.

Thus the conjecture that sacrificial animals were originally treated as kinsmen, is simply equivalent to the conjecture that sacrifices were drawn from animals of a holy kind, whose lives were ordinarily protected by religious scruples and sanctions; and in support of this position a great mass of evidence can be adduced, not merely for Semitic sacrifice, but for ancient sacrifice generally.

In the later days of heathenism, when animal food

---

animals, and holy things generally, are primarily conceived, not as belonging to the deity, but as being themselves instinct with divine power or life. Thus a holy animal is one which has a divine life; and if it be holy to a particular god, the meaning must be that its life and his are somehow bound up together. From what is known of primitive ways of thought we may infer that this means that the sacred animal is akin to the god, for all valid and permanent relation between individuals is conceived as kinship.

19

was commonly eaten, and the rule that all legitimate slaughter must be sacrificial was no longer insisted on, sacrifices were divided into two classes; ordinary sacrifices, where the victims were sheep, oxen or other beasts habitually used for food, and extraordinary sacrifices, where the victims were animals whose flesh was regarded as forbidden meat. The Emperor Julian [1] tells us that in the cities of the Roman Empire such extraordinary sacrifices were celebrated once or twice a year in mystical ceremonies, and he gives as an example the sacrifice of the dog to Hecate. In this case the victim was the sacred animal of the goddess to which it was offered; Hecate is represented in mythology as accompanied by demoniac dogs, and in her worship she loved to be addressed by the name of Dog.[2] Here, therefore, the victim is not only a sacred animal, but an animal kindred to the deity to which it is sacrificed. The same principle seems to lie at the root of all exceptional sacrifices of unclean animals, *i.e.* animals that were not ordinarily eaten, for we have already seen that the idea of uncleanness and holiness meet in the primitive conception of taboo. I leave it to classical scholars to follow this out in its application to Greek and Roman sacrifice; but as regards the Semites it is worth while to establish the point by going in detail through the sacrifices of unclean beasts that are known to us.

1. *The swine.* According to Al-Nadīm the heathen Harranians sacrificed the swine and ate swine's flesh once a year.[3] This ceremony is ancient, for it appears in Cyprus in connection with the worship of the Semitic Aphrodite and Adonis. In the ordinary worship of

---

[1] *Orat.* v. p. 176.

[2] Porph., *De Abst.* iii. 17, iv. 16. Mr. Bury has suggested that etymologically Ἑκάτη = Hund, hound, as ἕκατον = hundert, hundred.

[3] *Fihrist*, p. 326, l. 3 *sq.*

Aphrodite swine were not admitted, but in Cyprus wild boars were sacrificed once a year on April 2.[1] The same sacrifice is alluded to in the Book of Isaiah as a heathen abomination,[2] with which the prophet associates the sacrifice of two other unclean animals, the dog and the mouse. We know from Lucian that the swine was esteemed sacrosanct by the Syrians,[3] and that it was specially sacred to Aphrodite or Astarte is affirmed by Antiphanes, *ap.* Athen. iii. 49.[4]

2. *The dog.* This sacrifice, as we have seen, is mentioned in the Book of Isaiah, and it seems also to be alluded to as a Punic rite in Justin, xviii. 1. 10, where we read that Darius sent a message to the Carthaginians forbidding them to sacrifice human victims and to eat the flesh of dogs: in the connection a religious meal must be understood. In this case the accounts do not connect the rite with any particular deity to whom the dog was sacred,[5] but we know from Al-Nadīm that the dog was sacred among the Harranians. They offered sacrificial gifts to it, and in certain mysteries dogs were solemnly declared to be the brothers of the mystæ.[6] A hint as to the identity of the god to whom the dog was sacred may perhaps be got from Jacob of Sarug, who mentions "the Lord with the dogs" as one of the deities of Carrhæ.[7] This god again may be compared with the huntsman

---

[1] Lydus, *De Mensibus*, Bonn ed., p. 80. Exceptional sacrifices of swine to Aphrodite also took place at Argos (Athen. iii. 49) and in Pamphylia (Strabo, ix. 5. 17), but the Semitic origin of these rites is not so certain as in the case of the Cyprian goddess. The sacrifice of a sow is represented on the rock sculptures of J'rapta (Renan, *Phén.* pl. 31 ; cf. Pietschmann, p. 219, also Baudissin, *Adonis*, p. 145).

[2] Isa. lxv. 4, lxvi. 3, 17.   [3] *Dea Syria*, liv.

[4] In a modern Syrian superstition we find that a demoniac swine haunts houses where there is a marriageable maiden, *ZDPV.* vii. 107.

[5] Movers, *Phoenizier*, i. 104, is quite unsatisfactory.

[6] *Fihrist*, p. 326, l. 27 ; cf. p. 323, l. 28 ; p. 324, l. 2.

[7] *ZDMG.* xxix. 110 ; cf. vol. xlii. p. 473.

Heracles of the Assyrians mentioned by Tacitus.[1] The Tyrian Heracles or Melcarth also appears accompanied by a dog in the legend of the invention of the purple dye preserved by Pollux (i. 46) and Malalas (p. 32).[2] In Mohammedan tradition a demoniac character is ascribed to black dogs, which probably implies that in heathenism they had a certain sanctity.[3]

3. *Fish*, or at least certain species of fish, were sacred to Atargatis and forbidden food to all the Syrians, her worshippers, who believed—as totem peoples do—that if they ate the sacred flesh they would be visited by ulcers.[4]

[1] Tacitus, *Ann.* xii. 13. A huntsman god accompanied by a dog is figured
★ on cylinders (*Gazette Archéol.* 1879, p. 178 *sqq.*), but Assyriologists seem not to be agreed as to his identity. There were probably more divine huntsmen than one.

[2] Whether the Sicilian god Adranus, whose sacred dogs are mentioned by Ælian, *Nat. An.* xi. 20 (confirmed by monumental evidence ; Ganneau, *Rec. d'Arch. Or.* i. 236), is of Semitic origin is very uncertain. He is generally identified with Adar (the Adrammelech of the Bible) ; see Holm, *Gesch. Sic.* i. 95, 377. But the very existence of an Assyrian god Adar is problematical, and the Hadran of Melito (*Spic. Syr.* p. 25), who is taken by others as the Semitic equivalent of Adranus, is a figure equally obscure.

If the conjecture that the Heracles worshipped by the νόθοι in the Cynosarges at Athens was really the Phœnician Heracles can be made out, the connection of this deity with the dog will receive further confirmation. For Cynosarges means "the dog's yard" (Wachsmuth, *Athen.* i. 461). Steph. Byz. *s.v.* explains the name by a legend that while Diomos was sacrificing to Heracles, a white dog snatched the sacrificial pieces and laid them down on the spot where the sanctuary afterwards stood. The dog is here the sacred messenger who declares the will of the god, like the eagle of Zeus in Malalas, p. 199 ; cf. Steph. Byz. *s.v.* γαλιῶται. The sanctity of the dog among the Phœnicians seems also to be confirmed by the proper names
★ כלבא, כלבאלים, and by the existence of a class of sacred ministers called "dogs" (*CIS.* No. 86, cf. Deut. xxiii. 18 [19]). Reinach and G. Hoffmann, *op. cit.* p. 17, are hardly right in thinking of literal dogs ; but in any case that would only strengthen the argument.

[3] Damîrî, ii. 223 ; Vloten in *Vienna Or. Journ.* vii. 240. See also the legend of the dog-demon of Riām, B. Hish. p. 18. In Moslem countries dogs are still regarded with a curious mixture of respect and contempt. They are unclean, but it is an act of piety to feed them, and especially to give them drink (Moslim, ii. 196, ed. of A. H. 1290); and to kill a dog, as I have observed at Jeddah, is an act that excites a good deal of feeling. See also *ZDPV.* vii. 93.

[4] See the evidence collected by Selden, *de Diis Syris, Synt.* ii. cap. 3.

Yet Mnaseas (*ap.* Athen. viii. 37) tells us that fish were daily cooked and presented on the table of the goddess, being afterwards consumed by the priests; and Assyrian cylinders display the fish laid on the altar or presented before it, while, in one example, a figure which stands by in an attitude of adoration is clothed, or rather disguised, in a gigantic fish skin.[1] The meaning of such a disguise is well known from many savage rituals; it implies that the worshipper presents himself as a fish, *i.e.* as a being kindred to his sacrifice, and doubtless also to the deity to which it is consecrated.

4. *The mouse* appears as an abominable sacrifice in Isa. lxvi. 17, along with the swine and the "abomination" (שֶׁקֶץ). The last word is applied in the Levitical law [2] to creeping vermin generally (שֶׁרֶץ = Arab. *ḥanash*), a term which included the mouse and other such small quadrupeds as we also call vermin. All such creatures were unclean in an intense degree, and had the power to communicate uncleanness to whatever they touched. So strict a taboo is hardly to be explained except by supposing that, like the Arabian *ḥanash*,[3] they had supernatural and demoniac qualities. And in fact, in Ezek. viii. 10, we find them as objects of superstitious adoration. On what authority Maimonides says that the Harranians sacrificed field-mice I do not know,[4] but the biblical evidence is sufficient for our purpose.

5. *The horse* was sacred to the Sun-god, for 2 Kings xxiii. 11 speaks of the horses which the kings of Judah had consecrated to this deity—a superstition to which Josiah put an end. At Rhodes, where religion is throughout of a Semitic type, four horses were cast into the sea as a sacrifice at the annual feast of the sun.[5] The

---

[1] Menant, *Glyptique*, ii. 53.   [2] Lev. xi. 41.   [3] *Supra*, p. 128.
[4] Ed. Munk, vol. iii. p. 64, or Chwolsohn, *Ssabier*, ii. 456.
[5] Festus, *s.v.* "October equus"; cf. Pausanias, iii. 20. 4 (sacrifice of horses to the Sun at Taygetus); *Kinship*, p. 242 *sq.*

winged horse (Pegasus) is a sacred symbol of the Carthaginians.

6. *The dove*, which the Semites would neither eat nor
touch, was sacrificed by the Romans to Venus;[1] and as the
Roman Venus-worship of later times was largely derived
from the Phœnician sanctuary of Eryx, where the dove had
peculiar honour as the companion of Astarte,[2] it is very
possible that this was a Semitic rite, though I have not
found any conclusive evidence that it was so. It must
certainly have been a very rare sacrifice; for the dove
among the Semites had a quite peculiar sanctity, and
Al-Nadīm says expressly that it was not sacrificed by
the Harranians.[3] It was, however, offered by the Hebrews,
in sacrifices which we shall by and by see reason to regard
as closely analogous to mystical rites; and in Juvenal, vi.
459 *sqq.*, the superstitious matrons of Rome are represented
as calling in an Armenian or Syrian (Commagenian)
haruspex to perform the sacrifice of a dove, a chicken,
a dog, or even a child. In this association an exceptional
and mystic sacrifice is necessarily implied.[4]

The evidence of these examples is unambiguous. When
an unclean animal is sacrificed it is also a sacred animal.
If the deity to which it is devoted is named, it is the
deity which ordinarily protects the sanctity of the victim,
and, in some cases, the worshippers either in words or by
symbolic disguise claim kinship with the victim and the
god. Further, the sacrifice is generally limited to certain
solemn occasions, usually annual, and so has the character
of a public celebration. In several cases the worshippers
partake of the sacred flesh, which at other times it would

---

[1] Propertius, iv. 5. 62.   [2] Ælian, *Nat. An.* iv. 2.

[3] *Fihrist,* p. 319, l. 21.

[4] Cf. the חזה, *CIS.* No. 165, l. 11. Some other sacrifices of wild
animals, which present analogies to these mystic rites, will be considered in
Additional Note F, *Sacrifices of Sacred Animals.*

be impious to touch.   All this is exactly what we find among totem peoples.   Here also the sacred animal is forbidden food, it is akin to the men who acknowledge its sanctity, and if there is a god it is akin to the god. And, finally, the totem is sometimes sacrificed at an annual feast, with special and solemn ritual.   In such cases the flesh may be buried or cast into a river, as the horses of the sun were cast into the sea,[1] but at other times it is eaten as a mystic sacrament.[2]   These points of contact with the most primitive superstition cannot be accidental; they show that the mystical sacrifices, as Julian calls them, the sacrifices of animals not ordinarily eaten, are not the invention of later times, but have preserved with great accuracy the features of a sacrificial ritual of extreme antiquity.

To a superficial view the ordinary sacrifices of domestic animals, such as were commonly used for food, seem to stand on quite another footing; yet we have been led, by an independent line of reasoning, based on the evidence that all sacrifice was originally the act of the

---

[1] Bancroft, iii. 168; Frazer, *Totem. and Exog.*, i. 44 *sq.*, iv. 230 *sq.*

[2] The proof of this has to be put together out of the fragmentary evidence which is generally all that we possess on such matters.   As regards America the most conclusive evidence comes from Mexico, where the gods, though certainly of totem origin, had become anthropomorphic, and the victim, who was regarded as the representative of the god, was human.   At other times paste idols of the god were eaten sacramentally.   But that the ruder Americans attached a sacramental virtue to the eating of the totem appears from what is related of the Bear clan of the Ouataouaks (*Lettres édif. et cur.* vi. 171), who when they kill a bear make him a feast of his own flesh, and tell him not to resent being killed; "tu as de l'esprit, tu vois que nos enfants souffrent la faim, ils t'aiment, ils veulent te faire entrer dans leur corps, n'est il pas glorieux d'être mangé par des enfans de Captaine?"   The bear feast of the Ainos of Japan (fully described by Scheube in *Mitth. Deutsch. Gesellsch. S. und S. O. Asiens*, No. 22, p. 44 *sq.*) is a sacrificial feast on the flesh of the bear, which is honoured as divine, and slain with many apologies to the gods, on the pretext of necessity.   The eating of the totem as medicine (Frazer, i. 22) belongs to the same circle of ideas.   See also *infra*, p. 314.

clan, to surmise that they also in their origin were
rare and solemn offerings of victims whose lives were
ordinarily deemed sacred, because, like the unclean sacred
animals, they were of the kin of the worshippers and of
their god.[1]

And in point of fact precisely this kind of respect and
reverence is paid to domestic animals among many pastoral
peoples in various parts of the globe. They are regarded
on the one hand as the friends and kinsmen of men, and
on the other hand as sacred beings of a nature akin to the
gods; their slaughter is permitted only under exceptional
circumstances, and in such cases is never used to provide
a private meal, but necessarily forms the occasion of a
public feast, if not of a public sacrifice. The clearest case
is that of Africa. Agatharchides,[2] describing the Troglodyte
nomads of East Africa, a primitive pastoral people in the
polyandrous stage of society, tells us that their whole
sustenance was derived from their flocks and herds. When
pasture abounded, after the rainy season, they lived on
milk mingled with blood (drawn apparently, as in Arabia,
from the living animal), and in the dry season they had
recourse to the flesh of aged or weakly beasts. But the
butchers were regarded as unclean. Further, " they gave
the name of parent to no human being, but only to the ox
and cow, the ram and ewe, from whom they had their
nourishment." [3] Here we have all the features which our
theory requires: the beasts are sacred and kindred beings,

---

[1] Strictly speaking the thing is much more than a surmise, even on the
evidence already before us. But I prefer to understate rather than overstate
the case in a matter of such complexity.

[2] The extracts of Photius and Diodorus are printed together in *Fr. Hist.
Gr.* i. 153. The former has some points which the latter omits. See also
Artemidorus, *ap.* Strabo, xvi. 4. 17.

[3] This reminds us of the peculiar form of covenant among the Gallas, in
which a sheep is introduced as the mother of the parties (Lobo in Pinkerton's
Collection ; *Africa*, i. 8).

for they are the source of human life and subsistence.
They are killed only in time of need, and the butchers are
unclean, which implies that the slaughter was an impious
act.

Similar institutions are found among all the purely
pastoral African peoples, and have persisted with more or
less modification or attenuation down to our own time.[1]
The common food of these races is milk or game;[2] cattle
are seldom killed for food, and only on exceptional
occasions, such as the proclamation of a war, the circumcision of a youth, or a wedding,[3] or in order to obtain a
skin for clothing, or because the creature is maimed or old.[4]

In such cases the feast is public, as among Nilus's
Saracens,[5] all blood relations and even all neighbours having
a right to partake. Further, the herd and its members
are objects of affectionate and personal regard,[6] and are
surrounded by sacred scruples and taboos. Among the
Caffres the cattle kraal is sacred; women may not enter

[1] For the evidence of the sanctity of cattle among modern rude peoples, I
am largely indebted to Mr. Frazer.

[2] Sallust, *Jugurtha*, 89 (Numidians); Alberti, *De Kaffers* (Amst. 1810),
p. 37; Lichtenstein, *Reisen*, i. 144. Out of a multitude of proofs I cite
these, as being drawn from the parts of the continent most remote from one
another.

[3] So among the Caffres (Fleming, *Southern Africa*, p. 260; Lichtenstein,
Reisen, i. 442). The Dinkas hardly kill cattle except for a funeral feast
(Stanley, *Darkest Africa*, i. 424).

[4] Alberti, p. 163 (Caffres); cf. Gen. iii. 21, and Herod. iv. 189. The
religious significance of the dress of skin, which appears in the last cited
passage, will occupy us later.

[5] So among the Zulus (*supra*, p. 284, note) and among the Caffres
(Alberti, *ut supra*).

[6] See in particular the general remarks of Munzinger on the pastoral
peoples of East Africa, *Ostafr. Studien* (2nd ed., 1883), p. 547: "The nomad
values his cow above all things, and weeps for its death as for that of a
child." Again: "They have an incredible attachment to the old breed of
cattle, which they have inherited from father and grandfather, and keep a
record of their descent"—a trace of the feeling of kinship between the herd
and the tribe, as in Agatharchides. See also Schweinfurth, *Heart of Africa*,
i. 59 (3rd ed., 1878), and compare 2 Sam. xii. 3.

it,[1] and to defile it is a capital offence.[2]　Finally, the notion that cattle are the parents of men, which we find in Agatharchides, survives in the Zulu myth that men, especially great chiefs, "were belched up by a cow."[3]

These instances may suffice to show how universally the attitude towards domestic animals, described by Agatharchides, is diffused among the pastoral peoples of Africa.　But I must still notice one peculiar variation of the view that the life of cattle is sacred, which occurs both in Africa and among the Semites.　Herodotus[4] tells us that the Libyans, though they ate oxen, would not touch the flesh of the cow.　In the circle of ideas which we have found to prevail throughout Africa, this distinction must be connected, on the one hand, with the prevalence of kinship through women, which necessarily made the cow more sacred than the ox, and, on the other, with the fact that it is the cow that fosters man with her milk. The same rule prevailed in Egypt, where the cow was sacred to Hathor-Isis, and also among the Phœnicians, who both ate and sacrificed bulls, but would as soon have eaten human flesh as that of the cow.[5]

The importance of this evidence for our enquiry is all the greater because there is a growing disposition among scholars to recognise an ethnological connection of a somewhat close kind between the Semitic and African races. But the ideas which I have attempted to unfold are not

---

[1] Fleming, p. 214.

[2] Lichtenstein, i. 479, who adds that the punishment will not seem severe if we consider how holy their cattle are to them.

[3] Lang, *Myth, Ritual*, etc. i. 179.

[4] Bk. iv. chap. 186.

[5] See Porphyry, *De Abst.* ii. 11, for both nations ; and, for the Egyptians, Herod. ii. 41.　The Phœnician usage can hardly be ascribed to Egyptian influence, for at least a preference for male victims is found among the Semites generally, even where the deity is a goddess.　See what Chwolsohn, *Ssabier*, ii. 77 *sqq.*, adduces in illustration of the statement of the *Fihrist*, that the Harranians sacrificed only male victims.

the property of a single race. How far the ancient holiness of cattle, and especially of the cow, among the Iranians, presents details analogous to those which have come before us, is a question which I must leave to the professed students of a very obscure literature; it seems at least to be admitted that the thing is not an innovation of Zoroastrianism, but common to the Iranians with their Indian cousins, so that the origin of the sacred regard paid to the cow must be sought in the primitive nomadic life of the Indo-European race. But to show that exactly such notions as we have found in Africa appear among pastoral peoples of quite different race, I will cite the case of the Todas of South India. Here the domestic animal, the milk-giver and the main source of subsistence, is the buffalo. "The buffalo is treated with great kindness, even with a degree of adoration,"[1] and certain cows, the descendants from mother to daughter of some remote sacred ancestor, are hung with ancient cattle bells and invoked as divinities.[2] Further, "there is good reason for believing the Todas' assertion that they have never at any time eaten the flesh of the female buffalo," and the male they eat only once a year, when all the adult males in the village join in the ceremony of killing and eating a young bull calf, which is killed with special ceremonies and roasted by a sacred fire. Venison, on the other hand, they eat with pleasure.[3] At a funeral one or two buffaloes are killed:[4] "as each animal falls, men,

[1] Marshall, *Travels among the Todas* (1873), p. 130.

[2] *Ibid.* p. 131.

[3] *Ibid.* p. 81. The sacrifice is eaten only by males. So among the Caffres certain holy parts of an ox must not be eaten by women; and in Hebrew law the duty of festal worship was confined to males, though women were not excluded. Among the Todas men and women habitually eat apart, as the Spartans did; and the Spartan blood-broth may be compared with the Toda animal sacrifice.

[4] *Ibid.* p. 176.

women and children group themselves round its head,
and fondle, caress, and kiss its face, then sitting in groups
of pairs . . . give way to wailing and lamentation." These
victims are not eaten, but left on the ground.

These examples may suffice to show the wide diffusion
among rude pastoral peoples of a way of regarding sacred
animals with which the Semitic facts and the inferences
I have drawn from them exactly correspond; let us now
enquire how far similar ideas can be shown to have
prevailed among the higher races of antiquity. In this
connection I would first of all direct your attention to
the wide prevalence among all these nations of a belief
that the habit of slaughtering animals and eating flesh
is a departure from the laws of primitive piety. Except
in certain ascetic circles, priestly or philosophical, this
opinion bore no practical fruit; men ate flesh freely
when they could obtain it, but in their legends of the
★ Golden Age it was told how in the earliest and happiest
days of the race, when man was at peace with the gods
and with nature, and the hard struggle of daily toil had
not begun, animal food was unknown, and all man's wants
were supplied by the spontaneous produce of the bounteous
earth. This, of course, is not true, for even on anatomical
grounds it is certain that our remote ancestors were carni-
vorous, and it is matter of observation that primitive
nations do not eschew the use of animal food in general,
though certain kinds of flesh are forbidden on grounds
of piety. But, on the other hand, the idea of the Golden
Age cannot be a mere abstract speculation without any
basis in tradition. The legend in which it is embodied
is part of the ancient folk-lore of the Greeks,[1] and the
practical application of the idea in the form of a

---

[1] Hesiod, *Works and Days*, 109 *sqq.* Cf. Preller-Robert, I. i. p. 87 *sqq.*,
for the other literature of the subject.

precept of abstinence from flesh, as a rule of perfection
or of ceremonial holiness, is first found, not among in-
novating and speculative philosophers, but in priestly
circles, *e.g.* in Egypt and India—whose lore is entirely
based on tradition, or in such philosophic schools as
that of Pythagoras, all whose ideas are characterised by
an extraordinary regard for ancient usage and superstition.

In the case of the Egyptian priests the facts set forth
by Porphyry in his book *De Abstinentia*, iv. 6 *sqq.*, on the
authority of Chæremon,[1] enable us to make out distinctly the
connection between the abstinence imposed on the priests
and the primitive beliefs and practice of the mass of the
people.

From ancient times every Egyptian had, according to
the nome he lived in, his own particular kind of forbidden
flesh, venerating a particular species of sacred animal,
exactly as totemistic savages still do. The priests
extended this precept, being in fact the ministers of a
national religion, which gathered into one system the
worships of the various nomes; but only some of them
went so far as to eat no flesh at all, while others, who
were attached to particular cults, ordinarily observed
abstinence only from certain kinds of flesh, though
they were obliged to confine themselves to a strictly
vegetable diet at certain religious seasons, when they were
specially engaged in holy functions. It is, however,
obvious that the multitude of local prohibitions could not
have resulted in a general doctrine of the superior piety of
vegetarianism, unless the list of animals which were sacred
in one or other part of the country had included those
domestic animals which in a highly cultivated country like
Egypt must always form the chief source of animal food.

[1] The authority is good ; see Bernays, *Theophrastos' Schrift Ueber Fröm-
migkeit* (Breslau, 1866), p. 21.

In Egypt this was the case, and indeed the greatest and
most widely recognised deities were those that had associations with domesticated animals. In this respect Egyptian
civilisation declares its affinity to the primitive usages
and superstitions of the pastoral populations of Africa
generally; the Calf-god Apis, who was supposed to be
incarnate in an actual calf at Memphis, and the Cow-
goddess Isis-Hathor, who is either represented in the form
of a cow, or at least wears a cow's horns, directly connect
the dominant cults of Egypt with the sanctity ascribed to
the bovine species by the ruder races of Eastern Africa,
with whom the ox is the most important domestic animal;
and it is not therefore surprising to learn that even in later
times the eating of cow's flesh seemed to the Egyptians
a practice as horrible as cannibalism. Cows were never
sacrificed; and though bulls were offered on the altar, and
part of the flesh eaten in a sacrificial feast, the sacrifice
was only permitted as a *piaculum*, was preceded by a
solemn fast, and was accompanied by public lamentation
as at the death of a kinsman.[1] In like manner, at the
annual sacrifice at Thebes to the Ram-god Amen, the
worshippers bewailed the victim, thus declaring its kinship with themselves; while, on the other hand, its kinship
or identity with the god was expressed in a twofold way,
for the image of Amen was draped in the skin of the
sacrifice, while the body was buried in a sacred coffin.[2]

In Egypt, the doctrine that the highest degree of holiness can only be attained by abstinence from all animal
food, was the result of the political fusion of a number of
local cults in one national religion, with a national priesthood that represented imperial ideas. Nothing of this sort
took place in Greece or in most of the Semitic lands,[3] and

[1] Herod. ii. 39 *sq*.   [2] Herod. ii. 42.
[3] Babylonia is perhaps an exception.

in these accordingly we find no developed doctrine of priestly asceticism in the matter of food.[1]

Among the Greeks and Semites, therefore, the idea of a Golden Age, and the trait that in that age man was vegetarian in his diet, must be of popular not of priestly origin. Now in itself the notion that ancient times were better than modern, that the earth was more productive, men more pious and their lives less vexed with toil and sickness, needs no special explanation; it is the natural result of psychological laws which apply equally to the memory of individuals and the memory of nations. But the particular trait of primitive vegetarianism, as a characteristic feature of the good old times, does not fall under this general explanation, and can only have arisen at a time when there was still some active feeling of pious scruple about killing and eating flesh. This scruple cannot have applied to all kinds of flesh, *e.g.* to game, but it must have covered the very kinds of flesh that were ordinarily eaten in the agricultural stage of society, to which the origin of the legend of the Golden Age undoubtedly belongs. Flesh, therefore, in the legend means the flesh of domestic animals, and the legend expresses a feeling of respect for the lives of these animals, and an idea that their slaughter for food was an innovation not consistent with pristine piety.

When we look into the details of the traditions which later writers cite in support of the doctrine of primæval vegetarianism, we see that in effect this, and no more than

[1] On the supposed case of the Essenes see Lucius's books on the Essenes and Therapeutæ, and Schürer, *Gesch. des Jüd. Volkes,* ii.⁴ 679. The Therapeutæ, whether Jews or Christian monks, appear in Egypt, and most probably they were Egyptian Christians. Later developments of Semitic asceticism almost certainly stood under foreign influences, among which Buddhism seems to have had a larger and earlier share than it has been usual to admit. In old Semitic practice, as among the modern Jews and Moslems, religious fasting meant abstinence from all food, not merely from flesh.

this, is contained in them. The general statement that
early man respected all animal life is mere inference, but
popular tradition and ancient ritual alike bore testimony
that the life of the swine and the sheep,[1] but above all of
the ox,[2] was of old regarded as sacred, and might not be
taken away except for religious purposes, and even then
only with special precautions to clear the worshippers from
the guilt of murder.

To make this quite plain, it may be well to go in some
detail into the most important case of all, that of the ox.
That it was once a capital offence to kill an ox, both in
Attica and in the Peloponnesus, is attested by Varro.[3] So
far as Athens is concerned, this statement seems to be
drawn from the legend that was told in connection with
the annual sacrifice of the Diipolia, where the victim was a
bull, and its death was followed by a solemn enquiry as to
who was responsible for the act.[4] In this trial every one
who had anything to do with the slaughter was called as a
party : the maidens who drew water to sharpen the axe
and knife threw the blame on the sharpeners, they put
it on the man who handed the axe, he on the man who
struck down the victim, and he again on the one who cut
its throat, who finally fixed the responsibility on the knife,
which was accordingly found guilty of murder and cast
into the sea. According to the legend, this act was a mere
dramatic imitation of a piacular sacrifice devised to expiate
the offence of one Sopatros, who killed an ox that he saw
eating the cereal gifts from the table of the gods. This
impious offence was followed by famine, but the oracle

---

[1] Porph., *De Abst.* ii. 9.

[2] *Ibid.* ii. 10, 29 *sq.*; Plato, *Leges*, vi. p. 782; Pausanias, viii. 2. 1 *sqq.*
compared with i. 28. 10 (bloodless sacrifices under Cecrops, sacrifice of an
ox in the time of Erechtheus).

[3] *R. R.* ii. 5.

[4] Pausanias, i. 24. 4 ; Theophrastus, *ap.* Porph., *De Abst.* ii. 30.

declared that the guilt might be expiated if the slayer
were punished and the victim raised up again in connection
with the same sacrifice in which it died, and that it would
then go well with them if they tasted of the flesh and did
not hold back.　Sopatros himself, who had fled to Crete,
undertook to return and devise a means of carrying out
these injunctions, provided that the whole city would share
the responsibility of the murder that weighed on his
conscience ; and so the ceremonial was devised, which continued to be observed down to a late date.[1]　Of course the
legend as such has no value ; it is derived from the ritual,
and not *vice versâ* ; but the ritual itself shows clearly that
the slaughter was viewed as a murder, and that it was felt
to be necessary, not only to go through the form of throwing the guilt on the knife, but to distribute the responsibility
as widely as possible, by employing a number of sacrificial
ministers—who, it may be observed, were chosen from
different kindreds—and making it a public duty to taste
of the flesh.　Here, therefore, we have a well-marked case
of the principle that sacrifice is not to be excused except
by the participation of the whole community.[2]　This rite
does not stand alone.　At Tenedos the priest who offered
a bull - calf to Dionysus ἀνθρωπορραίστης was attacked
with stones and had to flee for his life ;[3] and at Corinth, in
the annual sacrifice of a goat to Hera Acræa, care was
taken to shift the responsibility of the death off the
shoulders of the community by employing hirelings as

[1] Aristophanes alludes to it as a very old-world rite (*Nubes*, 985), but the
observance was still kept up in the days of Theophrastus in all its old
quaintness.　In Pausanias's time it had undergone some simplification,
unless his account is inaccurate.

[2] The further feature that the ox chooses itself as victim, by approaching
the altar and eating the gifts laid on it, is noticeable, both because a similar
rite recurs at Eryx, as will be mentioned presently, and because in this way
the victim eats of the table of the gods, *i.e.* is acknowledged as divine.

[3] Ælian, *Nat. An.* xii. 34.

20

ministers. Even they did no more than hide the knife in such a way that the goat, scraping with its feet, procured its own death.[1] But indeed the idea that the slaughter of a bull was properly a murder, and only to be justified on exceptional sacrificial occasions, must once have been general in Greece; for βουφόνια (βουφονεῖν, βουφόνος) or "ox-murder," which in Athens was the name of the peculiar sacrifice of the Diipolia, is in older Greek a general term for the slaughter of oxen for a sacrificial feast.[2] And that the "ox-murder" must be taken quite literally appears in the sacrifice at Tenedos, where the bull-calf wears the cothurnus and its dam is treated like a woman in childbed. Here the kinship of the victim with man is clearly expressed, but so also is his kinship with the "man-slaying" god to whom the sacrifice is offered, for the cothurnus is proper to Bacchus, and that god was often represented and invoked as a bull.[3]

The same combination of ideas appears in the Hebrew and Phœnician traditions of primitive abstinence from flesh and of the origin of sacrifice. The evidence in this case requires to be handled with some caution, for the Phœnician traditions come to us from late authors, who are gravely suspected of tampering with the legends they record, and the Hebrew records in the Book of Genesis, though they are undoubtedly based on ancient popular lore, have been recast under the influence of a higher faith, and purged of such elements as were manifestly inconsistent

---

[1] Hesychius, s.v. αἴξ αἶγα; Zenobius on the same proverb; Schol. on Eurip., Medea.

[2] See Iliad, vii. 466; the Homeric hymn to Mercury, 436, in a story which seems to be one of the many legends about the origin of sacrifice; Æsch., Prom. 530.

[3] See especially Plutarch, Qu. Gr. 36. Another example to the same effect is that of the goat dressed up as a maiden, which was offered to Artemis Munychia (Parœmiogr. Gr. i. 402, and Eustathius as there cited by the editors).

with Old Testament monotheism.　As regards the Hebrew accounts, a distinction must be drawn between the earlier Jahvistic story and the post-exile narrative of the priestly historian.　In the older account, just as in the Greek fable of the Golden Age, man, in his pristine state of innocence, lived at peace with all animals,[1] eating the spontaneous fruits of the earth; but after the Fall he was sentenced to earn his bread by agricultural toil.　At the same time his war with hurtful creatures (the serpent) began, and domestic animals began to be slain sacrificially, and their skins used for clothing.[2]　In the priestly history, on the other hand, man's dominion over animals, and seemingly also the agricultural life, in which animals serve man in the work of tillage, are instituted at the creation.[3]　In this narrative there is no Garden of Eden, and no Fall, except the growing corruption that precedes the Flood.　After the Flood man receives the right to kill and eat animals, if their blood is poured upon the ground,[4] but sacrifice begins only with the Mosaic dispensation.　Now, as sacrifice and slaughter were never separated, in the case of domestic animals, till the time of Deuteronomy, this form of the story cannot be ancient; it rests on the post-Deuteronomic law of sacrifice, and especially on Lev. xvii. 10 *sq.*　The original Hebrew tradition is that of the Jahvistic story, which agrees with Greek legend in connecting the sacrifice of domestic animals with a fall from the state of pristine innocence.[5]　This, of course, is not the main feature in the

---

[1] Cf. Isa. xi. 6 *sq.*

[2] Gen. ii. 16 *sqq.*, iii. 15, 21, iv. 4.　I am disposed to agree with Budde (*Bibl. Urgeschichte*, p. 83), that the words of ii. 15, "to dress it and to keep it," are by a later hand.　They agree with Gen. i. 26 *sqq.* (priestly), but not with iii. 17 (Jahvistic).

[3] Gen. i. 28, 29, where the use of corn as well as of the fruit of trees is implied.

[4] Gen. ix. 1 *sq.*

[5] The Greek legend in the *Works and Days* agrees with the Jahvistic

biblical story of the Fall, nor is it one on which the narrator
lays stress, or to which he seems to attach any special
significance.   But for that very reason it is to be presumed
that this feature in the story is primitive, and that it must
be explained, like the corresponding Greek legend, not by
the aid of principles peculiar to the Old Testament revelation, but by considerations of a more general kind.   There
are other features in the story of the Garden of Eden—
especially the tree of life—which prove that the original
basis of the narrative is derived from the common stock of
North Semitic folk-lore ; and that this common stock included the idea of primitive vegetarianism is confirmed by
Philo Byblius,[1] whose legend of the primitive men, who
lived only on the fruits of the soil and paid divine honour
to these, has too peculiar a form to be regarded as a mere
transcript either from the Bible or from Greek literature.

It is highly improbable that among the ancient Semites
the story of a Golden Age of primitive fruit-eating can have
had its rise in any other class of ideas than those which
led to the formation of a precisely similar legend in Greece.
The Greeks concluded that primitive man did not eat the
flesh of domestic animals, because their sacrificial ritual
regarded the death of a victim as a kind of murder, only to
be justified under special circumstances, and when it was
accompanied by special precautions, for which a definite
historical origin was assigned.   And just in the same way
the Cypro-Phœnician legend which Porphyry [2] quotes from
Asclepiades, to prove that the early Phœnicians did not eat

story also in ascribing the Fall to the fault of a woman.   But this trait does
not seem to appear in all forms of the Greek story (see Preller-Robert, i. 94
sq.), and the estrangement between gods and men is sometimes ascribed to
Prometheus, who is also regarded as the inventor of fire and of animal
sacrifice.

[1] *Ap.* Eus., *Pr. Ev.* i. 106 (*Fr. Hist. Gr.* iii. 565).

[2] *De Abst.* iv. 15.

flesh, turns on the idea that the death of a victim was originally a surrogate for human sacrifice, and that the first man who dared to taste flesh was punished with death. The details of this story, which exactly agree with Lamb's humorous account of the discovery of the merits of roast sucking pig, are puerile and cannot be regarded as part of an ancient tradition, but the main idea does not seem to be mere invention. We have already seen that the Phœnicians would no more eat cow-beef than human flesh; it can hardly, therefore, be questioned that in ancient times the whole bovine race had such a measure of sanctity as would give even to the sacrifice of a bull the very character that our theory requires. And when Asclepiades states that every victim was originally regarded as a surrogate for a human sacrifice, he is confirmed in a remarkable way by the Elohistic account of the origin of burnt-sacrifice in Gen. xxii., where a ram is accepted in lieu of Isaac. This narrative presents another remarkable point of contact with Phœnician belief. Abraham says that God Himself will provide the sacrifice (ver. 8), and at ver. 13 the ram presents itself unsought as an offering. Exactly this principle was observed down to late times at the great Astarte temple at Eryx, where the victims were drawn from the sacred herds nourished at the sanctuary, and were believed to offer themselves spontaneously at the altar.[1] This is quite analogous to the usage at the Diipolia, where a number of cattle were driven round the sacred table, and the bull was selected for slaughter that approached it and ate of the sacred *popana*, and must be regarded as one of the many forms and fictions adopted to free the worshippers

[1] Ælian, *Nat. An.* x. 50; cf. Isa. liii. 7; Jer. xi. 19 (R. V.); but especially 1 Sam. vi. 14, where the kine halt at the sacrificial stone (Diog. Laert. i. 10. 3); also Ibn Hishām, p. 293, l. 14. That the victim presents itself spontaneously or comes to the altar willingly is a feature in many worships (*Mir. Ausc.* 137; Porph., *De Abst.* i. 25).

of responsibility for the death of the victim. All this
goes to show that the animal sacrifices of the Phœnicians
were regarded as quasi-human. But that the sacrificial
kinds were also viewed as kindred to the gods may be concluded from the way in which the gods were represented.
The idolatrous Israelites worshipped Jehovah under the
form of a steer, and the second commandment implies that
idols were made in the shape of many animals. So too
the bull of Europa, Zeus Asterius, is, as his epithet implies,
the male counterpart of Astarte, with whom Europa was
★ identified at Sidon.[1] Astarte herself was figured crowned
with a bull's head,[2] and the place name Ashteroth Karnaim [3]
is probably derived from the sanctuary of a horned Astarte.
It may indeed be questioned whether this last is identical
with the cow-Astarte of Sidon, or is rather a sheep-
goddess; for in Deut. vii. 13 the produce of the flock
is called the "Ashtaroth of the sheep"—an antique
expression that must have a religious origin. This sheep-
Aphrodite was specially worshipped in Cyprus, where
her annual mystic or piacular sacrifice was a sheep,
and was presented by worshippers clad in sheepskins, thus
declaring their kinship at once with the victim and with
the deity.[4]

It is well to observe that in the most ancient nomadic

---

[1] *De Dea Syria*, iv.; *Kinship*, p. 308.

[2] Philo Byb., *fr.* 24 (*Fr. Hist. Gr.* iii. 569).

[3] Gen. xiv. 5. Kuenen, in his paper on *De Melecheth des Hemels*, p. 37,
thinks it possible that the true reading is "Ashteroth and Karnaim."
But the identity of the later Carnain or Carnion with Ashtaroth or בעשתרה,
"the temple of Astarte" (Josh. xxi. 27), is confirmed by the fact that there
was a τέμινος or sacred enclosure there (1 Macc. v. 43). See further *ZDMG.*
xxix. 431, note 1. The ancient sanctity of the Astarte-shrine has been
transferred to the sepulchre of Job; cf. *S. Silviæ Peregrinatio* (Rome, 1887),
56 *sqq.* A Punic Baal-Carnaim has lately been discovered in the sanctuary
of Saturnus Balcaranensis on Jebel Bū Curnein near Tunis. This, however,
may probably be a local designation derived from the ancient name of the
double-topped mountain (*Mélanges d'Archéol. etc.*, Rome, 1892, p. 1 *sq.*).

[4] See *Additional Note* G, *The Sacrifice of a Sheep to the Cyprian Aphrodite.*

times, to which the sanctity of domestic animals must be referred, the same clan or community will not generally be found to breed more than one kind of domestic animal. Thus in Arabia, though the lines of separation are not so sharp as we must suppose them to have formerly been, there is still a broad distinction between the camel - breeding tribes of the upland plains and the shepherd tribes of the mountains ; and in like manner sheep and goats are the flocks appropriate to the steppes of Eastern Palestine, while kine and oxen are more suitable for the well-watered Phœnician mountains. Thus in the one place we may expect to find a sheep-Astarte, and in another a cow-goddess, and the Hebrew idiom in Deut. vii. 13 agrees with the fact that before the conquest of agricultural Palestine, the Hebrews, like their kinsmen of Moab, must have been mainly shepherds, not cowherds.[1]

I have now, I think, said enough about the sanctity of domestic animals ; the application to the doctrine of sacrifice must be left for another lecture.

---

[1] The great ancestress of the house of Joseph is Rachel, "the ewe." For ★ the Moabites see 2 Kings iii. 4.

LECTURE IX

THE SACRAMENTAL EFFICACY OF ANIMAL SACRIFICE, AND COGNATE ACTS OF RITUAL — THE BLOOD COVENANT —BLOOD AND HAIR OFFERINGS

IN the course of the last lecture we were led to look with some exactness into the distinction drawn in the later ages of ancient paganism between ordinary sacrifices, where the victim is one of the animals commonly used for human food, and extraordinary or mystical sacrifices, where the significance of the rite lies in an exceptional act of communion with the godhead, by participation in holy flesh which is ordinarily forbidden to man. Analysing this distinction, and carrying back our examination of the evidence to the primitive stage of society in which sacrificial ritual first took shape, we were led to conclude that in the most ancient times all sacrificial animals had a sacrosanct character, and that no kind of beast was offered to the gods which was not too holy to be slain and eaten without a religious purpose, and without the consent and active participation of the whole clan.

For the most primitive times, therefore, the distinction drawn by later paganism between ordinary and extraordinary sacrifices disappears. In both cases the sacred function is the act of the whole community, which is conceived as a circle of brethren, united with one another and with their god by participation in one life or life-blood. The same blood is supposed to flow also in the veins of the victim, so that its death is at once a shedding of the tribal blood and a violation of the sanctity of the divine life that is transfused through every member, human or irrational, of the sacred circle. Nevertheless the slaughter of such a victim is permitted or required on solemn occasions, and all the tribesmen partake of its flesh, that they may thereby cement and seal their mystic unity with one another and with their god. In later times we find the conception current that any food which two men partake of together, so that the same substance enters into their flesh and blood, is enough to establish some sacred unity of life between them ; but in ancient times this significance seems to be always attached to participation in the flesh of a sacrosanct victim, and the solemn mystery of its death is justified by the consideration that only in this way can the sacred cement be procured which creates or keeps alive a living bond of union between the worshippers and their god. This cement is nothing else than the actual life of the sacred and kindred animal, which is conceived as residing in its flesh, but especially in its blood, and so, in the sacred meal, is actually distributed among all the participants, each of whom incorporates a particle of it with his own individual life.

The notion that, by eating the flesh, or particularly by drinking the blood, of another living being, a man absorbs its nature or life into his own, is one which appears among primitive peoples in many forms. It lies at the root of the widespread practice of drinking the fresh blood of enemies—a practice which was familiar to certain tribes of the Arabs before Mohammed, and which tradition still ascribes to the wild race of Caḥṭān [1]—and also of the

---

[1] See the evidence in *Kinship*, p. 296 ; and cf. Doughty, ii. 41, where the better accounts seem to limit the drinking of human blood by the Caḥṭān to the blood covenant. See Wellh. 125, n. 6.

habit observed by many savage huntsmen of eating some
part (*e.g.* the liver) of dangerous carnivora, in order
that the courage of the animal may pass into them.
And in some parts of the world, where men have the
privilege of choosing a special kind of sacred animal
either in lieu of, or in addition to, the clan totem,
we find that the compact between the man and the
species that he is thenceforth to regard as sacred is
sealed by killing and eating an animal of the species,
which from that time forth becomes forbidden food to
him.[1]

But the most notable application of the idea is in the
rite of blood brotherhood, examples of which are found all
over the world.[2]   In the simplest form of this rite, two
men become brothers by opening their veins and sucking
one another's blood.   Thenceforth their lives are not two
but one.   This form of covenant is still known in the
Lebanon[3] and in some parts of Arabia.[4]   In ancient
Arabic literature there are many references to the blood
covenant, but instead of human blood that of a victim slain
at the sanctuary is employed.   The ritual in this case is
that all who share in the compact must dip their hands
into the gore, which at the same time is applied to the
sacred stone that symbolises the deity, or is poured forth
at its base.   The dipping of the hands into the dish

[1] Frazer (*Totemism and Exogamy*, i. 44 *sq.*) has collected some evidence
of the killing, but not of the eating.   For the latter he refers me to Cruick-
shank, *Gold Coast* (1853), p. 133 *sq.*

[2] See the collection of evidence in Trumbull, *The Blood Covenant* (New
York, 1885); and compare, for the Arabs, *Kinship*, pp. 57 *sqq.*, 59 n. ;
Wellhausen, p. 125 *sqq.* ; Goldziher, *Literaturbl. f. or. Phil.* 1886, p. 24,
Muh. Stud. p. 67.   In what follows I do not quote examples in detail for
things sufficiently exemplified in the books just cited.

[3] Trumbull, p. 5 *sq.*

[4] Doughty, ii. 41.   The value of the evidence is quite independent of
the accuracy of the statement that the Caḥtān still practise the rite ; at
least the tradition of such a rite subsists.   See also Trumbull, p. 9.

implies communion in an act of eating,[1] and so the ★
members of the bond are called "blood-lickers."   There
seems to be no example in the old histories and poems of
a covenant in which the parties lick one another's blood.
But we have seen that even in modern times the use of
human blood in covenants is not unknown to the Semites,
and the same thing appears for very early times from
Herodotus's account of the form of covenant used by the
Arabs on the borders of Egypt.[2]   Blood was drawn with
a sharp stone from the thumbs of each party, and smeared
on seven sacred stones with invocations of the gods.   The
smearing makes the gods parties to the covenant, but
evidently the symbolical act is not complete unless at the
same time the human parties taste each other's blood.   It
is probable that this was actually done, though Herodotus
does not say so.   But it is also possible that in course of
time the ritual had been so far modified that it was deemed
sufficient that the two bloods should meet on the sacred
stone.[3]   The rite described by Herodotus has for its object
the admission of an individual stranger [4] to fellowship with
an Arab clansman and his kin ; the compact is primarily
between two individuals, but the obligation contracted by
the single clansman is binding on all his "friends," *i.e.*
on the other members of the kin.   The reason why it is so
binding is that he who has drunk a clansman's blood is no
longer a stranger but a brother, and included in the mystic
circle of those who have a share in the life-blood that is
common to all the clan.   Primarily the covenant is not a

---

[1] Matt. xxvi. 23.   [2] Herod. iii. 8.

[3] Some further remarks on the various modifications of covenant ceremonies among the Semites will be found in *Additional Note* H.

[4] The ceremony might also take place between an Arab and his "towns-
man" (ἀστός), which, I apprehend, must mean another Arab, but one of a
different clan.   For if a special contract between two clansmen were meant,
there would be no meaning in the introduction to the "friends" who agree
to share the covenant obligation.

special engagement to this or that particular effect, but a
bond of troth and life-fellowship to all the effects for which
kinsmen are permanently bound together.   And this being
so, it is a matter of course that the engagement has a
religious side as well as a social, for there can be no
brotherhood without community of *sacra*, and the sanction
of brotherhood is the jealousy of the tribal deity, who
sedulously protects the holiness of kindred blood.   This
thought is expressed symbolically by the smearing of the
two bloods, which have now become one, upon the sacred
stones, which is as much as to say that the god himself is
a third blood-licker, and a member of the bond of brotherhood.[1]   It is transparent that in ancient times the deity
so brought into the compact must have been the kindred
god of the clan to which the stranger was admitted ; but
even in the days of Herodotus the old clan religion had
already been in great measure broken down ; all the Arabs
of the Egyptian frontier, whatever their clan, worshipped
the same pair of deities, Orotal and Alilat (Al-Lāt), and
these were the gods invoked in the covenant ceremony.
If, therefore, both the contracting parties were Arabs, of
different clans but of the same religion, neither could feel
that the covenant introduced him to the *sacra* of a new
god, and the meaning of the ceremony would simply be
that the gods whom both adored took the compact under
their protection.   This is the ordinary sense of covenant
with sacrifice in later times, *e.g.* among the Hebrews, but
also among the Arabs, where the deity invoked is ordinarily
Allah at the Caaba or some other great deity of more
than tribal consideration.   But that the appeal to a god
already acknowledged by both parties is a departure from

---

[1] Compare the blood covenant which a Mosquito Indian used to form with
the animal kind he chose as his protectors ;   Bancroft, i. 740 *sq.* (Frazer,
Totemism and Exogamy, i. 50).

the original sense of the rite, is apparent from the application of the blood, not only to the human contractors, but to the altar or sacred stone, which continued to be an invariable feature in covenant sacrifice; for this part of the rite has its full and natural meaning only in a ceremony of initiation, where the new tribesman has to be introduced to the god for the first time and brought into life-fellowship with him, or else in a periodical clan sacrifice held for the purpose of refreshing and renewing a bond between the tribesmen and their god, which by lapse of time may seem to have been worn out.

In Herodotus the blood of the covenant is that of the human parties; in the cases known from Arabic literature it is the blood of an animal sacrifice. At first sight this seems to imply a progress in refinement and an aversion to taste human blood. But it may well be doubted whether such an assumption is justified by the social history of the Arabs,[1] and we have already seen that the primitive form of the blood covenant has survived into modern times. Rather, I think, we ought to consider that the ceremony described by Herodotus is a covenant between individuals, without that direct participation of the whole kin, which, even in the time of Nilus, many centuries later, was essential in those parts of Arabia to an act of sacrifice involving the death of a victim. The covenants made by sacrifice are generally if not always compacts between whole kins, so that here sacrifice was appropriate, while at the same time a larger supply of blood was necessary than could well be obtained without slaughter. That the blood of an animal was accepted in lieu of the tribesmen's own blood, is generally passed over by modern writers without explanation. But an explanation is certainly required,

---

[1] See the examples of cannibalism and the drinking of human blood cited in *Kinship*, p. 296 *sq.*

and is fully supplied only by the consideration that, the victim being itself included in the sacred circle of the kin, whose life was to be communicated to the new-comers, its blood served quite the same purpose as man's blood. On this view the rationale of covenant sacrifice is perfectly clear.

I do not, however, believe that the origin of sacrifice can possibly be sought in the covenant between whole kins—a kind of compact which in the nature of things cannot have become common till the tribal system was weak, and which in primitive times was probably unknown. Even the adoption of individuals into a new clan, so that they renounced their old kin and *sacra*, is held by the most exact students of early legal custom to be, comparatively speaking, a modern innovation on the rigid rules of the ancient blood-fellowship; much more, then, must this be true of the adoption or fusion of whole clans. I apprehend, therefore, that the use of blood drawn from a living man for the initiation of an individual into new *sacra*, and the use of the blood of a victim for the similar initiation of a whole clan, must both rest in the last resort on practices that were originally observed within the bosom of a single kin.

To such sacrifice the idea of a covenant, whether between the worshippers mutually or between the worshippers and their god, is not applicable, for a covenant means artificial brotherhood, and has no place where the natural brotherhood of which it is an imitation already subsists. The Hebrews, indeed, who had risen above the conception that the relation between Jehovah and Israel was that of natural kinship, thought of the national religion as constituted by a formal covenant-sacrifice at Mount Sinai, where the blood of the victims was applied to the altar on the one hand, and to the people on the other,[1] or even

[1] Ex. xxiv. 4 *sqq.*

by a still earlier covenant rite in which the parties were
Jehovah and Abraham.[1] And by a further development
of the same idea, every sacrifice is regarded in Ps. 1. 5
as a covenant between God and the worshipper.[2] But in
purely natural religions, where the god and his community
are looked upon as forming a physical unity, the idea that
religion rests on a compact is out of place, and acts of
religious communion can only be directed to quicken and
confirm the life-bond that already subsists between the
parties. Some provision of this sort may well seem to be
necessary where kinship is conceived in the very realistic
way of which we have had so many illustrations. Physical
unity of life, regarded as an actual participation in one
common mass of flesh and blood, is obviously subject to
modification by every accident that affects the physical
system, and especially by anything that concerns the
nourishment of the body and the blood. On this ground
alone it might well seem reasonable to reinforce the sacred
life from time to time by a physical process. And this
merely material line of thought naturally combines itself
with considerations of another kind, which contain the
germ of an ethical idea. If the physical oneness of the

[1] Gen. xv. 8 *sqq.*

[2] That Jehovah's relation to Israel is not natural but ethical, is the doctrine of the prophets, and is emphasised, in dependence on their teaching, in the Book of Deuteronomy. But the passages cited show that the idea has its foundation in pre-prophetic times ; and indeed the prophets, though they give it fresh and powerful application, plainly do not regard the conception as an innovation. In fact, a nation like Israel is not a natural unity like a clan, and Jehovah as the national God was, from the time of Moses downward, no mere natural clan god, but the god of a confederation, so that here the idea of a covenant religion is entirely justified. The worship of Jehovah throughout all the tribes of Israel and Judah is probably older than the genealogical system that derives all the Hebrews from one natural parent ; cf. *Kinship*, p. 34 n. Mohammed's conception of heathen religion as resting on alliance (Wellh. p. 127) is also to be explained by the fact that the great gods of Arabia in his time were not the gods of single clans.

deity and his community is impaired or attenuated, the
help of the god can no longer be confidently looked for.
And conversely, when famine, plague or other disaster
shows that the god is no longer active on behalf of his
own, it is natural to infer that the bond of kinship with
him has been broken or relaxed, and that it is necessary
to retie it by a solemn ceremony, in which the sacred life
is again distributed to every member of the community.
From this point of view the sacramental rite is also an
atoning rite, which brings the community again into
harmony with its alienated god, and the idea of sacrificial
communion includes within it the rudimentary conception
of a piacular ceremony.   In all the older forms of Semitic
ritual the notions of communion and atonement are bound
up together, atonement being simply an act of communion designed to wipe out all memory of previous
estrangement.

The actual working of these ideas may be seen in two
different groups of ritual observance.   Where the whole
community is involved, the act of communion and atonement takes the shape of sacrifice.   But, besides this
communal act, we find what may be called private acts
of worship, in which an individual seeks to establish a
physical link of union between himself and the deity,
apart from the sacrifice of a victim, either by the use of
his own blood in a rite analogous to the blood covenant
between private individuals, or by other acts involving
an identical principle.   Observances of this kind are
peculiarly instructive, because they exhibit in a simple
form the same ideas that lie at the root of the complex
system of ancient sacrifice ; and it will be profitable to
devote some attention to them before we proceed further
with the subject of sacrifice proper.   By so doing we shall
indeed be carried into a considerable digression, but I hope

that we shall return to our main subject with a firmer grasp ★
of the fundamental principles involved.[1] (See p. 336.)

In the ritual of the Semites and other nations, both
ancient and modern, we find many cases in which the
worshipper sheds his own blood at the altar, as a means
of recommending himself and his prayers to the deity.[2] A
classical instance is that of the priests of Baal at the
contest between the god of Tyre and the God of Israel
(1 Kings xviii. 28). Similarly at the feast of the Syrian
goddess at Mabbog, the Galli and devotees made gashes in
their arms, or offered their backs to one another to beat,[3]
exactly as is now done by Persian devotees at the annual
commemoration of the martyrdom of Hasan and Hosain.[4] ★
I have elsewhere argued that the general diffusion of
this usage among the Aramæans is attested by the Syriac
word *ethkashshaph*, "make supplication," literally "cut ★
oneself." [5]

The current view about such rites in modern as in
ancient times has been that the effusion of blood without
taking away life is a substitute for human sacrifice,[6] an
explanation which recommends itself by its simplicity, and
probably hits the truth with regard to certain cases. But,

---

[1] For the subject discussed in the following paragraphs, compare especially
the copious collection of materials by Dr. G. A. Wilken, *Ueber das
Haaropfer, etc.*, Amsterdam, 1886-7.

[2] Cf. Spencer, *Leg. Rit. Heb.* ii. 13. 2.   [3] *Dea Syria*, 1.

[4] This seems to be a modern survival of the old rites of Anaitis-worship,
for the similar observances in the worship of Bellona at Rome under the
empire were borrowed from Cappadocia, and apparently from a form of the
cult of Anaitis (see the refs. in Roscher, *s.v.*). The latter, again, was closely
akin to the worship of the Syrian goddess, and appears to have been
developed to a great extent under Semitic influence. See my paper on
"Ctesias and the Semiramis Legend," *English Hist. Rev.*, April 1887.

[5] *Journ. Phil.* xiv. 125 ; cf. Nöldeke in *ZDMG.* xl. 723.

[6] See Pausanias, iii. 16. 10, where this is the account given of the bloody
flagellation of the Spartan ephebi at the altar of Artemis Orthia. Similarly
Euripides, *Iph. Taur.* 1458 *sqq.*; cf. also Bourke, *Snake Dance of the Moquis
of Arizona*, p. 196 ; and especially Wilken, *op. cit.* p. 68 *sqq.*

as a general explanation of the offering of his own blood by a suppliant, it is not quite satisfactory. Human sacrifice is offered, not on behoof of the victim, but at the expense of the victim on behoof of the sacrificing community, while the shedding of one's own blood is in many cases a means of recommending oneself to the godhead. Further, there is an extensive class of rites prevalent among savage and barbarous peoples in which blood-shedding forms part of an initiatory ceremony, by which youths, at or after the age of puberty, are admitted to the status of a man, and to a full share in the social privileges and *sacra* of the community. In both cases the object of the ceremony must be to tie, or to confirm, a blood-bond between the worshipper and the god by a means more potent than the ordinary forms of stroking, embracing or kissing the sacred stone. To this effect the blood of the man is shed at the altar, or applied to the image of the god, and has exactly the same efficacy as in the forms of blood covenant that have been already discussed.[1] And that this is so receives strong confirmation from the identical practices observed among so many nations in mourning for deceased kinsmen. The Hebrew law forbade mourners to gash or puncture themselves in honour of the dead,[2] evidently associating this practice, which nevertheless was common down to the close of the old kingdom,[3] with heathenish rites. Among the Arabs

---

[1] That the blood must fall on the altar, or at its foot, is expressly attested in certain cases, *e.g.* in the Spartan worship of Artemis Orthia, and in various Mexican rites of the same kind ; see Sahagun, *Nouvelle Espagne* (French Tr., 1880), p. 185. In Tibullus's account of Bellona worship (Lib. i. El. 6, vv. 45 *sqq.*) the blood is sprinkled on the idol ; the church-fathers add that those who shared in the rite drank one another's blood.

[2] Lev. xix. 28, xxi. 5 ; Deut. xiv. 1.

[3] Jer. xvi. 6. The funeral feast which Jeremiah mentions in the following verse (see the Revised Version, and compare Hos. ix. 4), and which has for its object to comfort the mourners, is, I apprehend, in its origin a feast of communion with the dead ; cf. Tylor, *Primitive Culture*[4], ii. 30 *sqq.* This

in like manner, as among the Greeks and other ancient nations, it was customary in mourning to scratch the face to the effusion of blood.[1]   The original meaning of this practice appears in the form which it has retained among certain rude nations.   In New South Wales, "several men stand by the open grave and cut each other's heads with a boomerang, and hold their heads over the grave so that the blood from the wound falls on the corpse."[2] Similarly in Otaheite the blood as well as the tears shed in mourning were received on pieces of linen, which were thrown on the bier.[3] Here the application of blood and tears to the dead is a pledge of enduring affection; and in Australia the ceremony is completed by cutting a piece of flesh from the corpse, which is dried, cut up and distributed among the relatives and friends of the deceased; some suck their portion " to get strength and courage."   The twosided nature of the rite in this case puts it beyond question that the object is to make an ★ enduring covenant with the dead.

Among the Hebrews and Arabs, and indeed among many other peoples both ancient and modern, the laceration of the flesh in mourning is associated with the practice of shaving the head or cutting off part of the hair and

act of communion consoles the survivors; but in the oldest times the consolation has a physical basis; thus the Arabian *solwān*, or draught that makes the mourner forget his grief, consists of water with which is mingled dust from the grave (Wellh. p. 163), a form of communion precisely similar in principle to the Australian usage of eating a small piece of the corpse. There is a tendency at present, in one school of anthropologists, to explain all death customs as due to fear of ghosts. But among the Semites, at any rate, almost all death customs, from the kissing of the corpse (Gen. l. 1) onwards, are dictated by an affection that endures beyond the grave.

[1] Wellh. p. 181, gives the necessary citations.   Cf. on the rites of mourning in general, Bokhārī, ii. 75 *sq.*, and Freytag in his Latin version of the *Ḥamāsa*, i. 430 *sq.*

[2] F. Bonney in *Journ. Anthrop. Inst.* xiii. (1884) p. 134.   For this and the following reference I am indebted to Mr. Frazer.

[3] *Cook's First Voyage*, Bk. i. chap. 19.

depositing it in the tomb or on the funeral pyre.[1] Here
also a comparison of the usage of more primitive races
shows that the rite was originally two-sided, and had
exactly the same sense as the offering of the mourner's
blood. For among the Australians it is permitted to
pull some hair from the corpse in lieu of a part of
its flesh. The hair, in fact, is regarded by primitive
peoples as a living and important part of the body, and
as such is the object of many taboos and superstitions.[2]

---

[1] See for the Arabs (among whom the practice was confined to women)
the authorities referred to above ; also Krehl, *Rel. der Araber*, p. 33, and
Goldziher, *Muh. Stud.* i. 248 ; note also the epithet *ḥalāc = ḥālica*,
"death." For the Hebrews—whose custom was not to shave the whole
head but only the front of it—see Jer. xvi. 6 ; Amos viii. 10 ; Ezek. vii. 18 ;
and the legal prohibitions, Lev. xix. 27 ; Deut. xiv. 1 ; cf. also Lev. xxi. 5 ;
Ezek. xliv. 20. In the Hebrew case it is not expressly said that the hair
was laid on the tomb, but in Arabia this was done in the times of heathenism,
and is still done by some Bedouin tribes, according to the testimony of
modern travellers. A notable feature in the Arabian custom is that after
shaving her head the mourner wrapped it in the *sicāb*, a cloth stained with
her own blood. See the verse ascribed to the poetess Al-Khansā in *Tāj*, *s. v.*

[2] See Frazer, *Golden Bough*, iii. 258 *sqq.* Wilken (*op. cit.* p. 78 *sqq.*, and
" De Simsonsage," *Gids*, 1888, No. 5) has collected many instances to show
that the hair is often regarded as the special seat of life and strength. It
may be conjectured that this idea is connected with the fact that the hair
continues to grow, and so to manifest life, even in mature age, and this conjecture is supported by the fact that the nails are among many peoples the
object of similar superstitious regard. The practice of cutting off the hair
of the head, or a part of it, is pretty widely diffused ; see Wilken, *Haaropfer*,
p. 74, and for the Arabs an isolated statement of a Mahūby Arab in Doughty,
i. 450, to which Mr. Doughty does not appear to attach much weight. Yet
it seems to me that a custom of cutting off the hair of the dead is implied
when we read that the Bekrites before the desperate battle of Ciḍḍa shaved
their heads as devoting themselves to death (Ham. 253, l. 17), and perhaps
also in Ibn Hishām, p. 254, l. 16 *sq.*, where a man dreams that his head is
shaven and accepts this as an omen of death. Wilken supposes that the
hair was originally cut away from the corpse, or from the dying man, to
facilitate the escape of the soul from the body. This notion might very well
recommend itself to the savage mind, inasmuch as the hair continues to grow
for some time after death. But when we find the hair of the dead used as a
means of divination, or as a charm, as is done among many peoples (Wilken,
Haaropfer, Anh. ii.), we are led to think that the main object in cutting it off
must be to preserve it as a means of continued connection with the dead.
The possession of hair from a man's head or of a shaving from his nails is, in

Thus, when the hair of the living is deposited with the dead, and the hair of the dead remains with the living, a permanent bond of connection unites the two.

Now among the Semites and other ancient peoples the hair-offering is common, not only in mourning but in the worship of the gods, and the details of the ritual in the two cases are so exactly similar that we cannot doubt that a single principle is involved in both. The hair of Achilles was dedicated to the river-god Spercheus, in whose honour it was to be shorn on his safe return from Troy; but, knowing that he should never return, the hero transferred the offering to the dead Patroclus, and laid his yellow locks in the hand of the corpse. Arab women laid their hair on the tomb of the dead; young men and maidens in Syria cut off their flowing tresses and deposited them in caskets of gold and silver in the temples.[1] The Hebrews shaved the fore part of the head in mourning; the Arabs of Herodotus habitually adopted a like tonsure in honour of their god Orotal, who was supposed to wear his hair in the same way.[2] To argue from these parallels

primitive magic, a potent means of getting and retaining a hold over him. This, I suppose, is the reason why an Arab before releasing a captive cut off his hair and put it in his quiver; see the authorities cited by Wilken, p. 111, and add Rasmussen, *Addit.* p. 70 *sq.*, *Agh.* xii. 128. 1. On the same principle Mohammed's hair was preserved by his followers and worn on their persons (*Muh. in Med.* 429, *Agh.* xv. 12. 13). One such hair is the famous relic in the mosque of the Companion at Cairawān.

[1] *Dea Syria*, lx., where modern editors, by a totally inadmissible conjecture, make it appear that maidens offered their locks, and youths only their beard. Cf. Ephraem Syrus, *Op. Syr.* i. 246; the Syriac version of Lev. xix. 27 renders "ye shall not let your hair grow long," and Ephraem explains that it was the custom of the heathen to let their hair grow for a certain time, and then on a fixed day to shave the head in a temple or beside a sacred fountain.

[2] The peculiar Arab tonsure is already referred to in Jer. xxv. 23, R.V. It is found elsewhere in antiquity, *e.g.* in Euboea and in some parts of Asia Minor (*Iliad*, ii. 542; Plut. *Thes.* 5; Strabo, x. 3. 6; Chœrilus, *ap.* Jos., *c. Ap.* i. 22; Pollux, ii. 28). At Delphi, where Greek ephebi were wont to offer the long hair of their childhood, this peculiar cut was called ὀνσκίς, for

between customs of mourning and of religion that the worship of the gods is based on the cult of the dead, would be to go beyond the evidence; what does appear is that the same means which were deemed efficacious to maintain an enduring covenant between the living and the dead were used to serve the religious purpose of binding together in close union the worshipper and his god.

Starting from this general principle, we can explain without difficulty the two main varieties of the hair-offering as it occurs in religion. In its nature the offering is a personal one, made on behalf of an individual, not of a community. It does not therefore naturally find a place in the stated and periodical exercises of local or tribal religion, where a group of men is gathered together in an ordinary act of communal worship. Its proper object is to create or to emphasise the relation between an individual and a god, and so it is in place either in ceremonies of initiation, by which a new member is incorporated into the circle of a particular religion, or in connection with special vows and special acts of devotion, by which a worshipper seeks to knit more closely the bond between himself and his god. Thus in Greek religion the hair-offering occurs either at the moment when a youth enters on manhood, and so takes up a full share in the religious as well as the political responsibilities of a citizen, or else in fulfilment of a vow made at some moment when a man is in special need of divine succour. The same thing is true of Semitic religion, but to make this clear requires some explanation.

Theseus was said to have shorn only his front locks at the temple. Among the Curetes this was the way in which warriors wore their hair; presumably, therefore, children let the front locks grow long, and sacrificed them on entering manhood, just as among the Arabs the two side locks are the distinguishing mark of an immature lad.

In early societies a man is destined by his birth to become a member of a particular political and social circle, which is at the same time a distinct religious community. But in many cases this destination has to be confirmed by a formal act of admission to the community. The child or immature stripling has not yet full civil privileges and responsibilities, and in general, on the principle that civil and religious status are inseparable, he has no full part either in the rights or in the duties of the communal religion. He is excluded from many religious ceremonies, and conversely he can do without offence things which on religious grounds are strictly forbidden to the full tribesman. Among rude nations the transition from ⋆ civil and religious immaturity to maturity is frequently preceded by certain probationary tests of courage and endurance; for the full tribesman must above all things be a warrior. In any case the step from childhood to manhood is too important to take place without a formal ceremony and public rites of initiation, importing the full and final incorporation of the neophyte into the civil and religious fellowship of his tribe or community.[1] It is clear from what has already been said, that the application of the blood of the youth to the sacred symbol, or the depositing of his hair at the shrine of his people's god, might form a significant feature in such a ritual; and among very many rude peoples one or other of these ceremonies is actually observed in connection with the rites which every young man must pass through before he attains the position of a warrior, and is allowed to marry and exercise the other prerogatives of perfect manhood. Among wholly barbarous races these initiation ceremonies have great importance,

---

[1] In some cases the rite seems to be connected with the transference of the lad from the mother's to the father's kin. But for the present argument it is not necessary to discuss this aspect of the matter.

and are often extremely repulsive in character. The blood-offering in particular frequently takes a form which makes it a severe test of the neophyte's courage—as in the cruel flagellation of Spartan ephebi at the altar of Artemis Orthia, or in the frightful ordeal which takes the place of simple circumcision in some of the wilder mountain tribes of Arabia.[1]   As manners become less fierce, and society ceases to be organised mainly for war, the ferocity of primitive ritual is naturally softened, and the initiation ceremony gradually loses importance, till at last it becomes a mere domestic celebration, which in its social aspect may be compared to the private festivities of a modern family when a son comes of age, and in its religious aspect to the first communion of a youthful Catholic.   When the rite loses political significance, and becomes purely religious, it is not necessary that it should be deferred to the age of full manhood ; indeed, the natural tendency of pious parents will be to dedicate their child as early as possible to the god who is to be his protector through life.   Thus circum-

★ cision, which was originally a preliminary to marriage, and so a ceremony of introduction to the full prerogative of manhood, is now generally undergone by Mohammedan boys before they reach maturity, while, among the Hebrews, infants were circumcised on the eighth day from birth.   Similar variations of usage apply to the Semitic hair-offering.   Among the Arabs in the time of Mohammed it was common to sacrifice a sheep on the birth of a child, and then to shave the head of the infant and daub the scalp with the blood of the victim.   This ceremony—callek 'acīca, or " the cutting off of the hair "—was designed to " avert evil from the child," and was evidently an act of dedication by which the infant was brought under the

---

[1] The connection between circumcision and the initiatory blood-offering will be considered more fully in another place.

protection of the god of the community.[1] Among Lucian's ★
Syrians, on the other hand, the hair of boys and girls was
allowed to grow unshorn as a consecrated thing from birth
to adolescence, and was cut off and dedicated at the
sanctuary as a necessary preliminary to marriage. In
other words, the hair-offering of youths and maidens
was a ceremony of religious initiation, through which
they had to pass before they were admitted to the
status of social maturity. The same thing appears to
have occurred, at least in the case of maidens, at
Phœnician sanctuaries; for the female worshippers at
the Adonis feast of Byblus, who, according to the author
just cited, were required to sacrifice either their hair or
their chastity,[2] appear from other accounts to have been ★
generally maidens, of whom this act of devotion was
exacted as a preliminary to marriage.[3] I apprehend that

[1] That the hair was regarded as an offering appears from the Moslem
practice, referred by tradition to the example of Fāṭima, of bestowing in
alms its weight of silver. Alms are a religious oblation, and in the similar
custom which Herod. ii. 65, Diod. i. 83, attest for ancient Egypt, the silver
was paid to the sanctuary. See for further details *Kinship*, p. 179 *sqq.*,
where I have dwelt on the way in which such a ceremony would facilitate
the change of the child's kin, when the rule that the son followed the
father and not the mother began to be established. I still think that
this point is worthy of notice, and that the desire to fix the child's
religion, and with it his tribal connection, at the earliest possible moment,
may have been one cause for performing the ceremony in infancy. But
Nöldeke's remarks in *ZDMG.* xl. 184, and a fuller consideration of the
whole subject of the hair-offering, have convinced me that the name 'acīca
is not connected with the idea of change of kin, but is derived from the
cutting away of the first hair. In this, however, I see a confirmation of the
view that among the Arabs, as among the Syrians, the old usage was to
defer the cutting of the first hair till adolescence, for 'acca is a very strong
term to apply to the shaving of the scanty hair of a new-born infant, while
it is quite appropriate to the sacrifice of the long locks characteristic of boy-
hood. Cf. also the use of the same verb in the phrases 'occat tamīmatuhu
(*Kāmil*, 405, 1. 19), 'acca 'l-shabābu tamīmatī (*Tāj, s.v.*), used of the cutting
away, when manhood was reached, of the amulet worn during childhood.
In modern Syria (Sidon district) a child's hair must not be cut till it is a
year old (*ZDPV.* vii. 85).

[2] *Dea Syria*, vi.

[3] Sozomen, v. 10. 7. Cf. Socrates, i. 18, and the similar usage in

among the Arabs, in like manner, the 'acīca was originally
a ceremony of initiation into manhood, and that the
transference of the ceremony to infancy was a later
innovation, for among the Arabs, as among the Syrians,
young lads let their hair grow long, and the sign of
immaturity was the retention of the side locks, which
adult warriors did not wear.[1]   The cutting of the side
locks was therefore a formal mark of admission into
manhood, and in the time of Herodotus it must also
have been a formal initiation into the worship of Orotal,
for otherwise the religious significance which the Greek
historian attaches to the shorn forehead of the Arabs is
unintelligible.   At that time, therefore, we must conclude
that a hair-offering, precisely equivalent to the 'acīca, took
place upon entry into manhood, and thereafter the front
hair was habitually worn short as a permanent memorial
of this dedicatory sacrifice.   It is by no means clear
that even in later times the initiatory ceremony was
invariably performed in infancy, for the name 'acīca, which
in Arabic denotes the first hair as well as the religious
ceremony of cutting it off, is sometimes applied to the
ruddy locks of a lad approaching manhood,[2] and figuratively to the plumage of a swift young ostrich or the
tufts of an ass's hair, neither of which has much resemblance to the scanty down on the head of a new-born
babe.[3]

It would seem, therefore, that the oldest Semitic usage,
both in Arabia and in Syria, was to sacrifice the hair of

Babylon, Herod. i. 199. We are not to suppose that participation in these
rites was confined to maidens before marriage (Euseb. *Vit. Const.* iii. 58. 1),
but it appears that it was obligatory on them.

[1] See Wellh., *Heid.* p. 198.

[2] Imraulcais, 3. 1; see also *Lisān*, xii. 129, l. 18, and Dozy, *s.v.*

[3] Zohair, 1. 17; *Diw. Hodh.* 232. 9. The sense of "down," which
Nöldeke, *ut supra*, gives to the word in these passages, is hardly appropriate.

childhood upon admission to the religious and social status of manhood.

The bond between the worshipper and his god which was established by means of the hair-offering had an enduring character, but it was natural to renew it from time to time, when there was any reason to fear that the interest of the deity in his votary might have been relaxed. Thus it was customary for the inhabitants of Ṭāïf in Arabia to shave their heads at the sanctuary of the town whenever they returned from a journey.[1] Here the idea seems to be that absence from the holy place might have loosened the religious tie, and that it was proper to bind it fast again. In like manner the hair-offering formed part of the ritual in every Arabian pilgrimage,[2] and also at the great feasts of Byblus and Bambyce,[3] which were not mere local celebrations, but drew worshippers from distant parts. The worshipper in these cases desired to attach himself as firmly as possible to a deity and a shrine with which he could not hope to keep up frequent and regular connection, and thus it was fitting that, when he went forth from the holy place, he should leave part of himself behind, as a permanent link of union with the temple and the god that inhabited it.

The Arabian and Syrian pilgrimages with which the hair-offering was associated were exceptional services ; in many cases their object was to place the worshipper under the protection of a foreign god, whose cult had no place in the pilgrim's local and natural religion, and in any case

---

[1] *Muh. in Med.* p. 381.

[2] Wellh. p. 123 *sq.* ; Goldziher, *op. cit.* p. 249. That the hair was shaved as an offering appears most clearly in the worship of Ocaiṣir, where it was mixed with an oblation of meal.

[3] *Dea Syria*, vi., lv. In the latter case the eyebrows also were shaved, and the sacrifice of hair from the eyebrow reappears in Peru, in the laws of the Incas. On the painted inscription of Citium (*CIS.* No. 86) barbers (גלבם) are enumerated among the stated ministers of the temple

the service was not part of a man's ordinary religious
duties, but was spontaneously undertaken as a work of
special piety, or under the pressure of circumstances that
made the pilgrim feel the need of coming into closer
touch with the divine powers. Among the Hebrews, at
least in later times, when stated pilgrimages to Jerusalem
were among the ordinary and imperative exercises of
every man's religion, the pilgrimage did not involve a hair-
offering, nor is it probable that in any part of antiquity
this form of service was required in connection with
ordinary visits to one's own local temple. The Pentateuchal law recognises the hair-offering only in the case
of the peculiar vow of the Nazarite, the ritual of which
is described in Num. vi. The details there given do
not help us to understand what part the Nazirate held
in the actual religious life of the Jews under the law,
but from Josephus[1] we gather that the vow was generally
taken in times of sickness or other trouble, and that it
was therefore exactly parallel to the ordinary Greek vow
to offer the hair on deliverance from urgent danger. From
the antique point of view, the fact that a man is in straits
or peril is a proof that the divine powers on which his life
is dependent are estranged or indifferent, and a warning to
bring himself into closer relation with the god from whom
he is estranged. The hair-offering affords the natural
means towards this end, and, if the offering cannot be
accomplished at the moment, it ought to be made the
subject of a vow, for a vow is the recognised way of
antedating a future act of service and making its efficacy
begin at once. A vow of this kind, aiming at the redin-
tegration of normal relations with the deity, is naturally
more than a bare promise; it is a promise for the performance of which one at once begins to make active

[1] *B. J.* ii. 15. 1.

preparation, so that the life of the votary from the time
when he assumes the engagement is taken out of the
ordinary sphere of secular existence, and becomes one
continuous act of religion.[1] As soon as a man takes
the vow to poll his locks at the sanctuary, the hair is a
consecrated thing, and as such, inviolable till the moment
for discharging the vow arrives ; and so the flowing locks
of the Hebrew Nazarite or of a Greek votary like Achilles
are the visible marks of his consecration. In like manner
the Arabian pilgrim, whose resolution to visit a distant
shrine was practically a vow,[2] was not allowed to poll
or even to comb and wash his locks till the pilgrimage
was accomplished ; and on the same principle the whole
course of his journey, from the day when he first set his
face towards the temple with the resolution to do homage
there, was a period of consecration (*iḥrām*),[3] during which
he was subject to a number of other ceremonial restrictions
or taboos, of the same kind with those imposed by actual
presence in the sanctuary.

The taboos connected with pilgrimages and other vows
require some further elucidation, but to go into the matter
now would carry us too far from the point immediately
before us. I will therefore reserve what I have still to say
on this subject for an additional note.[4] What has been
said already covers all the main examples of the hair-offering among the Semites.[5] They present considerable variety

[1] Of course, if the vow is conditional on something to happen in the future,
the engagement does not necessarily come into force till the condition is
fulfilled.

[2] In Mohammedan law it is expressly reckoned as a vow.

[3] Under Islam the consecration of the pilgrim need not begin till he
reaches the boundaries of the sacred territory. But it is permitted, and
according to many authorities preferable, to assume the *iḥrām* on leaving
one's home ; and this was the ancient practice.

[4] See *Additional Note* I, *The Taboos incident to Pilgrimages and Vows.*

[5] Quite distinct from the hair-offering are the cases in which the hair is
shaved off (but not consecrated) as a means of purification after pollution ;

of aspect, but the result of our discussion is that they can
be referred to a single principle. In their origin the hair-
offering and the offering of one's own blood are precisely
similar in meaning. But the blood - offering, while it
presents the idea of life-union with the god in the strongest
possible form, is too barbarous to be long retained as an
ordinary act of religion. It continued to be practised
among the civilised Semites, by certain priesthoods and
societies of devotees; but in the habitual worship of laymen it either fell out of use or was retained in a very
attenuated form, in the custom of tatooing the flesh with
★ punctures in honour of the deity.[1] The hair-offering, on
the other hand, which involved nothing offensive to civilised

e.g. Lev. xiv. 9 (purification of leper); *Dea Syria*, liii. (after defilement by
the dead); Deut. xxi. 12. In such cases the hair is cut off because defilement is specially likely to cling to it.

[1] For the στίγματα on the wrists and necks of the heathen Syrians the
classical passage is *Dea Syria*, lix.; compare for further evidence the discussion in Spencer, *Leg. Rit. Heb.* ii. 14; and see also *Kinship*, p. 249 *sqq*.
The tattooed marks were the sign that the worshipper belonged to the god ;
thus at the temple of Heracles at the Canobic mouth of the Nile, the fugitive
slave who had been marked with the sacred stigmata could not be reclaimed
by his master (Herod. ii. 113). The practice therefore stands on one line
with the branding or tattooing of cattle, slaves and prisoners of war. But in
Lev. xix. 28, where tattooing is condemned as a heathenish practice, it is
immediately associated with incisions in the flesh made in mourning or in
honour of the dead, and this suggests that in their ultimate origin the
stigmata are nothing more than the permanent scars of punctures made to
draw blood for a ceremony of self-dedication to the deity. Among the Arabs
I find no direct evidence of a religious significance attached to tattooing, and
the practice appears to have been confined to women, as was also the habitual
use of amulets in mature life. The presumption is that this coincidence is
not accidental, but that the tattooed marks were originally sacred stigmata
like those of the Syrians, and so were conceived to have the force of a charm.
Pietro della Valle (ed. 1843), i. 395, describes the Arabian tattooing, and says
that it is practised all over the East by men as well as by women. But so
far as I have observed, it is only Christian men that tattoo in Syria, and
with them the pattern chosen is a sacred symbol, which has been shown to
me as a proof that a man was exempt from the military service to which
Moslems are liable. In Farazdac, ed. Boucher, p. 232, l. 9, a tattooed hand
is the mark of a foreigner. In Egypt men of the peasant class are sometimes tattooed.

feelings, continued to play an important part in religion to the close of paganism, and even entered into Christian ritual in the tonsure of priests and nuns.[1]

Closely allied to the practice of leaving part of oneself —whether blood or hair—in contact with the god at the sanctuary, are offerings of part of one's clothes or other things that one has worn, such as ornaments or weapons. In the *Iliad,* Glaucus and Diomede exchange armour in token of their ancestral friendship; and when Jonathan makes a covenant of love and brotherhood with David, he invests him with his garments, even to his sword, his bow, and his girdle.[2] Among the Arabs, he who seeks protection lays hold of the garments of the man to whom he appeals, or more formally ties a knot in the head-shawl of his protector.[3] In the old literature, " pluck away my garments from thine " means " put an end to our attachment."[4] The clothes are so far part of a man that they can serve as a vehicle of personal connection. Hence the religious significance of suspending on an idol or *Dhāt Anwāt,* not only weapons, ornaments and complete garments, but mere shreds from one's raiment. These rag - offerings are still to be seen hanging on the sacred

[1] The latter was practised in Jerome's time in the monasteries of Egypt and Syria (*Ep.* 147 ad Sabinianum).

[2] 1 Sam. xviii. 3 *sq.* I presume that by ancient law Saul was bound to acknowledge the formal covenant thus made between David and his son, and that this ought to be taken into account in judging of the subsequent relations between the three.

[3] Wellhausen, *Heidenthum,* p. 109, note 3 ; Burckhardt, *Bed. and Wah.* i. 130 *sq.* ; Blunt, *Bedouin Tribes of the Euphrates,* i. 42. The knot, says Burckhardt, is tied that the protector may look out for witnesses to prove the act, and " the same custom is observed when any transaction is to be witnessed." But primarily, I apprehend, the knot is the symbolic sign of the engagement that the witnesses are called to prove, and I was told in the Ḥijāz that the suppliant gets a fragment of the fringe of the shawl to keep as his token of the transaction. In the covenant sacrifice, Herod. iii. 8, the blood is applied to the sacred stones with threads from the garments of the two contracting parties.

[4] Imraulc., *Moall.* l. 21

trees of Syria and on the tombs of Mohammedan saints;
they are not gifts in the ordinary sense, but pledges of
attachment.[1] It is possible that the rending of garments
in mourning was originally designed to procure such an
offering for the dead, just as the tearing of the hair on the
like occasion is not a natural sign of mourning, but a relic
of the hair-offering. Natural signs of mourning must not
be postulated lightly; in all such matters habit is a second
nature.[2]

Finally, I may note in a single word that the counterpart of the custom of leaving part of oneself or of one's
clothes with the deity at the sanctuary, is the custom of
wearing sacred relics as charms, so that something belonging
to the god remains always in contact with one's person.[3]

The peculiar instructiveness of the series of usages
which we have been considering, and the justification for
the long digression from the subject of sacrifice into which
they have led us, is that the ceremonies designed to
establish a life-bond between the worshipper and his god
are here dissociated from the death of a victim and from
every idea of penal satisfaction to the deity. They have

[1] A masterful man, in the early days of Islam, reserves a water for his
own use by hanging pieces of fringe of his red blanket on a tree beside it, or
by throwing them into the pool; Farazdac, p. 195, *Agh.* viii. 159. 10 *sqq.*

[2] It is to be noted that most of the standing methods of expressing
sorrow and distress are derived from the formal usages employed in primitive
times in mourning for the dead. These usages, however, are not all to be
derived from one principle. While the rudest nations seek to keep up their
connection with the beloved dead, they also believe that very dangerous
influences hover round death-beds, corpses, and graves, and many funeral
ceremonies are observed as safeguards against these, as has been well shown
by Mr. Frazer, *Journ. Anthr. Inst.* xv. 64 *sqq.*; though I think he has not
sufficiently allowed for another principle that underlies many such customs,
namely, the affectionate desire of even the rudest peoples to keep up a friendly
intercourse with their dead friends and relations. Compare below, p. 370.

[3] Thus in Palestine, at the present time, the man who hangs a rag on a
sacred tree takes with him in return, as a preservative against evil, one of
the rags that have been sanctified by hanging there for some time before
(*PEF. Qu. St.* 1893, p. 204).

indeed an atoning force, whenever they are used to renew
relations with a god who is temporarily estranged, but
this is merely a consequence of the conception that the
physical link which they establish between the divine and
human parties in the rite binds the god to the man as
well as the man to the god. Even in the case of the
blood-offering there is no reason to hold that the pain
of the self-inflicted wounds had originally any significant
place in the ceremony. But no doubt, as time went on,
the barbarous and painful sacrifice of one's own blood
came to be regarded as more efficacious than the simpler
and commoner hair-offering; for in religion what is unusual always appears to be more potent, and more fitted to
reconcile an offended deity.

The use of the Syriac word *ethkashshaph* seems to show
that the sacrifice of one's own blood was mainly associated
among the Aramæans with deprecation or supplication to
an angry god, and though I cannot point among the Semites
to any formal atoning ceremony devised on this principle,
the idea involved can be well illustrated by a rite still
sometimes practised in Arabia, as a means of making atonement to a man for offences short of murder. With bare ★
and shaven head the offender appears at the door of the
injured person, holding a knife in each hand, and, reciting a
formula provided for the purpose, strikes his head several
times with the sharp blades. Then, drawing his hands over
his bloody scalp, he wipes them on the doorpost. The
other must then come out and cover the suppliant's head
with a shawl, after which he kills a sheep, and they sit
down together at a feast of reconciliation. The characteristic point in this rite is the application of the blood to the
doorpost, which, as in the passover service, is equivalent
to applying it to the person of the inmates. Here, therefore, we still see the old idea at work, that the reconciling

22

value of the rite lies, not in the self-inflicted wounds, but in the application of the blood to make a life-bond between the two parties.

On the same analogy, when we turn to those blood-rites in which a whole community takes part, and in which therefore a victim has to be slaughtered to provide the material for the ceremony, we may expect to find that, at least in old times, the significant part of the ceremony does not lie in the death of the victim, but in the application of its life or life-blood; and in this expectation we shall not be disappointed.

Of all Semitic sacrifices those of the Arabs have the rudest and most visibly primitive character; and among the Arabs, where there was no complicated fire-ceremony at the altar, the sacramental meal stands out in full relief as the very essence of the ritual. Now, in the oldest known form of Arabian sacrifice, as described by Nilus, the camel chosen as the victim is bound upon a rude altar of stones piled together, and when the leader of the band has thrice led the worshippers round the altar in a solemn procession accompanied with chants, he inflicts the first wound, while the last words of the hymn are still upon the lips of the congregation, and in all haste drinks of the blood that gushes forth. Forthwith the whole company fall on the victim with their swords, hacking off pieces of the quivering flesh and devouring them raw with such wild haste, that in the short interval between the rise of the day star which marked the hour for the service to begin, and the disappearance of its rays before the rising sun, the entire camel, body and bones, skin, blood and entrails, is wholly devoured.[1] The plain meaning of this is that the victim was

---

[1] This must not be regarded as incredible. According to Artemidorus, *ap.* Strabo, xvi. 4. 17, the Troglodytes ate the bones and skin as well as the flesh of cattle.

devoured before its life had left the still warm blood and
flesh,—raw flesh is called "living" flesh in Hebrew and
Syriac,—and that thus in the most literal way all those who
shared in the ceremony absorbed part of the victim's life ★
into themselves.   One sees how much more forcibly than
any ordinary meal such a rite expresses the establishment
or confirmation of a bond of common life between the
worshippers, and also, since the blood is shed upon the
altar itself, between the worshippers and their god.

In this sacrifice, then, the significant factors are two : the
conveyance of the living blood to the godhead, and the
absorption of the living flesh and blood into the flesh and
blood of the worshippers.   Each of these is effected in the
simplest and most direct manner, so that the meaning
of the ritual is perfectly transparent.   In later Arabian
sacrifices, and still more in the sacrifices of the more
civilised Semitic nations, the primitive crudity of the
ceremonial was modified, and the meaning of the act is
therefore more or less disguised, but the essential type of
the ritual remains the same.

In all Arabian sacrifices except the holocaust—which
occurs only in the case of human victims—the godward
side of the ritual is summed up in the shedding of the
victim's blood, so that it flows over the sacred symbol, or
gathers in a pit (*ghabghab*) at the foot of the altar idol.
An application of the blood to the summit of the sacred
stone may be added, but that is all.[1]   What enters the
ghabghab is held to be conveyed to the deity ; thus at
certain Arabian shrines the pit under the altar was the
place where votive treasures were deposited.   A pit to
receive the blood existed also at Jerusalem under the
altar of burnt-offering, and similarly in certain Syrian
sacrifices the blood was collected in a hollow, which

---

[1] Zohair, x. 24.

apparently bore the name of *mashkan,* and thus was designated as the habitation of the godhead.[1]

In Arabia, accordingly, the most solemn act in the ritual is the shedding of the blood, which in Nilus's narrative takes place at the moment when the sacred chant comes to an end. This, therefore, is the crisis of the service, to which the choral procession round the altar leads up.[2] In later Arabia, the *ṭawāf,* or act of circling the sacred stone, was still a principal part of religion; but even before Mohammed's time it had begun to be dissociated from sacrifice, and become a meaningless ceremony. Again, the original significance of the *wocūf,* or "standing," which in the ritual of the post-Mohammedan pilgrimage has in like manner become an unmeaning ceremony, is doubtless correctly explained by Wellhausen, who compares it with the scene described by more than one old poet, where the worshippers stand round the altar idol, at a respectful distance, gazing with rapt attention, while the slaughtered victims lie stretched on the ground. The moment of this act of adoration must be that when the slaughter of the victims is just over, or still in progress, and their blood is draining into the *ghabghab,* or being applied by the priest to the head of the *noṣb.*[3]

In the developed forms of North Semitic worship, where fire-sacrifices prevail, the slaughter of the victim loses its importance as the critical point in the ritual.

---

[1] See the text published by Dozy and De Goeje in the *Actes* of the Leyden Congress of Orientalists, 1883, vol. iii. pp. 337, 363. For the *ghabghab,* see p. 198 *supra,* and Wellhausen, p. 103. Compare also the Persian ritual, Strabo, xv. 3. 14, and that of certain Greek sacrifices, Plutarch, *Aristides,* xxi. : τὸν ταῦρον εἰς τὴν πυρὰν σφάξας.

[2] The festal song of praise (הלל, *tahlil*) properly goes with the dance round the altar (cf. Ps. xxvi. 6 *sq.*), for in primitive times song and dance are inseparable. (Cf. Wellh. 110 *sq.*)

[3] Wellh. p. 61 *sq.* ; Yācūt, iii. 94, l. 13 *sq.* (cf. Nöldeke in *ZDMG.* 1887, p. 721) ; *ibid.* p. 182, l. 2 *sq.* (*supra,* p. 228).

The altar is above all things a hearth, and the burning of
the sacrificial fat is the most solemn part of the service.

This, however, is certainly not primitive; for even in
the period of fire - sacrifice the Hebrew altar is called
מזבח, that is, "the place of slaughter,"[1] and in ancient
times the victim was slain on or beside the altar, just as
among the Arabs, as appears from the account of the
sacrifice of Isaac, and from 1 Sam. xiv. 34.[2] The
latter passage proves that in the time of Saul the Hebrews
still knew a form of sacrifice in which the offering was
completed in the oblation of the blood. And even in
the case of fire-sacrifice the blood was not cast upon the
flames, but dashed against the sides of the altar or poured
out at its foot; the new ritual was not able wholly to
displace the old. Nay, the sprinkling of the blood continued to be regarded as the principal point of the ritual
down to the last days of Jewish ritual; for on it the
atoning efficacy of the sacrifice depended.[3]

As regards the manward part of the ritual, the revolting details given by Nilus have naturally no complete
parallel in the worship of the more civilised Semites, or
even of the later Arabs. In lieu of the scramble described
by Nilus—the wild rush to cut gobbets of flesh from the
still quivering victim—we find among the later Arabs a
partition of the sacrificial flesh among all who are present
at the ceremony. Yet it seems possible that the *ijāza*, or
" permission," that is, the word of command that terminates
the *wocūf*, was originally the permission to fall upon the

---

[1] Aram. *madbaḥ*, Arab. *madhbaḥ* ; the latter means also a trench in the
ground, which is intelligible from what has been said about the *ghabghab*.

[2] *Supra*, p. 202. In Ps. cxviii. 27 the festal victim is bound with
cords to the horns of the altar, a relic of ancient usage which was no
longer intelligible to the Septuagint translators or to the Jewish traditional
expositors. Cf. the sacrificial stake to which the victim is bound in Vedic
sacrifices.

[3] Heb. ix. 22 ; Reland, *Ant. Heb.* p. 300 (Gem. on *Zeb.* xlii. 1).

slaughtered victim.   In the Meccan pilgrimage the *ijāza*
which terminates the *wocūf* at 'Arafa was the signal for
a hot race to the neighbouring sanctuary of Mozdalifa,
where the sacred fire of the god Cozaḥ burned; it was, in
fact, not so much the permission to leave 'Arafa as to draw
near to Cozaḥ.   The race itself is called *ifāḍa*, which may
mean either " dispersion " or " distribution."   It cannot
★ well mean the former, for 'Arafa is not holy ground, but
merely the point of assemblage, just outside the Ḥaram,
at which the ceremonies began, and the station at 'Arafa
is only the preparation for the vigil at Mozdalifa.   On
the other hand, if the meaning is " distribution," the *ifāḍa*
answers to the rush of Nilus's Saracens to partake of the
sacrifice.   The only difference is that at Mozdalifa the
crowd is not allowed to assemble close to the altar, but
has to watch the performance of the solemn rites from
afar; compare Ex. xix. 10–13.[1]

The substitution of an orderly division of the victim
for the scramble described by Nilus does not touch the
meaning of the ceremonial.   Much more important, from
its effect in disguising an essential feature in the ritual,
is the modification by which, in most Semitic sacrifices, the
flesh is not eaten " alive " or raw, but sodden or roasted.
It is obvious that this change could not fail to establish
itself with the progress of civilisation; but it was still
possible to express the idea of communion in the actual
life of the victim by eating its flesh " with the blood."

---

[1] It may be noted that the ceremonies at Mozdalifa lay wholly between
sunset and sunrise, and that there was apparently one sacrifice just at or
after sunset and another before sunrise,—another point of contact with the
ritual described by Nilus.   The *wocūf* corresponding to the morning sacrifice
was of course held at Mozdalifa within the Ḥaram, for the pilgrims were
already consecrated by the previous service.   Nābigha in two places speaks
of a race of pilgrims to a place called Ilāl.   If the reference is to the Meccan
ḥajj, Ilāl must be Mozdalifa not, as the geographers suppose, a place at
'Arafa.

That bloody morsels were consumed by the heathen in
Palestine, and also by the less orthodox Israelites, is
apparent from Zech. ix. 7 ; Ezek. xxxiii. 25 ;[1] Lev. xix. 26 ;
and the context of these passages, with the penalty of
excommunication attached to the eating of blood in Lev.
vii. 27, justify us in assuming that this practice had a
directly religious significance, and occurred in connection
with sacrifice.　That it was in fact an act of communion
with heathen deities, is affirmed by Maimonides, not as a
mere inference from the biblical texts, but on the basis of
Arabic accounts of the religion of the Harranians.[2]　It
would seem, however, that in the northern Semitic lands
the ritual of blood-eating must already have been rare in
the times to which our oldest documents belong; presumably, indeed, it was confined to certain mystic initiations,
and did not extend to ordinary sacrifices.[3]

[1] I cannot comprehend why Cornill corrects Ezek. xxxiii. 25 by Ezek.
xviii. 6, xxii. 9, and not conversely ; cf. LXX. on Lev. xix. 26, where the
same mistake occurs.

[2] *Dalālat al-Ḥāirīn*, iii. 46, vol. iii. p. 104 of Munk's ed. (Paris, 1866)
and p. 371 of his translation.　That Maimonides had actual accounts of the
Harranians to go on appears by comparing the passage with that quoted
above from an Arabic source in the *Actes* of the Leyden Congress ; but
there may be a doubt whether his authorities attested blood-eating among
the Harranians, or only supplied hints by which he interpreted the biblical
evidence.

[3] For the mystic sacrifices of the heathen Semites, see above, p. 290 *sqq.*
That these sacrifices were eaten with the blood appears from a comparison
of Isa. lxv. 4, lxvi. 3, 17.　All these passages refer to the same circle of
rites, in which the victims chosen were such animals as were strictly
taboo in ordinary life—the swine, the dog, the mouse and vermin (שקץ)
generally.　To such sacrifices, as we learn from lxvi. 17, a peculiar consecrating and purifying efficacy was attached, which must be ascribed to
the sacramental participation in the sacrosanct flesh.　The flesh was eaten
in the form of broth, which in lxv. 4 is called broth of *piggŭlīm, i.e.* of
carrion, or flesh so killed as to retain the blood in it (Ezek. iv. 14 ; cf. Zech.
ix. 7).　We are to think, therefore, of a broth made with the blood, like
the black broth of the Spartans, which seems also to have been originally a
sacred food, reserved for warriors.　The dog-sacrifice in lxvi. 3 is killed by
breaking its neck, which agrees with this conclusion.　Similarly in the
mysteries of the Ainos, the sacred bear, which forms the sacrifice, is killed

In the legal sacrifices of the Hebrews blood was never eaten, but in the covenant sacrifice of Ex. xxiv. it is sprinkled on the worshippers, which, as we have already learned by a comparison of the various forms of the blood covenant between men, has the same meaning. In later forms of sacrifice this feature disappears, and the communion between god and man, which is still the main thing in ordinary sacrifices, is expressed by burning part of the flesh on the altar, while the rest is cooked and eaten by the worshippers. But the application of the living blood to the worshipper is retained in certain special cases—at the consecration of priests and the purification of the leper [1]—where it is proper to express in the strongest way the establishment of a special bond between the god and his servant,[2] or the restitution of one who has been cut off from religious fellowship with the deity and the community of his worshippers. In like manner, in the forms of sin-offering described in Lev. iv., it is at least required that the priest should dip his finger in the blood of the victim ; and in this kind of ritual, as is expressly stated in Lev. x. 17, the priest acts as the representative of the sinner or bears his sin. Again, the blood of the Paschal lamb is applied to the doorposts, and so extends its efficacy to all within the dwelling—the " house " in all the Semitic languages standing for the household or family.[3]

without effusion of blood ; cf. the Indian rite, Strabo, xv. 1. 54 (Satapatha Brahmana, tr. Eggeling, ii. 190), and the Cappadocian, *ibid.* xv. 3. 15 ; also the Finnish sacrifice, Mannhardt, *Ant. Wald- u. Feldkulte*, p. 160, and other cases of the same kind, *Journ. R. Geog. Soc.* vol. iii. p. 283, vol. xl. p. 171. Spencer compares the πνικτά of Acts xv. 20.

[1] Lev. viii. 23, xiv. 6, 14.

[2] The relation between God and His priests rests on a covenant (Deut. xxxiii. 9 ; Mal. ii. 4 *sqq.*).

[3] In modern Arabia " it is the custom to slaughter at the tent door and sprinkle the camels with the blood " (Blunt, *Nejd*, i. 203 ; also Doughty, i. 499). This protects the camels from sickness. Also the live booty from a foray is sprinkled with sacrificial blood—presumably to incorporate it with the tribal

The express provision that the flesh of the lamb must not
be eaten raw seems to be directed against a practice similar
to what Nilus describes ; and so also the precept that the
passover must be eaten in haste, in ordinary outdoor attire,
and that no part of it must remain till the morning, becomes intelligible if we regard it as having come down
from a time when the living flesh was hastily devoured
beside the altar before the sun rose.[1]　From all this it
is apparent that the ritual described by Nilus is by no
means an isolated invention of the religious fancy, in one
of the most barbarous corners of the Semitic world, but
a very typical embodiment of the main ideas that underlie
the sacrifices of the Semites generally.　Even in its
details it probably comes nearer to the primitive form
of Semitic worship than any other sacrifice of which we
have a description.

　　We may now take it as made out that, throughout the
Semitic field, the fundamental idea of sacrifice is not that
of a sacred tribute, but of communion between the god and
his worshippers by joint participation in the living flesh
and blood of a sacred victim.　We see, however, that in
the more advanced forms of ritual this idea becomes
attenuated and tends to disappear, at least in the commoner
kinds of sacrifice.　When men cease to eat raw or living
flesh, the blood, to the exclusion of the solid parts of the
body, comes to be regarded as the vehicle of life and the
true *res sacramenti*.　And the nature of the sacrifice as a
sacramental act is still further disguised when—for reasons

cattle (*tilād*) ; Doughty, i. 452.　An obscure reference to the smearing of a
camel with blood is found in Azracī, p. 53, l. 13, *Agh.* xiii. 110, l. 6, but the
variations between the two texts make it hazardous to attempt an explanation.
Cp. on the whole subject of blood-sprinkling, Kremer, *Studien*, p. 45 *sqq.*

[1] There is so much that is antique about the Paschal ritual, that one is
tempted to think that the law of Ex. xii. 46, "neither shall ye break a
bone thereof," may be a prohibition of some usage descended from the rule
given by Nilus, that the bones as well as the flesh must be consumed.

that will by and by appear more clearly—the sacramental
blood is no longer drunk by the worshippers but only
sprinkled on their persons, or finally finds no manward
application at all, but is wholly poured out at the altar,
so that it becomes the proper share of the deity, while the
flesh is left to be eaten by man.   This is the common
form of Arabian sacrifice, and among the Hebrews the
same form is attested by 1 Sam. xiv. 34.   At this stage,
at least among the Hebrews, the original sanctity of the
life of domestic animals is still recognised in a modified
form, inasmuch as it is held unlawful to use their flesh for
food except in a sacrificial meal.   But this rule is not
strict enough to prevent flesh from becoming a familiar
luxury.   Sacrifices are multiplied on trivial occasions of
religious gladness or social festivity, and the rite of eating
at the sanctuary loses the character of an exceptional
sacrament, and means no more than that men are invited
to feast and be merry at the table of their god, or that no
feast is complete in which the god has not his share.

This stage in the evolution of ritual is represented by
the worship of the Hebrew high places, or, beyond the
Semitic field, by the religion of the agricultural communities
of Greece.   Historically, therefore, it coincides with the
stage of religious development in which the deity is conceived as the king of his people and the lord of the land,
and as such is habitually approached with gifts and tribute.
It was the rule of antiquity, and still is the rule in the
East, that the inferior must not present himself before his
superior without a gift "to smooth his face" and make
him gracious.[1]   The same phrase is habitually applied in
the Old Testament to acts of sacrificial worship, and in Ex.

---

[1] חִלָּה פְנֵי, Prov. xix. 6 ; Ps. xlv. 13 (12), E.V., "intreat his favour."
In the Old Testament the phrase is much oftener used of acts of worship
addressed to the deity, e.g. 1 Sam. xiii. 12, of the burnt-offering.

xxiii. 15 the rule is formulated that no one shall appear before Jehovah empty-handed. Δῶρα θεοὺς πείθει, δῶρ' αἰδοίους βασιλῆας.

As the commonest gifts in a simple agricultural state of society necessarily consisted of grain, fruits and cattle, which served to maintain the open hospitality that prevailed at the courts of kings and great chiefs, it was natural that animal sacrifices, as soon as their sacramental significance fell into the background, should be mainly regarded as gifts of homage presented at the court of the divine king, out of which he maintained a public table for his worshippers. In part they were summed up along with the cereal oblations of first-fruits as stated tributes, which everyone who desired to retain the favour of the god was expected to present at fixed seasons; in part they were special offerings with which the worshipper associated special petitions, or with which he approached the deity to present his excuses for a fault and request forgiveness.[1] In the case where it is the business of the worshipper to make satisfaction for an offence, the gift may assume rather the character of a fine payable at the sanctuary; for in the oldest free communities personal chastisement is reserved for slaves, and the offences of freemen are habitually wiped out by the payment of an amercement.[2] But in the older Hebrew custom the fines paid to the sanctuary do not appear to have taken the form of victims for sacrifice, but rather of payments in money to the priest,[3] and the atoning effect ascribed to gifts

---

[1] 1 Sam. xxvi. 19 : "If Jehovah hath stirred thee up against me, let Him be gratified by an oblation."'

[2] The reason of this is that not even a chief can strike or mutilate a freeman without exposing himself to retaliation. This is still the case among the Bedouins, and so it was also in ancient Israel; see *The Old Testament in the Jewish Church*, 2nd ed., p. 368.

[3] 2 Kings xii. 16 ; cf. Amos ii. 8 ; Hos. iv. 8.

and sacrifices of all kinds seems simply to rest on the general principle that a gift smooths the face and pacifies anger.

It has sometimes been supposed that this is the oldest form of the idea of atoning sacrifice, and that the elaborate piacula, which begin to take the chief place in the altar ritual of the Semites from the seventh century onwards, are all developed out of it. The chief argument that appears to support this view is that the whole burnt-offering, which is entirely made over to the deity, the worshipper retaining no part for his own use, is prominent among piacular sacrifices, and may even be regarded as the piacular sacrifice *par excellence*. In the later forms of Syrian heathenism the sacrificial meal practically disappears, and almost the whole altar service consists of piacular holocausts,[1] and among the Jews the highest sin-offerings, whose blood was brought into the inner sanctuary, were wholly consumed, but not upon the altar,[2] while the flesh of other sin-offerings was at least withdrawn from the offerer and eaten by the priests.

We have seen, however, that a different and profounder conception of atonement, as the creation of a life-bond between the worshipper and his god, appears in the most primitive type of Semitic sacrifices, and that traces of it can still be found in many parts of the later ritual. Forms of consecration and atonement in which the blood of the victim is applied to the worshipper, or the blood of the worshipper conveyed to the symbol of godhead, occur in all stages of heathen religion, not only among the Semites but among the Greeks and other races; and even on *à priori* grounds it seems probable that when the Northern Semites,

---

[1] That the Harranians never ate sacrificial flesh seems to be an exaggeration, but one based on the prevalent character of their ritual; see Chwolsohn ii. 89 *sq.*

[2] Lev. vi. 23 (30), xvi. 27, iv. 11, 20.

in the distress and terror produced by the political convulsions of the seventh century, began to cast about for
rites of extraordinary potency to conjure the anger of the
gods, they were guided by the principle that ancient and
half obsolete forms of ritual are more efficacious than the
everyday practices of religion.

Further, it is to be observed that in the Hebrew ritual
both of the holocaust and of the sin-offering, the victim
is slain at the altar " before Jehovah," a phrase which is
wanting in the rule about ordinary sacrifices, and implies
that the act of slaughter and the effusion of the blood
beside the altar have a special significance, as in the
ancient Arabian ritual.   Moreover, in the sin - offering
there is still—although in a very attenuated form—a
trace of the manward application of the blood, when
the priest dips his finger in it, and so applies it to the
horns of the altar, instead of merely dashing it against
the sides of the altar from a bowl;[1] and also, as regards
the destination of the flesh, which is eaten by the priests
in the holy place, it is clear from Lev. x. 17 that the
flesh is given to the priests because they minister as the
representatives of the sinful people, and that the act of
eating it is an essential part of the ceremony, exactly as in
the old ritual of communion.   In fact the law expressly
recognises that the flesh and blood of the sin-offering is a
sanctifying medium of extraordinary potency; whosoever
touches the flesh becomes holy, the garment on which the
blood falls must be washed in a holy place, and even the
vessel in which the flesh is sodden must be broken or
scoured to remove the infection of its sanctity.[2]   That
this is the reason why none but the priests are allowed

---

[1] Lev. iv. 6, 17, 34, compared with chap. iii. 2. זרק is to sprinkle or
dash from the bowl, מזרק.

[2] Lev. vi. 20 (27).

to eat of it has been rightly discerned by Ewald;[1] the flesh, like the sacramental cup in the Roman Catholic Church, was too sacred to be touched by the laity. Thus the Levitical sin-offering is essentially identical with the ancient sacrament of communion in a sacred life; only the communion is restricted to the priests, in accordance with the general principle of the priestly legislation, which surrounds the holy things of Israel by fence within fence, and makes all access to God pass through the mediation of the priesthood.

I am not aware that anything quite parallel to the ordinary Hebrew sin - offering occurs among the other Semites; and indeed no other Semitic religion appears to have developed to the same extent the doctrine of the consuming holiness of God, and the consequent need for priestly intervention between the laity and the most holy things. But among the Romans the flesh of certain piacula was eaten by the priests, and in the piacular sacrifice of the Arval Brothers the ministrants also partook of the blood.[2] Among the Greeks, again, piacular victims —like the highest forms of the Hebrew sin-offering— were not eaten at all, but either burned, or buried, or cast into the sea, or carried up into some desert mountain far from the foot of man.[3] It is commonly supposed that this was done because they were unclean, being laden with the sins of the guilty worshippers; but this explanation is excluded, not only by the analogy of the Hebrew sin-offering, which is a *códesh codashīm*, or holy thing of the first class, but by various indications in Greek myth and ritual. For to the Greeks earth and sea are not impure but holy, and at Trœzen a sacred laurel was

[1] *Alterthümer*, 3rd ed., p. 87 *sq.* ; cf. the Syrian fish-sacrifices of which only the priests partook, *supra*, p. 293.

[2] Marquardt, *Sacralwesen*, p. 185 ; Servius on Æn. iii. 231.

[3] Hippocrates, ed. Littré, vi. 362.

believed to have grown from the buried carcase of the victim used in the atonement for Orestes.[1]   Further, the favourite piacular victims were sacred animals, *e.g.* the swine of Demeter and the dog of Hecate, and the essential part of the lustration consisted in the application of the blood of the offering to the guilty person, which is only intelligible if the victim was a holy sacrament.   The blood was indeed too holy to be left in permanent contact with a man who was presently to return to common life, and therefore it was washed off again with water.[2] According to Porphyry, the man who touched a sacrifice designed to avert the anger of the gods was required to bathe and wash his clothes in running water before entering the city or his house,[3] an ordinance which recurs in the case of such Hebrew sin-offerings as were not eaten, and of the red heifer whose ashes were used in lustrations.   These were burnt " without the camp," and both the ministrant priest and the man who disposed of the body had to bathe and wash their clothes exactly as in the Greek ritual.[4]

From all this it would appear that the sin-offering and other forms of piacula, including the holocaust, in which there is no sacrificial meal of which the sacrificer himself partakes, are yet lineally descended from the ancient ritual of sacrificial communion between the worshippers and their god, and at bottom rest on the same principle with those ordinary sacrifices in which the sacrificial meal played a chief part.   But the development of this part of our

---

[1] Pausanias, ii. 31. 8.

[2] Apoll. Rhod., *Argon.* iv. 702 *sqq.* Cf. Schoemann, *Gr. Alterth.* II. v. 13.

[3] *De Abst.* ii. 44.

[4] Lev. xvi. 24, 28 ; Num. xix. 7–10. In the *Fihrist,* p. 319, l. 12, after it has been explained that the sacrifices of the Harranians were not eaten but burned, it is added, "and the temple is not entered on that day."

subject must be reserved for another lecture, in which I will try to explain how the original form of sacrifice came to be differentiated into two distinct types of worship, and gave rise on the one hand to the "honorific" or ordinary, and on the other to the "piacular" or exceptional sacrifices of later times.

LECTURE X

THE DEVELOPMENT OF SACRIFICIAL RITUAL— FIRE-SACRIFICES AND PIACULA

WE have come to see that the sin-offering as well as the ordinary sacrificial meal is lineally descended from the primitive sacrifice of communion, in which the victim is a sacred animal that may not ordinarily be killed or used for food. But while in the one case the notion of the special holiness and inviolable character of the victim has gradually faded away, in the other this aspect of the sacrifice has been intensified, till even a religious participation in the flesh is regarded as an impiety. Each of these opposite processes can to a certain extent be traced from stage to stage. As regards the sacrificial meal, we find, both in the case of Nilus's Saracens and in that of African peoples, with whom the ox has a sanctity similar to that which the Arabs ascribed to the camel, that the sacramental flesh begins to be eaten as food under the pressure of necessity; and when this is done, it also begins to be cooked like other food. Then we have the stage, represented by the early Hebrew religion, in which domestic animals are freely eaten, but only on condition that they are presented as sacrifices at the altar and consumed in a sacred feast. And, finally, a stage is reached in which, as in Greece in the time of the Apostle Paul, sacrificial meat is freely sold in the shambles, or, as in Arabia before Mohammed, nothing more is required than that the beast

23

designed for food shall be slain in the name of a god.   In piacular sacrifices, on the other hand, we find, in a variety of expressions, a struggle between the feeling that the victim is too holy to be eaten or even touched, and the principle that its atoning efficacy depends on the participation of the worshippers in its life, flesh and blood.   In one rite the flesh may be eaten, or the blood drunk, but only by consecrated priests; in another, the flesh is burned, but the blood is poured on the hands or body of the sinner; in another, the lustration is effected with the ashes of the victim (the red heifer of the Jewish law); or, finally, it is enough that the worshipper should lay his hands on the head of the victim before its slaughter, and that then its life-blood should be presented at the altar.

The reasons for the gradual degradation of ordinary sacrifice are not far to seek; they are to be found, on the one hand, in the general causes which make it impossible for men above the state of savagery to retain a literal faith in the consanguinity of animal kinds with gods and men, and, on the other hand, in the pressure of hunger, and afterwards in the taste for animal food, which in a settled country could not generally be gratified except by eating domestic animals.   But it is not so easy to understand, *first*, why in spite of these influences certain sacrifices retained their old sacrosanct character, and in many cases became so holy that men were forbidden to touch or eat of them at all; and, *second*, why it is to this particular class of sacrifices that a special piacular efficacy is assigned.

In looking further into this matter, we must distinguish between the sacred domestic animals of pastoral tribes— the milk-givers, whose kinship with men rests on the principle of fosterage—and those other sacred animals of wild or half-domesticated kinds, such as the dove and the swine, which even in the later days of Semitic heathenism were surrounded by strict taboos, and looked upon as in some sense partakers of a divine nature. The latter are undoubtedly the older class of sacred beings; for observation of savage life in all parts of the world shows that the belief in sacred animals, akin to families of men, attains its highest development in tribes which have not yet learned to breed cattle and live on their milk. Totemism pure and simple has its home among races like the Australians and the North American Indians, and seems always to lose ground after the introduction of pastoral life. It would appear that the notion of kinship with milk-giving animals through fosterage has been one of the most powerful agencies in breaking up the old totem-religions, just as a systematic practice of adoption between men was a potent agency in breaking up the old exclusive system of clans. As the various totem clans began to breed cattle and live on their milk, they transferred to their herds the notions of sanctity and kinship which formerly belonged to species of wild animals, and thus the way was at once opened for the formation of religious and political communities larger than the old totem kins. In almost all ancient nations in the pastoral and agricultural stage, the chief associations of the great deities are with the milk-giving animals; and it is these animals, the ox, the sheep, the goat, or in Arabia the camel, that appear as victims in the public and national worship. But experience shows that primitive religious beliefs are practically indestructible, except by the destruction of the race in which they are ingrained, and thus we find that the new ideas of what I may call pastoral religion overlaid the old notions, but did not extinguish them. For example, the Astarte of the Northern Semites is essentially a goddess of flocks and herds, whose symbol and sacred animal is the cow, or (among the sheep-rearing tribes of the Syro-

Arabian desert) the ewe.[1] But this pastoral worship appears to have come on the top of certain older faiths, in which the goddess of one kindred of men was associated with fish, and that of another kindred with the dove. These creatures, accordingly, though no longer prominent in ritual, were still held sacred and surrounded by taboos, implying that they were of divine nature and akin to the goddess herself. The very fact that they were not regularly sacrificed, and therefore not regularly eaten even in religious feasts, tended to preserve their antique sanctity long after the sacrificial flesh of beeves and sheep had sunk almost to the rank of ordinary food; and thus, as we have seen in considering the case of the mystic sacrifices of the Roman Empire, the rare and exceptional rites, in which the victim was chosen from a class of animals ordinarily tabooed as human food, retained even in later paganism a sacramental significance, almost absolutely identical with that which belonged to the oldest sacrifices. It was still felt that the victim was of a divine kind, and that, in partaking of its flesh and blood, the worshippers enjoyed a veritable communion with the divine life. That to such sacrifices there was ascribed a special cathartic and consecrating virtue requires no explanation, for how can the impurity of sin be better expelled than by a draught of sacred life ? and how can man be brought nearer to his god than by physically absorbing a particle of the divine nature ?

It is, however, to be noted that piacula of this kind, in which atonement is effected by the use of an exceptional victim of sacred kind, do not rise into prominence till the national religions of the Semites fall into decay. The public piacular sacrifices of the independent Semitic states appear, so far as our scanty information goes, to

[1] *Supra*, p. 310.

have been mainly drawn from the same kinds of domestic
animals as supplied the ordinary sacrifices, except where
an exceptional emergency demanded a human victim.
Among the Hebrews, in particular, there is no trace of
anything answering to the later mystic sacrifices up to the
time of the captivity.   At this epoch, when the national
religion appeared to have utterly broken down, and the
judgment of those who were not upheld by the faith of
the prophets was that "Jehovah had forsaken His land,"[1]
all manner of strange sacrifices of unclean creatures—the
swine, the dog, the mouse and other vermin—began to
become popular, and were deemed to have a peculiar
purifying and consecrating power.[2]   The creatures chosen ★
for these sacrifices are such as were unclean in the first
degree, and surrounded by strong taboos of the kind which
in heathenism imply that the animal is regarded as divine;
and in fact the sacrifices of vermin described in the Book
of Isaiah have their counterpart in the contemporary
worship of all kinds of vermin described by Ezekiel.[3] ★
Both rites are evidently part of a single superstition,
the sacrifice being a mystical communion in the body
and blood of a divine animal.   Here, therefore, we have
a clear case of the re-emergence into the light of day of
a cult of the most primitive totem type, which had been
banished for centuries from public religion, but must have
been kept alive in obscure circles of private or local
superstition, and sprang up again on the ruins of the
national faith, like some noxious weed in the courts of
a deserted temple.   But while the ritual and its interpretation are still quite primitive, the resuscitated totem
mysteries have this great difference from their ancient

---

[1] Ezek. viii. 12.
[2] Isa. lxv. 3 *sqq.*, lxvi. 3, 17 ; see above, p. 291 *sq.*, p. 343, note 3.
[3] Ezek. viii. 10.

models, that they are no longer the exclusive possession
of particular kins, but are practised, by men who desert
the religion of their birth, as means of initiation into a
new religious brotherhood, no longer based on natural
kinship, but on mystical participation in the divine life held
forth in the sacramental sacrifice.   From this point of view
the obscure rites described by the prophets have a vastly
greater importance than has been commonly recognised ;
they mark the first appearance in Semitic history of the
tendency to found religious societies on voluntary association and mystic initiation, instead of natural kinship and
nationality.   This tendency was not confined to the
Hebrews, nor did it reach its chief development among
them.   The causes which produced a resuscitation of obsolete
mysteries among the Jews were at work at the same period
among all the Northern Semites ; for everywhere the old
national deities had shown themselves powerless to resist
the gods of Assyria and Babylon.   And among these
nations the tendency to fall back for help on primitive
superstitions was not held in check, as it was among the
Hebrews, by the counter-influence of the Prophets and
the Law.   From this period, therefore, we may date with
great probability the first rise of the mystical cults which
★ played so large a part in the later developments of
ancient paganism, and spread their influence over the
whole Græco-Roman world.   Most of these cults appear
to have begun among the Northern Semites, or in the
parts of Asia Minor that fell under the empire of the
Assyrians and Babylonians.   The leading feature that
distinguishes them from the old public cults, with which
they entered into competition, is that they were not based
on the principle of nationality, but sought recruits from
men of every race who were willing to accept initiation
through the mystic sacraments ; and in pursuance of this

object they carried on a missionary propaganda in all parts
of the Roman Empire, in a way quite alien to the spirit
of national religion.   The nature of their sacramental sacrifices, so far as it is known to us, indicates that they were
of a like origin with the Hebrew superstitions described
by Isaiah ; they used strange victims, invoked the gods by
animal names, and taught the initiated to acknowledge
kinship with the same animals.[1]   To pursue this subject
further would carry us beyond the limits of our present
task ; for a full discussion of mystical sacrifices cannot
be confined to the Semitic field.   These sacrifices, as we
have seen, lie aside from the main development of the
national religions of the Semites, and they acquire public
importance only after the collapse of the national systems.
In later times they were much sought after, and were
held to have a peculiar efficacy in purging away sin, and
bringing man into living union with the gods.   But
their atoning efficacy proceeds on quite different lines
from that of the recognised piacular rites of national
religion.   In the latter the sinner seeks reconciliation
with the national god whom he has offended, but in
mystic religion he takes refuge from the divine wrath
by incorporating himself in a new religious community.
Something of the same kind takes place in more primitive
society, when an outlaw, who has been banished from the
social and religious fellowship of his clan for shedding
kindred blood, is received by the covenant of adoption
into another clan.   Here also the act of adoption, which
is a religious as well as a civil rite, is in so far an act
of atonement, that the outlaw has again a god to receive
his worship and his prayers ; but he is not reconciled to
the god of his former worship, for it is only in a somewhat advanced stage of polytheism that acceptance by one

[1] Porph., *De Abst.* iv. 16, compared with *Fihrist*, p. 326, l. 25 *sq.*

god puts a man right with the gods as a whole. Among the Greeks, where the gods formed a sort of family circle, and were accessible to one another's influence, the outlaw, like Orestes, wanders about in exile, till he can find a god willing to receive him and act as his sponsor with the other deities ; and here, therefore, as in the mystical rites of the Semites, the ceremony of purification from bloodshed is essentially a ceremony of initiation into the cult of some god who, like the Apollo of Trœzen, makes it his business to receive suppliants. But among the older Semites there was no kinship or friendship between the gods of adjacent tribes or nations, and there was no way of reconciliation with the national god through the mediation of a third party, so that all atoning sacrifices were necessarily offered to the national god himself, and drawn, like ordinary sacrifices, from the class of domestic animals appropriated to his worship.

In the oldest stage of pastoral religion, when the tribal herd possessed inviolate sanctity, and every sheep or camel —according as the tribe consisted of shepherds or camelherds—was regarded as a kinsman, there was no occasion and no place for a special class of atoning sacrifices. The relations between the god and his worshippers were naturally as good and intimate as possible, for they were based on the strongest of all ties, the tie of kinship. To secure that this natural good understanding should continue unimpaired, it was only necessary that the congenital bond of kinship should not wear out, but continue strong and fresh. And this was provided for by periodical sacrifices, of the type described by Nilus, in which a particle of the sacred life of the tribe was distributed, between the god and his worshippers, in the sacramental flesh and blood of an animal of the holy stock of the clan. To make the sacrifice effective, it was only necessary that the victim should be perfect and without fault—a point which is strongly insisted upon in all ancient sacrifice—*i.e.*, that the sacred life should be completely and normally embodied in it. In the later ages of antiquity there was a very general belief — the origin of which will be explained as we proceed—that in strictness the oldest rituals demanded a human victim, and that animal sacrifices were substitutes for the life of a man. But in the oldest times there could be no reason for thinking a man's life better than that of a camel or a sheep as a vehicle of sacramental communion; indeed, if we may judge from modern examples of that primitive habit of thought which lies at the root of Semitic sacrifice, the animal ★ life would probably be deemed purer and more perfect than that of man.

On the other hand, there is every reason to think that even at this early stage certain impious crimes, notably murder within the kin, were expiated by the death of the offender. But the death of such a criminal cannot with any justice be called a sacrifice. Its object was simply to eliminate the impious person from the society whose sanctity he had violated, and outlawry was accepted as an alternative to execution.

As time went on, the idea of the full kinship of men with their cattle began to break down. The Saracens of Nilus killed and ate their camels in time of hunger, but we may be sure that they would not in similar circumstances have eaten one another. Thus even in a society where the flesh of the tribal camel was not ordinary food, and where private slaughter was forbidden, a camel's life was no longer as sacred as that of a man; it had begun to be recognised that human life, or rather the life of a tribesman, was a thing of unique sanctity. At the same time the old forms of sacrifice were retained, and the tradition of their old meaning cannot have been lost, for the ritual forms were too plainly significant to be misinterpreted. In short, the life of a camel, which no longer had the full value of a tribesman's life for ordinary purposes, was treated as a tribesman's life when it was presented at the altar; so that here we have already a beginning of the idea that the victim *quâ* victim possesses a sacrosanct character which does not belong to it merely in virtue of its natural kind. But now also, let it be noted, it is expressly attested that the sacrificial camel is regarded as the substitute for a human victim. The favourite victims of the Saracens were young and beautiful captives,[1] but if these were not to be had they contented themselves with a white and faultless camel. As to the veracity of this account there is no question : Nilus's own son, Theodulus, when a captive in the hands of these barbarians, escaped being sacrificed only by the accident that, on the appointed morning, his captors did not awake till the sun rose, and the lawful hour for the rite was past; and there are well-authenticated instances of the sacrifice of captives to Al-'Ozzā by the Lakhmite king of Al-Ḥīra at least a century later.[2]

It is true that in these cases the victims are aliens and not tribesmen, as in strictness the sense of the ritual requires; but the older Semites, when they had recourse to human sacrifice, were more strictly logical, and held with rigour to the fundamental principle that the life of the victim must be a kindred life.[3] The modification accepted

[1] The sacrifice of choice captives occurs also among the Carthaginians (Diod. xx. 65), and perhaps a trace of the same thing appears among the Hebrews in the slaying of Agag "before the LORD, at the sanctuary of Gilgal" (1 Sam. xv. 33).

[2] Nöldeke's *Tabari*, p. 171 (Procop., *Pers.* ii. 28; Land, *Anecd.* iii. 247); Isaac of Antioch, i. 220.

[3] See, for the Hebrews, Gen. xxii. ; 2 Kings xxi. 6 ; Micah vi. 7 : for the Moabites, 2 Kings iii. 27 : for the Phœnicians, Philo Byblius in *Fr. Hist.*

by the Saracens was one for which there was the strongest motive, and accordingly all over the world we find cases of human sacrifice in which an alien is substituted for a tribesman. This was not done in accordance with any change in the meaning of the ritual, for originally the substitution was felt to be a fraud on the deity; thus Diodorus tells us that the Carthaginians, in a time of trouble, felt that their god was angry because slave boys had been privily substituted for the children of their best families; and elsewhere we find that it is considered necessary to make believe that the victim is a tribesman, or even, as in the human sacrifices of the Mexicans, to dress and treat him as the representative of the deity to whom he is to be offered. Perhaps something of this kind was in the mind of Nilus's Saracens when they drank with prisoners destined to death, and so admitted them to boon fellowship.[1]

Gr. iii. 570 (Eus., *Pr. Ev.* 156 D) ; Porph., *De Abst.* ii. 56 : for the Carthaginians, Porph., *ibid.* ii. 27 ; Diodorus, xx. 14 ; Plutarch, *De Superst.* 13 : for the Syrians, *Dea Syr.* lviii.; Lampridius, *Vita Heliog.* 8, "pueri nobiles et decori . . . patrimi et matrimi": for the Babylonians, 2 Kings xvii. 31. For the Arabs the well-known story of ʿAbd al-Moṭṭalib's vow (B. Hish. p. 97), though of doubtful authenticity, may probably be accepted as based on actual custom. Another example of a vow to sacrifice a son is given in Mālik's Mowaṭṭa, Tunis ed., p. 176 (Kremer, *Stud. z. vergl. Culturg.* p. 44).

[1] Nilus, p. 66, where, however, the slaughter is not formally a sacrifice. The narrative represents the offer of drink as mere mockery, but it is difficult to reconcile this with known Arabian custom ; see above, p. 270. A more serious attempt to adopt Theodulus into the Saracen community seems to have been made after his providential escape from death ; he was invited to eat unclean things and sport with the women (p. 117). The combination is significant, and as μιαροφαγεῖν must refer to the eating of idolatrous meats, presumably camel's flesh,—which Symeon Stylites forbade to his Arab converts,—the question arises whether γυναιξὶ προσπαίζειν has not also a reference to some religious practice, and whether Wellhausen[1], p. 40, has not been too hasty in supposing that the orgies of the Arabian Venus renounced by the converts just mentioned are mere rhetorical orgies ; cf. *Kinship*, p. 301.

It has been suggested to me by an eminent scholar that the sacrifice of choice captives after a victory may be a form of *naciʾa* and properly a thank-offering from the spoil ; cf. the slaying of Agag. This is not impossible, for

From a purely abstract point of view it seems plausible
enough that the Saracens, who accepted an alien as a
substitute for a tribesman, might also accept a camel as
a substitute for a man. The plan of substituting an
offering which can be more readily procured or better
spared, for the more costly victim which traditional
ritual demands, was largely applied throughout antiquity,
and belongs to the general system of make-believe by
which early nations, while entirely governed by regard
for precedents, habitually get over difficulties in the
strict carrying out of traditional rules. If a Roman
rite called for a stag as victim, and a stag could not
be had, a sheep was substituted and feigned to be a stag
(*cervaria ovis*), and so forth. The thing was really a fraud,
but one to which the gods were polite enough to shut
their eyes rather than see the whole ceremony fail. But
in the particular case before us it is difficult to believe
that the camel was substituted for a man, and ultimately
for a tribesman. In that case the ritual of the camel-
sacrifice would have been copied from human sacrifice,
but in reality this was not so. The camel was eaten,
but the human victim was burned, after the blood had
been poured out as a libation,[1] and there can be no

different ideas often find their embodiment in identical ceremonies; but the
case of Jephthah's daughter and the express testimony of Diodorus appear to
me to weigh strongly against such a view.

[1] This appears from what we read of the preparations for the sacrifice of
Theodulus, among which are mentioned frankincense (the accompaniment of
fire-offerings) and a bowl for the libation, p. 110 ; and, at p. 113, Theodulus
prays: "Let not my blood be made a libation to demons, nor let unclean
spirits be made glad with the sweet smoke of my flesh." See Wellhausen[1],
p. 113, who conjectures that in Arabia human sacrifices were generally
burned, citing Yācūt, iv. 425, who tells that every clan of Rabī'a gave a son
to the god Moḥarric, "the burner," at Salmān (in 'Irāc, on the pilgrim road
from Cufa). Nöldeke, in *ZDMG.* xli. 712, doubts whether the reference is
to human sacrifice ; for Yācūt (*i.e.* Ibn al-Kalbī) presently cites examples
of men of different clans called "sons of Moḥarric," which may imply that
the sons were not sacrificed, but consecrated as children of the god. This,

question that the former is the more primitive rite. I
apprehend, therefore, that human sacrifice is not more
ancient than the sacrifice of sacred animals, and that
the prevalent belief of ancient heathenism, that animal
victims are an imperfect substitute for a human life,
arose by a false inference from traditional forms of
ritual that had ceased to be understood. In the oldest
rituals the victim's life is manifestly treated as sacred,
and in some rites, as we have seen in our examination
of the Attic *Buphonia*, the idea that the slaughter is
really a murder, *i.e.* a shedding of kindred blood, was
expressed down to quite a late date. When the full
kinship of animals with men was no longer recognised
in ordinary life, all this became unintelligible, and was
explained by the doctrine that at the altar the victim
took the place of a man.

This doctrine appears all over the ancient world in
connection with atoning sacrifices, and indeed the false
inference on which it rests was one that could not fail
to be drawn wherever the old forms of sacrifice had been
shaped at a time when cattle were revered as kindred

however, is so peculiar an institution for Arabia that it still remains probable
that the consecration was a substitute for sacrifice. At Salmān, in the
neighbourhood of Al-Ḥīra, we are in the region of the human sacrifices of the
Lakhmite kings. And these were probably burnt-offerings ; cf. the legend
of the holocaust of one hundred prisoners by ʿAmr b. Hind, *Kāmil*, p. 97 ;
Agh. xix. 129. Hence this king is said to have been called Moḥarriɔ, or,
according to another tradition, because he burned Yemāma (Mofaḍḍal
al-Ḍabbī, *Amthāl*, p. 68) ; but, as Nöldeke observes (*Ghassan. Fürsten* [1887],
p. 7), Moḥarriɔ without the article is hardly a mere epithet (*lacab*), and I
apprehend that the Lakhmite family was called "the family of Moḥarriɔ"
after their god, presumably Lucifer, the morning star, who afterwards
became feminine as al-ʿOzzā (*supra*, p. 56, note 3). The Ghassanid princes
of the house of Jafna were also called "the family of Moḥarriɔ," Ibn Cot.
p. 314 ; Ibn Dor. p. 259, and here the tradition is that their ancestor was
the first Arab who burned his enemies in their encampment. This, however,
is obviously a form of *ḥérem*, and must, I take it, be a religious act. For
the "family" (*āl*) of a god, as meaning his worshippers, see *Kinship*, p.
44.

beings. And this appears to have been the case in the
beginnings of every pastoral society. Accordingly, to
cite but a few instances, the notion that animal sacrifice
is accepted in lieu of an older sacrifice of the life of a
man appears among the Hebrews, in the story of Isaac's
sacrifice,[1] among the Phœnicians,[2] among the Egyptians,
where the victim was marked with a seal bearing the
image of a man bound, and with a sword at his throat,[3]
and also among the Greeks, the Romans, and many other
nations.[4] As soon, however, as it came to be held that
cattle were merely substitutes, and that the full sense of
the sacrifice was not brought out without an actual human
victim, it was naturally inferred that the original form
of offering was more potent, and was indicated on all
occasions of special gravity. Wherever we find the
doctrine of substitution of animal life for that of man,
we find also examples of actual human sacrifice, sometimes confined to seasons of extreme peril, and sometimes
practised periodically at solemn annual rites.[5]

---

[1] Gen. xxii. 13 ; cf. Lev. xvii. 11.　　　　　[2] Porph., *De Abst.* iv. 15.

[3] Plut., *Is. et Os.* xxxi. According to Wiedemann, *Herodots Zweites
Buch*, p. 182, these symbols are simply the hieroglyphic determinant of the
word *sema*, "slay."

[4] See the examples in Porph., *De Abst.* ii. 54 *sqq.*, and for the Romans,
Ovid, *Fasti*, vi. 162. We have had before us Greek rites where the victim
is disguised as a man ; but conversely human sacrifices are often dressed up
as animals, or said to represent animals : an example, from the worship at
Hierapolis-Bambyce, is found in *Dea Syria*, lviii., where fathers sacrificing
their children say that they are not children but beeves.

[5] Examples of human sacrifices, many of which subsisted within the
Roman Empire down to the time of Hadrian, are collected by Porphyry,
ut supra, on whom Eusebius, *Præp. Ev.* iv. 16, *Laus Const.* xiii. 7, depends.
See also Clem. Alex., *Coh. ad Gentes*, p. 27 (p. 36, Potter) ; cf. Hermann,
Gr. Alth. ii. § 27. In what follows I confine myself to the Semites ; it may
therefore be noted that, in antiquity generally, human victims were buried,
burned, or cast into the sea or into a river (cf. Mannhardt's essay on the
Lityerses legend). Yet indications survive that they were originally
sacrifices of communion, and as such were tasted by the worshippers :
notably in the most famous case of all, the human sacrifice offered in
Arcadia to Zeus Lycæus—the wolf-god—where a fragment of the *exta* was

I apprehend that this is the point from which the special development of piacular sacrifices, and the distinction between them and ordinary sacrifices, takes its start. It was impossible that the sacrificial customs should continue unmodified where the victim was held to represent a man and a tribesman, for even savages commonly refuse to eat their own kinsfolk, and to growing civilisation the idea that the gods had ordained meals of human flesh, or of flesh that was as sacred as that of a man, was too repulsive to be long retained. But when I say " repulsive," I put the matter rather in the light in which it appears to us, than in that wherein it presented itself to the first men who had scruples about cannibalism. Primarily the horror of eating human flesh was no doubt superstitious; it was felt to be dangerous to eat so sacrosanct a thing, even with all the precautions of religious ceremonial. Accordingly, in human sacrifices, and also in such other offerings as continued to be performed with a ritual simulating human sacrifice, the sacrificial meal tended to fall out of use; while, on the other hand, where the sacrificial meal was retained, the tendency was to drop such features in the ritual as suggested the disgusting idea of cannibalism.[1] ★ And so the apparent paradox is explained, that precisely in those sacrifices in which the victim most fully retained its original theanthropic character, and was therefore most efficacious as a vehicle of atonement, the primitive idea of

placed among the portions of sacrificial flesh derived from other victims that were offered along with the human sacrifice, and the man who tasted it was believed to become a were-wolf (Plato, *Rep.* viii. 15, p. 565 D; Pausanias, viii. 2).

Of the human sacrifices of rude peoples those of the Mexicans are perhaps the most instructive, for in them the theanthropic character of the victim comes out most clearly.

[1] Of course neither tendency was consistently carried out in every detail of ritual; there remains enough that is common to honorific and piacular sacrifice to enable us to trace them back to a common source.

atonement by communion in the sacred flesh and blood
was most completely disguised. The modifications in the
form of ritual that ensued when sacrifices of a certain
class were no longer eaten, can be best observed by
taking the case of actual human sacrifice and noting
how other sacrifices of equivalent significance follow its
model.

Whether the custom of actually eating the flesh survived
in historical times in any case of human sacrifice is more
than doubtful,[1] and even in the case of animal piacula—
apart from those of mystic type, in which the idea of
initiation into a new religion was involved—the sacrificial
meal is generally wanting or confined to the priests. The
custom of drinking the blood, or at least of sprinkling it
on the worshippers, may have been kept up longer; there
is some probability that it was observed in the human
sacrifices of Nilus's Saracens;[2] and the common Arabian

---

[1] According to Mohammedan accounts, the Harranians in the Middle Ages
annually sacrificed an infant, and, boiling down its flesh, baked it into cakes,
of which only freeborn men were allowed to partake (*Fihrist*, p. 323, l. 6 *sqq.*;
cf. Chwolsohn's *Excursus on Human Sacrifice*, vol. ii. p. 142). But in regard
to the secret mysteries of a forbidden religion, such as Syrian heathenism
was in Arabian times, it is always doubtful how far we can trust a hostile
narrator, who, even if he did not merely reproduce popular fictions, might
easily take for a real human sacrifice what was only the mystic offering of a
theanthropic animal. The new-born infant corresponds to the Arabian *fara'*,
offered while its flesh was still like glue, and to the Hebrew piaculum of a
sucking lamb in 1 Sam. vii. 9.

[2] The reason for thinking this is that on the Arabian mode of sacrifice a
bowl was not required to convey the blood to the deity, while it would be
necessary if the blood was drunk by the worshippers or sprinkled upon them.
It is true that the narrative speaks also of the preparation of a libation,—
whether of water or of wine does not appear,—but this in the Arabian ritual
can hardly be more than a vehicle for the more potent blood, just as the
blood was mixed with water in Greek sacrifices to heroes. Water as a
vehicle for sacrificial ashes appears in the Hebrew ritual of the red heifer
(Num. xix. 9), and is prescribed as a vehicle for the blood of lustration in
Lev. xiv. 5 *sq.* In the legends cited in the next note we find the notion
that if the blood of a human victim touches the ground, vengeance will be
taken for it. That the drinking of human blood, *e.g.* from an enemy slain
in battle, was a Saracen practice, is attested by Ammianus and Procopius

belief that the blood of kings, and perhaps also of other men of noble descent, is a cure for hydrophobia and demoniacal possession, seems to be a reminiscence of blood-drinking in connection with human sacrifice, for the Greeks in like manner, who ascribed epilepsy to demoniacal possession, sought to cure it by piacular offerings and purifications with blood.[1]

When the sacrosanct victim ceased to be eaten, it was necessary to find some other way of disposing of its flesh. It will be remembered that, in the sacrificial meals of Nilus's Saracens, it was a point of religion that the whole carcase should be consumed before the sun rose; the victim was so holy that no part of it could be treated as mere waste. The problem of disposing of the sacred carcase was in fact analogous to that which occurs whenever a kinsman dies. Here, too, the point is to find a way of dealing with the body consistent with the respect due to the dead—a respect which does not rest on sentimental grounds, but on the belief that the corpse is taboo, a source

(see *Kinship*, p. 296 *sqq.*) ; and the anecdote given by Wellh. p. 126, from *Agh.* xii. 144, where a husband, unable to save his wife from the enemy, kills her, anoints himself with her blood, and fights till he is slain, illustrates the significance which the Arabs attached to human blood as a vehicle of communion.

[1] Hippocrates, ed. Littré, vi. 362. The evidence for this Arabian superstition is collected by Freytag in his notes to the *Ḥamāsa*, ii. 583, and by We.[1] 142, [2] 162. It consists in poetical and proverbial allusions, to which may be added a verse in Mas'ūdī, iii. 193, and in a legend from the mythical story of Queen Zabbā (*Agh.* xiv. 74 ; Ṭabari, i. 760 ; Maidānī, i. 205 *sqq.*), where a king is slain by opening the veins of his arms, and the blood, to be used as a magical medicine, is gathered in a bowl. Not a drop must fall on the ground, otherwise there will be blood-revenge for it. I cannot but suspect that the legend is based on an old form of sacrifice applied to captive chiefs (cf. the case of Agag) ; it is described as the habitual way of killing kings ; cf. *Agh.* xv. 75. 4, where 'Abd Yaghūth is killed by opening his veins. The rule that not a drop of the blood must fall on the ground appears also in Caffre sacrifice ; Maclean, *Caffre Laws*, p. 81. According to later authorities, cited in the *Tāj al-'Arūs* (i. 3. 181 of the old edition), it was enough for this cure to draw a drop of blood from the finger of a noble, and drink it mixed with water.

24

of very dangerous supernatural influences of an infectious
kind. In later times this infectiousness is expressed as
uncleanness; but in the primitive taboo, as we know,
sanctity and uncleanness meet and are indistinguishable.
Now, as regards the kindred dead generally, we find a great
range of funeral customs, all directed to make sure that
the corpse is properly disposed of, and can no longer be a
source of danger to the living, but rather of blessing.[1]   In
certain cases it is the duty of the survivors to eat up their
dead, just as in Nilus's sacrifice.   This was the use of the
Issedones, according to Herodotus (iv. 26).   At other times
the dead are thrown outside the kraal, to be eaten by wild
beasts (Masai land), or are deposited in a desert place
which men must not approach; but more commonly the
body is buried or burned.   All these practices reappear in
the case of such sacrifices as may not be eaten.   Mere
exposure on the soil of the sanctuary was perhaps the use
in certain Arabian cults;[2] but this, it is plain, could not
suffice unless the sacred enclosure was an adyton forbidden
to the foot of man.   Hence at Duma the annual human
victim is buried at the foot of the altar idol,[3] and elsewhere,
perhaps, the corpse is hung up between earth and heaven
before the deity.[4]   Or else the sacrosanct flesh is carried

[1] This subject has been fully handled by Mr. J. G. Frazer in *Journ.*
Anthrop. Inst. xv. 64 *sqq.*, to which I refer for details.   I think Mr. Frazer
goes too far in supposing that mere fear of ghosts rules in all these observances.   Not seldom we find also a desire for continued fellowship with
the dead, under such conditions as make the fellowship free from danger.
In the language of physics, sanctity is a *polar* force, it both attracts and
repels.

[2] *Supra*, p. 225 *sqq.*

[3] Porph., *De Abst.* ii. 56.   In old Arabia little girls were often buried
alive by their fathers, apparently as sacrifices to the goddesses; see *Kinship*,
p. 291.   A similar form of human sacrifice probably lies at the root of the
legend about the tombs of the lovers whom Semiramis buried alive (Syncellus,
i. 119, from John of Antioch), for though these lovers are gods, all myths of
the death of gods seem to be derived from sacrifices of theanthropic victims.

[4] Deut. xxi. 21; cf. 1 Sam. xxxi. 10.   The execution of criminals con-

away into a desert place in the mountains, as was done in
the Greek piacula of which Hippocrates speaks, or is
simply flung down (a precipice) from the vestibule of the
temple, as was the use of Hierapolis.[1]   Among the Hebrews,
on the same principle, the heifer offered in atonement
for an untraced murder was sacrificed by breaking (or,
perhaps, severing) its neck in a barren ravine.[2]

Most commonly, however, human sacrifices, and in
general all such sacrifices as were not eaten, were burned;
and this usage is found not only among the Hebrews and
Phœnicians, with whom fire-sacrifices were common, but
among the Arabs, who seem to have admitted the fire-
offering in no other case.   In the more advanced rituals
the use of fire corresponds with the conception of the gods
as subtle beings, moving in the air, whose proper nourishment is the fragrant smoke of the burning flesh, so that
the burnt-offering, like the fat of the vitals in ordinary
victims, is the food of the gods, and falls under the head of
sacrificial gifts.   But in the Levitical ritual this explanation is sedulously excluded in the case of the sin-offering;
the fat is burned on the altar, but the rest of the flesh, so
far as it is not eaten by the priests, is burned outside the
camp, *i.e.* outside the walls of Jerusalem, so that in fact
the burning is merely an additional precaution added to

stantly assumes sacrificial forms, for the tribesman's life is sacred even if he
be a criminal, and he must not be killed in a common way.   This principle
is finally extended to all religious executions, in which, as the Hebrews and
Moabites say, the victim is devoted, as a *ḥerem*, to the god (Stele of Mesha,
l. 17).   In one peculiar sacrifice at Hierapolis (*Dea Syr.* xlix.) the victims
were suspended alive from trees, and the trees were then set on fire.   The
fire is perhaps a later addition, and the original rite may have consisted in
suspension alone.   The story of a human victim hung up in the temple
at Carrhæ by the Emperor Julian (Theod., *H. E.* iii. 21), and the similar
stories in the Syriac Julian-romances (ed. Hoffm. p. 247, etc.), are too
apocryphal to be used, though they probably reflect some obsolete popular
superstition.

[1] *Dea Syria*, lviii.   [2] Deut. xxi. 4.

the older rule that the sacred flesh must not be left
exposed to human contact. Now the Levitical sin-offering
is only a special development of the old piacular holocaust,
and thus the question at once suggests itself whether in its
first origin the holocaust was a subtle way of conveying a
gift of food to the god; or whether rather the victim was
burned, because it was too sacred to be eaten and yet must
not be left undisposed of. In the case of the Arabian
holocaust, which is confined to human victims, this is
certainly the easiest explanation; and even among the
Hebrews and their neighbours it would seem that human
sacrifices were not ordinarily burned on the altar or even
within the precincts of the sanctuary, but rather outside
the city. It is plain from various passages of the prophets,
that the sacrifices of children among the Jews before the
captivity, which are commonly known as sacrifices to
Moloch, were regarded by the worshippers as oblations to
Jehovah, under the title of king,[1] yet they were not presented at the temple, but consumed outside the town at
the Tophet in the ravine below the temple.[2] From Isa.
xxx. 33 it appears that Tophet means a pyre, such as is
prepared for a king. But the Hebrews themselves did not
burn their dead, unless in very exceptional cases,[3] and

---

[1] Jer. vii. 31, xix. 5, xxxii. 35 ; Ezek. xxiii. 39 ; Mic. vi. 7. The form
Moloch (LXX.), or rather Molech (Heb.), is nothing but *Melech*, "king,"
read with the vowels of *bosheth*, "shameful thing"; see Hoffmann in
Stade's *ZATW*. iii. (1883) p. 124. In Jer. xix. 5 delete עלות לבעל
with LXX.

[2] The valley of Hinnom is the Tyropœon ; see *Enc. Bib.*, arts. " Jerusalem " and " Hinnom."

[3] Saul's body was burned (1 Sam. xxxi. 12), possibly to save it from the
risk of exhumation by the Philistines, but perhaps rather with a religious
intention, and almost as an act of worship, since his bones were buried
under the sacred tamarisk at Jabesh. In Amos. vi. 10 the victims of a
plague are burned, which is to be understood by comparing Lev. xx. 14,
xxi. 9 ; Amos ii. 1, and remembering that plague was a special mark of
divine wrath (2 Sam. xxiv.), so that its victims might well be regarded as
intensely taboo.

burial was equally the rule among their Phœnician neighbours, as is plain from researches in their cemeteries,[1]
and apparently among all the Semites.   Thus, when the
prophet describes the deep and wide pyre "prepared for
the king," he does not draw his figure from ordinary life,
nor is it conceivable that he is thinking of the human
sacrifices in the valley of Hinnom, a reference which would
bring an utterly discordant strain into the imagery.   What
he does refer to is a rite well known to Semitic religion,
which was practised at Tarsus down to the time of Dio
Chrysostom, and the memory of which survives in the
Greek legend of Heracles - Melcarth,[2] in the story of
Sardanapalus, and in the myth of Queen Dido.   At Tarsus
there was an annual feast at which a very fair pyre was
erected, and the local Heracles or Baal burned on it in
effigy.[3]   This annual commemoration of the death of the
god in fire must have its origin in an older rite, in which
the victim was not a mere effigy but a theanthropic sacrifice, *i.e.* an actual man or sacred animal, whose life, according
to the antique conception now familiar to us, was an
embodiment of the divine-human life.

The significance of the death of the god in Semitic
religion is a subject on which I must not enter in this
connection ; we are here concerned with it only in so far
as the details, scenic or mythical, of the death of the god
throw light on the ritual of human sacrifice.   And for

---

[1] This is true also of Carthage ; Tissot, *La Prov. d'Afrique*, i. 612 ;
Justin, xix. 1.   But at Hadrumetum in the second century B.C. the dead
were burned ; see Berger in *Revue archéol.*, Juillet–Décembre, 1889, p. 375.

[2] For the burning of the Tyrian Heracles, cf. *Clem. Recog.* x. 24, where
we read that the sepulchre of the god was shown "apud Tyrum, ubi igni
crematus est."   It is a plausible conjecture, very generally accepted, that in
Herod. vii. 167 the legend of the self-immolation of Melcarth has got mixed
up with the story of the death of Hamilcar.

[3] See O. Müller, "Sandon und Sardanapal," in *Rhein. Mus.*, Ser. i,
Bd. iii.

this purpose it is well to cite also the legend of the death of Dido as it is related by Timæus,[1] where the pyre is erected outside the walls of the palace, *i.e.* of the temple of the goddess, and she leaps into it from the height of the edifice. According to Justin, the pyre stood " at the end of the town "; in fact the sanctuary of Cœlestis, which seems to represent the temple of Dido, stood a little way outside the citadel or original city of Carthage, on lower ground, and, at the beginning of the fourth century of our era, was surrounded by a thorny jungle, which the popular imagination pictured as inhabited by asps and dragons, the guardians of the sanctuary.[2] It can hardly be doubted that the spot at which legend placed the self-sacrifice of Dido to her husband Sicharbas was that at which the later Carthaginian human sacrifices were performed.[3]

We have therefore a series of examples all pointing to human sacrifice beneath and outside the city. At Hierapolis the victims are cast down from the temple, but we do not read that they are burned; at Jerusalem they are burned in the ravine below the temple, but not cast down. At Carthage the two rites meet, the sacrifice is outside the city and outside the walls of the temple; but the divine victim leaps into the pyre, and later victims, as Diodorus tells us,[4] were allowed to roll into a fiery pit from a sort of scaffold in the shape of an image of the god with outstretched arms. In this last shape of the rite the object plainly is to free the worshippers from the guilt of

---

[1] *Fr. Hist. Gr.* i. 197 ; cf. Justin, xviii. 6. On Dido as identical with Tanith (Tent), ἡ δαίμων τῆς Καρχηδόνος, see the ingenious conjectures of G. Hoffmann, *Phœn. Inschr.* p. 32 *sq*.

[2] Tissot, i. 653. Silius Ital., i. 81 *sqq.*, also describes the temple of Dido as enclosed in a thick grove, and surrounded by awful mystery.

[3] The name Sichar-bas, סכר־בעל, " commemoration of Baal," is not a divine title, but is to be understood from Ex. xx. 24. סכר is the Phœnician form of Heb. זכר.

[4] Diod. xx. 14.

bloodshed ; the child was delivered alive to the god, and he committed it to the flames. For the same reason, at the so-called sacrifice of the pyre at Hierapolis, the holocausts were burned alive,[1] and so was the Harranian sacrifice of a bull to the planet Saturn described by Dimashcī.[2] This last sacrifice is the lineal descendant of the older human sacrifices of which we have been speaking ; for the Carthaginian Baal or Moloch was identified with Saturn, and at Hierapolis the sacrificed children are called oxen. But in the more ancient Hebrew rite the children offered to Moloch were slaughtered before they were burned.[3] And that the burning is secondary, and was not the original substance of the rite, appears also from the use of Hierapolis, where the sacrifice is simply flung from the temple. So, too, although Dido in Timæus flings herself into the fire, there are other forms of the legend of the sacrifice of a Semite goddess, in which she simply casts herself down into water.[4]

When the burning came to be the essence of the rite, the spot outside the city where it was performed might naturally become itself a sanctuary, though it is plain from the descriptions of the temple of Dido that the sanctuary was of a very peculiar and awful kind, and separated from contact with man in a way not usual in the shrines of ordinary worship. And when this is so, the deity of this awful sanctuary naturally comes to be regarded as a separate divinity, rejoicing in a cult which

---

[1] *Dea Syria*, xlix.   [2] Ed. Mchren, p. 40 (Fr. trans. p. 42).

[3] Ezek. xvi. 20, xxiii. 39 ; Gen. xxii. 10. The inscriptions in Gesenius, *Mon. Phœn.* p. 448 *sq.*, which have sometimes been cited in this connection, are now known to have nothing to do with human sacrifice.

[4] The Semiramis legend at Hierapolis and Ascalon ; the legend of the death of Astarte at Aphaca (Meliton), which must be identified with the falling of the star into the water at the annual feast, just as in another legend Aphrodite after the death of Adonis throws herself from the Leucadian promontory (Ptol., *Nov. Hist.* vii. p. 198, West.).

the other gods abhor. But originally, we see, the human
sacrifice is offered to the ordinary god of the community,
only it is not consumed on the altar in the sanctuary, but
cast down into a ravine outside, or burned outside. This
rule appears to be universal, and I may note one or two
other instances that confirm it. Mesha burns his son as a
holocaust to Chemosh, not at the temple of Chemosh, but
on the wall of his beleaguered city ;[1] being under blockade,
he could not go outside the wall. Again, at Amathus the
human sacrifices offered to Jupiter Hospes were sacrificed
" before the gates,"[2] and here the Jupiter Hospes of the
Roman narrator can be none other than the Amathusian
Heracles or Malika, whose name, preserved by Hesychius,
identifies him with the Tyrian Melcarth. Or, again,
Malalas[3] tells us that the 22nd of May was kept as the
★ anniversary of a virgin sacrificed at the foundation of
Antioch, at sunrise, " half-way between the city and the
river," and afterwards worshipped like Dido as the Fortune
of the town.

All this is so closely parallel to the burning of the flesh
of the Hebrew sin-offerings outside the camp, that it seems
hardly doubtful that originally, as in the Hebrew sin-
offering, the true sacrifice, *i.e.* the shedding of the blood,
took place at the temple, and the burning was a distinct
act. An intermediate stage is exhibited in the sacrifice
of the red heifer, where the whole ceremony takes place
outside the camp, but the blood is sprinkled in the direction
of the sanctuary (Num. xix. 4). And in support of this
view let me press one more point that has come out in
our evidence. The human holocaust is not burned on an
altar, but on a pyre or fire-pit constructed for the occasion.
This appears both in the myths of Dido and Heracles and

---

[1] 2 Kings iii. 27.　　　[2] Ovid, *Metaph.* **x.** 224 ; cf. Movers, i. 408 *sq.*
[3] P. 200 of the Bonn ed.

in actual usage. At Tarsus a very fair pyre is erected yearly for the burning of Heracles; in the Carthaginian sacrifice of boys the victims fall into a pit of flame, and in the Harranian ox-sacrifice the victim is fastened to a grating placed over a vault filled with burning fuel; finally, Isaiah's Tophet is a broad and deep excavation filled with wood exactly like the fiery trench in which, according to Arabic tradition, the victims of 'Amr b. Hind and the martyrs of Nejrān found their end.[1] All these arrangements are totally unlike the old Semitic altar or sacred stone, and are mere developments of the primitive fireplace, made by scooping a hollow in the ground.[2] It appears, then, that in the ritual of human sacrifice, and therefore by necessary inference in the ritual of the holocaust generally, the burning was originally no integral part of the ceremony, and did not take place on the altar or even within the sanctuary, but in a place apart, away from the habitations of man. For human sacrifices and for solemn

---

[1] Aghāni, xix. 129; Ibn Hishām, p. 24 (Tab. i. 925; Sūra, 85, 4 sqq.).

[2] It seems to me that חפת is properly an Aramaic name for a fireplace, or for the framework set on the fire to support the victim, which appears in the Harranian sacrifice and, in a modified form, at Carthage. For we are not to think of the brazen Saturn as a shapely statue, but as a development of the dogs of a primitive fireplace. I figure it to myself as a pillar or cone with a rude head and arms, something like the divine symbol so often figured on Carthaginian Tanith cippi. Now the name for the stones on which a pot is set, and then for any stand or tripod set upon a fire, is in Arabic أُثْفِيَة Othfīyā, in Syriac ܠܐܦܐ, Tfāyā, of which we might, according to known analogies, have a variant tfāth. The corresponding Hebrew word is אַשְׁפֹּת (for shfāth), which means an ashpit or dunghill, but primarily must have denoted the fireplace, since the denominative verb שָׁפַת is "to set on a pot." In nomad life the fireplace of one day is the ash-heap of the next. Now, at the time when the word חפת first appears in Hebrew, the chief foreign influence in Judæan religion was that of Damascus (2 Kings xvi.), and there is therefore no improbability in the hypothesis that תֹּפֶת is an Aramaic word. The pronunciation tofeth is quite precarious, for LXX. has ταφιθ, and the Massorets seem to have given the loathsome thing the points of bosheth.

piacula this rule continued to be observed even to a late date, but for ordinary animal holocausts the custom of burning the flesh in the court of the sanctuary must have established itself pretty early. Thus, as regards the Hebrews, both the early narrators of the Pentateuch (the Jahvist and the Elohist) presuppose the custom of burning holocausts and other sacrifices on the altar,[1] so that the fusion is already complete between the sacred stone to receive the blood, and the hearth on which the flesh was burned. But the oldest history still preserves traces of a different custom. The burnt-sacrifices of Gideon and Manoah are not offered on an altar, but on the bare rock;[2] and even at the opening of Solomon's temple the fire-offerings were not burned on the altar, but in the middle of the court in front of the *naos*, as was done many centuries later at Hierapolis on the day of the Pyre-sacrifice. It is true that in 1 Kings viii. 64 this is said to have been done only because "the brazen altar that was before the Lord" was not large enough for so great an occasion; but, according to 1 Kings ix. 25, the holocausts and ordinary sacrifices which Solomon offered three times in the year were in like manner offered (not on the brazen altar, but) on an altar "built" by the king, *i.e.* a structure of stones; and indeed we have no unambiguous notice of a permanent altar of burnt-offering in the temple of Jerusalem till the reign of Ahaz, who had one constructed on the model of the altar of Damascus. This altar, and not the brazen altar, was again the model for the altar of the second temple, which was of stone, not of brass, and it is plain from the narrative of 2 Kings xvi., especially in the form of the text which has been preserved by the Septuagint,

---

[1] Gen. viii. 20, xxii. 9. Ex. xx. 24 makes the holocaust be slaughtered on the altar, but does not expressly say that it was burned on it.

[2] Judg. vi. 20, xiii. 19 ; Judg. vi. 26, the more modern story of Gideon's offering, gives the modern ritual.

that Ahaz's innovation was not merely the introduction of a new architectural pattern, but involved a modification of the whole ritual.[1]

We may now pass on to the case of ordinary fire-offerings, in which only the fat of the vitals is consumed on the altar. It is easy to see that when men began to shrink from the eating of sacrificial flesh, they would not necessarily at once take refuge in entire abstinence. The alternative was to abstain from partaking of those parts in which the sacred life especially centred. Accordingly we find that in ordinary Hebrew sacrifices the whole blood is poured out at the altar as a thing too sacred to be eaten.[2] Again, the head is by many nations regarded as a special seat of the soul, and so, in Egyptian sacrifice, the head was not eaten, but thrown into the Nile,[3] while among the Iranians the head of the victim was dedicated to Haoma, that the immortal part of the animal might return to him. But a not less important seat of life, according to Semitic ideas, lay in the viscera, especially in the kidneys and the liver, which in the Semitic dialects are continually named as the seats of emotion, or more broadly in the fat of the omentum and the organs that lie in and near it.[4] Now it is precisely this part of the

[1] See *Additional Note* K, *The Altar at Jerusalem.* I may add that, in 1 Kings xviii., Elijah's altar does not seem to be a raised structure, but simply a circle marked out by twelve standing stones and a trench.

[2] Among the Hottentots blood is allowed to men but not to women; the female sex being among savages excluded from many holy privileges. Similarly the flesh of the Hebrew sin-offering must be eaten only by males (Lev. vi. 22 [29]), and among the Caffres the head, breast and heart are man's part (Lichtenstein, p. 451).

[3] Herod. ii. 39. The objection to eating the head is very widely spread; *e.g.*, in Bavaria, as late as the fifteenth century (Usener, *Religionsgesch. Untersuchungen*, ii. 84). Some Arabs objected to eating the heart (Wustenfeld, *Reg.* p. 407).

[4] The Arabic *Khilb* (Heb. חֶלֶב, Syr. *ḥelbā*) primarily denotes the omentum or midriff, but includes the fat or suet connected therewith; see Lev. iii. 3. An Arab says of a woman who has inspired him with passion,

victim, the fat of the omentum with the kidneys and
the lobe of the liver, which the Hebrews were forbidden to eat, and, in the case of sacrifice, burned on
the altar.

The ideas connected with the kidney fat and its appurtenances may be illustrated by the usages of primitive
peoples in modern times. When the Australians kill an
enemy in blood revenge, " they always abstract the kidney
fat, and also take off a piece of the skin of the thigh " [or
a piece of the flank].[1] " These are carried home as trophies.
. . . The caul fat is carefully kept by the assassin, and
used to lubricate himself "; he thinks, we are told, that
thus the strength of the victim enters into him.[2] When
the Basutos offer a sacrifice to heal the sick, as soon as
the victim is dead, " they hasten to take the epiploon or
intestinal covering, which is considered the most sacred

" she has overturned my heart and torn my midriff " (Lane, p. 782). So
in Ps. xvii. 10 the sense is not " they have closed their fat (unfeeling)
heart," but "they have shut up their midriff," and thus are insensible to pity.
From this complex of fat parts the fat of the kidneys is particularly selected
by the Arabs, and by most savages, as the special seat of life. One says,
" I found him with his kidney fat," meaning I found him brisk and all
alive (Lane, p. 1513). In Egypt, according to Burckhardt (*Ar. Prov.* No.
301), "when a sheep is killed by a private person, some of the bystanders
often take away the kidneys, or at least the fat that incloses them, as due
to the public from him who slaughters the sheep." This, I take it, is a relic
of old sacrificial usage; what used to be given to the god is now given in
charity. For Greek ideas about the kidney fat see Mr. Platt's note on *Iliad*,
φ. 204, in *Journ. Phil.* xix. (1890) 46.

[1] The thigh is a seat of life and especially of procreative power, as
appears very clearly in the idiom of the Semites (*Kinship*, p. 38). From
this may be explained the sacredness of the *nervus ischiadicus* among the
Hebrews (Gen. xxxii. 33), and similar superstitions among other nations.
Is this also the reason why the "fat thigh bones " are an altar-portion
among the Greeks? The nature of the lameness produced by injury to the
sinew of the thigh socket is explained by the Arabic lexx., *s.v.* حَارِقَة ;
the man can only walk on the tips of his toes. This seems to have been a
common affection, for poetical metaphors are taken from it.

[2] Brough Smyth, ii. 289, i. 102 ; cf. Lumholtz, *Among Cannibals* (Lond.
1889), p. 272.

part, and put it round the patient's neck. . . . The gall
is then poured on the head of the patient. After a sacrifice the gall bladder is invariably fastened to the hair of
the individual for whom the victim has been slain, and
becomes a sign of purification." [1]

The importance attached by various nations to these
vital parts of the body is very ancient, and extends to
regions where sacrifice by fire is unknown. The point
of view from which we are to regard the reluctance to eat
of them is that, being more vital, they are more holy
than other parts, and therefore at once more potent and
more dangerous. All sacrificial flesh is charged with an
awful virtue, and all *sacra* are dangerous to the unclean
or to those who are not duly prepared; but these are so
holy and so awful that they are not eaten at all, but dealt
with in special ways, and in particular are used as powerful
charms. [2]

We see from the case of the Basuto sacrifice that it is
by no means true that all that man does not eat must be
given to the god, and the same thing appears in other
examples. The Hebrews pour out the blood at the altar,
but the Greeks use it for lustration and the old Arabs as
a cure for madness. The Persians restore the head and
with it the life to Haoma, while the Tauri, according to
Herodotus (iv. 103), in their human sacrifices, bury the
body or cast it down from the cliff on which the temple
stands, but fix the head on a pole above their houses as
a sacred guardian. Among the Semites, too, the magical
use of a dried head had great vogue. This sort of charm

---

[1] Casalis, p. 250.

[2] This may be illustrated by the case of the blood of sacrificial victims.
Among the Greeks bull's blood was regarded as a poison; but for this belief
there is no physiological basis: the danger lay in its sacred nature. But
conversely it was used under divine direction as a medicine; Ælian, *N. A.*
xi. 35. On blood as a medicine see also Pliny, *H. N.* xxviii. 43, xxvi. 8;
and Adams's *Paulus Ægineta*, iii. 25 *sq.*

is mentioned by Jacob of Edessa,[1] and hares' heads were worn as amulets by Arab women.[2] So, too, when we find bones, and especially dead men's bones, used as charms,[3] we must think primarily of the bones of sacrifices. Nilus's Saracens at least broke up the bones and ate the marrow, but the solid osseous tissue must from the first have defied most teeth unless it was pounded, and so it was particularly likely to be kept and used as a charm. Of course the sacred bones may have been often buried, and when fire was introduced they were likely to be burned, as is the rule with the Caffres.[4] As the sacrifices of the Caffres are not fire-sacrifices, it is clear that in this case the bones are burned to dispose of the holy substance, not to provide food for the gods. But even when the bones or the whole carcase of a sacrosanct victim are burned, the sacred virtue is not necessarily destroyed. The ashes of sacrifice are used, like the blood, for lustrations of various kinds, as we see in the case of the red heifer among the Hebrews ; and in agricultural religions such ashes are very commonly used to give fertility to the land. That is, the sacred elements, after they cease to be eaten, are still used in varied forms as a means of communicating the divine life and life-giving or protective virtue to the worshippers, their houses, their lands, and all things connected with them.

In the later fire-rituals, the fat of the victim, with its blood, is quite specially the altar food of the gods. But between the practice which this view represents and the

---

[1] Qu. 43 ; see more examples in Kayser's notes, p. 142, and in a paper by Jahn, *Ber. d. sächs-Ges. d. Wiss.* 1854, p. 48. For the magical human head, of which we read so much in the latest forms of Semitic heathenism, see Chwolsohn, ii. 150 *sqq.*, and the *Actes* of the Leyden Congress, ii. 365 *sq.*

[2] *Diw. Hudh.* clxxx. 9 ; *ZDMG.* xxxix. 329.

[3] Examples, *infra, Additional Note* B, p. 448. The very dung of cattle was a charm in Syria (Jacob of Edessa, Qu. 42), to which many parallels exist, not only in Africa, but among the Aryans of India.

[4] Maclean, p. 81.

primitive practice, in which the whole body was eaten, we
must, I think, in accordance with what has just been said,
insert an intermediate stage, which can still be seen and
studied in the usage of primitive peoples. Among the
Damaras the fat of particular animals " is supposed to
possess certain virtues, and is carefully collected and kept
in vessels of a particular kind. A small portion dissolved
in water is given to persons who return home safely after
a lengthened absence; . . . the chief makes use of it as
an unguent for his body." [1] So too " dried flesh and fat "
are used as amulets by the Namaquas.[2] Among the
Bechuanas lubrication with grease is part of the ceremony
of admission of girls into womanhood, and among the
Hottentots young men on their initiation into manhood are
daubed with fat and soot.[3] Grease is the usual unguent
all over Africa, and from these examples we see that its
use is not merely hygienic, but has a sacred meaning.
Indeed, the use of various kinds of fat, especially human
fat, as a charm, is common all over the world, and we learn
from the Australian superstition, quoted above, that the
reason of this is that the fat, as a special seat of life, is a
vehicle of the living virtue of the being from which it
is taken. Now we have seen, in speaking of the use of
unguents in Semitic religion,[4] that this particular medium
has in some way an equivalent value to blood, for which it
may be substituted in the covenant ceremony, and also in
the ceremony of bedaubing the sacred stone as an act of
homage. If, now, we remember that the oldest unguents
are animal fats, and that vegetable oil was unknown to
the Semitic nomads,[5] we are plainly led to the conclusion

---

[1] C. J. Andersson, *Lake Ngami*, p. 223.

[2] *Ibid.* p. 330. The dried flesh reminds us of the Arabian custom of
drying strips of sacrificial flesh on the days of Minā (Wellh. p. 80).

[3] *Ibid.* p. 465 ; Kolben, i. 121.　　　　[4] *Supra*, p. 233.

[5] Fränkel, *Fremdwörter*, p. 147.

that unction is primarily an application of the sacrificial fat, with its living virtues, to the persons of the worshippers. On this view the anointing of kings, and the use of unguents on visiting the sanctuary, are at once intelligible.[1]

The agricultural Semites anointed themselves with olive oil, and burned the sacrificial fat on the altar. This could be done without any fundamental modification of the old type of sacred stone or altar pillar, simply by making a hollow on the top to receive the grease; and there is some reason to think that fire-altars of this simple kind, which in certain Phœnician types are developed into altar candle-sticks, are older than the broad platform-altar proper for receiving a burnt-offering.[2] But there are evidences even in the Old Testament that it was only gradually that the burning of the fat came to be an integral part of the altar ritual. In 1 Sam. ii. 15 we find a controversy between the priests and the people on this very topic. The worshippers maintain that the priest has no claim to his fee of flesh till the fat is burned; but the priests assert their right to have a share of raw flesh at once. It is assumed in the argument that if the priests held back their claim till they had burned the fat, the flesh would be already cooked—so the worshippers at least did not wait to see the fat burned. And probably the priests had precedent on their side, for the old law of Ex. xxiii. 18 only requires that the fat of a festal sacrifice shall be burned before daybreak—the sacrifice itself having taken place in the evening.

I fear that these details may seem tedious, but the cumulative evidence which they afford that the burning of

[1] The use of unguents by witches when they desire to transform them-selves into animal shape,—as we find it, for example, in Apuleius's novel,—belongs to the same region of superstition, and to that most primitive form of the superstition which turns on the kinship of men with animals.

[2] See below, *Additional Note K.*

the flesh or fat held quite a secondary place in ancient
sacrifice, and was originally no integral part of the oblation
at the altar, is of the greatest importance for the history of
sacrificial ideas.　They show how impossible it is to regard
animal sacrifices as primarily consisting in a gift of food to
the gods, and how long it was before this notion superseded
the original notion of communion between men and their
gods in the life of the sacrifice.

I do not suppose that it is possible, on the basis of the
evidences that have come before us, to reconstruct from
step to step the whole history of the development of fire-
sacrifices.　But we can at least see in a general way how the
chief modifications of sacrificial ritual and idea came in.

Originally neither the flesh nor the life of the victim
could be regarded as a gift or tribute—*i.e.* as something
which belonged to the worshipper, and of which he
divested himself in order to make it over to the object of
his worship.　It is probable that sacrifice is older than
the idea of private property, and it is certain that its
beginnings go back to a time when the owner of a sheep,
an ox, or a camel had no right to dispose of its life
according to his own good pleasure.　Such an animal
could only be slain in order that its life might be distributed between all the kin and the kindred god.　At this
stage the details of the ritual are shaped by the rule that
no part of the life must be lost, and that therefore the
whole body, which is the vehicle of the life, must be
distributed and used up in the holy ritual.　In the first
instance, therefore, everything must be eaten up, and eaten
while it is still alive—fresh and raw.　Gradually this
rule is modified, partly because it is difficult to insist,
in the face of growing civilisation, on the rule that
even bones, skin and offal must be devoured, and partly
because there is increasing reluctance to partake of the

25

holy life. This reluctance again is connected with the growth of the distinction between degrees of holiness. Not every man is holy enough to partake of the most sacred sacraments without danger. What is safe for a consecrated chief or priest is not safe for the mass of the people. Or even it is better that the most sacred parts of the victim should not be eaten at all; the blood and the fat are medicines too powerful to be taken internally, but they may be sprinkled or daubed on the worshippers, while the sacrificial meal is confined to the parts of the flesh in which the sacred life is less intensely present. Or, finally, it is most seemly and most safe to withdraw the holiest things from man's use altogether, to pour out the whole blood at the altar, and to burn the fat. All this applies to ordinary sacrifices, in which the gradual concentration of the holiness of the victim in its fat and blood tends to make the rest of the flesh appear less and less holy, till ultimately it becomes almost a common thing. But, on special occasions, where the old ritual is naturally observed with antique rigidity, and where, therefore, the victim is treated at the altar as if it were a tribesman, the feeling of sacred horror against too close an approach to things most holy extends to the whole flesh, and develops itself, especially in connection with actual human sacrifice, into the rule that no part of such victims may be eaten, but that the whole must be reverently burned.

If we may generalise from the case of Arabia, where the holocaust was confined to human victims and the fat of ordinary sacrifices was not burned, it would appear that it was human sacrifice that first gave rise to the use of fire as a safe means of disposing of the bodies of the holiest victims. From this practice that of burning the fat in common sacrifices may very well have been derived. But the evidence is not sufficient to justify a positive con-

clusion on the matter, and it is quite possible that the use
of fire began among the Northern Semites in connection
with ordinary sacrifices, simply as a means of dealing with
such parts of the victim as were not or could not be eaten,
and yet were too holy to be left undisposed of. The
Hebrew ritual of ordinary sacrifices is careful to prescribe
that what is not eaten on the first or second day shall be
burned.[1] This is evidently a mere softening of the old
rule that the flesh of the victim must be consumed without
delay, while it is still alive and quivering, into the rule
that it must not be allowed to putrefy and decompose;
and this again, since the close connection between putrefaction and fermentation is patent even to the unscientific
observer, seems also to be the principle on which ferments
are excluded from the altar. The use of fire in sacrifice,
as the most complete and thorough means of avoiding
putrefaction in whatever part of the victim cannot or may
not be eaten, must have suggested itself so naturally
wherever fire was known, that no other reason is necessary
to explain its wide adoption. The burial of the sacrificial
flesh, of which we have found one or two examples, does
not appear to have met with so much favour, and indeed
was not so satisfactory from the point of view indicated by
the rules of Hebrew ritual.[2]

The use of fire in this sense does not involve any
fundamental modification in the ideas connected with
sacrifice. The critical point in the development is when
the fat of ordinary victims, or still more, the whole flesh
of the holocaust, is burned within the sanctuary or on the
altar, and is regarded as being thus made over to the deity.
This point claims to be examined more fully, and must be
reserved for consideration at our next meeting.

[1] Lev. vii. 15 *sqq.*   [2] See *Additional Note* L, *High Places.*

LECTURE XI

In connection with the later Semitic sacrifices, fire is employed for two purposes, apparently quite independent of one another. Its ordinary use is upon the altar, where it serves to sublimate, and so to convey to deities of an ethereal nature, gifts of solid flesh, which are regarded as the food of the gods. But in certain Hebrew piacula the sacrificial flesh is burned without the camp, and is not regarded as the food of the gods. The parts of the victim which in the highest form of piacula are burned outside the camp are the same which in lower forms of the sin-offering were eaten by the priests as representatives of the worshippers, or which in ordinary sacrifices would have been eaten by the worshippers themselves. Here, therefore, the fire seems to play the same part that is assigned to it under the rule that, if an ordinary sacrifice is not eaten up within one or two days, the remnant must be burned. All sacrificial flesh is holy, and must be dealt with according to fixed ritual rules, one of which is that it must not be allowed to putrefy. Ordinary sacrificial flesh may be either eaten or burned, but sin-offerings are too holy to be eaten except by the priests, and in certain cases are too holy to be eaten even by them, and therefore must be burned, not as a way of conveying them to the deity, but simply as a way of fitly disposing of them.

388

It is commonly supposed that the first use of fire was upon the altar, and that the burning outside the camp is a later invention, expressing the idea that, in the case of a sacrifice for sin, the deity does not desire a material gift, but only the death of the offender. The ritual of the Hebrew sin-offering lends itself to such an interpretation readily enough, but it is impossible to believe that its origin is to be explained on any such view. If the sin-offering is merely a symbolical representation of a penal execution, why is the flesh of the victim holy in the first degree? and why are the blood and fat offered upon the altar? But it is unnecessary to press these minor objections to the common view, which is refuted more conclusively by a series of facts that have come before us in the course of the last lecture. There is a variety of evidence that fire was applied to sacrifices, or to parts of sacrifices, as an alternative to their consumption by the worshippers, before the altar became a hearth, and before it came to be thought that what was burned was conveyed, as etherealised food, to the deity. The Hebrew piacula that were burned out-side the camp represent an older form of ritual than the holocaust on the altar, and the thing that really needs explanation is the origin of the latter.

Originally all sacrifices were eaten up by the worshippers. By and by certain portions of ordinary sacrifices, and the whole flesh of extraordinary sacrifices, ceased to be eaten. What was not eaten was burned, and in process of time it came to be burned on the altar and regarded as made over to the god. Exactly the same change took place with the sacrificial blood, except that here there is no use of fire. In the oldest sacrifices the blood was drunk by the worshippers, and after it ceased to be drunk it was all poured out at the altar. The tendency evidently was to convey directly to the godhead every portion of a sacrifice that was not consumed by the worshipper; but how did this tendency arise?

I daresay that some of you will be inclined to say that I am making a difficulty of a matter that needs no explanation. Is it not obvious that a sacrifice is a consecrated thing, that consecrated things belong to the god, and that the altar is their proper place? No doubt this seems to be obvious, but it is precisely the things that seem obvious which in a subject like ours require the most careful scrutiny. You say that consecrated things belong to the god, but we saw long ago that this is not the primitive idea of holiness. A holy thing is taboo, *i.e.* man's contact with it and use of it are subject to certain restrictions, but this idea does not in early society rest on the belief that it is the property of the gods. Again, you say that a sacrifice is a consecrated thing, but what do you mean by this? If you mean that the victim became holy by being selected for sacrifice and presented at the altar, you have not correctly apprehended the nature of the oldest rites. For in them the victim was naturally holy, not in virtue of its sacrificial destination, but because it was an animal of holy kind. So long as the natural holiness of certain animal species was a living element in popular faith, it was by no means obvious that holy things belong to the god, and should find their ultimate destination at the altar.

In later heathenism the conception of holy kinds and the old ideas of taboo generally had become obsolete, and the ritual observances founded upon them were no longer understood. And, on the other hand, the comparatively modern idea of property had taken shape, and began to play a leading part both in religion and in social life. The victim was no longer a naturally sacred thing, over which man had very limited rights, and which he was required to treat as a useful friend rather than a chattel, but was drawn from the absolute property of the worshipper, of which he had a right to dispose as he pleased. Before its presentation the victim was a common thing, and it was only by being selected for sacrifice that it became holy. If, therefore, by presenting his sheep or ox at the altar, the owner lost the right to eat or sell its flesh, the explanation could no longer be sought in any other way than by the assumption that he had surrendered his right of property to another party, viz. to the god. Consecration was inter-preted to mean a gift of man's property to the god, and everything that was withdrawn by consecration from the free use of man was conceived to have changed its owner. The blood and fat of ordinary sacrifices, or the whole flesh in the case of the holocaust, were withdrawn from human use; it was held, therefore, that they had become the property of the god, and were reserved for his use. This being so, it was inevitable that the burning of the flesh and fat should come to be regarded as a method of convey-ing them to the god; and as soon as this conclusion was drawn, the way was open for the introduction of the modern practice, in which the burning took place on the altar. The transformation of the altar into the hearth, on which the sacrificial flesh was consumed, marks the final establishment of a new view of holiness, based on the doctrine of property, in which the inviolability of holy things is no longer made to rest on their intrinsic super-natural quality, but upon their appropriation to the use and service of the gods. The success of this new view is not surprising, for in every department of early society we find that as soon as the notion of property, and of transfers of property from one person to another, gets firm footing, it begins to swallow up all earlier formulas for the relations of persons and things. But the adaptation of old institutions to new ideas can seldom be effected without leaving internal contradictions between the old and the new, which ultimately bring about the complete dissolution of the incongruous system. The new wine bursts the old bottles, and the new patch tears the old garment asunder.

In the case of ordinary sacrifices, the theory that holy things are the property of the deity, and that the consecration of things naturally common implies a gift from man to his god, was carried out with little difficulty. It was understood that at the altar the whole victim is made over to the deity and accepted by him, but that the main part of the flesh is returned to the worshipper, to be eaten sacrificially as a holy thing at the table of the god. This explanation went well enough with the conception of the deity as a king or great lord, whose temple was the court at which he sat to receive the homage of his subjects and tenants, and to entertain them with princely hospitality. But it did not satisfactorily account for the most characteristic feature in sacrifice, the application of the blood to the altar, and the burning of the fat on the sacred hearth. For these, according to the received interpretation, were the food of the deity; and so it appeared that the god was dependent on man for his daily nourishment, although, on the other hand, all the good things that man enjoyed he owed to the gift and favour of his god. This is the weak point in the current view of sacrifice which roused the indignation of the author of Psalm l., and afforded so much merriment to later satirists like Lucian. The difficulty might be explained away by a spiritualising interpretation, which treated the material altar gift as a mere symbol, and urged that the true value of the offering lay in the homage of the worshipper's heart, expressed in the traditional oblation. But the religion of the masses never took so subtle a view as this, and to the majority of the worshippers even in Israel, before the exile, the dominant idea in the ritual was that the material oblation afforded a physical satisfaction to the god, and that copious offerings were an infallible means of keeping him in good humour. So long as sacrifice was exclusively or mainly a social service, performed by the community, the crassness of this conception found its counterpoise in the ideas of religious fellowship that have been expounded in Lecture VII.[1] But in private sacrifice there was little or nothing to raise the transaction above the level of a mere bargain, in which no ethical consideration was involved, but the good understanding between the worshipper and his god was maintained by reciprocal friendly offices of a purely material kind. This superficial view of religion served very well in times of prosperity, but it could not stand the strain of serious and prolonged adversity, when it became plain that religion had to reckon with the sustained displeasure of the gods. In such circumstances men were forced to conclude that it was useless to attempt to appease the divine wrath by gifts of things which the gods, as lords of the earth, already possessed in abundance. It was not only Jehovah who could say, " I will take no bullock out of thy house, nor he-goats from thy folds ; for every beast of the forest is Mine, and the cattle on a thousand hills." The Baalim too were in their way lords of nature, and even from the standpoint of heathenism it was absurd to suppose that they were really dependent on the tribute of their worshippers. In short, the gift-theory of sacrifice was not enough to account for the rule that sacrifice is the sole and sufficient form of every act of worship, even in religions which had not realised, with the Hebrew prophets, that what the true God requires of

[1] *Supra*, p. 263 *sqq.*

His worshippers is not a material oblation, but "to do justice, and love mercy, and walk humbly with thy God."

If the theory of sacrifice as a gift or tribute, taken from man's property and conveyed to the deity, was inadequate even as applied to ordinary oblations, it was evidently still more inadequate as applied to the holocaust, and especially to human sacrifice. It is commonly supposed that the holocaust was more powerful than ordinary sacrifices, because the gift to the god was greater. But even in ordinary sacrifices the whole victim was consecrated and made over to the god; only in the holocaust the god kept everything to himself, while in ordinary sacrifices he invited the worshipper to dine with him. It does not appear that there is any good reason, on the doctrine of sacrificial tribute, why this difference should be to the advantage of the holocaust. In the case of human sacrifices the gift-theory led to results which were not only absurd but revolting—absurd, since it does not follow that because a man's firstborn son is dearer to himself than all his wealth, the life of that son is the most valuable gift that he can offer to his god; and revolting, when it came to be supposed that the sacrifice of children as fire-offerings was a gift of food to a deity who delighted in human flesh.[1] So detestable a view of the nature of the gods cannot fairly be said to correspond to the general character of the old Semitic religions, which ought to be judged of by the ordinary forms of worship and not by exceptional rites. If the gods had been habitually conceived as cannibal monsters, the general type of ritual would have been gloomy and timorous, whereas really it was full of joyous and even careless confidence. I conclude, therefore, that the child-devouring King of the later Moloch-worship owes his cannibal attributes, not to

[1] Ezek. xvi. 20, xxiii. 37.

the fundamental principles of Semitic religion, but to false logic, straining the gift-theory of sacrifice to cover rites to which it had no legitimate application. And this conclusion is justified when we find that, though human sacrifices were not unknown in older times, the ancient ritual was to burn them without the camp—a clear proof that their flesh was not originally regarded as a food-offering to the deity.[1]

On the whole, then, the introduction of ideas of property into the relations between men and their gods ★ seems to have been one of the most fatal aberrations in the development of ancient religion. In the beginnings of human thought, the natural and the supernatural, the material and the spiritual, were confounded, and this confusion gave rise to the old notion of holiness, which turned on the idea that supernatural influences emanated, like an infection, from certain material things. It was necessary to human progress that this crude conception should be superseded, and at first sight we are disposed to see nothing but good in the introduction of the notion that holy things are forbidden to man because they are reserved for the use of the gods, and that the danger associated with illegitimate invasion of them is not due to any deadly supernatural influence, directly proceeding from the holy object, but to the wrath of a personal god, who will not suffer his property to be tampered with. In one direction this modification was undoubtedly beneficial, for the vague dread of the unknown supernatural, which in savage society is so strong that it paralyses progress of every kind, and turns man aside from his legitimate task of subduing nature to his use, receives a fatal blow as soon as all supernatural processes are referred to the will and

[1] Compare the remarks on the sacrifice of the firstborn, *infra, Additional Note* E.

powers of known deities, whose converse with man is guided by fixed laws. But it was in the last degree unfortunate that these fixed laws were taken to be largely based on the principle of property; for the notion of property materialises everything that it touches, and its introduction into religion made it impossible to rise to spiritual conceptions of the deity and his relations to man on the basis of traditional religion. On the other hand, the more ancient idea of living communion between the god and his worshippers, which fell more and more into the background under the theory of sacrificial gifts, contained an element of permanent truth wrapped up in a very crude embodiment, and to it therefore all the efforts of ancient heathenism towards a better way of converse with the divine powers attach themselves, taking hold of those forms and features of sacrifice which evidently involved something more than the mere presentation to the deity of a material tribute. And as the need for something more than the ordinary altar gifts supplied was not habitually present to men's minds, but forced itself upon them in grave crises of life, and particularly in times of danger, when the god seemed to be angry with his people, or when at any rate it was of importance to make sure that he was not angry, all the aspects of worship that go beyond the payment of gifts and tribute came to be looked upon as having a special atoning character, that is, as being directed not so much to maintain a good understanding with the deity, as to renew it when it was interrupted.

When the idea of atonement is taken in this very general form, there is obviously no sharp line between atoning and ordinary sacrifices; for in ordinary life the means that are used to keep a man in good humour will often suffice to restore him to good humour, if they are sedulously employed. On this analogy a mere gift, presented at a suitable moment, or of greater value than usual, was often thought sufficient to appease the divine wrath; a general atoning force was ascribed to all sacrifices, and the value of special piacula was often estimated simply by the consideration that they cost the worshipper more than an everyday offering. We have seen that even human sacrifices were sometimes considered from this point of view; and in general the idea that every offence against the deity can be appraised, and made good by a payment of a certain value, was not inconsistent with the principles of ancient law, which deals with offences against persons on the doctrine of retaliation, but admits to an almost unlimited extent the doctrine that the injured party may waive his right of retaliation in consideration of a payment by the offender. But it is not the doctrine of ancient law that an injured party can be compelled to accept material compensation for an offence; and therefore, even on ordinary human analogies, no religious system could be regarded as complete which had not more powerful means of conjuring the divine displeasure than were afforded by the mere offer of a gift or payment. In point of fact, all ancient religions had sacrificial ceremonies of this more powerful kind, in which the notion of pleasing the god by a gift either found no expression at all, or evidently did not exhaust the significance of the ritual; and these are the sacrifices to which the distinctive name of *piacula* is properly applied.

It is sometimes supposed that special piacula did not exist in the older Semitic religions, and were invented for the first time when the gift-theory of sacrifice began to break down. But this supposition is incredible in itself, and is not consistent with the historical evidence. It is incredible that a gift should have been the oldest known

way of reconciling an offended god, for in ordinary life
atonement by fine came in at a relatively late date, and
never entirely superseded the *lex talionis*; and it is
certain, from what we have learned by observing the old
form of piacular holocausts, that these sacrifices were not
originally regarded as payments to the god, but arose on
quite different lines, as an independent development of the
primitive sacrifice of communion, whose atoning efficacy
rested on the persuasion that those in whose veins the
same life-blood circulates cannot be other than friends,
bound to serve each other in all the offices of brotherhood.

It has appeared in the course of our inquiry that two
kinds of sacrifice, which present features inconsistent with
the gift-theory, continued to be practised by the ancient
Semites; and to both kinds there was ascribed a special
efficacy in persuading or constraining the favour of the
gods. The first kind is the mystic sacrifice, represented by
a small class of exceptional rites, in which the victim was
drawn from some species of animals that retained even in
modern times their ancient repute of natural holiness.
Sacrifices of this sort could never fall under the gift-theory,
for creatures naturally holy are not man's property, but, so
far as they have an owner at all, are the property of the
god. The significance attached to these sacrifices and the
nature of their peculiar efficacy, has already received
sufficient attention. The other kind of offering which was
thought of as something more than a mere gift, consisted
of holocausts, and other sacrifices, whose flesh was not conveyed to the god and eaten at his table, but burned without
the camp, or buried, or cast away in a desert place. This
kind of service we have already studied from a formal
point of view, considering the way in which its ritual was
differentiated from the old communion sacrifice, and also

the way in which most sacrifices of the kind were ultimately brought under the class of sacrificial gifts, by the
introduction of the practice of burning the flesh on the
altar or burying it in the *ghabghab*; but we have not yet
considered how these successive modifications of ritual
were interpreted and made to fit into the general progress
of social institutions and ideas. Some notice of this side
of the subject is necessary to complete our study of the
principles of ancient sacrifice, and to it the remainder of
the present lecture will be devoted.

It must, however, be remembered that in ancient religion
there was no authoritative interpretation of ritual. It was
imperative that certain things should be done, but every
man was free to put his own meaning on what was done.
Now the more complicated ritual prestations, to which
the elaborate piacular services of later times must be
reckoned, were not forms invented, once for all, to express a
definite system of ideas, but natural growths, which were
slowly developed through many centuries, and in their
final form bore the imprint of a variety of influences, to
which they had been subjected from age to age under the
changing conditions of human life and social order. Every
rite therefore lent itself to more than one interpretation,
according as this or that aspect of it was seized upon as
the key to its meaning. Under such circumstances we
must not attempt to fix a definite interpretation on any of
the developments of ancient ritual; all that we can hope
to do is to trace in the ceremonial the influence of successive phases of thought, the presence of which is attested
to us by other movements in the structure of ancient society,
or conversely to show how features in ritual, of which the
historical origin had been forgotten, were accounted for on
more modern principles, and used to give support to new
ideas that were struggling for practical recognition.

From the analysis of the ritual of holocausts and other
piacula given in the last two lectures, it appears that
through all the varieties of atoning ceremony there runs
a common principle: the victim is sacrosanct, and the
peculiar value of the ceremony lies in the operation performed on its life, whether that life is merely conveyed to
the god on the altar, or is also applied to the worshippers
by the sprinkling of the blood, or some other lustral
ceremony.   Both these features are nothing more than
inheritances from the most primitive form of sacramental
communion; and in the oldest sacrifices their meaning
is perfectly transparent and unambiguous, for the ritual
exactly corresponds with the primitive ideas, that holiness
means kinship to the worshippers and their god, that
all sacred relations and all moral obligations depend on
physical unity of life, and that unity of physical life can
be created or reinforced by common participation in living
flesh and blood.   At this earliest stage the atoning force
of sacrifice is purely physical, and consists in the redin-
tegration of the congenital physical bond of kinship, on
which the good understanding between the god and his
worshippers ultimately rests.   But in the later stage of
religion, in which sacrifices of sacrosanct victims and
purificatory offerings are exceptional rites, these antique
ideas were no longer intelligible; and in ordinary sacrifices
those features of the old ritual were dropped or modified
which gave expression to obsolete notions, and implied
a physical transfer of holy l fe from the victim to the
worshippers.   Here, therefore, the question arises why
that which had ceased to be intelligible was still preserved in a peculiar class of sacrifices.   The obvious
answer is that it was preserved by the force of use and
precedent.

It is common, in discussions of the significance of

piacular ritual, to begin with the consideration that piacula are atonements for sin, and to assume that the ritual was devised with a view to the purchase of divine forgiveness. But this is to take the thing by the wrong handle. The characteristic features in piacular sacrifice are not the invention of a later age, in which the sense of sin and divine wrath was strong, but are features carried over from a very primitive type of religion, in which the sense of sin, in any proper sense of the word, did not exist at all, and the whole object of ritual was to maintain the bond of physical holiness that kept the religious community together. What we have to explain is not the origin of the sacrificial forms that later ages called piacular, but the way in which the old type of sacrifice came to branch off into two distinct types. And here we must consider that, even in tolerably advanced societies, the distinction between piacular and ordinary offerings long continued to be mainly one of ritual, and that the former were not so much sacrifices for sin, as sacrifices in which the ceremonial forms, observed at the altar, continued to express the original idea that the victim's life was sacrosanct, and in some way cognate to the life of the god and his worshippers. Thus, among the Hebrews of the pre-prophetic period, it certainly appears that a peculiar potency was assigned to holocausts and other exceptional sacrifices, as a means of conjuring the divine displeasure; but a certain atoning force was ascribed to all sacrifices; and, on the other hand, sacrifices of piacular form and force were offered on many occasions when we cannot suppose the sense of sin or of divine anger to have been present in any extraordinary degree. For example, it was the custom to open a campaign with a burnt-offering, which in old Israel was the most solemn piaculum; but this did not imply any feeling that war was a divine judgment and a

26

sign of the anger of Jehovah.[1]   It appears rather that the
sacrifice was properly the consecration of the warriors; for
the Hebrew phrase for opening war is " to consecrate war "
★ (קדש מלחמה), and warriors are consecrated persons, subject
to special taboos.[2]   Here, therefore, it lies near at hand to
suppose that the holocaust is simply the modification, on
lines which have been already explained, of an ancient
form of sacramental communion.[3]   The Greeks in like
manner commenced their wars with piacular sacrifices of
the most solemn kind; indeed, according to Phylarchus,[4]
a human victim was at one time customary, which is
certainly not true for historical times; but I have no
doubt that the statement of Phylarchus corresponds to a
wide-spread tradition such as might easily arise if the
offerings made on occasion of war were of the exceptional
and sacrosanct character with which legends of actual
human sacrifice are so frequently associated.[5]   One illus-

[1] The burnt-offering at the opening of a campaign appears in Judg. vi 20
(cf. ver. 26), xx. 26; 1 Sam. vii. 9, xiii. 10.   In Judg. xi. 31 we have,
instead of a sacrifice before the war, a vow to offer a holocaust on its successful termination.   The view taken by the last redactor of the historical
books (Judg., Sam., Kings), that the wars of Israel with its neighbours
were always chastisements for sin, is not ancient; cf. Gen. xxvii. 29, xlix. 8;
Num. xxiv. 24; Deut. xxxiii. 29.

[2] Isa. xiii. 3; Jer. vi. 4, li. 28; Joel iv. [iii.] 9; Mic. iii. 5.   See *supra*,
p. 158, and *Additional Note* C.

[3] I conjecture that the form of gathering warriors together by sending
round portions of a victim that has been hewn into pieces (1 Sam. xi. 7;
cf. Judg. xix. 29) had originally a sacramental sense, similar to that
expressed by the covenant form in which the victim is cut in twain; cf.
Additional Note H, and the Scythian custom noticed by Lucian, *Toxaris*,
§ 48.   A covenant by hewing an ox into small pieces was also in use among
the Molossians; Zenobius, ii. 83.

[4] *Ap.* Porph., *De Abst.* ii. 56.

[5] Even in the palmy days of Hellenic civilisation we find evidence of a
deeply-rooted belief in the potency of human sacrifice to ensure victory in
war.   So late as the time of Pelopidas, the propriety of such sacrifice was
formally discussed, and upheld by historical as well as mythical precedents
(Plutarch, *Pelopidas*, 21).   But the historical precedents reduce themselves,
on closer examination, to the single and wholly exceptional case of the
sacrifice of three captives before the battle of Salamis.   On the other hand,

tration of Phylarchus's statement will occur to everyone, viz. the sacrifice of Iphigenia; and here it is to be noted that, while all forms of the legend are agreed that Agamemnon must have committed some deadly sin before so terrible an offering was required of him, there is no agreement as to what his sin was. It is not therefore unreasonable to think that in the original story the piaculum was simply the ordinary preliminary to a campaign, and that later ages could not understand why such a sacrifice should be made, except to atone for mortal guilt.[1]

If, now, it be asked why the ordinary preliminary to a campaign was a sacrifice of the exceptionally solemn kind which in later times was deemed to have a special reference to sin, the answer must be that the ritual was fixed by immemorial precedent, going back to the time when all sacrifices were of the sacramental type, and involved the shedding of a sacrosanct life. At that time every sacrifice was an awful mystery, and not to be performed except on great occasions, when it was most necessary that the bond of kindred obligation between every member of the community, divine and human, should be as strong and fresh as possible. The outbreak of war was plainly such an occasion, and it is no hazardous conjecture that the rule of commencing a campaign with sacrifice dates from the most primitive times.[2] Accordingly the ceremonial to be observed in sacrifice on such an occasion would be protected by well-established tradition, and the victim would

additions might easily be made to the list of legendary precedents, *e.g.* the case of Bombus (Zenobius, ii. 84).

[1] The opening of a campaign appears also in Africa as one of the rare occasions that justify the slaughter of a victim from the tribal herds; see above, p. 297.

[2] There is also some reason to think that in very ancient times a sacrifice was appointed to be offered after a victory. See *Additional Note* M, *Sacrifice by Victorious Warriors.*

continue to be treated at the altar with all the old ritual forms which implied that its blood was holy and akin to man's, long after the general sanctity of all animals of sacrificial kind had ceased to be acknowledged in daily life. And in the same way sacrifices of exceptional form, in which the victim was treated as a human being, or its blood was applied in a primitive ceremonial to the persons of the worshippers, or its flesh was regarded as too sacred to be eaten, would continue to be offered on all occasions which were marked out as demanding a sacrifice, by some very ancient rule, dating from the time when the natural sanctity of sacrificial kinds was still recognised. In such cases the ancient ceremonial would be protected by immemorial custom; while, on the other hand, there would be nothing to prevent a more modern type of ritual from coming into use on occasions for which there was no ancient sacrificial precedent, *e.g.* on such occasions as arose for the first time under the conditions of agricultural life, when the old sanctity of domestic animals was very much broken down. Sacrifices were vastly more frequent with the agricultural than with the pastoral nations of antiquity, but, among the older agricultural Semites, the occasions that called for sacrifices of exceptional or piacular form were not numerous, and may fairly be regarded as corresponding in the main to the rare occasions for which the death of a victim was already prescribed by the rules of their nomadic ancestors.

This, it may be said, is no more than a hypothesis, but it satisfies the conditions of a legitimate hypothesis, by postulating the operation of no unknown or uncertain cause, but only of that force of precedent which in all times has been so strong to keep alive religious forms of which the original meaning is lost. And in certain cases, at any rate, it is very evident that rites of exceptional

form, which later ages generally connected with ideas of
sin and atonement, were merely the modern representatives
of primitive sacraments, kept up through sheer force of
habit, without any deeper meaning corresponding to the
peculiar solemnity of their form.   Thus the annual piacula
that were celebrated, with exceptional rites, by most nations
of antiquity, are not necessarily to be regarded as having
their first origin in a growing sense of sin or fear of divine
wrath,—although these reasons operated in later times to
multiply such acts of service and increase the importance
attached to them,—but are often nothing more than survivals of ancient annual sacrifices of communion in the
body and blood of a sacred animal.   For in some of these
rites, as we have seen in Lecture VIII.,[1] the form of communion in flesh too holy to be eaten except in a sacred
mystery is retained ; and where this is not the case, there
is at least some feature in the annual piaculum which
reveals its connection with the oldest type of sacrifice.
It is a mistake to suppose that annual religious feasts date
only from the beginnings of agricultural life, with its
yearly round of seed-time and harvest; for in all parts of
the world annual sacraments are found, and that not
merely among pastoral races, but even in rude hunting
tribes that have not emerged from the totem stage.[2]   And
though some of these totem sacraments involve actual communion in the flesh and blood of the sacred animal, the
commoner case, even in this primitive stage of society,
is that the theanthropic victim is deemed too holy to be
eaten, and therefore, as in the majority of Semitic piacula,
is burned, buried, or cast into a stream.[3]   It is certainly

---

[1] *Supra*, p. 290 *sqq.*

[2] For examples of annual sacraments by sacrifice of the totem, see Frazer,
Totemism and Exogamy, i. 44 *sq.* (iv. 232 *sq.*), and *supra*, p. 295, note 2.

[3] I apprehend that in most climates the vicissitudes of the seasons are
certainly not less important to the savage huntsman or to the pastoral

illegitimate to connect these very primitive piacula with any explicit ideas of sin and forgiveness; they have their origin in a purely naturalistic conception of holiness, and mean nothing more than that the mystic unity of life in the religious community is liable to wear out, and must be revived and strengthened from time to time.

Among the annual piacula of the more advanced Semites which, though they are not mystical sacrifices of an " unclean " animal, yet bear on their face the marks of ★ extreme antiquity, the first place belongs to the Hebrew Passover, held in the spring month Nisan, where the primitive character of the offering appears not only from the details of the ritual,[1] but from the coincidence of its season with that of the Arabian sacrifices in the month Rajab. Similarly in Cyprus, on the first of April, a sheep was offered to Astarte (Aphrodite) with ritual of a character evidently piacular.[2] At Hierapolis, in like manner, the chief feast of the year was the vernal ceremony of the Pyre, in which animals were burned alive—an antique ritual which has been illustrated in the last lecture. And again, among the Harranians, the first half of Nisan was

barbarian than to the more civilised tiller of the soil. From Doughty's account of the pastoral tribes of the Arabian desert, and also from what Agatharchides tells us of the herdsmen by the Red Sea, we perceive that in the purely pastoral life the seasons when pasture fails are annual periods of semi-starvation for man and beast. Among still ruder races, like the Australians, who have no domestic animals, the difference of the seasons is yet more painfully felt; so much so, indeed, that in some parts of Australia children are not born except at one season of the year; the annual changes of nature have impressed themselves on the life of man to a degree hardly conceivable to us. In pastoral Arabia domestic cattle habitually yean in the brief season of the spring pasture (Doughty, i. 429), and this would serve to fix an annual season of sacrifice. Camels calve in February and early March; Blunt, *Bed. Tribes*, ii. 166.

[1] *Supra*, p. 344. Note also that the head and the inwards have to be eaten, *i.e.* the special seats of life (Ex. xii. 9).

[2] Lydus, *De Mens.* iv. 45; cf. *Additional Note* G. The κώδιον marks the sacrifice as piacular, whether my conjecture κωδίῳ ἐσκεπασμένοι for κωδίῳ ἐσκεπασμένον is accepted or not.

marked by a series of exceptional sacrifices of piacular colour.[1]

So remarkable a concurrence in the season of the great annual piacular rites of Semitic communities leaves little doubt as to the extreme antiquity of the institution. Otherwise the season of the annual piacula is not material to our present purpose, except in so far as its coincidence with the yeaning time appears to be connected with the frequent use of sucking lambs and other very young animals as piacular victims. This point, however, seems to be of some importance as an indirect evidence of the antiquity of annual piacula. The reason often given for the sacrifice of very young animals, that a man thus got rid of a sacred obligation at the very cheapest rate, is not one that can be seriously maintained; while, on the other hand, the analogy of infanticide, which in many savage countries is not regarded as murder if it be performed immediately after birth, makes it very intelligible that, in those primitive times when a domestic animal had a life as sacred as that of a tribesman, new-born calves or lambs should be selected for sacrifice. The selection of an annual season of sacrifice coincident with the yeaning-time may therefore be plausibly referred to the time when sacrificial slaughter was still a rare and awful event, involving responsibilities which the worshippers were anxious to reduce, by every device, within the narrowest possible limits.

The point which I took a little time ago, that sacrifices of piacular form are not necessarily associated with a sense of sin, comes out very clearly in the case of annual piacula. Among the Hebrews, under the Law, the annual expiation

---

[1] *Fihrist*, p. 322. Traces of the sacredness of the month Nisan are found also at Palmyra (*Enc. Brit.*[9] xviii. 199. note 2), and among the Nabatæans, as Berger has inferred from a study of the inscriptions of Madāïn-Ṣāliḥ.

on the great Day of Atonement was directed to cleanse
the people from all their sins,[1] *i.e.* according to the Mishnic
★ interpretation, to purge away the guilt of all sins, committed
during the year, that had not been already expiated by
penitence, or by the special piacula appointed for particular
offences ;[2] but there is little trace of any such view
in connection with the annual piacula of the heathen
Semites ; and even in the Old Testament this interpretation appears to be modern.   The Day of Atonement is a
much less ancient institution than the Passover ; and in
the Passover, though the sprinkled blood has a protecting
efficacy, the law prescribes no forms of humiliation and
contrition, such as are enjoined for the more modern rite.
Again, the prophet Ezekiel, whose sketch of a legislation
for Israel, on its restoration from captivity, is older than
the law of Leviticus, does indeed provide for two annual
atoning ceremonies, in the first and in the seventh
month ;[3] but the point of these ceremonies lies in an
elaborate application of the blood to various parts of the
temple, with the object of "reconciling the house." This
reference of the sacrifice reappears also in Lev. xvi. ;
the sprinkling of the blood on the great Day of Atonement "cleanses the altar, and makes it holy from all the
uncleanness of the children of Israel."[4] Here an older
and merely physical conception of the ritual breaks through,
which has nothing to do with the forgiveness of sin ; for
uncleanness in the Levitical ritual is not an ethical conception.   It seems that the holiness of the altar is liable to
be impaired, and requires to be annually refreshed by an
application of holy blood—a conception which it would be
hard to justify from the higher teaching of the Old Testa-

---

[1] Lev. xvi. 30.   [2] *Yoma*, viii. 8, 9.

[3] Ezek. xlv. 19, 20 (LXX.).

[4] Lev. xvi. 19 ; cf. ver. 33, where the atonement extends to the whole
sanctuary.

ment, but which is perfectly intelligible as an inheritance from primitive ideas about sacrifice, in which the altar-idol on its part, as well as the worshippers on theirs, is periodically reconsecrated by the sprinkling of holy (*i.e.* kindred) blood, in order that the life-bond between the god it represents and his kindred worshippers may be kept fresh. This is the ultimate meaning of the yearly sprinkling with a tribesman's blood, which, as Theophrastus tells us, was demanded by so many altars of antiquity,[1] and also of the yearly sprinkling where the victim was not a man, but a sacrosanct or theanthropic animal.

Of all this, however, the later ages of antique religion understood no more than that ancient tradition prescribed certain annual rites of peculiar and sometimes of awful character as indispensable to the maintenance of normal relations between the gods and the worshipping community. The neglect of these rites, it was believed, entailed the wrath of the gods ; the Carthaginians, for example, in their distress in the war with Agathocles, believed that Cronus was angry because slaves had been substituted for the noble boys that were his proper victims. But it does not appear that they looked behind this and concluded that the god could not demand periodical sacrifices of such price except as an atonement for the ever-recurring sins of the nation. Ancient religion was so entirely ruled by precedent, that men did not deem it necessary to have an adequate moral explanation even of the most exorbitant demands of traditional ritual; they were content to explain them by some legend that told how the ritual first came to be set up. Thus Diodorus,

---

[1] Examples of annual human sacrifice in the Semitic field at Carthage, Porph., *De Abst.* ii. 27 (from Theophrastus), Pliny, *H. N.* xxxvi. 29 ; at Dumætha, or Duma, in Arabia, *De Abst.* ii. 56. At Laodicea in Syria the annual sacrifice of a deer was held to be a substitute for the more ancient sacrifice of a virgin. (See below, *Additional Note* F.)

when he mentions the Carthaginian human sacrifices, suggests the probability that they preserve the memory of
Cronus devouring his children;[1] and the Phœnicians
themselves appear, from the fragments of Philo Byblius,
to have traced back the custom of sacrificing children to
a precedent set by the God El, whom the Greeks identify
with Cronus.[2]

Indeed, among the Semites the most current view of
annual piacula seems to have been that they commemorate
a divine tragedy—the death of some god or goddess.[3] The
origin of such myths is easily explained from the nature
of the ritual. Originally the death of the god was nothing
else than the death of the theanthropic victim; but when
this ceased to be understood it was thought that the
piacular sacrifice represented an historical tragedy in
which the god was killed. Thus at Laodicea the annual
sacrifice of a deer in lieu of a maiden, which was offered
to the goddess of the city, is associated with a legend that
the goddess was a maiden who had been sacrificed to
consecrate the foundation of the town, and was thenceforth worshipped as its Fortune, like Dido at Carthage; it
was therefore the death of the goddess herself that was
annually renewed in the piacular rite. The same explanation applies to such scenic representations as were
spoken of in the last lecture,[4] where the deity is annually
burned in effigy, since the substitution of an effigy for a

[1] Diod. xx. 14.

[2] Euseb., *Præp. Ev.* i. 10. 21, 33. Thus it would seem that even the
unenlightened Israelites addressed in Mic. vi. 7 had a profounder sense of
sin than was current among the heathen Semites.

[3] I have not noted any Semitic example of another type of explanatory
legend of which there are various instances in Greece, viz. that the annual
piaculum was appointed as the punishment of an ancient crime for which
satisfaction had to be made from generation to generation: Pausan. ix. 8. 2
(at Potniæ), vii. 19 *sq.* (at Patræ in Achaia). In both cases, according to
the legend, the sacrifice was originally human.

[4] *Supra,* p. 364 *sqq.*

human sacrifice, or for a victim representing a god, is very
common in antique and barbarous religions.[1] And in like
manner the annual mourning for Tammuz or Adonis, which
supplies the closest parallel in point of form to the fasting and humiliation on the Hebrew Day of Atonement, is
the scenic commemoration of a divine tragedy in which
the worshippers take part with appropriate wailing and
lamentation.   That the rites of the Semitic Adonia[2] were
connected with a great sacrificial act, may safely be inferred
on general principles ; and that the sacrifice was piacular in
form, follows from Lucian's account of the ritual of Byblus :
" When they have done wailing they first burn a sacrifice [3]
to Adonis as to one dead "—the offering therefore was a
holocaust as in other annual piacula, and probably corresponds to the annual sacrifice of swine on April 2, at Cyprus,
which Joannes Lydus connects with the Adonis legend.[4]

The Adonia therefore seem to me to be only a special
form of annual piaculum, in which the sacrifice has come
to be overshadowed by its popular and dramatic accompaniments.[5]   The legend, the exhibition of the dead god in
effigy,[6] the formal act of wailing, which filled all the streets

[1] Thus the Romans substituted puppets of rushes or wool for human
offerings in the Argea and the worship of Mania.   In Mexico, again, human
victims were habitually regarded as incarnations of the deity, but also paste
images of the gods were made and eaten sacramentally.

[2] I use this word as a convenient general term describing a particular
type of ritual, without committing myself to the opinion that all rites of the
type were in connection with the worship of the same god.   It is not even
certain that there was a god Adonis.   What the Greeks took for a proper
name is perhaps no more than a title, *Adon*, "lord," applicable to various
deities, *CIL.* viii. 1211.

[3] Καταγίζουσι ; for the sense of the word compare Lucian, *De Luctu*, 19.

[4] *Supra*, p. 290 *sq.*   If this be so, the Cyprian Adonis was originally the
Swine-god, and in this as in many other cases the sacred victim has been
changed by false interpretation into the enemy of the god.   Cf. Frazer,
The Golden Bough, viii. 22 *sq.*, 31.

[5] In Greece, where the Adonia were no part of the State religion, the
celebration seems to have been limited to these.

[6] This is part of the genuine Semitic ritual, not merely Greek or

and was not confined to the sanctuary, took much greater
hold of the imagination than the antique piaculum at the
temple, and became one of the most deeply rooted parts
of popular religion.[1]   Late in the Middle Ages, in A.D
1064 and again in 1204, the Arabic historian Ibn al-
Athīr[2] records sporadic revivals, on a great scale, of the
ancient lament for the dead god.   In the former case a
mysterious threat was circulated from Armenia to Chuzistan,
that every town which did not lament the dead "king of
the Jinn" should utterly perish; in the latter a fatal disease
raged in the parts of Mosul and Irac, "and it was divulged
that a woman of the Jinn called Omm 'Oncōd (Mother of
the Grape-cluster) had lost her son, and that everyone who
would not make lamentation for him would fall a victim
to the epidemic."   In this case the form of the lamentation
is recorded : " O Omm 'Oncōd, excuse us, 'Oncōd is dead,
we knew it not."

   It seems to me that one characteristic feature in these
late observances is entirely true to the spirit of the old
Semitic heathenism.   The mourning is not a spontaneous
expression of sympathy with the divine tragedy, but obligatory and enforced by fear of supernatural anger.   And
a chief object of the mourners is to disclaim responsibility
for the god's death—a point which has already come before
us in connection with theanthropic sacrifices, such as the
" ox-murder at Athens."

   When the original meaning of the theanthropic ritual
was forgotten, and the death of the god was explained by

Alexandrian; see Lampridius, *Heliog.* vii. : "Salambonam etiam omni
planctu et iactatione Syriaci cultus exhibuit."   As it is not disputed that
Salambo or Salambas = בעל צלם, "the image of Baal," it is strange that
scholars should have been misled by Hesychius and the *Etym. Magn.* into
making Salambo a name of the Oriental Aphrodite.

   [1] *Dea Syria*, 6 (Byblus); Ammianus, xx. 9. 15 (Antioch).
   [2] Ed. Tornberg, x. 28; cf. Bar Hebræus, *Chron. Syr.* ed. Bedjan,
p. 242.

legendary history as a thing of the far past, the obligatory mourning at the annual piaculum was continued by force of usage, and presumably gave rise to various speculations which can only be matter of conjecture to us. But it is reasonable to suppose that ceremonies which were currently interpreted as the commemoration of a mythical tragedy could not suggest to the mass of the worshippers any ethical ideas transcending those embodied in the myth. The legends of the deaths of Semitic gods that have come down to us are singularly devoid of moral significance, and it is difficult to believe that they could excite any deeper feeling than a vague sentimental sympathy, or a melancholy conviction that the gods themselves were not exempt from the universal law of suffering and death. And with the common crowd I apprehend that the main feeling involved was generally that which we have seen to survive in the latest manifestations of heathen sentiment—the feeling that a bereaved deity is an angry deity, who may strike blindly all round at those who are not careful to free themselves from the suspicion of blame.

Among the agricultural Semites, where the Baal was mainly worshipped as the giver of vegetative increase and the quickening spirit of vegetative life, the annual mourning for the dead god seems often to have been brought into relation to agriculture and the cycle of agricultural feasts. In the Baal religion all agricultural operations, but particularly the harvest and vintage, are necessarily viewed as in some degree trenching on the holy things of the god, and must be conducted with special religious precautions.[1] Thus among the Hebrews the spring piaculum of the Passover, which in its origin belongs to the pre-agricultural stage of Semitic society, was connected in the Pentateuchal system with the opening of the corn-harvest,

[1] *Supra*, p. 158.

and in like manner the great Day of Atonement precedes
the vintage feast. Mr. Frazer has brought together a good
deal of evidence connecting the Adonia—or rather certain
forms of the Adonia [1]—with the corn-harvest; the death of
the god being held to be annually repeated in the cutting
of the divine grain.[2] Similarly the wailing for 'Oncŏd, the
divine Grape-cluster, seems to be the last survival of an old
vintage piaculum. I can only touch on this point here,
since the developments of religion connected with agriculture
lie beyond the scope of the present volume. The dread of
the worshippers, that the neglect of the usual ritual would
be followed by disaster, is particularly intelligible if they
regarded the necessary operations of agriculture as involving
the violent extinction of a particle of divine life. Here,
in fact, the horror attending the service is much the same
as in the case of the original theanthropic sacrifice, only
it is a holy fruit that suffers instead of a holy animal.

In the brighter days of Semitic heathenism, the annual
celebration of the god's death hardly suggested any serious
thought that was not presently drowned in an outburst of
mirth saluting the resurrection of the Baal on the following
morning; and in more distressful times, when the gloomier
aspects of religion were those most in sympathy with the
prevailing hopelessness of a decadent nation,—such times
as those in which Ezekiel found the women of Jerusalem

---

[1] The rites of Byblus cannot be connected either with vintage or harvest,
for both of these fall in the dry season, and the Byblian god died when his
sacred river was swollen with rain. Here the pre-agricultural spring piaculum
seems to have retained its old place in the yearly religious cycle.

[2] *The Golden Bough*, vol. v. chap. ix. The evidence adduced by Mr.
Frazer is not all applicable without limitation to the Semitic Adonia—
Greek and Alexandrian forms of the mourning were probably coloured by
Greek and Egyptian influence. The Semitic evidence points to Babylonia
as the source of the Semitic corn piaculum; it is therefore worth noting
that Bezold finds Tammuz and the following month Ab designated as the
harvest months of N. Babylonia in the fourteenth century B.C. (*Tell el-
Amarna Tablets*, Brit. Mus. 1892, p. xxix).

mourning for Tammuz,—the idea that the gods themselves
were not exempt from the universal law of death, and had
ordered this truth to be commemorated in their temples
by bloody, or even human sacrifices, could only favour the
belief that religion was as cruel as the relentless march of
adverse fate, and that man's life was ruled by powers that
were not to be touched by love or pity, but, if they could
be moved at all, would only be satisfied by the sacrifice of
man's happiness and the surrender of his dearest treasures.
The close psychological connection between sensuality and
cruelty, which is familiar to students of the human mind,
displays itself in ghastly fashion in the sterner aspects of
Semitic heathenism; and the same sanctuaries which, in
prosperous times, resounded with licentious mirth and
carnal gaiety, were filled in times of distress with the
cowardly lamentations of worshippers, who to save their
own lives were ready to give up everything they held dear,
even to the sacrifice of a firstborn or only child.

On the whole the annual piacula of Semitic heathenism
appear theatrical and unreal, when they are not cruel and
repulsive. The stated occurrence of gloomy rites at fixed
seasons, and without any direct relation to human conduct,
gave the whole ceremony a mechanical character, and so
made it inevitable that it should be either accepted as a
mere scenic tragedy, whose meaning was summed up in a
myth, or interpreted as a proof that the divine powers
were never thoroughly reconciled to man, and only tolerated
their worshippers in consideration of costly atonements
constantly renewed. I apprehend that even in Israel the
annual piacula, which were observed from an early date,
had little or no share in the development of the higher
sense of sin and responsibility which characterises the
religion of the Old Testament. The Passover is a rite of
the most primæval antiquity; and in the local cults,

annual mournings, like the lamentation for Jephthah's daughter, — which undoubtedly was connected with an annual sacrifice, like that which at Laodicea commemorated the mythical death of the virgin goddess,—had been yearly repeated from very ancient times. Yet, only after the exile, and then only by a sort of afterthought, which does not override the priestly idea that the annual atonement is above all a reconsecration of the altar and the sanctuary, do we find the annual piaculum of the Day of Atonement interpreted as a general atonement for the sins of Israel during the past year. In the older literature, when exceptional and piacular rites are interpreted as satisfactions for sin, the offence is always a definite one, and the piacular rite has not a stated and periodical character, but is directly addressed to the atonement of a particular sin or course of sinful life.

The conception of piacular rites as a satisfaction for sin appears to have arisen after the original sense of the theanthropic sacrifice of a kindred animal was forgotten, and mainly in connection with the view that the life of the victim was the equivalent of the life of a human member of the religious community. We have seen that when the victim was no longer regarded as naturally holy, and equally akin to the god and his worshippers, the ceremony of its death was still performed with solemn circumstances, not appropriate to the slaughter of a mere common beast. It was thus inevitable that the victim should be regarded either as a representative of the god, or as the representative of a tribesman, whose life was sacred to his fellows. The former interpretation predominated in the annual piacula of the Baal religions, but the latter was that naturally indicated in such atoning sacrifices as were offered on special emergencies and did not lend themselves to a mythical interpretation. For in old times the circumstances of the slaughter were those of a death which could only be justified by the consent, and even by the active participation, of the whole community, *i.e.* of the judicial execution of a kinsman.[1]   In later times this rule was modified, and in ordinary sacrifices the victim was slain either by the offerer, or by professional slaughterers, who formed a class of inferior ministers at the greater sanctuaries.[2]   But communal holocausts and piacula continued to be slain by the chief priests, or by the heads of the community or by their chosen representatives, so that the slaughter retained the character of a solemn public act.[3]   Again, the feeling that the slaying involves a grave responsibility, and must be justified by divine permission, was expressed by the Arabs, even in ordinary slaughter, by the use of the *bismillah, i.e.* by the slaughterer striking the victim in the name of his god.[4] But in many piacula this feeling was carried much further, and care was taken to slay the victim without bloodshed, or to make believe that it had killed itself.[5]   Certain

---

[1] *Supra*, p. 284 *sq.*

[2] In *CIS.* No. 86, the ministers of the temple include a class of slaughterers (זבחן), and so it was at Hierapolis (*Dea Syria*, xliii.).   Among the Jews, at the second temple, the Levites often acted as slaughterers; but before the captivity the temple slaughterers were uncircumcised foreigners (Ezek. xliv. 6 *sqq.*; cf. *O.T. in J. Ch.* 2nd ed., p. 260 *sqq.*).

[3] Thus in the Old Testament we find young men as sacrificers in Ex. xxiv. 5; the elders in Lev. iv. 15, Deut. xxi. 4; Aaron in Lev. xvi. 15; cf. *Yoma*, iv. 3.   All sacrifices, except the last named, might, according to the Rabbins, be killed by any Israelite.

The choice of "young men," or rather "lads," as sacrificers in Ex. xxiv. is curiously analogous to the choice of lads as executioners.   Judg. viii. 20 is not an isolated case, for Nilus also (p. 67) says that the Saracens charged lads with the execution of their captives.

[4] The same feeling is expressed in Lev. xvii. 11; Gen. viii. 3 *sqq.*

[5] The blood that calls for vengeance is blood that falls on the ground (Gen. iv. 10).   Hence blood to which vengeance is refused is said to be trodden under foot (Ibn Hishām, p. 79, *ult.*, p. 861, l. 5), and forgotten blood is covered by the earth (Job xvi. 18).   And so we often find the idea that a death in which no blood is shed, or none falls upon the ground, does not call for vengeance; while, on the other hand, a simple blow calls for

holocausts, like those of the Pyre-festival at Hierapolis, were burned alive; and other piacula were simply pushed over a height, so that they might seem to kill themselves by their fall. This was done at Hierapolis, both with animals and with human victims; and, according to the Mishna, the Hebrew scapegoat was not allowed to go free in the wilderness, but was killed by being pushed over a precipice.[1] The same kind of sacrifice occurs in Egypt, in a rite which is possibly of Semitic origin,[2] and in Greece, in more than one case where the victims were human.[3]

All such forms of sacrifice are precisely parallel to those which were employed in sacred executions, *i.e.* in the judicial slaying of members of the community. The criminal in ancient times was either stoned by the whole congregation, as was the usual form of the execution among the ancient Hebrews; or strangled, as was commonly done among the later Jews; or drowned, as in the Roman punishment for parricide, where the kin in the narrower sense is called on to execute justice on one of its own members; or otherwise disposed of in some way which either avoids bloodshed or prevents the guilt of blood from being fixed on an individual. These coincidences between the ritual of sacrifice and of execution are not accidental; in each case they had their origin in the scruple against shedding

blood-revenge, if it happens to draw blood through the accident of its falling on a sore (Moffaddal al-Dabbī, *Amthāl*, p. 10, ed. Constant. AH. 1300). Infanticide in Arabia was effected by burying the child alive; captive kings were slain by bleeding them into a cup, and if one drop touched the ground it was thought that their death would be revenged (*supra*, p. 369, note 1). Applications of this principle to sacrifices of sacrosanct and kindred animals are frequent; they are strangled or killed with a blunt instrument (*supra*, p. 343; note also the club or mallet that appears in sacrificial scenes on ancient Chaldean cylinders, Menant, *Glyptique*, i. 151), or at least no drop of their blood must fall on the ground (Bancroft, iii. 168).

[1] *Dea Syria*, lviii. ; *Yoma*, vi. 6.

[2] Plutarch, *Is. et Os.* § 30; cf. *Additional Note* F.

[3] At the Thargelia, and in the Leucadian ceremony.

kindred blood; and, when the old ideas of the kinship of man and beast became unintelligible, they helped to establish the view that the victim whose life was treated as equivalent to that of a man was a sacrifice to justice, accepted in atonement for the guilt of the worshippers. The parallelism between piacular sacrifice and execution came out with particular clearness where the victim was wholly burnt, or where it was cast down a precipice; for burning was the punishment appointed among the Hebrews and other ancient nations for impious offences,[1] and casting from a cliff is one of the commonest forms of execution.[2]

The idea originally connected with the execution of a tribesman is not exactly penal in our sense of the word: the object is not to punish the offender, but to rid the community of an impious member—ordinarily a man who has shed the sacred tribal blood. Murder and incest, or offences of a like kind against the sacred laws of blood, are in primitive society the only crimes of which the community as such takes cognisance; the offences of man against man are matters of private law, to be settled between the parties on the principle of retaliation or by the payment of damages. But murder, to which as the typical form of crime we may confine our attention, is an inexpiable offence, for which no compensation can be taken; the man who has killed his kinsman or his covenant ally, whether of design or by chance, is impious,

---

[1] Gen. xxxviii. 24; Lev. xx. 14, xxi. 9; Josh. vii. 15.

[2] The Tarpeian rock at Rome will occur to everyone. Among the Hebrews we find captives so killed (2 Chron. xxv. 12), and in our own days the Sinai Arabs killed Prof. Palmer by making him leap from a rock; cf. also 2 Kings viii. 12, Hos. x. 14, from which it would seem that this was the usual way of killing non-combatants. I apprehend that the obscure form of execution "before the Lord," mentioned in 2 Sam. xxi. 9 (and also Num. xxv. 4), is of the same sort, for the victims fall and are killed; הוקע will answer to

وَقَفَ. Note that this religious execution takes place at the season of the Paschal piaculum.　　　　　　　　　　　　　　　★

and must be cut off from his community by death or
outlawry.   And in such a case the execution or banish-
ment of the culprit is a religious duty, for if it is not
performed the anger of the deity rests on the whole kin
or community of the murderers.

In the oldest state of society the punishment of a
murderer is not on all fours with a case of blood-revenge.
Blood-revenge applies to manslaughter, *i.e.* to the killing of
a stranger.   And in that case the dead man's kin make no
effort to discover and punish the individual slayer; they
hold his whole kin responsible for his act, and take
vengeance on the first of them on whom they can lay
hands.   In the case of murder, on the other hand, the
point is to rid the kin of an impious person, who has
violated the sanctity of the tribal blood, and here therefore it is important to discover and punish the criminal
himself.   But if he cannot be discovered, some other means
must be taken to blot out the impiety and restore the
harmony between the community and its god, and for this
purpose a sacramental sacrifice is obviously indicated, such
as Deut. xxi. provides for the purging of the community
from the guilt of an untraced murder.[1]   In such a case it
was inevitable that the sacrifice, performed as it was with
circumstances closely akin to those of an execution, should
come to be regarded as a surrogate for the death of the
true culprit.   And this interpretation was all the more
readily established because, from an early date, the alliance
of different kins had begun to give rise to cases of homicide in which the line of distinction was no longer clear
between murder and manslaughter, between the case where
the culprit himself must die, and the case where any life

---

[1] Here the responsibility for the bloodshed falls on the nearest town
(ver. 2); cf. *Agh.* ix. 178, l. 26 *sq.*, where the blood-wit for a man slain is
charged to the nearest homestead.

kindred to his may suffice. Thus in the time of David [1]
the Israelites admit that a crime calling for expiation was
committed by Saul when he slew the Gibeonites, who were
the sworn allies of Israel. But, on the other hand, the
Gibeonites claim satisfaction under the law of blood-
revenge, and ask that in lieu of Saul himself certain
members of his house shall be given up to them. And in
this way the idea of substitution is brought in, even in a
case which is, strictly speaking, one of murder.

In all discussion of the doctrine of substitution as
applied to sacrifice, it must be remembered that private
sacrifice is a younger thing than clan sacrifice, and that
private piacula offered by an individual for his own sins
are of comparatively modern institution. The mortal sin
of an individual—and it is only mortal sin that has to be
considered in this connection—was a thing that affected
the whole community, or the whole kin of the offender.
Thus the inexpiable sin of the sons of Eli is visited on
his whole clan from generation to generation; [2] the sin of
Achan is the sin of Israel, and as such is punished by the
defeat of the national army; [3] and the sin of Saul and
" his bloody house " (i.e. the house involved in the bloodshed) leads to a three years' famine. Accordingly it is
the business of the community to narrow the responsibility
for the crime, and to free itself of the contagious taint by
fixing the guilt either on a single individual, or at least on
his immediate kin, as in the case of Achan, who was stoned
and then buried with his whole family. Hence, when a
tribesman is executed for an impious offence, he dies on
behalf of the community, to restore normal relations
between them and their god; so that the analogy with
sacrifice is very close in purpose as well as in form. And
so the cases in which the anger of the god can be traced

[1] 2 Sam. xxi.   [2] 1 Sam. ii. 27 *sqq.*   [3] Josh. vii. 1, 11

to the crime of a particular individual, and atoned for by his death, are very naturally seized upon to explain the cases in which the sin of the community cannot be thus individualised, but where, nevertheless, according to ancient custom, reconciliation is sought through the sacrifice of a theanthropic victim.   The old explanation, that the life of the sacrosanct animal is used to retie the life-bond between the god and his worshippers, fell out of date when the kinship of races of men with animal kinds was forgotten.   A new explanation had to be sought; and none lay nearer than that the sin of the community was concentrated on the victim, and that its death was accepted as a sacrifice to divine justice. This explanation was natural, and appears to have been widely adopted, though it hardly became a formal dogma, for ancient religion had no official dogmas, but contented itself with continuing to practise antique rites, and letting everyone interpret them as he would.   Even in the Levitical law the imposition of hands on the head of the victim is not formally interpreted as a laying of the sins of the people on its head, except in the case of the scape-goat.[1] And here the carrying away of the people's guilt to an isolated and desert region (ארץ גזרה) has its nearest analogies, not in ordinary atoning sacrifices, but in those physical methods of getting rid of an infectious taboo which characterise the lowest forms of superstition.   The same form of disinfection recurs in the Levitical legislation, where a live bird is made to fly away with the contagion of leprosy,[2] and in Arabian custom, when a widow before remarriage makes a bird fly away with the uncleanness of her widowhood.[3]   In ordinary burnt-

---

[1] Lev. xvi. 21.   [2] Lev. xiv. 7, 53 ; cf. Zech. v. 5 *sqq.*

[3] *Tāj al-'Arūs*, *s.v.* فضّ, VIII. (Lane, *s.v.* ; *O. T. in J. Ch.*, 1st ed., p. 439 ; Wellh.[1] p. 156).   An Assyrian parallel in *Records of the Past*, ix. 151.   It is indeed probable that in the oldest times the outlawry of a

offerings and sin-offerings the imposition of hands is not officially interpreted by the Law as a transference of sin to the victim, but rather has the same sense as in acts of blessing or consecration,[1] where the idea no doubt is that the physical contact between the parties serves to identify them, but not specially to transfer guilt from the one to the other.

In the Levitical ritual, all piacula, both public and private, refer only to sins committed unwittingly. As regards the sin-offering for the people this is quite intelligible, in accordance with what has just been said; for if the national sin can be brought home to an individual, he of course must be punished for it. But the private sin-offerings presented by an individual, for sins committed unwittingly, and subsequently brought to his knowledge, appear to be a modern innovation; before the exile the private offences for which satisfaction had to be made at the sanctuary were not mortal sins, and gave no room for the application of the doctrine of life for life, but were atoned for by a money payment, on the analogy of the satisfaction given by payment of a fine for the offences of man against man (2 Kings xii. 16). And, on the whole, while there can be no doubt that public piacula were often regarded as surrogates for the execution of an offender, who either was not known or whom the community hesitated to bring to justice, I very much doubt whether private offerings were often viewed in this light; even the sacrifice of a child, as we have already seen, was conceived rather as the greatest and most exorbitant gift that a man can offer.[2] The very idea of an execution implies a

criminal meant nothing more than freeing the community, just in this way, from a deadly contagion.

[1] Gen. xlviii. 14 ; Num. viii. 10 ; Deut. xxxiv. 9 ; cf. 2 Kings ii. 13 *sqq.*

[2] The Greek piacula for murder were certainly not regarded as executions, but as cathartic rites.

public function, and not a private prestation, and so I apprehend that the conception of a satisfaction paid to divine justice could not well be connected with any but public piacula. In these the death of the victim might very well pass for the scenic representation of an execution, and so represent the community as exonerating itself from all complicity in the crime to be atoned for. Looked at in this view, atoning rites no doubt served in some measure to keep alive a sense of divine justice and of the imperative duty of righteousness within the community. But the moral value of such scenic representation was probably not very great; and where an actual human victim was offered, so that the sacrifice practically became an execution, and was interpreted as a punishment laid on the community by its god, the ceremony was so wholly deficient in distributive justice that it was calculated to perplex, rather than to educate, the growing sense of morality.

Christian theologians, looking on the sacrifices of the Old Testament as a type of the sacrifice on the cross, and interpreting the latter as a satisfaction to divine justice, have undoubtedly over-estimated the ethical lessons embodied in the Jewish sacrificial system; as may be inferred even from the fact that, for many centuries, the official theology of the Church was content to interpret the death of Christ as a ransom for mankind paid to the devil, or as a satisfaction to the divine honour (Anselm), rather than as a recognition of the sovereignty of the moral law of justice. If Christian theology shows such variations in the interpretation of the doctrine of substitution, it is obviously absurd to expect to find a consistent doctrine on this head in connection with ancient sacrifice;[1]

---

[1] Jewish theology has a great deal to say about the acceptance of the merits of the righteous on behalf of the wicked, but very little about atonement through sacrifice.

and it may safely be affirmed that the influence of piacular sacrifices, in keeping the idea of divine justice before the minds of ancient nations, was very slight compared with the influence of the vastly more important idea that the gods, primarily as the vindicators of the duties of kinship, and then also of the wider morality which ultimately grew up on the basis of kinship, preside over the public exercise of justice, give oracles for the detection of hidden offences, and sanction or demand the execution of guilty tribesmen. Of these very real functions of divine justice the piacular sacrifice, when interpreted as a scenic execution, is at best only an empty shadow.

Another interpretation of piacular sacrifice, which has great prominence in antiquity, is that it purges away guilt. The cleansing effect of piacula is mainly associated with the application to the persons of the worshippers of sacrificial blood or ashes, or of holy water and other thing of sacred virtue, including holy herbs and even the fragrant smoke of incense. This is a topic which it would be easy to illustrate at great length and with a variety of curious particulars; but the principle involved is so simple that little would be gained by the enumeration of all the different substances to which a cathartic value was ascribed, either by themselves or as accessories to an atoning sacrifice. A main point to be noted is that ritual purity has in principle nothing to do with physical cleanliness, though such a connection was ultimately established by the common use of water as a means of lustration. Primarily, purification means the application to the person of some medium which removes a taboo, and enables the person purified to mingle freely in the ordinary life of his fellows. It is not therefore identical with consecration, for the latter often brings special taboos with it. And so we find that the ancients used purifica-

tory rites after as well as before holy functions.[1]   But as
the normal life of the member of a religious community
is in a broad sense a holy life, lived in accordance with
certain standing precepts of sanctity, and in a constant
relation to the deity of the community, the main use of
purificatory rites is not to tone down, to the level of
ordinary life, the excessive holiness conveyed by contact
with sacrosanct things, but rather to impart to one who
has lost it the measure of sanctity that puts him on the
level of ordinary social life.   So much indeed does this
view of the matter predominate, that among the Hebrews
all purifications are ordinarily reckoned as purification
from uncleanness; thus the man who has burned the red
heifer or carried its ashes, becomes ceremonially unclean,
though in reality the thing that he has been in contact
with was not impure but most holy;[2] and similarly the
handling of the Scriptures, according to the Rabbins,
defiles the hands, *i.e.* entails a ceremonial washing.   Purifications, therefore, are performed by the use of any of
the physical means that re-establish normal relations with
the deity and the congregation of his worshippers—in
short, by contact with something that contains and can
impart a divine virtue.   For ordinary purposes the use
of living water may suffice, for, as we know, there is a
sacred principle in such water.   But the most powerful
cleansing media are necessarily derived from the body and
blood of sacrosanct victims, and the forms of purification
embrace such rites as the sprinkling of sacrificial blood
or ashes on the person, anointing with holy unguents, or
fumigation with the smoke of incense, which from early
times was a favourite accessory to sacrifices.   It seems
probable, however, that the religious value of incense was

---

[1] See *infra, Additional Note* B, p. 446 *sq.*, and *supra*, p. 351 *sq.*
[2] Num. xix. 8, 10.

originally independent of animal sacrifice, for frankincense was the gum of a very holy species of tree, which was collected with religious precautions.[1]　Whether, therefore, the sacred odour was used in unguents or burned like an altar sacrifice, it appears to have owed its virtue, like the gum of the *samora* tree,[2] to the idea that it was the blood of an animate and divine plant.

It is easy to understand that cathartic media, like holiness itself, were of various degrees of intensity, and were sometimes used, one after another, in an ascending scale.　All contact with holy things has a dangerous side ; and so, before a man ventures to approach the holiest sacraments, he prepares himself by ablutions and other less potent cathartic applications.　On this principle ancient religions developed very complicated schemes of purificatory ceremonial, but in all grave cases these culminated in piacular sacrifice ; " without shedding of blood there is no remission of sin." [3]

In the most primitive form of the sacrificial idea the blood of the sacrifice is not employed to wash away an impurity, but to convey to the worshipper a particle of holy life.　The conception of piacular media as purificatory, however, involves the notion that the holy medium not only adds something to the worshipper's life, and refreshes its sanctity, but expels from him something that is impure.　The two views are obviously not inconsistent, if we conceive impurity as the wrong kind of life, which is dispossessed by inoculation with the right kind.　Some idea of this sort is, in fact, that which savages associate with the uncleanness of taboo, which they commonly

---

[1] Pliny, xii. 54.　The right even to see the trees was reserved to certain holy families, who, when engaged in harvesting the gum, had to abstain from all contact with women and from participation in funerals.

[2] *Supra*, p. 133.　　　　[3] Heb. ix. 22.

ascribe to the presence, in or about the man, of "spirits" or
living agencies; and the same idea occurs in much higher
forms of religion, as when, in mediæval Christianity, exor-
cisms to expel devils from the catechumen are regarded as
a necessary preliminary to baptism.

Among the Semites the impurities which were thought
of as cleaving to a man, and making him unfit to mingle
freely in the social and religious life of his community,
were of very various kinds, and often of a nature that
we should regard as merely physical, *e.g.* uncleanness from
contact with the dead, from leprosy, from eating forbidden
food, and so forth. All these are mere survivals of savage
taboos, and present nothing instructive for the higher
developments of Semitic religion. They were dealt with,
where the uncleanness was of a mild form, mainly by
ablutions; or where the uncleanness was more intense, by
more elaborate ceremonies involving the use of sacrificial
blood,[1] of sacrificial ashes,[2] or the like. Sometimes, as we
have seen, the Hebrews and Arabs conveyed the impurity
to a bird, and allowed it to fly away with it.[3]

There is, however, one form of impurity, viz. that of
bloodshed, with which important ethical ideas connected
themselves. Here also the impurity is primarily a physical
one; it is the actual blood of the murdered man, staining
the hands of the slayer, or lying unatoned and unburied
on the ground, that defiles the murderer and his whole
community, and has to be cleansed away. We have

---

[1] Lev. xiv. 17, 51.   [2] Num. xix. 17.

[3] *Supra*, p. 422. In the Arabian case the woman also threw away a piece
of camel's dung, which must also be supposed to have become the receptacle
for her impurity; or she cut her nails or plucked out part of her hair (cf.
Deut. xxi. 12), in which, as specially important parts of the body (*supra*, p.
324, note 2), the impure life might be supposed to be concentrated; or she
anointed herself with perfume, *i.e.* with a holy medium, or rubbed herself
against an ass, sheep or goat, presumably in order to transfer her uncleanness to the animal.

already seen[1] that the Semitic religions provide no atonement for the murderer himself, that can restore him to his
original place in his tribe, and this principle survives in
the Hebrew law, which does not admit piacula for mortal
sins.   The ritual idea of cleansing from the guilt of blood
is only applicable to the community, which disavows the
act of its impious member, and seeks the restoration of
its injured holiness by a public sacrificial act.   Thus
in Semitic antiquity the whole ritual conception of the
purging away of sin is bound up with the notion of the
solidarity of the body of worshippers—the same notion
which makes the pious Hebrews confess and lament not
only their own sins, but the sins of their fathers.[2]   When
the conception that the community, as such, is responsible
for the maintenance of holiness in all its parts, is combined
with the thought that holiness is specially compromised by
crime,—for in early society bloodshed within the kin is the
typical form, to the analogy of which all other crimes are
referred,—a solid basis is laid for the conception of the
religious community as a kingdom of righteousness, which
lies at the root of the spiritual teaching of the Hebrew
prophets.   The stricter view of divine righteousness which ★
distinguishes Hebrew religion from that of the Greeks even
before the prophetic period, is mainly connected with the
idea that, so far as individuals are concerned, there is no
atonement for mortal sin.[3]   This principle indeed is
common to all races in the earliest stages of law and
religion ; but among the Greeks it was early broken
down, for reasons that have been already explained,[4] while
among the Hebrews it subsisted, without change, till a date
when the conception of sin was sufficiently developed to

[1] *Supra,* pp. 359 *sq.,* 423.
[2] Hos. x. 9 ; Jer. iii. 25 ; Ezra ix. 7 ; Ps. cvi. 6.
[3] Ex. xxi. 14.   [4] *Supra,* p. 360

permit of its being interpreted, as was done by the prophets, in a way that raised the religion of Israel altogether out of the region of physical ideas with which primitive conceptions of holiness are bound up.

We had occasion a moment ago to glance at the subject of confession of sin and lamentation over it. The connection of this part of religion with piacular sacrifice is important enough to deserve a separate consideration.

Among the Jews the great Day of Expiation was a day of humiliation and penitent sorrow for sin, for which a strict fast and all the outward signs of deep mourning were prescribed.[1] Similar forms of grief were observed in all solemn supplications at the sanctuary, not only by the Hebrews,[2] but by their neighbours.[3] On such occasions, where the mourners assemble at a temple or high place, we must, according to the standing rules of ancient religion, assume that a piacular sacrifice formed the culminating point of the service;[4] and conversely it appears probable that forms of mourning, more or less accentuated, habitually went with piacular rites, not only when they were called for by some great public calamity, but on other occasions too. For we have already seen that in the annual piacula of the Baal religion there was also a formal act of mourning, which, however, was not an expression of penitence for sin, but a lament over the dead god. In this last case the origin and primary significance of the obligatory lamentation is sufficiently transparent; for the death of the god is originally nothing else than

---

[1] According to *Yoma*, viii. 1, washing, unguents, and the use of shoes were forbidden.

[2] 1 Sam. vii. 6 ; Isa. xxxvii. 1 ; Joel ii. 12 *sqq.*   [3] Isa. xv. 2 *sqq.*

[4] In Hos. vii. 14 the mourners who howl upon their beds are engaged in a religious function. And as ordinary mourners lie on the ground, I take it that the beds are the couches on which men reclined at a sacrificial banquet (Amos ii. 8, vi. 4), which here has the character, not of a joyous feast, but of an atoning rite.

the death of the theanthropic victim, which is bewailed by
those who assist at the ceremony, exactly as the Todas
bewail the slaughter of the sacred buffalo.[1]　On the same
principle the Egyptians of Thebes bewailed the death of
the ram that was annually sacrificed to the god Amen,
and then clothed the idol in its skin and buried the
carcase in a sacred coffin.[2]　Here the mourning is for the
death of the sacrosanct victim, which, as the use of the
skin indicates, represents the god himself.　But an act
of lamentation was not less appropriate in cases where
the victim was thought of rather as representing a man
of the kindred of the worshippers; and primarily, as we
know, the theanthropic victim was equally akin to the
god and to the sacrificers.

I think it can be made probable that a form of
lamentation over the victim was part of the oldest
sacrificial ritual, and that this is the explanation of such
rites as the howling (ὀλολυγή) which accompanied Greek
sacrifices, and in which, as in acts of mourning for the
dead, women took the chief part.　Herodotus (iv. 189)
was struck with the resemblance between the Greek
practice and that of the Libyans, a race among whom
the sacredness of domestic animals was very marked.
The Libyans killed their sacrifices without bloodshed,
by throwing them over their huts[3] and then twisting
their necks.　Where bloodshed is avoided in a sacrifice,
we may be sure that the life of the victim is regarded
as human or theanthropic, and the howling can be nothing
else than an act of mourning.　Among the Semites, in like
manner, the shouting (*hallel, tahlīl*) that accompanied

---

[1] *Supra*, p. 299 *sq*,

[2] Herod. ii. 42. In Egypt an act of mourning went also with other
sacrifices, notably in the great feast at Busiris ; Herod. ii. 40, 61.

[3] This is analogous to the Paschal sprinkling of blood on the lintel and
doorposts.

sacrifice may probably, in its oldest shape, have been a wail over the death of the victim, though it ultimately took the form of a chant of praise (Hallelujah), or, among the Arabs, degenerated into a meaningless repetition of the word *labbaika*. For it is scarcely legitimate to separate the Semitic *tahlīl* from the Greek and Libyan ὀλολυγή, and indeed the roots הלל and ילל (Ar. ولول), " to chant praises " and " to howl," are closely connected.[1]

Another rite which admits of a twofold interpretation is the sacrificial dance. Dancing is a common expression of religious joy, as appears from many passages of the Old Testament, but the limping dance of the priests of Baal in ★ 1 Kings xviii. 26 is associated with forms of mournful supplication, and in Syriac the same verb, in different conjugations, means " to dance " and " to mourn."

In ordinary sacrificial service, the ancient attitude of awe at the death of the victim was transformed into one of gladness, and the shouting underwent a corresponding change of meaning.[2] But piacular rites continued

---

[1] On this topic consult, but with caution, Movers, *Phoen.* i. 246 *sq.* The Arabic *ahalla, tahlīl*, is primarily connected with the slaughter of the victim (*supra*, p. 340). Meat that has been killed in the name of an idol is *mā ohilla lighairi 'llāh*, and the *tahlīl* includes (1) the *bismillāh* of the sacrificer, (2) the shouts of the congregation accompanying this act, (3) by a natural extension, all religious shouting. If, now, we note that the *bismillāh* is the form by which the sacrificer excuses his bold act, and that *tahlīl* also means "shrinking back in terror" (see Nöldeke in *ZDMG.* xli. 723), we can hardly doubt that the shouting was originally not joyous, but an expression of awe and anguish. The derivation of اهل from هلال, the new moon (Lagarde, *Orientalia*, ii. 19 ; Snouck-Hurgronje, *Het mek-kaansche Feest*, p. 75), is tempting, but must be given up. Compare on the whole matter, Wellh. p. 110 *sqq.* Cf. Gaudefroy-Demombynes, 180, note 4.

[2] This transition was probably much easier than it seems to us ; for shouting in mourning and shouting in joy seem both to be primarily directed to drive away evil influences. Of course, men, like children, are noisy when they are glad, but the conventional shrill cries of women in the East (*zaghārīt*) are not natural expressions of joy, and do not differ materi-ally from the sound made in wailing. The Hebrew word *rinna* is used both of shouts of joy and of the cry of suppliants at a religious fast (Jer.

to be conducted with signs of mourning, which were interpreted, as we have seen, sometimes as a lamentation for the death of the god, and sometimes as forms of penitent supplication, and deprecation of divine wrath.

That feelings of contrition find an expression in acts of mourning, is an idea so familiar to us that at first sight it seems to need no explanation; but a little reflection will correct this impression, and make it appear by no means unreasonable to suppose that the forms of mourning observed in supplicatory rites were not primarily expressions of sorrow for sin, or lamentable appeals to the compassion of the deity, but simply the obligatory wailing for the death of a kindred victim. The forms prescribed are identical with those used in mourning for the dead; and if it be urged that this is merely an expression of the most pungent grief, I reply that we have already found reason to be chary in assuming that certain acts are natural expressions of sorrow, and to recognise that the customs observed in lamentation for the dead had originally a very definite meaning, and could not become general expressions of grief till that meaning was forgotten.[1] And it is surely easier to suppose that the ancient rites of lamentation for the victim changed their sense, when men fell out of touch with the original meaning of them, than that they were altogether dropped for a time, and then resumed with a new meaning.

Again, the idea that the gods have a kindred feeling with their worshippers, and are touched with compassion when they see them to be miserable, is no doubt familiar even to early religions. But formal acts of worship in antiquity,

xiv. 12). In Arabic the root is used mainly of plaintive cries, as of mourning women.

[1] *Supra*, p. 322 *sq.*, p. 336 *sq.*

28

as we have seen from our analysis of sacrificial rites, are
directed, not merely to appeal to the sentiment of the deity,
but to lay him under a social obligation.   Even in the
theology of the Rabbins, penitence atones only for light
offences, all grave offences demanding also a material
prestation.[1]   If this is the view of later Judaism, after all
that had been taught by the prophets as to the worthless-
ness of material offerings, in the eyes of a God who looks
at the heart, it is hardly to be thought that in heathen
religions elaborate forms of mourning and supplication
were nothing more than appeals to divine compassion.
And, in fact, there is no doubt that some of the forms
which we are apt to take as expressions of intense grief or
self-abasement before the god, had originally quite another
meaning.   For example, when the worshippers gash their
own flesh in rites of supplication, this is not an appeal to
the divine compassion, but a purely physical means of
establishing a blood-bond with the god.[2]   Again, the usage
of religious fasting is commonly taken as a sign of sorrow,
the worshippers being so distressed at the alienation of
their god that they cannot eat; but there are very strong
reasons for believing that, in the strict Oriental form in
which total abstinence from meat and drink is prescribed,
fasting is primarily nothing more than a preparation for
the sacramental eating of holy flesh.   Some savage nations
not only fast, but use strong purges before venturing to eat
holy meat;[3] similarly the Harranians fasted on the eighth
of Nisan, and then broke their fast on mutton, at the same
time offering sheep as holocausts;[4] the modern Jews fast
from ten in the morning before eating the Passover; and

---

[1] *Yoma,* viii. 8, ‏תשובה מכפרת על עבירות קלות‎.

[2] *Supra,* p. 321 *sqq.*   [3] Thomson, *Masai Land,* p. 430.

[4] *Fihrist,* p. 322.   In Egypt a fast preceded the sacrificial meal at the
great feast of Busiris, where the victim is clearly theanthropic, Herod. ii.
40, 61.

even a modern Catholic must come to the communion with an empty stomach. On the whole, then, the conclusion seems to be legitimate, that the ritual of penitent confession and humiliation for sin follows the same law that we have found to hold good in other departments of ritual observance; the original interpretation turns on a physical conception of holiness, and it is only gradually and incompletely that physical ideas give way to ethical interpretation.

To the account that has been given of various aspects of the atoning efficacy of sacrifice, and of ritual observances that go with sacrifice, I have still to add some notice of a very remarkable series of ceremonies, in which the skin of the sacrosanct victim plays the chief part. In Nilus's sacrifice the skin and hair of the victim are eaten up like the rest of the carcase, and in some piacula, *e.g.* the Levitical red heifer, the victim is burned skin and all. Usually, however, it is flayed; and in later rituals, where rules are laid down determining whether the skin shall belong to the sacrificer or be part of the priest's fee, the hide is treated merely as an article of some commercial value which has no sacred significance.[1] But we have seen that in old times all parts of the sacrosanct victim were intensely holy, even down to the offal and excrement, and whatever was not eaten or burned was used for other sacred purposes, and had the force of a charm. The skin, in particular, is used in antique rituals either to clothe the idol or to clothe the worshippers. The meaning

---

[1] By the Levitical law (Lev. vii. 8) the skin of the holocaust goes to the ministrant priest; in other cases it must be inferred that it was retained by the owner. In the Carthaginian tariffs the usage varies, one temple giving the hides of victims to the priests and another to the owner of the sacrifice (*CIS.* Nos. 165, 167). At Sippar in Babylonia the sacrificial dues paid to the priest included the hide (*Beiträge zur Assyriologie*, vol. i. (1890) pp. 274, 286).

of both these rites was sufficiently perspicuous at the stage of religious development in which the god, his worshippers, and the victim were all members of one kindred.

As regards the draping of the idol or sacred stone in the skin, it will be remembered that in Lecture V. we came to the conclusion that in most cases sacred stones are not naturally holy, but are arbitrary erections which become holy because the god consents to dwell in them. We also find a widespread idea, persisting even in the ritual of the Jewish Day of Atonement, that the altar (which is only a more modern form of the sacred stone) requires to be consecrated with blood, and periodically reconsecrated in the same way.[1] In fact it is the sacred blood that makes the stone holy and a habitation of divine life; as in all the other parts of ritual, man does not begin by persuading his god to dwell in the stone, but by a theurgic process he actually brings divine life to the stone. All sanctuaries are consecrated by a theophany; but in the earliest times the sacrifice is itself a rudimentary theophany, and the place where sacred blood has once been shed is the fittest place to shed it again. From this point of view it is natural, not only to pour blood upon the altar-idol, but to anoint it with sacred fat, to fix upon it the heads and horns of sacrifices, and so forth. All these things are done in various parts of the world,[2] and when the sacred stone is on the way to become an idol, and primarily an animal-idol, it is peculiarly appropriate to dress it in the skin of the divine victim.

On the other hand, it is equally appropriate that the

---

[1] Ezek. xliii. 18 *sqq.*; Lev. viii. 15; Ezek. xlv. 18 *sqq.*; Lev. xvi. 33.

[2] The heads of oxen are common symbols on Greek altars, and this is only a modern surrogate for the actual heads of victims. The horns of the Semitic altar have perhaps the same origin.

worshipper should dress himself in the skin of a victim, and so, as it were, envelop himself in its sanctity. To ★ rude nations dress is not merely a physical comfort, but a fixed part of social religion, a thing by which a man constantly bears on his body the token of his religion, and which is itself a charm and a means of divine protection. Among African nations, where the sacredness of domestic animals is still acknowledged, one of the few purposes for which a beast may be killed is to get its skin as a cloak; and in the Book of Genesis (iii. 21) the primitive coat of skin is given to the first men by the Deity Himself. Similarly Herodotus, when he speaks of the sacrifices and worship of the Libyans,[1] is at once led on to observe that the ægis or goat-skin, worn by the statues of Athena, is nothing else than the goat-skin, fringed with thongs, which was worn by the Libyan women; the inference implies that it was a sacred dress.[2] When the dress of sacrificial skin, which at once declared a man's religion and his sacred kindred, ceased to be used in ordinary life, it was still retained in holy and especially in piacular functions. We have several examples of this within the Semitic field : the Assyrian Dagon-worshipper who offers the mystic fish-sacrifice to the Fish-god draped in a fish-skin ; the old Phœnician sacrifice of game by men clothed in the skin of

---

[1] Herod. iv. 188 *sqq.*; that the victims were goats is suggested by the context, but becomes certain by comparison of Hippocrates, ed. Littré, vi. 356.

[2] The thongs correspond to the fringes on the garment prescribed by Jewish law, which had a sacred significance (Num. xv. 38 *sqq.*). One of the oldest forms of the fringed garment is probably the *raht* or *hauf*, a girdle or short kilt of skin slashed into thongs, which was worn by Arab girls, by women in their courses, and also, it is said, by worshippers at the Caaba. From this primitive garment are derived the thongs and girdles with lappets that appear as amulets among the Arabs (*barīm, morassa'a* ; the latter is pierced, and another thong passed through it); compare the magical thongs of the Luperci, cut from the skin of the piaculum, whose touch cured sterility.

their prey; the Cyprian sacrifice of a sheep to the Sheep-goddess, in which sheep-skins are worn.[1] Similar examples are afforded by the Dionysiac mysteries and other Greek rites, and by almost every rude religion; while in later cults the old rite survives at least in the religious use of animal masks.[2] When worshippers present themselves at the sanctuary, already dressed in skins of the sacred kind, the meaning of the ceremony is that they come to worship as kinsmen of the victim, and so also of the god. But when the fresh skin of the victim is applied to the worshipper in the sacrifice, the idea is rather an imparting to him of the sacred virtue of its life. Thus in piacular and cathartic rites the skin of the sacrifice is used in a way quite similar to the use of the blood, but

★ dramatically more expressive of the identification of the worshipper's life with that of the victim. In Greek piacula the man on whose behalf the sacrifice was performed simply put his foot on the skin ($\kappa\dot{\omega}\delta\iota\sigma\nu$); at Hierapolis the pilgrim put the head and feet over his own head while he knelt on the skin;[3] in certain late Syrian rites a boy is initiated by a sacrifice in which his feet are clothed in slippers made of the skin of the sacrifice.[4] These rites do not appear to have suggested any idea, as to the meaning of piacular sacrifice, different from those that have already come before us; but as the skin of a sacrifice is the oldest form of a sacred garment, appropriate to the performance of holy functions, the figure of a "robe of righteousness," which is found both in the Old Testa-

---

[1] *Supra*, pp. 293, 310; and *Additional Notes* F and G. Note also that the hereditary priests of the Palmetum were dressed in skins (Strabo, xvi. 4. 18). Cf. the "girdle," or rather "kilt of skin," worn by the prophet Elijah (2 Kings i. 8).

[2] Such masks were used by the Arabs of Nejrān in rites which the Bishop Gregentius, in the laws he made for his flock (chap. xxxiv.), denounces as heathenish (Boissonade, *Anecd. Gr.* vol. v.).

[3] *Dea Syria*, lv.   [4] *Actes* of the Leyden Congress, ii. 1. 336 (361).

ment and in the New, and still supplies one of the commonest theological metaphors, may be ultimately traced back to this source.

On the whole it is apparent, from the somewhat tedious discussion which I have now brought to a close, that the various aspects in which atoning rites presented themselves to ancient worshippers have supplied a variety of religious images which passed into Christianity, and still have currency. Redemption, substitution, purification, atoning blood, the garment of righteousness, are all terms ★ which in some sense go back to antique ritual. But in ancient religion all these terms are very vaguely defined; they indicate impressions produced on the mind of the worshipper by features of the ritual, rather than formulated ethico-dogmatical ideas; and the attempt to find in them anything as precise and definite as the notions attached to the same words by Christian theologians is altogether illegitimate. The one point that comes out clear and strong is that the fundamental idea of ancient sacrifice is sacramental communion, and that all atoning rites are ultimately to be regarded as owing their efficacy to a communication of divine life to the worshippers, and to the establishment or confirmation of a living bond between them and their god. In primitive ritual this conception is grasped in a merely physical and mechanical shape, as indeed, in primitive life, all spiritual and ethical ideas are still wrapped up in the husk of a material embodiment. To free the spiritual truth from the husk was the great task that lay before the ancient religions, if they were to maintain the right to continue to rule the minds of men. That some progress in this direction was made, especially in Israel, appears from our examination. But on the whole it is manifest that none of the ritual systems of antiquity was able by mere natural development to shake itself free from the congenital defect inherent in every attempt to embody spiritual truth in material forms. A ritual system must always remain materialistic, even if its materialism is disguised under the cloak of mysticism.

ADDITIONAL NOTES

———◆———

ADDITIONAL NOTE A (p. 138)

GODS, DEMONS, AND PLANTS OR ANIMALS

THE object of this note is to consider some difficulties that may be felt with regard to the argument in the text.

1. The importance which I have attached to Arabian superstitions about the *jinn*, as affording a clue to the origin of local sanctuaries, may appear to be excessive when it is observed that the facts are almost all drawn from one part of the Semitic field. What evidence is there, it may be asked, that these Arabian superstitions are part of the common belief of the Semitic race? To this I reply, in the first place, that the Arabian conception proves upon analysis to have nothing peculiar about it. It is the ordinary conception of all primitive savages, and involves ideas that only belong to the savage mind. To suppose that it originated in Arabia, for special and local reasons, after the separation of the other Semites, is therefore to run in the teeth of all probability. Again, the little we do know about the goblins of the Northern Semites is in full agreement with the Arabian facts. The demons were banished from Hebrew religion, and hardly appear in the Old Testament except in poetic imagery. But the שְׂעִירִים or hairy ones, the לִילִית or nocturnal goblin, are exactly like the Arabian *jinn* (Wellhausen, p. 148).

The main point, however, is that the savage view of nature, which ascribes to plants and animals discourse of reason, and supernatural or demoniac attributes, can be shown to have prevailed among the Northern Semites as well as the Arabs. The savage point of view is constantly found to survive, in connection with practices of magic, after it has been superseded in religion proper; and the superstitions of the vulgar in modern civilised countries are not much more advanced than those of the rudest nations. So too among the Semites, magical rites and vulgar superstitions are not so much survivals from the higher official heathenism of the great sanctuaries as from a lower and more primitive stage of belief, which the higher forms of heathen worship overshadowed but did not extinguish. And the view of nature that pervades Semitic magic is precisely that savage view which we have found to underlie the Arabian belief in the *jinn*. Of the magical practices of the ancient Syrians, which persisted long after the introduction of Christianity, some specimens are preserved in the *Canons* of Jacob of Edessa, edited in Syriac by Lagarde, *Rel. iur. eccl. ant.* (Leipz. 1856), and translated by Kayser, *Die Canones Jacob's von Edessa* (Leipz. 1886). One of these, used in cases of sickness, was to dig up the root of a certain kind of thorn called "ischiac," and make an offering to it, eating and drinking beside the root, which was treated as a guest at the feast (Qu. 38). Another demoniac plant of the Northern Semites is the Baaras, described by Josephus, *B. J.* vii. 6. 3, which flees from those who try to grasp it, and whose touch is death so long as it is rooted in the ground. This plant seems to be the mandrake (Ar. *yabrūh*), about which the Arabs tell similar stories, and which even the ancient Germans thought to be inhabited by a spirit. When the plants in Jotham's parable speak and act like men, this is mere personification; but the dispute of the mallow and the mandrake, which Maimonides relates from the forged *Nabatœan Agriculture* (Chwolsohn, *Ssabier*, ii. 459, 914), and which prevents the mallow from supplying her prophet with responses, is a genuine piece of old Semitic superstition. In matters of this sort we cannot doubt that even a forger correctly represents popular beliefs. As regards animals, the demoniac character of the serpent in the Garden of Eden is unmistakable; the serpent is not a mere temporary disguise of Satan, otherwise its punishment would be meaningless.[1] The practice of serpent charming, repeatedly referred to in the Old Testament, is also connected with the demoniac character of the creature; and in general the idea that animals can be constrained by spells, *e.g.* prevented from injuring flocks and vineyards (Jacob of Ed., Qu. 46), rests on the same

---

[1] So in the legends of Syriac saints, the proper form of Satan, which he is compelled to resume when met with the name of Christ or the sign of the cross, is that of a black snake (*Mar Ḳardagh*, ed. Abbeloos, p. 39; Hoffmann, *Syr. Akten*, p. 76).

view, for the power of wizards is over demons and beings that are subject to the demons.

One of the most curious of the Syrian superstitions is as follows:—When caterpillars infest a garden, the maidens are assembled; a single caterpillar is taken, and one of the girls is constituted its mother. The insect is then bewailed and buried, and the mother is conducted to the place where the other caterpillars are, amidst lamentations for her bereavement. The whole of the caterpillars will then disappear (*op. cit.* Qu. 44). Here it is clearly assumed that the insects understand and are impressed by the tragedy got up for their benefit. The Syriac legends of Tūr 'Abdīn, collected by Prym and Socin (Gött. 1881), are full of beasts with demoniac powers. In these stories each kind of beast forms a separate organised community; they speak and act like men, but have supernatural powers, and close relations to the *jinn* that also occur in the legends. In conclusion, it may be observed that the universal Semitic belief in omens and guidance given by animals belongs to the same range of ideas. Omens are not blind tokens; the animals know what they tell to men.

2. If the argument in the text is correct, it may be asked why there are not direct and convincing evidences of Semitic totemism. You argue, it may be said, that traces of the old savage view of nature, which corresponds to totemism, are still clearly visible in the Semitic view of demons. But in savage nations that view is habitually conjoined with the belief that one kind of demon— or, more correctly, one kind of plants or animals endowed with demoniac qualities—is allied by kinship with each kindred of men. How does this square with the Arabian facts, in which all demons or demoniac animals habitually appear as man's enemies? The general answer to this difficulty is that totems, or friendly demoniac beings, rapidly develop into gods when men rise above pure savagery; whereas unfriendly beings, lying outside the circle of man's organised life, are not directly influenced by the social progress, and retain their primitive characteristics unchanged. When men deem themselves to be of the same blood with a particular animal kind, every advance in their way of thinking about themselves reacts on their ideas about the sacred animals. When they come to think of their god as the ancestor of their race, they must also think of him as the ancestor of their totem animals, and, so far as our observation goes, they tend to figure him as having animal form. The animal god concentrates on his

own person the respect that used to be paid to all animals of the totem kind, or at least the respect paid to them is made to depend on the worship he receives. Finally, the animal god, who, as a demoniac being, has many human attributes, is transformed into an anthropomorphic god, and his animal connections fall quite into the background. But nothing of this sort can happen to the demoniac animals that are left outside, and not brought into fellowship with men. They remain as they were, till the progress of enlightenment—a slow progress among the mass of any race— gradually strips them of their supernatural attributes. Thus it is natural that the belief in hostile demons of plant or animal kinds should survive long after the friendly kinds have given way to individual gods, whose original totem associations are in great measure obliterated. At the stage which even the rudest Semitic peoples had reached when they first become known to us, it would be absurd to expect to find examples of totemism pure and simple. What we may expect to find is the fragmentary survival of totem ideas, in the shape of special associations between certain kinds of animals on the one hand, and certain tribes or religious communities and their gods on the other hand. And of evidence of this kind there is, we shall see, no lack in Semitic antiquity. For the present I will only cite some direct evidences of kinship or brotherhood between human communities and animal kinds. Ibn al-Mojāwir relates that when the B. Hārith, a tribe of South Arabia, find a dead gazelle, they wash it, wrap it in cerecloths and bury it, and the whole tribe mourns for it seven days (Sprenger, *Postrouten*, p. 151). The animal is buried like a man, and mourned for as a kinsman.[1] Among the Arabs of Sinai the *wabr* (the coney of the Bible) is the brother of man, and it is said that he who eats his flesh will never see father and mother again. In the Harranian mysteries the worshippers acknowledged dogs, ravens and ants as their brothers (*Fihrist*, p. 326, l. 27). At Baalbek, the γενναῖος, or ancestral god of the town, was worshipped in the form of a lion (Damascius, *Vit. Isid.* § 203 ; cf. גד בעל, "leontopodion," Löw, *Aram. Pflanzennamen*, p. 406 ; G. Hoffmann, *Phoen.*

---

[1] Similarly we are told by Sohailī in his com. on Ibn Hishām (ed. Wüst. ii. 41 *sq.*) of more than one instance in which an orthodox Muslim wrapped a dead snake in a piece of his cloak and buried it. 'Omar II. is said to have done so. In this case the snake was " a believing Jinnī," an explanation that seems to be devised to justify an act of primitive superstition ; cf. Damīrī. i. 233.

Inschr. 1889, p. 27). On the banks of the Euphrates, according to *Mir. Ausc.* 149 *sq.*, there was found a species of small serpents that attacked foreigners, but did not molest natives, which is just what a totem animal is supposed to do.

3. If the oldest sanctuaries of the gods were originally haunts of a multiplicity of *jinn,* or of animals to which demoniac attributes were ascribed, we should expect to find, even in later times, some trace of the idea that the holy place is not inhabited by a single god, but by a plurality of sacred denizens. If the relation between the worshipping community and the sanctuary was formed in the totem state of thought, when the sacred denizens were still veritable animals, all animals of the sacred species would multiply unmolested in the holy precincts, and the individual god of the sanctuary, when such a being came to be singled out from the indeterminate plurality of totem creatures, would still be the father and protector of all animals of his own kind. And accordingly we do find that Semitic sanctuaries gave shelter to various species of sacred animals,—the doves of Astarte, the gazelles of Tabāla and Mecca, and so forth. But, apart from this, we may expect to find traces of vague plurality in the conception of the godhead as associated with special spots, to hear not so much of the god as of the gods of a place, and that not in the sense of a definite number of clearly individualised deities, but with the same indefiniteness as characterises the conception of the *jinn.* I am inclined to think that this is the idea which underlies the Hebrew use of the plural אלהים, and the Phœnician use of אלם, in a singular sense, on which cf. Hoffmann, *op. cit.* p. 17 *sqq.* Merely to refer this to primitive polytheism, as is sometimes done, does not explain how the plural form is habitually used to designate a single deity. But if the *Elōhīm* of a place originally meant all its sacred denizens, viewed collectively as an indeterminate sum of indistinguishable beings, the transition to the use of the plural in a singular sense would follow naturally, as soon as this indeterminate conception gave way to the conception of an individual god of the sanctuary. Further, the original indeterminate plurality of the *Elōhīm* appears in the conception of angels as *Bnē Elōhīm,* "sons of Elohim," which, according to linguistic analogy, means "beings of the Elohim kind." In the Old Testament the "sons of God" form the heavenly court, and ordinarily when an angel appears on earth he appears alone and on a special mission. But, in some of the oldest Hebrew traditions, angels

frequent holy places, such as Bethel and Mahanaim, when they
have no message to deliver (Gen. xxviii. 12, xxxii. 2). That
the angels, as "sons of God," form part of the old Semitic
mythology, is clear from Gen. vi. 2, 4, for the sons of God who
contract marriages with the daughters of men are out of place in
the religion of the Old Testament, and the legend must have been
taken over from a lower form of faith ; perhaps it was a local
legend connected with Mount Hermon (B. Enoch vi. 6 ; Hilary
on Ps. cxxxiii.). Ewald (*Lehre der Bibel*, ii. 283) rightly observes
that in Gen. xxxii. 28-30 the meaning is that an angel has no
name, *i.e.* no distinctive individuality ; he is simply one of a class ;
cf. p. 126, note, *supra.* Yet in wrestling with him Jacob wrestles
with אלהים (cf. Hos. xii. 4).

That the Arabic *jinn* is not a loan-word, as has sometimes
been supposed, is shown by Nöldeke, *ZDMG.* xli. 717.

ADDITIONAL NOTE B (p. 153)

HOLINESS, UNCLEANNESS AND TABOO

VARIOUS parallels between savage taboos, and Semitic rules of
holiness and uncleanness, will come before us from time to time ;
but it may be useful to bring together at this point some detailed
evidences that the two are in their origin indistinguishable.

Holy and unclean things have this in common, that in both
cases certain restrictions lie on men's use of and contact with
them, and that the breach of these restrictions involves supernatural dangers. The difference between the two appears, not in
their relation to man's ordinary life, but in their relation to the
gods. Holy things are not free to man, because they pertain to
the gods ; uncleanness is shunned, according to the view taken in
the higher Semitic religions, because it is hateful to the god, and
therefore not to be tolerated in his sanctuary, his worshippers, or
his land. But that this explanation is not primitive can hardly
be doubted, when we consider that the acts that cause uncleanness
are exactly the same which among savage nations place a man
under taboo, and that these acts are often involuntary, and often
innocent, or even necessary to society. The savage, accordingly,

imposes a taboo on a woman in childbed, or during her courses, and on the man who touches a corpse, not out of any regard for the gods, but simply because birth and everything connected with the propagation of the species on the one hand, and disease and death on the other, seem to him to involve the action of super-human agencies of a dangerous kind. If he attempts to explain, he does so by supposing that on these occasions spirits of deadly power are present; at all events the persons involved seem to him to be sources of mysterious danger, which has all the characters of an infection, and may extend to other people unless due pre-cautions are observed. This is not scientific, but it is perfectly intelligible, and forms the basis of a consistent system of practice; whereas, when the rules of uncleanness are made to rest on the will of the gods, they appear altogether arbitrary and meaningless. The affinity of such taboos with laws of uncleanness comes out most clearly when we observe that uncleanness is treated like a contagion, which has to be washed away or otherwise eliminated by physical means. Take the rules about the uncleanness pro-duced by the carcases of vermin in Lev. xi. 32 *sqq.*; whatever they touch must be washed; the water itself is then unclean, and can propagate the contagion; nay, if the defilement affect an (unglazed) earthen pot, it is supposed to sink into the pores, and cannot be washed out, so that the pot must be broken. Rules like this have nothing in common with the spirit of Hebrew religion; they can only be remains of a primitive superstition, like that of the savage who shuns the blood of uncleanness, and such like things, as a supernatural and deadly virus. The antiquity of the Hebrew taboos, for such they are, is shown by the way in which many of them reappear in Arabia; cf. for example Deut. xxi. 12, 13, with the Arabian ceremonies for removing the impurity of widowhood (*supra*, pp. 422, 428, n.). In the Arabian form the ritual is of purely savage type; the danger to life that made it unsafe for a man to marry the woman was transferred in the most materialistic way to an animal, which it was believed generally died in consequence, or to a bird. So too in the law for cleansing the leper (Lev. xiv. 4 *sqq.*) the impurity is transferred to a bird, which flies away with it; compare also the ritual of the scape-goat. So, again, the impurity of menstruation was recognised by all the Semites,[1] as in fact it is by all primitive

[1] The precept of the Coran, ii. 222, rests on ancient practice; see Baiḍāwī on the passage, *Ḥamāsa*, p. 107, last verse, and *Agh.* xvi. 27, 31.

and ancient peoples. Now among savages this impurity is distinctly connected with the idea that the blood of the *menses* is dangerous to man, and even the Romans held that " nihil facile reperiatur mulierum profluuio magis mirificum," or more full of deadly qualities (Pliny, *H. N.* vii. 64). Similar superstitions are current with the Arabs, a great variety of supernatural powers attaching themselves to a woman in this condition (Cazwīnī, i. 365). Obviously, therefore, in this case the Semitic taboo is exactly like the savage one; it has nothing ·to do with respect for the gods, but springs from mere terror of the supernatural influences associated with the woman's physical condition. That unclean things are tabooed on account of their inherent supernatural powers or associations, appears further from the fact that just these things are most powerful in magic; menstruous blood in particular is one of the strongest of charms in most countries, and so it was among the Arabs (Cazwīnī, *ut supra*). Wellhausen has shown how closely the ideas of amulet and ornament are connected (*Heid.*p.164 *sq.*),but has not brought out the equally characteristic fact that unclean things are not less potent. Such amulets are called by the Arabs *tanjīs, monajjasa*; and it is explained that the heathen Arabs used to tie unclean things, dead men's bones and menstruous rags, upon children, to avert the *jinn* and the evil eye (*Cāmūs, s.v.*); cf. Jacob of Edessa, *op. cit* Qu. 43.

We have seen, in the example of the swine, that prohibitions against using, and especially eating, certain animals belong in the higher Semitic religions to a sort of doubtful ground between the unclean and the holy. This topic cannot be fully elucidated till we come to speak of sacrifice, when it will appear probable that most of these restrictions, if not all of them, are parallel to the taboos which totemism lays on the use of sacred animals as food. Meantime it may be observed that such prohibitions, like those

For the Syrian heathen, *Fihrist*, p. 319, l. 18. According to Wāhidī, *Asbāb*, women in their courses were not allowed to remain in the house, which is a common savage rule. According to Mofaḍḍal al-Ḍabbī, *Amthāl*, p. 24, l. 20, the *'ārik* was isolated from her people in a hut, which, as may be inferred from the story, was on the outskirts of the hamlet or encampment. The same custom is indicated in the legend of the fall of Ḥaṭra, Tab. i. 829. 3. Girls at their first menstruation seem to have been strictly confined to a hut or tent; see the *Lisān* on the term *mo'ṣir*. This is also common all over the world. Widows were similarly confined; see the Lexx *s.v.* حفش. See Goldziher, *Abhand.* i. 207 *sq.*

that have been already considered, manifest their savage origin by the nature of the supernatural sanction attached to them. As the elk clan of the Omahas believe that they cannot eat the elk without boils breaking out on their bodies, so the Syrians, with whom fish were sacred to Atargatis, thought that if they ate a sprat or an anchovy they were visited with ulcers, swellings and wasting disease.[1] In both cases the punishment of the impious act is not a divine judgment, in our sense of that word, but flows directly from the malignant influences resident in the forbidden thing, which, so to speak, avenges itself on the offender. With this it agrees that the more notable unclean animals possess magical powers; the swine, for example, which the Saracens as well as the Hebrews and Syrians refused to eat (Sozomen, vi. 38), supplies many charms and magical medicines (Cazwīnī, i. 393).

The irrationality of laws of uncleanness, from the standpoint of spiritual religion or even of the higher heathenism, is so manifest, that they must necessarily be looked on as having survived from an earlier form of faith and of society. And this being so, I do not see how any historical student can refuse to class them with savage taboos. The attempts to explain them otherwise, which are still occasionally met with, seem to be confined to speculative writers, who have no knowledge of the general features of thought and belief in rude societies. As regards holy things in the proper sense of the word, i.e. such as are directly connected with the worship and service of the gods, more difficulty may reasonably be felt; for many of the laws of holiness may seem to have a good and reasonable sense even in the higher forms of religion, and to find their sufficient explanation in the habits and institutions of advanced societies. At present the most current view of the meaning of restrictions on man's free use of holy things is that holy things are the god's property, and I have therefore sought (supra, p. 142 sqq.) to show that the idea of property does not suffice to explain the facts of the case. A man's property consists of things to which he has an exclusive right; but in holy things the worshippers have rights as well as the gods, though their rights are subject to definite restrictions. Again, an owner is bound to respect other people's property while he preserves his own; but

---

[1] Menander, ap. Porph., De Abst. iv. 15 ; Plut., De Superst. x.; Selden, De Diis Syris, Synt. ii. Cap. 3. For savage parallels, see Frazer, Totemism and Exogamy, i. 16 sq. (cf. iv. 291, 294).

the principle of holiness, as appears in the law of asylum, can be used to override the privileges of human ownership. In this respect holiness exactly resembles taboo. The notion that certain things are taboo to a god or a chief means only that he, as the stronger person, and not only stronger but invested with supernatural power, and so very dangerous to offend, will not allow anyone else to meddle with them. To bring the taboo into force it is not necessary that there should be prior possession on the part of god or chief ; other people's goods may become taboo, and be lost to their original owner, merely by contact with the sacred person or with sacred things. Even the ground on which a king of Tahiti trod became taboo, just as the place of a theophany was thenceforth holy among the Semites. Nor does it follow that because a thing is taboo from the use of man, it is therefore in any real sense appropriated to the use of a god or sacred person ; the fundamental notion is merely that it is not safe for ordinary people to use it ; it has, so to speak, been touched by the infection of holiness, and so becomes a new source of supernatural danger. In this respect, again, the rules of Semitic holiness show clear marks of their origin in a system of taboo ; the distinction that holy things are employed for the use of the gods, while unclean things are simply forbidden to man's use, is not consistently carried out, and there remain many traces of the view that holiness is contagious, just as uncleanness is, and that things which are to be retained for ordinary use must be kept out of the way of the sacred infection. Of things undoubtedly holy, but not in any way used for the divine service, the consecrated camels of the Arabs afford a good example. But in old Israel also we find something of the same kind. By the later law (Lev. xxvii. 27) the firstling of a domestic animal that could not be sacrificed, and which the owner did not care to redeem, was sold for the benefit of the sanctuary, but by the old law (Ex. xiii. 13, xxxiv. 20) its neck was broken—a less humane rule than that of Arabia, where animals tabooed from human use were allowed to run free.[1]

Of the contagiousness of holiness there are many traces exactly similar to taboo. Among the Syrians the dove was most holy, and he who touched it became taboo for a day (*Dea Syria*, liv.). In Isa. lxv. 5 the heathen *mystæ* warn the bystander not to

[1] This parallel shows that the Arabian institution is not a mere degenerate form of an older consecration to positive sacred uses.

approach them lest he become taboo.[1] The flesh of the Hebrew
sin-offering, which is holy in the first degree, conveys a taboo to
everyone who touches it, and if a drop of the blood falls on a
garment, this must be washed, *i.e.* the sanctity must be washed
out, in a holy place, while the earthen pot in which the sacrifice
is sodden must be broken, as in the case where dead vermin falls
in a vessel and renders it unclean (Lev. vi. 27 *sq.* [Heb. ver. 20 *sq.*];
cf. Lev. xvi. 26, 28). At Mecca, in the times of heathenism,
the sacred circuit of the Caaba was made by the Bedouins either
naked, or in clothes borrowed from one of the *Ḥoms*, or religious
community of the sacred city. Wellhausen has shown that this
usage was not peculiar to Mecca, for at the sanctuary of Al-Jalsad ★
also it was customary for the sacrificer to borrow a suit from the
priest; and the same custom appears in the worship of the Tyrian
Baal (2 Kings x. 22), to which it may be added that, in 2 Sam.
vi. 14, David wears the priestly ephod at the festival of the in-
bringing of the ark. He had put off his usual clothes, for Michal
calls his conduct a shameless exposure of his person; see also
1 Sam. xix. 24. The Meccan custom is explained by saying that
they would not perform the sacred rite in garments stained with
sin, but the real reason is quite different. It appears that sometimes a man did make the circuit in his own clothes, but in that
case he could neither wear them again nor sell them, but had
to leave them at the gate of the sanctuary (Azracī, p. 125; B.
Hishām, p. 128 *sq.*). They became taboo (*ḥarīm*, as the verse
cited by Ibn Hishām has it) through contact with the holy place
and function. If any doubt remains as to the correctness of this
explanation, it will, I trust, be dispelled by a quotation from
Shortland's *Southern Districts of New Zealand* (p. 293 *sq.*),
which has been given to me by Mr. Frazer. " A slave or other
person not sacred would not enter a ' wahi tapu,' or sacred place,
without having first stripped off his clothes; for the clothes, having
become sacred the instant they entered the precincts of the ' wahi
tapu,' would ever after be useless to him in the ordinary business
of his life." [2]

[1] The suffix shows that the verb is transitive; not "for I am holier than
thou," but " for I would sanctify thee." We should therefore point it as
Piel, and compare Ezek. xliv. 19, xlvi. 12, where precautions are laid down
to prevent the people from being consecrated by approach to holy garments
and holy flesh.

[2] It is perhaps on this principle that a man found encroaching on a
ḥimā is punished by being stripped of his clothes, etc.; *Muḥ in Med.* p. 385

In the case of the garment stained by the blood of the sin-offering, we see that taboos produced by contact with holy things, like those due to uncleanness, can be removed by washing. In like manner, among the Jews the contact of a sacred volume or a phylactery "defiled the hands," and called for an ablution, and the high priest on the Day of Atonement washed his flesh with water, not only when he put on the holy garments of the day, but when he put them off (Lev. xvi. 24; cf. Mishna, *Yōmā*, viii. 4). In savage countries such ablutions are taken to be a literal physical removal of the contagious principle of the taboo, and all symbolical interpretations of them are nothing more than an attempt, in higher stages of religious development, to justify adhesion to traditional ritual.

These examples may suffice to show that it is impossible to separate the Semitic doctrine of holiness and uncleanness from the system of taboo. If anyone is not convinced by them, I am satisfied that he will not be convinced by an accumulation of evidence. But as the subject is curious in itself, and may possibly be found to throw light on some obscure customs, I will conclude this part of the subject by some additional remarks, of a more conjectural character, on the costume worn at the sanctuary.

The use of special vestments by priestly celebrants at religious functions is very widespread, and has relations which cannot be illustrated till we come to speak of sacrifice.[1] But it is certain that originally every man was his own priest, and the ritual observed in later times by the priests is only a development of what was originally observed by all worshippers. As regards the matter of vestments, it was an early and widespread custom to make a difference between the dress of ordinary life and that donned on sacred occasions. The ancient Hebrews, on approaching the presence of the Deity, either washed their clothes (Ex. xix. 10) or changed them (Gen. xxxv. 2), that is, put on their best clothes, and the women also wore their jewels (Hos. ii. 13 [15]; cf. Sozomen's account of the feast at Mamre, *H. E.* ii. 4).

The washing is undoubtedly to remove possible uncleanness,

(Wajj), Belādhorī, p. 9 (Naci'). The story that 'Amr Mozaiciā tore his clothes every night, that no one else might wear them (Ibn Doraid, p. 258), is perhaps a reminiscence of an old taboo attached to royalty.

[1] See what is said of the skin of the victim as furnishing a sacred dress, *supra*, p. 437 *sq.*

and in Gen. xxxv. 2 the change of garments has the same association. But the instances given above show that, if it was important not to carry impurity into the sanctuary, it was equally necessary not to carry into ordinary life the marks of contact with holy places and things. As all festive occasions in antiquity were sacred occasions, it may be presumed that best clothes were also holy clothes, reserved for festal purposes. They were perfumed (Gen. xxvii. 15, 27), and perfume among the Semites is a very holy thing (Pliny, xii. 54), used in purifications (Herod. i. 198), and applied, according to Phœnician ritual, to all those who stood before the altar, clad in the long byssus robes, with a single purple stripe, which were appropriated to religious offices (Silius, iii. 23 *sqq.*; cf. Herodian, v. 6. 10). Jewels, too, such as women wore in the sanctuary, had a sacred character; the Syriac word for an earring is *c'dāshā*, "the holy thing,"[1] and generally speaking jewels serve as amulets.[2] On the whole, therefore, holy dress and gala dress are one and the same thing, and it seems, therefore, legitimate to suppose that in early times best clothes meant clothes that were taboo for the purposes of ordinary life. But of course the great mass of people in a poor society could not keep a special suit for sacred occasions. Such persons would either wash their clothes after as well as before any specially sacred function (Lev. vi. 27, xvi. 26, 28), or would have to borrow sacred garments. Shoes could not well be washed, unless they were mere linen stockings, as in the Phœnician sacred dress described by Herodian; they were therefore put off before treading on holy ground (Ex. iii. 5; Josh. v. 15, etc.).[3]

Another Hebrew usage that may be noted here is the ban (Heb. *ḥérem*), by which impious sinners, or enemies of the com-

---

[1] The Arabic *codās* is doubtless an ancient loanword from this; but *cadīs*, an old Yemenite name for pearls (see *Tāj*, *s.v.*), is probably an independent expression of the same idea.

[2] As amulets, jewels are mainly worn to protect the chief organs of action (the hands and the feet), but especially the orifices of the body (ear-rings; nose-rings, hanging over the mouth; jewels on the forehead, hanging down and protecting the eyes). In Doughty, ii. 199, a man stuffs his ears with cotton before venturing to descend a well haunted by *jinn*. Similarly the lower orifices of the trunk are protected by clothing, which has a sacred meaning (*supra*, p. 437, note 2). Similar remarks apply to tattooing, staining with stibium and henna, etc.

[3] [A person about to consult the oracle of Trophonius, after being washed and anointed, put on a linen shirt and *shoes of the country*, ὑποδησάμενοι ἐπιχωρίας κρηπῖδας (Pausanias, ix. 39).—J. G. Frazer.]

munity and its god, were devoted to utter destruction. The ban
is a form of devotion to the deity, and so the verb " to ban " is
sometimes rendered "consecrate" (Micah iv. 13) or "devote"
(Lev. xxvii. 28 sq.). But in the oldest Hebrew times it involved
the utter destruction, not only of the persons involved, but of
their property; and only metals, after they had passed through
the fire, were added to the treasure of the sanctuary (Josh. vi.
24, vii. 24; 1 Sam. xv.). Even cattle were not sacrificed, but
simply slain, and the devoted city must not be rebuilt (Deut.
xiii. 16; Josh. vi. 26).[1] Such a ban is a taboo, enforced by
the fear of supernatural penalties (1 Kings xvi. 34), and, as
with taboo, the danger arising from it is contagious (Deut. vii.
26; Josh. vii.); he that brings a devoted thing into his house
falls under the same ban himself.

ADDITIONAL NOTE C (p. 158)

TABOOS ON THE INTERCOURSE OF THE SEXES

ACCORDING to Herodotus, ii. 64, almost all peoples, except the
Greeks and Egyptians, μίσγονται ἐν ἱροῖσι καὶ ἀπὸ γυναικῶν
ἀνιστάμενοι ἄλουτοι ἐσέρχονται ἐς ἱρόν. This is good evidence of
what the Greeks and Egyptians practised; but the assertion about
other nations is incorrect, at least as regards the Semites and
parts of Asia Minor,[2] whose religion had much in common with
theirs. As regards the evidence, it comes to the same thing
whether we are told that certain acts were forbidden at the
sanctuary, or to pilgrims bound for the sanctuary, or that no one
could enter the sanctuary without purification after committing
them. We find that among the Arabs sexual intercourse was
forbidden to pilgrims to Mecca. The same rule obtained among

[1] In Judg. ix. 45 the site is sown with salt, which is ordinarily explained
with reference to the infertility of saline ground. But the strewing of salt
has elsewhere a religious meaning (Ezek. xliii. 24), and is a symbol of
consecration. Similarly Hesychius explains the phrase, ἀρὰς ἐπισπείραι· ἔθος
Κυπρίων σπειρόντων κριθὰς μεθ' ἁλὸς καταρᾶσθαί τισιν.

[2] See the inscription of Apollo Lermenus, *Journ. Hell. Studies*, viii. 380
sqq.; this was not a Greek cult.

the Minæans in connection with the sacred office of collecting frankincense (Pliny, *H. N.* xii. 54). Among the Hebrews we find the restriction in connection with the theophany at Sinai (Ex. xix. 15) and the use of consecrated bread (1 Sam. xxi. 5); Sozomen, ii. 4, attests it for the heathen feast at Mamre ; and Herodotus himself tells us that among the Babylonians and Arabs every conjugal act was immediately followed, not only by an ablution, but by such a fumigation as is still practised in the Sūdān (Herod. i. 198). This restriction is not directed against immorality, for it applies to spouses ; nor does it spring from asceticism, for the temples of the Semitic deities were thronged with sacred prostitutes ; who, however, were careful to retire with their partners outside the sacred precincts (Herod. i. 199, ἔξω τοῦ ἱροῦ; cf. Hos. iv. 14, which curiously agrees in expression with *Ḥam.* p. 599, second verse, where the reference is to the love-making of the Arabs just outside the *himā*).

The extension of this kind of taboo to warriors on an expedition is common among rude peoples, and we know that it had place among the Arabs, and was not wholly obsolete as late as the second century of Islām ; see *Agh.* xiv. 67 (Ṭabarī, ed. Kosegarten, i. 144), xv. 161 ; Al-Akhṭal, *Dīw.* p. 120, l. 2 ; cf. Masʿūdī, vi. 63–65, *Fr. Hist. Ar.* p. 247 *sq.* See also Note I, *infra,* p. 481 *sqq.* In the Old Testament, war and warriors are often spoken of as consecrated,—a phrase which seems to be connected, not merely with the use of sacred ceremonies at the opening of a campaign, but with the idea that war is a holy function, and the camp a holy place (Deut. xxiii. 10–15). That the taboo on sexual intercourse applied to warriors in old Israel cannot be positively affirmed, but is probable from Deut. xxiii. 10, 11, compared with 1 Sam. xxi. 5, 6 [E.V. 4, 5]; 2 Sam. xi. 11. The passage in 1 Sam., which has always been a *crux interpretum,* calls for some remark. It seems to me that the text can be translated as it stands, if only we take יקדש as a plural, which is possible without adding ו. David says, " Nay, but women are forbidden to us, as has always been my rule when I go on an expedition, so that the gear (clothes, arms, etc.) of the young men is holy even when it is a common (not a sacred) journey ; how much more so when [Prov. xxi. 27] to-day they will be consecrated, gear and all." David distinguishes between expeditions of a common kind, and campaigns which were opened by the consecration of the warriors and their gear. He hints that his present excursion is of the second kind, and that the ceremony of consecration will take place as soon as he joins his men; but he reminds the priest that his custom has been to enforce the rules of sanctity even on ordinary expeditions. יקדש should perhaps be pointed as *Pual*. The word עצרה might more exactly be rendered "taboo," for it is evidently a technical expression. So in Jer. xxxvi. 5, "I am עצור, I cannot go into the temple," does not mean "I am imprisoned" (cf. ver. 19), but "I am restrained from entering the sanctuary by a ceremonial impurity." It seems to me that the proverbial עצור ועזוב, one of those phrases which name two categories, under one or other of which everybody is included, means "he who is under taboo, and he who is free"; cf. also נעצר, 1 Sam. xxi. 7 [8], and עצרה, "tempus clausum." The same sense

★ appears in Arabic *mo'sir*, applied to a girl who is shut up under the taboo which, in almost all early nations, affects girls at the age of puberty.

ADDITIONAL NOTE D (p. 212)

★　　THE SUPPOSED PHALLIC SIGNIFICANCE OF SACRED POSTS AND
PILLARS

THAT sacred posts and pillars among the Semites are phallic symbols is an opinion which enjoys a certain currency, mainly through the influence of Movers; but, as is so often the case with the theories of that author, the evidence in its favour is of the slenderest. For the pre-Hellenistic period Movers relies on 1 Kings xv. 13, 2 Chron. xv. 16, taking מפלצת, after the Vulgate, to mean *simulacrum Priapi*; but this is a mere guess, not supported by the other ancient versions. He also appeals to Ezek. xvi. 17, which clearly does not refer to phallic worship, but to images of the Baalim; the passage is imitated from Hos. ii. Many recent commentators suppose that יד, "hand," in Isa. lvii. 8, means the phallus. This is the merest conjecture, and even if it were certain, the use of יד in the sense of cippus, sign-post, would still have to be explained, not by supposing that every monument or road mark was a phallic pillar, but from the obvious symbolism which gives us the word finger-post. The Phœnician cippi dedicated to Tanith and Baal Hamman often have a hand figured on them, but a real hand, not a phallus.

In ancient times obscene symbols were used without offence to denote sex, and female symbols of this kind are found in many Phœnician grottoes scratched upon the rock. Herodotus, ii. 106, says that he saw in Syria Palæstina stelæ engraved with γυναικὸς αἰδοῖα, presumably *massēboth* dedicated to female deities; but how this can support the view that the *massēba* represents ἀνδρὸς αἰδοῖον I am at a loss to see. Indeed, the whole phallic theory seems to be wrecked on the fact that the *massēba* represents male and female deities indifferently. At a later date the two great pillars that stood in the Propylæa of the temple of Hierapolis are called *phalli* by Lucian (*Dea Syr.* xvi.). Such twin pillars are very common at Semitic temples; even the temple at Jerusalem had them, and they are shown on coins representing the temple at Paphos; so that Lucian's evidence seems important, especially as he tells us that they bore an inscription to the effect that "these phalli were set up by Dionysus to his mother Hera." But the inscription appears to have been in Greek, and proves only that the Greeks, who were accustomed to phallic symbols in Dionysus-worship, and habitually regarded the licentious sacred feasts of the Semites as Dionysiac, put their own interpretation on the pillars. In § xxviii. of Lucian's work it clearly appears that the meaning and use of the pillars was an open question. Men were accustomed to ascend them, and spend a week on the top—like the Christian Stylites of the same region. Lucian thinks that this too was done because of Dionysus, but the natives said either that at the immense height (which is stated at 30 fathoms) they held near converse with the gods and prayed for the good of all Syria, or that the practice was a memorial of the Flood, when men were driven by fear to ascend trees and mountains. It is not easy to extract anything phallic out of these statements.

Besides this, Movers (i. 680) cites the statement of Arnobius, *Adv. Gentes*, v. 19 (p. 212), that phalli, as signs of the grace of the deity, were presented to the *mystæ* of the Cyprian Venus; but the use of the phallus as an amulet—which was very widespread in antiquity—can throw no light on the origin of sacred pillars. Everything else that he adduces is purely fantastic, and without a particle of evidence, and I have not found anything in more recent writers to strengthen his argument.

ADDITIONAL NOTE E (p. 245)

SACRED TRIBUTE IN ARABIA—THE GIFT OF FIRSTLINGS

I HAVE stated in the text that the idea of sacred tribute has little
or no place among the nomadic Arabs, and it will hardly be disputed that, broadly speaking, this statement accords with the
facts. But it is important to determine, with as much precision
as possible, whether the conception of tribute and gifts of homage
paid to the deity had any place at all in the old religion of the
purely nomadic Semites, and if it had, to define that place with
exactness. As the full discussion of this question touches on
matters which go beyond the subject of Lecture VII., I have
reserved the topic for an Additional Note.

Among the agricultural Semites the idea of a sacred tribute
appears mainly in connection with first-fruits and tithes of agricultural produce. Animal sacrifices were ultimately brought
under the category of gifts of homage; and so, when they were
not presented as freewill offerings, but in accordance with ritual
laws that demanded certain definite oblations for definite occasions,
they also came to be looked upon as a kind of tribute. But we
have seen that, even in the later rituals, there was a clear
distinction between cereal oblations, which were simply payments to the god, and animal sacrifices, which were used to
furnish a feast for the god and his worshippers together. The
explanation that the victim is wholly given up to the god, who
then gives back part of it to the worshipper, that he may feast
at the temple as the guest of his deity, is manifestly too artificial
to be regarded as primitive; and if, on the other hand, we look
on a sacrifice simply as a feast provided by the worshipper, at
which the god is the chief guest, it does not appear that,
according to ancient ideas, any payment of tribute, or even any
gift, is involved. Hospitality is not placed by early nations
under the category of a gift; when a man slaughters an animal,
everyone who is present has his share in the feast as a matter
of course, and those who eat do not feel that any present has
been made to them. And in like manner it seems very doubtful
whether the oblations of milk which were poured out before
certain Arabian idols can in any proper sense be called gifts,—*i.e.*
transfers of valuable property,—for in the desert it is still a shame

to sell milk (Doughty, i. 215, ii. 443), and a draught from the milk-bowl is never refused to anyone. In a society where milk and meat are never sold, and where only a churl refuses to share these articles of food with every by-passer, we must not look to the sacrificial meal as a proof that the Arabs paid tribute to their gods.

The agricultural tribute of first-fruits and tithes is a charge on the produce of the land, paid to the gods as Baalim or landlords. In this form tribute cannot appear among pure nomads. But tribute is also paid to kings who are not landlords, by subjects who are not their tenants. An example of such a tribute is the royal tithe in Israel, which was paid by the free landowners ; and on this analogy it seems quite conceivable that a sacred tribute paid to the god, as king or chief of his worshippers, might arise in a purely nomadic community. In examining this possibility, however, we must have regard to the actual constitution of Arabian society.

Among the free tribes of the Arabian desert there is no taxation, and the chiefs derive no revenue from their tribesmen, but, on the contrary, are expected to use their wealth with generosity for the public benefit. A modern sheikh or emir, according to Burckhardt's description (*Bed. and Wah.* i. 118), is expected to treat strangers in a better style than any other member of the tribe, to maintain the poor, and to divide among his friends whatever presents he may receive. " His means of defraying these expenses are the tribute he exacts from the Syrian villages, and his emoluments from the Mecca pilgrim caravan,"—in short, black-mail. Black-mail is merely a regulated form of pillage, and the gains derived from it correspond to those which in earlier times came directly from the plundering of enemies and strangers. In ancient Arabia the chief took the fourth part of the spoils of war (*Ham.* p. 336, last verse ; Wācidī, ed. Kremer, p. 10), and had also certain other perquisites, particularly the right to select for himself, before the division, some special gift, such as a damsel or a sword (the so-called *ṣafāyā*, *Ham.* p. 458, last verse , and Abū 'Obaida, *ap.* Reiske, *An. Musl.* i. 26 *sqq.* of the notes).[1] Among the Hebrews, in like manner, the chief received a liberal share of the booty (1 Sam. xxx. 20), including some choice gift corresponding to the *ṣafāyā* (Judg. v. 30, viii. 24). In the

---

[1] Among the Arabs, a sacrifice (*nacī'a*) preceded the division of the spoil ; see below, *Additional Note* M.

Levitical law a fixed share of the spoil is assigned to the
sanctuary (Num. xxxi. 28 *sqq.*), just as in the Moslem theocracy
the chief's fourth is changed to a fifth, payable to Allah and his
prophet, but partly used for the discharge of burdens of charity
and the like, such as in old times fell upon the chiefs (Sura
viii. 42).   These fixed sacred tributes are modern, both in Arabia
and in Israel; but even in old times the spoils of war were a chief
source of votive offerings.   The votive offerings of the Arabs
frequently consisted of weapons (Wellh. p. 112; cf. 1 Sam. xxi.
9); and, among the Hebrews, part of the chief's booty was generally consecrated (Judg. viii. 27; 2 Sam. viii. 10 *sq.*; Micah iv. 13).
Similarly, Mesha of Moab dedicates part of his spoil to Chemosh;
and in Greece the sacred tithe occurs mainly in the form of a
percentage on the spoils of war.   It is obvious, however, that the
apportionment of a share of booty to the chief or to the god does
not properly fall under the category of tribute.   And on the
general Arabian principle that a chief must not tax his own
tribesmen, it does not appear that there was any room for the
development of a system of sacred dues, so long as the gods were
tribal deities worshipped only by their own tribe.   Among the
Arabs tribute is a payment to an alien tribe or to its chiefs,
either by way of black-mail, or in return for protection.   A king
who receives gifts and tribute is a king reigning over subjects
who are not of his own clan, and whom, therefore, he is not
bound to help and protect at his own expense.   I apprehend
that the oldest Hebrew taxation rested on this principle; for
even Solomon seems to have excluded the tribe of Judah from
his division of the kingdom for fiscal purposes (1 Kings iv. 7 *sqq.*),
while David, as a prosperous warrior, who drew vast sums from
conquered nations, probably raised no revenue from his Israelite
subjects.   As regards Saul, we know nothing more than that he
enriched his own tribesmen (1 Sam. xxii. 7).   The system of
taxation described in 1 Sam. viii. can hardly have been in full
force till the time of Solomon at the earliest, and its details seem
to indicate that, in fiscal as in other matters, the developed
Hebrew kingship took a lesson from its neighbours of Phœnicia,
and possibly of Egypt.

To return, however, to the Arabs: the tributes which chiefs
and kings received from foreigners were partly transit dues from
traders (Pliny, *H. N.* xii. 63 *sqq.*).   In such tribute the gods had
their share, as Pliny expressly relates for the case of the incense

traffic, and as Azracī (p. 107) appears to imply for the case of Greek merchants at Mecca. Commerce and religion were closely connected in all the Semitic lands; the greatest and richest temples are almost always found at cities which owed their importance to trade.

Of the other kind of tribute, paid by a subject tribe to a prince of alien kin, a lively picture is afforded by *Agh.* x. 12, where we find Zohair b. Jadhīma sitting in person at the fair of 'Okāẓ to collect from the Hawāzin, who frequented this annual market, their gifts of ghee, curds and small cattle. In like manner the tribute of the pastoral Moabites to the kings of the house of 'Omri was paid in sheep (2 Kings iii. 4); and on such analogies we can very well conceive that sacrificial oblations of food might be regarded as tribute, wherever the worshippers were not the tribesmen but the clients of their god. But to suppose that sacrifices generally were regarded by the ancient Semitic nomads as tributes and gifts of homage, is to suppose that the typical form of Semitic religion is clientship, a position which is altogether untenable.

Thus it would seem that all we know of the social institutions of the Arabs is in complete accordance with the results, obtained in the text of these lectures, with regard to the original meaning of sacrifice. The conclusion to which the ritual points, viz. that the sacrifice was in no sense a payment to the god, but simply an act of communion of the worshippers with one another and their god, is in accord with the relations that actually subsisted between chiefs and their tribesmen; and when we read that in the time of Mohammed the ordinary worship of household gods consisted in stroking them with the hand as one went out and in (*Muh. in Med.* p. 350), we are to remember that reverent salutation was all that, in ordinary circumstances, a great chieftain would expect from the meanest member of his tribe. At the pilgrimage feasts of the Arabs, as of the Hebrews, no man appeared without a gift; but this was in the worship of alien gods.

In a payment of tribute two things are involved—(1) a transfer of property, and (2) an obligation, not necessarily to pay on a fixed scale, but at least to pay something. That an Arabian sacrifice cannot without straining be conceived as a transfer of property, has appeared in the course of this note, and is shown from another point of view in Lecture XI. (*supra,* p. 390 *sqq.*). And in most sacrifices the second condition is also unfulfilled, for in Arabia it is left to a man's free will whether he will appear before the god and do sacrifice, even in the sacred month of Rajab.

It seems, however, to be probable that the absolute freedom of the individual will in matters of religious duty, as it appears among the Arabs in the generations immediately preceding Islam, was in part due to the breaking up of the old religion. There can, for example, be hardly a doubt that the ascetic observances during a war of blood-revenge, which in the time of the prophet were assumed by a voluntary vow, were at one time imperatively demanded by religious custom (*infra*, *Note I*). Again, there were certain religious restrictions on the use of a man's property which, even in later times, do not seem to have been purely optional, *e.g.* the prohibition of using for common work a camel which had produced ten female foals. But, in older times at least, such a camel was not given over in property to the god; the restriction was simply a taboo (*supra*, p. 149).

There is, however, one Arabian sacrifice which has very much the aspect of a fixed due payable to the god, viz. the sacrifice of firstlings (فَرَع, *fara‘*). It has already been remarked (*supra*, p. 227, note 3) that the accounts which have been handed down to us about the *fara‘* are confused and uncertain; but although the word seems to have been extended to cover other customary sacrifices, it appears properly to denote "the foal or lamb which is first cast." This is the definition given in the *ḥadīth*, which in such matters has always great weight, and it is confirmed by the proverb in Maidānī, ii. 20 (Freytag, *Ar. Pr.* ii. 212). As we also learn from the *ḥadīth* (*Lisān, s.v.*) that the custom was to sacrifice the *fara‘* when it was still so young that the flesh was like glue and stuck to the skin, it would seem that this sacrifice must be connected with the Hebrew sacrifice of the firstborn of kine and sheep, which according to the oldest law (Ex. xxii. 30) was to be offered on the eighth day from birth. There is an unfortunate ambiguity about the definition of the Arabian *fara‘*, for the first birth may mean either the first birth of the dam, or the first birth of the year, and Maidānī takes it in the latter sense, making *fara‘* a synonym of *roba‘*, *i.e.* a foal which, being born in the *rabī‘*, or season of abundant grass, when the mother was well fed, naturally grew up stronger and better than foals born later (cf. Gen. iv. 4). But apart from the analogy of the Hebrew firstlings, which are quite unambiguously explained as firstborn (פטר רחם, Ex.

xxxiv. 19), there are other uses of the Arabic word *fara'* which make Maidānī's interpretation improbable; and the presumption is that, however the rule may have been relaxed or modified in later times, there was a very ancient Semitic custom, anterior to the separation of the Arabs and Hebrews, of sacrificing the first-born of domestic animals. The conclusion that this offering was, for nomadic life, what the offering of first-fruits was among agricultural peoples, viz. a tribute paid to the gods, seems so obvious that it requires some courage to resist it. Yet, from what has been already said, it seems absolutely impossible that, at the very early date when the Hebrews and Arabs lived together, any tribute could have been paid to the god as chief or king; and, even in the form of the sacrifice of firstlings which is found among the Hebrews, there seem to be indications that the parallelism with the offering of first-fruits is less complete than at first sight it seems to be.

The first-fruits are an annual gift of the earliest and choicest fruits of the year, but the firstlings are the first offspring of an animal. Their proper parallel in the vegetable kingdom is therefore found in the law of Lev. xix. 23 *sqq.*, which ordains that for three years the fruit of a new orchard shall be treated as "uncircumcised," and not eaten, that the fourth year's fruit shall be consecrated to Jehovah, and that thereafter the fruit shall be common. The characteristic feature in this ordinance, from which its original meaning must be deduced, is the taboo on the produce of the first three years, not the offering at the temple paid in the fourth year. And that some form of taboo lies also at the bottom of the sacrifice of firstlings, appears from the provision of the older Hebrew law that, if a firstling ass is not redeemed by its owner, its neck shall be broken (Ex. xxxiv. 20). We see, however, that the tendency was to bring all such offerings under the category of sacred tribute; for by the later law (Lev. xxvii. 27) the ass that is not redeemed is to be sold for the benefit of the sanctuary, and even in the older law all the firstborn of men must be redeemed.

Primarily, a thing that is taboo is one that has supernatural qualities or associations, of a kind that forbid it to be used for common purposes. This is all that is involved, under the older law, in the holiness of the firstling ass; it is such an animal as the Arabs would have allowed to go free, instead of killing it. But in the very earliest times all domestic animals had a certain measure of holiness, and were protected by certain taboos which prevented them from being used by man as mere chattels; and so it would appear that the holiness of the firstborn, which is congenital (Lev. xxvii. 26), is only a higher form of the original sanctity of domestic animals. The correctness of this conclusion can be verified by a practical test; for if firstlings are animals of special intrinsic holiness, the sacrifices to which they are appropriate will be special acts of communion, piacular holocausts or the like, and not mere common sacrificial meals. And this is actually the case in the oldest Hebrew times; for the Passover, which is the sacrifice of firstlings *par excellence*, is an atoning rite of a quite exceptional kind (*supra*, p. 406).[1]

Further, there is a close connection between the firstlings and the piacular holocaust; both are limited to males, and the holocaust of Samuel (1 Sam. vii. 9) is a sucking lamb, while from Ex. xxii. 30 we see that firstlings were offered on the eighth day (or, probably, as soon after it as was practicable ; cf. Lev. xxii. 27).

The consecration of first-born male children (**Ex. xiii. 13,** xxii. 28, xxxiv. 20) has always created a difficulty. The legal usage was to redeem the human firstlings, and in Num. iii. this redemption is further connected in a very complicated way with the consecration of the tribe of Levi. It appears, however, that in the period immediately before the exile, when sacrifices of first-born children became common, these grisly offerings were supposed to fall under the law of firstlings (Jer. vii. 31, xix. 5 ; Ezek. xx. 26). To conclude from this that at one time the Hebrews actually sacrificed all their first born sons is absurd ; but, on the other hand, there must have been some point of attachment in ancient custom for the belief that the deity asked for such a sacrifice. In point of fact, even in old times, when exceptional circumstances called for a human victim, it was a child, and by preference a first-born or only child, that was selected by the peoples in and around Palestine.[2] This is

---

[1] That the paschal sacrifice was originally a sacrifice of firstlings is clearly brought out by Wellhausen, *Prolegomena*, chap. iii. § 1, 1. Ultimately the paschal lamb and the firstlings fell apart ; the former was retained, with much of its old and characteristic ritual, as a domestic sacrifice, while the latter continued to be presented at the sanctuary and offered on the altar, the whole flesh being the perquisite of the priest (Num. xviii. 18). But in the law of Deuteronomy (xii. 17 *sqq.*, xv. 19 *sqq.*) the firstlings have not yet assumed the character of a sacred tribute.

[2] 2 Kings iii. 27 ; Philo Byblius in *Fr. Hist. Gr.* iii. 571 ; cf. Porph., *De Abst.* ii. 56, τῶν φιλτάτων τινά.

commonly explained as the most costly offering a man can make; but it is rather to be regarded as the choice, for a special purpose, of the most sacred kind of victim. I apprehend that all the prerogatives of the firstborn among Semitic peoples are originally ★ prerogatives of sanctity; the sacred blood of the kin flows purest and strongest in him (Gen. xlix. 3; Deut. xxi. 17). Neither in the case of children, nor in that of cattle, did the congenital holiness of the first-born originally imply that they must be sacrificed or given to the deity on the altar, but only that if sacrifice was to be made they were the best and fittest, because the holiest, victims. But when the old ideas of holiness became unintelligible, and holy beasts came to mean beasts set aside for sacrifice, an obvious extension of this new view of holiness demanded that the human first-born should be redeemed, by the substitution of an animal victim (Gen. xxii.); and from this usage, again, the Moloch sacrifices were easily developed in the seventh century, when ordinary means seemed too weak to conjure the divine anger.

In the Passover we find the sacrifice of firstlings assuming the form of an annual feast, in the spring season. Such a combination is possible only when the yeaning time falls in spring. So far as sheep are concerned, there were two lambing times in ancient Italy, some sheep yeaning in spring, others in autumn. That the same thing was true of Palestine may perhaps be inferred from the old versions of Gen. xxx. 41, 42.[1] But in Arabia all cattle, small and great, yean in the season of the spring pasture, so that here we have the necessary condition for a spring sacrifice of firstlings,[2] and also a reason, more conclusive than the assertion of the *Lisān* (*supra*, p. 228), for identifying the Arabian Rajab sacrifices with the sacrifice of firstlings.

[1] Not from the text itself; cf. Bochart, Pars I. Lib. ii. cap. 46.

[2] Doughty, *Arabia Deserta*, i. 429; Blunt, *Bedouin Tribes*, ii. 166: "The calving time for camels is in February and early March." Of course there are exceptions to this rule; but the *ṣaifī* or summer foal is held by the Arabs to be a weakling (*Ḥamāsa*, p. 389, l. 25).

30

ADDITIONAL NOTE F (p. 294)

SACRIFICES OF SACRED ANIMALS

IN the text I have spoken only of animals corresponding to Julian's definition of the creatures suited for mystical piacula, viz. that they were such as were ordinarily excluded from human diet. But there are other animals which, though not strictly forbidden food in the times of which we have record, retained a certain reputation of natural holiness, which gave them a peculiar virtue when used in sacrifice. Of course, when the sacredness of an animal species ceases to be marked by the definite taboos that we find in the case of the swine, the dog, or the dove, the proof that it was once held to be holy in a particular religious circle becomes dependent on circumstantial evidence, and more or less vague. But it seems worth while to cite one or two examples in which the point can be fairly well made out, or at least made sufficiently probable to deserve further examination.

1. Deer and antelopes of various kinds were sacred animals in several parts of the Semitic field; see *Kinship*, p. 227 *sq.* They were not, indeed, forbidden food, but they had special relations to various deities. Troops of sacred gazelles occur down to a late date at sanctuaries, *e.g.* at Mecca and Tabāla (Wellh. p. 106), and in the island spoken of by Arrian, vii. 20. Moreover, stags or gazelles occur as sacred symbols in South Arabia, in connection with ʿAthtar-worship; at Mecca, probably in connection with the worship of Al-ʿOzzā; and in Phœnicia, both on gems and on coins of Laodicea ad Mare. Further, Ibn Mojāwir speaks of a South Arab tribe which, when a gazelle was found dead, solemnly buried it and mourned for seven days (see p. 444).

No kind of wild quadruped was an ordinary sacrificial animal among the Semites, and even the Arabs regard a gazelle as a mean substitute for a sheep; but in certain rituals we find the stag or gazelle as an exceptional sacrifice. The most notable case is the annual stag sacrifice at Laodicea on the Phœnician coast, which was regarded as a substitute for a more ancient sacrifice of a maiden, and was offered to a goddess whom Porphyry calls Athena (*De Abst.* ii. 56), while Pausanias (iii. 16. 8) identifies her with the Brauronian Artemis, and supposes that the cult was introduced by Seleucus. But the town (Ramitha in Phœnician, according to Philo, *ap.* Steph. Byz.) is much older than its re-christening by Seleucus, and if the goddess had really been Greek, she would not have been identified with Athena as well as with Artemis. She was, in fact, a form of Astarte, the ancient Tyche of the city, who, according to the usual manner of the later euhemeristic Syrians, was supposed to have been a virgin, immolated when the city was founded, and thereafter worshipped as a deity (Malalas, p. 203). Here, therefore, we have one of the many legends of the death of a deity which are grafted on a rite of annual human sacrifice, or on the annual sacrifice of a sacred animal, under circumstances that showed its life to be taken as having the value of a human life on the one hand, or of the life of the deity on the other. The stag, whose death has such significance, is a theanthropic victim, exactly as in the mystic sacrifices discussed in the text.

Of the stag or gazelle as a Phœnician sacrifice we have further evidence from Philo Byblius (Euseb., *Pr. Ev.* i. 10. 10) in the legend of the god Usous, who first taught men to clothe themselves in the skins of beasts taken in hunting, and to pour out their blood sacrificially before sacred stones. This god was worshipped at the sanctuary he instituted, at an annual feast, and doubtless with the ceremonies he himself devised, *i.e.* with libations of the blood of a deer or antelope—for these are the important kinds of game in the district of the Lebanon—presented by worshippers clad in deer-skins. The wearing of the skin of the victim, as we have seen at p. 438, is characteristic of mystical and piacular rites. Most scholars, from Scaliger downwards, have compared Usous with Esau; but it has not been observed that the scene of Isaac's blessing, where his son must first approach him with the savoury flesh of a gazelle, has all the air of a sacrificial scene. Moreover, Jacob, who substitutes kids for gazelles, wears their skin upon his arms and neck. The goat, which here appears as a substitute for the game offered by the huntsman Esau, was one of the chief Hebrew piacula, if not the chief of all. In Babylonia and Assyria also it has an exceptional place among sacrifices; see the representation in Menant, *Glyptique*, vol. i. p. 146 *sqq.*, vol. ii. p. 68. What is obsolete in common life often survives in poetic phrase and metaphor, and I am tempted to see in the opening words of David's dirge on Saul ("The gazelle, O Israel, is slain on thy high places," 2 Sam. i. 19) an allusion to some ancient sacrifice of

similar type to that which so long survived at Laodicea. The
sacred deer of Icarus, according to Arrian, could only be taken
for sacrifice.

2. The wild ass was eaten by the Arabs, and must have been
eaten with a religious intention, since its flesh was forbidden to
his converts by Symeon the Stylite. Conversely, among the
Harranians the ass was forbidden food, like the swine and the
dog; but there is no evidence that, like these animals, it was
sacrificed or eaten in exceptional mysteries. Yet when we
find one section of Semites forbidden to eat the ass, while
another section eats it in a way which to Christians appears
idolatrous, the presumption that the animal was anciently sacred
becomes very strong. An actual ass-sacrifice appears in Egypt
in the worship of Typhon (Set or Sutech), who was the chief
god of the Semites in Egypt, though Egyptologists doubt whether
he was originally a Semitic god. The ass was a Typhonic animal,
and in certain religious ceremonies the people of Coptus sacrificed
asses by casting them down a precipice, while those of Lycopolis,
in two of their annual feasts, stamped the figure of a bound ass
on their sacrificial cakes (Plut., *Is. et Os.* § 30); see, for the
meaning of these cakes, *supra*, pp. 225, note 3, 240, note 1; and
for sacrifice by casting from a precipice, *supra*, pp. 374, 418. Both
forms indicate a mystic or piacular rite, and stand on one line
with the holocausts of living men to Typhon mentioned by
Manetho (*ibid.* § 73). If it could be made out that these rites
were really of Semitic origin, the ass would be a clear case of
an ancient mystic piaculum within our field; but meantime the
matter must rest doubtful. It may, however, be noted that the
old clan name Hamor ("he-ass") among the Canaanites in
Shechem, seems to confirm the view that the ass was sacred
with some of the Semites; and the fables of ass-worship among
the Jews (on which compare Bochart, *Hierozoicon*, Pars I. Lib.
ii. cap. 18) probably took their rise, like so many other false
statements of a similar kind, in a confusion between the Jews
and their heathen neighbours. As regards the eating of wild
asses' flesh by the Arabs, I have not found evidence in Arabic
literature that in the times before Mohammed it had any religious
meaning, though Cazwīnī tells us that its flesh and hoofs supplied
powerful charms, and this is generally a relic of sacrificial use.
On the religious associations of the ass in classical antiquity, and
the uses of the ass's head as a charm, see the *Compte-rendu de la*

Comm. Imp. Archéol. (St. Petersburg) for 1863, and the *Berichte d. sächs. Ges. d. Wiss.*, 1854, p. 48.

It has been supposed that the "golden" Set, worshipped by the Semitic Hyksos in the Delta, was a Sun-god (E. Meyer, *Gesch. des Alt.* i. p. 135). If this be so, the horses of the sun may have succeeded to the older sanctity of the ass; for the ass is much more ancient than the horse in the Semitic lands.

3. To these two examples of sacred quadrupeds I am inclined to add one of a sacred bird. The quail sacrifice of the Phœnicians is said by Eudoxus (*ap.* Athen. ix. 47) to commemorate the resurrection of Heracles. But this was an annual festival at Tyre, in the month Peritius (February—March), *i.e.* just at the time when the quail returns to Palestine, immense crowds appearing in a single night (Jos., *Ant.* viii. 5. 3, compared with Tristram, *Fauna*, p. 124). An annual sacrifice of this sort, connected with a myth of the death of the god, can hardly be other than the mystical sacrifice of a sacred animal; and it is to be noted that the ancients regard quail's flesh as dangerous food, producing vertigo and tetanus, while on the other hand an ointment made from the brain is a cure for epilepsy (Bochart, II. i. 15). Lagarde (*Gr. Uebers. der Provv.* p. 81) once proposed to connect the Arabic سماني, "quail," with the god Eshmun-Iolaos, who restored Heracles to life by giving him a quail to smell at; if this be right, the god-name must be derived from that of the bird, and not *vice versâ.*

ADDITIONAL NOTE G (p. 310)

THE SACRIFICE OF A SHEEP TO THE CYPRIAN APHRODITE

INSTEAD of a note on this subject, I here print a paper read before the Cambridge Philological Society in 1888, of which only a brief abstract has hitherto been published:—

The peculiar rite which forms the subject of the present paper is known to us from a passage in Joannes Lydus, *De Mensibus*, iv. 45, which has been often referred to by writers on ancient religion, but, so far as my reading goes, without any notice being taken of a most serious difficulty, which it seems impossible to overcome without a change of the text. Lydus in the chapter in question begins by describing the practices by which women of the higher and lower classes respectively did honour to Venus on the Calends of April. Here, of course, he is speaking of Roman usage, as is plain from the general plan of his book and from the ceremonies he specifies. The honourable women did service to Venus ὑπὲρ ὁμονοίας καὶ βίου σώφρονος. This agrees with the worship of Venus *verticordia*, the patroness of female virtue, whose worship Ovid connects with the Calends of April (*Fasti*, iv. 155 *sq.*), and Mommsen conjectures to have been mentioned under that day in the *Fasti Prœn.* Again, Lydus says that the women of the common sort bathed in the men's baths, crowned with myrtle, which agrees with Ovid (*ibid.* 139 *sq.*), Plutarch (*Numa*, c. 19), and the service of *Fortuna virilis* in the *Fast. Prœn.* The transition from this Roman worship of Venus to the Cyprian ritual of the same day, is made by a remark as to the victims proper to the goddess. Venus, he says, was worshipped with the same sacrifices as Juno, but in Cyprus πρόβατον κωδίῳ ἐσκεπασμένον συνέθυον τῇ Ἀφροδίτῃ· ὁ δὲ τρόπος τῆς ἱερατείας ἐν τῇ Κύπρῳ ἀπὸ τῆς Κορίνθου παρῆλθέ ποτε. As Lydus goes on to say that thereafter (εἶτα δέ), on the second of April, they sacrificed wild boars to the goddess, on account of the attack of that animal on Adonis, it is clear that the sacrifice of a sheep took place on the first of April, and that Engel (*Kypros*, ii. 155) entirely overlooks the context when he says that, according to Lydus, the ordinary sacrifices of Aphrodite were the same as those of Hera, but that in Cyprus a favourite sacrifice to the former goddess was a sheep with a woolly fleece. Lydus does not say that a sheep was a favourite Cyprian sacrifice to Aphrodite, but that it was the sacrifice appropriated to the first of April. The very point of the passage is that the Roman feast of the first of April appears in Cyprus with variations in detail.

This coincidence cannot be accidental, and the explanation is not far to seek. The Cyprian Aphrodite is the Semitic Astarte, and her ritual is throughout marked with a Semitic stamp. It is to Semitic ritual, therefore, that we must look for the origin of the April feast. Now, among the Syrians, Nisan is the month corresponding to April, and on the first three days of Nisan, as we learn from the *Fihrist*, the Syrians of Harran, who clung to

the ancient Astarte-worship far into the Middle Ages, visited the
temple of the goddess in groups (Lydus's σύνεθνον), offered sacrifices, and burned living animals.   The burning of living animals
answers to the ceremonies observed at Hierapolis in the great
feast of the Syrian goddess at the incoming of spring, when, as
we read in Lucian, goats, sheep and other living creatures were
suspended on a pyre, and the whole was consumed.   The feast,
therefore, is an annual spring feast of Semitic origin.   The Roman
observance was less solemn, and of a popular kind rather than
part of the State religion.   Macrobius (*Sat.* i. 12. 12–15) tells us,
indeed, that at Rome this festival was not ancient, but was introduced for an historical reason which he omits to record.   Now, a
new ritual at Rome was almost certainly a borrowed one, and
there is ample evidence (for which it is enough to refer to
Preller's *Römische Mythologie*) that the most influential centre of
Venus-worship in the West, and that which had most to do with
the development of her cult in Italy, was the great temple at
Eryx, the ארך of the Carthaginians.   From Phœnician inscriptions it is certain that the goddess of Eryx (עשתרת ארך, *CIS.*
No. 140, cf. No. 135) was Astarte; and thus it is easily understood that the Asiatic festival found its way to Rome.   A festival
so widespread, and one which held its ground so long, is well
worthy of careful examination.

When Lydus, in passing from the Roman to the Cyprian rite,
says ἐτιμᾶτο δὲ ἡ Ἀφροδίτη τοῖς αὐτοῖς οἷς καὶ ἡ Ἥρα, I cannot
find with Engel that he makes any general statement that, as a
rule, the same sacrifices were appropriate to Venus and to Juno.
Oriental worships allowed a far greater range in the choice of
victims for a single deity or temple than was customary in Greece
or Rome.   For the Carthaginian temples of Baal this appears
from extant inscriptions; and as regards Astarte-Aphrodite, Tacitus
(*Hist.* iii. 2) tells us that at Paphos, and Ælian (*Nat. An.* x. 50)
that at Eryx, the worshipper chose any kind of sacrifice he pleased.
This liberty, which was evidently surprising to the Romans and
the Greeks, was probably due to the syncretism which established
itself at an early date at all the great Semitic sanctuaries; one
deity, as we see in the case of Hierapolis, combining a number of
characters which originally belonged to different gods, and uniting
at a single temple a corresponding variety of ancient rituals.
Such syncretism was probably very ancient among the cosmopolitan Phœnicians; and throughout the Semitic world it received

a great impulse by the breaking up of the old small States through Assyrian, Babylonian and Persian conquests. The political and religious cosmopolitanism of the East under the Macedonians rested on a basis which had been prepared centuries before.

In the West no such powerful political agencies were at work to develop an early tendency to syncretism, nor was it so easy tc confound the well-marked individualities of the Western Pantheon as to combine the hazy personalities of different Baals or Astartes. When the need for cosmopolitan forms of worship arose, Eastern gods and rituals were borrowed, as in the case of Sarapis; and the old acknowledged worships still retained their individual peculiarities. It is known that neither Juno nor Hera admitted such a free choice of victims for her shrine as was permitted at Eryx and Paphos. Their ordinary sacrifice was a cow; for, like other goddesses, they preferred victims of their own sex (Arnobius, vii. 19). But, so far as the Oriental Aphrodite had a preference, it was for male victims. So Tacitus tells us for Paphos, and Plautus also in the *Pœnulus* has " sex agnos immolavi Veneri." This preference was presumably connected with the androgynous character ascribed to the Eastern goddess in Cyprus and elsewhere, and of itself is sufficient to separate her sacrifices, as a whole, from those of Juno and Hera.[1] Besides, the favourite victim of Aphrodite was the goat (Tac. *Hist.* iii. 2), which, except at Sparta (Pausanias, iii. 15. 9) and in the annual piacular sacrifice of Hera Acræa at Corinth (Hesychius, *s.v.* αἲξ αἴγα; Zenobius on the same proverb; Schol. on Eurip., *Medea*), was excluded from the altars of Hera. Juno has relations to the goat at Lanuvium, but at Rome her cultus was closely related to that of Jupiter, from whose offerings the goat was strictly excluded (Arnobius, vii. 21).

I have perhaps spent too much time on this argument, for surely the context itself is sufficient to show that Lydus is not speaking of Venus-worship in general. What he says is that on the Calends of April—a special occasion—Venus was worshipped at Rome with the sacrifices of Juno. And as he is speaking of a ritual in which the worshippers were women, I think we may gc a step further, and recall the fact that the Calends of every month were sacred to Juno Lucina, to whom on that day the *regina*

---

[1] The preference for male victims seems, however, to have other connec-tions also; see p. 299, *supra*.

sacrorum offered in the Regia a sow or ewe-lamb (Macrob. i. 15. 19). The functions of Lucina, as the patroness of virtuous matrons and the family life of women, were so nearly identical with those of Venus *verticordia*, that their sacrifices might well be the same. And if this be so, it was natural for Lydus to pass on as he does to a remark on the Cyprian ritual, where the same sacrifices occur with characteristic variations. The sex of the victims is different, for a reason already explained, and the sacrifices are divided between two days. But the victims are still the sheep and the pig, so that the fundamental identity of the Roman and the Eastern service of the day receives fresh confirmation.

So far all is plain; but now we come to the unsolved difficulty. It lies in the phrase πρόβατον κωδίῳ ἐσκεπασμένον. These words describe the characteristic peculiarity, for the sake of which our author turns aside to mention the Cyprian rite, and it seems to be in relation to this feature that he observes that "the manner of the priestly service" was derived from Corinth. Unfortunately we know nothing of the Corinthian ritual referred to. The Corinthian Aphrodite-worship was Oriental in type, and any feature in it which reappears at Cyprus is almost certainly Phœnician. That Cyprus borrowed from Corinth is far less likely than that both borrowed from the East, and the authority of Lydus is not enough to outweigh this probability. The allusion to Corinth, however, is of value as teaching us that the peculiar rite was not merely local; and further, the allusion to "priestly service" shows that the sacrifice in question—as indeed is implied in the word συνέθυον—was not a private offering, but a public rite performed at a great temple. But this does not explain the words κωδίῳ ἐσκεπασμένον. It is plain that the meaning cannot be "a sheep with a woolly fleece," as Engel renders, nor does it seem possible to understand with the Duc de Luynes (*Num. et Insc. Cypr.* p. 6), "un bélier couvert de toute sa toison." If the words could bear this meaning, the rendering would be plausible enough, for we have seen that in the Syrian form of the festival the victims were given to the flames alive. But if Lydus had meant that the victim was consumed by fire, skin and all, he would have given κωδίῳ the article, and would have used a more precise word than συνέθυον. And can κώδιον be used of the sheep-skin on the sheep, or ἐσκεπασμένον of the natural coat? The plain sense of the words is that the sheep was wrapped in a sheep-skin when it was presented for sacrifice, not that its skin was left upon it, or wrapped round the sacrificial flesh before it was laid on the altar.

If the skin had been that of a different kind of animal, we might have explained the rite by the same principle of make-believe which we find in the Roman offering of the *cervaria ovis*, the sheep that was made to pass for a stag; for the ordinary meaning of skin-wearing in early religion is to simulate identification with the animal whose skin is worn. But to wrap a sheep in a sheep-skin is like gilding gold. I propose therefore to change a single letter, and read ἐσκεπασμένοι, a change which produces a sense good in itself and strongly recommended by the context and by analogy.

The significance of the κώδιον or sheep-skin in ancient ritual has been illustrated by Lobeck in his *Aglaophamus*, and by Preller in his commentary on Polemo. It always appears in connection with atoning and mystic rites, and in the majority of Greek examples the practice appears to have been that the person to be purged of guilt set his feet, or his left foot, upon the skin of a sacrificed ram. But this was not the only way of using the κώδιον. In Thessaly there was, according to Dicæarchus, a ceremony, observed at the greatest heat of summer, in which the worshippers ascended Mount Pelion to the temple of Zeus Acræus, clad in new sheep-skins (*Fr. Hist. Gr.* ii. 262). When Pythagoras was purified by the priests of Morgus in Crete, he was made to lie beside water (the sea by day, the river by night), wrapped in the fleece of a black lamb, and descended to the tomb of Zeus clad in black wool (Porph., *Vita Pyth.* § 17). Again, the first sacrifice of every worshipper at Hierapolis was a sheep. Having partaken of the flesh, the sacrificer laid the skin on the ground, and knelt on it, taking up the feet and head over his own head. In this posture he besought the deity to accept his offering. Here it is evident that the ceremony expresses the identification of the sacrificer with the victim. He has taken its flesh into his body, and he covers himself with its skin. It is, as it were, the idea of substitution turned outside in. The direct symbolism of vicarious sacrifice, where an animal's life is accepted in place of the life of a human being, is to treat the victim as if it were a man. At Tenedos, for example, the bull-calf sacrificed to Bacchus wears the cothurnus, and the mother cow is treated like a woman in child-bed. But in our case the symbolism is inverted; instead of making believe that the victim is a man, the ritual makes believe that the man is the victim, and so brings the atoning force of the sacrifice into immediate application to him.

It is evident that if this kind of symbolism be applied, not to purification of an individual, but to a general and public atoning service, the priests, as the representatives of the community on whose behalf the rite is performed, are the persons to whom the skin of the victim must be applied.   And if there are many priests and only one victim, it will be convenient not to use the actual skin of the sacrifice, which only one can wear at a time, but to clothe all the ministers in skins of the same kind.   This, according to my conjecture, is what was done in Cyprus.   And here I would ask whether the context, which alludes to the manner of the priestly service, does not show that some reference to the priests has been already made or implied.   Such a reference the proposed emendation supplies.

Upon this view of the passage it is necessarily involved that the rite described was expiatory.   And that it was so seems to appear from several arguments.   The sacrifice of the following day consisted in wild boars, and was explained in connection with the Adonis myth, so that its Semitic origin is not doubtful. Even in Greece the pig is the great purificatory sacrifice ; but in Semitic religion the offering of this animal is not a mere ordinary *piaculum*, but a mystic rite of the most exceptional kind (*supra*, p. 290).   Now, if the sacrifice of the second day of the feast was mystic, and therefore piacular in the highest degree, we may be sure that the first day's sacrifice was no ordinary sacrificial meal of a joyous character.   For a man must first be purified, and then sit down gladly at the table of the gods, and not conversely. Again, the Syrian and Roman rites, which we have found reason to regard as forms of the same observance, were plainly piacular or purificatory.   In Rome we have the women bathing, which is a form of lustration, and wearing myrtle, which had purifying virtues, for it was with myrtle twigs that the Romans and Sabines in the time of Romulus purged themselves at the temple of Venus Cloacina (Preller, *Röm. Myth.* 3rd ed., i. 439).   And in the Syrian rite, where animals are burnt alive to the goddess, the atoning nature of the sacrifice is unmistakable, and the idea of a mere sacrificial feast is entirely excluded.

A further argument for the atoning character of the rite may be derived from the choice of the victim, for next to the swine the ram was perhaps the commonest sin-offering in antiquity (cf

Hesychius, *s.v.* Ἀφροδισία ἄγρα); so much so, that Stephani, in the *Compte-rendu,* 1869, p. 130 *sqq.*, explains the frequent occurrence of rams' heads and the like in ancient ornament as derived from the association of the animal with the power of averting calamity. Such ornaments are in fact ἀποτρόπαια. It is always dangerous to apply general arguments of this kind to the interpretation of a particular ritual; for the same victim may be an atoning sacrifice in one rite and an ordinary sacrifice in another, and it by no means follows that because, for example, a piacular bull was offered to Zeus, the same piaculum would be appropriate to the Eastern Aphrodite. But in the case of the sheep used as a sin-offering, we have evidence that there was no limitation to a single deity; for when Epimenides was brought to Athens to check the plague, he suffered black and white sheep to stray at will from the Areopagus, and ordered each to be sacrificed, where it lay down, to the nameless deity of the spot (Diog. Laert. i. 10). This form of atonement came from Crete, which was one of the stepping-stones by which Oriental influence reached Greece, so that the example is the more appropriate to our present argument. And that, in point of fact, sheep or rams were offered as piacular sacrifices at the altars of the Eastern Aphrodite, seems to follow from the Hierapolitan ritual already mentioned. The same thing is implied for Carthage in the *Pœnulus* of Plautus, where the sacrifice of six male lambs is directed to propitiate the angry goddess.

These considerations will, I hope, be found sufficient to justify my general view of the Cyprian rite, and to support the proposed correction of the text. The sacrifice was piacular, and the κώδιον was therefore appropriate to the ritual; but on the received text the use of it is entirely unintelligible, whereas the correction ἐσκεπασμένοι restores a sense which gives to this feature the same character as it possesses in analogous ceremonies. But the most interesting aspect of the ceremony is only brought out when we connect it with a fact which I have hitherto kept in the background, because its significance depends on a theory of piacular and mystic sacrifice which is not yet generally accepted. A sheep, or a sheep's head, is a religious symbol of constant occurrence on Cyprian coins; and some of these coins show us a figure, which experts declare to be that of Aphrodite, clinging to the neck and fleece of a running ram. This device has been compared with others, which appear to be Eastern though not Cyprian, in which Aphrodite rides on a ram (see De Luynes, *Num. Cypr.* Pl. v. 3, vi. 5, and the references in Stephani, *Compte-rendu* for 1869, p. 87). The inference is that in Cyprus the sheep was the sacred animal of Aphrodite-Astarte. In this connection it is important to note that the sheep is of frequent occurrence on Semitic votive cippi of the class dedicated to Tanith (a form of Astarte) and Baal-Ḥammān. Examples will be found in *CIS.* Pt. I. Nos. 398, 419, and in a cippus from Sulci, figured in Perrot and Chipiez, iii. 253. The figures on this class of cippi are of various kinds, and sometimes convey allusions to sacrifices (*CIS.* p. 282 *sq.*), but it appears to have been essential to introduce a figure or symbol of the deity. And when animals are figured, they appear to be such symbols. Thus we find fish, which are known to have been sacred to Astarte, and forbidden food to her worshippers ; a bull or cow couching, the symbol of the Sidonian Astarte ; the elephant, which was not a sacrifice ; the horse, which appears so often on the coins of Carthage, and is certainly a divine symbol, as it is sometimes winged. On these analogies I conclude that among the Carthaginians, as in Cyprus, the sheep was sacred to and symbolic of Astarte. To speak quite exactly, one ought to say to a particular type of Astarte ; for as this goddess, in the progress of syncretism so characteristic of Semitic religion, absorbed a great number of local types, she had a corresponding multiplicity of sacred animals, each of which was prominent at particular sanctuaries or in particular rites. Thus the dove-Aphrodite is specially associated with Ascalon, and the Cow-goddess with Sidon, where she was identified with Europa, the bride of the bull-Zeus (*Dea Syria*, iv.), and, according to Philo Byblius, placed the head of a bull upon her own. The sheep-Astarte is another type, but it also seems to have its original home in Canaan, for in Deut. vii. 13 the produce of the flock is called "the Ashtaroth of the sheep." A phrase like this, which has descended from religion into ordinary life, and is preserved among the monotheistic Hebrews, is very old evidence for the association of Astarte with the sheep ; and it is impossible to explain it except by frankly admitting that Astarte, in one of her types, had originally the form of a sheep, and was a sheep herself, just as in other types she was a dove or a fish.

To this it may be objected that the ram or sheep is not the symbol of Tanith, but of the associated male deity Baal-Ḥammān, who in a terra-cotta of the Barre collection (Perrot et Chipiez, iii,

73) is represented with ram's horns, and laying his hand on the head of a sheep. But the inscription (*CIS*. No. 419), cited above, is dedicated to Tanith, not to Tanith and Baal-Ḥammān conjointly, from which it appears that the accompanying symbol was appropriate to the goddess as well as to her male partner.

It is reasonable that the same animal symbol should belong to the male and female members of a syzygy; and in the case of a goddess who was often represented as androgynous, it is not even necessary to suppose that her symbol would be the ewe and her partner's the ram. But in fact the sheep-symbols on the Tanith cippi, which are commonly called rams, are hornless, and so presumably stand for ewes. On the other hand, all wild sheep and many domestic breeds are horned in both sexes, so that there is no difficulty about a horned Sheep-goddess. The triangle surmounted by a circle, with horns bent outwards, which is commonly found on Tanith cippi, is probably a symbol of the god or the goddess indifferently. And here the horns, being concave outwards, can neither be bull's horns nor the horns of the crescent moon, but must be the horns of sheep.

The Cypriote coins of Aphrodite, in which she clings in a swimming attitude to a running ram, recall the legend of Helle and the golden ram, but they also are obviously parallel to the type of Europa and the bull. On this analogy we ought to remember that the male god specially associated with the ram is Hermes, and that the Cyprian goddess was worshipped in an androgynous form, to which Theophrastus gives the name of Hermaphroditus. I have already cited this androgynous character to explain why the Paphian (and apparently the Punic) Aphrodite preferred male victims; it now supplies an additional reason for supposing that it was the androgynous or bearded Astarte that was specially connected with the ram. On one of the cippi already cited, in which Tanith is figured under the symbol of a sheep (*CIS*. 419), the inscription is not, as usually, "to the Lady Tanith," but "to my Lord Tanith." If this is not a sculptor's error it points in the same direction. And it seems not unlikely that the standing title, תנת פן בעל, which has given rise to so much discussion, means nothing more than Tanith with Baal's face—the bearded goddess.

If, now, the Cyprian goddess was a Sheep-deity, our rite presents us with a piacular sacrifice in which priests, disguised as sheep, offer to the Sheep-goddess an animal of her own kind. The ceremony, therefore, is exactly parallel to the Roman Lupercalia, a purificatory sacrifice to Faunus under the name of Lupercus. The image of Lupercus at the Lupercal was naked, and was clad in a goat-skin (Justin, xliii. 1. 7). Here, at the great lustration of 15th February, the Luperci, who have the same name as their god, sacrifice goats and run about the city naked, daubed with mud and girt with goat-skins, applying to the women who desire to participate in the benefits of the rite strokes of thongs which were cut from the skins of the victims, and were called *februa.* Both sacrifices are complete types of that most ancient form of sacramental and piacular mystery in which the worshippers attest their kinship with the animal-god, and offer in sacrifice an animal of the same kind, which, except on these mystical occasions, it would be impious to bring upon the altar.

ADDITIONAL NOTE H (p. 315)

FURTHER REMARKS ON THE BLOOD COVENANT

AN evidence for the survival among the Arabs of the form of covenant described by Herodotus, in which blood is drawn from the parties themselves, seems to lie in the expression *miḥāsh,* "scarified," for "confederates" (Nābigha, xxiv. 1, ed. Ahlw. = xvii. 1, ed. Derenb.). Goldziher, in an interesting review of my *Kinship* (*Litbl.f. or. Phil.* 1886, p. 25 [see *Kin.*[2] 58, n.1]), thinks the term properly means "the burnt ones," which is the traditional interpretation, and suggests that we have in it an example of a covenant by fire, such as Jauharī (see Wellh.[1] p. 124) and Nowairī (Rasm., *Add.* p. 75, l. 11 *sqq.*) speak of under the head of *nār al-ḥūla.* It does not, however, seem that in the latter case the fire touched the parties; what we are told is that every tribe had a sacred fire, and that, when two men (obviously two tribesmen) had a dispute, they were made to swear beside the fire, while the priests cast salt on it. An oath by ashes and salt is mentioned by Al-Aʿshā in a line cited by Wellhausen from *Agh.* xx. 139, and as the ashes of the cooking pot (*ramād al-cidr*) are a metonym for hospitality, there is perhaps nothing more in the

oath by fire and salt than an appeal to the bond of common food
that unites tribesmen. This does not indeed fully account for
the fact that the fire is called " the fire of terror," and that the
poetical references to it show the oath to have really been a terrible
one, *i.e.* dangerous to the man that perjured himself ; but it is to
be remembered that, according to Arabian belief, a man who
broke an oath of purgation was likely to die by divine judgment
(Bokhārī, iv. 219 *sq.*, viii. 40 *sq.*). I think, therefore, that in
the present state of the evidence we must not attempt to connect
the *miḥāsh* with the *nār al-hūla*. If the former term really means
"burnt ones," we must rather suppose that the reference is to the
practice of branding with the tribal mark or *wasm* (which is also
called *nār*, Rasm., *Add.* p. 76) ; for we learn from *Agh.* vii. 110,
l. 26, that the *wasm* was sometimes applied to men as well as to
cattle. But مكهش primarily means "to scarify," and as it is
plain from the article in the *Lisān* that the traditional explanation
of the word was uncertain, I take it that the best and most
natural view is to interpret *miḥāsh* as " scarified ones."

In process of time the Arabs came to use various substitutes
for the blood of covenant, *e.g.* *robb*, *i.e.* inspissated fruit juice
(or perhaps the lees of clarified butter), perfumes, and even holy
water from a sacred spring (*Kinship*, p. 259 ; Wellh.[1] p. 121).
In all these cases we can still see that there was something about
the substitute which made it an equivalent for blood. As regards
"living water," this is obvious from what has been said in Lecture
V. p. 173 *sqq.* on the holiness of sacred springs. Again, perfumes
were habitually used in the form of unguents ; and unguents—
primarily sacred suet—are equivalent to blood, as has appeared in
Lecture X. p. 383 *sqq.* If *robb* in this connection means lees of
butter, the use of it in covenant making is explained by the
sacredness of unguents ; but if, as the traditions imply, it is fruit
juice, we must remember that, in other cases also, vegetable juices
are looked upon as a kind of blood (*supra*, pp. 133, 230). Compare what Lydus, *De mensibus*, iv. 29, says of the use of bean
juice for blood in a Roman ceremony, with the explanation that
the bean (κύαμος) κύει αἷμα: the whole passage is notable, and
helps to explain the existence of a bean-clan, the *gens Fabia*, at
Rome ; cf. also the Attic hero Κυαμίτης.

The Hebrew phrase כרת ברית, "to make (*literally*, to cut) a
covenant," is generally derived from the peculiar form of sacrifice
mentioned in Gen. xv., Jer. xxxiv. 18, where the victim is cut in

twain and the parties pass between the pieces; and this rite again is explained as a symbolic form of imprecation, as if those who ★ swore to one another prayed that, if they proved unfaithful, they might be similarly cut in pieces. But this does not explain the characteristic feature in the ceremony—the passing between the pieces; and, on the other hand, we see from Ex. xxiv. 8, "this is the blood of the covenant which Jehovah hath cut with you," that the dividing of the sacrifice and the application of the blood to both parties go together. The sacrifice presumably was divided into two parts (as in Ex. *l.c.* the blood is divided into two parts), when both parties joined in eating it; and when it ceased to be eaten, the parties stood between the pieces, as a symbol that they were taken within the mystical life of the victim. This interpretation is confirmed by the usage of Western nations, who practised the same rite with dogs and other extraordinary victims, as an atoning or purificatory ceremony; see the examples collected by Bochart, *Hierozoicon*, lib. ii. capp. 33, 56. There are many examples of a sacrifice being carried, or its blood sprinkled, round the place or persons to which its efficacy is to extend.

ADDITIONAL NOTE I (p. 333)

THE TABOOS INCIDENT TO PILGRIMAGES AND VOWS

THE subject of the taboos, or sacred restrictions, imposed on a pilgrim or other votary, is important enough to deserve a detailed examination. These restrictions are sometimes optional, so that they have to be expressed when the vow is taken; at other times they are of the nature of fixed and customary rules, to which every one who takes a vow is subject. To the latter class belong, *e.g.* the restrictions imposed upon every Arab pilgrim—he must not cut or dress his hair, he must abstain from sexual intercourse, and from bloodshed and so forth; to the former class belong the special engagements to which the Hebrews give the name of *ĕsār* or *issār* (obligatio), *e.g.* Ps. cxxxii. 3 *sq.*, "I will not enter my house or sleep on my bed until," etc.; Acts xxiii. 14, "We will not eat until we have killed Paul." It is to be observed that

31

restrictions of the optional class are evidently more modern than
the other, and only come in when the fixity of ancient custom
begins to break down; in old Arabia it was the rule that one
who was engaged on a blood-feud must abstain from women,
wine and unguents, but in the time of the prophet we find these
abstinences made matter of special engagements, e.g. Wācidī, ed.
Kremer, 182. 6 = Ibn Hishām, 543. 8; *Agh.* vi. 99. 24, 30. Where
the engagement is optional, it naturally assumes the character of
an incentive to prompt discharge of the vow; the votary stimulates
his own zeal by imposing on himself abstinence from certain of the
comforts of life till his task is discharged; see Marzūcī as quoted
by Reiske, Abulfeda, vol. i. p. 18 of the *Adnotationes*, where the
phrase *mā taktarithu 'l-nafsu bihi* may be compared with the אסר
נפש לעֲנוֹת of Num. xxx. 14. But the stated abstinences which go
as a matter of course with certain vows cannot be explained on
this principle, and when they are examined in detail it becomes
manifest that they are simply taboos incident to a state of consecration, the same taboos, in fact, which are imposed, without a
vow, on everyone who is engaged in worship or priestly service
in the sanctuary, or even everyone who is present in the holy
place. Thus the Hebrew Nazarite was required to abstain from
wine, and from uncleanness due to contact with the dead, and
the same rules applied to priests, either generally or when they
were on service (Lev. x. 9, xxi. 1 *sqq.*). Again, the taboo on
sexual intercourse which lay on the Arabian pilgrim applies,
among the Semites generally, to everyone who is engaged in
an act of worship or present in a holy place (see above, p. 454);
and the prohibition of bloodshed, and therefore also of hunting
and killing game, is only an extension of the general rule that
forbids bloodshed on holy ground. Further, when the same
taboos that attach to a pilgrim apply also to braves on the war-
path, and especially to men who are under a vow of blood-
revenge (*Diw. Hodh.* cvi. 14), it is to be remembered that with
the Semites, and indeed with all primitive peoples, war is a sacred
function, and the warrior a consecrated person (cf. pp. 402, 455).
The Arabic root *ḥalla* (Heb. חלל) applied to the discharge (*lit.* the
untying) of a vow, is the same which is regularly used of emergence from a state of taboo (the *iḥrām*, the *'idda* of widowhood,
etc.) into ordinary life.

     Wellhausen observes that the Arabic *nadhara* and the Hebrew
נזר both mean primarily "to consecrate." In an ordinary vow a

man consecrates some material thing, in the vow of pilgrimage or war he consecrates himself for a particular purpose. The Arabs have but one root to express both forms of vow, but in Hebrew and Syriac the root is differentiated into two: נדר, نذر, "to vow," but נזיר, ܢܙܪ, "a consecrated person." The Syriac *nĕzīr*, notwithstanding its medial *z*, is not a mere loan-word from the Old Testament, but is applied, for example, to maidens consecrated to the service of Belthis (Is. Ant. i. 212, l. 130).

In the case of pilgrimage, it seems that the votary consecrates himself by devoting his hair, which is part of himself, as an offering at the sanctuary. Whether the consecration of the warrior was originally effected in the same way, and the discharge of the vow accomplished by means of a hair-offering, can only be matter of conjecture, but is at least not inconceivable. If it was so, the deity to whom the hair was dedicated must have been the kindred god of the clan, who alone, in primitive religion, could be conceived as interested in the avenging of the tribal blood; and we may suppose that the hair-offering of the warriors took place in connection with the "sacrifice of the home-comers," to be spoken of in Note M, *infra*. It must, however, be observed that all over the world the head and hair of persons under taboo are peculiarly sacred and inviolable, and that the primitive notions about the hair as a special seat of life, which have been spoken of at p. 324, are quite sufficient to account for this, without reference to the hair-offering, which is only one out of many applications of these ideas. It is easy, for example, to understand why, if an important part of the life resides in the hair, a man whose whole life is consecrated—*e.g.* a Maori chief, or the Flamen Dialis, or in the Semitic field such a person as Samuel or Samson—should either be forbidden to cut his hair at all, or should be compelled, when he does so, to use special precautions against the profanation of the holy growth. From Ezek. xliv. 20 we may conclude that some Semitic priests let their hair grow unpolled, like Samuel, and that others kept it close shaved, like the priests of Egypt; both usages may be explained on a single principle, for the risk of profaning the hair could be met by not allowing it to grow at all, as well as by not allowing it to be touched. Among the Hebrews, princes as well as priests were consecrated persons, and *nazīr* sometimes means a prince, while *nezer*, "consecration," means "a diadem." As a diadem is in its origin nothing more than a fillet to confine hair that is worn long, I apprehend that in old times the hair of Hebrew princes, like that of a Maori chief, was taboo, and that Absalom's long locks (2 Sam. xiv. 26) were the mark of his political pretensions, and not of his vanity. When the hair of a Maori chief was cut, it was collected and buried in a sacred place or hung on a tree; and it is noteworthy that Absalom's hair was cut annually at the end of the year—*i.e.* in the sacred season of pilgrimage, and that it was collected and weighed, which suggests a religious rite similar to that mentioned by Herod. ii. 65.

While the general principle is clear, that the restrictions laid on persons under a vow were originally taboos, incident to a state of consecration, it is not to be supposed that we can always explain these taboos in detail; for, in the absence of direct evidence, it is often almost impossible for modern men to divine the workings of the primitive mind.

Something, however, may be said about two or three rules which seem, at first sight, to lend colour to the notion that the restrictions are properly privations, designed to prevent a man from delaying to fulfil his vow. The Syrian pilgrim, during his whole journey, was forbidden to sleep on a bed. With this rule Wellhausen compares the custom of certain Arabs, who, during the *iḥrām*, did not enter their houses by the door, but broke in from behind,—a practice which is evidently an evasive modification of an older rule that forbade the house to be entered at all. The link required to connect the Syrian and Arabian rules is supplied by Ps. cxxxii. 3, and with the latter may also be compared the refusal of Uriah to go down to his house during a campaign (2 Sam. xi. 11), and perhaps also the Hebrew usage of living in booths at the Feast of Tabernacles, to which there are many parallels in ancient religion. From the point of view of taboo, this rule is susceptible of two interpretations: it may either be a precaution against uncleanness, or be meant to prevent the house and bed from becoming taboo, and unfit for profane use, by contact with the consecrated person. In favour of the second view may be cited the custom of Tahiti, where the kings habitually abstained from entering an ordinary house, lest it should become taboo, and be lost to its owner. However this may be, the Syrian practice can hardly be separated from the case of priests like the Selli at Dodona, who were ἀνιπτόποδες χαμαιεῦναι, nor the rule against entering a house from the similar restriction imposed on the religious order of the Rechabites (Jer. xxxv. 9 *sq.*). The

Rechabites, like the Nazarites and Arabian votaries, abstained also from wine, and the same abstinence was practised by Egyptian priests (Porph., *De Abst.* iv. 6) and by the Pythagoreans, whose whole life was surrounded by a network of taboos. These parallels leave no doubt that the rule of abstinence is not an arbitrary privation, but a taboo incident to the state of consecration. From Judg. xiii. 4 it would seem that fermented drinks fall into the same class with unclean meats ; compare the prohibition of ferments in sacrifice. Again, the Arabian rule against washing or anointing the head is not ascetic, but is simply a consequence from the inviolability of the head, which must not be touched in a way that might detach hairs. The later Arabs did not fully understand these rules, as appears from the variations of the statements by different authorities about one and the same vow ; cf., for example, the references given at the beginning of this note for the vow of Abū Sofyān. Finally, the peculiar dress prescribed to the Arabian pilgrim is no doubt a privation to the modern Moslem, but the dress is really nothing else than the old national garb of Arabia, which became sacred under the influence of religious conservatism, combined with the principle already explained (*supra*, p. 451), that a man does not perform a sacred function in his everyday clothes, for fear of making them taboo.

ADDITIONAL NOTE K (pp. 379, 384)

THE ALTAR AT JERUSALEM

THAT there was always an altar of some kind before the temple at Jerusalem might be taken for granted, even without the express mention of it in 2 Kings xi. 11, xii. 9 [10], (1 Kings viii. 22, 54) ; but this passage throws no light on the nature of the altar. Let us consider separately (*a*) the altar of burnt-offering, (*b*) the brazen altar.

(*a*) According to 1 Kings x. 25, Solomon *built* an altar of burnt-offering, and offered on it three times a year. A built altar is an altar of stone, such as Ahaz's altar and the altar of the second temple were. There is no other trace of the existence of

such an altar before the time of Ahaz, and the verse, which is
omitted by the Septuagint, belongs to a series of fragmentary
notices, which form no part of the original narrative of Solomon's
reign, and are of various dates and of uncertain authority. Apart
from this passage, we first read of a built altar in 2 Kings xvi.,
viz. that which Ahaz erected on the model of the altar (*i.e.* the
chief altar) at Damascus. Ahaz's innovation evidently proved
permanent, for the altar of the second temple was also a platform
of stone. According to the Massoretic text of 2 Kings xvi. 14, as
it is usually translated, a brazen altar was removed to make way
for Ahaz's altar, but this sense is got by straining a corrupt text;
ויקרב cannot govern the preceding accusative, and to get sense we
must either omit ואת המזבח at the beginning of the verse or read
על for את. The former course, which has the authority of the
LXX., seems preferable; but in either case it follows that we must
point וַיִּקְרַב, and that the whole verse is an elaborate description
of the new ritual introduced by the king. The passage in fact
now runs thus (ver. 12): "The king went up upon the new altar
(ver. 13) and burned his holocaust and his cereal oblation, and
poured out his libation; and he dashed the blood of the
peace-offerings that were for himself against the altar (ver. 14) of
brass that was before Jehovah, and drew nigh from before the
naos, between the *naos* and the (new) altar (cf. Ezek. viii. 16;
Joel ii. 17) and applied it (*i.e.* some of the blood) to the northern
flank of the altar." The brazen altar, therefore, stood quite close
to the *naos*, and the new altar stood somewhat further off, presumably in the middle of the court, which since Solomon's time
had been consecrated as the place of burnt-offering. Further,
it appears that the brazen altar was essentially an altar for the
sprinkling of blood; for the king dashes the blood of his *shelāmīm*
against it before applying the blood to the new altar. But,
according to ver. 15, he ordains that in future the blood of
sacrifices shall be applied to the new or great altar, while the
brazen altar is reserved for one particular kind of offering by the
king himself (לי לבקר, E.V. "for me to inquire by"). The nature
of this offering is not clear from the words used in ver. 15, but from
ver. 14 it appears that it consisted of *shelāmīm* offered by the
king in person. In short, the old altar is not degraded but
reserved for special use; henceforth none but the king himself is
to pour sacrificial blood upon it.

(*b*) It appears, then, that the brazen altar was an ancient and sacred thing, which had existed long before Ahaz, and continued after his time. Yet there is no separate mention of a brazen altar either in the description of Solomon's temple furniture (1 Kings vii.) or in the list of brazen utensils carried off by the Chaldæans. The explanation suggested by Wellhausen (*Prolegomena*, Eng. tr., p. 44, n. 1), that the making of the brazen altar has been omitted from 1 Kings vii. by some redactor, who did not see the need of a new brazen altar in addition to that which the priestly author of the Pentateuch ascribes to Moses, does not fully meet the case, and I can see no way out of the difficulty except to suppose that the brazen altar of 2 Kings xvi. is identical with one of the two pillars Jachin and Boaz. In the old time there was no difference between an altar and a sacred stone or pillar, and the brazen pillars are simply the ancient sacred stones—which often occur in pairs—translated into metal. Quite similarly in Strabo (iii. 5. 5), the brazen pillars of Hercules at Gades, which were twelve feet high, are the place at which sailors do sacrifice. Of course an altar of this type belongs properly to the old fireless type of sacrifice; but so long as the holocaust was a rare offering, it was not necessary to have a huge permanent hearth altar; it was enough to erect from time to time a pyre of wood in the middle of the court. It is true that 2 Kings xvi. speaks only of one brazen altar used for the sprinkling of the sacrificial blood, but it is intelligible that usage may have limited this function to one of the two pillars.

I am inclined therefore to think that the innovation of Ahaz lay in the erection of a permanent altar hearth, and in the introduction of the rule that in ordinary cases this new altar should serve for the blood ritual as well as for the fire ritual. One can thus understand the fulness with which the ritual of the new altar is described, for the rule of Ahaz was that which from his time forward was the law of the sanctuary of Jerusalem. I feel, however, that there still remains a difficulty as regards the burning of the fat of the *shelāmīm*, which was practised in Israel even before the royal period (1 Sam. ii. 16). In great feasts it would appear that the fat of ordinary offerings was burned, along with the holocaust, on the pavement of the court (1 Kings viii. 64), but what was done with it on other occasions it is not so easy to say. It is very noteworthy, however, that the details of the capitals of the brazen pillars are those of huge candlesticks or cressets. They had bowls (1 Kings vii. 41) like those of the golden candlestick (Zech. iv. 3), and gratings like those of an altar hearth. They seem therefore to have been built on the model of those altar candlesticks which we find represented on Phœnician monuments; see *CIS*. Pt. I. pl. 29, and Perrot and Chipiez, *Hist. de l'Art*, vol. iii. figs. 81 *sqq*. The similarity to a candlestick, which strikes us in the description of the Hebrew pillars, is also notable in the twin detached pillars which are represented on coins as standing before the temple at Paphos. See the annexed figure. Similar cressets, with worshippers before them in the act of adoration, are figured on Assyrian engraved stones; see, for example, Menant, *Glyptique Orient.* vol. ii. fig. 46. In most of the Assyrian examples it is not easy to draw the line between the candelabrum and the sacred tree crowned with a star or crescent moon. The Hebrew pillar altars had also associations with the sacred tree, as appears from their adornment of pomegranates, but so had the golden candlestick, in which the motive of the ornament was taken from the almond tree (Ex. xxxvii. 17 *sqq.*).

It seems difficult to believe that the enormous pillars of Solomon's temple, which, if the measures are not exaggerated, were twenty-seven feet high, were actually used as fire altars; but if they were, the presumption is that the cressets were fed with the suet of the sacrifices. And perhaps this is after all a less violent supposition than that the details of a Phœnician altar candelabrum were reproduced in them in a meaningless way. At any rate there can be no doubt that one type of fire altar among the Phœnicians and Assyrians was a cresset rather than a hearth, and as this type comes much nearer to the old cippus than the broad platform fitted to receive a holocaust, I fancy that it must be regarded as the oldest type of fire altar. In other words, the permanent fire altar began by adding to the sacred stone an arrangement for consuming the fat of ordinary sacrifices, at a time when holocausts were still burned on a pyre. If the word "Ariel," "hearth of El," originally meant such a pillar altar, we get rid of a serious exegetical difficulty in 2 Sam. xxiii. 20; for on this view it will appear that Benaiah's exploit was to overthrow the twin fire pillars of the national sanctuary of Moab—an act which in these days probably needed more

courage than to kill two "lion-like men," as the English Version
has it.   On the stele of Mesha (l. 12), an *Ariel* appears as something that can be moved from its place, which accords with the
view now suggested.   Compare the twin pillars of the Tyrian
Baal, one of which shone by night (Herod. ii. 44).   It will be
observed that this line of argument lends some plausibility to
Grotius's suggestion that the *ḥammānim* of Isa. xvii. 8, xxvii. 9,
etc., are πυρεῖα.

Finally, it may be noted that Amos ix. 1 becomes far more
intelligible if the altar at Bethel was a pillar crowned by a sort of
capital bearing a bowl like those at Jerusalem.   For then it will
be the altar itself that is overthrown, as the context and the
parallelism of chap. iii. 14 seem to require : "smite the capital
till the bowls ring again, and dash them in pieces on the heads
of the worshippers."

[See G. B. Gray, *Sacrifice in the Old Testament*, 130 *sqq.* (Oxford, 1925).]

ADDITIONAL NOTE L (p. 387)

HIGH PLACES

In the text of the lectures I have tried to work out the history
of the fire altar, and show how the place of slaughter and the
pyre ultimately met in the altar hearth.   In the present note I
will give some reasons for thinking that the gradual change of
view, which made the burning and not the slaughter the chief
thing in sacrifice, also left its mark in another way, by influencing
the choice of places for worship.

It has been observed in Lecture V. (p. 172) that the
sanctuaries of the Northern Semites commonly lay outside and
above the town.   This does not seem to have been the case in
Arabia, where, on the contrary, most sanctuaries seem to have
lain in moist hollows, beside wells and trees.   And even in the
Northern Semitic lands we have found traces of sanctuaries
beside fountains, beneath the towns, which were older than
the high places on the hills.   At Jerusalem the sanctity of
Gihon and En-rogel is older than that of the waterless plateau
of Zion above the town.

Now, in the discussion of the natural marks of holy places, we

saw how well-watered spots, thickets and the like, might naturally
come to be taken as sanctuaries, and we also found it to be
intelligible that mountain ranges should be holy tracts; but we
have not found any natural reason for fixing a sanctuary on a
bare and barren eminence. It is often supposed that altars were
built on such spots because they were open to the heaven, and
nearer than other points of earth to the heavenly gods; but this
explanation takes a great deal for granted that we have no right
to assume. On the other hand, if the explanation of the origin
of burnt-offering given above is correct, it is obvious that the
barren and unfrequented hill-top above a town would be one of
the most natural places to choose for burning the holocaust. In
process of time a particular point on the hill would become the
established place of burning, and, as soon as the burnt flesh began
to be regarded as a food-offering presented to the deity, the place
of burning would be itself a sanctuary. Ultimately it would
become the chief sanctuary of the town, and be fitted up with
all the ancient apparatus of sacred posts and sacrificial pillars.

That the high places, or hill sanctuaries, of the Semites were
primarily places of burnt-sacrifice cannot be proved by direct
evidence, but may, I think, be made probable, quite apart from
the argument that has just been sketched. In Arabia we read of
only one sanctuary that had "a place of burning," and this is the
hill of Cozah at Mozdalifa. Among the Hebrews the sacrifice of
Isaac takes place on a mountain (Gen. xxii. 2), and so does the
burnt-sacrifice of Gideon. The annual mourning on the mountains
at Mizpah in Gilead must have been connected with a sacrifice on
the mountains, which, like that of Laodicea, was thought to
represent an ancient human sacrifice (Judg. xi. 40). In Isa.
xv. 2 the Moabites in their distress go up to the high places to
mourn, and presumably to offer atoning holocausts. It is to offer
burnt-sacrifice that Solomon visits the high place at Gibeon
(1 Kings iii. 4), and in general, קטר, "to burn sacrificial flesh"
(not as E.V., "to burn incense"), is the usual word applied to the
service of the high places. A distinction between a high place
(bāma) and an altar (mizbĕăḥ) is acknowledged in the Old
Testament down to the close of the kingdom (2 Kings xxiii. 15;
Isa. xxxvi. 7); but ultimately bāma is the name applied to any
idolatrous shrine or altar.

ADDITIONAL NOTE M (p. 403)

SACRIFICE BY VICTORIOUS WARRIORS

ACCORDING to Abū 'Obaida, the Arabs, after a successful foray, sacrificed one beast from the spoil, and feasted upon it before the division of the booty (*Ḥam.* p. 458 ; Reiske, *An. Musl.* i. 26 *sqq.* of the notes ; cf. *Lisān*, x. 240). This victim is called *nacī̆a*, or more fully *nacī̆at al-coddām*, "the *nacī̆a* of the home-comers." The verb نقع is used generally of sacrificing for a guest, but its primary sense is to split or rend, so that the name of *nacī̆a* seems to denote some peculiar way of killing the victim. Now it appears from the narrative of Nilus that the victims of the Saracens were derived from the choicest part of the booty, from which they selected for sacrifice, by preference a handsome boy, or, if no boys had been captured, a white and immaculate camel. The camel exactly corresponds to the *nacī̆a* of the Arabs, and the name probably means a victim torn to pieces in the way described by Nilus It seems probable, therefore, that the sacrifice made for warriors on their return from a foray was not an ordinary feast, but an antique rite of communion, in which the victim was a sacred animal, or might even be an actual man.

That the warriors on their return should unite in a solemn act of service is natural enough ; the thing falls under the same category with the custom of shaving one's head at the sanctuary on returning from a journey, and is, in its oldest meaning, simply a retying of the sacred links of common life, which may have grown weak through absence from the tribal seat. But of course a sacrifice of this kind would in later times appear to be piacular or lustral, and accordingly, in the Levitical law, an elaborate purification is prescribed for warriors returning from battle, before they are allowed to re-enter their homes (Num. xxxi. 19 *sqq.*). In ancient Arabia, on the other hand, where warriors were under the same taboos as a man engaged on pilgrimage, the *nacī̆a* was no doubt the means of untying the taboo, and so returning to ordinary life.

These remarks enable us to put the sacrifice of captives, or of certain chosen captives, in a somewhat clearer light. This sacrifice is not an act of blood-revenge, for revenge is taken in hot blood on the field of battle. The captive is simply, as Nilus

puts it, the choicest part of the prey, chosen for a religious
purpose; and the custom of preferring a human victim to a
camel is probably of secondary growth, like other customs of
human sacrifice.   It seems, however, to be very ancient, for
Saul undoubtedly spares Agag in order that he may be sacrificed, and Samuel actually accomplishes this offering by slaying
him "before the Lord" in Gilgal.   And in this, as in other cases
of human sacrifice, the choice of an alien instead of a tribesman
is not of the essence of the rite, for Jephthah looses his vow on
his return from smiting the Ammonites by the sacrifice of his
own daughter.

According to the Arabian lexicographers, the term *nacī̆a* may
be applied to sacrifices made on various occasions other than
return from war, *e.g.* to a coronation feast, or that which a man
makes for his intimates on his marriage; while ultimately the
word appears to assume a very general sense, and to be applied to
any slaughter to entertain a guest.   For the occasions on which
the Arabs were wont to kill a victim, which are very much the
same as those on which slaughter of the sacred cattle is permitted
by African peoples (*supra*, p. 298), note the verse cited in *Lisān*,
vi. 226, x. 240 (and with a variation, *Tāj*, v. 519, l. 2), where
the desirable meats include the *khors*, the *ī̆dhār*, and the *nacī̆a*.
The first, which is the name applied to the broth given to women
in child-bed, denotes also the feast made at a birth; the *ī̆dhār* is
the feast at a circumcision.   In *Journ. Phil.* xiv. 124, I have
connected the *khors* with the Hebrew חרשים, "charms."   Charmed
food is of course primarily holy food.

NOTES TO THE THIRD EDITION

BY

STANLEY A. COOK, Litt.D.

FELLOW OF GONVILLE AND CAIUS COLLEGE, CAMBRIDGE
UNIVERSITY LECTURER IN HEBREW AND ARAMAIC

NOTES TO THE THIRD EDITION

P. 1. THE SEMITES.[1]—The term, conveniently applied to the group of closely related peoples occupying a well-defined area (see p. 5 *sq.*), is derived from a classification in Gen. x. which is neither ethnographical nor linguistic, but, rather, political or cultural. So, the very intimate connexion between Egypt and the Phœnician coast (and notably the city of Gebal or Byblus) goes back to the third millennium B.C.; the history of Elam was powerfully influenced by its western (Semitic) neighbours, and the combination of Elam and Lud (p. 6)—which were naturally connected by the trade route between Susa and Sardes—could be justified at all events when both were under Assyrian domination in the seventh century B.C. (see G. R. Driver, p. 76). As regards the Hittites and Philistines (p. 10 *sq.*), what is now known of the Hatti in Asia Minor and of the Ægean civilization has opened new chapters in history. The influence of both upon Syria and Palestine can be clearly recognized; and " non-Semitic " though the Ægeans and Hittites were, it is not incorrect, on the strength of the Aramaic inscriptions found in North Syria and the references to the Philistines and Hittites in the Old Testament, to agree that on settling down they were speedily " Semitized." [2] As a matter of fact, it is simpler to determine Semitic *language* than Semitic *culture*, and the term is preferably used as a purely linguistic one.[3] There is less readiness now to look for " Phœnician " influence, for example, in Caria (p. 175 n. 2 end), or Lycia (p. 178 n. 4 end), or Delos (pp. 200 n. 1, 202 n. 1), or to discern it in the sacrifice of swine at Argus and Pamphylia (p. 291 n. 1). The various problems of influence, Phœnician and other, are found to be much more complex. It is necessary to recognize (*a*) a very ancient and close interconnexion between the Semitic and other areas, and (*b*) a considerable similarity of custom throughout South-West Asia, Egypt, and along North Africa; and to allow for some decisive waves of influence

[1] See G. A. Barton, *Sketch of Semitic Origins, Social and Religious*, chs. i. ii. (New York, 1902); Lagrange, *Études sur les Religions Sémitiques*[2], ch. i. (Paris, 1905); Nöldeke, art. " Semitic Languages," *Ency. Brit.*[11] (1911); S. A. Cook, *Cambridge Ancient History*, i.[2] (1924), ch. v., and Bibliography, *ib.* p. 630 *sqq.*; G. R. Driver, *People and the Book*, ch. iii. (ed. Peake, 1925); and in general, F. Hommel, *Ethnologie und Geographie des Alten Orients* (Munich, 1926).

[2] See articles " Philistines " in *E.Bi.* and *Ency. Brit.*; *Camb. Anc. Hist.*, vol. ii. ch. xii., vol. iii. ch. vi.

[3] Richardson, *American Journ. of Sem. Lang.*, xli. 10.

passing more forcefully now in one direction and now in another.[1] The "comparative" method of research has brought to light most striking parallels among Semitic, Egyptian, Old Indian, Greek, and other beliefs and customs, and it is necessary to allow, as in the case of languages, for (1) actual borrowing, due to migration, trade, war, etc., (2) a common ancestry, whether more immediate and obvious or more remote and hypothetical, and (3) those elementary physiological and psychological processes which are admittedly the common possession of all mankind.

The *linguistic* relationship that has been claimed between (a) Semitic and Sumerian, and between (b) the latter and Bantu, or Chinese, or Turkish, or Basque, etc., is uncertain.[2] On the other hand, that between Semitic and Egyptian is self-evident and far more significant.[3] Besides a broad ethnological connexion between Semites and Hamites (cf. p. 298, and Seligman, *JRAI*. xliii. 593), there is close cultural affinity between the tribes of North Africa and Arabia, areas which are geologically one. And while natives of North-East Africa can freely cross over into South Arabia, the influence of Syrians, Arabs, and other " Semites " upon Egypt (and North-East Africa) has at one time or another been decisive. Indeed, just as Coptic betrays the influence, though of course at a relatively late date, of " exchanges with Semitic neighbours " (Griffith, *Ency. Brit.* ix. 60), so, at a very remote date, before the rise of the language we call " Egyptian," intercourse between Egypt and the Semitic area may account for the remarkable points of contact between the two linguistic types. A suggestive analogy may perhaps be furnished by Amharic, whose Semitic features " give one the impression of having been superimposed on an alien (possibly) Hamitic basis " (Ambruster, *Initia Amharica*, i. 2 *sq.*). This language has diverged more than any other known Semitic tongue from the old Semitic type. A non-Semitic mode of thought is blended

---

[1] Cf. S. Eitrem, *Opferritus und Voropfer der Griechen und Römer*, 2; the theory of direct borrowing does not explain the facts.

[2] See, for (a) Ball, *Proc. of the British Academy*, 1915, vii., and his commentary on Job (Oxford, 1922), especially Burney's Preface. For (b) cf. Drexel in the *Semaine d'Ethnologie Religieuse*, 1922 (Enghien, 1923), 171 *sqq.*, and the literature in C. Autran, *Sumérien et Indo-Européen* (1925).

[3] Erman (see F. Ll. Griffith in *Ency. Brit.* ix. 59 *sq.*) ; for other discussions see Nöldeke, *Ency. Brit.* xxiv. 619d, and his *Beitrage z. Semit. Sprachwissenschaft*, i. (1905), 29 ; W. F. Albright, " Notes on Egypto-Semitic Etymology," *AJSL.* xxxiv. 81–94, 215–55 (p. 97 ; the resemblance is closer with Assyrian and South Arabian than the other Semitic languages) ; A. Ember (*Oriens*, ii.) ; C. Brockelmann, *Grundriss der vergleich. Grammatik d. Semit. Sprachen*, i. (1908), 3 *sq.* ; Hestermann, *Sprachen u. Völker i. Afrika*, viii. (1913), 221 ; for the older literature see Stübe, p. 6 n. 2.

with Semitic linguistic usage, so that Amharic construction is more difficult to the student of Semitic than to one ignorant of it. Apart from Arabic, no Semitic tongue is spoken by so large a number of people ; and the rise and prominence of this partly Semitic and partly African language, suggest how, in a prehistoric age, long before the history of the Egyptian language can be traced, a Semitic wave could so influence the current language of North-East Africa as to account for the " Semitic " elements in the Egyptian language, and not the language alone. Such an hypothesis would at least be in accordance with known processes, whereas the theory of a single ancestor —an Egypto-Semitic linguistic type, and an Afrcan home of the Semites—goes beyond the available evidence, and relies upon too simple a view of the origin of parallels and analogies, linguistic and other. The search after ultimate origins, whether of races, or languages, or elements of culture or religion, lies outside the scope of scientific research ; although theories of such origins are required by philosophical students.

The title and scope of the *Religion of the Semites* have sometimes been adversely criticized. The task of sketching the development of the main features of Semitic religion, or religions, is complicated by the evidence for the presence, within the Semitic area, of the most varied non-Semitic elements—Sumerian, Egyptian, Ægean, Hittite, and Iranian—before, to name a date, the Israelite monarchy. Moreover, even before this date Palestine and Syria possessed fairly high and well-organized systems of belief and practice, which would naturally influence Israelite or other tribes entering from the desert outside.[1] Consequently, the development of the religion of Israel, or rather of that of Palestine, which is so essential a part of the history of Semitic religion, now stands upon a new footing. Further, the conflicting claims of Arabia and of Babylonia-Assyria (see p. 13 *sq.*) have been repeatedly discussed ; and, whereas Robertson Smith, with Wellhausen, Stade, and others, took the relatively simple conditions of Arabia for their starting-point, scholars now give more prominence to the abundant evidence for the antiquity and richness of the civilization of the old Mesopotamian lands.

But much of what Robertson Smith wrote is not only untouched, but can actually be supplemented by the Babylonian material.[2]

---

[1] On the pre-Israelite (or pre-monarchical) culture of Palestine, see *CAH.* ii. ch. xiii.

[2] See Lagrange, *Études sur les Religions Sémitiques*; Winckler and Zimmern, *Keilinschriften und das Alte Testament* (1903) ; R. Campbell Thompson, *Semitic Magic, its Origins and Development* (1908) ; A. Jeremias, *Handbuch d. altorient. Geisteskultur* (Leipzig, 1913), and especially the works of Jastrow.

32

Moreover, even as regards Arabia itself, he was fully aware of the higher culture in early Arabia to which the Minæan and Sabæan inscriptions testify, and he did not fail to point out that the Arabia of the old poets, the Arabia of the generations immediately preceding the rise of Islam, was one where the old religion was breaking up (p. 462), an age of extreme decadence and disintegration (pp. 46, 71, 282; cf. *Kinship*, p. 272 *sq.*). Similarly, there is an age of disintegration at and after the sweeping Assyrian conquests of the eighth and seventh centuries B.C. : it is of the greatest importance for an estimate of the vicissitudes of Semitic religion (see pp. 35, 55, 65, 258, 358, 472). Further, the post-exilic Levitical sacrificial system is, in spite of its date, " primitive " (p. 240).[1] Properly speaking, nowhere can one find an absolutely *pure* society and an actually *primitive* stage of social and religious development. Theories of the development of religions naturally depend upon data selected from diverse social levels, of different ages, and at different stages of development ; and Robertson Smith was concerned with the more permanent features, which " recur with striking uniformity " and " govern the evolution of faith and worship down to a late date " (p. 15; see the whole paragraph). Such features, he says, are of the greatest interest to the " philosophical student," and his method of inquiry—which has sometimes been misunderstood—leads to the more subtle problems of the science and theory of religion.

In the simpler life of Arabia, in contrast to the more complex and more sophisticated social systems of Babylonia and Assyria, Robertson Smith looks for the main elements of the religious life. Periods of decadence and disintegration manifest the lack of those factors that make for a coherent and progressive society ; new creative ages reveal the pregnant ideas and beliefs which usher in new series of stages. So, " in many respects the religion of heathen Arabia . . . displays an extremely primitive type . . ." (p. 14). But this no more represents the actual primitive religion than " Classical Arabic," while preserving forms that have been further developed or have decayed in the cognate languages, represents the earliest form of Semitic.[2] The analogy is instructive. In certain respects the relation between modern Arab dialects and Classical Arabic resembles that between the old Semitic languages and their presumed ancestor. But in other respects the ancient South Arabian inscriptions (as might be expected) and also Hebrew and even Aramaic, are linguistically as well as historically older than Arabic. In Classical Arabic we find (after

---

[1] Jastrow (*Religious Belief in Bab. and Ass.*, 289 n.) comments on the preference in the Old Testament " for the lower form of culture over the higher."

[2] See *CAH*. i.[2] 188.

Nöldeke) an " excess of wealth," a modification of primitive forms, and a certain monotony that would not be found in a truly primitive tongue. Further, in the history of the Semitic languages similar processes recur as regards the decay of gutturals, the loss of case-endings, and the formation of the perfect; but in none of these examples are the genetic processes identical.

The facts of cultural development as a whole are obviously far more complex than those of language. They show that an essential similarity of type or process may lurk beneath the most striking differences, and that the points of resemblance and those of difference have each their own appropriate value. So, repeatedly a very similar attitude will recur in very different forms (e.g. the attitude to animals in totemism, theriomorphism, etc.). Again, a feature relatively primitive in some respects will recur amid conditions which in other respects are relatively advanced. Law and custom in the Old Testament represent a level sociologically less advanced than that in the earlier Babyonian code of Hammurabi, even as pre-Islamic Arabia is in various respects below the level of the Minæan and Sabæan culture. Finally, where genetic processes recur, the first step is neither absolutely primitive nor does it necessarily correspond in all respects to the first step elsewhere.[1] Accordingly, while Robertson Smith clearly admits the prominence of the " gift " idea in sacrifice, he is more concerned to determine the governing feature, namely, " communion," even as he considers the feeling of fear, however prominent in religion, to be less fundamental than the sentiment of kinship and alliance. But he no more attempts to reconstruct the actual primitive form of communion-sacrifice than one could venture to reconstruct, from the vicissitudes of the Semitic languages, the actual primitive and original Semitic tongue.

The history of the diverse elements of culture and of their inter-action, as illustrated in the vicissitudes of an alphabet, or the textual history of manuscripts, or the development of a branch of learning, is excessively complicated. Only from the more intelligible and tangible examples can one hope to throw light upon those that are more obscure or abstruse. The Semitic languages themselves show how, as one goes back, the problems of origin increase in intricacy. The Classical Arabic, which stands at the head of a fairly long linguistic development, was once only one of other current Semitic dialects;

---

[1] To generalize : the process l^1, m^1, n^1, will recur in the form l^2, m^2, n^2, etc., and it may be possible to postulate an older L, M, N ; but l^1, l^2, l^3, etc., although similar, are not identical; and the development l^1, l^2, l^3, etc., m^1, m^2, m^3, etc., is naturally not to be confused with l^1, m^1, n^1, etc. A common type of development is that symbolized by l^1, m^2, n^3.

and the Egyptian language, which has a much longer linguistic history, was once obviously neither Egyptian as known to us, and much less was it Semitic. Thus, the "Semites" as regards language and culture raise questions not merely of facts but of the treatment of facts, and Robertson Smith's leading theories soon involve questions of method. In the course of research one comes to see what problems seem tractable and what are insoluble, although the conditions of their solution may sometimes be recognized. The study of religion has become much more difficult in the thirty years and more that have elapsed since Robertson Smith's death, and it is symptomatic of the present situation that the rude totemism of Central Australia,[1] which has so remarkably confirmed his theory of the communion-sacrifice, has been regarded as "magic" rather than "religion," and, in any case, tends, along with much other new and important evidence, to force an entire reconsideration of the nature of "religion" and of its development.

P. 17 *sq.* MYTH AND RITUAL. — W. R. S.'s discussion of the relative value of myth and ritual is classical. As a general principle, religious ceremonial is prior to reflexion upon it, even as "political institutions are older than political theories" (p. 20). The practical religious life of a group is of greater value for the student than myth or dogma. The study of the "nature of the gods" is therefore of relatively less significance than is often recognized (p. 81 *sq.*); and, from the highest religious point of view no less than from the point of view of the critical study of religions, the really effective elements in a religion are not necessarily those that appear on the surface or are most clamant. Marett observes: "That ritual, or in other words a routine of external forms, is historically prior to dogma, was proclaimed years ago by W. R. S. and others; yet Social Anthropology is but to-day beginning to appreciate the psychological implications of this cardinal truth." [2] Similarly it has been remarked that the religious cult is "the centre which offers a relatively stable material upon which reflexion is exercised and out of which religious doctrines are fashioned. They express the meaning and value which the community attaches to its religious activity." [3]

When W. R. S. wrote he was protesting, as seems periodically to be necessary, against certain methods of interpreting myths.[4] There

---

[1] See, in the first instance, Sir Baldwin Spencer and F. J. Gillen, *Native Tribes of Central Australia* (1899), and *Northern Tribes of Central Australia* (1904).

[2] R. R. Marett, *The Birth of Humility*, 13; cf. *Threshold of Religion*, ix. ("religion in its psychological aspect is, fundamentally, a mark of social behaviour").

[3] See more fully, G. Galloway, *The Philosophy of Religion* (1914), 47 *sq.*

[4] Cf. Andrew Lang's notable article "Mythology" in the *Ency. Brit.*[11] vol. xix.

was the risk of going to another extreme and of making the distinction between myth and ritual too absolute ; and since his day it has often been pointed out that myths are not necessarily derived from ritual, and that myth and ritual often react upon each other.[1] Numerous myths are undeniably of quite secondary value. They are based upon misunderstandings (*e.g.* of images, words, names) ; they are explanations of explanations, the key to an old tradition having been lost. Or they are the elaborate product of the more intelligent and sophisticated individuals, and are out of touch with the thought of the great mass of their contemporaries. Or they have been purified of earlier crudities ; and fancy and imagination have played upon them, transforming them into a pleasing tale. But whether they acquire an antiquarian value in some cases or an æsthetic charm in others, the human interest of all such myths is not that which characterizes the myths of the simpler classes or communities. Thus, in Egypt it is instructive to contrast the homely myths of Osiris, Isis, and Horus, and the ideals of wifely affection and filial devotion which they contain, with those myths which reflect clearly enough political and theological tendencies to explain or simplify the interrelations of gods and of their domains.

" The myth that is an essential fact for the student of religion is that which enshrines some living religious idea or institution, or which proves the survival of some ritual or faith that belonged to an older system." [2] The ceremonial dance of certain North American Indians for the purpose of curing disease includes the dramatic rehearsal of a complicated myth which, in effect, invokes the unseen powers.[3] Frequently the recital of the god's great achievements is intended to strengthen the religion of the worshippers and encourage them to invoke or await his aid. Hence not only are the traditions of the god's deeds preserved, but knowledge is power, and to know how things happen is often felt to increase one's power (cf. Farnell, 190 *sq.*). And since there are occasions when talking about things brings them realistically to the mind, there are myths which are felt

[1] Reference may be made, *e.g.*, to D. G. Brinton, *Religions of Primitive Peoples*, 112 *sq.* (New York, 1897) ; C. H. Toy, *Introd. to the History of Religions* (Boston, 1916), ch. vii. ; and, most recently, Bronislaw Malinowski, *Myth in Primitive Psychology* (1926).

[2] R. Farnell, *Evolution of Religion*, 27. Malinowski (note above) illustrates myths as a direct expression of their subject-matter, statements of reality, products of a living faith, intimately connecting word and deed, legal charters, literature filling an emotional void—myths which are not, in any sense, mere theories, or merely intellectual explanations.

[3] Irving King, *The Development of Religion : a Study in Anthropology and Social Psychology*, 127 *sq.*

to be too " sacred " to be lightly mentioned.   Thus, in a variety
of ways the oral myths of a people will virtually correspond to the
sacred writings of the more advanced stages of religion.[1]   In general,
when myth (belief, doctrine, etc.) and ritual (cult, etc.) converge
or coalesce, it is at a stage prior to that where the myth is a more
detached story or explanation, and is less in touch with its *milieu*.
By " ritual " is meant properly what is social-religious and not solely
religious.   *Religious* ritual can undergo a change of value.   No
doubt the correct performance of such ritual was more important
than a man's belief concerning its origin (p. 17) ; but empty ritual
devoid of any organic meaning for the performer can hardly be of
any psychological worth, nor can it, as such, lead to any progressive
development.

Broadly speaking, myths deal with the powers of the gods, their
life-history, and their past or present functions, and they range from
the extremes of naïve anthropomorphism to the most highly specialized
interests.   They are specifically of *personal* interest, but, in general,
they appeal differently to the different types of mind in normal mixed
communities.   Every myth admits of analysis.   If by a myth is
meant " a story of the gods, originating in an impression produced
on the primitive mind by the more imposing phenomena of nature "
(Skinner, *Genesis*, viii.), a distinction may be drawn between its value
(*a*) for the light it throws upon ideas respecting the gods, and (*b*) as
an example of the knowledge of its day.   All myths reflect in varying
forms and in varying degree the thought of their age, and for this
reason they may be said to correspond, *mutatis mutandis*, to the more
specialized types of literature of more advanced peoples.   Especially
instructive is the testimony of myths to characteristic modes of
thought and regulative theories of the past.   Among these is the
" myth," if not, rather, the " theory," of a primitive Golden Age
(see above, p. 300) ; and of particular importance for W. R. S.'s
inquiry is the persistent conviction of an animal surrogate for an
original human sacrifice (p. 365).   Not unnaturally have writers sometimes spoken of certain recent sweeping theories as the modern representatives of the old-time " myth."   Among such have been included
the theory of a primitive " social contract (or compact)," " primitive
promiscuity " (cf. Crawley, *The Mystic Rose*, 483), and even W. R. S.'s
theory of the totem-sacrifice !   Perhaps the common tendency to
trace simple ancestries where peoples, languages, and the elements
of civilizations are concerned is no less along the lines of early " mytho-

[1] Cf. Jane Harrison, *Themis*, 329 ; Durkheim, *Elementary Forms of the Religious Life*, 82 *sq.*, 101 (on the necessity of distinguishing between myths and
fables).

logical " modes of thought.[1] In either case there is a tendency to go outside empirical data and to extend the explanation of a limited number of facts in order to cover larger fields. Obviously it is hazardous to look for clear-cut and more or less rationalized systems of belief and custom among communities who are devoid of the powers of reflexion, detachment, and systematization that characterize the modern mind ; but all modern scientific or critical studies of the data of religion sooner or later pass from mere strings of facts to a treatment of them which betrays a conscious or unconscious philosophy of religion. The really important question is whether the philosophy or the methodology is the most effective one for the purpose. It must suffice to say that the most serious objections brought against W. R. S.'s methods (including his treatment of myth and ritual) appear to reflect theological or philosophical presuppositions and regulative principles opposed to his and no less in need of criticism.

The real value of the myth is to be tested by its place in the life and thought of its environment. At one time myth, ritual, and even ideas of gods, men, and the world are parts of one organic system ; at another, they are no organic part of their environment, thought is more specialized, and there are specialized individuals. None the less, a purely secondary myth—just like some highly specialized theory—may contribute to a subsequent stage of development, while the rite, once an effective part of the life of a community and a guide for the modern interpreter, may become mechanical or fall out of touch with the movement of thought and thus lose the value it once had. Vicissitudes of this sort are always recurring in the actual history of religions, and, as W. R. S.'s argument shows, it is the constantly recurring stage, where myth and *social-religious* ritual are one and where the latter expresses the normal thought of the communty, which is of fundamental importance as a starting-point for the apprehension of the great permanent and pregnant steps in the history of religion.[2]

P. 31. TENTYRA.—See *Ency. Brit.* s.v. " Dendera," and cf. Juvenal, *Sat.* xv. 35 *sqq.*, 75 *sq.*

P. 32. THE UNITY OF GODS AND WORSHIPPERS.—The idea of a social system embracing all aspects of life and thought—social, economic, political, and religious—and connecting gods and men,

---

[1] Cf. *CAH.* i.[2] 224 *sq.*, iii. 422 (on the " ancestor " of all alphabetical types), 425 *sq.*

[2] In a characteristic lecture, given in 1875, on " Theology and the Church " (*Lectures and Essays*, 309 *sqq.*), W. R. S. had already dealt with the relation between a living religion and a theology which is no longer in touch with the trend of thought ; see the Introduction above.

stamps the whole book, and in the form in which W. R. S. develops it, is one of the most brilliant contributions to the study of religion.[1] Men are born into a system, an organism, a group-unit, which confers certain rights and entails certain obligations (p. 29). In every social group, with its common interests and aims, and dependent for its welfare on the welfare of its members, there is a moral and ethical unity. Early societies often have very definite notions of responsibility and retribution ;[2] but although ideas of social justice and righteousness spontaneously arose even at an early age, the generous ideals did not usually extend beyond the borders of the group's immediate interests. Further, since the gods were " part and parcel of the same natural community with their worshippers " (p. 255), and were also guardians of morality (p. 268), the gods vindicated morality (p. 425), and religion was a moral force (p. 53). But it was not necessarily religion of a very high standard (p. 256 sq.). Disasters might be an indication that the solidarity of gods and men was broken, but there were well-understood ways of remedying evils (p. 320). The gods were supposed to look after their group of worshippers as a matter of course, and they needed them even as they themselves were needed. Such group-religion engendered confidence if not a self-centred complacence (cf. p. 266 sq.) ; and we have in it typical social religious conditions which throw into strongest relief the Hebrew prophets' teaching of the absolute righteousness of God (pp. 74, 81).

Defeat and disaster easily shake or destroy the group-unit with its system of social, political, and religious beliefs and practices ; and the states of unrest and disorganization stand in striking contrast to the relatively coherent states which had preceded, and which follow when equilibrium is restored. It is this relative unity or solidarity which can be so often recognized and more often postulated that W. R. S. is emphasizing ; and in the history of peoples or tribes or even individuals, states whether of unity or disunity are characterized throughout by typical related phenomena. To a certain extent, then, there is an elementary psychological similarity, varying in degree, among all groups : family or tribal, local or national, sex and age groups, economic and specialist groups or guilds. Each

---

[1] In the lecture referred to above, W. R. S. says : " Every society is bound together by a common aim and common principles. [A Christian] society must be bound together by its common Christianity " (p. 326) ; " Organized fellowship implies common interests, a common aim, some function in which the whole society visibly combines " (p. 329). Both passages are significant for his later ideas on religion in general.

[2] Cf. Maine, *Ancient Law* (ed. Pollock, 1907), 135. On the social group as a moral force, see especially Durkheim, 206 *sqq.*

group is held together by the beliefs and usages proper to its scope and purpose. Each group is more than the sum of its members, and can be regarded as a unit, and, as frequently in the Old Testament, as a person (*e.g.* Edom, Num. xx. 14 *sqq.*). It will feel as one.[1] There are rites to enhance or renew group-unity (cf. the commensality, pp. 269, 274), to arouse collective enthusiasm, or to manifest collective grief. There is apt to be, throughout, a very similar attitude to those outside the group ; and there are initiation rites before the outsider can become a member of a self-conscious group.[2] There is a common responsibility and a common participation in both ills and benefits, so that in tribal groups the religion is essentially that of the whole group, and, to take a particular case, tribute is primarily for the common good, for the public feasts and sacrifices (pp. 247 *sqq.*).

Accordingly, group unity or disunity is essentially unity or disunity of sentiments, ideas, and interests, and the vicissitudes of groups and of the systems that unite them move *pari passu*. Even the rude totem-groups of Central Australia have their systems of beliefs and practices ; and Durkheim has shown that whether totemism is to be called " religion " or " magic " depends upon preliminary definitions, and that where any social group has a certain social coherence and effectiveness it is meaningless to expatiate upon the " errors " or " delusions " upon which its system might seem to be based.[3]

The social group united by blood-ties appears as the most primitive of groups, but (*a*) there have been different types of kinship, and (*b*) a group-unit of blood-relatives is not necessarily a group-unit as regards certain social and religious duties. Further (*c*), the members of a cult-group or brotherhood, though not akin, will readily claim a relationship which at times is a very close one.[4] As pointed out by Crawley, *relation* is more fundamental than *relationship*, and friendship can be a stronger tie than blood-kinship. There is, in fact, what may be called a psychical bond, which can be superior to physical kinship ; and it is instructive to observe that the feeling of closest unity can lead (*a*) to rites of union (sexual intercourse and marriage), or (*b*) to the absolute repudiation of marriage as being, so to speak,

---

[1] As in Paraguay where, if a child falls ill, all the relatives refrain from the food which is supposed to be injurious to it (Crawley, *The Mystic Rose*, 423).

[2] Cf. Hutton Webster, *Secret Societies*, Eitrem, 465.

[3] *Op. cit.* bk. ii. ch. iii. On the interrelation between a social organization and its ideas (religious and other), see I. King, *op. cit.* 74, 92, *et passim* ; cf. also Compte's remarks upon international anarchy and the absence of any general agreement on first principles (*Fundamental Principles*, i. § 70).

[4] See, *e.g.*, Cumont, *Oriental Religions in Roman Paganism*, ch. v., n. 82 : the *fratres carissimos* among the votaries of Jupiter Dolichenus.

incestuous.[1] Kinship was not necessarily a matter of birth, it could be acquired (p. 273). Blood-relationship and the blood-covenant might seem the most elemental and powerful type of unity, and W. R. S. makes the social group the starting-point of religious development (cf. *Kinship*, 259); but the psychical factors are clearly not less powerful than the physiological, and it is convenient to regard all group-units psychologically as systems, the social group of kinsfolk being the most elemental.

Among the more primitive societies the social group is relatively unspecialized and undifferentiated, although men of outstanding personality are by no means wanting (see p. 591). More advanced communities are distinguished by specialization of thought and function, and of belief and of custom, and individuals come to belong to a number of special groups each with its appropriate interests. How the growing complexity of the social order affects the earlier religious system can be easily followed. Properly, every group is, of course, held together by its unifying ideas, and among simple social groups the group and the cult are one. In totemism the animal or plant species—usually edible—unites the group in such a way that without this symbol there could be no totemic clan (Durkheim, 150). How essentially the group and its religion or cult are one is seen when the group and the god bear the same name (cf. Gad, Atar-Samain, and see p. 509). One life, human and divine, runs through the religious group (cf. *Kinship*, index, s.v. *ḥayy*; also John xv. 4). But whereas at the bottom of the scale all the members of the simple social groups are equal—or, rather, appear to be equal—as regards religious privileges and obligations, in course of social development there are representative individuals (*e.g.* priest-kings) and classes (*e.g.* priests), and these stand in a closer relationship than the rest of the community to the god or gods of the now more complex society (cf. pp. 44, 48).

Primarily there is an interdependence of men and the gods, each needs the other, and there is much truth in the observation that the *do ut des* formula expresses the mechanism of the sacrificial system, especially when, as in totemism, the totem-class and the totem-species are, so to say, of the same substance (Durkheim, 341, 346 *sq.*). It is instructive, therefore, to contrast the two stages: (*a*) where there is an intimate interrelationship between the men and god(s) of the

[1] So, *e.g.*, among allies, Crawley, *Mystic Rose*, 264 *sq.*, 451; see W. R. S., *Kinship*, 196 n. 1 (a boy and girl who have been suckled together may not marry). Among primitive peoples it is sometimes felt that a youth should not marry the sister of his mate, because he is as his own brother. On an East European rule forbidding the groomsman to marry into the family of the bride, see Westermarck, *Origin and Development of the Moral Ideas*, ii. 377 *sq.* (with other examples of prohibition of marriage on account of certain notions of what constitutes intimate relationship).

group, and (*b*), where individuals—whether as prominent representatives or as humbler personages—claim the privileges without the responsibilities of the group-system, and where men retain one-sided conceptions of the relation between gods and men, forgetful of the more complete and self-sustaining system of beliefs and practices of which these conceptions are the fragmentary survivals.

But while W. R. S. shows how the effective system of convergent institutions and beliefs is of more importance than secondary myths and doctrines, and while the conception of a group-unit comprising gods and their worshippers has thrown new light upon the problems of religion, the unit or system is an essentially abstract or simple concept of immense methodological value. So far from complex groups being derived from some simple, pure, or homogeneous ancestor, it is as impossible to construct an absolutely undifferentiated group-system as it is to construct an undifferentiated Semitic or Egypto-Semitic ancestor of the Semitic or of the Semitic and Egyptian languages (p. 499). Such is the continuous flux everywhere, even among rudimentary peoples, that a certain elasticity is required in estimating groups.[1] Thus, in Australia, although the totem-clans are natural units, each with considerable autonomy, the tribe is both a larger unit and a complex system, rather than a commonwealth, of totem-clans. Moreover, different conditions prevail as regards groups of contiguous tribes and those more remote. Indeed, as a general rule it is possible to distinguish between the cults of individual clans and those of the tribe as a whole, between the spirits (or gods) of separate localities and those of the area as a whole (the " national " gods), and between the latter and the spirits or gods of more remote tribes and areas. Thus there are always factors outside any one group-system which are relevant for its earlier or later vicissitudes ; and no system can be regarded as ultimately a closed one, although for practical methodological purposes it may be necessary to treat it as such.

The group with its members, its traditions, and its outlook, is a unit in space and time. It transcends the present and the visible. It is a spiritual or psychical unit, and that which makes it effective lies both within the empirical group and outside it.[2] In all practical

[1] Cf. Hobhouse, Wheeler, and Ginsberg, *Material Culture*, 3 n., 8 *sqq.* (on the " unit social group ") ; also Marett, *Anthropology*, 170 (the " group " as a methodological necessity).

[2] As this paradox is true even of Central Australian totemism, Durkheim's definition of Religion may be quoted : " A religion is a unified system of beliefs and practices relative to sacred things, that is to say, things set apart and forbidden— beliefs and practices which unite into one single moral community called a Church, all those who adhere to them " (p. 47). Besides Durkheim, Irving King (*Development of Religion*) has suggestively developed the theory of the social-religious group.

and effective social-religious groups there is a fusion of the " sacred "
and " divine " (the supernatural, supersensuous, etc.) and the " secular " and " human," the god or gods are both within the group-
system and outside it, and this paradox marks the development of
ideas of Immanence and Transcendence (cf. p. 565).

P. 37 and n. 5. PORTABLE SHRINES.—For the *'otfa* (also the related
maḥmal and *merkab*), see Schwally, *Semitische Kriegsaltertümer*, i. 9 *sqq.*;
Jaussen, *Coutumes des Arabes du pays de Moab*, 173 *sq.* (Paris, 1908);
and Mrs. B. Z. Seligman, " Sacred Litters among the Semites," in
Sudan Notes and Records, i. 268–282 (Cairo, 1918). The main features
are : their sacred character, the sacrifice to them of a camel, their
function in battle (as a palladium), and the part played by the sheikh's
daughter who, dressed as a bride, sits in the litter and inspires the men
to battle. According to Curtiss (*Bibl. World*, xxiii. 97), the Ruala offer
a preliminary sacrifice to Abu'd-Ḍuhur for victory, and sprinkle the
blood upon the *merkab* of the camel on which is seated the sheikh's
daughter or sister, who, perfumed and with exposed bosom, stirs the
young warriors' enthusiasm (cf. R. C. Thompson, *Sem. Magic*, 158).
While the portable shrine naturally recalls the Ark of the Israelites,
the boat-shaped *ḍollah* (Jaussen, 173) recalls the boats represented on
Mesopotamian seals and the custom of transporting deities in boats
and chariots (cf. Thureau-Dangin, *Rituels Accad.* 147). In view of
the religious duties of the modern sheikh as the guardian of the cult
(Jaussen, 173, 296 *sq.*, 305, 314 *sqq.*, 326, 328, 362), and as the local
Arab *weli* or saint is often regarded as originally a sheikh, it is possible
that not only is the *'otfa* a survival, but that the part played by the
female is also a survival of a more elaborate cult. A link in the chain
may perhaps be found in the models of images of the female *Tyche*,
sometimes in pairs, and seated on camels, discussed by Cumont,
Études Syriennes, 270 *sqq.* (1917).

P. 42 and n. 4. COMPOUNDS OF *'abd*.—Cf. the Babylonian names
compounded with *warad* and a divine name (Ranke, *Early Bab.
Personal Names*, 174 *sqq.*). The Arabian compounds of *'abd* (on which
see Wellh., 2–4) are well distributed over the whole peninsula. In
several cases the second element is an ordinary personal name, and
Wellhausen observes that it may be that of a venerated ancestor or
primarily of a god (see also *Kinship*, 53 n. 1). For the name Obed-
Edom (always written defectively, except 2 Chron. xxv. 24), cf. Phœn.
עבדאדם, and perhaps the Safa personal name אדם.[1] Esau, too, is
possibly a divine name (cf. the Phœnician Usōos), and, besides the
apparently feminine form in the Egyptian war-goddess Asit (W. M.

---

[1] The Phœn. מלכאדם may be otherwise explained (Lidzbarski, *Ephemeris*, i.
42).

Müller, *Asien und Europa*, 316 *sq.*), there are Egyptian references to a warrior-god " Edom " (Atum, *'tm*) and to a North Palestinian place-name " Shamash-atum," or the like.[1] This evidence would suggest that both Edom and Esau were divine names not originally or neces-sarily confined to the South of Palestine ;[2] for analogies, cf. the wide distribution of the divine name Gad with its restriction as a tribal name to a particular part of Israel, also the Arab tribe named after the Queen of Heaven (Atar-Samain) mentioned along with the men of Kedar among the enemies of Ashurbanipal (*c.* 640 B.C.).   For Uz (Uṣ, 'Auḍ), see Wellh., *Heid.*[1] 19, 58,[2] 66, Nöldeke, *Ency. of Religion and Ethics*, i. 662 ; and for abstract names like Gad (Τύχη), Saʿd (Luck), Manāt (Fate), Wadd (? Friendship), see Wellh.[2] 28, Hehn, *Bibl. und Bab. Gottesidee*, 140 *sq.*, Nöldeke, *op. cit.* 661.[3]   On the identification of Yeush with Yaghuth, accepted by Nöldeke, *ZDMG.* xl. 184 and Wellh. *Heid.*[1] 17 *sqq.*,[2] 19 *sqq.* (on his citation from Yacut consult Fischer, *ZDMG.* lviii. 869), see now Meyer, *Israeliten*, 351 (Safa, Nabatæan, and other references).   In the late Ptolemaic inscription from Memphis the form is Ιεγουθος, whereas the Septuagint form of Yeush is Ιεους, etc.   On the South Arabian god Cain(an), with Naba-tæan and other parallels, see Meyer, *op. cit.* 397 n.

P. 45 *sq.* KINSHIP OF GODS AND MEN.[4]—On the subject in general see Nöldeke, *E.Bi.* " Names " §§ 44–48, and his *Beiträge zur semit. Sprachwissenschaft*, i. 90 *sqq.* ; on the filial relation in particular, see N. Schmidt, *E.Bi.* " Son of God " §§ 3–5.   For the corresponding Babylonian names of the type Marduk(Shamash, etc.)-abī, also Abum-ili and Ishtar-ummi, see Ranke, *Early Bab. Personal Names*, 189, 249; Baudissin, *Adonis und Esmun*, 4ᴐ n. 1 ; and for the com-pounds of *abil* (son), *mār* and *mārtum* (child), see the latter, 43 n. 1.[5] In Egypt the idea of the kinship, if not the essential identity of ruler and god—with the queen as Isis—is realistically elaborated (cf. Sir J. G. Frazer, *The Golden Bough*[3], ii. 131), and the god's love for his royal son or for the king's newborn heir is familiar.[6]   Such names as Thotmes

---

[1] Cf. Ed. Meyer (and B. Luther), *Die Israeliten und ihre Nachbarstamme*, 278 *sq.*, 298.

[2] See Nöldeke, *E.Bi.* col. 1182 n. 1, on a common origin of the legends of Esau and Usōos.

[3] Cf. in Egypt, Shay " Fate," see A. Gardiner, *ERE.* *s.v.* Personification (Egyp-tian).   The conception of Fate is old (see Fichtner-Jeremias, *MVAG.* 1922, ii.), that of Time or Age (Æon) is relatively late.

[4] To p. 45 n. 1 (cf. p. 57, l. 5) add Dhorme, *La Religion Assyro-Babylonienne* (Paris, 1910), 166 *sqq.*, 185.

[5] Semitic names denoting the relationship of the god to the worshipper are classified by M. Noth, *ZDMG.* lxxxi. 1–45.

[6] On the persistence of this, see Norden, *Geburt des Kindes*, 132 *sq.*

(Thut-mose), usually interpreted " child of Thoth," can now be explained as " T. is born " (Sethe, *ZDMG*. 1926, p. 50). The name אמאשמן (n. 2, l. 10), like אמעשתרת in the Eshmunazar inscription (*CIS*. i. 3, l. 14) is taken to be an error for אמתע' (" handmaid of A."); but Lidzbarski interprets the second name as " my mother is Astarte." Baudissin (*Adonis*, 42, 517 n.) observes that, generally speaking, the names compounded with Astarte do not reflect any ethical idea ; the goddess—in contrast to the Babylonian Ishtar— is more of a productive nature-power, and is far less interested in mankind than are the male deities.

To the South Arabian compounds of אב (end of n. 2) add the female אבנעם (*CIS*. iv. 194). Names indicating relationship with a deity are rare in Arabia, with the exception of the old compounds of *'am*, " kinsman," or more specifically " paternal uncle " ; on the Babylonian compounds of *ammi* (? of West Semitic origin), see *KAT*. 480 *sqq*. This rarity is remarkable, but it is possible that Arab nomenclature, as handed down, is the result of a secondary development (so Nöldeke ; see Baudissin, 43 n. 2). Buchanan Gray, in turn (*Hebrew Proper Names*, 255), notes that there is a tendency for names indicating Yahweh as father, brother, or kinsman, to fall out of use ; though in this case it is because " the earlier idea of man's kinship with the gods faded away even from popular thought before the higher prophetic conceptions of man's unlikeness to Yahweh." While the *disappearance* of such names may thus be explained, their *construction*—obviously under appropriate religious and psychological conditions—is well illustrated in the Abyssinian names cited by Nöldeke (*Beit.*, i. 103). Here are such names as Walda(or Sartsa)-Krĕstōs " son of Christ," Walda-Amlāk " son of God," W.-Sellāsē " son of the Trinity," Sartsa-Dengel " offspring of the Virgin," W.-Maryām, W.-Gabriel, etc., Walatta-Sellāsē (or Amlāk), Aḥwa(or Eḥta)-Krĕstōs " brother (or sister) of Christ " ; also other terms indicating close connexion, *e.g.* lips, neck, sweat, etc., of Christ, shoes of St. George, etc. etc.[1]

The custom of naming the eldest son after his grandfather (to which W. R. S. refers) is frequent in Palestine (*JPOS*. v. 197). It does not seem to be traceable before the papyri of the Jewish or Palestinian colony in Elephantine of the fifth century B.C. It is found among the Jews of Palestine a couple of centuries later.[2]

---

[1] Specifically Phœnician are the compounds of בד (" limb, member ") and the divine names Eshmun, Melkart, Astarte, and Ṣid ; cf. Cooke, *North Semitic Inscriptions*, 41, 95.

[2] See G. B. Gray in the *Wellhausen-Festschrift, ZATW*. (1914), pp. 161 *sqq*.; cf. his *Heb. Prop. Names*, 3 *sqq*.

Nöldeke's analogies (n. 2 end) refer rather to compounds of *abu* in the sense of protector; cf. Gen. xlv. 8 (*ZDMG.* xlii. 480 n. 1), and hardly meet the case.[1] Terms of relationship are, of course, used in a highly metaphorical manner.[2] In modern Egypt " mother " and " sister " are terms for female friends who are of an earlier or of a contemporary generation, as the case may be ; and elsewhere, not only is the term " mother " often used of the women of the same generation or class as a man's mother, but all the terms of kinship are employed systematically in a classificatory manner, and the " mother " or " father " is the woman whom his father might otherwise have married, or the man who might otherwise have taken his mother.[3]

When W. R. S. emphasizes the " literal " kinship of gods and men in the " congenital physical bond " (pp. 30, l. 2 ; 50, l. 2 ; 400), it is to be understood that the convictions of kinship were developed to an extreme that would seem incredible were it not that the grossly anthropomorphic ideas of Allah in Mohammedan countries and the systematic development of the ideas in all their implications (*e.g.* the marriage of gods and men ; below, p. 513) prove that, what clearly can only be regarded as psychical or spiritual, could be interpreted, expressed, or grasped only in crude physical terms by people at relatively early stages of mental development.

Further, although his remarks on the kinship of gods and men are strictly independent of the problem of totemism (contrast Lagrange, *Études*, 112), it is necessary to raise the very important question whether the god as " father " represents an idea earlier or more primitive than the god as " brother." In totemism the " totem " is so much on an equality with the members of the clan that the profound difference between it and a god who is feared, reverenced, and invoked in case of need, has often been felt by scholars to be a fatal defect in W. R . S.'s arguments. Yet the view that, under certain conditions, gods are more likely to be thought of as brothers than as fathers cannot be set aside, although the once prevalent theory of widespread primitive polyandry can no longer be held (see further below, p. 610 *sq.*). Favourable to the idea of the " brotherhood " of the god is, *e.g.*, the belief that earth is the common mother of gods and men (p. 517). Sometimes a god is specifically called

---

[1] On *abu*, cf. S. A. Cook, *Moses and Hammurabi*, 12 n. 1.

[2] Thus, the Wapokomo of British East Africa speak of the river Tana (Tsana), upon which their existence depends and which is an integral part of their life and thought, as their brother (Miss A. Werner, *Journ. of African Soc.* (1913), p. 361.

[3] Crawley, *Mystic Rose*, 450 *sq.* ; see further, Mrs. Brenda Z. Seligman, " Studies in Semitic Kinship," in the *Bulletin of the School of Oriental Studies* (London), iii. i. (1923) 51 n., 54, 67.

" brother." [1] In Sumerian, Shamash is identified with a god whose
name means " great brother " (Nielsen, *op. cit.* 265 ; see Schollmeyer,
Sum.-bab. Hymnen, 12), and in his code Hammurabi is the brother
(*tālim*) of the god Zamama. In the Hymn of Victory of Thotmes III.,
in the " Utterance of Amon-Re, lord of Thebes," it is said, " I have
caused (thy enemies) to see thy majesty as thy two brothers (*i.e.*
Horus and Set) . . . thy two sisters (*i.e.* Isis and Nephthys), I have
set them as a protection behind thee " (Breasted, *Ancient Records
of Egypt,* ii. 266). In certain types of monarchical religion where the
rulers are at least quasi-divine the deities could easily be regarded
as fathers or as brothers ; and under the influence of ideas of divine
kingship Julia Sohæmia, the mother of Elgabalus, is styled Mater
Deum, Venus Cœlestis, etc. (see Baudissin, 48 n. 2). Such régimes
would foster ideas of hierarchies of greater or national deities and
of lesser deities.[2] In fact, not only is the relative inferiority of certain
deities and other supernatural beings recognized already in the
" Pyramid Texts " of Egypt (*c.* 2800 B.C.), but the relative and at
times absolute superiority of certain individuals over the rest, by
reason of their religious or other pre-eminence, would place them
in a uniquely close relationship with the great god or gods and set
them upon a more equal footing with the lesser ones. How far
difference of divine rank can be recognized in the Israelite conceptions of Yahweh is uncertain ; but a distinction has sometimes been
drawn between Yahweh as the national god of Israel and the less
restricted Elohim, God of Nature and of the whole world, though
the difference has often been exaggerated.[3] In any event, the
apparent equality of the totem and the rest of the totem group is not
without parallels in the higher stages, and the conception of a Supreme
God to be feared and reverenced solely from afar is not the only one
prevalent in the higher religions. See further on Immanence and
Transcendence, pp. 563 *sqq.*

 [1] Babylonian examples are cited by Dhorme, 197, and Nielsen, *Dreieinige Gott,*
79 *sq.*, 93 *sq.* (*e.g.* the name Aḫu-ṭab). On Heb. ii. 11 (Christ's brethren), see the
commentary of Moffatt.

 [2] In the Amarna Letters the kings who are on equal terms are " brothers."
When kings enter into the relation of " fatherhood " and " sonship," there is a
recognition of the supremacy of the superior and of the allegiance due to him ; cf.
the Scandinavian example cited by H. M. Chadwick, *The Heroic Age,* 374 (Cambridge, 1912). Frazer (*GB.* v. 50 *sq.*) suggests that religious prostitution in the rites
of the marriage of Astarte and Adonis could lead to " sons " and " daughters "
of the deities, who would have brother, sister, and parent deities like their fathers
and mothers before them.

 [3] See Kuenen, *Hexateuch,* 58 *sq.*, n. 19 ; Driver, *Lit. of the Old Test.* 13 n. ; Orr,
Problem of the Old Test. 225.

P. 50. MARRIAGE OF GODS AND MEN.—The belief in supernatural parentage is widespread and ancient ; and the evidence is so abundant and impressive as to give rise to the theory that early man was ignorant of the physiological processes of conception and birth.[1] On the other hand, the evidence goes to show that (a) only the more exceptional or abnormal births are supposed to be of non-human origin, or that (b) only part of the babe is of human origin, the rest being due, e.g., to an ancestral spirit, or (c) that both human and non-human factors are involved, conception being, in some cases, not the direct result of intercourse, or, as among the A-kam-ba, women being supposed to have, in addition to their husbands, spiritual spouses to whom are due their offspring (Frazer, Tot. Ex. ii. 423 sq.). Finally (d) the explicit conviction that the god can grant child-birth or restrain it (Gen. xv. 3, xvi. 2, xxv. 21, etc.) is typical; cf. the numerous personal names denoting a child as a gift (above, p. 108 n. 2).

On the most obvious interpretation of Gen. iv. 1, Eve " got " (produced or created, קנה) a man with (the co-operation of) Yahweh " (cf. Skinner, ad loc.) ; and in the saying of the Talmud (Kiddush. 30 b), " there are three partners in every human birth : God, father, and mother." [2] The innumerable beliefs in some essential spiritual or supernatural factor in conception and birth range from the crudest ideas to the most elaborate discussions of traducianism and creationism (see Toy, Introd. to the Hist. of Rel., §§ 32 sqq.). The evidence as a whole points rather to the persisting predominance of particular sentiments and ideas of a spiritual character than to any persisting ignorance of the significance of the physical processes.[3] In Central Australia the spirit of an animal or plant totem-species enters a woman and a child is born ; in Melanesia a spirit-animal or plant enters and the child that is born is identified with the species. When, at the other end of the scale, the old Greeks speak of human beings originating through the operations of trees and rocks upon passing women, and when men spring up from the stones dropped by Deucalion and Pyrrha, and the men of Ægina are descended from ants, it is evident that they can hardly be said to differ in kind from the beliefs of the totem

[1] See, in general, Hartland, Primitive Paternity, esp. ch. i. (Spiritual Conception) ; Frazer, Totemism and Exogamy, iv. 61 sq.; Saint-Yves, Les Vierges mères et les naissances miraculeuses (1908) ; cf. also ERE. art. " Religion," 678, § 23 ; Malinowski, Psyche, iv. 110 sqq.

[2] I. Abrahams, Studies in Pharisaism and the Gospels, 2nd ser. (Camb., 1924), 150, 176. On the meaning of קנה, see Burney, Journ. of Theol. Stud. xxvii. 162 sqq.

[3] That conception and birth were mysterious phenomena is seen, e.g., in Job x. 10 sq. ; Eccles. xi. 5 ; cf. H. Wheeler Robinson in The People and the Book (ed. Peake, 1925), 369 sq.

33

tribes of Australia.[1] In the modern East procreative powers are freely attributed to the *jinn,* to spirits of the dead, and to the *welis.* The *jinn* are believed to intermarry with men and women, or to disturb their conjugal life ; and it would seem that in Babylonia tormented victims offered male or female images to evil spirits in order that they themselves might be left alone (Lagrange, 230). Women still visit the tombs of saints and *welis,* and other sacred shrines, in the hope of offspring, and the spirit of the saint or sacred ancestor is the reputed father of the child. Whatever may be due to whole-hearted faith, not in olden times alone has the part of the powerful spirit been played by some " sacred " man.[2]

The idea of a conjugal relationship between a deity and a land, people, or ruler is familiar ; and Jahweh's marriage relationship with his people is realistically developed when, in Ezek. xxiii. 4, he is represented as having children by two wives, Oholah (Samaria), and Oholibah (Jerusalem). W. R. S. (*Prophets of Israel,* 170 *sq.,* 410 *sq.*), describing the marriage symbolism in Israelite religion, observes that the physical usage was the earlier, otherwise the allegorical use (in Hosea, etc.) could hardly be explained. It is also obvious on psychological grounds that what is really fundamental is a conviction of a relationship between people and god, so intimate as to find only in the marriage symbolism its most suggestive and fruitful expression.

Gods are " married " to other gods, (*a*) to provide them with consorts, on the human analogy, (*b*) to enhance their functions by the addition of particular female attributes, or (*c*) to unite different cults. Of particular significance is (*d*) Yahweh's " marriage " relation with Israel which was believed to guarantee her prosperity. Similarly the marriage of the Queen-Archon with the bull-god Dionysus in the festival of the Anthesteria was presumably to benefit the land by uniting the god and—in this case—its leading representative. In Babylonia the marriage of Ninurta and Gula or Bau was an important spring festival celebrating the union of the young sun-god with the goddess of vegetation. With this more or less magical fertility rite may be compared the *hieros gamos* of Zeus and Hera, where, however,

---

[1] J. L. Myres, in *Anthropology and the Classics,* 128.

[2] See Curtiss, *Primitive Semitic Religion,* 107, 116 *sqq.,* 123 ; Frazer, *GB.* v. 76 *sq.,* 79 *sqq.* In the Syriac story of the " Merchant of Harran " the barren woman is cured by a stone which she imagines to be from the block which Jacob had rolled from the well near Harran, and which could cure barrenness ; and the merchant who has deceived her, marvels at her faith and can only wonder what a genuine fragment would have accomplished (Burkitt, *Euphemia and the Goth,* 155 *sqq.*).

other *motifs* may participate, *e.g.*, an idealization and symbol of the marriage of ordinary mortals.[1]

Not uncommon is the marriage of girls (*a*) to rivers, lakes, etc. (even fishing-nets), to ensure the productivity and fertility of the latter, and (*b*) to images, etc., for their own benefit (Frazer, *GB.* ii. 147 *sq.*). Virgins were frequently dedicated, betrothed, or married to deities (cf. the Phœnician name אַרשתבעל " espoused of Baal "); and in such cases the bride might be (1) set apart for the god, or (2) a sacrificial victim, or (3) appropriated by the men who administer the cult.[2] When a vow is made on behalf of a girl she cannot be married until the vow is paid (Canaan, *JPOS.* vi. 59); and, according to Curtiss, *Prim. Sem. Rel.* 167 *sq.*, if a girl is dedicated to a saint it is a question whether or no she may marry. At Remtha in Hauran when a man is dangerously ill a daughter or sister may be vowed to ez-Zab'i, and when she is of marriageable age, she is dressed as a bride, taken to his shrine, and the first of the saint's descendants who sees her can take her as his wife, or dispose of her in marriage to any suitor who will pay him a dowry (Curtiss, *Expositor*, Dec. 1904, p. 464). Other gods than Bel of Babylon were provided with couches (see Frazer on Pausanias ii. 17, 3).[3] The consecration of the couch of Nebo at Calah on the occasion of his annual marriage is minutely described.[4] In Babylon the *entu* or bride of the god was of the highest caste, the wife of the patron god of the city (*CAH.* 1[2], 536); the great Sargon, who " knew not his father," and had for mother an *enitu*, was apparently the offspring of a " sacred " marriage.[5] Generally speaking, when a girl is dedicated it is not always clear whether it is to temple-harlotry or to absolute chastity.[6]

When Antiochus Epiphanes proposed to marry the goddess

[1] Farnell, *Cults*, i. 184, 192; *Greece and Babylon*, 263 *sq.* On the marriage of Adonis and Aphrodite celebrated at Alexandria in 273 B.C., see Frazer, *GB.* v. 224; Gressmann, *Expositor*, iii. (1921), 426 *sqq.* The Egyptian dynastic marriage was both divine and human, the queen being the " god's wife " (Moret, *Du Caractère Relig. de la Royauté Pharaonique*).

[2] See for (2) Farnell, *Greece and Bab.* 266; cf. the " Bride of the Nile," Frazer, *GB.* vi. 38 *sqq.*; and for (3) *GB.* ii. 150 *sq.* and v. 67 *sq.* (in Kikuyu the offspring are regarded as the deity's children).

[3] Apollo was nightly closeted with his prophetess during the months when he gave oracles at Patara (*GB.* ii. 135).

[4] *Journ. of Amer. Or. Soc.* xviii. 1897; i. 153; see *GB.* ii. 130.

[5] See further p. 613. The story of Paulina and the god Anubis (Josephus, *Antiq.* xviii. 3) at least shows what was considered credible; cf. also the stories of Nectanebus and Olympias, and see O. Weinreich's monograph (*Der Trug des Nektanebos*, Leipzig, 1911).

[6] For the latter, see in general Fehrle, *Die kultische Keuschheit im Altertum* (Giessen, 1910), and p. 614 below.

Nanæa in Elymais in order to seize the temple treasures as a " dowry "
(2 Macc. i. 14)—a trick he is said to have tried at Hierapolis—and
when Demetrius, son of Antigonus (c. 300 B.C.), had rooms at the
back of the Parthenon, and was entertained by Athene, and when
Anthony agreed to marry Athene at Athens for her dowry of a thousand
talents, each as the " husband " of the goddess could legitimatize
his claims.[1] Such marriages would be as intelligible in their day
as when Reuben, Absalom, and Adonijah by their several actions
laid claim to the rights and privileges of their fathers (see *Lectures*,
467 n. 2 ; *Kinship*, 109 *sq.*). In other words, the more conspicuous
ideas associated with marriage are those not only of fertility and
productivity, but also of appropriation and transmission of rights,
the woman being the vehicle (even as parentage is at times ascribed
solely to the father, the mother being the nurturer of the child), or
the one in whom rights or powers are vested.[2] See further below,
pp. 613, 637 *sq.*

P. 52. CHANGE OF SEX.—For examples of such changes see
Kinship, 304 *sqq.* (Allat, Sowā, etc.). The male Ruḍa (רצו) becomes
female (Lidzbarski, *Ephemeris*, iii. 92). Shamash, the sun-god, is
treated as feminine in one of the Amarna Letters (Knudtzon, No. 323,
from Askalon), also in South Arabia (*KAT*. 139 ; Nielsen, 321). In
the treaty between Shubbiluliuma of Hatti and Mattiuaza of Mitanni,
the goddess Shamash of Arinna, before whom a copy is placed,
" grants kingship and queenship," and was presumably the patroness
of the dynasty. 'Athtar in South Arabia was both *baal* and mother
(Barton, *Semitic Origins*, 125 *sqq.*), and in Babylonia Ishtar was male
as morning-star and female as evening-star. The god Tammuz has
at times feminine titles (Jastrow, *Rel. Belief in Bab. and Ass.* 347 n. ;
Burney, *Judges*, xix.).

The goddesses of Babylonia are mostly colourless—merely feminines
(Jastrow, 124 *sq.*), and Wellhausen remarks that the Semitic male
and female deities are not, primarily at least, married couples. The

---

[1] In the Twenty-fifth Dynasty marriage with the Theban royal priestess, the
" adoratrix of the god," secured the Pharaoh's position (*CAH*. iii. 268, 273;
GB. ii. 134).

[2] Among the Garos of Assam " a woman is merely the vehicle by which property
descends from one generation to another " (Frazer, *Tot. Ex.* iv. 297, citing
Playfair, *The Garos*, 71 *sq.*). On an African custom for the eldest son to inherit
all his father's wives, see *FOT.*, i. 541 and n. 3. The mock king at the Babylonian
Sacæa took the king's concubines (*GB*. ix. 355), and the supposed incarnation
of the dead king in Bunyoro during his reign of a week had the royal widows
(Frazer, *GB*. abbreviated ed., p. vi, citing Roscoe, *Soul of Central Africa*, 200).
In Mexico the youth who represented the god Tezcatlipoca was married to four
girls representing the four seasons, and was subsequently sacrificed (*GB*. ix. 278 *sq.*).

causes of change of sex are not necessarily due to change in type of kinship. The desire to possess a deity with feminine attributes will account for the transformation, in the Far East, of the male Avalo-kiteshvara into the Chinese and Japanese Kuanyin, the goddess of mercy (Bertholet and Lehmann, *Lehrbuch d. Rel. gesch.* i. 238). But the deity can be alike male and female. Thus Gudea addresses the mother-goddess Gatumdag as mother and father (Dhorme, 166), Ningirsu is both " mother " and " lord " (*CAH.* i.[2] 208), and Ikhnaton's sun-god is mother and father—in that order.[1] Besides the bi-sexual references to Yahweh (Deut. xxxii. 18 ; Isa. xlvi. 3), there are striking phrases in the Odes of Solomon (in xix. the Father is milked by the Holy Spirit).[2] But whereas impassioned religious feeling finds in its deity the highest male and female attributes, only at a secondary stage does art represent it as hermaphrodite (cf. Lagrange, 139).[3]

P. 52. MOTHER EARTH.—Pindar's belief (*Nem.* vi. i. 2 ; cf. Hesiod, *Works,* 108) finds its parallel in Ecclesiasticus xl. 1, less clearly in Job i. 21. Greek influence might be suspected in these passages, but, in its more undeveloped forms, the idea is not strange to the Semites.[4] After all, the Semites were at an early date in touch with Hittite, Mitannian, and other northern peoples, and the line between Semitic and Greek thought must not be drawn too rigidly (cf. p. 495 *sq.*). As against Dieterich (*Mutter Erde*), Nilsson (*Greek Rel.* 122) argues that Earth as " all mother," represents the idea of Nature rather than a real divinity. Her person is that of a woman whose lower limbs are hidden in the ground ; it is the conception that seems to lie behind Ps. cxxxix. 15. Man is formed from the earth.[5] He is moulded— the Hebrew verb is used of the potter's craft ; cf. Prometheus, and

---

[1] Breasted, *Rel. and Thought in Ancient Egypt,* 318, 330, 334 ; cf. Farnell, *Evol. of Rel.* 180 (from a North American tribe, " Who is my mother, who is my father ? Only Thou, O God ").

[2] Cf. the hymns of Namdev and Tukaram to Vithoba (Krishna) ; see Bouquet, in *Theology,* viii. 203, Macnicol, *Indian Theism,* 123, 218.

[3] Sex is secondary when, elsewhere, the bull-roarer is used in connexion with fertility-rites : in New Guinea it is produced when the yams are ready for digging, and is then called "mother of yams " (Haddon, *Study of Man,* 305 *sq.*). In another case it is differentiated into male and female (*Journ. of Royal Anthrop. Inst.* xiv. 312). Frazer also cites the use of " male " and "female " flutes used after circumcision rites in German North Guinea (Schellong, *Internat. Archiv f. Ethnog.* ii. 156).

[4] See Nöldeke, *Archiv f. Relig.* viii. 161 *sq.* ; Baudissin, 20 n. 1, 443 *sq.,* 505 *sq.*

[5] For Berosus (p. 43 above) see Lagrange, 386, and for other Bab. evidence, *ib.* 229, 385 ; *KAT.* 497 ; Dhorme, *Archiv f. Relig.* viii. 550 *sq.* ; L. W. King, *Seven Tablets of Creation,* i. xxxiii *sq.* Ea made men of clay, and of clay Aruru made Engidu. Proper names meaning " son (daughter) of the earth " (*abil, mār [mārat] irṣitim*) are cited by Ranke.

Khnum of Egypt; Ishtar is also called the potter. The metaphorical use of the word "seed," and the common association of human life with the rest of nature, is perhaps of more significance than the difference which is drawn between animal or human life and vegetable life, and which is emphasized by W. R. S. when he seeks to trace the development of the primitive sacrifice.

That the account of creation, as it stands in Gen. ii., is absolutely more primitive than that in ch. i. (p. 106 n. 1) is not easily determined. Already in ii. 5 *sq.* two conceptions can be distinguished (flood [?] and rain as sources of fertility, Skinner, *Gen.* 55 *sq.*). In ch. i. plants and animals are produced from the earth by the divine command. "The earth itself is conceived as endowed with productive power" (Skinner, 23). Similarly, Yahweh "calls" for the corn in Ezek. xxxvi. 29, and it responds; while the Babylonian Tablet of Creation opens with a reference to the time when neither heaven nor earth nor the gods had been "named." In Babylonian speculation a mental image (*zikru*) seems to precede physical creation (Skinner, 31 *sq.*, see Hehn in the *Sachau-Festschrift*, 46)—that the Platonic archetypal ideas have their forerunner among early and primitive peoples was observed long ago by Tylor (*Primitive Culture*[4], ii. 244 *sq.*). Evidently some intrinsic or immanent productive power is implied in Gen. i., as also in the case of the processes of birth which the god is believed to control (p. 513). It is noteworthy that the brooding (?) spirit in Gen. i. 2 plays no further part in the biblical cosmogony; it may have come in from another (? Phœnician) cosmogony.[1] Skinner (*Gen.* 18) suggests that the spirit perhaps symbolizes "an immanent principle of life and order in the as yet undeveloped chaos." It is, in effect, difficult to grasp with precision the ideas of growth and production that prevailed among ancient and primitive peoples, and precisely how far processes were natural or supernatural, or merely taken for granted (see pp. 535, 586). At all events, the idea that the earth has a certain inherent power or life of its own, and that man is in some way bound up therewith, explains how, in Manichæan dualism, when all the "light" has been separated from the "dark," there remains the Dark Matter, the Clod (*Bōlos*) (Burkitt, *Rel. of the Manichees*, 65 *sq.*; S. A. Cook, *Journ. of Theol. Stud.* xxvi. 389).

P. 54. FEAR AND THE GODS.—The "eloquent French writer," Renan (*Hist. d'Israel*, i. 29), quoting Statius (*Theb.* iii. 661), endorses

---

[1] See Meyer, *Israeliten*, 213 and n.; and on the way in which the idea of the creative efficacy of the divine spirit ($rū^a h$) verges on immanence and pantheism, see Baudissin, 443 *sq.*, 505 *sq.*

a view current among the Epicurean philosophers, found in Lucretius, and still frequently reiterated. To some extent it is well founded.[1] Fear is undoubtedly a powerful element in Semitic religion.[2] Gloom is characteristic (see p. 258), and Baudissin (57 *sq.*) considers that fear of the gods and dependence upon them are typically Semitic. Yet W. R. S. finds divine immanence as well as " transcendence " among the Semites (p. 194). Fear of ghosts and of the dead is undoubtedly prominent in religion (pp. 323 n., 370 n. 1), and there is fear of the *jinn* (p. 123 *sq.*) ; but W. R. S. maintains that fear of the supernatural paralyses progress (pp. 154, 395), and is the negation of moral order. A working relationship with unseen forces appears in the most primitive societies (pp. 53, 137) ; and certainly, where fear predominates among primitive peoples, the communities are unstable and unprogressive. Ignorance of causes and ignorance of the important physiological functions are common sources of fear, and although fear is dormant and easily aroused, the conquest of nature and the victory over fear of the unknown are the beginning of social development (p. 121 *sq.*).

Anthropology and psychology support W. R. S. " The maxim that fear first made gods in the universe is certainly not true in the light of anthropology " (Malinowski, in *Science, Religion, and Reality,* ed. Needham, 82). Durkheim (224) positively asserts that the primitive regards his gods as friends, kinsmen, and protectors. So usual is this that in due course only the uncertain, arbitrary, and hostile spirits are respected. " Although fear is a cause, it is certainly not the sufficient reason of religion " (Galloway, *Philosophy of Rel.* 75). " There is no quality in fear that fits it to be the so-called original religious emotion " (Leuba, *Psychological Study of Rel.* 129). Fear is a running away, it is harmful ; there is an emotional progression in religion, and fear yields to awe (*id.* 132). " Fear " does not explain the history of religion, whereas " awe " is another feeling, a recognition of greatness and a sense of a not unfriendly relation with the cosmos (*id.* 146 *sq.*). Fear is only true if we admit wonder, admiration, respect, and even love ; though " reverence . . . or the sense of discipline would be impossible but for the dash of fear that they contain." [3] This is not

---

[1] The words are also found in Petronius, *Frag.* xxvii. 1 (cf. Servius, *ad* Virg. *Æn.* ii. 715), though Statius has the better claim. (So Mr. W. T. Vesey of Gonville and Caius College, Cambridge, in a private communication.)

[2] See Nöldeke, *ERE.*, " Arabs," 660a, and *Arch. f. Rel.*, 1898, pp. 361 *sqq.* ; cf. Ar. *ittacā,* " be pious," etc., properly " be on one's guard." On the suggested connexion between *ilāh,* " god," and *'aliha,* " fear, dread," see Kautzsch, *E.Bi.* col. 3324, § 115 ; Fischer, *Islamica,* i. 391.

[3] Marett, *Psychol. and Folk-lore,* 160 ; *Threshold of Rel.* 13.

inhibition but self-restraint. Fear can crush and kill; but it is not the ignorance of peril, it is the consciousness of it, the renewal of self-confidence, the act of readjustment as a mental and moral growth, which mark the progressive steps (Crawley, *Tree of Life*, 291 *sq.*; cf. Durkheim, 223 *sq.*). The subject is of extreme methodological importance, and W. R. S. treats it dynamically; for the history of religions and of religion in general, the phases of awe, confidence, etc., are throughout more significant than those of fear, dread, etc.

P. 56. AL-LAT, MOTHER OF THE GODS.—The great mother-goddess Ishtar, patroness of birth (as her name Mylitta indicates, Herod. i. 131, 199), was "creator" (*bânat*), and "mistress" (*belit*) of the gods, and is ideographically described as a potter. The well-known type represents her with open breast and a suckling on her left arm. With another "mistress of the gods," Damkina (the Δαύκη of Damascius), the wife of Ea and mother of Marduk, and with Isis, the mother of Horus, Ishtar is a powerful intercessor in Assyria, and a prototype of the Madonna, and of the figure in the vision in Rev. xii.[1] Among the great "mothers" (Anahita, Cybele, etc.) is Lāt or rather Allat.[2] Apparently a sun-goddess (Wellh. 33), in Palmyra she is found coupled with Shamash (Cooke, 275 *sq.*), and the equation לת(א)והב—'Aθηνόδωρος (the son of Zenobia) points to her identification with Athene, who is named in Greek inscriptions from Hauran (Wadd. 2203, etc.), appears on coins of Gabala, etc., and was worshipped at Emesa. An altar found at Cordova names, among Syrian deities, νάζαια (Al-'Ozzā) and ('A)θηνᾶ 'Αλλαθ (*Arch. f. Rel.* xxii. 127). As "Αλιλατ—Urania (Herod. iii. 8) she is mother of Orotal—Dionysus, to whom corresponds the Nabatæan Dushara. The mother and son are associated at Petra; but at Hejra (*CIS.* ii. 198) she stands second. For Allat as a chthonic goddess, see p. 566.

The Petra festival has been much discussed.[3] Mithraic and Christian influence has been suspected. Wellhausen and Lagrange urge that the cult of a child-god is contrary to Semitic feeling (cf. *De Syria Dea*, xxxv.). On the other hand, 'Aziz (עזיז) or Ares, venerated at Edessa, and named with Arṣu (ארצו) on a Palmyrene inscription (Cooke, 295 *sq.*), is the *bonus puer* of a Greek inscription at Soada and of Dacian inscriptions (see *Kinship*, 302).[4] Youthful gods

---

[1] *KAT.* 360 *sq.*, 428 *sq.*, 440; Nielsen, *Der dreieinige Gott*, i. 337 *sqq.*

[2] Nabatæan inscription from Ṣalḥad, Vogüé 8=*CIS.* ii. 185.

[3] See Wellhausen, 49; Lagrange, 189 n.; Cumont, *CR.* of the *Acad. d. Inscr.*, 1911, p. 293; W. Weber, *Arch. f. Rel.* xix. 331 *sqq.*

[4] With the Palmyrene inscription is the representation of various figures, including a woman with a child on her knees, *Beit. z. Assyriol.*, 1902, p. 221; Cumont, *Études Syr.* 272; Nielsen, 122 *sq.*

are by no means unknown (Baudissin, *Adonis*, Index, *s.v.* " jugendliche götter "), and the influence of Isis and Harpocrates is possible. Of greater interest is the relief found at Petra itself, representing a winged child contending with winged lion-headed monsters, which Dalman is tempted to associate with the cult of Dusares.[1]

Al-'Ozzā (p. 57 n.), with Allāt and Manāt, the three " daughters of Allah," in the Coran, is the " lady 'Ozzai " to whom a man in a South Arabian inscription offers a golden image on behalf of his sick daughter Amath-Ozzai (Nielsen, *Der dreieinige Gott*, 318). Human sacrifice and licentious practices distinguish her cult. Isaac of Antioch identified her with Beltis, and calls her the " Star " (see *Kinship*, 300 *sq.*, Wellh. 40 *sq.*).

P. 58. FEMALE DEITIES.—The prominence of female deities is also explained by the considerable share of women in labour and management (cf. Wellhausen, 208 *sq.*, and, on women's part in primitive agriculture, Frazer, *GB*. vii. 113 *sqq.*). There are many examples of mother-right (see the summary by E. Meyer, *Gesch. des Alt.* i. 1, § 10); but fluctuations in the position of women and recurring transitions from one type of kinship to another are to be recognized rather than any single sociological development. The position of women is not necessarily the measure to a people's civilization ; and while, on the one hand, females in subjection to their husbands were not necessarily without rights and responsibilities, on the other hand, in Assyrian law, where the woman remains in her father's house, she has not the freedom that this type of marriage might have led us to expect.[2] The superior position of the mother's brother among the Bedouins,[3] and the Talmudic references to the resemblance between children and the mother's brother (*Kinship*, 195 n. 1), are among the elements that go to distinguish mother-kinship, though in themselves they are not necessarily derived from any such system ; and in general the question of the relation between female deities and the treatment of women is much more complicated than when W. R. S. wrote.[4]

---

[1] Dalman (*Petra und seine Felsheiligtümer* [Leipzig, 1908], 355 *sq.*) refers to the winged Horus on the Louvre seal of Baal-nathan (Lidzbarski, *Ephem.* i. 140 n.), and the boy holding a serpent, on the Taanach altar (Sellin, *Tell Ta'annek*, i. 77 ; Vincent, *Canaan*, 185). See further Nielsen, *Handbuch d. altarab-Altertumskunde*, 230 *sq.*

[2] Koschaker, *MVAG*. 1921, pp. 60 *sqq.* ; Ebeling in Gressmann, *Altorient. Texte z. A.T.*[2], 415, §§ 25 *sqq.* ; cf. the much stronger Californian and other cases cited by Westermarck, *Origin and Development of Moral Ideas*, i. 657.

[3] See G. Jacob, *Studien*, iii.: *Leben d. vorislam. Bed.*[2] 40.

[4] It may be added that in Palestine many a modern shrine is consecrated to a female who is sometimes associated with a male, whose sister or daughter she is (Schumacher, *Jaulan*, 209 ; *Qy. St.* of the Palestine Explor. Fund, 1875, p. 209 ; 1877, p. 99).

P. 58 n. 1.—See *Keilinschrift Bibliothek*, ii. 251 ; cf. the now well-known hymn, L. W. King, *Seven Tablets of Creation*, i. 222 *sqq.* ; Gressmann, *Altorient. Texte z. Alten Test.*[1], 85 *sq.*, [2] 257 *sqq.* ; and excerpts in Peake, *People and the Book*, 50 *sq.*, Wardle, *Israel and Babylon*, 76 *sqq.*

P. 60. AUTHORITY.—W. R. S. is dealing with the ideas of government, administration and authority, human and divine, and the relationship between rulers and subjects. The " king " is properly a counsellor (p. 62 n.)—cf. the title *Sayyid* (speaker) and the Heb. *sôd* (counsel)—and had typical religious or priestly duties. Similarly the modern sheikh has certain religious duties : when there is war he will make vows to the ancestral *weli* or saint, offer sacrifices at the tomb venerated by the tribe, and proclaim a fast in case of drought. There was no absolute monarchy, and, except in so far as his special functions were concerned, even a Babylonian king had no more rights than a private citizen.[1] The authority of parents was, and is, weak (*Kinship*, 68 *sq.*), and Westermarck (*Moral Ideas*, i. 599 *sq.*, 607) contrasts this weakness among rudimentary peoples with the parental authority among those more civilized. None the less, an Arab father may expect an almost servile deference (*Lectures*, 563) ; there might be stern treatment of children (Prov. xix. 18, with Toy's note), and a rebellious son might be stoned (Deut. xxi. 21 ; cf. Targum on Eccles. iii. 2). Yet even as regards the wife there was no *patria potestas* in the Roman sense ; she did not change her kin on marriage (*Kinship*, 66 n., 77, 122, 142, 203) ; and as regards the *'ebed* (servant), care must be taken not to read too much into the term (p. 68 *sq.*).

In the absence of an explicit constitution or organization, things are left to the will of a few individuals on the one hand, to custom on the other. For Arabia " the words *noblesse oblige* are no mere phrase but the complete truth." [2] In Israel there were things that ought or ought not to be done ; and a distinction was drawn between the days of unrestrained individuality and the unifying tendency of the monarchy. As for Arabia, Wellhausen lays stress upon the *secular* ideas of Right : the religious root has withered away ; Right is profane, and not, as in Israel, bound up with religion (*op. cit.* 14 *sq.*). In the Babylonian Code of Hammurabi, law has been almost severed from religion, society is divided into classes, and the general conditions are more advanced than those presupposed by the Israelite collections of laws. Neither among the loosely knit Arabian tribes nor in a Babylonia shortly to fall before invading Kassites, can we expect to find a

---

[1] Jastrow, *Rel. Beliefs of Bab. and Ass.*, 384 *sq.* (with which cf. *CAH.*[2] i. 412). On the restriction of monarchical power in Israel, see Day, *AJSL.* xl. 98 *sqq.*

[2] Wellhausen, *Ein Gemeinwesen ohne Obrigkeit*, 7 (Göttingen, 1900).

starting-point for our conception of ancient authority, and another approach must be sought.

It would seem that self-redress is more marked among the lower and simpler stages of society (viz. the Lower and Higher Hunters), whereas among Agriculturists more attention is paid to the maintenance of order, and public control is more in evidence. The development of social order may be roughly correlated with advance in economic culture ; and, as we advance from the Lower Hunters, we get larger societies, and by degrees provision is made for the administration of justice within these extended groups.[1] Periodical gatherings for religious, social, and judicial purposes are found among many primitive peoples (I. King, *Development of Religion*, 89 *sq.*, 100) ; and systematic lawlessness and lynch law, or the general absence of customary restraint, may be regarded not as a primary stage in the evolution of order, but as a transition between the decline and fall of one period of development and the inauguration of another. What is fundamental is the stage where religious custom and social custom are more or less closely interrelated parts of one organism or system.

In ordeals and oaths, in curses and blessings, and in regulative and restrictive taboos there is an implicit mechanism which is for the systematization of society.[2] W. R. S. himself (p. 162 *sq.*) comments upon the " instrinic power of holy things to vindicate themselves," and on the difference between man's confidence in it and the conviction that it is not safe to wait until the god vindicates himself (see below, p. 550). The difference is important, for here is to be sought the root of authority : the mechanism already implicit in the social structure and its development, on the one side, and, on the other, the individuals who by virtue of rank or ability are representatives, in one sense, of the group, and, in another, of this mechanism (see p. 591). Nowhere does there exist any vaguely abstract " group-mind " ; and even in Australia, where there is a " common consent to the observance of certain rules " over very large tracts, it is the elders who commonly uphold and enforce the customary law.[3] The headmen will form a council, and at the great initiation ceremonies there will be an exchange of ideas leading to modification and uniformity.[4] Even among rudimentary peoples, where the group-mind, the social mechanism,

[1] Hobhouse, Wheeler, and Ginsberg, *The Material Culture of the Simpler Peoples*, 46 *sqq.*, 82.

[2] See, *e.g.*, Frazer, *Psyche's Task*[2] (1913 ; with the sub-title, " a discourse concerning the influence of superstitition on the growth of institutions ").

[3] G. P. Wheeler, *The Tribe*, 9.

[4] Wheeler, 81 ; Crawley, *Mystic Rose*, 143 *sqq.*, 181 *sqq.* ; Westermarck, *Moral Ideas*, i. 603 *sqq.*, 619.

and the absence of individual enterprise seem most predominant, important changes can be made. Spencer and Gillen (*Native Tribes of Central Australia*, 12 *sq.*, 14 *sq.*) comment on the authority exercised by powerful men in introducing changes that are felt to be beneficial to the tribe ; and among the Omaha the words " and the people thought " are the preamble to every change, which, of course, is due not to an abstract " group-mind," but to the " authorities " for the time being (Hartland, *Primitive Law*, 204 *sqq.*, esp. 209).

Continuity amid change, and with the maintenance of the idea of authority—this is the fundamental conception the discussion of which W. R. S. opens. The great changes in the past can be ascribed to men who, by their superior personality, have wielded an authority which was above local vanity and rivalry. They were pre-eminently religious leaders (*e.g.* Moses and Mohammed, see p. 70), or primarily religious teachers or reformers like the prophets, or they were outstanding rulers, men whose rise was attended with significant social or political developments. Throughout, owing to the personal influence of such men, there was apt to be extreme arbitrariness and caprice, and an absence of stability (cf. W. R. S., *Prophets of Israel*, 94 ; *CAH.* i.[2] 210 *sq.*, 216) ; and owing to the divine authority claimed by or freely granted to them, the problem of " true " or " false " in the sphere of religion (*e.g.* as regards prophets, " sacred " men, or Messiahs) quickly arose. In Babylonia the divine authority of rulers, priests, and judges meant that misfortune and wrong-doing could shake confidence alike in the representative individuals or in the god or gods whose mouthpiece, vehicle, or representative they were supposed to be (cf. Jastrow, *Rel. Beliefs*, 275 *sq.*). In the old Egyptian tale of the " Eloquent Peasant," the underlying idea is that " the norm of just procedure is in the hands of the ruling class ; if they fail, where else shall it be found ? " [1] When reliance is placed upon some pre-eminent authority, forged sayings may be attributed to him and circulated by interested though conflicting parties (as in the case of Mohammed, *Ency. Brit.* xvii. 414*c*, *d*). But authority is also found in the principle *vox populi vox dei* ; and, says a tradition of Mohammed, " my people will never agree in an error " (*loc. cit.* 416*a*). The Coran remains the norm and authority of Islam ; [2] but a written authority needs supplementing, and by the side of the Jewish " written law " there grew up the " oral law " (see W. R. S., *Old Test. in the Jewish Church*, 45 *sqq.*). The sacred myths and traditions of a people represent, strictly speaking, only the particular stage

---

[1] Breasted, *Development of Religion and Thought in Ancient Egypt*, 221.

[2] See C. H. Toy, "The Semitic Conception of Absolute Law," *Nöldeke-Festschrift*, 802.

of thought at which they severally arose ; but a canonical literature extending—like the Old Testament, and more especially the whole Bible—over centuries of most vital development, affords a more objective basis for a dynamic conception of authority. The Bible, together with the apocryphal and pseudepigraphical writings of Jews and early Christians, presents a unique example of what has been called " the law of religious historiography "—the renovation and transformation of earlier authoritative sources in order to make them comply with the requirements of the present.[1] Renovation or re-writing is succeeded in course of time by reinterpretation ; and it is proper to refer to W. R. S.'s anxiety in his *Old Testament in the Jewish Church* (especially the Preface and opening chapter) to show that there can be continuity in reinterpretation, however revolutionary the new stage might seem to be.

Society, viewed as a whole, is a moral force (cf. Wellhausen, *Heid.* 226) ; and, as W. R. S. points out, the group-unit includes the gods. But ultimate authority does not lie in the empirical and visible group which is developed by its more energetic and critical constituents, nor does it lie precisely in the system of ideas uniting the group and its outstanding individuals with the sphere of the supernatural or super-sensuous as understood at the time. The great prophets, it is true, spoke as though they were recalling the people to an earlier ideal from which they had fallen, but the ideal of which they themselves became conscious did not, in the most conspicuous cases, lead back to an actual event of ancient history, but to a reinterpretation of it which was pregnant for the future. The system of ideas was enlarged, and, this being a general truth, ultimate authority is seen to lie in the ultimate whole of which the several groups and systems of ideas are the imperfectly developed parts. Ideas of governance and authority are apt to be undifferentiated among ancient or primitive peoples, and accordingly there is a relation between social order and the world order which often amounts to an identity. This accounts alike for the most impressive of religious beliefs and for the most extraordinary of magical practices. W. R. S. is mainly con-cerned with the ideas of social organization and of the organization of gods and worshippers ; but the question of order in the social sphere and in the external world is of exceptional interest for the history of ideas, both of right and righteousness, and of the natural powers and functions of gods and of their human representatives. See below, p. 658.

P. 67 n. 3.—See further *KAT.* 470 *sqq.* ; Lagrange, 99 *sqq.* The

---

[1] Kuenen, " The Critical Method," in the *Modern Review,* i. (1880), 705 ; cf. S. A. Cook, *Notes on O.T. History,* 62.

name of the Edomite king (Malik-ramu) is uncertain; see *KAT.*
467.

P. 68 n. 3.—The Phœnician reference is to Plautus, *Pœnulus*,
994, 1001, 1141 *sq.*—*auo auo donni hau amma silli hauon bene
silli*, " hail, hail my lord ! hail my mother ! hail my son ! " For
another explanation, see L. H. Gray, *Amer. Journ. of Sem. Lang.*
xxxix. 83. With the salutation compare (with Stübe) Meleager
of Gadara :

$$\text{'Αλλ'εἰ μὲν Σύρος ἐσσί, Σελόμ· εἰ δ'οὖν σύγε φοίνιξ,}$$
$$\text{Αὐδονίς· εἰ δ'''Ελλην, χαῖρε· τὸ δ'αὐτὸ φράσον,}$$

where Αὐδονίς is Scaliger's emendation (Wex, *Melet.* 29).

P. 70. COMPOUNDS OF IMR, AMR.—On such compounds, see A.
Fischer, *Islamica*, i. 4, 380 *sqq.* In the Hebrew Amariah, in S. Arabian
names of the type אבאמר, עמאמר, and in the Palmyrene אמרישא
(αμρισαμσος) another interpretation has been suggested : Yahweh
(etc.) promises or commands (see *E.Bi.* " Amariah " ; Cooke, 267).
The Phœn. אשתנת " man of Tanith " is doubtful (*CIS.* i. 542). In
the corresponding Babylonian names Amel-Sin (*KAT.* 537, 540),
Amel-Marduk (Evīl-Merodach), Amel-Nusku, etc., the second element
is a divine name. In S. Arabian אדם is used of one who belongs to
a god (Hartmann, *Islam. Orient,* ii. 405). Methushael (Gen. iv. 18)
is usually interpreted " man of god " (*mutu-sha-il*) ; but the relative
particle is a difficulty (Gray, *Heb. Prop. Names,* 165 n.). Methuselah
may be a deliberate alteration, as though " armed man " (Budde ; see
Skinner on Gen. v. 25). Apart from *mu-ut-Baal* in the Amarna
Letters, 255 l. 3, the clearest example is the name of the Tyrian king
of *circ.* 900 B.C., Μεθουάσταρτος, " man of Astarte " (Jos. *c. Ap.* i. 18 ;
Nöldeke, *E.Bi.* col. 3286, § 42).

P. 74. MONOTHEISM.—W. R. S. consistently denied that the
Semites had any particular capacity for monotheism ; see *Lectures and
Essays,* 425 *sq.* (an article written in 1877), 612 (a review of Renan's
Histoire, 1887). On the other hand, Nöldeke (*Sketches from Eastern
History,* 5 [1892]) considers that there are strong tendencies to monotheism among the Semites, Baudissin (*ZDMG.* 1903, p. 836) holds
that a clearer recognition of divine unity characterizes Semitic religion,
and, not to mention other names, the division of opinion indicates
that the problem of monotheism in general and of Semitic monotheism
in particular stands in need of restatement.

In the first place, there are certain tendencies which make for
polytheism (polydæmonism, etc.) and for monotheism (henotheism,
etc.). So, as regards the former, (*a*) specialization of function provides
deities with helpers and subordinates ; (*b*) deities (spirits, etc.) are

postulated to account for new or strange phenomena that lie outside the usual activities of the known gods ; (c) keener analysis of processes multiplies the gods (like the twelve Indigitamenta of Rome who presided over the twelve successive stages in the labours of the agriculturist); (d) personifications and abstractions multiply even to the extent of describing every phenomenon of the emotional or mental life as a " god " ;[1] (e) gods are differentiated, with the result that epithets, or manifestations, or embodiments become separate and distinct deities ; (f) impersonal processes are replaced or supplemented by personal agencies (e.g., the Indian wind-gods Vayu and Surya are more personal than Vata and Savitar) ; (g) gods are introduced from elsewhere by reformers, etc. ; and (h) new gods arise when the old traditional gods are felt to be remote or useless.

Among the tendencies which make for monotheism are (a) co-ordination of attributes or functions, when one god takes over those of others ; (b) the recognition of the points of similarity among different local, national, or functional gods ; (c) the disinclination to tolerate rival powers ; (d) social or political alliance or fusion, involving the co-ordination or fusion of gods ; (e) the rise through historical circumstances of one god above others through pre-eminence of a city, priesthood, or ruler, or through spread of cult ; and (f) the introduction of a new god who drives out or supersedes the rest. The rise of Re of Heliopolis in the Fifth Dynasty, and in Babylonia of Enlil of Nippur, later of Marduk (in the First Babylonian Dynasty), and later still of Asshur, are illustrations of (e). In the royal names Shamshi-Adad and in a divine name like Ishtar-Chemosh are unifying tendencies which make for monotheism (or rather henotheism) ; a combination of deities of different sexes may also perhaps be recognized in the Sabæan אלאלת (see Meyer, Israel. 212 n.). On the oft-cited tablet where Ninib (Ninurta) is Marduk of strength, Shamash Marduk of justice, and Adad, Nergal, etc., Marduk of rain, battle, etc., see Wardle, Israel and Babylon, 136.

Next, in the ebb and flow of religion there is a tendency for the masses to find the national religion—that of the rulers and priests—unintelligible, or out of touch with popular needs. The Great Gods, though not ignored or unknown, become remote, and the practical religion in the Mohammedan East is not that of Allah but of the local

---

[1] Cf. Nilsson, Greek Religion, 270, and ERE. s.v. " Personification." How to draw the line between a personification which is mythological and polytheistic and one that is purely poetical is a problem of methodology ; for a recevt discussion of the data, see Paul Heinisch, Personifikationen und Hypostasen im A.T. und im Alten Orient (Biblische Zeitfragen, ix. 10–12, Münster i. W., 1921).

saints.[1] All sorts of local and private beliefs and practices will flourish; outstanding men impress themselves upon the popular imagination, a remarkable case being the Sicilian cult of the Decollati or Executed Criminals.[2] Efforts, it is true, will be made to render the local cults orthodox, and everywhere typical problems arise touching the relation between the higher forms of religion (orthodox, national, etc.) and the lower (popular, private, etc.); see *CAH*. iii. 432 *sqq*. Again, besides the condemnation of a religion by reformers, there is the repeated recognition that the god is not to be restricted locally, nationally, or dogmatically. Indeed, Yahweh himself is said to be known to, though not explicitly recognized by, other peoples than his own (Isa. lxv. 1), and it is impressively set forth that the recognized worshippers of a god are not necessarily true ones (Matt. vii. 22 *sq*., xxv. 41 *sqq*.; Lk. xiii. 25 *sqq*.). In other words, the history of the vicissitudes of religion is the constantly recurring consciousness that what at any time passes for religion is not final.

There are degrees of deity. At times pre-eminent individuals are regarded as at least semi-divine, or as more truly divine than the unseen, intangible gods of tradition; and, at times, gods are thought of as little more than supermen. But there is also an intense consciousness of a Divine Power for whom human symbolism is imperfect, and ordinary anthropomorphism too meanly human. There are, from time to time, great movements which give a new impetus to a religion; and when they can be analysed, it is seen that sooner or later they take account of popular needs. The usual adjustment between the more individualistic reformers, or the men of outstanding spiritual ability, and the environment as a whole, with its variety of needs and capabilities, will explain those steps which, viewed from the outside, look like a compromise, a deterioration, and a lapse from the original spiritual idealism (cf. *CAH*. iii. 470, 486 *sq*.). The ethical monotheism of the prophets did not by any means exclude later stages of henotheism, or even a virtual polytheism, and the prevalence of superstitions such as commonly rule among the simpler minds. To be sure, the prophets had introduced a new wave of religious idea'ism; but a distinction is to be drawn between the positive contri utions of fresh spiritual movements and the subsequent systematization which makes the religion of a group seem closely akin to the earlier system prior to that movement, although it is vastly different owing to the new influences.

---

[1] Cf. also Lagrange, 25: " Dans la religion catholique . . . il faut que l'autorité lutte sans cesse contre la tendance qui frustrerait le Créateur du culte qui n'est dû qu'à lui. . . ."

[2] At Palermo. E. S. Hartland, *Folk-lore*, xxi. 172 *sqq*.

In such reforming movements, instead of a new god, an old one may be brought forward, and in a new dress (*e.g.* the Egyptian Aton, Apollo). Sometimes, the attributes of existing gods are so fixed that this is impossible : for the meanings of words cannot always be adjusted to suit new tendencies in religion. In the history of religion, besides the various changes of supreme importance which can be clearly recognized, others can certainly be assumed, as in the introduction of the fine ethical god Varuna of the Rig-Veda, who was known to the Hatti and Mitannians (*c.* fourteenth century), and subsequently became the Ahura-Mazda of Zoroastrianism. But the sort of reformation that can often be traced or definitely postulated must also be postulated to explain all other significant developments which have occurred in the history of religion. Besides the particular tendencies to polytheism and to monotheism, there are, then, the great vicissitudes of religion in history, and in particular, the numerous creative movements—naturally varying greatly in significance— which indicate the sort of process that, *mutatis mutandis*, must have been in operation, on however humble a scale, ages before the history of religion can be traced. Not only is the religion of any one period not final, but behind the recognized god or gods of any age is the Power which man has been seeking to formulate.

Hence, although much has been written on primitive monotheism, or on the Great Gods who are found among rudimentary peoples, the facts have not precisely the value set upon them.[1] These Supreme Beings are guardians of morality, founders of institutions, sometimes recognized by several tribes in common (*e.g.* in Australia; Durkheim, 285 *sq.*). At times they have a mythological rather than a religious value (Nilsson, 72), or they have a theoretical significance (Söderblom, 123), or they are found in circles where the crudest beliefs and practices are normal.[2] The belief in a Supreme Being or All-Father does not seem to depend upon the stage of social progress ; in Borneo a low-grade tribe in the interior believes in a Supreme God while more advanced tribes on the coast are polytheists (I. King, 211 *sq.*). The really cardinal fact is threefold : (*a*) the insignificant place which the belief in a Supreme God often holds in the normal beliefs and customs of very rudimentary peoples ; (*b*) the unique influence which theistic conceptions can have and have had in the

---

[1] See Westermarck, *Moral Ideas*, ii. 670 *sqq.* ; Söderblom, *Das Werden des Gottesglaubens* (1923) ; K. Th. Preuss, *Die höchste Gottheit bei den kulturarmen Völkern* (*Psych. Forsch.*, 1922).

[2] *e.g.* among the Yagans whom Darwin visited, and the Marinds of New Guinea. See *Semaine d'Ethnologie Religieuse à Tilbourg*, 1922 (1923), 316 *sqq.*, 384 *sqq.*, and Index, *s.v.* Monothéisme.

34

history of life and thought ; and (c) the very secondary place which the belief in a Supreme Being can come to hold even in advanced societies, and its inability to exclude effective beliefs and practices encircling other gods, deified ancestors, etc.

Accordingly, monarchical monotheism in itself has not even the religious sentiment of the henotheist who places his own god above the rest (Lagrange, 24). Monotheism in itself is not necessarily the outcome of a deep religious spirit, but rather of philosophic thought (Jastrow, *Rel. Belief in Bab. and Ass.* 104 *sq.*, 417). The temperament and religious experience which makes for monotheism cannot be denied to primitive peoples.[1] Among the Semites one can trace gods behind the gods, *e.g.* Anu, Enlil, and Ea are above and behind the Great Gods (Jastrow, 247) ; and it was possible, as in the Code of Hammurabi, to speak of *Ilu* as distinct from the recognized and specified gods. There is a similar ambiguity in Egypt as regards God, *the* god, or *a* god.[2] But the use of *ilu, el,* etc., among the Semites cannot be claimed in support of a primitive Semitic monotheism,[3] although the distribution of the term testifies to the consciousness that there was some common element among the gods. On the other hand, Semitic religion reflects a subjective unity, a unity of feeling and purpose, not a unity of composition (cf. *Lectures,* 418 *sq.,* 426). There was not that systematizing power upon which monotheism as a doctrine depends ; and ethical monotheism, the worship of the God of the national group, a God who was righteous and holy himself and demanded righteousness and holiness in the life of his people, more naturally deserves to be called monotheism than the more sporadic and more isolated examples which have not affected the historical development of the tribes among whom they are found.

A very important methodological principle is at stake. On the one hand there are the miscellaneous data for monotheisms and monotheistic movements ; on the other, W. R. S.'s tendency (a) to emphasize the quality of the data of religion,[4] and (b) to sever sharply Christianity and the Bible from all other religion. On his view, the practical working of a religious belief, *i.e.* the social-religious system, is far more significant for the *systematic* treatment of religions

---

[1] Paul Radin, *Monotheism among Primitive Peoples* (1924)—a useful study.

[2] F. Ll. Griffith (" The Teaching of Amenophis," *Journ. of Eg. Arch.* xii. 230) observes that the commonest expression for an unspecified deity is "the god" the term " god " or possibly " a god " is not uncommon, and the two terms seem to belong to different phrases rather than different ideas.

[3] Bevan, *The Critical Review,* 1897, p. 413 *sq.* ; Meyer, *Gesch. d. Alt.* i. § 346 n. ; Jastrow, 105 ; Lidzbarski, *Ephem.* ii. 38 ; Hehn. 150 *sqq.*

[4] Cf. *Prophets,* 88, 184, on the difference between the attitudes of Elisha and of Hosea to the religious movement at the rise of Jehu.

than either the more isolated and occasional data, or those which lay outside the development of religion—as he understood it. The earliest conceivable systems are therefore of greater value than isolated beliefs, however sublime in themselves—like the belief in a Supreme Being— unless these can be shown to have left their mark upon the system. Ultimate problems arise of methodology and theology which W. R. S. ignored ; and it may be urged that it is easier to perceive how systema- tized *animal*-cults (as totemism) can flourish by the side of and in spite of unsystematized beliefs in an All-Father, than to treat such cults as derivations from or degradations of a systematized social-religious cult in which the All-Father had an organic part, or to regard the idea of a Supreme Being as a *gradual* promotion of a cult-object to supremacy. Whatever consciousness there may have been among rudimentary peoples in prehistoric ages of a Supreme Being, the social-religious system of the day must always have been in an intelligible relationship with the current physical, economic, moral, mental, and all other *non-religious* conditions. See further below, pp. 669 *sqq.*

P. 76 n. 1.—See also Fraenkel, " Schutzrecht d. Araber," *Nöldeke- Festschrift,* 293 *sqq.*

P. 79 and n. 1. THE GĒR.[1]—Cf. the Phœnician names נראהל, נרהבל, among the graffiti of Abydos (Lidzbarski, *Ephem.* iii. 99 *sq.*), which describe the bearers as clients of the Tent and of the Temple. In *CIS.* i. 50 (נרמלך בן אהלמלך) the editors compare with the father's name the Phœn. אהלבעל and the S. Arab. אהלאל (add also אהלעתחר, and cf. the Heb. Oholah and Oholibamah), and they suggest that such names mean " tent of the god," *i.e.* sharing the same tent (similarly Lagrange, 118 n.). But, on the analogy of Shecaniah, " Yahweh dwells " (among his worshippers), the com- pounds would indicate rather that the bearer is the habitation of the god. The *gēr* can claim the help of his god, and at the present day a man passing a shrine will cry : " *anā ṭanīb 'alēkī, yā sittī, yā Badrīyeh,*" " I am a *ṭanīb* to you, O my lady, O Badriyeh." For *ṭanīb*, he who touches the tent-rope and invokes and expects protection, see *Kin- ship*, 49 n., and above, p. 76. In names of the type κοσγηρος the god (Cos) is, of course, the patron : " Allah is the *jār* of the righteous " (*Kinship*, p. 50 n. 1 ; cf. Nöldeke, *Sitz. Ber.*, Berlin, 1882, p. 1187 n. 6). On the *'ār* as a conditional curse, a means of forcing a covenant re- lation whereby the weak gains the protection of others, see Wester- marck, *Morocco*, i. 518 *sqq.*, and below, p. 692.

P. 80 n. 3.—*CIS.* ii. 904 does not recognize Euting's reading.

P. 80 n. 4.—For the Meccan custom Stübe refers to Snouck-

---

[1] For the Larnaca inscription (p. 77), see Cooke, 67 *sq.* ; Lagrange, 478 *sq.*

Hurgronje, *Mekka*, ii. 28 *sqq.*, 79 *sq.*, 151); see also Gaudefroy-Demombynes, *Pèlerinage à la Mekke*, 201 *sqq.*

P. 92 n. 2.—It is still disputed whether Nimrod is a Libyan figure (E. Meyer, *Gesch. d. Alt.* i. § 361 n.), or Babylonian (Skinner, *Gen.* 209; Kraeling, *AJSL.* xxxviii. 214; Prince, *JAOS.* xl. 202; Hommel, *Eth. u. Geog.* 184 n., and many others).

P. 93 n.—Much older than these are the recently discovered Phœnician inscriptions of Abibaal and Elbaal, kings of Gebal (Byblus). For the usage, cf. the numerous local "kings" in the Amarna Letters (*e.g.* Gezer, Lachish, etc., Megiddo, Taanach, etc).

P. 94, etc. BAAL.[1]—W. R. S.'s pages have been found to need some modification. The name Baal is known in Arabia (p. 109 n. 1), but it was not necessarily taken there by Aramæans (Wellh. 146, Lagr. 90), at least as the name of a god.[2] It is not a divine element in South Arabian nomenclature, El being used instead (Nielsen, *Dreieinige Gott*, 97 *sq.*); though Nöldeke is of opinion that a *god* Baal had once been known there (*ERE.* i. 664).[3] "Baal" could be applied at an early date to a heaven or sky god : a Baal of Heaven or Sky Baal occurs as the chief god in the Hamath inscription of *c.* 800 B.C. (Pognon, *Inscr. Sem.* No. 86), and in a treaty between Esarhaddon and Baal, king of Tyre (seventh century); and he is prominent in the Persian age.[4] Sky-gods are of long standing ; in Egypt there are gods who are lords in heaven, and in Babylonia Damkina, wife of Ea, is queen (*sharrat*) of heaven and earth (*KAT.* 360), and Ishtar is queen or lady (*belit*) of heaven (*ib.* 425 ; cf. Amarna Letters, 23 l. 26). In Hittite treaties Teshub (a god of the Addu–Hadad–Ramman type) is lord of heaven and earth, and this title is borne by Sin and Shamash. In the Egypto-Hittite treaty the "Lord of Heaven" (Re-Sutekh [Set]) has with him a "queen of heaven." In the Amarna Letters Baal proper corresponds to Addu (or Hadad), and in Egyptian texts (especially of the thirteenth century) Baal is well known as a war-god, causing terror, and associated with the mountains. Here he is god of rain and storm, and evidently to be equated with Set.[5] He also has solar attri-

---

[1] See Lagrange, 83 *sqq.*; Paton, *ERE.* s.v.; Baudissin, *Adonis*, 25 *sqq.* On place-names compounded with Baal (p. 94 n. 6), see Gray, *Heb. Prop. Names*, 125 *sqq.*; *E.Bi.* col. 3312.

[2] Nor, according to Barton (75 n., 104 n. 5), is there reason to believe that the date-palm was of purely North Semitic origin.

[3] See now Nielsen, *Handbuch d. Altarab. Altertumskunde* (Copenhagen, 1927), i. 240 *sq.*

[4] Lidzbarski, *Ephem.* i. 243 *sqq.* (see first ii. 122); Hehn, 117 *sq.*; Nielsen, 297 *sqq.*

[5] Gressmann, *Baudissin-Festschrift*, 191 *sqq.* In Ptolemaic Egypt a denominative of the word *ba'al* is used in the sense *böse sein, freveln* (202, No. 48 ; cf. above,

butes, and the imagery associates with him the bull, who was elsewhere associated with Baal and Yahweh—in Babylonia with Enlil (" the sturdy bull "). The bull, a symbol of strength, prowess, and the roaring storm, was also a symbol of the power of the sun. The combination of solar and taurine epithets occurs with both the god and the Pharaoh; the latter " cries like Addu in the sky " and is also a sun-god. The Assyrian name Shamshi-Adad reflects the same tendency to connect the two chief gods and their attributes ; it is a syncretizing, monotheizing tendency, and it suggests that Baal (Hadad) of Palestine would be a god of outstanding importance before he was succeeded by the Israelite Yahweh (see *CAH*. ii. 348 *sq.*).

In the Amarna Letters Baal is " *in* Heaven," perhaps the first stage in the title " Baal *of* Heaven." [1] Gods of the sky could none the less be localized on earth (Wellh. 211), and the Sky Baal in due course is worshipped by the side of other gods and becomes the god of particular cities. The Baal of Harran was Sin, the moon-god ; but the particular attributes of the Baals afford no clue to the primary meaning of the term, and local Baals could have special attributes and functions as readily as do the modern *welis*. The distribution of the Baals as divine names would show that a certain similarity or connexion was felt to exist everywhere between them ; but it does not follow that the local Baals gave rise to the conviction that there was a single supreme and clearly defined Baal, or that they are secondary differentiations of an original (prehistoric) Baal. The local saints, *welis*, and Madonnas are commonly the later forms of earlier local beings, and the relations between local or specialized deities and the Great Gods, whether rulers or merely otiose, would be as variable in the unknown past as they are in those periods where they can be more or less clearly recognized (cf. *CAH*. iii. 433).

A distinction may be drawn between *ba'al*, used of men and gods, and *'ēl*, used of the gods alone (Lagrange, 83 *sq.*, 97). But it may be questioned whether the primary meaning of *ba'al* is " inhabitant " or " owner " (above, p. 95 n. end). The idea of domination, at all events, does not necessarily involve a servile relationship (p. 94, cf. 109), although ideas of ownership and overrule (*e.g.* over a wife, *Kinship*, 92) are found, especially in the more complex society of Babylonia. On the other hand, property-rights come by " quickening " a place (p. 95 *sq.*)—the Baal " donne la fécondité du sol " (Lagrange, 98), or a man builds on the soil or cultivates it (p. 143). In other words, he makes things naturally effective. Already Toy (on Prov. iii. 27) has

p. 112 n.). " Waters of B." occurs from the Nineteenth Dynasty onwards (Gressmann, *op. cit.* Nos. 44–47).

[1] Gressmann, *op. cit.* 213. Shamash is also " *in* " (*ina, ishtu*) heaven.

suggested that *ba'al* signifies one who employs or controls a thing; and the compound expressions *ba'al* of tongue, wisdom, city, etc., suggest further that the primary idea of *ba'al* is that of a productive, effective agent, and, on this account, a possessor of rights (cf. p. 637).

The Baal " of " a place may be supposed to " own " it, but he is properly the god to be invoked when one is in his locality or requires his help. Gods are not merely to be feared or served, they are also to be used; and the conception of gods as *effective* causes is so common elsewhere, and so self-evident, as to lead us to expect it among the Semites. Gods are frequently causes of prosperity in general, or of particular activities, as when the earth becomes sterile and fertility ceases when Tammuz and Ishtar are in the Lower World. There are many nuances : the Greek *dæmon* causes a man to be what he is, and the Latin *genius* makes for the efficiency of people and the stability of things.[1] Among primitive peoples there are " species deities," archetypes, creators and sustainers of the various species of animals (in one case the guardian is an " elder brother ") and of various objects of nature.[2] So, too, there are presiding " angels," tutelary and other similar deities, and στοιχεῖα (see *E.Bi.* art. " Elements "). Throughout, the fundamental notion seems to be that of the power which makes things effective, causes them to act as they should, and preserves their nature. Accordingly, the Baal-Berith, as W. R. S. says, " presides over covenants " (p. 95 n.), though it is significant that this function is elsewhere ascribed to specific gods (the Aryan Varuna and Mitra),[3] or there is an immanent process, when, by means of vague imprecations, covenants are safeguarded by unspecified powers or some implied mechanism (p. 555).

But kings are also effective powers. When Rameses II., hailed by his courtiers as " lord of heaven, lord of earth, Re," is also " lord of food, plentiful in grain," *i.e.* he is a veritable food-baal (cf. p. 537). The king is the visible god and the source of the land's fruitfulness (Breasted, *Eg. Records*, iii. § 265); the " magical " powers of chiefs and kings are well known (see Frazer, *GB.* i. ch. vi.). It is, to be sure, difficult to say that the Pharaoh or the god is an actual immanent principle, although in the Pyramid Texts the dead king is a veritable cosmic principle : he becomes " the outflow of the rain," while in the Twelfth Dynasty a dead king is said to rejoin the Sun and his " divine limbs " mingle with him that begat him.[4] The evidence is

[1] Nilsson, 283 *sq.* ; cf. W. Warde Fowler, *Roman Ideas of Deity*, 17 *sqq.*

[2] Tylor, *Primitive Culture*[4], ii. 244 (cf. the " patrons " or " patterns ").

[3] Meillet, *Journ. Asiat.* 1907, ii. 143 ; Bertholet-Lehmann, *Lehrbuch d. Rel. gesch.*, ii. 21.

[4] Breasted, *Development of Eg. Thought*, 125 ; *Eg. Rec.* i. § 491, ii. § 592.

more intelligible when the god or the divine king exercises control from outside. So, Yahweh gives command (Gen. i.) and he " calls " for the corn (p. 518) ; and the Aryan Varuna is an ethical god, the guardian of an immanent principle of cosmic and social order (p. 657). Among primitive peoples the ability to get, control, or multiply the vital things of life (food, rain, etc.) is often associated with special individuals whose powers are either general or specialized. In typical cases an essential substantial relationship is believed to subsist between the controller and the controlled. The most remarkable are the ceremonies recorded by Spencer and Gillen among certain totem-clans of Central Australia. They are of extreme interest (1) for their contribution to our knowledge of primitive social-religious cults and totemism in particular, and (2) for the illustration they afford of W. R. S.'s fundamental theory of the totem communion-sacrifice.[1] Here, (a) each of the clans is of the same essence or substance as its totem-species, and the difference between the clans-men and the species (emu, kangaroo, etc.) is ignored so far as the cult is concerned—a criterion of totemism ; and (b) each clan, through its elders, is supposed, under appropriate conditions, to multiply or otherwise exercise control over its totem.[2] Thus it appears that where the idea prevails of some effective control there is between con-troller and controlled a unique relationship which, in the most striking examples, is a virtual or an actual identity. Hence the Semitic Baal-conception can hardly be isolated from the related ideas elsewhere.

Semitic Baalism is at the agricultural stage (pp. 113, 244). But this is not the earliest stage of society : the very notion of sacred places is earlier than the beginning of settled life (p. 118). For the primitive conceptions we are directed to the simpler Arab life (p. 101), or, with Lagrange (p. 98), to the cuneiform inscriptions of thousands of years earlier—the difference in method is highly typical. In any case, the Arab data are complex. Still, a distinction is drawn between

---

[1] Totemism has been defined as the cult of a social group, especially an exogamous one, which stands to a species of animal or plant (generally edible), or to an object or class of objects, in an intimate relationship ; the totem is treated as a cognate to be respected, and not to be eaten or used, or at least only under certain restrictions. See W. H. Rivers, *The History of Melanesian Society*, ii. 75 (Cambridge, 1914).

[2] In order that the ceremonies may be successful, the clansmen, who usually refrain from eating their own totem, must on this occasion eat a little. Frazer (*Tot. Ex.* iv. 231) observes that the ceremony is utilitarian and magical, and the animal in no sense divine, a criticism which of course turns upon his definition of religion and magic. (The researches of Spencer and Gillen have been in some respects modified by those of Strehlow ; but the main facts, so far as W. R. S.'s arguments are involved, are not affected.) See below, p. 586.

" Baal's land " and the " land " belonging to Athtar (*i.e.* Astarte
or Ishtar, p. 99 n. 2), and it is possible to regard the land that bears
fruit under the influence of the fertilizing power of Baal as his wife
(*Prophets*, 172, 411). If so, it is easy to see that, under the marriage
symbolism (the importance of which is indicated by W. R. S. *l.c.*),
different views could prevail touching the respective functions of the
male element and of the female element, and also of the power behind
or over these (see p. 513).[1] With Lagrange (97 *sq.*) it is unnecessary
to endeavour to restrict the nuances and developments of the idea
of the Baal, although it is difficult to agree with him that " l'idée de
propriété et par suite de domination rend compte de toutes ses
nuances." For the most primitive or fundamental conception we
seek some more pregnant and effective idea, in harmony with the
practical character of early religion.

P. 99 n.—On the terms *ba'l, ghail*, see the *Kitāb al-kharāj* of Yaḥyā
ibn Ādam (ed. Juynboll, 1896), 80 *sq.*—A. A. B.

P. 100 n.—See *CIS*. iv. 47; Barton, *Semitic Origins*, 86 *sq.*, 127, 128
n. 1; and, on water rights in South Arabia, Rhodokanakis, *Sitz. Ber.*
of the Vienna Academy, 185, No. 3 (1917), 86, 97, 108.

P. 107. APHACA.—See Lagrange, 129 n. 1, 159; Baudissin, *Adonis*,
80, 363 n. 1; Frazer, *GB.* v. 259 (and his description of the place,
28 *sq.*). On the local survival of cults associated with a female spirit
or deity, see Rouvier, *Bullet. Arch.* 1900, p. 170; Curtiss, *Prim. Sem.
Rel.* 153 *sq.* (a sacred fig-tree growing out of the ruins is known as " our
lady Venus "). Paton (*Annual of the American School of Oriental
Research in Jerusalem*, 1920, i. 56) refers to a fig-tree, a ruined shrine,
and a spring, the abode of Sa'īdat Afkā, of whom is told a story evidently
derived from the myth of Astarte and Adonis. In such cases, however,
it is difficult to decide whether the story goes back to pre-Christian
times, or has been from time to time resurrected by learned monks
or travellers, and in this way impressed upon the peasantry.

P. 108 and n. 3. THE HUSBAND OF THE LAND.—As W. R. S. shows
in more detail elsewhere (*Prophets*, 172 *sq.*, 410 *sq.*), land and people
form a natural unity, and it is the same whether the god marries the
land and makes it productive or marries the stock of the nation.[2]

---

[1] Dusares, who is a North Arabian Baal (Wellhausen, 51), is " he of the *shara*,"
a term given to districts which, as it seems, were moist and luxuriant (cf. Nöldeke,
ERE. i. 663). Although a connexion between the word and Ishtar is excluded
by the guttural, the goddess does seem to represent the fertility of nature and
to be the goddess of the fertilizing moisture of the soil (Baudissin, 21, 27; cf.
ZDMG. lvii. 824).

[2] See on Mother-Earth (p. 518). Among the Yuin of Australia the notion is
that a man owns the district where he was born (Hobhouse, Wheeler, and Ginsberg,
248 *sq.*).

The woman as land or field is a familiar notion; cf. Hartland, *Primitive Paternity*, i. 309 *sq.* (Vedic Law). In the Amarna Letters, Rib-Addi, lamenting the famine, says, " My field is like a woman without a husband " ; parallels to this are found in Old Egyptian, in the Talmudic " virgin soil " (קרקע בתולה), and *Taanith 6b*, " rain is the *ba'al* of the earth." [1] Rulers of a city are frequently compared to a bridegroom or husband.[2] Rameses II. is called " husband of Egypt," rescuing her from every enemy (Breasted, *Eg. Rec.* iii. § 490) ; and Rameses III. is an " abundant Nile " (iv. § 92), and " the great Nile, the great harvest-goddess of Egypt " (iv. p. 7 note *d*). Such kings both claim to be, and are recognized as, the cause of the land's material prosperity. Rameses II. is hailed as " lord of food, plentiful in grain, in whose footsteps is the harvest goddess." His word brings rain upon the mountains, for he is the incarnation of the god Re (iii. §§ 265, 268) ; and the god Ptah gives him " a great Nile," good harvests, and all prosperity (iii. §§ 404, 409). Similarly Amenemhet I. says, " I cultivated grain and loved the harvest-god " (i. § 483).

In general, the earth needs fertilization, and this comes through the god or a nature-god, or his representative. The procedure is sometimes most realistic.[3] Often fertility depends upon the conduct of the representative individual : the evil influence of a bad ruler upon nature and the agricultural prosperity of his country is familiar in ancient religion. But the fundamental belief in this interrelation or identity of man and nature is otherwise expressed when, at a more democratic stage, Israel's material prosperity depends upon the behaviour of the people, or when, at a more priestly stage, it depends upon the cultus, and upon the strict observance of the necessary religious rites. Social order and the order of nature are *in theory* one, but *in practice* special members of society are supposed to possess unique powers over nature, or by their conduct can exercise direct or indirect influence upon all that makes for human welfare.[4] The " husband " of

[1] Knudtzon, No. 74, rec. 7 *sq.*; *Alte Orient*, viii. 30 ; Sarowsky, *ZATW.* xxxii. 303 *sqq.*, xxxiii. 81 *sq.*

[2] Stübe refers to Schack, *Poesie u. Kunst d. Araber in Spanien u. Sicilien*, ii. 117 *sqq.* ; G. Jacob, *Altarab. Parellelen z. A.T.* 16.

[3] The union of sky-god and earth-mother can be traced through the Mediterranean area: so A. B. Cook, *Zeus*, i. 779 *sq.*, ii. 677. In the isles of Leti, etc., Mr. Sun comes down once a year to fertilize the earth (Frazer, *GB.* ii. 99) ; and the Pueblo Indians entreat the Sun Father to embrace the Earth Mother (Frazer, *Tot. Ex.* ii. 237). Farnell (*Evol. Rel.* 194) cites an early English prayer: " Hail be thou, Earth, Mother of Men ; wax fertile in the embrace of God, fulfilled with fruit for the use of men " (Grein, *Bibl. d. angel-sächs. Poesie*, ed. Wülcker, i. 316).

[4] For the interconnexion of man and " nature " (a conception which is by no means a primitive one), see also Aptowitzer, *MGWJ.* lxiv. 227, 305, lxv. 71, 164.

the land or people is therefore a particular form of various interrelated ideas of the cause of growth and fertility.

P. 119 *sqq.* (cf. 441 *sqq.*). THE JINN AND TOTEMISM.[1]—In contrast to the more or less systematized cults of settled communities are the miscellaneous beliefs in supernatural beings of vague individuality and, in particular, animal in form. They thus find analogies in some of the characteristics of totemism, and the question is raised, Are the *jinn* potential totems ? It is to be noticed that (1) W. R. S.'s evidence for *jinn* and demons is not peculiar to any part of the Semitic field, to any period of its history, or to the Semitic area itself.[2] (2) No sharp dividing line can be drawn between *jinn* and other more or less related beings : the *jinn* of both ancient and modern times often recall the fairies, trolls, and goblins of western lands (*e.g.* they will help the poor), and it may even be questioned whether such beings should be called *jinn* (Lang, *JRAI.* xxx. No. 17). (3) There is no great gulf between the *jinn* and wild beasts on the one hand (p. 121 n. 1) and human beings on the other—the failure to distinguish clearly between human and animal is common among primitive peoples.[3]

The *jinn*, like " demons " and their kind, serve conveniently to explain whatever is not due to " natural " causes, or that has a supernatural origin, and cannot be associated with any of the known gods or spirits. The *jinn* are by reputation harmful and Satanic ; they are hostile, whereas there are other animal beings which will give omens, assist in ordeals, and be generally helpful. Unusual phenomena will be ascribed either to *jinn* or demons, or to more friendly beings, according to the particular circumstances of each; so that sometimes the native is at a loss to whose charge to lay some more ambiguous occurrence. Of the springs in Palestine inhabited by supernatural beings, some are the centre of cults ; the water has creative properties, and the " saint " is accepted as orthodox and Islamic. But sometimes there is a *jinn* who takes the shape of an animal, a

---

[1] On the *jinn*, see also Wellhausen, 208 *sqq.*; Goldziher, *Abhand.* i. 107 *sqq.*, 201 ; Jaussen, 318 *sqq.*; Nöldeke, *ERE.* i. 669 *sq.*; Geyer in the *Nöldeke-Festschrift*, i. 66 *sqq.*; Einszler, *ZDPV.* x. 160 *sqq.* For criticisms of W. R. S., see Westermarck, *JRAI.* 1899, pp. 252–68 (the nature of the Arab jinn as illustrated by the present beliefs of the people of Morocco), now superseded by his *Ritual and Belief in Morocco*, i. 262–413.

[2] For Assyrian parallels, see R. Campbell Thompson, *Semitic Magic*, 57 *sq.*

[3] To the Gilyak of Alaska every animal is as much a man as a Gilyak, and perhaps greater and wiser (*G.B.* viii. 206). Australians see no difficulty in drawing an emu or a kangaroo with a shield (R. H. Matthews, *Queensland Geog. Journal*, xvi. [1900–1] p. 81, cf. xiv. 10 *sq.*; cf. also Frazer, *Tot. Ex.* i. 131 *sq.* and 119). Jastrow, *Bab. Ass. Birth Omens* (Giessen, 1914, p. 70 *sq.*) deals with the birth of monsters and other data which would foster ideas of the identity of human and animal nature.

monster, or a negro; he may injure people, and must be placated, driven off by prayers (*JPOS.* iv. 64). Again, there are springs which have no cult, but are the abode of vague beings varying according to the particular traditions that encircle each.

The relation between the *jinn* and the " god " resembles that between the δαίμων and the θεός at another cultural stage. The *dæmon* is essentially undefined and has no real individuality, it is the suprasensual explanation of phenomena which a man is unable to explain from his ordinary experience; whereas a " god " is developed by religious need, and, through the cult, into a characteristic individuality.[1] Accordingly, the terms *jinn*, demon, *dæmon*, god, etc., are properly used to denote different sorts of powers, agencies, etc., the " god " being distinguished by his having a personality and a relative permanence, and by being the centre of a cult and of a system of ideas (cf. Meyer, *Gesch. Alt.* i. § 50 *sq.*). Of course, care must be taken not to draw the line too rigorously, ignoring transitional forms : the Babylonian " demons " appear to be more systematized figures than the *jinn*, there are well-understood relations between them and men, whereas the *jinn* is rather a class-god or species. The history of all these beings is the history of beliefs, ideas, etc. In this way, " gods " become degraded into " demons." [2] But the reverse development cannot, on psychological grounds, be so easily followed, and W. R. S. is careful to speak only of the development of *friendly* " demoniac beings " (p. 443).

It is necessary to distinguish, where possible, between totemic features, and those which are at most totemistic, and those which can only be called theriomorphic. The striking local animal cults of Egypt in the period of her decline hardly represent the " purely totemic " stage (p. 226 ; cf. p. 578). In West African Secret Societies the " Human Leopards " or " Human Lions " periodically act as though they were these animals. In Nigeria Mohammedan families have each a sacred animal (camel, goat, etc.) known as the " head " or the " source " of the house ; it is never eaten, and is supposed to contain the spirits of the forefathers and to have witnessed the foundations of the house.[3] And this is in the midst of Islam ! But what forms actual totemism took among ancient and rudimentary peoples it is impossible to guess ; and the theory of totemism and its relation

---

[1] Cf. Nilsson, 164 *sqq.* All δαίμονες are θεῖοι, but very few are promoted to the rank of θεοί ; see Lightfoot's note on Col. ii. 9.

[2] P. 120 ; cf. Goldziher, *Abhand.* i. 113 *sq.* (Cozah, etc.); *ZA.* viii. 333. Cf. the Ishtars as female idols in Mandæan (Lidzbarski, *Ephem.* i. 101 and n. 12) and the Reshaphim as demons in later Hebrew (Bacher, *REJ.* xxviii. 151).

[3] C. K. Meek, *Northern Tribes of Nigeria*, i. 174 (Oxford, 1925).

to religion is really a methodological one. To some extent all animal symbolism and imagery is a refuge from anthropomorphism when ordinary human imagery is inadequate ; and Farnell, in some important pages, comments on the " unstable anthropomorphism " of Babylon and Assyria.[1] The problem of totemism is bound up with that of anthropomorphism, in that the animal imagery, etc., is either a reaction against the latter, or represents a stage prior to anthropomorphism itself. Naturally, animal cults cannot be derived from trees, springs, and stones, which, when regarded as sacred, are often thought of more or less along anthropomorphic lines. On the other hand, animals, by reason of their bodily and other characteristics (strength, cunning, etc.), are far more impressive, and have much more to contribute to man's growing knowledge of himself. In totemism there are rudimentary forms of these elements which recur in a more developed form where there are anthropomorphic deities ; [2] and even when there are " All-Fathers " or " Supreme Gods " in rudimentary areas, these are often as little an integral part of the social cult as they are in more advanced societies (p. 529 *sq.*). Again, not only are there sometimes tendencies to regard the totem as an at least semi-divine being, but " individual totems," " spirit guardians," and " naguals " are on the road to become personal gods.[3] Hence the questions arise, (*a*) Into what does totemism develop ? and (*b*) Is anthropomorphism primary, or, if not, what sort of cult (whether it deserves to be called " religious " or not) preceded it ?

W. R. S. lays the strongest emphasis upon the necessity of overcoming fear and terror of the unknown (p. 122); ideas of friendliness, relationship, and kinship necessarily characterize the earliest and most primitive types of religious cult (p. 137). The *jinn* are essentially unfriendly, but they illustrate some typical varieties of theriomorphism. On the other hand, friendly demoniacal beings, theriomorphic or other, capable of becoming " gods," can hardly be called *jinn*. The *jinn*, like the totem, are a " species "; they illustrate the material of which totemism is made, and in this sense it can be said that if they had human kinsfolk they would be " potential totems " (cf. p. 130). The elements which constitute totemism are, taken separately, not strange to the Semites ; [4] but this fact does not prove that *all* the Semitic peoples

[1] *Greece and Babylon*, 14 *sq.*, 54 *sqq.* ; cf. *Attributes of God*, 22 *sqq.*

[2] Cf. S. A. Cook, *ERE.* " Religion," § 17 *sq.*

[3] Frazer, *Tot. Ex.* ii. 18 *sq.*; cf. 151, and i. 81 *sq.*, also ii. 139 *sq.*, 166, iv. 30 *sq.* The Wollunqua snake-totem of the Warramunga " seems to be a totem on the high road to become a god " (*ib.* i. 145). For Frazer's evidence for the *worship* of totems, see the Introduction, above, p. xli.

[4] For instance, in the district of Dan in Palestine the late Lord Kitchener found the tomb of a dog which had become transformed into a holy place under the

passed through that stage of animal cults which we call totemic.
W. R. S.'s careful sentences on p. 125 (italicized in this edition) speak
not of an actual evolution, say from A to B, but of ideas and usages in
B which also find a more rudimentary expression in A. The difference is essential. He points out that primitive religious institutions
are not to be explained by conceptions belonging to a more advanced
stage beyond the " totem stage of thought " (p. 445, l. 11), because
new gods, sanctuaries, cults, etc., can spring up at a later and post-
totemic stage (p. 138). Of this earlier postulated totemic stage, there
can only be survivals ; but the postulate accounts for the triangular
relationship between gods, men, and animals of which there are so
many miscellaneous examples (p. 287 *sq.*).[1] It is true that W. R. S.
is thought to have exaggerated the significance of totemism, but it
is difficult, if not impossible, to point to any other theory which affords
a better explanation of those religious data with which he is concerned.

P. 121 n. 1.—The association between demons and wild beasts
may be illustrated by a verse of Ḥātim aṭ-Ṭā'ī (ed. Schulthess, 1897),
Banu-l-jinni lam yuṭbakh bicidrin jazūruhā (p. 27, line 18, of the Arabic
text ; p. 46 of the translation), " the sons of the Jinn whose victim is
not cooked in a cauldron." This conception of the *jinn* as eaters of raw
flesh agrees remarkably with what Spencer and Gillen say of the
Australian beliefs : " The spirits kill and eat all manner of game, but
always uncooked, for they are not supposed to have any fires " (*Native
Tribes of Central Australia*, 516).—A. A. B.

P. 135. ASTRAL RELIGION.[2]—Although there is evidence for a
widespread interest in the heavenly bodies—and the Pleiades in
particular were often carefully observed by primitive peoples (*G.B.*
vii. 308 *sqq.*)—astral cults have not that prevalence or antiquity

name of the Sheikh Merzuk (*PEF. Qy. St.* 1877, p. 171). Men named " dog " and
" whelp " are connected with the story of a shrine at Ma'alul, near Nazareth
(Tyrwhitt Drake, *ib.* 1873, p. 58). In Syria and Egypt every one has a double,
often in the form of an animal (Seligman, *Ridgeway Presentation Volume*, 138 *sq.*).
For saints in animal form, see *JPOS.* vii. 12 sq.

[1] Similarly, F. B. Jevons, *Introd. to the History of Rel.* 127, speaks of the *disjecta
membra* of totemism among Semites and Aryans. According to Meek (*op. cit.* ii.
186), the Nigerian tribes whose titles mean simply " Men " may be asserting that
they have passed beyond those who are called Lions, Frogs, Buffaloes, etc. It is
also possible that the familiar Cretan and other old Oriental representations of
the subjugation of beasts (cf. Nilsson, 20) may refer to that consciousness of the
difference between man and beast which also marks the Babylonian story of Engidu
(*CAH.* iii. 228).

[2] See *Kinship*, 255 *sq.* Astral cults among the Arabs have been rather under-
estimated (*e.g.* by Wellhausen, *Heid.*[1] 175, 217 ; cf. 2nd ed. 211), see G. Jacob, *Bed.
Leben*[2], 158. For the data, see Nöldeke, *ERE.* i. 660, and in general G. F. Moore,
E.Bi. " Nature Worship," § 5.

sometimes ascribed to them. The relative prominence of cults of the heavenly bodies in religion and mythology " differs widely among peoples upon the same plane of culture and even of the same stock ; they had a different significance to the settled population of Arabia from that which they had for the Arab nomad (in South Arabia the worship of the sun and moon is strikingly prevalent), and besides this economic reason there are doubtless historical causes for the diversity which are in great part concealed from us " (Moore). The indications of astral cults among the Western Semites certainly prove more numerous than was thought; but the references in the O.T. to the cults of the *later* Assyrian period stand in contrast to the scantiness in the literature referring to *earlier* periods, which, however, may come from late though simpler circles.[1]

In Babylonia the keen observation of the stars was bound up with the conviction that the will of the gods was reflected in them and could be discovered ; and an elaborate system of astrology arose, based on the belief that occurrences in the heavens and occurrences on earth were ruled by the same laws—that is, that heaven and earth were part of one harmonious system. To adopt a modern formula, " heaven and earth are each the image or reflexion of the other " (*Himmelsbild*= *Weltbild*).[2] A modern theory also urges that numerous *motifs* of astral religion permeated ancient tradition.[3] But in general, when astral, mythical, and legendary *motifs* are supposed to occur in the stories of personages or events, it is obvious (1) that their presence does not prove that we have myth or legend, and (2) that, even in the latter, normal human traits could naturally be utilized, especially when stories of the heavenly bodies were concerned. The " anthropomorphic " treatment of things celestial is based upon terrestrial experience ; the remote and the supersensuous (whether divine beings or planets regarded as divine) are spoken of in terms of the near and the known.

What is really important here is the emotional effect of myth and legend—of all that is supersensuous, idealizing, sublime, or artistic. It is in this respect that the myth or legend, with its peculiar treatment of nature or history, exercises so powerful an influence, and a " New

[1] Seals and other archæological data in Palestine point to a certain prevalence of astral ideas. See also G. B. Gray, *Sacrifice*, 297 *sq.* (lunar influence on the feasts), 148–178 (the later ideas of the sacrificial service in heaven).

[2] See especially Alfred Jeremias, *The O.T. in the Light of the Ancient East* (2 vols., 1911); *Handbuch der Altorient. Geisteskultur* (Leipzig, 1913) ; and for criticisms, Wardle, *Israel and Babylon*, ch. xii.

[3] The four wives of Jacob are the four phases of the moon ; Abraham and Lot are Dioscuri and must separate ; like Jacob and Esau, they are also respectively lunar and solar characters.

Jerusalem " appeals otherwise than does the Old.[1] The characteristic colouring which makes such tradition and literature effective stands in contrast to the secondary euhemerizing, rationalizing, and other processes which wash it out. Similarly, there is a characteristic tendency to de-divinize and de-spiritualize (p. 546). Both are typically *secondary* stages, although it is obvious that the material which receives the emotional, spiritual, or religious colouring had already undergone vicissitudes which in most cases cannot be recovered or reconstructed. It is not to be supposed that the *primary* stages are absolutely so ; but, as in W. R. S.'s theory of the " communion " origin of sacrifice, it is the beginning of a fresh development, and not some absolute stage in the evolution of religion which we look for (cf. p. 499 and note 1).

P. 145 n. 1.—See Floyer, *Journ. Royal Asiatic Society*, 1892, p. 813. The clause cited from Bekrī reads " and (the tribe of) Thacīf have most right to Wajj."—A. A. B.

P. 148. RIGHT OF ASYLUM.—See Quatremère, " Les Asyles chez les Arabes," *Mem. Acad. Inscr.* xv. (1845), 307 *sqq.*; Goldziher, *Muh. Stud.* i. 236 *sqq.*; Jacob, *Altarab. Parallelen z. A.T.*, 12 ; Wellhausen, 184 ; Landberg, *Arabica*, ii. 1781 ; Westermarck, *Origin and Devel. of Moral Ideas*, ii. 628 *sqq.*; *ERE.* ii. 161 *sqq.*; and Frazer, *Tot. Ex.* i. 96 *sqq* (who refers to A. Hellwig's monographs on the subject, Berlin, 1903, Stuttgart, 1906), iv. 267 *sq.*, and *id. FOT.* iii. 19 *sq.* (on Ps. lxxxiv. 3). See next note.

P. 150 and n. 2. SACRED AREAS.—The South Arabian *ḏāt-ḥmy*, " she of the sacred enclosure " (Hommel ; see Lagrange, 184 n. 3), is otherwise rendered " she of the burning heat " (Höyer, see Nielsen, 251 n.). With the " wall " as the watcher, cf. the Babylonian custom of giving significant names to gates, walls, etc., and the lustrations of the citadel in Iguvium, with prayer and sacrifice at each gate (Warde Fowler).[2]

As regards the protection of sacred animals (cf. pp. 142 n., 160), the Egyptian, in the so-called " Negative Confession," will testify that he has not taken away the birds or fishes of the gods ; and in the Saïte age a man declares, " I gave food to the ibis, the hawk, the cat, and the jackal " (Breasted, *Anc. Rec.* i. 126, note c). Even in Central Australia there are, besides the sacred totem species, spots (generally caves) containing the objects of cult ; everything there is sacred—no

---

[1] Cf. Cook in Peake's *People and the Book*, 60 *sq.*

[2] See *Kinship*, 162, on the root ḥ-m-y, and the *ḥām* as a term of relationship (the group which protects the woman against encroachment). From the root ḥ-r-m are derived the S. Arab. חרמת, מחרם, and the Nab. מחרמתא (sanctuary). See Cooke, 220 ; Lagrange, 184 ; G. R. Driver, *Journ. of Theol. Stud.* xxv. 294, 296.

plant may be pulled, no branch broken, even the animals that stray thither are safe (Frazer, *Tot. Ex.* i. 96). The sanctity of the saint's tomb in Palestine is well known ; objects can be deposited there temporarily, and a man of authority was once beaten to death for cutting down a thorn-tree in the *weli's* ground.[1] As a general rule, the *weli* is expected to protect his own property (cf. the story, *JPOS.* v. 174), or the sanctity of the place is vindicated by his people, or there is, as it were, an inherent protecting force. Further, the sanctity of a place sanctifies everything ; or something therein is especially sacred, so that *either* there seems to be a diffused sanctity, and everything participates in the sacred quality (cf. p. 156), *or* the sacred power is or can be localized, and any sound or movement in the area may be interpreted as a sign of the presence or response of the power invoked. Moreover, objects which are in the sacred area can retain their sanctity when taken outside. Conversely, the sacred object can sanctify a place, and it is presumably a survival of the sacred character of the horse in Persia when a stable is an asylum.[2]

P. 152 n. 2.—See now, *GB.* iii., and the articles on taboo in *Ency. Brit.* (N. W. Thomas) and *ERE.* (Marett).

P. 155 n. 1.—Cf. also Sir G. A. Smith, *E.Bi.* " Hermon," § 2 ; and E. Hommel, *JSOR.* x. 34 *sqq.*

P. 156 n. 1.—See Sir G. A. Smith, *E.Bi.* " Carmel," § 4 *sq.* On mountain cults in general, see *E.Bi.* col. 2065, § 2 and n. 3. A large proportion of the shrines in Palestine are on hilltops (Canaan, *JPOS.* iv. 4–7), and in time of drought people ascend the roof of a shrine in order to approach nearer to the deity (*id.* vi. 144 n. 1) ; cf. above, p. 230 n. 4.

P. 157 and note. ANCESTOR CULTS.—This subject, over which W. R. S. passes rapidly, is bound up with (*a*) the deification of men who are not necessarily ancestors, or who may be only reputed ancestors, (*b*) the tendency to think of a supernatural being as a parent or ancestor (cf. p. 509 *sq.*), and (*c*) the old and recurrent theory that all deities were originally deified men. Euhemerist tendencies come to the fore when there is little difference between gods and pre-eminent men (cf. p. 43), when such men are treated as semi-divine (cf. Lagrange, 463 *sq.*), when respect, veneration, or love are felt for ancestors, or

---

[1] Canaan, *JPOS.* v. 175. The Turks are supposed to have lost the battle of Gaza in the Great War because they cut down a sacred tree and destroyed a certain shrine (*ib.*).

[2] *Folk-lore*, xii. 269. The horse was worshipped in Bahrein—a Persian cult ? See *Kinship*, 243. It may perhaps be associated with the cult of Semiramis (see *GB.* ix. 407 n. 2). The horse was also sacred in the Vedic religion ; see E. Meyer, *GA.* i. § 580 ; Loisy, *Sacrifice*, 397 *sq.* ; *Camb. Hist. of India*, i. 119 *sq.*

when deities and ancestors are ceremonially represented by living representatives (see *GB.* ix. 385 *sq.*), or perhaps even as a reaction against theriomorphic ideas of divinity. In the case of the actual deification or divinization of great figures, especially kings (cf. pp. 44 *sq.*, 66), a distinction may be drawn between the rise of the cult after their death, and the practice of some sort of cult during their lifetime ; psychological differences between meditation upon the dead in a supersensuous realm and upon the living should not be overlooked. Further, although there is typically the closest and most intimate relationship between a sacred man and his deity, as *e.g.* in Egypt where the Pharaoh is the god incarnate and his " son " in the flesh, there is also typically a recognized difference between the man and his god, even though it is apt at times to be obscured. Already in the early Pyramid Texts the Pharaoh is man, son of the god, and a god ; and it is probable that the Divine Kingship throughout Egypt and South-West Asia involved a similar coexistence of most intimate relationship by the side of an essential difference.[1] The denunciation of the spiritual arrogance of Nebuchadrezzar (Dan. iv. 30 *sqq.*; cf. Judith iii. 8, vi. 2–4) and of the king of Tyre (Ezek. xxviii. 11 *sqq.*), and the " Fall of Lucifer " (Isa. xiv. 12), testify both to the persistence of the idea of the man-god and to the characteristic attitude of those teachers of Israel who were jealous of the sovereignty and supremacy of Yahweh. Such an attitude in Israel would be no less opposed to the deification of their own kings and to the worship of ancestors.

In the North Syrian inscription of Panammu, inscribed upon a colossal statue of the god Hadad, the dead king requests that his successor shall make mention of the name of the god and of himself, and shall pray that the soul of Panammu may eat and drink with the god (Cooke, No. 61 ; Lagrange, 492 *sqq.*). That Panammu could mediate on behalf of the living is not hinted ; and, speaking generally, it is constantly an open question (1) whether prayers and sacrifices are made to the god (in this case, to Hadad) on behalf of the dead, or in the hope that the grateful dead will use their good services on behalf of the living ; or (2) whether they are intended directly for the dead, either as a token of love or piety, or because the dead are, in a sense, more accessible and intelligible than the great and remote gods. For, when the powerful deities are felt to be afar off, a past ruler, leader, or holy man, powerful, helpful, and kindly, will be a far more historical

---

[1] Thus, the reforming king Ikhnaton is the beloved son of the self-begotten Aton, who makes him like himself and hears what is in his heart; he assigns to him his own length of years, and begets him every morning (Breasted, *Anc. Rec.* ii. §§ 991, 1010, etc.).

35

figure, and a more vivid nucleus of the god-idea in popular imagination and speculation.

In the vicissitudes of religion, divinization and de-divinization are typically alternating processes (see Toy, §§ 350 *sqq.*). The Babylonian god Tammuz appears in a list of primeval kings of Erech along with Gilgamesh the hero of the epic, and they rule for 100 and 126 years respectively (*CAH.* i.² 366 *sq.*). It is of course possible that an actual king Tammuz, becoming deified, was clothed in the characteristic garb of a vegetation god ; but it is equally possible that a still earlier god had already in some circles become the victim of euhemerism. The stories of the patriarch Jacob are sometimes thought to be derived from a heroic figure of a de-divinized god, in which case there has been a certain rationalizing process, for which there are analogies. Otherwise, traits of a mythical and supernatural character have certainly attached themselves to an originally historical figure.[1] The complexity of such inquiries as these can be illustrated from the modern cults of Palestinian saints and *welis* where (1) there are clans and families who claim to have sprung from one or other of these ; (2) where the well-known ancestor of a living sheikh is made a saint (Jaussen, 305), or where in this or in other ways a new cult springs into being, ready made ; and (3) where the identity of the saint or *weli* has clearly undergone change in the course of ages. As a general rule, specific tendencies (to divinize *or* to rationalize) can be more clearly apprehended than the actual origin of the local beings who are, in a sense, the lineal descendants of the Baals—and in a few cases of the Astartes—of the past.[2]

The predominant part played by local, family, and somewhat private cults testifies to the imperious demand for readily accessible supernatural powers. Such cults are often made tolerably orthodox and are affiliated to the national religion ; and although they may be repudiated, if not put down, by strict reforming movements (" Deuteronomic," Wahhabite, etc.), they come to the front again—though not in all their earlier form—because of the psychological needs they serve. Even on general principles, the cult of sacred beings who were regarded as ancestors, and of ancestors who were gods or heroic beings, is only to be expected in ancient times and among the Semites. The evidence has no doubt been exaggerated ; hence perhaps Lagrange's

---

[1] E. Meyer now decides that Jacob was primarily a god; see *Israeliten*, 109 (Luther), 282 ; *Gesch. Alt.* i. §§ 308, 343 *sq.* Rachel's continued interest in her children, and the unexpected indifference of Abraham and Israel (Isa. lxiii. 16), may point to an earlier and fuller cult of the great ancestral figures.

[2] Cf. the Anatolian *dede*, the heroized ancestor who to most is nameless (Ramsay, *Expositor*, Nov. 1906, p. 460.

not unnecessary reaction (ch. ix.). To Vincent (*Canaan*, ch. iv., see 288 *sqq.*, 295), the archæological data suggest care for the dead, rather than a cult. But there was evidently a belief in their continued existence, and the denunciation of mourning customs by the Israelite reformers is highly significant.

The modern custom of burying the dead in the vicinity of a sacred tomb or shrine is partly in order to preclude interference, and partly also to secure a blessing (*JPOS.* iv. 7). Sacrifices are made at graves, and there are gatherings with distribution of food and prayers for the dead.[1] Of special interest are the annual assemblies at the synagogue of R. Meir near Tiberias and the burnings at Meiron at the tomb of R. Simeon ben Yochai.[2] The desire to keep one's name alive (*e.g.* by a monument, 2 Sam. xviii. 18) would also involve some ceremony (*CAH.* iii. 445). Throughout, we find the idea of the continuance of the individual by himself, or as part of his group, or by virtue of his relationship with the god (see p. 555). Even Abraham and Aaron are gathered each to his " people " ('*am*, Gen. xxv. 8 ; Num. xx. 24) ; and not only is '*am* also a divine name, but when the group itself bears a divine name (Gad, etc.) the one life which pervades the whole group is, in a sense, more explicitly divine than when its god stands apart, *e.g.* as a " father." Theoretically, the union of the group and its sacred being is essentially of the closest ; the whole kindred conceives itself as having a single life in space and time (see above, p. 504 *sq.*). But in practice distinctions are made, and everywhere there are varying relations between the god, the group (as a whole), and special individuals. In Australian totemism the ancestors of the " Alcheringa times " are alike totem (animal or plant) and human (*Tot. Ex.* i. 188 *sq.*) ; ideas of human personality are undeveloped, and the visible totem-group and its ancestors are substantially one. With the growth of ideas of human nature, with increase of individuality, and especially with enhanced family or group sentiments there is a tendency to recognize supernatural beings of a more exclusive, more personal character, and ancestor cults easily arise. See pp. 591, 670.

The tendencies to replace a remote god by a human one, to find the link with the supernatural in specific dead individuals, and to think of gods along anthropomorphic lines have had so powerful an influence upon the development of social-religious ideas that ancestor worship has frequently commended itself as an explanation of the origin of religion. But there is always the question (see Crawley, *Tree of Life,* 174), Why " deify " a man, however much his character has won fear, respect, or love ? There are elements in religion which can hardly be

---

[1] Doughty, i. 240; Canaan, *JPOS.* vi. 65 *sq.*; Jaussen, 313 *sqq.*

[2] Cf. Ewing, *Life of J. E. H. Thomson,* 146 *sqq.*, 151.

derived from ancestor worship, or which are independent of anthropomorphic forms (*e.g.* cults of trees, stones, springs); and whereas the
broad developments in anthropomorphism have been towards more
elevated ideas of human personality, in totemism—and even animals
can be " ancestors "—the development has been towards anthropomorphism rather than away from it. The tendency to " deify " lies
behind both theriomorphism and anthropomorphism; and the experience of a " sacred " person or thing is not to be confused with the
way in which that experience has been formulated. See next note.

P. 161 and Additional Note B. THE SACRED.[1]—Here property
rights are secondary because (1) they are subordinated to the claims of a
sacred power, *e.g.* when animals stray upon a sacred area (cf. p. 543 *sq.*);
(2) a holy thing as such is not necessarily the god's property, it may
be a man's private cult-object; (3) even that which is the god's property may be a public rather than a private possession (cf. p. 147);
and (4), in general, all worshippers have access, subject to certain
restrictions, to what is sacred. The sacred is " restricted." The
" holiness " of the gods rather than their intolerance is their distinctive mark; it is a specifically Semitic attribute (Cumont, ch. v.
n. 47, after Clermont-Ganneau). Things are *either* sacred and holy
or common and profane; they are also divided into *either* clean *or*
unclean. The difference between the two classes of terms is very
important (see p. 446). Sanctity or holiness is something intrinsic,
inherent; and the " sacred " and " unclean " agree in their mechanical,
automatic, and physical character. A man carries the " unclean "
into the sanctuary, and can bring back the " sacred " into ordinary
life (p. 453). Things become unwittingly " sacred " or " unclean ";
and these states, induced by contagion, by physical means, etc., can
be remedied physically (*e.g.* by washing). Certain acts set in motion,
as it were, the " sacred " and " unclean." [2] Bloodshed is a sort of
miasma, and in Athens homicides were tried in an unroofed court in
order that the case might be conducted in a purer atmosphere.[3]

There is, of course, an essential distinction between the holy and the
unclean (p. 153 *sq.*), and the question arises whether this difference,
which Lagrange (150 *sq.*) properly emphasizes, is to be taken back to
the beginning, or whether both may be supposed to have sprung from

---

[1] Wellhausen, 168 *sqq.*; G. A. Simcox, *E.Bi.* art. " Clean "; Lagrange, ch. iv.;
Söderblom and Whitehouse, *ERE.* art. " Holiness "; Williger, *Hagios* (Giessen,
1922).

[2] It is as in a coal mine where fire-damp, when it comes in contact with a flame,
explodes and brings death to the careless and to the innocent alike; see R. H.
Kennett (and others) in *Early Ideals of Righteousness*, 10 (Edinburgh, 1910).

[3] Farnell, *Evolution of Religion*, 149.

the taboos of primitive peoples (cf. above, p. 446 foot; and see p. 152). Fear and irrational taboos have always been prejudicial to progress, whereas restrictions due to respect or awe for friendly powers " contain with them germinant principles of social progress and moral order " (p. 154). Admitted that the distinction between the holy and the unclean " marks a real advance above savagery " (*ib.*), we must draw a line between (1) this distinction, which is vital for very development, and (2) the confusion of blind fear and reverence which occurs repeatedly and precludes progress (p. 519 *sq.*). Hence it is simpler to start with a stage where religion, involving friendly relations (such as W. R. S. finds in totemism), can be recognized, than with some prior one where this distinction has not been made, even as it is simpler to start from a stage with both religion and its antithesis magic than from an assumed absolute priority of magic.

The unity of gods and men within the group is a fundamental part of W. R. S.'s argument. " The principle of sanctity and that of kinship are identical " (p. 289); " holiness means kinship to the worshippers and their god " (p. 400). In other words, the consciousness of the reality of the supersensuous power was characteristically one that united man to it in a way that could be formulated only in terms of most intimate relationship. In mysticism there are the well-known experiences of (*a*) a loss of the self, which approaches (*b*) identity with the unseen power; though the doctrine of an actual identity of the Self and the Other meets with condemnation at the hands of mystics themselves. Similarly, among rudimentary peoples there are rites of imitation of, and even of identification with, unseen powers, which are essentially only the more elemental and physical expression of experiences analogous to those in the spiritual and mystical religions at more advanced levels. Among rudimentary peoples these rites easily take forms and lead to consequences which must be regarded as contrary to the progressive development of religion; but " aberrations " are by no means wanting also at the higher stages. Theoretically, the entire group of gods and worshippers should be holy—this is the ideal (Ex. xix. 6, Num. xvi. 3). But in the history of religion distinctions are made. Among rudimentary peoples lines are drawn (1) between the full members and women, uninitiated and slaves; (2) between the special group in its ordinary, normal life and the " sacred " state when certain ceremonies are being performed collectively and various taboos are in force.[1]

There are ceremonies to confirm or to intensify the unity of gods

[1] The transition from one state to another, or from the " normal " to the " supernormal " and back again, has been handled at length by Van Gennep, *Les Rites de Passage* (1909).

and men, and there are offences which destroy it. Holiness and (ceremonial) cleanness are incompatible with uncleanness; and although men act as though there were a sort of automatic, self-vindicating process (pp. 162, 425 l. 5), they must also act on its behalf (p. 163). Both ritual and ethical offences weaken the unity ; but the specifically ethical aspect of divine holiness, as taught by the Hebrew prophets, though it reshaped the earlier religion, was followed, even as it had been preceded, by a preponderating emphasis upon ceremonial holiness. Such a succession of stages—alternately ritual and ethical—is probably normal. Some types of uncleanness (*e.g.* sexual), though perfectly natural, are thought to stand in need of purificatory rites, and peoples or lands which do not conform to them are, on this account, " unclean." [1] Although, theoretically, one's own land is " sacred " and the group participates in the sacred life (cf. p. 160), in practice there are definite holy places, or new centres of sacred power will manifest themselves (tree, spring, etc.). Life tends to be systematized into sacred places, times, and individuals (who, *e.g.*, will assert the doctrine of divine proprietorship), and sacred states. [2] But the readiness to experience what is sacred or holy is logically prior to the particular experience, which is at once shaped and interpreted according to the circumstances.

Since W. R. S. wrote, the subject has been considerably extended by the study of ideas of Mana. Among many peoples there is explicit recognition of some supersensuous cause of all phenomena that are striking, marvellous, abnormal, etc., or that are beyond man's power, or that are impressive because of their significance and regularity. A power manifests itself in unusual forms of what is otherwise usual (special strength, cunning, productivity), or in natural phenomena essential to human welfare. Many specific terms have been collected from different parts of the world—the North American Orenda, Manitu, etc., the Oudah of the Pygmies, the Petara of the Sea Dyaks of Sarawak, and so forth. [3] Throughout, the reference is to some power, whether vague, or more precisely connected with a god or with powerful ancestors. If impersonal, it tends to become personal when venerated.

---

[1] An " unclean " land was a foreign one (p. 93), and Gentile women who did not perform the usual Jewish purificatory rites were " unclean " themselves, and communicated the state to their husbands (Büchler, *Jew. Quart. Rev.* xvii. [1926], 67 *sq.*, 79 *sq.*).

[2] The importance of this (largely unconscious) systematization is especially emphasized by Durkheim, who illustrates it in the most rudimentary, though highly efficacious forms in Central Australian totemism.

[3] Marett, *Threshold of Religion*, 13, 120 *sqq.*, and *ERE*. " Mana " ; Durkheim, 192 *sqq.*; Crawley, *Idea of the Soul*; Hartland, *Ritual and Belief*, 36–160; I. King, ch. vi.

It is the power that is manifested in men of outstanding personality, and it is as the power of the mighty dead that it is most readily explained. Of the many terms with various nuances found among most widely severed peoples the Melanesian Mana is commonly adopted, but on the understanding that the particular Melanesian type of Mana is not the norm. It is properly a convenient term for co-ordinating great masses of related facts ancient and modern.[1]

The data of " Mana " range between the vague and more indefinite causes where, e.g., sacred stones have curative properties, though there is no tradition or explanation of their efficacy, and the more specific gods. A bull-roarer may be effective in a general way in promoting fertility ; but elementary reasoning enters when female fertility is combined with that of the soil, or, e.g., the liver of a fierce animal imparts fierceness to the eater.[2] Further, a distinction must be drawn between Mana according as it is used in a good or in a bad way. Thus, the translation of the Egyptian ḥike' by " magic " obscures the fact (a) that it is a power used also by the friendly and helpful gods, and (b) that there were anti-social, " irreligious," and harmful practices which would more naturally deserve that name. Even low down in the scale, among the Arunta of Central Australia, besides the power which is helpful and beneficent there is arunkulta, the evil influence, or an embodiment or manifestation of it.[3] It is therefore

[1] Thus, it includes the Indian Brahman, the Greek δύναμις (θεοῦ, χριστοῦ), the holy πνεῦμα, φῶς and χάρις, the ancient Egyptian ḥike', and the modern Arab baraka. See also Orient. Lit. zeit. 1923, col. 378 sq. ; Nilsson, 81 sq. The baraka is a mysterious force vouchsafed to sacred men or to objects (oil, stones, bones) which have been in contact with sacred shrines, tombs, etc. It comes directly from living sheikhs or from dead spirits (JPOS. v. 177, 179). Westermarck (Morocco, i. 35–261) calls it " holiness " or " blessed virtue." On ḥike', magical arts, power, and mysterious ways of doing things, see A. H. Gardiner, Proc. Soc. Bibl. Arch. xxxvii. (1915), 253 sqq., xxxviii. 52 ; Peet, CAH. i.[2], 354, ii: 199 sqq. In the Syriac Apocryphal Acts (ed. Wright, ii. 191, 258), the prayer of Judas Thomas enables divine power to enter water which heals the withered hands of a boy ; and the " power of Jesus " enters anointing oil and gives it curative properties.

[2] On the question whether Êl means " numen, mana," see Beth, ZATW. xxxvi. 129 sqq., xxxviii. 87 sqq. The objection that in orthodox Yahwism it is not Mana (Kleinert, Baudissin-Festschrift, 283 sq.) seems to miss the point ; the reflective and more orthodox view of an Êl, as e.g. one that shows compassion (Jerahmeel), does not exclude the vaguer ideas of power (personal or impersonal) where the Êl is less an object of close attention.

[3] Mana is powerful for life or for death ; cf. W. R. Halliday, Greek Divination, a Study of its Methods and Principles, 99 sqq. (1913). See Marett, Psychology and Folklore, 64, 67, 163, 166 sqq. : the savage gets Mana only by observing strict chastity, or undergoing discipline ; it is bestowed by an act of grace ; received with fear and wonder, it can be lost if he becomes a drunkard ; in the Iroquois

necessary to avoid the confusion of (1) the evidence for the recognition of power which could be used in a way contrary to the interests of a tribe with (2) the more theoretical if not controversial question of the best employment of such terms as Magic, Mana, etc.

Mana and Taboo are complementary.[1] The taboo arises out of precaution, heed, fear. Many typical taboos reflect an almost mystical detestation of what is felt to be offensive or repulsive ; a few would prove suicidal if persisted in (cf. 640). Some are essentially in the interests of a particular class. In general, they range between the vaguest fears of consequences, the dread of offending some one or something, and the most intelligible of prohibitions. Taboo by itself is restrictive, whereas Mana connotes a power to be utilized. Mana by itself leads to the belief that the power lies wholly in man's hand, and can be set in motion by man. The data of Mana refer to the power which man can employ, the bad use of which is harmful and dangerous ; the data of Taboo refer characteristically to the appropriate attitude that man must adopt where " sacred " things are concerned. Together, Mana and Taboo direct attention to the pragmatic side of religion—religion partly as an attitude that enables the man to face life, partly as a means of effective living. This practical aspect runs through all religion (e.g. Matt. vi. 32 sq.) ; and in the Old Testament the holy and righteous Yahweh is not merely the recipient of his people's prayers but acts on behalf of a people that complies with the conditions of the relationship between him and them. There is much truth in the distinction drawn by Malinowski,[2] that Religion is not a means to an end but an end in itself, whereas Magic is progressive, with a clear, definite aim—a " pseudo-science." But Religion fits a man to face any future, and it can lead to quietism ; whereas typical Magic seeks to forestall or to compel the future, and tends to become the worst enemy of Religion. Yet this antithesis must not be pressed too far, for there are innumerable beliefs and practices which can be called " magico-religious," because they combine imitative and other seemingly irrelevant and irrational practices for the welfare of the group with a spirit of reverence and awe, and with regulative taboos conducive to the stability of the group. Mana alone and Taboo alone become, on psychological grounds, stagnant and devoid of progressive elements ; whereas in combination the two are complementary, and stand at the head of series of developments. It is difficult to conceive the one without the other save in the secondary

phrase, if a man " lays down his own power " in its presence, he will be filled with a new power which is good, but if used for exploitation is bad.

[1] See especially Marett, *Threshold of Religion*.

[2] *Science, Religion, and Reality* (ed. Needham), 38, 81.

stages, and in this respect Mana and Taboo find an analogy in the equally complementary ideas of Divine Immanence and Transcendence (p. 564).

The widespread conception of Mana emphasizes the fact that man's attention is commonly directed first to the strange, mysterious, and abnormal phenomena ; a cause is demanded primarily for them, and only later, as it seems, for those more regular, but vital or impressive. Inquiry into the relation between (a) the cause of both these classes of phenomena and (b) the cause of all other and more familiar activities could not arise until the dawn of Science ; and the equally important question of the relation between religious data and the non-religious but otherwise comparable data still attracts little attention. Similarly, attention is commonly directed more readily to all that evokes feelings of fascination, admiration, etc., than to its quality. The distinction between the *jinn* and the saint, between the devilish and the divine, between the blasphemous and the holy, has already been drawn by these terms themselves ; but there remain the phenomena which are not, or cannot be, immediately evaluated.[1] The difference between the application of the term " sacred " to the *ḳedēshīm* of Israel and the prophets' doctrine of Yahweh's holiness is one of the most striking examples of an *ethical* development vital for the progress of religion ; but the early history of the Church at Corinth shows how quickly a " sacred " ceremony can lose spiritual value.

The paradoxical character of religion turns in large measure upon the coexistence of the good and the harmful aspects of " powerful " things. Salt preserves and kills ; sun and rain are life-giving and destructive ; the blood of women is taboo, but it is effective in magic ; blood gives a higher life to those who partake of it, but is highly dangerous to those who are not entitled, or who act heedlessly ; the king is taboo, his touch can kill or it can cure ; the dead corpse is dreaded as something " unclean," but a relic is an effective charm. The psychology of desire and disgust, of attraction and repulsion, accounts for some paradoxes. Further, there are topics so delicate and " sacred " that, although the discussion of them is necessary, a careless or improper mishandling of them is shocking. The Sacred is double-edged and must be safeguarded. The individual who trespasses here runs the risk of causing serious offence to others as well as himself ; and the history of Taboos is, in part, that of the

---

[1] Cf. the fascination of crime, etc., the unreflecting attitude to genius (perverse or other), and the readiness to distinguish the religious (or mystical) from the non-religious (or non-mystical) rather than to appraise the value (ethical, etc.) of religious (or mystical) data (*e.g.* true or false prophets, Messiahs, etc.).

effort to regularize the treatment of the sacred and holy in ways recognized to be socially beneficial.

Experiences that take men out of themselves have constantly been interpreted as necessarily taking them into the realm of the sacred, or bringing them into communion with supernatural beings (cf. p. 575). In man's ignorance of the world and of himself, when imagination and reality interpenetrated, and such activities as playing, dancing, and other releases of energy could have an at least quasi-divine meaning, the idea of the " sacred " had almost boundless extension. This is now more accurately recognized, and a wider concept has been coined in Rudolf Otto's " Numinous." [1] Here are included all that is uncanny, weird, eerie, awful, fascinating, majestic, sublime, ecstatic. It thus extends into religion, mysticism, spiritualism, occultism, poetry, art, drama, and all else where a man is taken away from the world of the senses and has a vivid consciousness of what is supersensuous but real, and often more real than the experiences of ordinary life. But even as Mana is logically neutral and Religion has its paradoxes, so the *mysterium tremendum et fascinosum* lies behind religion, and not religion alone. Without taking into account the subjective " numinous " states, it would be impossible to understand the presence, persistence, and progressive development of religion. But the " numinous " as such is not religious, even as the " sacred," and much that is placed in the category of " religion " lies outside that more objective estimate of religion which a systematic treatment of the data requires. There are times when " the religious consciousness, bursting its too narrow confines, seems at once to soar upward and to plunge downward " (Cornford, *CAH*. iv. 533 *sq.*). But the main stream of development is more important ; and the extraordinary range of data that claim to belong to the " sacred " and the " holy " demand a methodology of the subject. W. R. S.'s conception of the group-system, of holiness as kinship, and of the moral interrelations between the members of groups and their gods, lays the necessary emphasis upon those experiences of the " numinous " which have been valuable for mental, ethical, and social development, and on this account appears to offer the best mode of approach to the profounder problems of religion.

P. 163 note.—See Frazer, *GB*. and *Tot. Ex.* s.v. " Incest," and his *Psyche's Task*[2], on the effect of religious and related sanctions upon the growth of society.

P. 164. Curses.—The gods, who of their own will are wont to defend the right and punish wrong and thus uphold social order, are also

---

[1] See Otto, *The Idea of the Holy* (transl. by J. W. Harvey; Oxford, 1925).

besought to curse the evil-doer ; and the entreaty sometimes becomes virtually a compulsion, whether through the words or the ritual or the agent employed. But even without gods or any specially named spirits there is frequent resort to a curse, whether with or without ceremonial ; and the curse, as it were, sets in motion a process which is believed to be effective. Both blessings and curses, in some of their characteristic forms at least, imply a process which either may be styled an inherent one, or is operated by powers, who, however, are not necessarily specified. The process or mechanism is such that the blessing once uttered cannot be taken back (Gen. xxvii. 33, 38), and the curse of the wise will be effective even against the innocent (Talm. Bab. *Makk.* 11a) ; contrast Prov. xxvi. 2.[1]

P. 167. LIFE, LIVING WATER.—(1) By " Life " is meant not merely physiological conditions, but the state of being alive and of having that which makes life worth living.[2] The Babylonian gods Inurta (Ninurta) and Gula are gods of healing and " cause the dead to live," and Marduk restores to life. But all the gods could do was to keep a man alive as long as possible (Jastrow, *Rel. Bel.* 365 *sq.*) ; resurrection of the dead is not meant, but rather a fresh lease of life, and " fulness of days." [3] There is also the hope of continuance in the god's presence.[4] It was enough that a man's name was remembered, or that he was written in Yahweh's " book of life " ; for with Yahweh was the " fountain of life," and " life " is essentially the most important attribute of the gods. In Egypt both the gods and the semi-divine Pharaoh have the life-giving breath ; the idea recurs in the Amarna Letters and was no doubt familiar throughout South-West Asia, where the divine-kingship ruled.[5] Life and Breath were understood physically. The " sign of life " is given to the Pharaoh on his accession ; and on other occasions it is depicted near his face in order that he can inhale or otherwise assimilate the " power " it

[1] See Goldziher, *Abhand.* i. 382, also *ib.* 29, and ii. p. civ; the comparative studies by W. S. Fox, *AJSL.* xxx. 111 *sqq.*, and G. L. Hendrickson, *Amer. Journ. Philol.* 1925, pp. 104 *sqq.* ; and the mass of material collected by J. Hempel, " die Israelit. Anschauungen von Segen u. Fluch," *ZDMG.* 1925, pp. 20–100. For Westermarck's views, see below, p. 692.

[2] See Baudissin, 480 *sqq.*, and in *Sachau-Festschrift,* 143 *sqq.* ; also Lindblom, *Das ewige Leben* (Upsala, 1914).

[3] Norden, *Geburt d. Kindes,* 120, cites Ammian. xvii. 421 (βίον ἀπρόσκορον, life of which one cannot have too much). The hopes of Abgar, priest of Nerab, were for a good name, length of days, children of the fourth generation, and mourners to lament him (Cooke, No. 65).

[4] See C. H. W. Johns, *Cambridge Biblical Essays* (ed. Swete), 40 *sq.*

[5] Knudtzon, *El-Amarna Tafeln,* 1195, 1606 ; Baudissin, 503 *sq.*; Gressmann, *Baud. Festschrift,* 208.

contains.[1] In certain ceremonies into which the " water of life " enters, the water is depicted with a string of symbols of the sign of life (Blackman, *PSBA*. xl. 87). Purely spiritual or psychical ideas could only be conceived in physical material terms, and in Hebrew, where *rūᵃḥ* denoted the energy of Life as distinct from mere existence, the " idea of personality is an animated body, and not an incarnated soul." [2]

Primitive psychology, as Crawley has shown (*The Idea of the Soul*), could readily conceive of inanimate objects being as animate as trees and animals. Several animating principles could even be recognized (life, soul, etc.) ; and in the primitive analyses of all that goes to make up a man, relatively complex results emerge, as when in Central Australia a man is born of totem-spirit stuff to which he will return, but yet has an individual soul of his own. The varying ideas of soul–spirit–life are everywhere very differently systematized, and the ability to entertain complex convictions of this sort in material forms holds good of all peoples who have not reached that stage where the differentiation of a tangible body and an intangible spirit has become a presupposition.[3] See p. 676 *sq.*

(2) Water, especially running water, is " instinct with divine life and energy " (p. 173).[4] It is " purifying, consecrating, healing " ; " on y vit l'action d'un pouvoir supérieur sans distinguer entre la naturel et le surnaturel." It is the abode of dead souls, and to the significant traditions of gods who were drowned (on which see Eitrem, 114) one must add the well-known sacrifices to water-spirits and the strange superstition that it is unlucky to rescue the drowning—*i.e.* to deprive the water-spirit of its lawful victim (see Gomme, *Ethnology in Folk-lore*, 73). In both Egypt and Babylonia water was life-giving and purifying—the two attributes converge.[5] In Egypt there are " waters of life " in both sky and on earth ; [6] in Babylonia water-gods are prominent in incantations, and ceremonies to ward off evil spirits were often held on the bank of a river.[7] Ishtar is sprinkled with the waters of life before her ascent from the underworld. Marduk was

---

[1] Cf. metaphors connected with breath, odour, and welfare, Eitrem, 212 *sq.*

[2] H. Wheeler Robinson, in Peake, *People and the Book*, 360, 362, 381.

[3] See Crawley, *Mystic Rose*, 79 *sq.*, *Tree of Life*, 236 ; Kreglinger, *Études sur l'origine et le développement de la vie religieuse*, i. 163 *sq.* (Brussels, 1919) ; cf. *ERE.* art. " Religion," § 23.

[4] See Lagrange, 158 *sqq.* (with criticisms of W. R. S.) ; Toy, §§ 306 *sqq.* ; Moore, *E.Bi.* " Idolatry," § 2.

[5] It is possible that the root-meaning of " holy " (קדש) is pure, bright, or clean (see *E.Bi.* " Clean," § 1).

[6] See, further, Breasted, *Rel. and Thought*, 19 ; Blackman, *PSBA.* xl. 57 *sqq.*, 86 *sqq.*; and *Arch. f. Rel.* 1904, p. 40 *sq.*

[7] Morgenstern, 60, cf. 29, 84.

lord of the deep (*apshu*, the ocean below the earth; Wardle, *Israel and Bab.* 147), and lord of springs (*bel nakbe*) ; and his sacred water healed men. In Zoroastrianism water is full of " glory " (*hvarenah*), and gives might and glory (Söderblom, *Werden d. Gottesglaubens*, 248). Waters are frequently regarded as impregnating, and fertility is caused by drinking or bathing.[1] In Palestine the *weli* is the reputed husband of the barren women who bathe in springs with success (Curtiss, 117). The power of sacred waters is ascribed to some traditional figure (*e.g.* a sheikh) or is explained by a legend; thus, it was in the basin of the Sitti Mariam in Jerusalem that the Virgin once bathed, and certain wells are sacred and have healing properties because once a year their waters are supposed to mingle with the holy well Zamzam (*JPOS.* iv. 65; cf. above, p. 167 *sq.*). The tenth of Moharram is an especially efficacious day for bathing, and at Askalon women still bathe in the sea at the festival of Hosain (*JPOS.* l.c.; see v. 198). On this festival, see p. 321 and note 4.

According to W. R. S., the sacred character of waters and springs is to be explained on general principles, the legends or deities associated with them being secondary (p. 184). The main criticisms, on the other hand, start from these; and it is observed, *e.g.*, that waters, springs, etc., have neither temples nor priesthood, and " the superstitions of the Semites have not prevailed against the fundamental principle which made gods, not of animated things, but of the forces which put them in movement " (Lagrange, 166). What is at issue is the question whether the Semites recognized an inherent power in things without reference to personal powers acting upon or in them; and the very history of sacred waters should show that the readiness to believe in their sanctity is more fundamental than the traditional saints or stories, which, however amply they justify the sanctity, are apt to change throughout the ages.[2]

P. 168 n. 1.—See Mordtmann and Müller, *Sab. Denkmäler*, 10; Gaudefroy-Demombynes, *Pèlerinage à la Mekke*, 73.

P. 169 and n. 1.—For the Palmyrene inscription referred to, see Lidzbarski, *Handbuch der nordsemit. Epigraphik* (Weimar, 1898), i. 153 n. 7, 476, No. 11 : לגדא די עינא בריכתא עב[ד] באסמלוטן תרתן בולנא בר עזיזו . . . די אשלמת על ידוה. Clermont-Ganneau (*Rev. Archéol.* xxviii. 138 *sqq.*) finds a reference to the " guardian "

---

[1] Farnell, *Cults*, v. 423; Hartland, *Primitive Paternity*, i. 23, 66, 80 *sqq.*, 136; Frazer, *GB.* ii. 160 *sqq.*; R. C. Thompson, *Semitic Magic*, 79 *sq.*; Canaan, *JPOS.* v. 193 (water cures impotence).

[2] Lagrange (165 n. 1), among other criticisms, objects to W. R. S., p. 170 n. 1, on the ground that the pool being one of the artificial reservoirs in the Hauran would dry up annually and could scarcely be the object of a cult.

of the well (ἐπιμελητής, reading בּאפמ׳); cf. the " guardianship " (אפמלטות) of Yarḥibol in the Paplmyrene inscription edited by Lidzbarski, *Ephemeris*, ii. 300.   For Bethesda and its inter-mittent bubbling springs, see E. W. G. Masterman, *Quart. Statements* of the Palestine Exploration Fund, 1921, p. 93 *sq.*, who refers to the popular belief that a dragon lives beneath the " Virgin's Fountain " ; also R. A. S. Macalister, *Century of Excavation in Palestine*, 141 *sq.*[1] On the association of serpents with springs, see Baudissin, 338 (n. 2), and his article " Drache" in *Protest. Real-Encycl.* For temples and springs, see Baudissin 244 (cult of Eshmun), Morgenstern 31 (Baby-lonia); and for the modern belief that Turkish baths are inhabited by *jinn*, see *JPOS.* iv. 65 n. 4.

P. 169 and n. 3.—The Tigris and Euphrates, as also the rivers of Phœnicia, had their gods (see Lagrange, 160 *sq.*, 165; *KAT.* 359, 525 n. 5). In the treaty between Rameses ii. and the Hatti, gods of rivers are among the witnesses (Breasted, *Anc. Rec.* iii. § 386).   In note 3 add the reading λιμένων (Grotius), adopted by Stübe (131 n.) and Lagrange (161 n. 5).

P. 170 n. 4.—Cais may mean " husband"; so Winckler, *Altorient. Forschungen*, ii. 321; *Arab.–Semit.–Orient.* (*MVAG.* 1901, iv.) 84 n. It is certainly not connected with Cozaḥ, and doubtfully (so Nöldeke, *ZDMG.* 1889, p. 714 n. 1) with the Edomite Cos, Caus.

P. 176. SACRED FISH.—For Edessa, see also Duval, *Journ. Asiat.* xviii. (1891) 92, 231, and in general see Frazer, *Pausanias*, iv. 153 ; *E.Bi.* " Fish " §§ 9–11 ; Garstang on Lucian, § 45 ; Reinach, *Cultes*, iii. 43 *sq.*, 515 *sq.*; Cumont, *Orient. Relig.* ch. v. notes 36 and 37 ; and F. J. Dölger, *Der heilige Fisch i. d. antik. Relig. u. i. Christentum* (1922).

P. 180. ORDEALS AND OATHS.—See Wellhausen, 186 *sq.*; Halliday, *Greek Divination*, 112; Morgenstern, *Heb. Union Coll., Jubilee Vol.* (Cincinatti, 1925), pp. 113 *sqq.* Eitrem (117 n. 1) cites parallels to the omen at Aphaca (above, p. 178 and n. 2). For the story of Hind (p. 180 n. 3), see *Kinship*, 123 ; and for the ordeal by the " waters of jealousy," see *E.Bi.* 2342 *sq.*; Gray, *Numbers*, 44 *sq.*; Halliday, 105 *sq.*; and, on the text, Bewer, *AJSL.* xxx. 36 *sqq.* In Num. v. 17 (" holy water ") the LXX reads " living water." Nöldeke's reference (p. 181 n. 3) is to Lagarde, *Reliq.* 134, and the Mandæan *Sidrā Rabbā*, i. 224, 8. In the Code of Hammurabi (§§ 2, 132) the person accused of witchcraft and the woman suspected of adultery are thrown to the Sacred River or River-god ; this was also the ancient German method

---

[1] Was the spring at 'Artās, guarded by a ram, supposed to be a gateway to the underworld ? (Prof. Halliday, in a private communication ; see his remarks in *Folk-lore*, 1923, p. 132).

of testing the legitimacy of children (Dareste, *Journ. des Savants*, 1902, p. 519 n. 1). On the quasi-mechanical principle underlying the curse and ordeal, where gods and spirits are not specifically mentioned, see above, p. 555.[1]

P. 182 n. 2.—The text of Amos is retained by Driver, Sir G. A. Smith, etc. In a song at the Nebī Musā festival (Canaan, *JPOS.* vi. 135 n. 2), the way leading to the Sanctuary of the Prophet (*ṭarīc en-nabī*) is called upon to rejoice. But the parallelism and the LXX (ὁ θεός σου) have suggested the reading אֵלֶךְ (so Dozy), בְּאֶרֶךְ (Wellhausen, Elhorst), and preferably דֹּדְךָ, "thy *numen*" (G. Hoffmann, Winckler [*Altor. Forsch.* i. 194 *sq.*]). With the last cf. the name name דּוֹדָוָהוּ (for דּוֹדְיָהוּ ?), "Yahu is friend (uncle, cousin, patron)," and the parallels in Assyrian (*KAT.* 483), South Arabian (דדכרב, etc.), and the obscure דודה on the inscription of Mesha (Cooke, 11). As regards the meaning of *d–d*, cf. the Abyssinian name *Arka Dengel*, *i.e.* Friend of the Virgin, cited by Nöldeke, *E.Bi.* col. 3289, § 47.

P. 183 n. 2. THE SONG TO THE WELL.—Gray (*Numbers*, 289) cites, *inter alia*, a parallel from Nilus, col. 648. Gressmann (*Mose*, 350) cites Musil, *Arab. Petrœa*, i. 298, a parallel from the Arnon district, where the modern sheikh has taken the place of the nobles in Numbers. In Egypt, well-digging was a royal duty ; see Breasted, *Anc. Rec.* iii. § 195 (with a prayer to Amon and to the gods dwelling in the well on behalf of Seti I., the good shepherd who dug the well), and § 292 (where the water in the nether world hearkens to Rameses II. when he digs the well).

P. 185 *sq.* SACRED TREES.[2]—On a connexion between the words for " tree " and " god " ('*ēl*)—both involving the idea of " power "—see, besides p. 196 n. 4, Baudissin, 433 *sq.*, who comments on the distinction drawn between human (or animal) and vegetable life, and on the points of contact (personification, etc.). As elsewhere, questions arise, (1) whether there is a sacred life or power intrinsic or " immanent " (p. 194) in the species or single tree, (2) whether this is due to " sacred " life-giving water (p. 192), or (3) whether the tree is an

---

[1] Otherwise, when lots are cast the actual decision (*mishpāṭ*) comes from God (Prov. xvi. 33), and the guilty may be asked to admit its justice (Josh. vii. 19). Westermarck (*Moral Ideas*, i. 626) gives as one of the reasons for the efficacy of the curses and blessings of fathers the mystery of old age and the nearness of death. That the dying are in touch with the supernatural realm has also accounted for the prolonged torture of unhappy victims from whom knowledge of the unseen could accordingly be extracted (Halliday).

[2] See art. Tree-worship in *E.Bi.* (G. F. Moore),*Ency. Brit.* (S. A. Cook) ; Lagrange, ch. v. § 2 ; Barton, *Semitic Origins*, 87 *sqq.* ; Toy, §§ 262 *sqq.*; Baudissin, *Adonis* (see his Index, 535) ; Frazer, *FOT.* iii. ch. xv.

embodiment or a vehicle of some external power, and (4) whether the specific tradition which explains its sanctity is of primary or even secondary value. At the present day it has been computed that about 60 per cent. of the Palestinian shrines have trees ; but the more modern *welis* tend to do without them (Canaan, *JPOS.* iv. 30 *sqq.*). Such trees are not to be harmed, and if one is cut down another is planted in its place. The fruit may be plucked to satisfy hunger ; but it is safer to recite the *fātiḥah* before one plucks, and it should not be carried away. Branches may be removed for festal purposes, or in order to cook meals in fulfilment of a vow. The practice of hanging rags and other portions of one's personal belongings upon a sacred tree, and of taking away others which have been hanging there and now serve as amulets, implies a belief in the inherent sanctity of the tree. This sanctity is usually explained as due to the *weli*, or there is some appropriate tradition. In early Christian times a sacred tree at Samosata was worshipped, and justifiably, as the wood of the Cross (Chwolson, i. 293) ; but another tree to which the villagers burnt incense, and which Thomas of Marga condemns, was the abode of a " demon " (ed. Budge, 242 ; cf. *ib.* 511). At Tell el-Ḳāḍī, two large trees by the side of a stream shade the tomb of Sheikh Merzuk, who has taken the place of a dog. The " Laurel Lady," with dripping sword, manifested herself in a terebinth in 1917, driving back the British troops in their advance (Canaan, *JPOS.* iv. 71). The olive-tree is especially holy (*JPOS.* vi. 18, 20 n. 3, 138). For a parallel to the acacia (p. 133 above), see *JPOS.* iv. 71 n. 1 ; and for the belief that the palm-tree is sacred because it was created from the earth with which God made Adam, see Canaan, *JPOS.* iv. 14. Many of the modern sacred trees seem to be survivors of woods or groves (*ib.* iv. 34), and the existence of sacred groves and gardens at Daphne and elsewhere (cf. Frazer, *FOT.* iii. 67 *sqq.*) may explain the tendency of the LXX and Vulg. to translate *ashērah* by " grove " (for details, see Burney, *Kings*, 191). See further next note.

P. 188. THE GODDESS ASHERAH.[1]—W. R. S.'s denial (with Wellhausen, Stade, etc.) that there was a goddess Asherah—although he did not deny that " in some places the general symbol of deity had become a special goddess "—was hardly an " arbitrary theory " (Lagrange, 120) ; and his reasons, even if inadequate, are at least worthy of notice. (*a*) He urged that the tree or stock was the symbol of a *god* (Jer. ii. 27) ; though the fact that tree and stone (*ēṣ* and *'eben*) are

---

[1] See Stübe, 145 ; Lagrange, 120 *sqq.* ; Burney, *Judges*, 196 *sqq.* For Kuenen's essay (p. 189 n. 1 l. 8), see the German translation in the volume edited by Budde (1894), and cf. Moore, *E.Bi.* col. 3991. In Micah v. 13 (see p. 188, middle), for " thy cities " read " thy idols " (as in 2 Chron. xxiv. 18).

respectively masculine and feminine may be merely a grammatical point (Baud. 176 n. 2). Next, (*b*) as the Astarte-cult of Ahab's day was Tyrian, the *asherah* which Jehu left standing (2 Kings xiii. 6) was therefore not Tyrian ; and (*c*) there is no evidence for a divine pair in Israel. On the other hand, apart from textual difficulties,[1] the trend of archæological and other contemporary evidence is to obliterate the line which W. R. S. draws between " Israelite " and " Canaanite " religion, between the higher elements of Semitic religion and the popular Yahwism " which had all the characters of Baal worship " (p. 194): though the similarity between the religion of Israel and that of surrounding peoples only enhances the uniqueness of the more spiritual and ethical monotheistic teaching of the great prophets.

Asherah was West Semitic, perhaps " Amorite " ; a dedication on behalf of Hammurabi calls her " bride of the king of heaven," " lady (*belit*) of vigour and joy (*kuzbi u ulṣi*), intercessor, etc. In a cuneiform tablet found at Taʿanach reference is made to an omen by the finger (*u-ba-an*) of the deity A-shi-rat; and in the Amarna Letters her name recurs in that of the great anti-Egyptian Amorite chief Abd-Ashirta (or Ashrat, also written Abd-Ashtarti, with the determinative of deity). Ashirat and Ishtar (Astarte, etc.), though akin in nature, are not etymologically connected, the derivation of Ishtar being quite uncertain, while the name Ashirat possibly connotes ideas of good fortune (like Gad, Tyche).[2]

The *asherah* is the tree or tree-trunk familiar throughout South-West Asia. Sometimes a tree is shorn of branches and lopped off short (Susa ; see Vincent, *Canaan*, 144 *sqq.*), and among the Kissil Bashi of the Upper Tigris a trimmed oak-trunk stands under a tree at the eastern end of the village within a railed-off space into which only the " father priest " can enter (*The Standard* of 19th September 1904). Similar objects of cult are familiar elsewhere.[3] In the Phœnician Maʿsub inscription (" the Astarte in the Asherah ") the object may be a sign-post set up to mark the boundary (Moore, *E.Bi.* col. 332; cf. Cooke, 50, Lagrange, 448 *sq.*); compare the stelæ set up as landmarks by Ikhnaton to mark the boundary of the holy city of Akhetaton (Breasted, *Anc. Rec.* ii. §§ 949 *sqq.* ; Baikie, *Amarna Age*, 265 *sqq.*).

---

[1] See comm. on 2 Kings x. 26 (and Lagrange, 123 n., 207 n.), where what was burnt was presumably an *asherah* and not a stone pillar.

[2] *KAT.* 432 *sq.* ; Sellin, *Taannek*, i. 114, cf. 108 (for " finger," cf. Ex. viii. 19[15]) ; Gressmann, *Altorient. Texte z. A.T.*[2] i. 371 ; Jirku, *Altorient. Kommentar zum Alt. Test.* 118.

[3] See F. B. Jevons, *Introd. to Hist. of Rel.* 134 *sq.*; Moore, *E.Bi.* col. 30 n. 2 Newberry (*Nature*, cxii. 942) compares the *neter* pole, and Sidney Smith (*Journ. of Eg. Arch.* viii. 41) the *sed* pillar of Egypt.

36

At all events, the question remains whether the name of the goddess or that of the tree-trunk as her symbol or as her embodiment is the older. For the treatment of sacred objects (*e.g.* royal regalia) as in themselves sacred, that is, virtually as effective as the gods themselves, there are many parallels ancient and modern.[1] Here are to be named the *Ekurrate* deities (*lit.* temples) in Assyrian (Delitzsch, *Handwörterbuch*), and in Mandæan magical texts, where male Ekurs (עכוריא) are mentioned with female Ishtars (Lidzb. *Ephem.* i. 100 *sq.*).[2] Bait-il (Bethel) is also the name of a god. The Nabatæan מותבה (*CIS.* ii. 198) is named with Dusares as (*a*) his seat or abode (cf. *ZDMG.* xxix. 107 *sq.* l. 135) or (*b*) " his wife " (in a secondary sense; Winckler, *Altor. Forsch.* ii. 62, 321). With this compare the Xααβου (above, p. 56 n.), Zeus Μάδβαχος, the cult of the βωμὸς μέγας (see Meyer, *Israel.* 295, and A. B. Cook, *Zeus,* i. 519 *sqq.*), and the widespread cult of the empty throne.[3] On the Jewish usage of the Shechinah (the " abode " of God) for the Deity Himself, see J. Abelson, *The Immanence of God in Rabbinical Literature,* 79.[4]

P. 191.—On the story of Osiris, see, in the first instance, Frazer, *GB.* vi. 9 *sq.*, 108 *sqq.*, and Baudissin's discussion in *Adonis und Esmun,* 174 *sqq.*, 185 *sqq.* On Adonis, see Baudissin, *ib.*, and Frazer, *GB.* v. and vi. *passim.*

P. 193.—On the Ambrosian rocks at Tyre, see Gressmann, *Mose,* 26 ; A. B. Cook, *Zeus,* iii. ; and S. A. Cook, *Schweich Lectures.* On the Arab belief that ghosts and the like appear in or accompanied with flames, see Goldziher, *Abhand.* i. 205 *sqq.* Stories of trees with mysterious lights or in flames are current in Palestine, *Qy. St. of the PEF.*, 1872, p. 179 ; 1893, p. 203 ; Curtiss, 93 ; Gressmann, *Mose,* 28 n. ; the practice of hanging lamps on trees may account for some of the beliefs. In Yemen in the nineteenth century a tree formed by two or three growing into one was regarded as sacred, sacrifices were offered to it, and a voice was heard speaking from its branches (A. S. Tritton,

---

[1] Frazer, *GB.* i. 362 *sqq.*, iv. 202. Seligman (British Association, Manchester, 1915) reported that in the Sudan, where the great Queen Soba is worshipped as an ancestress, a stone or " throne " is the chair of the kingdom, and rocks associated with her are called after her name ; the prayers made to " grandmother Soba " testify to a confusion between the goddess and the particular stone invoked.

[2] Moore (*E.Bi.*, 332) compares the Phœn. names נרהכל, ברהכל, עבד, client or servant of the temple (*i.e.* the god) ; cf. above, p. 531.

[3] Add the divine צלם or " image " (see p. 587) and the Mandæan demon פתברא or " idol." See Gressmann, *Zeit. f. d. Neutest. Wissenschaft,* xx. (1921) 224 *sq.* ; and S. A. Cook, *Schweich Lectures* (on the god Bethel).

[4] At more advanced stages, instead of the cult-object, the attribute, emanation, name, etc., become separate entities ; see Farnell, *Evol. of Rel.* 74, on the veneration of the Fravashi or Soul of Ahura and the Θεοῦ Πρόνοια.

Calcutta Oriental Conference, 1922 [published 1923], 580). On trees that speak, sing, or prophesy, see also M. R. James, *Testament of Abraham* (1892), 59 *sqq.* (the cypress is specially sacred); Marmorstein, *Arch. f. Rel.* xvii. 132. As to what is said of Mamre the old reports differ : Syncellus speaks of the terebinth of Shechem (see Gressmann, *Mose*, loc. cit.; Bacher, *ZATW*. xxix. 148 *sqq.* ; Krauss, *ib.* 296 *sqq.*; and Frazer, *FOT*. iii. 57 *sqq.*).

P. 194. IMMANENCE AND TRANSCENDENCE.—The not uncommon view that the Jewish or the Semitic idea of deity was solely transcendent has often been denied.[1] Characteristic differences between Semitic and Greek religion have been emphasized, *e.g.* by Farnell (*Higher Aspects of the Greek Religion*, 132 *sq.*). But although in the former there is what has been styled a slave-temper, the latter has not the warmth and confidence which distinguish Semitic religion. Semitic religion has extraordinary extremes (*CAH*. i.[2] 197 *sqq.*). But the contrast between the exclusiveness of the Semitic gods and the universality of the Indo-European (Meyer, *Gesch. Alt.* i. §§ 557, 582) must not obscure the debt to the Semites for the development of the conception of the intimate relationship between the gods and the members of the group (social, religious, or ecclesiastical). The Semites' conviction of divine supremacy never prevented them from adopting the attitudes they would assume to a powerful ruler to whose good nature— and sense of duty and prestige—they could appeal (cf. Num. xiv. 14 *sqq.*, Josh. vii. 9). In Ezekiel, Divine Transcendence is most prominent ; but it is only one aspect of the Divine Nature (W. H. Bennett, *Rel. of the Post-Exilic Prophets* [1907], 30 *sq.*). What was said of a wrathful Yahweh did not exclude the chastening love of a Father. And, to take another case, the insistent demand of Ḥoni (Onias) for rain was denounced as unreasonable and sinful, but God accepted his prayer and treated him—in the words of Simeon ben Shetaḥ—" as a son that acts as a sinner to his father, but he grants his request." [2] See also p. 588.

In both Jewish and Mohammedan prayer there is an element of importunity if not of compulsion ;[3] and as a general rule it is frequently difficult to draw the line between propitiation and persuasion and coercion (Crawley, *Tree of Life*, 188). In fact, besides the way in

[1] See, *e.g.*, G. F. Moore, *History of Religions*, ii. 73 ; C .G. Montefiore, *Hibbert Lectures* (ed. of 1897), 424 *sqq.* (for post-exilic Judaism) ; J. Abelson, *The Immanence of God in Rabbinical Literature* (1912) ; and I. Abrahams, *Studies in Pharisaism and the Gospels* (2nd Ser. 1924), 149 *sq.*

[2] Büchler, *Types of Jewish Palestinian Piety* (1922), 252 *sqq.*, cf. 246 *sq.*

[3] See Goldziher, *Nöldeke-Festschrift*, 314, who cites the Talm. Bab. Sanhed. 105*a*: " boldness (חוצפא) avails even against Heaven."

which the Egyptians would threaten their sacred animals (Plut. *Is.* 73), gods and saints are often treated badly in order to force them to remove drought or other peril. They will be taunted (cf. 1 Kings xviii. 27) ; and steps may be taken to irritate a modern *weli*, in order to arouse him to manifest his power.[1] Such evidence indicates that problems of Immanence and Transcendence involve the varying degree of divinity attributed to the gods and spirits. For often these are little more than supermen, doing " easily " what is difficult for men—the Homeric ῥεῖα (Nilsson, 157) ; while, on the other hand, there are outstanding individuals, supermen, scarcely if at all inferior to the gods, and adequate embodiments of ideas of divinity.

The ideas of Immanence and of Transcendence are complementary. When gods are felt to be remote and no longer in touch with men, they lose their authority. Typically, the sacred beings must not be approached save by the sacred, they must be treated with respect, and intermediaries may be necessary. Such gods will become the gods of a special class or caste ; and the nature of the cult, or the myths, or the doctrines, will sever them from the community and make them accessible only to the few. Internal social changes, the movement of thought, or disasters which seem to prove the helplessness of the gods, combine to make them more or less negligible (cf. Zeph. i. 12). When more accessible and more intelligible beings arise, they are nearer at hand, and they, better than the " remote " gods, understand human needs. On the other hand, when gods are felt to be near at hand, and in close touch with men, they may lose their distinctive sanctity and cease to be the gods they once were. They may be easily manageable by prayers and charms, or too well known to be feared ; the key of the religious mechanism lies wholly in human hands. The gods then become so completely one with their visible abodes, so entirely comprehensible, that they virtually cease to exist, and need no distinctive term : they are lost in their embodiment.

The history of religion is, broadly speaking, that of efforts to escape from the two extremes : the god who is so remote, so unknown or unknowable as to be negligible, and the god so completely known as to be unnecessary. There are some highly instructive vicissitudes. Contrast, *e.g.*, the popular idea of a Yahweh who could be put to the test with the severe condemnation of such familiarity and lack of faith (see *CAH*. iii. 485). Constantly the god has come to be confused with his symbol or vehicle (p. 562), the metaphor has been taken literally, and the religious system treated as final. It is thus possible to distinguish the more primary and the more secondary developments, and to

---

[1] *JPOS*. vi. 5 (*e.g.* filth is put on the tomb) ; cf. *GB*. i. 300 *sq.*, 307 *sq.*

contrast the more creative movements with those tendencies along the extremes, either of Immanence or of Transcendence, which would lead nowhere. Accordingly, the combination of the two conceptions is seen to be of primary significance, and it may fairly be said to correspond to the combination of Mana and Taboo among rudimentary peoples, where man feels that he can utilize a power, but must be heedful (see p. 551 n. 3).[1] In Central Australian totemism the ceremonies for the control or multiplication of the totem species (commonly an edible animal or plant) are conducted as though those processes, which among less rudimentary peoples are usually associated directly or indirectly with the gods, lay within the power of the officiants. Yet at the same time they are in the " sacred " state psychologically akin to that which elsewhere accompanies the consciousness of, and fellowship with, a sacred and transcendent power. Again, special individuals (priests, priestly kings, rain-makers, etc.) constantly act, for the time being at least, as the embodiments or vehicles or representatives of a sacred power ; but although the divine and human thus converge, and the divine power is, in a sense, immanent in the man, the difference between the sacred man and the sacred power is not necessarily obliterated (p. 545). The group-system, uniting gods and their worshippers, did not necessarily involve the lowering of the god-idea, although, as W. R. S. points out, there was a tendency in this direction, and, as far as Israel was concerned, it was corrected by the prophets (p. 74). Here it must be recognized that W. R. S. makes a very important point. In the group-system the insistence upon the sacredness of the gods tended to prevent them from being wholly immanent ; none the less, the teaching of the prophets shows that even a national religious system could be a dangerously " closed " one because of the inadequate conception of Yahweh and of his " righteousness." The danger lay in the imperfect ideas of the most vital concepts—the " transcendental " concepts, in fact. No actual living system of beliefs and practices is really a closed one; outside it is that which makes for the further development of conceptions of God, Man, and the Universe. Cf. pp. 508, 525.

Whether such terms as Immanence and Transcendence should be used in reference to the simpler and older religions may seem doubtful in view of the absence among them of explicit conceptions of Nature. It was, of course, possible to distinguish between what was felt to be normal, natural, or intelligible, and the opposite. But primitive

---

[1] Cf. Marett, *Psychology and Folklore*, 166 : " It is the common experience of man that he can draw on a power that makes for, and in its most typical forms wills righteousness, the sole condition being that a certain fear, a certain shyness and humility accompany the effort so to do."

man, it may be said, would co-operate with the supernatural world, or would claim to do what elsewhere are the recognized functions of " gods," or are subsequently regarded as " natural " processes. He located the supernatural power where he happened to experience it, and the difficulty for us is to understand, not so much the varying conceptions of the supernatural, but the varying and contradictory interrelations between the supernatural and " natural." In the case of the Semites, pantheism was avoided because material things were symbols rather than realities (W. R. S., *Lectures*, 425). The god was behind or over " nature," his breath animated life ; and when a divine power was felt to be " immanent " in sacred hills, waters, etc. (above, pp. 173, 190, 194), this was not derived from a specific belief in a Supreme God which had been watered down and degraded; the explanation lies rather in the subjectivity of the Semite, as W. R. S. had already pointed out in a brilliant essay on the " Poetry of the O.T." (*Lectures*, 400 *sqq.*).

P. 197 n. ADONIS RODS.—See Frazer, *GB.* v. 236 *sqq.* Baudissin (87 *sq.*) questions their use as omens. Rods are also used in divination (above, p. 196 n. ; see, on the subject, Halliday, *Greek Divination*, 226 *sq.*), or for working witchcraft; cf. the story of Circe, etc., also the pointing-stick of the wonder-worker in Australia and the Torres Straits.

P. 198. SEMITIC CHTHONIC DEITIES.—Chthonic cults are associated partly with earth-dwelling powers and partly, as Baudissin argues (31, 53), with the youthful god who rises and returns to the underworld. A chthonic power is not necessarily limited to terrestrial attributes, and in Greece, thund r, if not also lightning, could be chthonian (A. B. Cook, *Zeus*, ii. 805 n. 6). Besides cults connected with chasms and with tombs (viz. libations poured on the ground, see p. 580), the Rephaim–" shades," were perhaps " healers " (cf. Lagrange, 318 *sq.*), though not all the dead were so regarded (Baud. 343). W. R. S. (in Driver, *Deuteronomy*, 40) agrees with Schwally (*Das Leben nach dem Tode*, 64 *sq.*) that there is some connexion between the Rephaim–" shades " or ghosts and extinct giants (such as were supposed to have haunted the district of Antioch) ; the Emim are to be connected with the Hebrew '*ēmah*, " terror " ; and the Zamzummim are " whisperers, murmurers." W. R. S. compares the Arabic '*azīf*, the eerie sound of the *jinn* (*Heid.* 150). Among special chthonic deities are Nergal, Molek (Milk), and Kronos: on their interrelations, see Lagrange, 104 *sqq.* ; but note A. B. Cook, *Zeus*, ii. 1107 *sqq.* Milkat is named on a Carthaginian *tabella devotionis* dedicated to the " Great Ones Ḥawwat, Allat, Milkat ..." (?)[1] To Allat

---

[1] . . . רבת חות אלת מלכת שיסכהא‎. See Clermont-Ganneau, *Recueil*, iii. 304, v. 87; Cooke, No. 50 ; Lidzbarski, *Ephem.* i. 26 *sqq.*

(on whom see p. 56) corresponds the Babylonian Ereshkigal, mistress of the underworld and wife of Nergal. The name of Ḥawwat is presumably to be compared with " Eve " and " serpent " ; the place of the serpent in chthonic cults needs no illustration.[1] With the three-fold invocation Clermont-Ganneau (*Rec.* iv. 90) compares the three-fold Hecate and her serpent attributes.

P. 198 n. 2. THE *ZAKKŪRĒ*.—In the passage cited, a young woman shortly about to give birth to a child is hung up and the babe cut out ; by means of magic the *zakkūrē* ascend from the middle of the earth, and agree to recognize their co-religionist, the Emperor Julian, as supreme king. More magic is performed by means of the child, which is restored to the body of its mother, who is laid upon the altar. Julian then makes his first ceremonial offering to the ruler of the world and to the powers above and below, and forthwith Satan enters into him as into a temple. For classical parallels, see Halliday, *Greek Divination*, 243 n. 1.

P. 199. CAVES, CHASMS, AND THE FLOOD.—In Palestine caves are sometimes found outside the tombs of saints ; but sometimes they are found or supposed to exist within the shrine, and it is believed that the saint's body lies concealed there. Among the famous caves are those of the Patriarchs at Machpelah, Elijah at Carmel and Horeb, Astarte at Kasimīyeh (Clermont-Ganneau, *Rec.* v. 333), and of Ablūn (Apollo) and el-Maḳdūra at Sidon, the former containing figures of Apollo, the latter, *inter alia,* a hideous female figure (Bädeker, *s.v.*). At Gezer there was current one of the not unfamiliar local traditions that the. Deluge rose in a *tannūr* or baking-oven (Clermont-Ganneau, *Archæo-logical Researches*, ii. 235, 237, 456, 480, 490) ; and it is tempting to associate with the story the great tunnel which was discovered there, and which in turn recalls the watercourse or tunnel (*ṣinnōr*) of Jeru-salem (2 Sam. v. 8).[2] (On Lucian [references in n. 2], see for discus-sions and parallels, Torge, *Seelen und Unsterblichkeitshoffnungen*, 134 [Leipzig, 1909].)

P. 200. MEGARON.—The word may be of independent (Cretan ? Ægean ?) origin (cf. λέσχη, p. 587 below). On the distinction in Greek between the underground cavern and the (Homeric) large hall, see

---

[1] On Eve as the mother-serpent, see Gressmann, *Harnack-Festschrift*, 37 *sq.* (contrast W. R. S., *Kinship*, 208, Eve as the great eponyma). Note the serpent deity of Dēr who was " lady of life " (*ib.*), and Nin-Azu the deity of healing and of vegetation and lord of the underworld (Morgenstern, 51). On a connexion between creeping animals and the spirits of the dead, see H. P. Smith, *Journ. of Bibl. Lit.* xxx. 55 *sqq.* ; *Amer. Journ. of Theol.* 1909, pp. 224 *sqq.*

[2] Vincent, *Qy. St. of the PEF.*, 1908, pp. 218 *sqq.* See R. A. S. Macalister, *Qy. St.* 1903, p. 218 (cf. 241) ; *Excavation of Gezer*, i. 264.

Frazer, *Pausanias*, iii. 15; Burney, *Judges*, xviii and xix n. The earliest inhabitants of Crete lived in caves, which continued to be used as centres of cult; and at Tiryns the *megaron* of the palace was converted into a temple to Hera (Nilsson, *Gr. Rel.* 12, 23 *sqq.*). With the difference of meaning cf. the צְרִיחַ of the temple of El-Berith at Shechem (Judg. ix. 46, 49), used of an underground cavern or chamber in 1 Sam. xiii. 6, and in Nabatæan inscriptions. Arabic distinguishes between صَر, tower or citadel, and ضَرِيح, grave, etc. See further, G. F. Moore on Judges, and Driver on Samuel. At Nablus (Shechem) the Arabic *ḍariḥ* is used of the holy place built over the remains of sundry prophets, sons of Jacob (Canaan, *JPOS.* iv. 24).

P. 200 *sqq.* SACRED STONES.[1]—Sacred stones include (1) those that have been deliberately and artificially made holy (see below, p. 572), and (2) those that are already so, perhaps because they arouse awe (a sense of the "numinous," see p. 554), or because of some tradition which professes to explain their sanctity (see p. 206). Sacred stones need not be portraits, or representations of any part of the body (on phallic symbols, see p. 687 *sq.*); there is not necessarily any self-evident connexion between them and what they stand for (p. 210). Nor need they have any intrinsic worth, like precious stones. It is remarkable that the cult of sacred stones is found on high levels,[2] and that among lower races the Central Australian *churinga* is of no little "spiritual value" because of the meaning it has for the native.[3] Fetishism is not necessarily "very savage and contemptible" (p. 209; cf. Lagrange, 215). It is easy to understand why certain stones or stone objects have been endowed with sacred power, *e.g.* aerolites and flints; and the black bituminous stones around Nebī Musā, before they are burnt on the fire, must first be addressed: "Permission, O son of Imrām, whose fire comes from his stones" (Canaan, *JPOS.* v. 166).[4] Stones as fertility charms will owe their efficacy, as the "Merchant of Harran" recognized, to the faith of the believer (see p. 514 n. 2); and at the present day women who desire children will resort to stones famed for their power, *e.g.* the Ḥajar el-Ḥāblah near Meirum,[5] or they

---

[1] See Wellhausen, 101 *sqq.*; Lagrange, 197 *sqq.*; Moore, *E.Bi.* "Massebah."

[2] Cf. Moore, *E.Bi.* 2979, § 2 and n. 9; Conybeare, *Oxford Congress of Rel.* ii. 177 *sqq.*; Frazer, *FOT.* ii. 73; and the oft-quoted modern example in A. C. Lyall's *Asiatic Studies* ("Religion of an Indian Province").

[3] Marett, *Ency. Brit.* xxiii. 66a, citing Spencer and Gillen, *Native Tribes of Central Australia*, 135, 165, *Northern Tribes*, 266.

[4] Prehistoric tools are sometimes treated as sacred on account of their obvious antiquity.

[5] Vincent, *Canaan*, 415 n. Cf. Bädeker, *Palest.* 356; Frazer, *FOT.* ii. 75.

will visit an old Egyptian monument and scrape off a little of the sand-stone, which they drink with water (*The Times*, 2nd October 1926).

As an object of cult the stone serves as a place where one can meet the god. When draped, carried about, hung with garments, it is virtually an idol (Wellh. 101 *sq.*). But instead of representing the god, a stone can be erected on behalf of a worshipper, and in this case it virtually represents *him* in the presence of the god. Among the Nabatæans the מישגדא seems to be, not so much the place of worship (cf. *mesjid*, "mosque") as the vehicle: it is a stela or column dedicated to a deity; but it may be shaped like an altar and may suggest an altar-table (Cooke, 238). When stones are set up by the childless, or as memorials of the worshipper, the desire to perpetuate the "name" suggests that it is the durability and permanence of the object which is the secret of the practice. It is on this account that the stone serves to commemorate; though, with W. R. S., it is questionable whether this is the true origin of stone-cults.

In Josh. xxii. the original narrative must have been changed (" an altar is a strange erection if it is only to be used as a monument"); and it is more probable that a Transjordanic altar was preserved by devoting it to a more innocent purpose, and through this compromise the narrative succeeds in emphasizing the unity of worship.[1] In Gen. xxviii. 12–22 (Jacob at Bethel) Lagrange (205 and n. 2) well compares the Assyrian practice of anointing foundation tablets. But why were such memorial tablets anointed? They bore the names of the founders; they must be anointed and sacrifices offered to them—to explain the ceremony as a mere act of commemoration seems inadequate (see p. 582 *sq.*) Moreover, the circumstances in Gen. *l.c.* go to show that Jacob's pillar was more than commemorative; the stone which was found to be sacred and was set up is a Massebah.[2] In Gen. xxxi. 44, the stone which commemorates the covenant between Jacob and Laban is regarded by Lagrange (206) as analogous to the Babylonian *kudurrus* or boundary stones. These stones bore the symbols of certain gods, who were not necessarily identical with those mentioned in the accompanying inscription; but in any event, divine powers, through the presence of these stones, were expected to act as a protection against evil-doers. The covenant feast (*v.* 46) recalls Gen. xxvi. 30; and the witness is God (*v.* 50 E), or the cairn itself (*v.* 48 J). The latter view underlies the explanation of the name

---

[1] Kennett, *Journal of Theol. Studies*, 1905, p. 175; cf. G. A. Cooke, *Joshua*, 210.

[2] See further Skinner, *Gen.* 377 *sqq.* Meyer (*Israel.* 283 *sqq.*) argues that the Bethel stone was the "rock of Israel," and the "steer of Jacob" (Gen. xlix. 24); cf. Jer. ii. 27, Is. li. 1. W. R. S. is guarded (p. 210 n.), presumably because he distinguishes "Israelite" from "Canaanite" religion.

Gal'ēd (Gilead), and finds a parallel in Josh. xxiv. 27 (E), where the stone at Shechem is a witness. Cairns are still built as witnesses of vows (Curtiss, 79 *sq.*), and stones convey ideas of stability where oaths and covenants are concerned (Frazer, *FOT*. ii. 403 *sqq.*). Stones are piled up as a " witness " or " confirmation " by the modern pilgrim when he prays, and on the Day of Judgment such stones will be among the testimonies to his piety (*JPOS*. iv. 75 *sq.*).

But even " commemorative " monuments readily have a sacred meaning, and they were condemned by the Puritan Wahhabites.[1] The *maṣṣebah* on the border of Egypt (Is. xix. 19) was, as Gray conjectured, perhaps an inscribed obelisk celebrating Yahweh's deeds. Boundaries were sacred, and Senusret (Sesostris) I. set up his statue at the boundary of Egypt that the people " might prosper because of it " (Breasted, i. § 660 ; cf. *CAH*. ii. 344). The treaty between Eannatum and the king of Lagash was commemorated by the " Stela of the Vultures " which was set up to mark the boundary ; it refers to the frontier shrines (*i.e.* presumably to the gods who were invoked to preserve the treaty), and the two kings took a solemn oath to respect the frontier, probably at the altars of the gods invoked.[2]

Sacred stones, rocks, and mountains seem to have been more prominent in the old Israelite religion than is commonly recognized (Meyer, *Israel.* 473) ; and with Lagrange (192 *sq.*) and Baudissin (*ZDMG*. 1903, p. 829) it is tempting to associate the Babylonian *zikkurat* towers and the cult of conical stones with the sanctity of mountains. Elagabalus of Emesa, then, may be the " deified mountain " (cf. Lagrange, 82 n.) ; and although Nöldeke has objected (see *ZDMG*. 1903, p. 817) that " Gebāl " is too specifically an Arabic word, he himself attributes to the Arab-speaking Nabatæans the name of Gebāl which was given to Mt. Seir (*E.Bi.* 1654), and in view of the constant movement of Arab tribes in Transjordania and the Arab connexions of the dynasty of Emesa the appearance of an El(a)-gabal is not difficult to explain. Further, since Mt. Seir is otherwise called " field of Edom," where " field " (*sādeh*), as in several other places in the O.T., should mean " mountain," like the Bab. *shadu* (Burney, *Judges*, 111 *sq.*), it would appear that Gebāl as a name for Edom corresponds to the earlier *sādeh*.[3]

In general, the various sorts of sacred stones, as also the meanings attached to them, easily shade off into one another (cf. Lagrange, 201,

---

[1] Hogarth, *Penetration of Arabia*, 73 ; G. B. Gray on Isa. xix. 19 (p. 338).

[2] L. W. King, *Sumer and Akkad*, 127 *sqq.* ; cf. *CAH*. i.[2] 380.

[3] Delitzsch's suggestion that the admittedly obscure title El Shaddai goes back to a " god-mountain " should perhaps be reconsidered. " Great mountain " (*shadū rabū*) is a title of Bel and Asshur ; *KAT*. 355, 358.

203). The stone can be an altar (cf. Wellhausen, 141) and at the same time a god, as in the stone at Duma (above, p. 205) and in *Zeus bōmos* (Cook, *Zeus*, i. 520 *sq.*). Gods are readily identified with their embodiments, vehicles, or symbols (p. 562), and even the merely " commemorative " stone can have a deep religious value. In such circumstances, what is absolutely primary and what secondary in the history of sacred stones can hardly be determined by reliance upon the *dates* of our evidence (against Lagrange, 207 *sq.*), especially when the evidence comes in turn from early Babylonia, the O.T., Herodotus, and Arab heathenism. Nor can one rely upon any preliminary distinction between the cults of savages and of civilized peoples (*id.* 215 *sq.*). The inanimate stone differs from the plant and more especially from the animal in that it does not in itself suggest, shape, or direct natural ideas of sacred life in the way that these can. It is on this account the more apt to be made the convenient centre of ideas from the vaguest to the most profound, and at different stages of culture. True, the stone has a certain permanence, the mountain points to the sky, or the environment of the sacred object awakens a sense of the sublime ; but by its very nature it stands outside the course of religious development and the growth of ideas of personality, human and divine. That sacred stones have bulked so largely in religion makes it all the more necessary to distinguish between a classification of the data of religion and the criteria by which the development of religion may be estimated.

P. 205. RITES OF TOUCHING, STROKING, ETC.—Such rites, for the purpose of acquiring or of transferring sanctity, have naturally a certain psychological significance, whether or no they include the special application of blood, oil, wine, fat, or anything supposed to contain some inherent efficacy. On taboos against touching sacred persons or things, see Frazer, *GB.* iii. 131 *sqq.* ; on charming by means of stroking, see E. Riess, *Amer. Journ. of Philol.*, 1925, pp. 226 *sqq.*, and for a typical Mohammedan custom, above, p. 461. On touching or pressing against the black stone at Mecca, see Wellhausen, 109, Gaudefroy-Demombynes, 209.[1] For kissing (1 Kings xix. 18 ; Hos. xiii. 2), cf. the kissing of the threshold and door-posts of churches in Abyssinia (Barton, *Sem. Origins*, 137). In an alignment of stones unearthed at Gezer, in what was evidently a sacred area, was one with small polished spots such as are still to be observed on the stones visited and kissed by pilgrims (R. A. S. Macalister, *Gezer*, ii. 388). On bodily contact with a teacher in order to acquire some of his

---

[1] The orthodox Palestinian Jew at the wall of Jerusalem presses against what is traditionally regarded as part of Solomon's temple (Jastrow, *Rel. Beliefs*, 266 n. 3).

knowledge, see the Rabbinical and other data by Eiseler, *Arch. f. Rel.*, 1914, p. 666 ; Kreglinger, 87 *sq.* In Syria men will touch a saint's tomb with their hand, and then wipe it over their face (A. S. Tritton, private communication), or they will rub the oil of the lamps over their hands and face (Canaan, *JPOS.* v. 177 *sq.*). Further, when a sacrifice is offered, he for whom it is made must come into contact with it, *e.g.* he must be marked with the blood of the victim. Or a man will smear a shrine in order to assure the saint that the sacrifice is made on his behalf (*JPOS.* vi. 48). The necessity of some physical or material accessory finds a curious illustration when the church of St. George, near Beit Jala, was connected by a wire with the hospital where the mental patients were kept, in order that the saint's healing power might be transmitted to the unfortunate inmates (v. 202).

P. 206. CONSECRATION, DIVINIZATION.—As distinct from inanimate or animate things already (naturally) sacred are those which are ceremonially made so ; and W. R. S. argues that the stage where an object already sacred is sacrificed to a god is prior to that where it is selected and sanctified for the purpose (p. 390). This view is rejected by Hubert and Mauss who, in their important monograph on sacrifice (cf. also Toy, § 1049), are more concerned with demonstrating the stage of " divinization" which W. R. S. considers secondary. For examples of divinization, see W. Crooke, " The Binding of the God," *Folk-lore,* viii. 325–355 (on the practices whereby gods are caused to enter into images); Hartland, *Ritual and Belief,* 55 (supernatural powers transferred by means of feathers); Cumont, *Oriental Religions in Roman Paganism,* ch. iv. n. 61.

In both Egypt and Babylonia there were rites whereby the images became inhabited by their respective gods.[1] In the daily ritual of the Egyptian temple the priest presented to the image of the deity the image of Maʿat, goddess of truth, right, etc., whereby it became, so to say, " truly and rightly " a god, and no longer a mere image (cf. *CAH.* i.[2] 346).[2] Such practices recall the story that Brahma taught a king how to restore a dead boy by painting a portrait, and then endowing it with life. Mohammedan thought is more explicit when the prohibition of making images is justified on the ground

---

[1] Rameses II. speaks of having performed such a rite (Breasted, *Anc. Rec.* iii. p. 179 note *c*).

[2] On the ceremony of " opening the mouth," see Blackman, *Journ. of Eg. Arch.* x. 47 *sqq.* (Bab.), 53 *sqq.* (Egypt) ; Zimmern, in the *Nöldeke-Festschrift,* 959 *sqq.* ; Sidney Smith, *Journ. of Royal Asiatic Soc.,* 1925, pp. 37 *sqq.* ; H. Bonnet, *Angelos,* 1925, pp. 103 *sqq.* On a ceremonial opening of the mouth as a sign that a man initiated into a sacred office has become fully ordained, see the West African example in Frazer, *GB.* v. 68.

that it is a sacrilegious assumption of the creative function of Allah, who alone possesses the life-giving breath.[1] Creation consists in the manufacture of the mould and the gift of life by blowing breath into the nostrils (cf. p. 555) ; and the Arab conviction reads as the echo of a monotheistic condemnation, which orthodox Jews would have shared, of the older practice of making gods.

In rites of consecration blood was especially used as a vehicle of life, if not as the life itself. Blood makes a stone holy ; it brings divine life into it (p. 436 above). An Abraxas papyrus speaks of the strangling of birds before an idol of Eros in order to endow it with life (*Class. Review*, 1896, p. 409). Primitive man feels the need of some instrument or vehicle as an embodiment of a " spirit," and instead of an image a corpse can serve (Halliday, *Greek Divination*, 243 *sq.*). A sacred or powerful man may be put to death in order that his spiritual presence shall benefit a district (cf. Hartland, *Folk-lore*, xxi. 176 *sq.*) ; and in the days of the Greek emigrations, " it became the established custom for the leader of a new pioneering enterprise to be buried in the market-place of the colony and honoured after death as its protecting hero " (Nilsson, 236). Between the utilization, the reinvigoration, and the construction of an abode for a powerful spirit it is not easy to draw the line, and W. R. S. and MM. Hubert and Mauss are really looking at different parts of the process : the latter made a most important contribution to certain types and uses of sacrifice, but the former goes to the more fundamental problem, *why* there is a desire to establish—or re-establish—communication with the " sacred " realm.

P. 210 n. 1.—The letters to the *Scotsman* are reprinted in *Lectures and Essays* (ed. J. S. Black and G. W. Chrystal), see *ib.* p. 544, and cf. p. 554.

P. 211 n. 1.—The verse cited by Wellhausen[1], 99, reads : " At a time when female children were not suffered to live, and when the people used to stand motionless by the sacred stones, round the *mudawwar*." The *mudawwar* is said to mean " an image which they used to circumambulate." The verse appears in the *Nacā'iḍ*, p. 950 l. 3 (ed. Bevan, Leiden, 1905).—A. A. B.

Pp. 214, 216, and 237 n.—On the terms " sacrifice " and " offering " (Luther, *schlacht-* and *speise-opfer*), etc., see Moore, *E.Bi.* " Sacrifice," § 11 ; Driver, *Hastings' Dict. Bible*, s.v. " Offer(ing), Oblation " ; G. Buchanan Gray, *Sacrifice in the O.T.*, 4 *sqq.* On the derivation of *minḥah* (מנח " give," or נחה a ritual S. Arab. term), see Lagrange,

---

[1] Sir T. W. Arnold, *Survivals of Sasanian and Manichaean Art in Persian Painting*, 4 (Oxford, 1924) ; Wensinck, " The Second Commandment," *Mededeelingen* of the Amsterdam University, lvii, A No. 6 (1925).

256 n., 269 n.; Hartmann, *Islam. Orient*, 208 n. 1; Gray, 14 *sqq.*; Hommel, *Ethnol. u. Geog. d. Alt. Orients*, 144, 162; and Dussaud, *Les Origines Cananéennes du Sacrifice Israélite*, 89 *sqq.*

P. 215 n.—Wellhausen's article "Pentateuch," famous in the annals of O.T. criticism, was reprinted in *E.Bi.* "Hexateuch" (with additions by Cheyne on later developments). Of subsequent tendencies (*a*) some (Kennett in *Journ. of Theol. Stud.*, 1905 *sq.*, Hölscher, etc.) place Deuteronomy *in its present form* after the seventh century B.C. (*b*) Others (Kosters, Torrey, etc.) reconstruct the history both of the Return from Exile (holding that there was no considerable return in the time of Zerubbabel) and of the work of Nehemiah and Ezra (in that order, the value of the account of Ezra being also open to doubt). Further (*c*), more attention is paid to the early elements in the law and ritual, especially in view of the antiquity of culture in Palestine centuries before the age of Moses. This latter fact, however, does not affect the problem of the approximate dates when the constituent sources of the Hexateuch and the Historical Books reached their present form, and for what purposes they were written down and combined. Since W. R. S. lays emphasis upon the archaic or primitive features of the priestly ritual, it is to be observed that, whereas on the "literary-critical" theory these appear in documents which are admittedly quite late (post-exilic), on the "conservative" or "traditional" view they are in documents of many centuries earlier, and the spiritual and ethical reforming movements of the great prophets did not prevent their persistence, survival, or re-emergence, and their prominence in post-exilic Judaism. Archaic and even crude features recur in Syria and Palestine in much later times, *e.g.* at the revival of Orientalism before and at the beginning of the Christian era; cf. the cults associated with Elagabalus and Emesa, and see also Cumont, *Oriental Religions in Roman Paganism* (Chicago, 1911). Conversely, relatively high ideas can be traced, not only among the neighbours of the Israelites outside Palestine, but also in Palestine before the age of the Israelite invasion and among the Canaanites amid whom the Israelites settled.

P. 218. For the camel as food, Stübe refers to Imrulcais, *Moall. vv.* 10–12. A particularly minute description of the slaughter of a camel for food is to be found in a poem of 'Amr ibn al-Ahtam (Mufaḍḍalīyāt, ed. Thorbecke, Poem xii. verses 12 *sq.*, Poem xxiii. in Lyall's edition).—A. A. B.

P. 220. WINE AND ECSTASY.—Certain abnormal states have readily been regarded as supernormal, and all that took a man out of himself was often supposed to take him into a supersensuous or sacred realm,

There have been many ways of producing the state : music, intona-
tion, and also awe-inspiring noises, notably the bull-roarer ; [1] dancing
and dreamy rhythmic movement (cf. below, p. 671 *sq.*) ; tobacco and the
inhalation of smoke ; eating of leaves (hashish, ivy, etc.) ; drinking
of blood, of wine and other intoxicating liquors. The sacred drink,
" sacred " because it is interpreted as bringing one under the influence
of or into the sphere of the supersensuous, will owe its discovery to
a god (Osiris, Dionysus).[2] The Indian *soma* was itself deified ; it
conferred immortality upon gods and men, and its appellation *amrita,*
" immortal," is the *ambrosia* of the Greek gods. Among other famous
drinks in religion are the *kava* ceremonial of the South Seas (*Folk-lore,*
xxxiii. 60) and the Mexican *peyote* (see Radin, *Crashing Thunder,*
169 *sqq.*). In Babylonia wine is ideographically the " food (or staff)
of life " (*KAT.* 526).

The opposition to wine in Gen. ix. 18 *sqq.* is to be read in the light
of Lamech's oracle on the birth of Noah (v. 29), where wine is a relief
from the curse of labour ; it " expresses the healthy recoil of primitive
Semitic morality from the licentious habits engendered by a civilization of which a salient feature was the use and abuse of wine "
(Skinner, *Genesis,* 185 *sqq.*, cf. 133 *sq.*). For restrictions on the use
of wine in religion, see, besides pp. 220 n. 5 and 485 above, Gray,
Numbers, 62 *sq.*, and Jastrow, *Journ. of Amer. Or. Soc.* xxxiii. 180 *sqq.*
The Egyptians abstained from wine because, on one view, it was the
blood, not of the gods, but of the enemies of the gods. Among the
Aztecs the native *pulque* was denounced because of the evils done
by men under its influence ; though, as they were supposed to be
possessed and inspired by the wine-god, such men were not to be
punished (Frazer, *GB.* iii. 249 *sq.*).[3] Analogous is the belief that
mentally abnormal men are—within certain limits—sacred (Canaan,
JPOS. vi. 10). Among the teetotal gods is the Nabatæan Shē'alḵūm
(שיעאלקום ; in Safa inscriptions שׁעהקם), *i.e.* the " protector of the
people," who is described as the " good and bountiful god who does
not drink wine " (טבא ושברא די לא שתא חמר). Interpreting this as
a protest against the cult of Dusares-Dionysus, Clermont-Ganneau
recalls the legendary " anti-Bacchic " god or king Lycurgus who

---

[1] Marett, *Threshold of Rel.* 156 *sq.* For singing (*carmen*=charm), cf. Gilbert
Murray, *Anthropology and the Classics,* 96, 105.

[2] On the " immortality of drunkenness," see further Frazer, *GB.* i. 378 *sqq.*,
iii. 248 *sqq.*, v. 52 *sq.*; also *FOT.* iii. 344 *sq.*; Hölscher, *Die Profeten,* 11 *sq.*; and
in general, Kircher, *Die sakrale Bedeutung des Weines im Altertum* (Giessen, 1910)
J. W. Hauer, *Die Religionen* (Tübingen, 1923), i. 69, 72 *sqq.*

[3] Similarly, crimes committed by the sacred men of the Gold Coast when in a
state of frenzy used to go unpunished (*GB.* v. 68 *sq.*).

strove with Dionysus in Arabia.[1] In general, the recognition of the
difference between the means of producing exhilaration, ecstsay,
and all else that was felt to be sacred, if not sacramental, and the
social, ethical, or other consequences of the means employed, is of
fundamental importance for the vicissitudes of religion.

P. 221. HONEY.—Honey was used at Harran (Chwolson, ii. 195,
230 *sq.*), in Greek cultus (Eitrem, 102 *sq.*), Egypt (*Journ. of Manch.
Eg. and Or. Soc.*, 1926, p. 15), and in Babylonia (milk and honey used
in the dedication of a new image).[2] For the explanation of the statement of Theophrastus (Porph. *de Abstin.* ii. 26) that much honey
was used at a certain rite by the Jews (*sic*, Idumæans ?), see Büchler,
ZATW. 1902, pp. 206 *sqq.* Honey was forbidden in sacrifices to
" Beelefarus " (Lafaye, *Rev. de l'Hist. des Rel.*, 1888, i. 218 *sqq.* ;
Dussaud, *Sacrifice*, 261, 324). Milk and honey are apotropaic
(Eitrem, 103), divine, and the typical food of the future Golden Age ;
cf. the heavenly honey and kine of Iranian mythology, and the curds
and honey of the infant Zeus.[3] In the *Odes of Solomon* (iv. 7) they
are God's blessings for the faithful. For honey as an intoxicant, see
A. B. Cook, *Zeus*, ii. 1027 l. 5, and as a special offering to chthonian
powers, *ib.* 1142 and n. 4. On milk in mystical rejuvenating and
other rites, see Moore, *E.Bi.* l.c., Eitrem, 101, 457.

P. 221 n. SEETHING THE KID.—This much-discussed prohibition
has, from Maimonides and St. Thomas Aquinas onward, been commonly
explained as directed against some Canaanite or, more particularly,
Dionysian rite.[4] There is elsewhere a singular compassionateness,
and a sentiment against brutality or even unseemliness (Lev. xxii. 28,
parent and young not to be killed on the same day) ; and Andrew
Lang (*Man*, 1907, No. 103), in this connexion, refers to the law of
the bird's nest (Deut. xxii. 6 *sq.*).[5] As often with taboos, much that
might be considered only undesirable is apt to be combined with much
that could justly be condemned or deprecated on entirely rational
or utilitarian grounds. But even benevolent and humanitarian
injunctions will have their supernatural or religious aspect or origin ;
e.g. the harvest law in Deut. xxiv. 19 (see Von Gall, *ZATW.* xxx. 96 ;

---

[1] Cooke, No. 140 B ; Clermont-Ganneau, *Rec.* iv. 384 *sq.*, 393 *sqq.* ; Lagrange,
507 ; Lidzb., *Ephem.* i. 345 *sq.*

[2] *KAT.* 526 ; Zimmern, *Nöldeke-Festschrift*, 962 n. 1 ; Gray, *Sacrifice*, 27 ;
Moore, *E.Bi.* col. 4193, n. 1.

[3] See Usener, *Rhein. Mus.* lvii. 177–192 ; Stade, *ZATW.* 1902, p. 321 *sq.* ;
Guidi, *Rev. Bibl.*, 1903, pp. 241 *sqq.*, and the discussions in the *ZDPV.* 1902–12
passim.

[4] Reinach (*Cultes*, etc., ii. 123) thinks of Dionysus Eriphus, and Radin (*AJSL.*
1924, p. 209) finds a trace of the cult at Raphia. See also *ERE.* ix. 905*b.*

[5] Cf. also Marett, *Psychology and Folklore*, 140.

Sir G. A. Smith, *Deut.* ad loc.). Among pastoral tribes in Africa there is a disinclination to boil milk : to do so would react harmfully upon the animals that yield it. Among the Beja tribes milk is something " sacrosanct " and not " common," and should not be mixed with meat.[1] Milk enters into rites of initiation and rebirth (where the " new-born " drinks milk), and essential foods are commonly bound up with religious rites and taboos. Accordingly, the prohibition will range between the denunciation of so monstrous an act as to cook a kid in what is, as it were, its own blood (Calvin ; see G. A. Smith), and the avoidance of a specific mystical rite which conveyed a definite meaning to the participants.[2]

P. 221 n. 3. HILLŪLĪM.—W. R. S. disputes the suggested connexion with the new moon (p. 432), and Jastrow (*Rel. Beliefs*, 214, 336), apropos of Bab., Arab, and Jewish ritual at the celebration of the new moon, suggests that the meaning of the word is " joy " (cf. above, *l.c.*). But it is possible that the root meaning is that of inaugurating or beginning. The Arabic *halla* is used of bursting forth, of breaking out into crying, of the child's first cry, of the new moon beginning to shine.[3] It thus denotes some commencement, cf. *tahlīl* as a consecration (p. 279 n. 5 above) ; and it is unnecessary, with Morgenstern, to read *hillūl* in Leviticus and Judges, although the ceremony in each case no doubt marks the transition from the " sacred " to the " profane." [4] On the importance of appropriate formulas or ceremonies when certain actions are done for the first time, see Westermarck, *Morocco*, i. 205 (the saying attributed to Mohammed, " Every matter of importance which is begun without mention of God is maimed "), 304 (water from a spring), ii. 6 *sq.*, 244 (the first corn fetched from the granary), etc., cf. the *bismillah* above, p. 432 n. 1, l. 4.

P. 222. ZÉBAḤ.—The Arabic root is still used of cutting the throat, *e.g.* at Aden, of a man still alive : " Have you seen the man with his throat cut ? " (المذبوح).[5] In Assyrian the word, though less common, is used loosely of an offering (*KAT.* 595 n. 4), and in Neo-Punic dedications the verb seems to mean " to offer or dedicate." In

---

[1] Frazer, *FOT.* iii. 117 *sqq.*, 163 ; A. B. Cook, *Zeus*, i. 676 ; C. G. Seligman, *JRAI.* xliii. 654 *sqq.* The Bahimas boil milk only as a solemn rite on certain occasions (J. Roscoe, *The Baganda*, 418).

[2] N. Schmidt (*JBL.* xlv. 278 n.) conjectures that the rite was originally a fertility one.

[3] Wellhausen[1], 108 *sq.*, [2] 110 n. 3 ; see Lagarde, *Orientalia*, ii. 19.

[4] *Journ. of Amer. Orient. Soc.* xxxvi. 328 *sq.* On the meaning of the root *halla*, see p. 482 above.

[5] A. S. Tritton : private communication.

37

Assyrian *nikū* " drink offering " has similarly come to have a general
meaning, as also has *nasaka* in Arabic (p. 229 above ; Wellh. 118
n. 1 ; Gray, *Sacrifice*, 401 n. 5).

P. 222 n.—For *Ṣ-d* cf. the name Sidon, explained as " fish-
town " (Justin, xviii. 3, etc.), and its occurrence apparently as a
divine name or title in Phœnician names (Ṣ-d—Tanith, Ṣ-d—Melkart,
Ṣ-d—Yāthōn, etc. Clermont-Ganneau conjectures that *Ṣ-d* was the
Baal of Lebanon, Adonis (*Rec.* i. 189 *sqq.*). Meyer (*E.Bi.* " Phœnicia,"
§ 12) maintains the old view that Ṣid (as he writes it) is Philo's Ἀγρεύς,
the hunter, or his brother Ἁλιεύς, the fisher (cf. Lagrange, 417). At
all events, a food-deity seems to recur in Dagon (Dagan), which in
place-names is not confined to the old Philistine area, and in personal
names is found in South Palestine (Dagan-takala, Amarna Letters,
c. 1400), and in other West Semitic names, the god himself standing
by the side of Anu.[1] The man-fish is found on coins of Arvad and
Askalon (cf. the earlier Assyrian Ea-Oannes), but in spite of the
Hebrew *dāg* (fish) there is no old evidence that Dagon was a fish-god
rather than one of corn (*dāgān*). Words for food easily admit
of differentiation or are used interchangeably, and *Ṣ-d* (fish or
game) and *D-g-n* (fish or corn) would find analogies in the
Arabic *laḥma*, flesh or meat, and Heb. *leḥem*, bread, but also food
of men, ants (Prov. vi. 8) and asses (Job xxiv. 5), and sacrificial
meat (Lev. iii. 11).[2]

P. 225 n. 3.—Nöldeke (*ERE.* i. 666 col. 1) agrees with Wellhausen (121 n. 1) that these birds were vultures. On the sacred doves
at Mecca, see *Kinship*, 229 and n. 1.

P. 226. EGYPTIAN TOTEMISM.—With this guarded statement,
cf. p. 301 *sq.* In pre-dynastic Egypt each tribal god was " the articulate expression of the inner cohesion and of the outward independence
of the tribe itself, but who outwardly manifested himself in the form
of some animal or took up his abode in some fetish of wood or stone "
(A. H. Gardiner, *Ency. Brit.* ix. 49 *sq.*). According to Peet, a large
number of Egyptian gods were " probably totemic in origin," *e.g.*
the ibis Thoth, the jackal (?) Anubis, the crocodile Sebek, the falcon
Horus. But by the side of these were nature gods. " In pre-
dynastic Egypt the tribes had each its totem animal or plant, and
the theory that Egypt passed through a true totemic stage *might*
explain why the Pharaoh is represented as a bull, lion, scorpion, or
hawk." " In historical times the true totemic stage has passed

[1] See especially Burney, *Judges*, 385 *sq.*, who compares, *inter alia*, Ceres and
Cerealia.

[2] The Assyrian deities of the Creation Myth, Laḥmu and Laḥāmu (the Λαχὸ,
καὶ Λαχόν of Damascius, reading Λ for Δ), are of other origin.

away and we are left with the worship of a god in human form with the head of the totem animal, while the domestication and sacrifice of animals, together with the sacredness of the whole totem species, still remains to testify to the origin of the system (*CAH.* i.² 246, 328). Seligman (*JRAI.* xliii. 653, 681 *sq.*) considers that the Egyptians were totemistic, and certainly given to animal cults. On the other side, see Foucart, *Hist. des Religions* (1913), 62 *sqq.*, and E. Meyer (*Gesch. Alt.* i. § 183), the latter of whom makes important remarks on the sanctity of the whole animal species.[1] See in general Wiedemann, *Tierkult d. alten Ägypter* (" Der alte Orient " series, xiv. 1912); T. Hopfner, in the *Denkschriften* of the Vienna Royal Academy, lvii. pt. ii. 328 *sq.*; Gressmann, *Vorträge d. Bibliothek Warburg*, iii. (1923-24) 179 *sqq.* (on the psychological aspect of Egyptian animal cults); and the critical survey by A. van Gennep, *L'État actuel du Problème Totémique*, 179 *sqq.*

P. 226 n. 3.—For the vulture, see Wellhausen, 23. F. C. Burkitt (*Journ. Theol. Stud.* xxv. 403) would read *Dushara* in *Abodah Zarah*, 11*b*, and Addai (Phillips, 24) in the place of the rare Nashra. In any event, Wellhausen (*l.c.*) cites a Syriac name meaning " Nashr-gave "; and, as for Arab cults in Syria, according to Isaac of Antioch (Bickell, xi. 97 *sq.*) the men of Harran, along with the Arabs, worshipped Uzza, and an Arab cult can also probably be recognized at Homs (Emesa); see above, p. 570. On the eagle cult in Syria, see Dussaud, *Notes de Mythol. Syr.* (1903), § 3.

P. 228 n.—It is not clear to what " scholiast " W. R. S. refers in line 7. Perhaps he had before him the explanation of the verse in question in the *Lisān*, vi. 211, 7. But the commentary on the same verse in the *Mo'allacāt* (ed. Arnold, p. 186) says " one sheep in each ten." This explanation, with a slight variation, is given also in Lyall's edition with the commentary of Tibrīzī, p. 136, 12 *sq.* It is difficult to see why Stübe (p. 172 n. 346), in his translation, speaks of the " sacrifice of an old beast." In his translation of p. 368 n. 1 (p. 281 n. 626) he explains *fara'* (firstling) as *Wildesel*, evidently a confusion with *fara'* (Heb. *pére'*). On the sacrificing of firstlings among the heathen Arabs, cf. also *Poems of 'Amr son of Qami'ah*, ed. Lyall (Cambridge, 1919), p. 21, note on verse 9.—A. A. B.

P. 230 n. 2.—In Ecclus. xxxix. 26 the Hebrew version has דם ענב (in Gen. xlix. 11, דם ענבים). In l. 15 it is wanting. For Arab parallels see Jacob, *Studien*, iv. (1897) 6 *sq.*; and for the " blood "

---

[1] Just as the divine kingship is maintained, in that every king on his death is replaced by another, so on the death of any of the sacred species the divine spirit is found in another, which is recognized by definite marks, and takes its place as the sacred animal.

of trees, see Frazer, *GB*. ii. 20, iii. 248. For the " juice " of grapes =
blood, cf. Isa. lxiii. 3 (*nêṣaḥ*).

P. 230 n. 4.—Sacrifices were offered to Ishtar on the roofs (Morgenstern, 110 *sq*., 143) ; they consisted of cakes (*kamānu*, see *E.Bi*. col.
3992) and bread. Isaac of Antioch tells of the women who, to increase
their beauty, went upon the roofs and made offerings to the stars
(Bickell, p. 240, l. 439). An inscription from Petra (*CIS*. ii. 354)
may refer to a family god set up on the roof (צהות) of a house (see
Cooke, 245 ; Clermont-Ganneau, *Rec*. ii. 370 *sqq*., iv. 338, v. 290). See
generally, on roof cults, Frazer, *Pausanias*, ii. 165 ; Boissier, *PSBA*.
1901, p. 118 *sq*. ; and H. J. Rose, *Folk-lore*, xxxiii. 34 *sqq*., 200.

P. 231. LIBATIONS OF WATER.—That of David (2 Sam. xxiii. 16 *sq*.)
explains itself ; the water brought at such risk is too sacred to drink.
Samuel's libation at the solemn convention at Mizpah (1 Sam. vii. 6)
is accompanied with fasting, confession, and invocation, and Yahweh's
thunder discomfits the Philistines (cf. the earthquake in 1 Sam. xiv.
15). The libation is generally interpreted as a pouring away of
sin, though this is hardly suggested by the context (Gray, *Sacrifice*,
400 *sq*.). But libations are also made at graves as an act of piety,
or more specifically in order to refresh the dead. The dead are
thirsty (see p. 235), the liquid disappears into the ground, whereas
dry food would be carried away by animals. On Egyptian monuments the prayer of the dead is for water ; and in Babylonia he who
is properly buried " rests on a couch and drinks pure waters," whereas
he whose shade has no rest eats of the pickings of the pot and the
food thrown into the street (Jastrow, *Rel. Beliefs*, 358 *sq*.). At the
present day it is sometimes believed that the soul of the dead visits
the tomb every Friday in the hope of finding water, or water is placed
in the cup-like holes, and the birds which drink of it will testify to
the merits of the dead (*JPOS*. iv. 27). See further Goldziher, *Arch.
f. Rel*. xiii. 45 *sq*. (post-Biblical and Mohammedan evidence) ;
Baudissin, 437 n. 3 ; and Torge, *Seelen u. Unsterblichkeitshoffnung*,
134 *sq*. (on 1 Sam. vii.).

P. 231. RAIN-CHARMS (cf. p. 211).—On the Feast of Tabernacles,
see *E.Bi*. " Sacrifice," § 36 ; " Tabernacles," § 7 ; Loisy, *Sacrifice*,
210 ; J. de Groot, *Theolog. Tijd*. 1918, pp. 38 *sqq*. Thackeray (*The
Septuagint and Jewish Origins*, 61 *sqq*.) observes that " with a solemn
public disclaimer of sun-worship the ceremony ended at cock-crow,"
i.e. the rising sun at the autumnal equinox. On the rite at Hierapolis
and the various parallels, see *Revue des Études Juives*, xxxvi. 317,
xliii. 195 ; Lagrange, 166 *sq*. (who distinguishes the libation as a rain-
charm from the " descent " of images to the water in order to purify
them) ; and Rieger, *JQR*. 1926, Jan., 232. According to Mariti,

the Tyrian ritual (see p. 232 n. 3) is called the marriage of the sea water to the land water ; he places the rite in October. On p. 231 n. 3, see, besides Wellhausen, 167 (who compares the Roman custom, *Ovid*, iv. 681 *sqq*.), Goldziher, *Muh. Stud.* i. 35, and Burney's discussion (*Judges*, 393 *sq*.).[1]

In the island of Imbros a prayer for the fertilizing dew is accompanied with a recitation of the Baptism of Christ, wherein St. John is the bestower of the life-giving dew.[2] In Palestine Christians, Jews, and Mohammedans take part in processions for rain (*Qy. St.* 1893, p. 218 ; *ZDPV*. vii. 94, No. 86). A puppet is often carried, and doggerel rhymes are sung to the Umm el-Ghēth, the "mother of rain" (*Qy. St.* 1925, p. 37). Father Antonin Jaussen denies that in Moab the puppet *'arūs* is called the "bride of Allah" (so Curtiss, 119), and Canaan (*JPOS*. vi. 144) could not verify the term "half (*nasf*) bride" which Jaussen heard in the Negeb. Intelligent opinion, at all events, repudiated the idea of a "bride of Allah" as a rain-maker, and no clear tradition seems to have survived.[3] At 'Ēn Karīm a cock is carried round and pinched in order that its cries for rain may be added to the rest.[4] In these ceremonies the head man will sprinkle the crowd with a little water, lack of rain is attributed to the sins of the elders or of specified families, while the younger people protest their own innocence.[5] In bad cases of drought the Imam proclaims a fast, even babes are not allowed to suckle ; the people put on their worst rags, they forgive one another and implore divine forgiveness (*JPOS*. vi. 157).

In prayers for rain not all shrines are equally effective, and in Rabbinical Judaism only men of outstanding merit were rain-makers. Among them were Ḥoni (Onias) and Nikodemos ben Gorion. The former of these, it has been said, "reminds one of a magician or a heathen priest praying for rain." A third, Joshua ben Levi, was

[1] An exploit like Samson's in Judg. xv. 3–5 is not always a mythological trait, it is also a device to destroy crops so that invaders should not feed on the district ; see Hartmann, *ZATW*. xxxi. 69 *sqq*., and Gaudefroy-Demombynes, *La Syrie à l'Époque des Mamelouks*, 262 *sq*.

[2] Jane Harrison, *Themis*, 17.

[3] There is said to be also an *Abū 'l-Ghēth* (*JPOS*. vi. 152 n. 5).

[4] On the cock in rain-charms, see Gressmann, *Marti-Festschrift*, 88 *sqq*. In Morocco children are pinched, their tears acting as a rain-charm (Westermarck, *Morocco*, ii. 265). For weeping as a rain-charm, see *GB*. vii. 248, viii. 91.

[5] *JPOS*. vi. 150. For sprinkling as a "survival" of drowning a victim, cf. *GB*. i. 277 *sq*. ; Westermarck, *op. cit.* 262 *sq*. The sacrifice of a human victim in order to procure rain is known to the Gemara on Abodah Zarah (iv. 7, f.55a), and is explained on the lines of Deut. iv. 19b and Prov. iii. 34. On human sacrifice for rain, see also Mader, 32.

successful only in his own town; and where the " merits " of the congregation did not deserve it, even his prayer would be unavailing.[1] As regards the story of Elijah at Mount Carmel, the Phœnician reference (in Menander) to the removal of the drought by the prayers of Ethbaal (the father-in-law of Ahab) suggests that the original Israelite version emphasized the tradition that it was not the priest-king of Astarte, but Elijah the servant of Yahweh who was the real rain-maker (*CAH*. iii. 369 *sq*.). Rameses II., when his sacrifices are accepted by the god, is supposed to be able to give rain to the Ḫatti or Hittites (Breasted, *Rec*. iii. § 426); and it is through Israel and because of Israel that the earth has sunshine and rain (Marmorstein, 129). Hence it is in accordance with the prevailing ideas that (*a*) drought is the result of such offences as the failure to rebuild the Temple (Hag. i.), or to make the accustomed offerings (Mal. iii. 10), or to keep the Feast of Tabernacles (Zech. xiv. 16 *sq*.), and (*b*) that the Temple with its round of festivals has an almost " magical " power. Nature, and in particular rain, can be controlled *either* by special gods *or* by special men or organizations (whether through their influence with the gods or in their own right), and the manner in which the fundamental ideas are shaped and systematized determines their effect upon the development of a group.[2]

P. 232. ANOINTING-OIL.—Oil, besides adding to the pleasure of Oriental life, has medicinal properties and, in certain climates, is indispensable (*E.Bi*. " Oil," § 4). Kings, priests, and prophets (1 Kings xix. 16) were anointed; the king and, later, the high priest being " *the* anointed *par excellence* " (see Gray, *Sacrifice*, 258 *sq*.). To the installation of the king as " Yahweh's anointed " corresponded the anointing of a prince by his suzerain, as when the King of Egypt anointed the head of the grandfather of Addu-nirari (Amarna Letters, No. 51). The anointing of images (and also of priests and worshippers) was both Babylonian and Egyptian custom.[3] The widespread practice of anointing stones (on which see Frazer, *FOT*. ii. 72 *sq*.) has been explained as merely an act of honour. This, however, hardly covers all the facts, seeing that Assyrian dedication tablets,

[1] A. Büchler, *Types of Jewish-Palestinian Piety*, 197 *sq*., 200, 246 *sq*., 254; Marmorstein, *Doctrine of Merits in old Rabb. Literature*, 71, 90, 251. On the trumpet-blowing (p. 231 above), cf. Büchler, 232 *sq*.

[2] On the rain-makers among the Nilotic Dinkas, see Seligman's article (*ERE. s.v.*, and cf. *JRAI*. xliii. 671 *sqq*.). On European rain-makers, see A. B. Cook, *Folk-lore*, xv. 371 *sqq*.

[3] Morgenstern, 63. The pure, bright, resplendent oil was valued in Babylonia or certain ceremonies; cf. " oil of life " (*Beiträge z. Ass.* iv. 160 l. 42). Oil was used in Bab. and Jewish divination (S. Daiches on Bab. oil magic; London, 1913), and in Greek (Farnell, *Greece and Babylon*, 301).

which were inscribed with the name of the founder, etc., were oiled and received sacrifices (cf. Harper, *Ass. and Bab. Lit.*, 80, etc.). Here the intention appears to be to preserve the name ; and that this is frequently true elsewhere is suggested (*a*) by the application of milk, butter, and of other forms of nourishment to stones, and (*b*) by the belief in the vital properties of oil, fat, etc. (cf. p. 379 *sq.*). Hence, anointing may often be regarded as a mode of transmitting either the sacred power of which the liquid was the symbol or vehicle, or the inherent nutritive and other properties with which it was credited. Indeed, to smear oneself with the remains of the dead, was one way of acquiring the qualities whether of man or animal—to eat the potent thing was another (see *GB.* viii. 162-5). See in general, Crawley and Jastrow, *ERE.* s.v. " Anointing " ; Weinel, *ZATW.* xviii. 1 *sqq.* ; Wellhausen, *Arch. f. Rel.* vii. 33 *sqq.*, and cf. ix. 140.

P. 241. FIRSTFRUITS AND FIRSTLINGS (cf. pp. 458 *sqq.*).—The parallel between the firstlings and the treatment of fruit-trees (Lev. xix. 23 *sqq.*) is important ; see pp. 159 n., 463. The trees are " sacred " and must not be touched ; similarly, when Israel is " sacred " to Yahweh, those who harm her suffer (Jer. ii. 3). Special precautions are necessary at the first use of things ; so, *e.g.*, at the opening up of new unbroken " virgin " land (p. 158), for which the Talmudic term is *bĕthūlah*, used also of untrimmed sycamores.[1] The conviction that the firstfruits or firstlings do not belong to those who might seem to have the first right takes many forms which are of interest for early ideas of ownership and property rights (p. 638). Usually, offerings must first be made to a god (or the gods), to the priest or the ruler—both primarily as representatives of the god(s)—or to the dead (ancestral spirits) ; or they are used for communal purposes, and more particularly for the poor (above, pp. 247, 253, 347).[2] Sometimes the firstfruits are eaten by the people themselves, not merely ceremonially but sacramentally ; or there are merely vague ideas, as among the Gallas, where the person who milks the cows should not drink of it before a sip has been taken by some one else.[3]

Various explanations of the offering of firstlings, etc., have been suggested. (*a*) It is an act of renunciation ; more positively it is the sacrifice of a portion in order to secure the rest. It is to suffer a willing loss in order to escape a worse one ; it is to propitiate Nemesis ; it is the price of success. . . . Intuitive feelings of this sort appear

---

[1] On the use of the Arabic *halla*, see p. 577.

[2] At the present day the proceeds of the firstfruits may be devoted to a feast in the name and to the honour of the *weli* (*JPOS.* vi. 25 n. 5).

[3] Miss A. Werner, *Journ. of the African Soc.* xiii. 130. See in general, *GB.* viii. ch. xi., and cf. Gray, *Numbers*, 225 *sqq.*

to be widespread and fundamental, and are too powerful to be ignored
(cf. Crawley, *Mystic Rose*, 366). More precisely (*b*), it is a thank-
offering and thanksgiving, gratitude for the past (see esp. Gray,
Sacrifice, 94 *et passim*). Yet, in any case, close at hand there lies
the hope of continued favours and future blessings ; and however
natural gratitude may seem to be, not far off are the ideas, however
indefinite, of the part played by the supernatural powers. So (*c*)
" God gave the increase " (1 Cor. iii. 6) ; and it is the typical belief
that the offerings belong properly to the gods. Sometimes the formula
is quite explicit : " What comes of thy hand we give thee " (1 Chron.
xxix. 14), or the modern " from thee and to thee " (*minnak u-ilēk*,
Canaan, *JPOS*. vi. 130). In these circumstances, to withhold offerings
and tithes is to rob (or overreach) God and bring disaster upon the
land (Mal. iii. 8–12) ; the gifts are " sacred " and must not be touched
by the people, still less may they be eaten.[1]

The first of a thing, like that which is unused and not as yet
profaned, is often believed to have superior sanctity and efficacy.[2]
Moreover, the first of any growth is also a guarantee of fertility and
continuity. As a " part " for a " whole," as an offering which released
the remainder of the produce from the taboo upon it, the practice
of firstfruits lent itself to highly developed teaching. Thus Philo
spiritualizes the offering of the first sheaf ; and the *aparche*, a communal
offering for the land, is for all mankind, and what the priest is to the
city so the Jewish people is to the whole human race.[3] Again, if the
Greek firstfruits are the sheaves, the source of next year's crop, the
offering of a part for the whole seems to be intended to secure the
continuity of produce.[4] In any event, it is a prevalent belief that a
" part " can stand for a " whole," and that through the " part " the
" whole " can be preserved or harmed ; even as the preservation of
the blood of a slain animal preserves the vital essence of the victim
so that it is not annihilated (cf. pp. 158, 379).

---

[1] Judith, xi. 12 *sq*. In Mal. iii. 8, Wellhausen and others read, after the LXX,
the verb '-*ḳ-b* for *ḳ-b-'*.

[2] Cf. the unused animal in Num. xix. 2 ; Deut. xxi. 3 ; 1 Sam. vi. 7 ; and the
firstling in Deut. xv. 19 ; see pp. 464 *sqq*. See also W. Warde Fowler (*Rel. Experience of the Roman People*, 172) on the festival on the Alban Mount, where the flesh
of a white heifer that had never felt the yoke was partaken of by the deputies of
the cities of the Latin League.

[3] See Gray, 324, 331, who observes that the resurrection of Jesus takes place
on 16th Nisan, when the *aparche* was presented at the Temple (388 *sq*.). Lightfoot
on Col. i. 18 points out that Christ as ἀρχή was the firstfruits of the dead and
also an " originating power . . . the source of life."

[4] See Cornford, *Ridgeway Presentation Volume*, 154 *sq*., 165 ; cf. 145 (following a
hint of Warde Fowler) ; Miss Jane Harrison, *Themis*, 292, 306 *sq*. ; Nilsson, 92, 123.

The necessity of securing continuity underlies many different practices which in one way or another are felt to preserve from extinction that which is vital. It may be enough that there is a god of whom the hunter must ask permission (pp. 158, 160). But among the Esquimaux of the Behring Straits a goddess preserves the " souls " of the animals that are hunted and killed, only hunters who observe certain taboos will be successful, and as the " souls " are reborn the continuity of the food-supply is ensured and the sanctity of life maintained.[1] This self-supporting system is an unusually interesting example of the widespread endeavour to preserve life by means of (1) some material or physical vehicle (blood, etc.), (2) the relation between it and a " living " deity, or (3) some idea or system of ideas which makes the individual life part of some more permanent whole. In the Esquimaux custom the seals and whales are perpetual reincarnations ; and it is essentially the same when an individual (or an animal) is a member of a group (or species) which remains intact in spite of the death of the individual—or even, what is more significant, is preserved through the death ; cf. p. 579 n.

Even in totemism the individual is born of a stock of " spirit-souls " which he rejoins at death ; and since in this most rudimentary of cults there are both animal and plant totems, the difference between firstborn and firstfruits, between animal and cereal, does not seem to be so important as W. R. S. argues. His distinction between the *zébaḥ*, where gods and men meet, and the *minḥah*, which is made over to the god (pp. 240, 244, etc.), is as well founded as it is natural to regard pastoral religion as earlier than agricultural. On the other hand, to suppose that the latter " borrowed " from the former (p. 243, end of note) seems to go too far ; it would be better, in the first instance, to recognize that similar fundamental ideas recur differently shaped owing to different conditions of life. W. R. S.'s suggested evolution of sacrificial cults has been adversely criticized by those who find that social religious development is too complex a process for simple theories such as he put forward. The differentiation into animal and vegetable life points to a higher stage than that found in totem-cults and in other more unsystematized forms among rudimentary peoples. Moreover, the stages where gods are anthropomorphic, and a similar life-blood runs through men and animals, are more systematized than those where the gods, if any, are scarcely part of the social system. Hence the idea of some essential oneness or unity takes very different forms according to the current convictions concerning men and the world of animal and plant life, even as in

[1] See Frazer *GB*. iii. 207 *sqq*., who calls it " animism, passing into religion " (213).

mysticism the feeling of oneness with something other than one's self is both shaped and expressed very differently by men differing as regards their particular religion or sect, or as regards their temperament (*e.g.* whether philosophical or nature mystics). But, fundamentally, the individual is part of a larger " whole," though what that " whole " is turns upon his system of thought. See p. 635.

In Australian totemism there are clans which perform ceremonies that are believed to control or multiply the edible animal or vegetable species in question. Although the clan does not eat, or at least only very sparingly, of its totem, on these occasions it is indispensable that it should partake of a little. Each clan controls its own totem animal or plant for the others, and the formal manner in which the officiants eat a small portion of the food is an integral part of what, throughout, is a very solemn ceremony. So, whereas elsewhere firstfruits may be handed over to a god or his representative, here there is no reference to a god, and the relation between the Australian and similar rites, on the one hand, and those where gods are immediately involved, on the other, raises a most important question of priority. Jevons suggests that the latter are primary : the Australian practices belong to a *later* stage, where " the reference to the god who is or was intended to partake of the firstfruits has, in the process of time and, we must add, in the course of religious decay, gradually dropped out." [1] On the other hand, the Australian rites do not resemble those where, as so commonly happens, an earlier god-idea has been washed away. The clan functions as a god might do on the anthropomorphic level, and the All-Fathers or Supreme Beings take no direct part. The clan officiates in a " sacred " condition, the clan and its totem are of the same substance, and to eat a portion of the food would be, so to say, cannibalism and akin to incest, both of which—very significantly —are at times more or less ceremonial acts. To all intents and purposes the very " soul " of the food lies within the members of the clan ; they are the sources of its existence and continuity. They alone are the producers of that which is their own. This seems fundamental. It is in other and less rudimentary communities that the question arises whether the firstfruits belong to the community as a whole or the poorer section of them, to the indispensable sacred officiants, to the responsible being, the god of the community, or to his own sacred representative. But, primarily, firstfruits and firstlings

---

[1] *Introd. to Comp. Rel.* 184 ; cf. *Idea of God*, 87, 90 *sq.* For general statements, and for discussions of the Australian evidence, see Jevons, *Introd.* 184 *sqq.*, 198 *sqq.* ; Toy, § 128, and, in the first instance, Frazer, *G.B.* i. 85 *sqq.* ; *Tot. Ex.* i. 104 *sqq.*, 230 *sqq.*, citing Spencer and Gillen, to whom the evidence is due ; see above, p. 535 and n. 2.

seem to arise out of the necessity for providing for the maintenance of the most fundamental needs of life.

P. 245 n. 2. TITHES.—In Babylonian religion the idea of tribute involved in offering animals appears to have been of a secondary character (Jastrow, *Rel. Bel.* 148). Tithes, too, are a relatively late institution, and first appear in a highly developed form in the time of Nebuchadrezzar II. (sixth century B.C.). According to Eissfeldt, more objects are tithed, and instead of tithes of natural objects, payments in money are not unusual and even money itself seems to be tithed; and tithing is less a personal and more of a business transaction (*Baudissin-Festschrift*, 166). See further W. R. S., *Prophets*, 383 *sq.*; *E.Bi.* " Taxation " (Benzinger), " Tithes " (Moore); Sir G. A. Smith, *Jerusalem*, i. ch. vi. *sq.*; Eissfeldt, *Erstlinge und Zehnten*, i. *A.T.* (Leipzig, 1917); *PW.* iv. 2306, 2423; and H. Schaeffer, *Social Legislation of the Primitive Semites* (New Haven, 1915), ch. xiii.

P. 247 n. 2.—On the inscription, see *PW.* ii. 2779, and A. B. Cook, *Zeus*, i. 565 n. 2.

P. 248 n.—Duval's interpretation of the Aramaic inscription at Taimā (*CIS.* ii. 113; Cooke, No. 69) is accepted by Lagrange, 503 *sq.* The text speaks of the " grant (?) " (צדקתא) of palm-trees which Ṣalm of Maḥram and Sin-galla and Ashīra (cf. Ashirat, p. 561), gods of Taimā, gave to Ṣalm of Hagam, and the priesthood which was conferred upon Ṣalm-Shēzeb, son of Peṭ-osiri, and his seed after him, ". . . (?) of the field, 16 palms, and of the treasure (שימתא) of the king 5 palms, in all 21 palms every year." Some (*e.g.* Hartmann, 464) explain Ṣalm (" image," cf. p. 562 n. 3) as the *numen*, and שימתא as an endowment. For ordinary endowments of trees, cf. the nut-trees with which a Christian church was endowed (Sir E. Budge, *Thomas of Marga*, 239, 653), and the renting of a vine belonging to a Palestine shrine to a man, the money going to its upkeep (*JPOS.* iv. 35); for Bab. examples see C. H. W. Johns, *Bab. and Ass. Laws, Contracts, etc.* (1904), 208 *sqq.*

P. 249.—On the Deuteronomic law, see Driver, *Deut.* 168 *sqq.* Chapman, *Introd. to the Pentateuch* (1911), 155 *sqq.*; A. H. M'Neile, *Deut.* (1912), 80 *sqq.*; and on the abuses against which the law is directed, cf. also W. R. S., *Prophets*, 98 *sqq.*

P. 254 n. 6.—λέσχη, like μέγαρον (p. 200), πάλλαξ (Heb. *pillégesh*), etc., may be neither Semitic nor Greek, but of some common Ægean origin (see Autran, *Les Phéniciens* [1920], 13, 46). On the use of the Heb. word, see Box, *E.Bi.* " Temple," § 32. The modern shrine (*maḳām*) will have one or more additional rooms for meals or festivals, for a kitchen or a dwelling-place for the attendant, for a schoolroom, guest-chamber, or for the pilgrims who spend a few days at the shrine. In such cases the building is mostly composed of two or at times of three storeys ; and they are dedicated to " Prophets " rather than to the *welis* (Canaan, *JPOS.* iv. 16 *sq.*). Such buildings recall the old synagogues (on which see Peritz, *E.Bi.* 4834 *sqq.*).[1]

P. 258. GLOOMY TYPES OF RELIGION.—Ed. Meyer (*Gesch. d. Alt.* i. § 191) comments upon the sinister note in Egyptian religion. In Babylonia this is much more marked. Babylonia is a land " not of laughter but of gloom and of serious meditation." " The fear of divine anger runs as an undercurrent throughout the entire religious literature of Babylonia and Assyria." [2] Gloom, it has been said, pervades Semitic religion, and distinguishes it from the healthy, happy tone that characterizes the religion of the *Rig Veda* as a whole, the latter in turn recalling, in several respects, the characteristics of the religion of the Viking period.[3] The profound difference between Greek and Semitic religion is strongly emphasized by Farnell.[4] Similarly Warde Fowler observes that in the Roman religion there is " no fear so long as the worship of the gods is performed exactly and correctly according to the rules of the state priesthoods ; there is no sense of sin or of pollution, of taboo irremediably broken, haunting the mind of the individual ; all is cheerfully serious, regular, ordered, ritualistic." [5] See also p. 563.

To be sure, every religion has its vicissitudes, and Farnell (*Evolution of Religion,* 113 *sq.*) notes the possibility that in Greece the " cathartic legislation emanating chiefly from Delphi and Crete may point to a religion which the intellectualism of Homeric civilization had happily suppressed for a time, but which reasserted itself, with renewed strength, when that civilization was overthrown." W. R. S. himself lays stress upon the changes which political disasters brought upon the old religion (p. 258, cf. p. 78), and Meyer summarizes concisely some typical changes in the history of religions (i. § 67 *sq.*). Further, difference of climate and difference of national temperament are obviously important factors ; and they are adduced to explain the fundamental divergence between the old Iranian ethical and practical religion and the pessimistic and mystical developments of post-Vedic

[1] Miss Jane Harrison compares the λέσχη to the " man's house " of the South Seas, etc. (*Themis,* 36 n. 3).

[2] See Jastrow, *Rel. Bel.* 326 *sqq.*, 333, 358 ; R. Campbell Thompson, *CAH.* i.[2] 533 ; Langdon, *ib.* 443 ; Cook, *ib.* 200.

[3] H. M. Chadwick, *The Heroic Age,* ch. xviii., who also compares Homeric Greece.

[4] *Greece and Babylon,* 263 ; *Higher Aspects of Greek Religion,* 132 *sq.* Halliday, *CAH.* ii. 606, speaks of the " friendliness " of Greek worship.

[5] *Anthropology and the Classics* (ed. Marett), 173.

religion in India.[1] Sensuality and cruelty go hand in hand (p. 415). Ashurbanipal, " the compassionate," after torturing and killing the rebels of Babylon, declares, " After I had performed these acts I softened the hearts of the Great Gods." The fanatical temper which found savage cruelty acceptable to the injured gods is akin to that bold anthropomorphism whereby Yahweh is said to comfort or appease himself by taking vengeance upon his enemies (Isa. i. 24). Not unnaturally, therefore, do men dread the arbitrary gods (Jastrow, 144, 326), even as Islam has an exaggerated consciousness of sin and fear of divine vengeance.[2]

The joyful and happy types of religion are psychologically no less significant ; and in Israel " sacrificial occasions were pre-eminently happy occasions " (Gray, *Sacrifice*, 93). This only makes the evidence for fear and gloom the more instructive. Throughout rudimentary religion high spirits and gaiety abound.[3] Shintoism has been described as a religion of happy social intercourse,[4] and among the Warramunga of Central Australia there is a totem of the " laughing boys " (Durkheim, 379 *sqq.*). No doubt the happy type of religion has a carelessness, and its mirth was not always innocent (Ex. xxxii. 6). Moreover, easy confidence in the god, particularly the god of one's own group, was not conducive to any depth of religion, and the light-heartedness of Samaria, denounced by Isaiah (ix. 8 *sqq.*), was, in view of the current conditions, unnatural. When there are recognized ways of maintaining the unity of gods and worshippers religion tends to be taken lightly ; and familiarity breeds a *camaraderie*, and an almost contemptuous estimate of the gods (cf. Chadwick, *op. cit.* 418, on Homer and the Viking Age). But while it is tempting to contrast the happy type in Israel with the later gloom and the undoubted timid notes of post-exilic Judaism, it can hardly be supposed that the Syro-Ephraimite wars before the rise of Jeroboam II., or the earlier Philistine and other crises, did not cloud the more cheerful type of religion. The Semitic readiness to pass from one extreme to another—already to be illustrated in the laments of Palestinian chiefs of the fourteenth century in their letters to Egypt—and the great events of early Palestinian history were of a sort to destroy any thoroughgoing optimistic religion, and they forbid simple theories of the development of religion

[1] G. F. Moore, *Hist. of Religions*, i. 359 *sqq.* ; for the Vedas, cf. J. N. Farquhar, *Outline of the Rel. Lit. of India* (1920), 13 *sq.* ; and for Indian pessimism, cf. Mrs. Sinclair Stevenson, *The Heart of Jainism*, 2, 4 (1915).

[2] R. A. Nicholson, *Literary History of the Arabs*, 211, 225.

[3] Irving King, *Development of Rel.* 58, 100, 241 *sq.*

[4] King, 114 *sq.*, citing Aston, *Shinto, the Way of the Gods*, 6. Against the criticism that Shinto has no ethics, see Moore, i. 107.

from one absolute type to another. In fact, a fuller knowledge of rudimentary peoples, with their gaiety, cruelty, and irresponsibility, warns one not to read more into the conception of " the childhood of humanity " (cf. p. 257) than the evidence warrants. The data upon which are based generalizations of gloomy and of happy types of religion are derived from different ages, stages, and classes of society. There are the obvious extremes of gloom, fanaticism, and dread, and of confidence, over-confidence, and indifference ; and the actual historical development of every religion has lain between them.

P. 263 *sqq*. THE RELIGION OF THE INDIVIDUAL AND OF THE GROUP. —W. R. S.'s pages have become classical. The difference between individualism and the conditions where the group is a unit with a " corporate personality " must not be made absolute. Group-unity " does not mean that no individual life is recognized, but simply that in a number of realms in which we have come to think individual-istically and to treat the single man as the unit, for punishment or reward, ancient thought envisaged the whole group of which he was part." [1] It means that a man does not exist except as a member of some group, clan, or tribe.[2] Early communities are relatively undifferentiated, there is less specialization of life and thought, and a man has less opportunity for developing along independent lines than in those more complex societies where religious, political, and other groupings do not necessarily coincide, and a man can belong to a number of different groups with group interests, traditions, and aims (see p. 506). In the simpler societies the individual has rights (*e.g.* as regards property and marriage) ; moreover, religion " is an affair of all in which every one takes an active and equivalent part." [3] What is in one sense a loss of individuality enables a man to find himself in a larger social circle and at another level. But the worth of the individual is subordinated to that of the group, and the security of the whole outweighs the welfare of the individual part. The group protects the individual so far as recognized group interests and custom demand ; but it is ready to treat with harshness the man marked out from the rest by reason of suffering, misfortune, abnor-mality, or some suspected sign of the displeasure of the supernatural powers. Group-religion is " this worldly," and social (p. 263); whereas in individual religion the man treads his own path, and sacrifice may be little more than a private bargain (p. 393). There

---

[1] H. Wheeler Robinson, in Peake, *The People and the Book*, 376.

[2] Cf. G. C. Wheeler, *The Tribe*, 16.

[3] Malinowski (ed. Needham), 81 *sq.* ; for general remarks, see *ib.* 53 *sq.*, where the extent of distinctively individual religious experience among savages is described.

is a tendency to deprecate the personal religion which severs a man from his group ; logically, such religion lies outside the system of the group, whether, with his private ideas, he may be proceeding along anti-social lines, or is contributing to the progressive development of his group.[1]

Group-religion is not a water-tight system. The group and its god may be regarded as a unit, but in practice certain individuals, objects, acts, and seasons are more sacred than others, and there is a tendency to specialization in both sacred and secular duties. Men of pre-eminent ability are readily credited with supernatural attributes ; men of position and experience become elders, and even among rudimentary peoples they are concerned in preserving or advancing group interests.[2] Specially irksome taboos will not be observed by the whole group, but restricted to and imposed upon a few ; and the specially sacred things are no longer for the group as a whole. Certain individuals become representative, and even among rudimentary peoples " individual totems," as distinct from the totems of whole clans, make for personal religion, as also do the sacred animal-guardians or protectors of the North American Indian.

While a group can be spoken of as a single individual, a single individual can for all intents and purposes represent a group. The " part " then stands for the whole, either occasionally, as in cases of collective responsibility, blood-feud, scapegoats, etc., or in the more permanent functions of ruler or priest. In the case of the priestly or sacred king the " representative " individual is the visible embodiment of the people and land, and no less of the god ; he represents, in one sense, the god to the people, and, in another sense, the people to the god. He is an intermediary and intercessor, responsible for benefits and evils, and the natural culprit or scapegoat when things go wrong (see *GB.* vol. ix.). In the solidarity of king–group–god the king is *the* individual, and his position and functions so vital that he is the centre of the national cult which grows up around him.[3] The growth of society has been marked by the increase of other significant functioning and representative individuals in religion (national, family, clan, and private cults) and in secular life. Accordingly, in most lands the communities are not a little complex : in

[1] Cf. Marett, *Ency. Brit.* xxii. 258a. Even at the higher stages of development silent prayers are discountenanced lest a man pray for that which he would be ashamed for others to know of (Farnell, *Evol. of Rel.* 206).

[2] Cf. Landtman, *The Primary Causes of Social Inequality*, 3 (Helsingfors. 1909) ; W. Beck, *Das Individuum bei den Australiern* (*Leipzig Instit. f. Völkerkunde*, 1924).

[3] Cf. Jastrow, *Rel. Bel.* 241 *sq.* ; Eitrem, 237 *sqq.* ; S. A. Cook (ed. Peake), 64 *sqq.*

Babylonia, for example, the line between public and private cults must not be too sharply drawn; there are both family and clan cults, and a man could have his own god who would, if necessary, approach a great god on his behalf.[1]

While the history of religions and the multiplication of sects by fission have recalled biological processes,[2] the vicissitudes of religious and secular groups would be much more intricate and unmanageable were it not for the concept of the group-unit (p. 504). The validity of W. R. S.'s generalizations can be tested by observing the ordinary facts of the history of social groups ; and they open up questions of far-reaching interest. Everywhere are tendencies that make for concentration and intensification and ultimate stagnation, and those that make for diffusion, cosmopolitanism, and ultimate weakening (cf. p. 264). One may compare the varying endogamous and exogamous tendencies in societies ; compulsory marriage *either* within *or* without a group or constellation of groups obviously affecting very differently the beliefs and customs of the groups involved. Periods of decadence and disintegration of earlier groups or group-systems, excessive individualism, and subsequent periods of organization, integration, and harmony of sentiment, are normal in the history of society. In Israel, at certain periods, as W. R. S. points out, " individuality stiffened into individualism . . . each man's feeling of personal worth asserted itself in refusal to acknowledge the rights of others and the supreme sovereignty of Yahweh." [3] Such a description is typical, and the inner history of the movement of religious and other thought from the decline of the monarchy of Judah to the inauguration of Judaism after the Exile is of supreme significance for the interrelation of the religion of individuals and that of groups, and for the growth of a new unity.

The Sumerian revival under Gudea of Lagash was marked by important religious and social movements, and during a seven days' Saturnalia " the maid was the equal of her mistress, and master and slave consorted together as friends." [4] Saturnalia, with the inversion of social ranks—and even with human sacrifice (*GB.* ix. 407) —are irregular manifestations of equality and unity which temporarily ignore those social conditions where differences in rank, ability, and function are normally recognized, as even among many rudimentary peoples. But, apart from Saturnalia, there are the more ordered social

---

[1] Jastrow, 300 ; cf. Morgenstern, 25.

[2] G. F. Moore, *Hist. of Religions*, ii. pp. x, 368.

[3] *Lectures*, 444. He refers to three periods of decay : (*a*) the time of the Judges, (*b*) before the Captivity, and (*c*) before the fall of Jerusalem.

[4] L. W. King, *History of Sumer and Akkad*, 271 *sq.* ; Langdon, *CAH.* i.[2] 429.

practices which manifest and cement the unity of the group, the sub-conscious unity which lies beneath the otherwise recognized differences. Unity is also fostered by the beliefs and rites of a levelling character, such as the absolute and unique supremacy of the god of the group, or of all interrelated groups, by symbols of a universal order (*e.g.* Sun and Sky-gods), by religious ideas which are universally intelligible, by a history which intimately unites all members of the group. Here the history of Israel is of cardinal value on account of the teaching of the great prophets before and at the Exile, and the subsequent reorganization, whereas centuries later at the rise of Christianity a Jewish sect arose from a Judaism which was unable to make a further advance, and the Jews ceased to be a nation. The facts of social and religious reorganization and decay are thus highly suggestive for the relations between groups and their constituent individuals.

When Gray (*Sacrifice*, 43 *sqq.*) remarks that the prophets " do not call the people back to a theory of sacrifice as a means of communion with God," he well observes that " the tenour of their teaching was, not gifts but fellowship," and that the road lay not through " the sacrificial system reinterpreted, but through conduct " (cf. 52). They demanded a self-renunciation, an obedience to a righteous God, not deprivation or the transference of property, or even particular rites whereby fellowship could be periodically manifested and realized in a physical or material sense. In the doctrine of the New Covenant (Jer. xxxi.), " the central truth," says Skinner, " is the inwardness of true religion, the spiritual illumination of the individual mind. . . ." There is a transition to a new individualism, for the Covenant is with each and every member of the community, and " the principle of nationalism is carried over from the Old dispensation to the New." [1] Accordingly in Deuteronomy, " one of the most noteworthy attempts in history to regulate the whole life of a people by its highest religious principle," [2] emphasis is laid upon the fact that Israel has come of age (xxix. 4, 13 ; cf. 1 Cor. xiii. 11), a new stage is inaugurated in the history of the people, and the immediacy and simplicity of the religious demands are the most striking features (Deut. xxx. 11–14). Similarly at the rise of Christianity, the appeal is to the individual, his worth is enhanced ; and, though a yoke must be borne, it is an easy one (Matt. xi. 30). As distinct from the most elemental or impressive or innocent of communion rites, the teachers of spiritual religion in addressing the individual emphasize the simplicity and directness of the new relationship, whether as a Covenant to be written on each man's heart, or as a Divine Presence where two or three are gathered

[1] J. Skinner, *Prophecy and Religion*, 329 (Cambridge, 1922).

[2] Moore, *E.Bi.* " Deuteronomy," col. 1093.

38

in His name. And the next step has been to apply the teaching to a group or people as a whole.

Long ago W. R. S. emphasized the difference between the Christian " conventicle," the group united only by " similarity of experience in details, identity of individual frames and habits of mind," and the Church as an " organic unity," uniting men of different types of religion and stages of spiritual growth (*Lectures*, 326 *sq.*). The distinction is important, because it is obvious that, where there is or has been regained a group-unity of men and their gods, the social-religious ideas have been systematized afresh. There has been a new co-ordination of corporate and individual habits and practices, a sufficient intelligibility of the most vital ideas, and a common consciousness which, despite all differences within the group, enable it to function as a unit. Whether W. R. S. was influenced by his own earlier ideals of an " organic unity " in Christianity, or not, he made powerful generalizations which are seen to be self-evident. Group-unity or corporate personality is constantly disintegrating, and new integrations are being formed ; the movements range from the supreme examples in the history of man to the vicissitudes of small parties and sects, from the most impressive reconstruction to the most casual recovery of social equilibrium. As far back as one can go, one can postulate an alternation between group coherence and incoherence, between the more collective and the more individual moments. In the history of religion there must, in the nature of the case, have been innumerable examples of social-religious reorganization even in the simplest and earliest societies. The farther back one goes, the more impossible is it to conceive the details of such prehistoric systems ; one is led, not to isolated beliefs or rites, or to isolated individuals, but rather to social *systems*, inconceivably rudimentary, but of a sort that could evolve ultimately into religion as we know it. Miscellaneous data, such as are still found among many rudimentary peoples (Andamanese, Veddahs, etc.), have of course their value ; but, for the systematic treatment of the religious data, the social-religious systems are the more important, even though, as in the case of the totemic systems of Central Australia, they have a history behind them and are no longer in their " original " shape.[1]

P. 270 and n. 2.—SALT is both destructive and life-giving, apotropaic and preservative. Ashurbanipal (Annals, vi. 79) scattered salt over the cities he had laid waste, and salt on the ground is a bad omen

---

[1] The more clearly the significance of collective religious rites for the social cohesion of primitive peoples is recognized (as by Malinowski, 64 *sq.*), the more necessary becomes the inquiry into the processes whereby periods of disintegration were succeeded by some new reconstruction.

(Jastrow, *Rel. Bab. u. Ass.* ii. 716). In Bab. ritual as in the Israelite it was strewn upon the sacrificial flesh (Ezek. xliii. 24 ; *KAT.* 598) ; and salt was among the things taboo to the Babylonian king on certain days of the month : viz. 7, 14, 21, 28, and (reckoned from the previous month) 49 (A. Jeremias, *Geisteskultur,* 170). Salt is impregnating (Eitrem, 329), and a symbol of life ; cf. Homer's " divine salt." It is still used in covenants (Landberg, *Dialectes,* ii. 303 *sqq.* ; *Arab.* v. 157 *sq.*), perhaps on account of its preservative virtues. It is rubbed into the new-born child (cf. Döller, 31 *sq.*, 282), and in Palestine is offered to the dead, or to a holy saint to enlist his favour (*JPOS.* v. 196). See W. R. S., *Ency. Brit.* s.v. " Salt " ; also W. R. S. and A. R. S. Kennedy, *E.Bi.* s.v. ; Eitrem, 309 *sqq.*

P. 274. BOND OF MILK.—On the validity of the bond of milk among the Bantu tribes, see Seligman, *JRAI.* xliii. 657. Such a bond unites ; but it can also make marriage impossible. A man will suck the milk of the woman who adopts him (*Rev. des l'Hist. des Rel.* liv. [1906], 391) ; but among the A-kamba, a Bantu tribe, there is " a special curse used for a bad wife. The husband draws a little milk from her breasts into his hand, and then licks it up; this is a curse which has no palliative; after it the husband can never again cohabit with the woman " (Seligman, citing Hobley, *The A-Kamba,* 105). Similarly, a boy and a girl who have been suckled together may not marry (*Kinship,* 196 n. 1). So also in the case of blood, a Palestinian woman will contrive that her indifferent husband drinks in his liquid a few drops of her blood in the belief that this will knit him more strongly to her (*JPOS.* vi. 49). On the other hand, in the Irish Saga of the wooing of Emer, when Cúchulainn wounded his love Dervorgil and sucked the wound, he was unable to marry her because he had tasted of her blood.[1] Cf. p. 506 n. 1.

P. 274 n. 1.—See *Kinship,* p. 39 and n. Among the Kabābīsh *laḥma* expresses a uterine relationship ; a man says, " I am the *laḥma* of such and such a tribe," naming his mother's (Seligman, *Harvard Studies,* 114).

P. 279.—" In India it is not the rule for Moslem men and women to eat separately ; as far as my observation goes, it is the universal rule in Syria " (A. S. Tritton ; private communication). Crawley (*Mystic Rose,* ch. vii. ; cf. 376 *sq.*, 379 *sq.*), discussing commensal relations, argues that the custom of not eating together is common even between brothers and sisters, and is due to a taboo between the sexes.

---

[1] A man who has drunk of the blood of another tribe is bound to support it against his own totem or kin group (Spencer and Gillen, *Native Tribes of Central Australia,* 461).

P. 290 n. 2.—Besides Prof. J. B. Bury's suggested connexion between Hecate and the dog (for which see Preller-Robert[4], i. 326 and n. 1), cf. that of Dr. H. R. Hall, *CAH*. iii. 309, deriving it from the Egyptian *ḥike'*, " magic " (on which term, see p. 551 n.).

P. 292 n. 1.—The cylinder (also in Lajard, *Culte de Mithra*, pl. xxix, no. 5) is explained by Hoffner (*Gaz. Arch.*, l.c.) as the representation of a god of the Heracles-Sandon type.

P. 292 n. 2.—To כלבא correspond the Tyrian χέλβης (Josephus, *contra Apion*. i. 21 [157]) and conceivably χάλβης, the herald slain by Heracles in Egypt (Apollodor. ii. 5, 11); see Lidzbarski, *Ephem*. ii. 10 and n. 1. With כלבאלם (so read) may be compared the New Bab. names Kalab-Ba'u, etc. (*PSBA*. xxi. 133; *E.Bi.* " Caleb," § 1), where the meaning may be " priest or servant " ; cf. in the Amarna Letters, *e.g.* 60₇, *kalbu sha bītishu*, " the (king's) house-dog," *CAH*. ii. 322 ; see also Lagrange, 221 n. 1; Hommel, *Ethnol.* 91 and n. 2.

P. 295. COMMENSALITY AND SACRAMENTAL MEALS.[1]—The difference between (*a*) eating in the presence of a god, (*b*) eating together with him (p. 270), and (*c*) eating the god himself, naturally affects the development of ideas (in myth, theology, philosophy, etc.) which can ensue in each case. But it is not always easy to draw a distinction. In meals for the dead, the dead are commonly supposed to join; and in those before the god, gods and men commonly participate.[2] At a modern Palestinian festival in fulfilment of a vow a prayer will be offered on behalf of the soul of the *weli*, the sacrifice is for him, and the saint is the host, dispensing hospitality ; the participants are his guests, and all passers-by may join in. To him belongs the " soul " of the food—a widespread belief when food is offered to supernatural beings.[3] In Deut. xii. 7, etc., the meal is in Yahweh's presence (cf. Driver on Ex. xviii. 12), and there is similar cautious wording in Ex. xxiv. 10 *sq.* (carried further in the LXX) ; but the prophets preserve the belief that Yahweh prepares his feast, issues his invitations, and sends the cup round among the guests (Isa. xxv. 6 ; Zeph. i. 7 ;

[1] Cf. A. Thomsen, *Archiv f. Rel.*, 1909, pp. 464 *sqq.*, 471 *sq.* A. A. Sykes, in his essay on the *Nature, Design, and Origin of Sacrifices* (1748), 59 *sqq.*, already observes that the common meal is a covenant, and that sacrifice is a friendship entered into and renewed with a god. He compares the alliance in *Æneid*, viii. 275 (" communemque vocate Deum," *i.e.* the god common to the two parties). Cf. below, pp. 665 *sqq.*

[2] Eitrem, 475 *sq.* ; W. Warde Fowler, *Rel. Experience of the Roman People*, 193 (and Index, *s.v.* " Meals " [sacrificial]).

[3] *JPOS*. vi. 43, 44 *sq.*, 61 *sq.*, 73 and n. 1. Where the food is definitely made over to the gods it may be admittedly used by the priests or distributed among the poor ; the story of Bel and the Dragon is ignorant of this.

Jer. xxv. 15 *sqq.*). Similarly, Paul in 1 Cor. x. 18 *sqq.* interprets the sacred meal as communion with the altar, *i.e.* the Deity.[1]

The common meal unites men as kin, or it strengthens or renews an existing union. The food may be " sanctified " for the occasion, like the guests ; or it is already " sacred." The divinity of life-giving food is well attested. The Babylonian Nisaba is both corn and a goddess ; Tammuz (later Ta-uz), like Adonis, was the divine corn in the same way that Ceres and Bacchus were corn and wine, and more than a common figure of speech.[2] In an Egyptian hymn to Osiris the god is invoked : " Thou art father and mother of men, they live by thy breath, they (eat) the flesh of thy body, thy name is Primeval God . . . thou breathest out breath into men's nostrils " (Erman, *Ægypt. Zeit.* xxxviii. 33). Here Osiris is more than a corn-god (for which see *GB.* vi. 89 *sqq.*) ; he is the life of the earth in which he is embedded, his sweat is the water, his breath the air. How readily ideas of divine food and fruit, or of a divine being immanent in the sustenance of life, transfer themselves can be seen when the African Manichee Faustus " claims that he and his held the true Christian doctrine, and that the suffering Jesus is not a Divine Man born from a human mother and the Holy Spirit, but the fruit which is man's food ' hanging on every tree, produced by the energy and power of the air that makes the earth conceive . . . wherefore our reverence for everything is like that of you Catholic Christians about the Bread and the Cup.' "[3] Such a conception finds a parallel in the pantheistic Logion, " Jesus saith, . . . raise the stone and there thou shalt find Me, cleave the wood and there am I," and more especially in a modern Greek (Eubœan) conviction during Holy Week that unless Christ rose there would be no corn that year.[4]

For the sacramental eating of firstfruits and of sacred food, Frazer has collected some evidence (*GB.* viii. 48 *sqq.* ; cf. 86 *sqq.*, 138 *sq.*), the most significant being the cases where the identity of the food with a god is explicit, as in the Aztec ceremony, the resemblance of which to the Christian Eucharist so impressed the early Spanish

[1] Cf. Gressmann, *Ursprung d. israel.-jüd. Eschatologie*, 129 *sqq.*, 136 *sqq.* ; *ZNTW.* xx. 224, 227, 230.

[2] *GB.* viii. 167 ; Lagrange, 240 n. 3 ; and Jastrow, *Rel. B. A.* ii. 670 ; Baudissin, 114, and Index, *s.v.* Tammuz ; for Adonis, see *ib.* 161 *sq.* (cf. Frazer, *GB.* v. 229 *sq.*). See above, p. 578, on *Ṣ-d* and *Dagan.*

[3] F. C. Burkitt, *The Religion of the Manichees* (Cambridge, 1925), 41 *sq.*, citing Augustine, *c. Faust.* xx. 2 (Jesus as a power of vegetation and the Divine Being in the Sun) ; cf. S. A. Cook, *Journ. of Theol. Stud.* xxvi. 387 *sq.*

[4] Lawson, *Modern Greek Folklore*, 573. Cf. an article on " Easter in Italy," *The Observer*, April 17, 1927 (association of the awakening of Nature with the Passion).

missionaries.[1] Examples of the ceremonial or sacramental eating of the totem are few : (1) the " leech " and " jute " folk of Assam must chew a bit of the totem (*Tot. Ex.* iv. 298, 319). (2) On certain occasions the totem is eaten in Southern Nigeria (*ib.* ii. 589 *sq.*). (3) Among the Zuni the turtle-ancestor is ceremonially killed, but it is not clear that it is a totem or eaten by the people (*ib.* i. 44 *sq.*, iv. 232). (4) A Bechuana tribe ceremonially kill the porcupine, whose flesh is supposed to have strengthening properties, but it is not eaten (*GB.* viii. 165). On the other hand, (5) the Central Australian evidence strikingly confirms W. R. S.'s totem sacrament theory ; although to Frazer and others (*Tot. Ex.* iv. 230 *sq.*) the discoveries of Spencer and Gillen have only added fresh difficulties (see above, pp. 535 n. 2, 586). Thus it is objected that, (*a*) instead of a religious rite, the Australian cere-monies are " magical "—in order to provide a plentiful supply of food ; (*b*) the animal is not regarded as divine ; (*c*) other clans can kill and eat it ; and (*d*) it would seem that the totem-clan itself once partook of it freely.

In reply to such objections it is obvious, in the first place, that whether the totem rites are magical or religious depends upon pre-liminary definitions of the terms. Sir Baldwin Spencer originally spoke of them as religious, though later he acquiesced in Sir James Frazer's view (*Tot. Ex.* i. 114 *sq.*). Marett (*Psychology and Folklore,* 196 *sqq.*), Durkheim (339 *sq.*), and Jevons (*Introd. to Comp. Rel.* 203 *sq.*) are among those who dissent from the label " magical." " Magico-religious " they may be styled, if necessary, in view of their significance for the group and the solemnity with which they are undertaken. Nor must it be overlooked (1) that the totem is sacred in a way that the members of the clan normally are not—except during the " sacred " ceremonies ; that (2) in more advanced stages of development gods are often far from being supreme beings far exalted above men (p. 563 *sq.*) ; and (3) that practical and utilitarian elements run through all religions. If the totem rites are to be styled " magical " or are examples of " departmental magic " (cf. Malinowski [ed. Needham], 45), one must not overlook the remarkable extent to which it has been believed that sacred rites affect not merely the relations between a group and its god, but even the world in which the group finds itself.[2]

The Australian totem sacrament cannot be severed from the

---

[1] Brinton, *Rel. of Primitive Peoples,* 189 *sq.* ; Frazer, *GB.* viii. 88 *sqq.* ; cf. above, p. 225 n. 3 (end).

[2] In reference to objections (*c*) and (*d*), it is not necessary to require that the totem of one clan should be taboo to other clans, or that the particular rites should always have been in vogue. If the totem was once freely eaten, the change is

beliefs elsewhere in the almost cosmic efficacy of sacrifice and sacramental meals. On the Brahman theory of the daily sacrifice, see *GB*. ix. 410 *sq*. (cf. i. 228 *sq*.), Eggeling (*Ency. Brit.* iv. 380*d*), and the monograph of Hubert and Mauss on Sacrifice (with special reference to ancient Indian and Jewish theory). The particular efficacy of a sacred meal is curiously seen in Manicheeism, where the elements of Light and Life, which are commingled with the dark and earthy, are one day to be separated. The Elect Manichee will not himself prepare food lest he injure the life contained in the grain, and " a sacramental, indeed an actual physical, benefit accrued to the Universe through his eating it." [1] The sacred " life " was to be found in high degree in the righteous, and by his taking into himself the " Light " that was in the food, there was, so to say, a cosmical effect, so much so that " the Manichees believed that even a couple of the highest class of Initiates would suffice for what the world needed." When such conceptions could prevail in a religion which, though not a social-religious cult, spread widely and was of some influence in the course of its career, other variations of the fundamental belief in the effect of sacred meals and ceremonies upon the cosmos, or some department of it, can be well understood. It became necessary, on the one hand, to safeguard their interpretation and significance and, on the other, to restrict participation in them. So, the most sacred and most important occasions become reserved for the professional sacred caste, or there are periodical mystical sacrifices in which only the members of exclusive guilds were brought near to the heart of things. [2]

It is not necessary to regard totemism as the " origin " of the beliefs and practices which are found elsewhere. Eating " sacred " food or the " divine " essence in food is an intense form of communion [3]; but not only is it a way of acquiring certain benefits, a sort of quasi-magical effect is, as we have seen, often produced, even as in another more elemental and intense form of communion, objective effects are sometimes anticipated (pp. 612 *sqq.*). Certain fundamental ideas

analogous to that from endogamy (marriage within the group) to exogamy ; cf. further below, p. 629.

[1] Burkitt, *op. cit.* 47. The Elect disclaims all responsibility for the destructive processes which turn the growing grain into bread (45) ; cf. the attitude to the killing of animals (p. 602).

[2] Cf. W. Warde Fowler, *op. cit.* 173, on a tendency of the early Roman priesthood to discourage participation in certain sacred rites.

[3] Cf. Chrysostom, *Hom. in Joann.* " He (Christ) hath given those who desire Him . . . to eat Him and fix their teeth in His flesh, and to embrace Him and satisfy all their love." As regards the relation between the Eucharist and the Mysteries, etc., the occurrence of a number of interrelated conceptions, ranging from the crude and sensual (cf., *inter alia*, the Odes of Solomon) to the most refined

can be traced throughout ; and a distinction can be drawn between the part they play in the social and moral development of the group and their place in the growth of man's knowledge of his ability to control his environment. That the totem ceremonies have a moral and biological value can be shown (see Malinowski, 46); and when the height of spiritual religion is reached in the doctrine of the " righteousness " which the God of the Universe requires of men, there are implicit therein ideas of the interrelations of social, moral, and cosmic order, the humblest and rudest beginnings of which can be recognized in the religious and magico-religious rites of primitive peoples. See p. 670 *sq.*

P. 296. SANCTITY OF DOMESTIC ANIMALS.—A possible trace of extreme respect can perhaps be found in Assyrian (R. Campbell Thompson, *Semitic Magic,* 210 n. 1). Reluctance to kill neat cattle except on special occasions has been observed in Arabia (Kremer, *Studien,* ii. 86 *sq.*), and cattle-killers was a term of reproach for the men of Jōbar (Wetzstein, *ZDMG.* xi. 488). In Phrygia it was a capital offence to kill a plough-ox (A. B. Cook, *Zeus,* i. 469). On the ox as a kinsman—in Hesiod—cf. Gilbert Murray, *Rise of Epic in Greece,* 62 (1907). In India the cow is regarded as the abode of all deities and sages, as sacred as the earth itself, and giver of all things necessary for man's sustenance (Enthoven, *Folk-lore of Bombay,* 213). Various forms and traces of cow-cult are found in Africa.[1] The case of the Todas (p. 299) is especially important, since, according to W. H. Rivers (*The Todas,* 1906), the dairy ritual is a secondary phase, the older religion has atrophied, and even the ritual itself has become degenerate. The old gods are remembered chiefly for their part in the dairy cult, and the practical religion has its centre in the practical interests of food and means of livelihood (see I. King, *Devel. of Rel.* 117–24, 236 *sq.*). As is the general rule, the effective religion is concerned with the essentials of life, in particular with the uncertainties of the food supply—unless, of course, life is easy; and conversely, where the religion becomes indifferent to the practical, social, and economic problems, the latter tend to become the centre of ideas which have a quasi-religious importance for those concerned. Cf. the problem (*a*) of the local Baalim, givers of food, and the national Yahweh, and (*b*) that of saints and *welis* and the Allah of Islam.[2]

and spiritual, finds a very significant analogy in the coexistence of diverse theriomorphic and anthropomorphic tendencies a few centuries earlier ; see p. 629.

[1] See J. Roscoe, *The Northern Bantu,* 10 *sqq.* (the royal cows of the Banyoro tribe); Frazer, *GB.* iii. 247, viii. 35, 37 *sqq.*; Seligman, *JRAI.* xliii. 654 *sqq.* Cf. below, p. 602, and the references by G. W. Murray, *Journ. of Eg. Arch.* xii. 249, to the veneration of the cow and the (grammatical) treatment of the cow as a person among the Beja.

[2] On the economic aspect of religion, see Malinowski, in the *Festskrift* to

On the possibility that totemism may have led to the domestication of animals and plants, see Frazer, *Tot. Ex.* iv. 20 n. 1, who refers to Jevons, *Introd. to Hist. of Rel.* 113 *sqq.*, 210 *sqq.*, and S. Reinach, *Cultes*, i. 86 *sqq.* It is quite possible that the " magical " control of part of nature was a step in social and intellectual progress (Frazer, *l.c.*, cf. *GB.* i. 245 *sq.*), and W. R. S. himself insists that an attitude, not of fear, but of confidence and *rapport*, was indispensable before man could have taken any upward step (see p. 137). A sympathetic *rapport* is, on psychological grounds, essential for any real knowledge of a process which it is desired to understand,[1] and this is precisely what happens when a close, intimate relationship is felt, or is believed to exist, between the one who exercises control over some part of nature and that which is controlled. See pp. 586, 658, 671.

P. 300. THE GOLDEN AGE (cf. pp. 303, 307).—According to the Gilgamesh epic, Engidu, the wild man, lived in the most intimate converse with the animals ; only after he had mated with one of Ishtar's maidens does enmity begin, and the beasts whom he was wont to save from the hunters now flee from his presence (*CAH.* iii. 228).[2] Old Jewish belief told of the age when man and beasts spoke a common language (Charles, on *Jubilees*, iii. 28). The conception of a Golden Age is that of a sympathy with the lower animals and the conviction that the world has passed from good to worse, with, in the Messianic ideas, the hope of the return of the primitive harmony (Skinner, *Genesis*, 35). Prometheus, who destroyed the Golden Age, was also the first to kill an ox (p. 307 n. 5 ; Roscher, *Lex.* iii. 3055) ; and sacrifice was inaugurated by him as also by the Indian fire-god Agni. The Phœnician myth of a deluge followed by sacrifice seems to be an echo of the post-exilic narrative in Gen. ix., the anointing of sacred stelæ with the blood of beasts corresponding to the legalizing of the slaughter of animals by the ceremonial restoration of the blood (Gen. ix. 4 ; see Lagrange, 417 ; Skinner, 159, 169).

P. 306. THE " MURDER " OF ANIMALS.—For parallels to the Buphonia, see Frazer, *Paus.* ii. 303, *GB.* viii. 5 *sqq.*, and the references in Stübe, 233 n., 501; on the mimic "resurrection," cf. Jane Harrison, *Themis*, 143, 182, who connects it with a rain-charm. For the rite at Tenedos (p. 305 and n. 3), see A. B. Cook, *Zeus*, i. 659, 711. In

Ed. Westermarck (Helsingfors, 1912), 81 *sqq.*, and I. King, *op. cit.*, Index, *s.v.* Food.

[1] Cf. C. Lloyd Morgan, *Instinct and Experience* (1912), 236 *sq.* (One must know " as it were from within," one must " *be* in some measure the object of close attention," etc.)

[2] See C. A. Williams, *Legend of the Hairy Anchorite* (Univ. of Illinois, 1925).

consequence of the sanctity of blood, various measures are as a rule taken to avoid responsibility for shedding blood, whether human or animal.[1] (1) Special care will be taken that blood does not fall upon the ground (pp. 369 n. 1, 417 n. 5).[2] (2) Effusion of blood will be avoided by stoning, forcing a man to leap from a height, pouring lead down his throat, starvation, suffocation, etc.[3] (3) Frequently hunters propitiate the animal they propose to kill and eat, or its death is bewailed ; so that in various ways the victim is pacified, appeased, and the risk of vengeance averted (*GB.* viii. ch. xiv.). Or (4) responsibility is shared by the whole community (cf. p. 417 and n. 1). Again (5) the animal procures its own death.[4] Or (6) the victim presents itself as a stranger.[5] (7) The victim is both conscious and willing : before the Khonds of Bengal sacrifice a human victim for the crops they stupefy him with opium or otherwise ensure that he shall not resist and appear unwilling (*GB.* vii. 247). Finally, (8) the task of shedding the blood is entrusted to another: the Shawiya-Berbers will call in a neighbour to kill an ox or a cow (*Folk-lore*, xxxiii. 193), and the Elect Manichee, in whom is the Light element that is also to be found in bread, will neither take nor break it; his food is prepared by a disciple (on whose behalf he prays), and he prays to the bread solemnly, " I neither reaped thee, nor winnowed thee, nor set thee in an oven" (Burkitt, *Rel. of the Manichees*, 23, 45)—vegetable life has also a soul (*e.g.* rice ; *GB.* vii. 189).

P. 310 and notes 1–3.—On Zeus Asterius, see Farnell, *Cults of the Greek States*, i. 44 ; A. B. Cook, *Zeus*, i. 545 *sq.* For Kuenen's paper (n. 3), see *Gesammelte Abhandlungen*, ed. Budde, 207. On the site of Ashteroth Karnaim, see Sir G. A. Smith, *E.Bi.* s.v. The double

---

[1] So even in the case of criminals, though here it may be lest their blood stain the earth ; see Kreglinger, *Études sur l'origine et le devel. de la vie relig.* i. 74.

[2] When a priest was officiating at the Holy Communion at the Church of St. George (el-Hadr), between Beit Jālā and the Pools of Solomon, he spilt some of the sacred wine on his foot, thereby wounding it. For his carelessness in handling the Saviour's Blood his wound never healed up and he died, and the stone on which it fell acquired wonderful healing properties, and by supernatural means repulsed every effort to carry it off (Canaan, *JPOS.* iv. 79 *sq.*, citing Hanauer, *Folk-lore*, 59).

[3] *GB.* iii. 243 *sq.* ; see also above, pp. 343 n. 3 (on the *Ainos*, cf. *GB.* viii. 183 *sq.*), 374 *sq.* (cf. 417 n. 5), 419, 431, and see Saalschütz, *Mosaisch. Recht*, 457 n., 580.

[4] See p. 309 n. 1, and the refs. in Stübe, 234 n. 505 ; cf. Wellhausen, *Muh. i. Med.* ; a willing victim (16) procures its own death (160). The victim comes unsought (above, p. 309 n. 1), and in Palestine a flock of sheep will be driven past the shrine, and the one that enters " has chosen it " (*JPOS.* vi. 34 ; a Sinaitic parallel, *ib.* 66).

[5] Cf. Gen. xxii. 13 *sq.*, and the story of Lityerses (*GB.* vii. 217 ; see *ib.* 225 on strangers, and below, p. 616 n. 4).

peaks have suggested to Schumacher and to G. F. Moore (*Journ. of Bib. Lit.* xvi. 155 *sqq.*) a simpler explanation, so perhaps already the Talmud. For the Punic Saturnus Balcaranensis (*c.* second century A.D.), see Toutain, *Mélanges,* l.c. (n. 3 end), and note that Saturn nowhere has horns; see also *Zeus,* ii. 554 *sq.* The " Ashtaroth of the sheep " (cf. p. 477) is unique. Ishtar as mother-goddess was symbol of creation, protector of flocks, patroness of birth; and *Ishtarāti* means " goddesses." Cf. " Hathors " as a title of goddesses of birth (Rameses II.; Breasted, *Anc. Rec.* iii. § 400 and n. *b*), also ἡ τῶν θεῶν Ἀρποκράτις (*deliciæ deorum*), Pap. Oxyr. xi. 1380 (see Norden, *Geburt d. Kindes,* 112 n. 2); and the Juno as the female counterpart of the Roman masculine Genius. The term may be a stereotyped and perhaps an original cult term for the young or for the dam (cf. Meyer, *Gesch. Alt.* i. § 346 n.).[1]

P. 311 n. 1.—See *Kinship,* 254, where W. R. S. remarks that " the most ancient division of the Israelites is between Rachel and Leah, both of whom are animal names—' ewe ' and ' bovine antelope,' " and that among the nomadic population of South Palestine, ultimately incorporated with Judah, the most important is Caleb the dog-tribe. On Leah, see also *ib.* 227 and n. 2. Meyer (*Israeliten,* 426 and n. 3) explains Leah as " serpent " (comparing Leviathan), pointing out that " Leah, like Rachel, is an ancient *numen* in animal shape." The question is complicated by the suggested connexion between Leah and Levi (*Kinship,* 34 n., 227), and between Levi and the Minæan priestly title *lawi'a(t),* on which see Gray, 243 *sqq.*

P. 315.—Classical parallels are cited by Meyer, *Israeliten,* 556 n. 1; Eitrem, 422 *sq.*

P. 316. OROTAL(T).—On Dionysus (Herod. iii. 8), *i.e.* Dusares, see Clermont-Ganneau, *Rec. d'Archéol. Orient.* v. 114. The derivation is quite uncertain: (*a*) οβοταλτ, *i.e.* עבדאלת (" servant of Allat "; Cumont, *Rev. Archéol.* 1902, p. 297 *sq.*);[2] (*b*) οροταν, *i.e.* Ruḍa (Wellh. 58 *sq.*), " favour, grace " (see Lidzb. *Ephem.* iii. 90 *sqq.*); the more Aramaic form of which is found in the Nabatæan god אערא (ααρρα), see Cooke, 239, though Lidzbarski (*Ephem.* ii. 262) would derive the latter from غَذِ, pointing out that " luxuriant " is an appropriate name for a god of fruitfulness. From a shrine (מסגדא) set up to

---

[1] How a proper name can become a common noun is illustrated in the use of " Mary " in pidgin-English for the female sex: women, girls, and dogs (C. W. Collinson, *Life and Laughter 'midst the Cannibals in South Sea Islands,* 86).

[2] Burrows, *JSOR.* xi. 77, suggests Obodat, and, explaining the name to mean " husbandman," notes that in an Assyrian list of gods (*ZA.* xxx. 284 *sqq.*), Du-shar-ra (*i.e.* Dusares) is called *uru-a* (=*erish*), which has the same meaning, and that Dusares=Orotal (Obodat).

Dusares—אערא—on the first of Nisan (see the Nab. inscr., Lidzb. *Ephem.* ii. 262), it is argued by Hommel (*Vogüé Florileg.* 300) that he was a god of light of the Marduk type. He, however, explains אערא to mean "having a white spot," while Littmann (*ib.* 385) compares the stone-block *ghariy* (cf. above, pp. 201, 210). (c) Meyer (*Israel.* 101 n. 3) rather favours the old view of Blau (*ZDMG.* xviii. 620 *sqq.*), that Orotal conceals the name of the tribe of the Garinda (Gharandel) north of Sinai and of Petra ; it was the name (according to Arab legend) of an idol ; see Hommel, *Ethnol.* 627 n. 3.

P. 321. REUNION OF GODS AND MEN.—Here the main argument, which is of the first importance, is suspended, to be resumed on p. 336. When, owing to disaster, defeat, etc., the group-unity of gods and men is broken, whatever brings the conviction of forgiveness brings the sense of a new unity. There may not be any intense experience of some immediate " communion " with the deity, but the restoration of the unity is fundamental in religion, and the actual vicissitudes of the history of religions imply that the bond between the worshippers and their gods, constantly weakened or broken, is constantly being renewed. The fundamental idea, as it occurs in Judaism, is thus stated by Abelson, *Immanence of God in Rabbinical Literature*, 140 : " Repentance is almost a synonym for Shechinah. It is a divine indwelling."

P. 321 and n. 4.—On the commemoration of Hasan and Hosain, see Eerdmans, *Zeit. f. Assyr.* ix. 280 *sqq.* ; Goldziher, *Moh. Stud.* ii. 331 ; Baudissin, 131 *sq.* ; Streck, *Sachau-Festschrift*, 393 *sqq.* ; all of whom find survivals of pre-Islamic beliefs.

P. 321 and n. 5.—From the Arabic *kasafa*, " cut," *kisf*, " piece, fragment," etc., W. R. S. conjectures that the Hebrew *kĕshāphīm* means herbs or drugs shredded into a magic brew. For Fleischer's derivation from *kasafa*, " to obscure," see Witton Davies, *E.Bi.* col. 2900(2). An exact analogy to the former etymology is התפלל, " pray," which Wellhausen (126 n. 5) explains from the Arabic *falla*, " to rend," *fall*, " the notch end of a sword " (*E.Bi.* " Prayer," § 1 ; cf. " Cuttings," § 1). That more physical meanings lie beneath the religious terms is seen further in עתר (העתיר), " make supplication," and Arabic *'atara*, "sacrifice" (Wellh. *loc. cit.*), and possibly in the Hebrew צלה, " roast flesh," Aram. " pray " (so Haupt, *Journ. of Bibl. Lit.* 1900, p. 78, but see the Oxford Heb. Lexicon). Praying is bound up with incense offering (see Eitrem, 229 *sq.*), and prayer and sacrifice are interwoven in early Christian thought (Gray, *Sacrifice*, 173). Between praying for a thing and appropriate sacrificial ritual (whether mimetic, as often in " magico-religious " rites, or other) there is no great gulf; see F. B. Jevons, *Introd. to the Study of Comp. Rel.* 176 *sqq.* (New York, 1908).

P. 323. MOURNING RITES.—Often, of course, these may be " merely ex ιggerated forms of the same emotional outbursts which lead nervous temperaments everywhere to wring the hands and tear the hair in moments of violent grief " (Brinton, *Religions of Primitive Peoples*, 213). Fear of the dead is regarded by Frazer as " a bulwark of morality and a bond of society," softening and humanizing manners (*Belief in Immortality*, i. 175, 392 ; cf. ii. 300) ; " the fear of the spirits of the dead has been one of the most powerful factors—perhaps, indeed, the most powerful of all—in shaping the course of religious evolution at every stage of social development from the lowest to the highest " (*GB.* viii. 36 *sq.*).[1] But W. R. S. disputes the significance of fear (pp. 322 n. 3, 336 n. 2, 370 n. 1) ; and Malinowski (ed. Needham, 47 *sqq.*), in a critical estimate of the psychological aspects of death, argues that in the mourning ceremonies " religion counteracts the centrifugal forces of fear, dismay, demoralization, and provides the most powerful means of reintegration of the group's shaken solidarity, and of the re-establishment of its morale."

When the Arab erects a tent on the grave of a venerated person and remains there, or the dead are buried in the house or near at hand, or there is resort to the dead and appeal to the ancestors, or there are periodic festivals of the dead (*GB.* vi. 51 *sqq.*, ix. 150 *sqq.*), fear is not the dominant element even though there be awe or respect. And where group or collective responsibility prevails, the living and the dead are virtually parts of one body. On the other hand, in the history of Israel individual responsibility and the denunciation of earlier mourning customs are among the marks of an age of social disintegration prior to the rise of a new reintegration.

In general, death arouses typical emotions which are variously directed by current usage. To-day the evil spirits, the cause of illness, surround the dead body and look for a living one in which to enter (*JPOS.* vi. 46), and the domestic rites are for the soul of the deceased (*ib.* 65). In one Bab. ritual, when a man is dying the room is swept, holy water sprinkled, lights are lit, a lamb is sacrificed, and ceremonies are performed for the family spirits (Morgenstern, 107 *sq.*). In Israel a man went to " his people " (Gen. xxv. 8). On the same principle the member of a totem-clan rejoins his ancestors at death, and sometimes will be buried in the skin of the totem-animal and marked with the clan mark (*Tot. Ex.* i. 35). Some deaths are specially grievous. In Assyria men and women who die prematurely cause harm unless they are laid to rest (R. C. Thompson, *Semitic Magic*, 17 *sqq.*).[2]

[1] Similarly, Marillier (*Rev. de l'histoire Rel.* xxxvi. 355), Wundt, and others.

[2] On the Bab. *eṭimmu*-demons, spirits of the dead, see A. Jeremias, *Handbuch d. altorient. Geisteskultur*, 318 *sqq.*

If the mourning is slight, the dead may be suspicious, and take vengeance ; hence the survivors will disclaim responsibility (above, p. 412), and otherwise mollify the dead. On the other hand, too much grief will disturb the dead.[1] In Central Australia, as Durkheim points out (391 *sqq.*), mourning is strictly regulated by etiquette ; it is a social and pious duty which forms a channel for the emotions, it assures the dead that he is not forgotten, establishes a new relation with the dead who is now a new kind of spirit, and strengthens the social unity which absence of mourning would weaken.[2]

On obligatory mourning (p. 430), see Wensinck in the *Sachau-Festschrift*, 26 *sqq.* ; and on the ὀλολυγή, in particular, see Eitrem, 461 *sq.*, and his *Beiträge*, iii. (1920), 44 *sqq.* ; also Jane Harrison, *Themis*, 160 (as an apotropaic lament).[3] As regards the blood-letting rites, Frazer (*FOT*. iii. 300) and Westermarck (*Morocco*, ii. 520) question whether they contain any idea of covenant ; the object is rather to benefit the dead, who are nourished by the blood (cf. Eitrem, 421). Blood contains, or rather blood *is* the life : Assyrian demons ceaselessly devour blood, and sacrificial slaughter—thought Origen— lures demons to the temples (R. C. Thompson, 195 *sq.*). But no single explanation of mourning rites need be sought. The evidence ranges from purely spontaneous emotion, with more or less vague ideas of death and the dead, to relatively coherent convictions of the efficacy of the rites ; and W. R. S.'s theory of the blood-covenant between living and dead gives a precision to the more elemental feelings in which the longing for continued relations does not necessarily come to the surface, but is justified by that unity of the living and dead members of a group which repeatedly expresses itself in many diverse ways.[4]

P. 325. HAIR-OFFERING.—Hair was shorn for rivers (Paus. viii. 41, 3 ; *GB.* i. 31), as a puberty rite (A. B. Cook, *Zeus*, i. 23 *sq.*), and as an offering for the dead (Frazer, *FOT*. iii. 274 ; Eitrem, 344 *sqq.*). It was cut for Osiris and other gods (Chwolson, ii. 307 *sq.*), *e.g.* for Heracles,

---

[1] See Hedwig Jahnow, *Das hebräische Leichenlied im Rahmen der Völkerdichtung* (Giessen, 1923), 48 n. 2 (with references).

[2] Cf. the elegant words of Tzŭ-yu (fourth–third century B.C.) : the ceremonial is a check upon undue emotion and a guarantee against any lack of proper respect —the due regulation of the emotions is the function of a set ceremonial (H. Giles, *Confucianism and its Rivals*, 116).

[3] On the " magic " of tears, cf. Canney, *Journ. of the Manchester Eg. and Or. Soc.*, 1926, p. 51.

[4] See, in general, Lagrange, 320 *sqq.*; Oesterley, *Immortality and the Unseen World* (1921), especially chs. ix.-xi. On laceration in particular, see *Kinship*, 77 n. 1 (3) ; Driver, *Deut.* 156 ; Frazer, *FOT*. iii. 270 *sqq.* ; Scheftelowitz, *Arch. f. Rel.* xix. 221 n. 2, 222 n. 4 ; Jahnow, *op. cit.* 4 *sqq.*, 12 *sqq.*, *et passim*.

the Tyrian Melkart, at Gades (Hölscher, *Profeten*, 144, citing Silius Italicus, iii. 21 *sqq.*).[1] Cut in honour of Orotal (Herod. iii. 8), this "imitation of the god" finds abundant parallels (masks, skins, etc., see p. 674 *sq.*), and the question why the god wore his hair in a particular way finds a parallel in the question why the gods limped (see p. 672). A man's hair contains his strength, vitality, or vital principle (*FOT*. ii. 484 *sqq.*), hence the various taboos (*GB*. iii. 258 *sqq.*). By means of it an enemy can injure a man by "magical" practices, and by retaining some of a man's hair one can ensure his remaining with one (*FOT*. iii. 254; cf. *GB*. xi. 103 *sq.*, 148; Cook, *Zeus*, i. 343 n. 4). Hence the sacrifice of one's hair is a very real one, no less than that demanded at Byblus (p. 329, see p. 616). While, on the one hand, among the Ewe the priest's hair must not be cut, because the god dwells in it (*FOT*. iii. 189); on the other, one can dedicate one's hair for a sacred person or purpose, in which case it is given to or saved for the god. It is preserved in order that the sacred power may occupy it; or it is renounced, virtually as a sacrifice of oneself.[2] The Nazarite's vow is a dedication of one's self; it being impossible, according to Philo, to pollute the altar with human blood (Gray, *Numbers*, 69).[3]

P. 327. FLAGELLATION AND INITIATION CEREMONIES.[4]—Herein are involved (1) the reluctance to admit a new comer into a privileged circle, (2) the desire to prove his worth, and (3) the psychology of ordeal, pain, and cruelty. Between initiation ceremonies and "hazing" there is ultimately no great gulf (Durkheim, 312 and n. 4). The trial, often a frightful one, is the characteristic feature; and the flagellation and other severities have been variously explained.[5] (1) They are to inspire awe, they are a test of a man's courage and fitness, or they are due to the genuine fear lest the youth should be effeminate (Crawley, *Mystic Rose*, 210 *sq.*). (2) When a special scourge or other instrument is used, it may be an actual transference—a "rubbing in"—of its sacred power. Thus among the Kamilaroi tribes the touch of the bull-roarer had fertilizing effects, the very sight of the

[1] On the shaven heads of Egyptians and Sumerians, see E. Meyer, *Gesch. d. Alt.* i. §§ 362, 368; and especially Gressmann, *Budde-Festschrift*, 61 *sqq.*

[2] Cf. *Qy. St.* 1893, p. 211 : a child whose hair is vowed is under the protection of the saint, and needs no amulet. When the hair is cut and sold the money is given to the poor; or it is for the *maḳām* (the shrine), and the family and relations eat together there.

[3] Eitrem (350 n. 2, 351 *sq.*) would treat hair-offerings as one of the many *rites de passage*.

[4] See Loisy, *Sacrifice*, ch. x.; Hocart, *Folk-lore*, xxxv. 308 *sqq.*

[5] Cf. Anton Thomsen, *Orthia* (Copenhagen, 1902); Miss Mudie Cooke, *Journ. of Roman Studies*, iii. (1913) 164 *sq.*; F. Schwenn, *Menschenopfer b. d. Griechen u. Römern*, 98 *sq.* (Giessen, 1915).

Dhurumbulum (? bull-roarer) imparted manly qualities (W. Ridley, *Kam. and other Australian Languages*, 140 *sq.*, 156). In the Sandwich Islands the newly installed king is struck in order to purify him (Crawley, 94). Nilsson (*Gr. Rel.* 94) holds that the power in the sacred bough passes over into the youth as truly as that of the " sowing cake " which was eaten ; it was fundamentally a sort of communion ; see also Reinach, *Cultes*, i. 173 *sqq.*, on the mystic virtues of the hazel rod. Psychologically, (3) the ordeal is a ritual purification, a *katharsis* ; suffering gives strength, sorrow has a sanctifying value. (4) More crudely, the belief runs that the *jinn* prefer stout and well-fed people, hence violent beating is necessary to drive out the demons (*JPOS.* v. 203). Psychologically again, (5) the ordeal from beginning to end serves to induce a unique state prior to the reception of the novice within the group. He is taught the customary morality of the tribe and learns the tribal legends.[1] He has been prepared for a new stage in life—a " renewal," according to the Kaffir term (Crawley, 271 *sq*). He has experienced the god's presence (Meek, ii. 88). Sometimes he is smeared with blood, or even fed with it (*Tot. Ex.* i. 42 *sq.*, 174). He has been introduced to the god (cf. Durkheim, 285) ; or there have been rites of death and rebirth, and he has died to live.[2] In Central Australia the boy pierces the veil ; he learns that the all-powerful being of the tribe is a " myth " ; he handles the bull-roarer and knows and sees the most sacred things (Spencer and Gillen, *Northern Tribes*, 491 *sqq.* ; cf. *Native Tribes*, 248). Similarly, in New Mexico the masked men who are representing the gods subsequently disclose their identity (Webster, *Primitive Secret Societies*, 187 *sqq.*). But the revelation of the mysteries does not necessarily destroy religious belief.[3]

P. 328. CIRCUMCISION.—For this practice (not found in Babylonia and Assyria) various reasons have been put forward (see Toy, §§ 153 *sqq.*) ; and it is necessary to distinguish afterthoughts from possible causes. If it were merely hygienic, it would be difficult to see why it was deferred until puberty—the supposition that hygienic reasons induced the alteration of date from puberty to infancy, like the idea of physical purification (Herodotus, ii. 37), is thought to imply more observation than is usually found. Phallicism (on which see p. 688)

---

[1] See Haddon on ethics among primitive peoples, *Expository Times*, June 1912 ; and on the general social value of initiation ceremonies, see Malinowski (ed. Needham) 38 *sqq.*, 60.

[2] Cf. *GB.* i. 76 n. 3 ; Hubert and Mauss, *Mélanges*, 131 *sq.*

[3] One may contrast the more psychological comments of Marett (*Threshold of Religion*, 157 *sqq.*, 164) upon the effect of the disclosures with those of Loisy (*Sacrifice*, 388 *sq.*).

is certainly an insufficient explanation. The same objection is urged against the later popular belief that it prepares for or facilitates sexual intercourse (Doughty, i. 341, 410; cf. Loisy, *Sacr.* 385). It does not necessarily entail very great suffering, though at times there are fearful ordeals, *e.g.* in Arabia among the Coraish and Hodhail.[1] It has been regarded as a dedication, the sacrifice of a part in order to ensure the safety of the whole (for such practices, cf. Crawley, *Mystic Rose*, 136, 300, 309); or it is supposed that by cutting off and preserving a part of oneself, one secures preservation after death, and reincarnation. The shedding of blood seems to be an essential part of the rite (cf. Lagrange, 243 *sq.*), and when, as in Australia, use is made of the skin and blood, or the blood is applied to others, ideas of covenant may perhaps be recognized.[2] So, among the Akikuyu circumcision is necessary before one can be a full member of the tribe and possess property; and the rite was at one time combined with a ceremony of rebirth (*FOT.* ii. 332 *sq.*). In Israel the metaphors of circumcision applied to heart, ear, and lips (Deut. x. 16, Jer. vi. 10, Ex. vi. 12) suggest that it meant allegiance, dedication, and an intimate relation with Yahweh, even as the rite itself was an initiation into the full tribal life.[3] The new prominence of circumcision in post-exilic Judaism, as a sign of the covenant relation (see Skinner, *Gen.* 297), coming as it does after the prophets' condemnation of ritual, will be due to the new social and religious equilibrium after the period of disintegration that had preceded. Cf. pp. 593, 664.

In the story of the Exodus the Israelites are circumcised before they keep the Passover, and eat of the produce of the land which they are about to conquer (Josh. v.; cf. Ex. xii. 43 *sq.*). Uncircumcised, they would be regarded as polluting Yahweh's land (on the analogy of Ezek. xliv. 7, 9). Both Circumcision and Passover mark new stages in the history of Israel, and they are associated in the very obscure story in Ex. iv. where Moses was attacked by Yahweh because the rite of circumcision had not been performed—on himself, or on his son (who is evidently the firstborn). The story is in a context where Israel is Yahweh's firstborn, and Pharaoh's firstborn is threatened with death (iv. 22 *sq.*). Ultimately Yahweh smites the firstborn of Egypt at the Passover, and " passes over " the houses smeared with blood

---

[1] W. R. S., *Lectures*, 577. Cf. We. [1]215, [2]174 *sqq.*; Landberg, *Dialectes*, i. 485–493, 1777 *sq.* For operations upon Arab women, see Seligman, *JRAI.* xliii. 642 *sqq.*; *Harvard Studies*, 149.

[2] H. P. Smith, *Journ. of Bibl. Lit.* xxv. (1906) 14; see Spencer and Gillen, *Native Tribes*, 250, 268 *sq.*, *Northern Tribes*, 334, 361, 372; Frazer, *GB.* i. 92 *sqq.*

[3] According to Westermarck (*Morocco*, ii. 433), circumcision is called " cleansing " (*ṭuhr*, etc.).

39

(Ex. xii.). When the Midianite wife of Moses circumcised her child, she touched his parts, presumably " to connect him with what she had done and to make her son's circumcision count as her husband's " (Driver, etc.). But it has also been suggested (Meyer, *Israel*. 59, Gressmann, *Mose*, 58) that Zipporah was supposed to touch this demon-like Yahweh who had sought Moses' life. Decision is difficult. Popular tradition may have retailed much that was primitive concerning Yahweh's marriage-relationship with his people, and in Gen. iv. 1, Eve " gets a man with Yahweh " (p. 513). With this archaic story may be connected the no less strange story of the wrestling at the Jabbok (Gen. xxxii. 24 *sqq.*), where the passage of Jacob (Israel) and his children over the Jordan is a parallel to the passage of the Children of Israel into Canaan (*CAH*. ii. 360), and the importance of the rite of circumcision is forthwith maintained at Shechem (Gen. xxxiv.). In his wrestling he (*i.e.* Jacob) was " touched " on the thigh, whence the " limping " (*vv.* 25^b, 31). But according to Hosea xii. 4 *sq.*, Jacob " prevailed " over his supernatural antagonist, and it has been conjectured that it was he who " struck the socket of his thigh," injuring his adversary (*v.* 25^a); see B. Luther, *ZATW*. xxi. 65 *sqq.*, and on the " limping " p. 671 *sq.* below.

P. 329 and n. 1. THE 'ACĪCA AND POLYANDRY.—C. and B. Seligman (*Harvard African Studies*, ii. 148) observe that among the Sudanese Kabābīsh the child's *'am* performed the ceremony of the *'icca* (as they heard the word). He and the mother eat separately, and he makes a present to the mother, which remains her own property. This, in their opinion, supports W. R. S.'s earlier view in *Kinship* (182) that it is a dissolving of the bond of kindred, and indicates a transition from matrilineal to patrilineal descent. According to Lane, the *'acīca* is a ransom, its blood (flesh, bone, skin, hair) being for his blood (flesh, bone, etc.); and in this respect it finds a parallel in the old Assyrian substitution ceremony for the sick—the head (neck, breast) for the head (neck, breast) of the man; see R. Campbell Thompson, *Semitic Magic*, 229; Gressmann, *Altorient. Texte z. A.T.*^{2}, 330.

The bearing of the *'acīca* ceremony upon polyandry is much more dubious since 1880–81, when W. R. S. (*Lectures*, 578), after M'Lennan, arranged exogamy, marriage by capture, female kinship, etc., in a line of development. Polyandry proves to be exceptional among simpler peoples.[1] It is confined to a few areas, or to more or less exceptional classes. The Levirate is not necessarily a survival of it, though there is " some reason to believe that among the Semites blood-brotherhood sometimes implied community of women," which, however, is not

---

[1] Hobhouse, Wheeler, and Ginsberg, *Material Culture and Social Institutions of the Simpler Peoples*, 163.

necessarily a relic of polyandry.[1] Strabo's story of the stick which a man left outside the woman's door as a signal for his brothers (*Kinship*, 158) is entirely in agreement with custom in South Malabar and elsewhere (Westermarck, 129, 138, where knives or weapons are left). The " absolute licence " that prevailed (*Kinship*, 206) is not necessarily a survival of earlier marriage customs or of promiscuity, and some (*e.g.* Nöldeke, *ZDMG*. xl. 155) would speak of it as looseness or " mere prostitution." In the South Arabian inscriptions there are cases where a man has two fathers,[2] while at the present day among the Shilluk a man has a qualified right of access to his brother's wife, and among the Bahima there are polyandrous practices among men too poor to get separate wives for themselves (as also in Arabia, see *Kinship*, 151 *sq.*). Hartmann (*Islam. Orient,* ii. 197 *sqq.*) is sceptical of the South Arabian evidence,[3] but C. and B. Seligman (*op. cit.* 141 n.) consider that the evidence for Arabian polyandry cannot be ignored, though it was local and occasional, and it is improbable that it was at all universal in Arabia.

P. 329. THE SACRIFICE OF CHASTITY.[4]—The compulsory sacrifice by virgins of either their hair or their chastity is, as Hartland has shown, not to be confused with ceremonial defloration, or with ceremonial prostitution, or licentious rites in connexion with a temple, or with prostitution as a recognized means of earning a dowry. This last is one of other indications of the slight value frequently attached to chastity before marriage, often to be followed by the strictest fidelity after marriage.[5] In fact, it sometimes happens that a girl who has been much sought after (and, among the Laplanders, especially by strangers) is the more highly esteemed. But money might be obtained in this way for a temple, and the *hieroi* or *hierodouloi* (see *ERE.* s.v.) dedicated to the temple were employed to work upon the temple-lands or in the manner indicated.[6] It is not clear whether the temple-harlots remained in the sacred precincts; in Gen. xxxviii.

---

[1] Westermarck, *History of Human Marriage* (1921), vol. iii. ch. xxix. *sq.*, and *ib.* pp. 208, 238.

[2] Cf. *Kinship*, 316; Landberg, *Arabica*, iv. (1897), 255 *sqq.*, *Dialectes*, ii. 367, 845 *sqq.*, 947 *sqq.*; Glaser and Weber, *MVAG*. 1923, ii. 41 *sqq.*

[3] Hartmann (ii. 200) would explain cases of the type, " X son of Y and Z," as Y the father and Z the uncle or some other near relative.

[4] See especially E. S. Hartland, in the *Tylor Essays* (1907), 189–222, reprinted in his *Ritual and Belief* (1914), 266 *sqq.*, also Frazer, *GB.* v. ch. iii. *sq.*; Meyer, *Gesch. Alt.* i. § 10 *sq.*; Farnell, *Greece and Babylon*, 269 *sqq.*; Crawley, *Mystic Rose*; Clemen in the *Baudissin-Festschrift*, 89 *sqq.*; Penzer, *Ocean of Story*, i. Appendix IV.; Briffault, *The Mothers* (1927), *passim*.

[5] On which cf. M. A. Potter, *Sohrab and Rustem*, 164 *sq.*, 167 *sqq.*

[6] Justin (xviii. 5) speaks of the virgins at Cyprus who were sent to the sea-shore

Tamar, the ḳedēshah, is in the street. Nor are the relevant Babylonian terms free from ambiguity : ḥarimtu, ḳadishtu, ishtaritu, though the first, unveiled and unmarried, is " of the street," and the second was a hierodule, veiled, and could nurse or adopt children.[1] At all events, as Jastrow suggests, the maidens of Ishtar (herself usually called by the second term) " may well be the prototypes of the houris with whom Mohammed peopled the paradise reserved for true believers " (Rel. Bel. 138).

The highly significant law in Deut. xxiii. 17 sq., forbidding the hire of a harlot (zonah) or a dog (kéleb) to be brought into the Temple, is to be supplemented by the prose appendix to the poem on Tyre (Isa. xxiii. 15 sqq.), where the city which once had commerce over the known world (cf. Ezek. xxvii.) becomes a forgotten harlot, subsequently to have fresh commerce with the kingdoms of the world, when her gains will be " sacred " to Yahweh and for the enrichment of his priestly people. The language, occurring as it does in a relatively late addition, is surprising ; but it testifies to a well-understood practice which may be interpreted possibly as prostitution on behalf of the funds of the temple, or as a reference to licentious rites at certain religious festivals perhaps due to certain ideas of the efficacy of intercourse with hierodules. Decision will often be difficult ; it must suffice to refer to the initial and concluding rites at Mecca (on which see Gaudefroy-Demombynes, 185 sq., 297 sq.. 306 sq.), the Pallades of Theban Ammon (GB. ii. 135), the " wives " of the Dahomey god (ii. 149), and the Tamil devadasis (v. 61).[2]

There is much miscellaneous evidence for the exchange of wives, among primitive peoples, as a means of welding together the group (Crawley, 248 sq., 479; Potter, 145 sqq.), also to avert some evil, ward off sickness, remove a threat, and more specifically to symbolize an entire change of circumstances and inaugurate a new life (Crawley, 280 sqq., 477 sq.). Licentious orgies thus served, on the one hand, to express the manifestation of group unity, the creation of feelings of absolute oneness, and a new strengthening of social ties ;[3] and, on the other, to annul existing conditions and initiate a new stage.[4] In Morocco maidens will be sent as a means of compelling a state of

to earn their dowry by prostitution, so as to pay a first-offering to Venus for their virtue henceforth—pro reliqua pudicitia libamenta Veneri soluturas (Farnell, 274).

[1] B. Brooks, AJSL. xxxix. 187 ; Jastrow, JAOS. xli. 36 n., 34 ; Campbell Thompson, CAH. i.² 538 sq.

[2] Tamar is spoken of as both ḳedēshah and " harlot " (Gen. xxxviii. 15). For references in the Minæan inscriptions to hierodules, see Hommel, Ethnol. 143, 603 sq., 683, and the translation in Gressmann, Altorient. Texte z. A.T.² 463 sq.

[3] Durkheim, 216 n., 383 nn. 1, 2 ; Malinowski (ed. Needham), 61.

[4] Hartland, Primitive Paternity, ii. 144 sqq., 150, 155, 175,

brotherhood with a family or tribe.[1] Through the woman a unity is established whether within the group itself or between two groups. Ideas of group-unity recur also in those endogamous communities where there is the closest intermarriage in order to preserve and strengthen all that which makes the group a single unit.   In certain cases all the male members of a group possess common rights over the women either of their group or of another clearly defined group ; thus when one of a Masai " age-grade " marries, the others may claim priority of intercourse.[2] The usage has been explained as a cere-monial access, a survival of original communal rights, or else as a removal of the dangers supposed to attend the first night of marriage (Crawley, 309, 349; see further below). But other ideas may have operated, enhancing the unity of the group of which she was a member.

The belief has prevailed that special benefits are to be derived from intercourse with " sacred " men ; e.g. with saints (Westermarck, *Morocco*, i. 198); while in childless families among the Karalits the *angekok* will be invited to sleep with the wife (Crawley, 350), and child-less women have ever continued to visit the shrines in the East.[3] Of another type is the statement that among the Takhtaji of the Adana district the " high priest " enters any house, and " the owner con-cedes to him during his stay all rights over property, children, and wives." [4] There are, broadly, two types of cases : in one the efficacy of sacred men (who are primarily in some way representatives of the supernatural powers) is pre-eminent; in the other, such individuals claim special rights which, in fact, are often quite freely granted to them. But ceremonial orgies, group-rights, and the efficacy of sacred men cannot be viewed apart from the utilitarian ideas that rule among primitive peoples as regards the fertility of nature. Sexual language and sympathetic ritual abound. A Sumerian liturgy invoking a flood of waters to bring rain is couched in the language of sexual inter-course (*JAOS*. xli. 143, 148). On beliefs and practices touching the sympathetic fertility of women and of nature, see Hartland, *Prim. Pat.* ii. 115 *sq.*, 151 *sq.*, 171 ; and on symbolic unions, *ib.* 210 *sq.*, 236 *sqq.*, and Frazer, *GB.* vii. 111.[5] Hence the many obscene agri-

---

[1] Westermarck, *Ritual and Belief in Morocco*, i. 529 *sq.*

[2] *Tot. Ex.* ii. 415 *sq.* ; Hartland, *Prim. Pat.* ii. 193 *sq.*, and *Prim. Law*, 64 ; Crawley, 348 *sq.*

[3] On all this as a story or *motif*, see Marmorstein, *Arch. f. Rel.* xxi. 502 *sqq.* ; and O. Weinreich, *Der Trug des Nektanebos* (Leipzig, 1911).

[4] See Sir William Ramsay (*The Expositor*, Nov. 1906, 466 *sqq.*), who observes that he is evidently the old priest king of primitive Anatolian religion, who " exer-cises in a vulgarized form the absolute authority of the god over all his people."

[5] See also *GB.* i. 140 *sqq.*, ii. 97, v. 67 (marriage of wives to an African serpent-god to make the crops sprout) ; cf. above, p. 515.

cultural rites, and the modern practice of the fellahin of Upper Egypt of placing in their vegetable patches figures (male, but more often male and female) emblematic of fertility. So, actual ceremonial licentious cults are practised to further the fertility of the soil (*GB.* v. 39 n. 3; Clemen, 95); it may be as part of the marriage of Sun-god and Mother-Earth (near North Guinea, *GB.* ii. 98 *sq.*), or for the general prosperity of the clan (*Tot. Ex.* ii. 602 *sq.*); cf. above, p. 514. And, whereas in departmental totemism certain clans have each a peculiar identity with a particular department of nature, here the ideas are vague and inchoate : man and nature are one, the group and its world form one unit, and the ideas of natural fertility and human welfare are not differentiated.

Yet, as has been seen, the ideas of sanctity and holiness can never be left out of the reckoning ; and ceremonial continence and chastity are no whit less conspicuous than sexual excess and orgy. "Contrary to what one would expect, in savagery sexual cults play an insignificant rôle" (Malinowski, 41). There is continence when warriors are at war (*GB.* iii. 164), on visiting a sanctuary, on trading-journeys, in times of crisis—in general there are " taboos " of this sort when the group is in a " sacred " state, or when supernatural help is required. There is abundant evidence for the belief in the superior efficacy of chaste and pure individuals as holders of " sacred " offices, or on occasions that are " sacred " from the group's point of view, *e.g.* when the cattle are at pasture among the Akamba and Akikuyu.[1] The devotee of the deity is chaste and devoted wholly to his (or her) service ; on the other hand, the " wife " of a god could be taken by those who served or represented the gods. It would be difficult to argue that ceremonial licentiousness was " earlier " than ceremonial chastity, or the reverse. The chaste individual was the abode of supernatural power, whereas the licentious rites could be regarded as an intensely emotional communion or identity of the individual with the supernatural power immanent in the group. While the licentious cults soon became more than obnoxious, the extremes of chastity have also tended to be anti-social; and between " ceremonial " and " magical " tendencies in each of these, progressive humanity has picked its way. It is a striking fact that, while the licentious cults were typically " magico-religious," viz. for the fertility of nature, chastity and continence were noticeably " taboos " on occasions when food-supply, success of expeditions, etc., were at stake ; and the former could not lead—as the latter actually did—to increased efficiency in the non-religious sphere.

[1] *FOT.* iii. 141 *sq.* See Fehrle, *Die Kultische Keuschheit im Altertum* (Giessen, 1910) ; A. D. Nock, *Arch. f. Rel.* xxiii. 27 n. 11, 28 n. 4, 30 nn. 8, 9, 32 n. 8, 33 n. 1.

Competent observers (cf. Westermarck, *History of Human Marriage*, i. 170 *sqq.*) agree that among rudimentary peoples feelings of delicacy and bashfulness (whether real or ceremonial) are by no means absent as regards sexual matters. Taboos where women are concerned are in some degree due to a fear both of the transmission of the weaker feminine characteristics and of one so psychologically different from men (cf. Marett, *Threshold*, 94). For a variety of reasons there is a general fear of the marriage night; for example, it is often believed that evil spirits are unusually active at marriages, and accordingly there are ceremonies, especially upon the first night and the following day, in order to ward off evil.[1] The inculcation of continence on the first night, enjoined by the Fourth Council of Carthage in 398 A.D., is in keeping with a practice of abstention found in many parts of the world, and justified on grounds ranging from good manners to the belief that the first night is dedicated to God.[2] In Brittany the first three nights were devoted respectively to God, the Virgin, and the husband's patron saint (*FOT.* i. 503), and elsewhere it has been believed that according to the duration of the continence will be the superiority of the child that is born. The Church of the Middle Ages interwove the inculcation of continence on the first night with the story of Tobit and Sarah in the Apocrypha (*FOT.* i. 497 *sq.*, 517 *sqq.*). But in return for certain payments the Church would allow newly married couples to ignore this rule. The bearing of this on the so-called *jus primæ noctis* is discussed at length by Sir James Frazer, who argues that there is no real basis for the " monstrous fable " that a feudal lord or ecclesiastical dignitary could claim the wives of his tenants or subordinates. There has been, he urges, a confusion of (*a*) the fine which a tenant or vassal paid to his feudal lord for the right of giving his daughter in marriage, and (*b*) the true *jus primæ noctis*, sold to the husband by an ecclesiastical authority, which permitted him to sleep with his wife on the wedding night (530). On the other hand, the former of these, the compensation for the loss of a woman's services, especially when she married away from the manor (493 *sq.*), is at the least a very noteworthy indication of the rights which could normally be claimed under what was known as the *merchet* (*marchet*). If there was room for abuse here, still more was there when chiefs took women with the greatest freedom from among their subjects, and the utmost

---

[1] Frazer, *FOT.* i. 520 *sqq.* ; Penzer, ii. 306 n. 1.

[2] Frazer, *FOT.* i. 485 *sqq.*, on the *jus primæ noctis*. Among the Narrinyeri of South Australia it is a point of decency for the couple to keep apart for the first two or three nights ; among earlier tribes of Canada such self-control was a proof that the couple married out of friendship and not to satisfy their passions (Frazer, 506, 512 *sqq.* ; Crawley, 344).

claims might be made to all marriageable women.[1] And as regards
the Church, in adding her blessing to the ceremony she normally
tended to remove from the superstitious all fear of untoward consequences, and the use made of the Story of Tobit goes to show how
powerful a part she played in the supernatural ideas (" religious " or
" magical ") which were centred upon the first night.

Sir James Frazer's analysis makes it increasingly improbable that
the *jus primæ noctis* ever prevailed as a recognized or established custom, but it does not follow that the *jus* in the popular sense was never
practised.   On the contrary, the rights of overlords and the powers
ascribed to or claimed by priests in touch with the supernatural realm
would favour the sporadic practice of what would be as much a scandal
and an abomination to some as it would be intelligible to others who
held cruder ideas of the ways of warding off evil, or of obtaining goodly
offspring—for, paradoxically, continence and ceremonial intercourse
could seem, each from its own point of view, equally efficacious.[2]   Indeed, such have been the feelings and fears touching the first night
that for this and other reasons there has been resort to ceremonial
defloration.[3]   Thus, a man was sometimes remunerated for performing
what was a dangerous service (*GB.* v. 59 n. 2); he is " sometimes
reported to be a priest " (60 n. 1).   Sometimes a stranger would be
preferred, and the fact that at the compulsory sacrifice of chastity at
Byblus, Babylon, and Cyprus the man is a stranger finds various
explanations.[4]

From the foregoing it will be seen that it is difficult to interpret the
exact meaning and implication of any single or isolated piece of evidence.   It is clear that the sacrifice of chastity was not necessarily
valued more highly than that of hair (as at Byblus, see p. 607), and the
fanaticism with which the licentious cults were maintained at Baalbek-
Heliopolis to the fourth century A.D. (see A. B. Cook, *Zeus,* i. 550, 554)

----

[1] For this, see Hartland, *Prim. Pat.* i. 123, 132 *sq.*, 188, 202, 240 ; cf. *ERE.* iii.
815.

[2] On the allegation that when the Jews were persecuted under Trajan and
Hadrian every bride was first given to the Roman στρατιώτης or *tiphsar*, see
J. Neubauer, *MVAG.* 1919, iii. 59 ; Krauss, *Rev. d'Études Juives,* xxx. 38 ;
I. Levi, *ib.* 220 *sq.*, 231.

[3] *GB.* v. 57 ; Toy, § 165 n. 1 ; *FOT.* i. 534 n. 1 ; Döller, 75.

[4] Thus, the stranger is less likely to take any further advantage ; he would not
have the same fear of supernatural consequences ; strangers as such are sometimes
feared, and sometimes regarded as divinely sent (Budge, *Book of Governors,* 557,
a fisherman casts his net into the Tigris in the name of strangers). See Farnell,
274 and n. 4 (note at Iconium the story of the strangers who are slain, 273 [*Et.
Mag.* s.v. Ἰκόνιον]).   For general ideas concerning strangers, see (besides *GB.*
index) Westermarck, *Moral Ideas,* ii. ch. xxiv. ; *Morocco,* i. 540 *sqq.*

indicates how deep-seated were the tendencies which, *mutatis mutandis*, had long before aroused the Hebrew prophets. Now the rites which the prophets condemn are associated with the cult of the Baalim, to whom was due the fertility of the land. Among the Hebrews religion and sexuality tended to be so intertwined as to become at times almost an obsession (Ezek. xvi.) : love of money and love of the beauty of women were the two great dangers for Israel—so wrote the late writer of the *Testament of Judah* (xvii. 2). Hence, in view of the usual relationship between sensuous language, eroticism, and religion (cf. the Song of Songs and its allegorical interpretation), if resort to other gods was harlotry, the cult of Yahweh (or of Baal as Yahweh) would be " marriage." With the god as the " husband " of people and land, and as the direct or indirect cause of birth, the rites which Hosea and other prophets denounce are no mere excrescences easily removed, but an integral part of the old religion. Buchanan Gray (*Sacrifice*, 95) does, it is true, call the offerings in Hosea ii. and iv. " eucharistic," and he comments on the " mirth " (Hos. ii. 11)— hardly an unambiguous word in itself. But if the functions of the " sacred " men and women, and the immoral cults as a whole, are not interpreted as gross immorality, they are to be regarded as in some sense practical and utilitarian from current points of view. Even the very sanctuary which the barren Hannah visited was served by priests of illustrious (Mosaic ?) origin whose conduct with the temple-women led to their downfall (1 Sam. ii. 22) ; and unless the prophets are to be charged with exaggerating the conditions, the less famous centres of cult of their day were no better.

Late tradition—scarcely an invention—even reports that a seven days' sacrifice of chastity before marriage was an " Amorite custom " (*Test. of Judah*, xii.). This goes much further than ritual licentiousness in connexion with agricultural festivals, and closely unites Palestine with Baalbek, Cyprus, and Babylon. There is no actual evidence that there was such a sacrifice—perhaps the counterpart of the circumcision of the male ; but it is tempting with Farnell (281, cf. 279) to compare the consecration of the firstfruits of the harvest in order to remove the taboo, a rite recognizably of the same world of ideas as circumcision (above p. 609). And there is much also to be said for his suggestion that the " sacred " men and women " were the human vehicles for diffusing through the community the peculiar virtue or potency of the (god or) goddess, the much-coveted blessing of human fertility." [1] If this were so, the firstborn would naturally be regarded as more sacred than the rest. And in fact the firstborn were Yahweh's,

[1] Farnell himself (282) confines his suggestion to the temple-women and the mother-goddess.

peculiarly his own, and to be redeemed ; and a connexion between the ḳedēshīm, etc., and the ideas concerning the firstborn may be suspected. The more spiritual and the more crude types of religion have their own convictions as to the way whereby marriages can be made fruitful ; and while the religion of the Old Testament lays emphasis upon Yahweh as the source of his people's increase and welfare, the prophets are an unintelligible phenomenon unless there were deep-rooted ideas utterly repugnant to their convictions of spiritual religion, and to the simpler stories which, with all their naïveté, inculcate spiritual ideas antagonistic to those more " magical " or " magico-religious " ideas which inform the rites and practices of the old religion (cf. *CAH*. iii. 473 *sq.*). The crude rites are the " physical " counterpart (or prototype) of the more " spiritual " conceptions of the interrelation of man and nature. The " sacred " officiants stood for ideas of holiness, and " holiness " means " kinship " (p. 549) ; these ideas the prophets spiritualized and the Jewish priesthood systematized.

The reformed religion (Judaism) was purged of its earlier grossness and excesses, but the Temple and Priesthood still maintained the almost " magico-religious " convictions of their supreme significance for the world. Rabbinical Judaism inherited them, with important modifications. The ideas were being cleansed ; but they go back to rude beginnings—the supreme importance of " sacred " individuals for the social or cosmic system of which they are part (see p. 658). If W. R. S.'s main position is sound, it is to be expected that the essential ideas of communion (fellowship, kinship, identity) were not confined to sacrifices, animal and vegetable, but that there would be an inter-relation between the " physical " rites and the " spiritual " ideas (cf. p. 439) ; there would be strange paradoxes (the sacrifice of chastity, and chastity as a sacrifice), and there would be a fundamental inter-connexion of " lower " and " higher " tendencies, although, on the other hand, the evolution is not so simple as he assumed.

P. 331. HAIR IN VOWS.—On the hair-offering by Arab pilgrims (*ḥalḳ*) see Gaudefroy-Demombynes, 291 *sqq.* W. R. S.'s explanation of *pāra'*, " let the hair grow loose " (Judg. v. 2 ; see especially Burney's commentary), revives an old conjecture (so Moore, *Judg*. 138), for which there is an Arab parallel (Bevan, cited by Wellh. 123 n. 2). Gilbert Murray (*Rise of Epic in Greece*, 123 [1907]) compares the descrip-tion of the Achæans in the *Iliad*, " letting their hair grow long " (κάρη κομόωντες), as a vow to take Troy.　　　On the cult of Ocaiṣir (note 2), see Wellh. 62 *sq.* ; Winckler, *Arab.–Semit.–Orient*. 132, *s.v.*　　In note 3 the Inca sacrifice has not been verified. Frazer (*GB*. i. 318) cites the custom of the Yucatan Indians of pulling out their eyelashes and blowing them towards the sun—but this is in order to stay its course.

For the shaving of the eyebrows, Eitrem (412) cites Roman parallels. In *CIS.* i. 257–259 a man is described as גלב אלם, an indication of the sacred calling of the barber in Phœnician temples. The shaving of the widow (Deut. xxi. 12) is one of various rites symbolizing the end of one stage and the beginning of another ; cf. also Wellh.[1] 156 (where W. R. S. adds in his copy references to Rasm. *Add.* 69 ; Rāghil, ii. 133). Another *rite de passage* is seen in the *iḥrām* (cf. We. 122, Gaudefroy-Demombynes, 170 *sqq.*).

P. 334. TATTOO MARKS.—These, when found among primitive peoples, though usually significant, are not necessarily *imitations* of totems, etc. (Frazer, *Tot. Ex.* i. 26–30, iv. 197 *sqq.*). But they will testify to the fact that all individuals similarly marked participate in the same rites (Durkheim, 232), or are members of the same group (social, secret, etc.). On the connexion between a tattoo or distinguishing mark and covenants, see *Kinship*, 250. So, the marks commonly denote devotion to, or possession by, a god, and the Egyptians would brand captives with the *name* of the god, or the (divine) king (Breasted, iii. § 414, iv. § 405). Slaves in Babylonia were tattooed with some name, and in the Elephantine papyri they are " marked " (שנת), apparently with a *yōd*.[1] The priests of Isis had cross-like marks on their foreheads (see Norden, *Geburt des Kindes*, 28 and n. 4), and Syrian Christians who have been to Jerusalem are tattooed with the cross (O. H. Parry, *Six Months in a Syrian Monastery*, 63). See further, p. 675 ; and for much useful material, Turnbull, *Blood Covenant*, 218 ; Frazer, *FOT.* i. 78 *sq.* ; Pedrizet, *Archiv f. Rel.* xiv. 54 *sqq.*, especially 100 *sq.*, 109, 112, 117.

P. 337.—The rite is called *nagā*, W. R. S., *Lectures*, 583 ; cf. Curtiss, 191 (an incident near Nablus).

P. 339. " LIVING " FLESH.—The general principle is that the sacrifice must be eaten while still alive and quivering, before its virtues have left it. Even when sacred food is not eaten fresh, it must not be allowed to putrefy or ferment (pp. 221 n., 387).[2] Though the much-quoted Saracenic rite stands alone, the principle is a simple one, and in Mexico the living representatives of the fire-god were thrown into the fire, taken out, and their still palpitating hearts torn from their bodies (*GB.* ix. 301). W. R. S. points out that either all share in and devour the sacrifice in its entirety (p. 338 n. 1), or there are modifications, some of which are due partly to a softening of manners (p. 342 *sq.*) ; the most sacred parts are reserved for the more sacred caste, or they

---

[1] See Code of Hammurabi, § 226 *sq.* ; Johns, *Bab. and Ass. Laws*, 177 ; S. A. Cook, *Moses and Hammurabi*, 159 ; Cowley, *Aramaic Papyri*, No. 28.

[2] Also the blood brought before the altar was stirred to prevent it from coagulating (cf. also Moore, *E.Bi.* " Sacrifice," § 46 and n. 3).

are otherwise disposed of in some special manner (p. 386), thus the entrails, etc., become the food of demons (see Eitrem, p. 424 *sq.*), who are supposed to eat raw flesh (cf. p. 541).

Properly, the victim must be complete and perfect. Tainted or imperfect victims should not be offered (Mal. i. 7 *sq.*, see *CAH.* iii. 449 *sq.*), and the sacrificial offering should be without blemish (Lev. xxii. 19 *sqq.*). That is to say, " the sacred life should be completely and normally embodied " (p. 361). The priest, too, should be without blemish (Lev. xxi. 17 *sqq.*); similarly in Babylonia.[1] The principle rules throughout that the more perfect is the more potent, and the sacred power resents contact with that which is not sacred. It enters only into the priest or the sacrificial victim, which, like itself, is " sacred." The fundamental idea is expressed in ways that range from the crudest to the most spiritual (Jer. xv. 19; Isa. lvii. 15). It lies at the bottom of liver-divination, where the animal selected for the purpose, pure and complete in every respect, becomes the embodiment of the deity, whose purposes are read by an expert examination of its liver, the organ of thought (Jastrow, *Rel. Bel.* 148, 155 *sq.*). And in the extremes of magic and of mysticism it will be believed that the correct ritual must necessarily secure the union of man and deity.

With the foregoing are bound up three distinct and far-reaching groups of ideas. (1) The conviction is widespread that the *physical* state at death determines the *physical* state in which one is reborn or lives in another existence.[2] Hence (*a*) the endeavours both to preserve intact the body of a dead friend and to mutilate a dead enemy; and (*b*) the spiritual counterpart: the moral state at death conditions the state after death. (2) Men whose physical powers are waning will sometimes desire to be put to death in order to ensure rebirth in a suitable physical condition.[3] (3) The physical condition of men is sometimes believed to be due to the good *or* bad relations between them and supernatural powers—*e.g.* remarkable strength and virility, *or* disease and suffering. And when certain men perform sacred functions (as priests, priestly kings, magicians) their strength is a matter of supreme importance. They must fulfil certain conditions (observe taboos, etc.) in order to be able to function successfully, and their failure or the occurrence of disasters can be ascribed to their impotence and interpreted as a proof that they no longer enjoy the

---

[1] J. Jeremias, *E.Bi.* col. 4119 ; Zimmern, *KAT.* 534 ; Lagrange, 223 *sq.*

[2] In Palestine the sacrificial sheep must be faultless and without mutilation, so that on the Day of Judgment it may reappear perfect and able to save the man on whose behalf it was offered (*JPOS.* vi. 41).

[3] Cf., *e.g.*, Procopius, *Goth.* ii. 14 (cited by Chadwick, *Heroic Age*, 411).

favour or help of the supernatural powers. The slaying of the " sacred king " has become, thanks to Frazer's *Golden Bough,* one of the most remarkable and significant discoveries of anthropological research.[1] The weakness—physical, ritual, or moral—of the " sacred " man is a danger to his group and land, and whatever is interpreted as an indication thereof will be regarded as a warning that his period of usefulness is over ; and conversely, steps will be taken to ensure that his condition is not likely to be prejudicial to people or land, hence his reign is a limited one, or he must defend himself against all comers, etc.[2] Theoretically, *all* members of the group are " sacred," and on their fitness depends the welfare of the group and all that is bound up with it ; but in *practice* particular individuals, by reason of their functions, have a heavier responsibility. Cf. pp. 549, 591.

P. 342.—On 'Arafa, see Wellhausen, 82 ; and on the *ifāḍa,* Gaude-froy-Demombynes, 260.

P. 357. UNCLEAN ANIMALS.—On the animals in question, see the Index, also *E.Bi.* s.vv. and art. " Clean," §§ 7 *sqq.* On the pig, see also Baudissin, 142 *sqq.,* 529, and the references in R. Campbell Thompson, *Devils and Evil Spirits of Babylonia,* ii. p. xlvii ; *Sem. Magic,* 208 ; G. Hölscher, *Die Profeten,* 376 *sq.* In Babylonia the pig was the sacred animal of Ninurta and Gula ; and, while eaten at certain special feasts, was taboo on the 30th of the fifth month (Prince, *J.B.L.* xliv. 156). The heart of a pig and of a dog formed part of a sacrifice to evil spirits (Morgenstern, 118, and n. 5). On the dog, see also Baudissin (*s.v.* Hund) and Zimmern in the *Nöldeke-Festschrift,* ii. 962 n. 3 (in the dedication of a new image to the Moon-god). For the Harranian " lord with the dogs " (above, p. 291), see *ZA.* xi. 242 *sq.* At the present day it is sometimes a sin to kill a dog (Parry, *Six Months in a Syrian Monastery,* 71), and the worship of a large black dog with annual licentious rites is found among the Kizil-Bashi (G. R. Driver, *Bulletin of the School of Or. Stud.,* London, ii. 2, 198). On the dog and mouse, see Hölscher, *op. cit.* 378 *sq.;* and on the latter, *ZA.* xiv. 206, 250 ; Jacob, *Altarab. Parallel.* 11. Camel's flesh is tabooed food (above, p. 283 *sq.*), and it is a great insult in Mosul to say that a man eats of it (Campbell Thompson, *Sem. Magic,* 210 n. 1).

[1] See, in addition, on the killing of the Khazar kings (in South Russia), Frazer, *Folk-lore,* xxviii. 382–407. For the important Dinka evidence, see Seligman, *JRAI.* xliii. 664 *sqq.,* 673, and *ERE.* s.v., and for evidence from the northern tribes of Nigeria, see C. K. Meek, i. 255, ii. 59 *sqq.;* the king must not be ill or grow old.

[2] See also Westermarck, *Moral Ideas,* ii. 609 *sq.* (in Morocco a pretender's *baraka* usually lasts only six months), and Landtman, *The Origin of Priesthood* (Ekenaes, Finland, 1905), 41 *sq.,* 64 *sq.,* 143 *sq.* (priests become chiefs through their supernatural powers ; losing them, they are deposed and killed).

P. 357. Totemism and Animal-Names.[1]—Besides the references
to the sacrifice and worship of animals described in the Deutero-Isaiah
and Ezekiel, of particular interest is the appearance, at about the same
age (viz. at the time of the discovery of the book of the Law in
Josiah's reign), of leading temple-personages bearing the names
Shaphan (coney or rather rock-badger), Achbor (mouse), and Huldah
(weasel or mole). It is, however, a recognized fact that animal-names
in themselves do not necessarily imply totemism or any systematized
animal-cult. To be more precise, it should be observed that, in general,
clans or tribes bearing such names undergo vicissitudes similar to those
of groups bearing other names, *e.g.* there will be tendencies to form
larger groupings or for the clans to be replaced by local and regional
groups. But more significant is the fact that groups with animal-
names will sometimes possess stocks of names peculiar to each, so that
it is possible to tell from the child's animal-name to which particular
group it belongs, even as, on higher levels, names compounded with
Marduk, Yahweh, or Apollo would, primarily at least, be an indication
of the original *milieu* of the bearer (see Frazer, *Tot. Ex.* ii. 344, 473 ;
iii. 13, 329, 360).

Further, there will sometimes be an appropriate connexion between
the animal-name of the group and the names of the constituent individuals ; *e.g.* among the Elk clan of the Omahas are such personal
names as Soft Horn, White Elk, Stumpy Tail (*Tot. Ex.* i. 58 *sqq.* ; iii.
35, 77, 101 *sq.*, 272). Such a practice, with which one may compare
and contrast the theophorous names distinctive of Babylonian,
Israelite, and other religions, is enhanced when it is a mark of piety to
employ the animal-names, as the animal whose name the group bears
would be angry if they fell out of use (the Wyandots, *Tot. Ex.* iii. 34 *sq.*).
In harmony with this is the fear of uttering the name of a mythical
animal-ancestor heedlessly or too often (the Warramunga of Australia,
Tot. Ex. i. 145; *GB.* iii. 384)—the name is " sacred," neither to be forgotten nor to be too freely used. Totem-animals, like animal-
guardians, are often supposed to benefit the men and women of their
group, provided they are duly invoked (*Tot. Ex.* i. 532 *sq.*) ; while, on
the other hand, the name is so " sacred " that sometimes the animal
(totem or other) must not be spoken of by its true name but by a
descriptive epithet (*Tot. Ex.* i. 16; *GB.* iii. 396 *sqq.*), and it is a serious
offence for the name of a totem to be publicly pronounced by a man of
another clan (the Tinnehs of North-West America, *Tot. Ex.* iii. 352 .

[1] See, in general, Jos. Jacobs, *Studies in Bibl. Archæology*, 64–103 (1894) ; G. B.
Gray, *Heb. Proper Names*, 101 *sqq.* ; Nöldeke, *ZDMG.* xl. 157 *sqq.*, and *Beiträge z.
Semit. Sprachwissenschaft*, i. 73 *sqq.* ; Zapletal, *Totemismus u. d. Rel. Israels*,
20 *sqq.* (1901).

Hence, the more significant the animal-name becomes, the more justly may it be said to function very similarly to that of anthropomorphic deities, though theophorous names, in their turn, constantly tend to lose their earlier force. And since the relation between the animals and the members of the group is essentially a " personal " one it is the more difficult to deny that such cults are religious, albeit of a very rudimentary type of religion. But only in proportion as the animal-name is an organic part of a significant system of social beliefs and practices can one begin to speak of true totemism.

Animal-names usually have *some* significance, for it is a common belief that people can be in some way influenced either by a name given to them or by the one who gives them the name. Animal-names are sometimes given to indicate the nature of the infant; they are supposed to frighten away demons and enemies or persuade them that the bearer is not worth their unwelcome attentions. In the same way, such personal names as " three (or five) cowries " among the Hindus will convince hostile spirits that such infants are beneath contempt.[1] It is true that some names may refer to bodily peculiarities (Meyer, *Israel.* 310 *sq.* ; *Gesch. Alt.* i. § 55) ; but more significant are those that denote some such attribute or quality as strength or swiftness which, it is hoped, the bearer will possess. It is a common belief that animals far surpass men in some useful ability. So, in order to protect a sickly child it will be given the name of a wild beast (Doughty, i. 329), and the name is, within its limits, as effective as is a significant theophorous name elsewhere which is thought to secure for the bearer the aid of a god.

Sometimes the names of both persons and places are those of animals which frequent a locality, and in this way make an impression upon the natives. Such cases might seem to be trifling, but often there are typical beliefs which connect the infant's character or nature with the animal seen by the mother before its birth. In Gujarat, where no totem organization can be traced, an infant may be called by the name of the animal (cat, dog, crow, etc.) which is heard to utter a cry at the time when the infant is born.[2] But with this inchoate usage contrast Central Australia, where the child is supposed to owe its origin to the proximity of its mother to the locality where the spirits or souls of the totem-species and of the totem-group are collected.[3] There is admittedly a wide range of possibilities as regards animal-names, but in the majority of cases the name in some way associates the bearer with the animal in question ; while in totemism

[1] Frazer, *FOT.* iii. 173 ; Clodd, *Magic in Names,* 102.

[2] R. E. Enthoven, *Folklore of Bombay,* 211.

[3] See Durkheim, 167 *sqq.,* 234 (discussion of the theories of the origin of totemism).

man and the totem-animal are of the same substance, even as, when gods and men are akin, some substantial identity is at least implicit in the relationship.[1]

Some writers on the " origin " of totemism hold that the system arose merely from the more or less fortuitous and non-significant bestowal of animal-names and from the mystical and transcendental ideas of a *rapport* between the individual and the animal which were in due course generated.[2] With this association granted, primitive man is supposed to believe that the animal, plant, or inanimate object or natural phenomenon is " in some hidden or mysterious way " connected with him, and this connexion " quite naturally " comes to be thought of in terms of relationship (I. King, 150). In more detail, Malinowski (ed. Needham, 45 *sq.*) points to man's keen interest in nature, the general affinity between man and the animals, the desire to control dangerous, useful, or edible animals, a desire which " must lead to a belief in special power over the species, affinity with it, a common essence between man and beast or plant." Such a belief " implies " certain restraints (*e.g.* the prohibition to kill and eat), and " endows man with the supernatural faculty of contributing ritually to the abundance of the species, . . ." and " this ritual leads to acts of a magical nature by which plenty is brought about."

All such explanations—if they can be so called—are of the greatest methodological interest both for the crucial *a priori* psychical elements which they are compelled to introduce, and for their bearing upon the problem of the relation between totemic (theriomorphic) and anthropomorphic cults. The psychological interrelation between such cults is such as to forbid us to sever them too rigidly ; and it is sounder to recognize, not that the " higher " cults have evolved from the " lower," but that they are the more evolved forms of beliefs and practices which appear in a more rudimentary state in totemic and totemistic

---

[1] Cf. pp. 506, 549. Of Frazer's theories of totemism, the third (the conceptional origin of totemism) is based on the Australian evidence (*Tot. Ex.* i. 157 *sqq.*, iv. 57 *sqq.*). He distinguishes (*a*) the Australian belief that what enters a woman at conception is—in his words—" the spirit of a human child which has an animal, a plant, a stone, or what not for its totem," and (*b*) the possible belief—*not as yet vouched for*—that an animal, plant, or stone entered and was born as that object in human form, a belief which *if it occurred* would be " a complete explanation of totemism " (iv. 58). On the other hand, it seems evident that the totem-species and totem-group are so related that what takes a human form in the group can take the form of the totem before and after its human life, and a clear difference between the two does not exist. The totem does not " become " human any more than totemism " becomes " anthropomorphism ; the true formula (that the *x* which appears in *l* reappears in another form in *m*) is a much more general one.

[2] Cf. Andrew Lang, *Ency. Brit.* " Totemism " ; *Folk-lore*, xxiv. 159 *sqq.*

cults—and whose still more rudimentary forms in prehistoric times cannot be conceived. That, as apart from problems of evolution or development, the problems of totemism and of theism cannot be ultimately severed is seen in the fact that beliefs in Supreme Beings have been found in totemic and other very simple environments (p. 529), and that the period of—to use W. R. S.'s words—" the re-emergence of a cult of the most primitive totem-type "—though it may be safer to call it totemistic or theriomorphic—is precisely the period which in the Deutero-Isaiah witnessed the high-water mark of Israelite theism.

P. 358. MYSTIC CULTS.—The significance of Ezek. viii. 10 *sq.* was first perceived ʋy W. R. S. in a famous article in the *Journal of Philology*, ix. (1880–81) 97 *sqq.*[1] Ed. Meyer (*Israeliten*, 309 n. 3 [1906]), while rejecting W. R. S.'s early arguments for David's supposed " serpent " connexions, attempts to explain Ezekiel's evidence on the lines of the bas-reliefs or paintings referred to in Ezek. xxiii. 14.[2] But it is clear that Ezekiel has in view more or less extensive cults due to the conviction that Yahweh had forsaken the land. A recent commentary (by Joh. Hermann, 60) recognizes a mystic cult, possibly Egyptian, though the mention of Tammuz could point to Babylon (viii. 14). It is very noteworthy, in any case, that one of the prominent officiants is the son of a Shaphan (badger), the name of one of the unclean animals, on whose Arabic equivalent the *wabr*, see p. 444, *Kinship*, 234, *Lectures*, 480 n. 1.[3] It is conceivable that the *shāphān*, the ʿ*achbōr* (mouse), and the *ḥuldah* (mole) were among the creatures connected with cults of the dead, in which case the prominence of these names in the story of the " Deuteronomic " reform attributed to King Josiah (2 Kings xxii.) is as striking as the condemnation of certain mourning customs in the Deuteronomic law ; cf. pp. 547, 605.

Animal-names recur also in the Edomite-Judæan genealogies. They are less marked in the northern tribes ; and whatever be the best explanation of their presence and distribution, " the second commandment, the cardinal precept of spiritual worship, is explicitly directed against the worship of the denizens of air, earth, and water " (*Lectures*, 470 *sqq.*). There is little doubt that theriomorphism, at all events, must have been more prevalent and deep-seated than is recognized by those writers who deny that there is any evidence for

---

[1] Reprinted in *Lectures*, 455 *sqq.* (see especially 479 *sq.*). On the interest—and storm—it excited, see *Life*, 332 *sq.*, 368 *sqq.*, 381 *sq.*

[2] W. R. S. himself never repeated the precarious argument on David and Nahash, even in *Kinship* (1st ed. 1885) ; and attention was drawn to this fact in a review of Zapletal's criticisms of W. R. S. (*Der Totemismus und die Religion Israels*, 1901), see S. A. Cook, *Jew. Quart. Rev.*, April 1902, p. 416 and n. 3.

[3] The *wabr* must not be killed ; see Musil, *Arab. Petræa*, iii. 324.

totemism of the sort that is found among rudimentary peoples of to-day. Further, it is no less noteworthy that Egypt—with which Palestine was in so many respects closely connected—is notorious both at the period under consideration, and later, for the persistence of extraordinary theriomorphic cults (see pp. 226, 578 *sq.*). It is also important to notice that, at this period of the collapse of social-religious systems and of the appearance of individualistic tendencies which naturally accompany and arise out of such conditions (cf. p. 592), we find not only new types of religious societies and mystical cults, but also guilds, unions, and other communities independent of the earlier social, political, and religious organizations, and possessing, in certain cases at least, more or less definite religious features of their own.

Some unions are distinctly industrial or economic, and they can be associated with the Temple of Jerusalem and, no doubt, the Second Temple dating from the latter part of the sixth century.[1] At the same time, there is independent evidence (*a*) for South Palestinian (semi-Edomitic) traditions of the origins of civilization and industry, (*b*) for the (late) Chronicler's interest in the Temple-guilds, and (*c*) for the probability that a semi-Edomite wave left its mark upon Palestine and upon the Biblical sources in and about the same age.[2] Obviously there are gaps between (1) the semi-Edomite and other animal-names, and the Temple and other guilds, and (2) the data in 2 Kings xxii., Isa. lxv. *sq.*, Ezek. viii. ; and for the present it can be regarded only as a coincidence that to the dog as a mystic sacrifice there corresponds the prominent semi-Edomite " dog "-clan Caleb in the constitution of Judah and, even at a late date, in the neighbourhood of Jerusalem.

Evidence of another sort is afforded by the communal festival מַרְזֵחַ in Amos vi. 7; Jer. xvi. 5. W. R. S. regarded it as some sort of atoning rite (p. 430 n. 4) ; but in the Talmud the term is used of a banquet or meal, and it is now well known from inscriptions.[3] On the Marseilles inscription (*CIS.* i. 165, l. 16, Cooke, No. 42) there are dues

---

[1] Cf. the craftsmen, potters, perfumers, and workers in linen in 1 Chron. iv. 14, 21, 23 ; Neh. iii. 8, 31 ; and in *CIS.* i. 86 A and B (from Citium) the builders, *velarii* (פרכם), barbers, masons, scribes, etc.; cf. the hereditary guilds at the Temple of Jerusalem, who possessed the secret of preparing the incense, etc. (*Yoma,* iii. 11). See in general P. Foucart, *Des Associations rel. chez les Grecs* (1873) ; Poland, *De Collegiis Artificum Dionysiacorum* (Dresden, 1895), *Gesch. d. griech. Vereinswesen* (Leipzig, 1909).

[2] See S. A. Cook, *CAH.* vi. 185 *sq.* ; cf. iii. 478–80.

[3] See Clermont-Ganneau, *Rec.* ii. 390, iii. 22, iv. 290, 339 ; *Qy. St. of the PEF.* 1901, pp. 239, 370 ; Gressmann, *Zeit. f. Neutest. Wissens.* xx. (1921) 228 *sqq.* ; and for the Talmudic data, see Dalman, *Neue Petra,* 93 *sq.*

for the מזרח (? the natives, a free society), the שפח the sept (cf.
the clan sacrifice in 1 Sam. xx. 6, וזבח משפחה), and the מרזח אלם
or gathering in honour of the gods. There was a *marzēaḥ* at
Altiburnus (Cooke, No. 55; twelve members and " their companions "),
and that at Maktar had thirty-two members and performed various
religious duties (Cooke, No. 59; Lidzb. i. 47 *sq.*). In a Piræus inscription (Cooke, No. 33), where a Sidonian community (בד) crown
Shama'ba'al president of the corporation (גו), it seems to be the
name of an annual festival. Among the Nabatæans it was connected
with the divine king Obedath.[1] In the temple of Bel, at Palmyra, nine
members erected an altar in Jan.–Feb. A.D. 132 to the gods Aglibol and
Malakbel (Cooke, No. 140A; Lidzb. i. 344). Also an image was set up
there in April A.D. 118 to a man during his presidency (רבנות מרזחותה)
among the priests of Bel (Lidzb. ii. 281 *sq.*). In a bilingual of April 203,
the president Shalmā was both symposiarch and ἀρχιερεύς (Lidzb. ii.
304); and the well-known Septimius Worod, viceroy of Palmyra in
the time of Gallienus, was stratēgos and symposiarch of the priests
of the god Bel (Cooke, 288, 303).

Another and more detailed Palmyrene inscription, of October
A.D. 243, refers to Yarḥai Agrippa, who in his presidency " served
the gods and presided over the divination (קסמא) all the year,"
and brought forth " old wine to the priests throughout the year from
his house, and brought no wine in wineskins from the west." Among
the officers enumerated are the scribe (כתובא), the cook (על בת דודא)
—corresponding to the ἀρχιμάγειρος of the temple of Jupiter at
Damascus (Wadd. 2549)—and Yarḥibola, the butler (ממזגנא).[2]
Yet another reference to the term has long been found in the place-
name βητομαρσεα (*i.e.* בית מרזח) on the mosaic map of Madeba
(Büchler, *Rev. des Ét. Juives*, 1901, p. 105). According to Musil, the
name may survive in el-Mezra', near Kerak. It is tempting to think
of the rites of Baal-Peor; and, in fact, *Siphrē*, 47b, speaks of the
orgiastic banquets (מרזיחים) with which the daughters of Moab
tempted the Israelites (see Cooke, 122 n. 1). When Rabbinical
tradition refers to the tents and booths which the women set up from
Beth-Yeshimoth to the " Snow Mountain " (טור תלנא), it is
preferable to read Mount Pisgah with Clermont-Ganneau, who adds
that if, following Conder, Baal Peor lay beside 'Ain Minyeh, the
adjacent Tal'at el-Benāt, with its old monuments of unhewn stone,
bears the suggestive name, " the ascent of the maidens " (*Qy. St.* 1901,
p. 372).

[1] עברת אלהא, Dalman, *op. cit.* 93 *sq.*; Lidzb. iii. 278. On the cult, cf. Cooke, 245.
[2] See further H. Ingholt, *Syria*, vii. (1926), 128 *sqq.*

If Lidzbarski's interpretation of an ostrakon from Elephantine be correct, mention is made of contributions for a מרחזא, whence it would appear that in this Jewish colony the word had no disreputable associations (*Ephem.* iii. 304). Nor is there necessarily any condemnation in Jer. xvi. 5 (LXX θίασος), whether the reference be to an occasion of lamentation or, as in Amos vi. 7, of revelry.[1] Some light is thrown on orgiastic cults by Hos. iv. 17–19 ;[2] and the work of Baudissin, Frazer, and Gressmann combines with the discoveries of curious cult-objects at Beisān (Beth-Shan) to support the probability that there were mystical cults in early Palestine.

In view of this scattered evidence, the statement of W. R. S. that old types of cult would be likely to be prominent in the period of unrest and stress in and about the sixth century B.C. gains fresh force ; and cults other than those of the Israelite nobles of Samaria whom Amos condemned, or of the colony of Elephantine, or of the Palmyrene priests can readily be imagined.[3] They would naturally be more in harmony with the internal economic and social conditions ; and the guilds, corporations, or brotherhoods, whether connected with the Temple or not, and whether or no they had their patron saints or other religious models, would readily tend to be religious societies with more or less practical aims.[4] As a general rule, the means of life, the food-supply, and all vital pursuits are invariably interwoven with religious or quasi-religious ideas.[5] Especially is this the case among primitive peoples and in periods of crisis. Apart from the usual religious or magico-religious ceremonies of a communal nature (see p. 586), sometimes it is the function of special secret societies to promote fertility.[6] In Central Australia totemism is " economic " : Nature is, so to say, subdivided among a number of clans, each of which is responsible for a special department ; the whole society is bound together by the economic interdependence of all the parts.[7] Although this is unique, the general principles are world-wide ; and with the break-up of the old religious systems in South-West Asia, and in the difficult economic conditions which can be traced, we are entitled to expect that the national and more orthodox beliefs and

---

[1] The latter interpretation is adopted by Duhm and Cornill ; for the former, see Peake. The ambiguity has analogies (see p. 432).

[2] Emended text ; see Gressmann, *ZNTW.* xx. 229 *sq.*

[3] The passage in Amos would seem to point to a musical guild, with David as the founder or patron of musical instruments ; cf. the South Palestinian tradition of Jubal, etc. (see Meyer, *Israel.* 218 *sq.* ; Cook, *CAH.* vi. 185 *sq.*).

[4] Cf. S. Angus, *Mystery Religions and Christianity*, 196 *sq.*

[5] See I. King, *Devel. of Rel.*, Index, *s.v.* " Food problem."

[6] *e.g.* among the Omahas, Hutton Webster, 182 *sq.* ; cf. 188.

[7] Cf. Malinowski in the *Westermarck-Festschrift*, 97, 100, 105, 107 *sq.*

practices relating to the care of the great gods for their people and land would give way to others in no degree less practical, but far more unsystematized and rudimentary.

Finally, the transitional period after the breakdown of the early religious systems is of universal importance for the history of religion in general, and in particular for the development in the Deutero-Isaiah of ideas of God and Man which mark an epoch in the evolution of religion.[1] Here, and in the strange Egyptian animal-cults, in the scattered Biblical data for mystic cults, etc., in the exhibitions of spiritual arrogance—of which the tradition of Nebuchadrezzar is only one—there are the most extraordinary extremes. Behind Isa. liii. lies a new era in religion, at a period which found its outlet in the most diverse manifestations, of which the testimony of Ezek. viii. 12, Isa. lxv. 3 *sqq.*, etc., is beyond all doubt. The evidence for theriomorphic, if not totemistic modes of thought, taken as a whole, though varying in value, confronts the sublime conception of the Servant of the Lord ; it is as though the deep-reaching disintegration of life and thought opened the way for unique developments in most contrary directions, and that roads led varyingly towards the " lowest " and the " highest " conceptions of spiritual nature. Cf. p. 554.

In both Egypt and South-West Asia the conditions of life and thought had passed far beyond those absolutely rudimentary conditions that characterize totemic societies *such as we know them.* W. R. S. has already pointed out that new cults can arise " at a later stage of human progress than that of which totemism is characteristic " (p. 138). It is now necessary to add that totemism can be seen in the making among the Bantu, and that among the no·thern tribes of Nigeria, Mohammedan families will venerate sacred animals as the embodiments of ancestral spirits.[2] But even in Central Australia totemism has had a history behind it (*Tot. Ex.* i. 238, 251). Hence, totemic and related phenomena represent tendencies which are not necessarily absolutely primitive, and which will vary in their issue according to the environment in which they emerge ; and no one specific totem-system (such as that in Australia) is necessarily to be regarded as the criterion, even as Melanesian Mana is not the touchstone for the many various interrelated forms of " Mana " (see p. 550 *sq.*). Precisely what shall be the criteria of totemism, and how the varieties of totemic, totemistic, and theriomorphic cults shall be classified, are problems of methodology ; but W. R. S.'s treatment of the Semitic

---

[1] Cf. G. F. Moore, *History of Religions,* i. viii *sq.* ; Cook, *CAH.* iii. 489, 499. See also pp. 592 *sqq.*

[2] See respectively J. T. Brown, *Among the Bantu Nomads* (cf. *Times Lit. Suppl.* 18th March 1926), and C. K. Meek, i. 174 *sq.*

data has, in any event, led to repeated discussion of the problems along most varied and fruitful lines.

P. 361 *sqq.* HUMAN SACRIFICE.[1]—Its prevalence among agricultural communities as against hunters and pastorals may be due to the association of ideas concerning bloodshed and fertility of soil. Infanticide is more common among hunters (due in large measure to their mode of life), but cannibalism declines as one passes on to settled peoples.[2] Among the reasons for human sacrifice are (1) the use of dead bodies for magical purposes (Mader, 55, 65). (2) Various psychological reasons—the desire to get into touch with the supersensuous, the feeling that the passage from life to death unites the seen and the unseen realm, and the like. (3) More precisely the object is to arouse the gods, to extort their aid (Westermarck, *Morocco,* i. 528 *sq.*) ; or it is to send a message by the victim to the supernatural realm. (4) It is to secure the presence of a human spirit, a man's *mana* or his sacred influence. (5) While a death is often regarded as something vicarious—on the conviction that another's death has saved one's own, the next step is deliberately to slay in order that another may live, and typically to strengthen or prolong the life of a " sacred " man, a chief, etc. (*GB.* iv. 160 *sq.,* vi. 221 *sqq.*). Here should probably be included the sacrifices to Moloch or Melek, the king-god.[3] That human sacrifice in some way invigorated the supernatural powers —who in their turn sustained human and other life—is a most fundamental idea, in that it is associated, on the one hand, with the belief that gods needed food, etc.—and primarily in order that *they* might perform their functions—and, on the other hand, with the more spiritual convictions of what it is that God really does require from men.[4]

The evidence for human sacrifice proves to be exceedingly impressive, pointing to an early prevalence and, at times, a systematization of ideas uniting men and the supernatural realm. Indeed, Frazer

[1] Wellhausen, 43, 115 *sq.* ; Lagrange, 101 *sqq.* ; Mannhardt's essay (see p. 366 n. 5) is in his *Mytholog. Forschungen* ; H. L. Strack, *Human Blood and Jewish Ritual* (1909) ; Mader, *Die Menschenopfer d. alten Hebräer u. d. benachbarten Völker* (Freiburg i. B., 1909) ; Westermarck, *Moral Ideas,* i. ch. xix. ; Schwenn, *Die Menschenopfer bei d. Griechen u. Römern* (Giessen, 1915).

[2] Hobhouse, Wheeler, and Ginsberg, 242.

[3] See Moore, *E.Bi.* 3187 *sqq.* ; Lagrange, 99 *sqq.,* 108 *sq.* ; Kennett and Frazer, *GB.* vi. 219 and note.

[4] For foundation sacrifices, see p. 633. The Egyptian kings sacrificed captives that their name might live ; on the Arab. *naci̯'a,* see p. 363 n. 1, and below, p. 641. On traces of the sacrifice of infants in South Arabian inscriptions, see *OLZ.* 1906, cols. 58–70 ; *Zeit. f. Ass.* xxix. 184 *sqq.* The supposed Phœnician references (*CIS.* i. 166, 194) are much too uncertain (cf. Mader, 78).

(*GB.* vii. 409) conjectures that there was a homogeneity of magico-religious ideas over a great part of South Europe and West Asia. Human sacrifice stamps relatively advanced and especially decadent peoples, among whom the difference between human and animal life is clearly understood; whereas, among rudimentary peoples the difference is only slightly grasped, and an animal victim might well be deemed a better victim than a man (cf. pp. 361, 623 *sq.*). As W. R. S. points out, the assumption that the animal victim is a surrogate for the human does not sufficiently explain the facts. If the change be due to a softening of manners, the re-emergence of the human victim enhanced religion; thus A. B. Davidson, speaking of the Servant of Yahweh in Isa. liii., well observes that " the prophet has taken the great step of lifting up the sacrificial idea out of the region of animal life into that of human life." [1] Human sacrifice (which became an obsession among certain peoples) and animal sacrifice alike admit of higher and lower interpretations; and any conviction that man was " higher " than the animals betokens a growth of human personality which involves the question of the relation between anthropomorphism and theriomorphism. See p. 670.

P. 366 n. 3.—Cf. Mader, 30. Prof. Peet points out (in a private communication) that the determinative throughout earlier times is simply a knife, with or without the addition of the sign of violent action, and that the determinative of the bound man with a knife at his throat is very late and degenerate. Whether so crude and, as it would seem, so primitive a meaning is to be expected in later times may seem doubtful, unless account is taken of the persistence of human sacrifice among the Phœnicians, and of other barbaric customs elsewhere in the old civilized world.

P. 366 n. 5.—On the possible Phœnician (Semitic) origin of Zeus Lycæus, see E. E. Sikes, *Classical Review*, ix. 68 *sq.*; on the wolf-god, see *Kinship*, 200, Frazer on Paus. viii. 2, 6 (and vol. iv. 189 *sq.*); Farnell, *Cults*, i. 41 ; A. B. Cook, *Zeus*, i. 63 n. 6.

P. 367. CANNIBALISM.—There is little evidence for cannibalistic ideas and usages in Palestine (*e.g.* " I slew him with my teeth," *Qy. St.* 1879, p. 85), Morocco (a symbolical practice by the blood-avenger, Westermarck, *Morocco*, i. 515), and Arabia (*Kinship*, 296); cf. also Lagrange, 259 and nn. 6 and 7). But cannibalism was primarily a mystical or sacred rite, and Malinowski (ed. Needham, 48) observes that among the Melanesians of New Guinea the custom of partaking of the flesh of the dead was a pious one, " done with extreme repugnance and dread," and at the same time felt to be " a supreme act of reverence, love, and devotion." Cf., in general, Westermarck, *Origin and*

[1] *O.T. Prophecy*, 430 (Edinburgh, 1903).

Development of the Moral Ideas, ii. ch. xlvi. Probably the most ancient, and certainly not the least interesting reference to it is found in the old " Pyramid Texts " (*c.* 2800 B.C.). These tell how the Pharaoh hunts, lassoes, and slaughters the gods in the celestial regions, makes an evening meal off them, and feeds on their internal organs in order to possess himself of their intelligence, skill, strength, etc. (see Breasted, *Rel. and Thought in Anc. Egypt*, 127 *sqq.*).

P. 372 *sqq.* BURNING THE VICTIM.[1]—For the ceremonial burnings at Hierapolis, see Clemen, *Baudissin-Festschrift*, 104 *sq.*, and cf. the destruction of garments, etc., at the festival of Simeon ben Yochai at Meiron (*Qy. St.* 1878, p. 24 ; *GB.* v. 178 *sq.*). On the Molech cult, see the references above, p. 630 n. 3 ; and on the flaming bull-shrines, A. B. Cook, *Zeus*, i. 722, 784 *sq.* Fire has its " spirit " inhabitants (*JPOS.* v. 165) ; like water, it is a purifying agent in Babylonia (*KAT.* 417 *sq.* ; Jastrow, *Rel. Bel.* 315 *sq.*), and a symbol of purity in Zoroastrianism. Passing through fire can thus be interpreted as a cleansing rite (Eitrem, 133 *sqq.*, 169 *sq.*, 174). Similarly, in New South Wales, Dhuramoolan is supposed to kill the youths, cut them up, burn them, and remould them into new beings (R. H. Matthews, *JRAI.* xxv. 297 *sq.*, xxvi. 336). Westermarck (*Morocco*, ii. 199 *sqq.*) explains Midsummer fire-ceremonies as purificatory and intended to remove harmful influences (see also Frazer, *GB.* x. pp. vii, 330 *sq.*). But a magical efficacy is also attached to the burning of animals (*e.g.* of a cock to make the year " white " or lucky, West., 203), and ideas of regeneration and re-creation seem to be fundamental. For the burning of Dido, Heracles of Tyre, Hamilcar, and others, see *GB.* ch. v.–vii. ; and as regards the so-called " pyre " of Sandan of Tarsus, see the criticisms of A. B. Cook, *Zeus*, i. 601. What was said of Sardanapalus seems to rest upon a confusion of Sin-shar-ishkun and the well-known fate of Shamash-shum-ukin ; unfortunately the British Museum text is illegible at the place where the fate of the former would be described (Gadd, *Fall of Nineveh*, 18 *sq.* ; Sidney Smith, *CAH.* iii. 129 *sq.*).

P. 376. FOUNDATION SACRIFICES.—On inaugural sacrifices, see p. 159 n. 1. At the present day, *dastūr* (" permission ") is asked on approaching the abode of any supernatural being ; and on commencing any undertaking it is usual to call on the name of Allah, the Virgin, and the Prophet (Canaan, *JPOS.* v. 166 *sq.*). The first or beginning of anything is crucial (cf. Crawley, *Mystic Rose*, 136, 191, 285), and ceremonies intended to carry one over an initial critical period are as common as they are psychologically intelligible (cf. Marett, *Threshold*,

---

[1] On burnt sacrifices in general, see G. F. Moore, *E.Bi.* art. "Sacrifice," §§ 12 *sq.*, 26 ; Lagrange, 261 ; and on cremation, see Sartori, *Zeit. d. Vereins f Volkskunde*, xvii. 361 *sqq.*

171 *sqq.*). On foundation sacrifices in particular, see especially Sartori, *Zeit. f. Ethnol.* xxx. 1–54.[1] For Malalas's story of Antioch ; see A. B. Cook, *Zeus*, ii. 1188. In the Arabic version of the Travels of John the Son of Zebedee (ed. Mrs. A. S. Lewis, 43) it is related that there was a Satanic power in the bath-house of the temple at Antioch ; when the foundations were laid, a living girl was buried in the ground and the foundation-stone laid over her, and thrice a year (at dates known to the keeper) this Satanic being would strangle a victim. The belief still survives that certain buildings, especially baths and houses erected near a spring, will not prosper unless the foundation has been erected upon blood ; and in the case of a Turkish bath a negro or Sudanese is the victim, whence such sayings as " The bath does not work except on a negro." [2] Of special interest is the evidence of Landtmann (*Acta Academiœ Abœnsis*, 1920, i. 5) on " Papuan Magic in the Building of Houses "—the lives of two old people, selected for the purpose, are forfeited when the building of the " men's house " is completed ; the actual cause of death is not clear, " there seems to be an understanding that the endowment of the house, with its various magical properties, has consumed their vitality " (12 *sq.*, 28).

" All sanctuaries are consecrated by a theophany " (p. 436) ; and in the closely related stories of the altars inaugurated by Gideon and by Manoah, the mysterious messenger who disappears (in xiii. 20 he ascends in the flame ; cf. Judg. xx. 40, of a burning city) may be the echo of a tradition of the burning of a sacred human victim (see S. A. Cook, *JTS.* 1927, No. 112). The human sacrifice at Duma (p. 370) to consecrate the altar finds a parallel in the similar sacrifice at the construction of altars of the Indian fire-god Agni (Loisy, 367), and in the Jewish and Christian belief that the souls of the righteous and of martyred saints are under the heavenly altar—martyrs being true sacrificial victims (see R.H.Charles on *Rev.* vi. 9). Evidence for ancient foundation sacrifices, illustrative of the story of Hiel's sacrifice (1 Kings xvi. 34), has been furnished by excavation in Palestine ; besides remains of actual sacrifices are figurines of men cut from laminæ of bronze and silver (Macalister, *Gezer*, ii. 426 *sqq.*). It may be remarked that the Babylonian ritual for the dedication of a house names the brick-god (*il libitti*), who, prominent during the work of building, is now expelled (Zimmern, *Zeit. f. Ass.* xxiii. 369). Foundation deposits, however, are found, nails terminating in a female bust, copper male figures

---

[1] See also Trumbull, *Threshold Covenant*, 45 *sqq.* ; Jaussen, 339, 343 ; Frazer, *GB*. iii. 89 *sqq.* ; *FOT.* i. 421 *sq.* ; and for the degeneration of the practice and the survivals, A. C. Haddon, *Study of Man*, 347–361.

[2] Canaan, *JPOS.* vi. 63 ; see also Hanauer, *Qy. St.* Jan. 1908, p. 77 *sq.* (if a man's shadow fall upon a foundation-stone that is being laid he will die within the year).

bearing the builder's basket, clay figures of the god Papsukal.[1] On the other hand, in Egypt the foundation deposits are under the corners of a building or the wall itself, and consist of objects intended to serve the deceased in his future life.

P. 381. VITAL PARTS OF THE BODY.—Among the Semites, as among other early peoples, the psychical (mental, ethical) and physical are one, " psychical and ethical functions are considered to be just as appropriate to the bodily organs as the physiological." [2] For the Bab. liver (*kabittu*) and reins (*kalitu, kalāte*) as seats of the emotions, see Dhorme, *Rev. Bibl.* xxxi. 506, 508 *sq.*, xxxii. 194. On the liver in Syriac and Arabic literature, see Merx, *Florilegium Vogüé*, 427 *sqq.* (citing, *inter alia*, Ibn Ezra, " the soul is in the liver "). The liver is of special interest for its use in divination (hepatoscopy), the pseudo-science which spread to the Etruscans, Greeks, and Romans, and turned on the belief that by appropriate means the liver of a sacrificial victim could be made to reflect the very soul or intention of the god.[3]

Any part of the body that was regarded as vital, indeed anything that seemed to be intimately connected with a man (*e.g.* his name or shadow), could be treated as an integral part of him, part of his personality in fact. In this way any part of a whole (*a*) could be used by an enemy, who would work magic by means of it [4]; or (*b*) it could be used as a charm or talisman, like a saint's relic,[5] and (*c*) it could be placed in security in order to preserve the owner's life.[6]

The " part " sufficiently represents the " whole." The under-

---

[1] See, further, L. W. King, *Records of the Reign of Tukulti-Ninib*, i. 15 *sqq.*

[2] H. Wheeler Robinson, in Peake's *People and Book*, 353 *sqq.* ; for O.T. data, see 362 *sqq.*

[3] For a concise account of Jastrow's researches in this field, see his *Religious Beliefs in Babylonia and Assyria*, 150 *sqq.* ; cf. also Halliday, *Gr. Div.* 187 *sqq.*, 198. On the erroneously styled " caul " (the " finger " or " lobe " of the liver), see Moore in the *Nöldeke-Festschrift*, 761 *sqq.* ; it was probably as a protest against divination that this significant part (the Roman *caput jecoris*) was commanded to be burnt (Lev. iii. 4 ; see Jastrow, 172 n. 2).

[4] For magical practices with parts of the body, see *GB.* i. 182–200. The belief in the danger of throwing away one's nail parings is old (see Seligsohn, *Jewish Ency.* " Nails " ; Daiches, *Oil Magic*, 32 n.).

[5] Cf. p. 382 n. 1. For the head as a trophy, see G. Jacob, *Das Leben d. vorislam. Beduinen*, 128 and n. 2 ; and as a relic, M. van Berchem, *Sachau-Festschrift*, 303 *sq.* ; Reinach, *Rev. de l'Hist. Rel.* lxiii. 25 ; *Cultes*, iv. 252 *sq.*

[6] The after-birth (*GB.* xi. 162) was viewed in Egypt as the physical or spiritual double of the child, and is still preserved among Arab tribes of the Sudan. At Kordofan a shrine is said to contain the placenta of a holy man ; see C. G. Seligman and Miss Margaret Murray, *Man* (1911), No. 97 (the Egyptian Sed festival and African parallels); Seligman, *JRAI.* xliii. 658 ; and the *Ridgeway Presentation Volume*, 451 *sq.*

lying principle recurs in ideas of group responsibility or corporate personality where the individual is part of a larger unit, which he can represent as a victim, scapegoat, mediator, etc. It is expressed (a) psychologically, in the ideas of preserving or of blotting out a *name*, and (b) physically, in rites for the preservation of blood, etc. Material vehicles are commonly required, as when a monument is set up to perpetuate the name, or the Ark and Temple of the Israelites testify to the presence and protection of Yahweh. The life of the people is wrapped up, as it were, in David the King (2 Sam. xxi. 17), but when David's life is bound up in the bundle of life with Yahweh (1 Sam. xxv. 29; Frazer, *FOT*. ii. 503 *sqq.*), the question arises whether there were appropriate symbols (*e.g.* like the Australian *churinga* or other material receptacles of life or soul). Similarly, when souls could be hunted or snared (Ezek. xiii. 17–21; *FOT*. ii. 510 *sqq.*), it is to be noted that among other peoples the belief that the soul has some concrete or material embodiment is a commonplace. In the various beliefs to the effect that (a) the individual has a life, soul, or vital principle which can be localized (in the blood, fat, etc.), and (b) that the larger group-unit can be represented adequately by a particular individual, are illustrated the ways in which early peoples endeavoured to express certain intuitive convictions of the " whole " of which the individual was a vital " part," and the relation between parts and wholes, whether of groups or of individuals. Frequently, the death or annihilation of a " part" does not affect the " whole." The man has an " external soul " or it is preserved elsewhere, and he is therefore safe (*GB*. xi. ch. x. *sq.*). An animal dies, but the species lives ; or it is killed, but certain appropriate beliefs and rites secure the continuity of the animal. The individual is bound up with that which is more permanent than himself—the group (through whom runs one common life), or the " living god," whose attribute guarantees the continuity of the group. The fundamental convictions of some unity and continuity transcend the particular ways in which we find them expressed ; and the fact that even in totemism they occur in remarkably systematized forms is far more important than the secondary question whether those are the " origin " of the more advanced forms.

P. 395 *sq.* PROPERTY.—Primitive ideas of property turn upon (1) the relations between the group and its god, (2) the group's land and livelihood, and (3) the relations between the group and the individual. Even among rudimentary peoples there is a certain amount of individuality and—where men have their own fetishes or their own personal totems—of individual religion, and consequently personal property is by no means rare (cf. p. 590). Thus, the Australian native will give away his weapons, tools, or even his *churinga*—the sacred object with which his soul or spirit is connected—though it is disposed of only according to certain rules (Wheeler, *The Tribe*, 36 *sq.*). Men can even possess dances ; there are proprietary rights in other than material objects, although when they are claimed or renounced, a certain reality and substance is given to the procedure by means of symbols ; cf. the story of Ruth (iii. 9, iv. 7), and see *Kinship*, 105. Naturally, individuality and individual property are less and ideas of communal or group property are greater among early, unspecialized, or relatively simple societies ; and when the religion encourages community of goods, this has sometimes meant, *e.g.* in Fiji, " the privilege of pilfering each other's goods with impunity." [1]

What is intimately connected with an individual is so much a part of him that it can serve as a potent relic or can be used to his hurt by the " magician." This might be his hair or his clothing, and sometimes the personal property of a man is so indistinguishable from him that it is destroyed at his death, not necessarily in the conviction that in this way it could accompany him to his new existence—prevalent though this belief has been—but rather from " the primitive extension of the man's personality to all the objects commonly associated with him in his lifetime." [2]

Among simple peoples, and hunters in particular, there is little divided ownership of land, and rights are shared by the tribe as a whole. But among so rude a folk as the Veddahs individuals will hold land, though they may not alienate it save with the permission of the group. Such a rule is common, and in Babylonia when Manishtusu bought an estate for his son, the leading men of each hamlet were the sellers (Johns, *Bab. and Ass. Laws*, 192). " Private ownership tends to increase in the higher agricultural stages, but partly in association with the communal principle, partly qualified by dependence on the chief, or, in some instances, by something of the nature of 'feudal tenure.' " [3]

The underlying ideas of property are of a semi-mystical nature in that the land belongs to the whole group and its sacred beings ; or, as in Israel, both land and people belong to the god (cf. pp. 95 *sqq.*, 536 *sq.*). In Australian totemism the totem-group who own land are virtually the reincarnations of their ancestors, and it is a typical conviction that the place where men are born is their own, and that they have a right to hunt over it. [4] Further, although ideas of property *seem* to lead

[1] J. F. M'Lennan, *Studies in Ancient History*, 2nd series, 217 ; to a similar effect, see R. A. S. Macalister, *Hist. of Civilisation in Palestine*, 127 *sqq.*

[2] E. S. Hartland, *Primitive Law*, 88 *sqq.*

[3] Hobhouse, Wheeler, and Ginsberg, 246, 253.

[4] Hobhouse, *Morals in Evolution*, 322, 325. Cf. p. 536 n. 2 above.

back to an absolute community, analogous to a primary promiscuity (cf. *Kinship*, 150 *sq.*), this is *theory* rather than *practice*, for there are representatives (chiefs, priests, etc.), and they have superior rights and privileges on account of their important functions or duties, which are primarily on behalf of the group. For example, they will receive a larger share of booty, etc. (see above, p. 495 *sq.*). Indeed, individuals may be said to have property-rights only as effective members of the group, and according to an old Arab rule, " none can be heirs who do not take part in battle, drive booty, and protect property " (*Kinship*, 66). However simple and intelligible in itself such a principle might be, it is a natural step from the rule that booty belonged only to the actual warriors (*ib.* 67) to the typical problem whether other members of the group were entitled to share in the distribution (1 Sam. xxx. 24 *sq.*, compared with Num. xxxi. 27 *sqq.*). And here arose the problem of the limits of groups. In general, the members of a group are bound together by initiation and other unifying ceremonies, by a common belief both in the validity of taboos, curses, and other supernatural sanctions, and in the function of the gods.[1] Property rights belonged to the full member of the group ; the man outside the group is as such rightless ; see further, p. 661.

Writers who suppose that primitive communities would escape the temptations to greed and avarice that beset modern societies, tend to forget that wives, children, and slaves were, in a sense, property. In fact, these certainly evoked early ideas of production and possession, even as the problems of the food-supply inevitably stimulated primitive speculation on growth and ownership. Even marital rights are property rights (*Kinship*, 105 ; cf. 132) ; but the rights of men over women are not absolute (cf. Westermarck, *Moral Ideas*, i. 631 *sqq.*, 637 *sqq.*). Women are commonly regarded as chattels ; but they have limited rights of property, even as slaves may have a right to their own earnings. Neither women nor slaves could dispose of their person ; and although their liberty is typically restricted as regards specific functions and duties, the menfolk, too, as full members of a group, are in their turn subject to the restrictions borne by the group. Hence the group-system is, as such, founded upon mutual restrictions which are for its welfare ; though in practice there is the invariable question whether such and such restrictions upon the disposal of oneself or one's possessions—in the widest sense—are for the advantage of particular individuals or of the group as a whole.

The feeling that production gives right of possession finds its most

---

[1] There are well-known gods of justice or righteousness (cf. p. 659 below) ; and in Senegambia two gods preside over Justice and Property respectively (Frazer, *FOT*, iii. 317). See, in general, Frazer, *Psyche's Task*.

characteristic expression in the question whether children, being gotten by the mother, belong to her kin-group, or, being begotten by the father, should be reckoned to his (cf. *CAH*. i.[2] 207 *sq*.). The difference, which is of the first importance in sociological development, not only involves primitive conceptions of production and ownership, but is also bound up with ideas of the supernatural factor in the processes of growth. As a general rule, much that could be reckoned among a man's possessions was seen to be due not solely to his own efforts ; and ideas of production and possession typically involved the supernatural powers as causes of fertility and prosperity, or even as owners and occupiers of the world at large. Thus, waste land had its occupants, it must not be opened up heedlessly ; and when the Hebrew *yārash* significantly covers both possession and dispossession, it agrees with the general feeling that things not already possessed by men are not without some possessor who has rights over them, or that they are " sacred " before they are taken by " sacred " individuals or are put to " profane " use after suitable precautions (above, p. 159 n.).[1]

The very practice of firstfruits, firstlings, and votive offerings, and the ceremonies believed to be indispensable for the maintenance and sustenance of the group, commonly reflect the primitive prototype of the later and more explicit conviction that, whatever be due to human activity, the increase is given by God. In the anxiety of primitive peoples concerning the fertility of man and of nature it is possible to perceive the underlying question—Do the gods (spirits, etc.) own, control, or exploit what they bestow upon men, much in the same way as men ? Or, as proprietors, agencies, producers, etc., are their activities in some way quite different from man's ? In other words, men's ideas of their own powers, and their ideas of what lies within the power of gods, spirits, and the like, interact ; and in the ideas of property, possession, rights, and so forth, the human and the supernatural or divine spheres interpenetrate. Moreover, sometimes the gods are obviously thought to possess complete rights over the processes upon which men rely ; but at other times they appear to be so immediately one with them as to be " immanent " in them. In either case men expect by appropriate appeal to gain the help of their gods. But, as apart from this, groups or special individuals are constantly performing ceremonies as though these processes were either completely under their control or immanent in themselves. That is to say, the data of religion represent gods and men alike as *controlling* from

---

[1] Hence, too, when the group-system has come to repudiate the widow and orphan it will be enunciated (as in O.T. religion) that these are under the care of the god of the group, thus extending the idea of the limits of the group and the group-god in question.

outside the processes upon which production, property, and wealth may be said to depend, or as being in intimate and immediate connexion with them, *immanent* in them.

W. R. S.'s fundamental theory is that holy things belong to the holy group and its god ; and when they are appropriated, it is by the representatives of the group and for the purposes of the group in its relation to the god (p. 147). This group, bound up with its past and its future, and with the god, is not the visible group limited in space and time ; and in agreement with this is his argument elsewhere to the effect that all property belongs to the group, and that individuals have only the usufruct (*Kinship*, 67). The latter view is instructive if only because such a law as that of the bird's nest in Deut. xxii. 6 *sq.* is no doubt meant to be a typical case of the " right of user." Complete possession cannot be claimed, especially by a people who, with its land, belongs to its god ; and even the ceremonial treatment of the blood of animals slain for food reflects the conviction that part of the victim must be restored to the giver of all things (p. 584 *sq.*).

W. R. S.'s strong remarks upon the evil effect of ideas of property in the development of religion are in keeping with his entire argument. A wrong notion of property obscures the elementary facts of the relation between the member of a group, his group, and the god. It is true that he seems to some writers to underrate the undeniable psychological value of benevolence and generosity (2 Cor. ix. 7) ; but he is concerned with the danger of false notions of the value of mere acts of transference, as though divine favour could be bought by payments (p. 396). The prophets condemn the assumption that heavy payments and costly gifts would purchase those practical manifestations of Yahweh's favour and assistance upon which the people's very existence depended (cf. G. B. Gray, *Sacrifice*, 43 *sq.*, 53 *sq.*). To cite Gray, " The prophets held forth the truth that God's favour is found by man's becoming like Himself, just and merciful . . . the tenour of their teaching was, not gifts but fellowship " (44). In other words, their ideal is the *imitatio Dei*, and this is no other than the spiritual counterpart of the primitive ideas that man's life, property, and welfare are secured by the ceremonial rites of communion or of identification with supernatural beings or with " natural " processes, which rites, however " magical " they tend to become, have in their primary stages those valuable characteristics which merit the term " magico-religious." Primitive religion—religion in its primary stages—is predominantly practical (cf. also Matt. vi. 25–33), and although W. R. S. appears to be dealing with abstract and theoretical questions, they are the ideas which are implicit, however imperfectly, in religious cults from totemism upwards.

P. 402. WAR.[1]—Among primitive peoples the objects of war are
mainly blood-revenge and vengeance, rather than booty or territorial
gains. At a more advanced stage, where religious, political, and other
considerations are interwoven, wars avenge affronts upon the god's
representative, people, or land ; they carry the god's name where it
was previously unknown, and among the old Oriental peoples wars, as
distinct from mere forays, will owe their driving force to religious
enthusiasm (or fanaticism), and the imperialism is a religious one.
Speaking generally, at the opening ceremonies of war means are taken
to consult oracles and enlist the gods (1 Sam. xxiii. 2, 4, 11 ; contrast xxviii. 6, 15 ; cf. Wellhausen, 132, 136 *sq.*). The familiar mimetic
rites of primitive peoples serve partly to concentrate attention upon
the coming fight, and no doubt partly also as a rehearsal. The
dramatic language of Ezekiel (ch. iv.), symbolizing the certainty of the
divine judgment, would find a distinctly " magical " counterpart in
the means commonly adopted to ensure, if not rather to compel, the
help of the gods ; cf. the story of Nectanebus (in Budge, *Alexander
the Great*, ii. 4 *sq.*). The mimetic ceremonies and the taboos of the
women, when the men are away fighting, have primarily a psychological
value ; they are " the spontaneous outflow of action along the line
of that which absorbed their attention " (I. King, *Devel. of Rel.* 179 *sq.*).
But while the knowledge of the women's interest could naturally
stimulate the absent menfolk, the activities tend to become regarded
as indispensable and automatically helpful, and thus gain a " magical "
efficacy. Similarly, the chastity both of the women at home and of
the warriors away, and the various taboos and vows, are primarily of
psychological value, being " religious," or rather " magico-religious,"
before they become mechanical methods of hastening victory. That
some taboos were likely to defeat their object is evident from what is
said of Saul's vow (1 Sam. xiv. 24 *sqq.*) and of the Jews' refusal to fight on
their Sabbath day (1 Macc. ii. 32 *sqq.*). Frazer cites cases of abstinence
from food, self-mutilation, and even the cutting off of fingers among
the Nootka Indians in order to ensure success (*GB.* iii. 160 *sqq.*).
Primarily, all such heroic measures are intended to gain if not to
force the assistance of the gods, and however " superstitious " or
" frivolous " they may seem, it is necessary to recognize that they
are psychologically explicable in their origin, and are very important
testimonies to the similarity of the religious consciousness everywhere,
and to the spontaneous conviction of the efficacy of restrictions,
restraints, mortifying practices, and self-inflicted pain.

[1] See Schwally, *Semit. Kriegsaltertümer* ; Holsti, " Some Superstitious Customs
in Primitive Warfare," *Westermarck-Festschrift*, 137 *sqq.* ; Sir G. A. Smith,
Deuteronomy, 243 *sqq.* ; S. A. Cook, *Rel. of Ancient Palestine*, s.v.

The order of encampment in Num. ii.—each tribe with its standard —finds a parallel in the Bedouin encampment " by kindreds " (Doughty, i. 414), and among North American Indians on the march, when " the members of each totem-clan camp together and the clans are arranged in a fixed order in camp " (Frazer, *Tot. Ex.* i. 75). When some Australian tribes go to war, the totem animal is carried, stuffed, as a standard.[1] Not only do the gods frequently accompany the army (p. 37 above), but men fight on behalf of their gods or what their gods stand for ; and they will be appropriately decorated with symbols or emblems of their totem or their god. They thus do more than merely imitate their gods : they are filled with a literal " enthusiasm." To warlike peoples correspond gods of war, and Egyptian references to the fierceness of Pharaoh, like " Baal in his wrath," etc., throw light upon the character of the Palestinian god (Hadad, see p. 532 *sq.*)—with which one may compare the attributes of Yahweh as a war-god—and point to the considerable body of relevant beliefs and practices concerning war and the gods which once prevailed (cf. *CAH.* ii. 349 ; iii. 431). The *ḥērem* is only theoretically absolute (Doughty, i. 335 ; Sir G. A. Smith on Deut. ii. 34). The slaughter of prisoners, especially chiefs, was a common practice in Egypt. In Assyria, of evil fame for its atrocities, Ashurnasirpal II. burns boys and girls (Annals, i. 109 ; ii. 19, 109 *sq.*) ; Ashurbanipal slays prisoners for the dead (*Keilinschrift. Bibliothek*, ii. 193, col. iv. 70), and kills the king of Elam on a board like a sheep (*KB.* ii. 257). On the *nacī'a*, see pp. 363 n., 491 *sq.*, and cf. the survival in Doughty, i. 452 ; and for the suggestion of the " eminent scholar," see Wellhausen, 121 n. 2, 127 n. 4. The splitting or rending (p. 491) recalls the use of *shāsaʿ* of the tearing open of the bird in Lev. i. 17 ; and when Samson similarly tears the lion down the middle, cf. the act of Engidu, and see further Burney, *Judges*, 358, and plate ii. (4).

The subsequent purificatory rites (p. 491) are on the same principle as those after other cases of bloodshed (see *GB.* iii. 157 *sqq.*, 165 *sqq.* ; *FOT.* i. 87 *sq.*, 93 *sqq.* ; Gray, *Num.* 243 *sq.*). Men pass through or under something, they wash away the stains of blood, they appease the spirits of the slain, and in one way or another ceremonially mark the cessation of the state of warfare which had been ceremonially inaugurated.

P. 406. SPRING FESTIVALS.—In the first lecture of the second series of the Burnett Lectures, " traces of the sanctity of the month of Nisan were shown to exist over a wide area, not only among the Arabs, but also among the northern Semites. The Hebrew Passover was older

---

[1] M'Lennan, *Studies in Ancient History*, ii. 301 ; cf. 380 (Aztecs), and Frazer, *Tot. Ex.* ii. 23 (Torres Straits).

than the settlement in Canaan, and preserved antique features similar to those of the most primitive Arabian sacrifices. In the later forms of Semitic religions, as elsewhere among the civilized peoples of antiquity, there gradually arose an elaborate cycle of annual feasts— a sacred calendar which ultimately was fixed astronomically." [1] On the Arab sacrifices in the month Rajab (pp. 227 *sq.* and n. 3, 465), see now Wellhausen, 97 *sqq.*; Winckler, *Altorient. Forsch.* ii. 344 *sq.*; Benzinger, *E.Bi.* " Passover " (especially col. 3594), and Moore, *ib.* " Sacrifice," § 4 *sq.* (on Spring Sacrifices).

Among other spring festivals are those of Harran : the first days of Nisan being a festival to Beltis (pp. 406 *sq.*, 470 *sq.*; Chwolson, ii. 25, 181); Hierapolis : annual holocausts (pp. 371 n., 375, 406, 471); and Cyprian Aphrodite (pp. 291, 470, 472). The Nabatæan and Palmyrene evidence (p. 407 n.) consists in the frequency with which inscriptions are dated in Nisan ; cf., for example, the "symposia" (p. 627), and see Lidzbarski, *Ephem.* ii. 304.

For modern spring circumcision festivals among the Arabs, see Doughty, i. 340 *sq.* (sacrifice of sheep, dancing, the young men select wives). The Neby Musā Easter festival, held a few miles to the south-west of Jericho, is a time of music and story-telling, of trading and of contests, vows are paid, the dead visited, and circumcision rites performed (Canaan, *JPOS.* vi. 117 *sqq.*). North Syrian Christians in the course of their solemn Easter ceremonies place food on the tombs (Parry, *Six Months in a Christian Monastery*, 382 *sq.*). At Malta a spring festival of St. John the Baptist seems to have taken the place of an Adonis rite (Baudissin, 129 *sqq.*, citing Wünsch's monograph, 50 *sq.* [1902]). For a spring festival with traces of fertility rites in Algeria, among the Shawiya, and some 150 miles away from the seat of the ancient Ausenses with their festival to Athena (Herod. iv. 180), see Hilton-Simpson, *Folk-lore*, xxxiii. 192, *Geog. Journ.* 1922, Jan., 32. For some traces of Easter vegetation rites in Italy and for a Greek association of the Resurrection with fertility in general, see above, p. 597. In modern Greece certain April dances have very archaic features; see Diels (*Harnack-Festschrift*, 69, 72 n. 4), who cites the condemnation by St. Basil of the shameless Easter dances of his day (Migne, *Patr. Gr.* xxxi. 446).

Possible indications of a spring festival among the Hittites, with horse-racing, etc., have been tentatively pointed out by Ehelolf (*SB.* of the Berlin Academy, 1925, p. 269). But by far the most valuable evidence is that of the Babylonian spring festival of the birth of the year and the union of the solar deity Inurta or (at Lagash)

---

[1] *Life*, 526. The second course (consisting of three lectures) was delivered from fragmentary notes.

Ningirsu with the goddess Gula or (at Nippur) Bau (*KAT.* 371 ; Jastrow, *Rel. Bel.* 130, 340 *sqq.*). Traces of specific fertility rites at the New Year (spring) are very ancient, to judge from the Assyrian festival in the garden of Nebo's temple in Assyria, where the king, priests in masks (evidently representing various gods), and Ishtar appear to perform ceremonies connected with the revival of vegetation. From a stela of Ur-Nammu (*c.* 2300 B.C.), it is possible that the ceremonial eating of fruit by the king was a significant part of these or similar rites.[1] Of special interest are the New Year festivals such as were held at Erech in Tishri (autumn) and at Babylon in Nisan (spring). Here, in the sixth and later centuries B.C., there was a celebration of the death and resurrection of Marduk-Bel, wherein the king and the priest took the part of that god and of Nebo respectively. On the evening of Nisan 4 there was a recital of the Creation Epic, with the birth of Marduk, his victory over the rebels, the establishment of the Divine Order, the theft of the Tablets of Destiny, Marduk's fall—Babylon is thrown into confusion in his absence—and his subsequent return.[2] Among the features of importance for this note and the following, are (1) the ceremonial entry of the Babylonian high priest into the very presence of the god on the second of Nisan. Similarly, the Jewish high priest goes behind the veil on the Jewish Day of Atonement, on the 10th of the (autumnal) New Year (Lev. xvi., Heb. ix. 7). To be allowed to see the face of the Pharaoh, the representative of the national god, was a sign of high favour (cf. the Amarna Letters, Nos. 148, 165, 286, etc. ; *CAH.* ii. 342). In like manner, it is the privilege of the king to be crowned by the god and to see the god in his holy chamber, and the Ethiopian Piankhi broke the seals and entered the most sacred abode of Re as an assertion of his position as legitimate Pharaoh.[3]

(2) On the fifth of Nisan the Babylonian king makes his first appearance and enters the shrine of Marduk alone. There follows a ritual act of humiliation and abdication. The high priest smites the king ; if he weeps, it is a good sign. After a humble prayer, the king is comforted by the priest and receives again the sceptre and other insignia of which he had been ceremonially deprived. It was a fateful time for the king, and omens were taken from his behaviour—if he

---

[1] See further, Sidney Smith, *Bulletin of the School of Oriental Studies* (1926), 72 *sq.* ; *Rev. d'Ass.* xxi. (1924), 84.

[2] See further, Langdon, *Bab. Epic of Creation*, 20 *sq.*, *JRAS.* 1924, p. 69 *sq.* ; Zimmern, *Das bab. Neujahrsfest* (*Der alte Orient*, 1926) ; Pallis, *The Babylonian Akîtu Festival* (Copenhagen, 1926). For the texts, see Gressmann, *Altorient. Texte z. A.T.*[2] 295–322.

[3] Breasted, *Anc. Rec.* ii. §§ 134, 221 *sqq.*, iv. §§ 806, 871 ; Hall, *CAH.* iii. 272 *sq.*

stumbled, it was unlucky. Certain traces of Jewish prayers for royalty at the spring or at the autumn New Year appear to indicate that the New Year as a time of confirming or renewing kingly majesty was known also in Judaism.[1]

(3) The New Year is a time of judgment. On Nisan 8 and 11 Marduk and the gods assemble in the Chamber of Destiny and decree the fates for the coming months. Similarly, at the New Year festival of the Yezīdis, the god sits on the throne issuing decrees for the year.[2] Survivals of the same belief attached themselves to the period of the Jewish Day of Atonement at the autumnal New Year. Late tradition differed as to whether the world was created in the first month (spring) or in the seventh (autumn). At all events, in the seventh month, on the anniversary of the creation of the world, God determines the lot of each land, whether it be for war or peace, for abundance or famine. According to popular belief, nine days are spent in fixing the destiny of individuals, and on the tenth the angels inscribe it in the book of fate.[3]

(4) It is a well-known belief that the opening day of the year will determine the rest (e.g. Nilsson, *Archiv f. Rel.* xix. 65, 69). References to fertility rites at Easter or the New Year have already been made. Their appropriateness at this season is obvious. Further, it is sometimes believed that (*a*) the decrees for the forthcoming year will affect the amount of rainfall, or (*b*) that the rain at the New Year is especially efficacious. Thus, as regards (*a*), it was a Jewish belief that at the beginning of the (autumnal) New Year rain was decreed in accordance with the merits of Israel. If Israel sinned, there was only little; if she repented, the amount could not be increased, but it would fall where it would do most good. If Israel was righteous, much rain would be decreed; if she sinned, the decree could not be revoked, but the rain would fall on seas and deserts, so that men would not profit from it.[4] As for (*b*), in Morocco the rain of April 27–May 3 has *baraka* and cures sterility, and in Palestine rain in Nisan is especially

---

[1] H. St. J. Thackeray, *Septuagint and Jewish Worship* (1921), 94; on the New Year prayers extolling divine majesty, see Bousset-Gressmann, *Rel. d. Judentums*[3], 371 *sq.* See further, H. Schmidt, *Die Thronfahrt Jahves am Fest der Jahreswende im Alten Israel* (Tübingen, 1927).

[2] Brockelmann, *ZDMG.* lv. 388 *sqq.*; cf. Chabot, *J. As.*, ninth series, vii. 123 *sq.*

[3] *Rosh ha-Shanah*, i. 9; see *KAT.* 515 nn. 9–10; *Jew. Encyc.* "Atonement (Day of)," "New Year"; G. B. Gray, *Sacrifice*, 303 *sq.* On the Hebrew parallel to the Babylonian "tablets of fate," cf. Pss. lxix. 28, lxxxvii. 6, cxxxix. 16, and Bousset-Gressmann, 258.

[4] Contrast Matt. v. 45, and see p. 663. In *Jubilees* xii. 16 *sq.*, Abraham is rebuked for his attempt, on the night of the New Moon of the seventh month, to determine from the stars the prospects of the year as regards rainfall.

valued (Westermarck, *Morocco*, ii. 177 *sqq.*). On a water ceremony at
the well Zamzam at the New Year, believed to affect the supply of
water throughout the year, see Gaudefroy-Demombynes, 84 *sq.*

Finally, (5) the beginning of the year is a new creation and inaugurates new conditions.[1] The belief that a new stage is introduced
underlies both the annual Day of Atonement in the autumnal New
Year (see p. 650) and the significance of the spring New Year at great
periods in Biblical tradition : (*a*) the birth of Israel as a nation
(Ex. xiii. 4), (*b*) the beginning of the return from exile under Ezra
(first of the first month, Ezra vii. 9), and (*c*) the return of Nehemiah
(Neh. ii. 1).[2]

P. 408. ATONEMENT.—When it is said that in primitive religion
" the sense of sin, in any proper sense of the word, did not exist at
all " (p. 401), a distinction is being drawn between the modern idea
of sin as specifically an ethical, moral, or spiritual failing or offence and
that wider connotation of words for sin, evil, wrong, etc., which characterizes early stages of thought. Here the infringement of some
recognized custom or rite is very keenly felt ; and men, overwhelmed
by the fear of the consequences which are expected to follow upon a
broken taboo, have been known to sicken and even to die. Early
ideas of " wrong " (a convenient term for " sin," in the widest sense)
are bound up with unanalysed conceptions of all evil, harm, or distress,
and enter into all departments of life and thought—illness, accidents,
loss, defeat, drought, etc. A misfortune is the first and surest sign
of some defect or offence. Broadly speaking, misfortune will be
ascribed (1) to a known or unknown fault of (*a*) the individual himself, or (*b*) of some other member of the group, whose offence reacts
upon the whole or some part of the group ; (2) to the deliberate malice
of another individual who has employed " magic " ; or (3) to some
supernatural cause. Moreover, apart from all positive ills, even fear,
uneasiness, and *malaise* are no less indications that something is wrong,
whereas when things are right there is confidence and relief. Hence
the problems of sin (wrong) and atonement must be viewed compre-
hensively along with ideas both of the sacred or holy and all that
infringes upon it (pp. 161 *sqq.*), and with ideas of right and righteousness and all that these involve (pp. 661, 663, 670 *sq.*).

Certain taboos and rites of propitiation in war-time have tended to be
suicidal (see p. 640) ; certain fears as to the consequence of destroying

---

[1] March 25 was the day of the resurrection of Attis (*GB.* v. 273), and a world-
birthday (see Norden, *Geburt des Kindes*, 14 *sqq.*).

[2] On the tradition that Joseph was born and was also liberated from prison on
the autumnal New Year, see Thackeray, *JTS.* xvi. 194. Ezekiel's vision of the
new Israel is on the tenth of the " beginning " of the year (Ezek. xl. 1).

animal and insect life, as found among the Jains, would make life impossible, were they acted on consistently. In Zoroastrianism there are most extreme notions of ritual uncleanness which, as Farnell says, must have been idle thunder, else Persia would have been depopulated.[1] Among the Aztecs there was a profound consciousness of sin (*ERE.* v. 637), and their gloomy and cruel rites are as instructive for the psychology of religion as those current among the Phœnicians (see p. 415). Especially in Babylonia was there a very deep sense of sin, an extreme sensitiveness—amounting almost to obsession—as regards unknown and unwitting offences or oversights. Though ethical ideas are by no means wanting, this consciousness of sin, even among advanced peoples, is that of wrong in a wide sense, and the passionate laments in Babylonian " Penitential Psalms " are, taken by themselves, no clue to the calamity which the penitent bewails.[2] But while the Babylonian hymn may specify the ritual which was overlooked or is now to be performed, the Hebrew psalms are conspicuous for the absence of the ritual note, so that in Ps. li. 18 *sq.* the question arises whether this is a later liturgical addition, or whether such passages have elsewhere been removed.[3]

The various methods of removing " sin " and of gaining relief, however mechanical they may become, must owe their rise, reappearance, and reshaping to their psychological efficacy. Among primitive peoples, confession of social or ethical wrong-doing is sometimes enjoined on critical occasions of illness or childbirth, or when on an expedition or at war.[4] Though not necessarily a systematized rite it affords relief, and it is important testimony to genuine sentiments of moral right and wrong, the absence of which would make the history of ideas of righteousness, sin, and atonement unintelligible. Sin is commonly conceived along physical lines, *e.g.* as filth, dirt, etc., and the remedial measures are directed upon the victim or sufferer, or to the removal of the presumed cause. Among such remedies are a pretended emetic (*GB.* iii. 214), some powerful " medicine " or pungent odour, or the burning of incense (on which cf. Eitrem, 215 *sqq.*)—evil has a bad smell (*ib.* 212 *sq.*). Rites of washing, cleansing, etc., are especially common. In Egypt the deceased Pharaoh was washed by

---

[1] *Evolution of Religion*, 127 *sqq.* (See *ib.* Lect. iii. on the ritual of purification.)

[2] Cf. Farnell, *Greece and Babylon*, 154 *sq.*; G. Driver (ed. D. C. Simpson), 170.

[3] The fine Babylonian prayer to Ishtar (p. 522) concludes with directions for the burning of fragrant woods, a drink-offering, the offering of a lamb, and the due recital of the prayer thrice, without turning round.

[4] Frazer, *GB.* iii. 191, 195, 211, 215 *sq.*; *Belief in Immortality*, ii. 189; Hartand, *Primitive Law*, 166.

various gods, and the ritual asserted that he was " righteous." [1] In Babylonia the washing with the pure water of Eridu cleansed a man of his evil. The usage is well illustrated in the Syriac story of the woman who, as she washed her body, cleansed her thoughts also.[2]

Water and fire are frequently employed in old Oriental cleansing rites. On gods of light and fire in purificatory ceremonies see Morgenstern, 95. As the sun-god is god of light and life and of right and righteousness (p. 659), the antitheses are darkness and evil ; and a man, praying that his sickness be consumed, adds, ' May I see the light " (Jastrow, 316). The fire-god cleanses the patient, making him bright like heaven (R. C. Thompson, *Sem. Magic*, 214). Fire tests and purifies (cf. צרף, and see *E.B.* s.v. Furnace). It expels and destroys evil or the cause thereof ; note the use, not necessarily always figurative in its practice, of בְּעֵר in Deuteronomy, and cf. p. 632. The " magical " practices in the Bab. *shurpu* and *maklu* ceremonies were intended to make a man's troubles disappear as things disappeared in the flames, or, as the magic of wizard or witch (*kashshapu, -ptu*) trembled, melted, and passed away in the fire, so might the sins of man. A demon or other cause of disease, ill, etc., will be gently or forcibly persuaded to leave a human body and enter a dead animal (R. C. Thompson, 180 *sqq.*) ; and in Palestine the *jinn* who is the cause of a child's convulsions may be induced by the gift of a pigeon to leave its victim (*JPOS.* vi. 46). Rites of transference are well known. In Babylonia a pig or a lamb is employed, especially the latter (Dhorme, 272 *sqq.*; Morgen. 111, cf. 115); in the case of a fever a kid is substituted (R. C. Thompson, 211), or the fleece of a young lamb may be applied to the body of the sick (Morgen. 75 *sq.*). Evil is transferred to something which is destroyed or thrown away ; and when transferred to a man, it may be to one who is destroyed (sometimes already a criminal), or to a " sacred " man able to overcome it.[3]

[1] With this " legitimation " or " justification," Norden (*Geburt des Kindes*, 127 *sq.*) compares 1 Tim. iii. 16.

[2] Burkitt, *Euphemia and the Goth*, 156. For Egypt, see Blackman, *PSBA.* xl. 62 *sq.*; for Babylonia, Jastrow, *Rel. Bel.* 306, and cf. Morgenstern, 43. With *salāḫu*, " sprinkle with water, remove uncleanness," cf. Heb. סלח " forgive." C. G. and B. Z. Seligman (*Harvard African Studies*, ii. 155 *sq.*) tell how Kabābīsh women, dancing in front of their master who had sacrificed a sheep and cleansed them of evil, sang a song the burden of which was " You are our soap." See, in general, Farnell, *Evol. of Rel.* 157 *sq.*; Eitrem, 78 *sq.*; and p. 556 above.

[3] For details consult *GB.* ix. (on the Scapegoat); *e.g.* a Brahman embraces a Rajah of Travancore, undertaking to bear away his sins and diseases (*GB.* ix. 423 ; Crawley, *Mystic Rose*, 94); and among the Bori the healer cures a man by becoming possessed by the demon, the cause of his disease (Tremearne, *Ban of the Bori*, 20).

Calamity and suffering are found to be cathartic ; hence pain and suffering will be inflicted to compel purgation or to anticipate and ward off some calamity assumed to be impending. The man who has lost one of his flock has perhaps thereby escaped death—it is a " ransom " (Ar. *fidu*, *JPOS.* vi. 62), and by appropriate and periodical sacrifice he may hope to avert doom henceforth. If evil must befall the community, let it fall where it is richly deserved ; hence the " wicked " should be a ransom (כֹּפֶר) for the righteous (Prov. xxi. 18). All misfortune has its cause, and the offender can be discovered by lot (Josh. vii. 13 *sqq.*) or by " magic " ; or means will be taken periodically to ward off the consequences of evil which has been committed, however unintentionally.

The terminology of forgiveness and the like is instructive (cf. *CAH.* iii. 447 *sq.*). Sin is a burden to be lifted off. The transgressor hides or conceals it, and confession is recommended.[1] One must not " cover " the face of the judge ; but God, whose eyes are too pure (" clean," *ṭ-h-r*) to look on evil (Hab. i. 13), may " cover " the sin— and " love covers all sins " (Ps. xxxii. 1, Prov. x. 12). The man who is forgiven has his face " lifted up " ; or he " sees the face " of his lord (cf. Driver, *l.c.* 133) ; or his sin can be blotted out (Jer. xviii. 23), and the tablet upon which it is written may be broken (Driver, 138 ; Morgen. 129). An action may be " reckoned " (חשב) evil, or the judge will " pass over it." Or the god is regarded as an irate avenger who must be " mollified " (p. 346 and n. 1), or placated with gifts or the smell of an offering ; one must hide from his anger (Job xiv. 13), unless he " turn away " from it, or he " return " to the people he had forsaken (cf. the moving entreaty to the absent god, Jastrow, *Rel. Bel.* 322). The god wreaks his wrath, and thus consoles himself (התנחם). Again, one must cause his heart to rest, appease it ;[2] and in Babylonia there was a day of rest for the heart of the god, when he was propitiated.[3] Or the god is besought not to accept the offering of the wicked, acceptance being a token of forgiveness.[4]

There are three main types of ideas involved : (1) the anthropomorphic or personal, where there are beings angry or pleased, who avenge evil or can turn evil into good ; (2) the impersonal, where there is, so to say, a mechanism such that sin is (*a*) the omission of what should be done, and what necessarily makes for good, or (*b*) the

[1] Prov. xxviii. 13. In the Amarna Letters, No. 137, it is called "opening" (*pitu*=פתח).

[2] נוח ; cf. the use of Bab. *nuḫḫu.* See Hehn, *Semaine d'Ethnol. Relig. à Tilbourg* (1923), 291 ; Driver, 157.

[3] *Um nuḫ libbi*, the 15th of the month ; see Wardle, *Israel and Babylon*, 244.

[4] Num. xvi. 15, Gen. iv. 5 *sq.* ; see Hehn, *l.c.* 291.

doing of that which is harmful and has necessary harmful consequences. Besides the emphasis laid either upon the supernatural powers or upon the processes, there are (3) intermediate types of idea, where the god works through the process, and the rites are the recognized means of preserving or restoring the relations between people and god. The first is characteristic of popular religion, the last of priestly ritualism ; while in the second the god recedes more and more into the background and disappears. "Sin," observes Skinner (*Gen.* 317), " is a violation of the objective moral order." But this is too narrow ; among peoples at an undifferentiated stage of thought both sin (or wrong) and right(-eousness) involve ideas of universal or cosmic order. Moral or spiritual wrong is only one side, though the most vital, of the wider conceptions which are at least implicit when convictions of right and wrong become oppressive and men feel their inability to escape from that chain of cause and effect or that entail of deeds which Indian religions so vividly depict.

According to the prophets of Palestine, the escape from the burden of evil, misfortune, and wrong lay in "return" (שׁוּב; cf. the later תְּשׁוּבָה) and μετάνοια. A "return" may be said to mark the sterile antiquarianism of Egypt (Twenty-sixth Dynasty) and Babylonia (sixth century B.C.); but whereas on the traditional view of the O.T., post-exilic Judaism is the re-establishment of, or "return" to Mosaism, on the modern standpoint there had been a change in the religious conditions, and instead of a "return" to the past there is rather a reassertion of the old in a new form, and the past has been re-viewed and re-written. In like manner, the continuity in the development from the O.T. to the N.T. and onwards appears not as any "return," but as a change or development in thought.[1] In either case there has been progress, though of progress there is no explicit idea.

When the prophet Ezekiel, calling for a "new" spirit or heart (Ezek. xi. 19, etc.),demands new energy, will, and mind, or when salvation comes in being "born again," it is to be observed that even among primitive peoples there are rites of renewal and especially of rebirth practised at initiation ceremonies and on other occasions when some entirely new stage in the life of the individual is realistically manifested and endorsed. Such practices are of the greatest psychological interest ; they testify to the consciousness of some break between old and new. They were developed by the observation of nature. Thus, in Egypt the sun-god was reborn every morning from the waters of the primeval ocean ; and the dead Pharaoh who was identified with him was daily

---

[1] On apparent "returns" in the history of thought, see S. A. Cook, *Study of Religions*, 126 *sq.*

reborn.[1]   The return of spring, the beginning of a new year, and finally
the birth of a new æon built up ideas of new development in history,
and such ideas culminated in the anticipation of an entirely new heaven
and earth.[2]   In this way men felt able to throw off the past and
hope for a new and unstained age.   There are simple and naïve
practices among primitive peoples to symbolize the removal of enmity
and ill-feeling, and there are periodic rites for the expulsion of evil.
The Day of Atonement shortly after the beginning of the (autumnal)
New Year, and the ideas of creation and the determination of fate at
that period, or in the spring New Year, are thus related to sweeping
conceptions of restoration and renewal ; and not without justice did
Franz Delitzsch call the Day of Atonement the Good Friday of the
Law (see *E.Bi.* col. 385 § 4).

In view of the supreme, if not cosmic importance of the leading
representative individuals, it is intelligible that the Babylonian king,
who, in a sense, stood for his land, should undergo atoning ceremonies
and make ritual lamentation in order that his land and people should
not suffer harm.   Such as he are *par excellence* the scapegoats in times
of misfortune and calamity.   Far more elaborate ideas are found in
India, in the Brahman theory of the daily sacrifice whereby the world
is daily created afresh by the self-sacrifice of the primordial Purusha out
of whom the world was made.   Maha-Purusha is the vast cosmic man
who both envelops the earth and transcends it ; he becomes the symbol
of creation, and is also one of the names for ultimate reality.[3]   On one
view, the world is made of god(s)—Prajapati is creator and produces
the world out of himself, upholding it and ruling it, as an immanent
divine power.   In less detail it is related how the Scandinavian giant
Ymir was dismembered by the gods, who created the world out of his
own body.   In Egypt, Osiris became the principle of life, immanent in
the world, and associated with the fertile soil and the life-giving
waters.[4]   Amid such ideas, the conviction of a renewal or regeneration
on a cosmic scale involved the renewal of the life or energy immanent
in the world.   In this way the Jewish anticipations of a Messiah and of
a Messianic age which all creation should enjoy find their later development in the Pauline conception both of a groaning creation longing for
regeneration and of a Christ who is not only the Saviour of Mankind,
but also the source and sustainer of nature.[5]

[1] Blackman, *PSBA.* xl. 60, 63, 65, 89 *sq.*

[2] See Charles, *Comment.* on Rev. xxi. 5 (pp. 174 *sq.*, 203 *sq.*) ; Bousset-Gressmann,
Rel. des Judentums[3], 243, 280 *sqq.* ; Norden, *Geburt des Kindes*, 33 *sqq.*

[3] Estlin Carpenter, *Theism in Medieval India* (1921), 43 *sq.*, 187.

[4] Breasted, *Religion and Thought*, 23 ; cf. p. 597.

[5] See p. 663. For the Messianic king who inaugurates a new age of peace

Such wider and more undifferentiated conceptions of right and wrong and of sin and atonement complicate the work of analysis which the progress of thought demands. But while W. R. S. is considered by some writers to have confused ideas of communion and of expiation or placation, on the other hand there has been a tendency to neglect those beliefs and practices—at times seemingly of a " magical " or " magico-religious " nature—with which the highly ethical and spiritual conceptions of sin and forgiveness have been interwoven. To suppose, with Buchanan Gray (*Sacrifice*, 95), that early sacrifice was more often eucharistic than propitiatory or expiatory is, surely, to overlook both the early undifferentiated and unspecialized ideas of evil and ill, and the fact that early Israel undoubtedly suffered disasters enough to call for apotropaic and other rites. But it does not follow that such rites were precisely those as described in the middle books of the Pentateuch, and it is noteworthy that the most significant of the Babylonian New Year inaugural ceremonies are of the age of Nebuchadrezzar II. (*c.* 605–562 B.C.) and later.

Highly instructive, on the other hand, is Gray's criticism (359) of W. R. S.'s remarks, p. 408 *sq.* above. Emphasizing the fact that חִטֵּא (Ezek. xlv. 18) is to cleanse of sin—to " unsin "—he explains the use of blood as a disinfectant rather than as a tonic. It is not that the altar is, as W. R. S. states, " annually refreshed by an application of blood " ; the ritual, asserts Gray, is " to rid what is naturally holy from intrusive contamination, not to impart fresh positive holiness." This, however, is W. R. S.'s meaning: sin breaks the sacred bond—the natural holiness—into which a man is born, and the atoning rites re-establish it and there is at-one-ment: " the holiness of the altar is liable to be impaired, and required to be annually *refreshed* . . ." The difference between the two scholars is possibly complicated by the choice of the word italicized ; but it involves a very important point : Does the blood *refresh* and make holy ? or does it " unsin " and *restore* the holiness ? Elsewhere W. R. S. remarks : " The notions of communion and atonement are bound up together " (p. 320) ; by partaking of what is holy the impurity of sin is expelled (p. 356) ; blood " refreshes " the sanctity of the worshipper's life and expels what is impure (p. 427). A more careful analysis may inquire whether the removal of sin thereby makes a man holy (*i.e.* forgiven, etc.), and whether the act of making a man holy thereby removes sin—contrast the medieval double rite : the expulsion of devils prior to baptism (on p. 428). For the study of sacrificial and other rites, these questions

and abundance, see the concise sketch by Hans Schmidt, *Der Mythos vom wiederkehrenden König im Alten Testament* (Giessen, 1925).

are of more than methodological importance.[1] No less important is
the question whether such analyses as these are primary. Certain
early attempts at analysis can be traced, though the difference between
the Jewish sin- and guilt-offerings is not altogether clear (cf. Gray,
57). Moreover, there are complicated ceremonies of consecration,
e.g. at the completion of an image in Babylonia, which seem to point
to attempts to bridge the gulfs between the profane, the sacred, and
its antithesis—the pollute. As a general rule, in all such matters as
these it is probable that priestly and popular opinion would be at
variance : certain rites (with the use of blood, etc.) would be specifically apotropaic : they kept away some power or influence ; or they
would be distinctively cathartic : they cleansed and purified. But
to the ordinary man the act of the removal of sin would mean the
entrance of good, and the cleansing ceremony that washed away evil
would have sanctifying virtue.[2] Everywhere there has been a tendency
for ceremonies to lose their primary significance ;[3] but, provided they
aroused the appropriate feelings of awe and solemnity, they tended
to afford convictions of relief, reassurance, and confidence which were
at least subjectively adequate.[4]

[1] In Isa. vi. the occasion that arouses a profound consciousness of sin brings the
cleansing act. How far W. R. S.'s treatment of ideas of atonement among primitive peoples may have been influenced, however unconsciously, by his Christology,
may perhaps be understood by reference to *Lectures and Essays.*

[2] In the purificatory rite in Lev. xiv. two pigeons are required : one is let loose,
the other sacrificed ; also in the ritual of the Scapegoat (Lev. xvi.) there are two
goats, one for Azazel, the other for Yahweh (see *E.Bi.* " Azazel "). There may
be here the explicit removal of impurity and the explicit sanctifying act. Further,
since Azazel, in later times at least, was the leader of the fallen angels, *i.e.* in effect
Satan, the old ritual may have suggested the antithesis between the prince of life
(ἀρχηγός, Acts iii. 15) and the prince of this world (ἄρχων, John xii. 31, xiv. 30)
who is to be cast out, and between the sacrificial death of Christ and the entry of
Satan into Judas (the διάβολος, John vi. 70) immediately after the communion rite
(xiii. 27). That the Paschal victim is a lamb (sheep) or goat is shown by Gray,
345 *sqq.*

[3] *e.g.* at the present day the sacrificed sheep has an atoning value : it will
appear on the Day of Judgment and carry the man into Paradise—hence the
saying, " Our sacrificial animals are our riding animals " (*daḥayānā maṭayānā,*
JPOS. vi. 41). Cf. *ZATW.* xxxv. 130, where the sheep or goat sacrificed seven
days after a man's death is eaten by the relatives and the bones buried, if possible,
in the grave so that the dead may ride (*r-k-b*) on it when the Day comes.

[4] At the annual ceremony of the Holy Fire in the Church of the Holy Sepulchre
in Jerusalem, children are brought in the belief that their presence at the ceremony
will preserve them against the ills of life or ensure their entrance to Paradise (*The
Near East,* June 24, 1926, p. 716). Similarly, the belief arose that all who kept the
Passover would escape death during the year (*Jubilees* xlix. 15 *sq.*). Gray (365,
381 *sq.*) argues that the Passover rite was not an act of communion but of com-

In view of the variation in the meaning and application of sacrificial atoning and other rites, the question of what—in the happy and extremely significant words of Gray (359 n.)—is the " actual creative idea " is one to which, whatever be thought of W. R. S.'s theory, the systematic study of religion demands an answer.[1] To regard the rites as primarily cathartic or apotropaic is unsatisfactory, because the notion of purifying or cleansing a man of evil, etc., or of removing untoward influences or the like, implies some considerable pre-existing body of beliefs. It is difficult to see how blood could be supposed, from any primitive standpoint, to have in itself the cathartic or apotropaic virtues which actually come to be ascribed to it. On the other hand, the assumption that the blood fed supernatural spirits, placating, sating, and otherwise inducing them to act as required, would be in accordance with primitive ideas ; but it neither follows nor is probable that this is the primary meaning. What seems to be of undoubted importance is (a) the extraordinary emotional significance of blood, and (b) the fact that the effect is *either* vague, diffused, though none the less powerful, *or* it is of the most intense significance, *e.g.* because it is the blood of a kinsman. Blood of the kin that is shed for intelligible, practical reasons in ceremonies wherein the life and welfare of the social group are concerned has a world of meaning. Such rites are an organic part of systems of life and thought ; and by reason of their very fulness and intensity it is easier to trace their weakening, deterioration, and disintegration than to conceive how any primary cathartic or apotropaic significance of blood could develop into a system.

Group blood-rites are the most elemental of all ceremonies associating men and their gods. On the other hand, spiritual religion—in the teaching of the prophets—treats sacrificial rites as of secondary value, if not, indeed, unnecessary. " Propitiation and expiation are to be wrought by well-doing alone " (Gray, 89). In contrast to the sacrificial ideas interconnecting man, god, and the world, it is enough that man should do his duty.[2] The history of religion in Palestine subsequent to the prophets illustrates the difficulty of determining wherein " well-doing " consists. Confronting a highly developed priestly ritual, the " Wisdom " literature presupposes the identity of divine wisdom and human wisdom, and inculcates reverence for the divine law. Further, " wickedness is folly, the bad man is a fool." [3] Sin

---

memoration, and was apotropaic; but the popular value of a religious ceremony is not necessarily so specialized as it might seem, viewed superficially (see Durkheim, 386).

[1] On the meaning of the root כפר in particular, see Moore, *E.Bi.* " Sacrifice," § 45, and Gray's discussion, 68 *sqq.*

[2] Cf. p. 663 on the " parallelism " which this implies.

[3] Toy, *E.Bi.* col. 5328, and his commentary on Prov. xv. 33.

is not only wicked, it is unnatural. Contrary to the will of Yahweh, contrary to social order, it was contrary to human nature, if not to Nature itself; for ideas of a " natural order" were spreading in the Greek age. Now when a man felt himself related to or bound up with a righteous god, a moral society, or with Nature, he could be conscious of order and disorder, right and wrong, and of good and evil. But in course of time ideas of what is specifically religious or spiritually wrong fade away, especially when it is believed that the god " could do neither good nor harm " (as earlier, in Zeph. i. 12). Corporate unity and social justice weaken until " righteousness " means merely " almsgiving" (p. 661). Even ideas of an order in Nature—if Nature is something quite apart from Man—do not and cannot *of themselves* move men to well-doing. The actual development of religion, so far as it can be traced in the Bible and in the history of thought that lies behind it, does not belong here ; but it is very striking because of the close relation between the atoning death of the Servant of the Lord in Isa. liii. and the death of Christ. For whereas the former is primarily of national import, and for Israel, the latter has also that universal or cosmic significance to which attention has been directed, and of which there is no hint in Isa. liii. It represents a far more comprehensive and undifferentiated interpretation of the Sacrifice, but could only have arisen out of Paul's conviction of the meaning of Christ. The combination, at this new stage in the history of religion, of the personal and of the cosmic meaning of the Sacrifice can hardly be adequately emphasized.

The more or less cosmic significance of Pharaohs and other representative personalities in early religion must arise, not of course from some independent conception of the constitution of the Universe, but from the impression they make upon men who both feel themselves akin to them and are conscious of unity with the world about them. It is through human personality that Nature has a new meaning for us. At once this seems to carry with it the priority of anthropomorphic types of religion. But the difference between the religion of individuals and that of the slow-moving environment with its many practical needs must be kept in mind. Ideas both of Right(eousness) and At-one-ment take more concrete form, especially among rudimentary peoples, where ideas of unity and oneness are not " spiritual " in the modern sense of the word, but are shaped by all that makes for material welfare. See further, pp. 657 *sqq.*, 671, 676 *sqq.*

P. 419 n.—The execution takes place at a time of drought and famine, and the bodies are left until the rain falls. It has been objected that the verb יקע is not used in 2 Chron. xxv. 12, where men are cast over a rock, and that the meaning suggested by W. R. S. hardly suits the preposition " *on* the mountain " (2 Sam. xxi. 9). In Gen. xxxii. 26, the verb seems to mean " rend " ; one may perhaps compare the use of *shāsa'* (p. 641). See Gray on Num. xxv. 4, and Skinner on Gen., and especially Driver on Sam. (Prof. E. H. Palmer, referred to in the note, was put to death in August 1892 ; see *Ency. Brit.* and *Dict. of Nat. Biog.*)

P. 420 n.—For parallels to Deut. *l.c.* in the Code of Hammurabi (§ 23 *sq.*) and elsewhere, see Cook, *Moses and Hammurabi*, 255 *sq.* ; *CAH.* i.² 512, ii. 343 ; for modern usage see also *Qy. St.* 1906, p. 14, and Sir G. A. Smith, *Deut.* 251.

P. 421.—The argument is not affected by the fact that 2 Sam. xxi. 1 should read " on Saul and on his house is bloodshed."

P. 422 n. 3.—See Wellhausen², 171, and *Götting. Gel. Nachr.* 1893, p. 455. For an Assyrian parallel, see Jastrow, *Rel. B.A.* ii. 95 (ills removed by means of bird, fish, etc.).

P. 426. DEFILING THE HANDS (cf. p. 452).—See Budde, *E.Bi.* " Canon," §§ 3 *sq.*, 53 ; Hölscher, *Kanonisch und Apokryph.* 4 *sq.* (Naumburg, 1905). In spite of the natural meaning of *ṭāmē'*, and the fact that the question was even asked whether the unwritten margins and outer covers defiled the hands, other explanations are still hazarded, *e.g.* that the reference is to the Levitical purity of the individual, who must avoid being defiled.

P. 429. RIGHTEOUSNESS.—The Semitic root *ṣ-d-ḳ* appears to connote congruence, fitness for purpose, conformity to an expected norm or standard.[1] Arabic derivatives are used of agreement with a conception or a statement ; a verbal form denotes earnest fighting, without pretence ; and the adjective means " genuine, what is as it should be " (whether of a javelin or of the date-fruit ; also of eyes and ears). The objection that such general ideas as being fit, true, *comme il faut*, etc., can hardly be primitive (so, *e.g.*, Skinner, *Hastings' D.B.* iv. 274*a*) confuses the perception of metaphysical facts with the capacity for metaphysical reasoning.[2] There can scarcely be anything more primitive than the intuitive recognition whether persons or things do or do not answer normal expectation or conform to their ordinary or expected behaviour. Again, when W. R. S. (*Prophets*, 389 ; cf. 71 *sq.*) holds that Kautzsch's idea of conformity " perhaps is too wide, and does not lay sufficient weight on the distinctly forensic element," it may be urged (*a*) that early conceptions of social right and

[1] See Kautzsch's oft-cited monograph on the subject (1881), 58 *sq.* ; cf. also Gordon, *ERE.* x. 780 n. 1.

[2] Cf. Momerie's reply to Matthew Arnold's objection that early Israel could have had no conception of the " personality " of God (*Inspiration and other Sermons*, 68), cited by T. H. Sprott, *Inspiration and the Old Testament*, 98 *sq.* (Camb. 1909).

wrong were closely bound up with ideas of what we call " natural " or " cosmic " order, (b) that specifically " forensic " conceptions imply a differentiation and a specialization which do not occur at the earliest stages of social development, and (c) that even so special a term as the Hebrew *mishpāṭ*, " judgment," is used of what is customary and characteristic. And the same reply may be made to Baudissin, who, in a survey of the distribution of the root, considers that, while it expresses the notion of correspondence to given conditions or expectations, the fundamental meaning is juridical.[1] It is essential, then, to bear in mind in this note that " righteousness " is only one of possible translations of *ṣedek* and other derivatives, and that " right," or " rightfulness " or " rightness " would often be preferable.

In fact, *ṣ-d-ḳ* belongs to a chain of ideas which are so far-reaching that T. W. Rhys Davids urged that a primitive " normalism," an intuitive consciousness of cause and effect, is more significant for early religion than theories of " animism " (*Proceedings of the British Academy*, 1917–18, pp. 279 *sqq.*). He illustrated his argument from Confucianism, with its recognition of a cosmic order (both physical and social), and Lao-Tsze's doctrine of the universal Tao in harmony with which man should live. In the Vedic Rita there is a cosmic order above and before the gods ; and in the Buddhist Dhamma lies a normalistic idea, the essence of the Buddhist reformation.[2] These and other interrelated ideas were independently treated by J. Estlin Carpenter, " Early Conceptions of Law in Nature," *Hibbert Journal*, 1923, July, 771 *sqq.* (cf. *Ency. Brit.*[11] xxiii. [1911], 71). Already Carnoy (*JAOS.* xxxvi. [1917], 306 *sqq.*) had observed the points of contact between Rita, the Zoroastrian Asha (Arta), and the Greek Moira; and Eduard Meyer had previously associated Rita and Asha with the Greek Themis and the Egyptian Maʿat or Meʿet (*Gesch. Alt.* i. [1907–9], §§ 75, 587, 590). Maʿat, whom Diodorus Siculus identified with Aletheia, with whom in turn Plutarch equated Asha, was goddess of truth, justice, right or righteousness ; the particular meaning varies according to the particular connexion in which it is used.[3] Further, James Drummond (*Hibbert Journal*, 1902, Oct., 83 *sq.*), on the " Righteousness of God," argued that δίκαιος meant properly " conformable to right " ; it was not primarily a forensic term, but implied some objective, external standard which righteous prophets and judges declare (cf. *E.Bi.* col. 4103 and n. 1). Δίκη, too, is the established way of things, the way they happen ; see Miss Jane Harrison, *Themis*, 516 *sq.* (Cambridge, 1912), who notes, after A. B. Cook, the use of δίκαιος, " breeding true " ; her book and that of F. M. Cornford, *From Religion to Philosophy* (*s.vv.* Dike, Rita, Tao [1912]), furnish good evidence for the

---

[1] See his essay, *Der gerechte Gott in altsemit. Rel.*, in the *Harnack-Festgabe*, 1–23 (Tübingen, 1921).

[2] See Mrs. Rhys Davids, *Buddhism : a Study of the Buddhist Norm* (1912), 32 *sqq.*, etc. (on *Dhamma* as moral law, ideal, standard, uniformity of sequence, etc.).

[3] Breasted, *Rel. and Thought in Ancient Egypt*, 116, 225 n.

use and distribution of all these and other interconnected conceptions, and recognize their importance for the early history of religion.[1]

The conception of an undifferentiated cosmic order—moral, social, physical, or natural—which makes things what they are, and as they should be, is perhaps seen most completely in the old Vedic term *Rita*.[2] In the corresponding Iranian Arta (Asha), social and moral order is singled out. But in both there is a world-order, which is partly inherent in things, and partly guarded, sustained, or fathered by specific gods who are of a marked ethical character (Varuna and Mitra ; Ahura-Mazda). These and the other interrelated terms have multifarious, but quite explicable, nuances. There are tendencies to make the order or principle an independent authority ; the gods themselves are subordinate to it, or it comes to be more or less of a deity in its own right. On the other hand, the emphasis may be laid, not upon the process, but upon the god who controls, contains, or informs it. Thus Ahura-Mazda becomes himself Righteousness and Justice ; and although there were tendencies to make the Indian Rita an independent deity, they were not pursued as they were in the case of the Chinese Tao.[3]

A survey of the data discloses a vast range of ideas concerning (a) the more undifferentiated or the more specialized ideas of Order— such Order being cosmic, departmental, social, etc. ; (b) the varying relations between the ideas of Order and the ruling gods ; and (c) the diverse powers and functions of such gods, who are, in turn, cosmic, departmental, tribal, etc. Certain developments are fairly clear. In the transition from the old Vedic cosmic Rita to the more specialized Iranian Asha, the Zoroastrian prayers are found to reflect a higher conception of righteousness (Farnell, *Evolution of Religion*, 216 *sq.*). Again, when the ideas of cosmic Order were divorced from the ideas of guardian or other gods (like Varuna and Rita), the way lay open for a more objective estimate of " natural " Order, as something distinct from the gods and their relations to man or nature, though the explicit idea of " nature " is late. Further, not all gods had the striking ethical traits of a Varuna ; and it was easy to feel that there was a cosmic Law or Order, heedless of man, uncontrolled by benevolent or

---

[1] For the inclusion of the Semitic *ṣ-d-ḳ* among these terms, see S. A. Cook, *CAH*. ii. 398. To the bibliography (*ib*. 669 *sq.*) may be added Bertholet-Lehmann, *Lehrbuch d. Rel. Gesch*. i. (1924), 80, on primitive ideas of right, law, necessity, etc.

[2] Besides the references already made, see A. B. Keith, *Religion and Philosophy of the Vedas and Upanishads*, i. 83, 246 (Harvard, 1925).

[3] Dikē is personified in Hesiod; see J. L. Myres, *Political Ideas of the Greeks*, 108 *sqq.* ; cf. also 100, 103, and his whole discussion of the meanings and fluctuations of Dikē, Themis, Physis, Arkhē, and other interrelated terms in Greek thought.

ethical gods, and without the moral qualities of Asha, and one beneath which man was helpless.

All the conceptions of Order, Norm, etc., were bound up with ideas of cause and effect. Even the most primitive races have a large stock of ordinary empirical knowledge as to how things are done ; and as all else belongs to the sphere of the " religious " or " magical," life's difficulties can be met by resort to appropriate " religious " or " magical " beliefs and practices. The question whether the processes necessary for life and welfare were " natural " or otherwise would turn upon the ordinary knowledge and upon the religious or magical ideas of the day ; but, throughout, men could only hope for success by conforming with current procedure. There is an Order of Things, a Way such that by the appropriate *Methodos* men can live. There are vital needs (fertility, growth, etc.) which can be satisfied directly or indirectly through the gods, etc. ; and men resort to special individuals who are helpful, either through their relation to the gods, or through the powers with which they themselves are credited. On the one hand, there are individuals who, by their influence with the gods or with certain " processes of nature "—as we might say—stand in a uniquely close relationship to all that which makes things act as they should. On the other, such individuals will come to be regarded as in some way responsible for the maintenance of this Order. Salt of the earth, pillars of society, they are in a sense the sustainers of things, and we can distinguish between those who are felt to be generally responsible for human welfare (the old priestly kings, for example) and those " specialists " who have special, not general powers, and are concerned with a special department of nature. But both classes must observe certain taboos—Mana and Taboo are complementary (p. 552). That Social Order (specifically " Righteousness "), the Order of the Universe, and Divine Order are in some way intimately related is the " theory " running through all religion : there are processes to be utilized, controlled, or exploited. So, the evil conduct of a representative *individual* (*e.g.* a king) or of a *people* (Israel) can have a prejudicial effect upon sources of life (cf. p. 537) ; the later Zoroastrian ritual not only gains the help of the gods but also assists them to work for good,[1] and the Lama whose praying-wheel is in sympathetic touch with the Cosmic Wheel would overthrow the processes of nature were he to turn it in the wrong direction.

Primarily, the conceptions of Order take a social or rather a mythological form. Ma'at, " truth, righteousness," etc., was associated with several Egyptian gods, and pre-eminently the Sun-god Re,

---

[1] G. F. Moore, *History of Religions*, i. 390 ; cf. the influence of the Brahman ritual, *ib.* 265.

who was its creator. Ma'at was the daughter of Re—cf. the relation of Dikē to Zeus ; and in Babylonia, where both the Moon-god Sin and the Sun-god Shamash have marked ethical traits, the children of the latter are Justice (*kettu*) and Uprightness (*mēsharu*) ; the first of these was also known as the child of the supreme god Anu.[1] In Babylonia, ideas of inflexible order and fate were interwoven partly with astral ideas, partly with arbitrary gods and spirits. As the old religion broke down, the spread of the ethical cult of Ahura-Mazda hastened the more objective study of the stars ; while its dualism, with the conflict of Good and Evil, Truth and Lie, was the natural development and more ethical restatement of earlier ideas of cosmic order and disorder.[2] What uprightness and justice meant from ancient though advanced social standpoints can be seen in the Code of Hammurabi (the " darling " of the Sun-god) with its rigorous *lex talio*, and in familiar Egyptian papyri.[3] While Ikhnaton reiterates his favourite title—an old one— " living in righteousness (or truth)," his age is conspicuous for a naturalism in art which delighted to depict things as they truly and rightly were—though not without some exaggeration (see Breasted, *CAH*. ii. 120 ; Hall, *ib.* 411). His solar monotheism inculcated a single pervading and benevolent life-giving principle, and of his god Aton he was the beloved son, issuing from the god's body and rays. The Egyptian kings, as earthly sons and representatives of the Sun-god, were sustainers of " righteousness " ; and, in view of primitive convictions of the disastrous results of wrong-doing, the " righteousness " of the ruler and representative of the group was vital. In Zoroastrianism the king must reign according to Order (Asha) and Glory (Hvarenah), and the fall of the latter into evil hands would cause desolation and disturbance. It is the Order with which Yima established the world, and confusion resulted when the Dragon carried it away, as also in the old Babylonian myth when the theft of the Tablets of Destiny imperilled mankind.

Of the Semitic uses of the root *ṣ-d-ḳ* the most striking is the term אצדק used in Nabatæan inscriptions enumerating those entitled to be buried in a tomb. A " legal kinsman " of some sort, it is not certain whether the emphasis lies on his *rights* or in the fact that he is one of

---

[1] Cf. the fine hymns to Shamash in Gressmann, *Altorient. Texte z. A.T.*[2] 244 *sqq.* ; also G. Driver in *The Psalmists* (ed. Simpson), 169. The old Sumerian solar Babbar of Larsa was also Lord of Justice. Apart from proper names (*e.g.* Ammizaduga), probably of western (Amorite) origin, the root *ṣ-d-ḳ* does not seem to occur in Babylonian.

[2] Jastrow, *Rel. Bel.* 60 *sqq.*, 252 *sqq.*, 257. For ideas of fate, see Fichtner Jeremias, *Schicksalsglaube bei d. Babyloniern* (Leipzig, 1922).

[3] Breasted, *op. cit.* ch. vii.

the near *kin*: thus Nöldeke compares the Syriac *zād'ḳē* " relations "
(Cooke, 226). Similarly, in Phœnician, צדק בן seems to denote a
" legitimate " prince, and צמח צדק, which is the " legitimate shoot "
in the Larnax Lapēthos inscription, in Jeremiah xxiii. 5 denotes
rather the " righteous shoot " to be raised up to David.[1] But when a
king of the neighbouring city of Lapēthos bears the name צדקמלך
(Cooke, 349 ; fifth century B.C.), its meaning is presumably, not that
the " king (or the god Milk) is legitimate," but rather that he is
" right(eous) " ; cf. the name J(eh)ozadaḳ, where the attribute is
applied to Yahweh.[2] A connexion can readily be found if the derivatives of the root *ṣ-d-ḳ*, like *kin* and *kind*, or *gens, genus*, and *generous*,
go back to ideas of group-unity and the appropriate behaviour among
the members of the group, which, of course, properly included the
group-god. Right(eous)ness, then, would be " conformity to the
obligations which bind together not merely the social unit, but that
organic unit of which the deity formed part." [3] More than *esprit de
corps*, it makes the group what it should be, and it involves a standard ;
the true member is " loyal " rather than " legal," and his " legitimacy "
carried with it a superior *noblesse oblige*. Such a view of *ṣ-d-ḳ* would
accord with W. R. S.'s fundamental theory of the group (*and* god)-
system and its significance for the development of religion. Indeed,
while preferring the forensic meaning of righteousness, he himself
observes that even " forensic righteousness " involves kindness and
truth, which are the basis of society; and he significantly explains
ḥésed (" loving-kindness ") as " the virtue that knits together society,"
citing the use of the Arabic *ḥashada* to connote combined hospitality.[4]

But *ṣ-d-ḳ* is no abstract righteousness, for all things that are done
rightly will turn out right. Things which are normal, right, true to
type, etc., have conformed with effective principles, and therefore any
action that is effective must meet with its inevitable consequences,
or—more neutrally—causes and effects are inevitably interconnected.
So תּוּשִׁיָּה, " wisdom," is also its result, " success," and the Syrian
zakkī " justify," issues in *zākūthā*, " victory " ; but no less does
" guilt " (עָוֹן) mean " punishment." Yahweh's universal righteousness

---

[1] Cooke, 86 ; see Clermont-Ganneau, *Rec.* v. 366, vi. 162 ; Lidzb. ii. 155.

[2] Similarly, Artaxerxes means the legitimate or true sovereignty.

[3] S. A. Cook, *JTS.* 1908, p. 632 n.; cf. *Expositor*, 1910, Aug., 120. Among
parallels, note the suggestion of Scheftelowitz that אריך in Ezra iv. 14 stands for
aryaka, " as befits an Aryan."

[4] *Prophets*, 408 *sq.* The more Aramaic *ḥesda* means " shame, reproach " ; cf.
Arab. *ḥasada*, " envy," and the relation between " jealous " and " zealous." The
root idea may mean combined or united action, differentiated into (1) hospitality
and (2) giving one, so to speak, the " cold shoulder."

made the punishment of an unrighteous Israel inevitable; but her subsequent conviction that she had paid the penalty and was "right(eous)" as against her enemies "constituted a claim on the righteousness of God for the vindication of Israel's right" (Skinner, *Comment. on Isa. xl.–lxvi.* p. 241). Good and evil are quasi-mechanical processes, and things which are felt to be good or evil have their corresponding causes; though in Israel the "righteousness" of Yahweh was the guarantee—so taught the prophets—that there was nothing arbitrary in his treatment of men. Later, the Jewish doctrine of "merits" continues to show how naturally causes and effects tended to be considered in terms of value, and how readily the convictions of inevitable consequences allowed the belief that there was, so to say, an inherent or immanent process which "meritorious" behaviour set in motion, utilized, or controlled.

The judge (*shōphēṭ*) acted in accordance with Yahweh's ordinances, the customary usages and standards (*mishpāṭ*), and the knowledge of what ought or ought not to be done in Israel. But to "judge" the righteous is to "deliver" him (cf. 1 Sam. xxiv. 15); and the "judges" of Israel deliver a penitent people from their oppressors (Judg. ii. 11 *sqq.*). "Righteousness" and "deliverance" become synonymous, and deliverance or salvation (ישע) means some "visible delivery and enlargement from distress" (*OTJC.*[2] 441). Righteous acts are those by which Yahweh manifests his "covenant faithfulness" (Burney on Judg. v. 11); he shows his righteousness in the "salvation" of his people (Kautzsch, *Hastings' D.B.* v. 633 n.). Israel's "righteousness" becomes, in effect, her material prosperity in token that her right is "acknowledged and declared by God" (Skinner, 242). In other words, Israel has her "rights," and she obtains them through Yahweh, even as the individual got his through Yahweh's representatives, the judges or *Elōhīm* (see Driver on 1 Sam. ii. 25). It is no mere play upon words, then, to say that a man's "rights" essentially turned primarily upon his "righteousness," *i.e.* upon his behaviour in the group of which he was an organic part (see p. 637). Such variations and developments are intelligible, and it is not surprising that in both Rabbinical Judaism and the Coran "righteousness" should manifest itself specifically in "almsgiving."

It is disputed whether, like the tendencies to deify Tao, Dikē, etc., there was actually a god *Ṣ-d-ḳ.*[1] "Righteousness" is naturally a most essential attribute of tribal or national gods, who safeguard the unity and welfare of their worshippers; and personal names predicate it of Yahweh, El, and the Syrian Rammān (*i.e.* Hadad). It is also attributed

[1] See Burney, *Judges*, 41 *sqq.*; and, in favour of the view, Baudissin in the *Harnack-Festgabe*, 8, 10, 15.

to the god Milk (or the king as the group-representative) and to 'Am,
i.e. the god of that name, or the " group," or the " uncle " as the
representative of the group.[1]   The last case is of special interest.   The
'*am* or group is knit together by a common life—the *ḥayy* (*Kinship*,
44, 46, and commentaries on 1 Sam. xviii. 18) ; and the corporate life
of a group is more recognizably divine when there is a god 'Am, or the
group bears a divine name, *e.g.* Gad (pp. 506, 547 ; cf. Meyer, *Gesch.
Alt.* i. § 343).   Names indicating that gods are brothers or fathers of
their worshippers are also highly significant for that close unity of
gods, men, and the world which appears to be implied in the root
ṣ-d-ḳ.   But these names tended to fall out of use (p. 510), the intimate
and natural bond between Israel and Yahweh was balanced by the
insistence upon his transcendence, and the familiarity and confidence
which characterized Israel's relations with Yahweh were checked by
the doctrine that Israel had no merits of her own.   That is to say,
against those tendencies which would have made Yahweh a god
immanent in his people, or in nature, a god who was the inherent
sustainer of all things, or even a food-god, a vegetation spirit, or a
nature-god (cf. pp. 578, 597)—tendencies which one would look for in
the Baal cults—there are those recurring and more characteristic
tendencies which make him independent of and above men and nature,
through whom he works, and his Transcendence and not his Immanence is the dominant note of the teaching of the prophets.   If, as the
prophets taught, Yahweh was bound by an Order or Law of " Righteousness " uniting people and their god, it was a transcendent principle
of which man had only imperfect knowledge.   The ethical god
Varuna may be compared ; but it is to be observed that the Semites
had no concept corresponding to the unidfferentiated Rita, and that
Yahweh—to the prophets—stood for social righteousness, and was
behind and over nature.[2]

In the N.T. the conceptions of Righteousness and the like are at
a more highly developed stage.   There is a Way—and as such it is
comparable to the Chinese Tao—and Christ both *teaches* the way and

---

[1] In Melchisedek, Adonizedek, Zadok, etc., the *ṣ-d-ḳ* idea is connected with
Jerusalem (*CAH*. ii. 397 *sq*., 400).   The connexion is more particularly with the
Lord (Ādōn), Yahweh (J[eh]ozadak), Milk or the king (? priest-king), also with the
Jerusalem priesthood (Zadokites), and, later, with the " Sadducean " aristocracy
(cf. *E.Bi*. 4106 n. 1).   That Jerusalem should be the seat of *ṣ-d-ḳ* (Isa. i. 26, Jer.
xxxi. 23) is in keeping with the significance attached to Zion as the source of uni-
versal right and religion (Isa. ii. 2–4), to the Temple as a mystical centre, and to the
Temple ritual.

[2] In Isa. xlv. 8, *ṣédeḳ* is poured down from above and *ṣedāḳah* springs up from the
earth ; a distinction between universal order and social order has been drawn by
Whitehouse (*Century Bible Commentary*).

is it. Christ is also head of the spiritual group, and an elder " brother " (Heb. ii. 11) ; He is one with the group (John xv. 4 *sqq.*), and kindness shown to the least of the group is done to Him (Matt. xxv. 40). But Christ is also the basis of existence, " the continuous immanent principle of order in the Universe." He is " the principle of cohesion in the Universe ; He impresses upon creation that unity and solidarity which makes it a cosmos instead of a chaos." [1] He is also a cosmic power regenerating at once man and nature (Rom. viii. 19 *sqq.*). Further developments along such lines explain the pantheistic Logion and the Manichæan conception of Jesus as virtually a vegetation spirit (above p. 597). But tendencies to a Christ immanent in nature were not developed. On the other hand, such a passage as Matt. vi. 25–33 (" Seek ye first . . . his righteousness ") reflects the explicitly spiritual conception which distinguishes Christianity as a social-religious movement. That is to say, spiritual religion with its *imitatio Dei* has all the practical consequences necessary for man's elementary needs, and stands in contrast to those less spiritual and more physical conceptions of the source of life and growth and to the magical or magico-religious ideas which in some way connect, if they do not virtually identify, man and part or whole of nature.[2]

In primitive religion, Mana and Taboo are correlative. Consequently, social disorder, or the failure to be " righteous," is commonly believed to disturb the order of nature upon which men depend. But in advanced spiritual religion there is implied what may be called a theory of " parallelism "—conformity to spiritual laws and the increasing recognition of all that makes for social order corresponding to the order which men find in the Cosmos. The belief that social disorder upsets cosmic order tends gradually to die : the rain falls alike on the righteous and the unrighteousness (Matt. v. 45 ; contrast Zech. xiv. 17 *sq.*, and see p. 644). Similarly, some centuries earlier, at an age of far-reaching social and political changes and the introduction of refined conceptions of Righteousness, Israel is assured that Yahweh will be true to His covenant and there will be no more destruction (Gen. viii. 21 *sq.*, ix. 11–17 ; Isa. liv. 9 *sq.* ; contrast Gen. vi. 5–7). A less ideal age is foreshadowed ; but inasmuch as man is no longer deterred from evil by the fear of catastrophic penalties, the development implies a very striking advance both in knowledge and in conceptions of man's increased free will and correspondingly increased

---

[1] See, respectively, Bishop Gore, *Reconstruction of Belief* (1926), 378, 389 (on the " activities of the Son of God in nature "), and Lightfoot on Col. i. 18.

[2] Indications of " spiritual " religion can be found in early Egypt : " more acceptable " in the sight of the Sun-god (*i.e.* the god of Truth, etc.) " is the nature of one just of heart than the ox of one that doeth iniquity " (Gardiner, *JEA.* i. 34).

responsibility. Accordingly, it is possible to trace some vital advances in the development of ideas of man's place in the Cosmos, and to contrast this evidence for an absolute development in the history of religious and related thought with the more primitive and persistent convictions of a more or less " magical " interpenetration of man and nature, and with other tendencies away from distinctively spiritual types of religion.

The higher ideal of δικαιοσύνη, which Jesus demanded (Matt. v. 20), marks a creative age with which it is legitimate to compare the prophets' teaching of Yahweh's demands upon his people Israel. Much earlier, at a period of disturbance—approximately the Mosaic age—traces of interrelated ideas of Truth and Order can be recognized in Egypt and South-West Asia (CAH. ii. 399 sqq.). But what ṣ-d-ḳ connoted in the fourteenth century can scarcely be determined ; though in one of the Amarna Letters Abdi-ḥiba, king of Jerusalem, assures the divine Pharaoh of Egypt that he is " loyal " (No. 287 saduk).[1] Nor, again, can one conjecture how Ammi-zaduga, who lived a century after the law-giver Hammurabi, would interpret his name, " 'Am (my 'Am ?) is righteous." All that need be said is that the interrelated terms of truth, order, righteousness, are such as to admit of continual restatement and reinterpretation.

The period from the age of the prophets and their doctrine of Yahweh's righteousness to the reconstruction of religion which subsequently ensued, is one of transition from social and political disturbance and unrest to what was ultimately a new reintegration (p. 592 sq.). The defects of all group-religion are obvious (pp. 256 sqq., 266 sq.), and from the weakness of the relationship between Israel and Yahweh one passes—though the steps are far from clear—to a new relationship which at length finds its expression in the Pentateuch and post-exilic Judaism.[2] A fixed social or national group-system is replaced by a legalistic religious system, and in due course the defects of narrow conceptions of " righteousness " again made themselves felt. Conformity to specified requirements, and an exaggerated estimate of the significance of the Torah for the world, induced a religious complacence and arrogance recalling that which the prophets had previously

[1] The king's name can be read Arta-ḫiba, to correspond to Zedek-iah (" Yah's righteousness ") ; see Burney, Judges, lxxxvi, after Hommel (cf. his Ethnol. 29 n. 3) and Dhorme (Revue Biblique, 1909, p. 72).

[2] The ideas are set forth in the Pentateuchal history of the deliverance from bondage, the discipline of people and leaders, and the inculcation of law and justice (cf. Prophets, 40). The ideas in this composite history have a value quite apart from the particular views which the writers have of the birth of Israel as a nation in or about the fourteenth century B.C.

condemned. Moreover, the Chinese belief that the study of the old Classics was indispensable for the maintenance of Tao or Universal Order would have found its parallel in Palestine, where Piety spelt Knowledge of the Torah.[1] On the one hand, then, the exaltation of the Torah and the possession of an infallible Way encouraged a false security. On the other hand, the consciousness that the Law was spiritual (Rom. vii. 12–14), but its requirements beyond man's unaided efforts, and that the alternative to group-righteousness was outlawry and expulsion, associates Paul's attitude to the Torah with the primitive and recurring conceptions of the place of the individual *either* within *or* without the group-system of men and their god.[2]

Baudissin (*op. cit.* 16 *sqq.*, 22), observing that *ṣ-d-ḳ* is the only certain early attribute of the gods—it is not applied to goddesses—looks for a social or tribal origin of the fundamental idea, and suggests that it grew up out of alliances. Undoubtedly the consciousness of disorder, injustice, and lawlessness drives home the need for order, justice, and law, and social and religious incoherence arouse the desire for a new state of cohesion. It is proper, therefore, to see in new social alliances, indeed in all new unifying efforts and their immediate results, the more explicit recognition of principles which, though they may have become conspicuously absent, are those upon which all social and religious systems must, as systems, necessarily be founded.

Every new unity is virtually a "confederation," based upon an agreement, rather than a *natio* which has come into being.[3] For in alliances (see above, pp. 316 *sqq.*) the parties are (*a*) the group (*or* individuals) and their god, or (*b*) the group (with or without the explicit inclusion of their god) and another group (*or* individuals). Now there are, as W. R. S. shows, well-known ceremonies whereby communion or fellowship is *either* renewed *or* it is created, the corporate spirit is *either* confirmed *or* it is extended. But while every group has in its possession ceremonies of a unifying character, a distinction must be drawn between the more ordinary and periodic rites and those more intense and impressive occasions when the situation demands some fresher and more effective and more compelling means of indicating its uniqueness, or of making it the inauguration of some new unity or fellowship.

---

[1] See Bousset-Gressmann, *Rel. des Judentums*³, 187 *sq.* Tao means "road." " If we were compelled to adopt a single word to represent the Tao of Lao-tsze, we should prefer the sense in which it is used by Confucius, ' the way,' *i.e.* μέθοδος " (R. Douglas, *Confucianism and Taouism*, 189).

[2] In contrast to the "loyalty" of Abdi-ḥiba of Jerusalem in the Amarna Letters is the " curse " (*araru*=ררא, Nos. 179, 193) on those guilty of " sin," *i.e.* disloyalty (*ḥiṭu*=אטח, Nos. 162 *sq.*, 353 *sq.*).

[3] On the use of *bĕrīth*, "covenant," for " nation, people," see *E.Bi.* 931.

Such ceremonies stand out above the rest for their impressiveness and effects. In course of time the impressiveness wears off, the sense of fellowship weakens, and the unity once more becomes impaired. In fact, there recur, not only in the great stages of religion in history, but in the vicissitudes of all social and religious systems, alternating periods of unity and disunity, differing obviously in duration and significance. Hence what may be called a " natural society " (p. 29 *sq.*) is hardly some absolute primary stage in human development, but an abstraction, a legitimate generalization of the normal conditions which have come into being, whose disintergation and subsequent reintegration may be followed, but whose prior stages and their inauguration are unknown or ignored.

W. R. S.'s analysis is concerned mainly with part only of the great recurring social-religious processes in history ; and although he starts from the " natural society," every such society has had its earlier inaugural stage. Now ceremonies of union, communion, and fellowship vary generally in significance and intensity, and the question arises whether there is any essential difference between them, or whether the most impressive and vital more closely resemble each other than those that are more normal and regular. The supreme importance of W. R. S.'s problem has always been recognized ; its interest is enhanced when it is remembered that it grew naturally out of his earlier years, when the Reformation and the need for a new formulation of Christian theology lay near his heart (see the *Introduction*). Consciously or not, he passed from the essentials of Christian communion and social unity to the more theoretical study of the fundamental ideas in atonement. His concern is with the creative moments in the history of all religion, and the question is whether such moments are more akin to one another than the intervening stages of decay or disintegration, and are distinguished by more primitive, more fundamental features.[1]

It would seem that every new and significant unity typically carries with it the consciousness that an earlier unity had been broken and repaired, or that the earlier unity has been developed further, or that there has been a realization of what was already potential. Nor is this strange, for in mystical and related experiences there is a persistent sense of ultimate unity or oneness which men have been unable to rationalize. Mysticism, with its experiences of a oneness with something pervasive lying beneath all life and thought, crude rites of social unity and oneness, and the ancient and primitive ideas of the interpenetration of man and nature—these reflect a sense of unity, communion, and undifferentiation which ordered thought tends to replace

---

[1] That is to say, if we assume the recurring series $l^1m^1n^1$, $l^2m^2n^2$, etc., does l^2 resemble l^1 more closely than m^1 or n^1 ? See p. 499 and n.

by differentiation, co-ordination, correlation, and the systematization of society and of knowledge. All such experiences, which naturally are not confined to any one age or land, are of primary significance ; they are by no means necessarily " religious " in any objective sense of the term (p. 554). The experiences typically produce or force an adjustment of one's thought, and must be regarded as logically more primary than the developments they initiate. They are subjectively far more intense than the systematization of life and thought which follow. But their content will be determined by the stage which had previously been reached, and the changes which ensue affect conditions which were already in existence.

It is through these primary experiences that things are " holy " or " sacred " before they become " profane " ; and it is simpler to say that the process of " sanctifying " brings out what was already potentially there, than to suppose that there is the absolute addition of a new quality; even as the conviction that something has been sanctified or divinized involves a qualitative change in the mind, and not the mere addition of a new idea. Similarly, a genuine conviction of the physical kinship of men and gods (as brothers or fathers) cannot be understood except as the outcome of genuine psychical experiences of unity which have been shaped by social conditions and by ideas concerning kins-men (or the terms to denote kinsmen) which already lay at hand. So, in the light of universal mystical and related experiences, it is possible to understand something of the vicissitudes in the conceptions of unity, order, truth, righteousness, and man's place in nature, and to recognize how naturally it would happen that practical social needs would control their development.

In so far as the fundamental idea of righteousness involves some new unity and the confirmation or extension of group-systems, the work of Moses and Mohammed illustrates how unity has been achieved by men who wield divine authority and are obeyed by jealous and conflicting tribes (p. 70 ; cf. *Lectures*, 617). Unity is effected by a god who becomes the god of a confederation (Yahweh, p. 319 n.), or who receives the veneration of scattered tribes (Orotal and Alilat, p. 316). The great ethical gods Varuna and Mitra, who are mentioned in certain old Hittite treaties, were essentially covenant gods (*CAH*. ii. 400); and the god of the border-city of Kadesh-Barnea, a meeting-place of different clans, was probably a covenant-god like the covenant-Baal of Shechem.[1] Such gods are primarily not narrowly tribal or national, but are more closely associated with the individuals who are

---

[1] Appropriately enough, the Phœnician gods Suduk (Righteousness) and Misor (Uprightness) are said to have discovered salt, the importance of which in covenant ceremonies is well known (p. 270, Num. xviii. 19 ; Burney, *Judges*, 42).

responsible for the alliance.[1] The gods that unite are behind or over the gods peculiar to the groups involved ; and the relations between local gods and the god(s) recognized by all the groups alike have always constituted a very delicate problem (see *CAH*. iii. 433 *sq*.). These higher gods seem to be less intimately a part of the unifying ceremonies and doctrines which persist after they themselves pass away. Varuna gives place to the more national Indra, and Yahweh found a serious rival in Baal, but was saved by the prophets ; Shamash, too, is not a national god in the sense that Marduk or Asshur are. The god of the dominant group tends to conquer the god of a system of groups. W. R. S. observes that when tribes were united in worshipping the same god, each retained its religious cult : " the circle of worship was still the kin, though the deity worshipped was not of the kin " (p. 48), and " they worshipped side by side, but not together " (p. 276). Even in Central Australia, the great gods belong to the larger systems rather than to the constituent groups (cf. p. 529).

It is obvious that to the acuteness and initiation of individuals must be due so remarkable a co-operative system as that in Australia (p. 586). Even among savages, the religion of the individual is a very genuine experience (Malinowski, ed. Needham, 54). Hence it is necessary to emphasize the contrast between men of initiative and of marked personality and their personal religion—whatever it was— and the several totem-clans who perform their own totem ceremonies for the mutual advantage of the whole body. The totem-clan (that is, the clan and the animal or plant totem), with its practical " magical " or " magico-religious " ceremonies, stands on quite another footing from the god(s) found in the tribe or tribal area, however important these may be for the tribe as a whole. But the clan or local cult possessed the machinery for more extensive cults. The clan-ceremonies were eminently practical and reinforced the clan-unity ; the collective ceremonies (*e.g.* initiation) strengthen the tribal feeling. Each clan formed a sort of mystical unity—which tended to break up whenever improved economic conditions made its ceremonies less vital—and totemism may fairly be described as a practical and " immanent " system in contrast to the more " transcendent " beings who are associated with the whole tribe and the leaders. The totem and clan are of the same essence ; and the totem (species), which is on a more equal footing with the clan, is indubitably more significant for the specific functions of the clan than the Supreme Being or Beings common to all the clans. The antithesis is typical : a group-god— tribal or national—tends to stand in an almost immanent relationship

[1] Cf. " thy God " in the appeal to Samuel, 1 Sam. xii. 19, and the words addressed to David, 1 Chron. xii. 18.

to the group. Even in Israel the national Yahweh, the god of the ancestors, and the deliverer of his own people, on the one side, and on the other the more universal God of all the earth, represent inevitable conflicting tendencies between the exclusive god of a group and the god of two or more groups who are aware that they are not one (p. 268). It is quite intelligible, therefore, that if the national god is to become universal the machinery of the national cult should be employed, and accordingly a universal Yahweh has his seat and his special priesthood at Jerusalem (cf. *CAH*. vi. 189).

There tends to be a correspondence between the nature of the god of the group and that of the group with its peculiar interests, temperament, history, economic conditions, etc. On the other hand, when groups are combined the god's nature must be one capable of uniting different groups ; it must go beneath and behind the conditions which sever individuals and groups, and appeal to that which they share collectively and in common (*i.e.* ideas of right, etc.). When the god is a sky- or sun-god it is the more fitted to be universal ; and a sun-god was especially appropriate as the symbol of regularity and order, purity and truth, and of hostility to darkness and evil. The consciousness of norm, order, right, etc., is *a priori*, like the experience of unity and oneness : neither is of abstract truths but of concrete particulars. Speculation concerning origins is futile ; but whereas analysis takes us back to the group-atom, which nowhere exists alone (p. 507) and we are tempted to build up conceptions of society from the smallest units, in actual history we encounter areas, peoples, tribes, or systems of units—systems which in course of time give place to other systems. Now since the systematizing efforts whereby these new combinations or systems arise must be ascribed to individuals, men of personality, it seems a natural assumption that their religion would be anthropomorphic rather than theriomorphic, and that the ideas of order, righteousness, etc., would be of an ethical character.

Personal religion, in the shape of Personal Totems and Guardian Spirits (see Frazer, *Tot. Ex.* s.vv.), is theriomorphic, but these are on the way to become personal gods of an increasingly anthropomorphic character. At higher stages the individual religion of the Pharaoh, impressive as it so often is, does not exclude striking animal symbolism, which, however, is not of an ethical stamp (p. 533). Further, against the assumption that animal gods could hardly serve to unite groups, could be set the distribution of certain totem-species—which, however, would unite only the scattered members of the particular totem-group ; or the extension, *e.g.*, of the Apis-bull of Memphis—though here, again, ethical ideas are missing. On the one hand, the ritual for a system of groups tends to be based upon one already in use among one or more single groups.[1] On the other, the eminence of the more conspicuous individuals could naturally lead to their being venerated, to the rise of ancestor-cults, and to anthropomorphic conceptions of Supreme Beings (p. 547). That is to say, the *ethical* ideas and ideals come primarily only through men.

Further, on the more exceptional and impressive occasions of some new union, when a sacrifice was required, the human victim might seem far more significant and valuable than an animal (cf. p. 361). An animal *surrogate* is not to be expected, though animals come to be the recognized sacrificial victims instead of man. But primarily, at least, the sacrificial animal must possess an inherent value of its own. In like manner, a " sacred " victim is to be expected rather than one that has been consecrated *ad hoc* (cf. p. 572); and as blood was the most elemental vehicle of life, the blood of one of the kin would primarily carry a profounder meaning than the blood of the victim which had ceremonially been made one of the kin. Here Central Australian totemism is extraordinarily suggestive, because (1) the clan and the totem are of the same kin and substance ; (2) the clan-ceremonies are curiously practical and " magico-religious," whereas the tribal system, composed of a number of mutually co-operating clans, owes its existence to the genius of individuals, and is profoundly interesting from a higher social and ethical point of view. In other words, while the cults are totemic—and the details have parallels and analogies on higher (anthropomorphic) levels—the creative factors are due to individuals. The environment always moves more slowly than the individual, and the difference between the gradual development of an environment and the growth of ideas among individuals is so invariable as to be anticipated at all ages and at all stages of human history. For these reasons both W. R. S. and his most convinced opponents are right if it be recognized that social-religious advance has been from the lowest forms, of which modern Central Australian totemism affords only one example, but advances are due to individuals whose private (religious) experience, even on the most rudimentary levels, was other than that of the group-system.

How this bears upon ideas of Right(eousness) and Wrong (sin, etc.) and Atonement (see pp. 654, 658) can now be seen. The fundamental ideas of man's control over nature range from (1) the most specialist, as in the totem ceremonies for the control or the multiplication of the special animal or plant totem, which is of the same substance as the

---

[1] See especially Durkheim, 384 *sqq.*, where the " multiplication " ceremonies are employed, *though not for their primary purpose*, when the novices are being initiated. A single rite may serve many ends, and different rites may be used to produce the same effect and can replace one another (*ib.* 386).

members of the clan, to (2) the most general and vague—though, as a matter of fact, the priestly kings themselves are more especially controllers of the weather. But in all the beliefs and practices wherein men utilize supernatural power there are conditions and restrictions : Mana and Taboo are complementary, and success depends upon the appropriate conduct (p. 565). In the totem ceremonies the behaviour of the officiants, the solemnity with which the rites are performed, and the atmosphere throughout combine to point to a psychological state which can only be styled a literal at-one-ment. Broken taboos and wrong-doing would frustrate the rites, which are for the benefit of others ; and there are implicit ideas of unity, right conduct, sociableness, which were capable of being grasped in their concrete form and extended. " In the O.T.," writes W. R. S., " the experience of forgiveness is no mere subjective feeling ; it rests on facts " (*OTJC.* 441). Primitive peoples have no explicit conceptions of Righteousness, Sin, and Atonement in any modern sense of the words. Their various social ceremonies meant (*a*) tribal unity and (*b*) the peculiar unity of each clan with some one department of nature ; and although modern Central Australian totemism cannot be supposed to represent actual primitive prehistoric religion, it enables us to understand how an extraordinarily rudimentary social-religious system may contain at least the germs of the great ideas which in the history of thought have been made explicit, differentiated, and developed.

P. 432. THE LIMPING DANCE.—Circumambulation is common, but sometimes a limping, hopping, or halting gait characterizes sacred or ceremonial dances ; see *Ency. Brit.* vii. 795*c* (India), Eitrem, 479 (Iceland), Hölscher, *Die Profeten*, 132, and Oesterley, *The Sacred Dance*, 117 *sq.*, citing Heliodorus, *Aeth.* iv. 16 *sq.* (the limping and leaping of Tyrian seafarers in the worship of Heracles of Tyre). For Gunkel's conjecture that the name Manasseh means " [the god] who causes to limp," see H. W. Hogg, *E.Bi.* col. 2921. The Arabic *takhalluj* denotes walking in a loose manner as though disjointed ; it is supposed to be the effect of contact with the jinn (Hogg, *ib.*). Here may be compared the place-name Beth-Ḥoglah, Jerome's *locus gyri*, which has been connected with Ar. *ḥajala*, " hobble or hop" (*E.Bi.* col. 557) ; it was perhaps the scene of a limping dance. Some hopping or limping dance seems to accompany the modern Syrian dirge *mā'id* (Jahnow, *Heb. Leichenlied*, 75 n. 6, citing Wetzstein). Jacob's limping, which is associated with a struggle with a supernatural being (and a victory, Hos. xii. 3 *sq.*), and with a " pass-over," may go back to some traditional limping ceremony at the Jordan (Gunkel, Oesterley) ; though it is said that the injury to the sinew of the thigh-socket such as he sustained, is a common affection, and causes a man to walk on tiptoe (cf. 380 n. 1, above ;

Skinner, *Gen.* 410 *sq.*).[1]   But the thigh is a seat of life and procreative power, and was sacred among the North American Choctaws for this reason (Frazer, *GB.* viii. 264 *sqq.*, especially 266) ; and the limping rite thus seems to connect itself with circumcision, possibly as a puberty rite.[2]   See above, p. 610.

When the Elema maskers, a secret society of New Guinea, " hop about as is characteristic of gods," [3] this comparison is presumably derived from earlier limping dances performed by men who were ceremonially representing or imitating the supernatural beings, and whose peculiar gait became fixed in tradition as that of the gods.   In the annual death-dance at Pulu in the Torres Straits, masked performers imitated the gait and actions of their deceased kinsmen (Webster, 162) ; and among the Kayans of Central Borneo, before the rice is sown, masked men imitate the spirits in order to ensure a good harvest (*GB.* vii. 186).   In a variety of ways men have gained their ideas of the gods from those who represented them or embodied them. On the stela with Hammurabi's Code of Laws the Sun-god resembles the king, who in his turn is " the Sun of the Land " ; [4] and, alternately, the gods are thought of and depicted after the patterns of outstanding individuals, and the accepted teaching concerning the gods subsequently provides the patterns for other men to follow.   Accordingly, it is necessary to distinguish (1) the imitation of gods and spirits by men who adopt a certain toilet, wear a disguise, or indulge in certain characteristic actions such as a " limping dance," and (2) the traditions, which have become " canonical," concerning the appearance, dress, gait, and other characteristics and attributes of the gods.   See further below, p. 674 *sq.*

P. 434.—Mr. C. G. Montefiore, in his Hibbert Lectures (1892) on the *Origin and Growth of Religion as illustrated by the Religion of the Ancient Hebrews* (ed. of 1897, pp. 333 *sq.*, 335 *sq.*), took exception to W. R. S.'s remarks here and also on p. 408 (as regards Lev. xvi. 30).   Still, as he remarks, the institution of the yearly Day of Atonement " was likely to lead, and did lead, to many fresh superstitions.   By the letter of the law, it was seemingly implied that the guilt of all sins . . . would

---

[1] For the " sacredness " of this sinew Wellhausen (168 n.) refers to Kamil, 552, 13.

[2] N. Schmidt (*JBL.* xlv. 275 *sq.*) conjectures that the *nāsheh* sinew was originally the pudic nerve, or rather the *membrum virile* itself.   The Shiahs do not eat the hare because, like the camel, it has " the sinew which shrank " (*The Near East*, February 10, 1927, p. 145).

[3] Hutton-Webster, *Primitive Secret Societies*, 101 *sq.* (cf. 106 for a limping dance) ; S. A. Cook, *Ridgeway Presentation Volume*, 397 *sq.*   On limping gods, cf. also Fries, *MVAG.* xv. 104.

[4] Similarly, the god Khons of Thebes is represented as an Egyptian prince, possibly Haremheb (Gressmann, *Vorträge*, Warburg, iii. 182).

be wiped out and atoned for by the ceremony of the Atonement-day."
He objects also that nothing is said in the Mishnah about " material
prestation," and argues that the atoning efficacy lay in the Day itself,
and that there was a formal suspension of forgiveness between the act
of repentance and the Day. Cf. also G. F. Moore, *E.Bi.* " Sacrifice,"
§ 51 *sq.*, who refers to R. Judah the patriarch, who seems to have
maintained that the Day of Atonement expiated sin without repentance,
though this was an exception to the prevailing view. W. R. S. (p. 434
l. 3) states that sacrificial rites lay the deity under a social obligation.
It is true that the trend of orthodox Rabbinical Judaism was to insist
upon the more ethical and spiritual conditions of atonement, but
" there are emphatic allusions to the Shechinah countenancing sin
and dwelling in contact with it. . . . God dwells in Israel at all costs "
(Abelson, *Immanence of God in Rabb. Lit.* 138). Gray (*Sacrifice*, 320)
observes that the institution of the Day of Atonement tended to foster
the growth of a very mechanical and unethical view of sin. He concludes : " Every ritual of expiation, every symbol of forgiveness, every
theory of atonement, is liable to abuse and to foster an unethical and
unspiritual conception of God's attitude to sin, and it would not be
difficult . . . to parallel from other religions such abuses as we have
observed of the Jewish Day of Atonement, and also of such protests in
favour of a more worthy one."

P. 434. FASTING BEFORE A SACRED MEAL.—See *GB.* viii. 73, 75,
76 *sq.*, 83, ix. 291 *sq.* The practice served to prepare the body for mystical experiences. It was a custom among the Jews of Philo's time
to fast during the day or to abstain from food and drink before the
Paschal meal, though scarcely for the reason given by some Rabbis—
to increase the appetite (so *Pesakh.* 99a ; Gray, 376). The early Syrian
Christians fasted before receiving the " Holy Mysteries " (Budge, *Book
of Governors*, ii. 666), and it was a practice at the Mysteries (cf. S. Angus,
The Mystery-Religions and Christianity, 85). From the complaint in
Isaiah lviii. 3, it would seem that fasting was supposed to ensure divine
attention (cf. Jer. xiv. 12); and although " to afflict oneself " (*'innah
néphesh*) might have been mainly psychological, it comes to denote
fasting ; see Cheyne, *E.Bi.* 386 n. 4 ; Benzinger, *ib.* 1507 (§ 5).

P. 435 n.—In the account of the sale of a priesthood in Babylonia
the sacrificial priest receives the intestines, ribs, reins, stomach, etc. ;
see further G. R. Driver, *Centenary Supplement of the Journ. of the
Royal Asiat. Soc.* 1924, Oct., 43. At the present day the ḳaiyam of
the Palestinian shrine generally receives the skin and the *saḳaṭ, i.e.*
extremities, head, abdominal organs (excluding the large omentum)
and the *maḏbaḥ* (the part of the throat where the knife has cut it) ; see
Canaan, *JPOS.* vi. 43.

43

P. 437. SACRED DRESS (cf. 451 *sq.*).—Garments frequently serve
as an indication of ownership (p. 336 n. 1) or of a claim (cf. Ezek.
xvi. 8; Ruth iii. 9),[1] as a token of protection, or as a covenant mark
(Landberg, *Arab.* v. 175 *sq.*); in the period of the First Babylonian
Dynasty the impression of the fringed border of a man's mantle
served instead of a seal or a signature (Thureau-Dangin, *Rituels Accad·*
57 n., 95). At the New Year's Festival in the cities of Bayblonia the
king would send his garments to represent himself (Langdon, *Epic
of Creation*, 29 n.). The clothes of "sacred" men naturally have
a special virtue (*e.g.* Mohammed's; Wellhausen, 196). Special and, in
particular, " clean " garments are commonly necessary on sacred
occasions, and (usually dark red and purple) were worn in Babylonia
both by the priests and laymen (Lagrange, 239 *sq.*; Morgenstern,
145 *sq.*). But such garments, besides being ritually " clean," were
sometimes in some way connected with the gods who were being
worshipped. A priest is said to wear the clothes of the city of Eridu
(Delitzsch, *Handwörterbuch*, 371*b*), and in general " the exorcising
priests donned special garments—often in imitation of the god in whose
name they acted " (Jastrow, *Rel. Bel.* 316). Centuries later, at Harran,
the worshipper who approached the various planetary gods wore a dress
appropriate to the god.[2] Presumably it was necessary to resemble
—externally, at least—the god to whom one was appealing (it was
a sort of identification or communion), and along these lines may
be explained the masks and other coverings of the worshippers of the
bull-deity in Asia Minor and elsewhere (A. B. Cook, *Zeus*, i. 490 *sq.*).
In Egypt, the man who presided over the rite of mummification is called
" Anubis the embalmer," and sometimes seems to have worn a jackal
mask.[3] But in general, masks are not necessarily to imitate gods, they
may also serve, like veils, to hide the face from the vulgar gaze or from
gazing upon the sacred. Cf. Exod. xxxiv. 33 *sqq.*

Here may be mentioned the use of skins (see p. 474). The skin of an
animal may be preserved as a token of, or as actually containing some
vital part of the animal (*GB.* viii. 173 *sq.*). Skins of sacrificial victims
are preserved as amulets, or they are used in ceremonies of rebirth
(in Kikuyu); *e.g.* a man wrapped in a skin or otherwise identified with

[1] See Wellhausen, *Archiv f. Rel.* 1904, p. 40 *sq.*; Goldziher, *Abhand.* i. 46 *sq.*

[2] De Goeje, *Leiden Oriental Congress*, 1883, ii. 341); cf. the special dress worn
when consulting oracles of Trophonius (Paus. ix. 39) and Delphi (Livy, xxiii. 11).

[3] Blackman, *Proc. of Soc. Bibl. Arch.* xl. 66. On masks, see Andrew Lang, *Myth,
Ritual, etc.* (1899), ii. 284; Crawley, *Mystic Rose*, 114 *sq.*, 330; Hoffman and
Gressmann, *ZATW.* 1922, pp. 78 *sqq.*, 94 *sq.* (on the teraphim, see further Sellin,
Alttest. Prophetismus, 203 *sq.*). On Gregentius, p. 438 n. 2 above, Stübe (note 760)
adds references to Migne, *Patr. Gr.* LXXXVI. i. 599, and *ZDMG.* xxxv. 1 *sqq.*,
693 *sqq.*

an animal undergoes symbolically a radical change in his status.[1] Such animals are not necessarily sacred, although, where this is the case, as in sleeping on a ram-skin to obtain a revelation (Paus. i. 34, 5), ideas of communion or identity are involved.

On some Babylonian representations of Marduk and Adad, the robes of the gods are adorned with astral symbols, which, it would seem, are intended to associate them with their celestial realm.[2] The cosmic interpretation of the dress of the Jewish high priest in Josephus (*Ant.* iii. 7. 1), in spite of its lateness, is explicable only if it points back to antique conceptions of the relation between the gods in their heavenly abodes and their human representatives on earth, which persisted (in varying forms) down to a very late period. On this, see Gray, *Sacrifice,* 143 *sqq.* (on the sacrificial service in heaven), and the rather speculative treatment by A. Jeremias in his *Handbuch* (*passim*).

P. 438. IMITATION AND IDENTIFICATION.—The desire to imitate or otherwise resemble a sacred being ranges from the loftiest spiritual injunction to imitate the perfection of a Heavenly Father (Matt. v. 48), or to be " holy " as Yahweh was holy (Lev. xix. 2), to the crudest efforts to imitate externally the animal or other sacred object with whom men felt themselves to be most intimately connected. Thus " Condor clans in Peru who believed themselves descended from the condor, adorned themselves with the feathers of the bird " (Frazer, *Tot. Ex.* i. 26). Among the Thompson Indians of North America, the boy who received a guardian spirit would paint his face with designs symbolic of this spirit (iii. 414). Among the Australian Arunta the newly initiated youth, after being told his secret name (which may be that of one of the famous departed, of whom he is the reincarnation), is painted on face and body with the device of his totem (i. 196). A new-born babe of the Deer clan of the Omaha Indians will be marked with red spots down the neck to indicate that it is a deer ; and when one of the Buffalo clan dies he is wrapped in a buffalo robe before rejoining his " ancestors " (iii. 103 *sq.*; cf. the Tlingit practices, *ib.* 269 *sq.,* and those of the Haidas, 289). In all such rites whereby the sacred being is imitated or an identity externally effected, the visible action has, primarily at least, a genuine psychological value. It manifests a communion with the sacred being (cf. Durkheim, 357 *sq.*), however conventional or mechanical this relationship may subsequently become.

[1] On skins in ritual, see Frazer, *FOT.* ii. 6 *sqq.* ; Eitrem, 386 *sqq.* (see *ib.* 401 *sq.,* 482 *sq.,* on clothes in ritual).

[2] Cf. A. Jeremias, *Old Test.* i. 106, fig. 33 (cf. ii. 190 n.), and *Handbuch d. Altorient. Geisteskultur,* 42, fig. 25 ; Gressmann, *Altorient. Bilder z. A.T.²,* figs. 314, 326 (with description, pp. 90, 93). Sellin, in the *Nöldeke-Festschrift,* 712, conjectures that the priestly shining dress in Babylonia reflects the shining majesty of the god (cf. Ps. civ. 1 *sq.*).

It represents the constantly recurrent stage where "spiritual" ideas are grasped only in a concrete and visible form; and it illustrates the characteristic difference between (a) the emphasis upon the outward act, as engendering, maintaining, and revealing a particular inward state, and (b) that upon the condition of mind of which the outward act is, at its highest, the natural fruit (cf. A. B. Davidson on Ezek. xviii. 9 [*Camb. Bible*]).   But however mystical the rites of imitation may be, they typically serve an essentially practical purpose.   In becoming like the god one acquired his powers and gained possession of his ability to control either things or else the processes which he operated.   The most striking cases of imitation are those in the Central Australian ceremonies, where certain totem-clans imitate in one way or another the totem in order to make it more abundant (as food) or otherwise control it.   The imitation sets in operation, as it were, a "mystic potency" (cf. I. King, 152 *sqq.*). However mystical imitative rites may seem, the religion of primitive peoples is predominantly practical; and the rites which seem to be crudely magical are better described as "magico-religious."   For the details, see Frazer, *GB.* i. 85 *sqq.*, *Tot. Ex.* i. 105 *sqq.*, 184 *sqq.*; Durkheim, 351 *sqq.*   See above on "limping," p. 672, and on imitation by means of dress, p. 674; also *ERE.* "Religion," § 19.

P. 439 *sq.* THE MATERIAL AND THE SPIRITUAL.—In his final paragraph, summing up the whole book, W. R. S. indicates the supreme problem of religion: (1) the real difference between primitive and advanced religions, and (2) the factors of the progressive development of religion.   Everywhere there is an invariable tendency for ideas to pass into movements, and attention to any movement readily evokes the tendency to copy it.   All primitive types of thought are at the perceptual rather than the conceptual stage: ideas are "bound," and cannot be grasped save in some physical, material, or concrete embodiment.   Some material object or action, more or less appropriate to the occasion, is commonly desired in order to give reality to what at higher stages is recognized as essentially mental; and purely psychological processes must be helped out by concrete rites.[1]   Primitive man, observes Kreglinger, has no internal life.   " Il est réaliste, découvre des réalistés objectives là même où il n'aperçoit en fait que les images subjectives nées dans sa propre pensée : il est matérialiste, tous les concepts se matérialisent dans sa pensée, sans d'ailleurs, cela

---

[1] Cf. Naaman in 2 Kings v. 10 *sqq.*   Canaan (*JPOS.* vi. 38 n. 4) cites a curious case where a mother cures her son of a very bad fright by acting as though he were dead; his alarm and anxiety dispel his fright, but he must eat of a hen which she has been boiling, and the hen is a black or white one according as the man had been frightened in the night-time or the day.   See above, pp. 84 *sqq.*

va de soi, que cette matérialisation soit vrai consciente." [1] Primitive religion, accordingly, is intensely practical, and centres on human life and on real human interests (above, pp. 16 *sqq.* ; cf. *Lectures*, 412).

The differences between the practical social-religious cults of rudimentary peoples and the more conceptual and abstract stages of thought at the higher levels constitute a common source of misunderstanding, and raise important questions. Misled by the concreteness of primitive religion, it is easy to overlook the ideas that lie behind or are implicit in primitive rites. On the other hand, since ideas of salvation, redemption, etc., would, as W. R. S. remarks, be primarily expressed in some concrete shape, it is often difficult in particular cases, *e.g.* in dealing with the O.T., to determine whether such ideas were reinforced by or expressed in concrete form, or had already become purely spiritual.[2] Ideas of spiritual imitation of a god have their more rudimentary physical counterpart (p. 675); and to spiritual rebirth or regeneration correspond realistic rites of rebirth (p. 649). Primarily, at least, such rites must have been of psychological value ; ideas of the kinship and marriage of gods and man, and other realistic modes of thought, must have been a genuine expression of the intimate relationship which men felt to subsist between their supernatural beings and themselves.

Now primitive men not only fail to recognize any essential difference between human and animal life, but can even aver a substantial identity between themselves and their totem (Frazer, *Tot. Ex.* i. 119 ; cf. above, 88 *sq.*). The Kangaroo man points to a photograph of himself and says, "That one is just the same as me; so is a kangaroo." The explanation of this lies in the meaning his totem has for him ; [3] and similarly, on a considerably higher level of civilization, when a Pharaoh, like Ikhnaton, is " son " of the solar disk Aton, it is obvious that the solar body is the embodiment of his god as truly as an image or other terrestrial object can be to its worshippers. So long as physical con-

---

[1] *Études sur l'origine et le développement de la vie religieuse* (Brussels, 1919), i. 160 *sqq.* Of course this type of thought occurs everywhere. In Rome, " Faunus *is* the wood and Vulturnus *is* the river, the name of the seed is *Ceres.*" " Dryads and Hamadryads *are* trees," and " whereas Naiads *are* sources, nixies and hags, and tree-spirits and brownies, are souls that are only bound to sources, trees, and houses, from which they long to be released " (Spengler, *The Decline of the West,* i. 403).

[2] So, *e.g.*, as concerns ideas of the safety of a man's " soul," see Cook in *People and the Book* (ed. Peake, 45 *sqq.*) ; cf. H. W. Robinson, *ib.* 353 *sqq.*, and for the connexion between " trust " (*b-ṭ-ḥ*) and prostration or throwing oneself upon another, see G. Driver, *ib.* 118, and cf. *JQR.* 1902, April, 447. See above, p. 635.

[3] Cf. Durkheim (188, 206): totemism is the religion, not of such and such animals, men, or images, but of the power found in them, though not to be confounded with them.

crete rites and modes of thought have a meaning which we can only describe as psychical or spiritual, the social and ethical value of much that seems purely ritual or material is psychologically explicable. In point of fact, the extent to which the " spiritual " lurks in seemingly crude and physical forms is astonishing. Ideas of " supernatural " birth, of the " spirits " or " souls " even of inanimate objects, or the ability of " spirits " to eat the " spirit " part of food, taken with the preponderance of religious or magical rites and practices in the life of primitive men, have given the impression that they must have passed all their time more or less in a mystical state. It is, however, truer to say that at the lower undifferentiated stages religious and related ideas permeated the greater part of life, and that through the very scanti-ness of positive knowledge the " supersensuous " was more immediate. Indeed, the reality of what we should call the spiritual or the super-senuous was such that even at higher stages of development, spirits and souls have concrete form, and spirit and matter instead of being antithetical are different qualities or modes of the same substance, being more refined or more coarse as the case may be. The immediate reality of the spiritual and psychical is the characteristic feature of early thought; the explicit distinction of the psychical and spiritual from the physical and material marks the great advance.

" The early Hebrews did not think about Yahweh, they believed in him and expressed the reality of his sovereignty in the great things which he did for his people " (*Prophets*, 42). The more detached objective and critical attitudes are secondary. It is then that names of things lose their concreteness and a distinction can be drawn between a name or a word and what it stands for, and meanings can be severed from the ways in which they are expressed. Differentiation takes place. In *Lectures*, 224 *sq.*, W. R. S. characteristically illustrates this in the "growth of the religious consciousness" at the Reformation. Rites like that which accompanies the prayer to Ishtar (p. 646 n. 3), or the ceremonial cited above (p. 676), have no real justification for their existence ; none the less it often proves difficult to sever rites from that with which they have no genetic connexion whatever. Similarly, a god will not be deemed to exist apart from the sacred object in which he is embodied, even as at the stage of conceptual thought ideas of a Supreme Being are treated in a quasi-physical way. And when the connexion between idea and ritual is of the closest, as in rites of purification, imitation, and rebirth, both the readiness with which the forms come to obscure the spiritual element which had given them their primary value, and the difficulty of modifying them, can be easily understood. Again, it often happens that the spiritual value of a rite is so slight that, properly speaking, it requires reinforcement which, however, is not provided for by any other rite ; or the rite has implications which, if developed—and there is a tendency to develop them—would impede ethical or intellectual progress. Upon the form in which an idea is clothed, or on the rite with which it is fused, will depend the advance of thought.[1]

The spiritual idea that can be found in some physical dress, *e.g.* the imitation of a god, is neither in isolation nor is it solely spiritual. Primarily, it has some real connexion with its environment. For this and other reasons it is proper to distinguish, where possible, between (*a*) the *magico-religious*, which has an evident value, even though it be interwoven with ideas of nature and the control of nature which are no longer held, and (*b*) the purely *magical*, wherein individuals profess to control nature in their own right, or there are amulets and other objects to which is ascribed an efficacy which is in no way inherent in them. The difference turns upon their psychological and social value. If, for example, the idea of scapegoats arose merely from a confusion between (1) the possibility of transferring actual physical burdens and (2) the supposition that bodily and mental ailments could be as readily shifted (see Frazer, *GB.* ix. Preface), the rise and persistence of the rites would be psychologically inexplicable. Hence, although numerous examples of a purely magical order could undoubtedly be cited, the rites must be regarded—when a long view is taken—as primarily " magico-religious." [2] Moreover, it is misleading to stamp religion at the physical stage as necessarily unethical. Early ideas of the Sacred and Holy had not that ethical or moral value which the Hebrew prophets gave them ; they were pre-ethical. They did not necessarily exclude an ethical meaning, but they were undifferentiated, being interwoven with what was non- and anti-ethical. And as the stress was not laid upon their ethical significance, they not only included but even emphasized (as in the *Ḳedēshōth*) what proved to be immoral and anti-social.[3]

[1] G. F. Moore (*Hist. of Religions*, i. 585), referring to the Roman deities Concordia, Spes, Pietas, etc., observes that modern authors often regard these as the deification of abstractions and a mark of advanced religious development ; but " it is only the modern who conceives them as abstract : the power which works harmony among citizens is for the antique apprehension no more abstract than the power that works the germination of grain in the earth." One sees how the treatment of ideas of Concord, Wisdom, etc., were hampered by their embodiment. The Semitic divine abstractions, in South Arabia, etc., are merely appellatives : *Ḥukm* is not Wisdom, but " the wise one " (Nielsen, *Handbuch*, i. 195 *sq.*).

[2] Incidentally, it should be noticed that the desire to relate primitive psychology to that of more advanced peoples is itself significant for the science and theory of religion ; cf. *ERE.* " Religion," § 12.

[3] Cf. p. 553. In the same way, ideas of " religion " can be at a pre-ethical stage

Differentiation and the development of some particular aspect are the most characteristic features in the history of religious thought, and a distinction has to be drawn between legitimate development, when a spiritual meaning is found in some rite, etc., and the tendencies to find some deeper meaning for which there is no justification—the notorious abuse of the allegorical method of interpretation. Spiritual development does not lie only in making explicit what was formerly implicit, but in processes of transmutation. In a singularly forcible passage, W. R. S. explains the spiritual ideas of Yahweh as a reaction against the passion of Semitic heathenism (*Lectures*, p. 425). Error and aberration will force a recognition of elemental ideas which need reshaping, even as gross evil will compel the recognition of the principles which it violates. Excesses in religion (phallicism, licentious cults, human sacrifice), and all else that is socially destructive, are to be regarded on this account, not as primary phenomena, but as late decadent tendencies. But it is often possible amid certain gross, irrational, and " superstitious " beliefs and practices to recover something germinal which needs transmuting, even as, at the conceptual level, an extreme theory, theology, or philosophy may contain elements which in another form are of permanent value.[1]

It is instructive to inquire why new spiritual teaching, such as that of the prophets, is ultimately assimilated. It may be found that it has developed and made explicit what was already implicit, or it has fitted in with current belief, or it has transmuted or reshaped it. But the spiritual ideas of great figures tend to be, like themselves, isolated and apart from practical life and thought. They need adjustment and systematization. There is always the danger that spiritual ideas will become merely verbal. Spiritual teaching is preserved by being systematized in tangible or concrete form, in individual or social life, in a doctrinal or other system. The teaching of the prophets became embodied in post-exilic Judaism, and " without those hard and ossified forms the preservation of its essential elements would have proved impossible." [2] The example is of the deepest interest as showing that the stage when religion has become " spiritual " (as in the individualistic prophets) is never the final stage. Many interesting points at once arise out of the relationship between the pre-spiritual and later stages. It may be asked, *e.g.*, whether the " priestly " account of the circumcision rite is recognizably post-prophetic, and whether the national history of Israel in its present form represents pre-prophetic or

when attention is directed to the intense subjective meaning that it has for the individual rather than upon its more objective aspects.

[1] Cf. Cook, *Study of Religions*, 211 *sqq.*
[2] Cf. Wellhausen, *Prolegomena*, 497 *sq.*, cited in *Ency. Brit.*[11] xv. 390*d*.

post-prophetic teaching. Moreover, false contrasts are frequently made. The Babylonian psalms, in spite of their many admirable features, *seem* unspiritual because of their material rewards or the absence of higher feelings of love for god or fellow-men. But a living religion is practical and apt to be material, notably that of Israel. The contrast is as misleading as that between the practical life and religion of Israelites and the height of idealism in the N.T.—as distinct from the troubled history of a worldly Christendom.

Religious experience must be made articulate, and therefore needs a theology—as W. R. S. was insisting in his earlier work (*Lectures*, cf. 323 *et passim*). So, too, spiritual religion must be in a system which is in a certain harmony with ordinary life and knowledge. In the development of religion the spiritual part, implicit or explicit, has invariably proved the most essential—conversely, that which has been developed is that which was " spiritual " ; and at the higher stages it must be embodied in order to preserve it, but it must not be suffocated. The " congenital defect inherent in every attempt to embody spiritual truth in material forms " (p. 440) is most obvious in rudimentary religion or in the priestly ritual of a post-exilic Judaism. But when W. R. S.—in the earlier part of his career, at least—reiterates his dissatisfaction with the theology of the day, and looks for a revival of the old Reformation spirit and principles, he is implying that even an explicitly theological system can lose its old spiritual power (see the *Introduction*). The transition from the physical or material stage through some spiritual movement to a new systematization at the conceptual level is not all ; and " spiritual " religion is not merely that which by reason of its terminology stands conspicuously opposed to material or ritual forms.

Gray (*Sacrifice*, 43 *sq.*, 52 *sqq.*) contrasts the spiritual demand of the prophets that men should be like God, with primitive communion rites and the offering of gifts. The root idea of both of the latter belongs, he asserts, to a " grossly material view of religion and of man's relation to God " (*ib.* 54). This is forcibly put. There are many practices whereby a man is taken out of himself into a " supersensuous " realm, and the occasions will be felt to be " sacred " ; but a distinction may well be drawn between those like the use of intoxicating drinks (p. 575 ; cf. also p. 612 *sq.*), and those whose demoralizing effects are less patent, notably material gifts (cf. p. 639). Again, even if man's gift of his own will to God be completely spiritual (Gray), must not this surrender be translated into action ? And if so, the question will arise, When is a man doing or not doing the will of his god ? If to do God's will is spiritual religion, it would seem that a distinction should be made between (*a*) the occasions when the individual is conscious of alternatives, one of which is definitely " higher," and may be regarded as in accordance with, or in submission to, a Divine Will ; and (*b*) all those where he is at least not consciously acting contrary to his highest ideals. There are other cases which need not be considered ; and it seems evident that in the latter (*b*) he is, consciously at least, not opposing God's will, though whether he is therefore doing it brings up questions which do not belong here. All that has to be said now is that one of the most characteristic features of primitive religion is not (1) " my will," the will of the all-powerful wonder-worker ; nor is it (2) " thy will," an explicit dependence upon and surrender to a higher power ; it may be called (3) " *our* will." In the last case men are admittedly or virtually or implicitly co-operating with their gods.[1] They are a " chosen people," or " representative " individuals ; they are symbols or vehicles of the recognized god(s), and it is frequently taken as a matter of course that the gods do the will of their adherents. Or men perform ceremonies to procure that for which elsewhere they appeal directly to the gods ; they act *qua* gods. This type readily develops, in one direction, into explicit subservience and quietism, and in the other, towards the crudest magical attitudes ; and for this reason it can be regarded as primary. " *Our* will " is the typical religion of the narrow group-system consisting of gods and their worshippers ; it is religion of an immanental and not transcendental character, and on this account is of the first importance for estimating the nature of " spiritual " religion.

W. R. S. clearly recognized that his researches bore directly on " the great problem of the origins of the spiritual religion of the Bible " (p. 2). Communion or At-one-ment with a Divine Power, as he had previously insisted, was a moral, a personal thing; it is an invisible bond, not an outward sign (*Lectures*, 223, 275, 319). It is enough for us to recall the New Covenant to be written on a man's heart, or the Divine Presence when two or three are gathered together in His Name —in the Talmud when men meet together to study the Torah the Shechinah is in their midst.[2] Now amid the many forms in which experiences and convictions of communion, at-one-ment, or fellowship have expressed themselves, we can distinguish (1) the fundamental experience without which the evidence would be unintelligible, and (2) the various forms which we may attempt to evaluate and arrange in some order of development. The x which we trace in l, m, and n is the " spiritual " element ; and ambiguity is caused when with x, the psychological origin of the forms and their primitive expression, is confused l, which, as the most rudimentary of forms, is regarded as the

[1] See *ERE*. " Religion," § 19 (3).
[2] *Bab. Berachoth*, 6a (Abelson, 145).

true origin. Moreover, even to say that *l* developed into *m* and *m* into *n* goes farther than to say that *n* can be traced back ultimately to *l* (cf. p. 541, top); and it is obvious that *l* can never represent actual prehistoric primitive data. So, as regards the theory of totem-origins, it is admittedly of extraordinary suggestiveness; it has drawn attention to the potentiality of some very rudimentary cults and to the persistence, recurrence, and constant reshaping of elements—of which the idea of communion is only one—which *for this reason* may be called " spiritual." W. R. S.'s theory of the " totem-origin " of sacrifice is true, therefore, in the sense that in totemism we find the most primitive types of belief and practice that we can well conceive, and that, as Durkheim clearly showed, it contains in rudimentary form some of the significant features which mark the higher religions.

It has been said somewhere that the most ancient religion would be the purest, the most recent the truest : at all events it is an important question whether primitive religion has any real value for or anything to contribute to modern knowledge. Has the " vision " of early types of religion any meaning for mature thought which admits of being rationalized ? Now, when Christianity arose, it did not cover the same ground and have the same *milieu* as pre-Christian Judaism ; and the same can be said of post-exilic Judaism in its relation to the old religion of Israel. In religious as in other thought a new stage will often be more intensive, but on a narrower basis, more idealist, less catholic. In the history of religions and of sects progress in one direction seems often to be accompanied by impoverishment in others. The development is at the cost of earlier material which had some value. It may be that this material is no longer compatible with the new movement, its interests or its *milieu*; or it is unsuitable for its members, who, it may be, are at a much less mature stage of intellectual growth. There are conspicuous occasions where religion has severed itself from non-religious material which it has not even transmuted, and characteristic of primitive religion is much that is of peculiar interest if only because of the profound gulf between it and modern thought.

The development of religion has been marked by the extension and differentiation of early ideas. What is true of a vital part of a system becomes true of every part, in both cases conditionally. What is true of the supreme representative individual applies—when allowance is made for differentiation of function—to all. We pass—in Egypt—from the eager hope that the great men must surely survive death to the belief that this may be true of all. The cosmic importance of the one or the few, by virtue of their relation to their god, gives way to the supreme value of every individual, and for the same reason.

Properly, everything is conditional, dependent upon a man's place in the system. The divine king and the anthropomorphic god expand conceptions of human personality and of man's place in the Universe. From the pre-eminent cosmic value of a divine king, and from the governance of the world for a Chosen People, we reach the presupposition that man is the centre of the Universe. It was a rationalizing, as it were, of the mystical experience of man's oneness or unity with all reality (p. 666 *sq*.). Further examples are unnecessary; it is enough to say that all early and undifferentiated stages of religious and other thought—the relationship between god and man and nature, the unity of the spiritual or psychical with the material or physical, and so forth—demand on our part a rational formulation of the relation between successive stages in the differentiation of thought and between the subsequently differentiated forms.

There is much in primitive religion that corresponds to " Divine Immanence " : the interrelation of gods and worshippers within the system, the " material reality of the spiritual," and the interpenetration where gods and men are alike one with nature. Where this realism prevails the actual world is both matter and spirit, and it seems probable that it is the origin of the dualist systems which have advanced beyond primitive religion and incorporate the learning and the science—or pseudo-science—of their age. This dualism may be said to mark the transition from ancient religion to the victorious Christianity which (1) was essentially a social religion rather than a theory of God, Man, and the Universe, and (2) explicitly preserved the teaching of Divine Transcendence. But whereas in this dualism the strictly transcendental aspect falls into the background, in early religion it can constantly be recognized. The divine king, in spite of his extraordinary powers, was subordinate to the supreme god (p. 545); the interpenetration of man and nature (man's power over and in nature) did not necessarily exclude the existence of supreme gods (often, no doubt, otiose), or of supreme principles; and in the early ideas of " holiness " moral elements were by no means always wanting. Even in totemism —which can be described as an " immanental " system—there are, as distinct from the clan-totems, gods of the tribe (cf. p. 668). In general, the tendencies that made for Immanence were, properly speaking, balanced by those that made for Transcendence (p. 564). Religion has struggled between a dual and a triple organization. (*a*) The world is physical or material *and* psychical; but the psychical is not necessarily spiritual, even as the " numinous " is not necessarily sacred, or theistic (p. 553 *sq*.). On the other hand (*b*) Yahweh is above nature, and therefore above this psychical principle in nature (cf. p. 662). Similarly, man is flesh (*sarx*) and *psyche*, but the *pneuma* is the transcendent, life-giving source; and without this transcendent element every system ceases to develop, becomes closed, decays and dies.

We must recognize, with W. R. S., that the central fact in religion is its progressive development. The difference between the vicissitudes of religions in general and the continuous explication of ideas up to the present day—no mere subjective conviction—is as vital for the world of thought as is man's place in the world of organic life. The spiritual teaching of the great creative ages is marked by an utter uncompromising insistence upon Divine Transcendence, and upon the futility of all human anticipations that the mere continuity of any religion hitherto is a guarantee that it will survive, should it lack the essential spirituality. True spiritual religion is not necessarily that which is at the conceptual stage, or is mystical, or expresses itself in psychological or spiritual terms—upon this the lengthy history of religion is decisive. Nor is that which is necessarily embodied—in order to make it effective—in practice or rite, in doctrine or system, necessarily physical, material, or mechanical. The spiritual elements are those which prove to be pregnant; upon them depends the further development of that which must have some embodiment and must be at least an implicit system. But outside every system is that which makes for its further growth; and without it progressive development sooner or later becomes impossible. Materialism is so far unavoidable that both the perceptual and the conceptual, the physical and the psychical, may belong to "matter." Even Pure Materialism seems methodologically necessary. But it becomes the closed system devoid of those pregnant elements which are fed from outside the system, and "matter," in this sense, is the fixed concept, the absolutely delimited, the data of the statistician, and—as brute matter—it can be weighed and measured.

Accordingly, the value of primitive religion lies in the fact that it reveals, not the historic origin, but the exceedingly rudimentary forms of the religious and other ideas from which modern thought has been derived. It shows us why they were true and effective for their environment, and how their strength lay in their interrelation one with another. The difference between the most primitive and the most advanced religion is precisely as instructive as that between the lowest and the highest organisms.[1] It is the permanent significance of

---

[1] Although emphasis must be laid upon the increase of differentiation and specialization in the history of thought—and therefore on the distinction between what belongs to Religion and what falls outside it—the periods of relative undifferentiation, when some real unity is found to lie beneath the differences, no less require emphasis, though the questions that arise therefrom are of a philosophical or methodological nature and do not belong here.

W. R. S.'s work that problems which are usually approached in the light of definite theological, philosophical, or other presuppositions were being treated *de novo* by a man of extraordinary attainments, who had a special knowledge of the area wherein the great progressive movements in religion took place, and who, while intensely religious, and with distinct theological interests, had from the first the conviction that a reformulation of religious doctrine was the need of his age.[1]

P. 445. ELOHIM.—Cf. Phœnician אלם, used of Nergal (*CIS*. i. 119$_2$) and of Astarte (Lidzbarski, *Ephem*. i. 155), and ηλειμ (Lidz. ii. 89). In the Hittite treaties Mitra and Varuna are *ilānu*, but not Indra, perhaps because he was more clearly individualized as the national god. In the Amarna Letters *ilānu* is used with a singular verb in No. 96$_4$; and the Pharaoh is addressed as " my god," *ilānu(-ia)*, and by Abimilk of Tyre as *(ilu)Shamshi-ia, ili-ia, ilāni-ia* (151$_1$). The plural in Semitic does not necessarily refer to a number of single persons or things (Gesenius-Cowley, *Heb. Gram*. § 124), and the so-called " broken plurals " are " in all probability . . . singular abstract forms which gradually came to be used in a concrete and collective sense, and hence pass for plurals " (Wm. Wright, *Comp. Gram. Semit. Lang*. 148). The plural does not necessarily serve the same function everywhere, and the view that the plural Elohim is derived from polytheism—as though it denoted the Pantheon—has difficulties. In contrast to individualization, tendencies " to pluralize the supernatural " are recurrent : W. Warde Fowler observes it even in the inscriptions of the Empire (*Roman Ideas of Deity*, 16 *sq*.); for Greece, cf. the " gentle gods," etc. (Nilsson, 111 *sq*., 120). Or the plural is indefinite—" They "—see Meyer, *Israel*. 212 n., who considers the *pluralis majestatis* an inadequate explanation of such cases as Teraphim, *Di Manes*, etc. At certain stages of religion the whole animal or tree species is sacred, and not the single specimen, which, in truth, is as eternal as the species and immanent in it. In such cases there is a very real " deity," though it is without clear-cut personality (Durkheim, 191, on the species-god of Samoa ; Crawley, *Tree of Life*, 252). Among the Australian Dieri the name for the supreme god Mura-Mura (" very holy ") designates the ancestral beings ; and the name Nuralie, the god of the tribes on the Murray River, is sometimes used as a collective expression for the primeval group of mythical beings (Durkheim, 290 ; cf. Marett, *Threshold of Rel*. 152 *sq*.).

---

[1] Though W. R. S. passed from being an ardent theologian to one of the most penetrating critics of Semitic religion and sociology, he did not himself attempt the necessary task of reformulating theological doctrine. On the contrary, towards the close of his life he found occasion to declare that he felt he never could have been a theologian (*Life*, p. 535). See the Introduction above.

P. 451. NAKED AND UNSHOD.—For nudity in religious ritual, cf. the use at Mecca (Wellh. 110; Gaudefroy-Demombynes, 172); on praying in a state of nudity, see Goldziher, *Nöldeke-Festschrift*, 328; for classical examples, besides the Lupercalia (p. 479 above), see Eitrem, 52, and in general J. Heckenbach, *De nuditate sacra sacrisque vinculis* (Giessen, 1911). At the present day, when Palestinian women implore the help of a god or saint they uncover the breast or go entirely naked as a sign of humiliation (*JPOS*. vi. 15); and in India they strip naked in a ploughing-rite where the rain deity is invoked (*JRAS*. 1897, pp. 475 *sq*., 478 *sq*.; 1898, p. 195). For other Indian examples, see R. E. Enthoven, *Folklore of Bombay*, 329 *sq*. (nudity in learning and in practising arts of incantation, fertility rites, etc.). In the Rossel island, off Papua, there are districts each of which (called *yaba*) is owned by a person of rank and controls some important process of nature (wind, birth, sago, sun and moon, etc.). Any untoward conduct would prevent the owner from exploiting this power of control, and people who visit the *yaba* always shed their clothing and take nothing with them (W. E. Armstrong, *Anthropos*, xviii.–xix. [1923–4]). Nudity rites are prehistoric, and the nude female image with crossed arms holding her breasts, etc., is taken to be a fertility charm or fertility goddess. In Palestine people at the present day will go in rags when they pray for rain (*JPOS*. vi. 157), and the custom of tearing the garment, laying bare arm or shoulder in mourning, may be interpreted, partly, as a survival of a nudity rite (see Jastrow, *JAOS*. xx. 133–150, xxi. 23–39; *ZATW*. 1902, pp. 117 *sqq*.), and partly and more psychologically as a mere impulsive action.[1]

As regards shoes, the modern peasant will remove them at the shrine of an important *weli* (Canaan, *JPOS*. i. 170, 171 n. 1). The custom was in vogue in Babylonian ritual (see Jirku, *ZATW*. xxxvii. 120); and in the Psalms of Solomon ii. 2 the writer complains that alien nations trample the altar with their sandals. For classical references, see Eitrem, 91 n. 6, 392 *sqq*.; Frazer, *Paus*. v. 202.

P. 456.—Cf. *uṣurtu*, taboo, R. Campbell Thompson, *Demons and Evil Spirits of Babylonia*, ii. pp. xli n. 1, 119, *Semitic Magic*, 126 n. 2. Muss-Arnolt gives the meaning " magical spell, curse."

P. 456. PHALLIC SYMBOLS.—Various phallic objects have been found in Palestine, *e.g.* at the foot of a pillar at Megiddo (G. Schumacher, *Tell el-Mutesellim*, i. 128), and at Taanach (E. Sellin, *Nachlese auf den Tell Ta'annek*, 1905, p. 9, fig. 7); one rudely carved to represent a man at Zakariya (Bliss and Macalister, *Excavations in Palestine*, 136,

---

[1] The Assyrian term for tearing off a garment in mourning is *sharaṭu* (see *KAT*. 603; Lagrange, 321; Winckler, *Altorient. Forsch.* ii. 29, 40). On its Arabic equivalent, used of a mark tattooed or cut on the person, see *Kinship*, 250.

plate lxvii. no. 7). They were found in " basketfuls " at the high place of Gezer along with Astarte plaques ; and one of the pillars is evidently itself phallic (Macalister, *Gezer*, ii. 394 ; Vincent, *Canaan*, 113). Besides some phallic objects at Petra, innumerable emblems were found at Nippur (Peters, *JAOS*. xli. 132, 141 *sq.* ; cf. *MDOG.* 1904, June, No. xxii. 26, a phallic-shaped pillar). The phallic origin of the boundary stones (*kudurru*) is doubtful. For the view that the ideogram IM=*rāmānu*=god of the phallus, see Ungnad, *ZA*. xxxvi. 272. Phallic emblems are rare on Babylonian seals (Ward, 65, 153), and they are not prominent in the cult of Adonis (Baudissin, 179). On the whole, indisputable female emblems on stone pillars are, in spite of arguments to the contrary, relatively rare ; and phallicism is a secondary phenomenon in religion. This is not to deny that at times it became extraordinarily prominent ; but phallicism never developed into an organized cult, even as phallic interpretations of religion have not succeeded in presenting any reasonable systematized theory of the history of religion.[1]

P. 465. FIRSTBORN.—There are few traces of birthright in Babylonia (see Meissner, *Beiträge z. altbab. Privatrecht*, 16 ; Johns, *Bab. and Ass. Laws*, 162). For ultimogeniture or junior-right in the O.T. and elsewhere, see Frazer, *FOT*. i. 429 *sqq.*, who discusses some of the causes which may have led to primogeniture. Reasons for the special treatment of firstborn can be found, *e.g.*, when a child is born to a childless couple or in response to a vow (cf. *GB*. iv. 181). Such is the anxiety touching the successful issue of a marriage that sometimes it is only after the birth of a child that a marriage is considered complete (Crawley, *Mystic Rose*, 432, 464). Children, and especially firstborn, have been sacrificed to cure barrenness or, more generally, to ensure health, good fortune, and fertility (Westermarck, *Moral Ideas*, i. 457, 460 ; *GB*. iv. 184). There are various savage rites—devouring the firstborn (New South Wales),[2] or killing them outright ; or the firstborn may be sacrificed to ensure the preservation of his successors (*FOT*. iii. 173). Sometimes the first few children are sacrificed (*GB*. iv. 181, Abyssinia). Men, and especially children, are slain by a king to restore to life a friend or to preserve the life of a king (Crawley, 277 *sq.* ; *GB*. vi. 226).

It is often believed that the father is reborn in his child ; [3] for this

---

[1] See Lagrange, 190 *sq.* ; Spoer, *ZATW*. xxviii. 271 ; Gressmann, xxix. 113–128 ; Sellin, *OLZ*. 1912, col. 119 *sq.* ; Budde, *ib*. 247 *sq.* ; and Ganszyniec, *Arch. f. Rel*. xxi. 499 *sqq.* (on Lucian, *Dea Syr*. xvi.).

[2] Frazer, *Belief in Immortality*, ii. 89 n. (refs.).

[3] In the Laws of Manu the husband is reborn as an embryo in the wife (*GB*. iv. 188 *sqq.* ; see *ERE*. vi. 332, and A. B. Cook, *Zeus*, ii. 294).

reason, at Tahiti and elsewhere, a chief should abdicate when a son is born (*GB.* iv. 190); hence the infant is put to death. The birth of a son may be an indication that the father will die (the Baganda, *FOT.* i. 562). Again, because the son is in some way his father over again, the father's name must not be given to the firstborn, and in Morocco the son is never called by the name of his father (if alive), unless that name be Mohammed. This name is frequently given to the first son, and the first daughter is called after the Prophet's daughter Fatima.[1] By a natural variation of the idea, a man is reborn not in his son but in his grandson. Commonly both have the same name (above, p. 510), and sometimes it is considered a misfortune for a chief to see his grandson (*FOT.* i. 479 *sq.*, 579 *sq.*). Throughout, the fundamental ideas turn upon the perpetuation of the stock.

In some social conditions it would be highly doubtful whether the firstborn was the true child of his mother's husband (C. E. Fox, *JRAI.* xlix. 119). This might be immaterial (*a*) where it was enough that he belonged to the group of which his mother was a member, and (*b*) where " a man is father of all the children of the woman by whom he has purchased the right to have offspring that shall be reckoned to his own kin " (*Kinship*, 132, where the husband calls in another man). Again, (*c*) where ceremonial defloration was practised the legitimacy of the firstborn might be doubtful. Among the Banaro of New Guinea this ceremony " takes place in the spirit or goblin house of the village," and the child is " the spirit-child or goblin-child " (*FOT.* i. 534); and elsewhere the firstborn will be of at least partly " sacred " origin. Does this throw light upon the " sacredness " of the firstborn in Palestine, with its *ḳedēshīm*, and its licentious cults ?[2] The evidence is admittedly incomplete (see p. 617 *sq.*): the firstborn were sacred to Yahweh and must be redeemed ; but infant sacrifice prevailed. The firstborn perpetuate the stock, and Yahweh was the spiritual father of Israel. *Spiritual* religion requires, not animal or human sacrifice, but " the souls of the righteous, and of children who have not yet sinned " (late Jewish ; Gray, *Sacrifice*, 172) ; and the Agadah of the third century A.D. developed the doctrine of the efficacious merits of pious children (Marmorstein, *Doctrine of Merits*, 95, 163). The new-born found interred in the sacred area at Gezer can hardly be proved, in view of the circumstances, to be sin-offerings (Micah, vi. 7), and it cannot, of course, be proved that they were firstborn; but whether they had died a natural death, or—as is more probable—

---

[1] Westermarck, *Morocco*, ii. 404. Of the same order is the conviction that the same name cannot be borne by any two persons of the same tribe (*GB.* iii. 370).

[2] Psellus (Migne, 832 *sq.*, cited by R. C. Thompson, *Sem. Magic*, 223) refers to the orgies of the Euchitæ and the sacrifice of their offspring nine months later.

had been sacrificed, the presence of the " spirits " of infants in a sacred locality may be associated with the common resort of women to shrines in the hope of obtaining offspring—a hope the more intelligible if " spirits " of infants were known to be there.

P. 469. SET AND THE ASS.—The " golden " Set is an old misinterpretation of " Set of Ombos " (Prof. T. E. Peet, private communication). Set's animal is uncertain ; it was perhaps the okapi, which became conventionalized and, in the Greek age, was identified with the ass.[1] The ass is generally reddish in colour (*E.Bi.* col. 344 and n. 1) ; and in Egypt the sacrifice of " red " men long persisted (Macalister, *ERE.* vi. 862 ; also Mader, 32 *sq.*, 120 *sqq.*). In the Sumerian pantheon Esignun, one of the subordinate gods, tended the sacred asses of the great god Ningirsu (L. W. King, *Sumer and Akkad,* 259, 268), and the ass was the animal of the god Labartu. It is possible that the special regard for the ass, in the case of the redemption of the firstling (Ex. xxxiv. 20), was because, as a beast of burden, it performed the work of the gods in the realm of the dead (Campbell Thompson, *Semitic Magic,* 234). In any case, as an older animal than the horse, and on the analogy of the " horses of the Sun " (cf. 2 Kings xxiii. 11), we might expect it to have been no less sacred in its day. But there is little to be said concerning the ass in Semitic lore (C. J. Ball, *PSBA.* xxxii. 64 *sqq.* ; cf. also A. B. Cook, *Journ. of Hell. Studies,* xiv. 81 *sqq.*). The Sumerian designation of Damascus as " ass city " can hardly be explained (see, *e.g.,* Haupt, *ZDMG.* lxix. 168 ; Winckler, *Arab. Semit. Orient.* 171 *sq.*). What Theophrastus (Porph. *de Abstin.* ii. 26) has to say about the ass and sacrifices may refer not to *Judæans* but *Idumæans* (Büchler, *ZATW.* 1902, pp. 206 *sqq.*). On the ass as a symbol of strength, cf. Wellh.[1] 157.[2]

P. 469. HERACLES AND THE QUAIL.—Heracles was slain by Typhon and brought to life by Iolaos ; see Frazer, *GB.* v. 111 *sq.* On Iolaos see *Kinship,* 226, 257, and on the " resurrection " of Heracles see Baudissin, 135, 172, Abel, *Rev. Bib.,* 1908, pp. 570, 577 *sq.* The meaning of the name Eshmun has been much discussed (see Lidzbarski, iii. 260 *sqq.*), but remains uncertain. The identity of Eshmun and the Arabic *sumāna* (quail) is favoured by Barton (267 n. 2) as against both Wellhausen (10) and Baudissin (208, 305 *sqq.*). Certainly, the meaning of the root (oily, fat, luxuriant, robust, etc. ; see Baud. 207) is not unsuitable

---

[1] Roeder, in Roscher's *Lex.* iv. 777 *sq.,* cf. 773, 776 ; see Kees, *MVAG.* 1924, i. 25 *sq.* Newberry (*Klio,* xii. 397) identified it with Ælian's wart-hog (*Phacochœrus africanus*).

[2] Among his numerous manuscript notes to his copy of Wellhausen's *Heidentum*[1] (in the Library of Christ's College, Cambridge), W. R. S. observes that, according to Cazwīnī (i. 377₁), riding backwards on an ass would cure scorpion bite ; see also *Heid.*[1] 216.

for a deity of the Baal type (though it does not seem to enter into theophorous names), and fits the quail, which is a fat, plump bird. Like the penguin, the bird when dead is apt to breed worms (*E.Bi.* col. 3991), and a characteristic malady produced by the bird was called *morbus Herculeus* (cf. Hommel, 730). Like the manna of the Israelites in the wilderness, the quail was divinely provided food, and the people, tired of manna and lusting after flesh, were " consecrated " in order to receive it (Num. xi. 18). But whereas the manna was not to be stored overnight (Ex. xvi. 19), the quails were eaten for a month, and with disastrous results. Further, whereas manna continued to be regarded as divine food and belongs to distinctively Israelite tradition, the quails had associations in both Phœnician and Greek mythology (cf. A. B. Cook, *Zeus*, i. 544 n.), and they were perhaps burnt alive to Melkart-Heracles at Tyre and to Sandan-Heracles at Tarsus (*GB.* v. 112, 126 n. 3). It is noteworthy that in another Biblical story (Num. xxi.), where the Israelites complain of the manna and of the lack of flesh, they are thereupon bitten by " serpents," and the bronze serpent set up to cure them recalls the connexion between the serpent and the healing god Eshmun.

P. 469. ADDITIONAL NOTE G.—For criticisms, see Stübe, 337 *sqq.* (with references and fuller details); Eitrem, 391 n. 1 ; Nilsson, *Griech. Feste*, 368 ; and Baudissin, 129, 144 (who questions whether Lydus knew of any Adonis festival in spring). Prof. W. R. Halliday (in a private communication) suggests that κωδίῳ ἐσκεπασμένον (see p. 473) may be a periphrasis for some term like ἄπεκτος, which meant technic ally an unshorn lamb less than a year old, and so taboo in Athenian sacrifice (Androtion, 41 ; Philochoros, 64). He compares ἐπίποκος Ἑκάτι ἐμ πόλει . . . οἰν ἐπίποκον τελέαν, *i.e.* a mature sheep with wool on or unshorn ; Paton and Hicks, *Inscriptions of Cos*, 401.[1] W. R. S.'s emendation would then become unnecessary.

P. 481. COVENANT CEREMONIES.—Two types are to be distinguished ; see Meyer and Luther, *Israeliten*, 556 *sqq.* (1) In Ex. xxiv. 3–8, the blood of the sacrifice is sprinkled over the people and over the altar (representing Yahweh). (2) In Gen. xv., Jer. xxxiv. 18 *sqq.*, the distinctive feature is the passage between the severed animal. The former is a familiar type (cf. Trumbull, *Blood Covenant*, 4 *sqq.*), but in the latter the significance of the severance and of the passage is not so clear. Parallels are found in purificatory and in imprecatory ceremonies (Frazer, *FOT*. i. 398 *sqq.*, 407 ; Meyer, 560 n. 1 ; Trumbull, 186). For the parallel Assyrian imprecatory ceremony, where the victim is not, however, a sacrifice, see Frazer, 401 *sq.*, *KAT*. 597, and *MVAG*. iii. 228 *sqq.* It has been thought that the passage between the divided

---

[1] See also Halliday, *Liverpool Annals of Art and Archæology*, xiv. 12.

victim may be a " rite of passage," symbolizing the emergence into a new state (cf. Pilcher, *PSBA*. xl. 8 *sqq.*) ; Crawley, however, recalls the " split token," the division of an object so that two contracting parties, by possessing each a half, are themselves parts, as it were, of a whole, and are thus most closely united (*Mystic Rose*, 238, 248, 258). On the Scythian custom (p. 402 n. 3), see Frazer, *FOT*. i. 394, 414 ; and on the origin of the term *bĕrīth*, see *E.Bi.* " Covenant," § 1 ; Lagrange, 234 *sq.*

Westermarck does not agree that the underlying idea of covenant ceremonies is that of communion.[1] He argues that the blood-covenant imposes duties upon the contracting parties and a penalty for their transgression ; and he invokes the Arabic ʽar and ʽahd where, in the former case, a ma exerts pressure upon a more powerful individual (or saint, etc.) in order to secure, if not rather to compel, his protection, and, in the latter, a man who undertakes a task " is believed to expose himself to supernatural danger in case of bad faith." As regards both, " their primary object was not to establish communion, but to transfer conditional curses both to the men and to the god." On the one hand, Westermarck rightly draws attention to certain forms of belief and practice which might easily be overlooked. On the other, there are gods who are believed to safeguard treaties and covenants (cf. Baal-Berith, p. 534) ; and when they are mentioned (*e.g.* in the Egypto-Hittite or the Hittite-Mitannian treaties), their ability to punish any infraction of the conditions is naturally not the only reason for their presence. In covenants and treaties the relationship between the parties and their gods is a more essential fact than the way in which the relationship is used, viz. in imprecations and curses. The very notion of transference of curses implies a relationship, and the object of exerting pressure upon gods (spirits, saints, etc.) is to utilize them in a way that is " magical " rather than " religious." Westermarck's argument involves the theory that the " magical " relation is more primary than the " religious," and that even if some covenant cere-monies are of a " religious " nature—which presumably would not be denied—the " magical " aspect is more essential than the " religious." But W. R. S. throughout argues from the priority of " religion." And if this is only a " theory," it will claim to deal both with the facts and with rival theories more adequately than does the " theory " of the priority of magic, and to provide a philosophy more true to human nature.

[1] *Origin and Development of Moral Ideas*, ii. 208 *sq.* ; *Ritual and Belief in Morocco*, i. 564, 569.

COMPARATIVE TABLE OF PAGINATION

In view of the use made by German and other continental scholars of Stübe's translation of *Religion of the Semites*, this adjustment of his table may be useful to English readers.

CHAPTER I.

German.	English.
1	1
1–2	2
2	3
3	4
3–4	5
4–5	6
5–6	7
6	8
6–7	9
8	10
8–9	11
9	12
10	13
10–11	14
11	15
12	16
12–3	17
13	18
14	19
14–5	20
15–6	21
16	22
16–7	23
17–8	24
18	25
18	26
18	27

CHAPTER II.

German.	English.
19	28
19–20	29
20–1	30
21	31
22	32
22–3	33
23	34
24	35
24–5	36
25	37
26	38
26–7	39
27	40
28	41
28–9	42
30	43
30–1	44
31–2	45
32–3	46
33–4	47
34	48
34–5	49
35–6	50
36	51
37	52
37–8	53
38	54
39	55
39–40	56
40–1	57
41	58
41–2	59
42–3	60
43	61
43–4	62
44–5	63
45	64
46	65
46–7	66
47	67
48	68
48–9	69
49–50	70
50	71
51	72
51–2	73
52–3	74
53	75
53–4	76
54–5	77
55	78
56	79
56–7	80
57	81
58	82
58–9	83

CHAPTER III.

German.	English.
60	84
60–1	85
61–2	86
62	87
62–3	88
63	89
64	90
64–5	91
65–6	92
66	93
66–7	94
68	95
68	96
69	97
69–70	98
70	99
71	100
71–2	101
72	102
73	103
74	104
74–5	105
75	106
76	107
77	108
77	109
78	110
78–9	111
79–80	112
80	113
80–81	114
81–2	115
82	116
82–3	117
83–4	118
84	119
85	120
85–6	121
86	122
86–7	123
87–8	124
88	125
88–9	126
89–90	127
90	128
91	129
91–2	130
92–3	131
93	132
93–4	133
94–5	134
95	135
96	136
96–7	137
97	138
97–8	441
98	442
99	443
99–100	444
100–1	445
101	446
101	139

CHAPTER IV.

German.	English.
102	140
102–3	141
103	142
104	143
105	144
105–6	145
106–7	146
107	147
107–8	148
108–9	149
109	150
110	151
110–1	152
111	153
112	446
112–3	447
113–4	448
114–5	449
115–6	450
116	451
117	452
117–8	453
118	454
119	154
119–20	155
120	156
121	157
121–2	158
122	454
122–3	455
123	456
123	158
124	159
124–5	160
125–6	161
126	162
127	163
127	164

CHAPTER V.

German.	English.
128	165
128–9	166
129–30	167
130	168
130–1	169
131–2	170
132	171
133	172
133–4	173
134–5	174
135	175
136	176
136–7	177
137	178
138	179
138–9	180
139	181
139–40	182
140–1	183
141	184
142	185
142–3	186
143	187
144	188
144–5	189
145–6	190
146	191
147	192
147–8	193
148	194
148–9	195
149–50	196
150	197
151	198
151–2	199
152	200
152	201
153–4	202
154	203
154–5	204
155	205
156	206
156–7	207
157	208

German.	English.
158	209
158–9	210
159, 161	211
160	456
160–1	457
161	212

CHAPTER VI.

German.	English.
162	213
162–3	214
163	215
164	216
164–5	217
165	218
166	219
166–7	220
167	221
168	222
168–9	223
169–70	224
170	225
171	226
171–2	227
172	228
173	229
173–4	230
174–5	231
175	232
176	233
176–7	234
177	235
178	236
178–9	237
179	238
179–80	239
180–81	240
181	241
181–2	242
182	243

CHAPTER VII.

German.	English.
183	244–5
184	458
184–5	459
185–6	460
186–7	461
187–8	462
188	463
189	464
189–90	465
190	245
191	246
191–2	247
192	248
193	249
193–4	250
194	251
195	252
195–6	253
196	254
197	255
197–8	256
198	257
199	258
199–200	259
200	260
201	261
201–2	262
202	263
203	264

German.	English.
203–4	265
204	266
205	267
205	268

CHAPTER VIII.

German.	English.
206	269
206–7	270
207	271
208	272
208–9	273
209–10	274
210	275
210–1	276
211–2	277
212	278
213	279
213–4	280
214	281
215	282
215–6	283
216	284
216–7	285
217–8	286
218	287
219	288
219–20	289
220	290
221	291
221–2	292
222	293
223	294
223–4	466
224–5	467
225–6	468
226	469, 294
226–7	295
227–8	296
228	297
228–9	298
229	299
230	300
230–1	301
231–2	302
232	303
232–3	304
233–4	305
234–5	306
235	307
236	308
236–7	309
237	310
238	311

CHAPTER IX.

German.	English.
239	312
239–40	313
240–1	314
241	315
241	479
241–2	480
242–3	481, 315
243–4	316
244	317
244–5	318
245	319
246	320
246–7	321
247	322
248	323

German.	English.
248–9	324
249	325
250	326
250–1	327
251–2	328
252	329
252–3	330
253–4	331
254	332
255	333
255	481
255–6	482
256–7	483
257–8	484
258	485
258–9	334
259–60	335
260–1	336
261	337
261–2	338
262	339
263	340
263–4	341
264	342
265	343
265–6	344
266	345
267	346
267–8	347
268	348
268–9	349
269	350
270	351
270	352

CHAPTER X.

German.	English.
271	353
271–2	354
272–3	355
273	356
273–4	357
274	358
275	359
275–6	360
276	361
277	362
277–8	363
278	364
279	365
279–80	366
280	367
281	368
281–2	369
282	370
283	371
283–4	372
284–5	373
285	374
285–6	375
286	376
287	377
287–8	378
288	485
289	486
289–90	487
290–2	488
292	489
292–3	379
293–4	380
294	381
295	382
295–6	383

German.	English.
296	384
296–7	385
297–8	386
298–9	387, 489–90

CHAPTER XI.

German.	English.
300	388
300–1	389
301–2	390
302	391
302–3	392
303	393
304	394
304–5	395
305	396
305–6	397
306–7	398
307	399
307–8	400
308–9	401
309	402
310	403
310–1	491
311	492
312	404
312–3	405
313	406
314	407
314–5	408
315	409
315–6	410
316–7	411
317	412
317–8	413
318–9	414
319	415
320	416
320–1	417
321–2	418
322	419
322–3	420
323–4	421
324	422
325	423
325–6	424
326	425
327	426
327–8	427
328	428
329	429
329–30	430
330	431
330–1	432
331–2	433
332	434
333	435
333–4	436
334–5	437
335	438
336	439
336	440
337	469
337–8	470
338–9	471
339–40	472
341	473
342	474
343	475
344	476
345–6	477
346–9	478
349	479

INDEX OF BIBLICAL PASSAGES

GENERAL INDEX

The references in Roman numerals are to the Introduction

45

---

[1] Explained to mean "ibex" (*MVAG.* 1923, ii. 69).